BLACKSTONE

The Companies Act 2006

BLACKSTONE'S GUIDE TO

The Companies Act 2006

Alan Steinfeld, Martin Mann, Richard Ritchie,
Elizabeth Weaver, Helen Galley, Stuart Adair, Neil
McLarnon, and Adam Cloherty

OXFORD
UNIVERSITY PRESS

OXFORD
UNIVERSITY PRESS

Great Clarendon Street, Oxford OX2 6DP

Oxford University Press is a department of the University of Oxford.
It furthers the University's objective of excellence in research, scholarship,
and education by publishing worldwide in

Oxford New York

Auckland Bangkok Buenos Aires Cape Town Chennai Dar es Salaam Delhi Hong Kong Istanbul Karachi
Kolkata Kuala Lumpur Madrid Melbourne Mexico City Mumbai Nairobi
São Paulo Shanghai Singapore Taipei Tokyo Toronto

with an associated company in Berlin

Oxford is a registered trade mark of Oxford University Press
in the UK and in certain other countries

Published in the United States
by Oxford University Press Inc., New York

British Library Cataloguing in Publication Data

Data available

Library of Congress Cataloging in Publication Data

Blackstone's guide to the Companies Act 2006 / Steinfeld ... [et al.].
    p. cm.—(Blackstone's guide)
    Includes bibliographical references and index.
    ISBN 978-0-19-921710-6 (pbk. : alk. paper) 1. Corporation law—Great Britain.
2. Great Britain. Companies Act 2006. I. Steinfeld, Alan, QC. II.
Title: Guide to the Companies Act 2006. III. Title: Companies Act 2006.
    KD2074. 54.B53 2007
    346.41'06602632—dc22

                                                    2007006858

Typeset by Laserwords Private Limited, Chennai, India
Printed in Great Britain
on acid-free paper by
Ashford Colour Press Limited, Gosport, Hampshire

ISBN 978–0–19–921710–6

1 3 5 7 9 10 8 6 4 2

Contents—Summary

CENTRE	Wrexh
CHECKED	AU
ZONE	Mawr
CLASS MARK/ SUFFIX	346.066R STE
LOAN PERIOD	Overnight Loan 1 month

Contents

Foreword

The Companies Act 2006 is the longest statute ever enacted. It has 1,300 sections and 16 schedules. About one-third of the sections restate earlier provisions and consolidate them into the new Act. But the remainder introduce a wide range of changes, great and small. They build on the work and recommendations of the Company Law Review Steering Group, which was appointed in March 1998 and produced its Final Report in two volumes in July 2001, following wide public consultation. Earlier reports by the Law Commission also played an influential part in the reforms introduced by the new Act.

Many of the changes are technical, but may prove the truth of the old adage that the devil is in the detail. Others, such as those relating to e-communications, align company law with modern realities, without any change in underlying principles. Still more, though shortly stated, may have a significant impact. An example is the abolition, as regards private companies, of the prohibition on a company giving financial assistance for the acquisition of its own shares. It remains, at least for the present, for public companies because of the requirements of EU law. The prohibition, originally introduced in 1929 on the recommendation of the Greene Committee to meet public concern resulting from well-publicized scandals, has loomed large in the life of the company lawyer advising on transactions. The Company Law Review Steering Group estimated in 1998 the annual cost in legal fees to be £20 million: probably then, and surely now, an under-estimate. Time will show whether by other means the law can prevent a recurrence of the scandals which originally inspired the prohibition.

The greatest changes lie in the codification of directors' duties and the new regime for derivative actions by shareholders. The pros and cons of codification, certainty and accessibility against flexibility, had been long debated. The result does not introduce fundamental changes in substantive law, but it eschews the simple elegance of past codifications such as the Sale of Goods Act 1893 for a more complex structure which seeks to marry existing principles and remedies with the newly codified duties.

The new regime for derivative actions replaces the relative certainty of the rule in *Foss v Harbottle* and its limited exceptions with an approach which depends to a far greater extent on judicial discretion in the circumstances of individual cases. This has led to no little anxiety in commercial circles. The Act contains provisions to guide the exercise of the discretion but, as the Attorney General made clear in the debates in the House of Lords, it is fundamentally a question of judicial control and his expectation was that the judiciary would be circumspect in reaching its decisions. We shall see how it develops in practice but at this stage I, of course, could not possibly comment.

With the new Act only recently enacted, and with most of its provisions yet to come into force, the task now is to get some understanding of its scope and of the changes it has made. Law firms and sets of chambers are already doing this for themselves and their clients. This book, written by well-respected practitioners from a single set of chambers, performs the same function for a wider audience. It breaks the subject-matter down into chapters of manageable size, grouping together related topics. It clearly summarizes the effect of the new provisions and the changes made by them. It also has a table of restated provisions. All this is combined with the text of the Act itself. The time for detailed exegesis has yet to come, but this book will, I believe, be a most valuable aid to the immediate need to get to grips with the Companies Act 2006.

David Richards
Royal Courts of Justice
February 2007

Preface

The reforms to company law to be made by what became the Companies Act 2006 (or "CA 2006" as it is referred to throughout this work) were heralded by the government as the greatest and most extensive to be made in a generation. Whilst not doubting that the changes to the pre-existing law are highly significant nor doubting this general proposition, many a practitioner might question whether in fact these changes are quite as significant or extensive as those that preceded it and which were consolidated in the great Companies Acts of the past, the 1929, 1948, and 1985 Companies Acts. Nevertheless the CA 2006 does undoubtedly mark a significant reform of company law and it will most surely rank as a milestone with those Acts at least for another generation.

The CA 2006 started and proceeded for most of its passage through Parliament as the Company Law Reform Bill. As such it dealt only with the changes to the pre-existing law which that Bill was intended to bring about, the government's intention at that time being to consolidate with the CA 1985 later. This work was accordingly originally conceived by Blackstone's, the publishers, as being restricted to a practical commentary on that Act (as it was to be) and hence restricted to the changes in the pre-existing law to be made by it. It was at that point that I was asked by Blackstone's to get together a team of expert company practitioners to set about preparing this work—and readily, but confessedly with some hesitation, agreed to do so. My hesitation and that of the team (all members of my Chambers at XXIV Old Buildings) would have been all the greater had I and they appreciated that at a very late stage in the passage of the Bill the government was to announce a radical change of plan. Instead of consolidating later it was now proposed to consolidate in one go. So there was now to be a wholly new Act which was to repeal virtually the whole of the CA 1985 and consolidate it with the new changes in an entirely new Act.

The result was the CA 2006, an Act that runs to no fewer than 1300 sections and 16 extensive Schedules, surely one of, if not the, lengthiest Acts on the statute book. The change of plan necessarily had its effect on the preparation of this work, not least because of the delay in being able to obtain from the government website a copy of the new Bill followed by an even further delay in obtaining a copy of the Act itself after it received its Royal assent on 8 November 2006. I must pay the highest possible tribute to the enthusiasm and skill of the team who were able to cope with these changes at such short notice, leaving me as consultant editor with little more to do than to check their manuscripts to ensure consistency and to add the occasional comment. The team consisted of the following:

Chapters 1, 2, 6, 10, 15, 16, and 19: Adam Cloherty
Chapters 3, 4, and 5: Neil McLarnon
Chapters 7, 8, and 9: Helen Galley
Chapters 11, 12, and 18: Elizabeth Weaver
Chapter 13: Richard Ritchie
Chapter 14: Stuart Adair
Chapter 17: Martin Mann QC

Despite the last minute change the purpose of this work remains what it was at the outset, namely to be a practical guide to and commentary upon the changes made to the pre-existing law. Whilst these changes affect almost every aspect of that law and are dealt with extensively in this work, the most significant one from the viewpoint of the company practitioner is probably the very much greater informality now permitted for the governance of private companies combined with a tightening up of the regulations governing public companies, particularly listed ones, with the aim of making their directors more accountable to their shareholders. The former has repercussions in all sorts of areas. They include the total abolition of the prohibition of the giving of financial assistance in relation to the purchase of shares in a private company and the removal of the procedural obstacles to the purchase by a private company of its own shares. No longer will a father be able to rely on some technical infringement of the applicable rules so as years later to be able to challenge a sale agreed by him and his son (the only shareholders) of his shares to the company and so deprive the son's widow of the fruits of her husband's subsequent endeavours (*Re R W Peak (Kings Lynn) Ltd* [1998] BCLC 193, surely a blot on the judicial landscape thankfully now statutorily buried). Another significant change is that for the first time the duties of directors are now statutorily and comprehensively set out.

As stated, the aim of this work is to provide a practical guide to the changes made by the CA 2006. As such it is primarily aimed at the company practitioner. Thus it assumes a certain degree of knowledge by the reader of the pre-existing law. It is not intended to be a substitute for the comprehensive treatment of company law by the well known textbooks—let alone a competitor to them. These works can be consulted for any more in-depth treatment of the subject (once they have come out with new editions/supplements to take in the provisions of the CA 2006).

Only a handful of the provisions of the CA 2006 came into effect immediately. The vast majority are to come into effect on dates to be appointed by statutory instrument. As at the date of publication the only substantive provisions already to have come into effect are Part 43 (implementing the transparency obligations directive), s 463 (making statutory provision for directors' reports to the market), provisions enabling greater investigation into interests in shares, provisions facilitating electronic communication with shareholders, and takeovers provisions. The government has announced its intention to bring all provisions of the CA 2006 into effect by October 2008. The delay is presumably to allow time for practitioners to absorb its changes.

I would finally express my thanks to the publishers and their staff for all their assistance at every stage in the preparation of this work, without whose assistance this work would be nowhere near to completion, and to the Honourable Mr Justice David Richards for having agreed to write the Foreword.

Table of Cases

References are to Paragraph Numbers

Table of Legislation

References are to Paragraph Numbers

EU Regulations and Directives

Regulations

Directives

List of Abbreviations and Glossary of Terms

1st Directive	1st Company Law Directive
CA 1985	Companies Act 1985
CA 1989	Companies Act 1989
CA 2006	Companies Act 2006
C(AICE)A 2004	Companies (Audit, Investigation and Community Enterprise) Act 2004
CLR	Company Law Review
CLRSG	Company Law Review Steering Group
FSA	Financial Services Authority
FSA 1986	Financial Services Act 1986
FSMA 2000	Financial Services and Markets Act 2000
IAS	International Accounting Standards
OFR	Operating and Financial Review

The Companies Acts—means the company law provisions of Parts 1–39 and 45–47 of CA 2006, Part 2 of C(AICE)A 2004 and the provisions of CA 1985 that remain in force (s 2 of CA 1985)

Subject to negative resolution procedure—means that the statutory instrument containing the regulations or order shall be subject to annulment in pursuance of a resolution of either House of Parliament (s 1289 of CA 2006)

Subject to affirmative resolution procedure—means that the draft regulations or order must not be made unless a draft of the statutory instrument containing them has been approved by a resolution of each House of Parliament (s 1290 of CA 2006)

1

INTRODUCTION AND OVERVIEW

A. GENESIS OF THE ACT

The Companies Act 2006 (CA 2006) has been a long time coming. The Company Law 1.01
Review (CLR), which 'provides the essential blueprint'[1] for CA 2006, was launched in
March 1998 by Margaret Beckett, then Secretary of State for Trade and Industry, with the
aim of developing a 'modern company law for a competitive economy'.[2] Some 11 reports,
two White Papers, and nearly nine years later, the project has finally come to fruition.

The CLR, overseen by a 'steering group' of eminent company lawyers and business-people 1.02
(CLRSG) and supported by 'working groups' of relevant specialists and interested persons,
submitted its final report in July 2001. The CLRSG's consultation process had proceeded in
three main stages[3] and involved a detailed dialogue with a wide range of interested parties.
Their recommendations were set out in a two-volume Final Report[4] which they believed
represented 'a major reworking of the whole framework of company law'.

'Modernising company law' became a commitment of the government in its manifesto 1.03
for the 2001 general election. The following year, the DTI responded to the CLR process
in a White Paper (published July 2002),[5] which also included further draft clauses for a
Companies Bill and which was itself subject to detailed consultation.

However, work then appeared to stall and nothing more was heard until a second, com- 1.04
prehensive, White Paper was published in March 2005. This was a substantial piece of work
and included in draft much of the Bill which the government eventually brought forward.

CA 2006 was introduced to Parliament in the House of Lords in November 2005 and 1.05
started its passage as the Company Law Reform Bill. Its name was, however, changed by a
Conservative amendment in the House of Commons in July 2006 by dropping the words

---

[1] *Company Law Reform White Paper* (Cm 6456, March 2005) 3.
[2] DTI, *Modern Company Law for a Competitive Economy* (March 1998).
[3] DTI, *The Strategic Framework*, URN 99/654 (February 1999), *Developing the Framework*, URN 00/656 (March 2000), and *Completing the Structure*, URN 00/1335 (November 2000) respectively. There were also various other specialized consultations.
[4] DTI, *Company Law Review: Final Report*, URN 01/942 (July 2001).
[5] *Modernising Company Law* (Cm 5553, July 2002).

'Law Reform' to maintain the 'traditional' nomenclature of companies legislation and to reflect the fact that the Bill as then proposed would partially consolidate, as well as reform, the law. Despite its size, consideration of the Bill by committee in the Commons was 'programmed', meaning that only a short period of about a month was available to consider the Bill in its entirety.

1.06　Reportedly the biggest Bill ever to have gone through Parliament, CA 2006 runs to some 1300 sections and 16 Schedules. Although—mercifully—many of those provisions either 'restate', or make relatively minor technical changes to, the existing law, CA 2006 does contain significant changes across all areas of company law which affect companies of all types. As such, it will be imperative for lawyers (both transactional and litigation) and others advising companies to have a good grasp of its content.

1.07　CA 2006 received Royal Assent on 8 November 2006.

B. SCOPE OF THE ACT

1. The Companies Acts

1.08　One of the main criticisms of the Bill from a practitioner's point of view was that there would be a division of core companies legislation across four major Acts: CA 1985, CA 1989, Companies (Audit, Investigation and Community Enterprise) Act 2004 (C(AICE)A 2004), and CA 2006. The government has, to a large extent, ameliorated this position by incorporating all of the 'company law' provisions of the other three Acts into CA 2006 (although restating those parts in consistent language) so that, it says, CA 2006 is a 'comprehensive statement of company law'.

1.09　However, parts of CA 1985, CA 1989, and C(AICE)A 2004 remain. These mostly relate to: Scots law provisions (which, since they are 'devolved matters', have to be dealt with by the Scottish Parliament); investigations (CA 1985); assisting overseas regulatory authorities (CA 1989); and community interest companies and provisions relating to the Financial Reporting Review Panel and the Financial Reporting Council (C(AICE) 2004).

1.10　It is still difficult to see why all of companies legislation could not finally have been consolidated in one place. The government's justification for retaining the provisions described in paragraph 1.09 above is that they are not 'core company law'. However, although the government has, for example, retained provision for investigations in CA 1985, Part 32 of CA 2006 makes provision on investigations too, ie CA 2006 already contains some of what, according to the government, is not 'core company law'.

2. Northern Ireland

1.11　One innovation in scope terms is to bring Northern Ireland within the ambit of the Companies Acts (see Part 45 of CA 2006) so that there will now be 'UK', rather than 'GB', company law. This is good news for Northern Ireland, which often had to wait even longer for new company law provision to be 'translated' by Order in Council.

3. Purely restated provisions

1.12　As indicated above, in addition to reform measures, some of CA 2006 merely 'restates' wholesale parts of CA 1985. It is clear that this is only intended to be a convenience measure and that the firm intention behind these 'restated' provisions is solely to consolidate, and not to change, the law.[6] Chapter 19 contains a table of purely restated provisions which are generally not comprehensively dealt with in this book.

C. KEY THEMES AND REFORMS

The 2005 White Paper sets out the government's four 'crucial objectives' for CA 2006: 1.13

(1) 'to enhance shareholder engagement and a long term investment culture';

(2) 'to ensure better regulation and a "Think Small First" approach';

(3) 'to make it easier to set up and run a company'; and

(4) 'to provide flexibility for the future'.

1. 'Think Small First' and ease

Objectives (2) and (3) are closely linked and are sought to be reflected throughout CA 2006, 1.14 so that companies legislation is 'reclaimed' for the 'average' smaller private company. The statutory language of this approach is to distinguish between 'larger' and 'smaller' companies (rather than simply as between 'public' and 'private'). Structurally, it adopts a 'tiered' system with three levels, proceeding on the assumption that all private companies are small and, as regards public companies, maintaining a difference between 'quoted' and 'other'. However, since the approach to private companies only creates a *default* position, the larger, more sophisticated, private companies can, if desired, opt for more intense regulation by providing it for themselves,[7] such as in their articles of association.

The approach described above is reflected in various ways. 1.15

(a) *Structure*

Structurally, CA 2006 generally states the provisions relating to small companies first and 1.16 groups them together so that they are easier to find. This contrasts with CA 1985 and previous Acts, which generally expressed the law relating to small/private companies as exceptions to that relating to large/public companies. For example, contrast the 'exemption' for small and medium-sized companies which is now outlined at the beginning of Part 15 of CA 2006, with the former 'exemption' placed in the middle of Part 7 of CA 1985.

(b) *Substance*

Substantively, CA 2006 seeks to 'remove unnecessary [regulatory] burdens on small firms'. 1.17 This is exemplified by the removal of the requirement for a company secretary, and the abolition of the financial assistance regime, for private companies—discussed further in Chapters 11 and 8 respectively.

Section 19 of CA 2006 also comprehends that there will now be different 'Table A' 1.18 default/model articles for different types of company, so that small private companies will benefit from their own, greatly pared down, version: see further, Chapter 4.

---

[6] See, eg, Secretary of State for Trade & Industry, *Hansard*, HC, cols 123 and 125 (6 June 2006).

[7] Secretary of State for Trade & Industry, *Hansard*, HC, col 132 (6 June 2006).

(c) *Practicality*

1.19   On a practical note, CA 2006 attempts to reflect the way in which the vast majority of companies (ie small private companies) work. Therefore, recognizing that such companies rarely, if ever, hold them, the *obligation* to hold AGMs is removed; conversely CA 2006 makes it easier for such companies to pass written resolutions by, inter alia, removing the unanimity requirement. We discuss meetings and resolutions more fully in Chapter 12. Finally, although essentially a non-statutory innovation, small companies are promised much more in the way of 'plain English guidance' from Companies House.

2. Other key themes and headline reforms

1.20   The main changes made by CA 2006 are highlighted more fully and by category in Chapter 2. A few introductory words are offered here on the other key themes behind the Act by reference to its 'headline' aspects.

(a) *Accessibility and flexibility*

1.21   Undoubtedly the most noteworthy aspect of CA 2006 is the introduction of a comprehensive codification of directors' general duties[8] in Part 10 of CA 2006. The fundamental driver for this is a desire to improve company law's 'accessibility', the government wanting to ensure 'that the duties are widely known and understood'.[9]

1.22   However, the approach adopted has not been universally popular—with the most significant opposition coming from, among others, the Law Society. In essence, opponents of the statement are concerned that it does not meet its stated aim of 'accessibility' and in fact results in the loss of 'flexibility' (another of the government's crucial objectives) inherent in the common law and equitable rules. On any view, the statement has the potential to spawn widespread litigation; we deal with it more fully in Chapter 13.

1.23   Further evidence of the government's desire to bring company law to a wider audience is found in Part 11 of CA 2006, which places the increasingly obsolescent derivative action on a statutory footing. This reform caused some concern during the Act's passage through Parliament—the main fear being its potential exploitation by rogue 'single-issue' shareholders who seek to paralyse companies with derivative litigation. We consider it more fully in Chapter 14.

1.24   The government's 'flexibility' agenda (part of its fourth 'crucial objective') suffered a serious blow when one of the most controversial proposals in the Bill, a generalized power to reform 'core company law' by secondary legislation, was roundly criticized and defeated in the House of Lords. The government did not reintroduce the measure in the Commons.

(b) *Transparency*

1.25   'Transparency' is, in company law as in other areas of life, much trumpeted. Indeed, EU corporate law now contains a whole directive on 'Transparency Obligations',[10] which Part 43 of CA 2006 (discussed further in Chapter 9) seeks to transpose.

---

[8] Described as 'the heart of the Bill' by the Secretary of State, *Hansard,* HC, col 125 (6 June 2006).

[9] 2005 White Paper [3.3].

[10] Council Directive (EC) 2004/109 on the harmonisation of transparency requirements in relation to information about issuers whose securities are admitted to trading on a regulated market and amending Directive 2001/34/EC [2004] OJ L390, (December 2004).

Underpinning much of the transparency agenda is a desire to encourage greater 'shareholder activism', hence the introduction of provisions making it easier for 'indirect investors' (ie those who 'stand behind' a nominee registered shareholder, such as an investment fund) to receive information and to exercise the various rights attaching to shares: see, eg, Part 9 of CA 2006, supplemented by the new provisions relating to proxies in ss 324–331, discussed in Chapters 6 and 12 respectively. The Secretary of State also takes a controversial[11] new power in s 1277 to require pension schemes, unit trusts, and other similar entities to disclose how they exercised voting rights attached to shares they hold whether directly or indirectly (see the fuller discussion in Chapter 9).   1.26

Yet, there is a tension between the goal of greater 'transparency' and another of the key themes, 'deregulation' (discussed below). That is evident from the repeal of the obligation for quoted companies to produce an Operating and Financial Review (OFR), touted as a great contribution to corporate transparency, before it had even got going. Its scrapping caused a wide degree of disgruntlement in Parliament and among many business people and others.[12] In place of the OFR comes the more narrowly focused 'business review' (see s 417) discussed along with other accounting and reporting provisions in Chapter 15.   1.27

(c) *Deregulation*
Many of the deregulatory measures have been introduced in the discussion of 'small' companies above. However, CA 2006's deregulatory zeal benefits not just companies themselves but external bodies too. CA 2006 relaxes the traditional rules prohibiting the limitation by auditors of their liability. Auditors may now enter into 'liability limitation agreements' with the companies they audit, so long as those agreements are authorized or approved by the company's members. Audit is discussed more fully in Chapter 16.   1.28

D. PROGNOSIS

CA 2006 will undoubtedly give rise to increased litigation as well as uncertainty for transactors—at least in the short to medium term. Largely, this will be the result of the various reforming measures but will also no doubt arise from what will have to be very complex transitional measures (which the government won't even begin consulting on until February 2007!). Inevitably there will also be at least an interim period of 'testing', as companies and their advisers, as well as external groups, try to take advantage of the ways in which previously malleable common law areas (such as derivative actions and directors' duties) are comprehensively set down in writing, as well as the way in which familiar old statutory provisions are 'restated'.   1.29

The government has indicated that the whole of CA 2006 will be fully in force by October 2008.[13]   1.30

However, some provisions came into force upon Royal Assent—the most important being provisions relating to transparency obligations (save for the new definition of 'regulated   1.31

---

[11] The clause was voted out during Committee Stage in the HL, but the government reintroduced it in the House of Commons.

[12] See, eg, *Hansard*, HC, cols 147, 152–3 and 161–2 (6 June 2006) and *Financial Times* (London 21 August 2006) 3.

[13] Statement made by Lord Sainsbury: see *Hansard*, HL, col 432 (2 November 2006) and statement by Secretary of State for Trade & Industry, *Hansard*, HC, col 126WS *et seq* (18 December 2006).

market' in the Financial Services and Markets Act 2000 (FSMA 2000)). Provisions relating to electronic communication with shareholders (discussed in Chapter 11) came into force on 20 January 2007 as did provisions relating to public companies' powers to investigate who is interested in their shares; the Secretary of State's powers to make regulations; and s 463 (which sets out directors' liabilities for reports to the market).

1.32   The government has also indicated that it intends to commence the following provisions from 6 April 2007: extension of the community interest companies regime to Northern Ireland; s 1281 allowing public authorities to disclose information they have obtained for the purposes of certain civil proceedings; and provisions implementing the Takeovers Directive in Part 28 of CA 2006.

1.33   Yet other provisions, such as those relating to auditors' resignation statements and sign-off of audit reports by a 'senior statutory auditor' will need to be commenced by June 2008 so as to comply with the amended 8th Company Law Directive.

1.34   As for the transitional regime, DTI are still consulting and, at the time of writing, had indicated that they would not have a proposed transitional scheme until at least February 2007. One major problem to be addressed is how the move from memorandum and articles to essentially a single constitutional document in the articles will apply to existing companies: this could involve transactional lawyers undertaking a serious amount of reviewing of existing arrangements. Then there is the vast array (thanks to the move away from Schedules in favour of regulations) of (often horrendously) complex regulations to be consulted on, drafted, and made. Again, consultation is not scheduled to happen before February 2007.[14] Therefore, there is still a great amount of work to be done—by government and by practitioners.

1.35   Modernizing company law has been a nine-year process and is still ongoing. That process alone, with its various iterations, must have been a hugely expensive exercise. It will also undoubtedly give rise to huge expense for companies and their advisers as they get to grips with the changes, incorporate them into transactions, and test them in the courts. Ultimately, though, only time can tell whether the benefits promised to be delivered by CA 2006—the Secretary of State proclaimed CA 2006 would save businesses £250m a year—justify those costs.

---

[14] Statement by Secretary of State for Trade & Industry, *Hansard*, HC, col 128WS (18 December 2006).

2

KEY CHANGES

There follows a list of the 'key' changes made by CA 2006 with an indication of where they are discussed in this book. 2.01

A. ALL COMPANIES

2.02

- Comprehensive statutory statement of directors' duties replacing common law/equitable duties (Chapter 13).
- 'Single' constitution: Memorandum of Association now simply a historical record and all constitutional provisions to be contained in Articles of Association (Chapter 4).
- Derivative actions on a statutory footing (Chapter 14).
- Companies able to communicate electronically with shareholders (Chapter 11).
- Auditors able to agree limitations of their liabilities to the companies they audit (Chapter 16).
- Ability for 'indirect investors' to receive information and exercise rights attached to shares (Chapter 6).
- Improved rights for proxies (Chapter 12).
- No requirement for companies to specify their objects (Chapter 4).
- New regime for company and business names (Chapter 5).
- Directors and shareholders able to specify service addresses on register (Chapters 11 and 6).
- New regime for company offences and 'officers in default' (Chapter 18).

B. PRIVATE COMPANIES

2.03

- Removal of obligation to hold an AGM (Chapter 12).
- Abolition of the financial assistance regime (Chapter 8).
- Removal of requirement to have a company secretary (Chapter 11).
- Separate version of 'Table A' model articles with small private companies in mind (Chapter 4).
- Easier to pass written resolutions (Chapter 12).
- Time for filing accounts and reports down from ten months to nine (Chapter 15).
- Removal of medium-sized group exemption from group accounts regime (Chapter 15).

C. PUBLIC AND QUOTED COMPANIES

2.04

- New requirement to publish accounts on a website (Chapter 15) and to publish members' concerns about audit on a website (Chapter 16).
- Increased reporting requirements for 'business review', including 'supply chain' information (Chapter 15).
- Takeovers Directive implemented in full and Takeovers Panel given statutory recognition and powers (Chapter 17).
- Takeovers: new disclosure requirements for directors' reports and new statutory basis for calculation of 'squeeze-out' and 'sell-out' thresholds (Chapter 17).
- Clarification of liability for reports to the market (Chapter 9).

D. OTHER

2.05

- Power for Secretary of State to require investors to disclose how they vote at company meetings (Chapter 9).
- Reversal of *Re Leyland Daf*[1]—liquidators now entitled to be paid out of floating charge assets (Chapter 18).

---

[1] [2004] UKHL 9; [2004] 2 AC 298.

3

NATURE AND FORMATION OF COMPANIES

A. TYPES OF COMPANY

The CLR recommended that the law should continue to provide for the formation of 3.01 companies of the types which were currently available at the time of its report (Final Report, paragraph 9.2). This recommendation was accepted by Parliament and CA 2006 retains all of the forms of companies which were current at the time of its enactment. Part 1 of CA 2006 provides for the different types of company which may exist in the UK. It lists seven types of company:

(1) limited companies;
(2) unlimited companies;
(3) private companies;
(4) public companies;
(5) companies limited by guarantee;
(6) companies having share capital; and
(7) community interest companies.

B. KEY DISTINCTIONS

A limited company is defined by s 3(1), which replaces s 1(2)(a), (b), and (c) of CA 3.02 1985, as a company whose members' liability is limited by its constitution; such liability may be limited by shares or limited by guarantee. Where the members' liability is limited to the amount, if any, unpaid on the shares held by the members, then the company is a company 'limited by shares' (s 3(2)). Where the members' liability is limited to such amount as the members undertake to contribute to the assets of the company in the event of its being wound up, then the company is a company 'limited by guarantee' (s 3(3)).

3.03   An unlimited company is a company whose members' liability is unlimited (s 3(4)).

3.04   A private company is defined by s 4(1) as a company that is not a public company which replaces s 1(3) of CA 1985.

3.05   A public company is defined in s 4(2) which replaces ss 1(3) and 735(2) of CA 1985 as a company limited by shares or limited by guarantee and having a share capital:

(a) whose certificate of incorporation states that it is a public company; and

(b) in relation to which the requirements of the Companies Acts, or the former Companies Acts, as to registration or re-registration as a public company have been complied with.

3.06   There are two major differences between public and private companies. These differences are dealt with in Part 20 of CA 2006. First, a private company limited by shares or limited by guarantee and having a share capital must not offer to the public any securities of the company or allot or agree to allot any securities of the company with a view to their being offered to the public. 'Securities' is defined in s 755(5) as meaning shares or debentures. 'Offer to the public' is defined in s 756. Second, a public company must have a minimum share capital of £50,000 (s 763).

3.07   A company limited by guarantee cannot have a share capital (s 5(1)) and any provision in the constitution of a company that purports to divide the company's undertaking into shares or interests is a provision for a share capital.

3.08   A community interest company (s 6) is one formed in accordance with Part 2 of the C(AICE)A 2004. A company limited by shares or a company limited by guarantee and not having a share capital may be formed as or become a community interest company. A company limited by guarantee and having a share capital may become a community interest company.

C. FORMATION OF A COMPANY

3.09   Part 2 of CA 2006 provides for company formation and registration. A company is formed by one or more persons subscribing their names to a memorandum of association (s 7(1)(a)) and complying with the requirements of CA 2006 as to registration (s 7(1)(b)). The memorandum of association is a memorandum stating that the subscribers wish to form a company under CA 2006 (s 8(1)(a)) and agree to become members of the company and, in the case of a company that is to have a share capital, to take at least one share each (s 8(1)(b)). The memorandum must be in the prescribed form and must be authenticated by each subscriber (s 8(2)).

3.10   Section 7 (method of forming a company) replaces s 1(1) and (3A) of CA 1985. The major change being that s 7(1) now enables one single person to form a company. Section 8 (memorandum of association) replaces s 2 of CA 1985. Whilst it retains the requirement under CA 1985 that individuals who wish to form a company must subscribe their names to the memorandum, under CA 2006 the memorandum serves a more limited, but nonetheless important, purpose: it evidences the intention of the subscribers to the memorandum to form a company and become members of that company on formation. In the case of a company that is to be limited by shares, the memorandum will also provide evidence of the members' agreement to take at least one share each in the company.

3.11   The memorandum of a company formed under CA 2006 will therefore look very different from that of a company formed under CA 1985 and it will not be possible to amend or update the memorandum of a company formed under CA 2006. Provisions in the memoranda of companies formed under previous Acts which are of a type that are not in the memoranda of companies formed under CA 2006 will be treated as provisions of the articles (s 28). Companies formed prior to the coming into force of the Act will be able to alter or update provisions in their constitution which are set out in their memoranda by amending their articles.

These changes to the memoranda are based on the CLR's recommendation that there   3.12
should be a single constitution (Final Report, paragraph 9.4). In line with the principles behind the recommendation, key information regarding the internal allocation of powers between the directors and members of a company formed under CA 2006 will be set out in one place: the articles of association. Companies formed prior to the coming into force of CA 2006 will not be required to amend their articles to reflect this change, but they may amend if they so wish.

D. REGISTRATION

Sections 9–16 deal with company registration and fall into two broad categories: ss 9–13   3.13
which deal with the requirements for registration and ss 14–16 which deal with the effects of registration.

Section 9 replaces ss 2 and 10 of CA 1985. It prescribes the types of information or   3.14
documents which must be delivered to the registrar when an application for registration is made and the manner in which that information must be delivered. Changes have been made to the way in which certain information is delivered to the registrar as a result of the changes that CA 2006 has brought to a company's memorandum. The memorandum must therefore be delivered along with an application for registration of the company (s 9(1)) which must also contain: in the case of a company which is to have a share capital, a statement of capital and initial shareholdings (s 9(4)(a)); in the case of a company that is to be limited by guarantee, a statement of guarantee (s 9(4)(b)); a statement of the company's proposed officers (s 9(4)(c)); a statement of the intended address of the company's registered office (s 9(5)(a)); a copy of the company's proposed articles of association, to the extent that these are not supplied by the default application of model articles (s 9(5)(b)); and a statement of compliance (s 13).

A major change brought by s 9 (registration of documents) is the requirement to file   3.15
a statement of capital and initial shareholdings. Under CA 1985, in the case of a limited company with a share capital, the memorandum was required to state the amount of the share capital with which the company proposed to be registered and the nominal amount of each of its shares. This was known as the 'authorised share capital'. The CLR recommended the abolition of the requirement that a company have an authorized share capital. CA 2006 gives effect to the recommendation. Under CA 2006, the memorandum will only contain a limited amount of information on its subscribers. Information about the shares subscribed for by the subscribers, which under CA 1985 was set out in the memorandum itself, will, under the Act, be provided to the registrar in the statement of share capital and initial shareholdings.

Section 14 (registration) replaces s 12 of CA 1985. Once the registrar is satisfied that   3.16
the requirements of the Act have been complied with, he must register the documents delivered to him. Upon registration, the registrar must give a certificate that the company is

incorporated. Section 12(3) and (3A) of CA 1985 which required a statutory declaration or, in the case of companies using electronic communications a statement of compliance, have been done away with and have been replaced with the statement of compliance, which does not need to be witnessed, required under s 13.

3.17   Section 15 replaces s 13(1), (2), (6), and (7) of CA 1985 and deals with the issue of the certificate of incorporation. There is only one change to the equivalent requirements of CA 1985, namely all certificates issued under the Act must include details of whether the company's registered office is situated in England and Wales (or in Wales), in Scotland, or in Northern Ireland. Whilst under CA 1985 it had been the registrar's practice to include this information in the certificate of incorporation there was no statutory requirement to do so.

3.18   Whilst s 16 provides for the effect of registration and replaces s 13(3)–(5) of CA 1985, it does not make any substantive changes to the equivalent provisions of CA 1985.

E. RE-REGISTRATION

3.19   Part 7 of CA 2006 deals with re-registration as a means of altering a company's status and covers five distinct situations:

(1) a private company altering its status to become a public company (ss 90–96);

(2) a public company altering its status to become a private company (ss 97–101);

(3) a private limited company altering its status to become an unlimited company (ss 102–104);

(4) a unlimited private company altering its status to become a limited company (ss 105–107); and

(5) a public company altering its status to become an unlimited private company (ss 109–111).

3.20   As recommended by the CLR (Final Report, paragraph 11.16), CA 2006 provides for the same re-registration situations as covered in CA 1985. However, CA 2006 has brought about one significant change to the CA 1985 regime. Under CA 2006, a public company will now be able to re-register as an unlimited private company without first having to re-register as a private limited company.

F. UNREGISTERED AND FOREIGN REGISTERED COMPANIES

1. Unregistered companies

3.21   Part 33 of CA 2006 deals with UK companies not formed under the Companies Acts. Chapter 1 of Part 33 deals with companies not formed under the Companies Acts but authorized to register. Chapter 2 of Part 33 deals with unregistered companies.

3.22   Chapter 1 contains ss 1040–1042. Section 1040 replaces s 680 of CA 1985. Companies incorporated within the UK, but not formed under the Companies Acts (or certain earlier companies legislation) may apply to register under the Act. The types of company that can take advantage of this provision are listed in s 1040(1). They are: companies formed before 2 November 1862; companies formed by private Act of Parliament; companies formed by letters patent; and companies otherwise constituted according to law. Such a company may apply to register as a company limited by shares, a company limited by guarantee, or an unlimited company subject to the restrictions imposed by s 1040(4) and (5). Section 1040 (4) provides that a company having the liability of its members limited by Act of Parliament or letters patent: (a) may not register under the section unless it is a joint stock company; and (b) may not register under the section as an unlimited company or a company limited by guarantee. Section 1040(5) provides that a company that is not a joint stock company may not register under the section as a company limited by shares.

Section 1041 replaces s 683 of CA 1985 and defines in the same terms what is meant by a 'joint stock company'.   3.23

Section 1042 gives the Secretary of State the power to make regulations in connection with the registration of a company following an application under s 1040. This is a new power which was not present in CA 1985 and regulations made under this power will replace the provisions made by ss 681, 682, 684–690, and Sch 21 of CA 1985. The regulations will cover the procedural requirements for registration, the conditions to be satisfied before registration, and the documents to be supplied on an application for registration. The regulations will also set out the consequences of registration, including the status of the company following registration and the application of the Companies Acts to such companies following registration. The regulations are subject to the negative resolution procedure.   3.24

Chapter 2 contains s 1043 (unregistered companies) which replaces s 718 of CA 1985. The section confers a power on the Secretary of State to apply provisions of the Companies Acts to certain unregistered companies. These are companies incorporated in the UK and having their principal place of business in the UK, but not formed or registered under the Companies Acts or any other public general Act of Parliament. Section 1043(1) exempts certain other companies from regulations under this section, including those exempted by direction of the Secretary of State.   3.25

Regulations under this section will replace the provision made by Sch 22 to CA 1985. The regulations may apply specified provisions of the Companies Acts to specified descriptions of an unregistered company, and may make limitations, adaptations, and modifications to the application of the Companies Act to unregistered companies. These regulations are also subject to the negative resolution procedure.   3.26

2. Foreign registered companies

Part 34 of CA 2006 deals with overseas companies and applies to companies incorporated outside the UK. It enables various registration, reporting, and disclosure requirements to be imposed on overseas companies. This Part together with the regulations to be made under it will replace the provisions made by Part 23 and Schs 21A–D of CA 1985. Regulations made under this Part will continue to implement the requirements of the Eleventh Company Law Directive[1] which imposes disclosure requirements on overseas companies that set up branches in the UK.   3.27

Prior to CA 2006, Part 23 of CA 1985 applied to companies incorporated outside Great Britain that established a place of business in Great Britain. Subsequently, the Eleventh Company Law Directive imposed a different set of disclosure requirements on Member   3.28

---

[1] Council Directive (EEC) 89/666 concerning disclosure requirements in respect of branches opened in a Member State by certain types of company governed by the law of another State [1989] OJ L395.

State companies with branches in the UK. Thus, the branch disclosure requirements differed depending on whether or not the overseas company was incorporated within another EEA state with the result that there were effectively two parallel regimes that applied to overseas companies.

3.29   The CLR set out their initial analysis of the rules for regulating companies formed abroad in Chapter 5.6 of the Strategic Framework and then put forward their provisional detailed conclusions in their consultation document of October 1999 entitled 'Reforming the law concerning overseas companies'. They presented their conclusions in paragraphs 11.21–11.33 of the Final Report.

3.30   The sections of Part 34 fall into three categories: those dealing with the registration of the particulars of overseas companies (ss 1046–1048); those dealing with the other requirements by which overseas companies have to abide (ss 1049–1053); and those dealing with supplementary matters (ss 1054–1059).

3.31   Section 1044 defines an 'overseas company' as a company incorporated outside the UK. This is wider than the definition of overseas company in s 744 of CA 1985 which it replaces. Section 744 of CA 1985 referred to companies incorporated outside Great Britain that establish a place of business in Great Britain. Under CA 2006, regulations made by the Secretary of State pursuant to his power under s 1046(1) will specify the connection with the UK that gives rise to the various disclosure obligations imposed under Part 34.

3. Registration

3.32   Section 1046 (duty to register particulars) provides that the regulations made by the Secretary of State may require overseas companies to register with the registrar of companies. The regulations may require particular information to be included in the registration; for example, an address for the company and details of its directors. The regulations may also require particular documents to be sent to the registrar, such as a copy of the company's constitution. Section 1046(2) ensures that the regulations implement the requirements of the Eleventh Company Law Directive under which an overseas Member State company must register if the company opens a branch in another Member State.

3.33   Section 1046(3) provides that regulations may require the overseas company to inform the registrar of companies of any changes in the details or documents it has registered. The regulations may also set deadlines for sending the information to the registrar of companies. They may also determine whether the overseas company should register with the registrar for England and Wales, the registrar for Scotland, or the registrar for Northern Ireland.

3.34   The Eleventh Company Law Directive imposed different disclosure requirements depending on where the overseas company setting up the branch is incorporated. Different reporting requirements are imposed on credit and financial institutions. Therefore, regulations under this section may make different provision according to the place where the company is incorporated and the activities carried on by it. Regulations made under this section are subject to the affirmative resolution procedure.

3.35   Section 1047 (registered name of overseas company) deals with overseas companies required to register with the registrar of companies by regulations made under s 1046. Overseas companies registered under that section will be required to provide a name for registration which will be entered on the index of company names.

3.36   The company may register its corporate name (ie its registered or legal name in its place of incorporation) or an 'alternative name'. All companies are free to choose whether to register their corporate name or an alternative name, subject to the restrictions imposed by s 1047(4) and (5). An alternative name can only be registered if it complies with the requirements imposed on the names of companies formed and registered under the Act. Likewise, unless the overseas company is incorporated in an EEA State, its corporate name can only be registered if it complies with these requirements. The only requirements of Chapters 1–4 of Part 5 (a company's name) that do not apply are the requirements for the names of certain types of company to end with certain words (ss 58–59); these rules are not appropriate for overseas companies as they are specific to the types of company formed under the Companies Act.

Subject to s 1047(5), where the overseas company is incorporated in an EEA State (defined in s 1170), it may always register its corporate name even if it does not comply with the requirements imposed on names of companies formed under the Act. Section 1047(5) states that the requirements relating to permitted characters to be found in s 57 of CA 2006 apply in every case. This section together with s 1048 replaces s 694 of CA 1985. 3.37

Section 1048 enables an overseas company to be registered under an alternative name rather than its corporate name. It also enables an overseas company to change the name by which it is registered. To do so, it must deliver a statement to the registrar of companies with its proposed new name for registration. As long as the proposed name complies with the requirements for registration under s 1047, the registrar of companies will enter it on the index of company names in place of the name previously registered. 3.38

The section also provides that whatever the name under which an overseas company is registered, whether its corporate name or an alternative, it is treated as being its corporate name for the purposes of the law in the UK. The change of name will not affect any legal proceedings that are continued or commenced by or against the company. 3.39

4. Other requirements

Section 1049 (accounts and reports: general) confers on the Secretary of State a power to make regulations requiring overseas companies to prepare accounts and directors' reports and to obtain an auditor's report. The requirements must be like those imposed on companies registered under CA 2006. The accounts, directors' report, and auditor's report requirements applying to companies formed and registered under CA 2006 appear in Part 15 (accounts and reports) and Part 16 (audit). 3.40

Regulations under this section may modify the requirements in their application to overseas companies as appropriate. Regulations under the section may require the overseas company to deliver to the registrar of companies copies of the accounts and reports prepared in accordance with the regulations; alternatively, the overseas company may be required to deliver to the registrar a copy of the accounts and reports that it prepared and had audited in accordance with the law of the country in which it is incorporated. The registrar will then place the accounts and reports on the public register. 3.41

Regulations under this section replace ss 699AA–703 of CA 1985 and Sch 21D to CA 1985. The regulations are subject to the negative resolution procedure. 3.42

Section 1050 applies only to credit or financial institutions (as defined by s 1173) incorporated or formed outside the UK and Gibraltar, with their head office outside the UK and Gibraltar but having a branch in the UK. The section gives the Secretary of State the power to make regulations specifically in respect of accounts and directors' reports by these credit or financial institutions. 3.43

3.44   Regulations under this clause will implement requirements of the Bank Branches Directive[2] of the Council of 13 February 1989. The definition of 'branch' in s 1050(2) is based on art 1(3) of the Directive[3] of the European Parliament and of the Council of 20 March 2000 relating to the taking up and pursuit of the business of credit institutions. The power to make regulations under this section takes the same pattern as under s 1049 (accounts and reports: general).

3.45   The regulations under this section replace s 699A and Sch 21c to CA 1985. The regulations are subject to the negative resolution procedure.

3.46   Section 1051 deals with trading disclosures and confers on the Secretary of State the power to make regulations as to the information that overseas companies must display in specified locations, include in specified documents or communications, or provide to those who make a request in the course of business. Regulations made under this section replace the provision made by s 693 of CA 1985. The section complements the similar power under s 82 to make regulations imposing trading disclosure obligations on companies formed and registered under the Companies Acts. The regulations are subject to the affirmative resolution procedure.

3.47   Section 1053 deals with delivery to the registrar of other returns. It confers on the Secretary of State the power to make regulations requiring companies which are required to register particulars under s 1046 to deliver returns to the registrar if they are being wound up or subjected to insolvency proceedings. The regulations may also require the liquidator of such a company to deliver returns to the registrar. They may also specify the circumstances in which a return is to be made to the registrar. They may also specify the information to be included in the return and set deadlines for sending it to the registrar (s 1053(3)). They may require notice to be given to the registrar of the appointment of a judicial factor in Scotland (s 1053(4)) and may to that end include any provision corresponding to the equivalent obligation placed on companies incorporated in the UK by s 1154 (duty to notify registrar of certain appointments etc) (s 1053(5)). The regulations replace ss 703P and 703Q of CA 1985 and are subject to the affirmative resolution procedure.

5. Supplementary matters

3.48   Section 1054 deals with offences and ensures that the regulations made under this Part are able to specify the person or persons who are to be responsible for complying with any specified requirement of the regulations. It allows regulations to provide for: an offence; who would be liable in the event of a contravention; and what might be considered a defence should a charge be brought. The maximum level of penalty permissible under the regulations on indictment is an unlimited fine and on a summary conviction a fine not exceeding level 5 on the standard scale, or, for continued contravention, a daily default fine not exceeding one-tenth of a level 5 fine.

3.49   Section 1055 deals with disclosure of an individual's residential address. It states that if the regulations under s 1046 (overseas companies: duty to register particulars) require an

---

[2] Council Directive (EEC) 89/117 on the obligations of branches established in a Member State of credit institutions and financial institutions having their head offices outside that Member State regarding the publication of annual accounting documents [1989] OJ L44.

[3] Council Directive (EC) 2000/12 relating to the taking up and pursuit of the business of credit institutions [2000] OJ L126.

overseas company to register an individual's usual residential address, then the regulations must also provide for its protection on the same basis as is provided for the directors' residential addresses in Chapter 8 of Part 10 (directors' residential addresses: protection from disclosure).

Section 1056 deals with the requirement to identify persons authorized to accept service   3.50 of documents and provides that every registered overseas company must register particulars identifying every person resident in the UK who is authorized to accept service of documents on the company's behalf or to make a statement that there is no such person. This section replaces the provisions made by s 691(1)(b)(ii) and para 3(e) of Sch 21A to CA 1985.

Section 1057 deals with which registrar to whom returns, notices, etc are to be delivered   3.51 and makes provision for the Secretary of State to have the power to make regulations in respect of overseas companies that are required to register, or have registered, particulars under s 1046 in more than one part of the UK. In such cases, regulations may set out what should happen, for example, if the overseas company has registered branches in Scotland and Northern Ireland; the regulations may require the returns or notices to be delivered to each registrar with which the company is registered, or to the registrar for such part or parts of the UK as the regulations may specify. Regulations made under this section are subject to the negative resolution procedure.

Section 1058 deals with an overseas company's duty to give notice of its ceasing to have   3.52 a registrable presence. It provides the Secretary of State with the power to make regulations requiring: (i) an overseas company to give notice to the registrar if it closes its UK branch; and (ii) an overseas company to give notice to the registrar if the circumstances that gave rise to the obligation to register particulars cease to obtain. The regulations made under this section are subject to the negative resolution procedure.

Section 1059 deals with the application of the provisions of this Part of CA 2006 where   3.53 a branch relocates from one part of the UK to another and provides that such situations are to be treated as the closing of the branch in one part and the opening of the branch in the other part. For example, if an overseas company moves a branch from Scotland to Wales, it must tell the registrar for Scotland that it is closing the branch and it must also tell the registrar for England and Wales that it is opening a branch in Wales. This section replaces the provision made by s 695A(4) of CA 1985.

4

COMPANY CONSTITUTIONS

A. INTRODUCTION

Part 3 of CA 2006 contains the provisions relating to a company's constitution. Part 4 of CA 2006 contains the provisions relating to a company's capacity and related matters. **4.01**

Part 3 consists of four chapters. Chapter 1 (s 17) is an introductory to Part 3. Chapter 2 (ss 18–28) deals with articles of association. Chapter 3 (ss 29 and 30) deals with resolutions and agreements affecting a company's constitution. Chapter 4 (ss 31–38) contains miscellaneous and supplementary provisions. **4.02**

Part 4 (ss 39–52) contains two main categories of provisions: the first (ss 39–42) governing the capacity of a company and the power of directors to bind the company and the second category (ss 43–47) which governs the formalities of doing business under the law of England and Wales or Northern Ireland. **4.03**

B. A COMPANY'S CONSTITUTION

Part 3 replaces similar provisions in CA 1985. Section 17 is new and had no equivalent in CA 1985. It sets out a definition of 'a company's constitution'. The definition is expressed to be non-exhaustive. **4.04**

Chapter 2 of Part 3 contains ss 18–28 which deal with a company's articles of association. A company's articles are rules, chosen by the company's members, which govern a company's internal affairs. They form a statutory contract between the members *inter se* and the company and its members. The articles of association are an integral part of a company's constitution. Under CA 1985, a company could divide its constitutional rules between its memorandum of association and its articles of association with the terms of its memorandum of association being capable of being altered in some respects but not in others after formation. However, under CA 2006 the memorandum of association is a very simple document of purely **4.05** historical significance. Under CA 2006, a memorandum only evidences an intention to form a company, all the company's key internal rules on matters such as the allocation of powers between the members of a company and its directors are set out in the articles of association (see s 8 (memorandum of association) and s 28 (existing companies: provision of memorandum treated as provisions of articles).

4.06   Section 18 (articles of association) replaces s 7 of CA 1985 and carries forward the requirement that all registered companies must have articles of association. Articles of association must be contained in a single document and must be divided into consecutively numbered paragraphs.

4.07   Section 19 (power of Secretary of State to prescribe model articles) gives the Secretary of State the power to prescribe by regulations model articles of association. For companies registered under previous Companies Acts the version of the model articles that was in force at the time it was registered will continue to apply (s 20(2)). Existing companies will, however, be free to adopt, wholly or in part, the model articles prescribed for companies of a particular description formed under CA 2006 (s 19(3)).

4.08   The adoption or otherwise of model articles of association by companies will be entirely a matter for the companies themselves. They will be able to incorporate (with or without amendment) provisions from the model articles and/or add to those provisions and/or exclude such provisions as they think fit.

4.09   Section 20 (default application of model articles) companies formed under CA 1985 had freedom to make such rules about their internal affairs as they thought fit, subject to the provision that if a company's articles contained anything that was contrary to the provisions of the Companies Acts, or against the general law, then it was to have no effect. Section 20 replaces s 8 of CA 1985 and carries forward the principle that where companies of certain descriptions fail to make provision for a particular matter in their registered articles (or fail to register articles at all) then the relevant model articles should apply by default to that company in the same way as Table A under CA 1985 applied to companies limited by shares.

4.10   Section 21 (amendment of articles) which replaces s 9 of CA 1985 provides that a company's articles can be amended by special resolution. Section 21 (2) and (3) make plain that this power is subject to certain rules in charities legislation about the ability of companies which are charities to change their constitutions and the effects which such changes have.

4.11   Section 22 (entrenched provisions of the articles) is a new provision which follows the recommendation of the CLR that the members of a company should be able to choose to entrench elements of the company's constitution in the articles (Final Report, paragraph 9.9). An 'entrenched' provision is one that may not be changed at all or may only be changed if certain conditions are met. Provision for 'entrenchment' may only be made on formation of a company or subsequently by unanimous consent of all of the company's members (s 22(2)). This new entrenchment mechanism replaces the practice provided for in s 17(2)(b) of CA 1985 whereby companies were able to entrench certain elements of their constitution by putting them in their memoranda and providing that they could not be altered.

4.12   Sections 23–24 stipulate the procedure that must be followed to notify the registrar of companies of entrenchment or removal of entrenched articles.

4.13   Section 31 (statement of company's objects) provides for a new approach to the question of a company's objects. Under CA 1985 all companies were required to have objects and these objects were specified in the company's memorandum of association. Based on a recommendation of the CLR (Final Report, paragraph 9.10), s 31 of CA 2006 provides that companies have unlimited objects unless the objects are specifically restricted by the articles of association.

C. CAPACITY OF A COMPANY

Section 39 (a company's capacity) provides that the validity of a company's acts is not to be questioned on the ground of lack of capacity because of anything in a company's constitution. It replaces s 35(1) of CA 1985 which made similar provision for restrictions of capacity contained in the memorandum. 4.14

D. POWER OF DIRECTORS TO BIND THE COMPANY

Section 40 (power of directors to bind the company) provides safeguards for a person dealing with a company in good faith. The section replaces s 35A of CA 1985. The power of the directors to bind the company, or authorize others to do so, is deemed not to be constrained by the company's constitution. This means that a third party dealing with a company in good faith need not concern itself about whether or not a company is acting within its constitution. Section 40(2)(b)(ii) replaces part of s 35B of CA 1985: an external party is not bound to enquire whether there are any limitations on the power of the directors. 4.15

Section 41 (constitutional limitations: transactions involving directors or their associates) retains the substance of s 322A of CA 1985. It applies to a transaction if, or to the extent that, its validity depends on s 40 (power of directors to bind the company) and provides that where the party to a transaction is an 'insider' then the protection afforded by s 40 will not apply (that is, the transaction may be avoided at the instance of the company). 4.16

Irrespective of whether the transaction is avoided, the 'insider' and any director who authorized the transaction is liable to account to the company for any gain he has made as a result of the transaction and to indemnify the company for any loss or damage that the company has suffered (s 41(3)). Under s 41(4) a transaction ceases to be voidable in certain circumstances, for example, if restitution of any money or asset that has been lost as a result of the transaction is no longer possible. 4.17

E. FORMALITIES FOR ENTERING INTO TRANSACTIONS

Section 43 (company contracts) re-enacts the provisions of s 36 of CA 1985 and provides that a contract may be entered into by a company itself by writing under its common seal or, on behalf of a company, by a person acting under its authority, express or implied. 4.18

Section 44 (execution of documents) replaces s 36A of CA 1985. It makes separate provision for private companies and public companies as the former are no longer required to have a company secretary (s 270). Section 44(1) and (2) provides that for private companies, a document may be executed by a company either by affixing its common seal or by the signature of two directors or by a single director in the presence of a witness. Section 44(3)provides a further option: signature by a director and a secretary. Section 44(5)–(8) replace s 36A(4A)–(7) of CA 1985 without change to their effect. 4.19

F. PRE-INCORPORATION TRANSACTIONS

4.20 Section 51 (pre-incorporation contracts, deeds and obligations) re-enacts s 36C of CA 1985. A company is not bound by a contract or deed purportedly made on its behalf before it came into existence unless the obligations are novated, that is a new contact must come into existence after incorporation on the same terms as the old one. Novation may be express or implied. In the absence of novation, the person purporting to act for the company or as agent for it is personally liable on the contract or deed.)

5

COMPANY AND BUSINESS NAMES

A. INTRODUCTION

CA 2006 contains two distinct Parts dealing with this area. Part 5 deals with a company's 5.01
name and Part 41 deals with business names.

Part 5 consists of six Chapters. Chapter 1 contains the general requirements relating 5.02
to a company's name. Chapter 2 deals with the requirements which need to be fulfilled
in relation to indicating company type or legal form. Chapter 3 deals with similarity
between company names. Chapter 4 deals with the power of the Secretary of State in
relation to misleading information. Chapter 5 deals with a company's change of name.
Chapter 6 deals with the requirements which a company must fulfil in relation to trading
disclosures.

Part 41 consists of three chapters. Chapter 1 deals with restricted or prohibited names. 5.03
Chapter 2 deals with the disclosure required of individuals or partnerships carrying on
business in the UK under a business name. Chapter 3 contains supplementary provisions
relating to business names.

B. COMPANY NAMES

1. Part 5, Chapter 1

(a) *General requirements*

Section 53 of CA 2006 deals with prohibited names and replaces s 26(1)(d) and (e) of CA 5.04
1985. It retains the prohibition under CA 1985 of companies registering names that cannot
be used without commission of an offence and of those that are offensive.

Section 54 deals with names suggesting a connection with government or public authority. 5.05
It replaces s 26(2)(a) of CA 1985 and it prevents a name being registered without the
Secretary of State's approval if it suggests a connection with Her Majesty's government, a
local authority, or—in a change from CA 1985—any part of the Scottish administration, or
Her Majesty's government in Northern Ireland. A new power allows similar protection to
be extended to other public authorities.

5.06   Section 55 deals with other sensitive words and expressions. It replaces ss 26(2)(b) and 29(1)(a) of CA 1985. Section 55(1) requires prior approval for the adoption of a name that includes words or expressions specified in regulations made by the Secretary of State under the section. Section 55(2) provides for the procedure to be used for making the regulations. The words and expressions protected under the Company and Business Names Regulations 1981[1] ('the 1981 regulations') included British, English, Scottish, and Welsh; chamber of commerce, charity, Her Majesty, midwife, police, and university.

5.07   Section 56 provides in certain circumstances for a duty upon an applicant to seek comment on the intended name of a government or other specified body. The section replaces s 29(1)(b), (2), (3), and (4) of CA 1985. Section 56(1) provides that the Secretary of State under his powers to make regulations under ss 54 and 55 may specify whose view must be sought when seeking approval for a name. Under the 1981 regulations, for example, the approval of the General Dental Council was required for the use of either 'dental' or 'dentistry'.

5.08   Section 57 (permitted characters) is a new provision and provides the Secretary of State with the power to make regulations specifying what letters, characters, signs or symbols, and punctuation may be used in a company's registered name. The regulations may also specify the standard or format for the name of a company for the purposes of registration. The regulations are subject to the negative resolution procedure.

2. Part 5, Chapter 2

(a) *Indications of company type or legal form*

5.09   Section 58 (public limited companies) replaces s 25(1) of CA 1985 (and also s 27(4)(b) and (d) in its application to s 25(2)). The section brings together in a single provision all the alternative statutory indicators of legal status that must be used by a public company as part of its registered name. The section does not, however, apply to community interest companies.

5.10   Section 59 (private limited companies) replaces s 25(2) of CA 1985 (and also s 27(4)(a) and (c) in their application to s 25(2)). The section brings together in a single provision all the alternative statutory indicators of legal status that must be used by a private company as part of its registered name. Again, the section does not apply to community interest companies.

5.11   Sections 60–62 of the Act replace s 30 of CA 1985. Section 30 exempted certain companies from the requirement for their names to conclude with 'limited'. Exempt companies under CA 1985 were also exempt from some of the requirements regarding the publication of their names though they still had to disclose their limited status in correspondence. Under CA 1985, exempt companies consisted of those with a licence granted under s 19 of CA 1948 and those which had delivered a statutory declaration to the registrar that the company complied with the requirements for exemption which, in effect, were that the company was non-profit-making and one or more of its objects were the promotion of commerce, art, science, education, religion, charity, or any profession.

5.12   Section 60 continues the above exemption to companies exempt under CA 1985 but, unlike CA 1985, extends it to charities and to other companies exempted by regulations made by the Secretary of State under the power granted to him by the section. So long as it

---

[1] SI 1981/1685.

continues to meet the conditions, a company formed under the earlier Acts will continue to be exempt unless and until it changes its registered name (ss 61 and 62).

Section 63 (exempt company: restriction on alteration of articles) replaces s 31(1) and (5) of CA 1985. It prohibits a company benefiting from an exemption under CA 1985 or CA 1948 (or their Northern Irish equivalents) from changing its articles in such a way that it no longer meets the requirements for the exemption. It is an offence under s 63(2) to change a company's articles in this way. 5.13

Section 64 (power to direct change of name in case of company ceasing to be entitled to exemption) replaces s 31(2)–(4) and (6) of CA 1985. The section gives the Secretary of State the power to withdraw a private company's exemption from the requirement for its name to conclude with 'limited' if the company no longer meets the criteria that applied when it was granted the exemption. 5.14

Section 65 (inappropriate use of indications of company type or legal form) replaces s 26(1)(a), (b), (bb) and (bbb) of CA 1985 which restricted the use of various words, expressions, and abbreviations which are indicators of legal status for the various types of commercial entity, eg plc, community interest company, open-ended investment company. The section provides the Secretary of State with the power to make regulations prohibiting the inclusion in a company's name of specified words, expressions, and abbreviations. The regulations under this section are subject to the negative resolution procedure. 5.15

3. Part 5, Chapter 3

(a) *Similarity to other names*

Section 66 (name not to be the same as another in the index) replaces s 26(1)(c) of CA 1985. Section 66(1) retains the prohibition which was found in s 26(1)(c) of CA 1985 on a company adopting a name that is already on the registrar's index of company names, which includes not only the names of Companies Act companies but also of various other business entities. Section 66(2) and (3) provides the Secretary of State with the power to make regulations to replace the detailed rules which were contained in s 26(3) of CA 1985 as to: (i) matters which are to be disregarded; and (ii) what words, expressions, signs, or symbols are, or are not, to be regarded as the same as each other. 5.16

Section 67 (power to direct change of name in case of similarity to existing name) replaces s 28(2) of CA 1985. The section gives the Secretary of State the power to direct a company to change its newly adopted name if the name is the same as or too like a name already on the registrar's index of company names or one which should have been there. The objective is to prevent the public being confused by the simultaneous appearance on the register of two very similar names when the similarity is such that the later name was not caught by the non-discretionary prohibition under s 67. 5.17

Section 67(2) and (3) provide power to make regulations, corresponding to that provided by s 66 to replace the detailed rules which were to be found in s 26(3) of CA 1985 as to: (i) what was to be disregarded; and (ii) what words, expressions, signs, or symbols are to be taken as the same as each other. As in s 66, s 67(4) provides for a power to make regulations permitting the use of names that would otherwise be regarded as 'too like' another name in certain circumstances or where consent is given. 5.18

Section 68 (direction to change name: supplementary provisions) replaces s 28(4) and (5) of CA 1985 as they applied to s 28(2) of CA 1985. The section provides deadlines for 5.19

the Secretary of State's giving of directions and for the company's compliance and makes failure to comply an offence.

(b) *Similarity to other name in which person has goodwill*

5.20 Sections 69–74 respond to the CLR's recommendation (Final Report, paragraph 11.50) that there be provision so that a person can apply for a company to be directed to change its name if the applicant can show that the name was chosen with the principal intention of seeking monies from him or preventing him using the name where it is one in which he has previously acquired reputation or goodwill.

5.21 Section 70 (company names adjudicators) provides the Secretary of State with the power to appoint company names adjudicators to adjudicate upon s 69 applications. Section 71 provides the Secretary of State with the power to make regulations governing proceedings before a company names adjudicator. Section 73 provides that if an objection under s 69 is upheld, then the adjudicator is to direct the company with the offending name to change its name to one that does not offend. A deadline will be set for the change and if the offending name is not changed, then the adjudicator will determine a new name for the company. Section 74 provides that a company which has received a direction from the company names adjudicator may appeal to court against the decision.

4. Part 5, Chapter 4

(a) *Other powers of the Secretary of State*

5.22 Section 75 (provision of misleading information) replaces s 28(3) of CA 1985 and, in so far as it supports that section, s 28(4)–(6) of CA 1985. Section 75 gives the Secretary of State the power to direct a company to change its name within a specified period in two circumstances: first, if misleading information was given to enable the adoption of the name; second, if an undertaking or assurance given to enable the adoption of the name has not been fulfilled. The direction, however, can only be made up to five years after the adoption of the name. The section provides that it is an offence not to comply with the Secretary of State's direction.

5.23 Section 76 (misleading indication of activities) replaces s 32 of CA 1985 and provides the Secretary of State with the power to direct a company to change its name, regardless of how long the company has had the name, in circumstances where the name gives a misleading indication of the nature of the company's activities with the result that the public are likely to suffer. The section also provides that it is an offence not to comply with the Secretary of State's direction. However, a company may within three weeks of the Secretary of State's direction appeal to the court, which can either confirm or set aside the direction.

5. Part 5, Chapter 5

(a) *Change of name*

5.24 Section 77 (change of name) replaces s 28(1) of CA 1985. Under CA 1985, companies could only change their names: (i) by special resolution; or (ii) by following a direction of the Secretary of State in the circumstances provided for by s 31 of CA 1985, which applied only to companies exempted from concluding their name with 'limited'. Section 77 provides, however, for four further circumstances: (i) where the means are provided for in the company's articles (meaning that the company will be able to determine the procedures for changing its own name); (ii) by an order of the company names adjudicator if an objection under s 73 has been upheld; (iii) on the determination of a new name by the court under s 74; and (iv) under s 1033 (company's name on restoration to the register). Sections 78–80 detail the procedures that need to be followed when and upon changing a company's name. Section 81 states the effect that a change of name has.

6. Part 5, Chapter 6

(a) *Trading disclosures*

Section 82 (requirement to disclose company name etc) replaces ss 348(1), 349(1) and 351(1)   5.25
and (2) of CA 1985 and, in so far as it applies to companies, s 4(1) of the Business Names Act 1985. Section 82 provides the Secretary of State with the power to make regulations requiring every company: (i) to display specified information in specified locations; (ii) to state specified information in specified descriptions of document or communication; and (iii) to provide specified information on request to those they deal with in the course of their business.

Section 83, which replaces s 349(4) of CA 1985 and, in so far as it applies to companies,   5.26
s 5 of the Business Names Act 1985, and s 84, which replaces ss 348(2), 349(2) and (3) and 351(5) of CA 1985 and, in so far as it applies to companies, Pt 7 of the Business Names Act 1985, deal with the civil and criminal consequences of a failure to make the required disclosures.

Section 85 is an altogether new provision and allows for a company's name as used   5.27
to comply with the disclosure requirements to be not exactly the same as the registered name. Permitted differences include case characters, diacritical marks, or punctuation and formatting style so long as there is no real likelihood of the names being taken to be different names.

C. BUSINESS NAMES

Part 41, as has been said, is divided into three chapters: the first chapter, ss 1192–1199,   5.28
which deals with restricted or prohibited names, is mainly divided between those sections dealing with sensitive words or expressions and those dealing with misleading names; the second chapter, ss 1200–1206, which deals with the disclosure required in the cases of individuals and partnerships, is mainly divided between the disclosure requirements and the consequences of a failure to make the required disclosure; and the third chapter, ss 1207 and 1208, which contain supplementary provisions relating to the Part.

1. Part 41, Chapter 1

(a) *Restricted or prohibited names*

Section 1192 (application of the Chapter) partly replaces s 1 of the Business Names Act   5.29
1985. It ensures that the restrictions on the use of names in the course of business apply to all persons carrying on business in the UK. As prior to the Act, the restrictions do not apply to individuals if they trade either alone or in partnership under their surnames augmented only by their forenames and/or initials. Sole traders and individuals carrying on business in partnership are also excluded from the scope of the Chapter if the only addition to their

name is to show that the business is carried on in succession to a former owner of the business.

5.30   Sections 1193–1195 replace ss 2, 3, 6, and 7 of the Business Names Act 1985. These sections require prior approval for the use of any name for carrying on a *business* in instances where a *company* would require approval before *it* could be registered.

5.31   Section 1197 (name containing inappropriate indication of company type or legal form) replaces ss 33, 34, and 34A of CA 1985 and gives the Secretary of State the power to make regulations prohibiting a person from carrying on business in the UK under a name consisting of or containing specified words, expressions, or other indications: (a) that are associated with a particular type of company or form of organization; or (b) that are similar to words, expressions, or other indications associated with a particular type of company or form of organization.

5.32   Section 1198 (name giving misleading indication of activities) makes it an offence for a person to carry on business in the UK under a name that gives so misleading an indication of the nature of its business activities as would be likely to cause harm to the public.

2. Part 41, Chapter 2

(a) *Disclosure required in the case of individual or partnership*

5.33   Chapter 2 re-enacts for individuals and partnerships the Business Names Act 1985 provisions relating to information which must be displayed at places of business and in correspondence. These sections ensure that a business's suppliers and customers can discover the legal identity of the person with which they are doing business and can serve documents upon it.

5.34   Section 1200 (application of this chapter) partly replaces s 1 of the Business Names Act 1985 and states that Chapter 2 applies to an individual or partnership carrying on business in the UK under a business name.

5.35   Section 1201 (information required to be disclosed) replaces s 4(1)(a)(i), (ii), and (iv) of the Business Names Act 1985 and specifies the information that is to be the subject of disclosure under the Chapter.

5.36   Sections 1202 (disclosure required: business documents etc) and 1203 (exemptions for large partnerships if certain conditions met) replace s 4(1)(a) and (2)–(7) of the Business Names Act 1985 and are designed to ensure that customers and suppliers:

(1) of sole traders know the true identity of the person with whom they are dealing and have an address for him/her which is effective for the service of documents relating to the business;

(2) of partnerships with 20 or fewer partners know the identity of every partner and the address which is effective for the service of documents relating to the business;

(3) of larger partnerships know the address which is effective for the service of documents relating to the business and either the identity of every partner of the address at which they can discover the identity of every partner.

5.37   Section 1204 (disclosure required: business premises) replaces s 4(1)(b) of the Business Names Act 1985 in so far as it applies to sole traders and partnerships and makes provision to enable customers and suppliers to discover the name(s) and the address for service of documents when visiting any business premises of the trader or partners.

Section 1205, which replaces s 7 of the Business Names Act 1985 in so far as it applies   5.38
to sole traders and partnerships, and s 1206, which replaces s 5 of the Business Names Act
1985 in so far as it applies to sole traders and partnerships, deal with the criminal and civil
consequences of a failure to make the required disclosures.

6

MEMBERSHIP OF A COMPANY

A. INTRODUCTION AND 'MEMBERSHIP'

Reforms in this area, along with changes in the law on proxies (discussed in Chapter 12, **6.01** paragraph 12.27 below), form the backbone of the government's 'enfranchising indirect investors'[1] agenda; and, although most of the previous provisions on membership and its consequences are restated, they are joined in Parts 8 and 9 of CA 2006 by a number of significant additions.

The definition of 'member', previously contained in the well-known s 22 of CA 1985, is **6.02** now found in s 112. Three new words in s 112(1)—'become members and ...'—provide clarification that subscribers to the memorandum immediately become members upon the company's incorporation.

The general prohibition on a subsidiary[2] being a member of its holding company[3] **6.03** (previously found in s 23(1) of CA 1985) is restated in s 136, while ss 138–140 and 141–142 restate, respectively, the exemptions for where: (i) in certain circumstances the subsidiary is only concerned as personal representative or trustee; and (ii) the subsidiary only holds the shares in the ordinary course of its business as intermediary. Section 137 restates the previous saving for shares acquired before the general prohibition came into force.

As under the previous law, a member is bound by the provisions of the constitution as **6.04** if 'there were covenants on the part of the company and of each member to observe those provisions' (s 33 of CA 2006, restating the troublesome s 14 of CA 1985).

B. REGISTER OF MEMBERS

Provisions regarding the register of members are restated in Chapter 2 of Part 8. Significant **6.05** changes arise from the vocal concerns expressed in some quarters about the need to protect shareholders from the dissemination of their personal details.

---

[1] See DTI, *Company Law Reform White Paper* (Cm 6456, March 2005), 18–20.
[2] Or a 'nominee' acting on its behalf: see s 144. By s 143, in companies limited by shares, references to shares are to the relevant interest of members in such companies.
[3] For 'subsidiary' and 'holding company' see s 1159.

1. The register and index of members

6.06 Most of the obligations (previously contained in s 352 of CA 1985) relating to the requirement to keep a register of members and its content are restated in s 113. A new provision in s 113(5) clarifies the position of joint holders of shares: although they must be treated as a single member and the register must show a single address, the register must also state the names of each joint holder.

6.07 Also restated is the requirement for companies with more than 50 members to keep an index of the names of members (unless the form of the register itself constitutes an index: see s 115).

6.08 As previously stated, no notice of any trust (whether express, implied, or constructive) is to be entered on the register of members (see now s 126), although practitioners should note the facilitation of rights given to persons standing 'behind' members discussed at paragraph 6.22 *et seq* below.

6.09 The register of members continues to be prima facie evidence of the matters entered on it (see s 127) and s 125 outlines the circumstances in which the court may rectify the register of members (restating s 359 of CA 1985).

6.10 By s 121, companies may now remove former members from the register 10 years after the cessation of membership rather than the previous 20, while s 128 reduces the time limit for the enforceability of claims arising out of an entry, non-entry, or deletion from the register from 20 to 10 years.

2. Content of the register of members

6.11 The obligation for a company holding its own shares in treasury[4] to be entered as a member (of itself) now merits its own section (see s 124).

6.12 A single member private company continues to require a statement in its register of members that it is such, either when the number of members falls to one (in which case it must record the date that occurred) or—which appears to be a new provision—where it is formed with one member (see s 123). That section also restates the requirement that the increase from one member to two or more (and the date it occurs) also needs to be recorded.

6.13 As before, the fact of the issue of share warrants must be entered in the register of members along with the date of issue and a statement of the shares which the warrants represent (see s 122). That section also restates the requirement to amend (if necessary) the register so that no person is named as holder of the shares represented by the warrant. In the latter regard, the new words 'if necessary' in s 122(1)(b) clarify that shares need not first be issued in registered form, but may instead be issued directly in warrant to bearer form.

3. Inspection of the register or index of members

6.14 A company's register of members must be 'kept available for inspection' either at its registered office or at some other place in the part of the UK where the company is registered (see s 114). This is a sensible change from the previous provision (s 353 of CA 1985) which required the register to be 'kept' at the registered office—albeit that if the work of maintaining the register was carried out elsewhere it could be kept there (so long as that place was in the

---

[4] On which see Chapter 6 of Part 18 and see Chapter 8, para 8.37 below.

same part of the UK as the registered office). The new provision recognizes that where the register is maintained is immaterial: it might, thanks to modern technology, be maintained anywhere in the world. Having the register available for inspection (eg by computer) is the important aspect.

The rights of any person to inspect the register and index of members, and to receive 6.15 copies of the register or parts of it, are restated in s 116. However, in response to concerns about member privacy, the person making any such request must now outline his name and address, the purpose for which the information will be used, and whether the information will be passed on to any other person (and, if so, that person's name, address, and their purpose for seeking the information).

It is an offence for a person knowingly or recklessly to make a misleading, false, or 6.16 deceptive request under s 116 (see s 119(1)).

On receiving a request for inspection or a copy, the company has two options. Within 6.17 five days it must either comply with the request or apply to the court seeking an order sanctioning non-disclosure (see s 117(1)). The court can make such an order where it is satisfied that the inspection or copy is not sought for a proper purpose (s 117(3))—and it may also prospectively order that the company need not comply with any similar requests in the future. Where the court makes no order under s 117, the company must immediately comply with the request.

Section 118 makes it an offence for the company (and every officer in default) to refuse 6.18 to allow inspection or supply a copy otherwise than in accordance with an order of the court as described above.

When granting inspection or providing a copy of the register, the company must state the 6.19 date to which it is made up (and that there are no further alterations to be made on that date): see s 120, responding to a CLR concern to ensure that those inspecting are properly informed about the accuracy of information obtained.

Once in receipt of the information under s 116, it is an offence for the person to disclose 6.20 the information, or fail to prevent its disclosure, to any other person knowing or having reason to suspect that that other person will use it for an improper purpose (see s 119(2)).

4. Overseas branch registers

Chapter 3 of Part 8 restates the regime (previously in s 362 and Sch 14 to CA 1985) allowing 6.21 companies with an overseas branch in specified countries to maintain in that country a register of members resident there. However, CA 2006 does not appear to have retained the power to apply the provisions relating to registers of members to the UK branches of foreign companies keeping their equivalent of overseas branch registers here (cf Part 3 of Sch 14 to CA 1985).

C. INDIRECT INVESTORS EXERCISING MEMBERS' RIGHTS

Part 9 of CA 2006 introduces a significant change to the previously hallowed rule that 6.22 companies were concerned only with their members as registered and not with those who were really interested in the shares—such as the investment fund using a nominee to hold its shares. It attempts to fill what is perceived to be an undesirable gap in corporate governance caused by the nominee member generally having no (financial) interest in exercising the rights attaching to shares and, for example, holding management to account. The Act sets out to achieve this in two ways.

1. Facilitating companies' recognition of indirect investors

6.23 The first applies to all companies. Section 145 facilitates the ability of companies to recognize 'indirect investors' by providing that where articles of association enable members to appoint others to enjoy or exercise their (member's) rights, references in CA 2006 to members and their rights shall include the nominated person. Thus, the nominated person, rather than the nominee member, becomes entitled to receive written resolutions or annual accounts. Likewise the nominated person is entitled to require the directors to call a general meeting.

6.24 However, this provision has one significant limitation: it does not create rights that the *nominated person* can *enforce* against the company (see s 145(4)(a)). Instead, if the company refuses to recognize the nominated person (eg it fails to send him the accounts), only the *member* can take enforcement action.[5] Nor do the provisions of s 145 affect the nominee member's ability to dispose of the shares (or any other relevant interest in the company) (see 145(4)(b)).

2. Traded companies: information rights

6.25 The second innovation relates only to 'traded companies'[6] and allows members of such companies who 'hold shares on behalf of another person' (such as nominees or intermediaries) to nominate that person to enjoy 'information rights' (see s 146).

6.26 Following nomination, all the provisions of CA 2006 and of the company's articles relating to communications with members then also have effect in relation to the nominated person (see s 150(3)).

6.27 Such a nomination is additional to, rather than instead of, the member's rights (see s 150(5)). It may be terminated at the request of either the member or the nominated person (s 148(2)) and terminates automatically on the bankruptcy (or, as appropriate, winding-up) of the nominated person (s 148(3)). It also terminates automatically if, following an enquiry from the company as to whether he wishes to remain nominated, the nominated person fails to respond within 28 days (s 148(7)).

6.28 As for the facilitative right discussed at paragraphs 6.23–6.24 above, a company's failure to recognize 'information rights' is only actionable by the *member* (and not by the nominated person) as if it were a breach of the articles (s 150(2)).

6.29 'Information rights' is comprehensively and exclusively defined in s 146(3) and includes a general right to receive all communications from the company to its members as well as the right to require copies of accounts and reports and the right to require hard copies of electronic documents.[7] The nomination should generally only be in respect of *all* the relevant rights, otherwise the company need not act on the nomination (s 146(5)).

6.30 The default means of providing information to the nominated person pursuant to these provisions is by a website, although nominated persons can opt for hard copies by

---

[5] Although it is likely that the contractual or other relationship between the nominee member and the nominated person will be such as to enable the nominated person to compel the member to take such enforcement action.

[6] Companies whose shares are admitted to trading on a regulated market.

[7] In s 1143 and Schs 4 and 5—discussed in Chapter 11, at para 11.21 *et seq.*

providing an address and directing the member to inform the company accordingly (see s 147).[8]

By s 149, any notice of a meeting sent to a nominated person must include a statement   6.31
that he may have a right: (i) to be appointed, or to have someone else appointed, as proxy
for the meeting; or (ii) to give instructions to the registered member on how to vote.

3. Exercising rights where shares held on behalf of others

Sections 152–153 supplement the provisions discussed above.   6.32

Nominee or intermediary members often hold large numbers of shares on behalf of various   6.33
different persons. Section 152 makes clear that not all the rights attaching to those shares
need be exercised in the same way (or indeed at all)—although a member intending to
exercise the rights in different ways must inform the company accordingly, failing which it
may assume they are being exercised in the same way.

Section 153 outlines rights for indirect investors to join together with each other (and   6.34
with members who hold shares on their own behalf)[9] so as to exercise various members'
rights, such as the power to require the circulation of resolutions prior to an AGM or the
power to require an independent report on a poll.[10]

---

[8] Though the provisions are also subject to the provisions allowing traded companies to agree to communicate electronically or by website—as to which see Parts 3 and 4 of Sch 5 to CA 2006.

[9] Section 153(2) contains minimum numbers requirements.

[10] Section 153(1) contains a full list of the powers.

7

SHARES

A. SHARE CAPITAL

Much of the previous law in relation to share capital is restated in Pt 17 of CA 2006. In some places the previous law is restated using the same words used in CA 1985 and in some sections different words are used but apparently to the same effect. The purpose of this Chapter is to draw attention to changes of significance made by CA 2006. — 7.01

The share capital of a company is divided into shares. Shares are personal as opposed to real property. Under the previous law it was possible to convert shares into stock. That will no longer be permitted after the commencement of CA 2006. This change applies to shares issued both before and after the commencement of CA 2006. Where shares have already been converted into stock under the prior law the company can, subject to authorization by ordinary resolution, convert the stock back to shares of any nominal value.[1] — 7.02

Previously, a company had to have an authorized share capital which acted as a ceiling on the amount of shares which a company might issue. This requirement has now been abolished. CA 2006 provides, however, by s 542 that the shares in a limited company must have a fixed nominal value, eg £1, 1p, or €1. An allotment of a share without a nominal value is void. Shares can be denominated in any currency and different classes of shares can be denominated in different currencies. Furthermore, if a company purports to allot shares in contravention of s 542 an offence is committed by every officer in default. — 7.03

The provisions of the previous law relating to the numbering of shares and to transferability of shares are restated in ss 543 and 544 with only minor alterations. — 7.04

Section 546 defines issued share capital and allotted share capital. Issued share capital will include allotted share capital. References to issued share capital or allotted share capital include shares taken on the formation of the company. The definitions of called-up share — 7.05

---

[1] See ss 540(3) and 620.

capital and equity share capital remain as under the previous law and are restated in more or less identical words in ss 547 and 548.

B. ISSUE AND ALLOTMENT OF SHARES

7.06　This section is concerned with the original issue of shares, ie the acquisition of new shares which have not previously been issued as opposed to 'second-hand' ones. The allotment of shares on behalf of the company is generally carried out by the directors, but currently they are only entitled to do so if they are authorized by ordinary resolution or by the articles of association. In addition, the extent and duration of the authority of the directors is currently constrained in various ways.

7.07　The underlying purpose of CA 2006 is to reduce the regulation of private companies whilst ensuring the protection of the public in relation to the workings of public companies. To this end CA 2006 relaxes, but does not remove in all cases, the requirement in relation to private companies under which an expiry date for the authority given to the directors to allot shares must be given. Thus, a private company can by resolution give the directors authority to allot shares either for an indefinite or for a fixed period. In some cases, referred to below, the need for prior authorization is removed altogether.

7.08　The way in which the change in the law is effected is to provide in s 549 of CA 2006 that the directors may not allot shares or grant rights to subscribe for shares or to convert any security into shares except in accordance with ss 550 and/or 551. There are exceptions to the requirement to comply with ss 550 and 551: (a) where the shares are to be allotted pursuant to an employee's share scheme;[2] and (b) where the right to subscribe for, or to convert any security into, shares already exists the directors may allot shares pursuant to that right.[3]

7.09　Section 550 provides that, where the company is a private company with only one class of shares and where it will only have one class of shares after the allotment there is generally no requirement to have the prior authority from the company's members to allot shares. This general power may be restricted or removed by the articles of association. The definition of 'classes of shares' is contained in s 629.

7.10　Section 551 replaces s 80(3)–(8) of CA 1985 and applies not only to private companies which will have more than one class of shares after the allotment but also to public companies. Section 551 provides that the directors may only allot shares (or grant rights to subscribe for shares or to convert any security into shares) if they have the prior authorization of the company to do so either by ordinary resolution of the company in general meeting or contained in the articles of association.

7.11　Section 551(2)–(5) sets out the way in which prior authorization (or a renewal of authorization) can be given. As under the previous law, the authorization may not be given for a period in excess of five years and must state the maximum amount of share capital which can be allotted pursuant to the authority given. The limit can be by reference to the number of shares or their nominal value.

7.12　Somewhat strangely an ordinary resolution will be effective for giving authorization even though it has the effect of altering the articles, something which could normally only be done by a special resolution.

---

[2] See s 549(2) which mirrors s 80(2) of CA 1985.　　[3] See s 549(3).

If the rules in relation to allotment contained in ss 550 and/or 551 referred to above are 7.13 not complied with any director who knowingly and wilfully allots shares in contravention of them is guilty of an offence[4] but the allotment is not invalidated.[5]

The rules on the prohibition of the payment of commissions, the giving of discounts and 7.14 the making of allowances set out in ss 552 and 553 remain, albeit differently drafted, the same as set out in CA 1985. The provisions of the previous law in this regard dealing with the contents of prospectuses is not retained as that is now a matter for Prospectus Rules made under Pt 6 of FSMA 2000.

C. REGISTRATION OF ALLOTMENT

A company (whether public or private) must register an allotment of shares as soon as 7.15 practicable and in any event within two months of the allotment itself.[6] This is a departure from the previous provisions under s 183A of CA 1985. A failure to comply with this requirement gives rise to an offence by the company and every director in default. Summary conviction gives rise to a liability to a fine not exceeding level 3 on the standard scale and, if the contravention continues, to a daily default fine. The company's duties in relation to the issue of share certificates, etc are set out in Part 21 of CA 2006.

Section 555 requires any company limited by shares or a company limited by guarantee 7.16 having a share capital to deliver to the registrar of companies within one month of the allotment a return of the allotment. The return must contain the prescribed information and be accompanied by a statement of capital. The 'statement of capital' is a new requirement and is, in essence, a snapshot of the company's total subscribed capital at a particular point in time, ie the date of the return. This requirement applies to both public and private companies and will mean that the register should contain more up-to-date information in relation to share capital than was previously the case.

The statement of capital will contain more than simply the total nominal value of the 7.17 subscribed capital. It must include, where there is more than one class of shares, the prescribed particulars of the rights attaching to each class of shares, the total number of shares of each class and the aggregate nominal value of the shares of each class, the amount paid up and the amount unpaid (if any) in relation to each share whether of the nominal value or by way of premium.[7]

Where a company is unlimited and it allots shares of a class with rights which are not 7.18 identical (save in relation to the right to dividends in the 12 months immediately following the allotment) to the rights attaching to shares already issued it must comply with s 556 by delivering a return of the allotment to the registrar for registration within one month of the allotment. The return must contain the prescribed particulars of the rights attaching to the shares.

Section 557 creates a new offence of failing to comply with ss 555 and/or 556. There 7.19 is power under s 555(3) to apply for relief where the default is in failing to file the return within the prescribed one-month period and the default was inadvertent or accidental. If the court is satisfied of the inadvertence or accidental nature of the default and considers it just and equitable to do so it can extend the period for delivery of the return for such period as it thinks proper.

---

[4] See s 549(5).   [5] See s 549(6).   [6] See s 554.   [7] See s 555(4).

D. PRE-EMPTION

7.20 Under the previous law and subject to certain exceptions, a company wishing to allot shares was required to offer them to existing shareholders first. The rationale behind this was that a shareholder should be entitled to protect his proportion of the equity in a company by having the opportunity to subscribe for any new issue in the same proportion as his existing shareholding bears to the existing total. This principle remains unchanged by CA 2006. The exemptions to the pre-emption rules and the ways in which the rules may be excluded remain as under the previous law. The major changes made by CA 2006 relate to the ways in which the pre-emption rights can be excluded or disapplied. The difference between 'exclusion' and 'disapplication' is essentially that the latter applies only to the particular allotment, whereas the former relates to allotments in general.

7.21 One minor change is that the pre-emption offer can be communicated to the existing shareholder by electronic means as an alternative to a hard copy (as under the previous law). Clearly this can only be done if the shareholder has provided an email address for service to the company. CA 2006 contains no requirement that a shareholder shall do so. This will make compliance with time periods easier, particularly where shareholders are resident overseas.

7.22 Section 569 provides that the directors of a company with only one class of shares can be given power by the articles or by special resolution to allot shares of that class as if the pre-emption provisions set out in s 561 either did not apply or applied with such modifications as the directors may determine.

7.23 Section 570 provides that where the directors have a general authorization to allot shares they may be given general power either by the articles or by special resolution pursuant to s 570 to allot shares as if s 561 did not apply or subject to such modifications as they may determine. The power once given will continue until the general authorization to allot shares is revoked or, if not renewed, expires. If the authorization is renewed the power may also be renewed by special resolution.

7.24 Where the directors are authorized to allot shares for the purposes of s 551 the company in general meeting can, pursuant to s 571, by special resolution give the directors the power to do so in relation to a particular allotment without following the pre-emption provisions in s 561 or with such modifications as are specified in the resolution. This power is more limited than the power in s 570. A special resolution under s 571 must not be proposed unless the directors recommend it and they have complied with the provisions in s 571(6)–(7), which require the directors to set out in writing their reasons for making the recommendation and to provide details of the amount payable in respect of the proposed allotment. This amount must be justified by the directors. A copy of the report must be circulated to every member who is entitled to vote on the proposed resolution in time for him to consider it before he exercises his right to vote. These rules mirror s 95(2) of CA 1985. The provisions in relation to misleading, false, or deceptive statements in such a report set out in s 95(6) of CA 1985 remain unchanged and are restated in s 572.

7.25 Under the previous law, if a company bought back its own shares it was normally required to cancel those shares. There were certain exceptions to this rule notably in relation to listed companies which could elect to hold them 'in treasury'. A share which is held in treasury can be sold at some future time. The directors can sell shares held 'in treasury' without obtaining the authorization of the company to do so but the pre-emption provisions still apply. Section 573 provides that the directors may be given power by the articles of association or by special resolution to sell treasury shares without applying the pre-emption provisions of s 561 or applying those provisions subject to such modifications as are specified in the resolution.

E. OFFERS TO THE PUBLIC

The general prohibition on private companies limited by shares or by guarantee offering   7.26
shares to the public or allotting shares with the intention that they be offered to the public is restated in Chapter 1 of Part 20 of CA 2006 with no significant amendment. Although public companies are not subject to any such prohibition the issue of shares to the public is regulated.

Public companies are subject to a minimum share capital requirement as set out in   7.27
Chapter 2 of Part 20 and if they fall below it they are required to register as private companies.

Section 578 deals with the situation where shares in a public company are offered for   7.28
subscription and not all the shares offered are taken up or other conditions specified in the offer are not met. In that event, unless the offer was made on the basis that it would still go ahead even if all the shares were not taken up or if the conditions were not met, a public company must not allot any of the shares offered. It is not possible for the terms of the offer to override the terms of this section. The purpose of this section is to protect persons who apply for shares. A public company will typically make such an offer when it has a particular need for capital. If only some of the shares offered are subscribed for, the capital may be insufficient for the company's needs. Those accepting the offer may be prejudiced in these circumstances if the offer could go ahead even though undersubscribed.

Section 578 provides that, if the offer remains undersubscribed for 40 days after it has   7.29
first been made, the money received from those who did apply must be returned. Interest will be payable after the expiration of 48 days from the date the offer was made. The rate of interest will be the same as applying on Civil Judgments, ie at present eight per cent per annum. Under CA 1985 the rate of interest was five per cent.

Under s 578 the time limits of 40 and 48 days run from the making of the offer   7.30
and not from the issue of the prospectus as was the case under CA 1985. In practice this may make little difference. As the need for and the contents of the prospectus are now a matter for securities law the provisions of ss 82 and 83 of CA 1985 have been repealed.

An allotment made in contravention of s 578 is voidable at the instance of the applicant   7.31
for the shares.[8] It remains voidable even where the company is in the course of being wound up. A director of a company who knowingly contravenes or permits or authorizes an allotment in contravention of s 578 is liable to compensate the company and the allottee for any loss, damages, costs, and expenses that they have respectively incurred. An action for recovery of such losses, etc may not be brought more than two years from the date of the allotment.[9]

---

[8] See s 579.   [9] See s 579(4).

F. CERTIFICATION AND TRANSFER OF SECURITIES

7.32 Under the previous law in England and Wales, a certificate under the common seal of the company was prima facie evidence of a shareholder's title to his shares. This remains the position. The rules in relation to certification and transfer of shares is largely restated using different wording but apparently to similar effect and in a different order than under CA 1985 in ss 768–782 of CA 2006.

G. PAPERLESS TRANSACTIONS

7.33 Chapter 2 of Pt 21 of CA 2006 deals with the ways in which title, including equitable title to, and the transfer of title in, securities (ie shares, debentures, debenture stock, stock, loan stock, bonds, etc as set out in s 783(a) of the Act) can be evidenced without written instrument. This Chapter largely restates the law in this regard previously set out in s 207 of CA 1989, but there are some significant additions. In accordance with the general trend in recent legislation the power to make regulations under the Chapter is reserved to the Secretary of State by virtue of ss 784 and 786 of CA 2006. The regulations anticipated by s 786 are related to specific topics whereas the regulations under s 784 are anticipated to be more general. The regulations anticipated by s 786 are intended to enable members of a company to decide, by ordinary resolution, to adopt arrangements under which title to securities or the transfer of title to securities is to be evidenced and transferred without written instrument. Section 787 reserves power to the Secretary of State or such other person who has the power to make regulations under Ch 2 of Pt 21 to make certain consequential orders and provisions relevant to this Chapter of CA 2006.

8

MAINTENANCE AND ALTERATION
OF CAPITAL

A. MAINTENANCE OF CAPITAL

Section 617 prohibits a limited company with a share capital from altering its share capital **8.01** save in the ways set out in CA 2006. A company may increase its capital by allotting new shares in accordance with Part 17 of CA 2006 and can reduce its share capital in accordance with Chapter 10 of Part 17.[1]

A company can subdivide or consolidate any of its share capital as set out in s 618. **8.02** Subdivision and consolidation has no effect on share capital per se. Shares can be subdivided into shares of a smaller nominal amount than its existing shares and can consolidate any of its share capital into shares of a larger nominal value than previously. It is essential in order to comply with the statutory provisions that the proportion between the amount paid and the amount (if any) unpaid on the shares remains the same before and after subdivision or consolidation. Before the company exercises the power to subdivide or consolidate shares an ordinary resolution of the members is required authorizing it to do so. The resolution may authorize the particular exercise of the power or powers at a particular time or in specific circumstances or on more than one occasion. The company's articles may exclude or restrict the exercise of the power to subdivide or consolidate shares.[2]

Section 619 provides that notice must be given to the registrar of companies of the exercise **8.03** of the powers conferred by s 618 within one month of their exercise. The notice must be accompanied by a statement of capital setting out the total number of shares of the company, the aggregate nominal value of the same and details in relation to each class of shares of the rights attaching to that class of shares, the total number of shares of that class, and the aggregate number of shares in that class. Details of the amount paid up and the amount (if any) unpaid on each share, whether on account of the nominal value or by way of premium,

---

[1] See paras 8.12 *et seq.*   [2] See s 618.

must also be given. A failure to comply with s 619 gives rise to an offence committed by the company and every officer of the company who is in default punishable by a fine as set out in s 619(5).

8.04 As is out in Chapter 7 of this guide CA 2006 repeals the previous ability of a company to convert paid up shares into stock. If a company had already done so before the commencement of CA 2006, s 620 empowers it to reconvert the stock into paid up shares of any nominal value subject to the passing of an ordinary resolution of the members as set out in s 620(2) and (3).

8.05 Notice of exercise of the power to reconvert stock must be given to the registrar of companies within one month of the exercise of the same pursuant to s 621. The notice must be accompanied by a statement of capital in the same form as under s 619 with the same consequences in the event of a default.

8.06 A company may, following an ordinary resolution to do so, convert shares having a nominal value in one currency into shares having a nominal value in another currency. This is referred to in s 622 of CA 2006 as 'redenomination'. The conversion must be made at the appropriate spot rate of exchange specified in the resolution which can be the rate prevailing on a day specified in the resolution or the average of the rates over a specified period of time. The day or period specified in the resolution must be within 28 days of the day before the resolution is passed. The resolution may impose conditions on the redenomination and if it does they must be complied with before the redenomination takes place. The redenomination can take effect on the day the resolution is passed or on such later date as is specified in or determined in accordance with the resolution. The resolution will lapse if the redenomination does not take effect within 28 days of the resolution. The power to redenominate shares can be prohibited or restricted by the articles.

8.07 Notice of the redenomination accompanied by a statement of capital in the same form as that referred to in paragraph 8.03 above and with the same consequences in the event of default is required by reason of s 625 of CA 2006.

8.08 A redenomination of shares may be coupled with a reduction in capital pursuant to s 626 if the company is of the opinion that a reduction is necessary for the purpose of adjusting the nominal value of the redenominated shares to obtain values which are more suitable.[3] A reduction of capital under s 626 requires the passing of a special resolution no more than three months after the resolution authorizing the redenomination.[4] The amount by which a company's capital can be reduced under this section cannot exceed ten per cent of the nominal value of the company's allotted share capital before the reduction.[5] A reduction under this section does not affect any liability in relation to shares which are not fully paid up.[6] This section is outside the general regime for reduction set out in Chapter 10 of Part 17 of CA 2006 and that Chapter does not have to be complied with.[7]

8.09 Notice of the reduction of capital accompanied by a statement of capital must be given to the registrar of companies under s 627. See paragraph 8.03 for the contents of a statement of capital and the consequences of default.

8.10 Section 626 does not define what is meant by 'suitable' but it is assumed that a reduction under this section will usually be considered 'suitable' when the redenomination would result in a share with a cumbersome nominal value such as $2.06. In such a case, the company could resolve to reduce capital by redenominating the shares with a nominal value of $2. In

---

[3] Section 626(1).   [4] Section 626(2) and (3).   [5] Section 626(4).
[6] Section 626(5).   [7] Section 626(6).

other words it will be used to round down values to an easy-to-use or round figure. Rounding up, of course, is possible without any resolution as the capital is maintained or increased rather than being reduced.

The amount by which the company's capital is reduced by the implementation of the procedure under s 626 must be transferred to a reserve account known as a redenomination reserve in accordance with s 628 and can be used in the manner therein set out.   8.11

Chapter 10 of CA 2006 sets out the ways other than in accordance with s 626 whereby a limited company can reduce its capital. In general terms the law remains unchanged from that set out in ss 135–140 of CA 1985. There are some changes of wording and some minor changes but essentially the procedure remains as in s 135 of CA 1985 in that a special resolution of a company's members is required and the reduction must be confirmed by the court. The circumstances in which a company may reduce its capital have been extended by the insertion of three additional subsections in s 641, which replaces s 135 of CA 1985. Section 641(1)(a) provides that a private company limited by shares will now be entitled to reduce its capital by special resolution supported by a solvency statement. For the procedure for such a reduction see ss 642–644. This procedure can only be used if there will be at least one member holding a non-redeemable share following the reduction.   8.12

Under the previous law a company could only reduce its capital under s 135 of CA 1985 if its articles authorized such a reduction. This requirement has been removed and now a company can utilize the power to reduce capital under ss 641 *et seq* unless it is prohibited from so doing or its right to do so is restricted by its articles.   8.13

Whether the solvency statement procedure introduced for private companies is used or the court authorization route is followed the company must pass a special resolution authorizing the reduction.   8.14

The procedure for an application to the court for approval of a reduction of capital remains as before and is restated in s 645. Creditors are entitled to object, as set out in s 646, and the court shall settle a list of creditors under s 646(2) unless the court directs in an appropriate case that this provision shall not apply. This will usually be where the court is satisfied that creditors will not be prejudiced by the reduction. In the event that s 646(2) does apply s 653 restates the previous law relating to the liability to creditors who are omitted from the list of creditors. The liability of members following a reduction in capital remains as under CA 1985 and is restated with slight changes of wording in s 652.   8.15

If the reduction is effected by special resolution and solvency statement, the resolution, the solvency statement, and other key documents have to be delivered to the registrar in accordance with s 644. Under the previous law, if the reduction was effected by special resolution and order of the court the order confirming the reduction and the minute of the reduction had to be registered with the registrar of companies before the reduction takes effect. This requirement has been updated by s 649 so as to replace the requirement to register a copy of the minute of the reduction with a requirement to register a statement of capital together with the order of the court. As to the contents of the statement of capital see paragraph 8.03. The resolution for the reduction of capital only takes effect in accordance with s 649(3) which in most cases will be on the registration of the order and statement of capital. The previous requirement of publication of the reduction in the manner directed by the court remains.[8] The registrar is required to certify registration[9] and the certificate   8.16

---

[8] Section 649(4).   [9] Section 649(5).

is conclusive evidence of compliance with the requirements of the Act and the company's share capital as stated in the statement of capital.[10]

8.17   The rules relating to a public company reducing its capital below the authorized minimum is restated with only very minor amendments in s 650. The procedure for the expedited re-registration of a public company as a private company is restated in s 651.

8.18   Chapter 11 of Part 17 of CA 2006 sets out miscellaneous and supplementary provisions relating to Part 17 which by and large restates the previous law. Section 657, however, gives power to the Secretary of State to make provision by regulation in relation to the specific but wide-ranging matters set out in the section including redenomination of share capital and reduction of capital.

B. ACQUISITION BY A LIMITED COMPANY OF ITS OWN SHARES

8.19   The general rule that a limited company must not acquire its own shares, whether by purchase, subscription, or otherwise and the general provision relating to or arising from this rule remain the same as set out in ss 143–150 and Sch 2 to CA 1985. The provisions are restated in similar language in ss 658–676 of CA 2006. The Act makes less use of schedules to set out substantive provisions which makes it clearer in some ways than previously. However, the prohibition is subject to s 690 (purchase by company of its own shares) considered in Section E below.

C. FINANCIAL ASSISTANCE WITH THE ACQUISITION OF SHARES

8.20   Chapter 2 of Part 18 deals with the provision of financial assistance by a company for the purchase of its own shares. Essentially the principles set out in CA 1985 remain unchanged. The definition of financial assistance is restated in s 677. The general prohibition on public companies providing financial assistance for the acquisition of their own shares is continued in s 678 as a result of the requirement of the Second Company Law Directive.[11] The general prohibition is lifted in relation to private companies in accordance with the underlying theme of relaxing the regulation of private companies where possible. As a result there is no need for the 'whitewash procedure' previously set out in ss 155–158. Even in relation to public companies there are unconditional and conditional exceptions to the general prohibition. These are set out in ss 681 and 682 respectively. Care must be taken in cases of re-registration of public companies as private companies and vice versa where there is, or arguably may have been, post-acquisition assistance. Where a private company re-registers as a public company between the date of the acquisition of the shares and the date of the assistance the prohibition will apply whereas if the company was a public company at the date of the acquisition but re-registers as a private company before the assistance is given the prohibition will not apply.[12]

---

[10] Section 649(6).

[11] Second Council Directive (EEC) 77/91 on coordination of safeguards which, for the protection of the interests of members and others, are required by Member States of companies within the meaning of the second paragraph of Article 58 of the Treaty, in respect of the formation of public limited liability companies and the maintenance and alteration of their capital, with a view to making such safeguards equivalent [1977] OJ L26.

[12] Section 678(3).

The rules relating to the provision of assistance by a subsidiary for the acquisition of   8.21
shares in its holding company are set out in s 679. A public company which is a subsidiary
of a private company is prohibited from giving assistance to a person acquiring shares in
the holding company directly or indirectly for the purpose of the acquisition before or at
the time of the acquisition.[13] Post-acquisition assistance is dealt with in s 679(3) referred
to above. Essentially the prohibition will apply if the 'assistor' is a public company at the
time the assistance is given. Exceptions in relation to post-acquisition assistance are set out
in s 679(4).

There is no prohibition on a company providing assistance for the acquisition of shares in   8.22
its holding company if the principal purpose of giving the assistance is not for the purpose of
any such acquisition or it is incidental to a larger purpose of the company and the assistance
is given in good faith in the interests of the company.[14] This restates the previous law.

The unconditional exceptions previously set out in s 153(3) of CA 1985 are restated with   8.23
necessary amendments to make reference to the relevant parts, chapters and sections of CA
2006. Section 682(1) sets out new exceptions. Section 682(1)(a) makes it plain that the
prohibition on financial assistance no longer applies at all in relation to private companies
and s 682(1)(b) extends that exception to public companies if the assistance does not reduce
the net assets of the company or, if the net assets are reduced, the assistance is given out of
distributable profits. Section 682(3) and (4) respectively deal with the definition of net assets
and how the value of assets and liabilities are to be determined for the purposes of s 682(1).
Section 682(2) restates the conditional exceptions previously set out in s 153(4) of CA 1985
relating to: (a) money lending companies; (b) employees' share schemes; (c) assistance by
companies in a group to employees, former employees, and spouses, civil partners, and other
close relatives of employees or former employees of the company or other company in the
group; and (d) making loans to employees to enable them to acquire shares in their employer
or another company in the employing company's group.

D. REDEEMABLE SHARES

Section 684 provides that a limited company having a share capital may issue redeemable   8.24
shares. The right is not unrestricted. The Act makes changes to the way in which companies
may issue redeemable shares and replaces ss 159 and 160 of CA 1985. For private companies
the requirement of prior authorization in the articles is removed. As in relation to other
powers conferred by CA 2006 a private company will now have the power to issue redeemable
shares unless the articles contain a prohibition or restriction on the exercise of the power.[15]
Under the previous law, the terms of redemption had to provide for payment on redemption
of any sums remaining unpaid on the shares to be redeemed. This requirement, contained
in s 159(3) of CA 1985, has now been removed. The new provision contained in s 686(2)
permits the terms of redemption to defer payment of the amount unpaid on redeemable
shares but, unless the terms do so provide, payment must be made on redemption.

There is a new provision setting out the terms and manner of redemption in s 685 of   8.25
CA 2006. This permits the directors of a company, whether private or public, to determine
the terms, conditions, and manner of redemption of redeemable shares. This power does,
however, require the prior authorization of the company either by resolution or by a

---

[13] Section 692(1).   [14] Section 693(2).   [15] Section 684(2).

provision in the articles. There is no longer any requirement for the terms and manner of the redemption to be set out in the articles if the directors are authorized to determine these matters. If the directors do not have such authorization the previous position requiring the terms and manner of the redemption to be set out in the articles applies.

8.26   The provisions of s 160 of CA 1985 setting out how the redemption of redeemable shares may be financed and how redeemed shares are to be treated is restated in ss 687 and 688 of CA 2006. In accordance with the general theme of the Act of providing notice of transactions relating to capital to the registrar of companies, s 689 provides for notice to be given accompanied by a statement of capital within the same period, containing the same information and having the same consequences in the event of a default as set out in paragraph 8.03 above.

E. PURCHASE OF OWN SHARES

8.27   Under s 162 of CA 1985 a company limited by shares or by guarantee and having a share capital could purchase its own shares provided it was authorized to do so by its articles. The new law is contained in s 690 of CA 2006 and removes the requirement for authorization in the articles even where the purchase is of redeemable shares. Instead, in common with the theme of the Act in relation to powers to deal with share capital generally, if a company is to be prohibited from purchasing its own shares or limited in its right to do so the articles can contain an express provision to that effect.

8.28   The other provisions of CA 2006 dealing with this topic restate the previous law applicable to a redemption of a company's own shares but making such adaptations as are necessary to ensure that the restated provisions work in the context of a purchase of shares.

8.29   Section 692 sets out the way in which a purchase of its own shares may be financed. Detailed provisions relating to the circumstances in which shares may be purchased out of capital are set out in Chapter 5 of Part 18. Subject to those provisions shares may only be purchased out of distributable profits or out of the proceeds of a fresh issue of shares made for the purpose of financing the purchase. Any premium payable on the purchase by a company of its own shares must be paid out of distributable profits save where the shares were originally issued at a premium (where s 692(3) applies).[16] In that event the shares can be purchased out of the proceeds of a new issue of shares up to an amount equivalent to the lesser of the total of the premiums received on the issue of the shares to be purchased or the amount standing to the credit of the share premium account.

8.30   Section 693 deals with the authority needed by a company for the purchase of its own shares. There is a difference between a 'market' purchase and an 'off-market' purchase. The nature of an 'off-market' purchase is defined by s 693(2) and the special rules relating to off-market purchases are set out in s 694. These rules restate those previously set out in ss 163 and 164 of CA 1985. A special resolution of the members is needed for an off-market purchase and the provisions relating to the obtaining of such a resolution are set out in ss 694–696 of CA 2006. Details of the proposed purchase contract must be disclosed to the members in the manner set out in s 696. Sections 695 and 696 restate what was previously in s 164(5) and (6) of CA 1985. Once the terms of an off-market purchase have been approved by resolution and the company is authorized to enter into the contract the terms can only be

---

[16] Section 705(2).

varied, revoked, or renewed by special resolution of the company under s 697 of CA 2006. On any variation, revocation, and renewal the procedures set out in ss 698–700 must be followed. The procedures therein are a restatement of the previous law.

Authority for a market purchase of its own shares must be obtained in accordance with s 701, which again restates the provisions in relation to the obtaining of a resolution of the members set out in s 166 of CA 1985. 8.31

Supplementary provisions setting out the requirement for a copy of the contract to be available for inspection by the members, the right of the members to enforce inspection rights, and the fact that the rights under a contract which has been authorized by the company as an off-market purchase or a market purchase cannot be assigned are contained in ss 702, 703, and 704 respectively. Section 705 provides that any payments connected with the purchase, such as payment for the acquisition of a right but not being the actual purchase price of the shares, must be paid out of distributable profits. 8.32

In common with other transactions involving share capital a return must be made to the registrar of companies. The return in this case is somewhat different from the other return and notices referred to above. The required contents are set out in s 707 which replaces with some amendment the provisions previously contained in s 169 of CA 1985. If shares have been cancelled or treated as cancelled following purchase a notice of cancellation must be given to the registrar in accordance with s 708, which restates, as amended, s 169(1A), (1B), and (1AA) of CA 1985. 8.33

Chapter 5 of Part 18 referred to at paragraph 8.29 above deals with the power of a private limited company to redeem or purchase its own shares out of capital and restates the previous law set out in ss 171–177 of CA 1985 with only minor amendments. The main changes are in accordance with the aim of the CA 2006 to reduce the regulation of private companies. The previous law only permitted a private company to purchase or redeem its own shares out of capital if its articles contained authority for it to do so. The new law under CA 2006 removes that requirement although the articles can prohibit or restrict the ability of the private company to acquire or redeem its own shares out of capital. Previously,[17] the directors had to make a statutory declaration specifying the matters set out in s 173(3) as a condition for payment out of capital. Under the new law, as set out in s 714, the company's directors have to make a 'statement' in accordance with the section. The required content of the statement is by and large the same as that previously required to be contained in the statutory declaration. The previous provision concerning the penalty for making a declaration which was unreasonable has been amended and expanded.[18] 8.34

The resolution requirements of the previous law are restated in ss 716 and 717 with s 716(3) making it plain that a resolution will only be effective if the voting rights requirements of s 717 are followed. The directors' statement and auditor's report produced under s 714 must be made available to members in advance of the resolution being passed as set out in s 718. The resolution will be ineffective if this section is not complied with. Notice must be given of the proposed payment out of capital within one week of the resolution being passed. The notice must be published in the *Gazette* and a national newspaper in accordance with s 719 which restates and replaces s 175 of CA 1985. The directors' statement and auditor's report must be kept available for inspection at the registered office for a period running from the date of publication of the notices under s 719 and the date five weeks after the resolution was passed. This requirement gives any disgruntled creditor the opportunity to 8.35

---

[17] Section 173(3) of CA 1985.   [18] Section 715.

inspect the documents and then apply to the court for the resolution to be cancelled under s 721. If an application to the court is made notice must be given by the person making the application to the registrar of companies under s 722. The company must also give notice to the registrar on being served with notice of the application. There are penalties for default. Sections 720, 721, and 722 restate provisions previously contained in s 175 of CA 1985 with only minor amendment.

8.36   Section 723 sets out when payment out of capital must be made, ie no earlier than five weeks and not later than seven weeks after the date of resolution under s 716. The only change from previously is that the court is given express power in s 721(5) to alter or extend time when the resolution has been confirmed following objection.

8.37   The special provisions operating where a company purchases its own shares and those shares are treasury shares are set out in Chapter 6 of Part 18. That Chapter makes very little amendment to the previous law and essentially restates the law set out in ss 162A–162G and 169A of CA 1985.

8.38   Supplementary provisions relating to Part 18 generally are contained in Chapter 6 and these are largely a restatement of previous law set out in ss 170, 171, and 178 of CA 1985. The only new provision is the reservation of the right for the Secretary of State in s 737 of the Act to modify the provisions of Part 18 by regulation which continues the trend towards legislation by the executive rather than by the legislature.

9

PROVISION AND DISCLOSURE
OF INFORMATION

A. DISCLOSURE OF INTERESTS IN SHARES

The provision of information to a company by shareholders or persons who are or who are 9.01 believed to be interested in the company's shares is governed by Part 22 of CA 2006. This part replaces ss 198–220 of CA 1985. As previously, the provisions only apply to public companies.

The emphasis of CA 2006 is completely different from that of the previous law. Part 22 9.02 applies to all shares carrying rights to vote at general meetings and includes treasury shares. Treasury shares were previously excluded.

The new law enables a public company to serve notice under s 793(1) on any person whom 9.03 the company knows or has reasonable cause to believe to be interested in the company's shares, or to have been interested in those shares in the three-year period immediately before the giving of the notice, to provide information about his interest in the shares as set out in s 793(2)–(6). The information required must be provided within such reasonable time as is specified in the notice.[1] Default in providing the information gives rise to the offence set out in s 795 subject to the defences therein set out. Previously, a person who acquired an interest in shares in a public company was, in certain circumstances, under an obligation to notify the company of his interests. This is no longer the case but the right to require information under CA 2006 applies more widely than the previous obligation to make a disclosure under CA 1985. The provisions of Part 15 of CA 1985 which gave a company a power to apply for an order imposing restrictions on shares where a notice requiring information to be provided about interests in shares has been served and there has been default in responding to the notice are restated in ss 794–802 of CA 2006.

Section 803 confers on the members of a public company the power to require the 9.04 company to exercise its powers to serve notice requiring information under s 793. The

---

[1] Section 793(7).

company is only required to act in accordance with the request of the members once it has received requests from members holding at least ten per cent of such of the paid-up capital as carries the right to vote at general meetings (but excluding any voting rights attached to treasury shares).[2]

9.05   A member's request can be in hard copy or electronic form and must set out the matters specified in s 803(3). The requests must be complied with[3] subject to the ten per cent rule referred to at paragraph 9.04. There are penalties for default.[4]

9.06   If the company carries out an investigation in accordance with the requests of its members then it is obliged to report on the outcome of the investigation in accordance with s 805. If the investigation is not concluded within three months the company must report to the members on the information obtained thus far.[5] Default in compliance with the reporting requirement of s 805 gives rise to an offence under s 806. A report produced by the company under s 805 is open to inspection by any person (not only shareholders) free of charge although a reasonable charge can be levied for a copy.[6] If inspection is refused or default is made in providing a copy an offence is committed by the company and each officer in default.[7]

9.07   Under s 808 the company is required to keep a register of the information provided. The information to be recorded and the manner of recording is set out in s 808(2)–(4). Again default leads to the commission of an offence.[8] The register is to be kept available for inspection as set out in s 809 and in default an offence is committed. Section 809 includes a requirement that unless the register is always kept at the registered office notice must be provided to the registrar of companies of the location at which the register is kept and any changes in that location. Unless the register is kept in such a way as to constitute an index a separate index of the names registered in it must be kept in accordance with s 810. The index must also be kept available for inspection as set out in s 810(4). Default gives rise to an offence under s 810(5).

9.08   Similar provisions are included in s 811 allowing any person to inspect the register and index kept under ss 808 and 810 as in relation to inspection of reports, etc referred to at paragraph 9.06 with similar provisions applying in default set out in s 809(4) and (5).

9.09   The right to inspect is subject to a proviso that it must be for a proper purpose. If a company refuses on the ground that the purpose is improper, the person who made the request is entitled to apply to the court. The rules and procedures relating to such an application are set out in s 812. Members making a request to a company to obtain information must not in so doing make statements which are misleading, false, or deceptive in a material particular. To do so gives rise to an offence under s 814(1). If a person gives information, obtained in exercise of the rights to request it, to another person or by inaction allows it to fall into the possession of another person who he knows or has reason to suspect may use it for an improper purpose he will be guilty of an offence under s 814(2).

9.10   Entries once made on the register must remain on it unless they are removed pursuant to s 816 as old entries or s 817 as incorrect entries relating to third parties.[9] If an entry is removed in any other circumstance an offence will be committed under s 815(3).

9.11   Section 818 deals with adjustments to entries in the register where an entry is made against a person as a party to a share acquisition agreement and that person ceases to be a party

---

² Section 803(2).   ³ Section 804(1).   ⁴ Section 804(2) and (3).   ⁵ Section 804(2).
⁶ Section 807(1) and (2).   ⁷ Section 807(3)–(5).   ⁸ Section 808(5)–(6).   ⁹ Section 815(1).

52

to the agreement. In that case he can apply to the company for inclusion of the relevant information to be included in the register. The register will still show that he was a party to a share acquisition agreement but will then show that he has ceased to be such a party.

If a company ceases to be a public company it must continue to keep the register of interests disclosed for a period of six years from when it ceased to be a public company.[10] Default leads to an offence.[11] **9.12**

Section 820 sets out what is meant by an interest in shares and makes it plain that it includes an interest of any kind, with any restrictions subject to which it is held or in relation to which the rights attaching to it may be exercised being disregarded. When a share is held on trust every beneficiary of the trust under which the share is held is regarded as having an interest in that share. It is unclear whether a discretionary beneficiary would be treated as having an interest as the section does not make this plain. If, however, a discretionary beneficiary was not treated as having an interest in the shares held by the trustees then it would be easy to circumvent the purpose of the statutory provisions. In addition, a person who has entered into a contract to acquire shares has an interest in them, as does a person who, although he is not the registered owner, is entitled to exercise any right conferred by the holding of such a share, eg the right to vote, or is able to control the exercise of any such right, eg the ability to direct the way in which a share is voted. A person who is entitled to call for delivery of shares to himself, or has a right to, or is under an obligation to take shares, has a sufficient interest in the shares. **9.13**

Section 822 provides that a person is to be regarded as having an interest in shares which are held by or in which his spouse, civil partner, or any infant child or stepchild of his is interested. In so far as spouses or civil partners are concerned this is perhaps somewhat strange in the twenty-first century. **9.14**

Section 823 deals with corporate interests by providing that if a company is interested in shares then a person on whose directions or instructions the company or its directors are accustomed to act will be regarded as having an interest in those shares. In the same way, if the person is entitled to exercise or control at least one-third of the voting power in a general meeting he will be treated as having an interest in the shares in which the company has an interest. This is a move away from the general principle of treating a company as a separate entity from its shareholders and the principle that a shareholder has no interest in the underlying assets of the company. **9.15**

Share acquisition agreements are dealt with by ss 824 and 825. An interest in shares can arise from an agreement between two or more persons which provides for the acquisition of shares or interests in shares in a public company by any one of them. Section 824(2) and (6) set out the requirements for an agreement to fall within the provision. More detailed provisions for the duration of the interest and similar matters are set out in s 824(3)–(6). Section 825 provides that each party to a share acquisition agreement which falls within the provisions is treated as having an interest in all the shares of the target company in which any other party to the agreement is interested apart from the agreement. Further detailed provisions are set out in the section. **9.16**

Supplementary provisions in ss 826–828 deal with the following matters: the protection of certain information from wider disclosure than specifically provided for by CA 2006; the reckoning of periods for fulfilling obligations imposed by Part 23; and the reservation of rights to make regulations. **9.17**

---

[10] Section 822(1).   [11] Section 822(2).

B. DISCLOSURE OF INFORMATION ABOUT VOTING AT MEETINGS

9.18   The provisions set out in s 1277 of Part 44 of CA 2006 introduce a power vested in the Secretary of State or the Treasury to make regulations requiring institutions to which the section applies to provide information about the exercise of voting rights attached to shares to which the section applies. These provisions have been introduced because of concerns about the extent to which those who are interested in public companies as shareholders become involved in its governance.

9.19   If an institution is subject to obligations to disclose information about the exercise of voting rights then that obligation can be enforced by civil proceedings brought by the person to whom the information should have been provided or a specified regulatory authority.[12] This is a rare example of a civil sanction being included in CA 2006 as opposed to the creation of a criminal offence.

9.20   The types of institutions to which the power relates are set out in s 1278. These are unit trust schemes as defined in FSMA 2000; open-ended investment companies incorporated under s 262 of FSMA 2000; investment trusts;[13] pension schemes;[14] undertakings authorized to carry on long-term insurance business under FSMA 2000; and collective investment schemes recognized by virtue of s 270 of FSMA 2000 being schemes authorized in designated countries or authorities. The regulations may provide that: (a) the section applies to other descriptions of institution; or (b) that the section does not apply to a specified description of institution. The regulations must specify in the case of any description of institution by whom the obligation imposed is to be fulfilled.

9.21   It can be seen from the description of the types of institution to which the power is expressly directed that it is in essence entities which carry on the business of investment of funds on behalf of others rather than carrying out a different type of business such as a manufacturing business. It is perhaps unsurprising that individuals who invest in such entities are only concerned with the performance of their investment and not in the day-to-day governance of the company in which all or part of their money is invested, at least until the investments take a nose dive or other events take place which have the effect of directly affecting the financial expectations of the investors. For that reason there is rarely any pressure on the institution to disclose information about how it has acted in relation to the voting of shares which it holds or in which it has an interest. The regulations enable such information to be obtained more easily and to be available to investors in the institutions to which the regulations apply.

9.22   The type of shares to which the information provisions apply are set out in s 1279 of CA 2006. These are shares of a description traded on a specified market and in which an institution has or is taken to have an interest. An institution has an interest in a share if the shares or a depositary certificate relating to them, are/is held by or on behalf of the institution. A depositary certificate is an instrument conferring rights (other than an option) in relation to shares held by another person and which can be transferred without the consent of that other person.

9.23   The information to be provided pursuant to the regulations is governed by s 1280 of CA 2006. The regulations may require that all or some of the information therein referred to

---

12 Section 1277(4)   13 For the purposes of s 842 of the Income and Corporation Taxes Act 1988.
14 As defined in s 1(5) of the Pension Schemes Act 1993 so far as England and Wales is concerned.

be provided. That information includes information about: the exercise or non-exercise of voting rights by the institution or its agent;[15] any instructions given by the institution or its agent in relation to the exercise or non-exercise of voting rights;[16] and any delegation of functions relating to the exercise or non-exercise of voting rights.[17] The regulations may provide information to be provided for a specified period or periods[18] and may require the disclosure of recommendations or advice given which led to the exercise or non-exercise of any voting rights where the institution has given instructions (whether general or specific, binding or non-binding, and whether acted on or not)[19] to act in accordance with recommendations or advice. The regulations may provide for the manner in which information is to be provided[20] including whether the institution can satisfy its obligations by referring to information provided on its behalf by a third party. It may be that a third party acts on behalf of more than one institution and if so the regulations may provide that information can be given in an aggregate form.[21]

9.24 This part also makes amendments to the provisions of the Enterprise Act 2002 relating to the disclosure of information.[22]

C. TRANSPARENCY OBLIGATIONS

9.25 The provisions in Part 43 of CA 2006 were inserted to give statutory effect to the Transparency Obligations Directive.[23] Section 1229 of CA 2006 inserts the definition of the Transparency Obligations Directive in s 103(1) of Part 6 of FSMA 2000.

9.26 Sections 1266–1268 insert new ss 89A–89N after s 89 of FSMA 2000. The so-called transparency rules again provide for legislation by regulation and empower the 'competent authority'[24] to make rules for the purposes of the Transparency Obligations Directive. Section 89A sets out what the rules may provide. A detailed exposition of these powers is beyond the scope of this book but in brief the regulations may contain provisions requiring the provision of voteholder information (this means information relating to the proportion of voting rights held by a person in relation to the voting shares in question)[25] to issuers and the provision of information by issuers to the public or the competent authority.[26] The terms 'issuer', 'securities', and 'regulated market' bear the same definitions as in Part 6 of FSMA 2000. The regulations can also contain rules for the purpose of ensuring that voteholder information relating to shares traded on a UK market other than a regulated market is made available to the competent authority. The regulations are likely, like the statutory provisions, to be extremely technical. The statutory provisions are largely enabling provisions and until the regulations are made there is little purpose in engaging in too much speculation as to their specific content.

9.27 The regulatory provisions are deliberately wide indicating an intention that the regulations will not necessarily simply implement the Directive but go beyond it to address the underlying purposes of the Directive. It is considered that the regulations impose three main types of obligation. These are:

---

[15] Section 1280(1)(a).   [16] Section 1280(1)(b).   [17] Section 1280(1)(c).   [18] Section 1280(2).
[19] Section 1280(3) and (6).   [20] Section 1280(4).   [21] Section 1280(5).   [22] Section 1281.
[23] Council Directive (EC) 2004/109 on the harmonisation of transparency requirements in relation to information about issuers whose securities are admitted to trading on a regulated market [2004] OJ L390.
[24] The FSA.   [25] See s 89B(2).   [26] See s 89A(3).

(a) to require issuers to make public their annual accounts and report prepared in accordance with EU International Accounts Standards Regulation and half yearly and interim management statements about their business;

(b) to require issuers to treat holders of the same securities equally;

(c) to require voteholders to disclose information about their holdings when the proportion of votes they hold reaches a specific proportion.

9.28   Section 89H to be inserted in FSMA 2000 by s 1267 of CA 2006 confers certain powers, which take effect on the date of commencement of Part 43 of CA 2006, on the competent authority to require persons to whom the section applies to provide information to it. The section applies to: issuers of securities to whom the transparency obligations apply; voteholders; auditors of issuers and voteholders; persons who control voteholders; persons controlled by voteholders; directors of issuers to which the section applies; and directors of voteholders (or in certain circumstances members of voteholders).

9.29   The right of the authority to require the provision of information is limited by s 89H(3) to that which is reasonably required in connection with the transparency rules. Section 89H(4) enables the authority to determine the time frame for the provision of information and the location for the information to be provided. Section 89H(5) makes it plain that any lien on a document is unaffected by the requirement to provide information.

9.30   Section 89I sets out the requirements connected with the competent authority's power to call for information. The authority will be empowered to request specific documents or information or information or documentation of a particular nature and may require authentication or verification. The authority is permitted under s 89I(3) to take copies of and extracts from documentation it receives and may also require the person submitting the information or any relevant person within the meaning of s 89I(4) to provide an explanation of the documentation produced. If a person fails to provide a document when required to do so the authority is permitted under s 89I(5) to require a person to state where it is.

9.31   Section 89J comprises supplementary provisions relating to the authority's power under ss 89H and 89I.

9.32   Section 1268 sets out four new provisions to be inserted in FSMA 2000 setting out the powers exercisable by the authority in case of an infringement of the transparency obligation. The competent authority can, under s 89K, make a public statement if an issuer fails to comply with the obligations. It may only do so after it has issued a warning to the issuer,[27] after the issuer has been given the opportunity to make representations, and after the authority has provided the issuer with a decision notice. The authority has to provide the issuer with a notice that it has a right to refer the matter to the Tribunal.[28]

9.33   The new s 89L inserted in FSMA 2000 gives the authority the power to require the market operator to suspend trading of issuers where they suspect that an applicable transparency obligation has been infringed,[29] or prohibit trading of issuers where they find such an infringement.[30] Section 89L(3) gives the authority powers to require the market operator to prohibit trading where the UK is not the home Member State of the issuer. The purpose behind this section is to enable the authority to take action to maintain market confidence. The new s 89M of FSMA 2000 sets out the relevant procedures for the exercise of the powers conferred by s 89L. Section 89N sets out the right of those who receive a decision notice

---

[27] Section 89L(2).   [28] See para 9.33.   [29] Section 89L(2).   [30] Section 89L(4).

(referred to in paragraph 9.31) or a notice under s 89K to refer matters to the Financial Services and Markets Tribunal.

Section 1269 of CA 2006 inserts a new s 89O into FSMA 2000 giving the competent authority power to make rules, referred to as 'corporate governance rules', for the purpose of implementing, enabling the implementation of, or dealing with matters arising out of or related to EU imposed obligations relating to the corporate governance of issuers who have requested or approved admission of their securities to trading on a regulated market. The rules can relate to issuers for whom the UK is the home Member State, issuers whose securities are traded on a regulated market in the UK or elsewhere in the EEA. What is included within the term 'corporate governance' is set out in s 89O(2). The regulations cannot impose greater burdens on issuers whose securities are traded outside the UK than those whose securities are traded on UK markets.[31]

9.34

Section 1270 inserts a new s 90A in FSMA 2000 which establishes a new regime of civil liability to third parties on issuers which make misleading statements in narrative reports or financial statements or other information provided in compliance with rules implementing the Transparency Obligations Directive. Articles 4 and 5 of the Directive provide for annual and half yearly reports, including management statements, to be made public, and requires that the statements contained in them give a true and fair view or in the case of management statements, a fair review of certain matters. In the case of a public company it is the directors who are responsible for making the statements. The Transparency Directive itself requires Member States to adopt a liability regime but leaves it to the individual Members States to determine the extent of the liability. The UK government has decided to establish an exhaustive regime in relation to ensuring the accuracy of the reports and statements which include criminal offences, administrative penalties, and civil claims for damages. Section 90M only deals with the liability of issuers to investors and leaves unchanged any other liability owed by directors to the issuer and other members of the company under UK and/or any other national law or under FSA rules. It also leaves unchanged any liability of the issuer in respect of loss and damage arising otherwise than as a result of acquiring securities in reliance on the relevant statement or report. There are powers to order directors to make restitution contained in ss 382 and 384 of FSMA 2000 on the application of the FSA or the Secretary of State.

9.35

The issuer will only be liable to the investor in relation to a misleading statement where the person responsible for making the statement (usually a director) knew the statement to be untrue or misleading or was reckless as to whether it was untrue or misleading or knew the statement to be a dishonest concealment of a material fact.[32] No loss is regarded as having been suffered as a result of the misleading statement unless the person suffering loss acquired the securities in reliance upon the information in the publication and at a time and in circumstances where it was reasonable for him to rely on the information.[33]

9.36

Section 1271 inserts a new s 100A in Part 6 of FSMA 2000 which sets out the competent authority's ability to exercise powers in relation to infringements of prospectus rules and transparency obligations or related provisions where issuers have chosen a home state other than the UK. The enforcement provisions extend only to cover infringements of provisions required by the relevant directive. If the authority finds that there has been an infringement by an issuer whose home state is not the UK it must give notice to the relevant authority of the issuer's home state requesting it to take enforcement measures and to inform the

9.37

---

[31] Section 89M(3).   [32] Section 90A(3).   [33] Section 90A(4).

authority of the measures it intends to take. The authority may take no further steps unless it is satisfied that the competent authority of the issuer's home state has failed or refused to take enforcement measures or that the measures taken are inadequate.[34]

9.38 Further and consequential amendments of FSMA 2000 and to C(AICE)A 2004 are set out in Sch 15 to CA 2006.

9.39 The Secretary of State is, by s 1273, given a power to make regulations in relation to company governance which is very similar to the power given to the FSA in s 1269 (the new s 89O of FSMA 2000). The section anticipates that regulations will be made for the purpose of implementing, enabling the implementation of, and dealing with matters arising out of community obligations on corporate governance for UK companies whose securities are traded on a regulated market in the UK or elsewhere in the EEA. Section 1273(3)(a) allows for regulations to be made by reference to any code regulating corporate governance. This could include, for example, the Combined Code on Corporate Governance issued by the Financial Reporting Council. Section 1273(4) provides that any criminal offence created by the regulations may not be subject to a greater penalty than an unlimited fine. Section 1273(5) allows for regulations to be made by negative resolution but it will also be possible to make regulations by affirmative resolution.

---

[34] Section 100A(3) and (4).

10

THE REGISTRAR AND REGISTER OF COMPANIES

A. THE REGISTRAR

Part 35 of CA 2006 makes provision regarding the registrar of companies. Although **10.01** significantly longer than its predecessor (Part 24 of CA 1985), it broadly restates most of those provisions—albeit elaborating them in greater detail—as well as making new provision regarding the register of companies and the powers and duties of the registrar.

Continuation of the office of registrar, performance by her of her functions, her seal, and **10.02** the payment of fees to the registrar are effected by ss 1060–1063 respectively.

The registrar continues to be obliged, by virtue of s 1064(1), to publish notice of **10.03** incorporation of a company, although s 1064(1)(b), together with section 1116, permits such notice to be otherwise than by way of, or in addition to, publication in the *Gazette*.[1]

B. ANNUAL RETURN

Part 24 of CA 2006 restates the requirements (previously contained in ss 363–365 of CA **10.04** 1985) for companies to submit annual returns to the registrar. The duty to deliver an annual return is contained in s 854, while s 858 restates the consequences of failing to comply.

The contents of the return are the subject of ss 855–857. The only change is that rather **10.05** than being comprehensively set out in the Act (cf ss 364 and 364A of CA 1985), some of the content will be prescribed in regulations.

---

[1] Although the government has said it has no intention in the foreseeable future of dispensing with *Gazette* publication: see *Hansard,* HC, col 407 (4 July 2006).

C. DELIVERY OF DOCUMENTS

10.06   As previously, s 1068 gives the registrar power to impose requirements as to the form of documents delivered to her, as well the means by which they are delivered (including electronically). As under CA 1985, a document will not be 'delivered' to the registrar until she 'receives' it: see s 1071, which also provides for the making of rules as to when a document is deemed to be 'received'.

10.07   With an eye to the future, the Secretary of State has also now taken a power (in s 1069) to enable him to require that certain documents *must* be delivered to the registrar electronically, although the government has said that it has no intention of using the power in the 'foreseeable future'.[2] In the meantime, s 1036 allows the registrar to agree with individual companies that they will make electronic delivery—the intention being that standard forms of agreement covering electronic communication between companies and the registrar will be devised.

10.08   Section 1072 provides that a document is not properly delivered unless all the requirements listed in s 1072(1) are met; and s 1072(2) provides that if a document is not properly delivered then it is not considered to be 'delivered' for the purposes of the provision which requires or authorizes delivery.

10.09   Section 1073 gives the registrar discretion nonetheless to accept and register such a document. This will be useful for those (rare) occasions when there is genuine doubt about whether a particular document complies or not.

10.10   Section 1074 deals with documents submitted which contain 'unnecessary material', ie material that was not necessary for compliance with the provision in question. If the unnecessary material can readily be separated, the registrar may register the document either as submitted or with the omission of the unnecessary material (s 1074(5)). However, if the unnecessary material cannot readily be separated then it is treated as not meeting the requirements of proper delivery:[3] see s 1074(4).

10.11   Companies can voluntarily remedy 'defective delivery' (ie which is not properly delivered) by replacing the relevant document: see s 1076.

10.12   Section 1093 provides for the registrar to give notice to companies of inconsistencies between documents filed and the register (eg filing a notice of resignation for a director whose appointment has not been recorded) and require correction within 14 days, failing which the company and every officer in default commits an offence.

10.13   Reflecting the convenience of modern communication methods, s 1075 contains a sensible new power for the registrar to 'informally' correct documents sent to her that appear incomplete, inconsistent, or containing unnecessary material after she has, for example, telephoned the company to clarify the position (the company must have previously consented to such informal communication). It is to be hoped that in practice this will become the general method for correcting defects.

10.14   Section 1113 provides for the registrar or any member or creditor to give notice to a company to make good any filing defaults within 14 days. If the company fails to do so, the

---

[2] *Hansard*, HC, col 409 (4 July 2006).   [3] On which see s 1072.

registrar, member, or creditor can apply to court for an order directing the company (or any specified officer of it) to make good the default within a specified time.

The general rule is that documents delivered to the registrar must be in English or Welsh as the case may be (see ss 1103 and 1104 respectively) although ss 1105–1107 make provision for the translation of documents into other languages. Sections 1108–1110 deal with the letters, characters, and symbols that are permitted as well as with transliteration of non-Roman characters. 10.15

Finally, ss 1077 and 1078 restate the current requirement for the registrar to give public notice of the receipt of certain documents, while s 1079 restates the rule (previously in s 42 of CA 1985) that companies cannot rely as against third parties on events which require notification to the registrar (such as an alteration of articles of association or the appointment of a liquidator) unless that event has been notified. 10.16

D. THE REGISTER[4]

Section 1080 continues the obligation to keep the register, ie records of all the documents, properly filed with the registrar and certificates of incorporation and registration of charge issued by her—and documents that are required to be disclosed by virtue of the EU Company Directives must be kept in electronic form.[5] In response to a specific CLR recommendation, the registrar is now empowered to 'annotate' the register with helpful details such as the date information was added or details of material that has been removed (see s 1081). 10.17

Section 1085 restates the right of the public to inspect the register, while s 1086 restates the right to take copies of information from the register. 10.18

The categories of information which are to be withheld from public inspection are listed in s 1087. In response to considerable concern raised in Parliament and elsewhere about the apparent risks created by the ready availability of shareholders' names and addresses, s 1088 adds to that list by providing for a regime whereby concerned shareholders can, as under the new regime for directors, apply to remove their address from the register and substitute a 'service address'. 10.19

Confusion in searching and other problems created by different directors, etc on the register having the same or similar names are sought to be solved by s 1082, which permits a system whereby reference numbers known as 'unique identifiers' are attached to each director, etc on the register. 10.20

Section 1083 reduces from ten years to three the length of time the registrar must retain original documents delivered to her (cf s 707A of CA 1985), while s 1084 restates the provision for records relating to dissolved companies to be transferred to the Public Record Office. 10.21

---

[4] Part 25 restates the provisions on registration of company charges (previously in Part 12 of CA 1985). It is understood that the government intends to pursue reform of this area in conjunction with the introduction of 'e-conveyancing' by the Land Registry.

[5] In response to Council Directive (EC) 2003/58 as regards disclosure requirements in respect of certain types of companies [2003] OJ L221, amending Council Directive 68/151/EEC (the First Company Law Directive).

E. ALTERATION OF THE REGISTER

10.22   Perhaps partly in response to recent case law strictly interpreting the powers of the registrar to deal with information on the register once it has been recorded even under court order,[6] CA 2006 provides various new powers for the alteration of the register.

10.23   Section 1094 allows the registrar to remove from the register anything that there was a power but not a duty to include, such as unnecessary material under s 1074, a defective document which has subsequently been replaced, or a previously inconsistent document that has been remedied in accordance with s 1093.

10.24   However, the main changes come in ss 1095 and 1096–1097, which create regimes whereby certain material can be removed from the register either by court order or by the registrar (following an application to her for that purpose) respectively. Removal applies to material that derives from anything that is (or is declared by the court to be) 'invalid' or 'ineffective' or that 'was done without the authority of the company'; or material that is (or declared by the court to be) 'factually inaccurate' or is 'derived from something that is factually inaccurate' or 'forged'.

F. FALSE INFORMATION OFFENCE

10.25   Section 1112 enacts a very widely drawn offence of knowingly or recklessly delivering or causing to be delivered false information to the registrar. The offence was a specific CLR recommendation and provides for a generalized 'false information offence' in place of the previous multitude of individual offences in relation to each filing requirement.

---

6 See, eg, *Halifax plc v Halifax Repossessions* [2004] EWCA Civ 331, [2004] BCC 281 (inability of court to direct the registrar to change company names infringing trademarks) and *Re A Company (No 007466 of 2003)* [2004] EWHC 35, [2004] 1 WLR 1357 (refusal to direct the removal of (extraneous) legally professionally privileged material disclosed in accounts that was recorded on the register). See also *igroup v Ocwen* [2004] 1 WLR 451 (no power to remove schedules to registered charge forms inadvertently containing sensitive personal information about lenders' customers).

11

MANAGEMENT AND ADMINISTRATION OF COMPANIES

A. DIRECTORS

CA 2006 makes a number of changes to the law concerning directors. As a general point, the existing definitions of director and shadow director are retained and now appear in ss 250 and 251. As regards numbers of directors, s 154 provides that a private company must have at least one director and all public companies must now have at least two directors. More significantly, all companies must now have at least one director who is a natural person: s 155(1). These requirements can now be enforced by the Secretary of State directing a company to remedy any breach by making the necessary appointment or appointments.   11.01

By s 157, only persons aged over 16 years are now eligible to be directors of companies (although the Secretary of State can make exceptions by regulation). Any existing director who is under the age of 16 years will cease to be a director when s 157 is brought into force.   11.02

However, acts of a person acting as a director will be valid despite any defect in his appointment because s 161 restates the previous saving provision which upholds acts by someone whose appointment as a director is subsequently found to be defective or void or to have terminated.   11.03

B. APPOINTMENT AND REMOVAL OF DIRECTORS

No changes of substance have been made to the provisions for the appointment or removal of directors which are now found in s 160 (appointments of public company directors to be voted on individually), s 168 (removal of directors by ordinary resolution at meeting),   11.04

and s 169 (right of director to protest removal). The provisions relating to directors' service contracts are considered in Chapter 13.

C. COMPANY SECRETARIES

1. Introduction

11.05 The major change in this area is that private companies no longer need to have a company secretary: s 270(1). Private companies do not need to take advantage of this exemption. CA 2006 therefore distinguishes between private companies without a secretary on the one hand and private companies with a secretary on the other.

2. Private companies

11.06 Section 270(3) provides that, in the case of a private company without a secretary, where anything is authorized or required to be sent or served on the secretary, it may be sent directly to the company and any act which needs to be done or may be done by the company's secretary can be done by a director or a person authorized to act by the directors.

3. Public companies only

11.07 Section 271 restates the requirement for a public company to have a secretary. That requirement can be enforced by the Secretary of State giving the company a direction to appoint a secretary. The directors remain under a duty to ensure that the secretary, who need not be an individual, has sufficient knowledge and experience to act and is duly qualified in accordance with the criteria in s 273 (which does not contain any material changes).

4. Private companies with a secretary and public companies

11.08 Section 274 contains a minor change from its CA 1985 counterpart. If there is no company secretary because the office is vacant or the secretary is unable to act, the directors can authorize any person to carry out the secretary's functions. Previously, only an officer of the company could be authorized to act.

D. REGISTER OF OFFICERS

1. Directors

11.09 The requirements for a company to keep a register of its directors (which must include specified information) at its registered office which is open to inspection by shareholders and the public are now found in ss 162 and 163 of the Act. CA 2006 contains a new provision (s 1136) by which the Secretary of State may make regulations under which the register may be kept at places other than the registered office. Section 162(4) therefore provides that if the register is not kept at the registered office, the company must notify the registrar of its location and of any change to that location. Section 164 sets out the particulars which have to be included in the register for corporate directors.

2. Directors' addresses

The most significant change is that companies' registers of directors are now required to include a service address for directors rather than the directors' usual residential address. A service address is defined by s 1141(1) as an address at which documents may effectively be served on a person and may be given as the company's registered office by virtue of s 163(5). However, mirroring this change, a company now must keep a separate register of directors' residential addresses, access to which is now restricted. These changes are considered in more detail in paragraph 11.12. Also, there is no longer any obligation to provide details of a director's other directorships. Section 163(2)– (4) makes minor changes to the information that has to be included where a director was formerly known for business purposes by another name. The requirement to notify the registrar of any changes to directors or their particulars is retained in s 167. 11.10

3. Secretaries

Section 275(1) requires a company to keep a register of its company secretaries. However, since the requirement for a private company to have a secretary has been abolished (see paragraph 11.05), it seems that this provision only applies to public companies and private companies which have not dispensed with their secretaries, as indicated by the side note preceding s 274. The register must be kept at the company's registered office or at a place specified in regulations made under s 1136 (in which case its location and any alteration to the location have to be notified to the registrar). The register must be open to inspection by shareholders and members of the public. The information which must be included is set out in ss 277–279. There is a duty under s 276 to notify the registrar of companies of any changes. One point to note is that there is no longer any requirement to include the home address of an individual company secretary in the register: that is the effect of s 277(5) which requires the register to contain a service address which may be the company's registered office. 11.11

E. NON-DISCLOSURE OF DIRECTORS' RESIDENTIAL ADDRESSES

As noted in paragraph 11.10, under CA 2006 a director may supply a service address which may but does not have to be the director's usual residential address. In consequence, the Act now requires companies to keep a parallel register of directors' residential addresses (although if the same as the service address (being an address other than the company's registered office) this register need only note that the addresses are the same). 11.12

This change is part of the new regime introduced to increase protection for individual directors because of previous abuse of the right of public access to their addresses, eg by political activists. Under the new regime (ss 240 and 241), information about a director's residential address and/or that the service address is the director's usual residential address is 'protected information' which cannot be used by the company, without the consent of the director, except for three purposes. Those purposes are: (a) communications between the company and the director; (b) disclosure to the registrar of companies under the Act; and (c) disclosure under a court order. By s 242, the registrar must not include the protected information in any publicly accessible part of the register. Section 243 prohibits the registrar from using or disclosing the information except for communications with the director or disclosure to 11.13

public authorities or credit reference agencies in accordance with regulations to be made by the Secretary of State. The information remains protected even after the individual ceases to be a director.

11.14　A director can lose the protection from disclosure in two situations. First, under s 244, on an application by a liquidator, creditor, shareholder of the company, or any other person with a sufficient interest, the court can order disclosure by the company if there is evidence that service of documents at a service address which is not the usual residential address is not effective to bring the documents to the director's notice or if disclosure is necessary in connection with the enforcement of a court order. If the company does not have the residential address or has been dissolved, the court can order the registrar to disclose the address.

11.15　The second situation, under ss 245 and 246, is that if communications from the registrar to the director at the director's service address have gone unanswered and there is evidence that using the service address is not effective to bring documents to the director's attention, the registrar can decide to put the director's usual residential address on the public record. Before doing so, the registrar must give notice to the company and the director and take account of any representations received. Once the registrar has put the director's residential address on the public record, he must notify the company which must then also include that address as the director's service address in its register of directors. If a director's address is made public by the registrar under these sections, the director cannot then register a service address except his residential address for the next five years.

11.16　The regime is reinforced by s 1142 which states that any requirement under the Companies Acts to give a person's address means (unless the contrary is expressly stated) to give a service address for that person.

11.17　The new regime replaces the existing scheme of confidentiality orders. It appears that the provisions are not retrospective so that, subject to any transitional provisions which may be made under the Act, residential addresses currently on the register of directors are not protected. However there is provision in s 1088 for the Secretary of State to make regulations to permit applications to the registrar to make addresses on the register unavailable for public inspection.

11.18　Section 1055 envisages that a similar regime of protection will apply to residential addresses for directors of registered overseas companies.

F. SERVICE OF DOCUMENTS

11.19　Section 1139 deals with the service of documents on companies. Section 1139(1) restates the existing position that a document can be served by leaving it at or sending it by post to the company's registered office. Service on registered overseas companies is dealt with in s 1139(2). There are no significant changes.

11.20　Section 1140 is a new provision dealing with service on directors, company secretaries, and designated representatives of registered overseas companies. It enables a document to be served by leaving it at, or sending it by post to, the person's registered address which is defined as any address shown as a current address in the publicly available register. Section 1139(3) should be noted as it provides that the registered address can be used even if the document is being served for a purpose unconnected with the person's position as director or secretary, so long as the person still holds the appointment in relation to which that address was registered (subsection (6)).

G. ELECTRONIC COMMUNICATION

Unlike the Companies Act 1985 (Electronic Communications) Order 2000[1] which allowed electronic communication by reference to specific provisions of CA 1985, CA 2006 brings in a regime which permits (but does not require) communication (ie the supply or sending of information and documents) in electronic form and by electronic means where that has been previously agreed. The company communications regime is one of the first parts of CA 2006 to be implemented, coming into operation by 20 January 2007.   11.21

The company communications regime is set out in ss 1143–1148 of Part 37 and Schs 4 and 5 to CA 2006. The starting point is ss 1143 and 1144. Section 1144 provides that: 11.22

(1) documents or information to be sent or supplied *to* a company must be sent or supplied in accordance with Sch 4;

(2) documents or information to be sent or supplied *by* a company must be sent or supplied in accordance with Sch 5;

(3) where documents or information are being sent by one company to another, Sch 5, not Sch 4, applies.

Section 1144 has to be read together with the interpretation and definition provisions in ss 1148 and 1168. In particular, s 1168 defines what is meant by 'hard copy form', 'electronic form' (essentially, email, fax, or disc), and 'electronic means'. There is a general requirement (s 1168(5) and (6)) that documents sent in electronic form must be capable of being read and retained by the recipient. Sections 1114(2) and 1132(7) make the company communications regime applicable to any sending, provision, or giving of information regardless of the precise verb used.   11.23

These general provisions are supplemented by three further sections. Section 1145 entitles a member or debenture holder of a company to request the company to send, free of charge, a hard copy of a document or information which he has received electronically. Sections 1146 and 1147 contain provisions dealing with the authentication of documents sent *to* a company by a person and the deemed delivery of material sent *by* a company.   11.24

As mentioned above, the mechanics of sending documents and information by hard or electronic means are set out in Schs 4 and 5, the operation of which is summarized in the following tables.   11.25

Material Supplied *to* a Company—Sch 4

Form of material	Means of supply	Address
hard copy	by hand or by prepaid post	address specified for that purpose by company or registered office or address authorized by Companies Acts
electronic form	electronic form by hand or post (eg delivering or sending a disc by post) or electronic means	address which would be valid if sent as hard copy address specified for that purpose by company or address deemed to have been so specified by Companies Acts

---

[1] SI 2000/3373.

Material Supplied *by* a Company—Sch 5

Form of material	Means of supply	Address	Remarks
hard copy	handed to recipient by prepaid post	address specified for that purpose by recipient or to a company at registered office or to a shareholder at the address in register of members or to a director at the address in the register of directors or to an address authorized by Companies Acts	if no address within these categories can be obtained the material can be sent to the recipient's last address known to the company
electronic form	electronic form by hand or post	personal delivery or to address that would be valid for hard copy	material can only be supplied to a person who has agreed (generally or specifically) to receive it in electronic form or to a company which is deemed by the Companies Acts to have agreed to receive it in electronic form
	electronic means	address specified by the recipient for that purpose or for a company address deemed by the Companies Act to have been specified for that purpose (eg s 333 of CA 2006)	
via website	being made available on a website in a form that enables the recipient to read it and retain a copy for a period either as specified by the Companies Acts or if no such period is specified for 28 days from the period when the recipient is notified of the presence of the material on the website		a website can only be used by a company to communicate information if a person has agreed or is taken to have agreed and that agreement has not been revoked. A member of a company will be taken to have agreed if: (a) the members have resolved that material can be supplied via a website; or (b) the company's articles have provision for that to happen and the member has been asked individually to agree to use of the website and has not responded within 28 days. Any request for agreement must specify what the effect of failure to respond is and only one request can be sent in any 12-month period in respect of any category of material. Similar provisions apply to communications with debenture holders if they have agreed by resolution or there is a provision in the instrument creating the debenture

Both Schedules contain supplementary provisions covering the supply of material in a form 11.26 other than hard copy, electronic copy, or by website. Schedule 5 also has provisions dealing with the supply of information and documents to joint holders of shares and debentures and following death or bankruptcy of a shareholder.

12

DECISION MAKING IN COMPANIES

A. DIRECTORS' MEETINGS

CA 2006 does not make any changes to the fundamental principle that the day-to-day 12.01 management of a company is, subject to any provisions in the articles, in the hands of the directors. CA 2006 also does not alter the law relating to resolutions by directors or board meetings, which remain regulated by the company's articles and case law.

The existing requirement for every company to keep minutes of all proceedings at 12.02 meetings of directors is now found in s 248(1) of CA 2006 which has also done away with the requirement to keep minutes of managers' meetings. Section 248(2) obliges companies to keep the minutes for ten years from the date of the meeting. Section 249 deals with the status of minutes as evidence of the holding of the meeting and the decisions taken at it.

B. COMPANY MEETINGS AND RESOLUTIONS

1. Overview

Company resolutions are dealt with in Chapters 1–3, 6, and 7 of Part 13 of CA 2006 which 12.03 replaces Chapter 4, Part 11 of CA 1985. Company meetings are covered in Chapters 3–5 of the same Part. The new provisions reflect Parliament's intention to make the running of private companies easier by proceeding on the basis that the main means of decision making by shareholders in a private company will be by written resolution rather than general meeting. Consequently, the requirement for private companies to hold annual general meetings is abolished.

Another theme which is said to underpin the Act is enhancing shareholder engagement 12.04 by improving the position of 'indirect shareholders', ie people who invest in a company through nominees and are not therefore registered members. Section 145(1) and (2) of CA 2006 therefore provide that, where a company's articles enable a member to nominate another person or persons to enjoy and exercise the rights of the member, rights conferred on members by the Act are to be regarded as conferred on the nominees. Section 145(3) highlights rights conferred in relation to resolutions and general meetings (eg the right to be sent proposed written resolutions or to require directors to call a general meeting) as prime examples where s 145 may operate. Section 153 provides for 'indirect shareholders' to be counted for the purposes of requests made by members to a company (eg a request to circulate a statement prior to a general meeting).

12.05 For companies whose shares are admitted to trading on a regulated market, s 146 provides that a member who holds shares on behalf of another can nominate that other to enjoy information rights which includes the right to receive copies of all communications sent by the company to its members or any class of members. That will include material relating to company resolutions and company meetings. The topic of the rights of indirect members is covered in more detail in Chapter 6.

12.06 Section 360 introduces the 'clear day rule' for computing the periods of time specified in relation to:

(1) notice required of general meeting (s 307);
(2) resolution requiring special notice (s 312);
(3) request to circulate members' statement (s 314);
(4) deposit of expenses of circulating statement (s 316);
(5) request to circulate statement at AGM (s 338);
(6) deposit of expenses of circulating statement (s 340).

The rule provides that both the day on which notice is given, the request is made, or the expenses are tendered (as the case may be) and the day of the meeting are excluded in determining the period of time.

2. Company resolutions

(a) General provisions

12.07 The new regime is encapsulated in s 281 which distinguishes between private companies which can pass a resolution either as a written resolution or at a members' meeting, and public companies which can only do so at a general meeting. The *Re Duomatic*[1] principle (whereby acts can be done with the unanimous informal agreement of all shareholders entitled to vote) is preserved by s 281(4)(a) as is the existing law on the circumstances in which a resolution is or is not treated as having been validly passed and cases in which a person is precluded from alleging that a resolution has not been duly passed.

12.08 Sections 282 and 283 restate the requirements for the passing of ordinary and special resolutions but with two key changes. First, unanimity is no longer required for a written resolution which may now be passed by a simple majority: s 282(2). Second, the requirement in s 378(2) of CA 1985 for 21 days' notice where a special resolution was to be passed at a meeting has been abolished: s 283(4)–(6). Section 281(3) stipulates that where a Companies Act provision refers to a resolution of a company or of the members without specifying what type of resolution is required, what is required is an ordinary resolution, ie a simple majority unless the company's articles impose a requirement for a higher majority or unanimity.

12.09 Sections 284–287 restate and expand various general provisions relating to voting on resolutions. The general rule (previously found in the Table A Regulations) that (subject to any contrary provision in the company's articles) a member has one vote for every share or

---

[1] [1969] 2 Ch 365.

£10 of stock held by him is now put on a statutory footing in s 284 which extends the rule to written resolutions.

Section 285 is a new provision. Section 285(1) invalidates any provision in a company's   12.10
articles under which a member voting by proxy has fewer votes than if the member votes in person. Section 285(3) addresses the point that written resolutions no longer need to be passed unanimously by providing that any provision in the articles whereby a member has a different number of votes in relation to a resolution which is passed as written resolution than if it were passed on a poll taken at a meeting is invalid. The provision (formerly reg 55 of Table A) that in the case of a jointly owned share, only the vote of the senior holder (ie the name which appears first in the register) counts is now s 286.

Section 287 upholds the effect of any provision in a company's articles which lays down a   12.11
procedure for objecting to a person's entitlement to vote.

(b) *Written resolutions*

Sections 288–300 of CA 2006 set out a more detailed framework for the use of written   12.12
resolutions by private companies than existed under CA 1985 so as to cater for the more extensive use of them which CA 2006 aims to encourage.

The previous prohibitions on using written resolutions to remove directors or auditors   12.13
before the expiration of their term of office remain and are now in s 288(2). These are now the only restrictions on the use of written resolutions by private companies and s 300 invalidates any provision in a company's articles which removes the right to use the written procedure for any resolution which could otherwise lawfully be passed as a written resolution.

Section 288(5) states that a written resolution of a private company has effect as if passed   12.14
by the company in a general meeting or by a meeting of a class of members, as applicable. The eligible members for the purposes of passing a written resolution are the members who would have been entitled to vote on the resolution on the circulation date, ie the earliest date on which copies of the resolution were sent to members: ss 289 and 290.

Further detailed provisions as to the powers of directors and members to circulate written   12.15
resolutions are set out in ss 291–295. In accordance with the general provisions in CA 2006 allowing communications between companies and their members by electronic means (which are dealt with in more detail at paragraphs 11.21–11.25), resolutions can be circulated in hard copy or in electronic form or by means of a website: ss 291 and 293.

To be effective, the written resolution procedure requires certainty and so s 296 provides   12.16
that a member cannot revoke his agreement to a written resolution once given. Section 297 imposes a default time limit of 28 days from the circulation date for the passing of a written resolution unless another period is specified in the company's articles.

3. Company meetings

(a) *Introduction*

CA 2006 makes a number of significant changes in relation to company meetings. The first   12.17
one to note is that private companies are no longer required to hold AGMs. As a consequence, the concept of an extraordinary general meeting also disappears from the new legislation. Instead, CA 2006 sets out general provisions applicable to both private and public companies for the passing of resolutions at general meetings. Those provisions are then supplemented by extra layers of regulation for public and quoted companies respectively.

(b) *General provisions*

12.18   Section 301 sets out the fundamental proposition that for a resolution of the members of a company to be validly passed at a general meeting, notice of the meeting and the resolution must be given and the meeting held and conducted in accordance with both the provisions of the Act (ie ss 301–335 and ss 336–340 for public companies) *and* the company's articles.

12.19   General meetings of companies can be called by: (a) the directors (under s 302 which is a statutory incorporation of Table A, reg 37); or (b) the members (under ss 303–305). Sections 303–305 restate the previous provisions about requisitions of meetings by members with the following changes. In the case of a private company, if more than 12 months have passed since the last general meeting at which members could circulate a resolution, a meeting can be requested by members holding five per cent of the voting shares (or five per cent of the voting rights in a company without a share capital). Otherwise, a request in a private company has to come from members holding ten per cent of the voting shares. In a public company, the required percentage remains at ten per cent as under CA 1985.

12.20   A request to call a meeting can include the text of a resolution intended to be moved at the meeting. The request can be made in hard copy form or electronic form.

12.21   The time limits for calling a meeting, the rights of the members to call a meeting if the directors fail to do so at the company's expense, and the court's powers to order a general meeting to be held are restated without any substantive changes in ss 303–306.

12.22   The notice periods for calling general meetings (except adjourned meetings) are unchanged at 14 days for private companies, 21 days for the AGM of a public company, and 14 days for another general meeting of a public company. As before, meetings can be called on shorter notice if agreed by the members but s 307 of CA 2006 introduces distinctions between private and public companies: in a private company the necessary majority to agree short notice is 90 per cent of the voting shares (or such higher percentage up to 95 per cent as specified in the articles) but for a public company, it remains at 95 per cent or in the case of the AGM unanimity (ss 307(6), (7), and 337(2)). The notice periods in respect of a resolution at a meeting requiring special notice are unchanged (as distinct from a special resolution as to which see s 283). The company must be given at least 28 days' notice and must give the members at least 14 days' notice: see s 312.

12.33   Sections 307–311 contain procedural points on the form of notice (which need to be read in conjunction with s 333 and the provisions on electronic communications dealt with in Chapter 11, Section G) and the persons to be notified and the content of the notice (by adopting the provisions of Table A, reg 38). The effect of accidental failure to give notice as required is dealt with by s 313 (based on Table A, reg 39) which states that such failure is normally to be disregarded unless the articles provide otherwise.

12.24   Four changes to the law on the circulation of members' statements prior to company meetings in ss 314–317 should be noted.

(1) If the statement refers to a resolution, it is the voting rights on that resolution which are relevant in assessing whether the required percentage of voting rights has been reached to trigger the obligation to circulate the statement.

(2) A person who is not a member of the company but for whom shares are held by a registered member can be included in the 100 persons who can request circulation of a statement if the conditions in s 153 are complied with.

(3) A request can be made in electronic form.

(4) In the case of a statement relating to the AGM of a public company, if sufficient requests to circulate the statement are received before the end of the financial year preceding the meeting, the members requesting circulation do not have to pay the expenses of circulation.

(c) *Procedure at meetings*

The provisions in relation to the quorum for a meeting are basically unchanged but the Act introduces the concept of a 'qualifying person'. A qualifying person is defined in s 318 as an individual who is a member of a company or a person authorized to act as a representative of a corporation in respect of the meeting or a person appointed as a proxy of a member. Subject to any contrary provisions in the company's articles, the quorum for a meeting is two qualifying persons (who cannot be representatives of the same corporation or proxies of the same member) except for a single member company when the proxy is one qualifying person.   12.25

A minor change has been made to the law in relation to the appointment of a representative by a corporation (now s 323 of CA 2006) by spelling out that more than one person can be appointed as representative but if the representatives do not exercise their votes or other powers in the same way, the company is treated as not having voted or exercised the power at all.   12.26

The following changes have been made to the rules relating to proxies by ss 324–331 by way of extension to the previous provision (s 372 of CA 1985).   12.27

(1) Members of both private and public companies now have the right to appoint more than one proxy provided that, in the case of a company with a share capital, each proxy is appointed in respect of the rights of different shares or blocks of shares. All proxies have the right to attend, speak, and vote at a meeting. Section 285 (considered in paragraph 12.09) ensures that members voting by proxies are not disadvantaged as against members voting in person. These rights (and any more extensive rights granted by a company's articles) must be set out in every notice calling a company meeting.

(2) In calculating the notice required to be given of an appointment of a proxy or the termination of a proxy's authority, only working days are now to be taken into account by virtue of s 327(2) and (3) and s 330(3), (6), and (7).

(3) There is a new provision (s 328) which permits a proxy to be elected as chairman of a general meeting (subject to the company's articles).

(4) Section 331 stipulates that none of the statutory provisions on proxies prevents a company from conferring more extensive rights on members and proxies by its articles.

The other general provisions relating to procedure at meetings, ie election of a chairman (s 319), declaration on a show of hands (s 320), right to demand a poll (s 321), voting on a poll (s 322), and date of resolution passed at an adjourned meeting (s 332), do not contain any substantive changes from CA 1985.   12.28

Sections 334 and 335 apply the provisions in relation to company meetings to meetings of a class of members with certain specified exceptions.   12.29

(d) *AGM of public company*

Sections 336–340 set out the requirements for public companies to hold an AGM and the procedure to be followed for giving notice of the AGM and circulating members'   12.30

resolutions. The key change is that a public company must hold an AGM within six months of its accounting reference date (or within three months of any notice under s 392 altering its accounting reference date). This linkage of the AGM with the end of the company's financial year is intended to put shareholders in a better position to hold the directors to account at the meeting. Although the threshold for requiring a resolution to be notified remains the same under the Act (members representing five per cent of the voting rights or 100 members holding paid up shares of £100 each), two minor changes have been made. First the requisitionists must have rights to vote on the resolution in question. Second, by s 153, a person who is not a member of the company but for whom shares are held by a member can be included in reckoning the 100 members.

(e) *Quoted companies*

12.31   By ss 341–354, CA 2006 imposes new obligations on quoted companies to disclose the results of polls at general meetings on their websites and to obtain an independent report on a poll if requested by the requisite number of members. A quoted company, for these purposes, is a company whose equity capital is included in the official list in the UK, officially in an EEA State or admitted to dealing on the New York Stock Exchange or Nasdaq (s 361 of CA 2006 applying s 385).

12.32   In brief, these are the new requirements. Where a poll has been taken at a general meeting (or a class meeting), the date of the meeting, the text of the resolution or a description of the subject matter for the poll, and the numbers of votes cast for and against must be put on a company website as soon as reasonably practicable and kept there for two years (although temporary unavoidable interruptions will be disregarded).

12.33   Where a poll is to be or has been taken at a general meeting (or a class meeting), either: (a) members representing five per cent of the total voting rights on the matter to which the poll relates; or (b) 100 members each holding paid up voting shares of not less than £100, can request the directors to appoint an independent assessor to report on whether the statutory requirements were observed, the procedure for the poll was conducted properly, and the votes counted accurately. The assessor must be appointed within a week of the request and his report must be posted on the website. The assessor is given rights to attend the meeting, consult the company's records and obtain information from the directors, employees, bankers, auditor, and solicitor of the company.

C. RECORD KEEPING

12.34   A company must keep minutes of all directors' meetings for a period of ten years (see paragraph 12.02). Section 355 imposes a similar obligation on companies to keep copies of resolutions, minutes of general meetings, and records of decisions of sole members notified under s 357. Section 356 provides that such records are evidence of the resolution or the proceedings at the meeting as the case may be and (unless the contrary is proved) that the meeting was validly held.

12.35   The records must be available for inspection at all times at the company's registered office or at a place specified in regulations made under s 1136 and must be open to inspection by members without charge. Members also have a right to have a copy of the records on payment of such fee as be may prescribed.

Section 1135 provides for company records (now defined in s 1134) to be kept in either **12.36** hard copy or electronic form. Section 1138 reproduces the requirement for a company to take adequate precautions to guard against falsification of records which are not kept in bound books and to facilitate discovery of such falsification, with a new proviso excluding copies of directors' service contracts or memoranda of terms and qualifying indemnity provisions from the scope of the section.

13

DIRECTORS' DUTIES

A. THE PRESENT LAW

Directors duties derive from two sources: 13.01

(1) statute; and
(2) the general law.

The main source is the general law. The memorandum and articles set out the general 13.02 powers of the directors but do not state the principles upon which they are to be exercised. Sometimes they impose specific restrictions on the directors, eg the need for sanction from shareholders before entering into certain transactions. Also, they often contain provisions relieving directors from liability or providing for indemnities. Statute is concerned with specific areas only. CA 1985 imposed particular duties on directors, such as the duty to cause the company to prepare and file accounts and dealt, in Part X, with the particular area of conflicts of interests and with contracts and transactions between the company and directors. In addition s 322A of CA 1985[1] reinforced the general law by providing specific remedies in respect of transactions with a director or a person connected or associated with him where the

---

[1] Inserted by CA 1989 and now s 41 of CA 2006.

board has exceeded any limitation on their powers in the company's constitution. Otherwise that Act left the directors' duties to be defined by the general law.

13.03   The basic principles that govern directors' conduct derive from the rules of common law and the principles of equity. These are based on two fundamental premises: (i) that the company is a separate person in law; and (ii) that as an artificial person it is only able to act through agents.

13.04   Duties are imposed on directors by analogy with other areas of law: (a) the law of agency, as directors act as agents for the company; and (b) the law of trusts, as directors are custodians of the company's property. Neither of these analogies is exact. Directors are not just agents of the company and are in fact subject to little control by their principles. They are not trustees in the strict sense because, unlike normal trustees, they are expected to risk the company's property in trade under their own management.

13.05   Their duties can be divided into fiduciary duties derived from equitable principles governing the roles of trustees and fiduciaries and non-fiduciary duties derived from common law principles (the duty to act with reasonable skill and care), though the same facts may rise to a breach of both a fiduciary and a non-fiduciary duty. The purpose of these duties is to protect the interests of the shareholders and to a lesser extent the creditors of the company, although they are often expressed as being owed to the company and the company is normally the proper person to claim any relief for breach of duty.

13.06   There is considerable overlap between the various duties imposed by the general law and these in turn can overlap with specific statutory provisions.

13.07   The main duties imposed by the general law are in outline:

(1) A duty to obey the company's constitution. Both at common law and in equity directors cannot do things they are not empowered to do and must act in accordance with the powers they are given. A failure to do so will often involve a misapplication of company property and where this occurs a director who authorized or participated in the transaction may be liable to account to the company for any loss sustained as a trustee of the company's property.

(2) A duty to act bona fide in what they, the directors, consider to be the interests of the company. In general it is for the directors, not the court, to decide what the interests of the company are but if the exercise of the relevant power could not possibly be considered by a reasonable man to be in the interests of the company it will not be valid.[2] A particular conundrum for directors is what is meant by 'the company'. Normally this means the shareholders (present and future) but this can change according to circumstance. If the company is insolvent, or in danger of becoming so, the interests of the creditors will replace those of the shareholders.[3] Section 309 of CA 1985 imposed a duty on directors to have regard to the interests of the employees in general, as well as the interests of the members, but that Act gave no further guidance on how this was to be done. Directors are probably not prevented from having regard to other interests, such as those of society at large or the local community, provided that it is likely to be in the interests of the company so to do, eg because it will enhance its reputation and prosperity.

(3) A duty to act for proper purposes and not for some 'collateral purpose'.[4] For example, directors cannot use their power to allot new shares to increase the votes of their

---

[2] *Gething v Kilner* [1972] 1 WLR 337, 342.   [3] *West Mercia Safetyware Ltd v Dodd* [1988] BCLC 250.
[4] *Re Smith and Fawcett Ltd* [1942] Ch 304, 306.

supporters[5] or to destroy an existing majority among the shareholders or create a new one that did not previously exist.[6]

(4) A duty to avoid conflicts of interest and duty. A fiduciary or agent cannot enter into engagements in which he has, or can have, a personal interest which conflicts or possibly may conflict with the interests of those whom he is bound to protect.[7] This rule gives rise to a number of associated rules:

(a) Disclosure.

Under the general law a director is under a duty to disclose the nature of any interest which he has in a contract, to which the company is or is to be a party, to the shareholders in a general meeting. The shareholders may sanction the contract. Disclosure to the board is not sufficient.

Statute in s 317 of CA 1985 also imposed a duty on a director, including a shadow director, who was in any way, directly or indirectly, interested in a contract or proposed contract with the company to declare the nature of his interest at a meeting of the directors.

The articles commonly contain provision releasing a director from the duty to disclose to the shareholders under the general law provided he complies with s 317 (see art 85 of the 1985 Table A).

(b) The duty not to make a secret profit. In common with other fiduciaries, any profit acquired by a director through holding his office as a director must be accounted for to the company. Again the shareholders can by ordinary resolution, or through acquiescence, permit him to retain the profit provided he has made full disclosure of it and the circumstances in which he acquired it.

(5) Duty to act with reasonable skill and care.

In addition to developments in the law of negligence, the jurisprudence surrounding ss 6 and 8 of the Directors Disqualification Act 1986 has defined more rigorous standards for directors. Further, s 214 of the Insolvency Act 1986 introduced a new liability of wrongful trading under which the standard for a director was that of:

... a reasonably diligent person having both—

(a) the general knowledge, skill and experience that may reasonably be expected of a person carrying out the same functions as are carried out by that director in relation to the company, and

(b) the general knowledge, skill and experience that that director has.

It would clearly be anomalous if the standard expected of a director at common law varied substantially from this standard and there is a body of first instance decisions which indicate that the applicable standard is now that laid down in s 214 of the Insolvency Act 1986.[8]

---

[5] *Hogg v Cramphorn Ltd* [1967] Ch 254.   [6] *Howard Smith Ltd v Ampol Petroleum Ltd* [1974] AC 821 (PC).

[7] See per Lord Cranworth in *Aberdeen Rly Co v Blaikie Bros* (1854) 1 Macq 461, 471; *Bhullar v Bhullar* [2003] 2 BCLC 241.

[8] *Re D'Jan of London* [1994] 1 BCLC 561; *Norman v Theodore Goddard* [1991] BCLC 1028; *Re Simmon Box (Diamonds) Ltd* [2000] BCC 275; *Westlowe Storage and Distribution Ltd* [2000] 2 BCLC 590.

B. INTRODUCTION TO THE NEW LAW

13.08 The main objects of the new law are:

(1) to provide a partial codification of directors' general duties; and

(2) to amend the existing law where required so that it corresponds with more modern business practices.

13.09 The codification is not entirely exhaustive or self-contained in that:

(1) it does not cover all the duties that a director may owe to the company—there is an express exception in respect of the director's duty to consider the interests of creditors in certain circumstances;

(2) it expressly provides for the duties to develop alongside and in accordance with the general law.

13.10 Among the amendments to the existing law are:

(1) The abolition of the rule that transactions between a director and the company have to be authorized by either the members or the board. Instead, the director's interest in the transactions or arrangement must, subject to certain exceptions, be declared under either ss 177 or 182.

(2) Most conflicts of interest arising from dealings between the director and third parties can now be authorized by the board, provided the conflicted directors have not participated in the decision or if the decision would have been valid even without their participation. Public companies that wish to adopt such board authorization will need to make specific provision for it in their constitution. One exception is acceptance of benefits from third parties which cannot be authorized by the board.

C. GENERAL DUTIES

1. General provisions

13.11 Chapter 2 of Part 10 of CA 2006 deals with directors' duties. Section 170 deals with the scope and nature of the general duties. Section 170(1) makes it clear that the director owes the duties set out in ss 171–177 of the Act to the company of which he is a director and not to anyone else. The general duties replace the common law rules and equitable principles upon which they are based (s 170(3)). Section 170(4) contains two important general principles:

(1) that the new general duties are to be interpreted and applied in the same way as the common law rules or equitable principles; and

(2) that regard shall be had to the corresponding common law rules or equitable principles in interpreting and applying the general duties.

This means that the new duties should be applied in the same way as the duties they replace and that their interpretation and application should be in line with developments in the general law. Thus, the new duties should not develop as a separate code divorced from developments in the general law but instead should develop alongside and in a manner consistent with it. The implication from this is that the choice of wording for the new duties is not intended to indicate any change or radical departure from the traditional formulations used to describe the particular duties. However, it is possible that the new formulations will impact on the interpretation of the new statutory duties.

The duties are cumulative and, except where otherwise provided, more than one duty may apply in any given case (s 179). One exception is conflicts of interest arising in relation to transactions with the company (s 175(3)). These are not caught by the 'no conflicts' duty in s 175 but only by the duty to declare the interest in either s 177 or s 182. Taking a bribe would be a breach of a number of duties. It is contrary to the express prohibition on accepting benefits from third parties in s 176. As regards the transaction between the third party and the company in respect of which he is being bribed, the director will have a declarable interest under s 177 and in so far as he was responsible for authorizing the transaction he would also be in breach of the duty to promote the success of the company (s 172) and the duty to exercise independent judgement (s 173).   13.12

As regards all the general duties, the ability of the members to authorize what would otherwise have been a breach of those duties is preserved in s 180(4)(a). In the case of authorization by directors to conflicts of interest under s 175 or where an interest in a proposed transaction or arrangement with the company is declared under s 177, the transaction cannot be set aside by virtue of any common law or equitable rule requiring members' consent or approval (s 180(1)), but this is without prejudice to any enactment or provision in the company's constitution requiring such consent or approval. Also, where the company's articles contain provisions dealing with conflicts of interest, the general duties are not infringed by anything done or omitted by the directors, or any of them, in accordance with those provisions (s 180(4)(b)).   13.13

As with CA 1985, a director includes any person occupying the position of director by whatever name called (s 250). The duties will apply to a de facto director. Section 170(5) provides that the new general duties apply to shadow directors[9] to the extent that the corresponding common law rules and principles so apply. Therefore there is no change in the law as regards shadow directors. Where the duty applied to them before, it will continue to do so and where it did not, it will not under the new regime.   13.14

The common law and equitable consequences of or remedies for breach (or threatened breach) of these duties are the same as those for breach of the duties under the corresponding common law rule or equitable principle (s 178(1)) and the fiduciary duties (namely, all those except the duty to exercise reasonable care, skill, and diligence in s 174) are enforceable in the same way as any other fiduciary duty owed to a company by its director (s 178(2)).   13.15

Some of the cases will fall within Chapter 4 (transactions requiring members' approval—such as substantial property transactions with a director) as well. Compliance with the general duties does not remove the need for approval under any applicable provision of Chapter 4 (s 180(3)). The general duties will still apply except that ss 175 (duty to avoid conflicts) and 176 (duty not to accept benefits from third parties) will not apply where   13.16

---

[9] Defined in s 251, as in CA 1985, as being a person in accordance with whose directions or instructions the directors are accustomed to act but that a person is not to be regarded as a shadow director by reason only that the directors act on advice given by him in a professional capacity. But a body corporate is not to be regarded as a shadow director of any of its subsidiaries for the purposes of Chapters 2, 4, and 6 by reason only that the directors of the subsidiary are accustomed to act in accordance with its directions or instructions.

Chapter 4 applies and either approval is given under Chapter 4 or the matter is one as to which it is provided that approval is not needed (s 180(2)).

13.17   The general duties have effect except as otherwise provided or as the context otherwise requires notwithstanding any enactment or rule of law (s 180(5)).

2. Duty to act within powers: s 171

13.18   Section 171 sets out the first of the general duties which is a duty:

(a) to act in accordance with the company's constitution, and

(b) to only exercise powers for the purposes for which they are conferred.

Formerly these would have been seen as two distinct duties, although in one sense the latter is part of the obligation to act within the company's constitution. There may be a question mark over whether the inclusion of the word 'only' is intended to prohibit mixed purposes; under the current law it is the primary purpose that matters. The company's constitution means more than simply the articles and any resolution or agreement to which Chapter 3 applies (s 17). It includes: (a) any resolution or other decision come to in accordance with the constitution; and (b) any decision by the members, or a class of members, that is treated by virtue of any enactment or rule of law as equivalent to a decision by the company (see s 257).

3. Duty to promote the success of the company: s 172

13.19   Section 172(1) provides that a director must act in the way he considers, in good faith, would most likely promote the success of the company for the benefit of its members as a whole. It also provides that in doing so the director must have regard (amongst other matters) to the following:

(a) the likely consequences of any decision in the long term,

(b) the interest of the company's employees,

(c) the need to foster the company's business relationships with suppliers, customers and others,

(d) the impact of the company's operations on the community and the environment,

(e) the desirability of the company maintaining a reputation for high standards of business conduct, and

(f) the need to act fairly as between members of the company.

This is a substantial reformulation of the duty to act bona fide in the interests of the company. Unlike the other formulations this goes further than the previous law. No doubt directors could take these matters into account under the old law, and frequently did, but with the exception of the interests of employees (s 309 of CA 1985), there was no express obligation on them to do so. The intention is to inject a certain amount of objectivity into the duty.

13.20   This formulation makes it clear that in this context the company means the shareholders and gives effect to the principle of 'enlightened shareholder value'. Further the concept of the 'interests of the company' is replaced with the concept of the success of the company, which may be more readily understandable by the business community. The new formulation as regards the interests of employees is clearer than s 309 of CA 1985, which it replaces. Employees are not stakeholders in the company ranking equally with the shareholders. The interests of employees are simply one of the matters to be taken into account as part of the duty to promote the success of the company for the benefit of the shareholders.

It would seem implicit that the directors only have to have regard to the matters listed in s 172(1) to the extent that they are relevant, though this is not expressly stated. Section 172 leaves it up to the directors to decide to what extent any particular matter is relevant and how it is to be taken into account. Consistently with the jurisprudence surrounding the old duty to act bona fide in the interests of the company, the courts should not interfere unless a reasonable director could not possibly have reached the same conclusion as the directors. The wording suggested by the CLR included a reference to practicality. The CLR had in mind that sometimes the directors would not have time to identify all relevant factors. Section 172 contains no such proviso but again this may be implicit. **13.21**

Section 172(2) deals with the situation where the company exists for purposes other than the benefit of its members, such as a charitable company. To the extent that the company's purposes consist of or include purposes other than the benefit of its members, the reference in s 172(1) to promoting the success of the company for the benefit of its members is replaced by achieving those purposes. **13.22**

Section 172(3) protects the interests of creditors by providing that the duty imposed by s 172 has effect subject to any enactment or rule of law requiring directors, in certain circumstances, to consider or act in the interests of creditors of the company. The section does not provide any guidance on what those circumstances are or how the interests of creditors are to be considered. These are left to the general law and the Insolvency Act 1986. Where the company is hopelessly insolvent the duty to promote its success would seem to be at an end. **13.23**

Section 247 of CA 2006, formerly s 719 of CA 1985, repeats the power for directors to make provision for employees or former employees on the cessation or transfer of all or part of the undertaking of the company or a subsidiary. This power is exercisable notwithstanding the general duty in s 172 (s 247(2)). In the case of a company that is a charity, it is exercisable notwithstanding any restrictions on the directors' powers or the company's capacity flowing from its objects (s 247(3)). The power can only be exercised (s 247(4)) if sanctioned either by a resolution of the members (ordinary resolution unless the articles require a higher majority or unanimity: s 281(3)) or of the directors. A directors' resolution has to be authorized by the company's articles and, unlike s 719 of CA 1985, the directors cannot now sanction payments to or for the benefit of themselves or former directors or shadow directors (s 247(6)). Any other requirements of the company's articles as to the exercise of this power must be complied with (s 247(7)) and any payment must be made before the commencement of any winding up of the company and out of profits available for dividend (s 247(8)). **13.24**

4. Duty to exercise independent judgment: s 173

A director must exercise independent judgement (s 173(1)). This duty is not infringed (s 173(2)) by acting: **13.25**

(a) in accordance with an agreement duly entered into by the company that restricts the future exercise of discretion by its directors, or

(b) in a way authorised by the company's constitution.

This duty is often not dealt with expressly in text books. This statement of the duty serves as a reminder to directors, especially of small companies and wholly owned subsidiaries, that the office of director requires them to decide questions for themselves and not to simply act at the direction of some other, such as the owner of the company. The first exception in (a) above gives recognition to cases such as *Fulham Football Club Ltd v Cabra Estates plc*,[10] which held that directors had not improperly fettered their discretion where, as part of a commercial transaction conferring benefits on the company, they had agreed to exercise their powers in a certain way. The section does not deal with the directors' power to delegate which will be governed by the company's constitution.

5. Duty to exercise reasonable care, skill, and diligence: s 174

13.26 Section 174(1) provides that a director has a duty to exercise reasonable care, skill, and diligence. Section 174(2), adopting a similar definition to that contained in s 214 of the Insolvency Act 1986, provides:

This means the care, skill and diligence that would be exercised by a reasonably diligent person with—

(a) the general knowledge, skill and experience that may reasonably be expected of a person carrying out the functions carried out by the director in relation to the company, and

(b) the general knowledge, skill and experience that the director has.

This means that the director's conduct is judged objectively under (a) but if he has any greater knowledge, skill, or experience than the ordinary director that will be taken into account against him under (b).

6. Duties concerning conflicts of interest—general

13.27 Sections 175–177 deal with conflicts of interest. Section 175 deals with conflicts of interest except those arising in relation to a transaction or arrangement with the company (s 175(3)). These will be caught instead by the duty to disclose in s 177, for a transaction/arrangement not yet entered into, and by s 182 if already entered into. The duties in ss 175 (duty to avoid conflicts of interest) and 176 (duty not to accept benefits from third parties) both apply to former directors, in the former case as regards the exploitation of any property, information, or opportunity of which he became aware at a time when he was a director and in the latter as regards things done or omitted by him before he ceased to be a director (s 170(2)(a) and (b)). Section 180(4)(b) preserves the company's ability to make express provision in its articles for dealing with conflicts of interest.

7. Duty to avoid conflicts of interest: s 175

13.28 Section 175(1) sets out the general duty that a director must avoid a situation in which he has, or can have, a direct or indirect interest that conflicts, or possibly may conflict, with the interests of the company. This is a direct transposition of the general equitable principle. Section 175(2) makes it clear that the duty applies in particular (but not exclusively) to the exploitation of any property, information, or opportunity and that it is immaterial whether the company could take advantage of it—a repetition of the existing law (see for example *Industrial Development Consultants Ltd v Cooley*[11]). Further, as a catch-all, s 175(7) states that any reference to a conflict of interest in s 175 includes a conflict of interest and duty and a conflict of duties.

13.29 Section 175(3) contains the exception for transactions or arrangements with the company and s 175(4) provides that the duty is not infringed:

---

[10] [1994] 1 BCLC 363.   [11] [1972] 1 WLR 443.

(a) if the situation cannot reasonably be regarded as likely to give rise to a conflict of interest; or

(b) if the matter has been authorised by the directors.

Presumably, in the light of s 175(2) the mere fact that the company could not have taken advantage of the opportunity itself does not mean that the opportunity can reasonably be regarded as not giving rise to a conflict of interest.

Authorization by the directors is new but is a recognition that most companies in fact   13.30
permit a director to have an interest in a proposed transaction with a company provided it has been declared and the view expressed by the CLR that the current strict rule relating to conflicts of interest in respect of personal exploitation of corporate opportunities fettered entrepreneurial activity by existing directors.

In the case of private companies authorization by directors is permitted unless the   13.31
company's constitution invalidates such authorization (s 175(5)(a)); but in the case of public companies it is only permitted if the company's constitution includes a provision enabling the directors to do so (s 175(5)(b)). This is in line with one of the Act's aims which is to make life simpler for private companies.

For the authorization to be effective, the requirement for a quorum at the directors'   13.32
meeting must be met excluding any interested directors and the matter must be agreed to without their votes being counted (or would have been agreed to if their votes had not been counted) (s 175(6)).

8. Duty not to accept benefits from third parties: s 176

Section 176(1) prohibits a director from accepting from a third party a benefit conferred by   13.33
reason of his (a) being a director or (b) his doing or not doing anything as a director. A 'third party' is a person other than the company, an associated body corporate,[12] or a person acting on behalf of the company or an associated body corporate (s 176(2)). Benefits received by the director from the person by whom his services (as a director or otherwise) are provided to the company are not regarded as conferred by a third party (s 176(3)). The duty is not infringed if the acceptance of the benefit could not reasonably be regarded as likely to give rise to a conflict of interest (s 176(4)) and/or a conflict of duties (s 176(5)). There is no provision for board authorization; authorization will have to come, if at all, from either the members or the articles under s 180(4). This prohibition would clearly cover matters such as bribes but, subject only to the exception in s 176(4), would also cover items like gifts at Christmas from suppliers or others who wish to curry favour with the directors.

9. Duty to declare interest in a proposed transaction or arrangement with the company: s 177

The requirement in s 317 of CA 1985 to declare interests in contracts (as defined) or   13.34
proposed contracts has now been split into two: proposed transactions, etc are dealt with in s 177 and existing contracts in s 182. The new regime clarifies a number of grey areas in the previous law and seeks to adopt a more practical approach.

Where a director is in any way, directly or indirectly, interested in a proposed transaction   13.35
or arrangement with the company, he must declare both the nature and the extent of

---

[12] For definition of 'associated body corporate' see s 256.

his interest to the other directors (s 177(1)). Unless the company's constitution otherwise requires, members' consent or approval is no longer required to proposed transactions or arrangements (s 180(1)). If the declaration proves to be or becomes inaccurate or incomplete the director must made a further declaration (s 177(3)). All declarations must be made before the company enters into the transaction or arrangement (s 177(4)). The formulation 'to the other directors' in s 177(1) means this section cannot apply to a sole director, unlike s 317 of CA 1985 which used the words 'at a meeting of the directors'.[13]

13.36   A director does not have to declare an interest:

(1) where he is not aware of the interest or of the transaction or arrangement but he is treated as being aware of matters of which he ought reasonably to be aware (s 177(5));

(2) where it cannot reasonably be regarded as likely to give rise to a conflict of interest (s 177(6)(a));

(3) if, or to the extent that, the other directors are already aware of it—and they too are treated as being aware of anything of which they ought reasonably to be aware (s 177(6)(b));

(4) if, or to the extent that, it concerns the terms of his service contract and these have been or are to be considered either by a meeting of the directors or by a directors' committee appointed for that purpose under the company's constitution.

13.37   The section does not lay down any rules as to how the declaration should be made except to say (s 177(2)) that it may (but need not) be made at a directors' meeting or by notice under either ss 184 (notice in writing) or 185 (general notice). There is no restriction on the conflicted director participating in the decision relating to the transaction. Any restriction would have to be found in the articles.

13.38   The director does not need to be personally involved in the proposed transaction in order to have an interest in it: an indirect interest, eg through his wife, will suffice. Treating a director as knowing matters of which he ought reasonably to be aware means that it is more difficult for a director to claim ignorance of the matters referred to in s 177(5) but it could mean that a director breaches this duty in genuine ignorance of the conflict in question.

D. MODIFICATION FOR CHARITABLE COMPANIES

13.39   There are four modifications in respect of charitable companies set out in s 181 (which does not apply to Scotland: s 181(5)):

(1) Whereas for ordinary companies the duty in s 175 to avoid conflicts of interest does not apply to conflicts arising in relation to a transaction or arrangement with the company, this only applies to charitable companies if or to the extent that the company's articles permit it, which they may do only in relation to descriptions of a transaction or arrangement specified in the company's articles (s 181(2)(a)).

(2) As with other companies the directors may give authorization to a transaction or arrangement in which a director has a conflict of interest under s 175 but in the case of a charitable company its constitution must contain a provision enabling them to do

---

[13] For the application of s 317 to a sole director see *Neptune (Vehicle Washing Equipment) Ltd v Fitzgerald* [1995] 1 BCLC 352 where it was held that in the case of a sole director the requirement was met if the director made the declaration at a 'meeting' consisting only of himself.

so by the matter being proposed to and authorized by them in accordance with the constitution (s 181(2)(b)).

(3) The exemption in s 180(2)(b)—from the necessity to comply with ss 175 (duty to avoid conflicts) and 176 (duty not to accept benefits from third parties) where the case falls within Chapter 4 and the matter is one to which it is provided that the approval of the members is not needed—only applies to a charitable company if, or to the extent that, the company's articles allow the duty to be disapplied, which they may do only in relation to descriptions of a transaction or arrangement specified in the company's articles.

(4) The final modification is to s 26(5) of the Charities Act 1993 which empowers the Charity Commissioners to authorize dealings with charity property, etc. A new s 26(5A) is to be inserted allowing the Commissioners to authorize an act where the charity is a company notwithstanding that it may involve a breach of a general duty of a director arising under Chapter 2 of Part 10 of CA 2006.

E. DECLARATION OF INTEREST IN EXISTING TRANSACTION OR ARRANGEMENT

The provisions relating to declarations of interest in existing transactions or arrangements, formerly contained in s 317 of CA 1985, are dealt with in Chapter 3. The new provisions are not identical to the old ones. Section 182(1) imposes a duty on a director who is in any way, directly or indirectly interested in a transaction or arrangement that has been entered into by the company to declare the nature and extent of his interest to the other directors in accordance with that section.   13.40

The duty does not apply in the following situations: 13.41

(1) If or to the extent that the interest has been declared under s 177 (duty to declare interest in proposed transactions) (see s 182(1)). Presumably, if the declaration under s 177 was found to be incomplete after the transaction had been entered into, a supplementary declaration would be required under s 182.

(2) If the director is not aware of (a) the interest or (b) the transaction or arrangement; but, as with s 177, the director is treated as being aware of matters of which he ought reasonably to be aware (s 182(5)).

(3) If the interest cannot reasonably be regarded as likely to give rise to a conflict of interest (s 182(6)(a)).

(4) If, or to the extent that, the other directors are already aware of it (and they are treated as being aware of anything of which they ought reasonably to be aware) (s 182(6)(b)).

(5) If, or to the extent that, it concerns the terms of his service contract which have been or are to be considered (a) by a meeting of the directors or (b) by a committee of them appointed for the purpose under the company's constitution (s 182(6)(c)).

If any declaration made under s 182 proves to be or becomes inaccurate or incomplete, the director must make a further declaration (s 182(3)).   13.42

The declaration must be made as soon as reasonably practicable but failure to comply with this requirement does not affect the underlying duty to make the declaration, ie it still has to be made, albeit late (s 182(4)).   13.43

13.44   The declaration must be made (s 182(2)):

(a) at a meeting of the directors, or
(b) by notice in writing (see section 184), or
(c) by general notice (see section 185).

13.45   The notice in writing under s 184 must be sent to the other directors (s 184(2)). It may be in hard copy form or in electronic form provided the recipient has agreed to receive it in that particular electronic form (s 184(3)). It may be sent by hand or post or the agreed electronic means (s 184(4)). Where the director makes a declaration in writing in accordance with this section it is deemed to form part of the proceedings at the next directors' meeting and the provisions of s 248 (minutes of directors' meetings) apply as if the declaration had been made at the meeting (s 184(5)).

13.46   A general notice under s 185 is treated as a sufficient declaration of the interest in relation to the matters to which it relates (s 185(1)). The notice is to the effect that the director either:

(a) has an interest (as member, officer, or otherwise) in a specified body corporate or firm; or

(b) is connected with some other specified person,

and is to be regarded as interested in any transaction or arrangement that may after the date of the notice be made with that body corporate, firm, or person (s 185(2)). The notice must state the nature and extent of the director's interest in the body corporate or firm or the nature of his connection with the person (s 185(3)). It is not effective unless given at a meeting of the directors or the director takes reasonable steps to secure that it is brought up and read at the next directors' meeting after it is given (s 185(4)).

13.47   Failure to comply with s 182 is a criminal offence (unlike s 177) and the director is liable to a fine, unlimited on indictment and subject to the statutory maximum (currently £5000) on summary conviction (s 183). Unlike s 177, there are no civil consequences for failure to comply with s 182 and the contract remains valid.

13.48   Where a company, required to have two directors, has only one director, he complies with s 182 by making a written record of the declaration; the declaration is deemed to form part of the proceedings at the next directors' meeting and the provisions of s 248 (minutes of directors' meetings) apply as if the declaration had been made at that meeting (s 186(1)).[14] Section 186 does not affect the operation of s 231 (contracts with sole member who is also a director not in the ordinary course of business to be recorded in writing). It follows on from s 186 and the requirement in s 182(1) for the declaration to be made to the other directors that s 182 does not apply to a sole director of a company only required to have one director.

13.49   Section 182 and Chapter 3 generally, like the old s 317, apply to a shadow director (s 187(1)) but, as he will not normally attend directors' meetings, he does not have the option of making the declaration at a director's meeting under s 182(2)(a) (see s 187(2)) nor of giving a general notice at a directors' meeting or having it brought up and read at a directors' meeting in accordance with s 185(4) (s 187(3)). A shadow director has either to give a written notice under s 184 or a general notice but a general notice by a shadow director has to be given in writing in accordance with s 184 (s 187(4)). This means his general notice must comply with ss 185(1)–(3) and 184.

---

[14] cf *Neptune (Vehicle Washing Equipment) Ltd v Fitzgerald* [1995] 1 BCLC 352.

F. TRANSACTIONS WITH DIRECTORS REQUIRING MEMBERS' APPROVAL

1. General

Chapters 4 and 5 of CA 2006 replacing the provisions formerly in Part X of CA 1985, are 13.50
designed to deal with specific situations in which a director has a conflict of interest; but
with a number of changes. These changes are designed:

(1) to be more readily comprehensible;

(2) to improve consistency; and

(3) to implement various recommendations of the Law Commission and the CLR.

There are two main categories: 13.51

(1) those matters requiring members' approval; and
(2) those merely requiring disclosure to members.

The matters requiring approval of members are: long-term service contracts; substantial 13.52
property transactions; loans, quasi-loans, and credit transactions; and payments for loss of
office. These are dealt with in Chapter 4.

The matters merely requiring disclosure to members are directors' service contracts 13.53
(Chapter 5) and qualifying third party indemnity provisions (Chapter 7). Chapter 6 deals
with contracts with sole members who are directors.

The requirements in Part X of CA 1985 to disclose and maintain a register of share 13.54
dealings by directors and their families are repealed. There are no longer criminal penalties
for failure to comply with the Chapter 4 requirements and the civil consequences for failure
to obtain members' approval to substantial property transactions and loans, quasi-loans, and
credit transactions have been made the same.

2. Members' approval

For all the transactions covered by Chapter 4 the members' approval by an ordinary resolution 13.55
is sufficient unless the company's articles require a higher majority or unanimity (s 281(3)).
Where approval is required under more than one provision of Chapter 4, the requirements
of each applicable provision must be met, but no separate resolution is required for the
purposes of each provision (s 225).

In the case of long-term service contracts (s 188), loans, etc (ss 197, 198, 200, 201, and 13.56
203), and payments for loss of office (ss 217, 218 and 219) a memorandum setting out
various matters must in the case of a written resolution be sent or submitted to every eligible
member at or before the time at which the proposed resolution is sent or submitted to
him and in the case of a resolution at a meeting, it must be made available to members
for inspection both at the company's registered office for not less than 15 days ending with
the day of the meeting and at the meeting itself.[15] Where approval is sought by written
resolution and a memorandum is required under Chapter 4 to be sent or submitted to

---

[15] Sections 188(5), 197(3), 198(4), 200(4), 201(4), 203(3), 217(3), 218(3), and 219(3).

eligible members before the resolution is passed any accidental failure to send or submit the memorandum is to be disregarded, subject to any provision in the company's articles (s 224).

13.57   The provisions in Chapter 4 apply where the transaction involves a director of the company or of its holding company.[16] In the latter case approval is required both from the members of the company and of the holding company.[17]

13.58   Members' approval is not required under Chapter 4 if that body corporate:

(a) is not a UK-registered company;[18] or

(b) is a wholly-owned subsidiary of another body corporate.[19]

13.59   Where the company is a charity the Charity Commissioners' prior written consent is required otherwise:

(a) any approval by the members under ss 188, 190, 197, 198, 200, 202, 203, 216, or 217; or

(b) any affirmation under ss 196 or 214

is ineffective (s 226 which substitutes a new s 66 of the Charities Act 1993). In addition, where there is an exception to any of the provisions referred to in (a) the charity must nonetheless not take advantage of the exception without the Charity Commissioners' prior written consent. If it does so the exception is treated as of no effect (s 226 inserting a new s 66A of the Charities Act 1993).

13.60   The provisions of Chapter 4 apply to a shadow director as they do to an ordinary director except that any reference to loss of office as a director does not apply to loss of his status as a shadow director (s 222).

3. Directors' long-term service contracts

13.61   Section 188 contains in clearer terms the provisions, formerly in s 319 of CA 1985, which require members' approval to a provision restricting the company's right to terminate the director's employment, the period during which the restriction applies now being called 'the guaranteed term'. Section 189 reproduces the provisions, previously contained in s 319(6) of the CA 1985, dealing with the consequences of failing to obtain members' approval: the provision is void to the extent of the contravention and the company is entitled to terminate the contract on reasonable notice. The only significant change is that the length of 'the guaranteed term' to which the section applies has been reduced from five years to two years. In addition, it is now expressly provided that in the case of employment terminable by the company by notice, the guaranteed term includes the period of notice.

---

[16] In many cases the transaction is caught whether it is with such a director or a person connected with him.

[17] Sections 188(2), 190(2), 197(2), 198(2), 200(2), 201(2), 203(2), 217(2), 218(2), and see also s 219(1) and (2), approval required from relevant shareholders, meaning shareholders of the shares or same class of shares to which the offer relates.

[18] For definition see s 1158—a company registered under CA 2006 excluding an overseas company that has registered particulars under s 1046.

[19] Sections 188(6), 190(4), 197(5), 198(6), 200(6), 201(6), 202(5), 217(4), 218(4), and 219(6).

4. Substantial property transactions

The provisions formerly in ss 320–322 of CA 1985 requiring members' consent to an arrangement whereby a company acquires or disposes of a non-cash asset over a certain value from or to a director or a person connected with him are now contained in ss 190–196. The substance is the same but set out in a more readily accessible format. **13.62**

The prohibition is set out in s 190(1). The remaining sections deal with the meaning of 'substantial' (s 191), various exceptions in ss 192–194, the civil consequences of contravention (s 195), and the effect of subsequent affirmation (s 196). Whereas previously the asset had to be worth a minimum of £2000, now it has to be worth more than £5000 and, as before, exceed ten per cent of the company's asset value (s 191(2)(a)). The alternative of exceeding £100,000 remains the same (s 191(2)(b)). It is now possible for the company to enter into such an arrangement conditionally on members' approval being obtained (s 190(1) and (2)). It is also now expressly provided that the company is not subject to any liability for failing to obtain members' approval (s 190(3)). **13.63**

Another new provision is that where the arrangement involves more than one non-cash asset or it is one of a series of arrangements the value of the non-cash assets is to be aggregated (s 190(5)). Also, s 190 does not apply to anything to which a director is entitled under his service contract or to payments for loss of office as defined in s 215 (s 190(6)). **13.64**

The company's asset value for this purpose is the value of the company's net assets, which are to be determined by reference to the most recent statutory accounts, provided statutory accounts have been prepared. 'Most recent' statutory accounts are now defined as those in relation to which the time for sending them out to members under s 424 is most recent (s 191(3) and (4)). If no statutory accounts have been prepared the company's asset value is the amount of the company's called-up share capital (s 191(3)(b)). **13.65**

The exemption for transactions between a company and a person in his character as member has now been extended to disposals by the member as well as to acquisitions by him (s 192(a)). The exception for winding-up[20] has been extended to administration and in both cases approval under s 190 is not required (a) by the members or (b) for an arrangement entered into by the company (s 193(2)). **13.66**

5. Loans, quasi-loans, etc

Sections 197–214 contain a substantial reworking of the provisions contained in ss 330–342 of CA 1985. Much of the material remains the same. Under the new regime none of the prohibitions is any longer absolute: all subject to members' approval. Subsequent ratification by the members is also possible provided it is given within a reasonable time (s 214). The criminal sanctions, formerly contained in s 342 of CA 1985, have been abolished. One proposed change was reversed at the last minute. In draft form, the prohibitions on quasi-loans and credit transactions were going to apply to all companies. The final form of CA 2006 reverts to the position under CA 1985 and these prohibitions only apply to a public company or a company associated with it. **13.67**

Under the new regime each prohibition is contained in a separate section and these are followed by exceptions which generally apply to all the prohibitions. This format contains **13.68**

---

[20] Excluding members' voluntary winding-up.

a certain amount of repetition as some provisions are repeated in each section containing a prohibition.

13.69   The prohibition on loans to directors or giving guarantees or providing security in connection with them without members' approval is now contained in s 197(1). The prohibition on a public company or a company associated with a public company[21] making quasi-loans to a director or giving a guarantee or providing security in connection with a quasi-loan is contained in s 198(1). As regards a public company or a company associated with a public company the prohibitions on loans and quasi-loans, etc extend to a person connected with the director of the company (or of its holding company) and this is dealt with separately in s 200. The proposal to extend the prohibition on loans by private companies to persons connected with a director was dropped at the last moment. The definition of 'quasi-loan' and related expressions[22] are retained and are contained in s 199, although the expanded definition of 'guarantee' to include indemnity (formerly s 331(1) of CA 1985) does not appear to have been repeated, probably being regarded as superfluous.

13.70   The prohibition on a public company (or a company associated with it) from entering into credit transactions (and guarantees and securities in connection with them) for the benefit of a director or a person connected with him, formerly in s 330(4) of CA 1985, is now contained in s 201(1). Whereas before it was absolute now it is subject to the approval of members. Section 202(1) repeats the definition of 'credit transaction' formerly contained in s 331(7) of CA 1985.[23]

13.71   The prohibition on a company entering into related transactions, formerly in s 330(6) and (7) of CA 1985, is now contained in s 203(1) and these transactions are now subject to members' approval.

13.72   For the purposes of ss 197–214 the definition of the person for whom a transaction or arrangement is entered into, formerly contained in s 331(9) of CA 1985, is repeated in s 212.[24]

13.73   The current exceptions where members' approval is not required under ss 197, 198, 200, or 201 are now:

(1) Expenditure on company business (s 204), formerly contained in s 337 of CA 1985. This exception is now extended to directors of a holding company and persons connected with the director. The requirement for members' approval for this expenditure has been abolished and the maximum aggregate amount of the transaction and other relevant transactions has been increased from £20,000 to £50,000.

(2) Expenditure on defending proceedings, etc (s 205), formerly s 337A of CA 1985.[25] This applies to directors and now directors of the holding company. The types of criminal and civil proceedings to which this exception applies are now limited to those in connection with any alleged negligence, default, breach of duty, or breach of trust by the director in relation to the company. The exception for applications for relief remains the same. As

---

[21] Section 256(b) defines a company as associated with another company if one is a subsidiary of the other or both are subsidiaries of the same body corporate. For the definition of subsidiary see s 1261(1) which in turn refers to s 1159 and Sch 6.

[22] Formerly s 331(3) and (4) of CA 1985.

[23] Other definitions such as 'services' and 'conditional sale agreement' and the person for whose benefit the credit transaction is entered into also remain the same (compare s 202(3) and (2) with s 331(8), (9)(b), and (10) of CA 1985.

[24] Section 212(b) is mirrored in s 202(2).

[25] Inserted by s 20 of the Companies (Audit, Investigations and Community Enterprise) Act 2004 with effect from 6 April 2005.

before, for these exceptions to apply the director must be required to repay in the event that the proceedings go against him.

(3) Expenditure in connection with regulatory action or investigation (s 206). This is new. It applies where the company does anything to provide a director or a director of its holding company with funds to meet expenditure (or to avoid meeting expenditure) incurred or to be incurred by him in defending himself either: (a) in an investigation by a regulatory authority; or (b) against action proposed by a regulatory authority in connection with any alleged negligence, default, breach of duty, or breach of trust by him in relation to the company. Unlike the previous exception there is no requirement that the director must be required to repay if his defence is not successful.

(4) Minor and business transactions.

(a) The small loan exception to s 197, formerly s 334 of CA 1985, is now also an exception to ss 198 and 200 and is no longer limited to directors of the company or its holding company (s 207(1)). The aggregate value of the transaction and of other relevant transactions for this exception is now £10,000[26] (s 207(1)).

(b) The limit on the exception to s 201, previously contained in s 335(1) of CA 1985, for transactions in aggregate not exceeding £10,000 is now £15,000 (s 207(2)).

(c) The exception for transactions under s 201 in the ordinary course of business, formerly in s 335(2) of CA 1985, is preserved in s 207(3).

(5) The exception for inter-group transactions (s 208). These were formerly contained in ss 333 and 336 of CA 1985. The exception has been simplified. No approval is required under ss 197, 198, or 200 in respect of transactions with or for the benefit of an associated body corporate. By virtue of s 256 a body corporate is associated with another if one is a subsidiary[27] of the other or both are subsidiaries of the same body corporate.

(6) Money-lending companies.

This exception, formerly in s 338 of CA 1985, which applies to ss 197, 198, and 200, has been retained (s 209). The limit of £100,000 has now been removed. The 'home loan' exception, which applied to directors and directors of the holding company, now also extends to employees of the company.

The short-term quasi-loan exception in s 332 of CA 1985 has been abolished. 13.74

Section 210 contains more simplified provisions for ascertaining other relevant transactions 13.75 for the purposes of any of the exceptions (formerly contained in s 339 of CA 1985). Section 211 contains the provisions for ascertaining the value of transactions or arrangements for the purposes of ss 197–214 (previously s 340 of CA 1985). The only major change is that where the value of the transaction or arrangement is not capable of being expressed in a sum of money its value is deemed to exceed £50,000 (formerly £100,000).

The provisions relating to the consequences of breaching ss 197, 198, 200, 201, or 203 are 13.76 set out in s 213. These are to substantially the same effect as s 341 of CA 1985. Section 214 introduces new provisions under which members of the company, and holding company if applicable, can ratify a breach of ss 197, 198, 200, 201, or 203 by resolution provided it is done within a reasonable period.

---

[26] Formerly £5000 (s 334). [27] For definition of 'subsidiary' see s 1261(1).

6. Payments for loss of office

13.77 The provisions contained in ss 312–316 of CA 1985 are expanded and are now set out in ss 215–222. The prohibition on making tax-free payments to directors in s 311 of CA 1985 is abolished.

13.78 Section 215 contains general definitions. References to compensation and consideration in Chapter 4 now include benefits other than in cash and payment has a corresponding meaning (s 215(2)). For the purposes of ss 217–221 indirect payments are now caught: payment to a person connected with a director or payment to any person at the direction of, or for the benefit of, a director or a person connected with him is treated as payment to the director (s 215(3)). References in those sections to payment by a person include payment to another person at the direction of, or on behalf of the person referred to (s 215(4)).

13.79 Section 215(1) contains a general definition for Chapter 4 of 'payment for loss of office'. This has now been expanded and no longer covers just loss of office as a director or retirement. It applies to a director or former director[28] and covers payment made:

(1) by way of compensation:
    (a) for loss of office as director of the company;
    (b) for loss, while a director of the company or in connection with ceasing to be a director of it, of:
        (i) any other office or employment in connection with the management of the affairs of the company;
        (ii) any office (as director or otherwise) or employment in connection with the management of the affairs of any subsidiary of the company;

(2) as consideration for or in connection with:
    (a) his retirement from office as director of the company; or
    (b) his retirement, while a director of the company or in connection with his ceasing to be a director of it, from:
        (i) any other office or employment in connection with the management of the affairs of the company, or
        (ii) any office (as director or otherwise) or employment in connection with the management of the affairs of any subsidiary undertaking of the company.

13.80 The prohibition on a company making a payment to a director for loss of office without members' approval is set out in s 217 (formerly s 312 of CA 1985). The prohibition on any person (not just the company) making a payment for loss of office in connection with the transfer of the whole or any part of the undertaking or property of the company or, which is new, of its subsidiary, without members' consent in now contained in s 218 (formerly s 313 of CA 1985).

13.81 The prohibition on any person (not just the company) making a payment to a director for loss of office in connection with the transfer of shares in the company or, which is new, a subsidiary, resulting from a takeover bid without members' approval is contained in s 219 (formerly s 314 of CA 1985). The reference to 'a takeover bid' simplifies and extends the previous provisions. The members' approval required in the case of s 219 is that of the

---

[28] As with the provisions of Chapter 4 generally payments by a subsidiary to a director of its holding company will also be caught and members' resolutions from both companies will be required (see eg s 217(2)).

holders of the shares to which the bid relates or any holders of shares of the same class (s 219(2)). Section 219(4) now prohibits the person making the offer or any associate of his (as defined in s 1260) from voting on the resolution but if otherwise so entitled:

(1) they are entitled to a copy of it if in writing;

(2) they are entitled to be given notice of the relevant meeting and to attend and speak and if present (in person or by proxy) to count towards the quorum (s 219(4)); and

(3) if the quorum is still not present after an adjournment, the payment is deemed (for the purposes of s 219) to have been approved (s 219(5)).

In the case of ss 217, 218, and 219 the provisions, formerly contained in s 316(2) of CA 1985, whereby any excess in the price obtained by the director over that which could have been obtained by other holders of the like shares or any valuable consideration given to the director by any person other than the company is deemed to have been a payment for loss of office, are repeated in s 216(2). Similarly, for these sections the rebuttable presumption, formerly in s 316(1) of CA 1985, that a payment made pursuant to an arrangement entered into as part of the agreement for the transfer in question of the whole or part of the undertaking of the company or its subsidiary or within one year before or two years afterwards is one to which the section applies is retained in ss 218(5) and 219(7).   **13.82**

The exceptions to ss 217, 218, and 219 for certain payments made in good faith, previously contained in s 316(3) of CA 1985, have been expanded in s 220 and now cover payments: **13.83**

(1) in discharge of a legal obligation (which in essence means an existing legal obligation not entered into, connected with, or in consequence of the event giving rise to the payment (for ss 217) or the transfer in question for ss 218 or 219[29]);

(2) by way of damages for breach of such an obligation;

(3) by way of settlement or compromise of any claim arising in connection with the termination of a person's office or employment; or

(4) by way of pension for past services.

Where the part of the payment falls within an exception and part does not, it is treated as if the parts were separate payments (s 220(5)).

There is now a new exception for small payments not exceeding £200 made by the company or any of its subsidiaries (s 221). These are to be aggregated with 'other relevant payments' as defined in s 221(3) and (4).   **13.84**

The consequences of making payments without approval (formerly ss 313(2) and 315 of CA 1985) have been simplified and made more coherent.   **13.85**

(1) If the payment contravenes s 217 (payment by the company for loss of office) it is held by the recipient on trust for the company making the payment and any director who authorized the payment is jointly and severally liable to indemnify the company for any loss (s 222(1)).

(2) If it is in contravention of s 218 (payment in connection with the transfer of undertaking etc) it is held by the recipient on trust for the company whose undertaking or property is or is proposed to be transferred (s 222(2)).

---

[29] See s 220(2), (3), and (4).

(3) If it is in contravention of s 219 (payment in connection with share transfer) it is held by the recipient on trust for the persons who have sold their shares as a result of the offer and the expenses incurred by the recipient in distribution of that sum among those persons is to be borne by him and not retained out of that sum (s 222(3)).

(4) If the payment contravenes ss 217 and 218, (2) above applies and not (1) above (s 222(4)).

(5) If the payment contravenes ss 217 and 219, (3) above applies and not (1) unless the court otherwise directs.

(6) The criminal offences formerly contained in s 314(3) of CA 1985 have been abolished.

G. DIRECTORS' SERVICE CONTRACTS

13.86   Chapter 5 now contains the provisions relating to the keeping of copies or memoranda of directors' contracts formerly contained in s 318 of CA 1985.

13.87   The term director's 'service contract' is now defined in s 227. The definition applies for the whole of Part 10 as well as for Chapter 5. The definition, which is new, covers a contract for whatever services a director, including a shadow director,[30] undertakes to perform personally, whether as a director or otherwise and whether for the company or a subsidiary. It also covers the situation where the director's services are made available by a third party. The provisions in Part 10 relating to directors' service contracts also apply to the terms of his appointment as a director.

13.88   Otherwise the provisions are to the same effect as those in s 318 of CA 1985 with the following exceptions:

(1) The copies and memoranda must be kept by the company for at least one year from the date the contract ends (s 228(3)).

(2) Defaults are no longer a criminal offence for the company but they remain so for every officer who is in default.

(3) Members are now entitled to be provided with a copy of the contract or memorandum within seven days on payment of the prescribed fee (s 229(2)) as well as being able to inspect it without charge, with power for the court to order performance.

(4) The exceptions for contracts requiring the director to work wholly or mainly outside the UK[31] and for contracts with less than 12 months to run[32] have been abolished. There are now no exceptions.

13.89   Under the new provisions all copies and memoranda must be kept at the company's registered office or at a place specified in regulations made under s 1136.

H. CONTRACTS WITH SOLE MEMBERS WHO ARE DIRECTORS

13.90   The provisions of s 322B of CA 1985 are now contained in Chapter 6 of Part 10, which in fact contains only one section: s 231. As the new Act permits public companies to have

---

[30] Section 230.   [31] Section 318(5) of CA 1985.   [32] Section 318(11) of CA 1985.

only one director, the provisions will now apply to public as well as private companies. It is no longer a criminal offence for the company to fail to comply with s 231 but it is for every officer who is in default; the validity of the contract is not affected. Section 231 requires that where a limited company, which has only one member who is also a director (including a shadow director), enters into an unwritten contract with that member, otherwise than in the ordinary course of business, the company must ensure that either there is a written memorandum of its terms or the terms are recorded in the minutes of the first board meeting after the making of the contract. This is in addition to any other enactment or rule of law that applies to contracts between a company and a director.

I. RESTRICTIONS ON PROVISIONS PROTECTING DIRECTORS FROM LIABILITY

The provisions in ss 232–238 of Chapter 7 stem from s 310 of CA 1985. In its original form, s 310(1) prohibited provisions, whether in the company's articles or in any contract with the company or otherwise, exempting or indemnifying any officer of the company or any auditor from any liability by virtue of any rule of law for any negligence, default, breach of duty, or breach of trust in relation to the company. Any such provision was void.[33] Section 19 of the Companies (Audit, Investigations and Community Enterprise) Act 2004[34] confined s 310 to auditors[35] and inserted new provisions as ss 309A–309C into CA 1985 dealing with the prohibition as regards directors, though the basic prohibitions remained the same. These did not repeat the reference to liability arising by virtue of any rule of law, thereby making it clear that it covered breaches of statutory provisions as well as breaches of the general law for negligence, default, etc.   13.91

In essence, the previous law, as contained in ss 309A–309C of CA 1985, is retained subject to: (a) a requirement on the company to retain a copy of a 'qualifying indemnity provision' (which is defined as either a qualifying third-party indemnity provision or a qualifying pension scheme indemnity provision: s 236(1)) or, if not in writing, the memorandum of it, for at least a year after its expiration; (b) a right for members to be provided with a copy on payment of the prescribed charge; and (c) the fact that it is now possible to have a qualifying pension scheme indemnity provision (see 13.96 below) as well as a qualifying third-party indemnity provision (essentially a provision whereby the company agrees to indemnify a director against liability incurred by him to third parties—ie not to the company or an associated company—subject to certain conditions: s 234); and (d) the abolition of any criminal liability on the company (as opposed to any officer) for failure to keep the copy or memorandum or allow inspection, etc of it.   13.92

The prohibition on exempting a director from liability for negligence, default, breach of duty, or breach of trust in relation to the company, formerly s 309A(2) of CA 1985, is now contained in s 232(1) and the prohibition on indemnities, formerly s 309(3) of CA 1985, in s 232(2). Section 232(4) provides that nothing in s 232 prevents a company's articles from making such provision as has previously been lawful for dealing with conflicts of interest.   13.93

---

[33] Section 310(2) of CA 1985.   [34] With effect from 6 April 2005.
[35] See now Chapter 6 of Part 17 of CA 2006.

This would seem to have the effect of preserving decisions like *Motivex v Bulfield*[36] which held that articles allowing a director to have interests in transactions which conflicted with the interests of the company, provided he disclosed the nature of his interest to the directors, were not prohibited (see also arts 78 and 84 of Table A to the 1948 Act, arts 85 and 94 of the 1985 Table A and art 15 of the draft Model Articles for Public Companies).

13.94   The prohibition on such indemnities is subject to three exemptions[37] (formerly two): (i) provisions permitting the company to take out insurance for a director (formerly s 309A(5)[38] of CA 1985, now s 233); (ii) qualifying third-party indemnity provisions (formerly s 309B of CA 1985, now s 234); and (iii) the new exemption for qualifying pension scheme indemnities contained in s 235.

13.95   The requirement for disclosure in the directors' report (formerly s 309C(1)–(3) of CA 1985) is retained in s 236 and now covers both qualifying third-party indemnity provisions and qualifying pension scheme indemnity provisions. Section 309C(5) of CA 1985 contained the requirement to keep a copy of the provision if in writing or, if not, a memorandum of its terms and to allow inspection by members and did so by applying s 318 of CA 1985 to those documents. CA 2006 does not adopt the method of cross-reference but sets out the provisions in full in s 237. Section 237(4) introduces the new requirement for the copy or memorandum to be retained for one year from the termination or expiry of the provision.[39] A member's right to inspect the copy or memorandum without charge is now contained in s 238(1) and s 238(2) introduces the new right of a member on payment of a prescribed fee to obtain a copy within seven days of receipt of the request by the company.

13.96   The qualifying pension scheme indemnity exception to the prohibition on indemnities (s 235) applies to a director of a company which is the trustee of an occupational pension scheme.[40] The permitted indemnity is against liability incurred in connection with the company's activities as trustee of the scheme. To qualify the indemnity must not cover any liability of the director to pay a fine imposed in criminal proceedings, a sum payable to a regulatory authority by way of penalty in respect of non-compliance with any requirement of a regulatory nature or any liability incurred by him in defending criminal proceedings in which he is convicted.

J. RATIFICATION

13.97   Section 239, which is new, preserves the general law principle that members may ratify acts of a director (including a former or shadow director). The section applies to conduct, which includes acts or omissions, of a director amounting to negligence, default, breach of duty, or breach of trust in relation to the company. Section 239(2) provides that the decision to ratify must be taken by the members. Generally, this may be taken by ordinary resolution, subject to anything in the company's articles requiring a higher majority or unanimity (s 281(3)).

[36] [1988] BCLC 104. The reasoning in that case that the no conflicts rule was not a duty has been doubted by the Court of Appeal in *Gwembe Valley Development Co Ltd v Koshy* [2004] 1 BCLC 131, but it was not suggested that such articles were invalid. The new statutory embodiment of this principle is expressly described as a duty (s 176(3)) but the general duties are to be interpreted and applied in the same way as the equitable principles.

[37] Section 232(2).

[38] Originally inserted as s 310(3)(a) in CA 1985 by the CA 1989.

[39] The copy or memorandum must be kept at the company's registered office or at a place specified in regulations made under s 1136.

[40] As defined in s 150(5) of the Finance Act 2004 (s 235(6)).

It is made clear by s 239(7) that the section does not address which acts can be ratified   13.98
and which cannot. Nor does it affect any other enactment or rule of law imposing additional
requirements for valid ratification. The section does not affect the validity of decisions taken
by unanimous consent nor the power of directors to agree not to sue or to settle or release
a claim by the company (s 239(6)). Therefore, the current position that there are some acts
which are incapable of being ratified, some that can only be ratified unanimously, and some
that can be ratified by ordinary resolution remains the same and is not clarified.

The section provides that the votes of the director, if a member of the company, and any   13.99
person connected with him are excluded. In the case of a written resolution the director
and any person connected with him are not eligible members (s 239(3)). This means that
the company does not have to send them a copy of the written resolution and they are
not counted when determining the number of votes required to pass the resolution. If the
resolution is proposed at a meeting, the director and any person connected with him may
attend the meeting, count towards the quorum, and take part in the meeting but their votes
are excluded when determining whether the necessary majority in favour has been obtained
(s 239(4)). The term 'connected person' is defined in s 252 but the definition is modified
for s 239. For the purposes of s 239, a director's fellow directors can be 'connected persons'
and the exception in s 252(3) does not apply (s 239(5)(d)).

K. CONNECTED PERSONS

The definition of a person being 'connected' with a director and vice versa for the purposes   13.100
of Part 10 is set out in ss 252–255 of CA 2006. Originally, these definitions were contained
in s 346 of CA 1985.[41] In the new Act these definitions have been split up so that s 252
defines when a person is connected with a director and vice versa. For the purposes of Part 10
the definition of what is meant by references to members of a director's family is contained
in s 253. Section 254 defines when a director is connected with a body corporate and s 255
defines when a director controls a body corporate.

The old law has otherwise been retained with the following exceptions: 13.101

(1) The reference to a director being 'associated' with a body corporate has been replaced by
    reference to a director being 'connected' with a body corporate.

(2) The reference to a Scottish firm in s 346(2)(e) of CA 1985 has been replaced in
    s 252(2)(e) by reference to a firm that is a legal person under the law of which it is
    governed.

(3) The definition of a director's family has been broadened. Under s 346(2)(a) of CA 1985
    that section only applied to a director's spouse, child, or stepchild and s 346(3) excluded
    children who had attained the age of 18. Under s 253 a director's family now includes
    in addition:

    (a) any civil partner;

    (b) any other person (whether of a different sex or the same sex) with whom the director
        lives as partner in an enduring family relationship but s 253(3) makes it clear that

---

[41] The rules for interpreting whether a person was interested in shares or debentures for the purposes of s 346(4)
and (5) were contained in Part 1 of Sch 13 to CA 1985. These are now contained in Sch 1 of the new Act.

      this does not apply to the director's grandparent or grandchild, sister, brother, aunt, uncle, or nephew or niece;

(c) the director's children or stepchildren over 18;

(d) any children or stepchildren of the director's partner in (b) above, who live with the director and are under 18, if not his children or stepchildren;

(e) the director's parents.

(4) There is an express exclusion for treasury shares in determining whether a director is connected with or controls a body corporate.

L. TRANSACTIONS UNDER FOREIGN LAW

13.102   Section 259 repeats the provision formerly contained in s 347 of CA 1985 that for the purposes of Part 10 it is immaterial whether the law (apart from the Act) that governs the arrangement or transaction is the law of the UK or not. This prevents any argument that because an arrangement or transaction is governed by foreign law it does not have to comply with Part 10.

M. RELIEF

13.103   The court's power to grant relief to officers (which will include directors) and auditors formerly contained in s 727 of CA 1985 is retained almost verbatim in s 1157.

14

DERIVATIVE CLAIMS

A. INTRODUCTION

A derivative action is an action brought by a member of a company on behalf of that 14.01
company. In 1997 the Law Commission recommended the introduction of a new statutory
derivative procedure 'with more modern, flexible and accessible criteria for determining
whether a shareholder can pursue' an action on behalf of a company.[1] Chapter 1 of Part 11
of CA 2006 gives effect to that recommendation by abolishing the common law derivative
action and replacing it with a statutory claim.

In placing the derivative action on a statutory footing the UK is following in the footsteps 14.02
of numerous other common law jurisdictions, including Canada, New Zealand, Australia,
Hong Kong, and Singapore. In those jurisdictions, as here, there have been essentially two
reasons for the introduction of a statutory derivative claim. First, a dissatisfaction with
the common law derivative action and the rule in *Foss v Harbottle*[2] which governs it and,
second, a desire to enable derivative claims to operate as a more effective tool of corporate
governance.

B. RULE IN *FOSS V HARBOTTLE*

The following three principles derived from the decisions in *Foss v Harbottle* and *Mozley v* 14.03
Alston[3] are compositely referred to as the rule in *Foss v Harbottle*:

(1) when a wrong is done to a company then only the company may sue for redress (the
Proper Plaintiff Principle);

---

[1] Law Commission, *Shareholders' Remedies* (Law Com No 246, Cm 3769, 1997), para 6.15.
[2] (1843) 2 Hare 461.   [3] (1847) 1 Ph 790.

(2) the court will not interfere with the internal management of a company acting intra vires (the Internal Management Principle); and

(3) a member cannot sue to rectify a mere irregularity if the act, when done regularly, would be within the powers of the company and if the intention of the majority of members is clear (the Irregularity Principle).

14.04   The strict application of the rule in *Foss v Harbottle* would preclude a member from bringing any proceedings on behalf of a company. However, there are exceptions to the rule, which were set out by the Court of Appeal in *Edwards v Halliwell*[4] in the following terms:

(1) where the alleged wrong is ultra vires the company;

(2) where the transaction complained of could be validly done or sanctioned only by a special resolution and could not, therefore, be sanctioned by a simple majority;

(3) where personal rights of members are infringed; and

(4) where what is complained of amounts to fraud and those responsible for the fraud are in control of the company.

14.05   Strictly speaking, only the fourth exception is a true exception to the rule in *Foss v Harbottle*. The other 'exceptions' are more properly described as situations in which the rule does not apply. It is within the scope of this exception, commonly referred to as 'a fraud on the minority', that the common law derivative action has operated.

14.06   The Law Commission criticized the rule in *Foss v Harbottle* for being 'complicated and unwieldy' and observed that 'there were situations which appeared to fall outside the fraud on the minority exception when it might be desirable for a member to be able to bring an action'.[5] The criticisms of the Law Commission echoed the observation of the Canadian Dickerson Committee that the rule engendered 'uncertainties' and 'obvious injustices'.[6]

C. COMMON LAW DERIVATIVE ACTION

14.07   At common law an action could be brought on behalf of a company by a registered member of that company in circumstances where conduct amounting to equitable fraud had caused the company to suffer a loss and the member was able to show that those responsible for such conduct were in control of the company.

14.08   In order to bring a common law derivative action it was necessary that those responsible for the conduct complained of had derived some benefit from such conduct. Thus, negligence by a director, who derived no benefit from his conduct, would probably not have been actionable by means of a derivative action. However, the common law did not impose any limitations regarding who could be a defendant to a derivative action.

14.09   At common law the ratification by a company of a wrong committed by a director of that company provided a complete bar to the commencement of a derivative action. Indeed, even if a formal ratification had not taken place, the fact that ratification might occur could preclude a derivative action.[7]

---

[4] [1950] 2 All ER 1064.   [5] *Shareholders' Remedies* (n 1 above) para 6.4.

[6] Proposal for a New Business Corporations Law for Canada (1971).

[7] *MacDougal v Gardiner* (1875) 1 Ch D 13.

The principle of judicial control of derivative actions was established by the Court of   14.10
Appeal in *Prudential Assurance Company Limited v Newman Industries Limited (No 2)*.[8] The
Court of Appeal held that, before proceeding with his action, a claimant ought to be required
to establish a prima facie case that the company is entitled to the relief sought and that the
action falls within the proper boundaries of the exception to the rule in *Foss v Harbottle*. The
prima facie case was to be established as a preliminary issue after the close of pleadings and
exchange of witness statements. In 1994 judicial control of derivative actions was tightened
by the introduction of RSC Ord 15, r 12A, which required a claimant to apply for leave to
continue the derivative action within 21 days of serving a statement of claim or receiving
notice of intention to defend (whichever was the later). With the introduction of the CPR,
RSC Ord 15, r 12A was replaced by CPR Part 19.9, which prevented a claimant taking any
further step in proceedings until an application for permission to continue the derivative
action had been made.

In *Wallersteiner v Moir (No 2)*[9] the Court of Appeal held that it was open to the court to   14.11
order that the company should indemnify the claimant against the costs incurred in pursuing
a derivative action. This jurisdiction was subsequently incorporated into RSC Ord 15,
r 12A(13) and then CPR Part 19.9(7). It is incumbent on a claimant applying for such an
order to show that it is genuinely needed.[10]

D. STATUTORY DERIVATIVE CLAIM

In line with the Law Commission's recommendation that a new statutory derivative   14.12
procedure should be introduced,[11] CA 2006 does not formulate a new rule to replace the
rule in *Foss v Harbottle*. Rather, it creates a new statutory derivative claim and lays down
procedural rules in accordance with which such claims are to be managed.

A statutory derivative claim is created by s 260(1) of CA 2006, which defines a 'derivative   14.13
claim' as proceedings brought by a member of a company:

(a) in respect of a cause of action vested in the company, and
(b) seeking relief on behalf of the company

CA 2006 effectively abolishes the common law derivative action by providing that a   14.14
derivative claim may only be brought under Chapter 1 of Part 11 of CA 2006 or pursuant
to an order of the court in proceedings brought for unfair prejudice under what was s 459 of
CA 1985 (now s 994 of CA 2006).[12]

CA 2006 widens the definition of 'member' for the purposes of a derivative claim by   14.15
providing that references to 'member' include persons, who are not registered as members, but
to whom shares in the company have been transferred by operation of law.[13] This provision
will enable trustees in bankruptcy and personal representatives of deceased members' estates
to bring derivative claims.

CA 2006 provides that a derivative claim may only be brought in respect of a cause of   14.16
action arising from an actual or proposed act or omission of a director involving negligence,
default, breach of duty, or breach of trust.[14] The ability to bring a derivative action in respect

---

[8] [1982] Ch 204.   [9] [1975] QB 373.   [10] *Smith v Croft (No 1)* [1986] 1 WLR 580.
[11] *Shareholders' Remedies* (n 1 above) para 6.15.   [12] Section 260(2).   [13] Section 260(5)(c).
[14] Section 260(3).

of negligence represents a significant widening of the scope of the remedy as compared with the position at common law. Furthermore, the wording clearly covers breaches of the extended and codified duties of company directors set out at Chapter 2 of Part 10 of CA 2006.[15] Thus, although the requirement that a derivative claim must be based on the unlawful conduct of a director serves to limit the circumstances in which a derivative claim might be brought, the scope of the conduct that might give rise to a derivative claim has been widened significantly. This is consistent with the policy of using the statutory derivative claim as tool of corporate governance.

14.17   Although a derivative claim may only be brought in respect of an unlawful act or omission of a director, the claim may be brought against a director or another person, or both.[16] Furthermore, CA 2006 makes clear that for the purposes of a derivative claim the term 'director' includes former directors, shadow directors, and de facto directors.[17]

E. JUDICIAL CONTROL

14.18   The Law Commission was of the view that 'tight judicial control' of derivative claims would preclude the risk of an enormous increase in litigation[18] and this view was repeated by the government during parliamentary debate of the Bill. The principal means by which CA 2006 establishes judicial control of derivative claims is the requirement that a member must apply for permission to continue a derivative claim, whether that member is commencing a new claim or continuing a claim commenced by another member or the company itself. The procedural aspects of such applications are dealt with below.

14.19   In its report the Law Commission made numerous recommendations regarding the case management powers of the court in respect of derivative claims. The following recommendations have not been enacted and may or may not find their way into the revised Civil Procedure Rules that will be necessary to regulate the new derivative claim:

(1) A prospective claimant should be required to give notice to the company of its intention to bring a derivative claim at least 28 days before the commencement of proceedings.[19]

(2) Where a derivative claim is brought, the court must fix a case management conference and, unless the court otherwise directs, the claimant must apply for permission to continue the derivative claim at that case management conference.[20]

(3) The rules should provide that any decision of the court is binding on the other shareholders on whose behalf the derivative claim is made.[21]

(4) No derivative claim may be discontinued or compromised without the permission of the court.[22]

14.20   The Law Commission's recommendation that applications for permission to continue should be made at a case management conference fixed by the court flows from its view that the application for permission should be dealt with at close of pleadings.[23] This would represent a loosening of judicial control from the position under both RSC ord 15, r 12A and CPR Part 19.9, which provided for such applications to be made before defendants

---

[15] See Chapter 13.   [16] Section 260(3).   [17] Section 260(5)(a) and (b); s 1261(1).
[18] *Shareholders' Remedies* (n 1 above) para 6.41.   [19] *Shareholders' Remedies*, para 6.59.
[20] *Shareholders' Remedies*, para 6.69.   [21] *Shareholders' Remedies*, para 6.94.
[22] *Shareholders' Remedies*, para 6.107.   [23] *Shareholders' Remedies*, para 6.66.

were required to file and serve defences to the claim. It remains to be seen whether this recommendation will be adopted.

F. PROCEDURE

1. Permission to continue

As was the case for a common law derivative action, CA 2006 provides that a member of a   14.21
company who issues a derivative claim must apply to the court for permission to continue the claim.[24] Section 261 of CA 2006 introduces a new two-stage process for this application, but does not state at what stage in proceedings this application is to be made. This will, no doubt, be dealt with in revised Civil Procedure Rules.

The first stage of the application requires the applicant to establish a prima facie case for   14.22
the court giving permission and involves the court considering only the application and the evidence filed by the applicant.[25] If, at this first stage, it does not appear to the court that such application and evidence disclose a prima facie case for the granting of permission to continue the claim, the court must dismiss the application[26] and may make any consequential orders it considers appropriate.[27] Such consequential orders might relate to costs or, in extreme circumstances, may be a civil restraint order.

In the event that the court is satisfied that a prima facie case is disclosed by the application   14.23
and supporting evidence, it may give directions for evidence to be filed by the company and may adjourn the proceedings to enable that evidence to be obtained.[28] The jurisdiction to grant an adjournment to enable the company to obtain evidence appears to give effect to the recommendation of the Law Commission that the court should have the power to adjourn a hearing to enable a meeting of shareholders to be convened.[29] Such a meeting might be for the purposes of consultation regarding the derivative claim or, alternatively, might serve to ratify alleged breaches of duty.

On the hearing of the second stage of the application the court may: (a) give permission   14.24
to continue the claim on such terms as it thinks fit; (b) refuse permission and dismiss the claim; or (c) adjourn the proceedings on the application and give such directions as it thinks fit.[30] The jurisdiction to adjourn the application and give directions is designed to meet the situation where the course that should be taken by the court is not yet clear. Such an adjournment may be ordered to permit a general meeting of the company to take place.

2. 'Change of carriage'

A derivative claim is a representative action, since it is brought on behalf of a company.   14.25
However, it is also analogous to a class action because it is ultimately for the benefit of all the (innocent) shareholders of the company in question. The nature of a derivative claim is reflected in the provisions of the Act entitling a member of a company to apply to the court for permission to (a) continue as a derivative claim a claim brought by that company;[31] and (b) continue a derivative claim brought by another member.[32] Although the phrase 'change

---

[24] Section 261(1).   [25] Section 261(2).   [26] Section 261(2)(a).
[27] Section 261(2)(b).   [28] Section 261(3).   [29] *Shareholders' Remedies* (n 1 above) para 6.103.
[30] Section 261(4).   [31] Section 262.   [32] Section 264.

of carriage' is not used in the Act, the provisions reflect, to a certain extent, the procedure for change of carriage of winding up and bankruptcy petitions.

3. Application to continue a claim commenced by the company

14.26 Section 262 of CA 2006 provides that, where a company has brought a claim that is based on a cause of action that could found a derivative claim,[33] a member of that company may apply to the court for permission to continue that claim as a derivative claim if:[34]

(a) the manner in which the company commenced or continued the claim amounts to an abuse of the process of the court,

(b) the company failed to prosecute the claim diligently, and

(c) it is appropriate for the member to continue the claim as a derivative claim.

14.27 The use of the word 'and' indicates that the three requirements set out above are cumulative and that all three must be satisfied if a member is to be permitted to continue the company's claim as a derivative claim. Thus, it is not sufficient that the claim has not been prosecuted diligently if, as commenced or continued, the claim was not an abuse of process. This drafting accurately reflects the recommendation of the Law Commission[35] and its view that:[36]

> We do not want individual shareholders to apply to take over current litigation being pursued by their company just because they are not happy with the progress being made. The provision is intended to deal with those situations where the company's real intention in commencing proceedings is to prevent a successful claim being brought. In the recent case of *Grovit v Doctor* [1997] 1 WLR 640 the court held that for a plaintiff to commence and to continue litigation which he had no intention to bring to a conclusion could amount to an abuse of process for the purposes of an application to strike out. We consider that an action commenced by a company for the purposes of preventing a shareholder bringing a derivative action and which it has no real intention of bringing to a conclusion would amount to an abuse of the process of the court for the purposes of the new rule we are proposing.

14.28 The requirement that the court be satisfied that it is 'appropriate' for a member to continue the company's claim as a derivative claim requires the court to have regard to the matters detailed at s 263 of CA 2006.

14.29 Section 262(3), (4), and (5) largely replicate s 261(2), (3), and (4) (with one or two necessary drafting differences) and apply the same two-stage process to applications for permission to continue, as a derivative claim, a claim commenced by the company. If the application and evidence in support of it do not disclose a prima facie case for giving permission, the court must dismiss the member's application and may make such consequential orders as it considers appropriate.

14.30 If a prima facie case is disclosed, the court may give directions for the company to provide evidence and adjourn the proceedings to enable that evidence to be obtained. On hearing the application the court may (a) give permission to continue the claim as a derivative claim on such terms as it thinks fit; (b) refuse permission and dismiss the member's application; or (c) adjourn the application and give such directions as it thinks fit. The important difference between applications under ss 261 and 262 of CA 2006 is that, where an application

---

[33] ie the cause of action arises from 'an actual or proposed act or omission involving negligence, default, breach of duty or breach of trust by a director of the company'—s 260(3) of CA 2006.

[34] Section 262(2).   [35] *Shareholders' Remedies* (n 1 above) para 6.65.

[36] *Shareholders' Remedies*, para 6.63.

under s 262 fails, the claim continues in the company's name and it is merely the application that is dismissed. If an application under s 261 fails the claim is dismissed.

4. Application to continue a derivative claim

By virtue of s 264 of CA 2006 a member may also apply to continue: 14.31

(1) a derivative claim brought by another member;

(2) a claim brought by the company and continued by another member as a derivative claim; or

(3) a derivative claim brought by one member and continued by another member.[37]

The difference between applications under this section and those made under ss 261 and   14.32
262 of CA 2006 is that, in the case of applications under s 264, the court has already permitted the proceedings to be continued as a derivative claim. In those circumstances one would have thought that the only issue would be the appropriateness of a 'change of carriage'. However, despite this fact, s 264(2), (3), (4), and (5) largely replicate s 262(2), (3), (4), and (5), applying the same two-stage process to the application and providing for evidence to be given by the company.

5. Matters relevant to the granting of permission to continue

As far as applications to continue are concerned, s 263 of CA 2006 sets out matters that must   14.33
result in the refusal of permission to continue[38] and other matters that must be considered by the court in coming to its decision as to whether or not it should grant permission to continue.[39] Section 263(1) of CA 2006 states that the section applies to applications under ss 261 and 262, but makes no mention of applications under s 264. This is logical since the court has already permitted proceedings that are the subject matter of a s 264 application to be continued as a derivative claim.

Section 263(2) of CA 2006 provides that an application under ss 261 or 262 for permission   14.34
to continue a claim must be refused if the court is satisfied:

(a) that a person acting in accordance with section 172 (duty to promote the success of the company) would not seek to continue the claim, or

(b) where the cause of action arises from an act or omission that is yet to occur, that act or omission has been authorised by the company, or

(c) where the cause of action arises from an act or omission that has already occurred, that act or omission—
    (i) was authorised by the company before it occurred, or
    (ii) has been ratified by the company since it occurred.

The first ground on which an application must be dismissed echoes the requirement   14.35
set out by Peter Gibson LJ in *Barrett v Duckett*[40] that to sue on behalf of a company a shareholder must bring a derivative action bona fide for the benefit of the company, but links it to the newly created statutory duty to promote the success of the company.[41]

---

[37] Section 264(1).   [38] Section 263(2).
[39] Section 263(3).   [40] [1995] 1 BCLC 243.
[41] Section 172.

14.36   The second and third grounds upon which an application for permission to continue must be dismissed apply either where the act or omission complained of has yet to occur, but has been authorized by the company, or where the act or omission has already occurred, but has been either authorized or ratified by the company. This preserves the common law position that: (a) an act or omission cannot amount to a wrong done to a company if that company has authorized it; and (b) the ratification of a breach of duty precludes a derivative action. However, CA 2006 imposes certain controls on the manner in which breaches of duties owed by directors may be authorized or ratified. These matters are dealt with in some detail in Chapter 13, but the following general points should be noted:

(1) Section 239 of CA 2006 requires that a decision to ratify conduct of a director amounting to negligence, default, breach of duty, or breach of trust must be taken by members by ordinary resolution (subject to any requirement in the articles of association for a larger majority) disregarding the votes of the director responsible for such conduct and the votes of any member connected with him.

(2) As far as authorization of breaches of duty is concerned, with certain exceptions, the common law position is preserved by s 180 of CA 2006.

(3) Section 175 of CA 2006, which deals with the duty to avoid a conflict of interest, expressly provides that a breach of that duty may be authorized by the board of directors of the company, provided that the vote of the director in question is not counted and his presence at a meeting is not counted as far as any requirement for a quorum is concerned.[42]

14.37   Assuming that an application to continue does not fall to be dismissed under s 263(2), the court must have regard to the following matters listed at s 263(3) of CA 2006:

(a) whether the member is acting in good faith in seeking to continue the claim;

(b) the importance that a person acting in accordance with section 172 (duty to promote the success of the company) would attach to continuing it;

(c) where the cause of action results from an act or omission that is yet to occur, whether the act or omission could be, and in the circumstances would be likely to be—
   (i) authorised by the company before it occurs, or
   (ii) ratified by the company after it occurs;

(d) where the cause of action arises from an act or omission that has already occurred, whether the act or omission could be, and in the circumstances would be likely to be ratified by the company;

(e) whether the company has decided not to pursue the claim;

(f) whether the act or omission in respect of which the claim is brought gives rise to a cause of action that the member could pursue in his own right rather than on behalf of the company.

14.38   Further, in considering whether or not to give permission to continue a claim, the court is required to have regard to any evidence before it as to the views of members of the company who have no direct or indirect personal interest in the matter.[43] This provision gives effect to the Law Commission's recommendation that the court should take account of the views of an independent organ. The phrase 'independent organ' was used by Knox J in *Smith v Croft (No 2)*[44] to describe a group of persons within the company whose votes would not be cast with a view to supporting the defendants rather than securing the benefit to the company.

---

[42] Section 175(4), (5), and (6).   [43] Section 263(4).   [44] [1988] Ch 114.

Section 263(5) and (6) provide that the Secretary of State may by regulation amend   14.39
s 263(2) and (3), but before so doing must consult with such persons as he considers
appropriate. Such regulations are to be subject to the affirmative resolution procedure.

6. Costs indemnity orders

The Law Commission recommended that the court's power to make costs indemnity orders in   14.40
relation to derivative actions should remain unchanged.[45] In line with this recommendation,
there is no mention of this jurisdiction in CA 2006. As previously stated, the jurisdiction
was first exercised in the case of *Wallersteiner v Moir (No 2)*[46] before being incorporated into
the Rules of the Supreme Court and then the Civil Procedure Rules. The jurisdiction is
presently to be found at Part 19.9(7) of the CPR and it is not anticipated that any significant
change will be made to the substance of that rule when revised Civil Procedure Rules are
produced to deal with the new statutory derivative claim.

---

[45] *Shareholders' Remedies* (n 1 above) para 6.104.   [46] [1975] QB 373.

15

ACCOUNTS AND REPORTS

A. INTRODUCTION

Part 15 of CA 2006 replaces the infamous Part 7 of CA 1985, although, apart from a relatively   15.01
small number of changes, it is essentially a restatement of the existing requirements.[1] The
new drafting style is certainly more user-friendly, as is the new numbering of provisions
(users will no longer have to contend with section numbers such as 234ZZB!)—at least for
those coming 'fresh' to the subject.

The part exemplifies the underlying 'think small first' approach of the new legislation by   15.02
adopting the three-tier structure, which is explicitly set out at the beginning in s 380. Where
provisions do not apply to all types of company, those relating to small companies are set out
first; provisions relating to private companies then appear before those for public companies;
and provisions relating to quoted companies appear last. This, it is said, will make it easier
for companies of all sizes and types to understand the accounting and reporting obligations
applying to them.

The headline changes in this area include: 15.03

(1) reduction in filing times: now nine months for private companies and six months for
    public companies;

(2) private companies no longer sending out accounts prior to, or laying them before, the
    general meeting;

(3) quoted companies to publish accounts and preliminary statements on websites;

(4) the 'business review' replacing in part the OFR.

Much of the detail of accounting and reporting requirements was previously contained in   15.04
(the somewhat impenetrable) Schs 4–11 to CA 1985, whereas now such requirements will

---

[1] For discussion of the provisions, see, eg, *Hansard,* HC, cols 681–715 (13 July 2006).

instead be detailed in regulations made by the Secretary of State: eg for Sch 4 to CA 1985, see now the power in s 396(3); for Sch 4A, the power in s 404(3); for Sch 5, the power in s 409(1); and so on. It is hoped that this innovation will provide for greater flexibility, especially as this area is the subject of frequent change.

B. DEFINITIONS

15.05   Sections 381–384 generally restate the 'qualifications' for benefiting from the small companies' regime. There is just one minor change, in relation to the eligibility of groups: a group is now ineligible if any of its members have their shares 'admitted to trading on a regulated market in an EEA state': see s 384(2)(b) (replacing s 247A(2) of CA 1985, which referred to 'power ... to offer ... shares or debentures to the public').

15.06   Section 385 defines 'quoted' and 'unquoted' companies in the same way as s 262 of CA 1985.

15.07   Sections 465–468 outline how companies qualify as 'medium sized'.

C. OBLIGATIONS OF ALL COMPANIES

1. Accounting records

15.08   Sections 386 and 388 replicate the duties to keep accounting records, and where and for how long they are to be kept, previously found in ss 221 and 222 of CA 1985 respectively. The offences for defaulting on these duties (previously in ss 221(5) and 222(6) of CA 1985) now have their own separate sections (ss 387 and 389 respectively).

2. Financial year, etc

15.09   Section 390 continues the definition of 'financial year' applied by s 223 of CA 1985, while ss 391 and 392 do the same for 'accounting reference periods/dates' and alteration of such periods/dates (previously ss 224 and 225 respectively). One minor consequential change appears in s 392(4) (inability to alter date if filing date has passed): the reference to 'laying and delivering accounts' is replaced with simply 'filing accounts', to reflect the fact that private companies are no longer obliged to lay accounts in a general meeting.

3. Annual accounts

15.10   Chapter 4 of Part 15 restates the annual accounts regime with some changes.

15.11   Section 393 outlines the overarching (and EU-wide) duty of directors to ensure that accounts, whether individual or group, give a 'true and fair view'. This is in addition to the specific 'true and fair' duties in relation to, for example, Companies Act individual accounts (restated in s 396) and Companies Act group accounts (restated in s 404). Section 393(2) contains a rather roundabout provision, requiring auditors to 'have regard to' the directors' 'true and fair' duties.

15.12   The individual accounts framework is found in ss 394–397. Companies still have a choice whether to produce individual accounts in accordance with the Companies Act framework or the IAS framework (see s 395)—subject of course to the general requirement of consistency of individual accounts within a group (now found in s 407) and the requirement for companies that are charities to use the Companies Act accounts regime (see s 395(2)).

By s 396(3), the detail of the form and content of individual Companies Act accounts **15.13** and the additional information required to be provided as notes thereto, will henceforth be contained in regulations made by the Secretary of State—rather than, as previously, in a Schedule.

Sections 398–408 comprise the group accounts regime. The old category of medium-sized **15.14** groups and its related exemption (see s 248 of CA 1985) has been abolished,[2] so that generally all parent companies must now produce group accounts unless they are small or otherwise exempt: see s 399; and, for the exemptions, ss 400–402. Parent companies that are 'small' still have the *option* to produce group accounts: see s 398.

Again, there is a choice of whether group accounts are produced in accordance with **15.15** the Companies Act framework or the IAS framework, save that parent companies that are charities must use the former (see s 403(3)) and those required to do so by the IAS regulation (ie those with publicly traded securities) *must* use the latter (see s 403(1)).[3]

Section 405 restates the general requirement (and exemptions thereto), previously found **15.16** in s 229 of CA 1985, for all subsidiaries in the group to be included in the consolidated accounts where those accounts follow the Companies Act regime. The circumstances in which a parent company can dispense with a separate individual profit and loss account are outlined in s 408 (replacing s 230 of CA 1985).

Section 409 restates requirements for extra information in respect of related undertakings **15.17** to be included in notes to accounts (and s 410 deals with 'alternative compliance')—though the detail will now be found in regulations made by the Secretary of State rather than in a Schedule (previously Sch 5 to CA 1985). The former s 231A of CA 1985, dealing with extra disclosure of information about employee numbers and costs, is now found in s 411.[4]

Former Part 1 of Sch 6 to CA 1985, which dealt with the detailed requirements in **15.18** respect of accounting disclosure of directors' remuneration, will also now be contained in regulations: see s 412(1). However, practitioners will be particularly pleased to note that what were formerly Parts 2 and 3 of Sch 6 to CA 1985, dealing with complex accounting disclosure requirements for directors and other officers in relation to advances, credit, and guarantees given by the company, have essentially been repealed and they need now only concern themselves with the (simplified) requirements of s 413 in this regard.

Finally, s 414 re-enacts s 233 of CA 1985 and provides for the approval of annual accounts **15.19** by the directors and the signature of the balance sheet on their behalf, as well as the offence of knowingly or recklessly approving accounts which do not comply with CA 2006's (or, if appropriate, the IAS Regulation's) requirements.

4. Directors' report

Chapter 5 of Part 15 (ss 415–419) restates the duty of companies to produce a directors' **15.20** report, as well as restating the requirements for its content, approval, and signature. The

---

[2] Though the 'medium-sized' concept continues to be relevant, eg for filing purposes: see para 15.31; and for benefiting from certain exemptions in relation to directors' reports: see s 417(7) of CA 2006.

[3] Transposing the requirements in the International Accounting Standards Regulation (Regulation EC 1606/2002).

[4] A proposed amendment to require information relating to the National Minimum Wage did not make it onto the statute book.

detail of these requirements has moved from the Act (previously Sch 7 to CA 1985) to regulations: see s 416(4). Each director continues to be obliged, by virtue of s 418, to make a statement as to disclosure of 'relevant audit information' to the auditors (cf s 234ZA of CA 1985).

15.21 Section 417 contains the requirement for the directors' report (other than in small companies)[5] to include a 'business review', previously contained in s 234ZZB of CA 1985. However, the requirements for the business review have been expanded so as to try and cover some of the ground previously covered by the short-lived OFR.[6] The 'business review' was hotly debated in Parliament and elsewhere.

15.22 The purpose of the business review is specifically stated to be to 'inform members ... and help them assess how directors have performed their duty ... to promote the success of the company'.[7]

15.23 As before, the business review must contain a fair review of the company's business and a description of the principal risks facing it. Likewise, it must continue to be a balanced and comprehensive analysis of the business's development and performance during the financial year, and its position at the end of that year, consistent with the business's size and complexity.

15.24 There are new requirements for quoted companies. By virtue of s 417(5), they must report on the main trends and factors likely to affect the business's future development, performance, and position; as well as providing information about environmental matters (including the impact of the company's business on the environment), the company's employees, and 'social and community issues' (whatever that may mean).

15.25 Most controversially, by virtue of a last-minute government amendment in the House of Commons, information about the company's supply chain, ie persons with whom the company has contractual or other arrangements which are essential to the company's business, must be included. The provision was fiercely resisted by the opposition in Parliament. Such disclosure need not be given where, in the directors' opinion, it would be seriously prejudicial to that person *and* contrary to the public interest.[8]

15.26 There is an element of materiality in these matters: the information need only be provided so far as necessary for an understanding of the business's development, performance, or positions. However, where information in any of the categories is not provided the review must say so.

5. Distribution and publication of accounts/reports

15.27 As a general rule, every company must continue to send its annual accounts and reports to members, debenture-holders, and those entitled to receive notice of meetings: see s 423. However, the time for such sending has changed (see generally s 424) to reflect the abolition

---

[5] The Accounts Modernisation Directive (EC) 2003/51 (amending the 4th and 7th Company Law Directives) requires all companies other than small companies to have a 'business review'.

[6] The Chancellor of the Exchequer announced (apparently unilaterally) in November 2005—less than a year after the OFR Regulations had been laid—that the OFR would be repealed as part of a deregulatory drive.

[7] Although s 417 does not 'dovetail' completely with the duty expressed in s 172. On the latter, see para 13.19. The business review will be the subject of updated ASB guidance, rather than statutory-based reporting standards—although the situation will be monitored (see *Hansard*, HC, col 915 (18 October 2006)).

[8] This limited exemption on supply chain information was the most the opposition could get out of the government. In particular, an amendment which would have sanctioned non-disclosure where it would not be prejudicial to the company's interest was defeated.

of the obligation for private companies to have general meetings (and therefore the need to 'lay' accounts): a private company must send the accounts/reports by the date it actually files them with the registrar or by the last date for so doing (whichever is the earlier); public companies must send out the accounts/reports no later than 21 days before the relevant accounts meeting.

However, the option for a company to provide those entitled to its accounts/reports (or, if appropriate, the person nominated to enjoy the relevant share's information rights)[9] with a summary financial statement instead is also preserved and the relevant regime comprises ss 426–429. The differing requirements for the summary statement's contents as regards 'unquoted' and 'quoted' companies are dealt with in ss 427 and 428 (and regulations made thereunder) respectively. There is a new power for the relevant regulations to provide that certain material, instead of being included in the statement, may be sent separately at the same time with it (see ss 427(5) and 428(5) respectively).[10]   15.28

Sections 431 and 432 restate the rights of members/debenture-holders of unquoted and quoted companies respectively to demand copies of the relevant last accounts/reports.   15.29

Sections 433–436 deal with the requirements in respect of accounts/reports which are 'published', ie made available for wider public consumption.   15.30

6. Filing accounts/reports

The obligations of companies as to filing accounts and reports with the registrar are dealt with in Chapter 10 of Part 16: requirements for small companies are outlined in s 444; medium-sized companies, which continue to have the option of filing abbreviated accounts,[11] are dealt with in s 445; unquoted companies are the subject of s 446; and the requirements for quoted companies appear in s 447. Unlimited companies continue to be generally exempt from filing accounts: see s 448. This simpler structuring of the requirements is much clearer than the previous scattering throughout Part 7 of CA 1985.   15.31

The now shorter period for filing accounts is dealt with in s 442, down from ten months from 'year end' to nine for private companies, and from seven months to six for public companies. Calculation of the period is further elucidated by s 443, clarifying the confusion caused by having months of unequal length: so it is clear that six months from year ending 28 February will in fact be 31 August (rather than 28 August).[12]   15.32

Sections 451–453 deal with the consequences of failing to file accounts. Sections 454–462 (Chapter 11 of Part 15) restate the comprehensive regime for the revision of defective accounts and reports, providing again for 'voluntary' revision, 'semi-voluntary' revision (ie following a notice of the defect), and 'compulsion', ie providing for the powers of the Financial Reporting Review Panel—the 'authorised person' in the language of this part of the Act—to investigate companies' financial reporting and to take appropriate action (including obtaining a court order for revision).   15.33

---

[9] See s 426(5). On information rights generally see para 6.25.

[10] So as to dovetail with the requirements of the Takeovers Directive regarding explanatory material (on which see para 17.39).

[11] Note also the requirements for abbreviated accounts now found in s 449 (auditor's report) and s 450 (approval and signing).

[12] Reversing the effect, for these purposes, of the so-called 'corresponding date rule': see *Dodds v Walker* [1981] 1 WLR 1027 (HL).

D. OBLIGATIONS OF PUBLIC COMPANIES ONLY

15.34   Sections 437–438 restate the requirement (previously in s 241 of CA 1985) to lay accounts and reports before the general meeting—although, in view of the fact that private companies are no longer obliged to hold them, the requirement is restricted to public companies.

E. OBLIGATIONS OF QUOTED COMPANIES ONLY

15.35   Quoted companies continue to be obliged to produce a directors' remuneration report, which is the subject of Chapter 6 of Part 15. The detail of the report, which was formerly outlined in Sch 7A to CA 1985, will now be contained in regulations pursuant to s 421(1), while ss 439–440 continue the requirement to have the report approved by members prior to the AGM.

15.36   An innovation of the Act as regards quoted companies is a requirement for them to publish their annual accounts on a website: see s 430. A requirement for preliminary statements also to be available on a website was removed during the Act's passage.

F. MISCELLANEOUS PROVISIONS

15.37   A relatively late addition to CA 2006 was s 463, which provides that directors are liable to compensate their companies for loss caused by knowingly or recklessly making misleading statements or omissions in directors' reports.

15.38   The generalized—and frequently used—power in s 257 of CA 1985 to amend accounts and reports provision is replaced with (an even broader) similar provision in s 468.

16

AUDIT AND AUDITORS

A. INTRODUCTION

Perhaps inevitably given the recent spate of financial scandals, the law of audit and auditors **16.01** has been in a continuing state of change in recent years. First came Part 1 of C(AICE)A 2004—the government's 'response' to Enron and WorldCom, etc. More recently, the EU Parliament and Council adopted the 8th Company Law Directive[1] on statutory audit. Now, significant changes are effected by CA 2006.

Provisions relating to the statutory audit and the appointment of auditors have, in CA **16.02** 2006, been brought together in one part (Part 16); this is a sensible change from CA 1985, where the relevant provisions were found within two different areas (Part 7 (accounts etc) and Part 11 (company administration)). The regulation of the audit profession (qualifications, independence etc), previously the subject of Part 2 of CA 1989, is now dealt with in Part 42 of CA 2006.

The headline reform in this area, however, is the controversial (partial) inroad into **16.03** the longstanding principle (previously enshrined in s 310 of CA 1985) that provisions exempting auditors from, or indemnifying them against, liability to the companies they audit are generally void. Auditors will now be able to enter into 'liability limitation agreements' with companies (discussed further at paras 16.22 *et seq*).

---

[1] Council Directive (EC) 2006/43 on statutory audits of annual accounts and consolidated accounts [2006] OJ L157.

B. AUDIT REQUIREMENT

16.04 Chapter 1 of Part 16[2] deals with the requirement for a statutory audit of accounts and reports. Section 475 restates the existing obligation for companies to have their accounts audited unless they are exempt. The exemptions for small companies and dormant companies continue; and the qualifications for such exemptions are outlined in ss 477–479 and 480–481 respectively.

16.05 A new exemption for public sector companies is introduced by ss 482–483. Henceforth, non-departmental public bodies that operate as registered companies will be able to be audited by public sector auditors (such as the Comptroller and Auditor General).

16.06 Members holding at least ten per cent of issued shares in an otherwise exempt company continue to be able to force an audit of its accounts: see s 476.

C. APPOINTMENT AND REMOVAL/RESIGNATION

1. Appointment

16.07 The appointment of auditors is the subject of Chapter 2 of Part 16, with ss 485–488 setting out the requirements for private companies; ss 489–491 dealing with public companies; and ss 492–494 outlining general provisions applying to both types of company.

16.08 The requirements are generally a restatement of the existing law, although with some changes for private companies. Since such companies are no longer obliged to hold meetings, they must now generally appoint an auditor by ordinary resolution within 28 days of the circulation of accounts (rather than at the meeting at which accounts are laid): see s 485(2).[3]

16.09 Another innovation is that where a private company fails to make such an appointment in time, the auditor in office is generally deemed to be reappointed (see s 487(2))—though the members can block this (see s 488).

16.10 The existing default powers of the Secretary of State to appoint auditors for private and public companies where they have failed to do so are restated in ss 486 and 490 respectively, while s 494 repeats his powers to require disclosure of all the services provided by an auditor or his associates to, and the remuneration it receives from, the company it audits. Section 493 introduces a new power to require disclosure of the terms of the audit appointment itself. Section 492 restates how auditor remuneration is to be fixed (generally, by members' ordinary resolution).

2. Removal/resignation

16.11 Sections 510–513 restate s 391 (and part of s 391A) of CA 1985 on the removal of auditors by ordinary resolution. The procedure which must be followed when failing to

---

[2] Section 498 provides a general power of amendment of Chapter 1.

[3] Unless, of course, the directors have resolved that audited accounts are unlikely to be required (see s 485(1)). Public companies must, if required, appoint an auditor by the end of the accounts meeting (see s 489(2)) and will generally do so at that meeting.

reappoint an existing auditor (previously in part of s 391 of CA 1985) is now found in ss 514–515.

The provisions on the resignation of auditors are found in ss 516–518. The method for resigning remains the same (see ss 516–517), as do the rights of resigning auditors (s 518). 16.12

3. Auditor's statement on ceasing to hold office

The main changes in this area concern the requirements for an auditor's statement when he ceases to hold office. Previously, a departing auditor for any type of company needed to make a statement regarding the circumstances of his departure only if he considered those circumstances ought to be brought to the attention of members/creditors. Now, in unquoted companies the auditor must in all cases make a statement—whether of the circumstances or of his opinion that there were none relevant (s 519(1) and (2)); and in quoted companies he must outline the circumstances (s 519(3)). 16.13

The statement must be deposited with the company, which must distribute it to members (s 520), unless it obtains a court order to the contrary. The auditor must also, in the absence of such a court order, send a copy to the registrar of companies (s 521). Finally, for 'major audits'[4] (essentially those of listed companies) the auditor must deposit the statement with the relevant 'audit authority'[5] whenever he ceases to hold office, while for 'non-major audits' this need only be done where he ceases to hold office before the end of his term: see s 522. 16.14

Similarly, the company must, in any case where an auditor ceases to hold office before the end of his term, notify the appropriate 'audit authority' (s 523). In any circumstances where an audit authority receives a statement, it must inform the Secretary of State and the Financial Reporting Review Panel (the intended 'authorised person'): s 524. 16.15

D. AUDITORS' FUNCTIONS/DUTIES

The functions, duties, and rights of auditors are the subject of Chapter 3 of Part 16. Sections 495–497 restate the existing requirements for an auditor's report on whether the annual accounts give a true and fair view, etc; whether the director's report is consistent with the financial statements; and whether the auditable part of the directors' remuneration report has been prepared in accordance with the Act's requirements. 16.16

As regards the 'business review' part of the directors' report this is, as regards quoted companies which were subject to the OFR, a change from the OFR audit requirement, which essentially required auditors to search out inconsistencies. Under CA 2006, the auditors need only say whether the business review is consistent with the financial statements. 16.17

Auditors' duties are set out in s 498 in the same terms as previously (cf s 237 of CA 1985), while auditors' rights of access and information are outlined, with greater elaboration than in CA 1985 but in substantially the same terms, in ss 499–502. 16.18

Signing-off the auditor's report is dealt with by s 503. Where the auditor is an individual, the position remains as under CA 1985: he must sign. However, where the auditor is a firm 16.19

---

[4] Defined in s 525(2)–(3).   [5] Defined in s 525(1).

there is a new requirement: the audit report must be signed by the 'senior statutory auditor'[6] (which in turn is defined by s 504).

16.20   Finally, despite strenuous opposition from former accountant MPs and peers, CA 2006 creates, in s 507, an offence of auditors knowingly or recklessly causing an audit report to include any matter that is 'misleading, false or deceptive in a material particular'.

E. QUOTED COMPANIES ONLY: AUDIT CONCERNS

16.21   Chapter 5 of Part 16 introduces a new right for members of quoted companies (either holding five per cent of total voting rights, or at least 100 members each holding shares with an average minimum paid-up sum of £100) to raise concerns, either about audit of accounts or an auditor's departure, at the next accounts meeting; and also to require the company to publish those concerns on a website prior to that meeting.

F. LIMITATION OF LIABILITY

16.22   Chapter 6 of Part 16 introduces one of the most controversial reforms in CA 2006: a regime allowing auditors to limit their liability to the companies they audit to a fair and reasonable amount. This is the government's response to intense lobbying by the 'big four' accountancy firms, who claimed to face potential extinction as a result of claims made against them in connection with big financial scandals such as Barings and Equitable Life.[7]

16.23   Section 532 voids any provision exempting auditors from, or directly or indirectly indemnifying them against, any liability to the companies they audit, save in so far as: it is an indemnity for successfully defending proceedings (which was already the case under s 310(3) of CA 1985, now the subject of s 533 of CA 2006); or (which is the reform) an effective 'liability limitation agreement is in place'.

16.24   Sections 534–536 outline the necessary ingredients for such an effective agreement: essentially, it can only relate to one financial year and it must be authorized by the members. There is also power, in s 535(2), for regulations to specify things which must be included, or things which cannot be included, in such agreements. Any liability limitation agreement must also be disclosed (eg in the accounts and reports) in the manner prescribed by regulations: see s 538.

16.25   By virtue of s 537, however, such agreements will not exclude liability completely. They may not limit liability to 'less than such an amount as is fair and reasonable in all the circumstances'—which circumstances include the auditor's duties under the Act as well as the professional standards expected of him. Such agreements can be prospectively terminated by the members withdrawing their authorization:[8] see s 536(1) and (6).

---

[6] This requirement transposes art 28(1) of the amended 8th Company Law Directive (EC) 2006/43 on statutory audit [2006] OJ L157.

[7] See, eg, *Barings v Coopers & Lybrand* [2003] EWHC 1319 (Ch) and *Equitable Life v Ernst & Young* [2003] 2 BCLC 603, the ultimate results of which arguably demonstrate that the courts were adequately equipped to meet these concerns.

[8] On authorization see para 16.24.

G. REGULATION OF AUDITORS

The regulation of the audit profession is outside the scope of this book. Suffice it to say   16.26
that Part 42 of and Schedules 10–14 to CA 2006 restate Part 2 of CA 1989, with various
modifications and additions which are largely calculated to transpose the 8th Company Law
Directive on Statutory Audit. The two main changes effected by Part 42 are: (i) to extend
audit regulation to so-called 'third country auditors', ie auditors of non-EU incorporated
companies with a UK listing (Chapter 5 of Part 42); and (ii) to permit so-called public-sector
auditors (such as the Comptroller and Auditor General) to act as statutory auditors (see
Chapter 3 of Part 42).

17

TAKEOVERS

A. PERSPECTIVE

Understanding the law of takeovers and mergers has in the past involved navigating relatively little statute law but quite a lot of regulation, making a straightforward topic seem overly complex. CA 2006 perpetuates this, which means it is no easier to gain a complete grasp of the law of takeovers and mergers with the coming into force of the Act than it has been hitherto.   17.01

Parliament has not legislated a great deal for takeovers, governments preferring in the past to leave regulation to the City of London's Panel on Takeovers and Mergers ('the Takeovers Panel') which, historically, exerted its discipline by means of the City Code on Takeovers and Mergers ('the Takeovers Code').   17.02

The Takeovers Panel and its modus operandi were described by Donaldson MR in *R v Panel on Takeovers and Mergers ex parte Datafin*,[1] as a body which: 17.03

… enjoys no contractual relationship with the financial market or with those who deal with the market, and which operates a system of self-regulation whereby a group of people, acting in concert, use their collective power to force themselves and others to comply with a code of conduct of their own devising.

Parliament stepped only hesitantly into this arena in 1948, with the enactment of s 209(2) and (3) of CA 1948 (acquisition of shares of a dissenting minority in order to facilitate company reconstruction or amalgamation), later stiffening these provisions with the enactment of s 428–430 of CA 1985, which it put in Part XIII (the part relating to arrangements and reconstructions).   17.04

Dedicated 'takeovers' provisions did not appear until rather later with the enactment by s 172 and Sch 12 of the Financial Services Act 1986 of replacement ss 428–430F, inserting them into a new Part XIIIA of CA 1985, the new s 428 introducing, for the first time, a   17.05

---

[1] [1987] QB 815, 825.

definition of a takeover offer, that is to say, an offer to acquire all the shares, or all the shares of any class or classes, in a company (other than shares which at the date of the offer were already held by the offeror), being an offer on terms which were the same in relation to all of the shares to which the offer related or, where those shares included shares of different classes, in relation to all the shares of each class.

17.06 Although some legislative refinements have been enacted since 1986 (introduced by subordinate legislation and CA 1989), and some bolt-ons (introduced by FSMA 2000, empowering the FSA to endorse the Takeovers Code, and making provision for the disclosure of information), these core takeover provisions remained substantially the same until their repeal by the Act, only to reappear, somewhat further refined but otherwise still substantially unreformed, in their present incarnation in Part 28 of CA 2006.

17.07 The seeds of a directive on takeovers which would in due course have to be carried into UK law had been sown as early as 1985, and in 1989 the European Commission proposed a directive on the topic. The Takeovers Directive[2] can therefore realistically be viewed as the principal catalyst for Part 28 and as perhaps the only or main reason for further reform.

B. THE TAKEOVERS DIRECTIVE

17.08 The Takeovers Directive was in fact heavily influenced by the Takeovers Code current during its lengthy period of gestation. It came as no surprise, therefore, that the UK government decided to designate the Takeovers Panel as the UK's supervisory body for the purposes of art 4 and to give to the Panel the statutory rule-making role which allowed it to adopt the edition of the Takeovers Code current immediately before the coming into force of the Act.

17.09 The Takeovers Panel currently describes its ethos and practices on its website <http://www.thetakeoverpanel.org.uk> in the following terms consonant with the credibility due to it in its now statutory role as the UK's supervisory body following implementation of the Takeovers Directive.

The Panel seeks to ensure compliance with the Code through a consensual approach with the parties engaged in takeover activity. It is the practice of the Panel, in discharging its functions under the Code, to focus on the specific consequences of breaches of the Code with the aim of providing appropriate remedial or compensatory action in a timely manner. Furthermore, in respect of certain breaches of the Code, disciplinary action may be appropriate. The Panel may issue compliance rulings and, in certain restricted circumstances, may require the payment of compensation.

17.10 The takeovers sections in Part 28 which substantially owe their existence to previous legislation (relating to 'squeeze-out' and 'sell-out') were already in large part in conformity with the minimum requirements of the Takeovers Directive even before its implementation.

17.11 The Takeovers Code was amended in readiness for implementation in a number of respects in order to conform to the Takeovers Directive. For example, key changes were made to the general principles, a new version of which was imported verbatim from art 3 of the Takeovers Directive.[3]

---

[2] Council Directive (EC) 2004/25 on takeover bids [2004] OJ L142.
[3] For other changes, see para 17.24.

The marriage between Part 28, the Code, and the Takeovers Directive means that the   17.12
reader of this work will on occasion find it as important to be able to access the Code
and/or the Directive as Part 28. The Takeovers Directive is accessible via the DTI website at
<http://www.dti.gov.uk/files/file10384.pdf>.

C. IMPLEMENTATION

Article 4 of the Takeovers Directive made it mandatory for Member States to designate an   17.13
authority or authorities competent to supervise bids for the purpose of the rules which it
required Member States to make in order to carry it into effect. The implementation date, 20
May 2006, was the date upon which Member States were required by the Takeovers Directive
to bring into force the laws, regulations, and administrative provisions. The Company Law
Reform Bill (as it was then known) was intended to be the vehicle for implementation
but as it would not have passed into law by the implementation date, regulations had
to be made in order to achieve implementation on an interim basis. These were the
Takeovers Directive (Interim Implementation) Regulations 2006[4] ('the Regulations'). It is
intended that the Regulations will cease to have effect when Part 28 of CA 2006 comes
into force.

Thus, the Takeovers Panel became a statutory body on 20 May 2006. Although the placing   17.14
of the Takeover Panel on a statutory basis as the UK's supervisory body can be viewed as
a compliment to the City, the truth is that in electing to designate the Takeovers Panel,
the UK government simply opted for the obvious, simplest, cheapest, and most convenient
course. The Regulations give statutory force to the Takeovers Code. The Takeovers Panel
published the eighth edition of the Takeovers Code on 20 May 2006, to coincide with
the implementation date. The Takeovers Code can be accessed by visiting the Takeovers
Panel's website at <http://www.thetakeoverpanel.org.uk>. Any changes to the Takeovers
Code after CA 2006 comes into force will be posted on the website and can be viewed there.[5]

It should be noted that while the core requirements of the Takeovers Directive are to   17.15
be found in either the Takeovers Code or Part 28, there are also to be found in Part 28
provisions which do not wholly owe their existence to the Takeovers Directive.[6]

D. THE TAKEOVERS PANEL

1. Functions, rules, powers, duties, and liabilities

Section 942 sets out the Takeovers Panel's functions and powers in wide terms. Sections 943   17.16
and 944 specify the rules it must make, and those which it is permissible for it to make and
how these may be made and evidenced. In this way, Parliament delegated to the Panel in its

---

[4] SI 2006/1183.
[5] The Regulations forbid any changes before the coming into force of the Act.
[6] There are at least two reasons for this, one of which is that the Takeovers Directive sets minimum standards,
leaving it to Member States to supplement these if they wish with stricter rules and regulations. Another is that
legislation which does not stem directly from the Takeovers Directive could not be passed into law via the Regulations
under powers in the European Communities Act 1972.

rule-making role the task of giving effect to arts 3.1, 4.2, 5, 6.1–6.3, 7–9, and 13 of the Takeovers Directive (as explained further in paragraphs 17.22–17.26).[7]

17.17　　Section 947, in conformity with art 6.5 of the Takeovers Directive, gives the Takeovers Panel power by notice in writing to require documents and information reasonably required in connection with the exercise of its functions. This means, and includes, documents and information concerning bids and mergers, and transactions that have, or may have, directly or indirectly, an effect on the ownership or control of companies.[8]

17.18　　By contrast, s 948 restricts disclosure of documents and information provided to the Panel which relates to the private affairs of an individual or to any particular business. This restriction is for the life of the individual or business. It does not apply to disclosure made by the FSA[9] and is disapplied where disclosure is made in accordance with prescribed rules, is in aid of the Panel's functions or to specified persons, and is of a specified description.[10] There is no saving for the consequences of disclosure in contravention of the Data Protection Act 1989.

17.19　　The Panel is under a duty to cooperate with the FSA and authorities, persons, or bodies specified pursuant to s 950(1). Section 950(2) provides for the sharing of information concerning which there is no restriction on disclosure.

17.20　　Parliament has left it to the Takeovers Panel to continue to make provision by rule for such matters as pre-bid information, the publishing of bids to the public, and generally the conduct of bids, giving effect, in this way, to the remaining obligations in art 6 of the Takeovers Directive.

17.21　　Section 961 gives the Takeovers Panel and personnel blanket exemptions from liability in damages for anything lawfully and properly done according to their office.

2. Hearings and appeals

17.22　　With the enactment of s 951, which requires the Takeovers Panel to establish by rule a procedure for the review of its decisions and appeals, the Takeovers Panel has for the first time a meaningful legal structure for enforcing its decisions and imposing penalties, if necessary, through the courts. There is a helpful synopsis in the introduction to the Takeovers Code (pp A10–A15, A18, and A19). The Hearings Committee also hears contested disciplinary proceedings which it conducts in accordance with the Rules of Procedure of the Hearings Committee. There is again a useful synopsis of the sanctions and other remedies for contraventions of the Code in the introduction (pp A19, A20). The Rules are accessible online via a link on the website. Appeals are to the Takeover Appeal Board. This is an independent body with its own website at <http://www.thetakeoverappealboard.org.uk>.

17.23　　Sections 952 and 954, by contrast, are permissive, simply empowering the Takeovers Panel to make provision by rule for the imposition of sanctions including the payment of

---

[7] It is not clear why the draftsman chose to differentiate between these articles and others such as article 6.5 when all might surely have been implemented by rule.

[8] Section 962 preserves the privilege from self-incrimination both in relation to the disclosure requirement under this section and where, under s 955 a court order enforcing a rule-based requirement is made.

[9] Section 948(7).

[10] See Parts 1–3 inclusive of Sch 2. The schedule may be amended by the Secretary of State by order subject to negative resolution procedure. Section 948(5) further circumscribes the power of amendment to ensure that persons who may be added are persons carrying out public functions and that the type of disclosure is limited to disclosure which will facilitate the exercise of a public function within the UK.

compensation for contravention of the Takeovers Code and any other rules it may make from time to time. At the time of writing, compensation rulings are limited to contraventions of rr 6, 9, 11, 14–16, and 35.3 of the Code. In these cases, the Panel can require a person to pay a restitutionary amount to the holders or former holders of securities of an offeree company who receive less than they would have received but for the contravention (see p A19 of the introduction to the Code).

E. THE TAKEOVERS CODE

Set out below is a non-exhaustive list of some of the changes introduced by the eighth edition of the Takeovers Code published on 20 May 2006, in large part to ensure the Code would conform with the minimum requirements set by the Takeovers Directive for rules to be made by the Takeovers Panel as the UK's supervisory authority.[11]   17.24

Location in Code	Topic	Change
Introduction		Totally replaces the previous introduction
Introduction (p B1)	General principles	Replaced by a new version uplifted verbatim from art 3.1 of the Takeovers Directive
Definitions (p C2)	'acting in concert'	Definition of affiliated persons (applicable to rr 9.1 and 24.2) significantly altered, the note relating to standstill agreements has been somewhat altered and a new note about irrevocable commitments has been inserted
Definitions (p C11)	Acquisitions of interests in securities	New, as made necessary by changes to mandatory bid rules (see next row)
Rule 9	Mandatory bid	Substantial changes to the rule and notes (see 17.25 and 17.26 below)
Rule 11.1	Consideration	Substantial changes to notes 1 (price), 2 (gross acquisitions), 10 (convertible securities, warrants and options)
Rule 21.1	Restrictions frustrating action when shareholders' consent is required	Substantial changes to this rule provide that the offeree board must secure the approval of shareholders in general meeting to any action, inter alia, which might result in any offer or bona fide possible offer being frustrated or in shareholders being denied the opportunity to decide on its merits. Also requires an offeree board to consult the Takeovers Panel in advance if there is any doubt as to whether any proposed action may fall within the

---

[11] These should also, in theory, satisfy the obligation referred to in 17.17 imposed on the Takeovers Panel by s 943(1) to make rules giving effect to arts 3.1, 4.2, 5, 6.1–6.3, 7–9, and 13.

17. Takeovers

(continued)

Location in Code	Topic	Change
		rule. Specifies when the Takeovers Panel must be consulted and its consent to proceed without a shareholder meeting obtained. (See also F1 below)
Rules 23, 24, 30.1, and 30.3	Offeror and offeree documents	Substantial changes re the general obligation to give information, eg about the offeror, identities of persons acting in concert, terms and manner of payment of the consideration, conditions, re types of specific information such as 'about the offeror', strategic plans, repercussions on employment, quantum of information and disclosure to shareholders (no relevant information to be withheld), timing and machinery (when the offer must be displayed, content of announcement, availability of information for inspection), offeree board's circulation of its opinion, distribution, compensation for the removal of breakthrough rights, method of assessment, and manner of payment
Rule 25.1	Views of the offeree's board on the offer and offeror's plans for offeree and employees	A new r 25.1(b) requires additional information to be given and reasons for the board's decision (see also the new r 30.2)
Rule 25.2	Financial information	Content of the first major circular from the offeree board advising on offer (whether recommending acceptance or rejection of the offer)
Rule 36	Takeover Panel's consent	Partial offers, acquisitions during and after the offer

1. Mandatory bid

17.25 The mandatory bid is so important an event in takeover situations that it will be briefly discussed here for completeness. Rule 9.1 of the Takeovers Code is the rule which makes a full bid mandatory when a person has attained a threshold level of shares which carry voting rights in shares of a company, hitherto 30 per cent or more. The Takeovers Directive did not lay down a specific percentage, preferring to leave it to Member States to decide this. The UK government concluded the 30 per cent threshold was about right in all the circumstances.[12] The Takeovers Panel has taken full advantage of the flexibility given it, now providing by

[12] Considering that the existing mandatory bid threshold in the UK strikes the right balance between ensuring an appropriate level of minority protection whilst not unduly restricting takeover bid activity (per explanatory memorandum to the Interim Implementation Regulations).

this rule that a mandatory bid is triggered (r 9.1(a)) if a person acquires, whether by a series of transactions over a period of time or not, an interest in shares which (taken together with shares in which persons acting in concert with him are interested) carry 30 per cent or more of the voting rights of a company. A mandatory bid is also triggered (r 9.1(b)) when a person, together with persons acting in concert with him, is interested in shares which in the aggregate carry not less than 30 per cent of the voting rights of a company but does not hold shares carrying more than 50 per cent of such voting rights, acquires, or any person acting in concert with him acquires, an interest in any other shares which increases the percentage of shares carrying voting rights in which he is interested. The offer must in these cases now be extended also to the holders of any other class of transferable securities carrying voting rights.[13] An offer is not required under this rule where control of the offeree company is acquired as a result of a voluntary offer made in accordance with the Code to all the holders of voting equity share capital and other transferable securities carrying voting rights.

Rule 9.5 of the Takeovers Code requires the consideration to be in cash or to be accompanied by a cash alternative not less than the highest price paid by the offeror or any person acting in concert during the period of 12 months prior to the announcement of that offer. The amended definition of 'acting in concert', referred to under 17.24, explains the meaning of acting in concert. There is no presumption that the trustees of an employee benefit trust are acting in concert with the directors but the Takeovers Panel should be consulted in advance of any proposed acquisition of an interest in shares if the aggregate number of shares in which the directors, any other persons acting, or presumed to be acting, in concert with any of the directors and the trustees of an employee trust are interested will, as a result of the acquisition, carry 30 per cent or more of the voting rights, or, if already carrying 30 per cent or more, will increase further.   17.26

F. THE NEW STATUTORY CODE

1. Impediments to takeovers

(a) *Definitions*

By s 971 a 'takeover bid' is stated to 'have the same meaning as the Takeovers Directive'. That meaning is given by art 2.1(a) as follows: 17.27

'takeover bid' or 'bid' shall mean a public offer (other than by the offeree company itself) made to the holders of the securities of a company to acquire all or some of those securities, whether mandatory or voluntary, which follows or has as its objective the acquisition of control of the offeree company in accordance with national law.

The definition of 'securities' is given by art 2.1(e) as follows:

'Securities' shall mean transferable securities carrying voting rights in a company

Section 971 refines this, so that, for the purposes of this chapter, securities are treated as shares in the company if they are convertible into or entitle the holder to subscribe for such shares, and debentures are treated as shares in the company if they carry voting rights.   17.28

---

[13] Note 10 describes the circumstances in which convertible securities and the like will fall to be treated as transferable securities for this purpose. In general, this will only be when and if conversion rights or options are exercised.

(b) *Purpose*

17.29 A principal reason for the protracted gestation of the Takeovers Directive was a dispute among Member States over the legitimacy of frustrating action. This was eventually resolved by a compromise (enshrined in art 12.1) enabling Member States to opt in or out of art 9.2, the requirement that a target company must secure shareholders' agreement in a meeting before taking frustrating action (ie with the intention of delaying or stopping a bid) without the prior authorization of shareholders at a general meeting during the period of acceptance of the bid, closely in line with the provisions in the Takeovers Code then current for minority shareholder protection. The UK government decided upon the opting-in option.

(c) *Opting-in, opting-out*

17.30 The opting-in and opting-out provisions in s 966–970 give effect to the UK government's decision and its consequences. The corresponding rule in the Takeovers Code is, principally, r 21, which includes provisions preventing action being taken by the management of the offeree company, without the agreement of shareholders at the time of the bid, to frustrate a takeover bid.

17.31 Section 966 lays down three conditions which must be satisfied before a company can opt-in. The first is that the company has voting shares admitted to trading on a regulated market. The second (a lazy piece of drafting) is that the company's articles do not contain any such restrictions as are mentioned in art 11 of the Takeovers Directive[14] or, if they do, provide for the restrictions not to apply at a time when, or in circumstances which, they would be disapplied by that article. Article 11 disapplies restrictions on the transfer of securities during the time allowed for the acceptance of a bid.[15] The third condition is unlikely to be relevant as it refers to golden shares and the like.

17.32 A company can opt-out by a further resolution opting-out of the section.[16] Section 967 requires resolutions under s 966 to specify an 'effective date' which may not be earlier than the date on which the resolution is passed.

17.33 The second and third conditions must be met at the time when the opting-in condition is passed, but the first one need not be met until the effective date. The effective date of an opting-out resolution cannot be earlier than the first anniversary of the date on which it was copied to the registrar.

17.34 Section 968 gives effect to art 11 of the Takeovers Directive by setting out the effect of an opting-in resolution in a takeover situation. This is 'breakthrough' in the jargon of the Directive. Section 968 invalidates any agreement which places a restriction on transfers of shares to or at the direction of an offeror during the offer period of a bid, on the transfers of shares to any other person at a time during the offer period when the offeror holds shares amounting to not less than 75 per cent in value of all of the voting shares in the company, on rights to vote at a general meeting of the company convened to decide upon frustrating action, and on rights to vote at a general meeting of the company that is the first such meeting to be held after the end of

---

[14] In case of doubt, reference should be made to art 11 for the types of restrictions which are caught by this provision.

[15] See para 17.38. A second limb of this condition to be aware of is that the articles must not contain any other provision which would be incompatible with that article.

[16] Section 966(5).

the offer period and which is held at a time when the offeror holds shares amounting to not less than 75 per cent in value of all of the voting shares in the company. 'Voting' shares, in this context, do not include debentures and shares in a company which under its articles of association do not normally carry rights to vote at its general meetings.

The section applies to agreements entered into between a person holding shares in the company and another such person on or after 24 April 2004 or entered into at any time between such person and the company. The proper law of the agreement is irrelevant for this purpose.   17.35

(d) *Compensation*

Section 968(6) gives anyone suffering loss occasioned by 'breakthrough' a right to compensation. This is a strange, ill-thought out provision stemming from art 11.3 which makes compensation mandatory where rights are removed. For instance, the paying party is not specified, the amount of compensation is in the discretion of the court, how a court would decide upon an amount which would be just and equitable in the circumstances is not explained. Besides, anyone entering into an invalidated agreement on or after 24 April 2004 ought surely to have been professionally advised about the possible consequences before doing so, and would, ex facie, be a contributory to any loss and damage (if any) occasioned. If, in these circumstances, he were to consider he had a claim one would think the only claim he could make would be against his adviser. This said, however, it seems the Takeovers Panel has, at least tentatively, formed the view that the payment of compensation will be the offeror's responsibility by requiring the offeror to specify in the offer documentation the compensation (if any) offered for the removal of breakthrough rights.[17] This is perhaps questionable, as the requirement is surely anti-competitive, and quite possibly challengeable. It will be interesting to see if at some time in the future a challenge is made to it, and, should there be a case in which no compensation is offered, how a court would tackle the problem that a challenge or 'non-offer' would pose, against whom and how the application would be pleaded and, should the application be successful, how a court would assesses the appropriate level of compensation.   17.36

2. 'Squeeze-out' and 'sell-out'

Section 991 defines a company for the purposes of this chapter as a company whose shares are the subject of a takeover offer. The definition of a takeover offer is in s 947 and differs from the meaning of 'takeover bid' in s 971, which, as we have seen, has exactly the same meaning as in the Takeovers Directive. The reason for this likely lies in the fact that art 5.3 of the Takeovers Directive leaves it to Members States to determine the percentage of voting rights which gives control for the purposes of art 5.1 (equitable price for minority shareholders where mandatory bid required). They are also given further flexibility by art 5.6. The UK government has taken advantage of these provisions in Chapter 3 by introducing a method of calculation of the squeeze-out and sell-out thresholds which differs from that in Part XIIIA of CA 1985.   17.37

Subject to this, ss 974–991 give effect to art 5 of the Takeovers Directive and largely mirror ss 428–430F in CA 1985.[18] In a nutshell, they describe the conditions which if   17.38

---

[17] Takeovers Code, r 24.2(d)(xv).   [18] As to these sections, see para 17.05.

satisfied will entitle and bind offerors and offerees respectively (as the case may be) to acquire ('squeeze-out') and sell ('sell-out') minority shareholdings, the means of enforcement and of providing the consideration. The new provisions differ from the previous ones, broadly, as follows:

(1) The 90 per cent condition must be satisfied both as to value and voting rights in a case where the offer relates to voting shares (ss 979(2), s 983(2)).[19]

(2) Squeeze-out and sell-out rights must be exercised by notice given in the prescribed manner not later than either the period of three months beginning with the day after the last day on which the offer can be accepted or the period of six months beginning with the date of the offer where that period ends earlier and the offer is not governed by the Takeovers Code.[20] Ascertaining the time allowed for acceptances necessitates turning up the relevant rule in the Takeovers Code, in cases where the Takeovers Code applies. This is r 31, which requires an offer to remain open for 21 days in the first instance following the date on which it is posted. Further closing dates may then be specified, subject, if the offer will remain open beyond the seventieth day following posting of the offer document, to at least 14 days' notice in writing being given to shareholders, who have not accepted the offer, of the final closing date. The offer remains open for 14 days after it becomes unconditional as to acceptances. Section 984(3) places an additional obligation on the offeree in a sell-out case to give notice within one month of the last day on which the offer can be accepted to all other shareholders who have not accepted the offer that sell-out rights are available and that the offer remains open in the meantime.

(3) The court cannot reduce the consideration to below the offer value.[21] On the other hand, the court can increase the consideration, although it cannot do so unless the holder of the shares shows that the offer value would be unfair (s 986(4)).

3. Disclosure

17.39   Article 10 of the Takeovers Directive makes it mandatory for companies to which the Directive applies to publish detailed information about themselves including, inter alia, any agreements between shareholders known to them which may result in restrictions on transfers of securities and/or voting rights. Most of the information not specifically mentioned here is already provided by or readily accessible to UK companies either in their articles of association or published accounts, and much of it is likely to be included in directors' reports. However, because it is unlikely that any company would voluntarily make a report on such information directly to its shareholders as required by art 10(3), the UK government decided to legislate for it. The result is s 992 of CA 2006, which sets out, by reference to a new Part 7 of Sch 7 to be inserted in CA 1985, the disclosure which is to be made 'by certain publicly traded companies' in a directors' report. The companies concerned are companies which had securities carrying voting rights admitted to trading on a regulated market at the end of the relevant financial year.

---

[19] In the case of 'sell-out', the calculation discounts debentures carrying voting rights which are to be treated as shares pursuant to s 990 and shares held in treasury are added in (s 983(5)).

[20] eg where the offer relates to shares in a private company.

[21] The provenance of this is art 7.1 of the Takeovers Directive.

4. Offences and enforcement by the court

(a) *Criminal offences*

Part 28 creates specific offences for contravention of: 17.40

(1) s 948 (restriction on disclosure by the Takeovers Panel);
(2) s 953 (knowing non-compliance with the rules in the Takeovers Code about bid documentation where a takeover bid is made for a company that has securities carrying voting rights admitted to trading on a regulated market in the UK);
(3) s 970 (failure to notify the Takeovers Panel that a company has passed an opting-in or an opting-out resolution);
(4) s 980(6)–(8) (failure to send a company whose shares are the subject of an offer a s 979 notice in the manner prescribed by s 980(4) or to provide a statutory declaration as required by that subsection);
(5) s 951(5) (failure by offeror to give a shareholder who has not accepted the offer notice in the prescribed manner of his minority rights).

(b) *Injunctions*

The Takeovers Panel can apply pursuant to s 955 for injunctions. The court can make any   17.41
order it thinks appropriate if satisfied that there is a reasonable likelihood that a person will contravene a rule-based requirement or that a person has contravened a rule-based requirement or a disclosure requirement. Only the Panel may make an application of this kind.

5. Breach of statutory duty, contravention of rules

By s 956, no action lies for breach of statutory duty. The section also provides that   17.42
a contravention of a rule-based requirement does not make any transaction void or unenforceable or (subject to any provision made by rules) affect the validity of any other thing.

18

OTHER CHANGES

A. POLITICAL DONATIONS

1. Overview

Part 14 of CA 2006 (ss 362–379) contains the provisions relating to the control of political   18.01
donations and political expenditure by companies. Essentially, the previous framework (ie a
prohibition on political donations and expenditure exceeding £5000 in any 12-month period
unless previously authorized by a resolution of the company and liability on directors to
compensate the company for unauthorized payments) has been retained but the provisions
have been restated in clearer language and simplified. A new specific exemption for trade
unions has been introduced by s 374 which is intended to ensure that donations (other than
contributions to a political fund) and other forms of assistance to trade unions are outside
the scope of the legislation.

2. Other changes

In line with the approach of CA 2006 of simplifying the running of private companies, there   18.02
is no longer any requirement for the authorization resolution to be passed at a meeting; it
can be a written resolution.

The position of subsidiary companies has been simplified. A donation or expenditure by   18.03
the wholly-owned subsidiary of a UK company need only be authorized by a resolution of
the members of that UK holding company. That resolution can relate to all subsidiaries
without naming them individually. In other cases, the donation or expenditure requires the
prior authorization of both the members of the subsidiary and the members of the relevant
holding company, ie the UK parent company highest up the chain of ownership.

Donations to or expenditure for the benefit of independent election candidates now fall   18.04
within the provisions.

The persons liable in respect of an unauthorized donation or expenditure are the directors   18.05
of the company and, where the company is the subsidiary of a relevant holding company,
the directors of the relevant holding company, but only if the holding company's directors

failed to take all reasonable steps to prevent the donation or expenditure being made. The defences set out in s 347H of CA 1985 are not reproduced. In the case of holding company directors they will now only be liable for failure to take reasonable steps. Directors of the company actually making the unauthorized payment will presumably be able to seek to be excused from liability under s 1157 of CA 2006 on the grounds that they have behaved honestly and reasonably.

B. COMPANY INVESTIGATIONS

18.06   Part 14 of CA 1985 (ss 431–453) gives the Secretary of State various powers to appoint inspectors to conduct investigations into and report on the affairs of companies, the membership and control of companies and share ownership, and dealings by directors and their families. These provisions are being retained in CA 1985 and not consolidated into CA 2006. However Part 32 of CA 2006 (ss 1035–1039) makes amendments to CA 1985 to enhance the powers of the Secretary of State. The Secretary of State can now give directions to the inspectors as to the steps to take in the investigation and matters to be covered in their report or as to the termination of the investigation. The amendments also deal with the resignation, removal, and replacement of inspectors and obtaining information and documents from former inspectors.

C. OFFENCES

18.07   Offences under the Companies Acts are dealt with in Part 36 (ss 1121–1133) of CA 2006. Previously, company legislation frequently provided that contravention of a statutory provision would be an offence by the company and every officer in default. According to the Explanatory Notes which accompanied the Company Law Reform Bill (as CA 2006 was originally known), the approach now adopted is that a company should only be liable for an offence if the class of potential victims goes wider than merely the company and its shareholders. The offences under the Companies Acts have been reviewed on that basis. So, for example, contravention of s 680(1) of CA 2006 (prohibited financial assistance) is an offence by the company and every officer in default whereas failure to comply with s 291(5) (circulation of written resolutions) results in only the officers of the company in default being guilty of an offence.

18.08   Section 1121 of CA 2006 now defines what is meant by 'an officer in default'. An officer is defined as a director, manager or secretary, or any person who is to be treated as an officer for the purposes of the provision in question. 'In default' means authorizing or permitting or participating in the contravention or failing to take all reasonable steps to prevent the contravention. Section 1123 applies those concepts to contraventions by bodies other than companies. Section 1122 now provides that where a company is an officer of another company, the first company is not liable as an officer in default unless one of its own officers is in default. Certain provisions (for instance, s 165(4) (requirement to keep register of directors' residential addresses)) expressly include shadow directors within the expression 'officer in default'.

18.09   Schedule 3 to CA 2006 contains a number of amendments to CA 1985 in relation to offences. Sections 1126–1132 contain a number of procedural matters relating to the investigation and prosecution of offences which largely restate existing provisions. There is no change to the level of fines. There is a provision in s 1132 permitting applications by the Director of Public Prosecutions, the Secretary of State, or chief police officers to the High Court ordering the production and inspection of documents in the control of a company which may contain evidence of the commission of an offence in connection with the management of the company's affairs. Except for s 1132, the provisions of CA 2006 relating to offences do not apply to offences committed before the commencement of the relevant provision by virtue of s 1133.

D. INSOLVENCY ACT AMENDMENT

One very important change to insolvency law is tucked away in Part 44 (miscellaneous **18.10** provisions) of CA 2006. Section 1282 reverses the House of Lords decision in *Buchler v Talbot*[1] about the payment of expenses in a company liquidation. The section provides that if the assets of the company available to meet the claims of unsecured creditors are insufficient to pay the expenses of winding up, those expenses have priority to and are to be paid out of any property subject to any floating charge created by the company. The amendment is made by inserting a new s 176ZA into the Insolvency Act 1986.

---

[1] [2004] UKHL 9, [2004] 2 AC 298.

19

TABLE OF RESTATED PROVISIONS

As indicated in Chapter 1, during the course of the Act's passage through Parliament, the government decided to consolidate 'core company law' into CA 2006. As a result, various parts of CA 1985 were restated wholesale in CA 2006 (in consistent language) without change of substance. A table of such provisions, which are generally not considered in this book, appears below.

CA 1985 provisions	Part of CA 2006	Brief description
ss 89–142	17	Share capital[1]
ss 143–179 and Sch 2 (para 35)	18	Acquisition by limited company of its own shares[2]
ss 190–197	19	Debentures
ss 183–189	21	Certification and transfer of securities
ss 263–281	23	Distributions
Pt 12	25	Registration of company charges
ss 425–427A and Parts of Sch 15B	26	Arrangements/reconstructions
ss 428–430F	Chapter 3 of Part 28	Takeover offers; squeeze-out/sell-out[3]
s 458	29	Fraudulent trading[4]
s 459–461	30	Protection from unfair prejudice
ss 652–657	31	Dissolution/restoration to the register
ss 103–110	ss 1149–1153 (in Part 37)	Valuation

---

[1] See Chapter 7 of this book.

[2] Though the financial assistance regime (previously in ss 151–158 of CA 1985) generally no longer applies to *private* companies: see Chapter 2 of Part 18 of the Act and Chapter 8.

[3] See Chapter 17 of this book.

[4] Note, however, the increase in maximum prison term from seven years to ten.

APPENDIX 1

Companies Act 2006

CHAPTER 46

CONTENTS

PART 3
A COMPANY'S CONSTITUTION

CHAPTER 1
INTRODUCTORY

CHAPTER 2
ARTICLES OF ASSOCIATION

General

Alteration of articles

Supplementary

CHAPTER 3
RESOLUTIONS AND AGREEMENTS AFFECTING A COMPANY'S
CONSTITUTION

CHAPTER 4
MISCELLANEOUS AND SUPPLEMENTARY PROVISIONS

Statement of company's objects

Other provisions with respect to a company's constitution

PART 8
A COMPANY'S MEMBERS

CHAPTER 1
THE MEMBERS OF A COMPANY

CHAPTER 2
REGISTER OF MEMBERS

General

Special cases

Supplementary

PART 10
A COMPANY'S DIRECTORS

CHAPTER 1
APPOINTMENT AND REMOVAL OF DIRECTORS

Requirement to have directors

Appointment

Register of directors, etc

Removal

CHAPTER 2
GENERAL DUTIES OF DIRECTORS

Introductory

The general duties

Supplementary provisions

CHAPTER 3
DECLARATION OF INTEREST IN EXISTING TRANSACTION OR ARRANGEMENT

CHAPTER 4
TRANSACTIONS WITH DIRECTORS REQUIRING APPROVAL OF MEMBERS

Service contracts

Substantial property transactions

Loans, quasi-loans and credit transactions

Payments for loss of office

Supplementary

CHAPTER 5

DIRECTORS' SERVICE CONTRACTS

CHAPTER 6

CONTRACTS WITH SOLE MEMBERS WHO ARE DIRECTORS

CHAPTER 7
DIRECTORS' LIABILITIES

CHAPTER 8
DIRECTORS' RESIDENTIAL ADDRESSES: PROTECTION FROM DISCLOSURE

CHAPTER 9
SUPPLEMENTARY PROVISIONS

CHAPTER 3
RESOLUTIONS AT MEETINGS

CHAPTER 6
RECORDS OF RESOLUTIONS AND MEETINGS

CHAPTER 7
SUPPLEMENTARY PROVISIONS

PART 14
CONTROL OF POLITICAL DONATIONS AND EXPENDITURE

Introductory

Donations and expenditure to which this Part applies

Authorisation required for donations or expenditure

Remedies in case of unauthorised donations or expenditure

Exemptions

CHAPTER 5
DIRECTORS' REPORT

CHAPTER 6
QUOTED COMPANIES: DIRECTORS' REMUNERATION REPORT

CHAPTER 7
PUBLICATION OF ACCOUNTS AND REPORTS

CHAPTER 8
PUBLIC COMPANIES: LAYING OF ACCOUNTS AND REPORTS BEFORE GENERAL MEETING

CHAPTER 9
QUOTED COMPANIES: MEMBERS' APPROVAL OF DIRECTORS' REMUNERATION REPORT

CHAPTER 10
FILING OF ACCOUNTS AND REPORTS

CHAPTER 11
REVISION OF DEFECTIVE ACCOUNTS AND REPORTS

CHAPTER 4
REMOVAL, RESIGNATION, ETC OF AUDITORS

CHAPTER 5
QUOTED COMPANIES: RIGHT OF MEMBERS TO RAISE AUDIT CONCERNS AT
ACCOUNTS MEETING

CHAPTER 2
ALLOTMENT OF SHARES: GENERAL PROVISIONS

Power of directors to allot shares

Prohibition of commission, discounts and allowances

Registration of allotment

Return of allotment

Supplementary provisions

CHAPTER 3
ALLOTMENT OF EQUITY SECURITIES: EXISTING SHAREHOLDERS' RIGHT OF PRE-EMPTION

Introductory

Existing shareholders' right of pre-emption

Exceptions to right of pre-emption

Exclusion of right of pre-emption

CHAPTER 7
SHARE PREMIUMS

The share premium account

Relief from requirements as to share premiums

Supplementary provisions

CHAPTER 8
ALTERATION OF SHARE CAPITAL

How share capital may be altered

Subdivision or consolidation of shares

CHAPTER 9
CLASSES OF SHARE AND CLASS RIGHTS

Introductory

Variation of class rights

Matters to be notified to the registrar

CHAPTER 10
REDUCTION OF SHARE CAPITAL

Introductory

Private companies: reduction of capital supported by solvency statement

CHAPTER 11
MISCELLANEOUS AND SUPPLEMENTARY PROVISIONS

PART 18
ACQUISITION BY LIMITED COMPANY OF ITS OWN SHARES

CHAPTER 1
GENERAL PROVISIONS

CHAPTER 2
FINANCIAL ASSISTANCE FOR PURCHASE OF OWN SHARES

CHAPTER 3
REDEEMABLE SHARES

CHAPTER 4
PURCHASE OF OWN SHARES

CHAPTER 5
REDEMPTION OR PURCHASE BY PRIVATE COMPANY OUT OF CAPITAL

PART 20
PRIVATE AND PUBLIC COMPANIES

CHAPTER 1
PROHIBITION OF PUBLIC OFFERS BY PRIVATE COMPANIES

CHAPTER 2
MINIMUM SHARE CAPITAL REQUIREMENT FOR PUBLIC COMPANIES

PART 21

CERTIFICATION AND TRANSFER OF SECURITIES

CHAPTER 1

CERTIFICATION AND TRANSFER OF SECURITIES: GENERAL

CHAPTER 2

EVIDENCING AND TRANSFER OF TITLE TO SECURITIES WITHOUT WRITTEN INSTRUMENT

PART 22
INFORMATION ABOUT INTERESTS IN A COMPANY'S SHARES

PART 23
DISTRIBUTIONS

CHAPTER 1
RESTRICTIONS ON WHEN DISTRIBUTIONS MAY BE MADE

Introductory

General rules

Distributions by investment companies

CHAPTER 2
JUSTIFICATION OF DISTRIBUTION BY REFERENCE TO ACCOUNTS

Justification of distribution by reference to accounts

PART 25

COMPANY CHARGES

CHAPTER 1

COMPANIES REGISTERED IN ENGLAND AND WALES OR IN NORTHERN
IRELAND

Requirement to register company charges

Special rules about debentures

Charges in other jurisdictions

Orders charging land: Northern Ireland

The register of charges

Avoidance of certain charges

Companies' records and registers

CHAPTER 2

COMPANIES REGISTERED IN SCOTLAND

Charges requiring registration

CHAPTER 3
POWERS OF THE SECRETARY OF STATE

PART 26
ARRANGEMENTS AND RECONSTRUCTIONS

Application of this Part

Meeting of creditors or members

Court sanction for compromise or arrangement

181

CHAPTER 4
SUPPLEMENTARY PROVISIONS

PART 28
TAKEOVERS ETC

CHAPTER 1
THE TAKEOVER PANEL

The Panel and its rules

Information

Co-operation

Hearings and appeals

Contravention of rules etc

Funding

Miscellaneous and supplementary

CHAPTER 2
IMPEDIMENTS TO TAKEOVERS

CHAPTER 3
"SQUEEZE-OUT" AND "SELL-OUT"

PART 35
THE REGISTRAR OF COMPANIES

The registrar

Certificates of incorporation

Registered numbers

Delivery of documents to the registrar

Requirements for proper delivery

Public notice of receipt of certain documents

PART 36
OFFENCES UNDER THE COMPANIES ACTS

Liability of officer in default

Offences under the Companies Act 1985

General provisions

Production and inspection of documents

Supplementary

PART 37
COMPANIES: SUPPLEMENTARY PROVISIONS

Company records

PART 38
COMPANIES: INTERPRETATION

Meaning of "UK-registered company"

Meaning of "subsidiary" and related expressions

Meaning of "undertaking" and related expressions

PART 39
COMPANIES: MINOR AMENDMENTS

PART 40
COMPANY DIRECTORS: FOREIGN DISQUALIFICATION ETC

CHAPTER 5
REGISTERED THIRD COUNTRY AUDITORS

CHAPTER 6
SUPPLEMENTARY AND GENERAL

Schedules:

COMPANIES ACT 2006

2006 CHAPTER 46

An Act to reform company law and restate the greater part of the enactments relating to companies; to make other provision relating to companies and other forms of business organisation; to make provision about directors' disqualification, business names, auditors and actuaries; to amend Part 9 of the Enterprise Act 2002; and for connected purposes. [8th November 2006]

B E IT ENACTED by the Queen's most Excellent Majesty, by and with the advice and consent of the Lords Spiritual and Temporal, and Commons, in this present Parliament assembled, and by the authority of the same, as follows:-

PART 1
GENERAL INTRODUCTORY PROVISIONS

Companies and Companies Acts

1. **Companies**
    (1) In the Companies Acts, unless the context otherwise requires—
        "company" means a company formed and registered under this Act, that is—
        (a) a company so formed and registered after the commencement of this Part, or
        (b) a company that immediately before the commencement of this Part—
            (i) was formed and registered under the Companies Act 1985 (c. 6) or the Companies (Northern Ireland) Order 1986 (S.I. 1986/1032 (N.I. 6)), or
            (ii) was an existing company for the purposes of that Act or that Order,
            (which is to be treated on commencement as if formed and registered under this Act).
    (2) Certain provisions of the Companies Acts apply to—
        (a) companies registered, but not formed, under this Act (see Chapter 1 of Part 33), and
        (b) bodies incorporated in the United Kingdom but not registered under this Act (see Chapter 2 of that Part).
    (3) For provisions applying to companies incorporated outside the United Kingdom, see Part 34 (overseas companies).

2. **The Companies Acts**
    (1) In this Act "the Companies Acts" means—

        (a) the company law provisions of this Act,

        (b) Part 2 of the Companies (Audit, Investigations and Community Enterprise) Act 2004 (c. 27) (community interest companies), and

        (c) the provisions of the Companies Act 1985 (c. 6) and the Companies Consolidation (Consequential Provisions) Act 1985 (c. 9) that remain in force.

    (2) The company law provisions of this Act are—
        (a) the provisions of Parts 1 to 39 of this Act, and
        (b) the provisions of Parts 45 to 47 of this Act so far as they apply for the purposes of those Parts.

Types of company

3. **Limited and unlimited companies**
    (1) A company is a "limited company" if the liability of its members is limited by its constitution. It may be limited by shares or limited by guarantee.
    (2) If their liability is limited to the amount, if any, unpaid on the shares held by them, the company is "limited by shares".

(3) If their liability is limited to such amount as the members undertake to contribute to the assets of the company in the event of its being wound up, the company is "limited by guarantee".

(4) If there is no limit on the liability of its members, the company is an "unlimited company".

4. **Private and public companies**

(1) A "private company" is any company that is not a public company.

(2) A "public company" is a company limited by shares or limited by guarantee and having a share capital—

(a) whose certificate of incorporation states that it is a public company, and

(b) in relation to which the requirements of this Act, or the former Companies Acts, as to registration or re-registration as a public company have been complied with on or after the relevant date.

(3) For the purposes of subsection (2)(b) the relevant date is—

(a) in relation to registration or re-registration in Great Britain, 22nd December 1980;

(b) in relation to registration or re-registration in Northern Ireland, 1st July 1983.

(4) For the two major differences between private and public companies, see Part 20.

5. **Companies limited by guarantee and having share capital**

(1) A company cannot be formed as, or become, a company limited by guarantee with a share capital.

(2) Provision to this effect has been in force—

(a) in Great Britain since 22nd December 1980, and

(b) in Northern Ireland since 1st July 1983.

(3) Any provision in the constitution of a company limited by guarantee that purports to divide the company's undertaking into shares or interests is a provision for a share capital.
This applies whether or not the nominal value or number of the shares or interests is specified by the provision.

6. **Community interest companies**

(1) In accordance with Part 2 of the Companies (Audit, Investigations and Community Enterprise) Act 2004 (c. 27)—

(a) a company limited by shares or a company limited by guarantee and not having a share capital may be formed as or become a community interest company, and

(b) a company limited by guarantee and having a share capital may become a community interest company.

(2) The other provisions of the Companies Acts have effect subject to that Part.

PART 2
COMPANY FORMATION

General

7. **Method of forming company**

(1) A company is formed under this Act by one or more persons—

(a) subscribing their names to a memorandum of association (see section 8), and

(b) complying with the requirements of this Act as to registration (see sections 9 to 13).

(2) A company may not be so formed for an unlawful purpose.

8. **Memorandum of association**

(1) A memorandum of association is a memorandum stating that the subscribers—

(a) wish to form a company under this Act, and

(b) agree to become members of the company and, in the case of a company that is to have a share capital, to take at least one share each.

(2) The memorandum must be in the prescribed form and must be authenticated by each subscriber.

Requirements for registration

9. **Registration documents**

(1) The memorandum of association must be delivered to the registrar together with an application for registration of the company, the documents required by this section and a statement of compliance.

(2) The application for registration must state—

(a) the company's proposed name,

(b) whether the company's registered office is to be situated in England and Wales (or in Wales), in Scotland or in Northern Ireland,

(c) whether the liability of the members of the company is to be limited, and if so whether it is to be limited by shares or by guarantee, and

(d) whether the company is to be a private or a public company.

(3) If the application is delivered by a person as agent for the subscribers to the memorandum of association, it must state his name and address.

(4) The application must contain—

(a) in the case of a company that is to have a share capital, a statement of capital and initial shareholdings (see section 10);

(b) in the case of a company that is to be limited by guarantee, a statement of guarantee (see section 11);

(c) a statement of the company's proposed officers (see section 12).

(5) The application must also contain—

(a) a statement of the intended address of the company's registered office; and

(b) a copy of any proposed articles of association (to the extent that these are not supplied by the default application of model articles: see section 20).

(6) The application must be delivered—

(a) to the registrar of companies for England and Wales, if the registered office of the company is to be situated in England and Wales (or in Wales);

(b) to the registrar of companies for Scotland, if the registered office of the company is to be situated in Scotland;

(c) to the registrar of companies for Northern Ireland, if the registered office of the company is to be situated in Northern Ireland.

10. **Statement of capital and initial shareholdings**

(1) The statement of capital and initial shareholdings required to be delivered in the case of a company that is to have a share capital must comply with this section.

(2) It must state—

(a) the total number of shares of the company to be taken on formation by the subscribers to the memorandum of association,

(b) the aggregate nominal value of those shares,

(c) for each class of shares—

(i) prescribed particulars of the rights attached to the shares,

(ii) the total number of shares of that class, and

(iii) the aggregate nominal value of shares of that class, and

(d) the amount to be paid up and the amount (if any) to be unpaid on each share (whether on account of the nominal value of the share or by way of premium).

(3) It must contain such information as may be prescribed for the purpose of identifying the subscribers to the memorandum of association.

(4) It must state, with respect to each subscriber to the memorandum—

(a) the number, nominal value (of each share) and class of shares to be taken by him on formation, and

(b) the amount to be paid up and the amount (if any) to be unpaid on each share (whether on account of the nominal value of the share or by way of premium).

(5) Where a subscriber to the memorandum is to take shares of more than one class, the information required under subsection (4)(a) is required for each class.

11. Statement of guarantee

(1) The statement of guarantee required to be delivered in the case of a company that is to be limited by guarantee must comply with this section.

(2) It must contain such information as may be prescribed for the purpose of identifying the subscribers to the memorandum of association.

(3) It must state that each member undertakes that, if the company is wound up while he is a member, or within one year after he ceases to be a member, he will contribute to the assets of the company such amount as may be required for—

(a) payment of the debts and liabilities of the company contracted before he ceases to be a member,

(b) payment of the costs, charges and expenses of winding up, and

(c) adjustment of the rights of the contributories among themselves,

not exceeding a specified amount.

12. Statement of proposed officers

(1) The statement of the company's proposed officers required to be delivered to the registrar must contain the required particulars of—

(a) the person who is, or persons who are, to be the first director or directors of the company;

(b) in the case of a company that is to be a private company, any person who is (or any persons who are) to be the first secretary (or joint secretaries) of the company;

(c) in the case of a company that is to be a public company, the person who is (or the persons who are) to be the first secretary (or joint secretaries) of the company.

(2) The required particulars are the particulars that will be required to be stated—

(a) in the case of a director, in the company's register of directors and register of directors' residential addresses (see sections 162 to 166);

(b) in the case of a secretary, in the company's register of secretaries (see sections 277 to 279).

(3) The statement must also contain a consent by each of the persons named as a director, as secretary or as one of joint secretaries, to act in the relevant capacity.
If all the partners in a firm are to be joint secretaries, consent may be given by one partner on behalf of all of them.

13. Statement of compliance

(1) The statement of compliance required to be delivered to the registrar is a statement that the requirements of this Act as to registration have been complied with.

(2) The registrar may accept the statement of compliance as sufficient evidence of compliance.

Registration and its effect

14. **Registration**

If the registrar is satisfied that the requirements of this Act as to registration are complied with, he shall register the documents delivered to him.

15. **Issue of certificate of incorporation**

(1) On the registration of a company, the registrar of companies shall give a certificate that the company is incorporated.

(2) The certificate must state—

(a) the name and registered number of the company,

(b) the date of its incorporation,

(c) whether it is a limited or unlimited company, and if it is limited whether it is limited by shares or limited by guarantee,

(d) whether it is a private or a public company, and

(e) whether the company's registered office is situated in England and Wales (or in Wales), in Scotland or in Northern Ireland.

(3) The certificate must be signed by the registrar or authenticated by the registrar's official seal.

(4) The certificate is conclusive evidence that the requirements of this Act as to registration have been complied with and that the company is duly registered under this Act.

16. **Effect of registration**

(1) The registration of a company has the following effects as from the date of incorporation.

(2) The subscribers to the memorandum, together with such other persons as may from time to time become members of the company, are a body corporate by the name stated in the certificate of incorporation.

(3) That body corporate is capable of exercising all the functions of an incorporated company.

(4) The status and registered office of the company are as stated in, or in connection with, the application for registration.

(5) In the case of a company having a share capital, the subscribers to the memorandum become holders of the shares specified in the statement of capital and initial shareholdings.

(6) The persons named in the statement of proposed officers—
(a) as director, or
(b) as secretary or joint secretary of the company,
are deemed to have been appointed to that office.

PART 3
A COMPANY'S CONSTITUTION

CHAPTER 1
INTRODUCTORY

17. **A company's constitution**

Unless the context otherwise requires, references in the Companies Acts to a company's constitution include—

(a) the company's articles, and

(b) any resolutions and agreements to which Chapter 3 applies (see section 29).

CHAPTER 2
ARTICLES OF ASSOCIATION

General

18. **Articles of association**
    (1) A company must have articles of association prescribing regulations for the company.
    (2) Unless it is a company to which model articles apply by virtue of section 20 (default application of model articles in case of limited company), it must register articles of association.
    (3) Articles of association registered by a company must—
        (a) be contained in a single document, and
        (b) be divided into paragraphs numbered consecutively.
    (4) References in the Companies Acts to a company's "articles" are to its articles of association.

19. **Power of Secretary of State to prescribe model articles**
    (1) The Secretary of State may by regulations prescribe model articles of association for companies.
    (2) Different model articles may be prescribed for different descriptions of company.
    (3) A company may adopt all or any of the provisions of model articles.
    (4) Any amendment of model articles by regulations under this section does not affect a company registered before the amendment takes effect.
        "Amendment" here includes addition, alteration or repeal.
    (5) Regulations under this section are subject to negative resolution procedure.

20. **Default application of model articles**
    (1) On the formation of a limited company—
        (a) if articles are not registered, or
        (b) if articles are registered, in so far as they do not exclude or modify the relevant model articles,
        the relevant model articles (so far as applicable) form part of the company's articles in the same manner and to the same extent as if articles in the form of those articles had been duly registered.
    (2) The "relevant model articles" means the model articles prescribed for a company of that description as in force at the date on which the company is registered.

Alteration of articles

21. **Amendment of articles**
    (1) A company may amend its articles by special resolution.
    (2) In the case of a company that is a charity, this is subject to—
        (a) in England and Wales, section 64 of the Charities Act 1993 (c. 10);
        (b) in Northern Ireland, Article 9 of the Charities (Northern Ireland) Order 1987 (S.I. 1987/2048 (N.I. 19)).
    (3) In the case of a company that is registered in the Scottish Charity Register, this is subject to—
        (a) section 112 of the Companies Act 1989 (c. 40), and
        (b) section 16 of the Charities and Trustee Investment (Scotland) Act 2005 (asp 10).

22. **Entrenched provisions of the articles**
    (1) A company's articles may contain provision ("provision for entrenchment") to the effect that specified provisions of the articles may be amended or repealed only if conditions are met, or procedures are complied with, that are more restrictive than those applicable in the case of a special resolution.
    (2) Provision for entrenchment may only be made—
        (a) in the company's articles on formation, or
        (b) by an amendment of the company's articles agreed to by all the members of the company.

(3) Provision for entrenchment does not prevent amendment of the company's articles—

    (a) by agreement of all the members of the company, or

    (b) by order of a court or other authority having power to alter the company's articles.

(4) Nothing in this section affects any power of a court or other authority to alter a company's articles.

23.   **Notice to registrar of existence of restriction on amendment of articles**

(1) Where a company's articles—

    (a) on formation contain provision for entrenchment,

    (b) are amended so as to include such provision, or

    (c) are altered by order of a court or other authority so as to restrict or exclude the power of the company to amend its articles,

the company must give notice of that fact to the registrar.

(2) Where a company's articles—

    (a) are amended so as to remove provision for entrenchment, or

    (b) are altered by order of a court or other authority—

        (i) so as to remove such provision, or

        (ii) so as to remove any other restriction on, or any exclusion of, the power of the company to amend its articles,

the company must give notice of that fact to the registrar.

24.   **Statement of compliance where amendment of articles restricted**

(1) This section applies where a company's articles are subject—

    (a) to provision for entrenchment, or

    (b) to an order of a court or other authority restricting or excluding the company's power to amend the articles.

(2) If the company—

    (a) amends its articles, and

    (b) is required to send to the registrar a document making or evidencing the amendment,

the company must deliver with that document a statement of compliance.

(3) The statement of compliance required is a statement certifying that the amendment has been made in accordance with the company's articles and, where relevant, any applicable order of a court or other authority.

(4) The registrar may rely on the statement of compliance as sufficient evidence of the matters stated in it.

25.   **Effect of alteration of articles on company's members**

(1) A member of a company is not bound by an alteration to its articles after the date on which he became a member, if and so far as the alteration—

    (a) requires him to take or subscribe for more shares than the number held by him at the date on which the alteration is made, or

    (b) in any way increases his liability as at that date to contribute to the company's share capital or otherwise to pay money to the company.

(2) Subsection (1) does not apply in a case where the member agrees in writing, either before or after the alteration is made, to be bound by the alteration.

26.   **Registrar to be sent copy of amended articles**

(1) Where a company amends its articles it must send to the registrar a copy of the articles as amended not later than 15 days after the amendment takes effect.

(2) This section does not require a company to set out in its articles any provisions of model articles that—

    (a) are applied by the articles, or

    (b) apply by virtue of section 20 (default application of model articles).

(3) If a company fails to comply with this section an offence is committed by—

(a) the company, and

(b) every officer of the company who is in default.

(4) A person guilty of an offence under this section is liable on summary conviction to a fine not exceeding level 3 on the standard scale and, for continued contravention, a daily default fine not exceeding one-tenth of level 3 on the standard scale.

27. **Registrar's notice to comply in case of failure with respect to amended articles**

(1) If it appears to the registrar that a company has failed to comply with any enactment requiring it—

(a) to send to the registrar a document making or evidencing an alteration in the company's articles, or

(b) to send to the registrar a copy of the company's articles as amended, the registrar may give notice to the company requiring it to comply.

(2) The notice must—

(a) state the date on which it is issued, and

(b) require the company to comply within 28 days from that date.

(3) If the company complies with the notice within the specified time, no criminal proceedings may be brought in respect of the failure to comply with the enactment mentioned in subsection (1).

(4) If the company does not comply with the notice within the specified time, it is liable to a civil penalty of £200.

This is in addition to any liability to criminal proceedings in respect of the failure mentioned in subsection (1).

(5) The penalty may be recovered by the registrar and is to be paid into the Consolidated Fund.

Supplementary

28. **Existing companies: provisions of memorandum treated as provisions of articles**

(1) Provisions that immediately before the commencement of this Part were contained in a company's memorandum but are not provisions of the kind mentioned in section 8 (provisions of new-style memorandum) are to be treated after the commencement of this Part as provisions of the company's articles.

(2) This applies not only to substantive provisions but also to provision for entrenchment (as defined in section 22).

(3) The provisions of this Part about provision for entrenchment apply to such provision as they apply to provision made on the company's formation, except that the duty under section 23(1)(a) to give notice to the registrar does not apply.

CHAPTER 3
RESOLUTIONS AND AGREEMENTS AFFECTING A COMPANY'S CONSTITUTION

29. **Resolutions and agreements affecting a company's constitution**

(1) This Chapter applies to—

(a) any special resolution;

(b) any resolution or agreement agreed to by all the members of a company that, if not so agreed to, would not have been effective for its purpose unless passed as a special resolution;

(c) any resolution or agreement agreed to by all the members of a class of shareholders that, if not so agreed to, would not have been effective for its purpose unless passed by some particular majority or otherwise in some particular manner;

(d) any resolution or agreement that effectively binds all members of a class of shareholders though not agreed to by all those members;

(e) any other resolution or agreement to which this Chapter applies by virtue of any enactment.

(2) References in subsection (1) to a member of a company, or of a class of members of a company, do not include the company itself where it is such a member by virtue only of its holding shares as treasury shares.

30. Copies of resolutions or agreements to be forwarded to registrar

(1) A copy of every resolution or agreement to which this Chapter applies, or (in the case of a resolution or agreement that is not in writing) a written memorandum setting out its terms, must be forwarded to the registrar within 15 days after it is passed or made.

(2) If a company fails to comply with this section, an offence is committed by—
(a) the company, and
(b) every officer of it who is in default.

(3) A person guilty of an offence under this section is liable on summary conviction to a fine not exceeding level 3 on the standard scale and, for continued contravention, a daily default fine not exceeding one-tenth of level 3 on the standard scale.

(4) For the purposes of this section, a liquidator of the company is treated as an officer of it.

CHAPTER 4
MISCELLANEOUS AND SUPPLEMENTARY PROVISIONS

Statement of company's objects

31. Statement of company's objects

(1) Unless a company's articles specifically restrict the objects of the company, its objects are unrestricted.

(2) Where a company amends its articles so as to add, remove or alter a statement of the company's objects—
(a) it must give notice to the registrar,
(b) on receipt of the notice, the registrar shall register it, and
(c) the amendment is not effective until entry of that notice on the register.

(3) Any such amendment does not affect any rights or obligations of the company or render defective any legal proceedings by or against it.

(4) In the case of a company that is a charity, the provisions of this section have effect subject to—
(a) in England and Wales, section 64 of the Charities Act 1993 (c. 10);
(b) in Northern Ireland, Article 9 of the Charities (Northern Ireland) Order 1987 (S.I. 1987/2048 (N.I. 19)).

(5) In the case of a company that is entered in the Scottish Charity Register, the provisions of this section have effect subject to the provisions of the Charities and Trustee Investment (Scotland) Act 2005 (asp 10).

Other provisions with respect to a company's constitution

32. Constitutional documents to be provided to members

(1) A company must, on request by any member, send to him the following documents—

   (a) an up-to-date copy of the company's articles;

   (b) a copy of any resolution or agreement relating to the company to which Chapter 3 applies (resolutions and agreements affecting a company's constitution) and that is for the time being in force;

   (c) a copy of any document required to be sent to the registrar under—
      (i) section 34(2) (notice where company's constitution altered by enactment), or
      (ii) section 35(2)(a) (notice where order of court or other authority alters company's constitution);

   (d) a copy of any court order under section 899 (order sanctioning compromise or arrangement) or section 900 (order facilitating reconstruction or amalgamation);

   (e) a copy of any court order under section 996 (protection of members against unfair prejudice: powers of the court) that alters the company's constitution;

   (f) a copy of the company's current certificate of incorporation, and of any past certificates of incorporation;

   (g) in the case of a company with a share capital, a current statement of capital;

   (h) in the case of a company limited by guarantee, a copy of the statement of guarantee.

(2) The statement of capital required by subsection (1)(g) is a statement of—

   (a) the total number of shares of the company,

   (b) the aggregate nominal value of those shares,

   (c) for each class of shares—
      (i) prescribed particulars of the rights attached to the shares,
      (ii) the total number of shares of that class, and
      (iii) the aggregate nominal value of shares of that class, and

   (d) the amount paid up and the amount (if any) unpaid on each share (whether on account of the nominal value of the share or by way of premium).

(3) If a company makes default in complying with this section, an offence is committed by every officer of the company who is in default.

(4) A person guilty of an offence under this section is liable on summary conviction to a fine not exceeding level 3 on the standard scale.

33. Effect of company's constitution

(1) The provisions of a company's constitution bind the company and its members to the same extent as if there were covenants on the part of the company and of each member to observe those provisions.

(2) Money payable by a member to the company under its constitution is a debt due from him to the company.
In England and Wales and Northern Ireland it is of the nature of an ordinary contract debt.

34. Notice to registrar where company's constitution altered by enactment

(1) This section applies where a company's constitution is altered by an enactment, other than an enactment amending the general law.

(2) The company must give notice of the alteration to the registrar, specifying the enactment, not later than 15 days after the enactment comes into force.

In the case of a special enactment the notice must be accompanied by a copy of the enactment.

(3) If the enactment amends—

    (a) the company's articles, or

    (b) a resolution or agreement to which Chapter 3 applies (resolutions and agreements affecting a company's constitution),

the notice must be accompanied by a copy of the company's articles, or the resolution or agreement in question, as amended.

(4) A "special enactment" means an enactment that is not a public general enactment, and includes—

    (a) an Act for confirming a provisional order,

    (b) any provision of a public general Act in relation to the passing of which any of the standing orders of the House of Lords or the House of Commons relating to Private Business applied, or

    (c) any enactment to the extent that it is incorporated in or applied for the purposes of a special enactment.

(5) If a company fails to comply with this section an offence is committed by—

    (a) the company, and

    (b) every officer of the company who is in default.

(6) A person guilty of an offence under this section is liable on summary conviction to a fine not exceeding level 3 on the standard scale and, for continued contravention, a daily default fine not exceeding one-tenth of level 3 on the standard scale.

35. **Notice to registrar where company's constitution altered by order**

(1) Where a company's constitution is altered by an order of a court or other authority, the company must give notice to the registrar of the alteration not later than 15 days after the alteration takes effect.

(2) The notice must be accompanied by—

    (a) a copy of the order, and

    (b) if the order amends—

        (i) the company's articles, or

        (ii) a resolution or agreement to which Chapter 3 applies (resolutions and agreements affecting the company's constitution),

    a copy of the company's articles, or the resolution or agreement in question, as amended.

(3) If a company fails to comply with this section an offence is committed by—

    (a) the company, and

    (b) every officer of the company who is in default.

(4) A person guilty of an offence under this section is liable on summary conviction to a fine not exceeding level 3 on the standard scale and, for continued contravention, a daily default fine not exceeding one-tenth of level 3 on the standard scale.

(5) This section does not apply where provision is made by another enactment for the delivery to the registrar of a copy of the order in question.

36. **Documents to be incorporated in or accompany copies of articles issued by company**

(1) Every copy of a company's articles issued by the company must be accompanied by—

    (a) a copy of any resolution or agreement relating to the company to which Chapter 3 applies (resolutions and agreements affecting a company's constitution),

(b) where the company has been required to give notice to the registrar under section 34(2) (notice where company's constitution altered by enactment), a statement that the enactment in question alters the effect of the company's constitution,

(c) where the company's constitution is altered by a special enactment (see section 34(4)), a copy of the enactment, and

(d) a copy of any order required to be sent to the registrar under section 35(2)(a) (order of court or other authority altering company's constitution).

(2) This does not require the articles to be accompanied by a copy of a document or by a statement if—
  (a) the effect of the resolution, agreement, enactment or order (as the case may be) on the company's constitution has been incorporated into the articles by amendment, or
  (b) the resolution, agreement, enactment or order (as the case may be) is not for the time being in force.

(3) If the company fails to comply with this section, an offence is committed by every officer of the company who is in default.

(4) A person guilty of an offence under this section is liable on summary conviction to a fine not exceeding level 3 on the standard scale for each occasion on which copies are issued, or, as the case may be, requested.

(5) For the purposes of this section, a liquidator of the company is treated as an officer of it.

Supplementary provisions

37. **Right to participate in profits otherwise than as member void**

In the case of a company limited by guarantee and not having a share capital any provision in the company's articles, or in any resolution of the company, purporting to give a person a right to participate in the divisible profits of the company otherwise than as a member is void.

38. **Application to single member companies of enactments and rules of law**

Any enactment or rule of law applicable to companies formed by two or more persons or having two or more members applies with any necessary modification in relation to a company formed by one person or having only one person as a member.

PART 4
A COMPANY'S CAPACITY AND RELATED MATTERS

Capacity of company and power of directors to bind it

39. **A company's capacity**

(1) The validity of an act done by a company shall not be called into question on the ground of lack of capacity by reason of anything in the company's constitution.

(2) This section has effect subject to section 42 (companies that are charities).

40. **Power of directors to bind the company**

(1) In favour of a person dealing with a company in good faith, the power of the directors to bind the company, or authorise others to do so, is deemed to be free of any limitation under the company's constitution.

(2) For this purpose—
  (a) a person "deals with" a company if he is a party to any transaction or other act to which the company is a party,

    (b) a person dealing with a company—

        (i)   is not bound to enquire as to any limitation on the powers of the directors to bind the company or authorise others to do so,

        (ii) is presumed to have acted in good faith unless the contrary is proved, and

        (iii) is not to be regarded as acting in bad faith by reason only of his knowing that an act is beyond the powers of the directors under the company's constitution.

(3) The references above to limitations on the directors' powers under the company's constitution include limitations deriving—

    (a) from a resolution of the company or of any class of shareholders, or

    (b) from any agreement between the members of the company or of any class of shareholders.

(4) This section does not affect any right of a member of the company to bring proceedings to restrain the doing of an action that is beyond the powers of the directors.

But no such proceedings lie in respect of an act to be done in fulfilment of a legal obligation arising from a previous act of the company.

(5) This section does not affect any liability incurred by the directors, or any other person, by reason of the directors' exceeding their powers.

(6) This section has effect subject to—

    section 41 (transactions with directors or their associates), and

    section 42 (companies that are charities).

41. Constitutional limitations: transactions involving directors or their associates

(1) This section applies to a transaction if or to the extent that its validity depends on section 40 (power of directors deemed to be free of limitations under company's constitution in favour of person dealing with company in good faith).

Nothing in this section shall be read as excluding the operation of any other enactment or rule of law by virtue of which the transaction may be called in question or any liability to the company may arise.

(2) Where—

    (a) a company enters into such a transaction, and

    (b) the parties to the transaction include—

        (i)   a director of the company or of its holding company, or

        (ii) a person connected with any such director,

the transaction is voidable at the instance of the company.

(3) Whether or not it is avoided, any such party to the transaction as is mentioned in subsection (2)(b)(i) or (ii), and any director of the company who authorised the transaction, is liable—

    (a) to account to the company for any gain he has made directly or indirectly by the transaction, and

    (b) to indemnify the company for any loss or damage resulting from the transaction.

(4) The transaction ceases to be voidable if—

    (a) restitution of any money or other asset which was the subject matter of the transaction is no longer possible, or

    (b) the company is indemnified for any loss or damage resulting from the transaction, or

    (c) rights acquired bona fide for value and without actual notice of the directors' exceeding their powers by a person who is not party to the transaction would be affected by the avoidance, or

    (d) the transaction is affirmed by the company.

(5) A person other than a director of the company is not liable under subsection (3) if he shows that at the time the transaction was entered into he did not know that the directors were exceeding their powers.

(6) Nothing in the preceding provisions of this section affects the rights of any party to the transaction not within subsection (2)(b)(i) or (ii).

But the court may, on the application of the company or any such party, make an order affirming, severing or setting aside the transaction on such terms as appear to the court to be just.

(7) In this section—

(a) "transaction" includes any act; and

(b) the reference to a person connected with a director has the same meaning as in Part 10 (company directors).

42. **Constitutional limitations: companies that are charities**

(1) Sections 39 and 40 (company's capacity and power of directors to bind company) do not apply to the acts of a company that is a charity except in favour of a person who—

(a) does not know at the time the act is done that the company is a charity, or

(b) gives full consideration in money or money's worth in relation to the act in question and does not know (as the case may be)—

(i) that the act is not permitted by the company's constitution, or

(ii) that the act is beyond the powers of the directors.

(2) Where a company that is a charity purports to transfer or grant an interest in property, the fact that (as the case may be)—

(a) the act was not permitted by the company's constitution, or

(b) the directors in connection with the act exceeded any limitation on their powers under the company's constitution,

does not affect the title of a person who subsequently acquires the property or any interest in it for full consideration without actual notice of any such circumstances affecting the validity of the company's act.

(3) In any proceedings arising out of subsection (1) or (2) the burden of proving—

(a) that a person knew that the company was a charity, or

(b) that a person knew that an act was not permitted by the company's constitution or was beyond the powers of the directors,

lies on the person asserting that fact.

(4) In the case of a company that is a charity the affirmation of a transaction to which section 41 applies (transactions with directors or their associates) is ineffective without the prior written consent of—

(a) in England and Wales, the Charity Commission;

(b) in Northern Ireland, the Department for Social Development.

(5) This section does not extend to Scotland (but see section 112 of the Companies Act 1989 (c. 40)).

Formalities of doing business under the law of England and Wales or Northern Ireland

43. **Company contracts**

(1) Under the law of England and Wales or Northern Ireland a contract may be made—

(a) by a company, by writing under its common seal, or

(b) on behalf of a company, by a person acting under its authority, express or implied.

(2) Any formalities required by law in the case of a contract made by an individual also apply, unless a contrary intention appears, to a contract made by or on behalf of a company.

44. **Execution of documents**

    (1) Under the law of England and Wales or Northern Ireland a document is executed by a company—

        (a) by the affixing of its common seal, or

        (b) by signature in accordance with the following provisions.

    (2) A document is validly executed by a company if it is signed on behalf of the company—

        (a) by two authorised signatories, or

        (b) by a director of the company in the presence of a witness who attests the signature.

    (3) The following are "authorised signatories" for the purposes of subsection (2)—

        (a) every director of the company, and

        (b) in the case of a private company with a secretary or a public company, the secretary (or any joint secretary) of the company.

    (4) A document signed in accordance with subsection (2) and expressed, in whatever words, to be executed by the company has the same effect as if executed under the common seal of the company.

    (5) In favour of a purchaser a document is deemed to have been duly executed by a company if it purports to be signed in accordance with subsection (2).

    A "purchaser" means a purchaser in good faith for valuable consideration and includes a lessee, mortgagee or other person who for valuable consideration acquires an interest in property.

    (6) Where a document is to be signed by a person on behalf of more than one company, it is not duly signed by that person for the purposes of this section unless he signs it separately in each capacity.

    (7) References in this section to a document being (or purporting to be) signed by a director or secretary are to be read, in a case where that office is held by a firm, as references to its being (or purporting to be) signed by an individual authorised by the firm to sign on its behalf.

    (8) This section applies to a document that is (or purports to be) executed by a company in the name of or on behalf of another person whether or not that person is also a company.

45. **Common seal**

    (1) A company may have a common seal, but need not have one.

    (2) A company which has a common seal shall have its name engraved in legible characters on the seal.

    (3) If a company fails to comply with subsection (2) an offence is committed by—

        (a) the company, and

        (b) every officer of the company who is in default.

    (4) An officer of a company, or a person acting on behalf of a company, commits an offence if he uses, or authorises the use of, a seal purporting to be a seal of the company on which its name is not engraved as required by subsection (2).

    (5) A person guilty of an offence under this section is liable on summary conviction to a fine not exceeding level 3 on the standard scale.

    (6) This section does not form part of the law of Scotland.

46. **Execution of deeds**

    (1) A document is validly executed by a company as a deed for the purposes of section 1(2)(b) of the Law of Property (Miscellaneous Provisions) Act 1989 (c. 34) and for the purposes of the law of Northern Ireland if, and only if—

        (a) it is duly executed by the company, and

        (b) it is delivered as a deed.

    (2) For the purposes of subsection (1)(b) a document is presumed to be delivered upon its being executed, unless a contrary intention is proved.

47. **Execution of deeds or other documents by attorney**

    (1) Under the law of England and Wales or Northern Ireland a company may, by instrument executed as a deed, empower a person, either generally or in respect of specified matters, as its attorney to execute deeds or other documents on its behalf.

    (2) A deed or other document so executed, whether in the United Kingdom or elsewhere, has effect as if executed by the company.

Formalities of doing business under the law of Scotland

48. **Execution of documents by companies**

    (1) The following provisions form part of the law of Scotland only.

    (2) Notwithstanding the provisions of any enactment, a company need not have a company seal.

    (3) For the purposes of any enactment—

    (a) providing for a document to be executed by a company by affixing its common seal, or

    (b) referring (in whatever terms) to a document so executed,

    a document signed or subscribed by or on behalf of the company in accordance with the provisions of the Requirements of Writing (Scotland) Act 1995 (c. 7) has effect as if so executed.

Other matters

49. **Official seal for use abroad**

    (1) A company that has a common seal may have an official seal for use outside the United Kingdom.

    (2) The official seal must be a facsimile of the company's common seal, with the addition on its face of the place or places where it is to be used.

    (3) The official seal when duly affixed to a document has the same effect as the company's common seal.

    This subsection does not extend to Scotland.

    (4) A company having an official seal for use outside the United Kingdom may—

    (a) by writing under its common seal, or

    (b) as respects Scotland, by writing subscribed in accordance with the Requirements of Writing (Scotland) Act 1995,

    authorise any person appointed for the purpose to affix the official seal to any deed or other document to which the company is party.

    (5) As between the company and a person dealing with such an agent, the agent's authority continues—

    (a) during the period mentioned in the instrument conferring the authority, or

    (b) if no period is mentioned, until notice of the revocation or termination of the agent's authority has been given to the person dealing with him.

    (6) The person affixing the official seal must certify in writing on the deed or other document to which the seal is affixed the date on which, and place at which, it is affixed.

50. **Official seal for share certificates etc**

    (1) A company that has a common seal may have an official seal for use—

    (a) for sealing securities issued by the company, or

    (b) for sealing documents creating or evidencing securities so issued.

    (2) The official seal—

    (a) must be a facsimile of the company's common seal, with the addition on its face of the word "Securities", and

    (b) when duly affixed to the document has the same effect as the company's common seal.

51. **Pre-incorporation contracts, deeds and obligations**

(1) A contract that purports to be made by or on behalf of a company at a time when the company has not been formed has effect, subject to any agreement to the contrary, as one made with the person purporting to act for the company or as agent for it, and he is personally liable on the contract accordingly.

(2) Subsection (1) applies—

(a) to the making of a deed under the law of England and Wales or Northern Ireland, and

(b) to the undertaking of an obligation under the law of Scotland,

as it applies to the making of a contract.

52. **Bills of exchange and promissory notes**

A bill of exchange or promissory note is deemed to have been made, accepted or endorsed on behalf of a company if made, accepted or endorsed in the name of, or by or on behalf or on account of, the company by a person acting under its authority.

PART 5

A COMPANY'S NAME

CHAPTER 1

GENERAL REQUIREMENTS

Prohibited names

53. **Prohibited names**

A company must not be registered under this Act by a name if, in the opinion of the Secretary of State—

(a) its use by the company would constitute an offence, or

(b) it is offensive.

Sensitive words and expressions

54. **Names suggesting connection with government or public authority**

(1) The approval of the Secretary of State is required for a company to be registered under this Act by a name that would be likely to give the impression that the company is connected with—

(a) Her Majesty's Government, any part of the Scottish administration or Her Majesty's Government in Northern Ireland,

(b) a local authority, or

(c) any public authority specified for the purposes of this section by regulations made by the Secretary of State.

(2) For the purposes of this section—

"local authority" means—

(a) a local authority within the meaning of the Local Government Act 1972 (c. 70), the Common Council of the City of London or the Council of the Isles of Scilly,

(b) a council constituted under section 2 of the Local Government etc. (Scotland) Act 1994 (c. 39), or

(c) a district council in Northern Ireland;

"public authority" includes any person or body having functions of a public nature.

(3) Regulations under this section are subject to affirmative resolution procedure.

55. **Other sensitive words or expressions**

   (1) The approval of the Secretary of State is required for a company to be registered under this Act by a name that includes a word or expression for the time being specified in regulations made by the Secretary of State under this section.

   (2) Regulations under this section are subject to approval after being made.

56. **Duty to seek comments of government department or other specified body**

   (1) The Secretary of State may by regulations under—

   (a) section 54 (name suggesting connection with government or public authority), or

   (b) section 55 (other sensitive words or expressions),

   require that, in connection with an application for the approval of the Secretary of State under that section, the applicant must seek the view of a specified Government department or other body.

   (2) Where such a requirement applies, the applicant must request the specified department or other body (in writing) to indicate whether (and if so why) it has any objections to the proposed name.

   (3) Where a request under this section is made in connection with an application for the registration of a company under this Act, the application must—

   (a) include a statement that a request under this section has been made, and

   (b) be accompanied by a copy of any response received.

   (4) Where a request under this section is made in connection with a change in a company's name, the notice of the change sent to the registrar must be accompanied by—

   (a) a statement by a director or secretary of the company that a request under this section has been made, and

   (b) a copy of any response received.

   (5) In this section "specified" means specified in the regulations.

Permitted characters etc

57. **Permitted characters etc**

   (1) The Secretary of State may make provision by regulations—

   (a) as to the letters or other characters, signs or symbols (including accents and other diacritical marks) and punctuation that may be used in the name of a company registered under this Act; and

   (b) specifying a standard style or format for the name of a company for the purposes of registration.

   (2) The regulations may prohibit the use of specified characters, signs or symbols when appearing in a specified position (in particular, at the beginning of a name).

   (3) A company may not be registered under this Act by a name that consists of or includes anything that is not permitted in accordance with regulations under this section.

   (4) Regulations under this section are subject to negative resolution procedure.

   (5) In this section "specified" means specified in the regulations.

CHAPTER 2
INDICATIONS OF COMPANY TYPE OR LEGAL FORM

Required indications for limited companies

58. **Public limited companies**

   (1) The name of a limited company that is a public company must end with "public limited company" or "p.l.c.".

(2) In the case of a Welsh company, its name may instead end with "cwmni cyfyngedig cyhoeddus" or "c.c.c.".

(3) This section does not apply to community interest companies (but see section 33(3) and (4) of the Companies (Audit, Investigations and Community Enterprise) Act 2004 (c. 27)).

59.   **Private limited companies**

(1) The name of a limited company that is a private company must end with "limited" or "ltd.".

(2) In the case of a Welsh company, its name may instead end with "cyfyngedig" or "cyf.".

(3) Certain companies are exempt from this requirement (see section 60).

(4) This section does not apply to community interest companies (but see section 33(1) and (2) of the Companies (Audit, Investigations and Community Enterprise) Act 2004)).

60.   **Exemption from requirement as to use of "limited"**

(1) A private company is exempt from section 59 (requirement to have name ending with "limited" or permitted alternative) if—

(a) it is a charity,

(b) it is exempted from the requirement of that section by regulations made by the Secretary of State, or

(c) it meets the conditions specified in—

section 61 (continuation of existing exemption: companies limited by shares), or

section 62 (continuation of existing exemption: companies limited by guarantee).

(2) The registrar may refuse to register a private limited company by a name that does not include the word "limited" (or a permitted alternative) unless a statement has been delivered to him that the company meets the conditions for exemption.

(3) The registrar may accept the statement as sufficient evidence of the matters stated in it.

(4) Regulations under this section are subject to negative resolution procedure.

61.   **Continuation of existing exemption: companies limited by shares**

(1) This section applies to a private company limited by shares—

(a) that on 25th February 1982—

(i)   was registered in Great Britain, and

(ii) had a name that, by virtue of a licence under section 19 of the Companies Act 1948 (c. 38) (or corresponding earlier legislation), did not include the word "limited" or any of the permitted alternatives, or

(b) that on 30th June 1983—

(i)   was registered in Northern Ireland, and

(ii) had a name that, by virtue of a licence under section 19 of the Companies Act (Northern Ireland) 1960 (c. 22 (N.I.)) (or corresponding earlier legislation), did not include the word "limited" or any of the permitted alternatives.

(2) A company to which this section applies is exempt from section 59 (requirement to have name ending with "limited" or permitted alternative) so long as—

(a) it continues to meet the following two conditions, and

(b) it does not change its name.

(3) The first condition is that the objects of the company are the promotion of commerce, art, science, education, religion, charity or any profession, and anything incidental or conducive to any of those objects.

(4) The second condition is that the company's articles—

(a) require its income to be applied in promoting its objects,

(b) prohibit the payment of dividends, or any return of capital, to its members, and

(c) require all the assets that would otherwise be available to its members generally to be transferred on its winding up either—

(i)   to another body with objects similar to its own, or

(ii) to another body the objects of which are the promotion of charity and anything incidental or conducive thereto,

(whether or not the body is a member of the company).

62. **Continuation of existing exemption: companies limited by guarantee**

(1) A private company limited by guarantee that immediately before the commencement of this Part—

(a) was exempt by virtue of section 30 of the Companies Act 1985 (c. 6) or Article 40 of the Companies (Northern Ireland) Order 1986 (S.I. 1986/1032 (N.I. 6)) from the requirement to have a name including the word "limited" or a permitted alternative, and

(b) had a name that did not include the word "limited" or any of the permitted alternatives,

is exempt from section 59 (requirement to have name ending with "limited" or permitted alternative) so long as it continues to meet the following two conditions and does not change its name.

(2) The first condition is that the objects of the company are the promotion of commerce, art, science, education, religion, charity or any profession, and anything incidental or conducive to any of those objects.

(3) The second condition is that the company's articles—

(a) require its income to be applied in promoting its objects,

(b) prohibit the payment of dividends to its members, and

(c) require all the assets that would otherwise be available to its members generally to be transferred on its winding up either—

(i) to another body with objects similar to its own, or

(ii) to another body the objects of which are the promotion of charity and anything incidental or conducive thereto,

(whether or not the body is a member of the company).

63. **Exempt company: restriction on amendment of articles**

(1) A private company—

(a) that is exempt under section 61 or 62 from the requirement to use "limited" (or a permitted alternative) as part of its name, and

(b) whose name does not include "limited" or any of the permitted alternatives,

must not amend its articles so that it ceases to comply with the conditions for exemption under that section.

(2) If subsection (1) above is contravened an offence is committed by—

(a) the company, and

(b) every officer of the company who is in default.

For this purpose a shadow director is treated as an officer of the company.

(3) A person guilty of an offence under this section is liable on summary conviction to a fine not exceeding level 5 on the standard scale and, for continued contravention, a daily default fine not exceeding one-tenth of level 5 on the standard scale.

(4) Where immediately before the commencement of this section—

(a) a company was exempt by virtue of section 30 of the Companies Act 1985 (c. 6) or Article 40 of the Companies (Northern Ireland) Order 1986 (S.I. 1986/1032 (N.I. 6)) from the requirement to have a name including the word "limited" (or a permitted alternative), and

(b) the company's memorandum or articles contained provision preventing an alteration of them without the approval of—

(i) the Board of Trade or a Northern Ireland department (or any other department or Minister), or

(ii) the Charity Commission,

that provision, and any condition of any such licence as is mentioned in section 61(1)(a)(ii) or (b)(ii) requiring such provision, shall cease to have effect.

This does not apply if, or to the extent that, the provision is required by or under any other enactment.

(5) It is hereby declared that any such provision as is mentioned in subsection (4)(b) formerly contained in a company's memorandum was at all material times capable, with the appropriate approval, of being altered or removed under section 17 of the Companies Act 1985 or Article 28 of the Companies (Northern Ireland) Order 1986 (S.I. 1986/1032 (N.I. 6)) (or corresponding earlier enactments).

64. **Power to direct change of name in case of company ceasing to be entitled to exemption**

(1) If it appears to the Secretary of State that a company whose name does not include "limited" or any of the permitted alternatives—

(a) has ceased to be entitled to exemption under section 60(1)(a) or (b), or

(b) in the case of a company within section 61 or 62 (which impose conditions as to the objects and articles of the company)—

(i) has carried on any business other than the promotion of any of the objects mentioned in subsection (3) of section 61 or, as the case may be, subsection (2) of section 62, or

(ii) has acted inconsistently with the provision required by subsection (4)(a) or (b) of section 61 or, as the case may be, subsection (3)(a) or (b) of section 62,

the Secretary of State may direct the company to change its name so that it ends with "limited" or one of the permitted alternatives.

(2) The direction must be in writing and must specify the period within which the company is to change its name.

(3) A change of name in order to comply with a direction under this section may be made by resolution of the directors.

This is without prejudice to any other method of changing the company's name.

(4) Where a resolution of the directors is passed in accordance with subsection (3), the company must give notice to the registrar of the change.

Sections 80 and 81 apply as regards the registration and effect of the change.

(5) If the company fails to comply with a direction under this section an offence is committed by—

(a) the company, and

(b) every officer of the company who is in default.

(6) A person guilty of an offence under this section is liable on summary conviction to a fine not exceeding level 5 on the standard scale and, for continued contravention, a daily default fine not exceeding one-tenth of level 5 on the standard scale.

(7) A company that has been directed to change its name under this section may not, without the approval of the Secretary of State, subsequently change its name so that it does not include "limited" or one of the permitted alternatives. This does not apply to a change of name on re-registration or on conversion to a community interest company.

Inappropriate use of indications of company type or legal form

65. **Inappropriate use of indications of company type or legal form**

(1) The Secretary of State may make provision by regulations prohibiting the use in a company name of specified words, expressions or other indications—

(a) that are associated with a particular type of company or form of organisation, or

(b) that are similar to words, expressions or other indications associated with a particular type of company or form of organisation.

(2) The regulations may prohibit the use of words, expressions or other indications—

(a) in a specified part, or otherwise than in a specified part, of a company's name;

(b) in conjunction with, or otherwise than in conjunction with, such other words, expressions or indications as may be specified.

(3) A company must not be registered under this Act by a name that consists of or includes anything prohibited by regulations under this section.

(4) In this section "specified" means specified in the regulations.

(5) Regulations under this section are subject to negative resolution procedure.

CHAPTER 3
SIMILARITY TO OTHER NAMES

Similarity to other name on registrar's index

66. **Name not to be the same as another in the index**

(1) A company must not be registered under this Act by a name that is the same as another name appearing in the registrar's index of company names.

(2) The Secretary of State may make provision by regulations supplementing this section.

(3) The regulations may make provision—

(a) as to matters that are to be disregarded, and

(b) as to words, expressions, signs or symbols that are, or are not, to be regarded as the same,

for the purposes of this section.

(4) The regulations may provide—

(a) that registration by a name that would otherwise be prohibited under this section is permitted—

(i) in specified circumstances, or

(ii) with specified consent, and

(b) that if those circumstances obtain or that consent is given at the time a company is registered by a name, a subsequent change of circumstances or withdrawal of consent does not affect the registration.

(5) Regulations under this section are subject to negative resolution procedure.

(6) In this section "specified" means specified in the regulations.

67. **Power to direct change of name in case of similarity to existing name**

(1) The Secretary of State may direct a company to change its name if it has been registered in a name that is the same as or, in the opinion of the Secretary of State, too like—

(a) a name appearing at the time of the registration in the registrar's index of company names, or

(b) a name that should have appeared in that index at that time.

(2) The Secretary of State may make provision by regulations supplementing this section.

(3) The regulations may make provision—

(a) as to matters that are to be disregarded, and

(b) as to words, expressions, signs or symbols that are, or are not, to be regarded as the same,

for the purposes of this section.

(4) The regulations may provide—

(a) that no direction is to be given under this section in respect of a name—

(i) in specified circumstances, or

(ii) if specified consent is given, and

(b) that a subsequent change of circumstances or withdrawal of consent does not give rise to grounds for a direction under this section.

(5) Regulations under this section are subject to negative resolution procedure.

(6) In this section "specified" means specified in the regulations.

68. **Direction to change name: supplementary provisions**

(1) The following provisions have effect in relation to a direction under section 67 (power to direct change of name in case of similarity to existing name).

(2) Any such direction—
    (a) must be given within twelve months of the company's registration by the name in question, and
    (b) must specify the period within which the company is to change its name.

(3) The Secretary of State may by a further direction extend that period.
Any such direction must be given before the end of the period for the time being specified.

(4) A direction under section 67 or this section must be in writing.

(5) If a company fails to comply with the direction, an offence is committed by—
    (a) the company, and
    (b) every officer of the company who is in default.
For this purpose a shadow director is treated as an officer of the company.

(6) A person guilty of an offence under this section is liable on summary conviction to a fine not exceeding level 3 on the standard scale and, for continued contravention, a daily default fine not exceeding one-tenth of level 3 on the standard scale.

Similarity to other name in which person has goodwill

69. Objection to company's registered name

(1) A person ("the applicant") may object to a company's registered name on the ground—
    (a) that it is the same as a name associated with the applicant in which he has goodwill, or
    (b) that it is sufficiently similar to such a name that its use in the United Kingdom would be likely to mislead by suggesting a connection between the company and the applicant.

(2) The objection must be made by application to a company names adjudicator (see section 70).

(3) The company concerned shall be the primary respondent to the application. Any of its members or directors may be joined as respondents.

(4) If the ground specified in subsection (1)(a) or (b) is established, it is for the respondents to show—
    (a) that the name was registered before the commencement of the activities on which the applicant relies to show goodwill; or
    (b) that the company—
        (i) is operating under the name, or
        (ii) is proposing to do so and has incurred substantial start-up costs in preparation, or
        (iii) was formerly operating under the name and is now dormant;
        or
    (c) that the name was registered in the ordinary course of a company formation business and the company is available for sale to the applicant on the standard terms of that business; or
    (d) that the name was adopted in good faith; or
    (e) that the interests of the applicant are not adversely affected to any significant extent.
If none of those is shown, the objection shall be upheld.

(5) If the facts mentioned in subsection (4)(a), (b) or (c) are established, the objection shall nevertheless be upheld if the applicant shows that the main purpose of the respondents (or any of them) in registering the name was to obtain money (or other consideration) from the applicant or prevent him from registering the name.

(6) If the objection is not upheld under subsection (4) or (5), it shall be dismissed.

(7) In this section "goodwill" includes reputation of any description.

70. Company names adjudicators

(1) The Secretary of State shall appoint persons to be company names adjudicators.

(2) The persons appointed must have such legal or other experience as, in the Secretary of State's opinion, makes them suitable for appointment.

(3) An adjudicator—
    (a) holds office in accordance with the terms of his appointment,
    (b) is eligible for re-appointment when his term of office ends,

(c) may resign at any time by notice in writing given to the Secretary of State, and

(d) may be dismissed by the Secretary of State on the ground of incapacity or misconduct.

(4) One of the adjudicators shall be appointed Chief Adjudicator.

He shall perform such functions as the Secretary of State may assign to him.

(5) The other adjudicators shall undertake such duties as the Chief Adjudicator may determine.

(6) The Secretary of State may—

    (a) appoint staff for the adjudicators;

    (b) pay remuneration and expenses to the adjudicators and their staff;

    (c) defray other costs arising in relation to the performance by the adjudicators of their functions;

    (d) compensate persons for ceasing to be adjudicators.

71. Procedural rules

(1) The Secretary of State may make rules about proceedings before a company names adjudicator.

(2) The rules may, in particular, make provision—

    (a) as to how an application is to be made and the form and content of an application or other documents;

    (b) for fees to be charged;

    (c) about the service of documents and the consequences of failure to serve them;

    (d) as to the form and manner in which evidence is to be given;

    (e) for circumstances in which hearings are required and those in which they are not;

    (f) for cases to be heard by more than one adjudicator;

    (g) setting time limits for anything required to be done in connection with the proceedings (and allowing for such limits to be extended, even if they have expired);

    (h) enabling the adjudicator to strike out an application, or any defence, in whole or in part—

        (i) on the ground that it is vexatious, has no reasonable prospect of success or is otherwise misconceived, or

        (ii) for failure to comply with the requirements of the rules;

    (i) conferring power to order security for costs (in Scotland, caution for expenses);

    (j) as to how far proceedings are to be held in public;

    (k) requiring one party to bear the costs (in Scotland, expenses) of another and as to the taxing (or settling) the amount of such costs (or expenses).

(3) The rules may confer on the Chief Adjudicator power to determine any matter that could be the subject of provision in the rules.

(4) Rules under this section shall be made by statutory instrument which shall be subject to annulment in pursuance of a resolution of either House of Parliament.

72. Decision of adjudicator to be made available to public

(1) A company names adjudicator must, within 90 days of determining an application under section 69, make his decision and his reasons for it available to the public.

(2) He may do so by means of a website or by such other means as appear to him to be appropriate.

73. Order requiring name to be changed

(1) If an application under section 69 is upheld, the adjudicator shall make an order—

    (a) requiring the respondent company to change its name to one that is not an offending name, and

    (b) requiring all the respondents—

        (i) to take all such steps as are within their power to make, or facilitate the making, of that change, and

        (ii) not to cause or permit any steps to be taken calculated to result in another company being registered with a name that is an offending name.

(2) An "offending name" means a name that, by reason of its similarity to the name associated with the applicant in which he claims goodwill, would be likely—

    (a) to be the subject of a direction under section 67 (power of Secretary of State to direct change of name), or

    (b) to give rise to a further application under section 69.

(3) The order must specify a date by which the respondent company's name is to be changed and may be enforced—

    (a) in England and Wales or Northern Ireland, in the same way as an order of the High Court;

    (b) in Scotland, in the same way as a decree of the Court of Session.

(4) If the respondent company's name is not changed in accordance with the order by the specified date, the adjudicator may determine a new name for the company.

(5) If the adjudicator determines a new name for the respondent company he must give notice of his determination—

    (a) to the applicant,

    (b) to the respondents, and

    (c) to the registrar.

(6) For the purposes of this section a company's name is changed when the change takes effect in accordance with section 81(1) (on the issue of the new certification of incorporation).

74. Appeal from adjudicator's decision

(1) An appeal lies to the court from any decision of a company names adjudicator to uphold or dismiss an application under section 69.

(2) Notice of appeal against a decision upholding an application must be given before the date specified in the adjudicator's order by which the respondent company's name is to be changed.

(3) If notice of appeal is given against a decision upholding an application, the effect of the adjudicator's order is suspended.

(4) If on appeal the court—

    (a) affirms the decision of the adjudicator to uphold the application, or

    (b) reverses the decision of the adjudicator to dismiss the application,

the court may (as the case may require) specify the date by which the adjudicator's order is to be complied with, remit the matter to the adjudicator or make any order or determination that the adjudicator might have made.

(5) If the court determines a new name for the company it must give notice of the determination—

    (a) to the parties to the appeal, and

    (b) to the registrar.

CHAPTER 4
OTHER POWERS OF THE SECRETARY OF STATE

75. Provision of misleading information etc

(1) If it appears to the Secretary of State—

    (a) that misleading information has been given for the purposes of a company's registration by a particular name, or

    (b) that an undertaking or assurance has been given for that purpose and has not been fulfilled,

the Secretary of State may direct the company to change its name.

(2) Any such direction—

    (a) must be given within five years of the company's registration by that name, and

    (b) must specify the period within which the company is to change its name.

(3) The Secretary of State may by a further direction extend the period within which the company is to change its name.

Any such direction must be given before the end of the period for the time being specified.

(4) A direction under this section must be in writing.

(5) If a company fails to comply with a direction under this section, an offence is committed by—

    (a) the company, and

    (b) every officer of the company who is in default.

For this purpose a shadow director is treated as an officer of the company.

(6) A person guilty of an offence under this section is liable on summary conviction to a fine not exceeding level 3 on the standard scale and, for continued contravention, a daily default fine not exceeding one-tenth of level 3 on the standard scale.

76. Misleading indication of activities

(1) If in the opinion of the Secretary of State the name by which a company is registered gives so misleading an indication of the nature of its activities as to be likely to cause harm to the public, the Secretary of State may direct the company to change its name.

(2) The direction must be in writing.

(3) The direction must be complied with within a period of six weeks from the date of the direction or such longer period as the Secretary of State may think fit to allow.

This does not apply if an application is duly made to the court under the following provisions.

(4) The company may apply to the court to set the direction aside.

The application must be made within the period of three weeks from the date of the direction.

(5) The court may set the direction aside or confirm it.

If the direction is confirmed, the court shall specify the period within which the direction is to be complied with.

(6) If a company fails to comply with a direction under this section, an offence is committed by—

    (a) the company, and

    (b) every officer of the company who is in default.

For this purpose a shadow director is treated as an officer of the company.

(7) A person guilty of an offence under this section is liable on summary conviction to a fine not exceeding level 3 on the standard scale and, for continued contravention, a daily default fine not exceeding one-tenth of level 3 on the standard scale.

CHAPTER 5
CHANGE OF NAME

77. Change of name

(1) A company may change its name—

    (a) by special resolution (see section 78), or

    (b) by other means provided for by the company's articles (see section 79).

(2) The name of a company may also be changed—

    (a) by resolution of the directors acting under section 64 (change of name to comply with direction of Secretary of State under that section);

    (b) on the determination of a new name by a company names adjudicator under section 73 (powers of adjudicator on upholding objection to company name);

    (c) on the determination of a new name by the court under section 74 (appeal against decision of company names adjudicator);

    (d) under section 1033 (company's name on restoration to the register).

78. Change of name by special resolution

(1) Where a change of name has been agreed to by a company by special resolution, the company must give notice to the registrar.

This is in addition to the obligation to forward a copy of the resolution to the registrar.

(2) Where a change of name by special resolution is conditional on the occurrence of an event, the notice given to the registrar of the change must—

    (a) specify that the change is conditional, and

    (b) state whether the event has occurred.

(3) If the notice states that the event has not occurred—

    (a) the registrar is not required to act under section 80 (registration and issue of new certificate of incorporation) until further notice,

    (b) when the event occurs, the company must give notice to the registrar stating that it has occurred, and

    (c) the registrar may rely on the statement as sufficient evidence of the matters stated in it.

79. **Change of name by means provided for in company's articles**

(1) Where a change of a company's name has been made by other means provided for by its articles—

    (a) the company must give notice to the registrar, and

    (b) the notice must be accompanied by a statement that the change of name has been made by means provided for by the company's articles.

(2) The registrar may rely on the statement as sufficient evidence of the matters stated in it.

80. **Change of name: registration and issue of new certificate of incorporation**

(1) This section applies where the registrar receives notice of a change of a company's name.

(2) If the registrar is satisfied—

    (a) that the new name complies with the requirements of this Part, and

    (b) that the requirements of the Companies Acts, and any relevant requirements of the company's articles, with respect to a change of name are complied with,

the registrar must enter the new name on the register in place of the former name.

(3) On the registration of the new name, the registrar must issue a certificate of incorporation altered to meet the circumstances of the case.

81. **Change of name: effect**

(1) A change of a company's name has effect from the date on which the new certificate of incorporation is issued.

(2) The change does not affect any rights or obligations of the company or render defective any legal proceedings by or against it.

(3) Any legal proceedings that might have been continued or commenced against it by its former name may be continued or commenced against it by its new name.

CHAPTER 6
TRADING DISCLOSURES

82. **Requirement to disclose company name etc**

(1) The Secretary of State may by regulations make provision requiring companies—

    (a) to display specified information in specified locations,

    (b) to state specified information in specified descriptions of document or communication, and

    (c) to provide specified information on request to those they deal with in the course of their business.

(2) The regulations—

    (a) must in every case require disclosure of the name of the company, and

    (b) may make provision as to the manner in which any specified information is to be displayed, stated or provided.

(3) The regulations may provide that, for the purposes of any requirement to disclose a company's name, any variation between a word or words required to be part of the name and a permitted abbreviation of that word or those words (or vice versa) shall be disregarded.

(4) In this section "specified" means specified in the regulations.

(5) Regulations under this section are subject to affirmative resolution procedure.

83. **Civil consequences of failure to make required disclosure**

(1) This section applies to any legal proceedings brought by a company to which section 82 applies (requirement to disclose company name etc) to enforce a right arising out of a contract made in the course of a business in respect of which the company was, at the time the contract was made, in breach of regulations under that section.

(2) The proceedings shall be dismissed if the defendant (in Scotland, the defender) to the proceedings shows—

(a) that he has a claim against the claimant (pursuer) arising out of the contract that he has been unable to pursue by reason of the latter's breach of the regulations, or

(b) that he has suffered some financial loss in connection with the contract by reason of the claimant's (pursuer's) breach of the regulations,

unless the court before which the proceedings are brought is satisfied that it is just and equitable to permit the proceedings to continue.

(3) This section does not affect the right of any person to enforce such rights as he may have against another person in any proceedings brought by that person.

84. **Criminal consequences of failure to make required disclosures**

(1) Regulations under section 82 may provide—

(a) that where a company fails, without reasonable excuse, to comply with any specified requirement of regulations under that section an offence is committed by—

(i) the company, and

(ii) every officer of the company who is in default;

(b) that a person guilty of such an offence is liable on summary conviction to a fine not exceeding level 3 on the standard scale and, for continued contravention, a daily default fine not exceeding one-tenth of level 3 on the standard scale.

(2) The regulations may provide that, for the purposes of any provision made under subsection (1), a shadow director of the company is to be treated as an officer of the company.

(3) In subsection (1)(a) "specified" means specified in the regulations.

85. **Minor variations in form of name to be left out of account**

(1) For the purposes of this Chapter, in considering a company's name no account is to be taken of—

(a) whether upper or lower case characters (or a combination of the two) are used,

(b) whether diacritical marks or punctuation are present or absent,

(c) whether the name is in the same format or style as is specified under section 57(1)(b) for the purposes of registration,

provided there is no real likelihood of names differing only in those respects being taken to be different names.

(2) This does not affect the operation of regulations under section 57(1)(a) permitting only specified characters, diacritical marks or punctuation.

PART 6

A COMPANY'S REGISTERED OFFICE

General

86. **A company's registered office**

A company must at all times have a registered office to which all communications and notices may be addressed.

87. **Change of address of registered office**

(1) A company may change the address of its registered office by giving notice to the registrar.

(2) The change takes effect upon the notice being registered by the registrar, but until the end of the period of 14 days beginning with the date on which it is registered a person may validly serve any document on the company at the address previously registered.

(3) For the purposes of any duty of a company—

(a) to keep available for inspection at its registered office any register, index or other document, or

(b) to mention the address of its registered office in any document,

a company that has given notice to the registrar of a change in the address of its registered office may act on the change as from such date, not more than 14 days after the notice is given, as it may determine.

(4) Where a company unavoidably ceases to perform at its registered office any such duty as is mentioned in subsection (3)(a) in circumstances in which it was not practicable to give prior notice to the registrar of a change in the address of its registered office, but—

(a) resumes performance of that duty at other premises as soon as practicable, and

(b) gives notice accordingly to the registrar of a change in the situation of its registered office within 14 days of doing so,

it is not to be treated as having failed to comply with that duty.

Welsh companies

88. **Welsh companies**

(1) In the Companies Acts a "Welsh company" means a company as to which it is stated in the register that its registered office is to be situated in Wales.

(2) A company—

(a) whose registered office is in Wales, and

(b) as to which it is stated in the register that its registered office is to be situated in England and Wales,

may by special resolution require the register to be amended so that it states that the company's registered office is to be situated in Wales.

(3) A company—

(a) whose registered office is in Wales, and

(b) as to which it is stated in the register that its registered office is to be situated in Wales,

may by special resolution require the register to be amended so that it states that the company's registered office is to be situated in England and Wales.

(4) Where a company passes a resolution under this section it must give notice to the registrar, who shall—

(a) amend the register accordingly, and

(b) issue a new certificate of incorporation altered to meet the circumstances of the case.

PART 7

RE-REGISTRATION AS A MEANS OF ALTERING A COMPANY'S STATUS

Introductory

89. **Alteration of status by re-registration**

A company may by re-registration under this Part alter its status—

(a) from a private company to a public company (see sections 90 to 96);

(b) from a public company to a private company (see sections 97 to 101);

(c) from a private limited company to an unlimited company (see sections 102 to 104);

(d) from an unlimited private company to a limited company (see sections 105 to 108);

(e) from a public company to an unlimited private company (see sections 109 to 111).

Private company becoming public

90. **Re-registration of private company as public**

(1) A private company (whether limited or unlimited) may be re-registered as a public company limited by shares if—

(a) a special resolution that it should be so re-registered is passed,

(b) the conditions specified below are met, and

(c) an application for re-registration is delivered to the registrar in accordance with section 94, together with—

(i) the other documents required by that section, and

(ii) a statement of compliance.

(2) The conditions are—

(a) that the company has a share capital;

(b) that the requirements of section 91 are met as regards its share capital;

(c) that the requirements of section 92 are met as regards its net assets;

(d) if section 93 applies (recent allotment of shares for non-cash consideration), that the requirements of that section are met; and

(e) that the company has not previously been re-registered as unlimited.

(3) The company must make such changes—

(a) in its name, and

(b) in its articles,

as are necessary in connection with its becoming a public company.

(4) If the company is unlimited it must also make such changes in its articles as are necessary in connection with its becoming a company limited by shares.

91. **Requirements as to share capital**

(1) The following requirements must be met at the time the special resolution is passed that the company should be re-registered as a public company—

(a) the nominal value of the company's allotted share capital must be not less than the authorised minimum;

(b) each of the company's allotted shares must be paid up at least as to one-quarter of the nominal value of that share and the whole of any premium on it;

(c) if any shares in the company or any premium on them have been fully or partly paid up by an undertaking given by any person that he or another should do work or perform services (whether for the company or any other person), the undertaking must have been performed or otherwise discharged;

(d) if shares have been allotted as fully or partly paid up as to their nominal value or any premium on them otherwise than in cash, and the consideration for the allotment consists of or includes an undertaking to the company (other than one to which paragraph (c) applies), then either—

(i) the undertaking must have been performed or otherwise discharged, or

(ii) there must be a contract between the company and some person pursuant to which the undertaking is to be performed within five years from the time the special resolution is passed.

(2) For the purpose of determining whether the requirements in subsection (1)(b), (c) and (d) are met, the following may be disregarded—

(a) shares allotted—

(i) before 22nd June 1982 in the case of a company then registered in Great Britain, or

(ii) before 31st December 1984 in the case of a company then registered in Northern Ireland;

(b) shares allotted in pursuance of an employees' share scheme by reason of which the company would, but for this subsection, be precluded under subsection (1)(b) (but not otherwise) from being re-registered as a public company.

(3) No more than one-tenth of the nominal value of the company's allotted share capital is to be disregarded under subsection (2)(a).

For this purpose the allotted share capital is treated as not including shares disregarded under subsection (2)(b).

(4) Shares disregarded under subsection (2) are treated as not forming part of the allotted share capital for the purposes of subsection (1)(a).

(5) A company must not be re-registered as a public company if it appears to the registrar that—
  (a) the company has resolved to reduce its share capital,
  (b) the reduction—
    (i) is made under section 626 (reduction in connection with redenomination of share capital),
    (ii) is supported by a solvency statement in accordance with section 643, or
    (iii) has been confirmed by an order of the court under section 648, and
  (c) the effect of the reduction is, or will be, that the nominal value of the company's allotted share capital is below the authorised minimum.

92. Requirements as to net assets

(1) A company applying to re-register as a public company must obtain—
  (a) a balance sheet prepared as at a date not more than seven months before the date on which the application is delivered to the registrar,
  (b) an unqualified report by the company's auditor on that balance sheet, and
  (c) a written statement by the company's auditor that in his opinion at the balance sheet date the amount of the company's net assets was not less than the aggregate of its called-up share capital and undistributable reserves.

(2) Between the balance sheet date and the date on which the application for re-registration is delivered to the registrar, there must be no change in the company's financial position that results in the amount of its net assets becoming less than the aggregate of its called-up share capital and undistributable reserves.

(3) In subsection (1)(b) an "unqualified report" means—
  (a) if the balance sheet was prepared for a financial year of the company, a report stating without material qualification the auditor's opinion that the balance sheet has been properly prepared in accordance with the requirements of this Act;
  (b) if the balance sheet was not prepared for a financial year of the company, a report stating without material qualification the auditor's opinion that the balance sheet has been properly prepared in accordance with the provisions of this Act which would have applied if it had been prepared for a financial year of the company.

(4) For the purposes of an auditor's report on a balance sheet that was not prepared for a financial year of the company, the provisions of this Act apply with such modifications as are necessary by reason of that fact.

(5) For the purposes of subsection (3) a qualification is material unless the auditor states in his report that the matter giving rise to the qualification is not material for the purpose of determining (by reference to the company's balance sheet) whether at the balance sheet date the amount of the company's net assets was not less than the aggregate of its called-up share capital and undistributable reserves.

(6) In this Part "net assets" and "undistributable reserves" have the same meaning as in section 831 (net asset restriction on distributions by public companies).

93. **Recent allotment of shares for non-cash consideration**

(1) This section applies where—

    (a) shares are allotted by the company in the period between the date as at which the balance sheet required by section 92 is prepared and the passing of the resolution that the company should re-register as a public company, and

    (b) the shares are allotted as fully or partly paid up as to their nominal value or any premium on them otherwise than in cash.

(2) The registrar shall not entertain an application by the company for re-registration as a public company unless—

    (a) the requirements of section 593(1)(a) and (b) have been complied with (independent valuation of non-cash consideration; valuer's report to company not more than six months before allotment), or

    (b) the allotment is in connection with—

        (i) a share exchange (see subsections (3) to (5) below), or

        (ii) a proposed merger with another company (see subsection (6) below).

(3) An allotment is in connection with a share exchange if—

    (a) the shares are allotted in connection with an arrangement under which the whole or part of the consideration for the shares allotted is provided by—

        (i) the transfer to the company allotting the shares of shares (or shares of a particular class) in another company, or

        (ii) the cancellation of shares (or shares of a particular class) in another company; and

    (b) the allotment is open to all the holders of the shares of the other company in question (or, where the arrangement applies only to shares of a particular class, to all the holders of the company's shares of that class) to take part in the arrangement in connection with which the shares are allotted.

(4) In determining whether a person is a holder of shares for the purposes of subsection (3), there shall be disregarded—

    (a) shares held by, or by a nominee of, the company allotting the shares;

    (b) shares held by, or by a nominee of—

        (i) the holding company of the company allotting the shares,

        (ii) a subsidiary of the company allotting the shares, or

        (iii) a subsidiary of the holding company of the company allotting the shares.

(5) It is immaterial, for the purposes of deciding whether an allotment is in connection with a share exchange, whether or not the arrangement in connection with which the shares are allotted involves the issue to the company allotting the shares of shares (or shares of a particular class) in the other company.

(6) There is a proposed merger with another company if one of the companies concerned proposes to acquire all the assets and liabilities of the other in exchange for the issue of its shares or other securities to shareholders of the other (whether or not accompanied by a cash payment). "Another company" includes any body corporate.

(7) For the purposes of this section—

    (a) the consideration for an allotment does not include any amount standing to the credit of any of the company's reserve accounts, or of its profit and loss account, that has been applied in paying up (to any extent) any of the shares allotted or any premium on those shares; and

    (b) "arrangement" means any agreement, scheme or arrangement, (including an arrangement sanctioned in accordance with—

        (i) Part 26 of this Act (arrangements and reconstructions), or

        (ii) section 110 of the Insolvency Act 1986 (c.45) or Article 96 of the Insolvency (Northern Ireland) Order 1989 (S.I. 1989/2405 (N.I. 19)) (liquidator in winding up accepting shares as consideration for sale of company's property)).

94. **Application and accompanying documents**
    (1) An application for re-registration as a public company must contain—
        (a) a statement of the company's proposed name on re-registration; and
        (b) in the case of a company without a secretary, a statement of the company's proposed secretary (see section 95).
    (2) The application must be accompanied by—
        (a) a copy of the special resolution that the company should re-register as a public company (unless a copy has already been forwarded to the registrar under Chapter 3 of Part 3);
        (b) a copy of the company's articles as proposed to be amended;
        (c) a copy of the balance sheet and other documents referred to in section 92(1); and
        (d) if section 93 applies (recent allotment of shares for non-cash consideration), a copy of the valuation report (if any) under subsection (2)(a) of that section.
    (3) The statement of compliance required to be delivered together with the application is a statement that the requirements of this Part as to re-registration as a public company have been complied with.
    (4) The registrar may accept the statement of compliance as sufficient evidence that the company is entitled to be re-registered as a public company.

95. **Statement of proposed secretary**
    (1) The statement of the company's proposed secretary must contain the required particulars of the person who is or the persons who are to be the secretary or joint secretaries of the company.
    (2) The required particulars are the particulars that will be required to be stated in the company's register of secretaries (see sections 277 to 279).
    (3) The statement must also contain a consent by the person named as secretary, or each of the persons named as joint secretaries, to act in the relevant capacity. If all the partners in a firm are to be joint secretaries, consent may be given by one partner on behalf of all of them.

96. **Issue of certificate of incorporation on re-registration**
    (1) If on an application for re-registration as a public company the registrar is satisfied that the company is entitled to be so re-registered, the company shall be re-registered accordingly.
    (2) The registrar must issue a certificate of incorporation altered to meet the circumstances of the case.
    (3) The certificate must state that it is issued on re-registration and the date on which it is issued.
    (4) On the issue of the certificate—
        (a) the company by virtue of the issue of the certificate becomes a public company,
        (b) the changes in the company's name and articles take effect, and
        (c) where the application contained a statement under section 95 (statement of proposed secretary), the person or persons named in the statement as secretary or joint secretary of the company are deemed to have been appointed to that office.
    (5) The certificate is conclusive evidence that the requirements of this Act as to re-registration have been complied with.

Public company becoming private

97. **Re-registration of public company as private limited company**
    (1) A public company may be re-registered as a private limited company if—
        (a) a special resolution that it should be so re-registered is passed,
        (b) the conditions specified below are met, and
        (c) an application for re-registration is delivered to the registrar in accordance with section 100, together with—
            (i) the other documents required by that section, and
            (ii) a statement of compliance.

(2) The conditions are that—

   (a) where no application under section 98 for cancellation of the resolution has been made—

     (i) having regard to the number of members who consented to or voted in favour of the resolution, no such application may be made, or

     (ii) the period within which such an application could be made has expired, or

   (b) where such an application has been made—

     (i) the application has been withdrawn, or

     (ii) an order has been made confirming the resolution and a copy of that order has been delivered to the registrar.

(3) The company must make such changes—

   (a) in its name, and

   (b) in its articles,

as are necessary in connection with its becoming a private company limited by shares or, as the case may be, by guarantee.

98. Application to court to cancel resolution

(1) Where a special resolution by a public company to be re-registered as a private limited company has been passed, an application to the court for the cancellation of the resolution may be made—

   (a) by the holders of not less in the aggregate than 5% in nominal value of the company's issued share capital or any class of the company's issued share capital (disregarding any shares held by the company as treasury shares);

   (b) if the company is not limited by shares, by not less than 5% of its members; or

   (c) by not less than 50 of the company's members;

but not by a person who has consented to or voted in favour of the resolution.

(2) The application must be made within 28 days after the passing of the resolution and may be made on behalf of the persons entitled to make it by such one or more of their number as they may appoint for the purpose.

(3) On the hearing of the application the court shall make an order either cancelling or confirming the resolution.

(4) The court may—

   (a) make that order on such terms and conditions as it thinks fit,

   (b) if it thinks fit adjourn the proceedings in order that an arrangement may be made to the satisfaction of the court for the purchase of the interests of dissentient members, and

   (c) give such directions, and make such orders, as it thinks expedient for facilitating or carrying into effect any such arrangement.

(5) The court's order may, if the court thinks fit—

   (a) provide for the purchase by the company of the shares of any of its members and for the reduction accordingly of the company's capital; and

   (b) make such alteration in the company's articles as may be required in consequence of that provision.

(6) The court's order may, if the court thinks fit, require the company not to make any, or any specified, amendments to its articles without the leave of the court.

99. Notice to registrar of court application or order

(1) On making an application under section 98 (application to court to cancel resolution) the applicants, or the person making the application on their behalf, must immediately give notice to the registrar.

This is without prejudice to any provision of rules of court as to service of notice of the application.

(2) On being served with notice of any such application, the company must immediately give notice to the registrar.

(3) Within 15 days of the making of the court's order on the application, or such longer period as the court may at any time direct, the company must deliver to the registrar a copy of the order.

(4) If a company fails to comply with subsection (2) or (3) an offence is committed by—
   (a) the company, and
   (b) every officer of the company who is in default.

(5) A person guilty of an offence under this section is liable on summary conviction to a fine not exceeding level 3 on the standard scale and, for continued contravention, a daily default fine not exceeding one-tenth of level 3 on the standard scale.

100. **Application and accompanying documents**

(1) An application for re-registration as a private limited company must contain a statement of the company's proposed name on re-registration.

(2) The application must be accompanied by—
   (a) a copy of the resolution that the company should re-register as a private limited company (unless a copy has already been forwarded to the registrar under Chapter 3 of Part 3); and
   (b) a copy of the company's articles as proposed to be amended.

(3) The statement of compliance required to be delivered together with the application is a statement that the requirements of this Part as to re-registration as a private limited company have been complied with.

(4) The registrar may accept the statement of compliance as sufficient evidence that the company is entitled to be re-registered as a private limited company.

101. **Issue of certificate of incorporation on re-registration**

(1) If on an application for re-registration as a private limited company the registrar is satisfied that the company is entitled to be so re-registered, the company shall be re-registered accordingly.

(2) The registrar must issue a certificate of incorporation altered to meet the circumstances of the case.

(3) The certificate must state that it is issued on re-registration and the date on which it is issued.

(4) On the issue of the certificate—
   (a) the company by virtue of the issue of the certificate becomes a private limited company, and
   (b) the changes in the company's name and articles take effect.

(5) The certificate is conclusive evidence that the requirements of this Act as to re-registration have been complied with.

Private limited company becoming unlimited

102. **Re-registration of private limited company as unlimited**

(1) A private limited company may be re-registered as an unlimited company if—
   (a) all the members of the company have assented to its being so re-registered,
   (b) the condition specified below is met, and
   (c) an application for re-registration is delivered to the registrar in accordance with section 103, together with—
      (i) the other documents required by that section, and
      (ii) a statement of compliance.

(2) The condition is that the company has not previously been re-registered as limited.

(3) The company must make such changes in its name and its articles—
   (a) as are necessary in connection with its becoming an unlimited company; and
   (b) if it is to have a share capital, as are necessary in connection with its becoming an unlimited company having a share capital.

(4) For the purposes of this section—
   (a) a trustee in bankruptcy of a member of the company is entitled, to the exclusion of the member, to assent to the company's becoming unlimited; and

(b) the personal representative of a deceased member of the company may assent on behalf of the deceased.

(5) In subsection (4)(a), "a trustee in bankruptcy of a member of the company" includes—

(a) a permanent trustee or an interim trustee (within the meaning of the Bankruptcy (Scotland) Act 1985 (c. 66)) on the sequestrated estate of a member of the company;

(b) a trustee under a protected trustee deed (within the meaning of the Bankruptcy (Scotland) Act 1985) granted by a member of the company.

103. Application and accompanying documents

(1) An application for re-registration as an unlimited company must contain a statement of the company's proposed name on re-registration.

(2) The application must be accompanied by—

(a) the prescribed form of assent to the company's being registered as an unlimited company, authenticated by or on behalf of all the members of the company;

(b) a copy of the company's articles as proposed to be amended.

(3) The statement of compliance required to be delivered together with the application is a statement that the requirements of this Part as to re-registration as an unlimited company have been complied with.

(4) The statement must contain a statement by the directors of the company—

(a) that the persons by whom or on whose behalf the form of assent is authenticated constitute the whole membership of the company, and

(b) if any of the members have not authenticated that form themselves, that the directors have taken all reasonable steps to satisfy themselves that each person who authenticated it on behalf of a member was lawfully empowered to do so.

(5) The registrar may accept the statement of compliance as sufficient evidence that the company is entitled to be re-registered as an unlimited company.

104. Issue of certificate of incorporation on re-registration

(1) If on an application for re-registration of a private limited company as an unlimited company the registrar is satisfied that the company is entitled to be so re-registered, the company shall be re-registered accordingly.

(2) The registrar must issue a certificate of incorporation altered to meet the circumstances of the case.

(3) The certificate must state that it is issued on re-registration and the date on which it is issued.

(4) On the issue of the certificate—

(a) the company by virtue of the issue of the certificate becomes an unlimited company, and

(b) the changes in the company's name and articles take effect.

(5) The certificate is conclusive evidence that the requirements of this Act as to re-registration have been complied with.

Unlimited private company becoming limited

105. Re-registration of unlimited company as limited

(1) An unlimited company may be re-registered as a private limited company if—

(a) a special resolution that it should be so re-registered is passed,

(b) the condition specified below is met, and

(c) an application for re-registration is delivered to the registrar in accordance with section 106, together with—

(i) the other documents required by that section, and

(ii) a statement of compliance.

(2) The condition is that the company has not previously been re-registered as unlimited.

(3) The special resolution must state whether the company is to be limited by shares or by guarantee.

(4) The company must make such changes—
(a) in its name, and
(b) in its articles,
as are necessary in connection with its becoming a company limited by shares or, as the case may be, by guarantee.

106. **Application and accompanying documents**

(1) An application for re-registration as a limited company must contain a statement of the company's proposed name on re-registration.

(2) The application must be accompanied by—
(a) a copy of the resolution that the company should re-register as a private limited company (unless a copy has already been forwarded to the registrar under Chapter 3 of Part 3);
(b) if the company is to be limited by guarantee, a statement of guarantee;
(c) a copy of the company's articles as proposed to be amended.

(3) The statement of guarantee required to be delivered in the case of a company that is to be limited by guarantee must state that each member undertakes that, if the company is wound up while he is a member, or within one year after he ceases to be a member, he will contribute to the assets of the company such amount as may be required for—
(a) payment of the debts and liabilities of the company contracted before he ceases to be a member,
(b) payment of the costs, charges and expenses of winding up, and
(c) adjustment of the rights of the contributories among themselves,
not exceeding a specified amount.

(4) The statement of compliance required to be delivered together with the application is a statement that the requirements of this Part as to re-registration as a limited company have been complied with.

(5) The registrar may accept the statement of compliance as sufficient evidence that the company is entitled to be re-registered as a limited company.

107. **Issue of certificate of incorporation on re-registration**

(1) If on an application for re-registration of an unlimited company as a limited company the registrar is satisfied that the company is entitled to be so re-registered, the company shall be re-registered accordingly.

(2) The registrar must issue a certificate of incorporation altered to meet the circumstances of the case.

(3) The certificate must state that it is issued on re-registration and the date on which it is so issued.

(4) On the issue of the certificate—
(a) the company by virtue of the issue of the certificate becomes a limited company, and
(b) the changes in the company's name and articles take effect.

(5) The certificate is conclusive evidence that the requirements of this Act as to re-registration have been complied with.

108. **Statement of capital required where company already has share capital**

(1) A company which on re-registration under section 107 already has allotted share capital must within 15 days after the re-registration deliver a statement of capital to the registrar.

(2) This does not apply if the information which would be included in the statement has already been sent to the registrar in—
(a) a statement of capital and initial shareholdings (see section 10), or
(b) a statement of capital contained in an annual return (see section 856(2)).

(3) The statement of capital must state with respect to the company's share capital on re-registration—
(a) the total number of shares of the company,
(b) the aggregate nominal value of those shares,

(c) for each class of shares—
  (i) prescribed particulars of the rights attached to the shares,
  (ii) the total number of shares of that class, and
  (iii) the aggregate nominal value of shares of that class, and
(d) the amount paid up and the amount (if any) unpaid on each share (whether on account of the nominal value of the share or by way of premium).

(4) If default is made in complying with this section, an offence is committed by—
  (a) the company, and
  (b) every officer of the company who is in default.

(5) A person guilty of an offence under this section is liable on summary conviction to a fine not exceeding level 3 on the standard scale and, for continued contravention, a daily default fine not exceeding one-tenth of level 3 on the standard scale.

Public company becoming private and unlimited

109. Re-registration of public company as private and unlimited

(1) A public company limited by shares may be re-registered as an unlimited private company with a share capital if—
  (a) all the members of the company have assented to its being so re-registered,
  (b) the condition specified below is met, and
  (c) an application for re-registration is delivered to the registrar in accordance with section 110, together with—
    (i) the other documents required by that section, and
    (ii) a statement of compliance.

(2) The condition is that the company has not previously been re-registered—
  (a) as limited, or
  (b) as unlimited.

(3) The company must make such changes—
  (a) in its name, and
  (b) in its articles,
as are necessary in connection with its becoming an unlimited private company.

(4) For the purposes of this section—
  (a) a trustee in bankruptcy of a member of the company is entitled, to the exclusion of the member, to assent to the company's re-registration; and
  (b) the personal representative of a deceased member of the company may assent on behalf of the deceased.

(5) In subsection (4)(a), "a trustee in bankruptcy of a member of the company" includes—
  (a) a permanent trustee or an interim trustee (within the meaning of the Bankruptcy (Scotland) Act 1985 (c. 66)) on the sequestrated estate of a member of the company;
  (b) a trustee under a protected trustee deed (within the meaning of the Bankruptcy (Scotland) Act 1985) granted by a member of the company.

110. Application and accompanying documents

(1) An application for re-registration of a public company as an unlimited private company must contain a statement of the company's proposed name on re-registration.

(2) The application must be accompanied by—
  (a) the prescribed form of assent to the company's being registered as an unlimited company, authenticated by or on behalf of all the members of the company, and
  (b) a copy of the company's articles as proposed to be amended.

(3) The statement of compliance required to be delivered together with the application is a statement that the requirements of this Part as to re-registration as an unlimited private company have been complied with.

(4) The statement must contain a statement by the directors of the company—

    (a) that the persons by whom or on whose behalf the form of assent is authenticated constitute the whole membership of the company, and

    (b) if any of the members have not authenticated that form themselves, that the directors have taken all reasonable steps to satisfy themselves that each person who authenticated it on behalf of a member was lawfully empowered to do so.

(5) The registrar may accept the statement of compliance as sufficient evidence that the company is entitled to be re-registered as an unlimited private company.

111. Issue of certificate of incorporation on re-registration

(1) If on an application for re-registration of a public company as an unlimited private company the registrar is satisfied that the company is entitled to be so re-registered, the company shall be re-registered accordingly.

(2) The registrar must issue a certificate of incorporation altered to meet the circumstances of the case.

(3) The certificate must state that it is issued on re-registration and the date on which it is so issued.

(4) On the issue of the certificate—

    (a) the company by virtue of the issue of the certificate becomes an unlimited private company, and

    (b) the changes in the company's name and articles take effect.

(5) The certificate is conclusive evidence that the requirements of this Act as to re-registration have been complied with.

PART 8
A COMPANY'S MEMBERS

CHAPTER 1
THE MEMBERS OF A COMPANY

112. The members of a company

(1) The subscribers of a company's memorandum are deemed to have agreed to become members of the company, and on its registration become members and must be entered as such in its register of members.

(2) Every other person who agrees to become a member of a company, and whose name is entered in its register of members, is a member of the company.

CHAPTER 2
REGISTER OF MEMBERS

General

113. Register of members

(1) Every company must keep a register of its members.

(2) There must be entered in the register—

    (a) the names and addresses of the members,

    (b) the date on which each person was registered as a member, and

    (c) the date at which any person ceased to be a member.

(3) In the case of a company having a share capital, there must be entered in the register, with the names and addresses of the members, a statement of—

      (a) the shares held by each member, distinguishing each share—

         (i) by its number (so long as the share has a number), and

         (ii) where the company has more than one class of issued shares, by its class, and

      (b) the amount paid or agreed to be considered as paid on the shares of each member.

(4) If the company has converted any of its shares into stock, and given notice of the conversion to the registrar, the register of members must show the amount and class of stock held by each member instead of the amount of shares and the particulars relating to shares specified above.

(5) In the case of joint holders of shares or stock in a company, the company's register of members must state the names of each joint holder.

In other respects joint holders are regarded for the purposes of this Chapter as a single member (so that the register must show a single address).

(6) In the case of a company that does not have a share capital but has more than one class of members, there must be entered in the register, with the names and addresses of the members, a statement of the class to which each member belongs.

(7) If a company makes default in complying with this section an offence is committed by—

      (a) the company, and

      (b) every officer of the company who is in default.

(8) A person guilty of an offence under this section is liable on summary conviction to a fine not exceeding level 3 on the standard scale and, for continued contravention, a daily default fine not exceeding one-tenth of level 3 on the standard scale.

114. Register to be kept available for inspection

(1) A company's register of members must be kept available for inspection—

      (a) at its registered office, or

      (b) at a place specified in regulations under section 1136.

(2) A company must give notice to the registrar of the place where its register of members is kept available for inspection and of any change in that place.

(3) No such notice is required if the register has, at all times since it came into existence (or, in the case of a register in existence on the relevant date, at all times since then) been kept available for inspection at the company's registered office.

(4) The relevant date for the purposes of subsection (3) is—

      (a) 1st July 1948 in the case of a company registered in Great Britain, and

      (b) 1st April 1961 in the case of a company registered in Northern Ireland.

(5) If a company makes default for 14 days in complying with subsection (2), an offence is committed by—

      (a) the company, and

      (b) every officer of the company who is in default.

(6) A person guilty of an offence under this section is liable on summary conviction to a fine not exceeding level 3 on the standard scale and, for continued contravention, a daily default fine not exceeding one-tenth of level 3 on the standard scale.

115. Index of members

(1) Every company having more than 50 members must keep an index of the names of the members of the company, unless the register of members is in such a form as to constitute in itself an index.

(2) The company must make any necessary alteration in the index within 14 days after the date on which any alteration is made in the register of members.

(3) The index must contain, in respect of each member, a sufficient indication to enable the account of that member in the register to be readily found.

(4) The index must be at all times kept available for inspection at the same place as the register of members.

(5) If default is made in complying with this section, an offence is committed by—

    (a) the company, and

    (b) every officer of the company who is in default.

(6) A person guilty of an offence under this section is liable on summary conviction to a fine not exceeding level 3 on the standard scale and, for continued contravention, a daily default fine not exceeding one-tenth of level 3 on the standard scale.

116. Rights to inspect and require copies

(1) The register and the index of members' names must be open to the inspection—

    (a) of any member of the company without charge, and

    (b) of any other person on payment of such fee as may be prescribed.

(2) Any person may require a copy of a company's register of members, or of any part of it, on payment of such fee as may be prescribed.

(3) A person seeking to exercise either of the rights conferred by this section must make a request to the company to that effect.

(4) The request must contain the following information—

    (a) in the case of an individual, his name and address;

    (b) in the case of an organisation, the name and address of an individual responsible for making the request on behalf of the organisation;

    (c) the purpose for which the information is to be used; and

    (d) whether the information will be disclosed to any other person, and if so—

        (i) where that person is an individual, his name and address,

        (ii) where that person is an organisation, the name and address of an individual responsible for receiving the information on its behalf, and

        (iii) the purpose for which the information is to be used by that person.

117. Register of members: response to request for inspection or copy

(1) Where a company receives a request under section 116 (register of members: right to inspect and require copy), it must within five working days either—

    (a) comply with the request, or

    (b) apply to the court.

(2) If it applies to the court it must notify the person making the request.

(3) If on an application under this section the court is satisfied that the inspection or copy is not sought for a proper purpose—

    (a) it shall direct the company not to comply with the request, and

    (b) it may further order that the company's costs (in Scotland, expenses) on the application be paid in whole or in part by the person who made the request, even if he is not a party to the application.

(4) If the court makes such a direction and it appears to the court that the company is or may be subject to other requests made for a similar purpose (whether made by the same person or different persons), it may direct that the company is not to comply with any such request.

The order must contain such provision as appears to the court appropriate to identify the requests to which it applies.

(5) If on an application under this section the court does not direct the company not to comply with the request, the company must comply with the request immediately upon the court giving its decision or, as the case may be, the proceedings being discontinued.

118. Register of members: refusal of inspection or default in providing copy

(1) If an inspection required under section 116 (register of members: right to inspect and require copy) is refused or default is made in providing a copy required under that section, otherwise than in accordance with an order of the court, an offence is committed by—

    (a) the company, and

    (b) every officer of the company who is in default.

(2) A person guilty of an offence under this section is liable on summary conviction to a fine not exceeding level 3 on the standard scale and, for continued contravention, a daily default fine not exceeding one-tenth of level 3 on the standard scale.

(3) In the case of any such refusal or default the court may by order compel an immediate inspection or, as the case may be, direct that the copy required be sent to the person requesting it.

119. Register of members: offences in connection with request for or disclosure of information

(1) It is an offence for a person knowingly or recklessly to make in a request under section 116 (register of members: right to inspect or require copy) a statement that is misleading, false or deceptive in a material particular.

(2) It is an offence for a person in possession of information obtained by exercise of either of the rights conferred by that section—

(a) to do anything that results in the information being disclosed to another person, or

(b) to fail to do anything with the result that the information is disclosed to another person, knowing, or having reason to suspect, that person may use the information for a purpose that is not a proper purpose.

(3) A person guilty of an offence under this section is liable—

(a) on conviction on indictment, to imprisonment for a term not exceeding two years or a fine (or both);

(b) on summary conviction—

(i) in England and Wales, to imprisonment for a term not exceeding twelve months or to a fine not exceeding the statutory maximum (or both);

(ii) in Scotland or Northern Ireland, to imprisonment for a term not exceeding six months, or to a fine not exceeding the statutory maximum (or both).

120. Information as to state of register and index

(1) When a person inspects the register, or the company provides him with a copy of the register or any part of it, the company must inform him of the most recent date (if any) on which alterations were made to the register and there were no further alterations to be made.

(2) When a person inspects the index of members' names, the company must inform him whether there is any alteration to the register that is not reflected in the index.

(3) If a company fails to provide the information required under subsection (1) or (2), an offence is committed by—

(a) the company, and

(b) every officer of the company who is in default.

(4) A person guilty of an offence under this section is liable on summary conviction to a fine not exceeding level 3 on the standard scale.

121. Removal of entries relating to former members

An entry relating to a former member of the company may be removed from the register after the expiration of ten years from the date on which he ceased to be a member.

Special cases

122. Share warrants

(1) On the issue of a share warrant the company must—

(a) enter in the register of members—

(i) the fact of the issue of the warrant,

(ii) a statement of the shares included in the warrant, distinguishing each share by its number so long as the share has a number, and

(iii) the date of the issue of the warrant,

and

(b) amend the register, if necessary, so that no person is named on the register as the holder of the shares specified in the warrant.

(2) Until the warrant is surrendered, the particulars specified in subsection (1)(a) are deemed to be those required by this Act to be entered in the register of members.

(3) The bearer of a share warrant may, if the articles of the company so provide, be deemed a member of the company within the meaning of this Act, either to the full extent or for any purposes defined in the articles.

(4) Subject to the company's articles, the bearer of a share warrant is entitled, on surrendering it for cancellation, to have his name entered as a member in the register of members.

(5) The company is responsible for any loss incurred by any person by reason of the company entering in the register the name of a bearer of a share warrant in respect of the shares specified in it without the warrant being surrendered and cancelled.

(6) On the surrender of a share warrant, the date of the surrender must be entered in the register.

123. Single member companies

(1) If a limited company is formed under this Act with only one member there shall be entered in the company's register of members, with the name and address of the sole member, a statement that the company has only one member.

(2) If the number of members of a limited company falls to one, or if an unlimited company with only one member becomes a limited company on re-registration, there shall upon the occurrence of that event be entered in the company's register of members, with the name and address of the sole member—

(a) a statement that the company has only one member, and

(b) the date on which the company became a company having only one member.

(3) If the membership of a limited company increases from one to two or more members, there shall upon the occurrence of that event be entered in the company's register of members, with the name and address of the person who was formerly the sole member—

(a) a statement that the company has ceased to have only one member, and

(b) the date on which that event occurred.

(4) If a company makes default in complying with this section, an offence is committed by—

(a) the company, and

(b) every officer of the company who is in default.

(5) A person guilty of an offence under this section is liable on summary conviction to a fine not exceeding level 3 on the standard scale and, for continued contravention, a daily default fine not exceeding one-tenth of level 3 on the standard scale.

124. Company holding its own shares as treasury shares

(1) Where a company purchases its own shares in circumstances in which section 724 (treasury shares) applies—

(a) the requirements of section 113 (register of members) need not be complied with if the company cancels all of the shares forthwith after the purchase, and

(b) if the company does not cancel all of the shares forthwith after the purchase, any share that is so cancelled shall be disregarded for the purposes of that section.

(2) Subject to subsection (1), where a company holds shares as treasury shares the company must be entered in the register as the member holding those shares.

Supplementary

125. Power of court to rectify register

(1) If—

(a) the name of any person is, without sufficient cause, entered in or omitted from a company's register of members, or

(b) default is made or unnecessary delay takes place in entering on the register the fact of any person having ceased to be a member,

the person aggrieved, or any member of the company, or the company, may apply to the court for rectification of the register.

(2) The court may either refuse the application or may order rectification of the register and payment by the company of any damages sustained by any party aggrieved.

(3) On such an application the court may decide any question relating to the title of a person who is a party to the application to have his name entered in or omitted from the register, whether the question arises between members or alleged members, or between members or alleged members on the one hand and the company on the other hand, and generally may decide any question necessary or expedient to be decided for rectification of the register.

(4) In the case of a company required by this Act to send a list of its members to the registrar of companies, the court, when making an order for rectification of the register, shall by its order direct notice of the rectification to be given to the registrar.

126. Trusts not to be entered on register

No notice of any trust, expressed, implied or constructive, shall be entered on the register of members of a company registered in England and Wales or Northern Ireland, or be receivable by the registrar.

127. Register to be evidence

The register of members is prima facie evidence of any matters which are by this Act directed or authorised to be inserted in it.

128. Time limit for claims arising from entry in register

(1) Liability incurred by a company—

    (a) from the making or deletion of an entry in the register of members, or

    (b) from a failure to make or delete any such entry,

is not enforceable more than ten years after the date on which the entry was made or deleted or, as the case may be, the failure first occurred.

(2) This is without prejudice to any lesser period of limitation (and, in Scotland, to any rule that the obligation giving rise to the liability prescribes before the expiry of that period).

CHAPTER 3
OVERSEAS BRANCH REGISTERS

129. Overseas branch registers

(1) A company having a share capital may, if it transacts business in a country or territory to which this Chapter applies, cause to be kept there a branch register of members resident there (an "overseas branch register").

(2) This Chapter applies to—

    (a) any part of Her Majesty's dominions outside the United Kingdom, the Channel Islands and the Isle of Man, and

    (b) the countries or territories listed below.

Bangladesh	Malaysia
Cyprus	Malta
Dominica	Nigeria
The Gambia	Pakistan
Ghana	Seychelles
Guyana	Sierra Leone
The Hong Kong Special Administrative Region of the People's Republic of China	Singapore
India	South Africa

Ireland	Sri Lanka
Kenya	Swaziland
Kiribati	Trinidad and Tobago
Lesotho	Uganda
Malawi	Zimbabwe

(3) The Secretary of State may make provision by regulations as to the circumstances in which a company is to be regarded as keeping a register in a particular country or territory.

(4) Regulations under this section are subject to negative resolution procedure.

(5) References—

    (a) in any Act or instrument (including, in particular, a company's articles) to a dominion register, or

    (b) in articles registered before 1st November 1929 to a colonial register,

are to be read (unless the context otherwise requires) as a reference to an overseas branch register kept under this section.

130. Notice of opening of overseas branch register

(1) A company that begins to keep an overseas branch register must give notice to the registrar within 14 days of doing so, stating the country or territory in which the register is kept.

(2) If default is made in complying with subsection (1), an offence is committed by—

    (a) the company, and

    (b) every officer of the company who is in default.

(3) A person guilty of an offence under subsection (2) is liable on summary conviction to a fine not exceeding level 3 on the standard scale and, for continued contravention, a daily default fine not exceeding one-tenth of level 3 on the standard scale.

131. Keeping of overseas branch register

(1) An overseas branch register is regarded as part of the company's register of members ("the main register").

(2) The Secretary of State may make provision by regulations modifying any provision of Chapter 2 (register of members) as it applies in relation to an overseas branch register.

(3) Regulations under this section are subject to negative resolution procedure.

(4) Subject to the provisions of this Act, a company may by its articles make such provision as it thinks fit as to the keeping of overseas branch registers.

132. Register or duplicate to be kept available for inspection in UK

(1) A company that keeps an overseas branch register must keep available for inspection—

    (a) the register, or

    (b) a duplicate of the register duly entered up from time to time,

at the place in the United Kingdom where the company's main register is kept available for inspection.

(2) Any such duplicate is treated for all purposes of this Act as part of the main register.

(3) If default is made in complying with subsection (1), an offence is committed by—

    (a) the company, and

    (b) every officer of the company who is in default.

(4) A person guilty of an offence under subsection (3) is liable on summary conviction to a fine not exceeding level 3 on the standard scale and, for continued contravention, a daily default fine not exceeding one-tenth of level 3 on the standard scale.

133. Transactions in shares registered in overseas branch register

(1) Shares registered in an overseas branch register must be distinguished from those registered in the main register.

(2) No transaction with respect to shares registered in an overseas branch register may be registered in any other register.

(3) An instrument of transfer of a share registered in an overseas branch register—

    (a) is regarded as a transfer of property situated outside the United Kingdom, and

    (b) unless executed in a part of the United Kingdom, is exempt from stamp duty.

134. Jurisdiction of local courts

(1) A competent court in a country or territory where an overseas branch register is kept may exercise the same jurisdiction as is exercisable by a court in the United Kingdom—

    (a) to rectify the register (see section 125), or

    (b) in relation to a request for inspection or a copy of the register (see section 117).

(2) The offences—

    (a) of refusing inspection or failing to provide a copy of the register (see section 118), and

    (b) of making a false, misleading or deceptive statement in a request for inspection or a copy (see section 119),

may be prosecuted summarily before any tribunal having summary criminal jurisdiction in the country or territory where the register is kept.

(3) This section extends only to those countries and territories to which paragraph 3 of Schedule 14 to the Companies Act 1985 (c. 6) (which made similar provision) extended immediately before the coming into force of this Chapter.

135. Discontinuance of overseas branch register

(1) A company may discontinue an overseas branch register.

(2) If it does so all the entries in that register must be transferred—

    (a) to some other overseas branch register kept in the same country or territory, or

    (b) to the main register.

(3) The company must give notice to the registrar within 14 days of the discontinuance.

(4) If default is made in complying with subsection (3), an offence is committed by—

    (a) the company, and

    (b) every officer of the company who is in default.

(5) A person guilty of an offence under subsection (4) is liable on summary conviction to a fine not exceeding level 3 on the standard scale and, for continued contravention, a daily default fine not exceeding one-tenth of level 3 on the standard scale.

CHAPTER 4

PROHIBITION ON SUBSIDIARY BEING MEMBER OF ITS HOLDING COMPANY

General prohibition

136. Prohibition on subsidiary being a member of its holding company

(1) Except as provided by this Chapter—

    (a) a body corporate cannot be a member of a company that is its holding company, and

    (b) any allotment or transfer of shares in a company to its subsidiary is void.

(2) The exceptions are provided for in—

section 138 (subsidiary acting as personal representative or trustee), and

section 141 (subsidiary acting as authorised dealer in securities).

137. Shares acquired before prohibition became applicable

(1) Where a body corporate became a holder of shares in a company—

    (a) before the relevant date, or

    (b) on or after that date and before the commencement of this Chapter in circumstances in which the prohibition in section 23(1) of the Companies Act 1985 or Article 33(1) of the Companies (Northern Ireland) Order 1986 (S.I. 1986/1032 (N.I. 6)) (or any corresponding earlier enactment), as it then had effect, did not apply, or

(c) on or after the commencement of this Chapter in circumstances in which the prohibition in section 136 did not apply,

it may continue to be a member of the company.

(2) The relevant date for the purposes of subsection (1)(a) is—

    (a) 1st July 1948 in the case of a company registered in Great Britain, and

    (b) 1st April 1961 in the case of a company registered in Northern Ireland.

(3) So long as it is permitted to continue as a member of a company by virtue of this section, an allotment to it of fully paid shares in the company may be validly made by way of capitalisation of reserves of the company.

(4) But, so long as the prohibition in section 136 would (apart from this section) apply, it has no right to vote in respect of the shares mentioned in subsection (1) above, or any shares allotted as mentioned in subsection (3) above, on a written resolution or at meetings of the company or of any class of its members.

Subsidiary acting as personal representative or trustee

138. Subsidiary acting as personal representative or trustee

(1) The prohibition in section 136 (prohibition on subsidiary being a member of its holding company) does not apply where the subsidiary is concerned only—

    (a) as personal representative, or

    (b) as trustee,

unless, in the latter case, the holding company or a subsidiary of it is beneficially interested under the trust.

(2) For the purpose of ascertaining whether the holding company or a subsidiary is so interested, there shall be disregarded—

    (a) any interest held only by way of security for the purposes of a transaction entered into by the holding company or subsidiary in the ordinary course of a business that includes the lending of money;

    (b) any interest within—

        section 139 (interests to be disregarded: residual interest under pension scheme or employees' share scheme), or

        section 140 (interests to be disregarded: employer's rights of recovery under pension scheme or employees' share scheme);

    (c) any rights that the company or subsidiary has in its capacity as trustee, including in particular—

        (i) any right to recover its expenses or be remunerated out of the trust property, and

        (ii) any right to be indemnified out of the trust property for any liability incurred by reason of any act or omission in the performance of its duties as trustee.

139. Interests to be disregarded: residual interest under pension scheme or employees' share scheme

(1) Where shares in a company are held on trust for the purposes of a pension scheme or employees' share scheme, there shall be disregarded for the purposes of section 138 any residual interest that has not vested in possession.

(2) A "residual interest" means a right of the company or subsidiary ("the residual beneficiary") to receive any of the trust property in the event of—

    (a) all the liabilities arising under the scheme having been satisfied or provided for, or

    (b) the residual beneficiary ceasing to participate in the scheme, or

    (c) the trust property at any time exceeding what is necessary for satisfying the liabilities arising or expected to arise under the scheme.

(3) In subsection (2)—

    (a) the reference to a right includes a right dependent on the exercise of a discretion vested by the scheme in the trustee or another person, and

     (b) the reference to liabilities arising under a scheme includes liabilities that have resulted, or may result, from the exercise of any such discretion.

  (4) For the purposes of this section a residual interest vests in possession—

     (a) in a case within subsection (2)(a), on the occurrence of the event mentioned there (whether or not the amount of the property receivable pursuant to the right is ascertained);

     (b) in a case within subsection (2)(b) or (c), when the residual beneficiary becomes entitled to require the trustee to transfer to him any of the property receivable pursuant to the right.

  (5) In this section "pension scheme" means a scheme for the provision of benefits consisting of or including relevant benefits for or in respect of employees or former employees.

  (6) In subsection (5)—

     (a) "relevant benefits" means any pension, lump sum, gratuity or other like benefit given or to be given on retirement or on death or in anticipation of retirement or, in connection with past service, after retirement or death; and

     (b) "employee" shall be read as if a director of a company were employed by it.

140. Interests to be disregarded: employer's rights of recovery under pension scheme or employees' share scheme

  (1) Where shares in a company are held on trust for the purposes of a pension scheme or employees' share scheme, there shall be disregarded for the purposes of section 138 any charge or lien on, or set-off against, any benefit or other right or interest under the scheme for the purpose of enabling the employer or former employer of a member of the scheme to obtain the discharge of a monetary obligation due to him from the member.

  (2) In the case of a trust for the purposes of a pension scheme there shall also be disregarded any right to receive from the trustee of the scheme, or as trustee of the scheme to retain, an amount that can be recovered or retained, under section 61 of the Pension Schemes Act 1993 (c. 48) or section 57 of the Pension Schemes (Northern Ireland) Act 1993 (c. 49) (deduction of contributions equivalent premium from refund of scheme contributions) or otherwise, as reimbursement or partial reimbursement for any contributions equivalent premium paid in connection with the scheme under Part 3 of that Act.

  (3) In this section "pension scheme" means a scheme for the provision of benefits consisting of or including relevant benefits for or in respect of employees or former employees.

"Relevant benefits" here means any pension, lump sum, gratuity or other like benefit given or to be given on retirement or on death or in anticipation of retirement or, in connection with past service, after retirement or death.

  (4) In this section "employer" and "employee" shall be read as if a director of a company were employed by it.

Subsidiary acting as dealer in securities

141. Subsidiary acting as authorised dealer in securities

  (1) The prohibition in section 136 (prohibition on subsidiary being a member of its holding company) does not apply where the shares are held by the subsidiary in the ordinary course of its business as an intermediary.

  (2) For this purpose a person is an intermediary if he—

     (a) carries on a bona fide business of dealing in securities,

     (b) is a member of or has access to a regulated market, and

     (c) does not carry on an excluded business.

  (3) The following are excluded businesses—

     (a) a business that consists wholly or mainly in the making or managing of investments;

     (b) a business that consists wholly or mainly in, or is carried on wholly or mainly for the purposes of, providing services to persons who are connected with the person carrying on the business;

    (c) a business that consists in insurance business;

    (d) a business that consists in managing or acting as trustee in relation to a pension scheme, or that is carried on by the manager or trustee of such a scheme in connection with or for the purposes of the scheme;

    (e) a business that consists in operating or acting as trustee in relation to a collective investment scheme, or that is carried on by the operator or trustee of such a scheme in connection with and for the purposes of the scheme.

(4) For the purposes of this section—

    (a) the question whether a person is connected with another shall be determined in accordance with section 839 of the Income and Corporation Taxes Act 1988 (c. 1);

    (b) "collective investment scheme" has the meaning given in section 235 of the Financial Services and Markets Act 2000 (c. 8);

    (c) "insurance business" means business that consists in the effecting or carrying out of contracts of insurance;

    (d) "securities" includes—

       (i) options,

       (ii) futures, and

       (iii) contracts for differences,

      and rights or interests in those investments;

    (e) "trustee" and "the operator" in relation to a collective investment scheme shall be construed in accordance with section 237(2) of the Financial Services and Markets Act 2000 (c. 8).

(5) Expressions used in this section that are also used in the provisions regulating activities under the Financial Services and Markets Act 2000 have the same meaning here as they do in those provisions.

See section 22 of that Act, orders made under that section and Schedule 2 to that Act.

142. Protection of third parties in other cases where subsidiary acting as dealer in securities

(1) This section applies where—

    (a) a subsidiary that is a dealer in securities has purportedly acquired shares in its holding company in contravention of the prohibition in section 136, and

    (b) a person acting in good faith has agreed, for value and without notice of the contravention, to acquire shares in the holding company—

       (i) from the subsidiary, or

       (ii) from someone who has purportedly acquired the shares after their disposal by the subsidiary.

(2) A transfer to that person of the shares mentioned in subsection (1)(a) has the same effect as it would have had if their original acquisition by the subsidiary had not been in contravention of the prohibition.

Supplementary

143. Application of provisions to companies not limited by shares

In relation to a company other than a company limited by shares, the references in this Chapter to shares shall be read as references to the interest of its members as such, whatever the form of that interest.

144. Application of provisions to nominees

The provisions of this Chapter apply to a nominee acting on behalf of a subsidiary as to the subsidiary itself.

PART 9

EXERCISE OF MEMBERS' RIGHTS

Effect of provisions in company's articles

145. **Effect of provisions of articles as to enjoyment or exercise of members' rights**

(1) This section applies where provision is made by a company's articles enabling a member to nominate another person or persons as entitled to enjoy or exercise all or any specified rights of the member in relation to the company.

(2) So far as is necessary to give effect to that provision, anything required or authorised by any provision of the Companies Acts to be done by or in relation to the member shall instead be done, or (as the case may be) may instead be done, by or in relation to the nominated person (or each of them) as if he were a member of the company.

(3) This applies, in particular, to the rights conferred by—

(a) sections 291 and 293 (right to be sent proposed written resolution);

(b) section 292 (right to require circulation of written resolution);

(c) section 303 (right to require directors to call general meeting);

(d) section 310 (right to notice of general meetings);

(e) section 314 (right to require circulation of a statement);

(f) section 324 (right to appoint proxy to act at meeting);

(g) section 338 (right to require circulation of resolution for AGM of public company); and

(h) section 423 (right to be sent a copy of annual accounts and reports).

(4) This section and any such provision as is mentioned in subsection (1)—

(a) do not confer rights enforceable against the company by anyone other than the member, and

(b) do not affect the requirements for an effective transfer or other disposition of the whole or part of a member's interest in the company.

Information rights

146. **Traded companies: nomination of persons to enjoy information rights**

(1) This section applies to a company whose shares are admitted to trading on a regulated market.

(2) A member of such a company who holds shares on behalf of another person may nominate that person to enjoy information rights.

(3) "Information rights" means—

(a) the right to receive a copy of all communications that the company sends to its members generally or to any class of its members that includes the person making the nomination, and

(b) the rights conferred by—

(i) section 431 or 432 (right to require copies of accounts and reports), and

(ii) section 1145 (right to require hard copy version of document or information provided in another form).

(4) The reference in subsection (3)(a) to communications that a company sends to its members generally includes the company's annual accounts and reports.

For the application of section 426 (option to provide summary financial statement) in relation to a person nominated to enjoy information rights, see subsection (5) of that section.

(5) A company need not act on a nomination purporting to relate to certain information rights only.

147. **Information rights: form in which copies to be provided**

(1) This section applies as regards the form in which copies are to be provided to a person nominated under section 146 (nomination of person to enjoy information rights).

(2) If the person to be nominated wishes to receive hard copy communications, he must—

    (a) request the person making the nomination to notify the company of that fact, and

    (b) provide an address to which such copies may be sent.

This must be done before the nomination is made.

(3) If having received such a request the person making the nomination—

    (a) notifies the company that the nominated person wishes to receive hard copy communications, and

    (b) provides the company with that address,

the right of the nominated person is to receive hard copy communications accordingly.

(4) This is subject to the provisions of Parts 3 and 4 of Schedule 5 (communications by company) under which the company may take steps to enable it to communicate in electronic form or by means of a website.

(5) If no such notification is given (or no address is provided), the nominated person is taken to have agreed that documents or information may be sent or supplied to him by the company by means of a website.

(6) That agreement—

    (a) may be revoked by the nominated person, and

    (b) does not affect his right under section 1145 to require a hard copy version of a document or information provided in any other form.

148. Termination or suspension of nomination

(1) The following provisions have effect in relation to a nomination under section 146 (nomination of person to enjoy information rights).

(2) The nomination may be terminated at the request of the member or of the nominated person.

(3) The nomination ceases to have effect on the occurrence in relation to the member or the nominated person of any of the following—

    (a) in the case of an individual, death or bankruptcy;

    (b) in the case of a body corporate, dissolution or the making of an order for the winding up of the body otherwise than for the purposes of reconstruction.

(4) In subsection (3)—

    (a) the reference to bankruptcy includes—

        (i) the sequestration of a person's estate, and

        (ii) a person's estate being the subject of a protected trust deed (within the meaning of the Bankruptcy (Scotland) Act 1985 (c. 66)); and

    (b) the reference to the making of an order for winding up is to—

        (i) the making of such an order under the Insolvency Act 1986 (c. 45) or the Insolvency (Northern Ireland) Order 1989 (S.I. 1989/2405 (N.I. 19)), or

        (ii) any corresponding proceeding under the law of a country or territory outside the United Kingdom.

(5) The effect of any nominations made by a member is suspended at any time when there are more nominated persons than the member has shares in the company.

(6) Where—

    (a) the member holds different classes of shares with different information rights, and

    (b) there are more nominated persons than he has shares conferring a particular right,

the effect of any nominations made by him is suspended to the extent that they confer that right.

(7) Where the company—

    (a) enquires of a nominated person whether he wishes to retain information rights, and

    (b) does not receive a response within the period of 28 days beginning with the date on which the company's enquiry was sent,

the nomination ceases to have effect at the end of that period.

Such an enquiry is not to be made of a person more than once in any twelve-month period.

(8) The termination or suspension of a nomination means that the company is not required to act on it.

It does not prevent the company from continuing to do so, to such extent or for such period as it thinks fit.

149. Information as to possible rights in relation to voting

(1) This section applies where a company sends a copy of a notice of a meeting to a person nominated under section 146 (nomination of person to enjoy information rights).

(2) The copy of the notice must be accompanied by a statement that—

(a) he may have a right under an agreement between him and the member by whom he was nominated to be appointed, or to have someone else appointed, as a proxy for the meeting, and

(b) if he has no such right or does not wish to exercise it, he may have a right under such an agreement to give instructions to the member as to the exercise of voting rights.

(3) Section 325 (notice of meeting to contain statement of member's rights in relation to appointment of proxy) does not apply to the copy, and the company must either—

(a) omit the notice required by that section, or

(b) include it but state that it does not apply to the nominated person.

150. Information rights: status of rights

(1) This section has effect as regards the rights conferred by a nomination under section 146 (nomination of person to enjoy information rights).

(2) Enjoyment by the nominated person of the rights conferred by the nomination is enforceable against the company by the member as if they were rights conferred by the company's articles.

(3) Any enactment, and any provision of the company's articles, having effect in relation to communications with members has a corresponding effect (subject to any necessary adaptations) in relation to communications with the nominated person.

(4) In particular—

(a) where under any enactment, or any provision of the company's articles, the members of a company entitled to receive a document or information are determined as at a date or time before it is sent or supplied, the company need not send or supply it to a nominated person—

(i) whose nomination was received by the company after that date or time, or

(ii) if that date or time falls in a period of suspension of his nomination; and

(b) where under any enactment, or any provision of the company's articles, the right of a member to receive a document or information depends on the company having a current address for him, the same applies to any person nominated by him.

(5) The rights conferred by the nomination—

(a) are in addition to the rights of the member himself, and

(b) do not affect any rights exercisable by virtue of any such provision as is mentioned in section 145 (provisions of company's articles as to enjoyment or exercise of members' rights).

(6) A failure to give effect to the rights conferred by the nomination does not affect the validity of anything done by or on behalf of the company.

(7) References in this section to the rights conferred by the nomination are to—

(a) the rights referred to in section 146(3) (information rights), and

(b) where applicable, the rights conferred by section 147(3) (right to hard copy communications) and section 149 (information as to possible voting rights).

151. Information rights: power to amend

(1) The Secretary of State may by regulations amend the provisions of sections 146 to 150 (information rights) so as to—

(a) extend or restrict the classes of companies to which section 146 applies,

(b) make other provision as to the circumstances in which a nomination may be made under that section, or

(c) extend or restrict the rights conferred by such a nomination.

(2) The regulations may make such consequential modifications of any other provisions of this Part, or of any other enactment, as appear to the Secretary of State to be necessary.

(3) Regulations under this section are subject to affirmative resolution procedure.

Exercise of rights where shares held on behalf of others

152. Exercise of rights where shares held on behalf of others: exercise in different ways

(1) Where a member holds shares in a company on behalf of more than one person—

(a) rights attached to the shares, and

(b) rights under any enactment exercisable by virtue of holding the shares,

need not all be exercised, and if exercised, need not all be exercised in the same way.

(2) A member who exercises such rights but does not exercise all his rights, must inform the company to what extent he is exercising the rights.

(3) A member who exercises such rights in different ways must inform the company of the ways in which he is exercising them and to what extent they are exercised in each way.

(4) If a member exercises such rights without informing the company—

(a) that he is not exercising all his rights, or

(b) that he is exercising his rights in different ways,

the company is entitled to assume that he is exercising all his rights and is exercising them in the same way.

153. Exercise of rights where shares held on behalf of others: members' requests

(1) This section applies for the purposes of—

(a) section 314 (power to require circulation of statement),

(b) section 338 (public companies: power to require circulation of resolution for AGM),

(c) section 342 (power to require independent report on poll), and

(d) section 527 (power to require website publication of audit concerns).

(2) A company is required to act under any of those sections if it receives a request in relation to which the following conditions are met—

(a) it is made by at least 100 persons;

(b) it is authenticated by all the persons making it;

(c) in the case of any of those persons who is not a member of the company, it is accompanied by a statement—

(i) of the full name and address of a person ("the member") who is a member of the company and holds shares on behalf of that person,

(ii) that the member is holding those shares on behalf of that person in the course of a business,

(iii) of the number of shares in the company that the member holds on behalf of that person,

(iv) of the total amount paid up on those shares,

(v) that those shares are not held on behalf of anyone else or, if they are, that the other person or persons are not among the other persons making the request,

(vi) that some or all of those shares confer voting rights that are relevant for the purposes of making a request under the section in question, and

(vii) that the person has the right to instruct the member how to exercise those rights;

(d) in the case of any of those persons who is a member of the company, it is accompanied by a statement—

(i) that he holds shares otherwise than on behalf of another person, or

(ii) that he holds shares on behalf of one or more other persons but those persons are not among the other persons making the request;

(e) it is accompanied by such evidence as the company may reasonably require of the matters mentioned in paragraph (c) and (d);

(f) the total amount of the sums paid up on—

(i) shares held as mentioned in paragraph (c), and

(ii) shares held as mentioned in paragraph (d),

divided by the number of persons making the request, is not less than £100;

(g) the request complies with any other requirements of the section in question as to contents, timing and otherwise.

PART 10
A COMPANY'S DIRECTORS

CHAPTER 1
APPOINTMENT AND REMOVAL OF DIRECTORS

Requirement to have directors

154. Companies required to have directors

(1) A private company must have at least one director.

(2) A public company must have at least two directors.

155. Companies required to have at least one director who is a natural person

(1) A company must have at least one director who is a natural person.

(2) This requirement is met if the office of director is held by a natural person as a corporation sole or otherwise by virtue of an office.

156. Direction requiring company to make appointment

(1) If it appears to the Secretary of State that a company is in breach of—

section 154 (requirements as to number of directors), or

section 155 (requirement to have at least one director who is a natural person),

the Secretary of State may give the company a direction under this section.

(2) The direction must specify—

(a) the statutory requirement the company appears to be in breach of,

(b) what the company must do in order to comply with the direction, and

(c) the period within which it must do so.

That period must be not less than one month or more than three months after the date on which the direction is given.

(3) The direction must also inform the company of the consequences of failing to comply.

(4) Where the company is in breach of section 154 or 155 it must comply with the direction by—

(a) making the necessary appointment or appointments, and

(b) giving notice of them under section 167,

before the end of the period specified in the direction.

(5) If the company has already made the necessary appointment or appointments (or so far as it has done so), it must comply with the direction by giving notice of them under section 167 before the end of the period specified in the direction.

(6) If a company fails to comply with a direction under this section, an offence is committed by—

(a) the company, and

(b) every officer of the company who is in default.

For this purpose a shadow director is treated as an officer of the company.

(7) A person guilty of an offence under this section is liable on summary conviction to a fine not exceeding level 5 on the standard scale and, for continued contravention, a daily default fine not exceeding one-tenth of level 5 on the standard scale.

Appointment

157. Minimum age for appointment as director

(1) A person may not be appointed a director of a company unless he has attained the age of 16 years.

(2) This does not affect the validity of an appointment that is not to take effect until the person appointed attains that age.

(3) Where the office of director of a company is held by a corporation sole, or otherwise by virtue of another office, the appointment to that other office of a person who has not attained the age of 16 years is not effective also to make him a director of the company until he attains the age of 16 years.

(4) An appointment made in contravention of this section is void.

(5) Nothing in this section affects any liability of a person under any provision of the Companies Acts if he—

(a) purports to act as director, or

(b) acts as a shadow director,

although he could not, by virtue of this section, be validly appointed as a director.

(6) This section has effect subject to section 158 (power to provide for exceptions from minimum age requirement).

158. Power to provide for exceptions from minimum age requirement

(1) The Secretary of State may make provision by regulations for cases in which a person who has not attained the age of 16 years may be appointed a director of a company.

(2) The regulations must specify the circumstances in which, and any conditions subject to which, the appointment may be made.

(3) If the specified circumstances cease to obtain, or any specified conditions cease to be met, a person who was appointed by virtue of the regulations and who has not since attained the age of 16 years ceases to hold office.

(4) The regulations may make different provision for different parts of the United Kingdom.
This is without prejudice to the general power to make different provision for different cases.

(5) Regulations under this section are subject to negative resolution procedure.

159. Existing under-age directors

(1) This section applies where—

(a) a person appointed a director of a company before section 157 (minimum age for appointment as director) comes into force has not attained the age of 16 when that section comes into force, or

(b) the office of director of a company is held by a corporation sole, or otherwise by virtue of another office, and the person appointed to that other office has not attained the age of 16 years when that section comes into force,

and the case is not one excepted from that section by regulations under section 158.

(2) That person ceases to be a director on section 157 coming into force.

(3) The company must make the necessary consequential alteration in its register of directors but need not give notice to the registrar of the change.

(4) If it appears to the registrar (from other information) that a person has ceased by virtue of this section to be a director of a company, the registrar shall note that fact on the register.

160. Appointment of directors of public company to be voted on individually

(1) At a general meeting of a public company a motion for the appointment of two or more persons as directors of the company by a single resolution must not be made unless a resolution

that it should be so made has first been agreed to by the meeting without any vote being given against it.

(2) A resolution moved in contravention of this section is void, whether or not its being so moved was objected to at the time.

But where a resolution so moved is passed, no provision for the automatic reappointment of retiring directors in default of another appointment applies.

(3) For the purposes of this section a motion for approving a person's appointment, or for nominating a person for appointment, is treated as a motion for his appointment.

(4) Nothing in this section applies to a resolution amending the company's articles.

161. Validity of acts of directors

(1) The acts of a person acting as a director are valid notwithstanding that it is afterwards discovered—

(a) that there was a defect in his appointment;

(b) that he was disqualified from holding office;

(c) that he had ceased to hold office;

(d) that he was not entitled to vote on the matter in question.

(2) This applies even if the resolution for his appointment is void under section 160 (appointment of directors of public company to be voted on individually).

Register of directors, etc

162. Register of directors

(1) Every company must keep a register of its directors.

(2) The register must contain the required particulars (see sections 163, 164 and 166) of each person who is a director of the company.

(3) The register must be kept available for inspection—

(a) at the company's registered office, or

(b) at a place specified in regulations under section 1136.

(4) The company must give notice to the registrar—

(a) of the place at which the register is kept available for inspection, and

(b) of any change in that place,

unless it has at all times been kept at the company's registered office.

(5) The register must be open to the inspection—

(a) of any member of the company without charge, and

(b) of any other person on payment of such fee as may be prescribed.

(6) If default is made in complying with subsection (1), (2) or (3) or if default is made for 14 days in complying with subsection (4), or if an inspection required under subsection (5) is refused, an offence is committed by—

(a) the company, and

(b) every officer of the company who is in default.

For this purpose a shadow director is treated as an officer of the company.

(7) A person guilty of an offence under this section is liable on summary conviction to a fine not exceeding level 5 on the standard scale and, for continued contravention, a daily default fine not exceeding one-tenth of level 5 on the standard scale.

(8) In the case of a refusal of inspection of the register, the court may by order compel an immediate inspection of it.

163. Particulars of directors to be registered: individuals

(1) A company's register of directors must contain the following particulars in the case of an individual—

(a) name and any former name;

(b) a service address;

(c) the country or state (or part of the United Kingdom) in which he is usually resident;

(d) nationality;

(e) business occupation (if any);

(f) date of birth.

(2) For the purposes of this section "name" means a person's Christian name (or other forename) and surname, except that in the case of—

(a) a peer, or

(b) an individual usually known by a title,

the title may be stated instead of his Christian name (or other forename) and surname or in addition to either or both of them.

(3) For the purposes of this section a "former name" means a name by which the individual was formerly known for business purposes.

Where a person is or was formerly known by more than one such name, each of them must be stated.

(4) It is not necessary for the register to contain particulars of a former name in the following cases—

(a) in the case of a peer or an individual normally known by a British title, where the name is one by which the person was known previous to the adoption of or succession to the title;

(b) in the case of any person, where the former name—

(i) was changed or disused before the person attained the age of 16 years, or

(ii) has been changed or disused for 20 years or more.

(5) A person's service address may be stated to be "The company's registered office".

164. **Particulars of directors to be registered: corporate directors and firms**

A company's register of directors must contain the following particulars in the case of a body corporate, or a firm that is a legal person under the law by which it is governed—

(a) corporate or firm name;

(b) registered or principal office;

(c) in the case of an EEA company to which the First Company Law Directive (68/151/EEC) applies, particulars of—

(i) the register in which the company file mentioned in Article 3 of that Directive is kept (including details of the relevant state), and

(ii) the registration number in that register;

(d) in any other case, particulars of—

(i) the legal form of the company or firm and the law by which it is governed, and

(ii) if applicable, the register in which it is entered (including details of the state) and its registration number in that register.

165. **Register of directors' residential addresses**

(1) Every company must keep a register of directors' residential addresses.

(2) The register must state the usual residential address of each of the company's directors.

(3) If a director's usual residential address is the same as his service address (as stated in the company's register of directors), the register of directors' residential addresses need only contain an entry to that effect.

This does not apply if his service address is stated to be "The company's registered office".

(4) If default is made in complying with this section, an offence is committed by—

(a) the company, and

(b) every officer of the company who is in default.

For this purpose a shadow director is treated as an officer of the company.

(5) A person guilty of an offence under this section is liable on summary conviction to a fine not exceeding level 5 on the standard scale and, for continued contravention, a daily default fine not exceeding one-tenth of level 5 on the standard scale.

(6) This section applies only to directors who are individuals, not where the director is a body corporate or a firm that is a legal person under the law by which it is governed.

166. **Particulars of directors to be registered: power to make regulations**

    (1) The Secretary of State may make provision by regulations amending—

        section 163 (particulars of directors to be registered: individuals),

        section 164 (particulars of directors to be registered: corporate directors and firms), or

        section 165 (register of directors' residential addresses),

        so as to add to or remove items from the particulars required to be contained in a company's register of directors or register of directors' residential addresses.

    (2) Regulations under this section are subject to affirmative resolution procedure.

167. **Duty to notify registrar of changes**

    (1) A company must, within the period of 14 days from—

        (a) a person becoming or ceasing to be a director, or

        (b) the occurrence of any change in the particulars contained in its register of directors or its register of directors' residential addresses,

        give notice to the registrar of the change and of the date on which it occurred.

    (2) Notice of a person having become a director of the company must—

        (a) contain a statement of the particulars of the new director that are required to be included in the company's register of directors and its register of directors' residential addresses, and

        (b) be accompanied by a consent, by that person, to act in that capacity.

    (3) Where—

        (a) a company gives notice of a change of a director's service address as stated in the company's register of directors, and

        (b) the notice is not accompanied by notice of any resulting change in the particulars contained in the company's register of directors' residential addresses,

        the notice must be accompanied by a statement that no such change is required.

    (4) If default is made in complying with this section, an offence is committed by—

        (a) the company, and

        (b) every officer of the company who is in default.

        For this purpose a shadow director is treated as an officer of the company.

    (5) A person guilty of an offence under this section is liable on summary conviction to a fine not exceeding level 5 on the standard scale and, for continued contravention, a daily default fine not exceeding one-tenth of level 5 on the standard scale.

Removal

168. **Resolution to remove director**

    (1) A company may by ordinary resolution at a meeting remove a director before the expiration of his period of office, notwithstanding anything in any agreement between it and him.

    (2) Special notice is required of a resolution to remove a director under this section or to appoint somebody instead of a director so removed at the meeting at which he is removed.

    (3) A vacancy created by the removal of a director under this section, if not filled at the meeting at which he is removed, may be filled as a casual vacancy.

    (4) A person appointed director in place of a person removed under this section is treated, for the purpose of determining the time at which he or any other director is to retire, as if he had become director on the day on which the person in whose place he is appointed was last appointed a director.

    (5) This section is not to be taken—

        (a) as depriving a person removed under it of compensation or damages payable to him in respect of the termination of his appointment as director or of any appointment terminating with that as director, or

(b) as derogating from any power to remove a director that may exist apart from this section.

169. Director's right to protest against removal

(1) On receipt of notice of an intended resolution to remove a director under section 168, the company must forthwith send a copy of the notice to the director concerned.

(2) The director (whether or not a member of the company) is entitled to be heard on the resolution at the meeting.

(3) Where notice is given of an intended resolution to remove a director under that section, and the director concerned makes with respect to it representations in writing to the company (not exceeding a reasonable length) and requests their notification to members of the company, the company shall, unless the representations are received by it too late for it to do so—

(a) in any notice of the resolution given to members of the company state the fact of the representations having been made; and

(b) send a copy of the representations to every member of the company to whom notice of the meeting is sent (whether before or after receipt of the representations by the company).

(4) If a copy of the representations is not sent as required by subsection (3) because received too late or because of the company's default, the director may (without prejudice to his right to be heard orally) require that the representations shall be read out at the meeting.

(5) Copies of the representations need not be sent out and the representations need not be read out at the meeting if, on the application either of the company or of any other person who claims to be aggrieved, the court is satisfied that the rights conferred by this section are being abused.

(6) The court may order the company's costs (in Scotland, expenses) on an application under subsection (5) to be paid in whole or in part by the director, notwithstanding that he is not a party to the application.

CHAPTER 2
GENERAL DUTIES OF DIRECTORS

Introductory

170. Scope and nature of general duties

(1) The general duties specified in sections 171 to 177 are owed by a director of a company to the company.

(2) A person who ceases to be a director continues to be subject—

(a) to the duty in section 175 (duty to avoid conflicts of interest) as regards the exploitation of any property, information or opportunity of which he became aware at a time when he was a director, and

(b) to the duty in section 176 (duty not to accept benefits from third parties) as regards things done or omitted by him before he ceased to be a director.

To that extent those duties apply to a former director as to a director, subject to any necessary adaptations.

(3) The general duties are based on certain common law rules and equitable principles as they apply in relation to directors and have effect in place of those rules and principles as regards the duties owed to a company by a director.

(4) The general duties shall be interpreted and applied in the same way as common law rules or equitable principles, and regard shall be had to the corresponding common law rules and equitable principles in interpreting and applying the general duties.

(5) The general duties apply to shadow directors where, and to the extent that, the corresponding common law rules or equitable principles so apply.

The general duties

171. **Duty to act within powers**

A director of a company must—

(a) act in accordance with the company's constitution, and

(b) only exercise powers for the purposes for which they are conferred.

172. **Duty to promote the success of the company**

(1) A director of a company must act in the way he considers, in good faith, would be most likely to promote the success of the company for the benefit of its members as a whole, and in doing so have regard (amongst other matters) to—

(a) the likely consequences of any decision in the long term,

(b) the interests of the company's employees,

(c) the need to foster the company's business relationships with suppliers, customers and others,

(d) the impact of the company's operations on the community and the environment,

(e) the desirability of the company maintaining a reputation for high standards of business conduct, and

(f) the need to act fairly as between members of the company.

(2) Where or to the extent that the purposes of the company consist of or include purposes other than the benefit of its members, subsection (1) has effect as if the reference to promoting the success of the company for the benefit of its members were to achieving those purposes.

(3) The duty imposed by this section has effect subject to any enactment or rule of law requiring directors, in certain circumstances, to consider or act in the interests of creditors of the company.

173. **Duty to exercise independent judgment**

(1) A director of a company must exercise independent judgment.

(2) This duty is not infringed by his acting—

(a) in accordance with an agreement duly entered into by the company that restricts the future exercise of discretion by its directors, or

(b) in a way authorised by the company's constitution.

174. **Duty to exercise reasonable care, skill and diligence**

(1) A director of a company must exercise reasonable care, skill and diligence.

(2) This means the care, skill and diligence that would be exercised by a reasonably diligent person with—

(a) the general knowledge, skill and experience that may reasonably be expected of a person carrying out the functions carried out by the director in relation to the company, and

(b) the general knowledge, skill and experience that the director has.

175. **Duty to avoid conflicts of interest**

(1) A director of a company must avoid a situation in which he has, or can have, a direct or indirect interest that conflicts, or possibly may conflict, with the interests of the company.

(2) This applies in particular to the exploitation of any property, information or opportunity (and it is immaterial whether the company could take advantage of the property, information or opportunity).

(3) This duty does not apply to a conflict of interest arising in relation to a transaction or arrangement with the company.

(4) This duty is not infringed—

(a) if the situation cannot reasonably be regarded as likely to give rise to a conflict of interest; or

(b) if the matter has been authorised by the directors.

(5) Authorisation may be given by the directors—

    (a) where the company is a private company and nothing in the company's constitution invalidates such authorisation, by the matter being proposed to and authorised by the directors; or

    (b) where the company is a public company and its constitution includes provision enabling the directors to authorise the matter, by the matter being proposed to and authorised by them in accordance with the constitution.

(6) The authorisation is effective only if—

    (a) any requirement as to the quorum at the meeting at which the matter is considered is met without counting the director in question or any other interested director, and

    (b) the matter was agreed to without their voting or would have been agreed to if their votes had not been counted.

(7) Any reference in this section to a conflict of interest includes a conflict of interest and duty and a conflict of duties.

176. Duty not to accept benefits from third parties

(1) A director of a company must not accept a benefit from a third party conferred by reason of—

    (a) his being a director, or

    (b) his doing (or not doing) anything as director.

(2) A "third party" means a person other than the company, an associated body corporate or a person acting on behalf of the company or an associated body corporate.

(3) Benefits received by a director from a person by whom his services (as a director or otherwise) are provided to the company are not regarded as conferred by a third party.

(4) This duty is not infringed if the acceptance of the benefit cannot reasonably be regarded as likely to give rise to a conflict of interest.

(5) Any reference in this section to a conflict of interest includes a conflict of interest and duty and a conflict of duties.

177. Duty to declare interest in proposed transaction or arrangement

(1) If a director of a company is in any way, directly or indirectly, interested in a proposed transaction or arrangement with the company, he must declare the nature and extent of that interest to the other directors.

(2) The declaration may (but need not) be made—

    (a) at a meeting of the directors, or

    (b) by notice to the directors in accordance with—

        (i) section 184 (notice in writing), or

        (ii) section 185 (general notice).

(3) If a declaration of interest under this section proves to be, or becomes, inaccurate or incomplete, a further declaration must be made.

(4) Any declaration required by this section must be made before the company enters into the transaction or arrangement.

(5) This section does not require a declaration of an interest of which the director is not aware or where the director is not aware of the transaction or arrangement in question.

For this purpose a director is treated as being aware of matters of which he ought reasonably to be aware.

(6) A director need not declare an interest—

    (a) if it cannot reasonably be regarded as likely to give rise to a conflict of interest;

    (b) if, or to the extent that, the other directors are already aware of it (and for this purpose the other directors are treated as aware of anything of which they ought reasonably to be aware); or

    (c) if, or to the extent that, it concerns terms of his service contract that have been or are to be considered—

        (i) by a meeting of the directors, or

(ii) by a committee of the directors appointed for the purpose under the company's constitution.

Supplementary provisions

178. Civil consequences of breach of general duties

(1) The consequences of breach (or threatened breach) of sections 171 to 177 are the same as would apply if the corresponding common law rule or equitable principle applied.

(2) The duties in those sections (with the exception of section 174 (duty to exercise reasonable care, skill and diligence)) are, accordingly, enforceable in the same way as any other fiduciary duty owed to a company by its directors.

179. Cases within more than one of the general duties

Except as otherwise provided, more than one of the general duties may apply in any given case.

180. Consent, approval or authorisation by members

(1) In a case where—

(a) section 175 (duty to avoid conflicts of interest) is complied with by authorisation by the directors, or

(b) section 177 (duty to declare interest in proposed transaction or arrangement) is complied with,

the transaction or arrangement is not liable to be set aside by virtue of any common law rule or equitable principle requiring the consent or approval of the members of the company.

This is without prejudice to any enactment, or provision of the company's constitution, requiring such consent or approval.

(2) The application of the general duties is not affected by the fact that the case also falls within Chapter 4 (transactions requiring approval of members), except that where that Chapter applies and—

(a) approval is given under that Chapter, or

(b) the matter is one as to which it is provided that approval is not needed,

it is not necessary also to comply with section 175 (duty to avoid conflicts of interest) or section 176 (duty not to accept benefits from third parties).

(3) Compliance with the general duties does not remove the need for approval under any applicable provision of Chapter 4 (transactions requiring approval of members).

(4) The general duties—

(a) have effect subject to any rule of law enabling the company to give authority, specifically or generally, for anything to be done (or omitted) by the directors, or any of them, that would otherwise be a breach of duty, and

(b) where the company's articles contain provisions for dealing with conflicts of interest, are not infringed by anything done (or omitted) by the directors, or any of them, in accordance with those provisions.

(5) Otherwise, the general duties have effect (except as otherwise provided or the context otherwise requires) notwithstanding any enactment or rule of law.

181. Modification of provisions in relation to charitable companies

(1) In their application to a company that is a charity, the provisions of this Chapter have effect subject to this section.

(2) Section 175 (duty to avoid conflicts of interest) has effect as if—

(a) for subsection (3) (which disapplies the duty to avoid conflicts of interest in the case of a transaction or arrangement with the company) there were substituted—

"(3) This duty does not apply to a conflict of interest arising in relation to a transaction or arrangement with the company if or to the extent that the company's articles allow that duty to be so disapplied, which they may do only in relation to descriptions of transaction or arrangement specified in the company's articles.";

    (b) for subsection (5) (which specifies how directors of a company may give authority under that section for a transaction or arrangement) there were substituted—

        "(5) Authorisation may be given by the directors where the company's constitution includes provision enabling them to authorise the matter, by the matter being proposed to and authorised by them in accordance with the constitution.".

(3) Section 180(2)(b) (which disapplies certain duties under this Chapter in relation to cases excepted from requirement to obtain approval by members under Chapter 4) applies only if or to the extent that the company's articles allow those duties to be so disapplied, which they may do only in relation to descriptions of transaction or arrangement specified in the company's articles.

(4) After section 26(5) of the Charities Act 1993 (c. 10) (power of Charity Commission to authorise dealings with charity property etc) insert—

    "(5A) In the case of a charity that is a company, an order under this section may authorise an act notwithstanding that it involves the breach of a duty imposed on a director of the company under Chapter 2 of Part 10 of the Companies Act 2006 (general duties of directors).".

(5) This section does not extend to Scotland.

CHAPTER 3
DECLARATION OF INTEREST IN EXISTING TRANSACTION OR ARRANGEMENT

182. Declaration of interest in existing transaction or arrangement

(1) Where a director of a company is in any way, directly or indirectly, interested in a transaction or arrangement that has been entered into by the company, he must declare the nature and extent of the interest to the other directors in accordance with this section.

This section does not apply if or to the extent that the interest has been declared under section 177 (duty to declare interest in proposed transaction or arrangement).

(2) The declaration must be made—

    (a) at a meeting of the directors, or

    (b) by notice in writing (see section 184), or

    (c) by general notice (see section 185).

(3) If a declaration of interest under this section proves to be, or becomes, inaccurate or incomplete, a further declaration must be made.

(4) Any declaration required by this section must be made as soon as is reasonably practicable. Failure to comply with this requirement does not affect the underlying duty to make the declaration.

(5) This section does not require a declaration of an interest of which the director is not aware or where the director is not aware of the transaction or arrangement in question.

For this purpose a director is treated as being aware of matters of which he ought reasonably to be aware.

(6) A director need not declare an interest under this section—

    (a) if it cannot reasonably be regarded as likely to give rise to a conflict of interest;

    (b) if, or to the extent that, the other directors are already aware of it (and for this purpose the other directors are treated as aware of anything of which they ought reasonably to be aware); or

    (c) if, or to the extent that, it concerns terms of his service contract that have been or are to be considered—

        (i) by a meeting of the directors, or

(ii) by a committee of the directors appointed for the purpose under the company's constitution.

183. Offence of failure to declare interest

(1) A director who fails to comply with the requirements of section 182 (declaration of interest in existing transaction or arrangement) commits an offence.

(2) A person guilty of an offence under this section is liable—

    (a) on conviction on indictment, to a fine;

    (b) on summary conviction, to a fine not exceeding the statutory maximum.

184. Declaration made by notice in writing

(1) This section applies to a declaration of interest made by notice in writing.

(2) The director must send the notice to the other directors.

(3) The notice may be sent in hard copy form or, if the recipient has agreed to receive it in electronic form, in an agreed electronic form.

(4) The notice may be sent—

    (a) by hand or by post, or

    (b) if the recipient has agreed to receive it by electronic means, by agreed electronic means.

(5) Where a director declares an interest by notice in writing in accordance with this section—

    (a) the making of the declaration is deemed to form part of the proceedings at the next meeting of the directors after the notice is given, and

    (b) the provisions of section 248 (minutes of meetings of directors) apply as if the declaration had been made at that meeting.

185. General notice treated as sufficient declaration

(1) General notice in accordance with this section is a sufficient declaration of interest in relation to the matters to which it relates.

(2) General notice is notice given to the directors of a company to the effect that the director—

    (a) has an interest (as member, officer, employee or otherwise) in a specified body corporate or firm and is to be regarded as interested in any transaction or arrangement that may, after the date of the notice, be made with that body corporate or firm, or

    (b) is connected with a specified person (other than a body corporate or firm) and is to be regarded as interested in any transaction or arrangement that may, after the date of the notice, be made with that person.

(3) The notice must state the nature and extent of the director's interest in the body corporate or firm or, as the case may be, the nature of his connection with the person.

(4) General notice is not effective unless—

    (a) it is given at a meeting of the directors, or

    (b) the director takes reasonable steps to secure that it is brought up and read at the next meeting of the directors after it is given.

186. Declaration of interest in case of company with sole director

(1) Where a declaration of interest under section 182 (duty to declare interest in existing transaction or arrangement) is required of a sole director of a company that is required to have more than one director—

    (a) the declaration must be recorded in writing,

    (b) the making of the declaration is deemed to form part of the proceedings at the next meeting of the directors after the notice is given, and

    (c) the provisions of section 248 (minutes of meetings of directors) apply as if the declaration had been made at that meeting.

(2) Nothing in this section affects the operation of section 231 (contract with sole member who is also a director: terms to be set out in writing or recorded in minutes).

187. **Declaration of interest in existing transaction by shadow director**

    (1) The provisions of this Chapter relating to the duty under section 182 (duty to declare interest in existing transaction or arrangement) apply to a shadow director as to a director, but with the following adaptations.

    (2) Subsection (2)(a) of that section (declaration at meeting of directors) does not apply.

    (3) In section 185 (general notice treated as sufficient declaration), subsection (4) (notice to be given at or brought up and read at meeting of directors) does not apply.

    (4) General notice by a shadow director is not effective unless given by notice in writing in accordance with section 184.

CHAPTER 4

TRANSACTIONS WITH DIRECTORS REQUIRING APPROVAL OF MEMBERS

Service contracts

188. **Directors' long-term service contracts: requirement of members' approval**

    (1) This section applies to provision under which the guaranteed term of a director's employment—

        (a) with the company of which he is a director, or

        (b) where he is the director of a holding company, within the group consisting of that company and its subsidiaries,

    is, or may be, longer than two years.

    (2) A company may not agree to such provision unless it has been approved—

        (a) by resolution of the members of the company, and

        (b) in the case of a director of a holding company, by resolution of the members of that company.

    (3) The guaranteed term of a director's employment is—

        (a) the period (if any) during which the director's employment—

            (i) is to continue, or may be continued otherwise than at the instance of the company (whether under the original agreement or under a new agreement entered into in pursuance of it), and

            (ii) cannot be terminated by the company by notice, or can be so terminated only in specified circumstances, or

        (b) in the case of employment terminable by the company by notice, the period of notice required to be given,

    or, in the case of employment having a period within paragraph (a) and a period within paragraph (b), the aggregate of those periods.

    (4) If more than six months before the end of the guaranteed term of a director's employment the company enters into a further service contract (otherwise than in pursuance of a right conferred, by or under the original contract, on the other party to it), this section applies as if there were added to the guaranteed term of the new contract the unexpired period of the guaranteed term of the original contract.

    (5) A resolution approving provision to which this section applies must not be passed unless a memorandum setting out the proposed contract incorporating the provision is made available to members—

        (a) in the case of a written resolution, by being sent or submitted to every eligible member at or before the time at which the proposed resolution is sent or submitted to him;

        (b) in the case of a resolution at a meeting, by being made available for inspection by members of the company both—

            (i) at the company's registered office for not less than 15 days ending with the date of the meeting, and

(ii) at the meeting itself.

(6) No approval is required under this section on the part of the members of a body corporate that—

(a) is not a UK-registered company, or

(b) is a wholly-owned subsidiary of another body corporate.

(7) In this section "employment" means any employment under a director's service contract.

189. **Directors' long-term service contracts: civil consequences of contravention**

If a company agrees to provision in contravention of section 188 (directors' long-term service contracts: requirement of members' approval)—

(a) the provision is void, to the extent of the contravention, and

(b) the contract is deemed to contain a term entitling the company to terminate it at any time by the giving of reasonable notice.

Substantial property transactions

190. **Substantial property transactions: requirement of members' approval**

(1) A company may not enter into an arrangement under which—

(a) a director of the company or of its holding company, or a person connected with such a director, acquires or is to acquire from the company (directly or indirectly) a substantial non-cash asset, or

(b) the company acquires or is to acquire a substantial non-cash asset (directly or indirectly) from such a director or a person so connected,

unless the arrangement has been approved by a resolution of the members of the company or is conditional on such approval being obtained.

For the meaning of "substantial non-cash asset" see section 191.

(2) If the director or connected person is a director of the company's holding company or a person connected with such a director, the arrangement must also have been approved by a resolution of the members of the holding company or be conditional on such approval being obtained.

(3) A company shall not be subject to any liability by reason of a failure to obtain approval required by this section.

(4) No approval is required under this section on the part of the members of a body corporate that—

(a) is not a UK-registered company, or

(b) is a wholly-owned subsidiary of another body corporate.

(5) For the purposes of this section—

(a) an arrangement involving more than one non-cash asset, or

(b) an arrangement that is one of a series involving non-cash assets,

shall be treated as if they involved a non-cash asset of a value equal to the aggregate value of all the non-cash assets involved in the arrangement or, as the case may be, the series.

(6) This section does not apply to a transaction so far as it relates—

(a) to anything to which a director of a company is entitled under his service contract, or

(b) to payment for loss of office as defined in section 215 (payments requiring members' approval).

191. **Meaning of "substantial"**

(1) This section explains what is meant in section 190 (requirement of approval for substantial property transactions) by a "substantial" non-cash asset.

(2) An asset is a substantial asset in relation to a company if its value—

(a) exceeds 10% of the company's asset value and is more than £5,000, or

(b) exceeds £100,000.

(3) For this purpose a company's "asset value" at any time is—

    (a) the value of the company's net assets determined by reference to its most recent statutory accounts, or

    (b) if no statutory accounts have been prepared, the amount of the company's called-up share capital.

(4) A company's "statutory accounts" means its annual accounts prepared in accordance with Part 15, and its "most recent" statutory accounts means those in relation to which the time for sending them out to members (see section 424) is most recent.

(5) Whether an asset is a substantial asset shall be determined as at the time the arrangement is entered into.

192. Exception for transactions with members or other group companies

Approval is not required under section 190 (requirement of members' approval for substantial property transactions)—

    (a) for a transaction between a company and a person in his character as a member of that company, or

    (b) for a transaction between—

        (i) a holding company and its wholly-owned subsidiary, or

        (ii) two wholly-owned subsidiaries of the same holding company.

193. Exception in case of company in winding up or administration

(1) This section applies to a company—

    (a) that is being wound up (unless the winding up is a members' voluntary winding up), or

    (b) that is in administration within the meaning of Schedule B1 to the Insolvency Act 1986 (c. 45) or the Insolvency (Northern Ireland) Order 1989 (S.I. 1989/2405 (N.I. 19)).

(2) Approval is not required under section 190 (requirement of members' approval for substantial property transactions)—

    (a) on the part of the members of a company to which this section applies, or

    (b) for an arrangement entered into by a company to which this section applies.

194. Exception for transactions on recognised investment exchange

(1) Approval is not required under section 190 (requirement of members' approval for substantial property transactions) for a transaction on a recognised investment exchange effected by a director, or a person connected with him, through the agency of a person who in relation to the transaction acts as an independent broker.

(2) For this purpose—

    (a) "independent broker" means a person who, independently of the director or any person connected with him, selects the person with whom the transaction is to be effected; and

    (b) "recognised investment exchange" has the same meaning as in Part 18 of the Financial Services and Markets Act 2000 (c. 8).

195. Property transactions: civil consequences of contravention

(1) This section applies where a company enters into an arrangement in contravention of section 190 (requirement of members' approval for substantial property transactions).

(2) The arrangement, and any transaction entered into in pursuance of the arrangement (whether by the company or any other person), is voidable at the instance of the company, unless—

    (a) restitution of any money or other asset that was the subject matter of the arrangement or transaction is no longer possible,

    (b) the company has been indemnified in pursuance of this section by any other persons for the loss or damage suffered by it, or

    (c) rights acquired in good faith, for value and without actual notice of the contravention by a person who is not a party to the arrangement or transaction would be affected by the avoidance.

(3) Whether or not the arrangement or any such transaction has been avoided, each of the persons specified in subsection (4) is liable—

(a) to account to the company for any gain that he has made directly or indirectly by the arrangement or transaction, and

(b) (jointly and severally with any other person so liable under this section) to indemnify the company for any loss or damage resulting from the arrangement or transaction.

(4) The persons so liable are—

(a) any director of the company or of its holding company with whom the company entered into the arrangement in contravention of section 190,

(b) any person with whom the company entered into the arrangement in contravention of that section who is connected with a director of the company or of its holding company,

(c) the director of the company or of its holding company with whom any such person is connected, and

(d) any other director of the company who authorised the arrangement or any transaction entered into in pursuance of such an arrangement.

(5) Subsections (3) and (4) are subject to the following two subsections.

(6) In the case of an arrangement entered into by a company in contravention of section 190 with a person connected with a director of the company or of its holding company, that director is not liable by virtue of subsection (4)(c) if he shows that he took all reasonable steps to secure the company's compliance with that section.

(7) In any case—

(a) a person so connected is not liable by virtue of subsection (4)(b), and

(b) a director is not liable by virtue of subsection (4)(d),

if he shows that, at the time the arrangement was entered into, he did not know the relevant circumstances constituting the contravention.

(8) Nothing in this section shall be read as excluding the operation of any other enactment or rule of law by virtue of which the arrangement or transaction may be called in question or any liability to the company may arise.

196. **Property transactions: effect of subsequent affirmation**

Where a transaction or arrangement is entered into by a company in contravention of section 190 (requirement of members' approval) but, within a reasonable period, it is affirmed—

(a) in the case of a contravention of subsection (1) of that section, by resolution of the members of the company, and

(b) in the case of a contravention of subsection (2) of that section, by resolution of the members of the holding company,

the transaction or arrangement may no longer be avoided under section 195.

Loans, quasi-loans and credit transactions

197. **Loans to directors: requirement of members' approval**

(1) A company may not—

(a) make a loan to a director of the company or of its holding company, or

(b) give a guarantee or provide security in connection with a loan made by any person to such a director,

unless the transaction has been approved by a resolution of the members of the company.

(2) If the director is a director of the company's holding company, the transaction must also have been approved by a resolution of the members of the holding company.

(3) A resolution approving a transaction to which this section applies must not be passed unless a memorandum setting out the matters mentioned in subsection (4) is made available to members—

(a) in the case of a written resolution, by being sent or submitted to every eligible member at or before the time at which the proposed resolution is sent or submitted to him;

    (b) in the case of a resolution at a meeting, by being made available for inspection by members of the company both—
        (i) at the company's registered office for not less than 15 days ending with the date of the meeting, and
        (ii) at the meeting itself.
(4) The matters to be disclosed are—
    (a) the nature of the transaction,
    (b) the amount of the loan and the purpose for which it is required, and
    (c) the extent of the company's liability under any transaction connected with the loan.
(5) No approval is required under this section on the part of the members of a body corporate that—
    (a) is not a UK-registered company, or
    (b) is a wholly-owned subsidiary of another body corporate.

198. Quasi-loans to directors: requirement of members' approval

(1) This section applies to a company if it is—
    (a) a public company, or
    (b) a company associated with a public company.
(2) A company to which this section applies may not—
    (a) make a quasi-loan to a director of the company or of its holding company, or
    (b) give a guarantee or provide security in connection with a quasi-loan made by any person to such a director,
    unless the transaction has been approved by a resolution of the members of the company.
(3) If the director is a director of the company's holding company, the transaction must also have been approved by a resolution of the members of the holding company.
(4) A resolution approving a transaction to which this section applies must not be passed unless a memorandum setting out the matters mentioned in subsection (5) is made available to members—
    (a) in the case of a written resolution, by being sent or submitted to every eligible member at or before the time at which the proposed resolution is sent or submitted to him;
    (b) in the case of a resolution at a meeting, by being made available for inspection by members of the company both—
        (i) at the company's registered office for not less than 15 days ending with the date of the meeting, and
        (ii) at the meeting itself.
(5) The matters to be disclosed are—
    (a) the nature of the transaction,
    (b) the amount of the quasi-loan and the purpose for which it is required, and
    (c) the extent of the company's liability under any transaction connected with the quasi-loan.
(6) No approval is required under this section on the part of the members of a body corporate that—
    (a) is not a UK-registered company, or
    (b) is a wholly-owned subsidiary of another body corporate.

199. Meaning of "quasi-loan" and related expressions

(1) A "quasi-loan" is a transaction under which one party ("the creditor") agrees to pay, or pays otherwise than in pursuance of an agreement, a sum for another ("the borrower") or agrees to reimburse, or reimburses otherwise than in pursuance of an agreement, expenditure incurred by another party for another ("the borrower")—
    (a) on terms that the borrower (or a person on his behalf) will reimburse the creditor; or
    (b) in circumstances giving rise to a liability on the borrower to reimburse the creditor.
(2) Any reference to the person to whom a quasi-loan is made is a reference to the borrower.

(3) The liabilities of the borrower under a quasi-loan include the liabilities of any person who has agreed to reimburse the creditor on behalf of the borrower.

200. Loans or quasi-loans to persons connected with directors: requirement of members' approval

(1) This section applies to a company if it is—

    (a) a public company, or

    (b) a company associated with a public company.

(2) A company to which this section applies may not—

    (a) make a loan or quasi-loan to a person connected with a director of the company or of its holding company, or

    (b) give a guarantee or provide security in connection with a loan or quasi-loan made by any person to a person connected with such a director,

unless the transaction has been approved by a resolution of the members of the company.

(3) If the connected person is a person connected with a director of the company's holding company, the transaction must also have been approved by a resolution of the members of the holding company.

(4) A resolution approving a transaction to which this section applies must not be passed unless a memorandum setting out the matters mentioned in subsection (5) is made available to members—

    (a) in the case of a written resolution, by being sent or submitted to every eligible member at or before the time at which the proposed resolution is sent or submitted to him;

    (b) in the case of a resolution at a meeting, by being made available for inspection by members of the company both—

        (i) at the company's registered office for not less than 15 days ending with the date of the meeting, and

        (ii) at the meeting itself.

(5) The matters to be disclosed are—

    (a) the nature of the transaction,

    (b) the amount of the loan or quasi-loan and the purpose for which it is required, and

    (c) the extent of the company's liability under any transaction connected with the loan or quasi-loan.

(6) No approval is required under this section on the part of the members of a body corporate that—

    (a) is not a UK-registered company, or

    (b) is a wholly-owned subsidiary of another body corporate.

201. Credit transactions: requirement of members' approval

(1) This section applies to a company if it is—

    (a) a public company, or

    (b) a company associated with a public company.

(2) A company to which this section applies may not—

    (a) enter into a credit transaction as creditor for the benefit of a director of the company or of its holding company, or a person connected with such a director, or

    (b) give a guarantee or provide security in connection with a credit transaction entered into by any person for the benefit of such a director, or a person connected with such a director,

unless the transaction (that is, the credit transaction, the giving of the guarantee or the provision of security, as the case may be) has been approved by a resolution of the members of the company.

(3) If the director or connected person is a director of its holding company or a person connected with such a director, the transaction must also have been approved by a resolution of the members of the holding company.

(4) A resolution approving a transaction to which this section applies must not be passed unless a memorandum setting out the matters mentioned in subsection (5) is made available to members—

(a) in the case of a written resolution, by being sent or submitted to every eligible member at or before the time at which the proposed resolution is sent or submitted to him;

(b) in the case of a resolution at a meeting, by being made available for inspection by members of the company both—

(i) at the company's registered office for not less than 15 days ending with the date of the meeting, and

(ii) at the meeting itself.

(5) The matters to be disclosed are—

(a) the nature of the transaction,

(b) the value of the credit transaction and the purpose for which the land, goods or services sold or otherwise disposed of, leased, hired or supplied under the credit transaction are required, and

(c) the extent of the company's liability under any transaction connected with the credit transaction.

(6) No approval is required under this section on the part of the members of a body corporate that—

(a) is not a UK-registered company, or

(b) is a wholly-owned subsidiary of another body corporate.

202. Meaning of "credit transaction"

(1) A "credit transaction" is a transaction under which one party ("the creditor")—

(a) supplies any goods or sells any land under a hire-purchase agreement or a conditional sale agreement,

(b) leases or hires any land or goods in return for periodical payments, or

(c) otherwise disposes of land or supplies goods or services on the understanding that payment (whether in a lump sum or instalments or by way of periodical payments or otherwise) is to be deferred.

(2) Any reference to the person for whose benefit a credit transaction is entered into is to the person to whom goods, land or services are supplied, sold, leased, hired or otherwise disposed of under the transaction.

(3) In this section—

"conditional sale agreement" has the same meaning as in the Consumer Credit Act 1974 (c. 39); and

"services" means anything other than goods or land.

203. Related arrangements: requirement of members' approval

(1) A company may not—

(a) take part in an arrangement under which—

(i) another person enters into a transaction that, if it had been entered into by the company, would have required approval under section 197, 198, 200 or 201, and

(ii) that person, in pursuance of the arrangement, obtains a benefit from the company or a body corporate associated with it, or

(b) arrange for the assignment to it, or assumption by it, of any rights, obligations or liabilities under a transaction that, if it had been entered into by the company, would have required such approval,

unless the arrangement in question has been approved by a resolution of the members of the company.

(2) If the director or connected person for whom the transaction is entered into is a director of its holding company or a person connected with such a director, the arrangement must also have been approved by a resolution of the members of the holding company.

(3) A resolution approving an arrangement to which this section applies must not be passed unless a memorandum setting out the matters mentioned in subsection (4) is made available to members—

    (a) in the case of a written resolution, by being sent or submitted to every eligible member at or before the time at which the proposed resolution is sent or submitted to him;

    (b) in the case of a resolution at a meeting, by being made available for inspection by members of the company both—

        (i) at the company's registered office for not less than 15 days ending with the date of the meeting, and

        (ii) at the meeting itself.

(4) The matters to be disclosed are—

    (a) the matters that would have to be disclosed if the company were seeking approval of the transaction to which the arrangement relates,

    (b) the nature of the arrangement, and

    (c) the extent of the company's liability under the arrangement or any transaction connected with it.

(5) No approval is required under this section on the part of the members of a body corporate that—

    (a) is not a UK-registered company, or

    (b) is a wholly-owned subsidiary of another body corporate.

(6) In determining for the purposes of this section whether a transaction is one that would have required approval under section 197, 198, 200 or 201 if it had been entered into by the company, the transaction shall be treated as having been entered into on the date of the arrangement.

204. Exception for expenditure on company business

(1) Approval is not required under section 197, 198, 200 or 201 (requirement of members' approval for loans etc) for anything done by a company—

    (a) to provide a director of the company or of its holding company, or a person connected with any such director, with funds to meet expenditure incurred or to be incurred by him—

        (i) for the purposes of the company, or

        (ii) for the purpose of enabling him properly to perform his duties as an officer of the company, or

    (b) to enable any such person to avoid incurring such expenditure.

(2) This section does not authorise a company to enter into a transaction if the aggregate of—

    (a) the value of the transaction in question, and

    (b) the value of any other relevant transactions or arrangements,

    exceeds £50,000.

205. Exception for expenditure on defending proceedings etc

(1) Approval is not required under section 197, 198, 200 or 201 (requirement of members' approval for loans etc) for anything done by a company—

    (a) to provide a director of the company or of its holding company with funds to meet expenditure incurred or to be incurred by him—

        (i) in defending any criminal or civil proceedings in connection with any alleged negligence, default, breach of duty or breach of trust by him in relation to the company or an associated company, or

        (ii) in connection with an application for relief (see subsection (5)), or

    (b) to enable any such director to avoid incurring such expenditure,

    if it is done on the following terms.

(2) The terms are—

    (a) that the loan is to be repaid, or (as the case may be) any liability of the company incurred under any transaction connected with the thing done is to be discharged, in the event of—

        (i) the director being convicted in the proceedings,

        (ii) judgment being given against him in the proceedings, or

        (iii) the court refusing to grant him relief on the application; and

    (b) that it is to be so repaid or discharged not later than—

        (i) the date when the conviction becomes final,

        (ii) the date when the judgment becomes final, or

        (iii) the date when the refusal of relief becomes final.

(3) For this purpose a conviction, judgment or refusal of relief becomes final—

    (a) if not appealed against, at the end of the period for bringing an appeal;

    (b) if appealed against, when the appeal (or any further appeal) is disposed of.

(4) An appeal is disposed of—

    (a) if it is determined and the period for bringing any further appeal has ended, or

    (b) if it is abandoned or otherwise ceases to have effect.

(5) The reference in subsection (1)(a)(ii) to an application for relief is to an application for relief under—

    section 661(3) or (4) (power of court to grant relief in case of acquisition of shares by innocent nominee), or

    section 1157 (general power of court to grant relief in case of honest and reasonable conduct).

206. Exception for expenditure in connection with regulatory action or investigation

Approval is not required under section 197, 198, 200 or 201 (requirement of members' approval for loans etc) for anything done by a company—

    (a) to provide a director of the company or of its holding company with funds to meet expenditure incurred or to be incurred by him in defending himself—

        (i) in an investigation by a regulatory authority, or

        (ii) against action proposed to be taken by a regulatory authority,

    in connection with any alleged negligence, default, breach of duty or breach of trust by him in relation to the company or an associated company, or

    (b) to enable any such director to avoid incurring such expenditure.

207. Exceptions for minor and business transactions

(1) Approval is not required under section 197, 198 or 200 for a company to make a loan or quasi-loan, or to give a guarantee or provide security in connection with a loan or quasi-loan, if the aggregate of—

    (a) the value of the transaction, and

    (b) the value of any other relevant transactions or arrangements,

    does not exceed £10,000.

(2) Approval is not required under section 201 for a company to enter into a credit transaction, or to give a guarantee or provide security in connection with a credit transaction, if the aggregate of—

    (a) the value of the transaction (that is, of the credit transaction, guarantee or security), and

    (b) the value of any other relevant transactions or arrangements,

    does not exceed £15,000.

(3) Approval is not required under section 201 for a company to enter into a credit transaction, or to give a guarantee or provide security in connection with a credit transaction, if—

    (a) the transaction is entered into by the company in the ordinary course of the company's business, and

(b) the value of the transaction is not greater, and the terms on which it is entered into are not more favourable, than it is reasonable to expect the company would have offered to, or in respect of, a person of the same financial standing but unconnected with the company.

208. Exceptions for intra-group transactions

(1) Approval is not required under section 197, 198 or 200 for—

    (a) the making of a loan or quasi-loan to an associated body corporate, or

    (b) the giving of a guarantee or provision of security in connection with a loan or quasi-loan made to an associated body corporate.

(2) Approval is not required under section 201—

    (a) to enter into a credit transaction as creditor for the benefit of an associated body corporate, or

    (b) to give a guarantee or provide security in connection with a credit transaction entered into by any person for the benefit of an associated body corporate.

209. Exceptions for money-lending companies

(1) Approval is not required under section 197, 198 or 200 for the making of a loan or quasi-loan, or the giving of a guarantee or provision of security in connection with a loan or quasi-loan, by a money-lending company if—

    (a) the transaction (that is, the loan, quasi-loan, guarantee or security) is entered into by the company in the ordinary course of the company's business, and

    (b) the value of the transaction is not greater, and its terms are not more favourable, than it is reasonable to expect the company would have offered to a person of the same financial standing but unconnected with the company.

(2) A "money-lending company" means a company whose ordinary business includes the making of loans or quasi-loans, or the giving of guarantees or provision of security in connection with loans or quasi-loans.

(3) The condition specified in subsection (1)(b) does not of itself prevent a company from making a home loan—

    (a) to a director of the company or of its holding company, or

    (b) to an employee of the company,

if loans of that description are ordinarily made by the company to its employees and the terms of the loan in question are no more favourable than those on which such loans are ordinarily made.

(4) For the purposes of subsection (3) a "home loan" means a loan—

    (a) for the purpose of facilitating the purchase, for use as the only or main residence of the person to whom the loan is made, of the whole or part of any dwelling-house together with any land to be occupied and enjoyed with it,

    (b) for the purpose of improving a dwelling-house or part of a dwelling-house so used or any land occupied and enjoyed with it, or

    (c) in substitution for any loan made by any person and falling within paragraph (a) or (b).

210. Other relevant transactions or arrangements

(1) This section has effect for determining what are "other relevant transactions or arrangements" for the purposes of any exception to section 197, 198, 200 or 201. In the following provisions "the relevant exception" means the exception for the purposes of which that falls to be determined.

(2) Other relevant transactions or arrangements are those previously entered into, or entered into at the same time as the transaction or arrangement in question in relation to which the following conditions are met.

(3) Where the transaction or arrangement in question is entered into—

    (a) for a director of the company entering into it, or

    (b) for a person connected with such a director,

the conditions are that the transaction or arrangement was (or is) entered into for that director, or a person connected with him, by virtue of the relevant exception by that company or by any of its subsidiaries.

(4) Where the transaction or arrangement in question is entered into—

(a) for a director of the holding company of the company entering into it, or

(b) for a person connected with such a director,

the conditions are that the transaction or arrangement was (or is) entered into for that director, or a person connected with him, by virtue of the relevant exception by the holding company or by any of its subsidiaries.

(5) A transaction or arrangement entered into by a company that at the time it was entered into—

(a) was a subsidiary of the company entering into the transaction or arrangement in question, or

(b) was a subsidiary of that company's holding company,

is not a relevant transaction or arrangement if, at the time the question arises whether the transaction or arrangement in question falls within a relevant exception, it is no longer such a subsidiary.

211. **The value of transactions and arrangements**

(1) For the purposes of sections 197 to 214 (loans etc)—

(a) the value of a transaction or arrangement is determined as follows, and

(b) the value of any other relevant transaction or arrangement is taken to be the value so determined reduced by any amount by which the liabilities of the person for whom the transaction or arrangement was made have been reduced.

(2) The value of a loan is the amount of its principal.

(3) The value of a quasi-loan is the amount, or maximum amount, that the person to whom the quasi-loan is made is liable to reimburse the creditor.

(4) The value of a credit transaction is the price that it is reasonable to expect could be obtained for the goods, services or land to which the transaction relates if they had been supplied (at the time the transaction is entered into) in the ordinary course of business and on the same terms (apart from price) as they have been supplied, or are to be supplied, under the transaction in question.

(5) The value of a guarantee or security is the amount guaranteed or secured.

(6) The value of an arrangement to which section 203 (related arrangements) applies is the value of the transaction to which the arrangement relates.

(7) If the value of a transaction or arrangement is not capable of being expressed as a specific sum of money—

(a) whether because the amount of any liability arising under the transaction or arrangement is unascertainable, or for any other reason, and

(b) whether or not any liability under the transaction or arrangement has been reduced,

its value is deemed to exceed £50,000.

212. **The person for whom a transaction or arrangement is entered into**

For the purposes of sections 197 to 214 (loans etc) the person for whom a transaction or arrangement is entered into is—

(a) in the case of a loan or quasi-loan, the person to whom it is made;

(b) in the case of a credit transaction, the person to whom goods, land or services are supplied, sold, hired, leased or otherwise disposed of under the transaction;

(c) in the case of a guarantee or security, the person for whom the transaction is made in connection with which the guarantee or security is entered into;

(d) in the case of an arrangement within section 203 (related arrangements), the person for whom the transaction is made to which the arrangement relates.

213. Loans etc: civil consequences of contravention

(1) This section applies where a company enters into a transaction or arrangement in contravention of section 197, 198, 200, 201 or 203 (requirement of members' approval for loans etc).

(2) The transaction or arrangement is voidable at the instance of the company, unless—

    (a) restitution of any money or other asset that was the subject matter of the transaction or arrangement is no longer possible,

    (b) the company has been indemnified for any loss or damage resulting from the transaction or arrangement, or

    (c) rights acquired in good faith, for value and without actual notice of the contravention by a person who is not a party to the transaction or arrangement would be affected by the avoidance.

(3) Whether or not the transaction or arrangement has been avoided, each of the persons specified in subsection (4) is liable—

    (a) to account to the company for any gain that he has made directly or indirectly by the transaction or arrangement, and

    (b) (jointly and severally with any other person so liable under this section) to indemnify the company for any loss or damage resulting from the transaction or arrangement.

(4) The persons so liable are—

    (a) any director of the company or of its holding company with whom the company entered into the transaction or arrangement in contravention of section 197, 198, 201 or 203,

    (b) any person with whom the company entered into the transaction or arrangement in contravention of any of those sections who is connected with a director of the company or of its holding company,

    (c) the director of the company or of its holding company with whom any such person is connected, and

    (d) any other director of the company who authorised the transaction or arrangement.

(5) Subsections (3) and (4) are subject to the following two subsections.

(6) In the case of a transaction or arrangement entered into by a company in contravention of section 200, 201 or 203 with a person connected with a director of the company or of its holding company, that director is not liable by virtue of subsection (4)(c) if he shows that he took all reasonable steps to secure the company's compliance with the section concerned.

(7) In any case—

    (a) a person so connected is not liable by virtue of subsection (4)(b), and

    (b) a director is not liable by virtue of subsection (4)(d),

    if he shows that, at the time the transaction or arrangement was entered into, he did not know the relevant circumstances constituting the contravention.

(8) Nothing in this section shall be read as excluding the operation of any other enactment or rule of law by virtue of which the transaction or arrangement may be called in question or any liability to the company may arise.

214. Loans etc: effect of subsequent affirmation

Where a transaction or arrangement is entered into by a company in contravention of section 197, 198, 200, 201 or 203 (requirement of members' approval for loans etc) but, within a reasonable period, it is affirmed—

(a) in the case of a contravention of the requirement for a resolution of the members of the company, by a resolution of the members of the company, and

(b) in the case of a contravention of the requirement for a resolution of the members of the company's holding company, by a resolution of the members of the holding company,

the transaction or arrangement may no longer be avoided under section 213.

Payments for loss of office

215. Payments for loss of office

(1) In this Chapter a "payment for loss of office" means a payment made to a director or past director of a company—

    (a) by way of compensation for loss of office as director of the company,

    (b) by way of compensation for loss, while director of the company or in connection with his ceasing to be a director of it, of—

        (i) any other office or employment in connection with the management of the affairs of the company, or

        (ii) any office (as director or otherwise) or employment in connection with the management of the affairs of any subsidiary undertaking of the company,

    (c) as consideration for or in connection with his retirement from his office as director of the company, or

    (d) as consideration for or in connection with his retirement, while director of the company or in connection with his ceasing to be a director of it, from—

        (i) any other office or employment in connection with the management of the affairs of the company, or

        (ii) any office (as director or otherwise) or employment in connection with the management of the affairs of any subsidiary undertaking of the company.

(2) The references to compensation and consideration include benefits otherwise than in cash and references in this Chapter to payment have a corresponding meaning.

(3) For the purposes of sections 217 to 221 (payments requiring members' approval)—

    (a) payment to a person connected with a director, or

    (b) payment to any person at the direction of, or for the benefit of, a director or a person connected with him,

is treated as payment to the director.

(4) References in those sections to payment by a person include payment by another person at the direction of, or on behalf of, the person referred to.

216. Amounts taken to be payments for loss of office

(1) This section applies where in connection with any such transfer as is mentioned in section 218 or 219 (payment in connection with transfer of undertaking, property or shares) a director of the company—

    (a) is to cease to hold office, or

    (b) is to cease to be the holder of—

        (i) any other office or employment in connection with the management of the affairs of the company, or

        (ii) any office (as director or otherwise) or employment in connection with the management of the affairs of any subsidiary undertaking of the company.

(2) If in connection with any such transfer—

    (a) the price to be paid to the director for any shares in the company held by him is in excess of the price which could at the time have been obtained by other holders of like shares, or

    (b) any valuable consideration is given to the director by a person other than the company, the excess or, as the case may be, the money value of the consideration is taken for the purposes of those sections to have been a payment for loss of office.

217. Payment by company: requirement of members' approval

(1) A company may not make a payment for loss of office to a director of the company unless the payment has been approved by a resolution of the members of the company.

(2) A company may not make a payment for loss of office to a director of its holding company unless the payment has been approved by a resolution of the members of each of those companies.

(3) A resolution approving a payment to which this section applies must not be passed unless a memorandum setting out particulars of the proposed payment (including its amount) is made available to the members of the company whose approval is sought—

    (a) in the case of a written resolution, by being sent or submitted to every eligible member at or before the time at which the proposed resolution is sent or submitted to him;

    (b) in the case of a resolution at a meeting, by being made available for inspection by the members both—

        (i) at the company's registered office for not less than 15 days ending with the date of the meeting, and

        (ii) at the meeting itself.

(4) No approval is required under this section on the part of the members of a body corporate that—

    (a) is not a UK-registered company, or

    (b) is a wholly-owned subsidiary of another body corporate.

218. Payment in connection with transfer of undertaking etc: requirement of members' approval

(1) No payment for loss of office may be made by any person to a director of a company in connection with the transfer of the whole or any part of the undertaking or property of the company unless the payment has been approved by a resolution of the members of the company.

(2) No payment for loss of office may be made by any person to a director of a company in connection with the transfer of the whole or any part of the undertaking or property of a subsidiary of the company unless the payment has been approved by a resolution of the members of each of the companies.

(3) A resolution approving a payment to which this section applies must not be passed unless a memorandum setting out particulars of the proposed payment (including its amount) is made available to the members of the company whose approval is sought—

    (a) in the case of a written resolution, by being sent or submitted to every eligible member at or before the time at which the proposed resolution is sent or submitted to him;

    (b) in the case of a resolution at a meeting, by being made available for inspection by the members both—

        (i) at the company's registered office for not less than 15 days ending with the date of the meeting, and

        (ii) at the meeting itself.

(4) No approval is required under this section on the part of the members of a body corporate that—

    (a) is not a UK-registered company, or

    (b) is a wholly-owned subsidiary of another body corporate.

(5) A payment made in pursuance of an arrangement—

    (a) entered into as part of the agreement for the transfer in question, or within one year before or two years after that agreement, and

    (b) to which the company whose undertaking or property is transferred, or any person to whom the transfer is made, is privy,

is presumed, except in so far as the contrary is shown, to be a payment to which this section applies.

219. Payment in connection with share transfer: requirement of members' approval

(1) No payment for loss of office may be made by any person to a director of a company in connection with a transfer of shares in the company, or in a subsidiary of the company, resulting from a takeover bid unless the payment has been approved by a resolution of the relevant shareholders.

(2) The relevant shareholders are the holders of the shares to which the bid relates and any holders of shares of the same class as any of those shares.

(3) A resolution approving a payment to which this section applies must not be passed unless a memorandum setting out particulars of the proposed payment (including its amount) is made available to the members of the company whose approval is sought—

    (a) in the case of a written resolution, by being sent or submitted to every eligible member at or before the time at which the proposed resolution is sent or submitted to him;

    (b) in the case of a resolution at a meeting, by being made available for inspection by the members both—

        (i) at the company's registered office for not less than 15 days ending with the date of the meeting, and

        (ii) at the meeting itself.

(4) Neither the person making the offer, nor any associate of his (as defined in section 988), is entitled to vote on the resolution, but—

    (a) where the resolution is proposed as a written resolution, they are entitled (if they would otherwise be so entitled) to be sent a copy of it, and

    (b) at any meeting to consider the resolution they are entitled (if they would otherwise be so entitled) to be given notice of the meeting, to attend and speak and if present (in person or by proxy) to count towards the quorum.

(5) If at a meeting to consider the resolution a quorum is not present, and after the meeting has been adjourned to a later date a quorum is again not present, the payment is (for the purposes of this section) deemed to have been approved.

(6) No approval is required under this section on the part of shareholders in a body corporate that—

    (a) is not a UK-registered company, or

    (b) is a wholly-owned subsidiary of another body corporate.

(7) A payment made in pursuance of an arrangement—

    (a) entered into as part of the agreement for the transfer in question, or within one year before or two years after that agreement, and

    (b) to which the company whose shares are the subject of the bid, or any person to whom the transfer is made, is privy,

is presumed, except in so far as the contrary is shown, to be a payment to which this section applies.

220. Exception for payments in discharge of legal obligations etc

(1) Approval is not required under section 217, 218 or 219 (payments requiring members' approval) for a payment made in good faith—

    (a) in discharge of an existing legal obligation (as defined below),

    (b) by way of damages for breach of such an obligation,

    (c) by way of settlement or compromise of any claim arising in connection with the termination of a person's office or employment, or

    (d) by way of pension in respect of past services.

(2) In relation to a payment within section 217 (payment by company) an existing legal obligation means an obligation of the company, or any body corporate associated with it, that was not entered into in connection with, or in consequence of, the event giving rise to the payment for loss of office.

(3) In relation to a payment within section 218 or 219 (payment in connection with transfer of undertaking, property or shares) an existing legal obligation means an obligation of the person making the payment that was not entered into for the purposes of, in connection with or in consequence of, the transfer in question.

(4) In the case of a payment within both section 217 and section 218, or within both section 217 and section 219, subsection (2) above applies and not subsection (3).

(5) A payment part of which falls within subsection (1) above and part of which does not is treated as if the parts were separate payments.

221. **Exception for small payments**

(1) Approval is not required under section 217, 218 or 219 (payments requiring members' approval) if—

(a) the payment in question is made by the company or any of its subsidiaries, and

(b) the amount or value of the payment, together with the amount or value of any other relevant payments, does not exceed £200.

(2) For this purpose "other relevant payments" are payments for loss of office in relation to which the following conditions are met.

(3) Where the payment in question is one to which section 217 (payment by company) applies, the conditions are that the other payment was or is paid—

(a) by the company making the payment in question or any of its subsidiaries,

(b) to the director to whom that payment is made, and

(c) in connection with the same event.

(4) Where the payment in question is one to which section 218 or 219 applies (payment in connection with transfer of undertaking, property or shares), the conditions are that the other payment was (or is) paid in connection with the same transfer—

(a) to the director to whom the payment in question was made, and

(b) by the company making the payment or any of its subsidiaries.

222. **Payments made without approval: civil consequences**

(1) If a payment is made in contravention of section 217 (payment by company)—

(a) it is held by the recipient on trust for the company making the payment, and

(b) any director who authorised the payment is jointly and severally liable to indemnify the company that made the payment for any loss resulting from it.

(2) If a payment is made in contravention of section 218 (payment in connection with transfer of undertaking etc), it is held by the recipient on trust for the company whose undertaking or property is or is proposed to be transferred.

(3) If a payment is made in contravention of section 219 (payment in connection with share transfer)—

(a) it is held by the recipient on trust for persons who have sold their shares as a result of the offer made, and

(b) the expenses incurred by the recipient in distributing that sum amongst those persons shall be borne by him and not retained out of that sum.

(4) If a payment is in contravention of section 217 and section 218, subsection (2) of this section applies rather than subsection (1).

(5) If a payment is in contravention of section 217 and section 219, subsection (3) of this section applies rather than subsection (1), unless the court directs otherwise.

Supplementary

223. **Transactions requiring members' approval: application of provisions to shadow directors**

(1) For the purposes of—

(a) sections 188 and 189 (directors' service contracts),

(b) sections 190 to 196 (property transactions),

(c) sections 197 to 214 (loans etc), and

(d) sections 215 to 222 (payments for loss of office),

a shadow director is treated as a director.

(2) Any reference in those provisions to loss of office as a director does not apply in relation to loss of a person's status as a shadow director.

224. **Approval by written resolution: accidental failure to send memorandum**

(1) Where—

(a) approval under this Chapter is sought by written resolution, and

(b) a memorandum is required under this Chapter to be sent or submitted to every eligible member before the resolution is passed, any accidental failure to send or submit the memorandum to one or more members shall be disregarded for the purpose of determining whether the requirement has been met.

(2) Subsection (1) has effect subject to any provision of the company's articles.

225. **Cases where approval is required under more than one provision**

(1) Approval may be required under more than one provision of this Chapter.

(2) If so, the requirements of each applicable provision must be met.

(3) This does not require a separate resolution for the purposes of each provision.

226. **Requirement of consent of Charity Commission: companies that are charities**

For section 66 of the Charities Act 1993 (c. 10) substitute—

"66 **Consent of Commission required for approval etc by members of charitable companies**

(1) Where a company is a charity—

(a) any approval given by the members of the company under any provision of Chapter 4 of Part 10 of the Companies Act 2006 (transactions with directors requiring approval by members) listed in subsection (2) below, and

(b) any affirmation given by members of the company under section 196 or 214 of that Act (affirmation of unapproved property transactions and loans),

is ineffective without the prior written consent of the Commission.

(2) The provisions are—

(a) section 188 (directors' long-term service contracts);

(b) section 190 (substantial property transactions with directors etc);

(c) section 197, 198 or 200 (loans and quasi-loans to directors etc);

(d) section 201 (credit transactions for benefit of directors etc);

(e) section 203 (related arrangements);

(f) section 217 (payments to directors for loss of office);

(g) section 218 (payments to directors for loss of office: transfer of undertaking etc).

66A **Consent of Commission required for certain acts of charitable company**

(1) A company that is a charity may not do an act to which this section applies without the prior written consent of the Commission.

(2) This section applies to an act that—

(a) does not require approval under a listed provision of Chapter 4 of Part 10 of the Companies Act 2006 (transactions with directors) by the members of the company, but

(b) would require such approval but for an exemption in the provision in question that disapplies the need for approval on the part of the members of a body corporate which is a wholly-owned subsidiary of another body corporate.

(3) The reference to a listed provision is a reference to a provision listed in section 66(2) above.

(4) If a company acts in contravention of this section, the exemption referred to in subsection (2)(b) shall be treated as of no effect in relation to the act.".

CHAPTER 5
DIRECTORS' SERVICE CONTRACTS

227. **Directors' service contracts**

(1) For the purposes of this Part a director's "service contract", in relation to a company, means a contract under which—

(a) a director of the company undertakes personally to perform services (as director or otherwise) for the company, or for a subsidiary of the company, or

    (b) services (as director or otherwise) that a director of the company undertakes personally to perform are made available by a third party to the company, or to a subsidiary of the company.

(2) The provisions of this Part relating to directors' service contracts apply to the terms of a person's appointment as a director of a company.

They are not restricted to contracts for the performance of services outside the scope of the ordinary duties of a director.

228. Copy of contract or memorandum of terms to be available for inspection

(1) A company must keep available for inspection—

    (a) a copy of every director's service contract with the company or with a subsidiary of the company, or

    (b) if the contract is not in writing, a written memorandum setting out the terms of the contract.

(2) All the copies and memoranda must be kept available for inspection at—

    (a) the company's registered office, or

    (b) a place specified in regulations under section 1136.

(3) The copies and memoranda must be retained by the company for at least one year from the date of termination or expiry of the contract and must be kept available for inspection during that time.

(4) The company must give notice to the registrar—

    (a) of the place at which the copies and memoranda are kept available for inspection, and

    (b) of any change in that place,

unless they have at all times been kept at the company's registered office.

(5) If default is made in complying with subsection (1), (2) or (3), or default is made for 14 days in complying with subsection (4), an offence is committed by every officer of the company who is in default.

(6) A person guilty of an offence under this section is liable on summary conviction to a fine not exceeding level 3 on the standard scale and, for continued contravention, a daily default fine not exceeding one-tenth of level 3 on the standard scale.

(7) The provisions of this section apply to a variation of a director's service contract as they apply to the original contract.

229. Right of member to inspect and request copy

(1) Every copy or memorandum required to be kept under section 228 must be open to inspection by any member of the company without charge.

(2) Any member of the company is entitled, on request and on payment of such fee as may be prescribed, to be provided with a copy of any such copy or memorandum.

The copy must be provided within seven days after the request is received by the company.

(3) If an inspection required under subsection (1) is refused, or default is made in complying with subsection (2), an offence is committed by every officer of the company who is in default.

(4) A person guilty of an offence under this section is liable on summary conviction to a fine not exceeding level 3 on the standard scale and, for continued contravention, a daily default fine not exceeding one-tenth of level 3 on the standard scale.

(5) In the case of any such refusal or default the court may by order compel an immediate inspection or, as the case may be, direct that the copy required be sent to the person requiring it.

230. Directors' service contracts: application of provisions to shadow directors

A shadow director is treated as a director for the purposes of the provisions of this Chapter.

CHAPTER 6
CONTRACTS WITH SOLE MEMBERS WHO ARE DIRECTORS

231. Contract with sole member who is also a director

(1) This section applies where—

(a) a limited company having only one member enters into a contract with the sole member,

(b) the sole member is also a director of the company, and

(c) the contract is not entered into in the ordinary course of the company's business.

(2) The company must, unless the contract is in writing, ensure that the terms of the contract are either—

(a) set out in a written memorandum, or

(b) recorded in the minutes of the first meeting of the directors of the company following the making of the contract.

(3) If a company fails to comply with this section an offence is committed by every officer of the company who is in default.

(4) A person guilty of an offence under this section is liable on summary conviction to a fine not exceeding level 5 on the standard scale.

(5) For the purposes of this section a shadow director is treated as a director.

(6) Failure to comply with this section in relation to a contract does not affect the validity of the contract.

(7) Nothing in this section shall be read as excluding the operation of any other enactment or rule of law applying to contracts between a company and a director of the company.

CHAPTER 7
DIRECTORS' LIABILITIES

Provision protecting directors from liability

232. Provisions protecting directors from liability

(1) Any provision that purports to exempt a director of a company (to any extent) from any liability that would otherwise attach to him in connection with any negligence, default, breach of duty or breach of trust in relation to the company is void.

(2) Any provision by which a company directly or indirectly provides an indemnity (to any extent) for a director of the company, or of an associated company, against any liability attaching to him in connection with any negligence, default, breach of duty or breach of trust in relation to the company of which he is a director is void, except as permitted by—

(a) section 233 (provision of insurance),

(b) section 234 (qualifying third party indemnity provision), or

(c) section 235 (qualifying pension scheme indemnity provision).

(3) This section applies to any provision, whether contained in a company's articles or in any contract with the company or otherwise.

(4) Nothing in this section prevents a company's articles from making such provision as has previously been lawful for dealing with conflicts of interest.

233. Provision of insurance

Section 232(2) (voidness of provisions for indemnifying directors) does not prevent a company from purchasing and maintaining for a director of the company, or of an associated company, insurance against any such liability as is mentioned in that subsection.

234. Qualifying third party indemnity provision

(1) Section 232(2) (voidness of provisions for indemnifying directors) does not apply to qualifying third party indemnity provision.

(2) Third party indemnity provision means provision for indemnity against liability incurred by the director to a person other than the company or an associated company.

Such provision is qualifying third party indemnity provision if the following requirements are met.

(3) The provision must not provide any indemnity against—

    (a) any liability of the director to pay—

        (i) a fine imposed in criminal proceedings, or

        (ii) a sum payable to a regulatory authority by way of a penalty in respect of non-compliance with any requirement of a regulatory nature (however arising); or

    (b) any liability incurred by the director—

        (i) in defending criminal proceedings in which he is convicted, or

        (ii) in defending civil proceedings brought by the company, or an associated company, in which judgment is given against him, or

        (iii) in connection with an application for relief (see subsection (6)) in which the court refuses to grant him relief.

(4) The references in subsection (3)(b) to a conviction, judgment or refusal of relief are to the final decision in the proceedings.

(5) For this purpose—

    (a) a conviction, judgment or refusal of relief becomes final—

        (i) if not appealed against, at the end of the period for bringing an appeal, or

        (ii) if appealed against, at the time when the appeal (or any further appeal) is disposed of; and

    (b) an appeal is disposed of—

        (i) if it is determined and the period for bringing any further appeal has ended, or

        (ii) if it is abandoned or otherwise ceases to have effect.

(6) The reference in subsection (3)(b)(iii) to an application for relief is to an application for relief under—

section 661(3) or (4) (power of court to grant relief in case of acquisition of shares by innocent nominee), or

section 1157 (general power of court to grant relief in case of honest and reasonable conduct).

235. Qualifying pension scheme indemnity provision

(1) Section 232(2) (voidness of provisions for indemnifying directors) does not apply to qualifying pension scheme indemnity provision.

(2) Pension scheme indemnity provision means provision indemnifying a director of a company that is a trustee of an occupational pension scheme against liability incurred in connection with the company's activities as trustee of the scheme.

Such provision is qualifying pension scheme indemnity provision if the following requirements are met.

(3) The provision must not provide any indemnity against—

    (a) any liability of the director to pay—

        (i) a fine imposed in criminal proceedings, or

        (ii) a sum payable to a regulatory authority by way of a penalty in respect of non-compliance with any requirement of a regulatory nature (however arising); or

    (b) any liability incurred by the director in defending criminal proceedings in which he is convicted.

(4) The reference in subsection (3)(b) to a conviction is to the final decision in the proceedings.

(5) For this purpose—

    (a) a conviction becomes final—

        (i) if not appealed against, at the end of the period for bringing an appeal, or

        (ii) if appealed against, at the time when the appeal (or any further appeal) is disposed of; and

(b) an appeal is disposed of—

    (i) if it is determined and the period for bringing any further appeal has ended, or

    (ii) if it is abandoned or otherwise ceases to have effect.

(6) In this section "occupational pension scheme" means an occupational pension scheme as defined in section 150(5) of the Finance Act 2004 (c. 12) that is established under a trust.

236. Qualifying indemnity provision to be disclosed in directors' report

(1) This section requires disclosure in the directors' report of—

    (a) qualifying third party indemnity provision, and

    (b) qualifying pension scheme indemnity provision.

Such provision is referred to in this section as "qualifying indemnity provision".

(2) If when a directors' report is approved any qualifying indemnity provision (whether made by the company or otherwise) is in force for the benefit of one or more directors of the company, the report must state that such provision is in force.

(3) If at any time during the financial year to which a directors' report relates any such provision was in force for the benefit of one or more persons who were then directors of the company, the report must state that such provision was in force.

(4) If when a directors' report is approved qualifying indemnity provision made by the company is in force for the benefit of one or more directors of an associated company, the report must state that such provision is in force.

(5) If at any time during the financial year to which a directors' report relates any such provision was in force for the benefit of one or more persons who were then directors of an associated company, the report must state that such provision was in force.

237. Copy of qualifying indemnity provision to be available for inspection

(1) This section has effect where qualifying indemnity provision is made for a director of a company, and applies—

    (a) to the company of which he is a director (whether the provision is made by that company or an associated company), and

    (b) where the provision is made by an associated company, to that company.

(2) That company or, as the case may be, each of them must keep available for inspection—

    (a) a copy of the qualifying indemnity provision, or

    (b) if the provision is not in writing, a written memorandum setting out its terms.

(3) The copy or memorandum must be kept available for inspection at—

    (a) the company's registered office, or

    (b) a place specified in regulations under section 1136.

(4) The copy or memorandum must be retained by the company for at least one year from the date of termination or expiry of the provision and must be kept available for inspection during that time.

(5) The company must give notice to the registrar—

    (a) of the place at which the copy or memorandum is kept available for inspection, and

    (b) of any change in that place,

unless it has at all times been kept at the company's registered office.

(6) If default is made in complying with subsection (2), (3) or (4), or default is made for 14 days in complying with subsection (5), an offence is committed by every officer of the company who is in default.

(7) A person guilty of an offence under this section is liable on summary conviction to a fine not exceeding level 3 on the standard scale and, for continued contravention, a daily default fine not exceeding one-tenth of level 3 on the standard scale.

(8) The provisions of this section apply to a variation of a qualifying indemnity provision as they apply to the original provision.

(9) In this section "qualifying indemnity provision" means—
    (a) qualifying third party indemnity provision, and
    (b) qualifying pension scheme indemnity provision.

238. Right of member to inspect and request copy

(1) Every copy or memorandum required to be kept by a company under section 237 must be open to inspection by any member of the company without charge.

(2) Any member of the company is entitled, on request and on payment of such fee as may be prescribed, to be provided with a copy of any such copy or memorandum.
The copy must be provided within seven days after the request is received by the company.

(3) If an inspection required under subsection (1) is refused, or default is made in complying with subsection (2), an offence is committed by every officer of the company who is in default.

(4) A person guilty of an offence under this section is liable on summary conviction to a fine not exceeding level 3 on the standard scale and, for continued contravention, a daily default fine not exceeding one-tenth of level 3 on the standard scale.

(5) In the case of any such refusal or default the court may by order compel an immediate inspection or, as the case may be, direct that the copy required be sent to the person requiring it.

Ratification of acts giving rise to liability

239. Ratification of acts of directors

(1) This section applies to the ratification by a company of conduct by a director amounting to negligence, default, breach of duty or breach of trust in relation to the company.

(2) The decision of the company to ratify such conduct must be made by resolution of the members of the company.

(3) Where the resolution is proposed as a written resolution neither the director (if a member of the company) nor any member connected with him is an eligible member.

(4) Where the resolution is proposed at a meeting, it is passed only if the necessary majority is obtained disregarding votes in favour of the resolution by the director (if a member of the company) and any member connected with him.
This does not prevent the director or any such member from attending, being counted towards the quorum and taking part in the proceedings at any meeting at which the decision is considered.

(5) For the purposes of this section—
    (a) "conduct" includes acts and omissions;
    (b) "director" includes a former director;
    (c) a shadow director is treated as a director; and
    (d) in section 252 (meaning of "connected person"), subsection (3) does not apply (exclusion of person who is himself a director).

(6) Nothing in this section affects—
    (a) the validity of a decision taken by unanimous consent of the members of the company, or
    (b) any power of the directors to agree not to sue, or to settle or release a claim made by them on behalf of the company.

(7) This section does not affect any other enactment or rule of law imposing additional requirements for valid ratification or any rule of law as to acts that are incapable of being ratified by the company.

CHAPTER 8
DIRECTORS' RESIDENTIAL ADDRESSES: PROTECTION FROM DISCLOSURE

240. Protected information

(1) This Chapter makes provision for protecting, in the case of a company director who is an individual—

    (a) information as to his usual residential address;

    (b) the information that his service address is his usual residential address.

(2) That information is referred to in this Chapter as "protected information".

(3) Information does not cease to be protected information on the individual ceasing to be a director of the company.

References in this Chapter to a director include, to that extent, a former director.

241. Protected information: restriction on use or disclosure by company

(1) A company must not use or disclose protected information about any of its directors, except—

    (a) for communicating with the director concerned,

    (b) in order to comply with any requirement of the Companies Acts as to particulars to be sent to the registrar, or

    (c) in accordance with section 244 (disclosure under court order).

(2) Subsection (1) does not prohibit any use or disclosure of protected information with the consent of the director concerned.

242. Protected information: restriction on use or disclosure by registrar

(1) The registrar must omit protected information from the material on the register that is available for inspection where—

    (a) it is contained in a document delivered to him in which such information is required to be stated, and

    (b) in the case of a document having more than one part, it is contained in a part of the document in which such information is required to be stated.

(2) The registrar is not obliged—

    (a) to check other documents or (as the case may be) other parts of the document to ensure the absence of protected information, or

    (b) to omit from the material that is available for public inspection anything registered before this Chapter comes into force.

(3) The registrar must not use or disclose protected information except—

    (a) as permitted by section 243 (permitted use or disclosure by registrar), or

    (b) in accordance with section 244 (disclosure under court order).

243. Permitted use or disclosure by the registrar

(1) The registrar may use protected information for communicating with the director in question.

(2) The registrar may disclose protected information—

    (a) to a public authority specified for the purposes of this section by regulations made by the Secretary of State, or

    (b) to a credit reference agency.

(3) The Secretary of State may make provision by regulations—

    (a) specifying conditions for the disclosure of protected information in accordance with this section, and

    (b) providing for the charging of fees.

(4) The Secretary of State may make provision by regulations requiring the registrar, on application, to refrain from disclosing protected information relating to a director to a credit reference agency.

(5) Regulations under subsection (4) may make provision as to—

    (a) who may make an application,

    (b) the grounds on which an application may be made,

(c) the information to be included in and documents to accompany an application, and

(d) how an application is to be determined.

(6) Provision under subsection (5)(d) may in particular—

(a) confer a discretion on the registrar;

(b) provide for a question to be referred to a person other than the registrar for the purposes of determining the application.

(7) In this section—

"credit reference agency" means a person carrying on a business comprising the furnishing of information relevant to the financial standing of individuals, being information collected by the agency for that purpose; and

"public authority" includes any person or body having functions of a public nature.

(8) Regulations under this section are subject to negative resolution procedure.

244. **Disclosure under court order**

(1) The court may make an order for the disclosure of protected information by the company or by the registrar if—

(a) there is evidence that service of documents at a service address other than the director's usual residential address is not effective to bring them to the notice of the director, or

(b) it is necessary or expedient for the information to be provided in connection with the enforcement of an order or decree of the court,

and the court is otherwise satisfied that it is appropriate to make the order.

(2) An order for disclosure by the registrar is to be made only if the company—

(a) does not have the director's usual residential address, or

(b) has been dissolved.

(3) The order may be made on the application of a liquidator, creditor or member of the company, or any other person appearing to the court to have a sufficient interest.

(4) The order must specify the persons to whom, and purposes for which, disclosure is authorised.

245. **Circumstances in which registrar may put address on the public record**

(1) The registrar may put a director's usual residential address on the public record if—

(a) communications sent by the registrar to the director and requiring a response within a specified period remain unanswered, or

(b) there is evidence that service of documents at a service address provided in place of the director's usual residential address is not effective to bring them to the notice of the director.

(2) The registrar must give notice of the proposal—

(a) to the director, and

(b) to every company of which the registrar has been notified that the individual is a director.

(3) The notice must—

(a) state the grounds on which it is proposed to put the director's usual residential address on the public record, and

(b) specify a period within which representations may be made before that is done.

(4) It must be sent to the director at his usual residential address, unless it appears to the registrar that service at that address may be ineffective to bring it to the individual's notice, in which case it may be sent to any service address provided in place of that address.

(5) The registrar must take account of any representations received within the specified period.

(6) What is meant by putting the address on the public record is explained in section 246.

246. **Putting the address on the public record**

(1) The registrar, on deciding in accordance with section 245 that a director's usual residential address is to be put on the public record, shall proceed as if notice of a change of registered particulars had been given—

(a) stating that address as the director's service address, and

(b) stating that the director's usual residential address is the same as his service address.

(2) The registrar must give notice of having done so—
  (a) to the director, and
  (b) to the company.

(3) On receipt of the notice the company must—
  (a) enter the director's usual residential address in its register of directors as his service address, and
  (b) state in its register of directors' residential addresses that his usual residential address is the same as his service address.

(4) If the company has been notified by the director in question of a more recent address as his usual residential address, it must—
  (a) enter that address in its register of directors as the director's service address, and
  (b) give notice to the registrar as on a change of registered particulars.

(5) If a company fails to comply with subsection (3) or (4), an offence is committed by—
  (a) the company, and
  (b) every officer of the company who is in default.

(6) A person guilty of an offence under subsection (5) is liable on summary conviction to a fine not exceeding level 5 on the standard scale and, for continued contravention, a daily default fine not exceeding one-tenth of level 5 on the standard scale.

(7) A director whose usual residential address has been put on the public record by the registrar under this section may not register a service address other than his usual residential address for a period of five years from the date of the registrar's decision.

CHAPTER 9
SUPPLEMENTARY PROVISIONS

Provision for employees on cessation or transfer of business

247. Power to make provision for employees on cessation or transfer of business

(1) The powers of the directors of a company include (if they would not otherwise do so) power to make provision for the benefit of persons employed or formerly employed by the company, or any of its subsidiaries, in connection with the cessation or the transfer to any person of the whole or part of the undertaking of the company or that subsidiary.

(2) This power is exercisable notwithstanding the general duty imposed by section 172 (duty to promote the success of the company).

(3) In the case of a company that is a charity it is exercisable notwithstanding any restrictions on the directors' powers (or the company's capacity) flowing from the objects of the company.

(4) The power may only be exercised if sanctioned—
  (a) by a resolution of the company, or
  (b) by a resolution of the directors,
in accordance with the following provisions.

(5) A resolution of the directors—
  (a) must be authorised by the company's articles, and
  (b) is not sufficient sanction for payments to or for the benefit of directors, former directors or shadow directors.

(6) Any other requirements of the company's articles as to the exercise of the power conferred by this section must be complied with.

(7) Any payment under this section must be made—
  (a) before the commencement of any winding up of the company, and
  (b) out of profits of the company that are available for dividend.

Records of meetings of directors

248. Minutes of directors' meetings

(1) Every company must cause minutes of all proceedings at meetings of its directors to be recorded.

(2) The records must be kept for at least ten years from the date of the meeting.

(3) If a company fails to comply with this section, an offence is committed by every officer of the company who is in default.

(4) A person guilty of an offence under this section is liable on summary conviction to a fine not exceeding level 3 on the standard scale and, for continued contravention, a daily default fine not exceeding one-tenth of level 3 on the standard scale.

249. Minutes as evidence

(1) Minutes recorded in accordance with section 248, if purporting to be authenticated by the chairman of the meeting or by the chairman of the next directors' meeting, are evidence (in Scotland, sufficient evidence) of the proceedings at the meeting.

(2) Where minutes have been made in accordance with that section of the proceedings of a meeting of directors, then, until the contrary is proved—

(a) the meeting is deemed duly held and convened,

(b) all proceedings at the meeting are deemed to have duly taken place, and

(c) all appointments at the meeting are deemed valid.

Meaning of "director" and "shadow director"

250. "Director"

In the Companies Acts "director" includes any person occupying the position of director, by whatever name called.

251. "Shadow director"

(1) In the Companies Acts "shadow director", in relation to a company, means a person in accordance with whose directions or instructions the directors of the company are accustomed to act.

(2) A person is not to be regarded as a shadow director by reason only that the directors act on advice given by him in a professional capacity.

(3) A body corporate is not to be regarded as a shadow director of any of its subsidiary companies for the purposes of—

Chapter 2 (general duties of directors),

Chapter 4 (transactions requiring members' approval), or

Chapter 6 (contract with sole member who is also a director),

by reason only that the directors of the subsidiary are accustomed to act in accordance with its directions or instructions.

Other definitions

252. Persons connected with a director

(1) This section defines what is meant by references in this Part to a person being "connected" with a director of a company (or a director being "connected" with a person).

(2) The following persons (and only those persons) are connected with a director of a company—

(a) members of the director's family (see section 253);

(b) a body corporate with which the director is connected (as defined in section 254);

(c) a person acting in his capacity as trustee of a trust—

(i) the beneficiaries of which include the director or a person who by virtue of paragraph (a) or (b) is connected with him, or

(ii) the terms of which confer a power on the trustees that may be exercised for the benefit of the director or any such person,

other than a trust for the purposes of an employees' share scheme or a pension scheme;

(d) a person acting in his capacity as partner—
  (i) of the director, or
  (ii) of a person who, by virtue of paragraph (a), (b) or (c), is connected with that director;

(e) a firm that is a legal person under the law by which it is governed and in which—
  (i) the director is a partner,
  (ii) a partner is a person who, by virtue of paragraph (a), (b) or (c) is connected with the director, or
  (iii) a partner is a firm in which the director is a partner or in which there is a partner who, by virtue of paragraph (a), (b) or (c), is connected with the director.

(3) References in this Part to a person connected with a director of a company do not include a person who is himself a director of the company.

253. Members of a director's family

(1) This section defines what is meant by references in this Part to members of a director's family.

(2) For the purposes of this Part the members of a director's family are—
(a) the director's spouse or civil partner;
(b) any other person (whether of a different sex or the same sex) with whom the director lives as partner in an enduring family relationship;
(c) the director's children or step-children;
(d) any children or step-children of a person within paragraph (b) (and who are not children or step-children of the director) who live with the director and have not attained the age of 18;
(e) the director's parents.

(3) Subsection (2)(b) does not apply if the other person is the director's grandparent or grandchild, sister, brother, aunt or uncle, or nephew or niece.

254. Director "connected with" a body corporate

(1) This section defines what is meant by references in this Part to a director being "connected with" a body corporate.

(2) A director is connected with a body corporate if, but only if, he and the persons connected with him together—
(a) are interested in shares comprised in the equity share capital of that body corporate of a nominal value equal to at least 20% of that share capital, or
(b) are entitled to exercise or control the exercise of more than 20% of the voting power at any general meeting of that body.

(3) The rules set out in Schedule 1 (references to interest in shares or debentures) apply for the purposes of this section.

(4) References in this section to voting power the exercise of which is controlled by a director include voting power whose exercise is controlled by a body corporate controlled by him.

(5) Shares in a company held as treasury shares, and any voting rights attached to such shares, are disregarded for the purposes of this section.

(6) For the avoidance of circularity in the application of section 252 (meaning of "connected person") —
(a) a body corporate with which a director is connected is not treated for the purposes of this section as connected with him unless it is also connected with him by virtue of subsection (2)(c) or (d) of that section (connection as trustee or partner); and
(b) a trustee of a trust the beneficiaries of which include (or may include) a body corporate with which a director is connected is not treated for the purposes of this section as connected with a director by reason only of that fact.

255. **Director "controlling" a body corporate**

(1) This section defines what is meant by references in this Part to a director "controlling" a body corporate.

(2) A director of a company is taken to control a body corporate if, but only if—

    (a) he or any person connected with him—

        (i) is interested in any part of the equity share capital of that body, or

        (ii) is entitled to exercise or control the exercise of any part of the voting power at any general meeting of that body, and

    (b) he, the persons connected with him and the other directors of that company, together—

        (i) are interested in more than 50% of that share capital, or

        (ii) are entitled to exercise or control the exercise of more than 50% of that voting power.

(3) The rules set out in Schedule 1 (references to interest in shares or debentures) apply for the purposes of this section.

(4) References in this section to voting power the exercise of which is controlled by a director include voting power whose exercise is controlled by a body corporate controlled by him.

(5) Shares in a company held as treasury shares, and any voting rights attached to such shares, are disregarded for the purposes of this section.

(6) For the avoidance of circularity in the application of section 252 (meaning of "connected person")—

    (a) a body corporate with which a director is connected is not treated for the purposes of this section as connected with him unless it is also connected with him by virtue of subsection (2)(c) or (d) of that section (connection as trustee or partner); and

    (b) a trustee of a trust the beneficiaries of which include (or may include) a body corporate with which a director is connected is not treated for the purposes of this section as connected with a director by reason only of that fact.

256. **Associated bodies corporate**

For the purposes of this Part—

(a) bodies corporate are associated if one is a subsidiary of the other or both are subsidiaries of the same body corporate, and

(b) companies are associated if one is a subsidiary of the other or both are subsidiaries of the same body corporate.

257. **References to company's constitution**

(1) References in this Part to a company's constitution include—

    (a) any resolution or other decision come to in accordance with the constitution, and

    (b) any decision by the members of the company, or a class of members, that is treated by virtue of any enactment or rule of law as equivalent to a decision by the company.

(2) This is in addition to the matters mentioned in section 17 (general provision as to matters contained in company's constitution).

General

258. **Power to increase financial limits**

(1) The Secretary of State may by order substitute for any sum of money specified in this Part a larger sum specified in the order.

(2) An order under this section is subject to negative resolution procedure.

(3) An order does not have effect in relation to anything done or not done before it comes into force.

Accordingly, proceedings in respect of any liability incurred before that time may be continued or instituted as if the order had not been made.

259. Transactions under foreign law

For the purposes of this Part it is immaterial whether the law that (apart from this Act) governs an arrangement or transaction is the law of the United Kingdom, or a part of it, or not.

PART 11
DERIVATIVE CLAIMS AND PROCEEDINGS BY MEMBERS

CHAPTER 1
DERIVATIVE CLAIMS IN ENGLAND AND WALES OR NORTHERN IRELAND

260. Derivative claims

(1) This Chapter applies to proceedings in England and Wales or Northern Ireland by a member of a company—
  (a) in respect of a cause of action vested in the company, and
  (b) seeking relief on behalf of the company.
  This is referred to in this Chapter as a "derivative claim".

(2) A derivative claim may only be brought—
  (a) under this Chapter, or
  (b) in pursuance of an order of the court in proceedings under section 994 (proceedings for protection of members against unfair prejudice).

(3) A derivative claim under this Chapter may be brought only in respect of a cause of action arising from an actual or proposed act or omission involving negligence, default, breach of duty or breach of trust by a director of the company.
  The cause of action may be against the director or another person (or both).

(4) It is immaterial whether the cause of action arose before or after the person seeking to bring or continue the derivative claim became a member of the company.

(5) For the purposes of this Chapter—
  (a) "director" includes a former director;
  (b) a shadow director is treated as a director; and
  (c) references to a member of a company include a person who is not a member but to whom shares in the company have been transferred or transmitted by operation of law.

261. Application for permission to continue derivative claim

(1) A member of a company who brings a derivative claim under this Chapter must apply to the court for permission (in Northern Ireland, leave) to continue it.

(2) If it appears to the court that the application and the evidence filed by the applicant in support of it do not disclose a prima facie case for giving permission (or leave), the court—
  (a) must dismiss the application, and
  (b) may make any consequential order it considers appropriate.

(3) If the application is not dismissed under subsection (2), the court—
  (a) may give directions as to the evidence to be provided by the company, and
  (b) may adjourn the proceedings to enable the evidence to be obtained.

(4) On hearing the application, the court may—
  (a) give permission (or leave) to continue the claim on such terms as it thinks fit,
  (b) refuse permission (or leave) and dismiss the claim, or
  (c) adjourn the proceedings on the application and give such directions as it thinks fit.

262. Application for permission to continue claim as a derivative claim

(1) This section applies where—
  (a) a company has brought a claim, and
  (b) the cause of action on which the claim is based could be pursued as a derivative claim under this Chapter.

(2) A member of the company may apply to the court for permission (in Northern Ireland, leave) to continue the claim as a derivative claim on the ground that—

    (a) the manner in which the company commenced or continued the claim amounts to an abuse of the process of the court,

    (b) the company has failed to prosecute the claim diligently, and

    (c) it is appropriate for the member to continue the claim as a derivative claim.

(3) If it appears to the court that the application and the evidence filed by the applicant in support of it do not disclose a prima facie case for giving permission (or leave), the court—

    (a) must dismiss the application, and

    (b) may make any consequential order it considers appropriate.

(4) If the application is not dismissed under subsection (3), the court—

    (a) may give directions as to the evidence to be provided by the company, and

    (b) may adjourn the proceedings to enable the evidence to be obtained.

(5) On hearing the application, the court may—

    (a) give permission (or leave) to continue the claim as a derivative claim on such terms as it thinks fit,

    (b) refuse permission (or leave) and dismiss the application, or

    (c) adjourn the proceedings on the application and give such directions as it thinks fit.

263. Whether permission to be given

(1) The following provisions have effect where a member of a company applies for permission (in Northern Ireland, leave) under section 261 or 262.

(2) Permission (or leave) must be refused if the court is satisfied—

    (a) that a person acting in accordance with section 172 (duty to promote the success of the company) would not seek to continue the claim, or

    (b) where the cause of action arises from an act or omission that is yet to occur, that the act or omission has been authorised by the company, or

    (c) where the cause of action arises from an act or omission that has already occurred, that the act or omission—

        (i) was authorised by the company before it occurred, or

        (ii) has been ratified by the company since it occurred.

(3) In considering whether to give permission (or leave) the court must take into account, in particular—

    (a) whether the member is acting in good faith in seeking to continue the claim;

    (b) the importance that a person acting in accordance with section 172 (duty to promote the success of the company) would attach to continuing it;

    (c) where the cause of action results from an act or omission that is yet to occur, whether the act or omission could be, and in the circumstances would be likely to be—

        (i) authorised by the company before it occurs, or

        (ii) ratified by the company after it occurs;

    (d) where the cause of action arises from an act or omission that has already occurred, whether the act or omission could be, and in the circumstances would be likely to be, ratified by the company;

    (e) whether the company has decided not to pursue the claim;

    (f) whether the act or omission in respect of which the claim is brought gives rise to a cause of action that the member could pursue in his own right rather than on behalf of the company.

(4) In considering whether to give permission (or leave) the court shall have particular regard to any evidence before it as to the views of members of the company who have no personal interest, direct or indirect, in the matter.

(5) The Secretary of State may by regulations—

(a) amend subsection (2) so as to alter or add to the circumstances in which permission (or leave) is to be refused;

(b) amend subsection (3) so as to alter or add to the matters that the court is required to take into account in considering whether to give permission (or leave).

(6) Before making any such regulations the Secretary of State shall consult such persons as he considers appropriate.

(7) Regulations under this section are subject to affirmative resolution procedure.

264. **Application for permission to continue derivative claim brought by another member**

(1) This section applies where a member of a company ("the claimant")—

(a) has brought a derivative claim,

(b) has continued as a derivative claim a claim brought by the company, or

(c) has continued a derivative claim under this section.

(2) Another member of the company ("the applicant") may apply to the court for permission (in Northern Ireland, leave) to continue the claim on the ground that—

(a) the manner in which the proceedings have been commenced or continued by the claimant amounts to an abuse of the process of the court,

(b) the claimant has failed to prosecute the claim diligently, and

(c) it is appropriate for the applicant to continue the claim as a derivative claim.

(3) If it appears to the court that the application and the evidence filed by the applicant in support of it do not disclose a prima facie case for giving permission (or leave), the court—

(a) must dismiss the application, and

(b) may make any consequential order it considers appropriate.

(4) If the application is not dismissed under subsection (3), the court—

(a) may give directions as to the evidence to be provided by the company, and

(b) may adjourn the proceedings to enable the evidence to be obtained.

(5) On hearing the application, the court may—

(a) give permission (or leave) to continue the claim on such terms as it thinks fit,

(b) refuse permission (or leave) and dismiss the application, or

(c) adjourn the proceedings on the application and give such directions as it thinks fit.

CHAPTER 2
DERIVATIVE PROCEEDINGS IN SCOTLAND

265. **Derivative proceedings**

(1) In Scotland, a member of a company may raise proceedings in respect of an act or omission specified in subsection (3) in order to protect the interests of the company and obtain a remedy on its behalf.

(2) A member of a company may raise such proceedings only under subsection (1).

(3) The act or omission referred to in subsection (1) is any actual or proposed act or omission involving negligence, default, breach of duty or breach of trust by a director of the company.

(4) Proceedings may be raised under subsection (1) against (either or both)—

(a) the director referred to in subsection (3), or

(b) another person.

(5) It is immaterial whether the act or omission in respect of which the proceedings are to be raised or, in the case of continuing proceedings under section 267 or 269, are raised, arose before or after the person seeking to raise or continue them became a member of the company.

(6) This section does not affect—

(a) any right of a member of a company to raise proceedings in respect of an act or omission specified in subsection (3) in order to protect his own interests and obtain a remedy on his own behalf, or

(b) the court's power to make an order under section 996 (2)(c) or anything done under such an order.

(7) In this Chapter—

    (a) proceedings raised under subsection (1) are referred to as "derivative proceedings",

    (b) the act or omission in respect of which they are raised is referred to as the "cause of action",

    (c) "director" includes a former director,

    (d) references to a director include a shadow director, and

    (e) references to a member of a company include a person who is not a member but to whom shares in the company have been transferred or transmitted by operation of law.

266. Requirement for leave and notice

(1) Derivative proceedings may be raised by a member of a company only with the leave of the court.

(2) An application for leave must—

    (a) specify the cause of action, and

    (b) summarise the facts on which the derivative proceedings are to be based.

(3) If it appears to the court that the application and the evidence produced by the applicant in support of it do not disclose a prima facie case for granting it, the court—

    (a) must refuse the application, and

    (b) may make any consequential order it considers appropriate.

(4) If the application is not refused under subsection (3)—

    (a) the applicant must serve the application on the company,

    (b) the court—

        (i) may make an order requiring evidence to be produced by the company, and

        (ii) may adjourn the proceedings on the application to enable the evidence to be obtained, and

    (c) the company is entitled to take part in the further proceedings on the application.

(5) On hearing the application, the court may—

    (a) grant the application on such terms as it thinks fit,

    (b) refuse the application, or

    (c) adjourn the proceedings on the application and make such order as to further procedure as it thinks fit.

267. Application to continue proceedings as derivative proceedings

(1) This section applies where—

    (a) a company has raised proceedings, and

    (b) the proceedings are in respect of an act or omission which could be the basis for derivative proceedings.

(2) A member of the company may apply to the court to be substituted for the company in the proceedings, and for the proceedings to continue in consequence as derivative proceedings, on the ground that—

    (a) the manner in which the company commenced or continued the proceedings amounts to an abuse of the process of the court,

    (b) the company has failed to prosecute the proceedings diligently, and

    (c) it is appropriate for the member to be substituted for the company in the proceedings.

(3) If it appears to the court that the application and the evidence produced by the applicant in support of it do not disclose a prima facie case for granting it, the court—

    (a) must refuse the application, and

    (b) may make any consequential order it considers appropriate.

(4) If the application is not refused under subsection (3)—

    (a) the applicant must serve the application on the company,

    (b) the court—

        (i) may make an order requiring evidence to be produced by the company, and

(ii) may adjourn the proceedings on the application to enable the evidence to be obtained, and

(c) the company is entitled to take part in the further proceedings on the application.

(5) On hearing the application, the court may—

(a) grant the application on such terms as it thinks fit,

(b) refuse the application, or

(c) adjourn the proceedings on the application and make such order as to further procedure as it thinks fit.

268. Granting of leave

(1) The court must refuse leave to raise derivative proceedings or an application under section 267 if satisfied—

(a) that a person acting in accordance with section 172 (duty to promote the success of the company) would not seek to raise or continue the proceedings (as the case may be), or

(b) where the cause of action is an act or omission that is yet to occur, that the act or omission has been authorised by the company, or

(c) where the cause of action is an act or omission that has already occurred, that the act or omission—

(i) was authorised by the company before it occurred, or

(ii) has been ratified by the company since it occurred.

(2) In considering whether to grant leave to raise derivative proceedings or an application under section 267, the court must take into account, in particular—

(a) whether the member is acting in good faith in seeking to raise or continue the proceedings (as the case may be),

(b) the importance that a person acting in accordance with section 172 (duty to promote the success of the company) would attach to raising or continuing them (as the case may be),

(c) where the cause of action is an act or omission that is yet to occur, whether the act or omission could be, and in the circumstances would be likely to be—

(i) authorised by the company before it occurs, or

(ii) ratified by the company after it occurs,

(d) where the cause of action is an act or omission that has already occurred, whether the act or omission could be, and in the circumstances would be likely to be, ratified by the company,

(e) whether the company has decided not to raise proceedings in respect of the same cause of action or to persist in the proceedings (as the case may be),

(f) whether the cause of action is one which the member could pursue in his own right rather than on behalf of the company.

(3) In considering whether to grant leave to raise derivative proceedings or an application under section 267, the court shall have particular regard to any evidence before it as to the views of members of the company who have no personal interest, direct or indirect, in the matter.

(4) The Secretary of State may by regulations—

(a) amend subsection (1) so as to alter or add to the circumstances in which leave or an application is to be refused,

(b) amend subsection (2) so as to alter or add to the matters that the court is required to take into account in considering whether to grant leave or an application.

(5) Before making any such regulations the Secretary of State shall consult such persons as he considers appropriate.

(6) Regulations under this section are subject to affirmative resolution procedure.

269. Application by member to be substituted for member pursuing derivative proceedings

(1) This section applies where a member of a company ("the claimant")—

(a) has raised derivative proceedings,

(b) has continued as derivative proceedings raised by the company, or

    (c) has continued derivative proceedings under this section.

  (2) Another member of the company ("the applicant") may apply to the court to be substituted for the claimant in the action on the ground that—

    (a) the manner in which the proceedings have been commenced or continued by the claimant amounts to an abuse of the process of the court,

    (b) the claimant has failed to prosecute the proceedings diligently, and

    (c) it is appropriate for the applicant to be substituted for the claimant in the proceedings.

  (3) If it appears to the court that the application and the evidence produced by the applicant in support of it do not disclose a prima facie case for granting it, the court—

    (a) must refuse the application, and

    (b) may make any consequential order it considers appropriate.

  (4) If the application is not refused under subsection (3)—

    (a) the applicant must serve the application on the company,

    (b) the court—

      (i) may make an order requiring evidence to be produced by the company, and

      (ii) may adjourn the proceedings on the application to enable the evidence to be obtained, and

    (c) the company is entitled to take part in the further proceedings on the application.

  (5) On hearing the application, the court may—

    (a) grant the application on such terms as it thinks fit,

    (b) refuse the application, or

    (c) adjourn the proceedings on the application and make such order as to further procedure as it thinks fit.

PART 12
COMPANY SECRETARIES

Private companies

270. Private company not required to have secretary

  (1) A private company is not required to have a secretary.

  (2) References in the Companies Acts to a private company "without a secretary" are to a private company that for the time being is taking advantage of the exemption in subsection (1); and references to a private company "with a secretary" shall be construed accordingly.

  (3) In the case of a private company without a secretary—

    (a) anything authorised or required to be given or sent to, or served on, the company by being sent to its secretary—

      (i) may be given or sent to, or served on, the company itself, and

      (ii) if addressed to the secretary shall be treated as addressed to the company; and

    (b) anything else required or authorised to be done by or to the secretary of the company may be done by or to—

      (i) a director, or

      (ii) a person authorised generally or specifically in that behalf by the directors.

Public companies

271. Public company required to have secretary
A public company must have a secretary.

272. **Direction requiring public company to appoint secretary**

(1) If it appears to the Secretary of State that a public company is in breach of section 271 (requirement to have secretary), the Secretary of State may give the company a direction under this section.

(2) The direction must state that the company appears to be in breach of that section and specify—

(a) what the company must do in order to comply with the direction, and

(b) the period within which it must do so.

That period must be not less than one month or more than three months after the date on which the direction is given.

(3) The direction must also inform the company of the consequences of failing to comply.

(4) Where the company is in breach of section 271 it must comply with the direction by—

(a) making the necessary appointment, and

(b) giving notice of it under section 276,

before the end of the period specified in the direction.

(5) If the company has already made the necessary appointment, it must comply with the direction by giving notice of it under section 276 before the end of the period specified in the direction.

(6) If a company fails to comply with a direction under this section, an offence is committed by—

(a) the company, and

(b) every officer of the company who is in default.

For this purpose a shadow director is treated as an officer of the company.

(7) A person guilty of an offence under this section is liable on summary conviction to a fine not exceeding level 5 on the standard scale and, for continued contravention, a daily default fine not exceeding one-tenth of level 5 on the standard scale.

273. **Qualifications of secretaries of public companies**

(1) It is the duty of the directors of a public company to take all reasonable steps to secure that the secretary (or each joint secretary) of the company—

(a) is a person who appears to them to have the requisite knowledge and experience to discharge the functions of secretary of the company, and

(b) has one or more of the following qualifications.

(2) The qualifications are—

(a) that he has held the office of secretary of a public company for at least three of the five years immediately preceding his appointment as secretary;

(b) that he is a member of any of the bodies specified in subsection (3);

(c) that he is a barrister, advocate or solicitor called or admitted in any part of the United Kingdom;

(d) that he is a person who, by virtue of his holding or having held any other position or his being a member of any other body, appears to the directors to be capable of discharging the functions of secretary of the company.

(3) The bodies referred to in subsection (2)(b) are—

(a) the Institute of Chartered Accountants in England and Wales;

(b) the Institute of Chartered Accountants of Scotland;

(c) the Association of Chartered Certified Accountants;

(d) the Institute of Chartered Accountants in Ireland;

(e) the Institute of Chartered Secretaries and Administrators;

(f) the Chartered Institute of Management Accountants;

(g) the Chartered Institute of Public Finance and Accountancy.

Provisions applying to private companies with a secretary and to public companies

274. **Discharge of functions where office vacant or secretary unable to act**

Where in the case of any company the office of secretary is vacant, or there is for any other reason no secretary capable of acting, anything required or authorised to be done by or to the secretary may be done—

(a) by or to an assistant or deputy secretary (if any), or

(b) if there is no assistant or deputy secretary or none capable of acting, by or to any person authorised generally or specifically in that behalf by the directors.

275. **Duty to keep register of secretaries**

(1) A company must keep a register of its secretaries.

(2) The register must contain the required particulars (see sections 277 to 279) of the person who is, or persons who are, the secretary or joint secretaries of the company.

(3) The register must be kept available for inspection—

(a) at the company's registered office, or

(b) at a place specified in regulations under section 1136.

(4) The company must give notice to the registrar—

(a) of the place at which the register is kept available for inspection, and

(b) of any change in that place,

unless it has at all times been kept at the company's registered office.

(5) The register must be open to the inspection—

(a) of any member of the company without charge, and

(b) of any other person on payment of such fee as may be prescribed.

(6) If default is made in complying with subsection (1), (2) or (3), or if default is made for 14 days in complying with subsection (4), or if an inspection required under subsection (5) is refused, an offence is committed by—

(a) the company, and

(b) every officer of the company who is in default.

For this purpose a shadow director is treated as an officer of the company.

(7) A person guilty of an offence under this section is liable on summary conviction to a fine not exceeding level 5 on the standard scale and, for continued contravention, a daily default fine not exceeding one-tenth of level 5 on the standard scale.

(8) In the case of a refusal of inspection of the register, the court may by order compel an immediate inspection of it.

276. **Duty to notify registrar of changes**

(1) A company must, within the period of 14 days from—

(a) a person becoming or ceasing to be its secretary or one of its joint secretaries, or

(b) the occurrence of any change in the particulars contained in its register of secretaries,

give notice to the registrar of the change and of the date on which it occurred.

(2) Notice of a person having become secretary, or one of joint secretaries, of the company must be accompanied by a consent by that person to act in the relevant capacity.

(3) If default is made in complying with this section, an offence is committed by every officer of the company who is in default.

For this purpose a shadow director is treated as an officer of the company.

(4) A person guilty of an offence under this section is liable on summary conviction to a fine not exceeding level 5 on the standard scale and, for continued contravention, a daily default fine not exceeding one-tenth of level 5 on the standard scale.

277. **Particulars of secretaries to be registered: individuals**

(1) A company's register of secretaries must contain the following particulars in the case of an individual—

(a) name and any former name;

(b) address.

(2) For the purposes of this section "name" means a person's Christian name (or other forename) and surname, except that in the case of—

(a) a peer, or

(b) an individual usually known by a title,

the title may be stated instead of his Christian name (or other forename) and surname or in addition to either or both of them.

(3) For the purposes of this section a "former name" means a name by which the individual was formerly known for business purposes.

Where a person is or was formerly known by more than one such name, each of them must be stated.

(4) It is not necessary for the register to contain particulars of a former name in the following cases—

(a) in the case of a peer or an individual normally known by a British title, where the name is one by which the person was known previous to the adoption of or succession to the title;

(b) in the case of any person, where the former name—

(i) was changed or disused before the person attained the age of 16 years, or

(ii) has been changed or disused for 20 years or more.

(5) The address required to be stated in the register is a service address.

This may be stated to be "The company's registered office".

278. Particulars of secretaries to be registered: corporate secretaries and firms

(1) A company's register of secretaries must contain the following particulars in the case of a body corporate, or a firm that is a legal person under the law by which it is governed—

(a) corporate or firm name;

(b) registered or principal office;

(c) in the case of an EEA company to which the First Company Law Directive (68/151/EEC) applies, particulars of—

(i) the register in which the company file mentioned in Article 3 of that Directive is kept (including details of the relevant state), and

(ii) the registration number in that register;

(d) in any other case, particulars of—

(i) the legal form of the company or firm and the law by which it is governed, and

(ii) if applicable, the register in which it is entered (including details of the state) and its registration number in that register.

(2) If all the partners in a firm are joint secretaries it is sufficient to state the particulars that would be required if the firm were a legal person and the firm had been appointed secretary.

279. Particulars of secretaries to be registered: power to make regulations

(1) The Secretary of State may make provision by regulations amending—

section 277 (particulars of secretaries to be registered: individuals), or

section 278 (particulars of secretaries to be registered: corporate secretaries and firms),

so as to add to or remove items from the particulars required to be contained in a company's register of secretaries.

(2) Regulations under this section are subject to affirmative resolution procedure.

280. Acts done by person in dual capacity

A provision requiring or authorising a thing to be done by or to a director and the secretary of a company is not satisfied by its being done by or to the same person acting both as director and as, or in place of, the secretary.

PART 13
RESOLUTIONS AND MEETINGS

CHAPTER 1
GENERAL PROVISIONS ABOUT RESOLUTIONS

281. **Resolutions**

(1) A resolution of the members (or of a class of members) of a private company must be passed—

(a) as a written resolution in accordance with Chapter 2, or

(b) at a meeting of the members (to which the provisions of Chapter 3 apply).

(2) A resolution of the members (or of a class of members) of a public company must be passed at a meeting of the members (to which the provisions of Chapter 3 and, where relevant, Chapter 4 apply).

(3) Where a provision of the Companies Acts—

(a) requires a resolution of a company, or of the members (or a class of members) of a company, and

(b) does not specify what kind of resolution is required,

what is required is an ordinary resolution unless the company's articles require a higher majority (or unanimity).

(4) Nothing in this Part affects any enactment or rule of law as to—

(a) things done otherwise than by passing a resolution,

(b) circumstances in which a resolution is or is not treated as having been passed, or

(c) cases in which a person is precluded from alleging that a resolution has not been duly passed.

282. **Ordinary resolutions**

(1) An ordinary resolution of the members (or of a class of members) of a company means a resolution that is passed by a simple majority.

(2) A written resolution is passed by a simple majority if it is passed by members representing a simple majority of the total voting rights of eligible members (see Chapter 2).

(3) A resolution passed at a meeting on a show of hands is passed by a simple majority if it is passed by a simple majority of—

(a) the members who, being entitled to do so, vote in person on the resolution, and

(b) the persons who vote on the resolution as duly appointed proxies of members entitled to vote on it.

(4) A resolution passed on a poll taken at a meeting is passed by a simple majority if it is passed by members representing a simple majority of the total voting rights of members who (being entitled to do so) vote in person or by proxy on the resolution.

(5) Anything that may be done by ordinary resolution may also be done by special resolution.

283. **Special resolutions**

(1) A special resolution of the members (or of a class of members) of a company means a resolution passed by a majority of not less than 75%.

(2) A written resolution is passed by a majority of not less than 75% if it is passed by members representing not less than 75% of the total voting rights of eligible members (see Chapter 2).

(3) Where a resolution of a private company is passed as a written resolution—

(a) the resolution is not a special resolution unless it stated that it was proposed as a special resolution, and

(b) if the resolution so stated, it may only be passed as a special resolution.

(4) A resolution passed at a meeting on a show of hands is passed by a majority of not less than 75% if it is passed by not less than 75% of—

(a) the members who, being entitled to do so, vote in person on the resolution, and

(b) the persons who vote on the resolution as duly appointed proxies of members entitled to vote on it.

(5) A resolution passed on a poll taken at a meeting is passed by a majority of not less than 75% if it is passed by members representing not less than 75% of the total voting rights of the members who (being entitled to do so) vote in person or by proxy on the resolution.

(6) Where a resolution is passed at a meeting—

    (a) the resolution is not a special resolution unless the notice of the meeting included the text of the resolution and specified the intention to propose the resolution as a special resolution, and

    (b) if the notice of the meeting so specified, the resolution may only be passed as a special resolution.

284. Votes: general rules

(1) On a vote on a written resolution—

    (a) in the case of a company having a share capital, every member has one vote in respect of each share or each £10 of stock held by him, and

    (b) in any other case, every member has one vote.

(2) On a vote on a resolution on a show of hands at a meeting—

    (a) every member present in person has one vote, and

    (b) every proxy present who has been duly appointed by a member entitled to vote on the resolution has one vote.

(3) On a vote on a resolution on a poll taken at a meeting—

    (a) in the case of a company having a share capital, every member has one vote in respect of each share or each £10 of stock held by him, and

    (b) in any other case, every member has one vote.

(4) The provisions of this section have effect subject to any provision of the company's articles.

285. Votes: specific requirements

(1) Where a member entitled to vote on a resolution has appointed one proxy only, and the company's articles provide that the proxy has fewer votes in a vote on a resolution on a show of hands taken at a meeting than the member would have if he were present in person—

    (a) the provision about how many votes the proxy has on a show of hands is void, and

    (b) the proxy has the same number of votes on a show of hands as the member who appointed him would have if he were present at the meeting.

(2) Where a member entitled to vote on a resolution has appointed more than one proxy, subsection (1) applies as if the references to the proxy were references to the proxies taken together.

(3) In relation to a resolution required or authorised by an enactment, if a private company's articles provide that a member has a different number of votes in relation to a resolution when it is passed as a written resolution and when it is passed on a poll taken at a meeting—

    (a) the provision about how many votes a member has in relation to the resolution passed on a poll is void, and

    (b) a member has the same number of votes in relation to the resolution when it is passed on a poll as he has when it is passed as a written resolution.

286. Votes of joint holders of shares

(1) In the case of joint holders of shares of a company, only the vote of the senior holder who votes (and any proxies duly authorised by him) may be counted by the company.

(2) For the purposes of this section, the senior holder of a share is determined by the order in which the names of the joint holders appear in the register of members.

(3) Subsections (1) and (2) have effect subject to any provision of the company's articles.

287. **Saving for provisions of articles as to determination of entitlement to vote**

Nothing in this Chapter affects—

(a) any provision of a company's articles—

    (i) requiring an objection to a person's entitlement to vote on a resolution to be made in accordance with the articles, and

    (ii) for the determination of any such objection to be final and conclusive, or

(b) the grounds on which such a determination may be questioned in legal proceedings.

CHAPTER 2
WRITTEN RESOLUTIONS

General provisions about written resolutions

288. **Written resolutions of private companies**

(1) In the Companies Acts a "written resolution" means a resolution of a private company proposed and passed in accordance with this Chapter.

(2) The following may not be passed as a written resolution—

    (a) a resolution under section 168 removing a director before the expiration of his period of office;

    (b) a resolution under section 510 removing an auditor before the expiration of his term of office.

(3) A resolution may be proposed as a written resolution—

    (a) by the directors of a private company (see section 291), or

    (b) by the members of a private company (see sections 292 to 295).

(4) References in enactments passed or made before this Chapter comes into force to—

    (a) a resolution of a company in general meeting, or

    (b) a resolution of a meeting of a class of members of the company,

have effect as if they included references to a written resolution of the members, or of a class of members, of a private company (as appropriate).

(5) A written resolution of a private company has effect as if passed (as the case may be)—

    (a) by the company in general meeting, or

    (b) by a meeting of a class of members of the company,

and references in enactments passed or made before this section comes into force to a meeting at which a resolution is passed or to members voting in favour of a resolution shall be construed accordingly.

289. **Eligible members**

(1) In relation to a resolution proposed as a written resolution of a private company, the eligible members are the members who would have been entitled to vote on the resolution on the circulation date of the resolution (see section 290).

(2) If the persons entitled to vote on a written resolution change during the course of the day that is the circulation date of the resolution, the eligible members are the persons entitled to vote on the resolution at the time that the first copy of the resolution is sent or submitted to a member for his agreement.

Circulation of written resolutions

290. **Circulation date**

References in this Part to the circulation date of a written resolution are to the date on which copies of it are sent or submitted to members in accordance with this Chapter (or if copies are sent or submitted to members on different days, to the first of those days).

291. **Circulation of written resolutions proposed by directors**

    (1) This section applies to a resolution proposed as a written resolution by the directors of the company.

    (2) The company must send or submit a copy of the resolution to every eligible member.

    (3) The company must do so—

        (a) by sending copies at the same time (so far as reasonably practicable) to all eligible members in hard copy form, in electronic form or by means of a website, or

        (b) if it is possible to do so without undue delay, by submitting the same copy to each eligible member in turn (or different copies to each of a number of eligible members in turn),

    or by sending copies to some members in accordance with paragraph (a) and submitting a copy or copies to other members in accordance with paragraph (b).

    (4) The copy of the resolution must be accompanied by a statement informing the member—

        (a) how to signify agreement to the resolution (see section 296), and

        (b) as to the date by which the resolution must be passed if it is not to lapse (see section 297).

    (5) In the event of default in complying with this section, an offence is committed by every officer of the company who is in default.

    (6) A person guilty of an offence under this section is liable—

        (a) on conviction on indictment, to a fine;

        (b) on summary conviction, to a fine not exceeding the statutory maximum.

    (7) The validity of the resolution, if passed, is not affected by a failure to comply with this section.

292. **Members' power to require circulation of written resolution**

    (1) The members of a private company may require the company to circulate a resolution that may properly be moved and is proposed to be moved as a written resolution.

    (2) Any resolution may properly be moved as a written resolution unless—

        (a) it would, if passed, be ineffective (whether by reason of inconsistency with any enactment or the company's constitution or otherwise),

        (b) it is defamatory of any person, or

        (c) it is frivolous or vexatious.

    (3) Where the members require a company to circulate a resolution they may require the company to circulate with it a statement of not more than 1,000 words on the subject matter of the resolution.

    (4) A company is required to circulate the resolution and any accompanying statement once it has received requests that it do so from members representing not less than the requisite percentage of the total voting rights of all members entitled to vote on the resolution.

    (5) The "requisite percentage" is 5% or such lower percentage as is specified for this purpose in the company's articles.

    (6) A request—

        (a) may be in hard copy form or in electronic form,

        (b) must identify the resolution and any accompanying statement, and

        (c) must be authenticated by the person or persons making it.

293. **Circulation of written resolution proposed by members**

    (1) A company that is required under section 292 to circulate a resolution must send or submit to every eligible member—

        (a) a copy of the resolution, and

        (b) a copy of any accompanying statement.

    This is subject to section 294(2) (deposit or tender of sum in respect of expenses of circulation) and section 295 (application not to circulate members' statement).

    (2) The company must do so—

        (a) by sending copies at the same time (so far as reasonably practicable) to all eligible members in hard copy form, in electronic form or by means of a website, or

(b) if it is possible to do so without undue delay, by submitting the same copy to each eligible member in turn (or different copies to each of a number of eligible members in turn),

or by sending copies to some members in accordance with paragraph (a) and submitting a copy or copies to other members in accordance with paragraph (b).

(3) The company must send or submit the copies (or, if copies are sent or submitted to members on different days, the first of those copies) not more than 21 days after it becomes subject to the requirement under section 292 to circulate the resolution.

(4) The copy of the resolution must be accompanied by guidance as to—

(a) how to signify agreement to the resolution (see section 296), and

(b) the date by which the resolution must be passed if it is not to lapse (see section 297).

(5) In the event of default in complying with this section, an offence is committed by every officer of the company who is in default.

(6) A person guilty of an offence under this section is liable—

(a) on conviction on indictment, to a fine;

(b) on summary conviction, to a fine not exceeding the statutory maximum.

(7) The validity of the resolution, if passed, is not affected by a failure to comply with this section.

294. Expenses of circulation

(1) The expenses of the company in complying with section 293 must be paid by the members who requested the circulation of the resolution unless the company resolves otherwise.

(2) Unless the company has previously so resolved, it is not bound to comply with that section unless there is deposited with or tendered to it a sum reasonably sufficient to meet its expenses in doing so.

295. Application not to circulate members' statement

(1) A company is not required to circulate a members' statement under section 293 if, on an application by the company or another person who claims to be aggrieved, the court is satisfied that the rights conferred by section 292 and that section are being abused.

(2) The court may order the members who requested the circulation of the statement to pay the whole or part of the company's costs (in Scotland, expenses) on such an application, even if they are not parties to the application.

Agreeing to written resolutions

296. Procedure for signifying agreement to written resolution

(1) A member signifies his agreement to a proposed written resolution when the company receives from him (or from someone acting on his behalf) an authenticated document—

(a) identifying the resolution to which it relates, and

(b) indicating his agreement to the resolution.

(2) The document must be sent to the company in hard copy form or in electronic form.

(3) A member's agreement to a written resolution, once signified, may not be revoked.

(4) A written resolution is passed when the required majority of eligible members have signified their agreement to it.

297. Period for agreeing to written resolution

(1) A proposed written resolution lapses if it is not passed before the end of—

(a) the period specified for this purpose in the company's articles, or

(b) if none is specified, the period of 28 days beginning with the circulation date.

(2) The agreement of a member to a written resolution is ineffective if signified after the expiry of that period.

Supplementary

298. **Sending documents relating to written resolutions by electronic means**
    (1) Where a company has given an electronic address in any document containing or accompanying a proposed written resolution, it is deemed to have agreed that any document or information relating to that resolution may be sent by electronic means to that address (subject to any conditions or limitations specified in the document).
    (2) In this section "electronic address" means any address or number used for the purposes of sending or receiving documents or information by electronic means.

299. **Publication of written resolution on website**
    (1) This section applies where a company sends—
        (a) a written resolution, or
        (b) a statement relating to a written resolution,
        to a person by means of a website.
    (2) The resolution or statement is not validly sent for the purposes of this Chapter unless the resolution is available on the website throughout the period beginning with the circulation date and ending on the date on which the resolution lapses under section 297.

300. **Relationship between this Chapter and provisions of company's articles**
    A provision of the articles of a private company is void in so far as it would have the effect that a resolution that is required by or otherwise provided for in an enactment could not be proposed and passed as a written resolution.

CHAPTER 3
RESOLUTIONS AT MEETINGS

General provisions about resolutions at meetings

301. **Resolutions at general meetings**
    A resolution of the members of a company is validly passed at a general meeting if—
    (a) notice of the meeting and of the resolution is given, and
    (b) the meeting is held and conducted,
    in accordance with the provisions of this Chapter (and, where relevant, Chapter 4) and the company's articles.

Calling meetings

302. **Directors' power to call general meetings**
    The directors of a company may call a general meeting of the company.

303. **Members' power to require directors to call general meeting**
    (1) The members of a company may require the directors to call a general meeting of the company.
    (2) The directors are required to call a general meeting once the company has received requests to do so from—
        (a) members representing at least the required percentage of such of the paid-up capital of the company as carries the right of voting at general meetings of the company (excluding any paid-up capital held as treasury shares); or
        (b) in the case of a company not having a share capital, members who represent at least the required percentage of the total voting rights of all the members having a right to vote at general meetings.
    (3) The required percentage is 10% unless, in the case of a private company, more than twelve months has elapsed since the end of the last general meeting—
        (a) called in pursuance of a requirement under this section, or

(b) in relation to which any members of the company had (by virtue of an enactment, the company's articles or otherwise) rights with respect to the circulation of a resolution no less extensive than they would have had if the meeting had been so called at their request,

in which case the required percentage is 5%.

(4) A request—

    (a) must state the general nature of the business to be dealt with at the meeting, and

    (b) may include the text of a resolution that may properly be moved and is intended to be moved at the meeting.

(5) A resolution may properly be moved at a meeting unless—

    (a) it would, if passed, be ineffective (whether by reason of inconsistency with any enactment or the company's constitution or otherwise),

    (b) it is defamatory of any person, or

    (c) it is frivolous or vexatious.

(6) A request—

    (a) may be in hard copy form or in electronic form, and

    (b) must be authenticated by the person or persons making it.

304. Directors' duty to call meetings required by members

(1) Directors required under section 303 to call a general meeting of the company must call a meeting—

    (a) within 21 days from the date on which they become subject to the requirement, and

    (b) to be held on a date not more than 28 days after the date of the notice convening the meeting.

(2) If the requests received by the company identify a resolution intended to be moved at the meeting, the notice of the meeting must include notice of the resolution.

(3) The business that may be dealt with at the meeting includes a resolution of which notice is given in accordance with this section.

(4) If the resolution is to be proposed as a special resolution, the directors are treated as not having duly called the meeting if they do not give the required notice of the resolution in accordance with section 283.

305. Power of members to call meeting at company's expense

(1) If the directors—

    (a) are required under section 303 to call a meeting, and

    (b) do not do so in accordance with section 304,

the members who requested the meeting, or any of them representing more than one half of the total voting rights of all of them, may themselves call a general meeting.

(2) Where the requests received by the company included the text of a resolution intended to be moved at the meeting, the notice of the meeting must include notice of the resolution.

(3) The meeting must be called for a date not more than three months after the date on which the directors become subject to the requirement to call a meeting.

(4) The meeting must be called in the same manner, as nearly as possible, as that in which meetings are required to be called by directors of the company.

(5) The business which may be dealt with at the meeting includes a resolution of which notice is given in accordance with this section.

(6) Any reasonable expenses incurred by the members requesting the meeting by reason of the failure of the directors duly to call a meeting must be reimbursed by the company.

(7) Any sum so reimbursed shall be retained by the company out of any sums due or to become due from the company by way of fees or other remuneration in respect of the services of such of the directors as were in default.

306. Power of court to order meeting

(1) This section applies if for any reason it is impracticable—

  (a) to call a meeting of a company in any manner in which meetings of that company may be called, or

  (b) to conduct the meeting in the manner prescribed by the company's articles or this Act.

(2) The court may, either of its own motion or on the application—

  (a) of a director of the company, or

  (b) of a member of the company who would be entitled to vote at the meeting,

order a meeting to be called, held and conducted in any manner the court thinks fit.

(3) Where such an order is made, the court may give such ancillary or consequential directions as it thinks expedient.

(4) Such directions may include a direction that one member of the company present at the meeting be deemed to constitute a quorum.

(5) A meeting called, held and conducted in accordance with an order under this section is deemed for all purposes to be a meeting of the company duly called, held and conducted.

Notice of meetings

307. Notice required of general meeting

(1) A general meeting of a private company (other than an adjourned meeting) must be called by notice of at least 14 days.

(2) A general meeting of a public company (other than an adjourned meeting) must be called by notice of—

  (a) in the case of an annual general meeting, at least 21 days, and

  (b) in any other case, at least 14 days.

(3) The company's articles may require a longer period of notice than that specified in subsection (1) or (2).

(4) A general meeting may be called by shorter notice than that otherwise required if shorter notice is agreed by the members.

(5) The shorter notice must be agreed to by a majority in number of the members having a right to attend and vote at the meeting, being a majority who—

  (a) together hold not less than the requisite percentage in nominal value of the shares giving a right to attend and vote at the meeting (excluding any shares in the company held as treasury shares), or

  (b) in the case of a company not having a share capital, together represent not less than the requisite percentage of the total voting rights at that meeting of all the members.

(6) The requisite percentage is—

  (a) in the case of a private company, 90% or such higher percentage (not exceeding 95%) as may be specified in the company's articles;

  (b) in the case of a public company, 95%.

(7) Subsections (5) and (6) do not apply to an annual general meeting of a public company (see instead section 337(2)).

308. Manner in which notice to be given

Notice of a general meeting of a company must be given—

(a) in hard copy form,

(b) in electronic form, or

(c) by means of a website (see section 309),

or partly by one such means and partly by another.

309. Publication of notice of meeting on website

(1) Notice of a meeting is not validly given by a company by means of a website unless it is given in accordance with this section.

(2) When the company notifies a member of the presence of the notice on the website the notification must—

    (a) state that it concerns a notice of a company meeting,

    (b) specify the place, date and time of the meeting, and

    (c) in the case of a public company, state whether the meeting will be an annual general meeting.

(3) The notice must be available on the website throughout the period beginning with the date of that notification and ending with the conclusion of the meeting.

310. Persons entitled to receive notice of meetings

(1) Notice of a general meeting of a company must be sent to—

    (a) every member of the company, and

    (b) every director.

(2) In subsection (1), the reference to members includes any person who is entitled to a share in consequence of the death or bankruptcy of a member, if the company has been notified of their entitlement.

(3) In subsection (2), the reference to the bankruptcy of a member includes—

    (a) the sequestration of the estate of a member;

    (b) a member's estate being the subject of a protected trust deed (within the meaning of the Bankruptcy (Scotland) Act 1985 (c. 66)).

(4) This section has effect subject to—

    (a) any enactment, and

    (b) any provision of the company's articles.

311. Contents of notices of meetings

(1) Notice of a general meeting of a company must state—

    (a) the time and date of the meeting, and

    (b) the place of the meeting.

(2) Notice of a general meeting of a company must state the general nature of the business to be dealt with at the meeting.

This subsection has effect subject to any provision of the company's articles.

312. Resolution requiring special notice

(1) Where by any provision of the Companies Acts special notice is required of a resolution, the resolution is not effective unless notice of the intention to move it has been given to the company at least 28 days before the meeting at which it is moved.

(2) The company must, where practicable, give its members notice of any such resolution in the same manner and at the same time as it gives notice of the meeting.

(3) Where that is not practicable, the company must give its members notice at least 14 days before the meeting—

    (a) by advertisement in a newspaper having an appropriate circulation, or

    (b) in any other manner allowed by the company's articles.

(4) If, after notice of the intention to move such a resolution has been given to the company, a meeting is called for a date 28 days or less after the notice has been given, the notice is deemed to have been properly given, though not given within the time required.

313. Accidental failure to give notice of resolution or meeting

(1) Where a company gives notice of—

    (a) a general meeting, or

    (b) a resolution intended to be moved at a general meeting,

any accidental failure to give notice to one or more persons shall be disregarded for the purpose of determining whether notice of the meeting or resolution (as the case may be) is duly given.

(2) Except in relation to notice given under—

    (a) section 304 (notice of meetings required by members),

    (b) section 305 (notice of meetings called by members), or

(c) section 339 (notice of resolutions at AGMs proposed by members),

subsection (1) has effect subject to any provision of the company's articles.

Members' statements

314. Members' power to require circulation of statements

(1) The members of a company may require the company to circulate, to members of the company entitled to receive notice of a general meeting, a statement of not more than 1,000 words with respect to—

    (a) a matter referred to in a proposed resolution to be dealt with at that meeting, or

    (b) other business to be dealt with at that meeting.

(2) A company is required to circulate a statement once it has received requests to do so from—

    (a) members representing at least 5% of the total voting rights of all the members who have a relevant right to vote (excluding any voting rights attached to any shares in the company held as treasury shares), or

    (b) at least 100 members who have a relevant right to vote and hold shares in the company on which there has been paid up an average sum, per member, of at least £100.

See also section 153 (exercise of rights where shares held on behalf of others).

(3) In subsection (2), a "relevant right to vote" means—

    (a) in relation to a statement with respect to a matter referred to in a proposed resolution, a right to vote on that resolution at the meeting to which the requests relate, and

    (b) in relation to any other statement, a right to vote at the meeting to which the requests relate.

(4) A request—

    (a) may be in hard copy form or in electronic form,

    (b) must identify the statement to be circulated,

    (c) must be authenticated by the person or persons making it, and

    (d) must be received by the company at least one week before the meeting to which it relates.

315. Company's duty to circulate members' statement

(1) A company that is required under section 314, to circulate a statement must send a copy of it to each member of the company entitled to receive notice of the meeting—

    (a) in the same manner as the notice of the meeting, and

    (b) at the same time as, or as soon as reasonably practicable after, it gives notice of the meeting.

(2) Subsection (1) has effect subject to section 316(2) (deposit or tender of sum in respect of expenses of circulation) and section 317 (application not to circulate members' statement).

(3) In the event of default in complying with this section, an offence is committed by every officer of the company who is in default.

(4) A person guilty of an offence under this section is liable—

    (a) on conviction on indictment, to a fine;

    (b) on summary conviction, to a fine not exceeding the statutory maximum.

316. Expenses of circulating members' statement

(1) The expenses of the company in complying with section 315 need not be paid by the members who requested the circulation of the statement if—

    (a) the meeting to which the requests relate is an annual general meeting of a public company, and

    (b) requests sufficient to require the company to circulate the statement are received before the end of the financial year preceding the meeting.

(2) Otherwise—

    (a) the expenses of the company in complying with that section must be paid by the members who requested the circulation of the statement unless the company resolves otherwise, and

(b) unless the company has previously so resolved, it is not bound to comply with that section unless there is deposited with or tendered to it, not later than one week before the meeting, a sum reasonably sufficient to meet its expenses in doing so.

317. **Application not to circulate members' statement**

(1) A company is not required to circulate a members' statement under section 315 if, on an application by the company or another person who claims to be aggrieved, the court is satisfied that the rights conferred by section 314 and that section are being abused.

(2) The court may order the members who requested the circulation of the statement to pay the whole or part of the company's costs (in Scotland, expenses) on such an application, even if they are not parties to the application.

Procedure at meetings

318. **Quorum at meetings**

(1) In the case of a company limited by shares or guarantee and having only one member, one qualifying person present at a meeting is a quorum.

(2) In any other case, subject to the provisions of the company's articles, two qualifying persons present at a meeting are a quorum, unless—

(a) each is a qualifying person only because he is authorised under section 323 to act as the representative of a corporation in relation to the meeting, and they are representatives of the same corporation; or

(b) each is a qualifying person only because he is appointed as proxy of a member in relation to the meeting, and they are proxies of the same member.

(3) For the purposes of this section a "qualifying person" means—

(a) an individual who is a member of the company,

(b) a person authorised under section 323 (representation of corporations at meetings) to act as the representative of a corporation in relation to the meeting, or

(c) a person appointed as proxy of a member in relation to the meeting.

319. **Chairman of meeting**

(1) A member may be elected to be the chairman of a general meeting by a resolution of the company passed at the meeting.

(2) Subsection (1) is subject to any provision of the company's articles that states who may or may not be chairman.

320. **Declaration by chairman on a show of hands**

(1) On a vote on a resolution at a meeting on a show of hands, a declaration by the chairman that the resolution—

(a) has or has not been passed, or

(b) passed with a particular majority,

is conclusive evidence of that fact without proof of the number or proportion of the votes recorded in favour of or against the resolution.

(2) An entry in respect of such a declaration in minutes of the meeting recorded in accordance with section 355 is also conclusive evidence of that fact without such proof.

(3) This section does not have effect if a poll is demanded in respect of the resolution (and the demand is not subsequently withdrawn).

321. **Right to demand a poll**

(1) A provision of a company's articles is void in so far as it would have the effect of excluding the right to demand a poll at a general meeting on any question other than—

(a) the election of the chairman of the meeting, or

(b) the adjournment of the meeting.

(2) A provision of a company's articles is void in so far as it would have the effect of making ineffective a demand for a poll on any such question which is made—

(a) by not less than 5 members having the right to vote on the resolution; or

(b) by a member or members representing not less than 10% of the total voting rights of all the members having the right to vote on the resolution (excluding any voting rights attached to any shares in the company held as treasury shares); or

(c) by a member or members holding shares in the company conferring a right to vote on the resolution, being shares on which an aggregate sum has been paid up equal to not less than 10% of the total sum paid up on all the shares conferring that right (excluding shares in the company conferring a right to vote on the resolution which are held as treasury shares).

322. **Voting on a poll**

On a poll taken at a general meeting of a company, a member entitled to more than one vote need not, if he votes, use all his votes or cast all the votes he uses in the same way.

323. **Representation of corporations at meetings**

(1) If a corporation (whether or not a company within the meaning of this Act) is a member of a company, it may by resolution of its directors or other governing body authorise a person or persons to act as its representative or representatives at any meeting of the company.

(2) Where the corporation authorises only one person, he is entitled to exercise the same powers on behalf of the corporation as the corporation could exercise if it were an individual member of the company.

(3) Where the corporation authorises more than one person, any one of them is entitled to exercise the same powers on behalf of the corporation as the corporation could exercise if it were an individual member of the company.

(4) Where the corporation authorises more than one person and more than one of them purport to exercise a power under subsection (3)—

(a) if they purport to exercise the power in the same way, the power is treated as exercised in that way,

(b) if they do not purport to exercise the power in the same way, the power is treated as not exercised.

Proxies

324. **Rights to appoint proxies**

(1) A member of a company is entitled to appoint another person as his proxy to exercise all or any of his rights to attend and to speak and vote at a meeting of the company.

(2) In the case of a company having a share capital, a member may appoint more than one proxy in relation to a meeting, provided that each proxy is appointed to exercise the rights attached to a different share or shares held by him, or (as the case may be) to a different £10, or multiple of £10, of stock held by him.

325. **Notice of meeting to contain statement of rights**

(1) In every notice calling a meeting of a company there must appear, with reasonable prominence, a statement informing the member of—

(a) his rights under section 324, and

(b) any more extensive rights conferred by the company's articles to appoint more than one proxy.

(2) Failure to comply with this section does not affect the validity of the meeting or of anything done at the meeting.

(3) If this section is not complied with as respects any meeting, an offence is committed by every officer of the company who is in default.

(4) A person guilty of an offence under this section is liable on summary conviction to a fine not exceeding level 3 on the standard scale.

326. **Company-sponsored invitations to appoint proxies**

(1) If for the purposes of a meeting there are issued at the company's expense invitations to members to appoint as proxy a specified person or a number of specified persons, the invitations must be issued to all members entitled to vote at the meeting.

(2) Subsection (1) is not contravened if—

(a) there is issued to a member at his request a form of appointment naming the proxy or a list of persons willing to act as proxy, and

(b) the form or list is available on request to all members entitled to vote at the meeting.

(3) If subsection (1) is contravened as respects a meeting, an offence is committed by every officer of the company who is in default.

(4) A person guilty of an offence under this section is liable on summary conviction to a fine not exceeding level 3 on the standard scale.

327. **Notice required of appointment of proxy etc**

(1) This section applies to—

(a) the appointment of a proxy, and

(b) any document necessary to show the validity of, or otherwise relating to, the appointment of a proxy.

(2) Any provision of the company's articles is void in so far as it would have the effect of requiring any such appointment or document to be received by the company or another person earlier than the following time—

(a) in the case of a meeting or adjourned meeting, 48 hours before the time for holding the meeting or adjourned meeting;

(b) in the case of a poll taken more than 48 hours after it was demanded, 24 hours before the time appointed for the taking of the poll;

(c) in the case of a poll taken not more than 48 hours after it was demanded, the time at which it was demanded.

(3) In calculating the periods mentioned in subsection (2) no account shall be taken of any part of a day that is not a working day.

328. **Chairing meetings**

(1) A proxy may be elected to be the chairman of a general meeting by a resolution of the company passed at the meeting.

(2) Subsection (1) is subject to any provision of the company's articles that states who may or who may not be chairman.

329. **Right of proxy to demand a poll**

(1) The appointment of a proxy to vote on a matter at a meeting of a company authorises the proxy to demand, or join in demanding, a poll on that matter.

(2) In applying the provisions of section 321(2) (requirements for effective demand), a demand by a proxy counts—

(a) for the purposes of paragraph (a), as a demand by the member;

(b) for the purposes of paragraph (b), as a demand by a member representing the voting rights that the proxy is authorised to exercise;

(c) for the purposes of paragraph (c), as a demand by a member holding the shares to which those rights are attached.

330. **Notice required of termination of proxy's authority**

(1) This section applies to notice that the authority of a person to act as proxy is terminated ("notice of termination").

(2) The termination of the authority of a person to act as proxy does not affect—

(a) whether he counts in deciding whether there is a quorum at a meeting,

(b) the validity of anything he does as chairman of a meeting, or

(c) the validity of a poll demanded by him at a meeting,

unless the company receives notice of the termination before the commencement of the meeting.

(3) The termination of the authority of a person to act as proxy does not affect the validity of a vote given by that person unless the company receives notice of the termination—

    (a) before the commencement of the meeting or adjourned meeting at which the vote is given, or

    (b) in the case of a poll taken more than 48 hours after it is demanded, before the time appointed for taking the poll.

(4) If the company's articles require or permit members to give notice of termination to a person other than the company, the references above to the company receiving notice have effect as if they were or (as the case may be) included a reference to that person.

(5) Subsections (2) and (3) have effect subject to any provision of the company's articles which has the effect of requiring notice of termination to be received by the company or another person at a time earlier than that specified in those subsections.

This is subject to subsection (6).

(6) Any provision of the company's articles is void in so far as it would have the effect of requiring notice of termination to be received by the company or another person earlier than the following time—

    (a) in the case of a meeting or adjourned meeting, 48 hours before the time for holding the meeting or adjourned meeting;

    (b) in the case of a poll taken more than 48 hours after it was demanded, 24 hours before the time appointed for the taking of the poll;

    (c) in the case of a poll taken not more than 48 hours after it was demanded, the time at which it was demanded.

(7) In calculating the periods mentioned in subsections (3)(b) and (6) no account shall be taken of any part of a day that is not a working day.

331. Saving for more extensive rights conferred by articles

Nothing in sections 324 to 330 (proxies) prevents a company's articles from conferring more extensive rights on members or proxies than are conferred by those sections.

Adjourned meetings

332. Resolution passed at adjourned meeting

Where a resolution is passed at an adjourned meeting of a company, the resolution is for all purposes to be treated as having been passed on the date on which it was in fact passed, and is not to be deemed passed on any earlier date.

Electronic communications

333. Sending documents relating to meetings etc in electronic form

(1) Where a company has given an electronic address in a notice calling a meeting, it is deemed to have agreed that any document or information relating to proceedings at the meeting may be sent by electronic means to that address (subject to any conditions or limitations specified in the notice).

(2) Where a company has given an electronic address—

    (a) in an instrument of proxy sent out by the company in relation to the meeting, or

    (b) in an invitation to appoint a proxy issued by the company in relation to the meeting,

it is deemed to have agreed that any document or information relating to proxies for that meeting may be sent by electronic means to that address (subject to any conditions or limitations specified in the notice).

(3) In subsection (2), documents relating to proxies include—

    (a) the appointment of a proxy in relation to a meeting,

    (b) any document necessary to show the validity of, or otherwise relating to, the appointment of a proxy, and

    (c) notice of the termination of the authority of a proxy.

(4) In this section "electronic address" means any address or number used for the purposes of sending or receiving documents or information by electronic means.

Application to class meetings

334. Application to class meetings

(1) The provisions of this Chapter apply (with necessary modifications) in relation to a meeting of holders of a class of shares as they apply in relation to a general meeting.

This is subject to subsections (2) and (3).

(2) The following provisions of this Chapter do not apply in relation to a meeting of holders of a class of shares—

    (a) sections 303 to 305 (members' power to require directors to call general meeting), and

    (b) section 306 (power of court to order meeting).

(3) The following provisions (in addition to those mentioned in subsection (2)) do not apply in relation to a meeting in connection with the variation of rights attached to a class of shares (a "variation of class rights meeting")—

    (a) section 318 (quorum), and

    (b) section 321 (right to demand a poll).

(4) The quorum for a variation of class rights meeting is—

    (a) for a meeting other than an adjourned meeting, two persons present holding at least one-third in nominal value of the issued shares of the class in question (excluding any shares of that class held as treasury shares);

    (b) for an adjourned meeting, one person present holding shares of the class in question.

(5) For the purposes of subsection (4), where a person is present by proxy or proxies, he is treated as holding only the shares in respect of which those proxies are authorised to exercise voting rights.

(6) At a variation of class rights meeting, any holder of shares of the class in question present may demand a poll.

(7) For the purposes of this section—

    (a) any amendment of a provision contained in a company's articles for the variation of the rights attached to a class of shares, or the insertion of any such provision into the articles, is itself to be treated as a variation of those rights, and

    (b) references to the variation of rights attached to a class of shares include references to their abrogation.

335. Application to class meetings: companies without a share capital

(1) The provisions of this Chapter apply (with necessary modifications) in relation to a meeting of a class of members of a company without a share capital as they apply in relation to a general meeting.

This is subject to subsections (2) and (3).

(2) The following provisions of this Chapter do not apply in relation to a meeting of a class of members—

    (a) sections 303 to 305 (members' power to require directors to call general meeting), and

    (b) section 306 (power of court to order meeting).

(3) The following provisions (in addition to those mentioned in subsection (2)) do not apply in relation to a meeting in connection with the variation of the rights of a class of members (a "variation of class rights meeting")—

(a) section 318 (quorum), and

(b) section 321 (right to demand a poll).

(4) The quorum for a variation of class rights meeting is—

(a) for a meeting other than an adjourned meeting, two members of the class present (in person or by proxy) who together represent at least one-third of the voting rights of the class;

(b) for an adjourned meeting, one member of the class present (in person or by proxy).

(5) At a variation of class rights meeting, any member present (in person or by proxy) may demand a poll.

(6) For the purposes of this section—

(a) any amendment of a provision contained in a company's articles for the variation of the rights of a class of members, or the insertion of any such provision into the articles, is itself to be treated as a variation of those rights, and

(b) references to the variation of rights of a class of members include references to their abrogation.

CHAPTER 4
PUBLIC COMPANIES: ADDITIONAL REQUIREMENTS FOR AGMS

336. **Public companies: annual general meeting**

(1) Every public company must hold a general meeting as its annual general meeting in each period of 6 months beginning with the day following its accounting reference date (in addition to any other meetings held during that period).

(2) A company that fails to comply with subsection (1) as a result of giving notice under section 392 (alteration of accounting reference date)—

(a) specifying a new accounting reference date, and

(b) stating that the current accounting reference period or the previous accounting reference period is to be shortened,

shall be treated as if it had complied with subsection (1) if it holds a general meeting as its annual general meeting within 3 months of giving that notice.

(3) If a company fails to comply with subsection (1), an offence is committed by every officer of the company who is in default.

(4) A person guilty of an offence under this section is liable—

(a) on conviction on indictment, to a fine;

(b) on summary conviction, to a fine not exceeding the statutory maximum.

337. **Public companies: notice of AGM**

(1) A notice calling an annual general meeting of a public company must state that the meeting is an annual general meeting.

(2) An annual general meeting may be called by shorter notice than that required by section 307(2) or by the company's articles (as the case may be), if all the members entitled to attend and vote at the meeting agree to the shorter notice.

338. **Public companies: members' power to require circulation of resolutions for AGMs**

(1) The members of a public company may require the company to give, to members of the company entitled to receive notice of the next annual general meeting, notice of a resolution which may properly be moved and is intended to be moved at that meeting.

(2) A resolution may properly be moved at an annual general meeting unless—

(a) it would, if passed, be ineffective (whether by reason of inconsistency with any enactment or the company's constitution or otherwise),

(b) it is defamatory of any person, or

(c) it is frivolous or vexatious.

(3) A company is required to give notice of a resolution once it has received requests that it do so from—

    (a) members representing at least 5% of the total voting rights of all the members who have a right to vote on the resolution at the annual general meeting to which the requests relate (excluding any voting rights attached to any shares in the company held as treasury shares), or

    (b) at least 100 members who have a right to vote on the resolution at the annual general meeting to which the requests relate and hold shares in the company on which there has been paid up an average sum, per member, of at least £100.

See also section 153 (exercise of rights where shares held on behalf of others).

(4) A request—

    (a) may be in hard copy form or in electronic form,

    (b) must identify the resolution of which notice is to be given,

    (c) must be authenticated by the person or persons making it, and

    (d) must be received by the company not later than—

        (i) 6 weeks before the annual general meeting to which the requests relate, or

        (ii) if later, the time at which notice is given of that meeting.

339. Public companies: company's duty to circulate members' resolutions for AGMs

(1) A company that is required under section 338 to give notice of a resolution must send a copy of it to each member of the company entitled to receive notice of the annual general meeting—

    (a) in the same manner as notice of the meeting, and

    (b) at the same time as, or as soon as reasonably practicable after, it gives notice of the meeting.

(2) Subsection (1) has effect subject to section 340(2) (deposit or tender of sum in respect of expenses of circulation).

(3) The business which may be dealt with at an annual general meeting includes a resolution of which notice is given in accordance with this section.

(4) In the event of default in complying with this section, an offence is committed by every officer of the company who is in default.

(5) A person guilty of an offence under this section is liable—

    (a) on conviction on indictment, to a fine;

    (b) on summary conviction, to a fine not exceeding the statutory maximum.

340. Public companies: expenses of circulating members' resolutions for AGM

(1) The expenses of the company in complying with section 339 need not be paid by the members who requested the circulation of the resolution if requests sufficient to require the company to circulate it are received before the end of the financial year preceding the meeting.

(2) Otherwise—

    (a) the expenses of the company in complying with that section must be paid by the members who requested the circulation of the resolution unless the company resolves otherwise, and

    (b) unless the company has previously so resolved, it is not bound to comply with that section unless there is deposited with or tendered to it, not later than—

        (i) six weeks before the annual general meeting to which the requests relate, or

        (ii) if later, the time at which notice is given of that meeting,

    a sum reasonably sufficient to meet its expenses in complying with that section.

CHAPTER 5
ADDITIONAL REQUIREMENTS FOR QUOTED COMPANIES

Website publication of poll results

341. Results of poll to be made available on website

(1) Where a poll is taken at a general meeting of a quoted company, the company must ensure that the following information is made available on a website—

(a) the date of the meeting,

(b) the text of the resolution or, as the case may be, a description of the subject matter of the poll,

(c) the number of votes cast in favour, and

(d) the number of votes cast against.

(2) The provisions of section 353 (requirements as to website availability) apply.

(3) In the event of default in complying with this section (or with the requirements of section 353 as it applies for the purposes of this section), an offence is committed by every officer of the company who is in default.

(4) A person guilty of an offence under subsection (3) is liable on summary conviction to a fine not exceeding level 3 on the standard scale.

(5) Failure to comply with this section (or the requirements of section 353) does not affect the validity of—

(a) the poll, or

(b) the resolution or other business (if passed or agreed to) to which the poll relates.

(6) This section only applies to polls taken after this section comes into force.

Independent report on poll

342. Members' power to require independent report on poll

(1) The members of a quoted company may require the directors to obtain an independent report on any poll taken, or to be taken, at a general meeting of the company.

(2) The directors are required to obtain an independent report if they receive requests to do so from—

(a) members representing not less than 5% of the total voting rights of all the members who have a right to vote on the matter to which the poll relates (excluding any voting rights attached to any shares in the company held as treasury shares), or

(b) not less than 100 members who have a right to vote on the matter to which the poll relates and hold shares in the company on which there has been paid up an average sum, per member, of not less than £100.

See also section 153 (exercise of rights where shares held on behalf of others).

(3) Where the requests relate to more than one poll, subsection (2) must be satisfied in relation to each of them.

(4) A request—

(a) may be in hard copy form or in electronic form,

(b) must identify the poll or polls to which it relates,

(c) must be authenticated by the person or persons making it, and

(d) must be received by the company not later than one week after the date on which the poll is taken.

343. Appointment of independent assessor

(1) Directors who are required under section 342 to obtain an independent report on a poll or polls must appoint a person they consider to be appropriate (an "independent assessor") to prepare a report for the company on it or them.

(2) The appointment must be made within one week after the company being required to obtain the report.

(3) The directors must not appoint a person who—

    (a) does not meet the independence requirement in section 344, or

    (b) has another role in relation to any poll on which he is to report (including, in particular, a role in connection with collecting or counting votes or with the appointment of proxies).

(4) In the event of default in complying with this section, an offence is committed by every officer of the company who is in default.

(5) A person guilty of an offence under this section is liable on summary conviction to a fine not exceeding level 5 on the standard scale.

(6) If at the meeting no poll on which a report is required is taken—

    (a) the directors are not required to obtain a report from the independent assessor, and

    (b) his appointment ceases (but without prejudice to any right to be paid for work done before the appointment ceased).

344. Independence requirement

(1) A person may not be appointed as an independent assessor—

    (a) if he is—

      (i) an officer or employee of the company, or

      (ii) a partner or employee of such a person, or a partnership of which such a person is a partner;

    (b) if he is—

      (i) an officer or employee of an associated undertaking of the company, or

      (ii) a partner or employee of such a person, or a partnership of which such a person is a partner;

    (c) if there exists between—

      (i) the person or an associate of his, and

      (ii) the company or an associated undertaking of the company,

    a connection of any such description as may be specified by regulations made by the Secretary of State.

(2) An auditor of the company is not regarded as an officer or employee of the company for this purpose.

(3) In this section—

    "associated undertaking" means—

    (a) a parent undertaking or subsidiary undertaking of the company, or

    (b) a subsidiary undertaking of a parent undertaking of the company; and

    "associate" has the meaning given by section 345.

(4) Regulations under this section are subject to negative resolution procedure.

345. Meaning of "associate"

(1) This section defines "associate" for the purposes of section 344 (independence requirement).

(2) In relation to an individual, "associate" means—

    (a) that individual's spouse or civil partner or minor child or step-child,

    (b) any body corporate of which that individual is a director, and

    (c) any employee or partner of that individual.

(3) In relation to a body corporate, "associate" means—

    (a) any body corporate of which that body is a director,

    (b) any body corporate in the same group as that body, and

    (c) any employee or partner of that body or of any body corporate in the same group.

(4) In relation to a partnership that is a legal person under the law by which it is governed, "associate" means—

    (a) any body corporate of which that partnership is a director,

    (b) any employee of or partner in that partnership, and

    (c) any person who is an associate of a partner in that partnership.

(5) In relation to a partnership that is not a legal person under the law by which it is governed, "associate" means any person who is an associate of any of the partners.

(6) In this section, in relation to a limited liability partnership, for "director" read "member".

346. **Effect of appointment of a partnership**

(1) This section applies where a partnership that is not a legal person under the law by which it is governed is appointed as an independent assessor.

(2) Unless a contrary intention appears, the appointment is of the partnership as such and not of the partners.

(3) Where the partnership ceases, the appointment is to be treated as extending to—

    (a) any partnership that succeeds to the practice of that partnership, or

    (b) any other person who succeeds to that practice having previously carried it on in partnership.

(4) For the purposes of subsection (3)—

    (a) a partnership is regarded as succeeding to the practice of another partnership only if the members of the successor partnership are substantially the same as those of the former partnership, and

    (b) a partnership or other person is regarded as succeeding to the practice of a partnership only if it or he succeeds to the whole or substantially the whole of the business of the former partnership.

(5) Where the partnership ceases and the appointment is not treated under subsection (3) as extending to any partnership or other person, the appointment may with the consent of the company be treated as extending to a partnership, or other person, who succeeds to—

    (a) the business of the former partnership, or

    (b) such part of it as is agreed by the company is to be treated as comprising the appointment.

347. **The independent assessor's report**

(1) The report of the independent assessor must state his opinion whether—

    (a) the procedures adopted in connection with the poll or polls were adequate;

    (b) the votes cast (including proxy votes) were fairly and accurately recorded and counted;

    (c) the validity of members' appointments of proxies was fairly assessed;

    (d) the notice of the meeting complied with section 325 (notice of meeting to contain statement of rights to appoint proxy);

    (e) section 326 (company-sponsored invitations to appoint proxies) was complied with in relation to the meeting.

(2) The report must give his reasons for the opinions stated.

(3) If he is unable to form an opinion on any of those matters, the report must record that fact and state the reasons for it.

(4) The report must state the name of the independent assessor.

348. **Rights of independent assessor: right to attend meeting etc**

(1) Where an independent assessor has been appointed to report on a poll, he is entitled to attend—

    (a) the meeting at which the poll may be taken, and

    (b) any subsequent proceedings in connection with the poll.

(2) He is also entitled to be provided by the company with a copy of—

    (a) the notice of the meeting, and

    (b) any other communication provided by the company in connection with the meeting to persons who have a right to vote on the matter to which the poll relates.

(3) The rights conferred by this section are only to be exercised to the extent that the independent assessor considers necessary for the preparation of his report.

(4) If the independent assessor is a firm, the right under subsection (1) to attend the meeting and any subsequent proceedings in connection with the poll is exercisable by an individual authorised by the firm in writing to act as its representative for that purpose.

349. Rights of independent assessor: right to information

(1) The independent assessor is entitled to access to the company's records relating to—

    (a) any poll on which he is to report;

    (b) the meeting at which the poll or polls may be, or were, taken.

(2) The independent assessor may require anyone who at any material time was—

    (a) a director or secretary of the company,

    (b) an employee of the company,

    (c) a person holding or accountable for any of the company's records,

    (d) a member of the company, or

    (e) an agent of the company,

to provide him with information or explanations for the purpose of preparing his report.

(3) For this purpose "agent" includes the company's bankers, solicitors and auditor.

(4) A statement made by a person in response to a requirement under this section may not be used in evidence against him in criminal proceedings except proceedings for an offence under section 350 (offences relating to provision of information).

(5) A person is not required by this section to disclose information in respect of which a claim to legal professional privilege (in Scotland, to confidentiality of communications) could be maintained in legal proceedings.

350. Offences relating to provision of information

(1) A person who fails to comply with a requirement under section 349 without delay commits an offence unless it was not reasonably practicable for him to provide the required information or explanation.

(2) A person guilty of an offence under subsection (1) is liable on summary conviction to a fine not exceeding level 3 on the standard scale.

(3) A person commits an offence who knowingly or recklessly makes to an independent assessor a statement (oral or written) that—

    (a) conveys or purports to convey any information or explanations which the independent assessor requires, or is entitled to require, under section 349, and

    (b) is misleading, false or deceptive in a material particular.

(4) A person guilty of an offence under subsection (3) is liable—

    (a) on conviction on indictment, to imprisonment for a term not exceeding two years or a fine (or both);

    (b) on summary conviction—

        (i) in England and Wales, to imprisonment for a term not exceeding twelve months or to a fine not exceeding the statutory maximum (or both);

        (ii) in Scotland or Northern Ireland, to imprisonment for a term not exceeding six months, or to a fine not exceeding the statutory maximum (or both).

(5) Nothing in this section affects any right of an independent assessor to apply for an injunction (in Scotland, an interdict or an order for specific performance) to enforce any of his rights under section 348 or 349.

351. Information to be made available on website

(1) Where an independent assessor has been appointed to report on a poll, the company must ensure that the following information is made available on a website—

    (a) the fact of his appointment,

    (b) his identity,

    (c) the text of the resolution or, as the case may be, a description of the subject matter of the poll to which his appointment relates, and

    (d) a copy of a report by him which complies with section 347.

(2) The provisions of section 353 (requirements as to website availability) apply.

(3) In the event of default in complying with this section (or with the requirements of section 353 as it applies for the purposes of this section), an offence is committed by every officer of the company who is in default.

(4) A person guilty of an offence under subsection (3) is liable on summary conviction to a fine not exceeding level 3 on the standard scale.

(5) Failure to comply with this section (or the requirements of section 353) does not affect the validity of—

(a) the poll, or

(b) the resolution or other business (if passed or agreed to) to which the poll relates.

Supplementary

352. Application of provisions to class meetings

(1) The provisions of—

section 341 (results of poll to be made available on website), and

sections 342 to 351 (independent report on poll),

apply (with any necessary modifications) in relation to a meeting of holders of a class of shares of a quoted company in connection with the variation of the rights attached to such shares as they apply in relation to a general meeting of the company.

(2) For the purposes of this section—

(a) any amendment of a provision contained in a company's articles for the variation of the rights attached to a class of shares, or the insertion of any such provision into the articles, is itself to be treated as a variation of those rights, and

(b) references to the variation of rights attached to a class of shares include references to their abrogation.

353. Requirements as to website availability

(1) The following provisions apply for the purposes of—

section 341 (results of poll to be made available on website), and

section 351 (report of independent observer to be made available on website).

(2) The information must be made available on a website that—

(a) is maintained by or on behalf of the company, and

(b) identifies the company in question.

(3) Access to the information on the website, and the ability to obtain a hard copy of the information from the website, must not be conditional on the payment of a fee or otherwise restricted.

(4) The information—

(a) must be made available as soon as reasonably practicable, and

(b) must be kept available throughout the period of two years beginning with the date on which it is first made available on a website in accordance with this section.

(5) A failure to make information available on a website throughout the period specified in subsection (4)(b) is disregarded if—

(a) the information is made available on the website for part of that period, and

(b) the failure is wholly attributable to circumstances that it would not be reasonable to have expected the company to prevent or avoid.

354. Power to limit or extend the types of company to which provisions of this Chapter apply

(1) The Secretary of State may by regulations—

(a) limit the types of company to which some or all of the provisions of this Chapter apply, or

(b) extend some or all of the provisions of this Chapter to additional types of company.

(2) Regulations under this section extending the application of any provision of this Chapter are subject to affirmative resolution procedure.

(3) Any other regulations under this section are subject to negative resolution procedure.

(4) Regulations under this section may—

    (a) amend the provisions of this Chapter (apart from this section);

    (b) repeal and re-enact provisions of this Chapter with modifications of form or arrangement, whether or not they are modified in substance;

    (c) contain such consequential, incidental and supplementary provisions (including provisions amending, repealing or revoking enactments) as the Secretary of State thinks fit.

CHAPTER 6
RECORDS OF RESOLUTIONS AND MEETINGS

355. Records of resolutions and meetings etc

(1) Every company must keep records comprising—

    (a) copies of all resolutions of members passed otherwise than at general meetings,

    (b) minutes of all proceedings of general meetings, and

    (c) details provided to the company in accordance with section 357 (decisions of sole member).

(2) The records must be kept for at least ten years from the date of the resolution, meeting or decision (as appropriate).

(3) If a company fails to comply with this section, an offence is committed by every officer of the company who is in default.

(4) A person guilty of an offence under this section is liable on summary conviction to a fine not exceeding level 3 on the standard scale and, for continued contravention, a daily default fine not exceeding one-tenth of level 3 on the standard scale.

356. Records as evidence of resolutions etc

(1) This section applies to the records kept in accordance with section 355.

(2) The record of a resolution passed otherwise than at a general meeting, if purporting to be signed by a director of the company or by the company secretary, is evidence (in Scotland, sufficient evidence) of the passing of the resolution.

(3) Where there is a record of a written resolution of a private company, the requirements of this Act with respect to the passing of the resolution are deemed to be complied with unless the contrary is proved.

(4) The minutes of proceedings of a general meeting, if purporting to be signed by the chairman of that meeting or by the chairman of the next general meeting, are evidence (in Scotland, sufficient evidence) of the proceedings at the meeting.

(5) Where there is a record of proceedings of a general meeting of a company, then, until the contrary is proved—

    (a) the meeting is deemed duly held and convened,

    (b) all proceedings at the meeting are deemed to have duly taken place, and

    (c) all appointments at the meeting are deemed valid.

357. Records of decisions by sole member

(1) This section applies to a company limited by shares or by guarantee that has only one member.

(2) Where the member takes any decision that—

    (a) may be taken by the company in general meeting, and

    (b) has effect as if agreed by the company in general meeting,

he must (unless that decision is taken by way of a written resolution) provide the company with details of that decision.

(3) If a person fails to comply with this section he commits an offence.

(4) A person guilty of an offence under this section is liable on summary conviction to a fine not exceeding level 2 on the standard scale.

(5) Failure to comply with this section does not affect the validity of any decision referred to in subsection (2).

358. Inspection of records of resolutions and meetings

(1) The records referred to in section 355 (records of resolutions etc) relating to the previous ten years must be kept available for inspection—

    (a) at the company's registered office, or

    (b) at a place specified in regulations under section 1136.

(2) The company must give notice to the registrar—

    (a) of the place at which the records are kept available for inspection, and

    (b) of any change in that place,

unless they have at all times been kept at the company's registered office.

(3) The records must be open to the inspection of any member of the company without charge.

(4) Any member may require a copy of any of the records on payment of such fee as may be prescribed.

(5) If default is made for 14 days in complying with subsection (2) or an inspection required under subsection (3) is refused, or a copy requested under subsection (4) is not sent, an offence is committed by every officer of the company who is in default.

(6) A person guilty of an offence under this section is liable on summary conviction to a fine not exceeding level 3 on the standard scale and, for continued contravention, a daily default fine not exceeding one-tenth of level 3 on the standard scale.

(7) In a case in which an inspection required under subsection (3) is refused or a copy requested under subsection (4) is not sent, the court may by order compel an immediate inspection of the records or direct that the copies required be sent to the persons who requested them.

359. Records of resolutions and meetings of class of members

The provisions of this Chapter apply (with necessary modifications) in relation to resolutions and meetings of—

    (a) holders of a class of shares, and

    (b) in the case of a company without a share capital, a class of members,

as they apply in relation to resolutions of members generally and to general meetings.

CHAPTER 7
SUPPLEMENTARY PROVISIONS

360. Computation of periods of notice etc: clear day rule

(1) This section applies for the purposes of the following provisions of this Part—

    section 307(1) and (2) (notice required of general meeting),

    section 312(1) and (3) (resolution requiring special notice),

    section 314(4)(d) (request to circulate members' statement),

    section 316(2)(b) (expenses of circulating statement to be deposited or tendered before meeting),

    section 338(4)(d)(i) (request to circulate member's resolution at AGM of public company), and

    section 340(2)(b)(i) (expenses of circulating statement to be deposited or tendered before meeting).

(2) Any reference in those provisions to a period of notice, or to a period before a meeting by which a request must be received or sum deposited or tendered, is to a period of the specified length excluding—

    (a) the day of the meeting, and

    (b) the day on which the notice is given, the request received or the sum deposited or tendered.

361. **Meaning of "quoted company"**
In this Part "quoted company" has the same meaning as in Part 15 of this Act.

PART 14
CONTROL OF POLITICAL DONATIONS AND EXPENDITURE

Introductory

362. **Introductory**
This Part has effect for controlling—
(a) political donations made by companies to political parties, to other political organisations and to independent election candidates, and
(b) political expenditure incurred by companies.

Donations and expenditure to which this Part applies

363. **Political parties, organisations etc to which this Part applies**
(1) This Part applies to a political party if—
(a) it is registered under Part 2 of the Political Parties, Elections and Referendums Act 2000 (c. 41), or
(b) it carries on, or proposes to carry on, activities for the purposes of or in connection with the participation of the party in any election or elections to public office held in a member State other than the United Kingdom.
(2) This Part applies to an organisation (a "political organisation") if it carries on, or proposes to carry on, activities that are capable of being reasonably regarded as intended—
(a) to affect public support for a political party to which, or an independent election candidate to whom, this Part applies, or
(b) to influence voters in relation to any national or regional referendum held under the law of the United Kingdom or another member State.
(3) This Part applies to an independent election candidate at any election to public office held in the United Kingdom or another member State.
(4) Any reference in the following provisions of this Part to a political party, political organisation or independent election candidate, or to political expenditure, is to a party, organisation, independent candidate or expenditure to which this Part applies.

364. **Meaning of "political donation"**
(1) The following provisions have effect for the purposes of this Part as regards the meaning of "political donation".
(2) In relation to a political party or other political organisation—
(a) "political donation" means anything that in accordance with sections 50 to 52 of the Political Parties, Elections and Referendums Act 2000—
(i) constitutes a donation for the purposes of Chapter 1 of Part 4 of that Act (control of donations to registered parties), or
(ii) would constitute such a donation reading references in those sections to a registered party as references to any political party or other political organisation,
and
(b) section 53 of that Act applies, in the same way, for the purpose of determining the value of a donation.
(3) In relation to an independent election candidate—
(a) "political donation" means anything that, in accordance with sections 50 to 52 of that Act, would constitute a donation for the purposes of Chapter 1 of Part 4 of that Act

(control of donations to registered parties) reading references in those sections to a registered party as references to the independent election candidate, and

(b) section 53 of that Act applies, in the same way, for the purpose of determining the value of a donation.

(4) For the purposes of this section, sections 50 and 53 of the Political Parties, Elections and Referendums Act 2000 (c. 41) (definition of "donation" and value of donations) shall be treated as if the amendments to those sections made by the Electoral Administration Act 2006 (which remove from the definition of "donation" loans made otherwise than on commercial terms) had not been made.

365. Meaning of "political expenditure"

(1) In this Part "political expenditure", in relation to a company, means expenditure incurred by the company on—

(a) the preparation, publication or dissemination of advertising or other promotional or publicity material—
  (i) of whatever nature, and
  (ii) however published or otherwise disseminated,
  that, at the time of publication or dissemination, is capable of being reasonably regarded as intended to affect public support for a political party or other political organisation, or an independent election candidate, or

(b) activities on the part of the company that are capable of being reasonably regarded as intended—
  (i) to affect public support for a political party or other political organisation, or an independent election candidate, or
  (ii) to influence voters in relation to any national or regional referendum held under the law of a member State.

(2) For the purposes of this Part a political donation does not count as political expenditure.

Authorisation required for donations or expenditure

366. Authorisation required for donations or expenditure

(1) A company must not—

(a) make a political donation to a political party or other political organisation, or to an independent election candidate, or

(b) incur any political expenditure,

unless the donation or expenditure is authorised in accordance with the following provisions.

(2) The donation or expenditure must be authorised—

(a) in the case of a company that is not a subsidiary of another company, by a resolution of the members of the company;

(b) in the case of a company that is a subsidiary of another company by—
  (i) a resolution of the members of the company, and
  (ii) a resolution of the members of any relevant holding company.

(3) No resolution is required on the part of a company that is a wholly-owned subsidiary of a UK-registered company.

(4) For the purposes of subsection (2)(b)(ii) a "relevant holding company" means a company that, at the time the donation was made or the expenditure was incurred—

(a) was a holding company of the company by which the donation was made or the expenditure was incurred,

(b) was a UK-registered company, and

(c) was not a subsidiary of another UK-registered company.

(5) The resolution or resolutions required by this section—

    (a) must comply with section 367 (form of authorising resolution), and

    (b) must be passed before the donation is made or the expenditure incurred.

(6) Nothing in this section enables a company to be authorised to do anything that it could not lawfully do apart from this section.

367. Form of authorising resolution

(1) A resolution conferring authorisation for the purposes of this Part may relate to—

    (a) the company passing the resolution,

    (b) one or more subsidiaries of that company, or

    (c) the company passing the resolution and one or more subsidiaries of that company.

(2) A resolution may be expressed to relate to all companies that are subsidiaries of the company passing the resolution—

    (a) at the time the resolution is passed, or

    (b) at any time during the period for which the resolution has effect,

    without identifying them individually.

(3) The resolution may authorise donations or expenditure under one or more of the following heads—

    (a) donations to political parties or independent election candidates;

    (b) donations to political organisations other than political parties;

    (c) political expenditure.

(4) The resolution must specify a head or heads—

    (a) in the case of a resolution under subsection (2), for all of the companies to which it relates taken together;

    (b) in the case of any other resolution, for each company to which it relates.

(5) The resolution must be expressed in general terms conforming with subsection (2) and must not purport to authorise particular donations or expenditure.

(6) For each of the specified heads the resolution must authorise donations or, as the case may be, expenditure up to a specified amount in the period for which the resolution has effect (see section 368).

(7) The resolution must specify such amounts—

    (a) in the case of a resolution under subsection (2), for all of the companies to which it relates taken together;

    (b) in the case of any other resolution, for each company to which it relates.

368. Period for which resolution has effect

(1) A resolution conferring authorisation for the purposes of this Part has effect for a period of four years beginning with the date on which it is passed unless the directors determine, or the articles require, that it is to have effect for a shorter period beginning with that date.

(2) The power of the directors to make a determination under this section is subject to any provision of the articles that operates to prevent them from doing so.

Remedies in case of unauthorised donations or expenditure

369. Liability of directors in case of unauthorised donation or expenditure

(1) This section applies where a company has made a political donation or incurred political expenditure without the authorisation required by this Part.

(2) The directors in default are jointly and severally liable—

    (a) to make good to the company the amount of the unauthorised donation or expenditure, with interest, and

    (b) to compensate the company for any loss or damage sustained by it as a result of the unauthorised donation or expenditure having been made.

(3) The directors in default are—
  (a) those who, at the time the unauthorised donation was made or the unauthorised expenditure was incurred, were directors of the company by which the donation was made or the expenditure was incurred, and
  (b) where—
    (i) that company was a subsidiary of a relevant holding company, and
    (ii) the directors of the relevant holding company failed to take all reasonable steps to prevent the donation being made or the expenditure being incurred,
    the directors of the relevant holding company.
(4) For the purposes of subsection (3)(b) a "relevant holding company" means a company that, at the time the donation was made or the expenditure was incurred—
  (a) was a holding company of the company by which the donation was made or the expenditure was incurred,
  (b) was a UK-registered company, and
  (c) was not a subsidiary of another UK-registered company.
(5) The interest referred to in subsection (2)(a) is interest on the amount of the unauthorised donation or expenditure, so far as not made good to the company—
  (a) in respect of the period beginning with the date when the donation was made or the expenditure was incurred, and
  (b) at such rate as the Secretary of State may prescribe by regulations.
  Section 379(2) (construction of references to date when donation made or expenditure incurred) does not apply for the purposes of this subsection.
(6) Where only part of a donation or expenditure was unauthorised, this section applies only to so much of it as was unauthorised.

370. Enforcement of directors' liabilities by shareholder action
(1) Any liability of a director under section 369 is enforceable—
  (a) in the case of a liability of a director of a company to that company, by proceedings brought under this section in the name of the company by an authorised group of its members;
  (b) in the case of a liability of a director of a holding company to a subsidiary, by proceedings brought under this section in the name of the subsidiary by—
    (i) an authorised group of members of the subsidiary, or
    (ii) an authorised group of members of the holding company.
(2) This is in addition to the right of the company to which the liability is owed to bring proceedings itself to enforce the liability.
(3) An "authorised group" of members of a company means—
  (a) the holders of not less than 5% in nominal value of the company's issued share capital,
  (b) if the company is not limited by shares, not less than 5% of its members, or
  (c) not less than 50 of the company's members.
(4) The right to bring proceedings under this section is subject to the provisions of section 371.
(5) Nothing in this section affects any right of a member of a company to bring or continue proceedings under Part 11 (derivative claims or proceedings).

371. Enforcement of directors' liabilities by shareholder action: supplementary
(1) A group of members may not bring proceedings under section 370 in the name of a company unless—
  (a) the group has given written notice to the company stating—
    (i) the cause of action and a summary of the facts on which the proceedings are to be based,
    (ii) the names and addresses of the members comprising the group, and
    (iii) the grounds on which it is alleged that those members constitute an authorised group; and

    (b) not less than 28 days have elapsed between the date of the giving of the notice to the company and the bringing of the proceedings.

(2) Where such a notice is given to a company, any director of the company may apply to the court within the period of 28 days beginning with the date of the giving of the notice for an order directing that the proposed proceedings shall not be brought, on one or more of the following grounds—

    (a) that the unauthorised amount has been made good to the company;

    (b) that proceedings to enforce the liability have been brought, and are being pursued with due diligence, by the company;

    (c) that the members proposing to bring proceedings under this section do not constitute an authorised group.

(3) Where an application is made on the ground mentioned in subsection (2)(b), the court may as an alternative to directing that the proposed proceedings under section 370 are not to be brought, direct—

    (a) that such proceedings may be brought on such terms and conditions as the court thinks fit, and

    (b) that the proceedings brought by the company—

        (i) shall be discontinued, or

        (ii) may be continued on such terms and conditions as the court thinks fit.

(4) The members by whom proceedings are brought under section 370 owe to the company in whose name they are brought the same duties in relation to the proceedings as would be owed by the company's directors if the proceedings were being brought by the company.
But proceedings to enforce any such duty may be brought by the company only with the permission of the court.

(5) Proceedings brought under section 370 may not be discontinued or settled by the group except with the permission of the court, which may be given on such terms as the court thinks fit.

372. Costs of shareholder action

(1) This section applies in relation to proceedings brought under section 370 in the name of a company ("the company") by an authorised group ("the group").

(2) The group may apply to the court for an order directing the company to indemnify the group in respect of costs incurred or to be incurred by the group in connection with the proceedings.
The court may make such an order on such terms as it thinks fit.

(3) The group is not entitled to be paid any such costs out of the assets of the company except by virtue of such an order.

(4) If no such order has been made with respect to the proceedings, then—

    (a) if the company is awarded costs in connection with the proceedings, or it is agreed that costs incurred by the company in connection with the proceedings should be paid by any defendant, the costs shall be paid to the group; and

    (b) if any defendant is awarded costs in connection with the proceedings, or it is agreed that any defendant should be paid costs incurred by him in connection with the proceedings, the costs shall be paid by the group.

(5) In the application of this section to Scotland for "costs" read "expenses" and for "defendant" read "defender".

373. Information for purposes of shareholder action

(1) Where proceedings have been brought under section 370 in the name of a company by an authorised group, the group is entitled to require the company to provide it with all information relating to the subject matter of the proceedings that is in the company's possession or under its control or which is reasonably obtainable by it.

(2) If the company, having been required by the group to do so, refuses to provide the group with all or any of that information, the court may, on an application made by the group, make an order directing—

(a) the company, and

(b) any of its officers or employees specified in the application,

to provide the group with the information in question in such form and by such means as the court may direct.

Exemptions

374. Trade unions

(1) A donation to a trade union, other than a contribution to the union's political fund, is not a political donation for the purposes of this Part.

(2) A trade union is not a political organisation for the purposes of section 365 (meaning of "political expenditure").

(3) In this section—

"trade union" has the meaning given by section 1 of Trade Union and Labour Relations (Consolidation) Act 1992 (c. 52) or Article 3 of the Industrial Relations (Northern Ireland) Order 1992 (S.I. 1992/807 (N.I. 5));

"political fund" means the fund from which payments by a trade union in the furtherance of political objects are required to be made by virtue of section 82(1)(a) of that Act or Article 57(2)(a) of that Order.

375. Subscription for membership of trade association

(1) A subscription paid to a trade association for membership of the association is not a political donation for the purposes of this Part.

(2) For this purpose—

"trade association" means an organisation formed for the purpose of furthering the trade interests of its members, or of persons represented by its members, and

"subscription" does not include a payment to the association to the extent that it is made for the purpose of financing any particular activity of the association.

376. All-party parliamentary groups

(1) An all-party parliamentary group is not a political organisation for the purposes of this Part.

(2) An "all-party parliamentary group" means an all-party group composed of members of one or both of the Houses of Parliament (or of such members and other persons).

377. Political expenditure exempted by order

(1) Authorisation under this Part is not needed for political expenditure that is exempt by virtue of an order of the Secretary of State under this section.

(2) An order may confer an exemption in relation to—

(a) companies of any description or category specified in the order, or

(b) expenditure of any description or category so specified (whether framed by reference to goods, services or other matters in respect of which such expenditure is incurred or otherwise),

or both.

(3) If or to the extent that expenditure is exempt from the requirement of authorisation under this Part by virtue of an order under this section, it shall be disregarded in determining what donations are authorised by any resolution of the company passed for the purposes of this Part.

(4) An order under this section is subject to affirmative resolution procedure.

378. **Donations not amounting to more than £5,000 in any twelve month period**
  (1) Authorisation under this Part is not needed for a donation except to the extent that the total amount of—
    (a) that donation, and
    (b) other relevant donations made in the period of 12 months ending with the date on which that donation is made,
    exceeds £5,000.
  (2) In this section—
    "donation" means a donation to a political party or other political organisation or to an independent election candidate; and
    "other relevant donations" means—
      (a) in relation to a donation made by a company that is not a subsidiary, any other donations made by that company or by any of its subsidiaries;
      (b) in relation to a donation made by a company that is a subsidiary, any other donations made by that company, by any holding company of that company or by any other subsidiary of any such holding company.
  (3) If or to the extent that a donation is exempt by virtue of this section from the requirement of authorisation under this Part, it shall be disregarded in determining what donations are authorised by any resolution passed for the purposes of this Part.

Supplementary provisions

379. **Minor definitions**
  (1) In this Part—
    "director" includes shadow director; and
    "organisation" includes any body corporate or unincorporated association and any combination of persons.
  (2) Except as otherwise provided, any reference in this Part to the time at which a donation is made or expenditure is incurred is, in a case where the donation is made or expenditure incurred in pursuance of a contract, any earlier time at which that contract is entered into by the company.

PART 15
ACCOUNTS AND REPORTS

CHAPTER 1
INTRODUCTION

General

380. **Scheme of this Part**
  (1) The requirements of this Part as to accounts and reports apply in relation to each financial year of a company.
  (2) In certain respects different provisions apply to different kinds of company.
  (3) The main distinctions for this purpose are—
    (a) between companies subject to the small companies regime (see section 381) and companies that are not subject to that regime; and
    (b) between quoted companies (see section 385) and companies that are not quoted.
  (4) In this Part, where provisions do not apply to all kinds of company—
    (a) provisions applying to companies subject to the small companies regime appear before the provisions applying to other companies,

(b) provisions applying to private companies appear before the provisions applying to public companies, and

(c) provisions applying to quoted companies appear after the provisions applying to other companies.

Companies subject to the small companies regime

381. **Companies subject to the small companies regime**

The small companies regime for accounts and reports applies to a company for a financial year in relation to which the company—

(a) qualifies as small (see sections 382 and 383), and

(b) is not excluded from the regime (see section 384).

382. **Companies qualifying as small: general**

(1) A company qualifies as small in relation to its first financial year if the qualifying conditions are met in that year.

(2) A company qualifies as small in relation to a subsequent financial year—

(a) if the qualifying conditions are met in that year and the preceding financial year;

(b) if the qualifying conditions are met in that year and the company qualified as small in relation to the preceding financial year;

(c) if the qualifying conditions were met in the preceding financial year and the company qualified as small in relation to that year.

(3) The qualifying conditions are met by a company in a year in which it satisfies two or more of the following requirements—

1. Turnover	Not more than £5.6 million
2. Balance sheet total	Not more than £2.8 million
3. Number of employees	Not more than 50

(4) For a period that is a company's financial year but not in fact a year the maximum figures for turnover must be proportionately adjusted.

(5) The balance sheet total means the aggregate of the amounts shown as assets in the company's balance sheet.

(6) The number of employees means the average number of persons employed by the company in the year, determined as follows—

(a) find for each month in the financial year the number of persons employed under contracts of service by the company in that month (whether throughout the month or not),

(b) add together the monthly totals, and

(c) divide by the number of months in the financial year.

(7) This section is subject to section 383 (companies qualifying as small: parent companies).

383. **Companies qualifying as small: parent companies**

(1) A parent company qualifies as a small company in relation to a financial year only if the group headed by it qualifies as a small group.

(2) A group qualifies as small in relation to the parent company's first financial year if the qualifying conditions are met in that year.

(3) A group qualifies as small in relation to a subsequent financial year of the parent company—

(a) if the qualifying conditions are met in that year and the preceding financial year;

(b) if the qualifying conditions are met in that year and the group qualified as small in relation to the preceding financial year;

(c) if the qualifying conditions were met in the preceding financial year and the group qualified as small in relation to that year.

(4) The qualifying conditions are met by a group in a year in which it satisfies two or more of the following requirements—

1. Aggregate turnover	Not more than £5.6 million net (or £6.72 million gross)
2. Aggregate balance sheet total	Not more than £2.8 million net (or £3.36 million gross)
3. Aggregate number of employees	Not more than 50

(5) The aggregate figures are ascertained by aggregating the relevant figures determined in accordance with section 382 for each member of the group.

(6) In relation to the aggregate figures for turnover and balance sheet total—

"net" means after any set-offs and other adjustments made to eliminate group transactions—

    (a) in the case of Companies Act accounts, in accordance with regulations under section 404,

    (b) in the case of IAS accounts, in accordance with international accounting standards; and

"gross" means without those set-offs and other adjustments.

A company may satisfy any relevant requirement on the basis of either the net or the gross figure.

(7) The figures for each subsidiary undertaking shall be those included in its individual accounts for the relevant financial year, that is—

    (a) if its financial year ends with that of the parent company, that financial year, and

    (b) if not, its financial year ending last before the end of the financial year of the parent company.

If those figures cannot be obtained without disproportionate expense or undue delay, the latest available figures shall be taken.

384. Companies excluded from the small companies regime

(1) The small companies regime does not apply to a company that is, or was at any time within the financial year to which the accounts relate—

    (a) a public company,

    (b) a company that—

        (i) is an authorised insurance company, a banking company, an e-money issuer, an ISD investment firm or a UCITS management company, or

        (ii) carries on insurance market activity, or

    (c) a member of an ineligible group.

(2) A group is ineligible if any of its members is—

    (a) a public company,

    (b) a body corporate (other than a company) whose shares are admitted to trading on a regulated market in an EEA State,

    (c) a person (other than a small company) who has permission under Part 4 of the Financial Services and Markets Act 2000 (c. 8) to carry on a regulated activity,

    (d) a small company that is an authorised insurance company, a banking company, an e-money issuer, an ISD investment firm or a UCITS management company, or

    (e) a person who carries on insurance market activity.

(3) A company is a small company for the purposes of subsection (2) if it qualified as small in relation to its last financial year ending on or before the end of the financial year to which the accounts relate.

Quoted and unquoted companies

385. Quoted and unquoted companies

(1) For the purposes of this Part a company is a quoted company in relation to a financial year if it is a quoted company immediately before the end of the accounting reference period by reference to which that financial year was determined.

(2) A "quoted company" means a company whose equity share capital—
  (a) has been included in the official list in accordance with the provisions of Part 6 of the Financial Services and Markets Act 2000 (c. 8), or
  (b) is officially listed in an EEA State, or
  (c) is admitted to dealing on either the New York Stock Exchange or the exchange known as Nasdaq.
In paragraph (a) "the official list" has the meaning given by section 103(1) of the Financial Services and Markets Act 2000.

(3) An "unquoted company" means a company that is not a quoted company.

(4) The Secretary of State may by regulations amend or replace the provisions of subsections (1) to (2) so as to limit or extend the application of some or all of the provisions of this Part that are expressed to apply to quoted companies.

(5) Regulations under this section extending the application of any such provision of this Part are subject to affirmative resolution procedure.

(6) Any other regulations under this section are subject to negative resolution procedure.

CHAPTER 2
ACCOUNTING RECORDS

386. Duty to keep accounting records

(1) Every company must keep adequate accounting records.

(2) Adequate accounting records means records that are sufficient—
  (a) to show and explain the company's transactions,
  (b) to disclose with reasonable accuracy, at any time, the financial position of the company at that time, and
  (c) to enable the directors to ensure that any accounts required to be prepared comply with the requirements of this Act (and, where applicable, of Article 4 of the IAS Regulation).

(3) Accounting records must, in particular, contain—
  (a) entries from day to day of all sums of money received and expended by the company and the matters in respect of which the receipt and expenditure takes place, and
  (b) a record of the assets and liabilities of the company.

(4) If the company's business involves dealing in goods, the accounting records must contain—
  (a) statements of stock held by the company at the end of each financial year of the company,
  (b) all statements of stocktakings from which any statement of stock as is mentioned in paragraph (a) has been or is to be prepared, and
  (c) except in the case of goods sold by way of ordinary retail trade, statements of all goods sold and purchased, showing the goods and the buyers and sellers in sufficient detail to enable all these to be identified.

(5) A parent company that has a subsidiary undertaking in relation to which the above requirements do not apply must take reasonable steps to secure that the undertaking keeps such accounting records as to enable the directors of the parent company to ensure that any accounts required to be prepared under this Part comply with the requirements of this Act (and, where applicable, of Article 4 of the IAS Regulation).

387. Duty to keep accounting records: offence

(1) If a company fails to comply with any provision of section 386 (duty to keep accounting records), an offence is committed by every officer of the company who is in default.

(2) It is a defence for a person charged with such an offence to show that he acted honestly and that in the circumstances in which the company's business was carried on the default was excusable.

    (3) A person guilty of an offence under this section is liable—

        (a) on conviction on indictment, to imprisonment for a term not exceeding two years or a fine (or both);

        (b) on summary conviction—

            (i) in England and Wales, to imprisonment for a term not exceeding twelve months or to a fine not exceeding the statutory maximum (or both);

            (ii) in Scotland or Northern Ireland, to imprisonment for a term not exceeding six months, or to a fine not exceeding the statutory maximum (or both).

388. Where and for how long records to be kept

    (1) A company's accounting records—

        (a) must be kept at its registered office or such other place as the directors think fit, and

        (b) must at all times be open to inspection by the company's officers.

    (2) If accounting records are kept at a place outside the United Kingdom, accounts and returns with respect to the business dealt with in the accounting records so kept must be sent to, and kept at, a place in the United Kingdom, and must at all times be open to such inspection.

    (3) The accounts and returns to be sent to the United Kingdom must be such as to—

        (a) disclose with reasonable accuracy the financial position of the business in question at intervals of not more than six months, and

        (b) enable the directors to ensure that the accounts required to be prepared under this Part comply with the requirements of this Act (and, where applicable, of Article 4 of the IAS Regulation).

    (4) Accounting records that a company is required by section 386 to keep must be preserved by it—

        (a) in the case of a private company, for three years from the date on which they are made;

        (b) in the case of a public company, for six years from the date on which they are made.

    (5) Subsection (4) is subject to any provision contained in rules made under section 411 of the Insolvency Act 1986 (c. 45) (company insolvency rules) or Article 359 of the Insolvency (Northern Ireland) Order 1989 (S.I. 1989/2405 (N.I. 19)).

389. Where and for how long records to be kept: offences

    (1) If a company fails to comply with any provision of subsections (1) to (3) of section 388 (requirements as to keeping of accounting records), an offence is committed by every officer of the company who is in default.

    (2) It is a defence for a person charged with such an offence to show that he acted honestly and that in the circumstances in which the company's business was carried on the default was excusable.

    (3) An officer of a company commits an offence if he—

        (a) fails to take all reasonable steps for securing compliance by the company with subsection (4) of that section (period for which records to be preserved), or

        (b) intentionally causes any default by the company under that subsection.

    (4) A person guilty of an offence under this section is liable—

        (a) on conviction on indictment, to imprisonment for a term not exceeding two years or a fine (or both);

        (b) on summary conviction—

            (i) in England and Wales, to imprisonment for a term not exceeding twelve months or to a fine not exceeding the statutory maximum (or both);

            (ii) in Scotland or Northern Ireland, to imprisonment for a term not exceeding six months, or to a fine not exceeding the statutory maximum (or both).

CHAPTER 3
A COMPANY'S FINANCIAL YEAR

390. A company's financial year

(1) A company's financial year is determined as follows.

(2) Its first financial year—

    (a) begins with the first day of its first accounting reference period, and

    (b) ends with the last day of that period or such other date, not more than seven days before or after the end of that period, as the directors may determine.

(3) Subsequent financial years—

    (a) begin with the day immediately following the end of the company's previous financial year, and

    (b) end with the last day of its next accounting reference period or such other date, not more than seven days before or after the end of that period, as the directors may determine.

(4) In relation to an undertaking that is not a company, references in this Act to its financial year are to any period in respect of which a profit and loss account of the undertaking is required to be made up (by its constitution or by the law under which it is established), whether that period is a year or not.

(5) The directors of a parent company must secure that, except where in their opinion there are good reasons against it, the financial year of each of its subsidiary undertakings coincides with the company's own financial year.

391. Accounting reference periods and accounting reference date

(1) A company's accounting reference periods are determined according to its accounting reference date in each calendar year.

(2) The accounting reference date of a company incorporated in Great Britain before 1st April 1996 is—

    (a) the date specified by notice to the registrar in accordance with section 224(2) of the Companies Act 1985 (c. 6) (notice specifying accounting reference date given within nine months of incorporation), or

    (b) failing such notice—

        (i) in the case of a company incorporated before 1st April 1990, 31st March, and

        (ii) in the case of a company incorporated on or after 1st April 1990, the last day of the month in which the anniversary of its incorporation falls.

(3) The accounting reference date of a company incorporated in Northern Ireland before 22nd August 1997 is—

    (a) the date specified by notice to the registrar in accordance with article 232(2) of the Companies (Northern Ireland) Order 1986 (S.I. 1986/1032 (N.I. 6)) (notice specifying accounting reference date given within nine months of incorporation), or

    (b) failing such notice—

        (i) in the case of a company incorporated before the coming into operation of Article 5 of the Companies (Northern Ireland) Order 1990 (S.I. 1990/593 (N.I. 5)), 31st March, and

        (ii) in the case of a company incorporated after the coming into operation of that Article, the last day of the month in which the anniversary of its incorporation falls.

(4) The accounting reference date of a company incorporated—

    (a) in Great Britain on or after 1st April 1996 and before the commencement of this Act,

    (b) in Northern Ireland on or after 22nd August 1997 and before the commencement of this Act, or

    (c) after the commencement of this Act,

is the last day of the month in which the anniversary of its incorporation falls.

(5) A company's first accounting reference period is the period of more than six months, but not more than 18 months, beginning with the date of its incorporation and ending with its accounting reference date.

(6) Its subsequent accounting reference periods are successive periods of twelve months beginning immediately after the end of the previous accounting reference period and ending with its accounting reference date.

(7) This section has effect subject to the provisions of section 392 (alteration of accounting reference date).

392. Alteration of accounting reference date

(1) A company may by notice given to the registrar specify a new accounting reference date having effect in relation to—

    (a) the company's current accounting reference period and subsequent periods, or

    (b) the company's previous accounting reference period and subsequent periods.

A company's "previous accounting reference period" means the one immediately preceding its current accounting reference period.

(2) The notice must state whether the current or previous accounting reference period—

    (a) is to be shortened, so as to come to an end on the first occasion on which the new accounting reference date falls or fell after the beginning of the period, or

    (b) is to be extended, so as to come to an end on the second occasion on which that date falls or fell after the beginning of the period.

(3) A notice extending a company's current or previous accounting reference period is not effective if given less than five years after the end of an earlier accounting reference period of the company that was extended under this section.

This does not apply—

    (a) to a notice given by a company that is a subsidiary undertaking or parent undertaking of another EEA undertaking if the new accounting reference date coincides with that of the other EEA undertaking or, where that undertaking is not a company, with the last day of its financial year, or

    (b) where the company is in administration under Part 2 of the Insolvency Act 1986 (c. 45) or Part 3 of the Insolvency (Northern Ireland) Order 1989 (S.I. 1989/2405 (N.I. 19)), or

    (c) where the Secretary of State directs that it should not apply, which he may do with respect to a notice that has been given or that may be given.

(4) A notice under this section may not be given in respect of a previous accounting reference period if the period for filing accounts and reports for the financial year determined by reference to that accounting reference period has already expired.

(5) An accounting reference period may not be extended so as to exceed 18 months and a notice under this section is ineffective if the current or previous accounting reference period as extended in accordance with the notice would exceed that limit.

This does not apply where the company is in administration under Part 2 of the Insolvency Act 1986 (c. 45) or Part 3 of the Insolvency (Northern Ireland) Order 1989 (S.I. 1989/2405 (N.I. 19)).

(6) In this section "EEA undertaking" means an undertaking established under the law of any part of the United Kingdom or the law of any other EEA State.

CHAPTER 4
ANNUAL ACCOUNTS

General

393. Accounts to give true and fair view

(1) The directors of a company must not approve accounts for the purposes of this Chapter unless they are satisfied that they give a true and fair view of the assets, liabilities, financial position and profit or loss—

    (a) in the case of the company's individual accounts, of the company;

    (b) in the case of the company's group accounts, of the undertakings included in the consolidation as a whole, so far as concerns members of the company.

(2) The auditor of a company in carrying out his functions under this Act in relation to the company's annual accounts must have regard to the directors' duty under subsection (1).

Individual accounts

394. Duty to prepare individual accounts

The directors of every company must prepare accounts for the company for each of its financial years.

Those accounts are referred to as the company's "individual accounts".

395. Individual accounts: applicable accounting framework

(1) A company's individual accounts may be prepared—

    (a) in accordance with section 396 ("Companies Act individual accounts"), or

    (b) in accordance with international accounting standards ("IAS individual accounts").

    This is subject to the following provisions of this section and to section 407 (consistency of financial reporting within group).

(2) The individual accounts of a company that is a charity must be Companies Act individual accounts.

(3) After the first financial year in which the directors of a company prepare IAS individual accounts ("the first IAS year"), all subsequent individual accounts of the company must be prepared in accordance with international accounting standards unless there is a relevant change of circumstance.

(4) There is a relevant change of circumstance if, at any time during or after the first IAS year—

    (a) the company becomes a subsidiary undertaking of another undertaking that does not prepare IAS individual accounts,

    (b) the company ceases to be a company with securities admitted to trading on a regulated market in an EEA State, or

    (c) a parent undertaking of the company ceases to be an undertaking with securities admitted to trading on a regulated market in an EEA State.

(5) If, having changed to preparing Companies Act individual accounts following a relevant change of circumstance, the directors again prepare IAS individual accounts for the company, subsections (3) and (4) apply again as if the first financial year for which such accounts are again prepared were the first IAS year.

396. Companies Act individual accounts

(1) Companies Act individual accounts must comprise—

    (a) a balance sheet as at the last day of the financial year, and

    (b) a profit and loss account.

(2) The accounts must—

    (a) in the case of the balance sheet, give a true and fair view of the state of affairs of the company as at the end of the financial year, and

(b) in the case of the profit and loss account, give a true and fair view of the profit or loss of the company for the financial year.

(3) The accounts must comply with provision made by the Secretary of State by regulations as to—

(a) the form and content of the balance sheet and profit and loss account, and

(b) additional information to be provided by way of notes to the accounts.

(4) If compliance with the regulations, and any other provision made by or under this Act as to the matters to be included in a company's individual accounts or in notes to those accounts, would not be sufficient to give a true and fair view, the necessary additional information must be given in the accounts or in a note to them.

(5) If in special circumstances compliance with any of those provisions is inconsistent with the requirement to give a true and fair view, the directors must depart from that provision to the extent necessary to give a true and fair view.

Particulars of any such departure, the reasons for it and its effect must be given in a note to the accounts.

397. IAS individual accounts

Where the directors of a company prepare IAS individual accounts, they must state in the notes to the accounts that the accounts have been prepared in accordance with international accounting standards.

Group accounts: small companies

398. Option to prepare group accounts

If at the end of a financial year a company subject to the small companies regime is a parent company the directors, as well as preparing individual accounts for the year, may prepare group accounts for the year.

Group accounts: other companies

399. Duty to prepare group accounts

(1) This section applies to companies that are not subject to the small companies regime.

(2) If at the end of a financial year the company is a parent company the directors, as well as preparing individual accounts for the year, must prepare group accounts for the year unless the company is exempt from that requirement.

(3) There are exemptions under-

section 400 (company included in EEA accounts of larger group),

section 401 (company included in non-EEA accounts of larger group), and

section 402 (company none of whose subsidiary undertakings need be included in the consolidation).

(4) A company to which this section applies but which is exempt from the requirement to prepare group accounts, may do so.

400. Exemption for company included in EEA group accounts of larger group

(1) A company is exempt from the requirement to prepare group accounts if it is itself a subsidiary undertaking and its immediate parent undertaking is established under the law of an EEA State, in the following cases—

(a) where the company is a wholly-owned subsidiary of that parent undertaking;

(b) where that parent undertaking holds more than 50% of the allotted shares in the company and notice requesting the preparation of group accounts has not been served on the company by shareholders holding in aggregate—

(i) more than half of the remaining allotted shares in the company, or

(ii) 5% of the total allotted shares in the company.

Such notice must be served not later than six months after the end of the financial year before that to which it relates.

(2) Exemption is conditional upon compliance with all of the following conditions—

    (a) the company must be included in consolidated accounts for a larger group drawn up to the same date, or to an earlier date in the same financial year, by a parent undertaking established under the law of an EEA State;

    (b) those accounts must be drawn up and audited, and that parent undertaking's annual report must be drawn up, according to that law—

        (i) in accordance with the provisions of the Seventh Directive (83/349/EEC) (as modified, where relevant, by the provisions of the Bank Accounts Directive (86/635/EEC)), or the Insurance Accounts Directive (91/674/EEC)), or

        (ii) in accordance with international accounting standards;

    (c) the company must disclose in its individual accounts that it is exempt from the obligation to prepare and deliver group accounts;

    (d) the company must state in its individual accounts the name of the parent undertaking that draws up the group accounts referred to above and—

        (i) if it is incorporated outside the United Kingdom, the country in which it is incorporated, or

        (ii) if it is unincorporated, the address of its principal place of business;

    (e) the company must deliver to the registrar, within the period for filing its accounts and reports for the financial year in question, copies of—

        (i) those group accounts, and

        (ii) the parent undertaking's annual report,

    together with the auditor's report on them;

    (f) any requirement of Part 35 of this Act as to the delivery to the registrar of a certified translation into English must be met in relation to any document comprised in the accounts and reports delivered in accordance with paragraph (e).

(3) For the purposes of subsection (1)(b) shares held by a wholly-owned subsidiary of the parent undertaking, or held on behalf of the parent undertaking or a wholly-owned subsidiary, shall be attributed to the parent undertaking.

(4) The exemption does not apply to a company any of whose securities are admitted to trading on a regulated market in an EEA State.

(5) Shares held by directors of a company for the purpose of complying with any share qualification requirement shall be disregarded in determining for the purposes of this section whether the company is a wholly-owned subsidiary.

(6) In subsection (4) "securities" includes—

    (a) shares and stock,

    (b) debentures, including debenture stock, loan stock, bonds, certificates of deposit and other instruments creating or acknowledging indebtedness,

    (c) warrants or other instruments entitling the holder to subscribe for securities falling within paragraph (a) or (b), and

    (d) certificates or other instruments that confer—

        (i) property rights in respect of a security falling within paragraph (a), (b) or (c),

        (ii) any right to acquire, dispose of, underwrite or convert a security, being a right to which the holder would be entitled if he held any such security to which the certificate or other instrument relates, or

        (iii) a contractual right (other than an option) to acquire any such security otherwise than by subscription.

401. Exemption for company included in non-EEA group accounts of larger group

(1) A company is exempt from the requirement to prepare group accounts if it is itself a subsidiary undertaking and its parent undertaking is not established under the law of an EEA State, in the following cases—

    (a) where the company is a wholly-owned subsidiary of that parent undertaking;

    (b) where that parent undertaking holds more than 50% of the allotted shares in the company and notice requesting the preparation of group accounts has not been served on the company by shareholders holding in aggregate—

        (i) more than half of the remaining allotted shares in the company, or

        (ii) 5% of the total allotted shares in the company.

    Such notice must be served not later than six months after the end of the financial year before that to which it relates.

(2) Exemption is conditional upon compliance with all of the following conditions—

    (a) the company and all of its subsidiary undertakings must be included in consolidated accounts for a larger group drawn up to the same date, or to an earlier date in the same financial year, by a parent undertaking;

    (b) those accounts and, where appropriate, the group's annual report, must be drawn up—

        (i) in accordance with the provisions of the Seventh Directive (83/349/EEC) (as modified, where relevant, by the provisions of the Bank Accounts Directive (86/635/EEC) or the Insurance Accounts Directive (91/674/EEC)), or

        (ii) in a manner equivalent to consolidated accounts and consolidated annual reports so drawn up;

    (c) the group accounts must be audited by one or more persons authorised to audit accounts under the law under which the parent undertaking which draws them up is established;

    (d) the company must disclose in its individual accounts that it is exempt from the obligation to prepare and deliver group accounts;

    (e) the company must state in its individual accounts the name of the parent undertaking which draws up the group accounts referred to above and—

        (i) if it is incorporated outside the United Kingdom, the country in which it is incorporated, or

        (ii) if it is unincorporated, the address of its principal place of business;

    (f) the company must deliver to the registrar, within the period for filing its accounts and reports for the financial year in question, copies of—

        (i) the group accounts, and

        (ii) where appropriate, the consolidated annual report, together with the auditor's report on them;

    (g) any requirement of Part 35 of this Act as to the delivery to the registrar of a certified translation into English must be met in relation to any document comprised in the accounts and reports delivered in accordance with paragraph (f).

(3) For the purpose of subsection (1)(b), shares held by a wholly-owned subsidiary of the parent undertaking, or held on behalf of the parent undertaking or a wholly-owned subsidiary, are attributed to the parent undertaking.

(4) The exemption does not apply to a company any of whose securities are admitted to trading on a regulated market in an EEA State.

(5) Shares held by directors of a company for the purpose of complying with any share qualification requirement shall be disregarded in determining for the purposes of this section whether the company is a wholly-owned subsidiary.

(6) In subsection (4) "securities" includes—

    (a) shares and stock,

    (b) debentures, including debenture stock, loan stock, bonds, certificates of deposit and other instruments creating or acknowledging indebtedness,

(c) warrants or other instruments entitling the holder to subscribe for securities falling within paragraph (a) or (b), and

(d) certificates or other instruments that confer—

    (i) property rights in respect of a security falling within paragraph (a), (b) or (c),

    (ii) any right to acquire, dispose of, underwrite or convert a security, being a right to which the holder would be entitled if he held any such security to which the certificate or other instrument relates, or

    (iii) a contractual right (other than an option) to acquire any such security otherwise than by subscription.

402. Exemption if no subsidiary undertakings need be included in the consolidation

A parent company is exempt from the requirement to prepare group accounts if under section 405 all of its subsidiary undertakings could be excluded from consolidation in Companies Act group accounts.

Group accounts: general

403. Group accounts: applicable accounting framework

(1) The group accounts of certain parent companies are required by Article 4 of the IAS Regulation to be prepared in accordance with international accounting standards ("IAS group accounts").

(2) The group accounts of other companies may be prepared—

    (a) in accordance with section 404 ("Companies Act group accounts"), or

    (b) in accordance with international accounting standards ("IAS group accounts").

This is subject to the following provisions of this section.

(3) The group accounts of a parent company that is a charity must be Companies Act group accounts.

(4) After the first financial year in which the directors of a parent company prepare IAS group accounts ("the first IAS year"), all subsequent group accounts of the company must be prepared in accordance with international accounting standards unless there is a relevant change of circumstance.

(5) There is a relevant change of circumstance if, at any time during or after the first IAS year—

    (a) the company becomes a subsidiary undertaking of another undertaking that does not prepare IAS group accounts,

    (b) the company ceases to be a company with securities admitted to trading on a regulated market in an EEA State, or

    (c) a parent undertaking of the company ceases to be an undertaking with securities admitted to trading on a regulated market in an EEA State.

(6) If, having changed to preparing Companies Act group accounts following a relevant change of circumstance, the directors again prepare IAS group accounts for the company, subsections (4) and (5) apply again as if the first financial year for which such accounts are again prepared were the first IAS year.

404. Companies Act group accounts

(1) Companies Act group accounts must comprise—

    (a) a consolidated balance sheet dealing with the state of affairs of the parent company and its subsidiary undertakings, and

    (b) a consolidated profit and loss account dealing with the profit or loss of the parent company and its subsidiary undertakings.

(2) The accounts must give a true and fair view of the state of affairs as at the end of the financial year, and the profit or loss for the financial year, of the undertakings included in the consolidation as a whole, so far as concerns members of the company.

(3) The accounts must comply with provision made by the Secretary of State by regulations as to—

    (a) the form and content of the consolidated balance sheet and consolidated profit and loss account, and

    (b) additional information to be provided by way of notes to the accounts.

(4) If compliance with the regulations, and any other provision made by or under this Act as to the matters to be included in a company's group accounts or in notes to those accounts, would not be sufficient to give a true and fair view, the necessary additional information must be given in the accounts or in a note to them.

(5) If in special circumstances compliance with any of those provisions is inconsistent with the requirement to give a true and fair view, the directors must depart from that provision to the extent necessary to give a true and fair view.

Particulars of any such departure, the reasons for it and its effect must be given in a note to the accounts.

405. Companies Act group accounts: subsidiary undertakings included in the consolidation

(1) Where a parent company prepares Companies Act group accounts, all the subsidiary undertakings of the company must be included in the consolidation, subject to the following exceptions.

(2) A subsidiary undertaking may be excluded from consolidation if its inclusion is not material for the purpose of giving a true and fair view (but two or more undertakings may be excluded only if they are not material taken together).

(3) A subsidiary undertaking may be excluded from consolidation where—

    (a) severe long-term restrictions substantially hinder the exercise of the rights of the parent company over the assets or management of that undertaking, or

    (b) the information necessary for the preparation of group accounts cannot be obtained without disproportionate expense or undue delay, or

    (c) the interest of the parent company is held exclusively with a view to subsequent resale.

(4) The reference in subsection (3)(a) to the rights of the parent company and the reference in subsection (3)(c) to the interest of the parent company are, respectively, to rights and interests held by or attributed to the company for the purposes of the definition of "parent undertaking" (see section 1162) in the absence of which it would not be the parent company.

406. IAS group accounts

Where the directors of a company prepare IAS group accounts, they must state in the notes to those accounts that the accounts have been prepared in accordance with international accounting standards.

407. Consistency of financial reporting within group

(1) The directors of a parent company must secure that the individual accounts of—

    (a) the parent company, and

    (b) each of its subsidiary undertakings,

are all prepared using the same financial reporting framework, except to the extent that in their opinion there are good reasons for not doing so.

(2) Subsection (1) does not apply if the directors do not prepare group accounts for the parent company.

(3) Subsection (1) only applies to accounts of subsidiary undertakings that are required to be prepared under this Part.

(4) Subsection (1) does not require accounts of undertakings that are charities to be prepared using the same financial reporting framework as accounts of undertakings which are not charities.

(5) Subsection (1)(a) does not apply where the directors of a parent company prepare IAS group accounts and IAS individual accounts.

408. Individual profit and loss account where group accounts prepared

(1) This section applies where—

    (a) a company prepares group accounts in accordance with this Act, and

    (b) the notes to the company's individual balance sheet show the company's profit or loss for the financial year determined in accordance with this Act.

(2) The profit and loss account need not contain the information specified in section 411 (information about employee numbers and costs).

(3) The company's individual profit and loss account must be approved in accordance with section 414(1) (approval by directors) but may be omitted from the company's annual accounts for the purposes of the other provisions of the Companies Acts.

(4) The exemption conferred by this section is conditional upon its being disclosed in the company's annual accounts that the exemption applies.

Information to be given in notes to the accounts

409. Information about related undertakings

(1) The Secretary of State may make provision by regulations requiring information about related undertakings to be given in notes to a company's annual accounts.

(2) The regulations—

    (a) may make different provision according to whether or not the company prepares group accounts, and

    (b) may specify the descriptions of undertaking in relation to which they apply, and make different provision in relation to different descriptions of related undertaking.

(3) The regulations may provide that information need not be disclosed with respect to an undertaking that—

    (a) is established under the law of a country outside the United Kingdom, or

    (b) carries on business outside the United Kingdom,

    if the following conditions are met.

(4) The conditions are—

    (a) that in the opinion of the directors of the company the disclosure would be seriously prejudicial to the business of—

        (i) that undertaking,

        (ii) the company,

        (iii) any of the company's subsidiary undertakings, or

        (iv) any other undertaking which is included in the consolidation;

    (b) that the Secretary of State agrees that the information need not be disclosed.

(5) Where advantage is taken of any such exemption, that fact must be stated in a note to the company's annual accounts.

410. Information about related undertakings: alternative compliance

(1) This section applies where the directors of a company are of the opinion that the number of undertakings in respect of which the company is required to disclose information under any provision of regulations under section 409 (related undertakings) is such that compliance with that provision would result in information of excessive length being given in notes to the company's annual accounts.

(2) The information need only be given in respect of—

    (a) the undertakings whose results or financial position, in the opinion of the directors, principally affected the figures shown in the company's annual accounts, and

    (b) where the company prepares group accounts, undertakings excluded from consolidation under section 405(3) (undertakings excluded on grounds other than materiality).

(3) If advantage is taken of subsection (2)—

    (a) there must be included in the notes to the company's annual accounts a statement that the information is given only with respect to such undertakings as are mentioned in that subsection, and

    (b) the full information (both that which is disclosed in the notes to the accounts and that which is not) must be annexed to the company's next annual return.

For this purpose the "next annual return" means that next delivered to the registrar after the accounts in question have been approved under section 414.

(4) If a company fails to comply with subsection (3)(b), an offence is committed by—

    (a) the company, and

    (b) every officer of the company who is in default.

(5) A person guilty of an offence under subsection (4) is liable on summary conviction to a fine not exceeding level 3 on the standard scale and, for continued contravention, a daily default fine not exceeding one-tenth of level 3 on the standard scale.

411. Information about employee numbers and costs

(1) In the case of a company not subject to the small companies regime, the following information with respect to the employees of the company must be given in notes to the company's annual accounts—

    (a) the average number of persons employed by the company in the financial year, and

    (b) the average number of persons so employed within each category of persons employed by the company.

(2) The categories by reference to which the number required to be disclosed by subsection (1)(b) is to be determined must be such as the directors may select having regard to the manner in which the company's activities are organised.

(3) The average number required by subsection (1)(a) or (b) is determined by dividing the relevant annual number by the number of months in the financial year.

(4) The relevant annual number is determined by ascertaining for each month in the financial year—

    (a) for the purposes of subsection (1)(a), the number of persons employed under contracts of service by the company in that month (whether throughout the month or not);

    (b) for the purposes of subsection (1)(b), the number of persons in the category in question of persons so employed;

and adding together all the monthly numbers.

(5) In respect of all persons employed by the company during the financial year who are taken into account in determining the relevant annual number for the purposes of subsection (1)(a) there must also be stated the aggregate amounts respectively of—

    (a) wages and salaries paid or payable in respect of that year to those persons;

    (b) social security costs incurred by the company on their behalf; and

    (c) other pension costs so incurred.

This does not apply in so far as those amounts, or any of them, are stated elsewhere in the company's accounts.

(6) In subsection (5)—

"pension costs" includes any costs incurred by the company in respect of—

    (a) any pension scheme established for the purpose of providing pensions for persons currently or formerly employed by the company,

    (b) any sums set aside for the future payment of pensions directly by the company to current or former employees, and

    (c) any pensions paid directly to such persons without having first been set aside;

"social security costs" means any contributions by the company to any state social security or pension scheme, fund or arrangement.

(7) Where the company prepares group accounts, this section applies as if the undertakings included in the consolidation were a single company.

412. Information about directors' benefits: remuneration

(1) The Secretary of State may make provision by regulations requiring information to be given in notes to a company's annual accounts about directors' remuneration.

(2) The matters about which information may be required include—

    (a) gains made by directors on the exercise of share options;

    (b) benefits received or receivable by directors under long-term incentive schemes;

    (c) payments for loss of office (as defined in section 215);

    (d) benefits receivable, and contributions for the purpose of providing benefits, in respect of past services of a person as director or in any other capacity while director;

    (e) consideration paid to or receivable by third parties for making available the services of a person as director or in any other capacity while director.

(3) Without prejudice to the generality of subsection (1), regulations under this section may make any such provision as was made immediately before the commencement of this Part by Part 1 of Schedule 6 to the Companies Act 1985 (c.6).

(4) For the purposes of this section, and regulations made under it, amounts paid to or receivable by—

    (a) a person connected with a director, or

    (b) a body corporate controlled by a director,

are treated as paid to or receivable by the director.

The expressions "connected with" and "controlled by" in this subsection have the same meaning as in Part 10 (company directors).

(5) It is the duty of—

    (a) any director of a company, and

    (b) any person who is or has at any time in the preceding five years been a director of the company,

to give notice to the company of such matters relating to himself as may be necessary for the purposes of regulations under this section.

(6) A person who makes default in complying with subsection (5) commits an offence and is liable on summary conviction to a fine not exceeding level 3 on the standard scale.

413. Information about directors' benefits: advances, credit and guarantees

(1) In the case of a company that does not prepare group accounts, details of—

    (a) advances and credits granted by the company to its directors, and

    (b) guarantees of any kind entered into by the company on behalf of its directors,

must be shown in the notes to its individual accounts.

(2) In the case of a parent company that prepares group accounts, details of—

    (a) advances and credits granted to the directors of the parent company, by that company or by any of its subsidiary undertakings, and

    (b) guarantees of any kind entered into on behalf of the directors of the parent company, by that company or by any of its subsidiary undertakings,

must be shown in the notes to the group accounts.

(3) The details required of an advance or credit are—

    (a) its amount,

    (b) an indication of the interest rate,

    (c) its main conditions, and

    (d) any amounts repaid.

(4) The details required of a guarantee are—

    (a) its main terms,

    (b) the amount of the maximum liability that may be incurred by the company (or its subsidiary), and

      (c) any amount paid and any liability incurred by the company (or its subsidiary) for the purpose of fulfilling the guarantee (including any loss incurred by reason of enforcement of the guarantee).

(5) There must also be stated in the notes to the accounts the totals—

      (a) of amounts stated under subsection (3)(a),

      (b) of amounts stated under subsection (3)(d),

      (c) of amounts stated under subsection (4)(b), and

      (d) of amounts stated under subsection (4)(c).

(6) References in this section to the directors of a company are to the persons who were a director at any time in the financial year to which the accounts relate.

(7) The requirements of this section apply in relation to every advance, credit or guarantee subsisting at any time in the financial year to which the accounts relate—

      (a) whenever it was entered into,

      (b) whether or not the person concerned was a director of the company in question at the time it was entered into, and

      (c) in the case of an advance, credit or guarantee involving a subsidiary undertaking of that company, whether or not that undertaking was such a subsidiary undertaking at the time it was entered into.

(8) Banking companies and the holding companies of credit institutions need only state the details required by subsections (3)(a) and (4)(b).

Approval and signing of accounts

414. Approval and signing of accounts

(1) A company's annual accounts must be approved by the board of directors and signed on behalf of the board by a director of the company.

(2) The signature must be on the company's balance sheet.

(3) If the accounts are prepared in accordance with the provisions applicable to companies subject to the small companies regime, the balance sheet must contain a statement to that effect in a prominent position above the signature.

(4) If annual accounts are approved that do not comply with the requirements of this Act (and, where applicable, of Article 4 of the IAS Regulation), every director of the company who—

      (a) knew that they did not comply, or was reckless as to whether they complied, and

      (b) failed to take reasonable steps to secure compliance with those requirements or, as the case may be, to prevent the accounts from being approved,

commits an offence.

(5) A person guilty of an offence under this section is liable—

      (a) on conviction on indictment, to a fine;

      (b) on summary conviction, to a fine not exceeding the statutory maximum.

CHAPTER 5
DIRECTORS' REPORT

Directors' report

415. Duty to prepare directors' report

(1) The directors of a company must prepare a directors' report for each financial year of the company.

(2) For a financial year in which—

      (a) the company is a parent company, and

      (b) the directors of the company prepare group accounts,

the directors' report must be a consolidated report (a "group directors' report") relating to the undertakings included in the consolidation.

(3) A group directors' report may, where appropriate, give greater emphasis to the matters that are significant to the undertakings included in the consolidation, taken as a whole.

(4) In the case of failure to comply with the requirement to prepare a directors' report, an offence is committed by every person who—

(a) was a director of the company immediately before the end of the period for filing accounts and reports for the financial year in question, and

(b) failed to take all reasonable steps for securing compliance with that requirement.

(5) A person guilty of an offence under this section is liable—

(a) on conviction on indictment, to a fine;

(b) on summary conviction, to a fine not exceeding the statutory maximum.

416. Contents of directors' report: general

(1) The directors' report for a financial year must state—

(a) the names of the persons who, at any time during the financial year, were directors of the company, and

(b) the principal activities of the company in the course of the year.

(2) In relation to a group directors' report subsection (1)(b) has effect as if the reference to the company was to the undertakings included in the consolidation.

(3) Except in the case of a company subject to the small companies regime, the report must state the amount (if any) that the directors recommend should be paid by way of dividend.

(4) The Secretary of State may make provision by regulations as to other matters that must be disclosed in a directors' report.

Without prejudice to the generality of this power, the regulations may make any such provision as was formerly made by Schedule 7 to the Companies Act 1985.

417. Contents of directors' report: business review

(1) Unless the company is subject to the small companies' regime, the directors' report must contain a business review.

(2) The purpose of the business review is to inform members of the company and help them assess how the directors have performed their duty under section 172 (duty to promote the success of the company).

(3) The business review must contain—

(a) a fair review of the company's business, and

(b) a description of the principal risks and uncertainties facing the company.

(4) The review required is a balanced and comprehensive analysis of—

(a) the development and performance of the company's business during the financial year, and

(b) the position of the company's business at the end of that year,

consistent with the size and complexity of the business.

(5) In the case of a quoted company the business review must, to the extent necessary for an understanding of the development, performance or position of the company's business, include—

(a) the main trends and factors likely to affect the future development, performance and position of the company's business; and

(b) information about—

(i) environmental matters (including the impact of the company's business on the environment),

(ii) the company's employees, and

(iii) social and community issues,

including information about any policies of the company in relation to those matters and the effectiveness of those policies; and

(c) subject to subsection (11), information about persons with whom the company has contractual or other arrangements which are essential to the business of the company.

If the review does not contain information of each kind mentioned in paragraphs (b)(i), (ii) and (iii) and (c), it must state which of those kinds of information it does not contain.

(6) The review must, to the extent necessary for an understanding of the development, performance or position of the company's business, include—

(a) analysis using financial key performance indicators, and

(b) where appropriate, analysis using other key performance indicators, including information relating to environmental matters and employee matters.

"Key performance indicators" means factors by reference to which the development, performance or position of the company's business can be measured effectively.

(7) Where a company qualifies as medium-sized in relation to a financial year (see sections 465 to 467), the directors' report for the year need not comply with the requirements of subsection (6) so far as they relate to non-financial information.

(8) The review must, where appropriate, include references to, and additional explanations of, amounts included in the company's annual accounts.

(9) In relation to a group directors' report this section has effect as if the references to the company were references to the undertakings included in the consolidation.

(10) Nothing in this section requires the disclosure of information about impending developments or matters in the course of negotiation if the disclosure would, in the opinion of the directors, be seriously prejudicial to the interests of the company.

(11) Nothing in subsection (5)(c) requires the disclosure of information about a person if the disclosure would, in the opinion of the directors, be seriously prejudicial to that person and contrary to the public interest.

418. Contents of directors' report: statement as to disclosure to auditors

(1) This section applies to a company unless—

(a) it is exempt for the financial year in question from the requirements of Part 16 as to audit of accounts, and

(b) the directors take advantage of that exemption.

(2) The directors' report must contain a statement to the effect that, in the case of each of the persons who are directors at the time the report is approved—

(a) so far as the director is aware, there is no relevant audit information of which the company's auditor is unaware, and

(b) he has taken all the steps that he ought to have taken as a director in order to make himself aware of any relevant audit information and to establish that the company's auditor is aware of that information.

(3) "Relevant audit information" means information needed by the company's auditor in connection with preparing his report.

(4) A director is regarded as having taken all the steps that he ought to have taken as a director in order to do the things mentioned in subsection (2)(b) if he has—

(a) made such enquiries of his fellow directors and of the company's auditors for that purpose, and

(b) taken such other steps (if any) for that purpose,

as are required by his duty as a director of the company to exercise reasonable care, skill and diligence.

(5) Where a directors' report containing the statement required by this section is approved but the statement is false, every director of the company who—

(a) knew that the statement was false, or was reckless as to whether it was false, and

(b) failed to take reasonable steps to prevent the report from being approved,

commits an offence.

(6) A person guilty of an offence under subsection (5) is liable—
  (a) on conviction on indictment, to imprisonment for a term not exceeding two years or a fine (or both);
  (b) on summary conviction—
    (i) in England and Wales, to imprisonment for a term not exceeding twelve months or to a fine not exceeding the statutory maximum (or both);
    (ii) in Scotland or Northern Ireland, to imprisonment for a term not exceeding six months, or to a fine not exceeding the statutory maximum (or both).

419. Approval and signing of directors' report
  (1) The directors' report must be approved by the board of directors and signed on behalf of the board by a director or the secretary of the company.
  (2) If the report is prepared in accordance with the small companies regime, it must contain a statement to that effect in a prominent position above the signature.
  (3) If a directors' report is approved that does not comply with the requirements of this Act, every director of the company who—
    (a) knew that it did not comply, or was reckless as to whether it complied, and
    (b) failed to take reasonable steps to secure compliance with those requirements or, as the case may be, to prevent the report from being approved,
    commits an offence.
  (4) A person guilty of an offence under this section is liable—
    (a) on conviction on indictment, to a fine;
    (b) on summary conviction, to a fine not exceeding the statutory maximum.

CHAPTER 6
QUOTED COMPANIES: DIRECTORS' REMUNERATION REPORT

420. Duty to prepare directors' remuneration report
  (1) The directors of a quoted company must prepare a directors' remuneration report for each financial year of the company.
  (2) In the case of failure to comply with the requirement to prepare a directors' remuneration report, every person who—
    (a) was a director of the company immediately before the end of the period for filing accounts and reports for the financial year in question, and
    (b) failed to take all reasonable steps for securing compliance with that requirement,
    commits an offence.
  (3) A person guilty of an offence under this section is liable—
    (a) on conviction on indictment, to a fine;
    (b) on summary conviction, to a fine not exceeding the statutory maximum.

421. Contents of directors' remuneration report
  (1) The Secretary of State may make provision by regulations as to—
    (a) the information that must be contained in a directors' remuneration report,
    (b) how information is to be set out in the report, and
    (c) what is to be the auditable part of the report.
  (2) Without prejudice to the generality of this power, the regulations may make any such provision as was made, immediately before the commencement of this Part, by Schedule 7A to the Companies Act 1985 (c. 6).
  (3) It is the duty of—
    (a) any director of a company, and
    (b) any person who is or has at any time in the preceding five years been a director of the company,

to give notice to the company of such matters relating to himself as may be necessary for the purposes of regulations under this section.

(4) A person who makes default in complying with subsection (3) commits an offence and is liable on summary conviction to a fine not exceeding level 3 on the standard scale.

422. Approval and signing of directors' remuneration report

(1) The directors' remuneration report must be approved by the board of directors and signed on behalf of the board by a director or the secretary of the company.

(2) If a directors' remuneration report is approved that does not comply with the requirements of this Act, every director of the company who—

    (a) knew that it did not comply, or was reckless as to whether it complied, and

    (b) failed to take reasonable steps to secure compliance with those requirements or, as the case may be, to prevent the report from being approved,

commits an offence.

(3) A person guilty of an offence under this section is liable—

    (a) on conviction on indictment, to a fine;

    (b) on summary conviction, to a fine not exceeding the statutory maximum.

CHAPTER 7

PUBLICATION OF ACCOUNTS AND REPORTS

Duty to circulate copies of accounts and reports

423. Duty to circulate copies of annual accounts and reports

(1) Every company must send a copy of its annual accounts and reports for each financial year to—

    (a) every member of the company,

    (b) every holder of the company's debentures, and

    (c) every person who is entitled to receive notice of general meetings.

(2) Copies need not be sent to a person for whom the company does not have a current address.

(3) A company has a "current address" for a person if—

    (a) an address has been notified to the company by the person as one at which documents may be sent to him, and

    (b) the company has no reason to believe that documents sent to him at that address will not reach him.

(4) In the case of a company not having a share capital, copies need not be sent to anyone who is not entitled to receive notices of general meetings of the company.

(5) Where copies are sent out over a period of days, references in the Companies Acts to the day on which copies are sent out shall be read as references to the last day of that period.

(6) This section has effect subject to section 426 (option to provide summary financial statement).

424. Time allowed for sending out copies of accounts and reports

(1) The time allowed for sending out copies of the company's annual accounts and reports is as follows.

(2) A private company must comply with section 423 not later than—

    (a) the end of the period for filing accounts and reports, or

    (b) if earlier, the date on which it actually delivers its accounts and reports to the registrar.

(3) A public company must comply with section 423 at least 21 days before the date of the relevant accounts meeting.

(4) If in the case of a public company copies are sent out later than is required by subsection (3), they shall, despite that, be deemed to have been duly sent if it is so agreed by all the members entitled to attend and vote at the relevant accounts meeting.

(5) Whether the time allowed is that for a private company or a public company is determined by reference to the company's status immediately before the end of the accounting reference period by reference to which the financial year for the accounts in question was determined.

(6) In this section the "relevant accounts meeting" means the accounts meeting of the company at which the accounts and reports in question are to be laid.

425. Default in sending out copies of accounts and reports: offences

(1) If default is made in complying with section 423 or 424, an offence is committed by—

    (a) the company, and

    (b) every officer of the company who is in default.

(2) A person guilty of an offence under this section is liable—

    (a) on conviction on indictment, to a fine;

    (b) on summary conviction, to a fine not exceeding the statutory maximum.

Option to provide summary financial statement

426. Option to provide summary financial statement

(1) A company may—

    (a) in such cases as may be specified by regulations made by the Secretary of State, and

    (b) provided any conditions so specified are complied with,

    provide a summary financial statement instead of copies of the accounts and reports required to be sent out in accordance with section 423.

(2) Copies of those accounts and reports must, however, be sent to any person entitled to be sent them in accordance with that section and who wishes to receive them.

(3) The Secretary of State may make provision by regulations as to the manner in which it is to be ascertained, whether before or after a person becomes entitled to be sent a copy of those accounts and reports, whether he wishes to receive them.

(4) A summary financial statement must comply with the requirements of—

    section 427 (form and contents of summary financial statement: unquoted companies), or

    section 428 (form and contents of summary financial statement: quoted companies).

(5) This section applies to copies of accounts and reports required to be sent out by virtue of section 146 to a person nominated to enjoy information rights as it applies to copies of accounts and reports required to be sent out in accordance with section 423 to a member of the company.

(6) Regulations under this section are subject to negative resolution procedure.

427. Form and contents of summary financial statement: unquoted companies

(1) A summary financial statement by a company that is not a quoted company must—

    (a) be derived from the company's annual accounts, and

    (b) be prepared in accordance with this section and regulations made under it.

(2) The summary financial statement must be in such form, and contain such information, as the Secretary of State may specify by regulations.

The regulations may require the statement to include information derived from the directors' report.

(3) Nothing in this section or regulations made under it prevents a company from including in a summary financial statement additional information derived from the company's annual accounts or the directors' report.

(4) The summary financial statement must—

    (a) state that it is only a summary of information derived from the company's annual accounts;

    (b) state whether it contains additional information derived from the directors' report and, if so, that it does not contain the full text of that report;

    (c) state how a person entitled to them can obtain a full copy of the company's annual accounts and the directors' report;

  (d) contain a statement by the company's auditor of his opinion as to whether the summary financial statement—

   (i) is consistent with the company's annual accounts and, where information derived from the directors' report is included in the statement, with that report, and

   (ii) complies with the requirements of this section and regulations made under it;

  (e) state whether the auditor's report on the annual accounts was unqualified or qualified and, if it was qualified, set out the report in full together with any further material needed to understand the qualification;

  (f) state whether, in that report, the auditor's statement under section 496 (whether directors' report consistent with accounts) was qualified or unqualified and, if it was qualified, set out the qualified statement in full together with any further material needed to understand the qualification;

  (g) state whether that auditor's report contained a statement under—

   (i) section 498(2)(a) or (b) (accounting records or returns inadequate or accounts not agreeing with records and returns), or

   (ii) section 498(3) (failure to obtain necessary information and explanations),

   and if so, set out the statement in full.

 (5) Regulations under this section may provide that any specified material may, instead of being included in the summary financial statement, be sent separately at the same time as the statement.

 (6) Regulations under this section are subject to negative resolution procedure.

428. Form and contents of summary financial statement: quoted companies

 (1) A summary financial statement by a quoted company must—

  (a) be derived from the company's annual accounts and the directors' remuneration report, and

  (b) be prepared in accordance with this section and regulations made under it.

 (2) The summary financial statement must be in such form, and contain such information, as the Secretary of State may specify by regulations.

  The regulations may require the statement to include information derived from the directors' report.

 (3) Nothing in this section or regulations made under it prevents a company from including in a summary financial statement additional information derived from the company's annual accounts, the directors' remuneration report or the directors' report.

 (4) The summary financial statement must—

  (a) state that it is only a summary of information derived from the company's annual accounts and the directors' remuneration report;

  (b) state whether it contains additional information derived from the directors' report and, if so, that it does not contain the full text of that report;

  (c) state how a person entitled to them can obtain a full copy of the company's annual accounts, the directors' remuneration report or the directors' report;

  (d) contain a statement by the company's auditor of his opinion as to whether the summary financial statement—

   (i) is consistent with the company's annual accounts and the directors' remuneration report and, where information derived from the directors' report is included in the statement, with that report, and

   (ii) complies with the requirements of this section and regulations made under it;

  (e) state whether the auditor's report on the annual accounts and the auditable part of the directors' remuneration report was unqualified or qualified and, if it was qualified, set out the report in full together with any further material needed to understand the qualification;

(f) state whether that auditor's report contained a statement under—

    (i) section 498(2) (accounting records or returns inadequate or accounts or directors' remuneration report not agreeing with records and returns), or

    (ii) section 498(3) (failure to obtain necessary information and explanations),

    and if so, set out the statement in full;

(g) state whether, in that report, the auditor's statement under section 496 (whether directors' report consistent with accounts) was qualified or unqualified and, if it was qualified, set out the qualified statement in full together with any further material needed to understand the qualification.

(5) Regulations under this section may provide that any specified material may, instead of being included in the summary financial statement, be sent separately at the same time as the statement.

(6) Regulations under this section are subject to negative resolution procedure.

429. Summary financial statements: offences

(1) If default is made in complying with any provision of section 426, 427 or 428, or of regulations under any of those sections, an offence is committed by—

(a) the company, and

(b) every officer of the company who is in default.

(2) A person guilty of an offence under this section is liable on summary conviction to a fine not exceeding level 3 on the standard scale.

Quoted companies: requirements as to website publication

430. Quoted companies: annual accounts and reports to be made available on website

(1) A quoted company must ensure that its annual accounts and reports—

(a) are made available on a website, and

(b) remain so available until the annual accounts and reports for the company's next financial year are made available in accordance with this section.

(2) The annual accounts and reports must be made available on a website that—

(a) is maintained by or on behalf of the company, and

(b) identifies the company in question.

(3) Access to the annual accounts and reports on the website, and the ability to obtain a hard copy of the annual accounts and reports from the website, must not be—

(a) conditional on the payment of a fee, or

(b) otherwise restricted, except so far as necessary to comply with any enactment or regulatory requirement (in the United Kingdom or elsewhere).

(4) The annual accounts and reports—

(a) must be made available as soon as reasonably practicable, and

(b) must be kept available throughout the period specified in subsection (1)(b).

(5) A failure to make the annual accounts and reports available on a website throughout that period is disregarded if—

(a) the annual accounts and reports are made available on the website for part of that period, and

(b) the failure is wholly attributable to circumstances that it would not be reasonable to have expected the company to prevent or avoid.

(6) In the event of default in complying with this section, an offence is committed by every officer of the company who is in default.

(7) A person guilty of an offence under subsection (6) is liable on summary conviction to a fine not exceeding level 3 on the standard scale.

Right of member or debenture holder to demand copies of accounts and reports

431. Right of member or debenture holder to copies of accounts and reports: unquoted companies

(1) A member of, or holder of debentures of, an unquoted company is entitled to be provided, on demand and without charge, with a copy of—

(a) the company's last annual accounts,

(b) the last directors' report, and

(c) the auditor's report on those accounts (including the statement on that report).

(2) The entitlement under this section is to a single copy of those documents, but that is in addition to any copy to which a person may be entitled under section 423.

(3) If a demand made under this section is not complied with within seven days of receipt by the company, an offence is committed by—

(a) the company, and

(b) every officer of the company who is in default.

(4) A person guilty of an offence under this section is liable on summary conviction to a fine not exceeding level 3 on the standard scale and, for continued contravention, a daily default fine not exceeding one-tenth of level 3 on the standard scale.

432. Right of member or debenture holder to copies of accounts and reports: quoted companies

(1) A member of, or holder of debentures of, a quoted company is entitled to be provided, on demand and without charge, with a copy of—

(a) the company's last annual accounts,

(b) the last directors' remuneration report,

(c) the last directors' report, and

(d) the auditor's report on those accounts (including the report on the directors' remuneration report and on the directors' report).

(2) The entitlement under this section is to a single copy of those documents, but that is in addition to any copy to which a person may be entitled under section 423.

(3) If a demand made under this section is not complied with within seven days of receipt by the company, an offence is committed by—

(a) the company, and

(b) every officer of the company who is in default.

(4) A person guilty of an offence under this section is liable on summary conviction to a fine not exceeding level 3 on the standard scale and, for continued contravention, a daily default fine not exceeding one-tenth of level 3 on the standard scale.

Requirements in connection with publication of accounts and reports

433. Name of signatory to be stated in published copies of accounts and reports

(1) Every copy of a document to which this section applies that is published by or on behalf of the company must state the name of the person who signed it on behalf of the board.

(2) In the case of an unquoted company, this section applies to copies of—

(a) the company's balance sheet, and

(b) the directors' report.

(3) In the case of a quoted company, this section applies to copies of—

(a) the company's balance sheet,

(b) the directors' remuneration report, and

(c) the directors' report.

(4) If a copy is published without the required statement of the signatory's name, an offence is committed by—

(a) the company, and

(b) every officer of the company who is in default.

(5) A person guilty of an offence under this section is liable on summary conviction to a fine not exceeding level 3 on the standard scale.

434. Requirements in connection with publication of statutory accounts

(1) If a company publishes any of its statutory accounts, they must be accompanied by the auditor's report on those accounts (unless the company is exempt from audit and the directors have taken advantage of that exemption).

(2) A company that prepares statutory group accounts for a financial year must not publish its statutory individual accounts for that year without also publishing with them its statutory group accounts.

(3) A company's "statutory accounts" are its accounts for a financial year as required to be delivered to the registrar under section 441.

(4) If a company contravenes any provision of this section, an offence is committed by—
   (a) the company, and
   (b) every officer of the company who is in default.

(5) A person guilty of an offence under this section is liable on summary conviction to a fine not exceeding level 3 on the standard scale.

(6) This section does not apply in relation to the provision by a company of a summary financial statement (see section 426).

435. Requirements in connection with publication of non-statutory accounts

(1) If a company publishes non-statutory accounts, it must publish with them a statement indicating—
   (a) that they are not the company's statutory accounts,
   (b) whether statutory accounts dealing with any financial year with which the non-statutory accounts purport to deal have been delivered to the registrar, and
   (c) whether an auditor's report has been made on the company's statutory accounts for any such financial year, and if so whether the report—
      (i) was qualified or unqualified, or included a reference to any matters to which the auditor drew attention by way of emphasis without qualifying the report, or
      (ii) contained a statement under section 498(2) (accounting records or returns inadequate or accounts or directors' remuneration report not agreeing with records and returns), or section 498(3) (failure to obtain necessary information and explanations).

(2) The company must not publish with non-statutory accounts the auditor's report on the company's statutory accounts.

(3) References in this section to the publication by a company of "non-statutory accounts" are to the publication of—
   (a) any balance sheet or profit and loss account relating to, or purporting to deal with, a financial year of the company, or
   (b) an account in any form purporting to be a balance sheet or profit and loss account for a group headed by the company relating to, or purporting to deal with, a financial year of the company,
otherwise than as part of the company's statutory accounts.

(4) In subsection (3)(b) "a group headed by the company" means a group consisting of the company and any other undertaking (regardless of whether it is a subsidiary undertaking of the company) other than a parent undertaking of the company.

(5) If a company contravenes any provision of this section, an offence is committed by—
   (a) the company, and
   (b) every officer of the company who is in default.

(6) A person guilty of an offence under this section is liable on summary conviction to a fine not exceeding level 3 on the standard scale.

(7) This section does not apply in relation to the provision by a company of a summary financial statement (see section 426).

436. **Meaning of "publication" in relation to accounts and reports**

(1) This section has effect for the purposes of—

section 433 (name of signatory to be stated in published copies of accounts and reports),

section 434 (requirements in connection with publication of statutory accounts), and

section 435 (requirements in connection with publication of non-statutory accounts).

(2) For the purposes of those sections a company is regarded as publishing a document if it publishes, issues or circulates it or otherwise makes it available for public inspection in a manner calculated to invite members of the public generally, or any class of members of the public, to read it.

CHAPTER 8
PUBLIC COMPANIES: LAYING OF ACCOUNTS AND REPORTS BEFORE GENERAL MEETING

437. **Public companies: laying of accounts and reports before general meeting**

(1) The directors of a public company must lay before the company in general meeting copies of its annual accounts and reports.

(2) This section must be complied with not later than the end of the period for filing the accounts and reports in question.

(3) In the Companies Acts "accounts meeting", in relation to a public company, means a general meeting of the company at which the company's annual accounts and reports are (or are to be) laid in accordance with this section.

438. **Public companies: offence of failure to lay accounts and reports**

(1) If the requirements of section 437 (public companies: laying of accounts and reports before general meeting) are not complied with before the end of the period allowed, every person who immediately before the end of that period was a director of the company commits an offence.

(2) It is a defence for a person charged with such an offence to prove that he took all reasonable steps for securing that those requirements would be complied with before the end of that period.

(3) It is not a defence to prove that the documents in question were not in fact prepared as required by this Part.

(4) A person guilty of an offence under this section is liable on summary conviction to a fine not exceeding level 5 on the standard scale and, for continued contravention, a daily default fine not exceeding one-tenth of level 5 on the standard scale.

CHAPTER 9
QUOTED COMPANIES: MEMBERS' APPROVAL OF DIRECTORS' REMUNERATION REPORT

439. **Quoted companies: members' approval of directors' remuneration report**

(1) A quoted company must, prior to the accounts meeting, give to the members of the company entitled to be sent notice of the meeting notice of the intention to move at the meeting, as an ordinary resolution, a resolution approving the directors' remuneration report for the financial year.

(2) The notice may be given in any manner permitted for the service on the member of notice of the meeting.

(3) The business that may be dealt with at the accounts meeting includes the resolution.
This is so notwithstanding any default in complying with subsection (1) or (2).

(4) The existing directors must ensure that the resolution is put to the vote of the meeting.

(5) No entitlement of a person to remuneration is made conditional on the resolution being passed by reason only of the provision made by this section.

(6) In this section—

"the accounts meeting" means the general meeting of the company before which the company's annual accounts for the financial year are to be laid; and

"existing director" means a person who is a director of the company immediately before that meeting.

440. Quoted companies: offences in connection with procedure for approval

(1) In the event of default in complying with section 439(1) (notice to be given of resolution for approval of directors' remuneration report), an offence is committed by every officer of the company who is in default.

(2) If the resolution is not put to the vote of the accounts meeting, an offence is committed by each existing director.

(3) It is a defence for a person charged with an offence under subsection (2) to prove that he took all reasonable steps for securing that the resolution was put to the vote of the meeting.

(4) A person guilty of an offence under this section is liable on summary conviction to a fine not exceeding level 3 on the standard scale.

(5) In this section—

"the accounts meeting" means the general meeting of the company before which the company's annual accounts for the financial year are to be laid; and

"existing director" means a person who is a director of the company immediately before that meeting.

CHAPTER 10
FILING OF ACCOUNTS AND REPORTS

Duty to file accounts and reports

441. Duty to file accounts and reports with the registrar

(1) The directors of a company must deliver to the registrar for each financial year the accounts and reports required by—

section 444 (filing obligations of companies subject to small companies regime),

section 445 (filing obligations of medium-sized companies),

section 446 (filing obligations of unquoted companies), or

section 447 (filing obligations of quoted companies).

(2) This is subject to section 448 (unlimited companies exempt from filing obligations).

442. Period allowed for filing accounts

(1) This section specifies the period allowed for the directors of a company to comply with their obligation under section 441 to deliver accounts and reports for a financial year to the registrar. This is referred to in the Companies Acts as the "period for filing" those accounts and reports.

(2) The period is—

(a) for a private company, nine months after the end of the relevant accounting reference period, and

(b) for a public company, six months after the end of that period.

This is subject to the following provisions of this section.

(3) If the relevant accounting reference period is the company's first and is a period of more than twelve months, the period is—

(a) nine months or six months, as the case may be, from the first anniversary of the incorporation of the company, or

(b) three months after the end of the accounting reference period,

whichever last expires.

(4) If the relevant accounting reference period is treated as shortened by virtue of a notice given by the company under section 392 (alteration of accounting reference date), the period is—

(a) that applicable in accordance with the above provisions, or

(b) three months from the date of the notice under that section,

whichever last expires.

(5) If for any special reason the Secretary of State thinks fit he may, on an application made before the expiry of the period otherwise allowed, by notice in writing to a company extend that period by such further period as may be specified in the notice.

(6) Whether the period allowed is that for a private company or a public company is determined by reference to the company's status immediately before the end of the relevant accounting reference period.

(7) In this section "the relevant accounting reference period" means the accounting reference period by reference to which the financial year for the accounts in question was determined.

443. Calculation of period allowed

(1) This section applies for the purposes of calculating the period for filing a company's accounts and reports which is expressed as a specified number of months from a specified date or after the end of a specified previous period.

(2) Subject to the following provisions, the period ends with the date in the appropriate month corresponding to the specified date or the last day of the specified previous period.

(3) If the specified date, or the last day of the specified previous period, is the last day of a month, the period ends with the last day of the appropriate month (whether or not that is the corresponding date).

(4) If—

(a) the specified date, or the last day of the specified previous period, is not the last day of a month but is the 29th or 30th, and

(b) the appropriate month is February,

the period ends with the last day of February.

(5) "The appropriate month" means the month that is the specified number of months after the month in which the specified date, or the end of the specified previous period, falls.

Filing obligations of different descriptions of company

444. Filing obligations of companies subject to small companies regime

(1) The directors of a company subject to the small companies regime—

(a) must deliver to the registrar for each financial year a copy of a balance sheet drawn up as at the last day of that year, and

(b) may also deliver to the registrar—

(i) a copy of the company's profit and loss account for that year, and

(ii) a copy of the directors' report for that year.

(2) The directors must also deliver to the registrar a copy of the auditor's report on those accounts (and on the directors' report).

This does not apply if the company is exempt from audit and the directors have taken advantage of that exemption.

(3) The copies of accounts and reports delivered to the registrar must be copies of the company's annual accounts and reports, except that where the company prepares Companies Act accounts—

(a) the directors may deliver to the registrar a copy of a balance sheet drawn up in accordance with regulations made by the Secretary of State, and

(b) there may be omitted from the copy profit and loss account delivered to the registrar such items as may be specified by the regulations.

These are referred to in this Part as "abbreviated accounts".

(4) If abbreviated accounts are delivered to the registrar the obligation to deliver a copy of the auditor's report on the accounts is to deliver a copy of the special auditor's report required by section 449.

(5) Where the directors of a company subject to the small companies regime deliver to the registrar IAS accounts, or Companies Act accounts that are not abbreviated accounts, and in accordance with this section—

(a) do not deliver to the registrar a copy of the company's profit and loss account, or

(b) do not deliver to the registrar a copy of the directors' report,

the copy of the balance sheet delivered to the registrar must contain in a prominent position a statement that the company's annual accounts and reports have been delivered in accordance with the provisions applicable to companies subject to the small companies regime.

(6) The copies of the balance sheet and any directors' report delivered to the registrar under this section must state the name of the person who signed it on behalf of the board.

(7) The copy of the auditor's report delivered to the registrar under this section must—

(a) state the name of the auditor and (where the auditor is a firm) the name of the person who signed it as senior statutory auditor, or

(b) if the conditions in section 506 (circumstances in which names may be omitted) are met, state that a resolution has been passed and notified to the Secretary of State in accordance with that section.

445. Filing obligations of medium-sized companies

(1) The directors of a company that qualifies as a medium-sized company in relation to a financial year (see sections 465 to 467) must deliver to the registrar a copy of—

(a) the company's annual accounts, and

(b) the directors' report.

(2) They must also deliver to the registrar a copy of the auditor's report on those accounts (and on the directors' report).

This does not apply if the company is exempt from audit and the directors have taken advantage of that exemption.

(3) Where the company prepares Companies Act accounts, the directors may deliver to the registrar a copy of the company's annual accounts for the financial year—

(a) that includes a profit and loss account in which items are combined in accordance with regulations made by the Secretary of State, and

(b) that does not contain items whose omission is authorised by the regulations.

These are referred to in this Part as "abbreviated accounts".

(4) If abbreviated accounts are delivered to the registrar the obligation to deliver a copy of the auditor's report on the accounts is to deliver a copy of the special auditor's report required by section 449.

(5) The copies of the balance sheet and directors' report delivered to the registrar under this section must state the name of the person who signed it on behalf of the board.

(6) The copy of the auditor's report delivered to the registrar under this section must—

(a) state the name of the auditor and (where the auditor is a firm) the name of the person who signed it as senior statutory auditor, or

(b) if the conditions in section 506 (circumstances in which names may be omitted) are met, state that a resolution has been passed and notified to the Secretary of State in accordance with that section.

(7) This section does not apply to companies within section 444 (filing obligations of companies subject to the small companies regime).

446. Filing obligations of unquoted companies

(1) The directors of an unquoted company must deliver to the registrar for each financial year of the company a copy of—

(a) the company's annual accounts, and

(b) the directors' report.

(2) The directors must also deliver to the registrar a copy of the auditor's report on those accounts (and the directors' report).

This does not apply if the company is exempt from audit and the directors have taken advantage of that exemption.

(3) The copies of the balance sheet and directors' report delivered to the registrar under this section must state the name of the person who signed it on behalf of the board.

(4) The copy of the auditor's report delivered to the registrar under this section must—

(a) state the name of the auditor and (where the auditor is a firm) the name of the person who signed it as senior statutory auditor, or

(b) if the conditions in section 506 (circumstances in which names may be omitted) are met, state that a resolution has been passed and notified to the Secretary of State in accordance with that section.

(5) This section does not apply to companies within—

(a) section 444 (filing obligations of companies subject to the small companies regime), or

(b) section 445 (filing obligations of medium-sized companies).

447. Filing obligations of quoted companies

(1) The directors of a quoted company must deliver to the registrar for each financial year of the company a copy of—

(a) the company's annual accounts,

(b) the directors' remuneration report, and

(c) the directors' report.

(2) They must also deliver a copy of the auditor's report on those accounts (and on the directors' remuneration report and the directors' report).

(3) The copies of the balance sheet, the directors' remuneration report and the directors' report delivered to the registrar under this section must state the name of the person who signed it on behalf of the board.

(4) The copy of the auditor's report delivered to the registrar under this section must—

(a) state the name of the auditor and (where the auditor is a firm) the name of the person who signed it as senior statutory auditor, or

(b) if the conditions in section 506 (circumstances in which names may be omitted) are met, state that a resolution has been passed and notified to the Secretary of State in accordance with that section.

448. Unlimited companies exempt from obligation to file accounts

(1) The directors of an unlimited company are not required to deliver accounts and reports to the registrar in respect of a financial year if the following conditions are met.

(2) The conditions are that at no time during the relevant accounting reference period—

(a) has the company been, to its knowledge, a subsidiary undertaking of an undertaking which was then limited, or

(b) have there been, to its knowledge, exercisable by or on behalf of two or more undertakings which were then limited, rights which if exercisable by one of them would have made the company a subsidiary undertaking of it, or

(c) has the company been a parent company of an undertaking which was then limited.

The references above to an undertaking being limited at a particular time are to an undertaking (under whatever law established) the liability of whose members is at that time limited.

(3) The exemption conferred by this section does not apply if—

    (a) the company is a banking or insurance company or the parent company of a banking or insurance group, or

    (b) the company is a qualifying company within the meaning of the Partnerships and Unlimited Companies (Accounts) Regulations 1993 (S.I. 1993/1820).

(4) Where a company is exempt by virtue of this section from the obligation to deliver accounts—

    (a) section 434(3) (requirements in connection with publication of statutory accounts: meaning of "statutory accounts") has effect with the substitution for the words "as required to be delivered to the registrar under section 441" of the words "as prepared in accordance with this Part and approved by the board of directors"; and

    (b) section 435(1)(b) (requirements in connection with publication of non-statutory accounts: statement whether statutory accounts delivered) has effect with the substitution for the words from "whether statutory accounts" to "have been delivered to the registrar" of the words "that the company is exempt from the requirement to deliver statutory accounts".

(5) In this section the "relevant accounting reference period", in relation to a financial year, means the accounting reference period by reference to which that financial year was determined.

Requirements where abbreviated accounts delivered

449. Special auditor's report where abbreviated accounts delivered

(1) This section applies where—

    (a) the directors of a company deliver abbreviated accounts to the registrar, and

    (b) the company is not exempt from audit (or the directors have not taken advantage of any such exemption).

(2) The directors must also deliver to the registrar a copy of a special report of the company's auditor stating that in his opinion—

    (a) the company is entitled to deliver abbreviated accounts in accordance with the section in question, and

    (b) the abbreviated accounts to be delivered are properly prepared in accordance with regulations under that section.

(3) The auditor's report on the company's annual accounts need not be delivered, but—

    (a) if that report was qualified, the special report must set out that report in full together with any further material necessary to understand the qualification, and

    (b) if that report contained a statement under—

        (i) section 498(2)(a) or (b) (accounts, records or returns inadequate or accounts not agreeing with records and returns), or

        (ii) section 498(3) (failure to obtain necessary information and explanations),

    the special report must set out that statement in full.

(4) The provisions of—

sections 503 to 506 (signature of auditor's report), and

sections 507 to 509 (offences in connection with auditor's report),

apply to a special report under this section as they apply to an auditor's report on the company's annual accounts prepared under Part 16.

(5) If abbreviated accounts are delivered to the registrar, the references in section 434 or 435 (requirements in connection with publication of accounts) to the auditor's report on the company's annual accounts shall be read as references to the special auditor's report required by this section.

450. Approval and signing of abbreviated accounts

(1) Abbreviated accounts must be approved by the board of directors and signed on behalf of the board by a director of the company.

(2) The signature must be on the balance sheet.

(3) The balance sheet must contain in a prominent position above the signature a statement to the effect that it is prepared in accordance with the special provisions of this Act relating (as the case may be) to companies subject to the small companies regime or to medium-sized companies.

(4) If abbreviated accounts are approved that do not comply with the requirements of regulations under the relevant section, every director of the company who—

(a) knew that they did not comply, or was reckless as to whether they complied, and

(b) failed to take reasonable steps to prevent them from being approved,

commits an offence.

(5) A person guilty of an offence under subsection (4) is liable—

(a) on conviction on indictment, to a fine;

(b) on summary conviction, to a fine not exceeding the statutory maximum.

Failure to file accounts and reports

451. Default in filing accounts and reports: offences

(1) If the requirements of section 441 (duty to file accounts and reports) are not complied with in relation to a company's accounts and reports for a financial year before the end of the period for filing those accounts and reports, every person who immediately before the end of that period was a director of the company commits an offence.

(2) It is a defence for a person charged with such an offence to prove that he took all reasonable steps for securing that those requirements would be complied with before the end of that period.

(3) It is not a defence to prove that the documents in question were not in fact prepared as required by this Part.

(4) A person guilty of an offence under this section is liable on summary conviction to a fine not exceeding level 5 on the standard scale and, for continued contravention, a daily default fine not exceeding one-tenth of level 5 on the standard scale.

452. Default in filing accounts and reports: court order

(1) If—

(a) the requirements of section 441 (duty to file accounts and reports) are not complied with in relation to a company's accounts and reports for a financial year before the end of the period for filing those accounts and reports, and

(b) the directors of the company fail to make good the default within 14 days after the service of a notice on them requiring compliance,

the court may, on the application of any member or creditor of the company or of the registrar, make an order directing the directors (or any of them) to make good the default within such time as may be specified in the order.

(2) The court's order may provide that all costs (in Scotland, expenses) of and incidental to the application are to be borne by the directors.

453. Civil penalty for failure to file accounts and reports

(1) Where the requirements of section 441 are not complied with in relation to a company's accounts and reports for a financial year before the end of the period for filing those accounts and reports, the company is liable to a civil penalty.

This is in addition to any liability of the directors under section 451.

(2) The amount of the penalty shall be determined in accordance with regulations made by the Secretary of State by reference to—

(a) the length of the period between the end of the period for filing the accounts and reports in question and the day on which the requirements are complied with, and

(b) whether the company is a private or public company.

(3) The penalty may be recovered by the registrar and is to be paid into the Consolidated Fund.

(4) It is not a defence in proceedings under this section to prove that the documents in question were not in fact prepared as required by this Part.

(5) Regulations under this section having the effect of increasing the penalty payable in any case are subject to affirmative resolution procedure.

Otherwise, the regulations are subject to negative resolution procedure.

CHAPTER 11
REVISION OF DEFECTIVE ACCOUNTS AND REPORTS

Voluntary revision

454. Voluntary revision of accounts etc

(1) If it appears to the directors of a company that—

    (a) the company's annual accounts,

    (b) the directors' remuneration report or the directors' report, or

    (c) a summary financial statement of the company,

did not comply with the requirements of this Act (or, where applicable, of Article 4 of the IAS Regulation), they may prepare revised accounts or a revised report or statement.

(2) Where copies of the previous accounts or report have been sent out to members, delivered to the registrar or (in the case of a public company) laid before the company in general meeting, the revisions must be confined to—

    (a) the correction of those respects in which the previous accounts or report did not comply with the requirements of this Act (or, where applicable, of Article 4 of the IAS Regulation), and

    (b) the making of any necessary consequential alterations.

(3) The Secretary of State may make provision by regulations as to the application of the provisions of this Act in relation to—

    (a) revised annual accounts,

    (b) a revised directors' remuneration report or directors' report, or

    (c) a revised summary financial statement.

(4) The regulations may, in particular—

    (a) make different provision according to whether the previous accounts, report or statement are replaced or are supplemented by a document indicating the corrections to be made;

    (b) make provision with respect to the functions of the company's auditor in relation to the revised accounts, report or statement;

    (c) require the directors to take such steps as may be specified in the regulations where the previous accounts or report have been—

        (i) sent out to members and others under section 423,

        (ii) laid before the company in general meeting, or

        (iii) delivered to the registrar,

    or where a summary financial statement containing information derived from the previous accounts or report has been sent to members under section 426;

    (d) apply the provisions of this Act (including those creating criminal offences) subject to such additions, exceptions and modifications as are specified in the regulations.

(5) Regulations under this section are subject to negative resolution procedure.

Secretary of State's notice

455. Secretary of State's notice in respect of accounts or reports

(1) This section applies where—

    (a) copies of a company's annual accounts or directors' report have been sent out under section 423, or

(b) a copy of a company's annual accounts or directors' report has been delivered to the registrar or (in the case of a public company) laid before the company in general meeting,

and it appears to the Secretary of State that there is, or may be, a question whether the accounts or report comply with the requirements of this Act (or, where applicable, of Article 4 of the IAS Regulation).

(2) The Secretary of State may give notice to the directors of the company indicating the respects in which it appears that such a question arises or may arise.

(3) The notice must specify a period of not less than one month for the directors to give an explanation of the accounts or report or prepare revised accounts or a revised report.

(4) If at the end of the specified period, or such longer period as the Secretary of State may allow, it appears to the Secretary of State that the directors have not—

(a) given a satisfactory explanation of the accounts or report, or

(b) revised the accounts or report so as to comply with the requirements of this Act (or, where applicable, of Article 4 of the IAS Regulation),

the Secretary of State may apply to the court.

(5) The provisions of this section apply equally to revised annual accounts and revised directors' reports, in which case they have effect as if the references to revised accounts or reports were references to further revised accounts or reports.

Application to court

456. **Application to court in respect of defective accounts or reports**

(1) An application may be made to the court—

(a) by the Secretary of State, after having complied with section 455, or

(b) by a person authorised by the Secretary of State for the purposes of this section,

for a declaration (in Scotland, a declarator) that the annual accounts of a company do not comply, or a directors' report does not comply, with the requirements of this Act (or, where applicable, of Article 4 of the IAS Regulation) and for an order requiring the directors of the company to prepare revised accounts or a revised report.

(2) Notice of the application, together with a general statement of the matters at issue in the proceedings, shall be given by the applicant to the registrar for registration.

(3) If the court orders the preparation of revised accounts, it may give directions as to—

(a) the auditing of the accounts,

(b) the revision of any directors' remuneration report, directors' report or summary financial statement, and

(c) the taking of steps by the directors to bring the making of the order to the notice of persons likely to rely on the previous accounts,

and such other matters as the court thinks fit.

(4) If the court orders the preparation of a revised directors' report it may give directions as to—

(a) the review of the report by the auditors,

(b) the revision of any summary financial statement,

(c) the taking of steps by the directors to bring the making of the order to the notice of persons likely to rely on the previous report, and

(d) such other matters as the court thinks fit.

(5) If the court finds that the accounts or report did not comply with the requirements of this Act (or, where applicable, of Article 4 of the IAS Regulation) it may order that all or part of—

(a) the costs (in Scotland, expenses) of and incidental to the application, and

(b) any reasonable expenses incurred by the company in connection with or in consequence of the preparation of revised accounts or a revised report,

are to be borne by such of the directors as were party to the approval of the defective accounts or report.

For this purpose every director of the company at the time of the approval of the accounts or report shall be taken to have been a party to the approval unless he shows that he took all reasonable steps to prevent that approval.

(6) Where the court makes an order under subsection (5) it shall have regard to whether the directors party to the approval of the defective accounts or report knew or ought to have known that the accounts or report did not comply with the requirements of this Act (or, where applicable, of Article 4 of the IAS Regulation), and it may exclude one or more directors from the order or order the payment of different amounts by different directors.

(7) On the conclusion of proceedings on an application under this section, the applicant must send to the registrar for registration a copy of the court order or, as the case may be, give notice to the registrar that the application has failed or been withdrawn.

(8) The provisions of this section apply equally to revised annual accounts and revised directors' reports, in which case they have effect as if the references to revised accounts or reports were references to further revised accounts or reports.

457. **Other persons authorised to apply to the court**

(1) The Secretary of State may by order (an "authorisation order") authorise for the purposes of section 456 any person appearing to him—

   (a) to have an interest in, and to have satisfactory procedures directed to securing, compliance by companies with the requirements of this Act (or, where applicable, of Article 4 of the IAS Regulation) relating to accounts and directors' reports,

   (b) to have satisfactory procedures for receiving and investigating complaints about companies' annual accounts and directors' reports, and

   (c) otherwise to be a fit and proper person to be authorised.

(2) A person may be authorised generally or in respect of particular classes of case, and different persons may be authorised in respect of different classes of case.

(3) The Secretary of State may refuse to authorise a person if he considers that his authorisation is unnecessary having regard to the fact that there are one or more other persons who have been or are likely to be authorised.

(4) If the authorised person is an unincorporated association, proceedings brought in, or in connection with, the exercise of any function by the association as an authorised person may be brought by or against the association in the name of a body corporate whose constitution provides for the establishment of the association.

(5) An authorisation order may contain such requirements or other provisions relating to the exercise of functions by the authorised person as appear to the Secretary of State to be appropriate.

No such order is to be made unless it appears to the Secretary of State that the person would, if authorised, exercise his functions as an authorised person in accordance with the provisions proposed.

(6) Where authorisation is revoked, the revoking order may make such provision as the Secretary of State thinks fit with respect to pending proceedings.

(7) An order under this section is subject to negative resolution procedure.

458. **Disclosure of information by tax authorities**

(1) The Commissioners for Her Majesty's Revenue and Customs may disclose information to a person authorised under section 457 for the purpose of facilitating—

   (a) the taking of steps by that person to discover whether there are grounds for an application to the court under section 456 (application in respect of defective accounts etc), or

   (b) a decision by the authorised person whether to make such an application.

(2) This section applies despite any statutory or other restriction on the disclosure of information. Provided that, in the case of personal data within the meaning of the Data Protection Act 1998 (c. 29), information is not to be disclosed in contravention of that Act.

(3) Information disclosed to an authorised person under this section—

  (a) may not be used except in or in connection with—

    (i) taking steps to discover whether there are grounds for an application to the court under section 456, or

    (ii) deciding whether or not to make such an application,

  or in, or in connection with, proceedings on such an application; and

  (b) must not be further disclosed except—

    (i) to the person to whom the information relates, or

    (ii) in, or in connection with, proceedings on any such application to the court.

(4) A person who contravenes subsection (3) commits an offence unless—

  (a) he did not know, and had no reason to suspect, that the information had been disclosed under this section, or

  (b) he took all reasonable steps and exercised all due diligence to avoid the commission of the offence.

(5) A person guilty of an offence under subsection (4) is liable—

  (a) on conviction on indictment, to imprisonment for a term not exceeding two years or a fine (or both);

  (b) on summary conviction—

    (i) in England and Wales, to imprisonment for a term not exceeding twelve months or to a fine not exceeding the statutory maximum (or both);

    (ii) in Scotland or Northern Ireland, to imprisonment for a term not exceeding six months, or to a fine not exceeding the statutory maximum (or both).

Power of authorised person to require documents etc

459. Power of authorised person to require documents, information and explanations

(1) This section applies where it appears to a person who is authorised under section 457 that there is, or may be, a question whether a company's annual accounts or directors' report comply with the requirements of this Act (or, where applicable, of Article 4 of the IAS Regulation).

(2) The authorised person may require any of the persons mentioned in subsection (3) to produce any document, or to provide him with any information or explanations, that he may reasonably require for the purpose of—

  (a) discovering whether there are grounds for an application to the court under section 456, or

  (b) deciding whether to make such an application.

(3) Those persons are—

  (a) the company;

  (b) any officer, employee, or auditor of the company;

  (c) any persons who fell within paragraph (b) at a time to which the document or information required by the authorised person relates.

(4) If a person fails to comply with such a requirement, the authorised person may apply to the court.

(5) If it appears to the court that the person has failed to comply with a requirement under subsection (2), it may order the person to take such steps as it directs for securing that the documents are produced or the information or explanations are provided.

(6) A statement made by a person in response to a requirement under subsection (2) or an order under subsection (5) may not be used in evidence against him in any criminal proceedings.

(7) Nothing in this section compels any person to disclose documents or information in respect of which a claim to legal professional privilege (in Scotland, to confidentiality of communications) could be maintained in legal proceedings.

(8) In this section "document" includes information recorded in any form.

460. **Restrictions on disclosure of information obtained under compulsory powers**

    (1) This section applies to information (in whatever form) obtained in pursuance of a requirement or order under section 459 (power of authorised person to require documents etc) that relates to the private affairs of an individual or to any particular business.

    (2) No such information may, during the lifetime of that individual or so long as that business continues to be carried on, be disclosed without the consent of that individual or the person for the time being carrying on that business.

    (3) This does not apply—

        (a) to disclosure permitted by section 461 (permitted disclosure of information obtained under compulsory powers), or

        (b) to the disclosure of information that is or has been available to the public from another source.

    (4) A person who discloses information in contravention of this section commits an offence, unless—

        (a) he did not know, and had no reason to suspect, that the information had been disclosed under section 459, or

        (b) he took all reasonable steps and exercised all due diligence to avoid the commission of the offence.

    (5) A person guilty of an offence under this section is liable—

        (a) on conviction on indictment, to imprisonment for a term not exceeding two years or a fine (or both);

        (b) on summary conviction—

            (i) in England and Wales, to imprisonment for a term not exceeding twelve months or to a fine not exceeding the statutory maximum (or both);

            (ii) in Scotland or Northern Ireland, to imprisonment for a term not exceeding six months, or to a fine not exceeding the statutory maximum (or both).

461. **Permitted disclosure of information obtained under compulsory powers**

    (1) The prohibition in section 460 of the disclosure of information obtained in pursuance of a requirement or order under section 459 (power of authorised person to require documents etc) that relates to the private affairs of an individual or to any particular business has effect subject to the following exceptions.

    (2) It does not apply to the disclosure of information for the purpose of facilitating the carrying out by the authorised person of his functions under section 456.

    (3) It does not apply to disclosure to—

        (a) the Secretary of State,

        (b) the Department of Enterprise, Trade and Investment for Northern Ireland,

        (c) the Treasury,

        (d) the Bank of England,

        (e) the Financial Services Authority, or

        (f) the Commissioners for Her Majesty's Revenue and Customs.

    (4) It does not apply to disclosure—

        (a) for the purpose of assisting a body designated by an order under section 46 of the Companies Act 1989 (c. 40) (delegation of functions of the Secretary of State) to exercise its functions under Part 2 of that Act;

        (b) with a view to the institution of, or otherwise for the purposes of, disciplinary proceedings relating to the performance by an accountant or auditor of his professional duties;

        (c) for the purpose of enabling or assisting the Secretary of State or the Treasury to exercise any of their functions under any of the following—

            (i) the Companies Acts,

            (ii) Part 5 of the Criminal Justice Act 1993 (c. 36) (insider dealing),

      (iii) the Insolvency Act 1986 (c. 45) or the Insolvency (Northern Ireland) Order 1989 (S.I. 1989/2405 (N.I. 19)),

      (iv) the Company Directors Disqualification Act 1986 (c. 46) or the Company Directors Disqualification (Northern Ireland) Order 2002 (S.I. 2002/3150 (N.I. 4)),

      (v) the Financial Services and Markets Act 2000 (c. 8);

  (d) for the purpose of enabling or assisting the Department of Enterprise, Trade and Investment for Northern Ireland to exercise any powers conferred on it by the enactments relating to companies, directors' disqualification or insolvency;

  (e) for the purpose of enabling or assisting the Bank of England to exercise its functions;

  (f) for the purpose of enabling or assisting the Commissioners for Her Majesty's Revenue and Customs to exercise their functions;

  (g) for the purpose of enabling or assisting the Financial Services Authority to exercise its functions under any of the following—

      (i) the legislation relating to friendly societies or to industrial and provident societies,

      (ii) the Building Societies Act 1986 (c. 53),

      (iii) Part 7 of the Companies Act 1989 (c. 40),

      (iv) the Financial Services and Markets Act 2000; or

  (h) in pursuance of any Community obligation.

(5) It does not apply to disclosure to a body exercising functions of a public nature under legislation in any country or territory outside the United Kingdom that appear to the authorised person to be similar to his functions under section 456 for the purpose of enabling or assisting that body to exercise those functions.

(6) In determining whether to disclose information to a body in accordance with subsection (5), the authorised person must have regard to the following considerations—

  (a) whether the use which the body is likely to make of the information is sufficiently important to justify making the disclosure;

  (b) whether the body has adequate arrangements to prevent the information from being used or further disclosed other than—

      (i) for the purposes of carrying out the functions mentioned in that subsection, or

      (ii) for other purposes substantially similar to those for which information disclosed to the authorised person could be used or further disclosed.

(7) Nothing in this section authorises the making of a disclosure in contravention of the Data Protection Act 1998 (c. 29).

462. Power to amend categories of permitted disclosure

(1) The Secretary of State may by order amend section 461(3), (4) and (5).

(2) An order under this section must not—

  (a) amend subsection (3) of that section (UK public authorities) by specifying a person unless the person exercises functions of a public nature (whether or not he exercises any other function);

  (b) amend subsection (4) of that section (purposes for which disclosure permitted) by adding or modifying a description of disclosure unless the purpose for which the disclosure is permitted is likely to facilitate the exercise of a function of a public nature;

  (c) amend subsection (5) of that section (overseas regulatory authorities) so as to have the effect of permitting disclosures to be made to a body other than one that exercises functions of a public nature in a country or territory outside the United Kingdom.

(3) An order under this section is subject to negative resolution procedure.

CHAPTER 12
SUPPLEMENTARY PROVISIONS

Liability for false or misleading statements in reports

463. **Liability for false or misleading statements in reports**
    (1) The reports to which this section applies are—
        (a) the directors' report,
        (b) the directors' remuneration report, and
        (c) a summary financial statement so far as it is derived from either of those reports.
    (2) A director of a company is liable to compensate the company for any loss suffered by it as a result of—
        (a) any untrue or misleading statement in a report to which this section applies, or
        (b) the omission from a report to which this section applies of anything required to be included in it.
    (3) He is so liable only if—
        (a) he knew the statement to be untrue or misleading or was reckless as to whether it was untrue or misleading, or
        (b) he knew the omission to be dishonest concealment of a material fact.
    (4) No person shall be subject to any liability to a person other than the company resulting from reliance, by that person or another, on information in a report to which this section applies.
    (5) The reference in subsection (4) to a person being subject to a liability includes a reference to another person being entitled as against him to be granted any civil remedy or to rescind or repudiate an agreement.
    (6) This section does not affect—
        (a) liability for a civil penalty, or
        (b) liability for a criminal offence.

Accounting and reporting standards

464. **Accounting standards**
    (1) In this Part "accounting standards" means statements of standard accounting practice issued by such body or bodies as may be prescribed by regulations.
    (2) References in this Part to accounting standards applicable to a company's annual accounts are to such standards as are, in accordance with their terms, relevant to the company's circumstances and to the accounts.
    (3) Regulations under this section may contain such transitional and other supplementary and incidental provisions as appear to the Secretary of State to be appropriate.

Companies qualifying as medium-sized

465. **Companies qualifying as medium-sized: general**
    (1) A company qualifies as medium-sized in relation to its first financial year if the qualifying conditions are met in that year.
    (2) A company qualifies as medium-sized in relation to a subsequent financial year—
        (a) if the qualifying conditions are met in that year and the preceding financial year;
        (b) if the qualifying conditions are met in that year and the company qualified as medium-sized in relation to the preceding financial year;
        (c) if the qualifying conditions were met in the preceding financial year and the company qualified as medium-sized in relation to that year.

(3) The qualifying conditions are met by a company in a year in which it satisfies two or more of the following requirements—

1. Turnover	Not more than £22.8 million
2. Balance sheet total	Not more than £11.4 million
3. Number of employees	Not more than 250

(4) For a period that is a company's financial year but not in fact a year the maximum figures for turnover must be proportionately adjusted.

(5) The balance sheet total means the aggregate of the amounts shown as assets in the company's balance sheet.

(6) The number of employees means the average number of persons employed by the company in the year, determined as follows—

    (a) find for each month in the financial year the number of persons employed under contracts of service by the company in that month (whether throughout the month or not),

    (b) add together the monthly totals, and

    (c) divide by the number of months in the financial year.

(7) This section is subject to section 466 (companies qualifying as medium-sized: parent companies).

466. **Companies qualifying as medium-sized: parent companies**

(1) A parent company qualifies as a medium-sized company in relation to a financial year only if the group headed by it qualifies as a medium-sized group.

(2) A group qualifies as medium-sized in relation to the parent company's first financial year if the qualifying conditions are met in that year.

(3) A group qualifies as medium-sized in relation to a subsequent financial year of the parent company—

    (a) if the qualifying conditions are met in that year and the preceding financial year;

    (b) if the qualifying conditions are met in that year and the group qualified as medium-sized in relation to the preceding financial year;

    (c) if the qualifying conditions were met in the preceding financial year and the group qualified as medium-sized in relation to that year.

(4) The qualifying conditions are met by a group in a year in which it satisfies two or more of the following requirements—

1. Aggregate turnover	Not more than £22.8 million net (or £27.36 million gross)
2. Aggregate balance sheet total	Not more than £11.4 million net (or £13.68 million gross)
3. Aggregate number of employees	Not more than 250

(5) The aggregate figures are ascertained by aggregating the relevant figures determined in accordance with section 465 for each member of the group.

(6) In relation to the aggregate figures for turnover and balance sheet total—

    "net" means after any set-offs and other adjustments made to eliminate group transactions—

        (a) in the case of Companies Act accounts, in accordance with regulations under section 404,

        (b) in the case of IAS accounts, in accordance with international accounting standards; and

    "gross" means without those set-offs and other adjustments.

A company may satisfy any relevant requirement on the basis of either the net or the gross figure.

(7) The figures for each subsidiary undertaking shall be those included in its individual accounts for the relevant financial year, that is—

    (a) if its financial year ends with that of the parent company, that financial year, and

(b) if not, its financial year ending last before the end of the financial year of the parent company.

If those figures cannot be obtained without disproportionate expense or undue delay, the latest available figures shall be taken.

467. Companies excluded from being treated as medium-sized

(1) A company is not entitled to take advantage of any of the provisions of this Part relating to companies qualifying as medium-sized if it was at any time within the financial year in question—

    (a) a public company,

    (b) a company that—

        (i) has permission under Part 4 of the Financial Services and Markets Act 2000 (c. 8) to carry on a regulated activity, or

        (ii) carries on insurance market activity, or

    (c) a member of an ineligible group.

(2) A group is ineligible if any of its members is—

    (a) a public company,

    (b) a body corporate (other than a company) whose shares are admitted to trading on a regulated market,

    (c) a person (other than a small company) who has permission under Part 4 of the Financial Services and Markets Act 2000 to carry on a regulated activity,

    (d) a small company that is an authorised insurance company, a banking company, an e-money issuer, an ISD investment firm or a UCITS management company, or

    (e) a person who carries on insurance market activity.

(3) A company is a small company for the purposes of subsection (2) if it qualified as small in relation to its last financial year ending on or before the end of the financial year in question.

General power to make further provision about accounts and reports

468. General power to make further provision about accounts and reports

(1) The Secretary of State may make provision by regulations about—

    (a) the accounts and reports that companies are required to prepare;

    (b) the categories of companies required to prepare accounts and reports of any description;

    (c) the form and content of the accounts and reports that companies are required to prepare;

    (d) the obligations of companies and others as regards—

        (i) the approval of accounts and reports,

        (ii) the sending of accounts and reports to members and others,

        (iii) the laying of accounts and reports before the company in general meeting,

        (iv) the delivery of copies of accounts and reports to the registrar, and

        (v) the publication of accounts and reports.

(2) The regulations may amend this Part by adding, altering or repealing provisions.

(3) But they must not amend (other than consequentially)—

    (a) section 393 (accounts to give true and fair view), or

    (b) the provisions of Chapter 11 (revision of defective accounts and reports).

(4) The regulations may create criminal offences in cases corresponding to those in which an offence is created by an existing provision of this Part.

The maximum penalty for any such offence may not be greater than is provided in relation to an offence under the existing provision.

(5) The regulations may provide for civil penalties in circumstances corresponding to those within section 453(1) (civil penalty for failure to file accounts and reports).

The provisions of section 453(2) to (5) apply in relation to any such penalty.

Other supplementary provisions

469. Preparation and filing of accounts in euros

(1) The amounts set out in the annual accounts of a company may also be shown in the same accounts translated into euros.

(2) When complying with section 441 (duty to file accounts and reports), the directors of a company may deliver to the registrar an additional copy of the company's annual accounts in which the amounts have been translated into euros.

(3) In both cases—

   (a) the amounts must have been translated at the exchange rate prevailing on the date to which the balance sheet is made up, and

   (b) that rate must be disclosed in the notes to the accounts.

(4) For the purposes of sections 434 and 435 (requirements in connection with published accounts) any additional copy of the company's annual accounts delivered to the registrar under subsection (2) above shall be treated as statutory accounts of the company.

   In the case of such a copy, references in those sections to the auditor's report on the company's annual accounts shall be read as references to the auditor's report on the annual accounts of which it is a copy.

470. Power to apply provisions to banking partnerships

(1) The Secretary of State may be regulations apply to banking partnerships, subject to such exceptions, adaptations and modifications as he considers appropriate, the provisions of this Part (and of regulations made under this Part) applying to banking companies.

(2) A "banking partnership" means a partnership which has permission under Part 4 of the Financial Services and Markets Act 2000 (c. 8).

   But a partnership is not a banking partnership if it has permission to accept deposits only for the purpose of carrying on another regulated activity in accordance with that permission.

(3) Expressions used in this section that are also used in the provisions regulating activities under the Financial Services and Markets Act 2000 have the same meaning here as they do in those provisions.

   See section 22 of that Act, orders made under that section and Schedule 2 to that Act.

(4) Regulations under this section are subject to affirmative resolution procedure.

471. Meaning of "annual accounts" and related expressions

(1) In this Part a company's "annual accounts", in relation to a financial year, means—

   (a) the company's individual accounts for that year (see section 394), and

   (b) any group accounts prepared by the company for that year (see sections 398 and 399).

   This is subject to section 408 (option to omit individual profit and loss account from annual accounts where information given in group accounts).

(2) In the case of an unquoted company, its "annual accounts and reports" for a financial year are—

   (a) its annual accounts,

   (b) the directors' report, and

   (c) the auditor's report on those accounts and the directors' report (unless the company is exempt from audit).

(3) In the case of a quoted company, its "annual accounts and reports" for a financial year are—

   (a) its annual accounts,

   (b) the directors' remuneration report,

   (c) the directors' report, and

   (d) the auditor's report on those accounts, on the auditable part of the directors' remuneration report and on the directors' report.

472. **Notes to the accounts**

(1) Information required by this Part to be given in notes to a company's annual accounts may be contained in the accounts or in a separate document annexed to the accounts.

(2) References in this Part to a company's annual accounts, or to a balance sheet or profit and loss account, include notes to the accounts giving information which is required by any provision of this Act or international accounting standards, and required or allowed by any such provision to be given in a note to company accounts.

473. **Parliamentary procedure for certain regulations under this Part**

(1) This section applies to regulations under the following provisions of this Part—

section 396 (Companies Act individual accounts),

section 404 (Companies Act group accounts),

section 409 (information about related undertakings),

section 412 (information about directors' benefits: remuneration, pensions and compensation for loss of office),

section 416 (contents of directors' report: general),

section 421 (contents of directors' remuneration report),

section 444 (filing obligations of companies subject to small companies regime),

section 445 (filing obligations of medium-sized companies),

section 468 (general power to make further provision about accounts and reports).

(2) Any such regulations may make consequential amendments or repeals in other provisions of this Act, or in other enactments.

(3) Regulations that—

(a) restrict the classes of company which have the benefit of any exemption, exception or special provision,

(b) require additional matter to be included in a document of any class, or

(c) otherwise render the requirements of this Part more onerous,

are subject to affirmative resolution procedure.

(4) Otherwise, the regulations are subject to negative resolution procedure.

474. **Minor definitions**

(1) In this Part—

"e-money issuer" means a person who has permission under Part 4 of the Financial Services and Markets Act 2000 (c. 8) to carry on the activity of issuing electronic money within the meaning of article 9B of the Financial Services and Markets Act 2000 (Regulated Activities) Order 2001 (S.I. 2001/544);

"group" means a parent undertaking and its subsidiary undertakings;

"IAS Regulation" means EC Regulation No. 1606/2002 of the European Parliament and of the Council of 19 July 2002 on the application of international accounting standards;

"included in the consolidation", in relation to group accounts, or "included in consolidated group accounts", means that the undertaking is included in the accounts by the method of full (and not proportional) consolidation, and references to an undertaking excluded from consolidation shall be construed accordingly;

"international accounting standards" means the international accounting standards, within the meaning of the IAS Regulation, adopted from time to time by the European Commission in accordance with that Regulation;

"ISD investment firm" has the meaning given by the Glossary forming part of the Handbook made by the Financial Services Authority under the Financial Services and Markets Act 2000;

"profit and loss account", in relation to a company that prepares IAS accounts, includes an income statement or other equivalent financial statement required to be prepared by international accounting standards;

"regulated activity" has the meaning given in section 22 of the Financial Services and Markets Act 2000, except that it does not include activities of the kind specified in any of the following provisions of the Financial Services and Markets Act 2000 (Regulated Activities) Order 2001 (S.I. 2001/544)—

(a) article 25A (arranging regulated mortgage contracts),

(b) article 25B (arranging regulated home reversion plans),

(c) article 25C (arranging regulated home purchase plans),

(d) article 39A (assisting administration and performance of a contract of insurance),

(e) article 53A (advising on regulated mortgage contracts),

(f) article 53B (advising on regulated home reversion plans),

(g) article 53C (advising on regulated home purchase plans),

(h) article 21 (dealing as agent), article 25 (arranging deals in investments) or article 53 (advising on investments) where the activity concerns relevant investments that are not contractually based investments (within the meaning of article 3 of that Order), or

(i) article 64 (agreeing to carry on a regulated activity of the kind mentioned in paragraphs (a) to (h));

"turnover", in relation to a company, means the amounts derived from the provision of goods and services falling within the company's ordinary activities, after deduction of—

(a) trade discounts,

(b) value added tax, and

(c) any other taxes based on the amounts so derived;

"UCITS management company" has the meaning given by the Glossary forming part of the Handbook made by the Financial Services Authority under the Financial Services and Markets Act 2000 (c. 8).

(2) In the case of an undertaking not trading for profit, any reference in this Part to a profit and loss account is to an income and expenditure account.

References to profit and loss and, in relation to group accounts, to a consolidated profit and loss account shall be construed accordingly.

PART 16

AUDIT

CHAPTER 1

REQUIREMENT FOR AUDITED ACCOUNTS

Requirement for audited accounts

475. Requirement for audited accounts

(1) A company's annual accounts for a financial year must be audited in accordance with this Part unless the company—

(a) is exempt from audit under—

section 477 (small companies), or

section 480 (dormant companies);

or

(b) is exempt from the requirements of this Part under section 482 (non-profit-making companies subject to public sector audit).

(2) A company is not entitled to any such exemption unless its balance sheet contains a statement by the directors to that effect.

(3) A company is not entitled to exemption under any of the provisions mentioned in subsection (1)(a) unless its balance sheet contains a statement by the directors to the effect that—

    (a) the members have not required the company to obtain an audit of its accounts for the year in question in accordance with section 476, and

    (b) the directors acknowledge their responsibilities for complying with the requirements of this Act with respect to accounting records and the preparation of accounts.

(4) The statement required by subsection (2) or (3) must appear on the balance sheet above the signature required by section 414.

476. Right of members to require audit

(1) The members of a company that would otherwise be entitled to exemption from audit under any of the provisions mentioned in section 475(1)(a) may by notice under this section require it to obtain an audit of its accounts for a financial year.

(2) The notice must be given by—

    (a) members representing not less in total than 10% in nominal value of the company's issued share capital, or any class of it, or

    (b) if the company does not have a share capital, not less than 10% in number of the members of the company.

(3) The notice may not be given before the financial year to which it relates and must be given not later than one month before the end of that year.

Exemption from audit: small companies

477. Small companies: conditions for exemption from audit

(1) A company that meets the following conditions in respect of a financial year is exempt from the requirements of this Act relating to the audit of accounts for that year.

(2) The conditions are—

    (a) that the company qualifies as a small company in relation to that year,

    (b) that its turnover in that year is not more than £5.6 million, and

    (c) that its balance sheet total for that year is not more than £2.8 million.

(3) For a period which is a company's financial year but not in fact a year the maximum figure for turnover shall be proportionately adjusted.

(4) For the purposes of this section—

    (a) whether a company qualifies as a small company shall be determined in accordance with section 382(1) to (6), and

    (b) "balance sheet total" has the same meaning as in that section.

(5) This section has effect subject to—

section 475(2) and (3) (requirements as to statements to be contained in balance sheet),

section 476 (right of members to require audit),

section 478 (companies excluded from small companies exemption), and

section 479 (availability of small companies exemption in case of group company).

478. Companies excluded from small companies exemption

A company is not entitled to the exemption conferred by section 477 (small companies) if it was at any time within the financial year in question—

(a) a public company,

(b) a company that—

    (i) is an authorised insurance company, a banking company, an e-money issuer, an ISD investment firm or a UCITS management company, or

    (ii) carries on insurance market activity, or

(c) a special register body as defined in section 117(1) of the Trade Union and Labour Relations (Consolidation) Act 1992 (c. 52) or an employers' association as defined in section 122 of that Act or Article 4 of the Industrial Relations (Northern Ireland) Order 1992 (S.I. 1992/807 (N.I. 5)).

479. **Availability of small companies exemption in case of group company**

(1) A company is not entitled to the exemption conferred by section 477 (small companies) in respect of a financial year during any part of which it was a group company unless—

    (a) the conditions specified in subsection (2) below are met, or

    (b) subsection (3) applies.

(2) The conditions are—

    (a) that the group—

        (i) qualifies as a small group in relation to that financial year, and

        (ii) was not at any time in that year an ineligible group;

    (b) that the group's aggregate turnover in that year is not more than £5.6 million net (or £6.72 million gross);

    (c) that the group's aggregate balance sheet total for that year is not more than £2.8 million net (or £3.36 million gross).

(3) A company is not excluded by subsection (1) if, throughout the whole of the period or periods during the financial year when it was a group company, it was both a subsidiary undertaking and dormant.

(4) In this section—

    (a) "group company" means a company that is a parent company or a subsidiary undertaking, and

    (b) "the group", in relation to a group company, means that company together with all its associated undertakings.

For this purpose undertakings are associated if one is a subsidiary undertaking of the other or both are subsidiary undertakings of a third undertaking.

(5) For the purposes of this section—

    (a) whether a group qualifies as small shall be determined in accordance with section 383 (companies qualifying as small: parent companies);

    (b) "ineligible group" has the meaning given by section 384(2) and (3);

    (c) a group's aggregate turnover and aggregate balance sheet total shall be determined as for the purposes of section 383;

    (d) "net" and "gross" have the same meaning as in that section;

    (e) a company may meet any relevant requirement on the basis of either the gross or the net figure.

(6) The provisions mentioned in subsection (5) apply for the purposes of this section as if all the bodies corporate in the group were companies.

Exemption from audit: dormant companies

480. **Dormant companies: conditions for exemption from audit**

(1) A company is exempt from the requirements of this Act relating to the audit of accounts in respect of a financial year if—

    (a) it has been dormant since its formation, or

    (b) it has been dormant since the end of the previous financial year and the following conditions are met.

(2) The conditions are that the company—

    (a) as regards its individual accounts for the financial year in question—

        (i) is entitled to prepare accounts in accordance with the small companies regime (see sections 381 to 384), or

        (ii) would be so entitled but for having been a public company or a member of an ineligible group, and

    (b) is not required to prepare group accounts for that year.

(3) This section has effect subject to—

section 475(2) and (3) (requirements as to statements to be contained in balance sheet),

section 476 (right of members to require audit), and

section 481 (companies excluded from dormant companies exemption).

481. Companies excluded from dormant companies exemption

A company is not entitled to the exemption conferred by section 480 (dormant companies) if it was at any time within the financial year in question a company that—

(a) is an authorised insurance company, a banking company, an e-money issuer, an ISD investment firm or a UCITS management company, or

(b) carries on insurance market activity.

Companies subject to public sector audit

482. Non-profit-making companies subject to public sector audit

(1) The requirements of this Part as to audit of accounts do not apply to a company for a financial year if it is non-profit-making and its accounts—

(a) are subject to audit—

(i) by the Comptroller and Auditor General by virtue of an order under section 25(6) of the Government Resources and Accounts Act 2000 (c. 20), or

(ii) by the Auditor General for Wales by virtue of section 96, or an order under section 144, of the Government of Wales Act 1998 (c. 38);

(b) are accounts—

(i) in relation to which section 21 of the Public Finance and Accountability (Scotland) Act 2000 (asp 1) (audit of accounts: Auditor General for Scotland) applies, or

(ii) that are subject to audit by the Auditor General for Scotland by virtue of an order under section 483 (Scottish public sector companies: audit by Auditor General for Scotland); or

(c) are subject to audit by the Comptroller and Auditor General for Northern Ireland by virtue of an order under Article 5(3) of the Audit and Accountability (Northern Ireland) Order 2003 (S.I. 2003/418 (N.I. 5)).

(2) In the case of a company that is a parent company or a subsidiary undertaking, subsection (1) applies only if every group undertaking is non-profit-making.

(3) In this section "non-profit-making" has the same meaning as in Article 48 of the Treaty establishing the European Community.

(4) This section has effect subject to section 475(2) (balance sheet to contain statement that company entitled to exemption under this section).

483. Scottish public sector companies: audit by Auditor General for Scotland

(1) The Scottish Ministers may by order provide for the accounts of a company having its registered office in Scotland to be audited by the Auditor General for Scotland.

(2) An order under subsection (1) may be made in relation to a company only if it appears to the Scottish Ministers that the company—

(a) exercises in or as regards Scotland functions of a public nature none of which relate to reserved matters (within the meaning of the Scotland Act 1998 (c. 46)), or

(b) is entirely or substantially funded from a body having accounts falling within paragraph (a) or (b) of subsection (3).

(3) Those accounts are—

(a) accounts in relation to which section 21 of the Public Finance and Accountability (Scotland) Act 2000 (asp 1) (audit of accounts: Auditor General for Scotland) applies,

(b) accounts which are subject to audit by the Auditor General for Scotland by virtue of an order under this section.

(4) An order under subsection (1) may make such supplementary or consequential provision (including provision amending an enactment) as the Scottish Ministers think expedient.

(5) An order under subsection (1) shall not be made unless a draft of the statutory instrument containing it has been laid before, and approved by resolution of, the Scottish Parliament.

General power of amendment by regulations

484. General power of amendment by regulations

(1) The Secretary of State may by regulations amend this Chapter or section 539 (minor definitions) so far as applying to this Chapter by adding, altering or repealing provisions.

(2) The regulations may make consequential amendments or repeals in other provisions of this Act, or in other enactments.

(3) Regulations under this section imposing new requirements, or rendering existing requirements more onerous, are subject to affirmative resolution procedure.

(4) Other regulations under this section are subject to negative resolution procedure.

CHAPTER 2
APPOINTMENT OF AUDITORS

Private companies

485. Appointment of auditors of private company: general

(1) An auditor or auditors of a private company must be appointed for each financial year of the company, unless the directors reasonably resolve otherwise on the ground that audited accounts are unlikely to be required.

(2) For each financial year for which an auditor or auditors is or are to be appointed (other than the company's first financial year), the appointment must be made before the end of the period of 28 days beginning with—

(a) the end of the time allowed for sending out copies of the company's annual accounts and reports for the previous financial year (see section 424), or

(b) if earlier, the day on which copies of the company's annual accounts and reports for the previous financial year are sent out under section 423.

This is the "period for appointing auditors".

(3) The directors may appoint an auditor or auditors of the company—

(a) at any time before the company's first period for appointing auditors,

(b) following a period during which the company (being exempt from audit) did not have any auditor, at any time before the company's next period for appointing auditors, or

(c) to fill a casual vacancy in the office of auditor.

(4) The members may appoint an auditor or auditors by ordinary resolution—

(a) during a period for appointing auditors,

(b) if the company should have appointed an auditor or auditors during a period for appointing auditors but failed to do so, or

(c) where the directors had power to appoint under subsection (3) but have failed to make an appointment.

(5) An auditor or auditors of a private company may only be appointed—

(a) in accordance with this section, or

(b) in accordance with section 486 (default power of Secretary of State).

This is without prejudice to any deemed re-appointment under section 487.

486. Appointment of auditors of private company: default power of Secretary of State

(1) If a private company fails to appoint an auditor or auditors in accordance with section 485, the Secretary of State may appoint one or more persons to fill the vacancy.

(2) Where subsection (2) of that section applies and the company fails to make the necessary appointment before the end of the period for appointing auditors, the company must within one week of the end of that period give notice to the Secretary of State of his power having become exercisable.

(3) If a company fails to give the notice required by this section, an offence is committed by—

(a) the company, and

(b) every officer of the company who is in default.

(4) A person guilty of an offence under this section is liable on summary conviction to a fine not exceeding level 3 on the standard scale and, for continued contravention, a daily default fine not exceeding one-tenth of level 3 on the standard scale.

487. Term of office of auditors of private company

(1) An auditor or auditors of a private company hold office in accordance with the terms of their appointment, subject to the requirements that—

(a) they do not take office until any previous auditor or auditors cease to hold office, and

(b) they cease hold office at the end of the next period for appointing auditors unless re-appointed.

(2) Where no auditor has been appointed by the end of the next period for appointing auditors, any auditor in office immediately before that time is deemed to be re-appointed at that time, unless—

(a) he was appointed by the directors, or

(b) the company's articles require actual re-appointment, or

(c) the deemed re-appointment is prevented by the members under section 488, or

(d) the members have resolved that he should not be re-appointed, or

(e) the directors have resolved that no auditor or auditors should be appointed for the financial year in question.

(3) This is without prejudice to the provisions of this Part as to removal and resignation of auditors.

(4) No account shall be taken of any loss of the opportunity of deemed reappointment under this section in ascertaining the amount of any compensation or damages payable to an auditor on his ceasing to hold office for any reason.

488. Prevention by members of deemed re-appointment of auditor

(1) An auditor of a private company is not deemed to be re-appointed under section 487(2) if the company has received notices under this section from members representing at least the requisite percentage of the total voting rights of all members who would be entitled to vote on a resolution that the auditor should not be re-appointed.

(2) The "requisite percentage" is 5%, or such lower percentage as is specified for this purpose in the company's articles.

(3) A notice under this section—

(a) may be in hard copy or electronic form,

(b) must be authenticated by the person or persons giving it, and

(c) must be received by the company before the end of the accounting reference period immediately preceding the time when the deemed reappointment would have effect.

Public companies

489. Appointment of auditors of public company: general

(1) An auditor or auditors of a public company must be appointed for each financial year of the company, unless the directors reasonably resolve otherwise on the ground that audited accounts are unlikely to be required.

(2) For each financial year for which an auditor or auditors is or are to be appointed (other than the company's first financial year), the appointment must be made before the end of the

accounts meeting of the company at which the company's annual accounts and reports for the previous financial year are laid.

(3) The directors may appoint an auditor or auditors of the company—

    (a) at any time before the company's first accounts meeting;

    (b) following a period during which the company (being exempt from audit) did not have any auditor, at any time before the company's next accounts meeting;

    (c) to fill a casual vacancy in the office of auditor.

(4) The members may appoint an auditor or auditors by ordinary resolution—

    (a) at an accounts meeting;

    (b) if the company should have appointed an auditor or auditors at an accounts meeting but failed to do so;

    (c) where the directors had power to appoint under subsection (3) but have failed to make an appointment.

(5) An auditor or auditors of a public company may only be appointed—

    (a) in accordance with this section, or

    (b) in accordance with section 490 (default power of Secretary of State).

490. Appointment of auditors of public company: default power of Secretary of State

(1) If a public company fails to appoint an auditor or auditors in accordance with section 489, the Secretary of State may appoint one or more persons to fill the vacancy.

(2) Where subsection (2) of that section applies and the company fails to make the necessary appointment before the end of the accounts meeting, the company must within one week of the end of that meeting give notice to the Secretary of State of his power having become exercisable.

(3) If a company fails to give the notice required by this section, an offence is committed by—

    (a) the company, and

    (b) every officer of the company who is in default.

(4) A person guilty of an offence under this section is liable on summary conviction to a fine not exceeding level 3 on the standard scale and, for continued contravention, a daily default fine not exceeding one-tenth of level 3 on the standard scale.

491. Term of office of auditors of public company

(1) The auditor or auditors of a public company hold office in accordance with the terms of their appointment, subject to the requirements that—

    (a) they do not take office until the previous auditor or auditors have ceased to hold office, and

    (b) they cease to hold office at the conclusion of the accounts meeting next following their appointment, unless re-appointed.

(2) This is without prejudice to the provisions of this Part as to removal and resignation of auditors.

General provisions

492. Fixing of auditor's remuneration

(1) The remuneration of an auditor appointed by the members of a company must be fixed by the members by ordinary resolution or in such manner as the members may by ordinary resolution determine.

(2) The remuneration of an auditor appointed by the directors of a company must be fixed by the directors.

(3) The remuneration of an auditor appointed by the Secretary of State must be fixed by the Secretary of State.

(4) For the purposes of this section "remuneration" includes sums paid in respect of expenses.

(5) This section applies in relation to benefits in kind as to payments of money.

493. Disclosure of terms of audit appointment

(1) The Secretary of State may make provision by regulations for securing the disclosure of the terms on which a company's auditor is appointed, remunerated or performs his duties. Nothing in the following provisions of this section affects the generality of this power.

(2) The regulations may—

    (a) require disclosure of—

        (i) a copy of any terms that are in writing, and

        (ii) a written memorandum setting out any terms that are not in writing;

    (b) require disclosure to be at such times, in such places and by such means as are specified in the regulations;

    (c) require the place and means of disclosure to be stated—

        (i) in a note to the company's annual accounts (in the case of its individual accounts) or in such manner as is specified in the regulations (in the case of group accounts),

        (ii) in the directors' report, or

        (iii) in the auditor's report on the company's annual accounts.

(3) The provisions of this section apply to a variation of the terms mentioned in subsection (1) as they apply to the original terms.

(4) Regulations under this section are subject to affirmative resolution procedure.

494. Disclosure of services provided by auditor or associates and related remuneration

(1) The Secretary of State may make provision by regulations for securing the disclosure of—

    (a) the nature of any services provided for a company by the company's auditor (whether in his capacity as auditor or otherwise) or by his associates;

    (b) the amount of any remuneration received or receivable by a company's auditor, or his associates, in respect of any such services.

Nothing in the following provisions of this section affects the generality of this power.

(2) The regulations may provide—

    (a) for disclosure of the nature of any services provided to be made by reference to any class or description of services specified in the regulations (or any combination of services, however described);

    (b) for the disclosure of amounts of remuneration received or receivable in respect of services of any class or description specified in the regulations (or any combination of services, however described);

    (c) for the disclosure of separate amounts so received or receivable by the company's auditor or any of his associates, or of aggregate amounts so received or receivable by all or any of those persons.

(3) The regulations may—

    (a) provide that "remuneration" includes sums paid in respect of expenses;

    (b) apply to benefits in kind as well as to payments of money, and require the disclosure of the nature of any such benefits and their estimated money value;

    (c) apply to services provided for associates of a company as well as to those provided for a company;

    (d) define "associate" in relation to an auditor and a company respectively.

(4) The regulations may provide that any disclosure required by the regulations is to be made—

    (a) in a note to the company's annual accounts (in the case of its individual accounts) or in such manner as is specified in the regulations (in the case of group accounts),

    (b) in the directors' report, or

    (c) in the auditor's report on the company's annual accounts.

(5) If the regulations provide that any such disclosure is to be made as mentioned in subsection (4)(a) or (b), the regulations may require the auditor to supply the directors of the company with any information necessary to enable the disclosure to be made.

(6) Regulations under this section are subject to negative resolution procedure.

CHAPTER 3
FUNCTIONS OF AUDITOR

Auditor's report

495. Auditor's report on company's annual accounts

(1) A company's auditor must make a report to the company's members on all annual accounts of the company of which copies are, during his tenure of office—

(a) in the case of a private company, to be sent out to members under section 423;

(b) in the case of a public company, to be laid before the company in general meeting under section 437.

(2) The auditor's report must include—

(a) an introduction identifying the annual accounts that are the subject of the audit and the financial reporting framework that has been applied in their preparation, and

(b) a description of the scope of the audit identifying the auditing standards in accordance with which the audit was conducted.

(3) The report must state clearly whether, in the auditor's opinion, the annual accounts—

(a) give a true and fair view—

(i) in the case of an individual balance sheet, of the state of affairs of the company as at the end of the financial year,

(ii) in the case of an individual profit and loss account, of the profit or loss of the company for the financial year,

(iii) in the case of group accounts, of the state of affairs as at the end of the financial year and of the profit or loss for the financial year of the undertakings included in the consolidation as a whole, so far as concerns members of the company;

(b) have been properly prepared in accordance with the relevant financial reporting framework; and

(c) have been prepared in accordance with the requirements of this Act (and, where applicable, Article 4 of the IAS Regulation).

Expressions used in this subsection that are defined for the purposes of Part 15 (see section 474) have the same meaning as in that Part.

(4) The auditor's report—

(a) must be either unqualified or qualified, and

(b) must include a reference to any matters to which the auditor wishes to draw attention by way of emphasis without qualifying the report.

496. Auditor's report on directors' report

The auditor must state in his report on the company's annual accounts whether in his opinion the information given in the directors' report for the financial year for which the accounts are prepared is consistent with those accounts.

497. Auditor's report on auditable part of directors' remuneration report

(1) If the company is a quoted company, the auditor, in his report on the company's annual accounts for the financial year, must—

(a) report to the company's members on the auditable part of the directors' remuneration report, and

(b) state whether in his opinion that part of the directors' remuneration report has been properly prepared in accordance with this Act.

(2) For the purposes of this Part, "the auditable part" of a directors' remuneration report is the part identified as such by regulations under section 421.

Duties and rights of auditors

498. Duties of auditor

(1) A company's auditor, in preparing his report, must carry out such investigations as will enable him to form an opinion as to—

(a) whether adequate accounting records have been kept by the company and returns adequate for their audit have been received from branches not visited by him, and

(b) whether the company's individual accounts are in agreement with the accounting records and returns, and

(c) in the case of a quoted company, whether the auditable part of the company's directors' remuneration report is in agreement with the accounting records and returns.

(2) If the auditor is of the opinion—

(a) that adequate accounting records have not been kept, or that returns adequate for their audit have not been received from branches not visited by him, or

(b) that the company's individual accounts are not in agreement with the accounting records and returns, or

(c) in the case of a quoted company, that the auditable part of its directors' remuneration report is not in agreement with the accounting records and returns,

the auditor shall state that fact in his report.

(3) If the auditor fails to obtain all the information and explanations which, to the best of his knowledge and belief, are necessary for the purposes of his audit, he shall state that fact in his report.

(4) If—

(a) the requirements of regulations under section 412 (disclosure of directors' benefits: remuneration, pensions and compensation for loss of office) are not complied with in the annual accounts, or

(b) in the case of a quoted company, the requirements of regulations under section 421 as to information forming the auditable part of the directors' remuneration report are not complied with in that report,

the auditor must include in his report, so far as he is reasonably able to do so, a statement giving the required particulars.

(5) If the directors of the company have prepared accounts and reports in accordance with the small companies regime and in the auditor's opinion they were not entitled so to do, the auditor shall state that fact in his report.

499. Auditor's general right to information

(1) An auditor of a company—

(a) has a right of access at all times to the company's books, accounts and vouchers (in whatever form they are held), and

(b) may require any of the following persons to provide him with such information or explanations as he thinks necessary for the performance of his duties as auditor.

(2) Those persons are—

(a) any officer or employee of the company;

(b) any person holding or accountable for any of the company's books, accounts or vouchers;

(c) any subsidiary undertaking of the company which is a body corporate incorporated in the United Kingdom;

(d) any officer, employee or auditor of any such subsidiary undertaking or any person holding or accountable for any books, accounts or vouchers of any such subsidiary undertaking;

(e) any person who fell within any of paragraphs (a) to (d) at a time to which the information or explanations required by the auditor relates or relate.

(3) A statement made by a person in response to a requirement under this section may not be used in evidence against him in criminal proceedings except proceedings for an offence under section 501.

(4) Nothing in this section compels a person to disclose information in respect of which a claim to legal professional privilege (in Scotland, to confidentiality of communications) could be maintained in legal proceedings.

500. Auditor's right to information from overseas subsidiaries

(1) Where a parent company has a subsidiary undertaking that is not a body corporate incorporated in the United Kingdom, the auditor of the parent company may require it to obtain from any of the following persons such information or explanations as he may reasonably require for the purposes of his duties as auditor.

(2) Those persons are—

    (a) the undertaking;

    (b) any officer, employee or auditor of the undertaking;

    (c) any person holding or accountable for any of the undertaking's books, accounts or vouchers;

    (d) any person who fell within paragraph (b) or (c) at a time to which the information or explanations relates or relate.

(3) If so required, the parent company must take all such steps as are reasonably open to it to obtain the information or explanations from the person concerned.

(4) A statement made by a person in response to a requirement under this section may not be used in evidence against him in criminal proceedings except proceedings for an offence under section 501.

(5) Nothing in this section compels a person to disclose information in respect of which a claim to legal professional privilege (in Scotland, to confidentiality of communications) could be maintained in legal proceedings.

501. Auditor's rights to information: offences

(1) A person commits an offence who knowingly or recklessly makes to an auditor of a company a statement (oral or written) that—

    (a) conveys or purports to convey any information or explanations which the auditor requires, or is entitled to require, under section 499, and

    (b) is misleading, false or deceptive in a material particular.

(2) A person guilty of an offence under subsection (1) is liable—

    (a) on conviction on indictment, to imprisonment for a term not exceeding two years or a fine (or both);

    (b) on summary conviction—

        (i) in England and Wales, to imprisonment for a term not exceeding twelve months or to a fine not exceeding the statutory maximum (or both);

        (ii) in Scotland or Northern Ireland, to imprisonment for a term not exceeding six months or to a fine not exceeding the statutory maximum (or both).

(3) A person who fails to comply with a requirement under section 499 without delay commits an offence unless it was not reasonably practicable for him to provide the required information or explanations.

(4) If a parent company fails to comply with section 500, an offence is committed by—

    (a) the company, and

    (b) every officer of the company who is in default.

(5) A person guilty of an offence under subsection (3) or (4) is liable on summary conviction to a fine not exceeding level 3 on the standard scale.

(6) Nothing in this section affects any right of an auditor to apply for an injunction (in Scotland, an interdict or an order for specific performance) to enforce any of his rights under section 499 or 500.

502. Auditor's rights in relation to resolutions and meetings

(1) In relation to a written resolution proposed to be agreed to by a private company, the company's auditor is entitled to receive all such communications relating to the resolution as, by virtue of any provision of Chapter 2 of Part 13 of this Act, are required to be supplied to a member of the company.

(2) A company's auditor is entitled—

(a) to receive all notices of, and other communications relating to, any general meeting which a member of the company is entitled to receive,

(b) to attend any general meeting of the company, and

(c) to be heard at any general meeting which he attends on any part of the business of the meeting which concerns him as auditor.

(3) Where the auditor is a firm, the right to attend or be heard at a meeting is exercisable by an individual authorised by the firm in writing to act as its representative at the meeting.

Signature of auditor's report

503. Signature of auditor's report

(1) The auditor's report must state the name of the auditor and be signed and dated.

(2) Where the auditor is an individual, the report must be signed by him.

(3) Where the auditor is a firm, the report must be signed by the senior statutory auditor in his own name, for and on behalf of the auditor.

504. Senior statutory auditor

(1) The senior statutory auditor means the individual identified by the firm as senior statutory auditor in relation to the audit in accordance with—

(a) standards issued by the European Commission, or

(b) if there is no applicable standard so issued, any relevant guidance issued by—

(i) the Secretary of State, or

(ii) a body appointed by order of the Secretary of State.

(2) The person identified as senior statutory auditor must be eligible for appointment as auditor of the company in question (see Chapter 2 of Part 42 of this Act).

(3) The senior statutory auditor is not, by reason of being named or identified as senior statutory auditor or by reason of his having signed the auditor's report, subject to any civil liability to which he would not otherwise be subject.

(4) An order appointing a body for the purpose of subsection (1)(b)(ii) is subject to negative resolution procedure.

505. Names to be stated in published copies of auditor's report

(1) Every copy of the auditor's report that is published by or on behalf of the company must—

(a) state the name of the auditor and (where the auditor is a firm) the name of the person who signed it as senior statutory auditor, or

(b) if the conditions in section 506 (circumstances in which names may be omitted) are met, state that a resolution has been passed and notified to the Secretary of State in accordance with that section.

(2) For the purposes of this section a company is regarded as publishing the report if it publishes, issues or circulates it or otherwise makes it available for public inspection in a manner calculated to invite members of the public generally, or any class of members of the public, to read it.

(3) If a copy of the auditor's report is published without the statement required by this section, an offence is committed by—

(a) the company, and

(b) every officer of the company who is in default.

(4) A person guilty of an offence under this section is liable on summary conviction to a fine not exceeding level 3 on the standard scale.

506. Circumstances in which names may be omitted

(1) The auditor's name and, where the auditor is a firm, the name of the person who signed the report as senior statutory auditor, may be omitted from—

(a) published copies of the report, and

(b) the copy of the report delivered to the registrar under Chapter 10 of Part 15 (filing of accounts and reports),

if the following conditions are met.

(2) The conditions are that the company—

(a) considering on reasonable grounds that statement of the name would create or be likely to create a serious risk that the auditor or senior statutory auditor, or any other person, would be subject to violence or intimidation, has resolved that the name should not be stated, and

(b) has given notice of the resolution to the Secretary of State, stating—

(i) the name and registered number of the company,

(ii) the financial year of the company to which the report relates, and

(iii) the name of the auditor and (where the auditor is a firm) the name of the person who signed the report as senior statutory auditor.

Offences in connection with auditor's report

507. Offences in connection with auditor's report

(1) A person to whom this section applies commits an offence if he knowingly or recklessly causes a report under section 495 (auditor's report on company's annual accounts) to include any matter that is misleading, false or deceptive in a material particular.

(2) A person to whom this section applies commits an offence if he knowingly or recklessly causes such a report to omit a statement required by—

(a) section 498(2)(b) (statement that company's accounts do not agree with accounting records and returns),

(b) section 498(3) (statement that necessary information and explanations not obtained), or

(c) section 498(5) (statement that directors wrongly took advantage of exemption from obligation to prepare group accounts).

(3) This section applies to—

(a) where the auditor is an individual, that individual and any employee or agent of his who is eligible for appointment as auditor of the company;

(b) where the auditor is a firm, any director, member, employee or agent of the firm who is eligible for appointment as auditor of the company.

(4) A person guilty of an offence under this section is liable—

(a) on conviction on indictment, to a fine;

(b) on summary conviction, to a fine not exceeding the statutory maximum.

508. Guidance for regulatory and prosecuting authorities: England, Wales and Northern Ireland

(1) The Secretary of State may issue guidance for the purpose of helping relevant regulatory and prosecuting authorities to determine how they should carry out their functions in cases where behaviour occurs that—

(a) appears to involve the commission of an offence under section 507 (offences in connection with auditor's report), and

(b) has been, is being or may be investigated pursuant to arrangements—

(i) under paragraph 15 of Schedule 10 (investigation of complaints against auditors and supervisory bodies), or

    (ii) of a kind mentioned in paragraph 24 of that Schedule (independent investigation for disciplinary purposes of public interest cases).

(2) The Secretary of State must obtain the consent of the Attorney General before issuing any such guidance.

(3) In this section "relevant regulatory and prosecuting authorities" means—

    (a) supervisory bodies within the meaning of Part 42 of this Act,

    (b) bodies to which the Secretary of State may make grants under section 16(1) of the Companies (Audit, Investigations and Community Enterprise) Act 2004 (c. 27) (bodies concerned with accounting standards etc),

    (c) the Director of the Serious Fraud Office,

    (d) the Director of Public Prosecutions or the Director of Public Prosecutions for Northern Ireland, and

    (e) the Secretary of State.

(4) This section does not apply to Scotland.

509. Guidance for regulatory authorities: Scotland

(1) The Lord Advocate may issue guidance for the purpose of helping relevant regulatory authorities to determine how they should carry out their functions in cases where behaviour occurs that—

    (a) appears to involve the commission of an offence under section 507 (offences in connection with auditor's report), and

    (b) has been, is being or may be investigated pursuant to arrangements—

        (i) under paragraph 15 of Schedule 10 (investigation of complaints against auditors and supervisory bodies), or

        (ii) of a kind mentioned in paragraph 24 of that Schedule (independent investigation for disciplinary purposes of public interest cases).

(2) The Lord Advocate must consult the Secretary of State before issuing any such guidance.

(3) In this section "relevant regulatory authorities" means—

    (a) supervisory bodies within the meaning of Part 42 of this Act,

    (b) bodies to which the Secretary of State may make grants under section 16(1) of the Companies (Audit, Investigations and Community Enterprise) Act 2004 (c. 27) (bodies concerned with accounting standards etc), and

    (c) the Secretary of State.

(4) This section applies only to Scotland.

CHAPTER 4
REMOVAL, RESIGNATION, ETC OF AUDITORS

Removal of auditor

510. Resolution removing auditor from office

(1) The members of a company may remove an auditor from office at any time.

(2) This power is exercisable only—

    (a) by ordinary resolution at a meeting, and

    (b) in accordance with section 511 (special notice of resolution to remove auditor).

(3) Nothing in this section is to be taken as depriving the person removed of compensation or damages payable to him in respect of the termination—

    (a) of his appointment as auditor, or

    (b) of any appointment terminating with that as auditor.

(4) An auditor may not be removed from office before the expiration of his term of office except by resolution under this section.

511. **Special notice required for resolution removing auditor from office**

(1) Special notice is required for a resolution at a general meeting of a company removing an auditor from office.

(2) On receipt of notice of such an intended resolution the company must immediately send a copy of it to the auditor proposed to be removed.

(3) The auditor proposed to be removed may make with respect to the intended resolution representations in writing to the company (not exceeding a reasonable length) and request their notification to members of the company.

(4) The company must (unless the representations are received by it too late for it to do so)—

    (a) in any notice of the resolution given to members of the company, state the fact of the representations having been made, and

    (b) send a copy of the representations to every member of the company to whom notice of the meeting is or has been sent.

(5) If a copy of any such representations is not sent out as required because received too late or because of the company's default, the auditor may (without prejudice to his right to be heard orally) require that the representations be read out at the meeting.

(6) Copies of the representations need not be sent out and the representations need not be read at the meeting if, on the application either of the company or of any other person claiming to be aggrieved, the court is satisfied that the auditor is using the provisions of this section to secure needless publicity for defamatory matter.

    The court may order the company's costs (in Scotland, expenses) on the application to be paid in whole or in part by the auditor, notwithstanding that he is not a party to the application.

512. **Notice to registrar of resolution removing auditor from office**

(1) Where a resolution is passed under section 510 (resolution removing auditor from office), the company must give notice of that fact to the registrar within 14 days.

(2) If a company fails to give the notice required by this section, an offence is committed by—

    (a) the company, and

    (b) every officer of it who is in default.

(3) A person guilty of an offence under this section is liable on summary conviction to a fine not exceeding level 3 on the standard scale and, for continued contravention, a daily default fine not exceeding one-tenth of level 3 on the standard scale.

513. **Rights of auditor who has been removed from office**

(1) An auditor who has been removed by resolution under section 510 has, notwithstanding his removal, the rights conferred by section 502(2) in relation to any general meeting of the company—

    (a) at which his term of office would otherwise have expired, or

    (b) at which it is proposed to fill the vacancy caused by his removal.

(2) In such a case the references in that section to matters concerning the auditor as auditor shall be construed as references to matters concerning him as a former auditor.

Failure to re-appoint auditor

514. **Failure to re-appoint auditor: special procedure required for written resolution**

(1) This section applies where a resolution is proposed as a written resolution of a private company whose effect would be to appoint a person as auditor in place of a person (the "outgoing auditor") whose term of office has expired, or is to expire, at the end of the period for appointing auditors.

(2) The following provisions apply if—

    (a) no period for appointing auditors has ended since the outgoing auditor ceased to hold office, or

    (b) such a period has ended and an auditor or auditors should have been appointed but were not.

(3) The company must send a copy of the proposed resolution to the person proposed to be appointed and to the outgoing auditor.

(4) The outgoing auditor may, within 14 days after receiving the notice, make with respect to the proposed resolution representations in writing to the company (not exceeding a reasonable length) and request their circulation to members of the company.

(5) The company must circulate the representations together with the copy or copies of the resolution circulated in accordance with section 291 (resolution proposed by directors) or section 293 (resolution proposed by members).

(6) Where subsection (5) applies—

(a) the period allowed under section 293(3) for service of copies of the proposed resolution is 28 days instead of 21 days, and

(b) the provisions of section 293(5) and (6) (offences) apply in relation to a failure to comply with that subsection as in relation to a default in complying with that section.

(7) Copies of the representations need not be circulated if, on the application either of the company or of any other person claiming to be aggrieved, the court is satisfied that the auditor is using the provisions of this section to secure needless publicity for defamatory matter.

The court may order the company's costs (in Scotland, expenses) on the application to be paid in whole or in part by the auditor, notwithstanding that he is not a party to the application.

(8) If any requirement of this section is not complied with, the resolution is ineffective.

515. **Failure to re-appoint auditor: special notice required for resolution at general meeting**

(1) This section applies to a resolution at a general meeting of a company whose effect would be to appoint a person as auditor in place of a person (the "outgoing auditor") whose term of office has ended, or is to end—

(a) in the case of a private company, at the end of the period for appointing auditors;

(b) in the case of a public company, at the end of the next accounts meeting.

(2) Special notice is required of such a resolution if—

(a) in the case of a private company—

(i) no period for appointing auditors has ended since the outgoing auditor ceased to hold office, or

(ii) such a period has ended and an auditor or auditors should have been appointed but were not;

(b) in the case of a public company—

(i) there has been no accounts meeting of the company since the outgoing auditor ceased to hold office, or

(ii) there has been an accounts meeting at which an auditor or auditors should have been appointed but were not.

(3) On receipt of notice of such an intended resolution the company shall forthwith send a copy of it to the person proposed to be appointed and to the outgoing auditor.

(4) The outgoing auditor may make with respect to the intended resolution representations in writing to the company (not exceeding a reasonable length) and request their notification to members of the company.

(5) The company must (unless the representations are received by it too late for it to do so)—

(a) in any notice of the resolution given to members of the company, state the fact of the representations having been made, and

(b) send a copy of the representations to every member of the company to whom notice of the meeting is or has been sent.

(6) If a copy of any such representations is not sent out as required because received too late or because of the company's default, the outgoing auditor may (without prejudice to his right to be heard orally) require that the representations be read out at the meeting.

(7) Copies of the representations need not be sent out and the representations need not be read at the meeting if, on the application either of the company or of any other person claiming to be aggrieved, the court is satisfied that the auditor is using the provisions of this section to secure needless publicity for defamatory matter.

The court may order the company's costs (in Scotland, expenses) on the application to be paid in whole or in part by the outgoing auditor, notwithstanding that he is not a party to the application.

Resignation of auditor

516. Resignation of auditor

(1) An auditor of a company may resign his office by depositing a notice in writing to that effect at the company's registered office.

(2) The notice is not effective unless it is accompanied by the statement required by section 519.

(3) An effective notice of resignation operates to bring the auditor's term of office to an end as of the date on which the notice is deposited or on such later date as may be specified in it.

517. Notice to registrar of resignation of auditor

(1) Where an auditor resigns the company must within 14 days of the deposit of a notice of resignation send a copy of the notice to the registrar of companies.

(2) If default is made in complying with this section, an offence is committed by—

    (a) the company, and

    (b) every officer of the company who is in default.

(3) A person guilty of an offence under this section is liable—

    (a) on conviction on indictment, to a fine;

    (b) on summary conviction, to a fine not exceeding the statutory maximum and, for continued contravention, a daily default fine not exceeding one-tenth of the statutory maximum.

518. Rights of resigning auditor

(1) This section applies where an auditor's notice of resignation is accompanied by a statement of the circumstances connected with his resignation (see section 519).

(2) He may deposit with the notice a signed requisition calling on the directors of the company forthwith duly to convene a general meeting of the company for the purpose of receiving and considering such explanation of the circumstances connected with his resignation as he may wish to place before the meeting.

(3) He may request the company to circulate to its members—

    (a) before the meeting convened on his requisition, or

    (b) before any general meeting at which his term of office would otherwise have expired or at which it is proposed to fill the vacancy caused by his resignation,

a statement in writing (not exceeding a reasonable length) of the circumstances connected with his resignation.

(4) The company must (unless the statement is received too late for it to comply)—

    (a) in any notice of the meeting given to members of the company, state the fact of the statement having been made, and

    (b) send a copy of the statement to every member of the company to whom notice of the meeting is or has been sent.

(5) The directors must within 21 days from the date of the deposit of a requisition under this section proceed duly to convene a meeting for a day not more than 28 days after the date on which the notice convening the meeting is given.

(6) If default is made in complying with subsection (5), every director who failed to take all reasonable steps to secure that a meeting was convened commits an offence.

(7) A person guilty of an offence under this section is liable—

    (a) on conviction on indictment, to a fine;

(b) on summary conviction to a fine not exceeding the statutory maximum.

(8) If a copy of the statement mentioned above is not sent out as required because received too late or because of the company's default, the auditor may (without prejudice to his right to be heard orally) require that the statement be read out at the meeting.

(9) Copies of a statement need not be sent out and the statement need not be read out at the meeting if, on the application either of the company or of any other person who claims to be aggrieved, the court is satisfied that the auditor is using the provisions of this section to secure needless publicity for defamatory matter.

The court may order the company's costs (in Scotland, expenses) on such an application to be paid in whole or in part by the auditor, notwithstanding that he is not a party to the application.

(10) An auditor who has resigned has, notwithstanding his resignation, the rights conferred by section 502(2) in relation to any such general meeting of the company as is mentioned in subsection (3)(a) or (b) above.

In such a case the references in that section to matters concerning the auditor as auditor shall be construed as references to matters concerning him as a former auditor.

Statement by auditor on ceasing to hold office

519. Statement by auditor to be deposited with company

(1) Where an auditor of an unquoted company ceases for any reason to hold office, he must deposit at the company's registered office a statement of the circumstances connected with his ceasing to hold office, unless he considers that there are no circumstances in connection with his ceasing to hold office that need to be brought to the attention of members or creditors of the company.

(2) If he considers that there are no circumstances in connection with his ceasing to hold office that need to be brought to the attention of members or creditors of the company, he must deposit at the company's registered office a statement to that effect.

(3) Where an auditor of a quoted company ceases for any reason to hold office, he must deposit at the company's registered office a statement of the circumstances connected with his ceasing to hold office.

(4) The statement required by this section must be deposited—

(a) in the case of resignation, along with the notice of resignation;

(b) in the case of failure to seek re-appointment, not less than 14 days before the end of the time allowed for next appointing an auditor;

(c) in any other case, not later than the end of the period of 14 days beginning with the date on which he ceases to hold office.

(5) A person ceasing to hold office as auditor who fails to comply with this section commits an offence.

(6) In proceedings for such an offence it is a defence for the person charged to show that he took all reasonable steps and exercised all due diligence to avoid the commission of the offence.

(7) A person guilty of an offence under this section is liable—

(a) on conviction on indictment, to a fine;

(b) on summary conviction, to a fine not exceeding the statutory maximum.

520. Company's duties in relation to statement

(1) This section applies where the statement deposited under section 519 states the circumstances connected with the auditor's ceasing to hold office.

(2) The company must within 14 days of the deposit of the statement either—

(a) send a copy of it to every person who under section 423 is entitled to be sent copies of the accounts, or

(b) apply to the court.

(3) If it applies to the court, the company must notify the auditor of the application.

(4) If the court is satisfied that the auditor is using the provisions of section 519 to secure needless publicity for defamatory matter—

   (a) it shall direct that copies of the statement need not be sent out, and

   (b) it may further order the company's costs (in Scotland, expenses) on the application to be paid in whole or in part by the auditor, even if he is not a party to the application.

   The company must within 14 days of the court's decision send to the persons mentioned in subsection (2)(a) a statement setting out the effect of the order.

(5) If no such direction is made the company must send copies of the statement to the persons mentioned in subsection (2)(a) within 14 days of the court's decision or, as the case may be, of the discontinuance of the proceedings.

(6) In the event of default in complying with this section an offence is committed by every officer of the company who is in default.

(7) In proceedings for such an offence it is a defence for the person charged to show that he took all reasonable steps and exercised all due diligence to avoid the commission of the offence.

(8) A person guilty of an offence under this section is liable—

   (a) on conviction on indictment, to a fine;

   (b) on summary conviction, to a fine not exceeding the statutory maximum.

521. Copy of statement to be sent to registrar

(1) Unless within 21 days beginning with the day on which he deposited the statement under section 519 the auditor receives notice of an application to the court under section 520, he must within a further seven days send a copy of the statement to the registrar.

(2) If an application to the court is made under section 520 and the auditor subsequently receives notice under subsection (5) of that section, he must within seven days of receiving the notice send a copy of the statement to the registrar.

(3) An auditor who fails to comply with subsection (1) or (2) commits an offence.

(4) In proceedings for such an offence it is a defence for the person charged to show that he took all reasonable steps and exercised all due diligence to avoid the commission of the offence.

(5) A person guilty of an offence under this section is liable—

   (a) on conviction on indictment, to a fine;

   (b) on summary conviction, to a fine not exceeding the statutory maximum.

522. Duty of auditor to notify appropriate audit authority

(1) Where—

   (a) in the case of a major audit, an auditor ceases for any reason to hold office, or

   (b) in the case of an audit that is not a major audit, an auditor ceases to hold office before the end of his term of office,

   the auditor ceasing to hold office must notify the appropriate audit authority.

(2) The notice must—

   (a) inform the appropriate audit authority that he has ceased to hold office, and

   (b) be accompanied by a copy of the statement deposited by him at the company's registered office in accordance with section 519.

(3) If the statement so deposited is to the effect that he considers that there are no circumstances in connection with his ceasing to hold office that need to be brought to the attention of members or creditors of the company, the notice must also be accompanied by a statement of the reasons for his ceasing to hold office.

(4) The auditor must comply with this section—

   (a) in the case of a major audit, at the same time as he deposits a statement at the company's registered office in accordance with section 519;

   (b) in the case of an audit that is not a major audit, at such time (not being earlier than the time mentioned in paragraph (a)) as the appropriate audit authority may require.

(5) A person ceasing to hold office as auditor who fails to comply with this section commits an offence.

(6) If that person is a firm an offence is committed by—

    (a) the firm, and

    (b) every officer of the firm who is in default.

(7) In proceedings for an offence under this section it is a defence for the person charged to show that he took all reasonable steps and exercised all due diligence to avoid the commission of the offence.

(8) A person guilty of an offence under this section is liable—

    (a) on conviction on indictment, to a fine;

    (b) on summary conviction, to a fine not exceeding the statutory maximum.

523. Duty of company to notify appropriate audit authority

(1) Where an auditor ceases to hold office before the end of his term of office, the company must notify the appropriate audit authority.

(2) The notice must—

    (a) inform the appropriate audit authority that the auditor has ceased to hold office, and

    (b) be accompanied by—

        (i) a statement by the company of the reasons for his ceasing to hold office, or

        (ii) if the copy of the statement deposited by the auditor at the company's registered office in accordance with section 519 contains a statement of circumstances in connection with his ceasing to hold office that need to be brought to the attention of members or creditors of the company, a copy of that statement.

(3) The company must give notice under this section not later than 14 days after the date on which the auditor's statement is deposited at the company's registered office in accordance with section 519.

(4) If a company fails to comply with this section, an offence is committed by—

    (a) the company, and

    (b) every officer of the company who is in default.

(5) In proceedings for such an offence it is a defence for the person charged to show that he took all reasonable steps and exercised all due diligence to avoid the commission of the offence.

(6) A person guilty of an offence under this section is liable—

    (a) on conviction on indictment, to a fine;

    (b) on summary conviction, to a fine not exceeding the statutory maximum.

524. Information to be given to accounting authorities

(1) The appropriate audit authority on receiving notice under section 522 or 523 of an auditor's ceasing to hold office—

    (a) must inform the accounting authorities, and

    (b) may if it thinks fit forward to those authorities a copy of the statement or statements accompanying the notice.

(2) The accounting authorities are—

    (a) the Secretary of State, and

    (b) any person authorised by the Secretary of State for the purposes of section 456 (revision of defective accounts: persons authorised to apply to court).

(3) If either of the accounting authorities is also the appropriate audit authority it is only necessary to comply with this section as regards any other accounting authority.

(4) If the court has made an order under section 520(4) directing that copies of the statement need not be sent out by the company, sections 460 and 461 (restriction on further disclosure) apply in relation to the copies sent to the accounting authorities as they apply to information obtained under section 459 (power to require documents etc).

525. **Meaning of "appropriate audit authority" and "major audit"**

(1) In sections 522, 523 and 524 "appropriate audit authority" means—

    (a) in the case of a major audit—

        (i) the Secretary of State, or

        (ii) if the Secretary of State has delegated functions under section 1252 to a body whose functions include receiving the notice in question, that body;

    (b) in the case of an audit that is not a major audit, the relevant supervisory body.

    "Supervisory body" has the same meaning as in Part 42 (statutory auditors) (see section 1217).

(2) In sections 522 and this section "major audit" means a statutory audit conducted in respect of—

    (a) a company any of whose securities have been admitted to the official list (within the meaning of Part 6 of the Financial Services and Markets Act 2000 (c. 8)), or

    (b) any other person in whose financial condition there is a major public interest.

(3) In determining whether an audit is a major audit within subsection (2)(b), regard shall be had to any guidance issued by any of the authorities mentioned in subsection (1).

Supplementary

526. **Effect of casual vacancies**

If an auditor ceases to hold office for any reason, any surviving or continuing auditor or auditors may continue to act.

CHAPTER 5
QUOTED COMPANIES: RIGHT OF MEMBERS TO RAISE AUDIT CONCERNS AT ACCOUNTS MEETING

527. **Members' power to require website publication of audit concerns**

(1) The members of a quoted company may require the company to publish on a website a statement setting out any matter relating to—

    (a) the audit of the company's accounts (including the auditor's report and the conduct of the audit) that are to be laid before the next accounts meeting, or

    (b) any circumstances connected with an auditor of the company ceasing to hold office since the previous accounts meeting,

that the members propose to raise at the next accounts meeting of the company.

(2) A company is required to do so once it has received requests to that effect from—

    (a) members representing at least 5% of the total voting rights of all the members who have a relevant right to vote (excluding any voting rights attached to any shares in the company held as treasury shares), or

    (b) at least 100 members who have a relevant right to vote and hold shares in the company on which there has been paid up an average sum, per member, of at least £100.

See also section 153 (exercise of rights where shares held on behalf of others).

(3) In subsection (2) a "relevant right to vote" means a right to vote at the accounts meeting.

(4) A request—

    (a) may be sent to the company in hard copy or electronic form,

    (b) must identify the statement to which it relates,

    (c) must be authenticated by the person or persons making it, and

    (d) must be received by the company at least one week before the meeting to which it relates.

(5) A quoted company is not required to place on a website a statement under this section if, on an application by the company or another person who claims to be aggrieved, the court is satisfied that the rights conferred by this section are being abused.

(6) The court may order the members requesting website publication to pay the whole or part of the company's costs (in Scotland, expenses) on such an application, even if they are not parties to the application.

528. Requirements as to website availability

(1) The following provisions apply for the purposes of section 527 (website publication of members' statement of audit concerns).

(2) The information must be made available on a website that—
   (a) is maintained by or on behalf of the company, and
   (b) identifies the company in question.

(3) Access to the information on the website, and the ability to obtain a hard copy of the information from the website, must not be conditional on the payment of a fee or otherwise restricted.

(4) The statement—
   (a) must be made available within three working days of the company being required to publish it on a website, and
   (b) must be kept available until after the meeting to which it relates.

(5) A failure to make information available on a website throughout the period specified in subsection (4)(b) is disregarded if—
   (a) the information is made available on the website for part of that period, and
   (b) the failure is wholly attributable to circumstances that it would not be reasonable to have expected the company to prevent or avoid.

529. Website publication: company's supplementary duties

(1) A quoted company must in the notice it gives of the accounts meeting draw attention to—
   (a) the possibility of a statement being placed on a website in pursuance of members' requests under section 527, and
   (b) the effect of the following provisions of this section.

(2) A company may not require the members requesting website publication to pay its expenses in complying with that section or section 528 (requirements in connection with website publication).

(3) Where a company is required to place a statement on a website under section 527 it must forward the statement to the company's auditor not later than the time when it makes the statement available on the website.

(4) The business which may be dealt with at the accounts meeting includes any statement that the company has been required under section 527 to publish on a website.

530. Website publication: offences

(1) In the event of default in complying with
   (a) section 528 (requirements as to website publication), or
   (b) section 529 (companies' supplementary duties in relation to request for website publication),
an offence is committed by every officer of the company who is in default.

(2) A person guilty of an offence under this section is liable—
   (a) on conviction on indictment, to a fine;
   (b) on summary conviction, to a fine not exceeding the statutory maximum.

531. Meaning of "quoted company"

(1) For the purposes of this Chapter a company is a quoted company if it is a quoted company in accordance with section 385 (quoted and unquoted companies for the purposes of Part 15) in relation to the financial year to which the accounts to be laid at the next accounts meeting relate.

(2) The provisions of subsections (4) to (6) of that section (power to amend definition by regulations) apply in relation to the provisions of this Chapter as in relation to the provisions of that Part.

CHAPTER 6
AUDITORS' LIABILITY

Voidness of provisions protecting auditors from liability

532. Voidness of provisions protecting auditors from liability

(1) This section applies to any provision—

  (a) for exempting an auditor of a company (to any extent) from any liability that would otherwise attach to him in connection with any negligence, default, breach of duty or breach of trust in relation to the company occurring in the course of the audit of accounts, or

  (b) by which a company directly or indirectly provides an indemnity (to any extent) for an auditor of the company, or of an associated company, against any liability attaching to him in connection with any negligence, default, breach of duty or breach of trust in relation to the company of which he is auditor occurring in the course of the audit of accounts.

(2) Any such provision is void, except as permitted by—

  (a) section 533 (indemnity for costs of successfully defending proceedings), or

  (b) sections 534 to 536 (liability limitation agreements).

(3) This section applies to any provision, whether contained in a company's articles or in any contract with the company or otherwise.

(4) For the purposes of this section companies are associated if one is a subsidiary of the other or both are subsidiaries of the same body corporate.

Indemnity for costs of defending proceedings

533. Indemnity for costs of successfully defending proceedings

Section 532 (general voidness of provisions protecting auditors from liability) does not prevent a company from indemnifying an auditor against any liability incurred by him—

(a) in defending proceedings (whether civil or criminal) in which judgment is given in his favour or he is acquitted, or

(b) in connection with an application under section 1157 (power of court to grant relief in case of honest and reasonable conduct) in which relief is granted to him by the court.

Liability limitation agreements

534. Liability limitation agreements

(1) A "liability limitation agreement" is an agreement that purports to limit the amount of a liability owed to a company by its auditor in respect of any negligence, default, breach of duty or breach of trust, occurring in the course of the audit of accounts, of which the auditor may be guilty in relation to the company.

(2) Section 532 (general voidness of provisions protecting auditors from liability) does not affect the validity of a liability limitation agreement that—

  (a) complies with section 535 (terms of liability limitation agreement) and of any regulations under that section, and

  (b) is authorised by the members of the company (see section 536).

(3) Such an agreement—

  (a) is effective to the extent provided by section 537, and

  (b) is not subject—

    (i) in England and Wales or Northern Ireland, to section 2(2) or 3(2)(a) of the Unfair Contract Terms Act 1977 (c. 50);

    (ii) in Scotland, to section 16(1)(b) or 17(1)(a) of that Act.

535. **Terms of liability limitation agreement**

(1) A liability limitation agreement—

   (a) must not apply in respect of acts or omissions occurring in the course of the audit of accounts for more than one financial year, and

   (b) must specify the financial year in relation to which it applies.

(2) The Secretary of State may by regulations—

   (a) require liability limitation agreements to contain specified provisions or provisions of a specified description;

   (b) prohibit liability limitation agreements from containing specified provisions or provisions of a specified description.

"Specified" here means specified in the regulations.

(3) Without prejudice to the generality of the power conferred by subsection (2), that power may be exercised with a view to preventing adverse effects on competition.

(4) Subject to the preceding provisions of this section, it is immaterial how a liability limitation agreement is framed.

In particular, the limit on the amount of the auditor's liability need not be a sum of money, or a formula, specified in the agreement.

(5) Regulations under this section are subject to negative resolution procedure.

536. **Authorisation of agreement by members of the company**

(1) A liability limitation agreement is authorised by the members of the company if it has been authorised under this section and that authorisation has not been withdrawn.

(2) A liability limitation agreement between a private company and its auditor may be authorised—

   (a) by the company passing a resolution, before it enters into the agreement, waiving the need for approval,

   (b) by the company passing a resolution, before it enters into the agreement, approving the agreement's principal terms, or

   (c) by the company passing a resolution, after it enters into the agreement, approving the agreement.

(3) A liability limitation agreement between a public company and its auditor may be authorised—

   (a) by the company passing a resolution in general meeting, before it enters into the agreement, approving the agreement's principal terms, or

   (b) by the company passing a resolution in general meeting, after it enters into the agreement, approving the agreement.

(4) The "principal terms" of an agreement are terms specifying, or relevant to the determination of—

   (a) the kind (or kinds) of acts or omissions covered,

   (b) the financial year to which the agreement relates, or

   (c) the limit to which the auditor's liability is subject.

(5) Authorisation under this section may be withdrawn by the company passing an ordinary resolution to that effect—

   (a) at any time before the company enters into the agreement, or

   (b) if the company has already entered into the agreement, before the beginning of the financial year to which the agreement relates.

Paragraph (b) has effect notwithstanding anything in the agreement.

537. **Effect of liability limitation agreement**

(1) A liability limitation agreement is not effective to limit the auditor's liability to less than such amount as is fair and reasonable in all the circumstances of the case having regard (in particular) to—

   (a) the auditor's responsibilities under this Part,

(b) the nature and purpose of the auditor's contractual obligations to the company, and

(c) the professional standards expected of him.

(2) A liability limitation agreement that purports to limit the auditor's liability to less than the amount mentioned in subsection (1) shall have effect as if it limited his liability to that amount.

(3) In determining what is fair and reasonable in all the circumstances of the case no account is to be taken of—

(a) matters arising after the loss or damage in question has been incurred, or

(b) matters (whenever arising) affecting the possibility of recovering compensation from other persons liable in respect of the same loss or damage.

538. Disclosure of agreement by company

(1) A company which has entered into a liability limitation agreement must make such disclosure in connection with the agreement as the Secretary of State may require by regulations.

(2) The regulations may provide, in particular, that any disclosure required by the regulations shall be made—

(a) in a note to the company's annual accounts (in the case of its individual accounts) or in such manner as is specified in the regulations (in the case of group accounts), or

(b) in the directors' report.

(3) Regulations under this section are subject to negative resolution procedure.

CHAPTER 7
SUPPLEMENTARY PROVISIONS

539. Minor definitions

In this Part—

"e-money issuer" means a person who has permission under Part 4 of the Financial Services and Markets Act 2000 (c. 8) to carry on the activity of issuing electronic money within the meaning of article 9B of the Financial Services and Markets Act 2000 (Regulated Activities) Order 2001 (S.I. 2001/544);

"ISD investment firm" has the meaning given by the Glossary forming part of the Handbook made by the Financial Services Authority under the Financial Services and Markets Act 2000;

"qualified", in relation to an auditor's report (or a statement contained in an auditor's report), means that the report or statement does not state the auditor's unqualified opinion that the accounts have been properly prepared in accordance with this Act or, in the case of an undertaking not required to prepare accounts in accordance with this Act, under any corresponding legislation under which it is required to prepare accounts;

"turnover", in relation to a company, means the amounts derived from the provision of goods and services falling within the company's ordinary activities, after deduction of—

(a) trade discounts,

(b) value added tax, and

(c) any other taxes based on the amounts so derived;

"UCITS management company" has the meaning given by the Glossary forming part of the Handbook made by the Financial Services Authority under the Financial Services and Markets Act 2000.

PART 17

A COMPANY'S SHARE CAPITAL

CHAPTER 1

SHARES AND SHARE CAPITAL OF A COMPANY

Shares

540. Shares

(1) In the Companies Acts "share", in relation to a company, means share in the company's share capital.

(2) A company's shares may no longer be converted into stock.

(3) Stock created before the commencement of this Part may be reconverted into shares in accordance with section 620.

(4) In the Companies Acts—

(a) references to shares include stock except where a distinction between share and stock is express or implied, and

(b) references to a number of shares include an amount of stock where the context admits of the reference to shares being read as including stock.

541. Nature of shares

The shares or other interest of a member in a company are personal property (or, in Scotland, moveable property) and are not in the nature of real estate (or heritage).

542. Nominal value of shares

(1) Shares in a limited company having a share capital must each have a fixed nominal value.

(2) An allotment of a share that does not have a fixed nominal value is void.

(3) Shares in a limited company having a share capital may be denominated in any currency, and different classes of shares may be denominated in different currencies.

But see section 765 (initial authorised minimum share capital requirement for public company to be met by reference to share capital denominated in sterling or euros).

(4) If a company purports to allot shares in contravention of this section, an offence is committed by every officer of the company who is in default.

(5) A person guilty of an offence under this section is liable—

(a) on conviction on indictment, to a fine;

(b) on summary conviction, to a fine not exceeding the statutory maximum.

543. Numbering of shares

(1) Each share in a company having a share capital must be distinguished by its appropriate number, except in the following circumstances.

(2) If at any time—

(a) all the issued shares in a company are fully paid up and rank *pari passu* for all purposes, or

(b) all the issued shares of a particular class in a company are fully paid up and rank *pari passu* for all purposes,

none of those shares need thereafter have a distinguishing number so long as it remains fully paid up and ranks *pari passu* for all purposes with all shares of the same class for the time being issued and fully paid up.

544. Transferability of shares

(1) The shares or other interest of any member in a company are transferable in accordance with the company's articles.

(2) This is subject to—

(a) the Stock Transfer Act 1963 (c. 18) or the Stock Transfer Act (Northern Ireland) 1963 (c.24 (N.I.)) (which enables securities of certain descriptions to be transferred by a simplified process), and

(b) regulations under Chapter 2 of Part 21 of this Act (which enable title to securities to be evidenced and transferred without a written instrument).

(3) See Part 21 of this Act generally as regards share transfers.

545. Companies having a share capital

References in the Companies Acts to a company having a share capital are to a company that has power under its constitution to issue shares.

546. Issued and allotted share capital

(1) References in the Companies Acts—

(a) to "issued share capital" are to shares of a company that have been issued;

(b) to "allotted share capital" are to shares of a company that have been allotted.

(2) References in the Companies Acts to issued or allotted shares, or to issued or allotted share capital, include shares taken on the formation of the company by the subscribers to the company's memorandum.

Share capital

547. Called-up share capital

In the Companies Acts—

"called-up share capital", in relation to a company, means so much of its share capital as equals the aggregate amount of the calls made on its shares (whether or not those calls have been paid), together with—

(a) any share capital paid up without being called, and

(b) any share capital to be paid on a specified future date under the articles, the terms of allotment of the relevant shares or any other arrangements for payment of those shares; and

"uncalled share capital" is to be construed accordingly.

548. Equity share capital

In the Companies Acts "equity share capital", in relation to a company, means its issued share capital excluding any part of that capital that, neither as respects dividends nor as respects capital, carries any right to participate beyond a specified amount in a distribution.

CHAPTER 2

ALLOTMENT OF SHARES: GENERAL PROVISIONS

Power of directors to allot shares

549. Exercise by directors of power to allot shares etc

(1) The directors of a company must not exercise any power of the company—

(a) to allot shares in the company, or

(b) to grant rights to subscribe for, or to convert any security into, shares in the company,

except in accordance with section 550 (private company with single class of shares) or section 551 (authorisation by company).

(2) Subsection (1) does not apply—

(a) to the allotment of shares in pursuance of an employees' share scheme, or

(b) to the grant of a right to subscribe for, or to convert any security into, shares so allotted.

(3) If this section applies in relation to the grant of a right to subscribe for, or to convert any security into, shares, it does not apply in relation to the allotment of shares pursuant to that right.

(4) A director who knowingly contravenes, or permits or authorises a contravention of, this section commits an offence.

(5) A person guilty of an offence under this section is liable—

    (a) on conviction on indictment, to a fine;

    (b) on summary conviction, to a fine not exceeding the statutory maximum.

(6) Nothing in this section affects the validity of an allotment or other transaction.

550. Power of directors to allot shares etc: private company with only one class of shares

Where a private company has only one class of shares, the directors may exercise any power of the company—

    (a) to allot shares of that class, or

    (b) to grant rights to subscribe for or to convert any security into such shares,

except to the extent that they are prohibited from doing so by the company's articles.

551. Power of directors to allot shares etc: authorisation by company

(1) The directors of a company may exercise a power of the company—

    (a) to allot shares in the company, or

    (b) to grant rights to subscribe for or to convert any security into shares in the company,

if they are authorised to do so by the company's articles or by resolution of the company.

(2) Authorisation may be given for a particular exercise of the power or for its exercise generally, and may be unconditional or subject to conditions.

(3) Authorisation must—

    (a) state the maximum amount of shares that may be allotted under it, and

    (b) specify the date on which it will expire, which must be not more than five years from—

        (i) in the case of authorisation contained in the company's articles at the time of its original incorporation, the date of that incorporation;

        (ii) in any other case, the date on which the resolution is passed by virtue of which the authorisation is given.

(4) Authorisation may—

    (a) be renewed or further renewed by resolution of the company for a further period not exceeding five years, and

    (b) be revoked or varied at any time by resolution of the company.

(5) A resolution renewing authorisation must—

    (a) state (or restate) the maximum amount of shares that may be allotted under the authorisation or, as the case may be, the amount remaining to be allotted under it, and

    (b) specify the date on which the renewed authorisation will expire.

(6) In relation to rights to subscribe for or to convert any security into shares in the company, references in this section to the maximum amount of shares that may be allotted under the authorisation are to the maximum amount of shares that may be allotted pursuant to the rights.

(7) The directors may allot shares, or grant rights to subscribe for or to convert any security into shares, after authorisation has expired if—

    (a) the shares are allotted, or the rights are granted, in pursuance of an offer or agreement made by the company before the authorisation expired, and

    (b) the authorisation allowed the company to make an offer or agreement which would or might require shares to be allotted, or rights to be granted, after the authorisation had expired.

(8) A resolution of a company to give, vary, revoke or renew authorisation under this section may be an ordinary resolution, even though it amends the company's articles.

(9) Chapter 3 of Part 3 (resolutions affecting a company's constitution) applies to a resolution under this section.

Prohibition of commissions, discounts and allowances

552. **General prohibition of commissions, discounts and allowances**

(1) Except as permitted by section 553 (permitted commission), a company must not apply any of its shares or capital money, either directly or indirectly, in payment of any commission, discount or allowance to any person in consideration of his—

    (a) subscribing or agreeing to subscribe (whether absolutely or conditionally) for shares in the company, or

    (b) procuring or agreeing to procure subscriptions (whether absolute or conditional) for shares in the company.

(2) It is immaterial how the shares or money are so applied, whether by being added to the purchase money of property acquired by the company or to the contract price of work to be executed for the company, or being paid out of the nominal purchase money or contract price, or otherwise.

(3) Nothing in this section affects the payment of such brokerage as has previously been lawful.

553. **Permitted commission**

(1) A company may, if the following conditions are satisfied, pay a commission to a person in consideration of his subscribing or agreeing to subscribe (whether absolutely or conditionally) for shares in the company, or procuring or agreeing to procure subscriptions (whether absolute or conditional) for shares in the company.

(2) The conditions are that—

    (a) the payment of the commission is authorised by the company's articles; and

    (b) the commission paid or agreed to be paid does not exceed—

        (i) 10% of the price at which the shares are issued, or

        (ii) the amount or rate authorised by the articles,

    whichever is the less.

(3) A vendor to, or promoter of, or other person who receives payment in money or shares from, a company may apply any part of the money or shares so received in payment of any commission the payment of which directly by the company would be permitted by this section.

Registration of allotment

554. **Registration of allotment**

(1) A company must register an allotment of shares as soon as practicable and in any event within two months after the date of the allotment.

(2) This does not apply if the company has issued a share warrant in respect of the shares (see section 779).

(3) If a company fails to comply with this section, an offence is committed by—

    (a) the company, and

    (b) every officer of the company who is in default.

(4) A person guilty of an offence under this section is liable on summary conviction to a fine not exceeding level 3 on the standard scale and, for continued contravention, a daily default fine not exceeding one-tenth of level 3 on the standard scale.

(5) For the company's duties as to the issue of share certificates etc, see Part 21 (certification and transfer of securities).

Return of allotment

555. **Return of allotment by limited company**

(1) This section applies to a company limited by shares and to a company limited by guarantee and having a share capital.

(2) The company must, within one month of making an allotment of shares, deliver to the registrar for registration a return of the allotment.

(3) The return must—

    (a) contain the prescribed information, and

    (b) be accompanied by a statement of capital.

(4) The statement of capital must state with respect to the company's share capital at the date to which the return is made up—

    (a) the total number of shares of the company,

    (b) the aggregate nominal value of those shares,

    (c) for each class of shares—

        (i) prescribed particulars of the rights attached to the shares,

        (ii) the total number of shares of that class, and

        (iii) the aggregate nominal value of shares of that class, and

    (d) the amount paid up and the amount (if any) unpaid on each share (whether on account of the nominal value of the share or by way of premium).

556. Return of allotment by unlimited company allotting new class of shares

(1) This section applies to an unlimited company that allots shares of a class with rights that are not in all respects uniform with shares previously allotted.

(2) The company must, within one month of making such an allotment, deliver to the registrar for registration a return of the allotment.

(3) The return must contain the prescribed particulars of the rights attached to the shares.

(4) For the purposes of this section shares are not to be treated as different from shares previously allotted by reason only that the former do not carry the same rights to dividends as the latter during the twelve months immediately following the former's allotment.

557. Offence of failure to make return

(1) If a company makes default in complying with—

section 555 (return of allotment of shares by limited company), or

section 556 (return of allotment of new class of shares by unlimited company),

an offence is committed by every officer of the company who is in default.

(2) A person guilty of an offence under this section is liable—

    (a) on conviction on indictment, to a fine;

    (b) on summary conviction, to a fine not exceeding the statutory maximum and, for continued contravention, a daily default fine not exceeding one-tenth of the statutory maximum.

(3) In the case of default in delivering to the registrar within one month after the allotment the return required by section 555 or 556—

    (a) any person liable for the default may apply to the court for relief, and

    (b) the court, if satisfied—

        (i) that the omission to deliver the document was accidental or due to inadvertence, or

        (ii) that it is just and equitable to grant relief,

    may make an order extending the time for delivery of the document for such period as the court thinks proper.

Supplementary provisions

558. When shares are allotted

For the purposes of the Companies Acts shares in a company are taken to be allotted when a person acquires the unconditional right to be included in the company's register of members in respect of the shares.

559. Provisions about allotment not applicable to shares taken on formation

The provisions of this Chapter have no application in relation to the taking of shares by the subscribers to the memorandum on the formation of the company.

CHAPTER 3

ALLOTMENT OF EQUITY SECURITIES: EXISTING SHAREHOLDERS'
RIGHT OF PRE-EMPTION

Introductory

560. Meaning of "equity securities" and related expressions

(1) In this Chapter—

"equity securities" means—

(a) ordinary shares in the company, or

(b) rights to subscribe for, or to convert securities into, ordinary shares in the company;

"ordinary shares" means shares other than shares that as respects dividends and capital carry a right to participate only up to a specified amount in a distribution.

(2) References in this Chapter to the allotment of equity securities include—

(a) the grant of a right to subscribe for, or to convert any securities into, ordinary shares in the company, and

(b) the sale of ordinary shares in the company that immediately before the sale are held by the company as treasury shares.

Existing shareholders' right of pre-emption

561. Existing shareholders' right of pre-emption

(1) A company must not allot equity securities to a person on any terms unless—

(a) it has made an offer to each person who holds ordinary shares in the company to allot to him on the same or more favourable terms a proportion of those securities that is as nearly as practicable equal to the proportion in nominal value held by him of the ordinary share capital of the company, and

(b) the period during which any such offer may be accepted has expired or the company has received notice of the acceptance or refusal of every offer so made.

(2) Securities that a company has offered to allot to a holder of ordinary shares may be allotted to him, or anyone in whose favour he has renounced his right to their allotment, without contravening subsection (1)(b).

(3) If subsection (1) applies in relation to the grant of such a right, it does not apply in relation to the allotment of shares in pursuance of that right.

(4) Shares held by the company as treasury shares are disregarded for the purposes of this section, so that—

(a) the company is not treated as a person who holds ordinary shares, and

(b) the shares are not treated as forming part of the ordinary share capital of the company.

(5) This section is subject to—

(a) sections 564 to 566 (exceptions to pre-emption right),

(b) sections 567 and 568 (exclusion of rights of pre-emption),

(c) sections 569 to 573 (disapplication of pre-emption rights), and

(d) section 576 (saving for certain older pre-emption procedures).

562. Communication of pre-emption offers to shareholders

(1) This section has effect as to the manner in which offers required by section 561 are to be made to holders of a company's shares.

(2) The offer may be made in hard copy or electronic form.

(3) If the holder—

(a) has no registered address in an EEA State and has not given to the company an address in an EEA State for the service of notices on him, or

(b) is the holder of a share warrant,

the offer may be made by causing it, or a notice specifying where a copy of it can be obtained or inspected, to be published in the Gazette.

(4) The offer must state a period during which it may be accepted and the offer shall not be withdrawn before the end of that period.

(5) The period must be a period of at least 21 days beginning—

(a) in the case of an offer made in hard copy form, with the date on which the offer is sent or supplied;

(b) in the case of an offer made in electronic form, with the date on which the offer is sent;

(c) in the case of an offer made by publication in the Gazette, with the date of publication.

(6) The Secretary of State may by regulations made by statutory instrument—

(a) reduce the period specified in subsection (5) (but not to less than 14 days), or

(b) increase that period.

(7) A statutory instrument containing regulations made under subsection (6) is subject to affirmative resolution procedure.

563. **Liability of company and officers in case of contravention**

(1) This section applies where there is a contravention of—

section 561 (existing shareholders' right of pre-emption), or

section 562 (communication of pre-emption offers to shareholders).

(2) The company and every officer of it who knowingly authorised or permitted the contravention are jointly and severally liable to compensate any person to whom an offer should have been made in accordance with those provisions for any loss, damage, costs or expenses which the person has sustained or incurred by reason of the contravention.

(3) No proceedings to recover any such loss, damage, costs or expenses shall be commenced after the expiration of two years—

(a) from the delivery to the registrar of companies of the return of allotment, or

(b) where equity securities other than shares are granted, from the date of the grant.

Exceptions to right of pre-emption

564. **Exception to pre-emption right: bonus shares**

Section 561 (1) (existing shareholders' right of pre-emption) does not apply in relation to the allotment of bonus shares.

565. **Exception to pre-emption right: issue for non-cash consideration**

Section 561 (1) (existing shareholders' right of pre-emption) does not apply to a particular allotment of equity securities if these are, or are to be, wholly or partly paid up otherwise than in cash.

566. **Exception to pre-emption right: securities held under employees' share scheme**

Section 561 (existing shareholders' right of pre-emption) does not apply to the allotment of securities that would, apart from any renunciation or assignment of the right to their allotment, be held under an employees' share scheme.

Exclusion of right of pre-emption

567. **Exclusion of requirements by private companies**

(1) All or any of the requirements of—

(a) section 561 (existing shareholders' right of pre-emption), or

(b) section 562 (communication of pre-emption offers to shareholders)

may be excluded by provision contained in the articles of a private company.

(2) They may be excluded—

(a) generally in relation to the allotment by the company of equity securities, or

(b) in relation to allotments of a particular description.

(3) Any requirement or authorisation contained in the articles of a private company that is inconsistent with either of those sections is treated for the purposes of this section as a provision excluding that section.

(4) A provision to which section 568 applies (exclusion of pre-emption right: corresponding right conferred by articles) is not to be treated as inconsistent with section 561.

568. Exclusion of pre-emption right: articles conferring corresponding right

(1) The provisions of this section apply where, in a case in which section 561 (existing shareholders' right of pre-emption) would otherwise apply—

    (a) a company's articles contain provision ("pre-emption provision") prohibiting the company from allotting ordinary shares of a particular class unless it has complied with the condition that it makes such an offer as is described in section 561 (1) to each person who holds ordinary shares of that class, and

    (b) in accordance with that provision—

        (i) the company makes an offer to allot shares to such a holder, and

        (ii) he or anyone in whose favour he has renounced his right to their allotment accepts the offer.

(2) In that case, section 561 does not apply to the allotment of those shares and the company may allot them accordingly.

(3) The provisions of section 562 (communication of pre-emption offers to shareholders) apply in relation to offers made in pursuance of the pre-emption provision of the company's articles. This is subject to section 567 (exclusion of requirements by private companies).

(4) If there is a contravention of the pre-emption provision of the company's articles, the company, and every officer of it who knowingly authorised or permitted the contravention, are jointly and severally liable to compensate any person to whom an offer should have been made under the provision for any loss, damage, costs or expenses which the person has sustained or incurred by reason of the contravention.

(5) No proceedings to recover any such loss, damage, costs or expenses may be commenced after the expiration of two years—

    (a) from the delivery to the registrar of companies of the return of allotment, or

    (b) where equity securities other than shares are granted, from the date of the grant.

Disapplication of pre-emption rights

569. Disapplication of pre-emption rights: private company with only one class of shares

(1) The directors of a private company that has only one class of shares may be given power by the articles, or by a special resolution of the company, to allot equity securities of that class as if section 561 (existing shareholders' right of pre-emption)—

    (a) did not apply to the allotment, or

    (b) applied to the allotment with such modifications as the directors may determine.

(2) Where the directors make an allotment under this section, the provisions of this Chapter have effect accordingly.

570. Disapplication of pre-emption rights: directors acting under general authorisation

(1) Where the directors of a company are generally authorised for the purposes of section 551 (power of directors to allot shares etc: authorisation by company), they may be given power by the articles, or by a special resolution of the company, to allot equity securities pursuant to that authorisation as if section 561 (existing shareholders' right of pre-emption)—

    (a) did not apply to the allotment, or

    (b) applied to the allotment with such modifications as the directors may determine.

(2) Where the directors make an allotment under this section, the provisions of this Chapter have effect accordingly.

(3) The power conferred by this section ceases to have effect when the authorisation to which it relates—

(a) is revoked, or

(b) would (if not renewed) expire.

But if the authorisation is renewed the power may also be renewed, for a period not longer than that for which the authorisation is renewed, by a special resolution of the company.

(4) Notwithstanding that the power conferred by this section has expired, the directors may allot equity securities in pursuance of an offer or agreement previously made by the company if the power enabled the company to make an offer or agreement that would or might require equity securities to be allotted after it expired.

571. Disapplication of pre-emption rights by special resolution

(1) Where the directors of a company are authorised for the purposes of section 551 (power of directors to allot shares etc: authorisation by company), whether generally or otherwise, the company may by special resolution resolve that section 561 (existing shareholders' right of pre-emption)—

(a) does not apply to a specified allotment of equity securities to be made pursuant to that authorisation, or

(b) applies to such an allotment with such modifications as may be specified in the resolution.

(2) Where such a resolution is passed the provisions of this Chapter have effect accordingly.

(3) A special resolution under this section ceases to have effect when the authorisation to which it relates—

(a) is revoked, or

(b) would (if not renewed) expire.

But if the authorisation is renewed the resolution may also be renewed, for a period not longer than that for which the authorisation is renewed, by a special resolution of the company.

(4) Notwithstanding that any such resolution has expired, the directors may allot equity securities in pursuance of an offer or agreement previously made by the company if the resolution enabled the company to make an offer or agreement that would or might require equity securities to be allotted after it expired.

(5) A special resolution under this section, or a special resolution to renew such a resolution, must not be proposed unless—

(a) it is recommended by the directors, and

(b) the directors have complied with the following provisions.

(6) Before such a resolution is proposed, the directors must make a written statement setting out—

(a) their reasons for making the recommendation,

(b) the amount to be paid to the company in respect of the equity securities to be allotted, and

(c) the directors' justification of that amount.

(7) The directors' statement must—

(a) if the resolution is proposed as a written resolution, be sent or submitted to every eligible member at or before the time at which the proposed resolution is sent or submitted to him;

(b) if the resolution is proposed at a general meeting, be circulated to the members entitled to notice of the meeting with that notice.

572. Liability for false statement in directors' statement

(1) This section applies in relation to a directors' statement under section 571 (special resolution disapplying pre-emption rights) that is sent, submitted or circulated under subsection (7) of that section.

(2) A person who knowingly or recklessly authorises or permits the inclusion of any matter that is misleading, false or deceptive in a material particular in such a statement commits an offence.

(3) A person guilty of an offence under this section is liable—

    (a) on conviction on indictment, to imprisonment for a term not exceeding two years or a fine (or both);

    (b) on summary conviction—

        (i) in England and Wales, to imprisonment for a term not exceeding twelve months or to a fine not exceeding the statutory maximum (or both);

        (ii) in Scotland or Northern Ireland, to imprisonment for a term not exceeding six months, or to a fine not exceeding the statutory maximum (or both).

573. Disapplication of pre-emption rights: sale of treasury shares

(1) This section applies in relation to a sale of shares that is an allotment of equity securities by virtue of section 560 (2) (b) (sale of shares held by company as treasury shares).

(2) The directors of a company may be given power by the articles, or by a special resolution of the company, to allot equity securities as if section 561 (existing shareholders' right of pre-emption)—

    (a) did not apply to the allotment, or

    (b) applied to the allotment with such modifications as the directors may determine.

(3) The provisions of section 570 (2) and (4) apply in that case as they apply to a case within subsection (1) of that section.

(4) The company may by special resolution resolve that section 561—

    (a) shall not apply to a specified allotment of securities, or

    (b) shall apply to the allotment with such modifications as may be specified in the resolution.

(5) The provisions of section 571 (2) and (4) to (7) apply in that case as they apply to a case within subsection (1) of that section.

Supplementary

574. References to holder of shares in relation to offer

(1) In this Chapter, in relation to an offer to allot securities required by—

    (a) section 561 (existing shareholders' right of pre-emption), or

    (b) any provision to which section 568 applies (articles conferring corresponding right),

a reference (however expressed) to the holder of shares of any description is to whoever was the holder of shares of that description at the close of business on a date to be specified in the offer.

(2) The specified date must fall within the period of 28 days immediately before the date of the offer.

575. Saving for other restrictions on offer or allotment

(1) The provisions of this Chapter are without prejudice to any other enactment by virtue of which a company is prohibited (whether generally or in specified circumstances) from offering or allotting equity securities to any person.

(2) Where a company cannot by virtue of such an enactment offer or allot equity securities to a holder of ordinary shares of the company, those shares are disregarded for the purposes of section 561 (existing shareholders' right of pre-emption), so that—

    (a) the person is not treated as a person who holds ordinary shares, and

    (b) the shares are not treated as forming part of the ordinary share capital of the company.

576. Saving for certain older pre-emption requirements

(1) In the case of a public company the provisions of this Chapter do not apply to an allotment of equity securities that are subject to a pre-emption requirement in relation to which section 96 (1) of the Companies Act 1985 (c. 6) or Article 106(1) of the Companies (Northern Ireland) Order 1986 (S.I. 1986/1032 (N.I. 6)) applied immediately before the commencement of this Chapter.

(2) In the case of a private company a pre-emption requirement to which section 96 (3) of the Companies Act 1985 or Article 106(3) of the Companies (Northern Ireland) Order 1986 applied immediately before the commencement of this Chapter shall have effect, so long as the company remains a private company, as if it were contained in the company's articles.

(3) A pre-emption requirement to which section 96(4) of the Companies Act 1985 or Article 106(4) of the Companies (Northern Ireland) Order 1986 applied immediately before the commencement of this section shall be treated for the purposes of this Chapter as if it were contained in the company's articles.

577. **Provisions about pre-emption not applicable to shares taken on formation**

The provisions of this Chapter have no application in relation to the taking of shares by the subscribers to the memorandum on the formation of the company.

CHAPTER 4
PUBLIC COMPANIES: ALLOTMENT WHERE ISSUE NOT FULLY SUBSCRIBED

578. **Public companies: allotment where issue not fully subscribed**

(1) No allotment shall be made of shares of a public company offered for subscription unless—
  (a) the issue is subscribed for in full, or
  (b) the offer is made on terms that the shares subscribed for may be allotted—
    (i) in any event, or
    (ii) if specified conditions are met (and those conditions are met).

(2) If shares are prohibited from being allotted by subsection (1) and 40 days have elapsed after the first making of the offer, all money received from applicants for shares must be repaid to them forthwith, without interest.

(3) If any of the money is not repaid within 48 days after the first making of the offer, the directors of the company are jointly and severally liable to repay it, with interest at the rate for the time being specified under section 17 of the Judgments Act 1838 (c. 110) from the expiration of the 48th day.

A director is not so liable if he proves that the default in the repayment of the money was not due to any misconduct or negligence on his part.

(4) This section applies in the case of shares as wholly or partly payable otherwise than in cash as it applies in the case of shares offered for subscription.

(5) In that case—
  (a) the references in subsection (1) to subscription shall be construed accordingly;
  (b) references in subsections (2) and (3) to the repayment of money received from applicants for shares include—
    (i) the return of any other consideration so received (including, if the case so requires, the release of the applicant from any undertaking), or
    (ii) if it is not reasonably practicable to return the consideration, the payment of money equal to its value at the time it was so received;
  (c) references to interest apply accordingly.

(6) Any condition requiring or binding an applicant for shares to waive compliance with any requirement of this section is void.

579. **Public companies: effect of irregular allotment where issue not fully subscribed**

(1) An allotment made by a public company to an applicant in contravention of section 578 (public companies: allotment where issue not fully subscribed) is voidable at the instance of the applicant within one month after the date of the allotment, and not later.

(2) It is so voidable even if the company is in the course of being wound up.

(3) A director of a public company who knowingly contravenes, or permits or authorises the contravention of, any provision of section 578 with respect to allotment is liable to

compensate the company and the allottee respectively for any loss, damages, costs or expenses that the company or allottee may have sustained or incurred by the contravention.

(4) Proceedings to recover any such loss, damages, costs or expenses may not be brought more than two years after the date of the allotment.

CHAPTER 5
PAYMENT FOR SHARES

General rules

580. Shares not to be allotted at a discount

(1) A company's shares must not be allotted at a discount.

(2) If shares are allotted in contravention of this section, the allottee is liable to pay the company an amount equal to the amount of the discount, with interest at the appropriate rate.

581. Provision for different amounts to be paid on shares

A company, if so authorised by its articles, may—

(a) make arrangements on the issue of shares for a difference between the shareholders in the amounts and times of payment of calls on their shares;

(b) accept from any member the whole or part of the amount remaining unpaid on any shares held by him, although no part of that amount has been called up;

(c) pay a dividend in proportion to the amount paid up on each share where a larger amount is paid up on some shares than on others.

582. General rule as to means of payment

(1) Shares allotted by a company, and any premium on them, may be paid up in money or money's worth (including goodwill and know-how).

(2) This section does not prevent a company—

(a) from allotting bonus shares to its members, or

(b) from paying up, with sums available for the purpose, any amounts for the time being unpaid on any of its shares (whether on account of the nominal value of the shares or by way of premium).

(3) This section has effect subject to the following provisions of this Chapter (additional rules for public companies).

583. Meaning of payment in cash

(1) The following provisions have effect for the purposes of the Companies Acts.

(2) A share in a company is deemed paid up (as to its nominal value or any premium on it) in cash, or allotted for cash, if the consideration received for the allotment or payment up is a cash consideration.

(3) A "cash consideration" means—

(a) cash received by the company,

(b) a cheque received by the company in good faith that the directors have no reason for suspecting will not be paid,

(c) a release of a liability of the company for a liquidated sum,

(d) an undertaking to pay cash to the company at a future date, or

(e) payment by any other means giving rise to a present or future entitlement (of the company or a person acting on the company's behalf) to a payment, or credit equivalent to payment, in cash.

(4) The Secretary of State may by order provide that particular means of payment specified in the order are to be regarded as falling within subsection (3)(e).

(5) In relation to the allotment or payment up of shares in a company—

(a) the payment of cash to a person other than the company, or

(b) an undertaking to pay cash to a person other than the company, counts as consideration other than cash.

This does not apply for the purposes of Chapter 3 (allotment of equity securities: existing shareholders' right of pre-emption).

(6) For the purpose of determining whether a share is or is to be allotted for cash, or paid up in cash, "cash" includes foreign currency.

(7) An order under this section is subject to negative resolution procedure.

Additional rules for public companies

584. **Public companies: shares taken by subscribers of memorandum**

Shares taken by a subscriber to the memorandum of a public company in pursuance of an undertaking of his in the memorandum, and any premium on the shares, must be paid up in cash.

585. **Public companies: must not accept undertaking to do work or perform services**

(1) A public company must not accept at any time, in payment up of its shares or any premium on them, an undertaking given by any person that he or another should do work or perform services for the company or any other person.

(2) If a public company accepts such an undertaking in payment up of its shares or any premium on them, the holder of the shares when they or the premium are treated as paid up (in whole or in part) by the undertaking is liable—

   (a) to pay the company in respect of those shares an amount equal to their nominal value, together with the whole of any premium or, if the case so requires, such proportion of that amount as is treated as paid up by the undertaking; and

   (b) to pay interest at the appropriate rate on the amount payable under paragraph (a).

(3) The reference in subsection (2) to the holder of shares includes a person who has an unconditional right—

   (a) to be included in the company's register of members in respect of those shares, or

   (b) to have an instrument of transfer of them executed in his favour.

586. **Public companies: shares must be at least one-quarter paid up**

(1) A public company must not allot a share except as paid up at least as to one-quarter of its nominal value and the whole of any premium on it.

(2) This does not apply to shares allotted in pursuance of an employees' share scheme.

(3) If a company allots a share in contravention of this section—

   (a) the share is to be treated as if one-quarter of its nominal value, together with the whole of any premium on it, had been received, and

   (b) the allottee is liable to pay the company the minimum amount which should have been received in respect of the share under subsection (1) (less the value of any consideration actually applied in payment up, to any extent, of the share and any premium on it), with interest at the appropriate rate.

(4) Subsection (3) does not apply to the allotment of bonus shares, unless the allottee knew or ought to have known the shares were allotted in contravention of this section.

587. **Public companies: payment by long-term undertaking**

(1) A public company must not allot shares as fully or partly paid up (as to their nominal value or any premium on them) otherwise than in cash if the consideration for the allotment is or includes an undertaking which is to be, or may be, performed more than five years after the date of the allotment.

(2) If a company allots shares in contravention of subsection (1), the allottee is liable to pay the company an amount equal to the aggregate of their nominal value and the whole of any premium (or, if the case so requires, so much of that aggregate as is treated as paid up by the undertaking), with interest at the appropriate rate.

(3) Where a contract for the allotment of shares does not contravene subsection (1), any variation of the contract that has the effect that the contract would have contravened the subsection, if the terms of the contract as varied had been its original terms, is void.

This applies also to the variation by a public company of the terms of a contract entered into before the company was re-registered as a public company.

(4) Where—

 (a) a public company allots shares for a consideration which consists of or includes (in accordance with subsection (1)) an undertaking that is to be performed within five years of the allotment, and

 (b) the undertaking is not performed within the period allowed by the contract for the allotment of the shares,

the allottee is liable to pay the company, at the end of the period so allowed, an amount equal to the aggregate of the nominal value of the shares and the whole of any premium (or, if the case so requires, so much of that aggregate as is treated as paid up by the undertaking), with interest at the appropriate rate.

(5) References in this section to a contract for the allotment of shares include an ancillary contract relating to payment in respect of them.

Supplementary provisions

588. Liability of subsequent holders of shares

(1) If a person becomes a holder of shares in respect of which—

 (a) there has been a contravention of any provision of this Chapter, and

 (b) by virtue of that contravention another is liable to pay any amount under the provision contravened,

that person is also liable to pay that amount (jointly and severally with any other person so liable), subject as follows.

(2) A person otherwise liable under subsection (1) is exempted from that liability if either—

 (a) he is a purchaser for value and, at the time of the purchase, he did not have actual notice of the contravention concerned, or

 (b) he derived title to the shares (directly or indirectly) from a person who became a holder of them after the contravention and was not liable under subsection (1).

(3) References in this section to a holder, in relation to shares in a company, include any person who has an unconditional right—

 (a) to be included in the company's register of members in respect of those shares, or

 (b) to have an instrument of transfer of the shares executed in his favour.

(4) This section applies in relation to a failure to carry out a term of a contract as mentioned in section 587 (4) (public companies: payment by long-term undertaking) as it applies in relation to a contravention of a provision of this Chapter.

589. Power of court to grant relief

(1) This section applies in relation to liability under—

section 585 (2) (liability of allottee in case of breach by public company of prohibition on accepting undertaking to do work or perform services),

section 587 (2) or (4) (liability of allottee in case of breach by public company of prohibition on payment by long-term undertaking), or

section 588 (liability of subsequent holders of shares),

as it applies in relation to a contravention of those sections.

(2) A person who—

 (a) is subject to any such liability to a company in relation to payment in respect of shares in the company, or

414

(b) is subject to any such liability to a company by virtue of an undertaking given to it in, or in connection with, payment for shares in the company,

may apply to the court to be exempted in whole or in part from the liability.

(3) In the case of a liability within subsection (2)(a), the court may exempt the applicant from the liability only if and to the extent that it appears to the court just and equitable to do so having regard to—

    (a) whether the applicant has paid, or is liable to pay, any amount in respect of—

        (i) any other liability arising in relation to those shares under any provision of this Chapter or Chapter 6, or

        (ii) any liability arising by virtue of any undertaking given in or in connection with payment for those shares;

    (b) whether any person other than the applicant has paid or is likely to pay, whether in pursuance of any order of the court or otherwise, any such amount;

    (c) whether the applicant or any other person—

        (i) has performed in whole or in part, or is likely so to perform any such undertaking, or

        (ii) has done or is likely to do any other thing in payment or part payment for the shares.

(4) In the case of a liability within subsection (2)(b), the court may exempt the applicant from the liability only if and to the extent that it appears to the court just and equitable to do so having regard to—

    (a) whether the applicant has paid or is liable to pay any amount in respect of liability arising in relation to the shares under any provision of this Chapter or Chapter 6;

    (b) whether any person other than the applicant has paid or is likely to pay, whether in pursuance of any order of the court or otherwise, any such amount.

(5) In determining whether it should exempt the applicant in whole or in part from any liability, the court must have regard to the following overriding principles—

    (a) a company that has allotted shares should receive money or money's worth at least equal in value to the aggregate of the nominal value of those shares and the whole of any premium or, if the case so requires, so much of that aggregate as is treated as paid up;

    (b) subject to that, where a company would, if the court did not grant the exemption, have more than one remedy against a particular person, it should be for the company to decide which remedy it should remain entitled to pursue.

(6) If a person brings proceedings against another ("the contributor") for a contribution in respect of liability to a company arising under any provision of this Chapter or Chapter 6 and it appears to the court that the contributor is liable to make such a contribution, the court may, if and to the extent that it appears to it just and equitable to do so having regard to the respective culpability (in respect of the liability to the company) of the contributor and the person bringing the proceedings—

    (a) exempt the contributor in whole or in part from his liability to make such a contribution, or

    (b) order the contributor to make a larger contribution than, but for this subsection, he would be liable to make.

590. Penalty for contravention of this Chapter

(1) If a company contravenes any of the provisions of this Chapter, an offence is committed by—

    (a) the company, and

    (b) every officer of the company who is in default.

(2) A person guilty of an offence under this section is liable—

    (a) on conviction on indictment, to a fine;

    (b) on summary conviction, to a fine not exceeding the statutory maximum.

591. Enforceability of undertakings to do work etc

(1) An undertaking given by any person, in or in connection with payment for shares in a company, to do work or perform services or to do any other thing, if it is enforceable by the

company apart from this Chapter, is so enforceable notwithstanding that there has been a contravention in relation to it of a provision of this Chapter or Chapter 6.

(2) This is without prejudice to section 589 (power of court to grant relief etc in respect of liabilities).

592. **The appropriate rate of interest**

(1) For the purposes of this Chapter the "appropriate rate" of interest is 5% per annum or such other rate as may be specified by order made by the Secretary of State.

(2) An order under this section is subject to negative resolution procedure.

CHAPTER 6
PUBLIC COMPANIES: INDEPENDENT VALUATION OF NON-CASH CONSIDERATION

Non-cash consideration for shares

593. **Public company: valuation of non-cash consideration for shares**

(1) A public company must not allot shares as fully or partly paid up (as to their nominal value or any premium on them) otherwise than in cash unless—

   (a) the consideration for the allotment has been independently valued in accordance with the provisions of this Chapter,

   (b) the valuer's report has been made to the company during the six months immediately preceding the allotment of the shares, and

   (c) a copy of the report has been sent to the proposed allottee.

(2) For this purpose the application of an amount standing to the credit of—

   (a) any of a company's reserve accounts, or

   (b) its profit and loss account,

   in paying up (to any extent) shares allotted to members of the company, or premiums on shares so allotted, does not count as consideration for the allotment.

   Accordingly, subsection (1) does not apply in that case.

(3) If a company allots shares in contravention of subsection (1) and either—

   (a) the allottee has not received the valuer's report required to be sent to him, or

   (b) there has been some other contravention of the requirements of this section or section 596 that the allottee knew or ought to have known amounted to a contravention,

   the allottee is liable to pay the company an amount equal to the aggregate of the nominal value of the shares and the whole of any premium (or, if the case so requires, so much of that aggregate as is treated as paid up by the consideration), with interest at the appropriate rate.

(4) This section has effect subject to—

   section 594 (exception to valuation requirement: arrangement with another company), and

   section 595 (exception to valuation requirement: merger).

594. **Exception to valuation requirement: arrangement with another company**

(1) Section 593 (valuation of non-cash consideration) does not apply to the allotment of shares by a company ("company A") in connection with an arrangement to which this section applies.

(2) This section applies to an arrangement for the allotment of shares in company A on terms that the whole or part of the consideration for the shares allotted is to be provided by—

   (a) the transfer to that company, or

   (b) the cancellation,

   of all or some of the shares, or of all or some of the shares of a particular class, in another company ("company B").

(3) It is immaterial whether the arrangement provides for the issue to company A of shares, or shares of any particular class, in company B.

(4) This section applies to an arrangement only if under the arrangement it is open to all the holders of the shares in company B (or, where the arrangement applies only to shares of a particular class, to all the holders of shares of that class) to take part in the arrangement.

(5) In determining whether that is the case, the following shall be disregarded—

    (a) shares held by or by a nominee of company A;

    (b) shares held by or by a nominee of a company which is—

        (i) the holding company, or a subsidiary, of company A, or

        (ii) a subsidiary of such a holding company;

    (c) shares held as treasury shares by company B.

(6) In this section—

    (a) "arrangement" means any agreement, scheme or arrangement (including an arrangement sanctioned in accordance with—

        (i) Part 26 (arrangements and reconstructions), or

        (ii) section 110 of the Insolvency Act 1986 (c. 45) or Article 96 of the Insolvency (Northern Ireland) Order 1989 (S.I. 1989/2405 (N.I. 19)) (liquidator in winding up accepting shares as consideration for sale of company property)), and

    (b) "company", except in reference to company A, includes any body corporate.

595. Exception to valuation requirement: merger

(1) Section 593 (valuation of non-cash consideration) does not apply to the allotment of shares by a company in connection with a proposed merger with another company.

(2) A proposed merger is where one of the companies proposes to acquire all the assets and liabilities of the other in exchange for the issue of shares or other securities of that one to shareholders of the other, with or without any cash payment to shareholders.

(3) In this section "company", in reference to the other company, includes any body corporate.

596. Non-cash consideration for shares: requirements as to valuation and report

(1) The provisions of sections 1150 to 1153 (general provisions as to independent valuation and report) apply to the valuation and report required by section 593 (public company: valuation of non-cash consideration for shares).

(2) The valuer's report must state—

    (a) the nominal value of the shares to be wholly or partly paid for by the consideration in question;

    (b) the amount of any premium payable on the shares;

    (c) the description of the consideration and, as respects so much of the consideration as he himself has valued, a description of that part of the consideration, the method used to value it and the date of the valuation;

    (d) the extent to which the nominal value of the shares and any premium are to be treated as paid up—

        (i) by the consideration;

        (ii) in cash.

(3) The valuer's report must contain or be accompanied by a note by him—

    (a) in the case of a valuation made by a person other than himself, that it appeared to himself reasonable to arrange for it to be so made or to accept a valuation so made,

    (b) whoever made the valuation, that the method of valuation was reasonable in all the circumstances,

    (c) that it appears to the valuer that there has been no material change in the value of the consideration in question since the valuation, and

    (d) that, on the basis of the valuation, the value of the consideration, together with any cash by which the nominal value of the shares or any premium payable on them is to be paid up, is not less than so much of the aggregate of the nominal value and the whole of any such premium as is treated as paid up by the consideration and any such cash.

(4) Where the consideration to be valued is accepted partly in payment up of the nominal value of the shares and any premium and partly for some other consideration given by the company, section 593 and the preceding provisions of this section apply as if references to the consideration accepted by the company included the proportion of that consideration that is properly attributable to the payment up of that value and any premium.

(5) In such a case—

    (a) the valuer must carry out, or arrange for, such other valuations as will enable him to determine that proportion, and

    (b) his report must state what valuations have been made under this subsection and also the reason for, and method and date of, any such valuation and any other matters which may be relevant to that determination.

597. Copy of report to be delivered to registrar

(1) A company to which a report is made under section 593 as to the value of any consideration for which, or partly for which, it proposes to allot shares must deliver a copy of the report to the registrar for registration.

(2) The copy must be delivered at the same time that the company files the return of the allotment of those shares under section 555 (return of allotment by limited company).

(3) If default is made in complying with subsection (1) or (2), an offence is committed by every officer of the company who is in default.

(4) A person guilty of an offence under this section is liable—

    (a) on conviction on indictment, to a fine;

    (b) on summary conviction, to a fine not exceeding the statutory maximum and, for continued contravention, a daily default fine not exceeding one-tenth of the statutory maximum.

(5) In the case of default in delivering to the registrar any document as required by this section, any person liable for the default may apply to the court for relief.

(6) The court, if satisfied—

    (a) that the omission to deliver the document was accidental or due to inadvertence, or

    (b) that it is just and equitable to grant relief,

may make an order extending the time for delivery of the document for such period as the court thinks proper.

Transfer of non-cash asset in initial period

598. Public company: agreement for transfer of non-cash asset in initial period

(1) A public company formed as such must not enter into an agreement—

    (a) with a person who is a subscriber to the company's memorandum,

    (b) for the transfer by him to the company, or another, before the end of the company's initial period of one or more non-cash assets, and

    (c) under which the consideration for the transfer to be given by the company is at the time of the agreement equal in value to one-tenth or more of the company's issued share capital,

unless the conditions referred to below have been complied with.

(2) The company's "initial period" means the period of two years beginning with the date of the company being issued with a certificate under section 761 (trading certificate).

(3) The conditions are those specified in—

    section 599 (requirement of independent valuation), and

    section 601 (requirement of approval by members).

(4) This section does not apply where—

    (a) it is part of the company's ordinary business to acquire, or arrange for other persons to acquire, assets of a particular description, and

    (b) the agreement is entered into by the company in the ordinary course of that business.

(5) This section does not apply to an agreement entered into by the company under the supervision of the court or of an officer authorised by the court for the purpose.

599. Agreement for transfer of non-cash asset: requirement of independent valuation

(1) The following conditions must have been complied with—

    (a) the consideration to be received by the company, and any consideration other than cash to be given by the company, must have been independently valued in accordance with the provisions of this Chapter,

    (b) the valuer's report must have been made to the company during the six months immediately preceding the date of the agreement, and

    (c) a copy of the report must have been sent to the other party to the proposed agreement not later than the date on which copies have to be circulated to members under section 601 (3).

(2) The reference in subsection (1)(a) to the consideration to be received by the company is to the asset to be transferred to it or, as the case may be, to the advantage to the company of the asset's transfer to another person.

(3) The reference in subsection (1)(c) to the other party to the proposed agreement is to the person referred to in section 598 (1) (a).

If he has received a copy of the report under section 601 in his capacity as a member of the company, it is not necessary to send another copy under this section.

(4) This section does not affect any requirement to value any consideration for purposes of section 593 (valuation of non-cash consideration for shares).

600. Agreement for transfer of non-cash asset: requirements as to valuation and report

(1) The provisions of sections 1150 to 1153 (general provisions as to independent valuation and report) apply to the valuation and report required by section 599 (public company: transfer of non-cash asset).

(2) The valuer's report must state—

    (a) the consideration to be received by the company, describing the asset in question (specifying the amount to be received in cash) and the consideration to be given by the company (specifying the amount to be given in cash), and

    (b) the method and date of valuation.

(3) The valuer's report must contain or be accompanied by a note by him—

    (a) in the case of a valuation made by a person other than himself, that it appeared to himself reasonable to arrange for it to be so made or to accept a valuation so made,

    (b) whoever made the valuation, that the method of valuation was reasonable in all the circumstances,

    (c) that it appears to the valuer that there has been no material change in the value of the consideration in question since the valuation, and

    (d) that, on the basis of the valuation, the value of the consideration to be received by the company is not less than the value of the consideration to be given by it.

(4) Any reference in section 599 or this section to consideration given for the transfer of an asset includes consideration given partly for its transfer.

(5) In such a case—

    (a) the value of any consideration partly so given is to be taken as the proportion of the consideration properly attributable to its transfer,

    (b) the valuer must carry out or arrange for such valuations of anything else as will enable him to determine that proportion, and

    (c) his report must state what valuations have been made for that purpose and also the reason for and method and date of any such valuation and any other matters which may be relevant to that determination.

601. Agreement for transfer of non-cash asset: requirement of approval by members

(1) The following conditions must have been complied with—

    (a) the terms of the agreement must have been approved by an ordinary resolution of the company,

    (b) the requirements of this section must have been complied with as respects the circulation to members of copies of the valuer's report under section 599, and

    (c) a copy of the proposed resolution must have been sent to the other party to the proposed agreement.

(2) The reference in subsection (1)(c) to the other party to the proposed agreement is to the person referred to in section 598 (1) (a).

(3) The requirements of this section as to circulation of copies of the valuer's report are as follows—

    (a) if the resolution is proposed as a written resolution, copies of the valuer's report must be sent or submitted to every eligible member at or before the time at which the proposed resolution is sent or submitted to him;

    (b) if the resolution is proposed at a general meeting, copies of the valuer's report must be circulated to the members entitled to notice of the meeting not later than the date on which notice of the meeting is given.

602. Copy of resolution to be delivered to registrar

(1) A company that has passed a resolution under section 601 with respect to the transfer of an asset must, within 15 days of doing so, deliver to the registrar a copy of the resolution together with the valuer's report required by that section.

(2) If a company fails to comply with subsection (1), an offence is committed by—

    (a) the company, and

    (b) every officer of the company who is in default.

(3) A person guilty of an offence under this section is liable on summary conviction to a fine not exceeding level 3 on the standard scale and, for continued contravention, to a daily default fine not exceeding one-tenth of level 3 on the standard scale.

603. Adaptation of provisions in relation to company re-registering as public

The provisions of sections 598 to 602 (public companies: transfer of non-cash assets) apply with the following adaptations in relation to a company re-registered as a public company—

    (a) the reference in section 598 (1) (a) to a person who is a subscriber to the company's memorandum shall be read as a reference to a person who is a member of the company on the date of re-registration;

    (b) the reference in section 598(2) to the date of the company being issued with a certificate under section 761 (trading certificate) shall be read as a reference to the date of re-registration.

604. Agreement for transfer of non-cash asset: effect of contravention

(1) This section applies where a public company enters into an agreement in contravention of section 598 and either—

    (a) the other party to the agreement has not received the valuer's report required to be sent to him, or

    (b) there has been some other contravention of the requirements of this Chapter that the other party to the agreement knew or ought to have known amounted to a contravention.

(2) In those circumstances—

    (a) the company is entitled to recover from that person any consideration given by it under the agreement, or an amount equal to the value of the consideration at the time of the agreement, and

    (b) the agreement, so far as not carried out, is void.

(3) If the agreement is or includes an agreement for the allotment of shares in the company, then—

    (a) whether or not the agreement also contravenes section 593 (valuation of non-cash consideration for shares), this section does not apply to it in so far as it is for the allotment of shares, and

    (b) the allottee is liable to pay the company an amount equal to the aggregate of the nominal value of the shares and the whole of any premium (or, if the case so requires, so much of that aggregate as is treated as paid up by the consideration), with interest at the appropriate rate.

Supplementary provisions

605. Liability of subsequent holders of shares

  (1) If a person becomes a holder of shares in respect of which—

    (a) there has been a contravention of section 593 (public company: valuation of non-cash consideration for shares), and

    (b) by virtue of that contravention another is liable to pay any amount under the provision contravened,

  that person is also liable to pay that amount (jointly and severally with any other person so liable), unless he is exempted from liability under subsection (3) below.

  (2) If a company enters into an agreement in contravention of section 598 (public company: agreement for transfer of non-cash asset in initial period) and—

    (a) the agreement is or includes an agreement for the allotment of shares in the company,

    (b) a person becomes a holder of shares allotted under the agreement, and

    (c) by virtue of the agreement and allotment under it another person is liable to pay an amount under section 604,

  the person who becomes the holder of the shares is also liable to pay that amount (jointly and severally with any other person so liable), unless he is exempted from liability under subsection (3) below.

  This applies whether or not the agreement also contravenes section 593.

  (3) A person otherwise liable under subsection (1) or (2) is exempted from that liability if either—

    (a) he is a purchaser for value and, at the time of the purchase, he did not have actual notice of the contravention concerned, or

    (b) he derived title to the shares (directly or indirectly) from a person who became a holder of them after the contravention and was not liable under subsection (1) or (2).

  (4) References in this section to a holder, in relation to shares in a company, include any person who has an unconditional right—

    (a) to be included in the company's register of members in respect of those shares, or

    (b) to have an instrument of transfer of the shares executed in his favour.

606. Power of court to grant relief

  (1) A person who—

    (a) is liable to a company under any provision of this Chapter in relation to payment in respect of any shares in the company, or

    (b) is liable to a company by virtue of an undertaking given to it in, or in connection with, payment for any shares in the company,

  may apply to the court to be exempted in whole or in part from the liability.

  (2) In the case of a liability within subsection (1)(a), the court may exempt the applicant from the liability only if and to the extent that it appears to the court just and equitable to do so having regard to—

    (a) whether the applicant has paid, or is liable to pay, any amount in respect of—

      (i) any other liability arising in relation to those shares under any provision of this Chapter or Chapter 5, or

      (ii) any liability arising by virtue of any undertaking given in or in connection with payment for those shares;

  (b) whether any person other than the applicant has paid or is likely to pay, whether in pursuance of any order of the court or otherwise, any such amount;

  (c) whether the applicant or any other person—

      (i) has performed in whole or in part, or is likely so to perform any such undertaking, or

      (ii) has done or is likely to do any other thing in payment or part payment for the shares.

(3) In the case of a liability within subsection (1)(b), the court may exempt the applicant from the liability only if and to the extent that it appears to the court just and equitable to do so having regard to—

  (a) whether the applicant has paid or is liable to pay any amount in respect of liability arising in relation to the shares under any provision of this Chapter or Chapter 5;

  (b) whether any person other than the applicant has paid or is likely to pay, whether in pursuance of any order of the court or otherwise, any such amount.

(4) In determining whether it should exempt the applicant in whole or in part from any liability, the court must have regard to the following overriding principles—

  (a) that a company that has allotted shares should receive money or money's worth at least equal in value to the aggregate of the nominal value of those shares and the whole of any premium or, if the case so requires, so much of that aggregate as is treated as paid up;

  (b) subject to this, that where such a company would, if the court did not grant the exemption, have more than one remedy against a particular person, it should be for the company to decide which remedy it should remain entitled to pursue.

(5) If a person brings proceedings against another ("the contributor") for a contribution in respect of liability to a company arising under any provision of this Chapter or Chapter 5 and it appears to the court that the contributor is liable to make such a contribution, the court may, if and to the extent that it appears to it, just and equitable to do so having regard to the respective culpability (in respect of the liability to the company) of the contributor and the person bringing the proceedings—

  (a) exempt the contributor in whole or in part from his liability to make such a contribution, or

  (b) order the contributor to make a larger contribution than, but for this subsection, he would be liable to make.

(6) Where a person is liable to a company under section 604 (2) (agreement for transfer of non-cash asset: effect of contravention), the court may, on application, exempt him in whole or in part from that liability if and to the extent that it appears to the court to be just and equitable to do so having regard to any benefit accruing to the company by virtue of anything done by him towards the carrying out of the agreement mentioned in that subsection.

607. Penalty for contravention of this Chapter

(1) This section applies where a company contravenes—

    section 593 (public company allotting shares for non-cash consideration), or

    section 598 (public company entering into agreement for transfer of non-cash asset).

(2) An offence is committed by—

  (a) the company, and

  (b) every officer of the company who is in default.

(3) A person guilty of an offence under this section is liable—

  (a) on conviction on indictment, to a fine;

  (b) on summary conviction, to a fine not exceeding the statutory maximum.

608. Enforceability of undertakings to do work etc

(1) An undertaking given by any person, in or in connection with payment for shares in a company, to do work or perform services or to do any other thing, if it is enforceable by the company apart from this Chapter, is so enforceable notwithstanding that there has been a contravention in relation to it of a provision of this Chapter or Chapter 5.

(2) This is without prejudice to section 606 (power of court to grant relief etc in respect of liabilities).

609. **The appropriate rate of interest**

(1) For the purposes of this Chapter the "appropriate rate" of interest is 5% per annum or such other rate as may be specified by order made by the Secretary of State.

(2) An order under this section is subject to negative resolution procedure.

CHAPTER 7

SHARE PREMIUMS

The share premium account

610. **Application of share premiums**

(1) If a company issues shares at a premium, whether for cash or otherwise, a sum equal to the aggregate amount or value of the premiums on those shares must be transferred to an account called "the share premium account".

(2) Where, on issuing shares, a company has transferred a sum to the share premium account, it may use that sum to write off—

 (a) the expenses of the issue of those shares;

 (b) any commission paid on the issue of those shares.

(3) The company may use the share premium account to pay up new shares to be allotted to members as fully paid bonus shares.

(4) Subject to subsections (2) and (3), the provisions of the Companies Acts relating to the reduction of a company's share capital apply as if the share premium account were part of its paid up share capital.

(5) This section has effect subject to—

 section 611 (group reconstruction relief);

 section 612 (merger relief);

 section 614 (power to make further provisions by regulations).

(6) In this Chapter "the issuing company" means the company issuing shares as mentioned in subsection (1) above.

Relief from requirements as to share premiums

611. **Group reconstruction relief**

(1) This section applies where the issuing company—

 (a) is a wholly-owned subsidiary of another company ("the holding company"), and

 (b) allots shares—

  (i) to the holding company, or

  (ii) to another wholly-owned subsidiary of the holding company,

  in consideration for the transfer to the issuing company of non-cash assets of a company ("the transferor company") that is a member of the group of companies that comprises the holding company and all its wholly-owned subsidiaries.

(2) Where the shares in the issuing company allotted in consideration for the transfer are issued at a premium, the issuing company is not required by section 610 to transfer any amount in excess of the minimum premium value to the share premium account.

(3) The minimum premium value means the amount (if any) by which the base value of the consideration for the shares allotted exceeds the aggregate nominal value of the shares.

(4) The base value of the consideration for the shares allotted is the amount by which the base value of the assets transferred exceeds the base value of any liabilities of the transferor company assumed by the issuing company as part of the consideration for the assets transferred.

(5) For the purposes of this section—
  (a) the base value of assets transferred is taken as—
    (i)   the cost of those assets to the transferor company, or
    (ii) if less, the amount at which those assets are stated in the transferor company's accounting records immediately before the transfer;
  (b) the base value of the liabilities assumed is taken as the amount at which they are stated in the transferor company's accounting records immediately before the transfer.

612. Merger relief

(1) This section applies where the issuing company has secured at least a 90% equity holding in another company in pursuance of an arrangement providing for the allotment of equity shares in the issuing company on terms that the consideration for the shares allotted is to be provided—
  (a) by the issue or transfer to the issuing company of equity shares in the other company, or
  (b) by the cancellation of any such shares not held by the issuing company.

(2) If the equity shares in the issuing company allotted in pursuance of the arrangement in consideration for the acquisition or cancellation of equity shares in the other company are issued at a premium, section 610 does not apply to the premiums on those shares.

(3) Where the arrangement also provides for the allotment of any shares in the issuing company on terms that the consideration for those shares is to be provided—
  (a) by the issue or transfer to the issuing company of non-equity shares in the other company, or

  (b) by the cancellation of any such shares in that company not held by the issuing company,

  relief under subsection (2) extends to any shares in the issuing company allotted on those terms in pursuance of the arrangement.

(4) This section does not apply in a case falling within section 611 (group reconstruction relief).

613. Merger relief: meaning of 90% equity holding

(1) The following provisions have effect to determine for the purposes of section 612 (merger relief) whether a company ("company A") has secured at least a 90% equity holding in another company ("company B") in pursuance of such an arrangement as is mentioned in subsection (1) of that section.

(2) Company A has secured at least a 90% equity holding in company B if in consequence of an acquisition or cancellation of equity shares in company B (in pursuance of that arrangement) it holds equity shares in company B of an aggregate amount equal to 90% or more of the nominal value of that company's equity share capital.

(3) For this purpose—
  (a) it is immaterial whether any of those shares were acquired in pursuance of the arrangement; and
  (b) shares in company B held by the company as treasury shares are excluded in determining the nominal value of company B's share capital.

(4) Where the equity share capital of company B is divided into different classes of shares, company A is not regarded as having secured at least a 90% equity holding in company B unless the requirements of subsection (2) are met in relation to each of those classes of shares taken separately.

(5) For the purposes of this section shares held by—
  (a) a company that is company A's holding company or subsidiary, or
  (b) a subsidiary of company A's holding company, or
  (c) its or their nominees,
  are treated as held by company A.

614. Power to make further provision by regulations

    (1) The Secretary of State may by regulations make such provision as he thinks appropriate—

        (a) for relieving companies from the requirements of section 610 (application of share premiums) in relation to premiums other than cash premiums;

        (b) for restricting or otherwise modifying any relief from those requirements provided by this Chapter.

    (2) Regulations under this section are subject to affirmative resolution procedure.

615. Relief may be reflected in company's balance sheet

    An amount corresponding to the amount representing the premiums, or part of the premiums, on shares issued by a company that by virtue of any relief under this Chapter is not included in the company's share premium account may also be disregarded in determining the amount at which any shares or other consideration provided for the shares issued is to be included in the company's balance sheet.

Supplementary provisions

616. Interpretation of this Chapter

    (1) In this Chapter—

        "arrangement" means any agreement, scheme or arrangement (including an arrangement sanctioned in accordance with—

        (a) Part 26 (arrangements and reconstructions), or

        (b) section 110 of the Insolvency Act 1986 (c. 45) or Article 96 of the Insolvency (Northern Ireland) Order 1989 (S.I. 1989/2405 (N.I. 19)) (liquidator in winding up accepting shares as consideration for sale of company property));

        "company", except in reference to the issuing company, includes any body corporate;

        "equity shares" means shares comprised in a company's equity share capital, and "non-equity shares" means shares (of any class) that are not so comprised;

        "the issuing company" has the meaning given by section 610 (6).

    (2) References in this Chapter (however expressed) to—

        (a) the acquisition by a company of shares in another company, and

        (b) the issue or allotment of shares to, or the transfer of shares to or by, a company,

        include (respectively) the acquisition of shares by, and the issue or allotment or transfer of shares to or by, a nominee of that company.

        The reference in section 611 to the transferor company shall be read accordingly.

    (3) References in this Chapter to the transfer of shares in a company include the transfer of a right to be included in the company's register of members in respect of those shares.

CHAPTER 8
ALTERATION OF SHARE CAPITAL

How share capital may be altered

617. Alteration of share capital of limited company

    (1) A limited company having a share capital may not alter its share capital except in the following ways.

    (2) The company may—

        (a) increase its share capital by allotting new shares in accordance with this Part, or

        (b) reduce its share capital in accordance with Chapter 10.

    (3) The company may—

        (a) sub-divide or consolidate all or any of its share capital in accordance with section 618, or

        (b) reconvert stock into shares in accordance with section 620.

(4) The company may redenominate all or any of its shares in accordance with section 622, and may reduce its share capital in accordance with section 626 in connection with such a redenomination.

(5) Nothing in this section affects—

(a) the power of a company to purchase its own shares, or to redeem shares, in accordance with Part 18;

(b) the power of a company to purchase its own shares in pursuance of an order of the court under—

    (i) section 98 (application to court to cancel resolution for re-registration as a private company),

    (ii) section 721 (6) (powers of court on objection to redemption or purchase of shares out of capital),

    (iii) section 759 (remedial order in case of breach of prohibition of public offers by private company), or

    (iv) Part 30 (protection of members against unfair prejudice);

(c) the forfeiture of shares, or the acceptance of shares surrendered in lieu, in pursuance of the company's articles, for failure to pay any sum payable in respect of the shares;

(d) the cancellation of shares under section 662 (duty to cancel shares held by or for a public company);

(e) the power of a company—

    (i) to enter into a compromise or arrangement in accordance with Part 26 (arrangements and reconstructions), or

    (ii) to do anything required to comply with an order of the court on an application under that Part.

Subdivision or consolidation of shares

618. Sub-division or consolidation of shares

(1) A limited company having a share capital may—

(a) sub-divide its shares, or any of them, into shares of a smaller nominal amount than its existing shares, or

(b) consolidate and divide all or any of its share capital into shares of a larger nominal amount than its existing shares.

(2) In any sub-division, consolidation or division of shares under this section, the proportion between the amount paid and the amount (if any) unpaid on each resulting share must be the same as it was in the case of the share from which that share is derived.

(3) A company may exercise a power conferred by this section only if its members have passed a resolution authorising it to do so.

(4) A resolution under subsection (3) may authorise a company—

(a) to exercise more than one of the powers conferred by this section;

(b) to exercise a power on more than one occasion;

(c) to exercise a power at a specified time or in specified circumstances.

(5) The company's articles may exclude or restrict the exercise of any power conferred by this section.

619. Notice to registrar of sub-division or consolidation

(1) If a company exercises the power conferred by section 618 (sub-division or consolidation of shares) it must within one month after doing so give notice to the registrar, specifying the shares affected.

(2) The notice must be accompanied by a statement of capital.

(3) The statement of capital must state with respect to the company's share capital immediately following the exercise of the power—
  (a) the total number of shares of the company,
  (b) the aggregate nominal value of those shares,
  (c) for each class of shares—
    (i) prescribed particulars of the rights attached to the shares,
    (ii) the total number of shares of that class, and
    (iii) the aggregate nominal value of shares of that class, and
  (d) the amount paid up and the amount (if any) unpaid on each share (whether on account of the nominal value of the share or by way of premium).

(4) If default is made in complying with this section, an offence is committed by—
  (a) the company, and
  (b) every officer of the company who is in default.

(5) A person guilty of an offence under this section is liable on summary conviction to a fine not exceeding level 3 on the standard scale and, for continued contravention, a daily default fine not exceeding one-tenth of level 3 on the standard scale.

Reconversion of stock into shares

620. Reconversion of stock into shares

(1) A limited company that has converted paid-up shares into stock (before the repeal by this Act of the power to do so) may reconvert that stock into paid-up shares of any nominal value.

(2) A company may exercise the power conferred by this section only if its members have passed an ordinary resolution authorising it to do so.

(3) A resolution under subsection (2) may authorise a company to exercise the power conferred by this section—
  (a) on more than one occasion;
  (b) at a specified time or in specified circumstances.

621. Notice to registrar of reconversion of stock into shares

(1) If a company exercises a power conferred by section 620 (reconversion of stock into shares) it must within one month after doing so give notice to the registrar, specifying the stock affected.

(2) The notice must be accompanied by a statement of capital.

(3) The statement of capital must state with respect to the company's share capital immediately following the exercise of the power—
  (a) the total number of shares of the company,
  (b) the aggregate nominal value of those shares,
  (c) for each class of shares—
    (i) prescribed particulars of the rights attached to the shares,
    (ii) the total number of shares of that class, and
    (iii) the aggregate nominal value of shares of that class, and
  (d) the amount paid up and the amount (if any) unpaid on each share (whether on account of the nominal value of the share or by way of premium).

(4) If default is made in complying with this section, an offence is committed by—
  (a) the company, and
  (b) every officer of the company who is in default.

(5) A person guilty of an offence under this section is liable on summary conviction to a fine not exceeding level 3 on the standard scale and, for continued contravention, a daily default fine not exceeding one-tenth of level 3 on the standard scale.

Redenomination of share capital

622. **Redenomination of share capital**

    (1) A limited company having a share capital may by resolution redenominate its share capital or any class of its share capital.

        "Redenominate" means convert shares from having a fixed nominal value in one currency to having a fixed nominal value in another currency.

    (2) The conversion must be made at an appropriate spot rate of exchange specified in the resolution.

    (3) The rate must be either—

        (a) a rate prevailing on a day specified in the resolution, or

        (b) a rate determined by taking the average of rates prevailing on each consecutive day of a period specified in the resolution.

        The day or period specified for the purposes of paragraph (a) or (b) must be within the period of 28 days ending on the day before the resolution is passed.

    (4) A resolution under this section may specify conditions which must be met before the redenomination takes effect.

    (5) Redenomination in accordance with a resolution under this section takes effect—

        (a) on the day on which the resolution is passed, or

        (b) on such later day as may be determined in accordance with the resolution.

    (6) A resolution under this section lapses if the redenomination for which it provides has not taken effect at the end of the period of 28 days beginning on the date on which it is passed.

    (7) A company's articles may prohibit or restrict the exercise of the power conferred by this section.

    (8) Chapter 3 of Part 3 (resolutions affecting a company's constitution) applies to a resolution under this section.

623. **Calculation of new nominal values**

    For each class of share the new nominal value of each share is calculated as follows:

    Step One

    Take the aggregate of the old nominal values of all the shares of that class.

    Step Two

    Translate that amount into the new currency at the rate of exchange specified in the resolution.

    Step Three

    Divide that amount by the number of shares in the class.

624. **Effect of redenomination**

    (1) The redenomination of shares does not affect any rights or obligations of members under the company's constitution, or any restrictions affecting members under the company's constitution.

        In particular, it does not affect entitlement to dividends (including entitlement to dividends in a particular currency), voting rights or any liability in respect of amounts unpaid on shares.

    (2) For this purpose the company's constitution includes the terms on which any shares of the company are allotted or held.

    (3) Subject to subsection (1), references to the old nominal value of the shares in any agreement or statement, or in any deed, instrument or document, shall (unless the context otherwise requires) be read after the resolution takes effect as references to the new nominal value of the shares.

625. **Notice to registrar of redenomination**

    (1) If a limited company having a share capital redenominates any of its share capital, it must within one month after doing so give notice to the registrar, specifying the shares redenominated.

    (2) The notice must—

        (a) state the date on which the resolution was passed, and

(b) be accompanied by a statement of capital.

(3) The statement of capital must state with respect to the company's share capital as redenominated by the resolution—

    (a) the total number of shares of the company,

    (b) the aggregate nominal value of those shares,

    (c) for each class of shares—

        (i) prescribed particulars of the rights attached to the shares,

        (ii) the total number of shares of that class, and

        (iii) the aggregate nominal value of shares of that class, and

    (d) the amount paid up and the amount (if any) unpaid on each share (whether on account of the nominal value of the share or by way of premium).

(4) If default is made in complying with this section, an offence is committed by—

    (a) the company, and

    (b) every officer of the company who is in default.

(5) A person guilty of an offence under this section is liable on summary conviction to a fine not exceeding level 3 on the standard scale and, for continued contravention, a daily default fine not exceeding one-tenth of level 3 on the standard scale.

626. Reduction of capital in connection with redenomination

(1) A limited company that passes a resolution redenominating some or all of its shares may, for the purpose of adjusting the nominal values of the redenominated shares to obtain values that are, in the opinion of the company, more suitable, reduce its share capital under this section.

(2) A reduction of capital under this section requires a special resolution of the company.

(3) Any such resolution must be passed within three months of the resolution effecting the redenomination.

(4) The amount by which a company's share capital is reduced under this section must not exceed 10% of the nominal value of the company's allotted share capital immediately after the reduction.

(5) A reduction of capital under this section does not extinguish or reduce any liability in respect of share capital not paid up.

(6) Nothing in Chapter 10 applies to a reduction of capital under this section.

627. Notice to registrar of reduction of capital in connection with redenomination

(1) A company that passes a resolution under section 626 (reduction of capital in connection with redenomination) must within 15 days after the resolution is passed give notice to the registrar stating—

    (a) the date of the resolution, and

    (b) the date of the resolution under section 622 in connection with which it was passed.

This is in addition to the copies of the resolutions themselves that are required to be delivered to the registrar under Chapter 3 of Part 3.

(2) The notice must be accompanied by a statement of capital.

(3) The statement of capital must state with respect to the company's share capital as reduced by the resolution—

    (a) the total number of shares of the company,

    (b) the aggregate nominal value of those shares,

    (c) for each class of shares—

        (i) prescribed particulars of the rights attached to the shares,

        (ii) the total number of shares of that class, and

        (iii) the aggregate nominal value of shares of that class, and

    (d) the amount paid up and the amount (if any) unpaid on each share (whether on account of the nominal value of the share or by way of premium).

(4) The registrar must register the notice and the statement on receipt.

(5) The reduction of capital is not effective until those documents are registered.

(6) The company must also deliver to the registrar, within 15 days after the resolution is passed, a statement by the directors confirming that the reduction in share capital is in accordance with section 626 (4) (reduction of capital not to exceed 10% of nominal value of allotted shares immediately after reduction).

(7) If default is made in complying with this section, an offence is committed by—

    (a) the company, and

    (b) every officer of the company who is in default.

(8) A person guilty of an offence under this section is liable—

    (a) on conviction on indictment to a fine, and

    (b) on summary conviction to a fine not exceeding the statutory maximum.

628. Redenomination reserve

(1) The amount by which a company's share capital is reduced under section 626 (reduction of capital in connection with redenomination) must be transferred to a reserve, called "the redenomination reserve".

(2) The redenomination reserve may be applied by the company in paying up shares to be allotted to members as fully paid bonus shares.

(3) Subject to that, the provisions of the Companies Acts relating to the reduction of a company's share capital apply as if the redenomination reserve were paid-up share capital of the company.

CHAPTER 9
CLASSES OF SHARE AND CLASS RIGHTS

Introductory

629. Classes of shares

(1) For the purposes of the Companies Acts shares are of one class if the rights attached to them are in all respects uniform.

(2) For this purpose the rights attached to shares are not regarded as different from those attached to other shares by reason only that they do not carry the same rights to dividends in the twelve months immediately following their allotment.

Variation of class rights

630. Variation of class rights: companies having a share capital

(1) This section is concerned with the variation of the rights attached to a class of shares in a company having a share capital.

(2) Rights attached to a class of a company's shares may only be varied—

    (a) in accordance with provision in the company's articles for the variation of those rights, or

    (b) where the company's articles contain no such provision, if the holders of shares of that class consent to the variation in accordance with this section.

(3) This is without prejudice to any other restrictions on the variation of the rights.

(4) The consent required for the purposes of this section on the part of the holders of a class of a company's shares is—

    (a) consent in writing from the holders of at least three-quarters in nominal value of the issued shares of that class (excluding any shares held as treasury shares), or

    (b) a special resolution passed at a separate general meeting of the holders of that class sanctioning the variation.

(5) Any amendment of a provision contained in a company's articles for the variation of the rights attached to a class of shares, or the insertion of any such provision into the articles, is itself to be treated as a variation of those rights.

(6) In this section, and (except where the context otherwise requires) in any provision in a company's articles for the variation of the rights attached to a class of shares, references to the variation of those rights include references to their abrogation.

631. Variation of class rights: companies without a share capital

(1) This section is concerned with the variation of the rights of a class of members of a company where the company does not have a share capital.

(2) Rights of a class of members may only be varied—

    (a) in accordance with provision in the company's articles for the variation of those rights, or

    (b) where the company's articles contain no such provision, if the members of that class consent to the variation in accordance with this section.

(3) This is without prejudice to any other restrictions on the variation of the rights.

(4) The consent required for the purposes of this section on the part of the members of a class is—

    (a) consent in writing from at least three-quarters of the members of the class, or

    (b) a special resolution passed at a separate general meeting of the members of that class sanctioning the variation.

(5) Any amendment of a provision contained in a company's articles for the variation of the rights of a class of members, or the insertion of any such provision into the articles, is itself to be treated as a variation of those rights.

(6) In this section, and (except where the context otherwise requires) in any provision in a company's articles for the variation of the rights of a class of members, references to the variation of those rights include references to their abrogation.

632. Variation of class rights: saving for court's powers under other provisions

Nothing in section 630 or 631 (variation of class rights) affects the power of the court under—

section 98 (application to cancel resolution for public company to be re-registered as private),

Part 26 (arrangements and reconstructions), or

Part 30 (protection of members against unfair prejudice).

633. Right to object to variation: companies having a share capital

(1) This section applies where the rights attached to any class of shares in a company are varied under section 630 (variation of class rights: companies having a share capital).

(2) The holders of not less in the aggregate than 15% of the issued shares of the class in question (being persons who did not consent to or vote in favour of the resolution for the variation) may apply to the court to have the variation cancelled.

For this purpose any of the company's share capital held as treasury shares is disregarded.

(3) If such an application is made, the variation has no effect unless and until it is confirmed by the court.

(4) Application to the court—

    (a) must be made within 21 days after the date on which the consent was given or the resolution was passed (as the case may be), and

    (b) may be made on behalf of the shareholders entitled to make the application by such one or more of their number as they may appoint in writing for the purpose.

(5) The court, after hearing the applicant and any other persons who apply to the court to be heard and appear to the court to be interested in the application, may, if satisfied having regard to all the circumstances of the case that the variation would unfairly prejudice the shareholders of the class represented by the applicant, disallow the variation, and shall if not so satisfied confirm it.

The decision of the court on any such application is final.

(6) References in this section to the variation of the rights of holders of a class of shares include references to their abrogation.

634. **Right to object to variation: companies without a share capital**

    (1) This section applies where the rights of any class of members of a company are varied under section 631 (variation of class rights: companies without a share capital).

    (2) Members amounting to not less than 15% of the members of the class in question (being persons who did not consent to or vote in favour of the resolution for the variation) may apply to the court to have the variation cancelled.

    (3) If such an application is made, the variation has no effect unless and until it is confirmed by the court.

    (4) Application to the court must be made within 21 days after the date on which the consent was given or the resolution was passed (as the case may be) and may be made on behalf of the members entitled to make the application by such one or more of their number as they may appoint in writing for the purpose.

    (5) The court, after hearing the applicant and any other persons who apply to the court to be heard and appear to the court to be interested in the application, may, if satisfied having regard to all the circumstances of the case that the variation would unfairly prejudice the members of the class represented by the applicant, disallow the variation, and shall if not so satisfied confirm it.

    The decision of the court on any such application is final.

    (6) References in this section to the variation of the rights of a class of members include references to their abrogation.

635. **Copy of court order to be forwarded to the registrar**

    (1) The company must within 15 days after the making of an order by the court on an application under section 633 or 634 (objection to variation of class rights) forward a copy of the order to the registrar.

    (2) If default is made in complying with this section an offence is committed by—

        (a) the company, and

        (b) every officer of the company who is in default.

    (3) A person guilty of an offence under this section is liable on summary conviction to a fine not exceeding level 3 on the standard scale and, for continued contravention, a daily default fine not exceeding one-tenth of level 3 on the standard scale.

Matters to be notified to the registrar

636. **Notice of name or other designation of class of shares**

    (1) Where a company assigns a name or other designation, or a new name or other designation, to any class or description of its shares, it must within one month from doing so deliver to the registrar a notice giving particulars of the name or designation so assigned.

    (2) If default is made in complying with this section, an offence is committed by—

        (a) the company, and

        (b) every officer of the company who is in default.

    (3) A person guilty of an offence under this section is liable on summary conviction to a fine not exceeding level 3 on the standard scale and, for continued contravention, a daily default fine not exceeding one-tenth of level 3 on the standard scale.

637. **Notice of particulars of variation of rights attached to shares**

    (1) Where the rights attached to any shares of a company are varied, the company must within one month from the date on which the variation is made deliver to the registrar a notice giving particulars of the variation.

    (2) If default is made in complying with this section, an offence is committed by—

        (a) the company, and

        (b) every officer of the company who is in default.

(3) A person guilty of an offence under this section is liable on summary conviction to a fine not exceeding level 3 on the standard scale and, for continued contravention, a daily default fine not exceeding one-tenth of level 3 on the standard scale.

638. Notice of new class of members

(1) If a company not having a share capital creates a new class of members, the company must within one month from the date on which the new class is created deliver to the registrar a notice containing particulars of the rights attached to that class.

(2) If default is made in complying with this section, an offence is committed by—
   (a) the company, and
   (b) every officer of the company who is in default.

(3) A person guilty of an offence under this section is liable on summary conviction to a fine not exceeding level 3 on the standard scale and, for continued contravention, a daily default fine not exceeding one-tenth of level 3 on the standard scale.

639. Notice of name or other designation of class of members

(1) Where a company not having a share capital assigns a name or other designation, or a new name or other designation, to any class of its members, it must within one month from doing so deliver to the registrar a notice giving particulars of the name or designation so assigned.

(2) If default is made in complying with this section, an offence is committed by—
   (a) the company, and
   (b) every officer of the company who is in default.

(3) A person guilty of an offence under this section is liable on summary conviction to a fine not exceeding level 3 on the standard scale and, for continued contravention, a daily default fine not exceeding one-tenth of level 3 on the standard scale.

640. Notice of particulars of variation of class rights

(1) If the rights of any class of members of a company not having a share capital are varied, the company must within one month from the date on which the variation is made deliver to the registrar a notice containing particulars of the variation.

(2) If default is made in complying with this section, an offence is committed by—
   (a) the company, and
   (b) every officer of the company who is in default.

(3) A person guilty of an offence under this section is liable on summary conviction to a fine not exceeding level 3 on the standard scale and, for continued contravention, a daily default fine not exceeding one-tenth of level 3 on the standard scale.

CHAPTER 10
REDUCTION OF SHARE CAPITAL

Introductory

641. Circumstances in which a company may reduce its share capital

(1) A limited company having a share capital may reduce its share capital—
   (a) in the case of a private company limited by shares, by special resolution supported by a solvency statement (see sections 642 to 644);
   (b) in any case, by special resolution confirmed by the court (see sections 645 to 651).

(2) A company may not reduce its capital under subsection (1)(a) if as a result of the reduction there would no longer be any member of the company holding shares other than redeemable shares.

(3) Subject to that, a company may reduce its share capital under this section in any way.

(4) In particular, a company may—
   (a) extinguish or reduce the liability on any of its shares in respect of share capital not paid up, or

(b) either with or without extinguishing or reducing liability on any of its shares—

    (i) cancel any paid-up share capital that is lost or unrepresented by available assets, or

    (ii) repay any paid-up share capital in excess of the company's wants.

(5) A special resolution under this section may not provide for a reduction of share capital to take effect later than the date on which the resolution has effect in accordance with this Chapter.

(6) This Chapter (apart from subsection (5) above) has effect subject to any provision of the company's articles restricting or prohibiting the reduction of the company's share capital.

Private companies: reduction of capital supported by solvency statement

642. Reduction of capital supported by solvency statement

(1) A resolution for reducing share capital of a private company limited by shares is supported by a solvency statement if—

    (a) the directors of the company make a statement of the solvency of the company in accordance with section 643 (a "solvency statement") not more than 15 days before the date on which the resolution is passed, and

    (b) the resolution and solvency statement are registered in accordance with section 644.

(2) Where the resolution is proposed as a written resolution, a copy of the solvency statement must be sent or submitted to every eligible member at or before the time at which the proposed resolution is sent or submitted to him.

(3) Where the resolution is proposed at a general meeting, a copy of the solvency statement must be made available for inspection by members of the company throughout that meeting.

(4) The validity of a resolution is not affected by a failure to comply with subsection (2) or (3).

643. Solvency statement

(1) A solvency statement is a statement that each of the directors—

    (a) has formed the opinion, as regards the company's situation at the date of the statement, that there is no ground on which the company could then be found to be unable to pay (or otherwise discharge) its debts; and

    (b) has also formed the opinion—

        (i) if it is intended to commence the winding up of the company within twelve months of that date, that the company will be able to pay (or otherwise discharge) its debts in full within twelve months of the commencement of the winding up; or

        (ii) in any other case, that the company will be able to pay (or otherwise discharge) its debts as they fall due during the year immediately following that date.

(2) In forming those opinions, the directors must take into account all of the company's liabilities (including any contingent or prospective liabilities).

(3) The solvency statement must be in the prescribed form and must state—

    (a) the date on which it is made, and

    (b) the name of each director of the company.

(4) If the directors make a solvency statement without having reasonable grounds for the opinions expressed in it, and the statement is delivered to the registrar, an offence is committed by every director who is in default.

(5) A person guilty of an offence under subsection (4) is liable—

    (a) on conviction on indictment, to imprisonment for a term not exceeding two years or a fine (or both);

    (b) on summary conviction—

        (i) in England and Wales, to imprisonment for a term not exceeding twelve months or to a fine not exceeding the statutory maximum (or both);

        (ii) in Scotland or Northern Ireland, to imprisonment for a term not exceeding six months, or to a fine not exceeding the statutory maximum (or both).

644. **Registration of resolution and supporting documents**

    (1) Within 15 days after the resolution for reducing share capital is passed the company must deliver to the registrar—

        (a) a copy of the solvency statement, and

        (b) a statement of capital.

    This is in addition to the copy of the resolution itself that is required to be delivered to the registrar under Chapter 3 of Part 3.

    (2) The statement of capital must state with respect to the company's share capital as reduced by the resolution—

        (a) the total number of shares of the company,

        (b) the aggregate nominal value of those shares,

        (c) for each class of shares—

            (i) prescribed particulars of the rights attached to the shares,

            (ii) the total number of shares of that class, and

            (iii) the aggregate nominal value of shares of that class, and

        (d) the amount paid up and the amount (if any) unpaid on each share (whether on account of the nominal value of the share or by way of premium).

    (3) The registrar must register the documents delivered to him under subsection (1) on receipt.

    (4) The resolution does not take effect until those documents are registered.

    (5) The company must also deliver to the registrar, within 15 days after the resolution is passed, a statement by the directors confirming that the solvency statement was—

        (a) made not more than 15 days before the date on which the resolution was passed, and

        (b) provided to members in accordance with section 642 (2) or (3).

    (6) The validity of a resolution is not affected by—

        (a) a failure to deliver the documents required to be delivered to the registrar under subsection (1) within the time specified in that subsection, or

        (b) a failure to comply with subsection (5).

    (7) If the company delivers to the registrar a solvency statement that was not provided to members in accordance with section 642 (2) or (3), an offence is committed by every officer of the company who is in default.

    (8) If default is made in complying with this section, an offence is committed by—

        (a) the company, and

        (b) every officer of the company who is in default.

    (9) A person guilty of an offence under subsection (7) or (8) is liable—

        (a) on conviction on indictment, to a fine;

        (b) on summary conviction, to a fine not exceeding the statutory maximum.

Reduction of capital confirmed by the court

645. **Application to court for order of confirmation**

    (1) Where a company has passed a resolution for reducing share capital, it may apply to the court for an order confirming the reduction.

    (2) If the proposed reduction of capital involves either—

        (a) diminution of liability in respect of unpaid share capital, or

        (b) the payment to a shareholder of any paid-up share capital,

    section 646 (creditors entitled to object to reduction) applies unless the court directs otherwise.

    (3) The court may, if having regard to any special circumstances of the case it thinks proper to do so, direct that section 646 is not to apply as regards any class or classes of creditors.

    (4) The court may direct that section 646 is to apply in any other case.

646. Creditors entitled to object to reduction

(1) Where this section applies (see section 645 (2) and (4)), every creditor of the company who at the date fixed by the court is entitled to any debt or claim that, if that date were the commencement of the winding up of the company would be admissible in proof against the company, is entitled to object to the reduction of capital.

(2) The court shall settle a list of creditors entitled to object.

(3) For that purpose the court—

   (a) shall ascertain, as far as possible without requiring an application from any creditor, the names of those creditors and the nature and amount of their debts or claims, and

   (b) may publish notices fixing a day or days within which creditors not entered on the list are to claim to be so entered or are to be excluded from the right of objecting to the reduction of capital.

(4) If a creditor entered on the list whose debt or claim is not discharged or has not determined does not consent to the reduction, the court may, if it thinks fit, dispense with the consent of that creditor on the company securing payment of his debt or claim.

(5) For this purpose the debt or claim must be secured by appropriating (as the court may direct) the following amount—

   (a) if the company admits the full amount of the debt or claim or, though not admitting it, is willing to provide for it, the full amount of the debt or claim;

   (b) if the company does not admit, and is not willing to provide for, the full amount of the debt or claim, or if the amount is contingent or not ascertained, an amount fixed by the court after the like enquiry and adjudication as if the company were being wound up by the court.

647. Offences in connection with list of creditors

(1) If an officer of the company—

   (a) intentionally or recklessly—

      (i) conceals the name of a creditor entitled to object to the reduction of capital, or

      (ii) misrepresents the nature or amount of the debt or claim of a creditor, or

   (b) is knowingly concerned in any such concealment or misrepresentation,

   he commits an offence.

(2) A person guilty of an offence under this section is liable—

   (a) on conviction on indictment, to a fine;

   (b) on summary conviction, to a fine not exceeding the statutory maximum.

648. Court order confirming reduction

(1) The court may make an order confirming the reduction of capital on such terms and conditions as it thinks fit.

(2) The court must not confirm the reduction unless it is satisfied, with respect to every creditor of the company who is entitled to object to the reduction of capital that either—

   (a) his consent to the reduction has been obtained, or

   (b) his debt or claim has been discharged, or has determined or has been secured.

(3) Where the court confirms the reduction, it may order the company to publish (as the court directs) the reasons for reduction of capital, or such other information in regard to it as the court thinks expedient with a view to giving proper information to the public, and (if the court thinks fit) the causes that led to the reduction.

(4) The court may, if for any special reason it thinks proper to do so, make an order directing that the company must, during such period (commencing on or at any time after the date of the order) as is specified in the order, add to its name as its last words the words "and reduced".

If such an order is made, those words are, until the end of the period specified in the order, deemed to be part of the company's name.

649. **Registration of order and statement of capital**

(1) The registrar, on production of an order of the court confirming the reduction of a company's share capital and the delivery of a copy of the order and of a statement of capital (approved by the court), shall register the order and statement.

This is subject to section 650 (public company reducing capital below authorised minimum).

(2) The statement of capital must state with respect to the company's share capital as altered by the order—

(a) the total number of shares of the company,

(b) the aggregate nominal value of those shares,

(c) for each class of shares—

(i) prescribed particulars of the rights attached to the shares,

(ii) the total number of shares of that class, and

(iii) the aggregate nominal value of shares of that class, and

(d) the amount paid up and the amount (if any) unpaid on each share (whether on account of the nominal value of the share or by way of premium).

(3) The resolution for reducing share capital, as confirmed by the court's order, takes effect—

(a) in the case of a reduction of share capital that forms part of a compromise or arrangement sanctioned by the court under Part 26 (arrangements and reconstructions)—

(i) on delivery of the order and statement of capital to the registrar, or

(ii) if the court so orders, on the registration of the order and statement of capital;

(b) in any other case, on the registration of the order and statement of capital.

(4) Notice of the registration of the order and statement of capital must be published in such manner as the court may direct.

(5) The registrar must certify the registration of the order and statement of capital.

(6) The certificate—

(a) must be signed by the registrar or authenticated by the registrar's official seal, and

(b) is conclusive evidence—

(i) that the requirements of this Act with respect to the reduction of share capital have been complied with, and

(ii) that the company's share capital is as stated in the statement of capital.

Public company reducing capital below authorised minimum

650. **Public company reducing capital below authorised minimum**

(1) This section applies where the court makes an order confirming a reduction of a public company's capital that has the effect of bringing the nominal value of its allotted share capital below the authorised minimum.

(2) The registrar must not register the order unless either—

(a) the court so directs, or

(b) the company is first re-registered as a private company.

(3) Section 651 provides an expedited procedure for re-registration in these circumstances.

651. **Expedited procedure for re-registration as a private company**

(1) The court may authorise the company to be re-registered as a private company without its having passed the special resolution required by section 97.

(2) If it does so, the court must specify in the order the changes to the company's name and articles to be made in connection with the re-registration.

(3) The company may then be re-registered as a private company if an application to that effect is delivered to the registrar together with—

(a) a copy of the court's order, and

(b) notice of the company's name, and a copy of the company's articles, as altered by the court's order.

(4) On receipt of such an application the registrar must issue a certificate of incorporation altered to meet the circumstances of the case.

(5) The certificate must state that it is issued on re-registration and the date on which it is issued.

(6) On the issue of the certificate—

   (a) the company by virtue of the issue of the certificate becomes a private company, and

   (b) the changes in the company's name and articles take effect.

(7) The certificate is conclusive evidence that the requirements of this Act as to re-registration have been complied with.

Effect of reduction of capital

652. Liability of members following reduction of capital

(1) Where a company's share capital is reduced a member of the company (past or present) is not liable in respect of any share to any call or contribution exceeding in amount the difference (if any) between—

   (a) the nominal amount of the share as notified to the registrar in the statement of capital delivered under section 644 or 649, and

   (b) the amount paid on the share or the reduced amount (if any) which is deemed to have been paid on it, as the case may be.

(2) This is subject to section 653 (liability to creditor in case of omission from list).

(3) Nothing in this section affects the rights of the contributories among themselves.

653. Liability to creditor in case of omission from list of creditors

(1) This section applies where, in the case of a reduction of capital confirmed by the court—

   (a) a creditor entitled to object to the reduction of share capital is by reason of his ignorance—

      (i) of the proceedings for reduction of share capital, or

      (ii) of their nature and effect with respect to his debt or claim,

      not entered on the list of creditors, and

   (b) after the reduction of capital the company is unable to pay the amount of his debt or claim.

(2) Every person who was a member of the company at the date on which the resolution for reducing capital took effect under section 649 (3) is liable to contribute for the payment of the debt or claim an amount not exceeding that which he would have been liable to contribute if the company had commenced to be wound up on the day before that date.

(3) If the company is wound up, the court on the application of the creditor in question, and proof of ignorance as mentioned in subsection (1)(a), may if it thinks fit—

   (a) settle accordingly a list of persons liable to contribute under this section, and

   (b) make and enforce calls and orders on them as if they were ordinary contributories in a winding up.

(4) The reference in subsection (1)(b) to a company being unable to pay the amount of a debt or claim has the same meaning as in section 123 of the Insolvency Act 1986 (c. 45) or Article 103 of the Insolvency (Northern Ireland) Order 1989 (S.I. 1989/2405 (N.I. 19)).

CHAPTER 11
MISCELLANEOUS AND SUPPLEMENTARY PROVISIONS

654. Treatment of reserve arising from reduction of capital

(1) A reserve arising from the reduction of a company's share capital is not distributable, subject to any provision made by order under this section.

(2) The Secretary of State may by order specify cases in which—

   (a) the prohibition in subsection (1) does not apply, and

   (b) the reserve is to be treated for the purposes of Part 23 (distributions) as a realised profit.

(3) An order under this section is subject to affirmative resolution procedure.

655. Shares no bar to damages against company

A person is not debarred from obtaining damages or other compensation from a company by reason only of his holding or having held shares in the company or any right to apply or subscribe for shares or to be included in the company's register of members in respect of shares.

656. Public companies: duty of directors to call meeting on serious loss of capital

(1) Where the net assets of a public company are half or less of its called-up share capital, the directors must call a general meeting of the company to consider whether any, and if so what, steps should be taken to deal with the situation.

(2) They must do so not later than 28 days from the earliest day on which that fact is known to a director of the company.

(3) The meeting must be convened for a date not later than 56 days from that day.

(4) If there is a failure to convene a meeting as required by this section, each of the directors of the company who—

(a) knowingly authorises or permits the failure, or

(b) after the period during which the meeting should have been convened, knowingly authorises or permits the failure to continue,

commits an offence.

(5) A person guilty of an offence under this section is liable—

(a) on conviction on indictment, to a fine;

(b) on summary conviction, to a fine not exceeding the statutory maximum.

(6) Nothing in this section authorises the consideration at a meeting convened in pursuance of subsection (1) of any matter that could not have been considered at that meeting apart from this section.

657. General power to make further provision by regulations

(1) The Secretary of State may by regulations modify the following provisions of this Part—

sections 552 and 553 (prohibited commissions, discounts and allowances),

Chapter 5 (payment for shares),

Chapter 6 (public companies: independent valuation of non-cash consideration),

Chapter 7 (share premiums),

sections 622 to 628 (redenomination of share capital),

Chapter 10 (reduction of capital), and

section 656 (public companies: duty of directors to call meeting on serious loss of capital).

(2) The regulations may—

(a) amend or repeal any of those provisions, or

(b) make such other provision as appears to the Secretary of State appropriate in place of any of those provisions.

(3) Regulations under this section may make consequential amendments or repeals in other provisions of this Act, or in other enactments.

(4) Regulations under this section are subject to affirmative resolution procedure.

PART 18

ACQUISITION BY LIMITED COMPANY OF ITS OWN SHARES

CHAPTER 1
GENERAL PROVISIONS

Introductory

658. General rule against limited company acquiring its own shares

(1) A limited company must not acquire its own shares, whether by purchase, subscription or otherwise, except in accordance with the provisions of this Part.

(2) If a company purports to act in contravention of this section—

    (a) an offence is committed by—

        (i) the company, and

        (ii) every officer of the company who is in default, and

    (b) the purported acquisition is void.

(3) A person guilty of an offence under this section is liable—

    (a) on conviction on indictment, to imprisonment for a term not exceeding two years or a fine (or both);

    (b) on summary conviction—

        (i) in England and Wales, to imprisonment for a term not exceeding twelve months or a fine not exceeding the statutory maximum (or both);

        (ii) in Scotland or Northern Ireland, to imprisonment for a term not exceeding six months or a fine not exceeding the statutory maximum (or both).

659. Exceptions to general rule

(1) A limited company may acquire any of its own fully paid shares otherwise than for valuable consideration.

(2) Section 658 does not prohibit—

    (a) the acquisition of shares in a reduction of capital duly made;

    (b) the purchase of shares in pursuance of an order of the court under—

        (i) section 98 (application to court to cancel resolution for re-registration as a private company),

        (ii) section 721(6) (powers of court on objection to redemption or purchase of shares out of capital),

        (iii) section 759 (remedial order in case of breach of prohibition of public offers by private company), or

        (iv) Part 30 (protection of members against unfair prejudice);

    (c) the forfeiture of shares, or the acceptance of shares surrendered in lieu, in pursuance of the company's articles, for failure to pay any sum payable in respect of the shares.

Shares held by company's nominee

660. Treatment of shares held by nominee

(1) This section applies where shares in a limited company—

    (a) are taken by a subscriber to the memorandum as nominee of the company,

    (b) are issued to a nominee of the company, or

    (c) are acquired by a nominee of the company, partly paid up, from a third person.

(2) For all purposes—

    (a) the shares are to be treated as held by the nominee on his own account, and

    (b) the company is to be regarded as having no beneficial interest in them.

(3) This section does not apply—

    (a) to shares acquired otherwise than by subscription by a nominee of a public company, where—

        (i) a person acquires shares in the company with financial assistance given to him, directly or indirectly, by the company for the purpose of or in connection with the acquisition, and

        (ii) the company has a beneficial interest in the shares;

    (b) to shares acquired by a nominee of the company when the company has no beneficial interest in the shares.

661. Liability of others where nominee fails to make payment in respect of shares

(1) This section applies where shares in a limited company—

    (a) are taken by a subscriber to the memorandum as nominee of the company,

     (b) are issued to a nominee of the company, or

     (c) are acquired by a nominee of the company, partly paid up, from a third person.

(2) If the nominee, having been called on to pay any amount for the purposes of paying up, or paying any premium on, the shares, fails to pay that amount within 21 days from being called on to do so, then—

     (a) in the case of shares that he agreed to take as subscriber to the memorandum, the other subscribers to the memorandum, and

     (b) in any other case, the directors of the company when the shares were issued to or acquired by him,

are jointly and severally liable with him to pay that amount.

(3) If in proceedings for the recovery of an amount under subsection (2) it appears to the court that the subscriber or director—

     (a) has acted honestly and reasonably, and

     (b) having regard to all the circumstances of the case, ought fairly to be relieved from liability,

the court may relieve him, either wholly or in part, from his liability on such terms as the court thinks fit.

(4) If a subscriber to a company's memorandum or a director of a company has reason to apprehend that a claim will or might be made for the recovery of any such amount from him—

     (a) he may apply to the court for relief, and

     (b) the court has the same power to relieve him as it would have had in proceedings for recovery of that amount.

(5) This section does not apply to shares acquired by a nominee of the company when the company has no beneficial interest in the shares.

Shares held by or for public company

662. Duty to cancel shares in public company held by or for the company

  (1) This section applies in the case of a public company—

     (a) where shares in the company are forfeited, or surrendered to the company in lieu of forfeiture, in pursuance of the articles, for failure to pay any sum payable in respect of the shares;

     (b) where shares in the company are surrendered to the company in pursuance of section 102C(1)(b) of the Building Societies Act 1986 (c. 53);

     (c) where shares in the company are acquired by it (otherwise than in accordance with this Part or Part 30 (protection of members against unfair prejudice)) and the company has a beneficial interest in the shares;

     (d) where a nominee of the company acquires shares in the company from a third party without financial assistance being given directly or indirectly by the company and the company has a beneficial interest in the shares; or

     (e) where a person acquires shares in the company, with financial assistance given to him, directly or indirectly, by the company for the purpose of or in connection with the acquisition, and the company has a beneficial interest in the shares.

  (2) Unless the shares or any interest of the company in them are previously disposed of, the company must—

     (a) cancel the shares and diminish the amount of the company's share capital by the nominal value of the shares cancelled, and

     (b) where the effect is that the nominal value of the company's allotted share capital is brought below the authorised minimum, apply for re-registration as a private company, stating the effect of the cancellation.

(3) It must do so no later than—

    (a) in a case within subsection (1)(a) or (b), three years from the date of the forfeiture or surrender;

    (b) in a case within subsection (1)(c) or (d), three years from the date of the acquisition;

    (c) in a case within subsection (1)(e), one year from the date of the acquisition.

(4) The directors of the company may take any steps necessary to enable the company to comply with this section, and may do so without complying with the provisions of Chapter 10 of Part 17 (reduction of capital).

    See also section 664 (re-registration as private company in consequence of cancellation).

(5) Neither the company nor, in a case within subsection (1)(d) or (e), the nominee or other shareholder may exercise any voting rights in respect of the shares.

(6) Any purported exercise of those rights is void.

663. Notice of cancellation of shares

(1) Where a company cancels shares in order to comply with section 662, it must within one month after the shares are cancelled give notice to the registrar, specifying the shares cancelled.

(2) The notice must be accompanied by a statement of capital.

(3) The statement of capital must state with respect to the company's share capital immediately following the cancellation—

    (a) the total number of shares of the company,

    (b) the aggregate nominal value of those shares,

    (c) for each class of shares—

        (i) prescribed particulars of the rights attached to the shares,

        (ii) the total number of shares of that class, and

        (iii) the aggregate nominal value of shares of that class, and

    (d) the amount paid up and the amount (if any) unpaid on each share (whether on account of the nominal value of the share or by way of premium).

(4) If default is made in complying with this section, an offence is committed by—

    (a) the company, and

    (b) every officer of the company who is in default.

(5) A person guilty of an offence under this section is liable on summary conviction to a fine not exceeding level 3 on the standard scale and, for continued contravention, a daily default fine not exceeding one-tenth of level 3 on the standard scale.

664. Re-registration as private company in consequence of cancellation

(1) Where a company is obliged to re-register as a private company to comply with section 662, the directors may resolve that the company should be so re-registered.

    Chapter 3 of Part 3 (resolutions affecting a company's constitution) applies to any such resolution.

(2) The resolution may make such changes—

    (a) in the company's name, and

    (b) in the company's articles,

    as are necessary in connection with its becoming a private company.

(3) The application for re-registration must contain a statement of the company's proposed name on re-registration.

(4) The application must be accompanied by—

    (a) a copy of the resolution (unless a copy has already been forwarded under Chapter 3 of Part 3),

    (b) a copy of the company's articles as amended by the resolution, and

    (c) a statement of compliance.

(5) The statement of compliance required is a statement that the requirements of this section as to re-registration as a private company have been complied with.

(6) The registrar may accept the statement of compliance as sufficient evidence that the company is entitled to be re-registered as a private company.

665. **Issue of certificate of incorporation on re-registration**

(1) If on an application under section 664 the registrar is satisfied that the company is entitled to be re-registered as a private company, the company shall be re-registered accordingly.

(2) The registrar must issue a certificate of incorporation altered to meet the circumstances of the case.

(3) The certificate must state that it is issued on re-registration and the date on which it is issued.

(4) On the issue of the certificate—

    (a) the company by virtue of the issue of the certificate becomes a private company, and

    (b) the changes in the company's name and articles take effect.

(5) The certificate is conclusive evidence that the requirements of this Act as to re-registration have been complied with.

666. **Effect of failure to re-register**

(1) If a public company that is required by section 662 to apply to be re-registered as a private company fails to do so before the end of the period specified in subsection (3) of that section, Chapter 1 of Part 20 (prohibition of public offers by private company) applies to it as if it were a private company.

(2) Subject to that, the company continues to be treated as a public company until it is so re-registered.

667. **Offence in case of failure to cancel shares or re-register**

(1) This section applies where a company, when required to do by section 662—

    (a) fails to cancel any shares, or

    (b) fails to make an application for re-registration as a private company,

within the time specified in subsection (3) of that section.

(2) An offence is committed by—

    (a) the company, and

    (b) every officer of the company who is in default.

(3) A person guilty of an offence under this section is liable on summary conviction to a fine not exceeding level 3 on the standard scale and, for continued contravention, a daily default fine not exceeding one-tenth of level 3 on the standard scale.

668. **Application of provisions to company re-registering as public company**

(1) This section applies where, after shares in a private company—

    (a) are forfeited in pursuance of the company's articles or are surrendered to the company in lieu of forfeiture,

    (b) are acquired by the company (otherwise than by any of the methods permitted by this Part or Part 30 (protection of members against unfair prejudice)), the company having a beneficial interest in the shares,

    (c) are acquired by a nominee of the company from a third party without financial assistance being given directly or indirectly by the company, the company having a beneficial interest in the shares, or

    (d) are acquired by a person with financial assistance given to him, directly or indirectly, by the company for the purpose of or in connection with the acquisition, the company having a beneficial interest in the shares,

the company is re-registered as a public company.

(2) In that case the provisions of sections 662 to 667 apply to the company as if it had been a public company at the time of the forfeiture, surrender or acquisition, subject to the following modification.

(3) The modification is that the period specified in section 662(3)(a), (b) or (c) (period for complying with obligations under that section) runs from the date of the re-registration of the company as a public company.

669. **Transfer to reserve on acquisition of shares by public company or nominee**

(1) Where—

(a) a public company, or a nominee of a public company, acquires shares in the company, and

(b) those shares are shown in a balance sheet of the company as an asset,

an amount equal to the value of the shares must be transferred out of profits available for dividend to a reserve fund and is not then available for distribution.

(2) Subsection (1) applies to an interest in shares as it applies to shares. As it so applies the reference to the value of the shares shall be read as a reference to the value to the company of its interest in the shares.

Charges of public company on own shares

670. **Public companies: general rule against lien or charge on own shares**

(1) A lien or other charge of a public company on its own shares (whether taken expressly or otherwise) is void, except as permitted by this section.

(2) In the case of any description of company, a charge is permitted if the shares are not fully paid up and the charge is for an amount payable in respect of the shares.

(3) In the case of a company whose ordinary business—

(a) includes the lending of money, or

(b) consists of the provision of credit or the bailment (in Scotland, hiring) of goods under a hire-purchase agreement, or both,

a charge is permitted (whether the shares are fully paid or not) if it arises in connection with a transaction entered into by the company in the ordinary course of that business.

(4) In the case of a company that has been re-registered as a public company, a charge is permitted if it was in existence immediately before the application for re-registration.

Supplementary provisions

671. **Interests to be disregarded in determining whether company has beneficial interest**

In determining for the purposes of this Chapter whether a company has a beneficial interest in shares, there shall be disregarded any such interest as is mentioned in—

section 672 (residual interest under pension scheme or employees' share scheme),

section 673 (employer's charges and other rights of recovery), or

section 674 (rights as personal representative or trustee).

672. **Residual interest under pension scheme or employees' share scheme**

(1) Where the shares are held on trust for the purposes of a pension scheme or employees' share scheme, there shall be disregarded any residual interest of the company that has not vested in possession.

(2) A "residual interest" means a right of the company to receive any of the trust property in the event of—

(a) all the liabilities arising under the scheme having been satisfied or provided for, or

(b) the company ceasing to participate in the scheme, or

(c) the trust property at any time exceeding what is necessary for satisfying the liabilities arising or expected to arise under the scheme.

(3) In subsection (2)—

(a) the reference to a right includes a right dependent on the exercise of a discretion vested by the scheme in the trustee or another person, and

(b) the reference to liabilities arising under a scheme includes liabilities that have resulted, or may result, from the exercise of any such discretion.

(4) For the purposes of this section a residual interest vests in possession—

(a) in a case within subsection (2)(a), on the occurrence of the event mentioned there (whether or not the amount of the property receivable pursuant to the right is ascertained);

(b) in a case within subsection (2)(b) or (c), when the company becomes entitled to require the trustee to transfer to it any of the property receivable pursuant to that right.

(5) Where by virtue of this section shares are exempt from section 660 or 661 (shares held by company's nominee) at the time they are taken, issued or acquired but the residual interest in question vests in possession before they are disposed of or fully paid up, those sections apply to the shares as if they had been taken, issued or acquired on the date on which that interest vests in possession.

(6) Where by virtue of this section shares are exempt from sections 662 to 668 (shares held by or for public company) at the time they are acquired but the residual interest in question vests in possession before they are disposed of, those sections apply to the shares as if they had been acquired on the date on which the interest vests in possession.

673. Employer's charges and other rights of recovery

(1) Where the shares are held on trust for the purposes of a pension scheme there shall be disregarded—

(a) any charge or lien on, or set-off against, any benefit or other right or interest under the scheme for the purpose of enabling the employer or former employer of a member of the scheme to obtain the discharge of a monetary obligation due to him from the member;

(b) any right to receive from the trustee of the scheme, or as trustee of the scheme to retain, an amount that can be recovered or retained—

(i) under section 61 of the Pension Schemes Act 1993 (c. 48), or otherwise, as reimbursement or partial reimbursement for any contributions equivalent premium paid in connection with the scheme under Part 3 of that Act, or

(ii) under section 57 of the Pension Schemes (Northern Ireland) Act 1993 (c. 49), or otherwise, as reimbursement or partial reimbursement for any contributions equivalent premium paid in connection with the scheme under Part 3 of that Act.

(2) Where the shares are held on trust for the purposes of an employees' share scheme, there shall be disregarded any charge or lien on, or set-off against, any benefit or other right or interest under the scheme for the purpose of enabling the employer or former employer of a member of the scheme to obtain the discharge of a monetary obligation due to him from the member.

674. Rights as personal representative or trustee

Where the company is a personal representative or trustee, there shall be disregarded any rights that the company has in that capacity including, in particular—

(a) any right to recover its expenses or be remunerated out of the estate or trust property, and

(b) any right to be indemnified out of that property for any liability incurred by reason of any act or omission of the company in the performance of its duties as personal representative or trustee.

675. Meaning of "pension scheme"

(1) In this Chapter "pension scheme" means a scheme for the provision of benefits consisting of or including relevant benefits for or in respect of employees or former employees.

(2) In subsection (1) "relevant benefits" means any pension, lump sum, gratuity or other like benefit given or to be given on retirement or on death or in anticipation of retirement or, in connection with past service, after retirement or death.

676. Application of provisions to directors

For the purposes of this Chapter references to "employer" and "employee", in the context of a pension scheme or employees' share scheme, shall be read as if a director of a company were employed by it.

CHAPTER 2
FINANCIAL ASSISTANCE FOR PURCHASE OF OWN SHARES

Introductory

677. **Meaning of "financial assistance"**

(1) In this Chapter "financial assistance" means—

    (a) financial assistance given by way of gift,

    (b) financial assistance given—

        (i) by way of guarantee, security or indemnity (other than an indemnity in respect of the indemnifier's own neglect or default), or

        (ii) by way of release or waiver,

    (c) financial assistance given—

        (i) by way of a loan or any other agreement under which any of the obligations of the person giving the assistance are to be fulfilled at a time when in accordance with the agreement any obligation of another party to the agreement remains unfulfilled, or

        (ii) by way of the novation of, or the assignment (in Scotland, assignation) of rights arising under, a loan or such other agreement, or

    (d) any other financial assistance given by a company where—

        (i) the net assets of the company are reduced to a material extent by the giving of the assistance, or

        (ii) the company has no net assets.

(2) "Net assets" here means the aggregate amount of the company's assets less the aggregate amount of its liabilities.

(3) For this purpose a company's liabilities include—

    (a) where the company draws up Companies Act individual accounts, any provision of a kind specified for the purposes of this subsection by regulations under section 396, and

    (b) where the company draws up IAS individual accounts, any provision made in those accounts.

Circumstances in which financial assistance prohibited

678. **Assistance for acquisition of shares in public company**

(1) Where a person is acquiring or proposing to acquire shares in a public company, it is not lawful for that company, or a company that is a subsidiary of that company, to give financial assistance directly or indirectly for the purpose of the acquisition before or at the same time as the acquisition takes place.

(2) Subsection (1) does not prohibit a company from giving financial assistance for the acquisition of shares in it or its holding company if—

    (a) the company's principal purpose in giving the assistance is not to give it for the purpose of any such acquisition, or

    (b) the giving of the assistance for that purpose is only an incidental part of some larger purpose of the company,

and the assistance is given in good faith in the interests of the company.

(3) Where—

    (a) a person has acquired shares in a company, and

    (b) a liability has been incurred (by that or another person) for the purpose of the acquisition,

it is not lawful for that company, or a company that is a subsidiary of that company, to give financial assistance directly or indirectly for the purpose of reducing or discharging the liability if, at the time the assistance is given, the company in which the shares were acquired is a public company.

(4) Subsection (3) does not prohibit a company from giving financial assistance if—

   (a) the company's principal purpose in giving the assistance is not to reduce or discharge any liability incurred by a person for the purpose of the acquisition of shares in the company or

   (b) the reduction or discharge of any such liability is only an incidental part of some larger purpose of the company,

and the assistance is given in good faith in the interests of the company.

(5) This section has effect subject to section 681 and 682 (unconditional and conditional exceptions to prohibition).

679. Assistance by public company for acquisition of shares in its private holding company

(1) Where a person is acquiring or proposing to acquire shares in a private company, it is not lawful for a public company that is a subsidiary of that company to give financial assistance directly or indirectly for the purpose of the acquisition before or at the same time as the acquisition takes place.

(2) Subsection (1) does not prohibit a company from giving financial assistance for the acquisition of shares in its holding company if—

   (a) the company's principal purpose in giving the assistance is not to give it for the purpose of any such acquisition, or

   (b) the giving of the assistance for that purpose is only an incidental part of some larger purpose of the company,

and the assistance is given in good faith in the interests of the company.

(3) Where—

   (a) a person has acquired shares in a private company, and

   (b) a liability has been incurred (by that or another person) for the purpose of the acquisition,

it is not lawful for a public company that is a subsidiary of that company to give financial assistance directly or indirectly for the purpose of reducing or discharging the liability.

(4) Subsection (3) does not prohibit a company from giving financial assistance if—

   (a) the company's principal purpose in giving the assistance is not to reduce or discharge any liability incurred by a person for the purpose of the acquisition of shares in its holding company, or

   (b) the reduction or discharge of any such liability is only an incidental part of some larger purpose of the company,

and the assistance is given in good faith in the interests of the company.

(5) This section has effect subject to sections 681 and 682 (unconditional and conditional exceptions to prohibition).

680. Prohibited financial assistance an offence

(1) If a company contravenes section 678(1) or (3) or section 679(1) or (3) (prohibited financial assistance) an offence is committed by—

   (a) the company, and

   (b) every officer of the company who is in default.

(2) A person guilty of an offence under this section is liable—

   (a) on conviction on indictment, to imprisonment for a term not exceeding two years or a fine (or both);

   (b) on summary conviction—

      (i) in England and Wales, to imprisonment for a term not exceeding twelve months or to a fine not exceeding the statutory maximum (or both);

      (ii) in Scotland or Northern Ireland, to imprisonment for a term not exceeding six months, or to a fine not exceeding the statutory maximum (or both).

Exceptions from prohibition

681. Unconditional exceptions

(1) Neither section 678 nor section 679 prohibits a transaction to which this section applies.

(2) Those transactions are—

(a) a distribution of the company's assets by way of—

(i) dividend lawfully made, or

(ii) distribution in the course of a company's winding up;

(b) an allotment of bonus shares;

(c) a reduction of capital under Chapter 10 of Part 17;

(d) a redemption of shares under Chapter 3 or a purchase of shares under Chapter 4 of this Part;

(e) anything done in pursuance of an order of the court under Part 26 (order sanctioning compromise or arrangement with members or creditors);

(f) anything done under an arrangement made in pursuance of section 110 of the Insolvency Act 1986 (c. 45) or Article 96 of the Insolvency (Northern Ireland) Order 1989 (S.I. 1989/2405 (N.I. 19)) (liquidator in winding up accepting shares as consideration for sale of company's property);

(g) anything done under an arrangement made between a company and its creditors that is binding on the creditors by virtue of Part 1 of the Insolvency Act 1986 or Part 2 of the Insolvency (Northern Ireland) Order 1989 (S.I. 1989/2405 (N.I. 19)).

682. Conditional exceptions

(1) Neither section 678 nor section 679 prohibits a transaction to which this section applies—

(a) if the company giving the assistance is a private company, or

(b) if the company giving the assistance is a public company and—

(i) the company has net assets that are not reduced by the giving of the assistance, or

(ii) to the extent that those assets are so reduced, the assistance is provided out of distributable profits.

(2) The transactions to which this section applies are—

(a) where the lending of money is part of the ordinary business of the company, the lending of money in the ordinary course of the company's business;

(b) the provision by the company, in good faith in the interests of the company or its holding company, of financial assistance for the purposes of an employees' share scheme;

(c) the provision of financial assistance by the company for the purposes of or in connection with anything done by the company (or another company in the same group) for the purpose of enabling or facilitating transactions in shares in the first-mentioned company or its holding company between, and involving the acquisition of beneficial ownership of those shares by—

(i) bona fide employees or former employees of that company (or another company in the same group), or

(ii) spouses or civil partners, widows, widowers or surviving civil partners, or minor children or step-children of any such employees or former employees;

(d) the making by the company of loans to persons (other than directors) employed in good faith by the company with a view to enabling those persons to acquire fully paid shares in the company or its holding company to be held by them by way of beneficial ownership.

(3) The references in this section to "net assets" are to the amount by which the aggregate of the company's assets exceeds the aggregate of its liabilities.

(4) For this purpose—

(a) the amount of both assets and liabilities shall be taken to be as stated in the company's accounting records immediately before the financial assistance is given, and

(b) "liabilities" includes any amount retained as reasonably necessary for the purpose of providing for a liability the nature of which is clearly defined and that is either likely to be incurred or certain to be incurred but uncertain as to amount or as to the date on which it will arise.

(5) For the purposes of subsection (2)(c) a company is in the same group as another company if it is a holding company or subsidiary of that company or a subsidiary of a holding company of that company.

Supplementary

683. **Definitions for this Chapter**

(1) In this Chapter—

"distributable profits", in relation to the giving of any financial assistance—

(a) means those profits out of which the company could lawfully make a distribution equal in value to that assistance, and

(b) includes, in a case where the financial assistance consists of or includes, or is treated as arising in consequence of, the sale, transfer or other disposition of a non-cash asset, any profit that, if the company were to make a distribution of that character would be available for that purpose (see section 846); and

"distribution" has the same meaning as in Part 23 (distributions) (see section 829).

(2) In this Chapter—

(a) a reference to a person incurring a liability includes his changing his financial position by making an agreement or arrangement (whether enforceable or unenforceable, and whether made on his own account or with any other person) or by any other means, and

(b) a reference to a company giving financial assistance for the purposes of reducing or discharging a liability incurred by a person for the purpose of the acquisition of shares includes its giving such assistance for the purpose of wholly or partly restoring his financial position to what it was before the acquisition took place.

CHAPTER 3
REDEEMABLE SHARES

684. **Power of limited company to issue redeemable shares**

(1) A limited company having a share capital may issue shares that are to be redeemed or are liable to be redeemed at the option of the company or the shareholder ("redeemable shares"), subject to the following provisions.

(2) The articles of a private limited company may exclude or restrict the issue of redeemable shares.

(3) A public limited company may only issue redeemable shares if it is authorised to do so by its articles.

(4) No redeemable shares may be issued at a time when there are no issued shares of the company that are not redeemable.

685. **Terms and manner of redemption**

(1) The directors of a limited company may determine the terms, conditions and manner of redemption of shares if they are authorised to do so—

(a) by the company's articles, or

(b) by a resolution of the company.

(2) A resolution under subsection (1)(b) may be an ordinary resolution, even though it amends the company's articles.

(3) Where the directors are authorised under subsection (1) to determine the terms, conditions and manner of redemption of shares—

    (a) they must do so before the shares are allotted, and

    (b) any obligation of the company to state in a statement of capital the rights attached to the shares extends to the terms, conditions and manner of redemption.

(4) Where the directors are not so authorised, the terms, conditions and manner of redemption of any redeemable shares must be stated in the company's articles.

686. Payment for redeemable shares

(1) Redeemable shares in a limited company may not be redeemed unless they are fully paid.

(2) The terms of redemption of shares in a limited company may provide that the amount payable on redemption may, by agreement between the company and the holder of the shares, be paid on a date later than the redemption date.

(3) Unless redeemed in accordance with a provision authorised by subsection (2), the shares must be paid for on redemption.

687. Financing of redemption

(1) A private limited company may redeem redeemable shares out of capital in accordance with Chapter 5.

(2) Subject to that, redeemable shares in a limited company may only be redeemed out of—

    (a) distributable profits of the company, or

    (b) the proceeds of a fresh issue of shares made for the purposes of the redemption.

(3) Any premium payable on redemption of shares in a limited company must be paid out of distributable profits of the company, subject to the following provision.

(4) If the redeemable shares were issued at a premium, any premium payable on their redemption may be paid out of the proceeds of a fresh issue of shares made for the purposes of the redemption, up to an amount equal to—

    (a) the aggregate of the premiums received by the company on the issue of the shares redeemed, or

    (b) the current amount of the company's share premium account (including any sum transferred to that account in respect of premiums on the new shares),

    whichever is the less.

(5) The amount of the company's share premium account is reduced by a sum corresponding (or by sums in the aggregate corresponding) to the amount of any payment made under subsection (4).

(6) This section is subject to section 735(4) (terms of redemption enforceable in a winding up).

688. Redeemed shares treated as cancelled

Where shares in a limited company are redeemed—

(a) the shares are treated as cancelled, and

(b) the amount of the company's issued share capital is diminished accordingly by the nominal value of the shares redeemed.

689. Notice to registrar of redemption

(1) If a limited company redeems any redeemable shares it must within one month after doing so give notice to the registrar, specifying the shares redeemed.

(2) The notice must be accompanied by a statement of capital.

(3) The statement of capital must state with respect to the company's share capital immediately following the redemption—

    (a) the total number of shares of the company,

    (b) the aggregate nominal value of those shares,

    (c) for each class of shares—

        (i) prescribed particulars of the rights attached to the shares,

        (ii) the total number of shares of that class, and

        (iii) the aggregate nominal value of shares of that class, and

(d) the amount paid up and the amount (if any) unpaid on each share (whether on account of the nominal value of the share or by way of premium).

(4) If default is made in complying with this section, an offence is committed by—

(a) the company, and

(b) every officer of the company who is in default.

(5) A person guilty of an offence under this section is liable on summary conviction to a fine not exceeding level 3 on the standard scale and, for continued contravention, a daily default fine not exceeding one-tenth of level 3 on the standard scale.

CHAPTER 4
PURCHASE OF OWN SHARES

General provisions

690. **Power of limited company to purchase own shares**

(1) A limited company having a share capital may purchase its own shares (including any redeemable shares), subject to—

(a) the following provisions of this Chapter, and

(b) any restriction or prohibition in the company's articles.

(2) A limited company may not purchase its own shares if as a result of the purchase there would no longer be any issued shares of the company other than redeemable shares or shares held as treasury shares.

691. **Payment for purchase of own shares**

(1) A limited company may not purchase its own shares unless they are fully paid.

(2) Where a limited company purchases its own shares, the shares must be paid for on purchase.

692. **Financing of purchase of own shares**

(1) A private limited company may purchase its own shares out of capital in accordance with Chapter 5.

(2) Subject to that—

(a) a limited company may only purchase its own shares out of—

(i) distributable profits of the company, or

(ii) the proceeds of a fresh issue of shares made for the purpose of financing the purchase, and

(b) any premium payable on the purchase by a limited company of its own shares must be paid out of distributable profits of the company, subject to subsection (3).

(3) If the shares to be purchased were issued at a premium, any premium payable on their purchase by the company may be paid out of the proceeds of a fresh issue of shares made for the purpose of financing the purchase, up to an amount equal to—

(a) the aggregate of the premiums received by the company on the issue of the shares purchased, or

(b) the current amount of the company's share premium account (including any sum transferred to that account in respect of premiums on the new shares),

whichever is the less.

(4) The amount of the company's share premium account is reduced by a sum corresponding (or by sums in the aggregate corresponding) to the amount of any payment made under subsection (3).

(5) This section has effect subject to section 735(4) (terms of purchase enforceable in a winding up).

Authority for purchase of own shares

693. Authority for purchase of own shares

(1) A limited company may only purchase its own shares—

    (a) by an off-market purchase, in pursuance of a contract approved in advance in accordance with section 694;

    (b) by a market purchase, authorised in accordance with section 701.

(2) A purchase is "off-market" if the shares either—

    (a) are purchased otherwise than on a recognised investment exchange, or

    (b) are purchased on a recognised investment exchange but are not subject to a marketing arrangement on the exchange.

(3) For this purpose a company's shares are subject to a marketing arrangement on a recognised investment exchange if—

    (a) they are listed under Part 6 of the Financial Services and Markets Act 2000 (c. 8), or

    (b) the company has been afforded facilities for dealings in the shares to take place on the exchange—

        (i) without prior permission for individual transactions from the authority governing that investment exchange, and

        (ii) without limit as to the time during which those facilities are to be available.

(4) A purchase is a "market purchase" if it is made on a recognised investment exchange and is not an off-market purchase by virtue of subsection (2)(b).

(5) In this section "recognised investment exchange" means a recognised investment exchange (within the meaning of Part 18 of the Financial Services and Markets Act 2000) other than an overseas exchange (within the meaning of that Part).

Authority for off-market purchase

694. Authority for off-market purchase

(1) A company may only make an off-market purchase of its own shares in pursuance of a contract approved prior to the purchase in accordance with this section.

(2) Either—

    (a) the terms of the contract must be authorised by a special resolution of the company before the contract is entered into, or

    (b) the contract must provide that no shares may be purchased in pursuance of the contract until its terms have been authorised by a special resolution of the company.

(3) The contract may be a contract, entered into by the company and relating to shares in the company, that does not amount to a contract to purchase the shares but under which the company may (subject to any conditions) become entitled or obliged to purchase the shares.

(4) The authority conferred by a resolution under this section may be varied, revoked or from time to time renewed by a special resolution of the company.

(5) In the case of a public company a resolution conferring, varying or renewing authority must specify a date on which the authority is to expire, which must not be later than 18 months after the date on which the resolution is passed.

(6) A resolution conferring, varying, revoking or renewing authority under this section is subject to—

section 695 (exercise of voting rights), and

section 696 (disclosure of details of contract).

695. Resolution authorising off-market purchase: exercise of voting rights

(1) This section applies to a resolution to confer, vary, revoke or renew authority for the purposes of section 694 (authority for off-market purchase of own shares).

(2) Where the resolution is proposed as a written resolution, a member who holds shares to which the resolution relates is not an eligible member.

(3) Where the resolution is proposed at a meeting of the company, it is not effective if—

    (a) any member of the company holding shares to which the resolution relates exercises the voting rights carried by any of those shares in voting on the resolution, and

    (b) the resolution would not have been passed if he had not done so.

(4) For this purpose—

    (a) a member who holds shares to which the resolution relates is regarded as exercising the voting rights carried by those shares not only if he votes in respect of them on a poll on the question whether the resolution shall be passed, but also if he votes on the resolution otherwise than on a poll;

    (b) any member of the company may demand a poll on that question;

    (c) a vote and a demand for a poll by a person as proxy for a member are the same respectively as a vote and a demand by the member.

696. Resolution authorising off-market purchase: disclosure of details of contract

(1) This section applies in relation to a resolution to confer, vary, revoke or renew authority for the purposes of section 694 (authority for off-market purchase of own shares).

(2) A copy of the contract (if it is in writing) or a memorandum setting out its terms (if it is not) must be made available to members—

    (a) in the case of a written resolution, by being sent or submitted to every eligible member at or before the time at which the proposed resolution is sent or submitted to him;

    (b) in the case of a resolution at a meeting, by being made available for inspection by members of the company both—

        (i) at the company's registered office for not less than 15 days ending with the date of the meeting, and

        (ii) at the meeting itself.

(3) A memorandum of contract terms so made available must include the names of the members holding shares to which the contract relates.

(4) A copy of the contract so made available must have annexed to it a written memorandum specifying such of those names as do not appear in the contract itself.

(5) The resolution is not validly passed if the requirements of this section are not complied with.

697. Variation of contract for off-market purchase

(1) A company may only agree to a variation of a contract authorised under section 694 (authority for off-market purchase) if the variation is approved in advance in accordance with this section.

(2) The terms of the variation must be authorised by a special resolution of the company before it is agreed to.

(3) That authority may be varied, revoked or from time to time renewed by a special resolution of the company.

(4) In the case of a public company a resolution conferring, varying or renewing authority must specify a date on which the authority is to expire, which must not be later than 18 months after the date on which the resolution is passed.

(5) A resolution conferring, varying, revoking or renewing authority under this section is subject to—

section 698 (exercise of voting rights), and

section 699 (disclosure of details of variation).

698. Resolution authorising variation: exercise of voting rights

(1) This section applies to a resolution to confer, vary, revoke or renew authority for the purposes of section 697 (variation of contract for off-market purchase of own shares).

(2) Where the resolution is proposed as a written resolution, a member who holds shares to which the resolution relates is not an eligible member.

(3) Where the resolution is proposed at a meeting of the company, it is not effective if—

    (a) any member of the company holding shares to which the resolution relates exercises the voting rights carried by any of those shares in voting on the resolution, and

    (b) the resolution would not have been passed if he had not done so.

(4) For this purpose—

    (a) a member who holds shares to which the resolution relates is regarded as exercising the voting rights carried by those shares not only if he votes in respect of them on a poll on the question whether the resolution shall be passed, but also if he votes on the resolution otherwise than on a poll;

    (b) any member of the company may demand a poll on that question;

    (c) a vote and a demand for a poll by a person as proxy for a member are the same respectively as a vote and a demand by the member.

699. Resolution authorising variation: disclosure of details of variation

(1) This section applies in relation to a resolution under section 697 (variation of contract for off-market purchase of own shares).

(2) A copy of the proposed variation (if it is in writing) or a written memorandum giving details of the proposed variation (if it is not) must be made available to members—

    (a) in the case of a written resolution, by being sent or submitted to every eligible member at or before the time at which the proposed resolution is sent or submitted to him;

    (b) in the case of a resolution at a meeting, by being made available for inspection by members of the company both—

        (i) at the company's registered office for not less than 15 days ending with the date of the meeting, and

        (ii) at the meeting itself.

(3) There must also be made available as mentioned in subsection (2) a copy of the original contract or, as the case may be, a memorandum of its terms, together with any variations previously made.

(4) A memorandum of the proposed variation so made available must include the names of the members holding shares to which the variation relates.

(5) A copy of the proposed variation so made available must have annexed to it a written memorandum specifying such of those names as do not appear in the variation itself.

(6) The resolution is not validly passed if the requirements of this section are not complied with.

700. Release of company's rights under contract for off-market purchase

(1) An agreement by a company to release its rights under a contract approved under section 694 (authorisation of off-market purchase) is void unless the terms of the release agreement are approved in advance in accordance with this section.

(2) The terms of the proposed agreement must be authorised by a special resolution of the company before the agreement is entered into.

(3) That authority may be varied, revoked or from time to time renewed by a special resolution of the company.

(4) In the case of a public company a resolution conferring, varying or renewing authority must specify a date on which the authority is to expire, which must not be later than 18 months after the date on which the resolution is passed.

(5) The provisions of—

section 698 (exercise of voting rights), and

section 699 (disclosure of details of variation),

apply to a resolution authorising a proposed release agreement as they apply to a resolution authorising a proposed variation.

Authority for market purchase

701. **Authority for market purchase**

    (1) A company may only make a market purchase of its own shares if the purchase has first been authorised by a resolution of the company.

    (2) That authority—

        (a) may be general or limited to the purchase of shares of a particular class or description, and

        (b) may be unconditional or subject to conditions.

    (3) The authority must—

        (a) specify the maximum number of shares authorised to be acquired, and

        (b) determine both the maximum and minimum prices that may be paid for the shares.

    (4) The authority may be varied, revoked or from time to time renewed by a resolution of the company.

    (5) A resolution conferring, varying or renewing authority must specify a date on which it is to expire, which must not be later than 18 months after the date on which the resolution is passed.

    (6) A company may make a purchase of its own shares after the expiry of the time limit specified if—

        (a) the contract of purchase was concluded before the authority expired, and

        (b) the terms of the authority permitted the company to make a contract of purchase that would or might be executed wholly or partly after its expiration.

    (7) A resolution to confer or vary authority under this section may determine either or both the maximum and minimum price for purchase by—

        (a) specifying a particular sum, or

        (b) providing a basis or formula for calculating the amount of the price (but without reference to any person's discretion or opinion).

    (8) Chapter 3 of Part 3 (resolutions affecting a company's constitution) applies to a resolution under this section.

Supplementary provisions

702. **Copy of contract or memorandum to be available for inspection**

    (1) This section applies where a company has entered into—

        (a) a contract approved under section 694 (authorisation of contract for off-market purchase), or

        (b) a contract for a purchase authorised under section 701 (authorisation of market purchase).

    (2) The company must keep available for inspection—

        (a) a copy of the contract, or

        (b) if the contract is not in writing, a written memorandum setting out its terms.

    (3) The copy or memorandum must be kept available for inspection from the conclusion of the contract until the end of the period of ten years beginning with—

        (a) the date on which the purchase of all the shares in pursuance of the contract is completed, or

        (b) the date on which the contract otherwise determines.

    (4) The copy or memorandum must be kept available for inspection—

        (a) at the company's registered office, or

        (b) at a place specified in regulations under section 1136.

    (5) The company must give notice to the registrar—

        (a) of the place at which the copy or memorandum is kept available for inspection, and

        (b) of any change in that place,

    unless it has at all times been kept at the company's registered office.

(6) Every copy or memorandum required to be kept under this section must be kept open to inspection without charge—

(a) by any member of the company, and

(b) in the case of a public company, by any other person.

(7) The provisions of this section apply to a variation of a contract as they apply to the original contract.

703. **Enforcement of right to inspect copy or memorandum**

(1) If default is made in complying with section 702(2), (3) or (4) or default is made for 14 days in complying with section 702(5), or an inspection required under section 702(6) is refused, an offence is committed by—

(a) the company, and

(b) every officer of the company who is in default.

(2) A person guilty of an offence under this section is liable on summary conviction to a fine not exceeding level 3 on the standard scale and, for continued contravention, a daily default fine not exceeding one-tenth of level 3 on the standard scale.

(3) In the case of refusal of an inspection required under section 702(6) the court may by order compel an immediate inspection.

704. **No assignment of company's right to purchase own shares**

The rights of a company under a contract authorised under—

(a) section 694 (authority for off-market purchase), or

(b) section 701 (authority for market purchase)

are not capable of being assigned.

705. **Payments apart from purchase price to be made out of distributable profits**

(1) A payment made by a company in consideration of—

(a) acquiring any right with respect to the purchase of its own shares in pursuance of a contingent purchase contract approved under section 694 (authorisation of off-market purchase),

(b) the variation of any contract approved under that section, or

(c) the release of any of the company's obligations with respect to the purchase of any of its own shares under a contract—

(i) approved under section 694, or

(ii) authorised under section 701 (authorisation of market purchase),

must be made out of the company's distributable profits.

(2) If this requirement is not met in relation to a contract, then—

(a) in a case within subsection (1)(a), no purchase by the company of its own shares in pursuance of that contract may be made under this Chapter;

(b) in a case within subsection (1)(b), no such purchase following the variation may be made under this Chapter;

(c) in a case within subsection (1)(c), the purported release is void.

706. **Treatment of shares purchased**

Where a limited company makes a purchase of its own shares in accordance with this Chapter, then—

(a) if section 724 (treasury shares) applies, the shares may be held and dealt with in accordance with Chapter 6;

(b) if that section does not apply—

(i) the shares are treated as cancelled, and

(ii) the amount of the company's issued share capital is diminished accordingly by the nominal value of the shares cancelled.

707. **Return to registrar of purchase of own shares**

(1) Where a company purchases shares under this Chapter, it must deliver a return to the registrar within the period of 28 days beginning with the date on which the shares are delivered to it.

(2) The return must distinguish—
  (a) shares in relation to which section 724 (treasury shares) applies and shares in relation to which that section does not apply, and
  (b) shares in relation to which that section applies—
    (i) that are cancelled forthwith (under section 729 (cancellation of treasury shares)), and
    (ii) that are not so cancelled.

(3) The return must state, with respect to shares of each class purchased—
  (a) the number and nominal value of the shares, and
  (b) the date on which they were delivered to the company.

(4) In the case of a public company the return must also state—
  (a) the aggregate amount paid by the company for the shares, and
  (b) the maximum and minimum prices paid in respect of shares of each class purchased.

(5) Particulars of shares delivered to the company on different dates and under different contracts may be included in a single return.

In such a case the amount required to be stated under subsection (4)(a) is the aggregate amount paid by the company for all the shares to which the return relates.

(6) If default is made in complying with this section an offence is committed by every officer of the company who is in default.

(7) A person guilty of an offence under this section is liable—
  (a) on conviction on indictment, to a fine;
  (b) on summary conviction to a fine not exceeding the statutory maximum and, for continued contravention, a daily default fine not exceeding one-tenth of the statutory maximum.

708. Notice to registrar of cancellation of shares

(1) If on the purchase by a company of any of its own shares in accordance with this Part—
  (a) section 724 (treasury shares) does not apply (so that the shares are treated as cancelled), or
  (b) that section applies but the shares are cancelled forthwith (under section 729 (cancellation of treasury shares)),
the company must give notice of cancellation to the registrar, within the period of 28 days beginning with the date on which the shares are delivered to it, specifying the shares cancelled.

(2) The notice must be accompanied by a statement of capital.

(3) The statement of capital must state with respect to the company's share capital immediately following the cancellation—
  (a) the total number of shares of the company,
  (b) the aggregate nominal value of those shares,
  (c) for each class of shares—
    (i) prescribed particulars of the rights attached to the shares,
    (ii) the total number of shares of that class, and
    (iii) the aggregate nominal value of shares of that class, and
  (d) the amount paid up and the amount (if any) unpaid on each share (whether on account of the nominal value of the share or by way of premium).

(4) If default is made in complying with this section, an offence is committed by—
  (a) the company, and
  (b) every officer of the company who is in default.

(5) A person guilty of an offence under this section is liable on summary conviction to a fine not exceeding level 3 on the standard scale and, for continued contravention, a daily default fine not exceeding one-tenth of level 3 on the standard scale.

CHAPTER 5

REDEMPTION OR PURCHASE BY PRIVATE COMPANY OUT OF CAPITAL

Introductory

709. Power of private limited company to redeem or purchase own shares out of capital

(1) A private limited company may in accordance with this Chapter, but subject to any restriction or prohibition in the company's articles, make a payment in respect of the redemption or purchase of its own shares otherwise than out of distributable profits or the proceeds of a fresh issue of shares.

(2) References below in this Chapter to payment out of capital are to any payment so made, whether or not it would be regarded apart from this section as a payment out of capital.

The permissible capital payment

710. The permissible capital payment

(1) The payment that may, in accordance with this Chapter, be made by a company out of capital in respect of the redemption or purchase of its own shares is such amount as, after applying for that purpose—

(a) any available profits of the company, and

(b) the proceeds of any fresh issue of shares made for the purposes of the redemption or purchase,

is required to meet the price of redemption or purchase.

(2) That is referred to below in this Chapter as "the permissible capital payment" for the shares.

711. Available profits

(1) For the purposes of this Chapter the available profits of the company, in relation to the redemption or purchase of any shares, are the profits of the company that are available for distribution (within the meaning of Part 23).

(2) But the question whether a company has any profits so available, and the amount of any such profits, shall be determined in accordance with section 712 instead of in accordance with sections 836 to 842 in that Part.

712. Determination of available profits

(1) The available profits of the company are determined as follows.

(2) First, determine the profits of the company by reference to the following items as stated in the relevant accounts—

(a) profits, losses, assets and liabilities,

(b) provisions of the following kinds—

(i) where the relevant accounts are Companies Act accounts, provisions of a kind specified for the purposes of this subsection by regulations under section 396;

(ii) where the relevant accounts are IAS accounts, provisions of any kind;

(c) share capital and reserves (including undistributable reserves).

(3) Second, reduce the amount so determined by the amount of—

(a) any distribution lawfully made by the company, and

(b) any other relevant payment lawfully made by the company out of distributable profits,

after the date of the relevant accounts and before the end of the relevant period.

(4) For this purpose "other relevant payment lawfully made" includes—

(a) financial assistance lawfully given out of distributable profits in accordance with Chapter 2,

(b) payments lawfully made out of distributable profits in respect of the purchase by the company of any shares in the company, and

(c) payments of any description specified in section 705 (payments other than purchase price to be made out of distributable profits) lawfully made by the company.

(5) The resulting figure is the amount of available profits.

(6) For the purposes of this section "the relevant accounts" are any accounts that—

    (a) are prepared as at a date within the relevant period, and

    (b) are such as to enable a reasonable judgment to be made as to the amounts of the items mentioned in subsection (2).

(7) In this section "the relevant period" means the period of three months ending with the date on which the directors' statement is made in accordance with section 714.

Requirements for payment out of capital

713. Requirements for payment out of capital

(1) A payment out of capital by a private company for the redemption or purchase of its own shares is not lawful unless the requirements of the following sections are met—

section 714 (directors' statement and auditor's report);

section 716 (approval by special resolution);

section 719 (public notice of proposed payment);

section 720 (directors' statement and auditor's report to be available for inspection).

(2) This is subject to any order of the court under section 721 (power of court to extend period for compliance on application by persons objecting to payment).

714. Directors' statement and auditor's report

(1) The company's directors must make a statement in accordance with this section.

(2) The statement must specify the amount of the permissible capital payment for the shares in question.

(3) It must state that, having made full inquiry into the affairs and prospects of the company, the directors have formed the opinion—

    (a) as regards its initial situation immediately following the date on which the payment out of capital is proposed to be made, that there will be no grounds on which the company could then be found unable to pay its debts, and

    (b) as regards its prospects for the year immediately following that date, that having regard to—

        (i) their intentions with respect to the management of the company's business during that year, and

        (ii) the amount and character of the financial resources that will in their view be available to the company during that year,

    the company will be able to continue to carry on business as a going concern (and will accordingly be able to pay its debts as they fall due) throughout that year.

(4) In forming their opinion for the purposes of subsection (3)(a), the directors must take into account all of the company's liabilities (including any contingent or prospective liabilities).

(5) The directors' statement must be in the prescribed form and must contain such information with respect to the nature of the company's business as may be prescribed.

(6) It must in addition have annexed to it a report addressed to the directors by the company's auditor stating that—

    (a) he has inquired into the company's state of affairs,

    (b) the amount specified in the statement as the permissible capital payment for the shares in question is in his view properly determined in accordance with sections 710 to 712, and

    (c) he is not aware of anything to indicate that the opinion expressed by the directors in their statement as to any of the matters mentioned in subsection (3) above is unreasonable in all the circumstances.

715. Directors' statement: offence if no reasonable grounds for opinion

(1) If the directors make a statement under section 714 without having reasonable grounds for the opinion expressed in it, an offence is committed by every director who is in default.

(2) A person guilty of an offence under this section is liable—

    (a) on conviction on indictment, to imprisonment for a term not exceeding two years or a fine (or both);

    (b) on summary conviction—

        (i) in England and Wales, to imprisonment for a term not exceeding twelve months or a fine not exceeding the statutory maximum (or both);

        (ii) in Scotland or Northern Ireland, to imprisonment for a term not exceeding six months or a fine not exceeding the statutory maximum (or both).

716. Payment to be approved by special resolution

(1) The payment out of capital must be approved by a special resolution of the company.

(2) The resolution must be passed on, or within the week immediately following, the date on which the directors make the statement required by section 714.

(3) A resolution under this section is subject to—

section 717 (exercise of voting rights), and

section 718 (disclosure of directors' statement and auditors' report).

717. Resolution authorising payment: exercise of voting rights

(1) This section applies to a resolution under section 716 (authority for payment out of capital for redemption or purchase of own shares).

(2) Where the resolution is proposed as a written resolution, a member who holds shares to which the resolution relates is not an eligible member.

(3) Where the resolution is proposed at a meeting of the company, it is not effective if—

    (a) any member of the company holding shares to which the resolution relates exercises the voting rights carried by any of those shares in voting on the resolution, and

    (b) the resolution would not have been passed if he had not done so.

(4) For this purpose—

    (a) a member who holds shares to which the resolution relates is regarded as exercising the voting rights carried by those shares not only if he votes in respect of them on a poll on the question whether the resolution shall be passed, but also if he votes on the resolution otherwise than on a poll;

    (b) any member of the company may demand a poll on that question;

    (c) a vote and a demand for a poll by a person as proxy for a member are the same respectively as a vote and a demand by the member.

718. Resolution authorising payment: disclosure of directors' statement and auditor's report

(1) This section applies to a resolution under section 716 (resolution authorising payment out of capital for redemption or purchase of own shares).

(2) A copy of the directors' statement and auditor's report under section 714 must be made available to members—

    (a) in the case of a written resolution, by being sent or submitted to every eligible member at or before the time at which the proposed resolution is sent or submitted to him;

    (b) in the case of a resolution at a meeting, by being made available for inspection by members of the company at the meeting.

(3) The resolution is ineffective if this requirement is not complied with.

719. Public notice of proposed payment

(1) Within the week immediately following the date of the resolution under section 716 the company must cause to be published in the Gazette a notice—

    (a) stating that the company has approved a payment out of capital for the purpose of acquiring its own shares by redemption or purchase or both (as the case may be),

    (b) specifying—

        (i) the amount of the permissible capital payment for the shares in question, and

        (ii) the date of the resolution,

    (c) stating where the directors' statement and auditor's report required by section 714 are available for inspection, and

    (d) stating that any creditor of the company may at any time within the five weeks immediately following the date of the resolution apply to the court under section 721 for an order preventing the payment.

(2) Within the week immediately following the date of the resolution the company must also either—

    (a) cause a notice to the same effect as that required by subsection (1) to be published in an appropriate national newspaper, or

    (b) give notice in writing to that effect to each of its creditors.

(3) "An appropriate national newspaper" means a newspaper circulating throughout the part of the United Kingdom in which the company is registered.

(4) Not later than the day on which the company—

    (a) first publishes the notice required by subsection (1), or

    (b) if earlier, first publishes or gives the notice required by subsection (2),

the company must deliver to the registrar a copy of the directors' statement and auditor's report required by section 714.

720. Directors' statement and auditor's report to be available for inspection

(1) The directors' statement and auditor's report must be kept available for inspection throughout the period—

    (a) beginning with the day on which the company—

        (i) first publishes the notice required by section 719(1), or

        (ii) if earlier, first publishes or gives the notice required by section 719(2), and

    (b) ending five weeks after the date of the resolution for payment out of capital.

(2) They must be kept available for inspection—

    (a) at the company's registered office, or

    (b) at a place specified in regulations under section 1136.

(3) The company must give notice to the registrar—

    (a) of the place at which the statement and report are kept available for inspection, and

    (b) of any change in that place,

unless they have at all times been kept at the company's registered office.

(4) They must be open to the inspection of any member or creditor of the company without charge.

(5) If default is made for 14 days in complying with subsection (3), or an inspection under subsection (4) is refused, an offence is committed by—

    (a) the company, and

    (b) every officer of the company who is in default.

(6) A person guilty of an offence under this section is liable on summary conviction to a fine not exceeding level 3 on the standard scale and, for continued contravention, a daily default fine not exceeding one-tenth of level 3 on the standard scale.

(7) In the case of a refusal of an inspection required by subsection (4), the court may by order compel an immediate inspection.

Objection to payment by members or creditors

721. Application to court to cancel resolution

(1) Where a private company passes a special resolution approving a payment out of capital for the redemption or purchase of any of its shares—

    (a) any member of the company (other than one who consented to or voted in favour of the resolution), and

    (b) any creditor of the company,

may apply to the court for the cancellation of the resolution.

(2) The application—

    (a) must be made within five weeks after the passing of the resolution, and

    (b) may be made on behalf of the persons entitled to make it by such one or more of their number as they may appoint in writing for the purpose.

(3) On an application under this section the court may if it thinks fit—

    (a) adjourn the proceedings in order that an arrangement may be made to the satisfaction of the court—

        (i) for the purchase of the interests of dissentient members, or

        (ii) for the protection of dissentient creditors, and

    (b) give such directions and make such orders as it thinks expedient for facilitating or carrying into effect any such arrangement.

(4) Subject to that, the court must make an order either cancelling or confirming the resolution, and may do so on such terms and conditions as it thinks fit.

(5) If the court confirms the resolution, it may by order alter or extend any date or period of time specified—

    (a) in the resolution, or

    (b) in any provision of this Chapter applying to the redemption or purchase to which the resolution relates.

(6) The court's order may, if the court thinks fit—

    (a) provide for the purchase by the company of the shares of any of its members and for the reduction accordingly of the company's capital, and

    (b) make any alteration in the company's articles that may be required in consequence of that provision.

(7) The court's order may, if the court thinks fit, require the company not to make any, or any specified, amendments of its articles without the leave of the court.

722. Notice to registrar of court application or order

(1) On making an application under section 721 (application to court to cancel resolution) the applicants, or the person making the application on their behalf, must immediately give notice to the registrar.

This is without prejudice to any provision of rules of court as to service of notice of the application.

(2) On being served with notice of any such application, the company must immediately give notice to the registrar.

(3) Within 15 days of the making of the court's order on the application, or such longer period as the court may at any time direct, the company must deliver to the registrar a copy of the order.

(4) If a company fails to comply with subsection (2) or (3) an offence is committed by—

    (a) the company, and

    (b) every officer of the company who is in default.

(5) A person guilty of an offence under this section is liable on summary conviction to a fine not exceeding level 3 on the standard scale and, for continued contravention, a daily default fine not exceeding one-tenth of level 3 on the standard scale.

Supplementary provisions

723. When payment out of capital to be made

(1) The payment out of capital must be made—

    (a) no earlier than five weeks after the date on which the resolution under section 716 is passed, and

    (b) no more than seven weeks after that date.

(2) This is subject to any exercise of the court's powers under section 721(5) (power to alter or extend time where resolution confirmed after objection).

CHAPTER 6
TREASURY SHARES

724. Treasury shares

(1) This section applies where—
  (a) a limited company makes a purchase of its own shares in accordance with Chapter 4,
  (b) the purchase is made out of distributable profits, and
  (c) the shares are qualifying shares.

(2) For this purpose "qualifying shares" means shares that—
  (a) are included in the official list in accordance with the provisions of Part 6 of the Financial Services and Markets Act 2000 (c. 8),
  (b) are traded on the market known as the Alternative Investment Market established under the rules of London Stock Exchange plc,
  (c) are officially listed in an EEA State, or
  (d) are traded on a regulated market.
  In paragraph (a) "the official list" has the meaning given in section 103(1) of the Financial Services and Markets Act 2000.

(3) Where this section applies the company may—
  (a) hold the shares (or any of them), or
  (b) deal with any of them, at any time, in accordance with section 727 or 729.

(4) Where shares are held by the company, the company must be entered in its register of members as the member holding the shares.

(5) In the Companies Acts references to a company holding shares as treasury shares are to the company holding shares that—
  (a) were (or are treated as having been) purchased by it in circumstances in which this section applies, and
  (b) have been held by the company continuously since they were so purchased (or treated as purchased).

725. Treasury shares: maximum holdings

(1) Where a company has shares of only one class, the aggregate nominal value of shares held as treasury shares must not at any time exceed 10% of the nominal value of the issued share capital of the company at that time.

(2) Where the share capital of a company is divided into shares of different classes, the aggregate nominal value of the shares of any class held as treasury shares must not at any time exceed 10% of the nominal value of the issued share capital of the shares of that class at that time.

(3) If subsection (1) or (2) is contravened by a company, the company must dispose of or cancel the excess shares, in accordance with section 727 or 729, before the end of the period of twelve months beginning with the date on which that contravention occurs.
  The "excess shares" means such number of the shares held by the company as treasury shares at the time in question as resulted in the limit being exceeded.

(4) Where a company purchases qualifying shares out of distributable profits in accordance with section 724, a contravention by the company of subsection (1) or (2) above does not render the acquisition void under section 658 (general rule against limited company acquiring its own shares).

726. Treasury shares: exercise of rights

(1) This section applies where shares are held by a company as treasury shares.

(2) The company must not exercise any right in respect of the treasury shares, and any purported exercise of such a right is void.

This applies, in particular, to any right to attend or vote at meetings.

(3) No dividend may be paid, and no other distribution (whether in cash or otherwise) of the company's assets (including any distribution of assets to members on a winding up) may be made to the company, in respect of the treasury shares.

(4) Nothing in this section prevents—

    (a) an allotment of shares as fully paid bonus shares in respect of the treasury shares, or

    (b) the payment of any amount payable on the redemption of the treasury shares (if they are redeemable shares).

(5) Shares allotted as fully paid bonus shares in respect of the treasury shares are treated as if purchased by the company, at the time they were allotted, in circumstances in which section 724(1) (treasury shares) applied.

727. Treasury shares: disposal

(1) Where shares are held as treasury shares, the company may at any time—

    (a) sell the shares (or any of them) for a cash consideration, or

    (b) transfer the shares (or any of them) for the purposes of or pursuant to an employees' share scheme.

(2) In subsection (1)(a) "cash consideration" means—

    (a) cash received by the company, or

    (b) a cheque received by the company in good faith that the directors have no reason for suspecting will not be paid, or

    (c) a release of a liability of the company for a liquidated sum, or

    (d) an undertaking to pay cash to the company on or before a date not more than 90 days after the date on which the company agrees to sell the shares, or

    (e) payment by any other means giving rise to a present or future entitlement (of the company or a person acting on the company's behalf) to a payment, or credit equivalent to payment, in cash.

For this purpose "cash" includes foreign currency.

(3) The Secretary of State may by order provide that particular means of payment specified in the order are to be regarded as falling within subsection (2)(e).

(4) If the company receives a notice under section 979 (takeover offers: right of offeror to buy out minority shareholders) that a person desires to acquire shares held by the company as treasury shares, the company must not sell or transfer the shares to which the notice relates except to that person.

(5) An order under this section is subject to negative resolution procedure.

728. Treasury shares: notice of disposal

(1) Where shares held by a company as treasury shares—

    (a) are sold, or

    (b) are transferred for the purposes of an employees' share scheme,

the company must deliver a return to the registrar not later than 28 days after the shares are disposed of.

(2) The return must state with respect to shares of each class disposed of—

    (a) the number and nominal value of the shares, and

    (b) the date on which they were disposed of.

(3) Particulars of shares disposed of on different dates may be included in a single return.

(4) If default is made in complying with this section an offence is committed by every officer of the company who is in default.

(5) A person guilty of an offence under this section is liable—

    (a) on conviction on indictment, to a fine;

(b) on summary conviction, to a fine not exceeding the statutory maximum and, for continued contravention, a daily default fine not exceeding one-tenth of the statutory maximum.

729. Treasury shares: cancellation

(1) Where shares are held as treasury shares, the company may at any time cancel the shares (or any of them).

(2) If shares held as treasury shares cease to be qualifying shares, the company must forthwith cancel the shares.

(3) For this purpose shares are not to be regarded as ceasing to be qualifying shares by virtue only of—

    (a) the suspension of their listing in accordance with the applicable rules in the EEA State in which the shares are officially listed, or

    (b) the suspension of their trading in accordance with—

        (i) in the case of shares traded on the market known as the Alternative Investment Market, the rules of London Stock Exchange plc, and

        (ii) in any other case, the rules of the regulated market on which they are traded.

(4) If company cancels shares held as treasury shares, the amount of the company's share capital is reduced accordingly by the nominal amount of the shares cancelled.

(5) The directors may take any steps required to enable the company to cancel its shares under this section without complying with the provisions of Chapter 10 of Part 17 (reduction of share capital).

730. Treasury shares: notice of cancellation

(1) Where shares held by a company as treasury shares are cancelled, the company must deliver a return to the registrar not later than 28 days after the shares are cancelled.

This does not apply to shares that are cancelled forthwith on their acquisition by the company (see section 708).

(2) The return must state with respect to shares of each class cancelled—

    (a) the number and nominal value of the shares, and

    (b) the date on which they were cancelled.

(3) Particulars of shares cancelled on different dates may be included in a single return.

(4) The notice must be accompanied by a statement of capital.

(5) The statement of capital must state with respect to the company's share capital immediately following the cancellation—

    (a) the total number of shares of the company,

    (b) the aggregate nominal value of those shares,

    (c) for each class of shares—

        (i) prescribed particulars of the rights attached to the shares,

        (ii) the total number of shares of that class, and

        (iii) the aggregate nominal value of shares of that class, and

    (d) the amount paid up and the amount (if any) unpaid on each share (whether on account of the nominal value of the share or by way of premium).

(6) If default is made in complying with this section, an offence is committed by—

    (a) the company, and

    (b) every officer of the company who is in default.

(7) A person guilty of an offence under this section is liable on summary conviction to a fine not exceeding level 3 on the standard scale and, for continued contravention, a daily default fine not exceeding one-tenth of level 3 on the standard scale.

731. Treasury shares: treatment of proceeds of sale

(1) Where shares held as treasury shares are sold, the proceeds of sale must be dealt with in accordance with this section.

(2) If the proceeds of sale are equal to or less than the purchase price paid by the company for the shares, the proceeds are treated for the purposes of Part 23 (distributions) as a realised profit of the company.

(3) If the proceeds of sale exceed the purchase price paid by the company—

    (a) an amount equal to the purchase price paid is treated as a realised profit of the company for the purposes of that Part, and

    (b) the excess must be transferred to the company's share premium account.

(4) For the purposes of this section—

    (a) the purchase price paid by the company must be determined by the application of a weighted average price method, and

    (b) if the shares were allotted to the company as fully paid bonus shares, the purchase price paid for them is treated as nil.

732. Treasury shares: offences

(1) If a company contravenes any of the provisions of this Chapter (except section 730 (notice of cancellation)), an offence is committed by—

    (a) the company, and

    (b) every officer of the company who is in default.

(2) A person guilty of an offence under this section is liable—

    (a) on conviction on indictment, to a fine;

    (b) on summary conviction to a fine not exceeding the statutory maximum.

CHAPTER 7
SUPPLEMENTARY PROVISIONS

733. The capital redemption reserve

(1) In the following circumstances a company must transfer amounts to a reserve, called the "capital redemption reserve".

(2) Where under this Part shares of a limited company are redeemed or purchased wholly out of the company's profits, the amount by which the company's issued share capital is diminished in accordance with—

    (a) section 688(b) (on the cancellation of shares redeemed), or

    (b) section 706(b)(ii) (on the cancellation of shares purchased),

must be transferred to the capital redemption reserve.

(3) If—

    (a) the shares are redeemed or purchased wholly or partly out of the proceeds of a fresh issue, and

    (b) the aggregate amount of the proceeds is less than the aggregate nominal value of the shares redeemed or purchased,

the amount of the difference must be transferred to the capital redemption reserve.

This does not apply in the case of a private company if, in addition to the proceeds of the fresh issue, the company applies a payment out of capital under Chapter 5 in making the redemption or purchase.

(4) The amount by which a company's share capital is diminished in accordance with section 729(4) (on the cancellation of shares held as treasury shares) must be transferred to the capital redemption reserve.

(5) The company may use the capital redemption reserve to pay up new shares to be allotted to members as fully paid bonus shares.

(6) Subject to that, the provisions of the Companies Acts relating to the reduction of a company's share capital apply as if the capital redemption reserve were part of its paid up share capital.

734. **Accounting consequences of payment out of capital**

(1) This section applies where a payment out of capital is made in accordance with Chapter 5 (redemption or purchase of own shares by private company out of capital).

(2) If the permissible capital payment is less than the nominal amount of the shares redeemed or purchased, the amount of the difference must be transferred to the company's capital redemption reserve.

(3) If the permissible capital payment is greater than the nominal amount of the shares redeemed or purchased—

  (a) the amount of any capital redemption reserve, share premium account or fully paid share capital of the company, and

  (b) any amount representing unrealised profits of the company for the time being standing to the credit of any revaluation reserve maintained by the company,

may be reduced by a sum not exceeding (or by sums not in total exceeding) the amount by which the permissible capital payment exceeds the nominal amount of the shares.

(4) Where the proceeds of a fresh issue are applied by the company in making a redemption or purchase of its own shares in addition to a payment out of capital under this Chapter, the references in subsections (2) and (3) to the permissible capital payment are to be read as referring to the aggregate of that payment and those proceeds.

735. **Effect of company's failure to redeem or purchase**

(1) This section applies where a company—

  (a) issues shares on terms that they are or are liable to be redeemed, or

  (b) agrees to purchase any of its shares.

(2) The company is not liable in damages in respect of any failure on its part to redeem or purchase any of the shares.

This is without prejudice to any right of the holder of the shares other than his right to sue the company for damages in respect of its failure.

(3) The court shall not grant an order for specific performance of the terms of redemption or purchase if the company shows that it is unable to meet the costs of redeeming or purchasing the shares in question out of distributable profits.

(4) If the company is wound up and at the commencement of the winding up any of the shares have not been redeemed or purchased, the terms of redemption or purchase may be enforced against the company.

When shares are redeemed or purchased under this subsection, they are treated as cancelled.

(5) Subsection (4) does not apply if—

  (a) the terms provided for the redemption or purchase to take place at a date later than that of the commencement of the winding up, or

  (b) during the period—

    (i) beginning with the date on which the redemption or purchase was to have taken place, and

    (ii) ending with the commencement of the winding up,

  the company could not at any time have lawfully made a distribution equal in value to the price at which the shares were to have been redeemed or purchased.

(6) There shall be paid in priority to any amount that the company is liable under subsection (4) to pay in respect of any shares—

  (a) all other debts and liabilities of the company (other than any due to members in their character as such), and

  (b) if other shares carry rights (whether as to capital or as to income) that are preferred to the rights as to capital attaching to the first-mentioned shares, any amount due in satisfaction of those preferred rights.

Subject to that, any such amount shall be paid in priority to any amounts due to members in satisfaction of their rights (whether as to capital or income) as members.

736. **Meaning of "distributable profits"**

In this Part (except in Chapter 2 (financial assistance): see section 683) "distributable profits", in relation to the making of any payment by a company, means profits out of which the company could lawfully make a distribution (within the meaning given by section 830) equal in value to the payment.

737. **General power to make further provision by regulations**

(1) The Secretary of State may by regulations modify the provisions of this Part.

(2) The regulations may—

(a) amend or repeal any of the provisions of this Part, or

(b) make such other provision as appears to the Secretary of State appropriate in place of any of the provisions of this Part.

(3) Regulations under this section may make consequential amendments or repeals in other provisions of this Act, or in other enactments.

(4) Regulations under this section are subject to affirmative resolution procedure.

PART 19

DEBENTURES

General provisions

738. **Meaning of "debenture"**

In the Companies Acts "debenture" includes debenture stock, bonds and any other securities of a company, whether or not constituting a charge on the assets of the company.

739. **Perpetual debentures**

(1) A condition contained in debentures, or in a deed for securing debentures, is not invalid by reason only that the debentures are made—

(a) irredeemable, or

(b) redeemable only—

(i) on the happening of a contingency (however remote), or

(ii) on the expiration of a period (however long),

any rule of equity to the contrary notwithstanding.

(2) Subsection (1) applies to debentures whenever issued and to deeds whenever executed.

740. **Enforcement of contract to subscribe for debentures**

A contract with a company to take up and pay for debentures of the company may be enforced by an order for specific performance.

741. **Registration of allotment of debentures**

(1) A company must register an allotment of debentures as soon as practicable and in any event within two months after the date of the allotment.

(2) If a company fails to comply with this section, an offence is committed by—

(a) the company, and

(b) every officer of the company who is in default.

(3) A person guilty of an offence under this section is liable on summary conviction to a fine not exceeding level 3 on the standard scale and, for continued contravention, a daily default fine not exceeding one-tenth of level 3 on the standard scale.

(4) For the duties of the company as to the issue of the debentures, or certificates of debenture stock, see Part 21 (certification and transfer of securities)

742. **Debentures to bearer (Scotland)**

Notwithstanding anything in the statute of the Scots Parliament of 1696, chapter 25, debentures to bearer issued in Scotland are valid and binding according to their terms.

Register of debenture holders

743. **Register of debenture holders**

   (1) Any register of debenture holders of a company that is kept by the company must be kept available for inspection—

   (a) at the company's registered office, or

   (b) at a place specified in regulations under section 1136.

   (2) A company must give notice to the registrar of the place where any such register is kept available for inspection and of any change in that place.

   (3) No such notice is required if the register has, at all times since it came into existence, been kept available for inspection at the company's registered office.

   (4) If a company makes default for 14 days in complying with subsection (2), an offence is committed by—

   (a) the company, and

   (b) every officer of the company who is in default.

   (5) A person guilty of an offence under this section is liable on summary conviction to a fine not exceeding level 3 on the standard scale and, for continued contravention, a daily default fine not exceeding one-tenth of level 3 on the standard scale.

   (6) References in this section to a register of debenture holders include a duplicate—

   (a) of a register of debenture holders that is kept outside the United Kingdom, or

   (b) of any part of such a register.

744. **Register of debenture holders: right to inspect and require copy**

   (1) Every register of debenture holders of a company must, except when duly closed, be open to the inspection—

   (a) of the registered holder of any such debentures, or any holder of shares in the company, without charge, and

   (b) of any other person on payment of such fee as may be prescribed.

   (2) Any person may require a copy of the register, or any part of it, on payment of such fee as may be prescribed.

   (3) A person seeking to exercise either of the rights conferred by this section must make a request to the company to that effect.

   (4) The request must contain the following information—

   (a) in the case of an individual, his name and address;

   (b) in the case of an organisation, the name and address of an individual responsible for making the request on behalf of the organisation;

   (c) the purpose for which the information is to be used; and

   (d) whether the information will be disclosed to any other person, and if so—

   (i) where that person is an individual, his name and address,

   (ii) where that person is an organisation, the name and address of an individual responsible for receiving the information on its behalf, and

   (iii) the purpose for which the information is to be used by that person.

   (5) For the purposes of this section a register is "duly closed" if it is closed in accordance with provision contained—

   (a) in the articles or in the debentures,

   (b) in the case of debenture stock in the stock certificates, or

   (c) in the trust deed or other document securing the debentures or debenture stock.

   The total period for which a register is closed in any year must not exceed 30 days.

   (6) References in this section to a register of debenture holders include a duplicate—

   (a) of a register of debenture holders that is kept outside the United Kingdom, or

   (b) of any part of such a register.

745. **Register of debenture holders: response to request for inspection or copy**

(1) Where a company receives a request under section 744 (register of debenture holders: right to inspect and require copy), it must within five working days either—

(a) comply with the request, or

(b) apply to the court.

(2) If it applies to the court it must notify the person making the request.

(3) If on an application under this section the court is satisfied that the inspection or copy is not sought for a proper purpose—

(a) it shall direct the company not to comply with the request, and

(b) it may further order that the company's costs (in Scotland, expenses) on the application be paid in whole or in part by the person who made the request, even if he is not a party to the application.

(4) If the court makes such a direction and it appears to the court that the company is or may be subject to other requests made for a similar purpose (whether made by the same person or different persons), it may direct that the company is not to comply with any such request.

The order must contain such provision as appears to the court appropriate to identify the requests to which it applies.

(5) If on an application under this section the court does not direct the company not to comply with the request, the company must comply with the request immediately upon the court giving its decision or, as the case may be, the proceedings being discontinued.

746. **Register of debenture holders: refusal of inspection or default in providing copy**

(1) If an inspection required under section 744 (register of debenture holders: right to inspect and require copy) is refused or default is made in providing a copy required under that section, otherwise than in accordance with an order of the court, an offence is committed by—

(a) the company, and

(b) every officer of the company who is in default.

(2) A person guilty of an offence under this section is liable on summary conviction to a fine not exceeding level 3 on the standard scale and, for continued contravention, a daily default fine not exceeding one-tenth of level 3 on the standard scale.

(3) In the case of any such refusal or default the court may by order compel an immediate inspection or, as the case may be, direct that the copy required be sent to the person requesting it.

747. **Register of debenture holders: offences in connection with request for or disclosure of information**

(1) It is an offence for a person knowingly or recklessly to make in a request under section 744 (register of debenture holders: right to inspect and require copy) a statement that is misleading, false or deceptive in a material particular.

(2) It is an offence for a person in possession of information obtained by exercise of either of the rights conferred by that section—

(a) to do anything that results in the information being disclosed to another person, or

(b) to fail to do anything with the result that the information is disclosed to another person, knowing, or having reason to suspect, that person may use the information for a purpose that is not a proper purpose.

(3) A person guilty of an offence under this section is liable—

(a) on conviction on indictment, to imprisonment for a term not exceeding two years or a fine (or both);

(b) on summary conviction—

(i) in England and Wales, to imprisonment for a term not exceeding twelve months or to a fine not exceeding the statutory maximum (or both);

(ii) in Scotland or Northern Ireland, to imprisonment for a term not exceeding six months, or to a fine not exceeding the statutory maximum (or both).

748. Time limit for claims arising from entry in register

   (1) Liability incurred by a company—

      (a) from the making or deletion of an entry in the register of debenture holders, or

      (b) from a failure to make or delete any such entry,

   is not enforceable more than ten years after the date on which the entry was made or deleted or, as the case may be, the failure first occurred.

   (2) This is without prejudice to any lesser period of limitation (and, in Scotland, to any rule that the obligation giving rise to the liability prescribes before the expiry of that period).

Supplementary provisions

749. Right of debenture holder to copy of deed

   (1) Any holder of debentures of a company is entitled, on request and on payment of such fee as may be prescribed, to be provided with a copy of any trust deed for securing the debentures.

   (2) If default is made in complying with this section, an offence is committed by every officer of the company who is in default.

   (3) A person guilty of an offence under this section is liable on summary conviction to a fine not exceeding level 3 on the standard scale and, for continued contravention, a daily default fine not exceeding one-tenth of level 3 on the standard scale.

   (4) In the case of any such default the court may direct that the copy required be sent to the person requiring it.

750. Liability of trustees of debentures

   (1) Any provision contained in—

      (a) a trust deed for securing an issue of debentures, or

      (b) any contract with the holders of debentures secured by a trust deed,

   is void in so far as it would have the effect of exempting a trustee of the deed from, or indemnifying him against, liability for breach of trust where he fails to show the degree of care and diligence required of him as trustee, having regard to the provisions of the trust deed conferring on him any powers, authorities or discretions.

   (2) Subsection (1) does not invalidate—

      (a) a release otherwise validly given in respect of anything done or omitted to be done by a trustee before the giving of the release;

      (b) any provision enabling such a release to be given—

         (i) on being agreed to by a majority of not less than 75% in value of the debenture holders present and voting in person or, where proxies are permitted, by proxy at a meeting summoned for the purpose, and

         (ii) either with respect to specific acts or omissions or on the trustee dying or ceasing to act.

   (3) This section is subject to section 751 (saving for certain older provisions).

751. Liability of trustees of debentures: saving for certain older provisions

   (1) Section 750 (liability of trustees of debentures) does not operate—

      (a) to invalidate any provision in force on the relevant date so long as any person—

         (i) then entitled to the benefit of the provision, or

         (ii) afterwards given the benefit of the provision under subsection (3) below,

      remains a trustee of the deed in question, or

      (b) to deprive any person of any exemption or right to be indemnified in respect of anything done or omitted to be done by him while any such provision was in force.

   (2) The relevant date for this purpose is—

      (a) 1st July 1948 in a case where section 192 of the Companies Act 1985 (c. 6) applied immediately before the commencement of this section;

(b) 1st July 1961 in a case where Article 201 of the Companies (Northern Ireland) Order 1986 (S.I. 1986/1032 (N.I. 6)) then applied.

(3) While any trustee of a trust deed remains entitled to the benefit of a provision saved by subsection (1) above the benefit of that provision may be given either—

(a) to all trustees of the deed, present and future, or

(b) to any named trustees or proposed trustees of it,

by a resolution passed by a majority of not less than 75% in value of the debenture holders present in person or, where proxies are permitted, by proxy at a meeting summoned for the purpose.

(4) A meeting for that purpose must be summoned in accordance with the provisions of the deed or, if the deed makes no provision for summoning meetings, in a manner approved by the court.

752. Power to re-issue redeemed debentures

(1) Where a company has redeemed debentures previously issued, then unless—

(a) provision to the contrary (express or implied) is contained in the company's articles or in any contract made by the company, or

(b) the company has, by passing a resolution to that effect or by some other act, manifested its intention that the debentures shall be cancelled,

the company may re-issue the debentures, either by re-issuing the same debentures or by issuing new debentures in their place.

This subsection is deemed always to have had effect.

(2) On a re-issue of redeemed debentures the person entitled to the debentures has (and is deemed always to have had) the same priorities as if the debentures had never been redeemed.

(3) The re-issue of a debenture or the issue of another debenture in its place under this section is treated as the issue of a new debenture for the purposes of stamp duty.

It is not so treated for the purposes of any provision limiting the amount or number of debentures to be issued.

(4) A person lending money on the security of a debenture re-issued under this section which appears to be duly stamped may give the debenture in evidence in any proceedings for enforcing his security without payment of the stamp duty or any penalty in respect of it, unless he had notice (or, but for his negligence, might have discovered) that the debenture was not duly stamped. In that case the company is liable to pay the proper stamp duty and penalty.

753. Deposit of debentures to secure advances

Where a company has deposited any of its debentures to secure advances from time to time on current account or otherwise, the debentures are not treated as redeemed by reason only of the company's account having ceased to be in debit while the debentures remained so deposited.

754. Priorities where debentures secured by floating charge

(1) This section applies where debentures of a company registered in England and Wales or Northern Ireland are secured by a charge that, as created, was a floating charge.

(2) If possession is taken, by or on behalf of the holders of the debentures, of any property comprised in or subject to the charge, and the company is not at that time in the course of being wound up, the company's preferential debts shall be paid out of assets coming to the hands of the persons taking possession in priority to any claims for principal or interest in respect of the debentures.

(3) "Preferential debts" means the categories of debts listed in Schedule 6 to the Insolvency Act 1986 (c. 45) or Schedule 4 to the Insolvency (Northern Ireland) Order 1989 (S.I. 1989/2405 (N.I. 19)).

For the purposes of those Schedules "the relevant date" is the date of possession being taken as mentioned in subsection (2).

(4) Payments under this section shall be recouped, as far as may be, out of the assets of the company available for payment of general creditors.

PART 20
PRIVATE AND PUBLIC COMPANIES

CHAPTER 1
PROHIBITION OF PUBLIC OFFERS BY PRIVATE COMPANIES

755. Prohibition of public offers by private company

(1) A private company limited by shares or limited by guarantee and having a share capital must not—

  (a) offer to the public any securities of the company, or

  (b) allot or agree to allot any securities of the company with a view to their being offered to the public.

(2) Unless the contrary is proved, an allotment or agreement to allot securities is presumed to be made with a view to their being offered to the public if an offer of the securities (or any of them) to the public is made—

  (a) within six months after the allotment or agreement to allot, or

  (b) before the receipt by the company of the whole of the consideration to be received by it in respect of the securities.

(3) A company does not contravene this section if—

  (a) it acts in good faith in pursuance of arrangements under which it is to re-register as a public company before the securities are allotted, or

  (b) as part of the terms of the offer it undertakes to re-register as a public company within a specified period, and that undertaking is complied with.

(4) The specified period for the purposes of subsection (3)(b) must be a period ending not later than six months after the day on which the offer is made (or, in the case of an offer made on different days, first made).

(5) In this Chapter "securities" means shares or debentures.

756. Meaning of "offer to the public"

(1) This section explains what is meant in this Chapter by an offer of securities to the public.

(2) An offer to the public includes an offer to any section of the public, however selected.

(3) An offer is not regarded as an offer to the public if it can properly be regarded, in all the circumstances, as—

  (a) not being calculated to result, directly or indirectly, in securities of the company becoming available to persons other than those receiving the offer, or

  (b) otherwise being a private concern of the person receiving it and the person making it.

(4) An offer is to be regarded (unless the contrary is proved) as being a private concern of the person receiving it and the person making it if—

  (a) it is made to a person already connected with the company and, where it is made on terms allowing that person to renounce his rights, the rights may only be renounced in favour of another person already connected with the company; or

  (b) it is an offer to subscribe for securities to be held under an employees' share scheme and, where it is made on terms allowing that person to renounce his rights, the rights may only be renounced in favour of—

    (i) another person entitled to hold securities under the scheme, or

    (ii) a person already connected with the company.

(5) For the purposes of this section "person already connected with the company" means—

  (a) an existing member or employee of the company,

473

    (b) a member of the family of a person who is or was a member or employee of the company,

    (c) the widow or widower, or surviving civil partner, of a person who was a member or employee of the company,

    (d) an existing debenture holder of the company, or

    (e) a trustee (acting in his capacity as such) of a trust of which the principal beneficiary is a person within any of paragraphs (a) to (d).

(6) For the purposes of subsection (5)(b) the members of a person's family are the person's spouse or civil partner and children (including step-children) and their descendants.

757. Enforcement of prohibition: order restraining proposed contravention

(1) If it appears to the court—

    (a) on an application under this section, or

    (b) in proceedings under Part 30 (protection of members against unfair prejudice),

that a company is proposing to act in contravention of section 755 (prohibition of public offers by private companies), the court shall make an order under this section.

(2) An order under this section is an order restraining the company from contravening that section.

(3) An application for an order under this section may be made by—

    (a) a member or creditor of the company, or

    (b) the Secretary of State.

758. Enforcement of prohibition: orders available to the court after contravention

(1) This section applies if it appears to the court—

    (a) on an application under this section, or

    (b) in proceedings under Part 30 (protection of members against unfair prejudice),

that a company has acted in contravention of section 755 (prohibition of public offers by private companies).

(2) The court must make an order requiring the company to re-register as a public company unless it appears to the court—

    (a) that the company does not meet the requirements for re-registration as a public company, and

    (b) that it is impractical or undesirable to require it to take steps to do so.

(3) If it does not make an order for re-registration, the court may make either or both of the following—

    (a) a remedial order (see section 759), or

    (b) an order for the compulsory winding up of the company.

(4) An application under this section may be made by—

    (a) a member of the company who—

        (i) was a member at the time the offer was made (or, if the offer was made over a period, at any time during that period), or

        (ii) became a member as a result of the offer,

    (b) a creditor of the company who was a creditor at the time the offer was made (or, if the offer was made over a period, at any time during that period), or

    (c) the Secretary of State.

759. Enforcement of prohibition: remedial order

(1) A "remedial order" is an order for the purpose of putting a person affected by anything done in contravention of section 755 (prohibition of public offers by private company) in the position he would have been in if it had not been done.

(2) The following provisions are without prejudice to the generality of the power to make such an order.

(3) Where a private company has—

    (a) allotted securities pursuant to an offer to the public, or

    (b) allotted or agreed to allot securities with a view to their being offered to the public, a remedial order may require any person knowingly concerned in the contravention of section 755 to offer to purchase any of those securities at such price and on such other terms as the court thinks fit.

(4) A remedial order may be made—

    (a) against any person knowingly concerned in the contravention, whether or not an officer of the company;

    (b) notwithstanding anything in the company's constitution (which includes, for this purpose, the terms on which any securities of the company are allotted or held);

    (c) whether or not the holder of the securities subject to the order is the person to whom the company allotted or agreed to allot them.

(5) Where a remedial order is made against the company itself, the court may provide for the reduction of the company's capital accordingly.

760. Validity of allotment etc not affected

Nothing in this Chapter affects the validity of any allotment or sale of securities or of any agreement to allot or sell securities.

CHAPTER 2
MINIMUM SHARE CAPITAL REQUIREMENT FOR PUBLIC COMPANIES

761. Public company: requirement as to minimum share capital

(1) A company that is a public company (otherwise than by virtue of re-registration as a public company) must not do business or exercise any borrowing powers unless the registrar has issued it with a certificate under this section (a "trading certificate").

(2) The registrar shall issue a trading certificate if, on an application made in accordance with section 762, he is satisfied that the nominal value of the company's allotted share capital is not less than the authorised minimum.

(3) For this purpose a share allotted in pursuance of an employees' share scheme shall not be taken into account unless paid up as to—

    (a) at least one-quarter of the nominal value of the share, and

    (b) the whole of any premium on the share.

(4) A trading certificate has effect from the date on which it is issued and is conclusive evidence that the company is entitled to do business and exercise any borrowing powers.

762. Procedure for obtaining certificate

(1) An application for a certificate under section 761 must—

    (a) state that the nominal value of the company's allotted share capital is not less than the authorised minimum,

    (b) specify the amount, or estimated amount, of the company's preliminary expenses,

    (c) specify any amount or benefit paid or given, or intended to be paid or given, to any promoter of the company, and the consideration for the payment or benefit, and

    (d) be accompanied by a statement of compliance.

(2) The statement of compliance is a statement that the company meets the requirements for the issue of a certificate under section 761.

(3) The registrar may accept the statement of compliance as sufficient evidence of the matters stated in it.

763. The authorised minimum

(1) "The authorised minimum", in relation to the nominal value of a public company's allotted share capital is—

    (a) £50,000, or

    (b) the prescribed euro equivalent.

(2) The Secretary of State may by order prescribe the amount in euros that is for the time being to be treated as equivalent to the sterling amount of the authorised minimum.

(3) This power may be exercised from time to time as appears to the Secretary of State to be appropriate.

(4) The amount prescribed shall be determined by applying an appropriate spot rate of exchange to the sterling amount and rounding to the nearest 100 euros.

(5) An order under this section is subject to negative resolution procedure.

(6) This section has effect subject to any exercise of the power conferred by section 764 (power to alter authorised minimum).

764. **Power to alter authorised minimum**

(1) The Secretary of State may by order—

    (a) alter the sterling amount of the authorised minimum, and

    (b) make a corresponding alteration of the prescribed euro equivalent.

(2) The amount of the prescribed euro equivalent shall be determined by applying an appropriate spot rate of exchange to the sterling amount and rounding to the nearest 100 euros.

(3) An order under this section that increases the authorised minimum may—

    (a) require a public company having an allotted share capital of which the nominal value is less than the amount specified in the order to—

        (i) increase that value to not less than that amount, or

        (ii) re-register as a private company;

    (b) make provision in connection with any such requirement for any of the matters for which provision is made by this Act relating to—

        (i) a company's registration, re-registration or change of name,

        (ii) payment for shares comprised in a company's share capital, and

        (iii) offers to the public of shares in or debentures of a company,

        including provision as to the consequences (in criminal law or otherwise) of a failure to comply with any requirement of the order;

    (c) provide for any provision of the order to come into force on different days for different purposes.

(4) An order under this section is subject to affirmative resolution procedure.

765. **Authorised minimum: application of initial requirement**

(1) The initial requirement for a public company to have allotted share capital of a nominal value not less than the authorised minimum, that is—

    (a) the requirement in section 761(2) for the issue of a trading certificate, or

    (b) the requirement in section 91(1)(a) for re-registration as a public company,

    must be met either by reference to allotted share capital denominated in sterling or by reference to allotted share capital denominated in euros (but not partly in one and partly in the other).

(2) Whether the requirement is met is determined in the first case by reference to the sterling amount and in the second case by reference to the prescribed euro equivalent.

(3) No account is to be taken of any allotted share capital of the company denominated in a currency other than sterling or, as the case may be, euros.

(4) If the company could meet the requirement either by reference to share capital denominated in sterling or by reference to share capital denominated in euros, it must elect in its application for a trading certificate or, as the case may be, for re-registration as a public company which is to be the currency by reference to which the matter is determined.

766. **Authorised minimum: application where shares denominated in different currencies etc**

(1) The Secretary of State may make provision by regulations as to the application of the authorised minimum in relation to a public company that—

    (a) has shares denominated in more than one currency,

    (b) redenominates the whole or part of its allotted share capital, or

    (c) allots new shares.

(2) The regulations may make provision as to the currencies, exchange rates and dates by reference to which it is to be determined whether the nominal value of the company's allotted share capital is less than the authorised minimum.

(3) The regulations may provide that where—

(a) a company has redenominated the whole or part of its allotted share capital, and

(b) the effect of the redenomination is that the nominal value of the company's allotted share capital is less than the authorised minimum,

the company must re-register as a private company.

(4) Regulations under subsection (3) may make provision corresponding to any provision made by sections 664 to 667 (re-registration as private company in consequence of cancellation of shares).

(5) Any regulations under this section have effect subject to section 765 (authorised minimum: application of initial requirement).

(6) Regulations under this section are subject to negative resolution procedure.

767. **Consequences of doing business etc without a trading certificate**

(1) If a company does business or exercises any borrowing powers in contravention of section 761, an offence is committed by—

(a) the company, and

(b) every officer of the company who is in default.

(2) A person guilty of an offence under subsection (1) is liable—

(a) on conviction on indictment, to a fine;

(b) on summary conviction, to a fine not exceeding the statutory maximum.

(3) A contravention of section 761 does not affect the validity of a transaction entered into by the company, but if a company—

(a) enters into a transaction in contravention of that section, and

(b) fails to comply with its obligations in connection with the transaction within 21 days from being called on to do so,

the directors of the company are jointly and severally liable to indemnify any other party to the transaction in respect of any loss or damage suffered by him by reason of the company's failure to comply with its obligations.

(4) The directors who are so liable are those who were directors at the time the company entered into the transaction.

PART 21
CERTIFICATION AND TRANSFER OF SECURITIES

CHAPTER 1
CERTIFICATION AND TRANSFER OF SECURITIES: GENERAL

Share certificates

768. **Share certificate to be evidence of title**

(1) In the case of a company registered in England and Wales or Northern Ireland, a certificate under the common seal of the company specifying any shares held by a member is prima facie evidence of his title to the shares.

(2) In the case of a company registered in Scotland—

(a) a certificate under the common seal of the company specifying any shares held by a member, or

(b) a certificate specifying any shares held by a member and subscribed by the company in accordance with the Requirements of Writing (Scotland) Act 1995 (c. 7),

is sufficient evidence, unless the contrary is shown, of his title to the shares.

Issue of certificates etc on allotment

769. Duty of company as to issue of certificates etc on allotment

(1) A company must, within two months after the allotment of any of its shares, debentures or debenture stock, complete and have ready for delivery—

    (a) the certificates of the shares allotted,

    (b) the debentures allotted, or

    (c) the certificates of the debenture stock allotted.

(2) Subsection (1) does not apply—

    (a) if the conditions of issue of the shares, debentures or debenture stock provide otherwise,

    (b) in the case of allotment to a financial institution (see section 778), or

    (c) in the case of an allotment of shares if, following the allotment, the company has issued a share warrant in respect of the shares (see section 779).

(3) If default is made in complying with subsection (1) an offence is committed by every officer of the company who is in default.

(4) A person guilty of an offence under subsection (3) is liable on summary conviction to a fine not exceeding level 3 on the standard scale and, for continued contravention, a daily default fine not exceeding one-tenth of level 3 on the standard scale.

Transfer of securities

770. Registration of transfer

(1) A company may not register a transfer of shares in or debentures of the company unless—

    (a) a proper instrument of transfer has been delivered to it, or

    (b) the transfer—

        (i) is an exempt transfer within the Stock Transfer Act 1982 (c. 41), or

        (ii) is in accordance with regulations under Chapter 2 of this Part.

(2) Subsection (1) does not affect any power of the company to register as shareholder or debenture holder a person to whom the right to any shares in or debentures of the company has been transmitted by operation of law.

771. Procedure on transfer being lodged

(1) When a transfer of shares in or debentures of a company has been lodged with the company, the company must either—

    (a) register the transfer, or

    (b) give the transferee notice of refusal to register the transfer, together with its reasons for the refusal,

as soon as practicable and in any event within two months after the date on which the transfer is lodged with it.

(2) If the company refuses to register the transfer, it must provide the transferee with such further information about the reasons for the refusal as the transferee may reasonably request.

This does not include copies of minutes of meetings of directors.

(3) If a company fails to comply with this section, an offence is committed by—

    (a) the company, and

    (b) every officer of the company who is in default.

(4) A person guilty of an offence under this section is liable on summary conviction to a fine not exceeding level 3 on the standard scale and, for continued contravention, a daily default fine not exceeding one-tenth of level 3 on the standard scale.

(5) This section does not apply—

    (a) in relation to a transfer of shares if the company has issued a share warrant in respect of the shares (see section 779);

    (b) in relation to the transmission of shares or debentures by operation of law.

772. **Transfer of shares on application of transferor**

On the application of the transferor of any share or interest in a company, the company shall enter in its register of members the name of the transferee in the same manner and subject to the same conditions as if the application for the entry were made by the transferee.

773. **Execution of share transfer by personal representative**

An instrument of transfer of the share or other interest of a deceased member of a company—

(a) may be made by his personal representative although the personal representative is not himself a member of the company, and

(b) is as effective as if the personal representative had been such a member at the time of the execution of the instrument.

774. **Evidence of grant of probate etc**

The production to a company of any document that is by law sufficient evidence of the grant of—

(a) probate of the will of a deceased person,

(b) letters of administration of the estate of a deceased person, or

(c) confirmation as executor of a deceased person,

shall be accepted by the company as sufficient evidence of the grant.

775. **Certification of instrument of transfer**

(1) The certification by a company of an instrument of transfer of any shares in, or debentures of, the company is to be taken as a representation by the company to any person acting on the faith of the certification that there have been produced to the company such documents as on their face show a prima facie title to the shares or debentures in the transferor named in the instrument.

(2) The certification is not to be taken as a representation that the transferor has any title to the shares or debentures.

(3) Where a person acts on the faith of a false certification by a company made negligently, the company is under the same liability to him as if the certification had been made fraudulently.

(4) For the purposes of this section—

(a) an instrument of transfer is certificated if it bears the words "certificate lodged" (or words to the like effect);

(b) the certification of an instrument of transfer is made by a company if—

(i) the person issuing the instrument is a person authorised to issue certificated instruments of transfer on the company's behalf, and

(ii) the certification is signed by a person authorised to certificate transfers on the company's behalf or by an officer or employee either of the company or of a body corporate so authorised;

(c) a certification is treated as signed by a person if—

(i) it purports to be authenticated by his signature or initials (whether handwritten or not), and

(ii) it is not shown that the signature or initials was or were placed there neither by himself nor by a person authorised to use the signature or initials for the purpose of certificating transfers on the company's behalf.

Issue of certificates etc on transfer

776. **Duty of company as to issue of certificates etc on transfer**

(1) A company must, within two months after the date on which a transfer of any of its shares, debentures or debenture stock is lodged with the company, complete and have ready for delivery—

(a) the certificates of the shares transferred,

(b) the debentures transferred, or

(c) the certificates of the debenture stock transferred.

(2) For this purpose a "transfer" means—

   (a) a transfer duly stamped and otherwise valid, or

   (b) an exempt transfer within the Stock Transfer Act 1982 (c. 41),

but does not include a transfer that the company is for any reason entitled to refuse to register and does not register.

(3) Subsection (1) does not apply—

   (a) if the conditions of issue of the shares, debentures or debenture stock provide otherwise,

   (b) in the case of a transfer to a financial institution (see section 778), or

   (c) in the case of a transfer of shares if, following the transfer, the company has issued a share warrant in respect of the shares (see section 779).

(4) Subsection (1) has effect subject to section 777 (cases where the Stock Transfer Act 1982 applies).

(5) If default is made in complying with subsection (1) an offence is committed by every officer of the company who is in default.

(6) A person guilty of an offence under this section is liable on summary conviction to a fine not exceeding level 3 on the standard scale and, for continued contravention, a daily default fine not exceeding one-tenth of level 3 on the standard scale.

777. Issue of certificates etc: cases within the Stock Transfer Act 1982

(1) Section 776(1) (duty of company as to issue of certificates etc on transfer) does not apply in the case of a transfer to a person where, by virtue of regulations under section 3 of the Stock Transfer Act 1982, he is not entitled to a certificate or other document of or evidencing title in respect of the securities transferred.

(2) But if in such a case the transferee—

   (a) subsequently becomes entitled to such a certificate or other document by virtue of any provision of those regulations, and

   (b) gives notice in writing of that fact to the company,

section 776 (duty to company as to issue of certificates etc) has effect as if the reference in subsection (1) of that section to the date of the lodging of the transfer were a reference to the date of the notice.

Issue of certificates etc on allotment or transfer to financial institution

778. Issue of certificates etc: allotment or transfer to financial institution

(1) A company—

   (a) of which shares or debentures are allotted to a financial institution,

   (b) of which debenture stock is allotted to a financial institution, or

   (c) with which a transfer for transferring shares, debentures or debenture stock to a financial institution is lodged,

is not required in consequence of that allotment or transfer to comply with section 769(1) or 776(1) (duty of company as to issue of certificates etc).

(2) A "financial institution" means—

   (a) a recognised clearing house acting in relation to a recognised investment exchange, or

   (b) a nominee of—

     (i) a recognised clearing house acting in that way, or

     (ii) a recognised investment exchange,

   designated for the purposes of this section in the rules of the recognised investment exchange in question.

(3) Expressions used in subsection (2) have the same meaning as in Part 18 of the Financial Services and Markets Act 2000 (c. 8).

Share warrants

779. Issue and effect of share warrant to bearer

(1) A company limited by shares may, if so authorised by its articles, issue with respect to any fully paid shares a warrant (a "share warrant") stating that the bearer of the warrant is entitled to the shares specified in it.

(2) A share warrant issued under the company's common seal or (in the case of a company registered in Scotland) subscribed in accordance with the Requirements of Writing (Scotland) Act 1995 (c. 7) entitles the bearer to the shares specified in it and the shares may be transferred by delivery of the warrant.

(3) A company that issues a share warrant may, if so authorised by its articles, provide (by coupons or otherwise) for the payment of the future dividends on the shares included in the warrant.

780. Duty of company as to issue of certificates on surrender of share warrant

(1) A company must, within two months of the surrender of a share warrant for cancellation, complete and have ready for delivery the certificates of the shares specified in the warrant.

(2) Subsection (1) does not apply if the company's articles provide otherwise.

(3) If default is made in complying with subsection (1) an offence is committed by every officer of the company who is in default.

(4) A person guilty of an offence under subsection (3) is liable on summary conviction to a fine not exceeding level 3 on the standard scale and, for continued contravention, a daily default fine not exceeding one-tenth of level 3 on the standard scale.

781. Offences in connection with share warrants (Scotland)

(1) If in Scotland a person—

(a) with intent to defraud, forges or alters, or offers, utters, disposes of, or puts off, knowing the same to be forged or altered, any share warrant or coupon, or any document purporting to be a share warrant or coupon issued in pursuance of this Act, or

(b) by means of any such forged or altered share warrant, coupon or document—

   (i) demands or endeavours to obtain or receive any share or interest in a company under this Act, or

   (ii) demands or endeavours to receive any dividend or money payment in respect of any such share or interest,

knowing the warrant, coupon or document to be forged or altered, he commits an offence.

(2) If in Scotland a person without lawful authority or excuse (of which proof lies on him)—

(a) engraves or makes on any plate, wood, stone, or other material, any share warrant or coupon purporting to be—

   (i) a share warrant or coupon issued or made by any particular company in pursuance of this Act, or

   (ii) a blank share warrant or coupon so issued or made, or

   (iii) a part of such a share warrant or coupon, or

(b) uses any such plate, wood, stone, or other material, for the making or printing of any such share warrant or coupon, or of any such blank share warrant or coupon or of any part of such a share warrant or coupon, or

(c) knowingly has in his custody or possession any such plate, wood, stone, or other material, he commits an offence.

(3) A person guilty of an offence under subsection (1) is liable on summary conviction to imprisonment for a term not exceeding six months or to a fine not exceeding level 5 on the standard scale (or both).

(4) A person guilty of an offence under subsection (2) is liable—

(a) on conviction on indictment, to imprisonment for a term not exceeding seven years or a fine (or both);

(b) on summary conviction, to imprisonment for a term not exceeding six months or a fine not exceeding the statutory maximum (or both).

Supplementary provisions

782. Issue of certificates etc: court order to make good default

(1) If a company on which a notice has been served requiring it to make good any default in complying with—

(a) section 769(1) (duty of company as to issue of certificates etc on allotment),

(b) section 776(1) (duty of company as to issue of certificates etc on transfer), or

(c) section 780(1) (duty of company as to issue of certificates etc on surrender of share warrant),

fails to make good the default within ten days after service of the notice, the person entitled to have the certificates or the debentures delivered to him may apply to the court.

(2) The court may on such an application make an order directing the company and any officer of it to make good the default within such time as may be specified in the order.

(3) The order may provide that all costs (in Scotland, expenses) of and incidental to the application are to be borne by the company or by an officer of it responsible for the default.

CHAPTER 2
EVIDENCING AND TRANSFER OF TITLE TO SECURITIES WITHOUT WRITTEN INSTRUMENT

Introductory

783. Scope of this Chapter

In this Chapter—

(a) "securities" means shares, debentures, debenture stock, loan stock, bonds, units of a collective investment scheme within the meaning of the Financial Services and Markets Act 2000 (c. 8) and other securities of any description;

(b) references to title to securities include any legal or equitable interest in securities;

(c) references to a transfer of title include a transfer by way of security;

(d) references to transfer without a written instrument include, in relation to bearer securities, transfer without delivery.

784. Power to make regulations

(1) The power to make regulations under this Chapter is exercisable by the Treasury and the Secretary of State, either jointly or concurrently.

(2) References in this Chapter to the authority having power to make regulations shall accordingly be read as references to both or either of them, as the case may require.

(3) Regulations under this Chapter are subject to affirmative resolution procedure.

Powers exercisable

785. Provision enabling procedures for evidencing and transferring title

(1) Provision may be made by regulations for enabling title to securities to be evidenced and transferred without a written instrument.

(2) The regulations may make provision—

(a) for procedures for recording and transferring title to securities, and

(b) for the regulation of those procedures and the persons responsible for or involved in their operation.

(3) The regulations must contain such safeguards as appear to the authority making the regulations appropriate for the protection of investors and for ensuring that competition is not restricted, distorted or prevented.

(4) The regulations may, for the purpose of enabling or facilitating the operation of the procedures provided for by the regulations, make provision with respect to the rights and obligations of persons in relation to securities dealt with under the procedures.

(5) The regulations may include provision for the purpose of giving effect to—

    (a) the transmission of title to securities by operation of law;

    (b) any restriction on the transfer of title to securities arising by virtue of the provisions of any enactment or instrument, court order or agreement;

    (c) any power conferred by any such provision on a person to deal with securities on behalf of the person entitled.

(6) The regulations may make provision with respect to the persons responsible for the operation of the procedures provided for by the regulations—

    (a) as to the consequences of their insolvency or incapacity, or

    (b) as to the transfer from them to other persons of their functions in relation to those procedures.

786. **Provision enabling or requiring arrangements to be adopted**

(1) Regulations under this Chapter may make provision—

    (a) enabling the members of a company or of any designated class of companies to adopt, by ordinary resolution, arrangements under which title to securities is required to be evidenced or transferred (or both) without a written instrument; or

    (b) requiring companies, or any designated class of companies, to adopt such arrangements.

(2) The regulations may make such provision—

    (a) in respect of all securities issued by a company, or

    (b) in respect of all securities of a specified description.

(3) The arrangements provided for by regulations making such provision as is mentioned in subsection (1)—

    (a) must not be such that a person who but for the arrangements would be entitled to have his name entered in the company's register of members ceases to be so entitled, and

    (b) must be such that a person who but for the arrangements would be entitled to exercise any rights in respect of the securities continues to be able effectively to control the exercise of those rights.

(4) The regulations may—

    (a) prohibit the issue of any certificate by the company in respect of the issue or transfer of securities,

    (b) require the provision by the company to holders of securities of statements (at specified intervals or on specified occasions) of the securities held in their name, and

    (c) make provision as to the matters of which any such certificate or statement is, or is not, evidence.

(5) In this section—

    (a) references to a designated class of companies are to a class designated in the regulations or by order under section 787; and

    (b) "specified" means specified in the regulations.

787. **Provision enabling or requiring arrangements to be adopted: order-making powers**

(1) The authority having power to make regulations under this Chapter may by order—

    (a) designate classes of companies for the purposes of section 786 (provision enabling or requiring arrangements to be adopted);

    (b) provide that, in relation to securities of a specified description—

        (i) in a designated class of companies, or

        (ii) in a specified company or class of companies,

specified provisions of regulations made under this Chapter by virtue of that section either do not apply or apply subject to specified modifications.

(2) In subsection (1) "specified" means specified in the order.

(3) An order under this section is subject to negative resolution procedure.

Supplementary

788. **Provision that may be included in regulations**

Regulations under this Chapter may—

(a) modify or exclude any provision of any enactment or instrument, or any rule of law;

(b) apply, with such modifications as may be appropriate, the provisions of any enactment or instrument (including provisions creating criminal offences);

(c) require the payment of fees, or enable persons to require the payment of fees, of such amounts as may be specified in the regulations or determined in accordance with them;

(c) empower the authority making the regulations to delegate to any person willing and able to discharge them any functions of the authority under the regulations.

789. **Duty to consult**

Before making—

(a) regulations under this Chapter, or

(b) any order under section 787,

the authority having power to make regulations under this Chapter must carry out such consultation as appears to it to be appropriate.

790. **Resolutions to be forwarded to registrar**

Chapter 3 of Part 3 (resolutions affecting a company's constitution) applies to a resolution passed by virtue of regulations under this Chapter.

PART 22

INFORMATION ABOUT INTERESTS IN A COMPANY'S SHARES

Introductory

791. **Companies to which this Part applies**

This Part applies only to public companies.

792. **Shares to which this Part applies**

(1) References in this Part to a company's shares are to the company's issued shares of a class carrying rights to vote in all circumstances at general meetings of the company (including any shares held as treasury shares).

(2) The temporary suspension of voting rights in respect of any shares does not affect the application of this Part in relation to interests in those or any other shares.

Notice requiring information about interests in shares

793. **Notice by company requiring information about interests in its shares**

(1) A public company may give notice under this section to any person whom the company knows or has reasonable cause to believe—

(a) to be interested in the company's shares, or

(b) to have been so interested at any time during the three years immediately preceding the date on which the notice is issued.

(2) The notice may require the person—

(a) to confirm that fact or (as the case may be) to state whether or not it is the case, and

(b) if he holds, or has during that time held, any such interest, to give such further information as may be required in accordance with the following provisions of this section.

(3) The notice may require the person to whom it is addressed to give particulars of his own present or past interest in the company's shares (held by him at any time during the three year period mentioned in subsection (1)(b)).

(4) The notice may require the person to whom it is addressed, where—

    (a) his interest is a present interest and another interest in the shares subsists, or

    (b) another interest in the shares subsisted during that three year period at a time when his interest subsisted,

to give, so far as lies within his knowledge, such particulars with respect to that other interest as may be required by the notice.

(5) The particulars referred to in subsections (3) and (4) include—

    (a) the identity of persons interested in the shares in question, and

    (b) whether persons interested in the same shares are or were parties to—

        (i) an agreement to which section 824 applies (certain share acquisition agreements), or

        (ii) an agreement or arrangement relating to the exercise of any rights conferred by the holding of the shares.

(6) The notice may require the person to whom it is addressed, where his interest is a past interest, to give (so far as lies within his knowledge) particulars of the identity of the person who held that interest immediately upon his ceasing to hold it.

(7) The information required by the notice must be given within such reasonable time as may be specified in the notice.

794. Notice requiring information: order imposing restrictions on shares

(1) Where—

    (a) a notice under section 793 (notice requiring information about interests in company's shares) is served by a company on a person who is or was interested in shares in the company, and

    (b) that person fails to give the company the information required by the notice within the time specified in it,

the company may apply to the court for an order directing that the shares in question be subject to restrictions.

For the effect of such an order see section 797.

(2) If the court is satisfied that such an order may unfairly affect the rights of third parties in respect of the shares, the court may, for the purpose of protecting those rights and subject to such terms as it thinks fit, direct that such acts by such persons or descriptions of persons and for such purposes as may be set out in the order shall not constitute a breach of the restrictions.

(3) On an application under this section the court may make an interim order. Any such order may be made unconditionally or on such terms as the court thinks fit.

(4) Sections 798 to 802 make further provision about orders under this section.

795. Notice requiring information: offences

(1) A person who—

    (a) fails to comply with a notice under section 793 (notice requiring information about interests in company's shares), or

    (b) in purported compliance with such a notice—

        (i) makes a statement that he knows to be false in a material particular, or

        (ii) recklessly makes a statement that is false in a material particular,

commits an offence.

(2) A person does not commit an offence under subsection (1)(a) if he proves that the requirement to give information was frivolous or vexatious.

(3) A person guilty of an offence under this section is liable—

    (a) on conviction on indictment, to imprisonment for a term not exceeding two years or a fine (or both);

    (b) on summary conviction—

        (i) in England and Wales, to imprisonment for a term not exceeding twelve months or to a fine not exceeding the statutory maximum (or both);

        (ii) in Scotland or Northern Ireland, to imprisonment for a term not exceeding six months, or to a fine not exceeding the statutory maximum (or both).

796. Notice requiring information: persons exempted from obligation to comply

(1) A person is not obliged to comply with a notice under section 793 (notice requiring information about interests in company's shares) if he is for the time being exempted by the Secretary of State from the operation of that section.

(2) The Secretary of State must not grant any such exemption unless—

    (a) he has consulted the Governor of the Bank of England, and

    (b) he (the Secretary of State) is satisfied that, having regard to any undertaking given by the person in question with respect to any interest held or to be held by him in any shares, there are special reasons why that person should not be subject to the obligations imposed by that section.

Orders imposing restrictions on shares

797. Consequences of order imposing restrictions

(1) The effect of an order under section 794 that shares are subject to restrictions is as follows—

    (a) any transfer of the shares is void;

    (b) no voting rights are exercisable in respect of the shares;

    (c) no further shares may be issued in right of the shares or in pursuance of an offer made to their holder;

    (d) except in a liquidation, no payment may be made of sums due from the company on the shares, whether in respect of capital or otherwise.

(2) Where shares are subject to the restriction in subsection (1)(a), an agreement to transfer the shares is void.

This does not apply to an agreement to transfer the shares on the making of an order under section 800 made by virtue of subsection (3)(b) (removal of restrictions in case of court-approved transfer).

(3) Where shares are subject to the restriction in subsection (1)(c) or (d), an agreement to transfer any right to be issued with other shares in right of those shares, or to receive any payment on them (otherwise than in a liquidation), is void.

This does not apply to an agreement to transfer any such right on the making of an order under section 800 made by virtue of subsection (3)(b) (removal of restrictions in case of court-approved transfer).

(4) The provisions of this section are subject—

    (a) to any directions under section 794(2) or section 799(3) (directions for protection of third parties), and

    (b) in the case of an interim order under section 794(3), to the terms of the order.

798. Penalty for attempted evasion of restrictions

(1) This section applies where shares are subject to restrictions by virtue of an order under section 794.

(2) A person commits an offence if he—

    (a) exercises or purports to exercise any right—

        (i) to dispose of shares that to his knowledge, are for the time being subject to restrictions, or

(ii) to dispose of any right to be issued with any such shares, or

(b) votes in respect of any such shares (whether as holder or proxy), or appoints a proxy to vote in respect of them, or

(c) being the holder of any such shares, fails to notify of their being subject to those restrictions a person whom he does not know to be aware of that fact but does know to be entitled (apart from the restrictions) to vote in respect of those shares whether as holder or as proxy, or

(d) being the holder of any such shares, or being entitled to a right to be issued with other shares in right of them, or to receive any payment on them (otherwise than in a liquidation), enters into an agreement which is void under section 797(2) or (3).

(3) If shares in a company are issued in contravention of the restrictions, an offence is committed by—

(a) the company, and

(b) every officer of the company who is in default.

(4) A person guilty of an offence under this section is liable—

(a) on conviction on indictment, to a fine;

(b) on summary conviction, to a fine not exceeding the statutory maximum.

(5) The provisions of this section are subject—

(a) to any directions under—

section 794(2) (directions for protection of third parties), or

section 799 or 800 (relaxation or removal of restrictions), and

(b) in the case of an interim order under section 794(3), to the terms of the order.

799. Relaxation of restrictions

(1) An application may be made to the court on the ground that an order directing that shares shall be subject to restrictions unfairly affects the rights of third parties in respect of the shares.

(2) An application for an order under this section may be made by the company or by any person aggrieved.

(3) If the court is satisfied that the application is well-founded, it may, for the purpose of protecting the rights of third parties in respect of the shares, and subject to such terms as it thinks fit, direct that such acts by such persons or descriptions of persons and for such purposes as may be set out in the order do not constitute a breach of the restrictions.

800. Removal of restrictions

(1) An application may be made to the court for an order directing that the shares shall cease to be subject to restrictions.

(2) An application for an order under this section may be made by the company or by any person aggrieved.

(3) The court must not make an order under this section unless—

(a) it is satisfied that the relevant facts about the shares have been disclosed to the company and no unfair advantage has accrued to any person as a result of the earlier failure to make that disclosure, or

(b) the shares are to be transferred for valuable consideration and the court approves the transfer.

(4) An order under this section made by virtue of subsection (3)(b) may continue, in whole or in part, the restrictions mentioned in section 797(1)(c) and (d) (restrictions on issue of further shares or making of payments) so far as they relate to a right acquired or offer made before the transfer.

(5) Where any restrictions continue in force under subsection (4)—

(a) an application may be made under this section for an order directing that the shares shall cease to be subject to those restrictions, and

(b) subsection (3) does not apply in relation to the making of such an order.

801. **Order for sale of shares**

(1) The court may order that the shares subject to restrictions be sold, subject to the court's approval as to the sale.

(2) An application for an order under subsection (1) may only be made by the company.

(3) Where the court has made an order under this section, it may make such further order relating to the sale or transfer of the shares as it thinks fit.

(4) An application for an order under subsection (3) may be made—

    (a) by the company,

    (b) by the person appointed by or in pursuance of the order to effect the sale, or

    (c) by any person interested in the shares.

(5) On making an order under subsection (1) or (3) the court may order that the applicant's costs (in Scotland, expenses) be paid out of the proceeds of sale.

802. **Application of proceeds of sale under court order**

(1) Where shares are sold in pursuance of an order of the court under section 801, the proceeds of the sale, less the costs of the sale, must be paid into court for the benefit of the persons who are beneficially interested in the shares.

(2) A person who is beneficially interested in the shares may apply to the court for the whole or part of those proceeds to be paid to him.

(3) On such an application the court shall order the payment to the applicant of—

    (a) the whole of the proceeds of sale together with any interest on them, or

    (b) if another person had a beneficial interest in the shares at the time of their sale, such proportion of the proceeds and interest as the value of the applicant's interest in the shares bears to the total value of the shares.

This is subject to the following qualification.

(4) If the court has ordered under section 801(5) that the costs (in Scotland, expenses) of an applicant under that section are to be paid out of the proceeds of sale, the applicant is entitled to payment of his costs (or expenses) out of those proceeds before any person interested in the shares receives any part of those proceeds.

Power of members to require company to act

803. **Power of members to require company to act**

(1) The members of a company may require it to exercise its powers under section 793 (notice requiring information about interests in shares).

(2) A company is required to do so once it has received requests (to the same effect) from members of the company holding at least 10% of such of the paid-up capital of the company as carries a right to vote at general meetings of the company (excluding any voting rights attached to any shares in the company held as treasury shares).

(3) A request—

    (a) may be in hard copy form or in electronic form,

    (b) must—

        (i) state that the company is requested to exercise its powers under section 793,

        (ii) specify the manner in which the company is requested to act, and

        (iii) give reasonable grounds for requiring the company to exercise those powers in the manner specified, and

    (c) must be authenticated by the person or persons making it.

804. **Duty of company to comply with requirement**

(1) A company that is required under section 803 to exercise its powers under section 793 (notice requiring information about interests in company's shares) must exercise those powers in the manner specified in the requests.

(2) If default is made in complying with subsection (1) an offence is committed by every officer of the company who is in default.

(3) A person guilty of an offence under this section is liable—

   (a) on conviction on indictment, to a fine;

   (b) on summary conviction, to a fine not exceeding the statutory maximum.

805. Report to members on outcome of investigation

(1) On the conclusion of an investigation carried out by a company in pursuance of a requirement under section 803 the company must cause a report of the information received in pursuance of the investigation to be prepared.

   The report must be made available for inspection within a reasonable period (not more than 15 days) after the conclusion of the investigation.

(2) Where—

   (a) a company undertakes an investigation in pursuance of a requirement under section 803, and

   (b) the investigation is not concluded within three months after the date on which the company became subject to the requirement,

   the company must cause to be prepared in respect of that period, and in respect of each succeeding period of three months ending before the conclusion of the investigation, an interim report of the information received during that period in pursuance of the investigation.

(3) Each such report must be made available for inspection within a reasonable period (not more than 15 days) after the end of the period to which it relates.

(4) The reports must be retained by the company for at least six years from the date on which they are first made available for inspection and must be kept available for inspection during that time—

   (a) at the company's registered office, or

   (b) at a place specified in regulations under section 1136.

(5) The company must give notice to the registrar—

   (a) of the place at which the reports are kept available for inspection, and

   (b) of any change in that place,

   unless they have at all times been kept at the company's registered office.

(6) The company must within three days of making any report prepared under this section available for inspection, notify the members who made the requests under section 803 where the report is so available.

(7) For the purposes of this section an investigation carried out by a company in pursuance of a requirement under section 803 is concluded when—

   (a) the company has made all such inquiries as are necessary or expedient for the purposes of the requirement, and

   (b) in the case of each such inquiry—

      (i) a response has been received by the company, or

      (ii) the time allowed for a response has elapsed.

806. Report to members: offences

(1) If default is made for 14 days in complying with section 805(5) (notice to registrar of place at which reports made available for inspection) an offence is committed by—

   (a) the company, and

   (b) every officer of the company who is in default.

(2) A person guilty of an offence under subsection (1) is liable on summary conviction to a fine not exceeding level 3 on the standard scale and, for continued contravention, a daily default fine not exceeding one-tenth of level 3 on the standard scale.

(3) If default is made in complying with any other provision of section 805 (report to members on outcome of investigation), an offence is committed by every officer of the company who is in default.

(4) A person guilty of an offence under subsection (3) is liable—

    (a) on conviction on indictment, to a fine;

    (b) on summary conviction, to a fine not exceeding the statutory maximum.

807. Right to inspect and request copy of reports

(1) Any report prepared under section 805 must be open to inspection by any person without charge.

(2) Any person is entitled, on request and on payment of such fee as may be prescribed, to be provided with a copy of any such report or any part of it.

The copy must be provided within ten days after the request is received by the company.

(3) If an inspection required under subsection (1) is refused, or default is made in complying with subsection (2), an offence is committed by—

    (a) the company, and

    (b) every officer of the company who is in default.

(4) A person guilty of an offence under this section is liable on summary conviction to a fine not exceeding level 3 on the standard scale and, for continued contravention, a daily default fine not exceeding one-tenth of level 3 on the standard scale.

(5) In the case of any such refusal or default the court may by order compel an immediate inspection or, as the case may be, direct that the copy required be sent to the person requiring it.

Register of interests disclosed

808. Register of interests disclosed

(1) The company must keep a register of information received by it in pursuance of a requirement imposed under section 793 (notice requiring information about interests in company's shares).

(2) A company which receives any such information must, within three days of the receipt, enter in the register—

    (a) the fact that the requirement was imposed and the date on which it was imposed, and

    (b) the information received in pursuance of the requirement.

(3) The information must be entered against the name of the present holder of the shares in question or, if there is no present holder or the present holder is not known, against the name of the person holding the interest.

(4) The register must be made up so that the entries against the names entered in it appear in chronological order.

(5) If default is made in complying with this section an offence is committed by—

    (a) the company, and

    (b) every officer of the company who is in default.

(6) A person guilty of an offence under this section is liable on summary conviction to a fine not exceeding level 3 on the standard scale and, for continued contravention, a daily default fine not exceeding one-tenth of level 3 on the standard scale.

(7) The company is not by virtue of anything done for the purposes of this section affected with notice of, or put upon inquiry as to, the rights of any person in relation to any shares.

809. Register to be kept available for inspection

(1) The register kept under section 808 (register of interests disclosed) must be kept available for inspection—

    (a) at the company's registered office, or

    (b) at a place specified in regulations under section 1136.

(2) A company must give notice to the registrar of companies of the place where the register is kept available for inspection and of any change in that place.

(3) No such notice is required if the register has at all times been kept available for inspection at the company's registered office.

(4) If default is made in complying with subsection (1), or a company makes default for 14 days in complying with subsection (2), an offence is committed by—

    (a) the company, and

    (b) every officer of the company who is in default.

(5) A person guilty of an offence under this section is liable on summary conviction to a fine not exceeding level 3 on the standard scale and, for continued contravention, a daily default fine not exceeding one-tenth of level 3 on the standard scale.

810. **Associated index**

(1) Unless the register kept under section 808 (register of interests disclosed) is kept in such a form as itself to constitute an index, the company must keep an index of the names entered in it.

(2) The company must make any necessary entry or alteration in the index within ten days after the date on which any entry or alteration is made in the register.

(3) The index must contain, in respect of each name, a sufficient indication to enable the information entered against it to be readily found.

(4) The index must be at all times kept available for inspection at the same place as the register.

(5) If default is made in complying with this section, an offence is committed by—

    (a) the company, and

    (b) every officer of the company who is in default.

(6) A person guilty of an offence under this section is liable on summary conviction to a fine not exceeding level 3 on the standard scale and, for continued contravention, a daily default fine not exceeding one-tenth of level 3 on the standard scale.

811. **Rights to inspect and require copy of entries**

(1) The register required to be kept under section 808 (register of interests disclosed), and any associated index, must be open to inspection by any person without charge.

(2) Any person is entitled, on request and on payment of such fee as may be prescribed, to be provided with a copy of any entry in the register.

(3) A person seeking to exercise either of the rights conferred by this section must make a request to the company to that effect.

(4) The request must contain the following information—

    (a) in the case of an individual, his name and address;

    (b) in the case of an organisation, the name and address of an individual responsible for making the request on behalf of the organisation;

    (c) the purpose for which the information is to be used; and

    (d) whether the information will be disclosed to any other person, and if so—

        (i) where that person is an individual, his name and address,

        (ii) where that person is an organisation, the name and address of an individual responsible for receiving the information on its behalf, and

        (iii) the purpose for which the information is to be used by that person.

812. **Court supervision of purpose for which rights may be exercised**

(1) Where a company receives a request under section 811 (register of interests disclosed: right to inspect and require copy), it must—

    (a) comply with the request if it is satisfied that it is made for a proper purpose, and

    (b) refuse the request if it is not so satisfied.

(2) If the company refuses the request, it must inform the person making the request, stating the reason why it is not satisfied.

(3) A person whose request is refused may apply to the court.

(4) If an application is made to the court—

    (a) the person who made the request must notify the company, and

    (b) the company must use its best endeavours to notify any persons whose details would be disclosed if the company were required to comply with the request.

(5) If the court is not satisfied that the inspection or copy is sought for a proper purpose, it shall direct the company not to comply with the request.

(6) If the court makes such a direction and it appears to the court that the company is or may be subject to other requests made for a similar purpose (whether made by the same person or different persons), it may direct that the company is not to comply with any such request.
The order must contain such provision as appears to the court appropriate to identify the requests to which it applies.

(7) If the court does not direct the company not to comply with the request, the company must comply with the request immediately upon the court giving its decision or, as the case may be, the proceedings being discontinued.

813. **Register of interests disclosed: refusal of inspection or default in providing copy**

(1) If an inspection required under section 811 (register of interests disclosed: right to inspect and requrie copy) is refused or default is made in providing a copy required under that section, otherwise than in accordance with an order of the court, an offence is committed by—
(a) the company, and
(b) every officer of the company who is in default.

(2) A person guilty of an offence under this section is liable on summary conviction to a fine not exceeding level 3 on the standard scale and, for continued contravention, a daily default fine not exceeding one-tenth of level 3 on the standard scale.

(3) In the case of any such refusal or default the court may by order compel an immediate inspection or, as the case may be, direct that the copy required be sent to the person requesting it.

814. **Register of interests disclosed: offences in connection with request for or disclosure of information**

(1) It is an offence for a person knowingly or recklessly to make in a request under section 811 (register of interests disclosed: right to inspect or require copy) a statement that is misleading, false or deceptive in a material particular.

(2) It is an offence for a person in possession of information obtained by exercise of either of the rights conferred by that section—
(a) to do anything that results in the information being disclosed to another person, or
(b) to fail to do anything with the result that the information is disclosed to another person, knowing, or having reason to suspect, that person may use the information for a purpose that is not a proper purpose.

(3) A person guilty of an offence under this section is liable—
(a) on conviction on indictment, to imprisonment for a term not exceeding two years or a fine (or both);
(b) on summary conviction—
(i) in England and Wales, to imprisonment for a term not exceeding twelve months or to a fine not exceeding the statutory maximum (or both);
(ii) in Scotland or Northern Ireland, to imprisonment for a term not exceeding six months, or to a fine not exceeding the statutory maximum (or both).

815. **Entries not to be removed from register**

(1) Entries in the register kept under section 808 (register of interests disclosed) must not be deleted except in accordance with—
section 816 (old entries), or
section 817 (incorrect entry relating to third party).

(2) If an entry is deleted in contravention of subsection (1), the company must restore it as soon as reasonably practicable.

(3) If default is made in complying with subsection (1) or (2), an offence is committed by—
(a) the company, and
(b) every officer of the company who is in default.

(4) A person guilty of an offence under this section is liable on summary conviction to a fine not exceeding level 3 on the standard scale and, for continued contravention of subsection (2), a daily default fine not exceeding one-tenth of level 3 on the standard scale.

816. **Removal of entries from register: old entries**

A company may remove an entry from the register kept under section 808 (register of interests disclosed) if more than six years have elapsed since the entry was made.

817. **Removal of entries from register: incorrect entry relating to third party**

(1) This section applies where in pursuance of an obligation imposed by a notice under section 793 (notice requiring information about interests in company's shares) a person gives to a company the name and address of another person as being interested in shares in the company.

(2) That other person may apply to the company for the removal of the entry from the register.

(3) If the company is satisfied that the information in pursuance of which the entry was made is incorrect, it shall remove the entry.

(4) If an application under subsection (3) is refused, the applicant may apply to the court for an order directing the company to remove the entry in question from the register.

The court may make such an order if it thinks fit.

818. **Adjustment of entry relating to share acquisition agreement**

(1) If a person who is identified in the register kept by a company under section 808 (register of interests disclosed) as being a party to an agreement to which section 824 applies (certain share acquisition agreements) ceases to be a party to the agreement, he may apply to the company for the inclusion of that information in the register.

(2) If the company is satisfied that he has ceased to be a party to the agreement, it shall record that information (if not already recorded) in every place where his name appears in the register as a party to the agreement.

(3) If an application under this section is refused (otherwise than on the ground that the information has already been recorded), the applicant may apply to the court for an order directing the company to include the information in question in the register.

The court may make such an order if it thinks fit.

819. **Duty of company ceasing to be public company**

(1) If a company ceases to be a public company, it must continue to keep any register kept under section 808 (register of interests disclosed), and any associated index, until the end of the period of six years after it ceased to be such a company.

(2) If default is made in complying with this section, an offence is committed by—

(a) the company, and

(b) every officer of the company who is in default.

(3) A person guilty of an offence under this section is liable on summary conviction to a fine not exceeding level 3 on the standard scale and, for continued contravention, a daily default fine not exceeding one-tenth of level 3 on the standard scale.

Meaning of interest in shares

820. **Interest in shares: general**

(1) This section applies to determine for the purposes of this Part whether a person has an interest in shares.

(2) In this Part—

(a) a reference to an interest in shares includes an interest of any kind whatsoever in the shares, and

(b) any restraints or restrictions to which the exercise of any right attached to the interest is or may be subject shall be disregarded.

(3) Where an interest in shares is comprised in property held on trust, every beneficiary of the trust is treated as having an interest in the shares.

(4) A person is treated as having an interest in shares if—

    (a) he enters into a contract to acquire them, or

    (b) not being the registered holder, he is entitled—

        (i) to exercise any right conferred by the holding of the shares, or

        (ii) to control the exercise of any such right.

(5) For the purposes of subsection (4)(b) a person is entitled to exercise or control the exercise of a right conferred by the holding of shares if he—

    (a) has a right (whether subject to conditions or not) the exercise of which would make him so entitled, or

    (b) is under an obligation (whether subject to conditions or not) the fulfilment of which would make him so entitled.

(6) A person is treated as having an interest in shares if—

    (a) he has a right to call for delivery of the shares to himself or to his order, or

    (b) he has a right to acquire an interest in shares or is under an obligation to take an interest in shares.

This applies whether the right or obligation is conditional or absolute.

(7) Persons having a joint interest are treated as each having that interest.

(8) It is immaterial that shares in which a person has an interest are unidentifiable.

821. **Interest in shares: right to subscribe for shares**

(1) Section 793 (notice by company requiring information about interests in its shares) applies in relation to a person who has, or previously had, or is or was entitled to acquire, a right to subscribe for shares in the company as it applies in relation to a person who is or was interested in shares in that company.

(2) References in that section to an interest in shares shall be read accordingly.

822. **Interest in shares: family interests**

(1) For the purposes of this Part a person is taken to be interested in shares in which—

    (a) his spouse or civil partner, or

    (b) any infant child or step-child of his,

is interested.

(2) In relation to Scotland "infant" means a person under the age of 18 years.

823. **Interest in shares: corporate interests**

(1) For the purposes of this Part a person is taken to be interested in shares if a body corporate is interested in them and—

    (a) the body or its directors are accustomed to act in accordance with his directions or instructions, or

    (b) he is entitled to exercise or control the exercise of one-third or more of the voting power at general meetings of the body.

(2) For the purposes of this section a person is treated as entitled to exercise or control the exercise of voting power if—

    (a) another body corporate is entitled to exercise or control the exercise of that voting power, and

    (b) he is entitled to exercise or control the exercise of one-third or more of the voting power at general meetings of that body corporate.

(3) For the purposes of this section a person is treated as entitled to exercise or control the exercise of voting power if—

    (a) he has a right (whether or not subject to conditions) the exercise of which would make him so entitled, or

    (b) he is under an obligation (whether or not subject to conditions) the fulfilment of which would make him so entitled.

824. **Interest in shares: agreement to acquire interests in a particular company**

(1) For the purposes of this Part an interest in shares may arise from an agreement between two or more persons that includes provision for the acquisition by any one or more of them of interests in shares of a particular public company (the "target company" for that agreement).

(2) This section applies to such an agreement if—

(a) the agreement includes provision imposing obligations or restrictions on any one or more of the parties to it with respect to their use, retention or disposal of their interests in the shares of the target company acquired in pursuance of the agreement (whether or not together with any other interests of theirs in the company's shares to which the agreement relates), and

(b) an interest in the target company's shares is in fact acquired by any of the parties in pursuance of the agreement.

(3) The reference in subsection (2) to the use of interests in shares in the target company is to the exercise of any rights or of any control or influence arising from those interests (including the right to enter into an agreement for the exercise, or for control of the exercise, of any of those rights by another person).

(4) Once an interest in shares in the target company has been acquired in pursuance of the agreement, this section continues to apply to the agreement so long as the agreement continues to include provisions of any description mentioned in subsection (2).

This applies irrespective of—

(a) whether or not any further acquisitions of interests in the company's shares take place in pursuance of the agreement;

(b) any change in the persons who are for the time being parties to it;

(c) any variation of the agreement.

References in this subsection to the agreement include any agreement having effect (whether directly or indirectly) in substitution for the original agreement.

(5) In this section—

(a) "agreement" includes any agreement or arrangement, and

(b) references to provisions of an agreement include—

(i) undertakings, expectations or understandings operative under an arrangement, and

(ii) any provision whether express or implied and whether absolute or not.

References elsewhere in this Part to an agreement to which this section applies have a corresponding meaning.

(6) This section does not apply—

(a) to an agreement that is not legally binding unless it involves mutuality in the undertakings, expectations or understandings of the parties to it; or

(b) to an agreement to underwrite or sub-underwrite an offer of shares in a company, provided the agreement is confined to that purpose and any matters incidental to it.

825. **Extent of obligation in case of share acquisition agreement**

(1) For the purposes of this Part each party to an agreement to which section 824 applies is treated as interested in all shares in the target company in which any other party to the agreement is interested apart from the agreement (whether or not the interest of the other party was acquired, or includes any interest that was acquired, in pursuance of the agreement).

(2) For those purposes an interest of a party to such an agreement in shares in the target company is an interest apart from the agreement if he is interested in those shares otherwise than by virtue of the application of section 824 (and this section) in relation to the agreement.

(3) Accordingly, any such interest of the person (apart from the agreement) includes for those purposes any interest treated as his under section 822 or 823 (family or corporate interests) or by the application of section 824 (and this section) in relation to any other agreement with respect to shares in the target company to which he is a party.

(4) A notification with respect to his interest in shares in the target company made to the company under this Part by a person who is for the time being a party to an agreement to which section 824 applies must—

    (a) state that the person making the notification is a party to such an agreement,

    (b) include the names and (so far as known to him) the addresses of the other parties to the agreement, identifying them as such, and

    (c) state whether or not any of the shares to which the notification relates are shares in which he is interested by virtue of section 824 (and this section) and, if so, the number of those shares.

Other supplementary provisions

826. Information protected from wider disclosure

(1) Information in respect of which a company is for the time being entitled to any exemption conferred by regulations under section 409(3) (information about related undertakings to be given in notes to accounts: exemption where disclosure harmful to company's business)—

    (a) must not be included in a report under section 805 (report to members on outcome of investigation), and

    (b) must not be made available under section 811 (right to inspect and request copy of entries).

(2) Where any such information is omitted from a report under section 805, that fact must be stated in the report.

827. Reckoning of periods for fulfilling obligations

Where the period allowed by any provision of this Part for fulfilling an obligation is expressed as a number of days, any day that is not a working day shall be disregarded in reckoning that period.

828. Power to make further provision by regulations

(1) The Secretary of State may by regulations amend—

    (a) the definition of shares to which this Part applies (section 792),

    (b) the provisions as to notice by a company requiring information about interests in its shares (section 793), and

    (c) the provisions as to what is taken to be an interest in shares (sections 820 and 821).

(2) The regulations may amend, repeal or replace those provisions and make such other consequential amendments or repeals of provisions of this Part as appear to the Secretary of State to be appropriate.

(3) Regulations under this section are subject to affirmative resolution procedure.

PART 23

DISTRIBUTIONS

CHAPTER 1

RESTRICTIONS ON WHEN DISTRIBUTIONS MAY BE MADE

Introductory

829. Meaning of "distribution"

(1) In this Part "distribution" means every description of distribution of a company's assets to its members, whether in cash or otherwise, subject to the following exceptions.

(2) The following are not distributions for the purposes of this Part—

    (a) an issue of shares as fully or partly paid bonus shares;

    (b) the reduction of share capital—

        (i) by extinguishing or reducing the liability of any of the members on any of the company's shares in respect of share capital not paid up, or

(ii) by repaying paid-up share capital;

(c) the redemption or purchase of any of the company's own shares out of capital (including the proceeds of any fresh issue of shares) or out of unrealised profits in accordance with Chapter 3, 4 or 5 of Part 18;

(d) a distribution of assets to members of the company on its winding up.

General rules

830. Distributions to be made only out of profits available for the purpose

(1) A company may only make a distribution out of profits available for the purpose.

(2) A company's profits available for distribution are its accumulated, realised profits, so far as not previously utilised by distribution or capitalisation, less its accumulated, realised losses, so far as not previously written off in a reduction or reorganisation of capital duly made.

(3) Subsection (2) has effect subject to sections 832 and 835 (investment companies etc: distributions out of accumulated revenue profits).

831. Net asset restriction on distributions by public companies

(1) A public company may only make a distribution—

(a) if the amount of its net assets is not less than the aggregate of its called-up share capital and undistributable reserves, and

(b) if, and to the extent that, the distribution does not reduce the amount of those assets to less than that aggregate.

(2) For this purpose a company's "net assets" means the aggregate of the company's assets less the aggregate of its liabilities.

(3) "Liabilities" here includes—

(a) where the relevant accounts are Companies Act accounts, provisions of a kind specified for the purposes of this subsection by regulations under section 396;

(b) where the relevant accounts are IAS accounts, provisions of any kind.

(4) A company's undistributable reserves are—

(a) its share premium account;

(b) its capital redemption reserve;

(c) the amount by which its accumulated, unrealised profits (so far as not previously utilised by capitalisation) exceed its accumulated, unrealised losses (so far as not previously written off in a reduction or reorganisation of capital duly made);

(d) any other reserve that the company is prohibited from distributing—

(i) by any enactment (other than one contained in this Part), or

(ii) by its articles.

The reference in paragraph (c) to capitalisation does not include a transfer of profits of the company to its capital redemption reserve.

(5) A public company must not include any uncalled share capital as an asset in any accounts relevant for purposes of this section.

(6) Subsection (1) has effect subject to sections 832 and 835 (investment companies etc: distributions out of accumulated revenue profits).

Distributions by investment companies

832. Distributions by investment companies out of accumulated revenue profits

(1) An investment company may make a distribution out of its accumulated, realised revenue profits if the following conditions are met.

(2) It may make such a distribution only if, and to the extent that, its accumulated, realised revenue profits, so far as not previously utilised by a distribution or capitalisation, exceed its

accumulated revenue losses (whether realised or unrealised), so far as not previously written off in a reduction or reorganisation of capital duly made.

(3) It may make such a distribution only—

    (a) if the amount of its assets is at least equal to one and a half times the aggregate of its liabilities to creditors, and

    (b) if, and to the extent that, the distribution does not reduce that amount to less than one and a half times that aggregate.

(4) For this purpose a company's liabilities to creditors include—

    (a) in the case of Companies Act accounts, provisions of a kind specified for the purposes of this subsection by regulations under section 396;

    (b) in the case of IAS accounts, provisions for liabilities to creditors.

(5) The following conditions must also be met—

    (a) the company's shares must be listed on a recognised UK investment exchange;

    (b) during the relevant period it must not have—

        (i) distributed any capital profits otherwise than by way of the redemption or purchase of any of the company's own shares in accordance with Chapter 3 or 4 of Part 18, or

        (ii) applied any unrealised profits or any capital profits (realised or unrealised) in paying up debentures or amounts unpaid on its issued shares;

    (c) it must have given notice to the registrar under section 833(1) (notice of intention to carry on business as an investment company)—

        (i) before the beginning of the relevant period, or

        (ii) as soon as reasonably practicable after the date of its incorporation.

(6) For the purposes of this section—

    (a) "recognised UK investment exchange" means a recognised investment exchange within the meaning of Part 18 of the Financial Services and Markets Act 2000 (c. 8), other than an overseas investment exchange within the meaning of that Part; and

    (b) the "relevant period" is the period beginning with—

        (i) the first day of the accounting reference period immediately preceding that in which the proposed distribution is to be made, or

        (ii) where the distribution is to be made in the company's first accounting reference period, the first day of that period,

    and ending with the date of the distribution.

(7) The company must not include any uncalled share capital as an asset in any accounts relevant for purposes of this section.

833. Meaning of "investment company"

(1) In this Part an "investment company" means a public company that—

    (a) has given notice (which has not been revoked) to the registrar of its intention to carry on business as an investment company, and

    (b) since the date of that notice has complied with the following requirements.

(2) Those requirements are—

    (a) that the business of the company consists of investing its funds mainly in securities, with the aim of spreading investment risk and giving members of the company the benefit of the results of the management of its funds;

    (b) that the condition in section 834 is met as regards holdings in other companies;

    (c) that distribution of the company's capital profits is prohibited by its articles;

    (d) that the company has not retained, otherwise than in compliance with this Part, in respect of any accounting reference period more than 15% of the income it derives from securities.

(3) Subsection (2)(c) does not require an investment company to be prohibited by its articles from redeeming or purchasing its own shares in accordance with Chapter 3 or 4 of Part 18 out of its capital profits.

    (4) Notice to the registrar under this section may be revoked at any time by the company on giving notice to the registrar that it no longer wishes to be an investment company within the meaning of this section.

    (5) On giving such a notice, the company ceases to be such a company.

834. Investment company: condition as to holdings in other companies

    (1) The condition referred to in section 833(2)(b) (requirements to be complied with by investment company) is that none of the company's holdings in companies (other than those that are for the time being investment companies) represents more than 15% by value of the company's investments.

    (2) For this purpose—

        (a) holdings in companies that—

            (i) are members of a group (whether or not including the investing company), and

            (ii) are not for the time being investment companies,

        are treated as holdings in a single company; and

        (b) where the investing company is a member of a group, money owed to it by another member of the group—

            (i) is treated as a security of the latter held by the investing company, and

            (ii) is accordingly treated as, or as part of, the holding of the investing company in the company owing the money.

    (3) The condition does not apply—

        (a) to a holding in a company acquired before 6th April 1965 that on that date represented not more than 25% by value of the investing company's investments, or

        (b) to a holding in a company that, when it was acquired, represented not more than 15% by value of the investing company's investments,

    so long as no addition is made to the holding.

    (4) For the purposes of subsection (3)—

        (a) "holding" means the shares or securities (whether or one class or more than one class) held in any one company;

        (b) an addition is made to a holding whenever the investing company acquires shares or securities of that one company, otherwise than by being allotted shares or securities without becoming liable to give any consideration, and if an addition is made to a holding that holding is acquired when the addition or latest addition is made to the holding; and

        (c) where in connection with a scheme of reconstruction a company issues shares or securities to persons holding shares or securities in a second company in respect of and in proportion to (or as nearly as may be in proportion to) their holdings in the second company, without those persons becoming liable to give any consideration, a holding of the shares or securities in the second company and a corresponding holding of the shares or securities so issued shall be regarded as the same holding.

    (5) In this section—

    "company" and "shares" shall be construed in accordance with section 99 and 288 of the Taxation of Chargeable Gains Act 1992 (c. 12);

    "group" means a company and all companies that are its 51% subsidiaries (within the meaning of section 838 of the Income and Corporation Taxes Act 1988 (c. 1)); and

    "scheme of reconstruction" has the same meaning as in section 136 of the Taxation of Chargeable Gains Act 1992.

835. Power to extend provisions relating to investment companies

    (1) The Secretary of State may by regulations extend the provisions of sections 832 to 834 (distributions by investment companies out of accumulated profits), with or without modifications, to other companies whose principal business consists of investing their funds

in securities, land or other assets with the aim of spreading investment risk and giving their members the benefit of the results of the management of the assets.

(2) Regulations under this section are subject to affirmative resolution procedure.

CHAPTER 2
JUSTIFICATION OF DISTRIBUTION BY REFERENCE TO ACCOUNTS

Justification of distribution by reference to accounts

836. **Justification of distribution by reference to relevant accounts**

(1) Whether a distribution may be made by a company without contravening this Part is determined by reference to the following items as stated in the relevant accounts—

(a) profits, losses, assets and liabilities;

(b) provisions of the following kinds—

(i) where the relevant accounts are Companies Act accounts, provisions of a kind specified for the purposes of this subsection by regulations under section 396;

(ii) where the relevant accounts are IAS accounts, provisions of any kind;

(c) share capital and reserves (including undistributable reserves).

(2) The relevant accounts are the company's last annual accounts, except that—

(a) where the distribution would be found to contravene this Part by reference to the company's last annual accounts, it may be justified by reference to interim accounts, and

(b) where the distribution is proposed to be declared during the company's first accounting reference period, or before any accounts have been circulated in respect of that period, it may be justified by reference to initial accounts.

(3) The requirements of—

section 837 (as regards the company's last annual accounts),

section 838 (as regards interim accounts), and

section 839 (as regards initial accounts),

must be complied with, as and where applicable.

(4) If any applicable requirement of those sections is not complied with, the accounts may not be relied on for the purposes of this Part and the distribution is accordingly treated as contravening this Part.

Requirements applicable in relation to relevant accounts

837. **Requirements where last annual accounts used**

(1) The company's last annual accounts means the company's individual accounts—

(a) that were last circulated to members in accordance with section 423 (duty to circulate copies of annual accounts and reports), or

(b) if in accordance with section 426 the company provided a summary financial statement instead, that formed the basis of that statement.

(2) The accounts must have been properly prepared in accordance with this Act, or have been so prepared subject only to matters that are not material for determining (by reference to the items mentioned in section 836(1)) whether the distribution would contravene this Part.

(3) Unless the company is exempt from audit and the directors take advantage of that exemption, the auditor must have made his report on the accounts.

(4) If that report was qualified—

(a) the auditor must have stated in writing (either at the time of his report or subsequently) whether in his opinion the matters in respect of which his report is qualified are material for determining whether a distribution would contravene this Part, and

      (b) a copy of that statement must—

         (i) in the case of a private company, have been circulated to members in accordance with section 423, or

         (ii) in the case of a public company, have been laid before the company in general meeting.

  (5) An auditor's statement is sufficient for the purposes of a distribution if it relates to distributions of a description that includes the distribution in question, even if at the time of the statement it had not been proposed.

838. Requirements where interim accounts used

  (1) Interim accounts must be accounts that enable a reasonable judgment to be made as to the amounts of the items mentioned in section 836(1).

  (2) Where interim accounts are prepared for a proposed distribution by a public company, the following requirements apply.

  (3) The accounts must have been properly prepared, or have been so prepared subject to matters that are not material for determining (by reference to the items mentioned in section 836(1)) whether the distribution would contravene this Part.

  (4) "Properly prepared" means prepared in accordance with sections 395 to 397 (requirements for company individual accounts), applying those requirements with such modifications as are necessary because the accounts are prepared otherwise than in respect of an accounting reference period.

  (5) The balance sheet comprised in the accounts must have been signed in accordance with section 414.

  (6) A copy of the accounts must have been delivered to the registrar.

      Any requirement of Part 35 of this Act as to the delivery of a certified translation into English of any document forming part of the accounts must also have been met.

839. Requirements where initial accounts used

  (1) Initial accounts must be accounts that enable a reasonable judgment to be made as to the amounts of the items mentioned in section 836(1).

  (2) Where initial accounts are prepared for a proposed distribution by a public company, the following requirements apply.

  (3) The accounts must have been properly prepared, or have been so prepared subject to matters that are not material for determining (by reference to the items mentioned in section 836(1)) whether the distribution would contravene this Part.

  (4) "Properly prepared" means prepared in accordance with sections 395 to 397 (requirements for company individual accounts), applying those requirements with such modifications as are necessary because the accounts are prepared otherwise than in respect of an accounting reference period.

  (5) The company's auditor must have made a report stating whether, in his opinion, the accounts have been properly prepared.

  (6) If that report was qualified—

      (a) the auditor must have stated in writing (either at the time of his report or subsequently) whether in his opinion the matters in respect of which his report is qualified are material for determining whether a distribution would contravene this Part, and

      (b) a copy of that statement must—

         (i) in the case of a private company, have been circulated to members in accordance with section 423, or

         (ii) in the case of a public company, have been laid before the company in general meeting.

  (7) A copy of the accounts, of the auditor's report and of any auditor's statement must have been delivered to the registrar.

Any requirement of Part 35 of this Act as to the delivery of a certified translation into English of any of those documents must also have been met.

Application of provisions to successive distributions etc

840. **Successive distributions etc by reference to the same accounts**
   (1) In determining whether a proposed distribution may be made by a company in a case where—
      (a) one or more previous distributions have been made in pursuance of a determination made by reference to the same relevant accounts, or
      (b) relevant financial assistance has been given, or other relevant payments have been made, since those accounts were prepared,
      the provisions of this Part apply as if the amount of the proposed distribution was increased by the amount of the previous distributions, financial assistance and other payments.
   (2) The financial assistance and other payments that are relevant for this purpose are—
      (a) financial assistance lawfully given by the company out of its distributable profits;
      (b) financial assistance given by the company in contravention of section 678 or 679 (prohibited financial assistance) in a case where the giving of that assistance reduces the company's net assets or increases its net liabilities;
      (c) payments made by the company in respect of the purchase by it of shares in the company, except a payment lawfully made otherwise than out of distributable profits;
      (d) payments of any description specified in section 705 (payments apart from purchase price of shares to be made out of distributable profits).
   (3) In this section "financial assistance" has the same meaning as in Chapter 2 of Part 18 (see section 677).
   (4) For the purpose of applying subsection (2)(b) in relation to any financial assistance—
      (a) "net assets" means the amount by which the aggregate amount of the company's assets exceeds the aggregate amount of its liabilities, and
      (b) "net liabilities" means the amount by which the aggregate amount of the company's liabilities exceeds the aggregate amount of its assets,
      taking the amount of the assets and liabilities to be as stated in the company's accounting records immediately before the financial assistance is given.
   (5) For this purpose a company's liabilities include any amount retained as reasonably necessary for the purposes of providing for any liability—
      (a) the nature of which is clearly defined, and
      (b) which is either likely to be incurred or certain to be incurred but uncertain as to amount or as to the date on which it will arise.

CHAPTER 3
SUPPLEMENTARY PROVISIONS

Accounting matters

841. **Realised losses and profits and revaluation of fixed assets**
   (1) The following provisions have effect for the purposes of this Part.
   (2) The following are treated as realised losses—
      (a) in the case of Companies Act accounts, provisions of a kind specified for the purposes of this paragraph by regulations under section 396 (except revaluation provisions);
      (b) in the case of IAS accounts, provisions of any kind (except revaluation provisions).
   (3) A "revaluation provision" means a provision in respect of a diminution in value of a fixed asset appearing on a revaluation of all the fixed assets of the company, or of all of its fixed assets other than goodwill.

(4) For the purpose of subsections (2) and (3) any consideration by the directors of the value at a particular time of a fixed asset is treated as a revaluation provided—

    (a) the directors are satisfied that the aggregate value at that time of the fixed assets of the company that have not actually been revalued is not less than the aggregate amount at which they are then stated in the company's accounts, and

    (b) it is stated in a note to the accounts—

        (i) that the directors have considered the value of some or all of the fixed assets of the company without actually revaluing them,

        (ii) that they are satisfied that the aggregate value of those assets at the time of their consideration was not less than the aggregate amount at which they were then stated in the company's accounts, and

        (iii) that accordingly, by virtue of this subsection, amounts are stated in the accounts on the basis that a revaluation of fixed assets of the company is treated as having taken place at that time.

(5) Where—

    (a) on the revaluation of a fixed asset, an unrealised profit is shown to have been made, and

    (b) on or after the revaluation, a sum is written off or retained for depreciation of that asset over a period,

an amount equal to the amount by which that sum exceeds the sum which would have been so written off or retained for the depreciation of that asset over that period, if that profit had not been made, is treated as a realised profit made over that period.

842. **Determination of profit or loss in respect of asset where records incomplete**

In determining for the purposes of this Part whether a company has made a profit or loss in respect of an asset where—

(a) there is no record of the original cost of the asset, or

(b) a record cannot be obtained without unreasonable expense or delay,

its cost is taken to be the value ascribed to it in the earliest available record of its value made on or after its acquisition by the company.

843. **Realised profits and losses of long-term insurance business**

(1) The provisions of this section have effect for the purposes of this Part as it applies in relation to an authorised insurance company carrying on long-term business.

(2) An amount included in the relevant part of the company's balance sheet that—

    (a) represents a surplus in the fund or funds maintained by it in respect of its long-term business, and

    (b) has not been allocated to policy holders or, as the case may be, carried forward unappropriated in accordance with asset identification rules made under section 142(2) of the Financial Services and Markets Act 2000 (c. 8),

is treated as a realised profit.

(3) For the purposes of subsection (2)—

    (a) the relevant part of the balance sheet is that part of the balance sheet that represents accumulated profit or loss;

    (b) a surplus in the fund or funds maintained by the company in respect of its long-term business means an excess of the assets representing that fund or those funds over the liabilities of the company attributable to its long-term business, as shown by an actuarial investigation.

(4) A deficit in the fund or funds maintained by the company in respect of its long-term business is treated as a realised loss.

For this purpose a deficit in any such fund or funds means an excess of the liabilities of the company attributable to its long-term business over the assets representing that fund or those funds, as shown by an actuarial investigation.

(5) Subject to subsections (2) and (4), any profit or loss arising in the company's long-term business is to be left out of account.

(6) For the purposes of this section an "actuarial investigation" means an investigation made into the financial condition of an authorised insurance company in respect of its long-term business—

(a) carried out once in every period of twelve months in accordance with rules made under Part 10 of the Financial Services and Markets Act 2000, or

(b) carried out in accordance with a requirement imposed under section 166 of that Act,

by an actuary appointed as actuary to the company.

(7) In this section "long-term business" means business that consists of effecting or carrying out contracts of long-term insurance.

This definition must be read with section 22 of the Financial Services and Markets Act 2000, any relevant order under that section and Schedule 2 to that Act.

844. **Treatment of development costs**

(1) Where development costs are shown or included as an asset in a company's accounts, any amount shown or included in respect of those costs is treated—

(a) for the purposes of section 830 (distributions to be made out of profits available for the purpose) as a realised loss, and

(b) for the purposes of section 832 (distributions by investment companies out of accumulated revenue profits) as a realised revenue loss.

This is subject to the following exceptions.

(2) Subsection (1) does not apply to any part of that amount representing an unrealised profit made on revaluation of those costs.

(3) Subsection (1) does not apply if—

(a) there are special circumstances in the company's case justifying the directors in deciding that the amount there mentioned is not to be treated as required by subsection (1),

(b) it is stated—

(i) in the case of Companies Act accounts, in the note required by regulations under section 396 as to the reasons for showing development costs as an asset, or

(ii) in the case of IAS accounts, in any note to the accounts,

that the amount is not to be so treated, and

(c) the note explains the circumstances relied upon to justify the decision of the directors to that effect.

Distributions in kind

845. **Distributions in kind: determination of amount**

(1) This section applies for determining the amount of a distribution consisting of or including, or treated as arising in consequence of, the sale, transfer or other disposition by a company of a non-cash asset where—

(a) at the time of the distribution the company has profits available for distribution, and

(b) if the amount of the distribution were to be determined in accordance with this section, the company could make the distribution without contravening this Part.

(2) The amount of the distribution (or the relevant part of it) is taken to be—

(a) in a case where the amount or value of the consideration for the disposition is not less than the book value of the asset, zero;

(b) in any other case, the amount by which the book value of the asset exceeds the amount or value of any consideration for the disposition.

(3) For the purposes of subsection (1)(a) the company's profits available for distribution are treated as increased by the amount (if any) by which the amount or value of any consideration for the disposition exceeds the book value of the asset.

(4) In this section "book value", in relation to an asset, means—

    (a) the amount at which the asset is stated in the relevant accounts, or

    (b) where the asset is not stated in those accounts at any amount, zero.

(5) The provisions of Chapter 2 (justification of distribution by reference to accounts) have effect subject to this section.

846. Distributions in kind: treatment of unrealised profits

(1) This section applies where—

    (a) a company makes a distribution consisting of or including, or treated as arising in consequence of, the sale, transfer or other disposition by the company of a non-cash asset, and

    (b) any part of the amount at which that asset is stated in the relevant accounts represents an unrealised profit.

(2) That profit is treated as a realised profit—

    (a) for the purpose of determining the lawfulness of the distribution in accordance with this Part (whether before or after the distribution takes place), and

    (b) for the purpose of the application, in relation to anything done with a view to or in connection with the making of the distribution, of any provision of regulations under section 396 under which only realised profits are to be included in or transferred to the profit and loss account.

Consequences of unlawful distribution

847. Consequences of unlawful distribution

(1) This section applies where a distribution, or part of one, made by a company to one of its members is made in contravention of this Part.

(2) If at the time of the distribution the member knows or has reasonable grounds for believing that it is so made, he is liable—

    (a) to repay it (or that part of it, as the case may be) to the company, or

    (b) in the case of a distribution made otherwise than in cash, to pay the company a sum equal to the value of the distribution (or part) at that time.

(3) This is without prejudice to any obligation imposed apart from this section on a member of a company to repay a distribution unlawfully made to him.

(4) This section does not apply in relation to—

    (a) financial assistance given by a company in contravention of section 678 or 679, or

    (b) any payment made by a company in respect of the redemption or purchase by the company of shares in itself.

Other matters

848. Saving for certain older provisions in articles

(1) Where immediately before the relevant date a company was authorised by a provision of its articles to apply its unrealised profits in paying up in full or in part unissued shares to be allotted to members of the company as fully or partly paid bonus shares, that provision continues (subject to any alteration of the articles) as authority for those profits to be so applied after that date.

(2) For this purpose the relevant date is—

    (a) for companies registered in Great Britain, 22nd December 1980;

    (b) for companies registered in Northern Ireland, 1st July 1983.

849. Restriction on application of unrealised profits

A company must not apply an unrealised profit in paying up debentures or any amounts unpaid on its issued shares.

850. **Treatment of certain older profits or losses**

(1) Where the directors of a company are, after making all reasonable enquiries, unable to determine whether a particular profit made before the relevant date is realised or unrealised, they may treat the profit as realised.

(2) Where the directors of a company, after making all reasonable enquiries, are unable to determine whether a particular loss made before the relevant date is realised or unrealised, they may treat the loss as unrealised.

(3) For the purposes of this section the relevant date is—

(a) for companies registered in Great Britain, 22nd December 1980;

(b) for companies registered in Northern Ireland, 1st July 1983.

851. **Application of rules of law restricting distributions**

(1) Except as provided in this section, the provisions of this Part are without prejudice to any rule of law restricting the sums out of which, or the cases in which, a distribution may be made.

(2) For the purposes of any rule of law requiring distributions to be paid out of profits or restricting the return of capital to members—

(a) section 845 (distributions in kind: determination of amount) applies to determine the amount of any distribution or return of capital consisting of or including, or treated as arising in consequence of the sale, transfer or other disposition by a company of a non-cash asset; and

(b) section 846 (distributions in kind: treatment of unrealised profits) applies as it applies for the purposes of this Part.

(3) In this section references to distributions are to amounts regarded as distributions for the purposes of any such rule of law as is referred to in subsection (1).

852. **Saving for other restrictions on distributions**

The provisions of this Part are without prejudice to any enactment, or any provision of a company's articles, restricting the sums out of which, or the cases in which, a distribution may be made.

853. **Minor definitions**

(1) The following provisions apply for the purposes of this Part.

(2) References to profit or losses of any description—

(a) are to profits or losses of that description made at any time, and

(b) except where the context otherwise requires, are to profits or losses of a revenue or capital character.

(3) "Capitalisation", in relation to a company's profits, means any of the following operations (whenever carried out)—

(a) applying the profits in wholly or partly paying up unissued shares in the company to be allotted to members of the company as fully or partly paid bonus shares, or

(b) transferring the profits to capital redemption reserve.

(4) References to "realised profits" and "realised losses", in relation to a company's accounts, are to such profits or losses of the company as fall to be treated as realised in accordance with principles generally accepted at the time when the accounts are prepared, with respect to the determination for accounting purposes of realised profits or losses.

(5) Subsection (4) is without prejudice to—

(a) the construction of any other expression (where appropriate) by reference to accepted accounting principles or practice, or

(b) any specific provision for the treatment of profits or losses of any description as realised.

(6) "Fixed assets" means assets of a company which are intended for use on a continuing basis in the company's activities.

PART 24
A COMPANY'S ANNUAL RETURN

854. **Duty to deliver annual returns**

(1) Every company must deliver to the registrar successive annual returns each of which is made up to a date not later than the date that is from time to time the company's return date.

(2) The company's return date is—

(a) the anniversary of the company's incorporation, or

(b) if the company's last return delivered in accordance with this Part was made up to a different date, the anniversary of that date.

(3) Each return must—

(a) contain the information required by or under the following provisions of this Part, and

(b) be delivered to the registrar within 28 days after the date to which it is made up.

855. **Contents of annual return: general**

(1) Every annual return must state the date to which it is made up and contain the following information—

(a) the address of the company's registered office;

(b) the type of company it is and its principal business activities;

(c) the prescribed particulars of—

(i) the directors of the company, and

(ii) in the case of a private company with a secretary or a public company, the secretary or joint secretaries;

(d) if the register of members is not kept available for inspection at the company's registered office, the address of the place where it is kept available for inspection;

(e) if any register of debenture holders (or a duplicate of any such register or a part of it) is not kept available for inspection at the company's registered office, the address of the place where it is kept available for inspection.

(2) The information as to the company's type must be given by reference to the classification scheme prescribed for the purposes of this section.

(3) The information as to the company's principal business activities may be given by reference to one or more categories of any prescribed system of classifying business activities.

856. **Contents of annual return: information about share capital and shareholders**

(1) The annual return of a company having a share capital must also contain—

(a) a statement of capital, and

(b) the particulars required by subsections (3) to (6) about the members of the company.

(2) The statement of capital must state with respect to the company's share capital at the date to which the return is made up—

(a) the total number of shares of the company,

(b) the aggregate nominal value of those shares,

(c) for each class of shares—

(i) prescribed particulars of the rights attached to the shares,

(ii) the total number of shares of that class, and

(iii) the aggregate nominal value of shares of that class, and

(d) the amount paid up and the amount (if any) unpaid on each share (whether on account of the nominal value of the share or by way of premium).

(3) The return must contain the prescribed particulars of every person who—

(a) is a member of the company on the date to which the return is made up, or

(b) has ceased to be a member of the company since the date to which the last return was made up (or, in the case of the first return, since the incorporation of the company).

The return must conform to such requirements as may be prescribed for the purpose of enabling the entries relating to any given person to be easily found.

(4) The return must also state—

    (a) the number of shares of each class held by each member of the company at the date to which the return is made up,

    (b) the number of shares of each class transferred—

        (i) since the date to which the last return was made up, or

        (ii) in the case of the first return, since the incorporation of the company,

    by each member or person who has ceased to be a member, and

    (c) the dates of registration of the transfers.

(5) If either of the two immediately preceding returns has given the full particulars required by subsections (3) and (4), the return need only give such particulars as relate—

    (a) to persons ceasing to be or becoming members since the date of the last return, and

    (b) to shares transferred since that date.

(6) Where the company has converted any of its shares into stock, the return must give the corresponding information in relation to that stock, stating the amount of stock instead of the number or nominal value of shares.

857. Contents of annual return: power to make further provision by regulations

(1) The Secretary of State may by regulations make further provision as to the information to be given in a company's annual return.

(2) The regulations may—

    (a) amend or repeal the provisions of sections 855 and 856, and

    (b) provide for exceptions from the requirements of those sections as they have effect from time to time.

(3) Regulations under this section are subject to negative resolution procedure.

858. Failure to deliver annual return

(1) If a company fails to deliver an annual return before the end of the period of 28 days after a return date, an offence is committed by—

    (a) the company,

    (b) subject to subsection (4)—

        (i) every director of the company, and

        (ii) in the case of a private company with a secretary or a public company, every secretary of the company, and

    (c) every other officer of the company who is in default.

(2) A person guilty of an offence under subsection (1) is liable on summary conviction to a fine not exceeding level 5 on the standard scale and, for continued contravention, a daily default fine not exceeding one-tenth of level 5 on the standard scale.

(3) The contravention continues until such time as an annual return made up to that return date is delivered by the company to the registrar.

(4) It is a defence for a director or secretary charged with an offence under subsection (1)(b) to prove that he took all reasonable steps to avoid the commission or continuation of the offence.

(5) In the case of continued contravention, an offence is also committed by every officer of the company who did not commit an offence under subsection (1) in relation to the initial contravention but is in default in relation to the continued contravention.

A person guilty of an offence under this subsection is liable on summary conviction to a fine not exceeding one-tenth of level 5 on the standard scale for each day on which the contravention continues and he is in default.

859. Application of provisions to shadow directors

For the purposes of this Part a shadow director is treated as a director.

PART 25
COMPANY CHARGES

CHAPTER 1
COMPANIES REGISTERED IN ENGLAND AND WALES OR IN NORTHERN
IRELAND

Requirement to register company charges

860. **Charges created by a company**

(1) A company that creates a charge to which this section applies must deliver the prescribed particulars of the charge, together with the instrument (if any) by which the charge is created or evidenced, to the registrar for registration before the end of the period allowed for registration.

(2) Registration of a charge to which this section applies may instead be effected on the application of a person interested in it.

(3) Where registration is effected on the application of some person other than the company, that person is entitled to recover from the company the amount of any fees properly paid by him to the registrar on registration.

(4) If a company fails to comply with subsection (1), an offence is committed by—
  (a) the company, and
  (b) every officer of it who is in default.

(5) A person guilty of an offence under this section is liable—
  (a) on conviction on indictment, to a fine;
  (b) on summary conviction, to a fine not exceeding the statutory maximum.

(6) Subsection (4) does not apply if registration of the charge has been effected on the application of some other person.

(7) This section applies to the following charges—
  (a) a charge on land or any interest in land, other than a charge for any rent or other periodical sum issuing out of land,
  (b) a charge created or evidenced by an instrument which, if executed by an individual, would require registration as a bill of sale,
  (c) a charge for the purposes of securing any issue of debentures,
  (d) a charge on uncalled share capital of the company,
  (e) a charge on calls made but not paid,
  (f) a charge on book debts of the company,
  (g) a floating charge on the company's property or undertaking,
  (h) a charge on a ship or aircraft, or any share in a ship,
  (i) a charge on goodwill or on any intellectual property.

861. **Charges which have to be registered: supplementary**

(1) The holding of debentures entitling the holder to a charge on land is not, for the purposes of section 860 (7)(a), an interest in the land.

(2) It is immaterial for the purposes of this Chapter where land subject to a charge is situated.

(3) The deposit by way of security of a negotiable instrument given to secure the payment of book debts is not, for the purposes of section 860 (7)(f), a charge on those book debts.

(4) For the purposes of section 860 (7)(i), "intellectual property" means—
  (a) any patent, trade mark, registered design, copyright or design right;
  (b) any licence under or in respect of any such right.

(5) In this Chapter—
  "charge" includes mortgage, and
  "company" means a company registered in England and Wales or in Northern Ireland.

862. **Charges existing on property acquired**

(1) This section applies where a company acquires property which is subject to a charge of a kind which would, if it had been created by the company after the acquisition of the property, have been required to be registered under this Chapter.

(2) The company must deliver the prescribed particulars of the charge, together with a certified copy of the instrument (if any) by which the charge is created or evidenced, to the registrar for registration.

(3) Subsection (2) must be complied with before the end of the period allowed for registration.

(4) If default is made in complying with this section, an offence is committed by—

(a) the company, and

(b) every officer of it who is in default.

(5) A person guilty of an offence under this section is liable—

(a) on conviction on indictment, to a fine;

(b) on summary conviction, to a fine not exceeding the statutory maximum.

Special rules about debentures

863. **Charge in series of debentures**

(1) Where a series of debentures containing, or giving by reference to another instrument, any charge to the benefit of which debenture holders of that series are entitled *pari passu* is created by a company, it is for the purposes of section 860 (1) sufficient if the required particulars, together with the deed containing the charge (or, if there is no such deed, one of the debentures of the series), are delivered to the registrar before the end of the period allowed for registration.

(2) The following are the required particulars—

(a) the total amount secured by the whole series, and

(b) the dates of the resolutions authorising the issue of the series and the date of the covering deed (if any) by which the series is created or defined, and

(c) a general description of the property charged, and

(d) the names of the trustees (if any) for the debenture holders.

(3) Particulars of the date and amount of each issue of debentures of a series of the kind mentioned in subsection (1) must be sent to the registrar for entry in the register of charges.

(4) Failure to comply with subsection (3) does not affect the validity of the debentures issued.

(5) Subsections (2) to (6) of section 860 apply for the purposes of this section as they apply for the purposes of that section, but as if references to the registration of a charge were references to the registration of a series of debentures.

864. **Additional registration requirement for commission etc in relation to debentures**

(1) Where any commission, allowance or discount has been paid or made either directly or indirectly by a company to a person in consideration of his—

(a) subscribing or agreeing to subscribe, whether absolutely or conditionally, for debentures in a company, or

(b) procuring or agreeing to procure subscriptions, whether absolute or conditional, for such debentures,

the particulars required to be sent for registration under section 860 shall include particulars as to the amount or rate per cent. of the commission, discount or allowance so paid or made.

(2) The deposit of debentures as security for a debt of the company is not, for the purposes of this section, treated as the issue of debentures at a discount.

(3) Failure to comply with this section does not affect the validity of the debentures issued.

865. **Endorsement of certificate on debentures**

(1) The company shall cause a copy of every certificate of registration given under section 869 to be endorsed on every debenture or certificate of debenture stock which is issued by the company, and the payment of which is secured by the charge so registered.

(2) But this does not require a company to cause a certificate of registration of any charge so given to be endorsed on any debenture or certificate of debenture stock issued by the company before the charge was created.

(3) If a person knowingly and wilfully authorises or permits the delivery of a debenture or certificate of debenture stock which under this section is required to have endorsed on it a copy of a certificate of registration, without the copy being so endorsed upon it, he commits an offence.

(4) A person guilty of an offence under this section is liable on summary conviction to a fine not exceeding level 3 on the standard scale.

Charges in other jurisdictions

866. Charges created in, or over property in, jurisdictions outside the United Kingdom

(1) Where a charge is created outside the United Kingdom comprising property situated outside the United Kingdom, the delivery to the registrar of a verified copy of the instrument by which the charge is created or evidenced has the same effect for the purposes of this Chapter as the delivery of the instrument itself.

(2) Where a charge is created in the United Kingdom but comprises property outside the United Kingdom, the instrument creating or purporting to create the charge may be sent for registration under section 860 even if further proceedings may be necessary to make the charge valid or effectual according to the law of the country in which the property is situated.

867. Charges created in, or over property in, another United Kingdom jurisdiction

(1) Subsection (2) applies where—

   (a) a charge comprises property situated in a part of the United Kingdom other than the part in which the company is registered, and

   (b) registration in that other part is necessary to make the charge valid or effectual under the law of that part of the United Kingdom.

(2) The delivery to the registrar of a verified copy of the instrument by which the charge is created or evidenced, together with a certificate stating that the charge was presented for registration in that other part of the United Kingdom on the date on which it was so presented has, for the purposes of this Chapter, the same effect as the delivery of the instrument itself.

Orders charging land: Northern Ireland

868. Northern Ireland: registration of certain charges etc. affecting land

(1) Where a charge imposed by an order under Article 46 of the 1981 Order or notice of such a charge is registered in the Land Registry against registered land or any estate in registered land of a company, the Registrar of Titles shall as soon as may be cause two copies of the order made under Article 46 of that Order or of any notice under Article 48 of that Order to be delivered to the registrar.

(2) Where a charge imposed by an order under Article 46 of the 1981 Order is registered in the Registry of Deeds against any unregistered land or estate in land of a company, the Registrar of Deeds shall as soon as may be cause two copies of the order to be delivered to the registrar.

(3) On delivery of copies under this section, the registrar shall—

   (a) register one of them in accordance with section 869, and

   (b) not later than 7 days from that date of delivery, cause the other copy together with a certificate of registration under section 869 (5) to be sent to the company against which judgment was given.

(4) Where a charge to which subsection (1) or (2) applies is vacated, the Registrar of Titles or, as the case may be, the Registrar of Deeds shall cause a certified copy of the certificate of satisfaction lodged under Article 132(1) of the 1981 Order to be delivered to the registrar for entry of a memorandum of satisfaction in accordance with section 872.

(5) In this section—

"the 1981 Order" means the Judgments Enforcement (Northern Ireland) Order 1981 (S.I. 1981/226 (N.I. 6));

"the Registrar of Deeds" means the registrar appointed under the Registration of Deeds Act (Northern Ireland) 1970 (c. 25);

"Registry of Deeds" has the same meaning as in the Registration of Deeds Acts;

"Registration of Deeds Acts" means the Registration of Deeds Act (Northern Ireland) 1970 and every statutory provision for the time being in force amending that Act or otherwise relating to the registry of deeds, or the registration of deeds, orders or other instruments or documents in such registry;

"the Land Registry" and "the Registrar of Titles" are to be construed in accordance with section 1 of the Land Registration Act (Northern Ireland) 1970 (c. 18);

"registered land" and "unregistered land" have the same meaning as in Part 3 of the Land Registration Act (Northern Ireland) 1970.

The register of charges

869. **Register of charges to be kept by registrar**

(1) The registrar shall keep, with respect to each company, a register of all the charges requiring registration under this Chapter.

(2) In the case of a charge to the benefit of which holders of a series of debentures are entitled, the registrar shall enter in the register the required particulars specified in section 863 sec(2).

(3) In the case of a charge imposed by the Enforcement of Judgments Office under Article 46 of the Judgments Enforcement (Northern Ireland) Order 1981, the registrar shall enter in the register the date on which the charge became effective.

(4) In the case of any other charge, the registrar shall enter in the register the following particulars—

(a) if it is a charge created by a company, the date of its creation and, if it is a charge which was existing on property acquired by the company, the date of the acquisition,

(b) the amount secured by the charge,

(c) short particulars of the property charged, and

(d) the persons entitled to the charge.

(5) The registrar shall give a certificate of the registration of any charge registered in pursuance of this Chapter, stating the amount secured by the charge.

(6) The certificate—

(a) shall be signed by the registrar or authenticated by the registrar's official seal, and

(b) is conclusive evidence that the requirements of this Chapter as to registration have been satisfied.

(7) The register kept in pursuance of this section shall be open to inspection by any person.

870. **The period allowed for registration**

(1) The period allowed for registration of a charge created by a company is—

(a) 21 days beginning with the day after the day on which the charge is created, or

(b) if the charge is created outside the United Kingdom, 21 days beginning with the day after the day on which the instrument by which the charge is created or evidenced (or a copy of it) could, in due course of post (and if despatched with due diligence) have been received in the United Kingdom.

(2) The period allowed for registration of a charge to which property acquired by a company is subject is—

(a) 21 days beginning with the day after the day on which the acquisition is completed, or

(b) if the property is situated and the charge was created outside the United Kingdom, 21 days beginning with the day after the day on which the instrument by which the charge is created or evidenced (or a copy of it) could, in due course of post (and if despatched with due diligence) have been received in the United Kingdom.

(3) The period allowed for registration of particulars of a series of debentures as a result of section 863 is—

    (a) if there is a deed containing the charge mentioned in section 863 (1), 21 days beginning with the day after the day on which that deed is executed, or

    (b) if there is no such deed, 21 days beginning with the day after the day on which the first debenture of the series is executed.

871. Registration of enforcement of security

(1) If a person obtains an order for the appointment of a receiver or manager of a company's property, or appoints such a receiver or manager under powers contained in an instrument, he shall within 7 days of the order or of the appointment under those powers, give notice of the fact to the registrar.

(2) Where a person appointed receiver or manager of a company's property under powers contained in an instrument ceases to act as such receiver or manager, he shall, on so ceasing, give the registrar notice to that effect.

(3) The registrar must enter a fact of which he is given notice under this section in the register of charges.

(4) A person who makes default in complying with the requirements of this section commits an offence.

(5) A person guilty of an offence under this section is liable on summary conviction to a fine not exceeding level 3 on the standard scale and, for continued contravention, a daily default fine not exceeding one-tenth of level 3 on the standard scale.

872. Entries of satisfaction and release

(1) Subsection (2) applies if a statement is delivered to the registrar verifying with respect to a registered charge—

    (a) that the debt for which the charge was given has been paid or satisfied in whole or in part, or

    (b) that part of the property or undertaking charged has been released from the charge or has ceased to form part of the company's property or undertaking.

(2) The registrar may enter on the register a memorandum of satisfaction in whole or in part, or of the fact part of the property or undertaking has been released from the charge or has ceased to form part of the company's property or undertaking (as the case may be).

(3) Where the registrar enters a memorandum of satisfaction in whole, the registrar shall if required send the company a copy of it.

873. Rectification of register of charges

(1) Subsection (2) applies if the court is satisfied—

    (a) that the failure to register a charge before the end of the period allowed for registration, or the omission or mis-statement of any particular with respect to any such charge or in a memorandum of satisfaction—

        (i) was accidental or due to inadvertence or to some other sufficient cause, or

        (ii) is not of a nature to prejudice the position of creditors or shareholders of the company, or

    (b) that on other grounds it is just and equitable to grant relief.

(2) The court may, on the application of the company or a person interested, and on such terms and conditions as seem to the court just and expedient, order that the period allowed for registration shall be extended or, as the case may be, that the omission or mis-statement shall be rectified.

Avoidance of certain charges

874. **Consequence of failure to register charges created by a company**
    (1) If a company creates a charge to which section 860 applies, the charge is void (so far as any security on the company's property or undertaking is conferred by it) against—
        (a) a liquidator of the company,
        (b) an administrator of the company, and
        (c) a creditor of the company,
    unless that section is complied with.
    (2) Subsection (1) is subject to the provisions of this Chapter.
    (3) Subsection (1) is without prejudice to any contract or obligation for repayment of the money secured by the charge; and when a charge becomes void under this section, the money secured by it immediately becomes payable.

Companies' records and registers

875. **Companies to keep copies of instruments creating charges**
    (1) A company must keep available for inspection a copy of every instrument creating a charge requiring registration under this Chapter, including any document delivered to the company under section 868 (3)(b) (Northern Ireland: orders imposing charges affecting land).
    (2) In the case of a series of uniform debentures, a copy of one of the debentures of the series is sufficient.

876. **Company's register of charges**
    (1) Every limited company shall keep available for inspection a register of charges and enter in it—
        (a) all charges specifically affecting property of the company, and
        (b) all floating charges on the whole or part of the company's property or undertaking.
    (2) The entry shall in each case give a short description of the property charged, the amount of the charge and, except in the cases of securities to bearer, the names of the persons entitled to it.
    (3) If an officer of the company knowingly and wilfully authorises or permits the omission of an entry required to be made in pursuance of this section, he commits an offence.
    (4) A person guilty of an offence under this section is liable—
        (a) on conviction on indictment, to a fine;
        (b) on summary conviction, to a fine not exceeding the statutory maximum.

877. **Instruments creating charges and register of charges to be available for inspection**
    (1) This section applies to—
        (a) documents required to be kept available for inspection under section 875 (copies of instruments creating charges), and
        (b) a company's register of charges kept in pursuance of section 876.
    (2) The documents and register must be kept available for inspection—
        (a) at the company's registered office, or
        (b) at a place specified in regulations under section 1136.
    (3) The company must give notice to the registrar—
        (a) of the place at which the documents and register are kept available for inspection, and
        (b) of any change in that place,
    unless they have at all times been kept at the company's registered office.
    (4) The documents and register shall be open to the inspection—
        (a) of any creditor or member of the company without charge, and
        (b) of any other person on payment of such fee as may be prescribed.

(5) If default is made for 14 days in complying with subsection (3) or an inspection required under subsection (4) is refused, an offence is committed by—

    (a) the company, and

    (b) every officer of the company who is in default.

(6) A person guilty of an offence under this section is liable on summary conviction to a fine not exceeding level 3 on the standard scale and, for continued contravention, a daily default fine not exceeding one-tenth of level 3 on the standard scale.

(7) If an inspection required under subsection (4) is refused the court may by order compel an immediate inspection.

CHAPTER 2
COMPANIES REGISTERED IN SCOTLAND

Charges requiring registration

878. Charges created by a company

(1) A company that creates a charge to which this section applies must deliver the prescribed particulars of the charge, together with a copy certified as a correct copy of the instrument (if any) by which the charge is created or evidenced, to the registrar for registration before the end of the period allowed for registration.

(2) Registration of a charge to which this section applies may instead be effected on the application of a person interested in it.

(3) Where registration is effected on the application of some person other than the company, that person is entitled to recover from the company the amount of any fees properly paid by him to the registrar on the registration.

(4) If a company fails to comply with subsection (1), an offence is committed by—

    (a) the company, and

    (b) every officer of the company who is in default.

(5) A person guilty of an offence under this section is liable—

    (a) on conviction on indictment, to a fine;

    (b) on summary conviction, to a fine not exceeding the statutory maximum.

(6) Subsection (4) does not apply if registration of the charge has been effected on the application of some other person.

(7) This section applies to the following charges—

    (a) a charge on land or any interest in such land, other than a charge for any rent or other periodical sum payable in respect of the land,

    (b) a security over incorporeal moveable property of any of the following categories—

        (i) goodwill,

        (ii) a patent or a licence under a patent,

        (iii) a trademark,

        (iv) a copyright or a licence under a copyright,

        (v) a registered design or a licence in respect of such a design,

        (vi) a design right or a licence under a design right,

        (vii) the book debts (whether book debts of the company or assigned to it), and

        (viii) uncalled share capital of the company or calls made but not paid,

    (c) a security over a ship or aircraft or any share in a ship,

    (d) a floating charge.

879. Charges which have to be registered: supplementary

(1) A charge on land, for the purposes of section 878 (7)(a), includes a charge created by a heritable security within the meaning of section 9 (8) of the Conveyancing and Feudal Reform (Scotland) Act 1970 (c. 35).

(2) The holding of debentures entitling the holder to a charge on (land is not, for the purposes of section 878 (7)(a), deemed to be an interest in land.

(3) It is immaterial for the purposes of this Chapter where land subject to a charge is situated.

(4) The deposit by way of security of a negotiable instrumentiven to secure the payment of book debts is not, for the purposes of section 878 (7)(b)(vii), to be treated as a charge on those book debts.

(5) References in this Chapter to the date of the creation of a charge are—

    (a) in the case of a floating charge, the date on which the instrument creating the floating charge was executed by the company creating the charge, and

    (b) in any other case, the date on which the right of the person entitled to the benefit of the charge was constituted as a real right.

(6) In this Chapter "company" means an incorporated company registered in Scotland.

880. **Duty to register charges existing on property acquired**

(1) Subsection (2) applies where a company acquires any property which is subject to a charge of any kind as would, if it had been created by the company after the acquisition of the property, have been required to be registered under this Chapter.

(2) The company must deliver the prescribed particulars of the charge, together with a copy (certified to be a correct copy) of the instrument (if any) by which the charge was created or is evidenced, to the registrar for registration before the end of the period allowed for registration.

(3) If default is made in complying with this section, an offence is committed by—

    (a) the company, and

    (b) every officer of it who is in default.

(4) A person guilty of an offence under this section is liable—

    (a) on conviction on indictment, to a fine;

    (b) on summary conviction, to a fine not exceeding the statutory maximum.

881. **Charge by way of ex facie absolute disposition, etc**

(1) For the avoidance of doubt, it is hereby declared that, in the case of a charge created by way of an *ex facie* absolute disposition or assignation qualified by a back letter or other agreement, or by a standard security qualified by an agreement, compliance with section 878 (1) does not of itself render the charge unavailable as security for indebtedness incurred after the date of compliance.

(2) Where the amount secured by a charge so created is purported to be increased by a further back letter or agreement, a further charge is held to have been created by the *ex facie* absolute disposition or assignation or (as the case may be) by the standard security, as qualified by the further back letter or agreement.

(3) In that case, the provisions of this Chapter apply to the further charge as if—

    (a) references in this Chapter (other than in this section) to a charge were references to the further charge, and

    (b) references to the date of the creation of a charge were references to the date on which the further back letter or agreement was executed.

Special rules about debentures

882. **Charge in series of debentures**

(1) Where a series of debentures containing, or giving by reference to any other instrument, any charge to the benefit of which the debenture-holders of that series are entitled *pari passu*, is created by a company, it is sufficient for purposes of section 878 if the required particulars, together with a copy of the deed containing the charge (or, if there is no such deed, of one of the debentures of the series) are delivered to the registrar before the end of the period allowed for registration.

(2) The following are the required particulars—

    (a) the total amount secured by the whole series,

    (b) the dates of the resolutions authorising the issue of the series and the date of the covering deed (if any) by which the security is created or defined,

    (c) a general description of the property charged,

    (d) the names of the trustees (if any) for the debenture-holders, and

    (e) in the case of a floating charge, a statement of any provisions of the charge and of any instrument relating to it which prohibit or restrict or regulate the power of the company to grant further securities ranking in priority to, or *pari passu* with, the floating charge, or which vary or otherwise regulate the order of ranking of the floating charge in relation to subsisting securities.

(3) Where more than one issue is made of debentures in the series, particulars of the date and amount of each issue of debentures of the series must be sent to the registrar for entry in the register of charges.

(4) Failure to comply with subsection (3) does not affect the validity of any of those debentures.

(5) Subsections (2) to (6) of section 878 apply for the purposes of this section as they apply for the purposes of that section but as if for the reference to the registration of the charge there was substituted a reference to the registration of the series of debentures.

883. Additional registration requirement for commission etc in relation to debentures

(1) Where any commission, allowance or discount has been paid or made either directly or indirectly by a company to a person in consideration of his—

    (a) subscribing or agreeing to subscribe, whether absolutely or conditionally, for debentures in a company, or

    (b) procuring or agreeing to procure subscriptions, whether absolute or conditional, for such debentures,

the particulars required to be sent for registration under section 878 shall include particulars as to the amount or rate per cent. of the commission, discount or allowance so paid or made.

(2) The deposit of debentures as security for a debt of the company is not, for the purposes of this section, treated as the issue of debentures at a discount.

(3) Failure to comply with this section does not affect the validity of the debentures issued.

Charges on property outside the United Kingdom

884. Charges on property outside United Kingdom

Where a charge is created in the United Kingdom but comprises property outside the United Kingdom, the copy of the instrument creating or purporting to create the charge may be sent for registration under section 878 even if further proceedings may be necessary to make the charge valid or effectual according to the law of the country in which the property is situated.

The register of charges

885. Register of charges to be kept by registrar

(1) The registrar shall keep, with respect to each company, a register of all the charges requiring registration under this Chapter.

(2) In the case of a charge to the benefit of which holders of a series of debentures are entitled, the registrar shall enter in the register the required particulars specified in section 882 (2).

(3) In the case of any other charge, the registrar shall enter in the register the following particulars—

    (a) if it is a charge created by a company, the date of its creation and, if it is a charge which was existing on property acquired by the company, the date of the acquisition,

(b) the amount secured by the charge,

(c) short particulars of the property charged,

(d) the persons entitled to the charge, and

(e) in the case of a floating charge, a statement of any of the provisions of the charge and of any instrument relating to it which prohibit or restrict or regulate the company's power to grant further securities ranking in priority to, or *pari passu* with, the floating charge, or which vary or otherwise regulate the order of ranking of the floating charge in relation to subsisting securities.

(4) The registrar shall give a certificate of the registration of any charge registered in pursuance of this Chapter, stating—

(a) the name of the company and the person first-named in the charge among those entitled to the benefit of the charge (or, in the case of a series of debentures, the name of the holder of the first such debenture issued), and

(b) the amount secured by the charge.

(5) The certificate—

(a) shall be signed by the registrar or authenticated by the registrar's official seal, and

(b) is conclusive evidence that the requirements of this Chapter as to registration have been satisfied.

(6) The register kept in pursuance of this section shall be open to inspection by any person.

886. The period allowed for registration

(1) The period allowed for registration of a charge created by a company is—

(a) 21 days beginning with the day after the day on which the charge is created, or

(b) if the charge is created outside the United Kingdom, 21 days beginning with the day after the day on which a copy of the instrument by which the charge is created or evidenced could, in due course of post (and if despatched with due diligence) have been received in the United Kingdom.

(2) The period allowed for registration of a charge to which property acquired by a company is subject is—

(a) 21 days beginning with the day after the day on which the transaction is settled, or

(b) if the property is situated and the charge was created outside the United Kingdom, 21 days beginning with the day after the day on which a copy of the instrument by which the charge is created or evidenced could, in due course of post (and if despatched with due diligence) have been received in the United Kingdom.

(3) The period allowed for registration of particulars of a series of debentures as a result of section 882 is—

(a) if there is a deed containing the charge mentioned in section 882(1), 21 days beginning with the day after the day on which that deed is executed, or

(b) if there is no such deed, 21 days beginning with the day after the day on which the first debenture of the series is executed.

887. Entries of satisfaction and relief

(1) Subsection (2) applies if a statement is delivered to the registrar verifying with respect to any registered charge—

(a) that the debt for which the charge was given has been paid or satisfied in whole or in part, or

(b) that part of the property charged has been released from the charge or has ceased to form part of the company's property.

(2) If the charge is a floating charge, the statement must be accompanied by either—

(a) a statement by the creditor entitled to the benefit of the charge, or a person authorised by him for the purpose, verifying that the statement mentioned in subsection (1) is correct, or

     (b) a direction obtained from the court, on the ground that the statement by the creditor mentioned in paragraph (a) could not be readily obtained, dispensing with the need for that statement.

(3) The registrar may enter on the register a memorandum of satisfaction (in whole or in part) regarding the fact contained in the statement mentioned in subsection (1).

(4) Where the registrar enters a memorandum of satisfaction in whole, he shall, if required, furnish the company with a copy of the memorandum.

(5) Nothing in this section requires the company to submit particulars with respect to the entry in the register of a memorandum of satisfaction where the company, having created a floating charge over all or any part of its property, disposes of part of the property subject to the floating charge.

888. Rectification of register of charges

(1) Subsection (2) applies if the court is satisfied—

     (a) that the failure to register a charge before the end of the period allowed for registration, or the omission or mis-statement of any particular with respect to any such charge or in a memorandum of satisfaction—

         (i) was accidental or due to inadvertence or to some other sufficient cause, or

         (ii) is not of a nature to prejudice the position of creditors or shareholders of the company, or

     (b) that on other grounds it is just and equitable to grant relief.

(2) The court may, on the application of the company or a person interested, and on such terms and conditions as seem to the court just and expedient, order that the period allowed for registration shall be extended or, as the case may be, that the omission or mis-statement shall be rectified.

Avoidance of certain charges

889. Charges void unless registered

(1) If a company creates a charge to which section 878 applies, the charge is void (so far as any security on the company's property or any part of it is conferred by the charge) against—

     (a) the liquidator of the company,

     (b) an administrator of the company, and

     (c) any creditor of the company

unless that section is complied with.

(2) Subsection (1) is without prejudice to any contract or obligation for repayment of the money secured by the charge; and when a charge becomes void under this section the money secured by it immediately becomes payable.

Companies' records and registers

890. Copies of instruments creating charges to be kept by company

(1) Every company shall cause a copy of every instrument creating a charge requiring registration under this Chapter to be kept available for inspection.

(2) In the case of a series of uniform debentures, a copy of one debenture of the series is sufficient.

891. Company's register of charges

(1) Every company shall keep available for inspection a register of charges and enter in it all charges specifically affecting property of the company, and all floating charges on any property of the company.

(2) There shall be given in each case a short description of the property charged, the amount of the charge and, except in the case of securities to bearer, the names of the persons entitled to it.

(3) If an officer of the company knowingly and wilfully authorises or permits the omission of an entry required to be made in pursuance of this section, he commits an offence.

(4) A person guilty of an offence under this section is liable—

    (a) on conviction on indictment, to a fine;

    (b) on summary conviction, to a fine not exceeding the statutory maximum.

892. Instruments creating charges and register of charges to be available for inspection

(1) This section applies to—

    (a) documents required to be kept available for inspection under section 890 (copies of instruments creating charges), and

    (b) a company's register of charges kept in pursuance of section 891.

(2) The documents and register must be kept available for inspection—

    (a) at the company's registered office, or

    (b) at a place specified in regulations under section 1136.

(3) The company must give notice to the registrar—

    (a) of the place at which the documents and register are kept available for inspection, and

    (b) of any change in that place,

unless they have at all times been kept at the company's registered office.

(4) The documents and register shall be open to the inspection—

    (a) of any creditor or member of the company without charge, and

    (b) of any other person on payment of such fee as may be prescribed.

(5) If default is made for 14 days in complying with subsection (3) or an inspection required under subsection (4) is refused, an offence is committed by—

    (a) the company, and

    (b) every officer of the company who is in default.

(6) A person guilty of an offence under this section is liable on summary conviction to a fine not exceeding level 3 on the standard scale and, for continued contravention, a daily default fine not exceeding one-tenth of level 3 on the standard scale.

(7) If an inspection required under subsection (4) is refused the court may by order compel an immediate inspection.

CHAPTER 3
POWERS OF THE SECRETARY OF STATE

893. Power to make provision for effect of registration in special register

(1) In this section a "special register" means a register, other than the register of charges kept under this Part, in which a charge to which Chapter 1 or Chapter 2 applies is required or authorised to be registered.

(2) The Secretary of State may by order make provision for facilitating the making of information-sharing arrangements between the person responsible for maintaining a special register ("the responsible person") and the registrar that meet the requirement in subsection (4).

"Information-sharing arrangements" are arrangements to share and make use of information held by the registrar or by the responsible person.

(3) If the Secretary of State is satisfied that appropriate information-sharing arrangements have been made, he may by order provide that—

    (a) the registrar is authorised not to register a charge of a specified description under Chapter 1 or Chapter 2,

    (b) a charge of a specified description that is registered in the special register within a specified period is to be treated as if it had been registered (and certified by the registrar as registered) in accordance with the requirements of Chapter 1 or, as the case may be, Chapter 2, and

(c) the other provisions of Chapter 1 or, as the case may be, Chapter 2 apply to a charge so treated with specified modifications.

(4) The information-sharing arrangements must ensure that persons inspecting the register of charges—

    (a) are made aware, in a manner appropriate to the inspection, of the existence of charges in the special register which are treated in accordance with provision so made, and

    (b) are able to obtain information from the special register about any such charge.

(5) An order under this section may—

    (a) modify any enactment or rule of law which would otherwise restrict or prevent the responsible person from entering into or giving effect to information-sharing arrangements,

    (b) authorise the responsible person to require information to be provided to him for the purposes of the arrangements,

    (c) make provision about—

        (i) the charging by the responsible person of fees in connection with the arrangements and the destination of such fees (including provision modifying any enactment which would otherwise apply in relation to fees payable to the responsible person), and

        (ii) the making of payments under the arrangements by the registrar to the responsible person,

    (d) require the registrar to make copies of the arrangements available to the public (in hard copy or electronic form).

(6) In this section "specified" means specified in an order under this section.

(7) A description of charge may be specified, in particular, by reference to one or more of the following—

    (a) the type of company by which it is created,

    (b) the form of charge which it is,

    (c) the description of assets over which it is granted,

    (d) the length of the period between the date of its registration in the special register and the date of its creation.

(8) Provision may be made under this section relating to registers maintained under the law of a country or territory outside the United Kingdom.

(9) An order under this section is subject to negative resolution procedure.

894. General power to make amendments to this Part

(1) The Secretary of State may by regulations under this section—

    (a) amend this Part by altering, adding or repealing provisions,

    (b) make consequential amendments or repeals in this Act or any other enactment (whether passed or made before or after this Act).

(2) Regulations under this section are subject to affirmative resolution procedure.

PART 26
ARRANGEMENTS AND RECONSTRUCTIONS

Application of this Part

895. Application of this Part

(1) The provisions of this Part apply where a compromise or arrangement is proposed between a company and—

    (a) its creditors, or any class of them, or

    (b) its members, or any class of them.

(2) In this Part—

"arrangement" includes a reorganisation of the company's share capital by the consolidation of shares of different classes or by the division of shares into shares of different classes, or by both of those methods; and "company"—

(a) in section 900 (powers of court to facilitate reconstruction or amalgamation) means a company within the meaning of this Act, and

(b) elsewhere in this Part means any company liable to be wound up under the Insolvency Act 1986 (c. 45) or the Insolvency (Northern Ireland) Order 1989 (S.I. 1989/2405 (N.I. 19)).

(3) The provisions of this Part have effect subject to Part 27 (mergers and divisions of public companies) where that Part applies (see sections 902 and 903).

Meeting of creditors or members

896. Court order for holding of meeting

(1) The court may, on an application under this section, order a meeting of the creditors or class of creditors, or of the members of the company or class of members (as the case may be), to be summoned in such manner as the court directs.

(2) An application under this section may be made by—

(a) the company,

(b) any creditor or member of the company, or

(c) if the company is being would up or an administration order is in force in relation to it, the liquidator or administrator.

897. Statement to be circulated or made available

(1) Where a meeting is summoned under section 896—

(a) every notice summoning the meeting that is sent to a creditor or member must be accompanied by a statement complying with this section, and

(b) every notice summoning the meeting that is given by advertisement must either—

(i) include such a statement, or

(ii) state where and how creditors or members entitled to attend the meeting may obtain copies of such a statement.

(2) The statement must—

(a) explain the effect of the compromise or arrangement, and

(b) in particular, state—

(i) any material interests of the directors of the company (whether as directors or as members or as creditors of the company or otherwise), and

(ii) the effect on those interests of the compromise or arrangement, in so far as it is different from the effect on the like interests of other persons.

(3) Where the compromise or arrangement affects the rights of debenture holders of the company, the statement must give the like explanation as respects the trustees of any deed for securing the issue of the debentures as it is required to give as respects the company's directors.

(4) Where a notice given by advertisement states that copies of an explanatory statement can be obtained by creditors or members entitled to attend the meeting, every such creditor or member is entitled, on making application in the manner indicated by the notice, to be provided by the company with a copy of the statement free of charge.

(5) If a company makes default in complying with any requirement of this section, an offence is committed by—

(a) the company, and

(b) every officer of the company who is in default.

This is subject to subsection (7) below.

(6) For this purpose the following are treated as officers of the company—
    (a) a liquidator or administrator of the company, and
    (b) a trustee of a deed for securing the issue of debentures of the company.

(7) A person is not guilty of an offence under this section if he shows that the default was due to the refusal of a director or trustee for debenture holders to supply the necessary particulars of his interests.

(8) A person guilty of an offence under this section is liable—
    (a) on conviction on indictment, to a fine;
    (b) on summary conviction, to a fine not exceeding the statutory maximum.

898. Duty of directors and trustees to provide information

(1) It is the duty of—
    (a) any director of the company, and
    (b) any trustee for its debenture holders,
to give notice to the company of such matters relating to himself as may be necessary for the purposes of section 897 (explanatory statement to be circulated or made available).

(2) Any person who makes default in complying with this section commits an offence.

(3) A person guilty of an offence under this section is liable on summary conviction to a fine not exceeding level 3 on the standard scale.

Court sanction for compromise or arrangement

899. Court sanction for compromise or arrangement

(1) If a majority in number representing 75% in value of the creditors or class of creditors or members or class of members (as the case may be), present and voting either in person or by proxy at the meeting summoned under section 896, agree a compromise or arrangement, the court may, on an application under this section, sanction the compromise or arrangement.

(2) An application under this section may be made by—
    (a) the company,
    (b) any creditor or member of the company, or
    (c) if the company is being wound up or an administration order is in force in relation it, the liquidator or administrator.

(3) A compromise or agreement sanctioned by the court is binding on—
    (a) all creditors or the class of creditors or on the members or class of members (as the case may be), and
    (b) the company or, in the case of a company in the course of being wound up, the liquidator and contributories of the company.

(4) The court's order has no effect until a copy of it has been delivered to the registrar.

Reconstructions and amalgamations

900. Powers of court to facilitate reconstruction or amalgamation

(1) This section applies where application is made to the court under section 899 to sanction a compromise or arrangement and it is shown that—
    (a) the compromise or arrangement is proposed for the purposes of, or in connection with, a scheme for the reconstruction of any company or companies, or the amalgamation of any two or more companies, and
    (b) under the scheme the whole or any part of the undertaking or the property of any company concerned in the scheme ("a transferor company") is to be transferred to another company ("the transferee company").

(2) The court may, either by the order sanctioning the compromise or arrangement or by a subsequent order, make provision for all or any of the following matters—

  (a) the transfer to the transferee company of the whole or any part of the undertaking and of the property or liabilities of any transferor company;

  (b) the allotting or appropriation by the transferee company of any shares, debentures, policies or other like interests in that company which under the compromise or arrangement are to be allotted or appropriated by that company to or for any person;

  (c) the continuation by or against the transferee company of any legal proceedings pending by or against any transferor company;

  (d) the dissolution, without winding up, of any transferor company;

  (e) the provision to be made for any persons who, within such time and in such manner as the court directs, dissent from the compromise or arrangement;

  (f) such incidental, consequential and supplemental matters as are necessary to secure that the reconstruction or amalgamation is fully and effectively carried out.

(3) If an order under this section provides for the transfer of property or liabilities—

  (a) the property is by virtue of the order transferred to, and vests in, the transferee company, and

  (b) the liabilities are, by virtue of the order, transferred to and become liabilities of that company.

(4) The property (if the order so directs) vests freed from any charge that is by virtue of the compromise or arrangement to cease to have effect.

(5) In this section—

"property" includes property, rights and powers of every description; and
"liabilities" includes duties.

(6) Every company in relation to which an order is made under this section must cause a copy of the order to be delivered to the registrar within seven days after its making.

(7) If default is made in complying with subsection (6) an offence is committed by—

  (a) the company, and

  (b) every officer of the company who is in default.

(8) A person guilty of an offence under subsection (7) is liable on summary conviction to a fine not exceeding level 3 on the standard scale and, for continued contravention, a daily default fine not exceeding one-tenth of level 3 on the standard scale.

Obligations of company with respect to articles etc

901. Obligations of company with respect to articles etc

(1) This section applies—

  (a) to any order under section 899 (order sanctioning compromise or arrangement), and

  (b) to any order under section 900 (order facilitating reconstruction or amalgamation) that alters the company's constitution.

(2) If the order amends—

  (a) the company's articles, or

  (b) any resolution or agreement to which Chapter 3 of Part 3 applies (resolution or agreement affecting a company's constitution),

the copy of the order delivered to the registrar by the company under section 899(4) or section 900(6) must be accompanied by a copy of the company's articles, or the resolution or agreement in question, as amended.

(3) Every copy of the company's articles issued by the company after the order is made must be accompanied by a copy of the order, unless the effect of the order has been incorporated into the articles by amendment.

(4) In this section—

    (a) references to the effect of the order include the effect of the compromise or arrangement to which the order relates; and

    (b) in the case of a company not having articles, references to its articles shall be read as references to the instrument constituting the company or defining its constitution.

(5) If a company makes default in complying with this section an offence is committed by—

    (a) the company, and

    (b) every officer of the company who is in default.

(6) A person guilty of an offence under this section is liable on summary conviction to a fine not exceeding level 3 on the standard scale.

PART 27
MERGERS AND DIVISIONS OF PUBLIC COMPANIES

CHAPTER 1
INTRODUCTORY

902. Application of this Part

(1) This Part applies where—

    (a) a compromise or arrangement is proposed between a public company and—

        (i) its creditors or any class of them, or

        (ii) its members or any class of them,

    for the purposes of, or in connection with, a scheme for the reconstruction of any company or companies or the amalgamation of any two or more companies,

    (b) the scheme involves—

        (i) a merger (as defined in section 904), or

        (ii) a division (as defined in section 919), and

    (c) the consideration for the transfer (or each of the transfers) envisaged is to be shares in the transferee company (or one or more of the transferee companies) receivable by members of the transferor company (or transferor companies), with or without any cash payment to members.

(2) In this Part—

    (a) a "new company" means a company formed for the purposes of, or in connection with, the scheme, and

    (b) an "existing company" means a company other than one formed for the purposes of, or in connection with, the scheme.

(3) This Part does not apply where the company in respect of which the compromise or arrangement is proposed is being wound up.

903. Relationship of this Part to Part 26

(1) The court must not sanction the compromise or arrangement under Part 26 (arrangements and reconstructions) unless the relevant requirements of this Part have been complied with.

(2) The requirements applicable to a merger are specified in sections 905 to 914. Certain of those requirements, and certain general requirements of Part 26, are modified or excluded by the provisions of sections 915 to 918.

(3) The requirements applicable to a division are specified in sections 920 to 930.
Certain of those requirements, and certain general requirements of Part 26, are modified or excluded by the provisions of sections 931 to 934.

CHAPTER 2
MERGER

Introductory

904. **Mergers and merging companies**

    (1) The scheme involves a merger where under the scheme—

        (a) the undertaking, property and liabilities of one or more public companies, including the company in respect of which the compromise or arrangement is proposed, are to be transferred to another existing public company (a "merger by absorption"), or

        (b) the undertaking, property and liabilities of two or more public companies, including the company in respect of which the compromise or arrangement is proposed, are to be transferred to a new company, whether or not a public company, (a "merger by formation of a new company").

    (2) References in this Part to "the merging companies" are—

        (a) in relation to a merger by absorption, to the transferor and transferee companies;

        (b) in relation to a merger by formation of a new company, to the transferor companies.

Requirements applicable to merger

905. **Draft terms of scheme (merger)**

    (1) A draft of the proposed terms of the scheme must be drawn up and adopted by the directors of the merging companies.

    (2) The draft terms must give particulars of at least the following matters—

        (a) in respect of each transferor company and the transferee company—

            (i) its name,

            (ii) the address of its registered office, and

            (iii) whether it is a company limited by shares or a company limited by guarantee and having a share capital;

        (b) the number of shares in the transferee company to be allotted to members of a transferor company for a given number of their shares (the "share exchange ratio") and the amount of any cash payment;

        (c) the terms relating to the allotment of shares in the transferee company;

        (d) the date from which the holding of shares in the transferee company will entitle the holders to participate in profits, and any special conditions affecting that entitlement;

        (e) the date from which the transactions of a transferor company are to be treated for accounting purposes as being those of the transferee company;

        (f) any rights or restrictions attaching to shares or other securities in the transferee company to be allotted under the scheme to the holders of shares or other securities in a transferor company to which any special rights or restrictions attach, or the measures proposed concerning them;

        (g) any amount of benefit paid or given or intended to be paid or given—

            (i) to any of the experts referred to in section 909 (expert's report), or

            (ii) to any director of a merging company,

        and the consideration for the payment of benefit.

    (3) The requirements in subsection (2)(b), (c) and (d) are subject to section 915 (circumstances in which certain particulars not required).

906. **Publication of draft terms (merger)**

    (1) The directors of each of the merging companies must deliver a copy of the draft terms to the registrar.

    (2) The registrar must publish in the Gazette notice of receipt by him from that company of a copy of the draft terms.

(3) That notice must be published at least one month before the date of any meeting of that company summoned for the purpose of approving the scheme.

907. **Approval of members of merging companies**

(1) The scheme must be approved by a majority in number, representing 75% in value, of each class of members of each of the merging companies, present and voting either in person or by proxy at a meeting.

(2) This requirement is subject to sections 916, 917 and 918 (circumstances in which meetings of members not required).

908. **Directors' explanatory report (merger)**

(1) The directors of each of the merging companies must draw up and adopt a report.

(2) The report must consist of—

(a) the statement required by section 897 (statement explaining effect of compromise or arrangement), and

(b) insofar as that statement does not deal with the following matters, a further statement—

(i) setting out the legal and economic grounds for the draft terms, and in particular for the share exchange ratio, and

(ii) specifying any special valuation difficulties.

(3) The requirement in this section is subject to section 915 (circumstances in which reports not required).

909. **Expert's report (merger)**

(1) An expert's report must be drawn up on behalf of each of the merging companies.

(2) The report required is a written report on the draft terms to the members of the company.

(3) The court may on the joint application of all the merging companies approve the appointment of a joint expert to draw up a single report on behalf of all those companies.

If no such appointment is made, there must be a separate expert's report to the members of each merging company drawn up by a separate expert appointed on behalf of that company.

(4) The expert must be a person who—

(a) is eligible for appointment as a statutory auditor (see section 1212), and

(b) meets the independence requirement in section 936.

(5) The expert's report must—

(a) indicate the method or methods used to arrive at the share exchange ratio;

(b) give an opinion as to whether the method or methods used are reasonable in all the circumstances of the case, indicate the values arrived at using each such method and (if there is more than one method) give an opinion on the relative importance attributed to such methods in arriving at the value decided on;

(c) describe any special valuation difficulties that have arisen;

(d) state whether in the expert's opinion the share exchange ratio is reasonable; and

(e) in the case of a valuation made by a person other than himself (see section 935), state that it appeared to him reasonable to arrange for it to be so made or to accept a valuation so made.

(6) The expert (or each of them) has—

(a) the right of access to all such documents of all the merging companies, and

(b) the right to require from the companies' officers all such information,

as he thinks necessary for the purposes of making his report.

(7) The requirement in this section is subject to section 915 (circumstances in which reports not required).

910. **Supplementary accounting statement (merger)**

(1) If the last annual accounts of any of the merging companies relate to a financial year ending more than seven months before the first meeting of the company summoned for the purposes of approving the scheme, the directors of that company must prepare a supplementary accounting statement.

(2) That statement must consist of—

    (a) a balance sheet dealing with the state of affairs of the company as at a date not more than three months before the draft terms were adopted by the directors, and

    (b) where the company would be required under section 399 to prepare group accounts if that date were the last day of a financial year, a consolidated balance sheet dealing with the state of affairs of the company and the undertakings that would be included in such a consolidation.

(3) The requirements of this Act (and where relevant Article 4 of the IAS Regulation) as to the balance sheet forming part of a company's annual accounts, and the matters to be included in notes to it, apply to the balance sheet required for an accounting statement under this section, with such modifications as are necessary by reason of its being prepared otherwise than as at the last day of a financial year.

(4) The provisions of section 414 as to the approval and signing of accounts apply to the balance sheet required for an accounting statement under this section.

911. Inspection of documents (merger)

(1) The members of each of the merging companies must be able, during the period specified below—

    (a) to inspect at the registered office of that company copies of the documents listed below relating to that company and every other merging company, and

    (b) to obtain copies of those documents or any part of them on request free of charge.

(2) The period referred to above is the period—

    (a) beginning one month before, and

    (b) ending on the date of,

the first meeting of the members, or any class of members, of the company for the purposes of approving the scheme.

(3) The documents referred to above are—

    (a) the draft terms;

    (b) the directors' explanatory report;

    (c) the expert's report;

    (d) the company's annual accounts and reports for the last three financial years ending on or before the first meeting of the members, or any class of members, of the company summoned for the purposes of approving the scheme; and

    (e) any supplementary accounting statement required by section 910.

(4) The requirements of subsection (3)(b) and (c) are subject to section 915 (circumstances in which reports not required).

912. Approval of articles of new transferee company (merger)

In the case of a merger by formation of a new company, the articles of the transferee company, or a draft of them, must be approved by ordinary resolution of the transferor company or, as the case may be, each of the transferor companies.

913. Protection of holders of securities to which special rights attached (merger)

(1) The scheme must provide that where any securities of a transferor company (other than shares) to which special rights are attached are held by a person otherwise than as a member or creditor of the company, that person is to receive rights in the transferee company of equivalent value.

(2) Subsection (1) does not apply if—

    (a) the holder has agreed otherwise, or

    (b) the holder is, or under the scheme is to be, entitled to have the securities purchased by the transferee company on terms that the court considers reasonable.

914. No allotment of shares to transferor company or its nominee (merger)

The scheme must not provide for shares in the transferee company to be allotted to a transferor company (or its nominee) in respect of shares in the transferor company held by it (or its nominee).

Exceptions where shares of transferor company held by transferee company

915. Circumstances in which certain particulars and reports not required (merger)

(1) This section applies in the case of a merger by absorption where all of the relevant securities of the transferor company (or, if there is more than one transferor company, of each of them) are held by or on behalf of the transferee company.

(2) The draft terms of the scheme need not give the particulars mentioned in section 905(2)(b), (c) or (d) (particulars relating to allotment of shares to members of transferor company).

(3) Section 897 (explanatory statement to be circulated or made available) does not apply.

(4) The requirements of the following sections do not apply—

section 908 (directors' explanatory report),

section 909 (expert's report).

(5) The requirements of section 911 (inspection of documents) so far as relating to any document required to be drawn up under the provisions mentioned in subsection (3) above do not apply.

(6) In this section "relevant securities", in relation to a company, means shares or other securities carrying the right to vote at general meetings of the company.

916. Circumstances in which meeting of members of transferee company not required (merger)

(1) This section applies in the case of a merger by absorption where 90% or more (but not all) of the relevant securities of the transferor company (or, if there is more than one transferor company, of each of them) are held by or on behalf of the transferee company.

(2) It is not necessary for the scheme to be approved at a meeting of the members, or any class of members, of the transferee company if the court is satisfied that the following conditions have been complied with.

(3) The first condition is that publication of notice of receipt of the draft terms by the registrar took place in respect of the transferee company at least one month before the date of the first meeting of members, or any class of members, of the transferor company summoned for the purpose of agreeing to the scheme.

(4) The second condition is that the members of the transferee company were able during the period beginning one month before, and ending on, that date—

(a) to inspect at the registered office of the transferee company copies of the documents listed in section 911(3)(a), (d) and (e) relating to that company and the transferor company (or, if there is more than one transferor company, each of them), and

(b) to obtain copies of those documents or any part of them on request free of charge.

(5) The third condition is that—

(a) one or more members of the transferee company, who together held not less than 5% of the paid-up capital of the company which carried the right to vote at general meetings of the company (excluding any shares in the company held as treasury shares) would have been able, during that period, to require a meeting of each class of members to be called for the purpose of deciding whether or not to agree to the scheme, and

(b) no such requirement was made.

(6) In this section "relevant securities", in relation to a company, means shares or other securities carrying the right to vote at general meetings of the company.

917. Circumstances in which no meetings required (merger)

(1) This section applies in the case of a merger by absorption where all of the relevant securities of the transferor company (or, if there is more than one transferor company, of each of them) are held by or on behalf of the transferee company.

(2) It is not necessary for the scheme to be approved at a meeting of the members, or any class of members, of any of the merging companies if the court is satisfied that the following conditions have been complied with.

(3) The first condition is that publication of notice of receipt of the draft terms by the registrar took place in respect of all the merging companies at least one month before the date of the court's order.

(4) The second condition is that the members of the transferee company were able during the period beginning one month before, and ending on, that date—

    (a) to inspect at the registered office of that company copies of the documents listed in section 911(3) relating to that company and the transferor company (or, if there is more than one transferor company, each of them), and

    (b) to obtain copies of those documents or any part of them on request free of charge.

(5) The third condition is that—

    (a) one or more members of the transferee company, who together held not less than 5% of the paid-up capital of the company which carried the right to vote at general meetings of the company (excluding any shares in the company held as treasury shares) would have been able, during that period, to require a meeting of each class of members to be called for the purpose of deciding whether or not to agree to the scheme, and

    (b) no such requirement was made.

(6) In this section "relevant securities", in relation to a company, means shares or other securities carrying the right to vote at general meetings of the company.

Other exceptions

918. Other circumstances in which meeting of members of transferee company not required (merger)

(1) In the case of any merger by absorption, it is not necessary for the scheme to be approved by the members of the transferee company if the court is satisfied that the following conditions have been complied with.

(2) The first condition is that publication of notice of receipt of the draft terms by the registrar took place in respect of that company at least one month before the date of the first meeting of members, or any class of members, of the transferor company (or, if there is more than one transferor company, any of them) summoned for the purposes of agreeing to the scheme.

(3) The second condition is that the members of that company were able during the period beginning one month before, and ending on, the date of any such meeting—

    (a) to inspect at the registered office of that company copies of the documents specified in section 911(3) relating to that company and the transferor company (or, if there is more than one transferor company, each of them), and

    (b) to obtain copies of those documents or any part of them on request free of charge.

(4) The third condition is that—

    (a) one or more members of that company, who together held not less than 5% of the paid-up capital of the company which carried the right to vote at general meetings of the company (excluding any shares in the company held as treasury shares) would have been able, during that period, to require a meeting of each class of members to be called for the purpose of deciding whether or not to agree to the scheme, and

    (b) no such requirement was made.

CHAPTER 3
DIVISION

Introductory

919. **Divisions and companies involved in a division**

(1) The scheme involves a division where under the scheme the undertaking, property and liabilities of the company in respect of which the compromise or arrangement is proposed are to be divided among and transferred to two or more companies each of which is either—

(a) an existing public company, or

(b) a new company (whether or not a public company).

(2) References in this Part to the companies involved in the division are to the transferor company and any existing transferee companies.

Requirements to be complied with in case of division

920. **Draft terms of scheme (division)**

(1) A draft of the proposed terms of the scheme must be drawn up and adopted by the directors of each of the companies involved in the division.

(2) The draft terms must give particulars of at least the following matters—

(a) in respect of the transferor company and each transferee company—

(i) its name,

(ii) the address of its registered office, and

(iii) whether it is a company limited by shares or a company limited by guarantee and having a share capital;

(b) the number of shares in a transferee company to be allotted to members of the transferor company for a given number of their shares (the "share exchange ratio") and the amount of any cash payment;

(c) the terms relating to the allotment of shares in a transferee company;

(d) the date from which the holding of shares in a transferee company will entitle the holders to participate in profits, and any special conditions affecting that entitlement;

(e) the date from which the transactions of the transferor company are to be treated for accounting purposes as being those of a transferee company;

(f) any rights or restrictions attaching to shares or other securities in a transferee company to be allotted under the scheme to the holders of shares or other securities in the transferor company to which any special rights or restrictions attach, or the measures proposed concerning them;

(g) any amount of benefit paid or given or intended to be paid or given—

(i) to any of the experts referred to in section 924 (expert's report), or

(ii) to any director of a company involved in the division,

and the consideration for the payment of benefit.

(3) The draft terms must also—

(a) give particulars of the property and liabilities to be transferred (to the extent that these are known to the transferor company) and their allocation among the transferee companies;

(b) make provision for the allocation among and transfer to the transferee companies of any other property and liabilities that the transferor company has acquired or may subsequently acquire; and

(c) specify the allocation to members of the transferor company of shares in the transferee companies and the criteria upon which that allocation is based.

921. **Publication of draft terms (division)**

(1) The directors of each company involved in the division must deliver a copy of the draft terms to the registrar.

(2) The registrar must publish in the Gazette notice of receipt by him from that company of a copy of the draft terms.

(3) That notice must be published at least one month before the date of any meeting of that company summoned for the purposes of approving the scheme.

(4) The requirements in this section are subject to section 934 (power of court to exclude certain requirements).

922. Approval of members of companies involved in the division

(1) The compromise or arrangement must be approved by a majority in number, representing 75% in value, of each class of members of each of the companies involved in the division, present and voting either in person or by proxy at a meeting.

(2) This requirement is subject to sections 931 and 932 (circumstances in which meeting of members not required).

923. Directors' explanatory report (division)

(1) The directors of the transferor and each existing transferee company must draw up and adopt a report.

(2) The report must consist of—

    (a) the statement required by section 897 (statement explaining effect of compromise or arrangement), and

    (b) insofar as that statement does not deal with the following matters, a further statement—

        (i) setting out the legal and economic grounds for the draft terms, and in particular for the share exchange ratio and for the criteria on which the allocation to the members of the transferor company of shares in the transferee companies was based, and

        (ii) specifying any special valuation difficulties.

(3) The report must also state—

    (a) whether a report has been made to any transferee company under section 593 (valuation of non-cash consideration for shares), and

    (b) if so, whether that report has been delivered to the registrar of companies.

(4) The requirement in this section is subject to section 933 (agreement to dispense with reports etc).

924. Expert's report (division)

(1) An expert's report must be drawn up on behalf of each company involved in the division.

(2) The report required is a written report on the draft terms to the members of the company.

(3) The court may on the joint application of the companies involved in the division approve the appointment of a joint expert to draw up a single report on behalf of all those companies. If no such appointment is made, there must be a separate expert's report to the members of each company involved in the division drawn up by a separate expert appointed on behalf of that company.

(4) The expert must be a person who—

    (a) is eligible for appointment as a statutory auditor (see section 1212), and

    (b) meets the independence requirement in section 936.

(5) The expert's report must—

    (a) indicate the method or methods used to arrive at the share exchange ratio;

    (b) give an opinion as to whether the method or methods used are reasonable in all the circumstances of the case, indicate the values arrived at using each such method and (if there is more than one method) give an opinion on the relative importance attributed to such methods in arriving at the value decided on;

    (c) describe any special valuation difficulties that have arisen;

    (d) state whether in the expert's opinion the share exchange ratio is reasonable; and

    (e) in the case of a valuation made by a person other than himself (see section 935), state that it appeared to him reasonable to arrange for it to be so made or to accept a valuation so made.

(6) The expert (or each of them) has—

    (a) the right of access to all such documents of the companies involved in the division, and

    (b) the right to require from the companies' officers all such information,

as he thinks necessary for the purposes of making his report.

(7) The requirement in this section is subject to section 933 (agreement to dispense with reports etc).

925. Supplementary accounting statement (division)

(1) If the last annual accounts of a company involved in the division relate to a financial year ending more than seven months before the first meeting of the company summoned for the purposes of approving the scheme, the directors of that company must prepare a supplementary accounting statement.

(2) That statement must consist of—

    (a) a balance sheet dealing with the state of affairs of the company as at a date not more than three months before the draft terms were adopted by the directors, and

    (b) where the company would be required under section 399 to prepare group accounts if that date were the last day of a financial year, a consolidated balance sheet dealing with the state of affairs of the company and the undertakings that would be included in such a consolidation.

(3) The requirements of this Act (and where relevant Article 4 of the IAS Regulation) as to the balance sheet forming part of a company's annual accounts, and the matters to be included in notes to it, apply to the balance sheet required for an accounting statement under this section, with such modifications as are necessary by reason of its being prepared otherwise than as at the last day of a financial year.

(4) The provisions of section 414 as to the approval and signing of accounts apply to the balance sheet required for an accounting statement under this section.

(5) The requirement in this section is subject to section 933 (agreement to dispense with reports etc).

926. Inspection of documents (division)

(1) The members of each company involved in the division must be able, during the period specified below—

    (a) to inspect at the registered office of that company copies of the documents listed below relating to that company and every other company involved in the division, and

    (b) to obtain copies of those documents or any part of them on request free of charge.

(2) The period referred to above is the period—

    (a) beginning one month before, and

    (b) ending on the date of,

the first meeting of the members, or any class of members, of the company for the purposes of approving the scheme.

(3) The documents referred to above are—

    (a) the draft terms;

    (b) the directors' explanatory report;

    (c) the expert's report;

    (d) the company's annual accounts and reports for the last three financial years ending on or before the first meeting of the members, or any class of members, of the company summoned for the purposes of approving the scheme; and

    (e) any supplementary accounting statement required by section 925.

(4) The requirements in subsection (3)(b), (c) and (e) are subject to section 933 (agreement to dispense with reports etc) and section 934 (power of court to exclude certain requirements).

927. **Report on material changes of assets of transferor company (division)**
   (1) The directors of the transferor company must report—
      (a) to every meeting of the members, or any class of members, of that company summoned for the purpose of agreeing to the scheme, and
      (b) to the directors of each existing transferee company,
      any material changes in the property and liabilities of the transferor company between the date when the draft terms were adopted and the date of the meeting in question.
   (2) The directors of each existing transferee company must in turn—
      (a) report those matters to every meeting of the members, or any class of members, of that company summoned for the purpose of agreeing to the scheme, or
      (b) send a report of those matters to every member entitled to receive notice of such a meeting.
   (3) The requirement in this section is subject to section 933 (agreement to dispense with reports etc).

928. **Approval of articles of new transferee company (division)**
   The articles of every new transferee company, or a draft of them, must be approved by ordinary resolution of the transferor company.

929. **Protection of holders of securities to which special rights attached (division)**
   (1) The scheme must provide that where any securities of the transferor company (other than shares) to which special rights are attached are held by a person otherwise than as a member or creditor of the company, that person is to receive rights in a transferee company of equivalent value.
   (2) Subsection (1) does not apply if—
      (a) the holder has agreed otherwise, or
      (b) the holder is, or under the scheme is to be, entitled to have the securities purchased by a transferee company on terms that the court considers reasonable.

930. **No allotment of shares to transferor company or its nominee (division)**
   The scheme must not provide for shares in a transferee company to be allotted to the transferor company (or its nominee) in respect of shares in the transferor company held by it (or its nominee).

Exceptions where shares of transferor company held by transferee company

931. **Circumstances in which meeting of members of transferor company not required (division)**
   (1) This section applies in the case of a division where all of the shares or other securities of the transferor company carrying the right to vote at general meetings of the company are held by or on behalf of one or more existing transferee companies.
   (2) It is not necessary for the scheme to be approved by a meeting of the members, or any class of members, of the transferor company if the court is satisfied that the following conditions have been complied with.
   (3) The first condition is that publication of notice of receipt of the draft terms by the registrar took place in respect of all the companies involved in the division at least one month before the date of the court's order.
   (4) The second condition is that the members of every company involved in the division were able during the period beginning one month before, and ending on, that date—
      (a) to inspect at the registered office of their company copies of the documents listed in section 926(3) relating to every company involved in the division, and
      (b) to obtain copies of those documents or any part of them on request free of charge.
   (5) The third condition is that—
      (a) one or more members of the transferor company, who together held not less than 5% of the paid-up capital of the company (excluding any shares in the company held as treasury shares) would have been able, during that period, to require a meeting of each

class of members to be called for the purpose of deciding whether or not to agree to the scheme, and

(b) no such requirement was made.

(6) The fourth condition is that the directors of the transferor company have sent—

(a) to every member who would have been entitled to receive notice of a meeting to agree to the scheme (had any such meeting been called), and

(b) to the directors of every existing transferee company,

a report of any material change in the property and liabilities of the transferor company between the date when the terms were adopted by the directors and the date one month before the date of the court's order.

Other exceptions

932. Circumstances in which meeting of members of transferee company not required (division)

(1) In the case of a division, it is not necessary for the scheme to be approved by the members of a transferee company if the court is satisfied that the following conditions have been complied with in relation to that company.

(2) The first condition is that publication of notice of receipt of the draft terms by the registrar took place in respect of that company at least one month before the date of the first meeting of members of the transferor company summoned for the purposes of agreeing to the scheme.

(3) The second condition is that the members of that company were able during the period beginning one month before, and ending on, that date—

(a) to inspect at the registered office of that company copies of the documents specified in section 926(3) relating to that company and every other company involved in the division, and

(b) to obtain copies of those documents or any part of them on request free of charge.

(4) The third condition is that—

(a) one or more members of that company, who together held not less than 5% of the paid-up capital of the company which carried the right to vote at general meetings of the company (excluding any shares in the company held as treasury shares) would have been able, during that period, to require a meeting of each class of members to be called for the purpose of deciding whether or not to agree to the scheme, and

(b) no such requirement was made.

(5) The first and second conditions above are subject to section 934 (power of court to exclude certain requirements).

933. Agreement to dispense with reports etc (division)

(1) If all members holding shares in, and all persons holding other securities of, the companies involved in the division, being shares or securities that carry a right to vote in general meetings of the company in question, so agree, the following requirements do not apply.

(2) The requirements that may be dispensed with under this section are—

(a) the requirements of—

(i) section 923 (directors' explanatory report),

(ii) section 924 (expert's report),

(iii) section 925 (supplementary accounting statement), and

(iv) section 927 (report on material changes in assets of transferor company); and

(b) the requirements of section 926 (inspection of documents) so far as relating to any document required to be drawn up under the provisions mentioned in paragraph (a)(i), (ii) or (iii) above.

(3) For the purposes of this section—

(a) the members, or holders of other securities, of a company, and

(b) whether shares or other securities carry a right to vote in general meetings of the company,

are determined as at the date of the application to the court under section 896.

934. Power of court to exclude certain requirements (division)

(1) In the case of a division, the court may by order direct that—

    (a) in relation to any company involved in the division, the requirements of—

        (i) section 921 (publication of draft terms), and

        (ii) section 926 (inspection of documents),

        do not apply, and

    (b) in relation to an existing transferee company, section 932 (circumstances in which meeting of members of transferee company not required) has effect with the omission of the first and second conditions specified in that section,

    if the court is satisfied that the following conditions will be fulfilled in relation to that company.

(2) The first condition is that the members of that company will have received, or will have been able to obtain free of charge, copies of the documents listed in section 926—

    (a) in time to examine them before the date of the first meeting of the members, or any class of members, of that company summoned for the purposes of agreeing to the scheme, or

    (b) in the case of an existing transferee company where in the circumstances described in section 932 no meeting is held, in time to require a meeting as mentioned in subsection (4) of that section.

(3) The second condition is that the creditors of that company will have received or will have been able to obtain free of charge copies of the draft terms in time to examine them—

    (a) before the date of the first meeting of the members, or any class of members, of the company summoned for the purposes of agreeing to the scheme, or

    (b) in the circumstances mentioned in subsection (2)(b) above, at the same time as the members of the company.

(4) The third condition is that no prejudice would be caused to the members or creditors of the transferor company or any transferee company by making the order in question.

CHAPTER 4

SUPPLEMENTARY PROVISIONS

Expert's report and related matters

935. Expert's report: valuation by another person

(1) Where it appears to an expert—

    (a) that a valuation is reasonably necessary to enable him to draw up his report, and

    (b) that it is reasonable for that valuation, or part of it, to be made by (or for him to accept a valuation made by) another person who—

        (i) appears to him to have the requisite knowledge and experience to make the valuation or that part of it, and

        (ii) meets the independence requirement in section 936,

    he may arrange for or accept such a valuation, together with a report which will enable him to make his own report under section 909 or 924.

(2) Where any valuation is made by a person other than the expert himself, the latter's report must state that fact and must also—

    (a) state the former's name and what knowledge and experience he has to carry out the valuation, and

    (b) describe so much of the undertaking, property and liabilities as was valued by the other person, and the method used to value them, and specify the date of the valuation.

936. Experts and valuers: independence requirement

(1) A person meets the independence requirement for the purposes of section 909 or 924 (expert's report) or section 935 (valuation by another person) only if—

    (a) he is not—

        (i) an officer or employee of any of the companies concerned in the scheme, or

        (ii) a partner or employee of such a person, or a partnership of which such a person is a partner;

    (b) he is not—

        (i) an officer or employee of an associated undertaking of any of the companies concerned in the scheme, or

        (ii) a partner or employee of such a person, or a partnership of which such a person is a partner; and

    (c) there does not exist between—

        (i) the person or an associate of his, and

        (ii) any of the companies concerned in the scheme or an associated undertaking of such a company,

    a connection of any such description as may be specified by regulations made by the Secretary of State.

(2) An auditor of a company is not regarded as an officer or employee of the company for this purpose.

(3) For the purposes of this section—

    (a) the "companies concerned in the scheme" means every transferor and existing transferee company;

    (b) "associated undertaking", in relation to a company, means—

        (i) a parent undertaking or subsidiary undertaking of the company, or

        (ii) a subsidiary undertaking of a parent undertaking of the company; and

    (c) "associate" has the meaning given by section 937.

(4) Regulations under this section are subject to negative resolution procedure.

937. Experts and valuers: meaning of "associate"

(1) This section defines "associate" for the purposes of section 936 (experts and valuers: independence requirement).

(2) In relation to an individual, "associate" means—

    (a) that individual's spouse or civil partner or minor child or step-child,

    (b) any body corporate of which that individual is a director, and

    (c) any employee or partner of that individual.

(3) In relation to a body corporate, "associate" means—

    (a) any body corporate of which that body is a director,

    (b) any body corporate in the same group as that body, and

    (c) any employee or partner of that body or of any body corporate in the same group.

(4) In relation to a partnership that is a legal person under the law by which it is governed, "associate" means—

    (a) any body corporate of which that partnership is a director,

    (b) any employee of or partner in that partnership, and

    (c) any person who is an associate of a partner in that partnership.

(5) In relation to a partnership that is not a legal person under the law by which it is governed, "associate" means any person who is an associate of any of the partners.

(6) In this section, in relation to a limited liability partnership, for "director" read "member".

Powers of the court

938. Power of court to summon meeting of members or creditors of existing transferee company

(1) The court may order a meeting of—

    (a) the members of an existing transferee company, or any class of them, or

    (b) the creditors of an existing transferee company, or any class of them,

    to be summoned in such manner as the court directs.

(2) An application for such an order may be made by—
    (a) the company concerned,
    (b) a member or creditor of the company, or
    (c) if an administration order is in force in relation to the company, the administrator.

939. Court to fix date for transfer of undertaking etc of transferor company

(1) Where the court sanctions the compromise or arrangement, it must—
    (a) in the order sanctioning the compromise or arrangement, or
    (b) in a subsequent order under section 900 (powers of court to facilitate reconstruction or amalgamation),
fix a date on which the transfer (or transfers) to the transferee company (or transferee companies) of the undertaking, property and liabilities of the transferor company is (or are) to take place.

(2) Any such order that provides for the dissolution of the transferor company must fix the same date for the dissolution.

(3) If it is necessary for the transferor company to take steps to ensure that the undertaking, property and liabilities are fully transferred, the court must fix a date, not later than six months after the date fixed under subsection (1), by which such steps must be taken.

(4) In that case, the court may postpone the dissolution of the transferor company until that date.

(5) The court may postpone or further postpone the date fixed under subsection (3) if it is satisfied that the steps mentioned cannot be completed by the date (or latest date) fixed under that subsection.

Liability of transferee companies

940. Liability of transferee companies for each other's defaults

(1) In the case of a division, each transferee company is jointly and severally liable for any liability transferred to any other transferee company under the scheme to the extent that the other company has made default in satisfying that liability.
This is subject to the following provisions.

(2) If a majority in number representing 75% in value of the creditors or any class of creditors of the transferor company, present and voting either in person or by proxy at a meeting summoned for the purposes of agreeing to the scheme, so agree, subsection (1) does not apply in relation to the liabilities owed to the creditors or that class of creditors.

(3) A transferee company is not liable under this section for an amount greater than the net value transferred to it under the scheme.
The "net value transferred" is the value at the time of the transfer of the property transferred to it under the scheme less the amount at that date of the liabilities so transferred.

Interpretation

941. Meaning of "liabilities" and "property"

In this Part—
"liabilities" includes duties;
"property" includes property, rights and powers of every description.

PART 28
TAKEOVERS ETC

CHAPTER 1
THE TAKEOVER PANEL

The Panel and its rules

942. The Panel

(1) The body known as the Panel on Takeovers and Mergers ("the Panel") is to have the functions conferred on it by or under this Chapter.

(2) The Panel may do anything that it considers necessary or expedient for the purposes of, or in connection with, its functions.

(3) The Panel may make arrangements for any of its functions to be discharged by—

(a) a committee or sub-committee of the Panel, or

(b) an officer or member of staff of the Panel, or a person acting as such.

This is subject to section 943(4) and (5).

943. Rules

(1) The Panel must make rules giving effect to Articles 3.1, 4.2, 5, 6.1 to 6.3, 7 to 9 and 13 of the Takeovers Directive.

(2) Rules made by the Panel may also make other provision—

(a) for or in connection with the regulation of—

(i) takeover bids,

(ii) merger transactions, and

(iii) transactions (not falling within sub-paragraph (i) or (ii)) that have or may have, directly or indirectly, an effect on the ownership or control of companies;

(b) for or in connection with the regulation of things done in consequence of, or otherwise in relation to, any such bid or transaction;

(c) about cases where—

(i) any such bid or transaction is, or has been, contemplated or apprehended, or

(ii) an announcement is made denying that any such bid or transaction is intended.

(3) The provision that may be made under subsection (2) includes, in particular, provision for a matter that is, or is similar to, a matter provided for by the Panel in the City Code on Takeovers and Mergers as it had effect immediately before the passing of this Act.

(4) In relation to rules made by virtue of section 957 (fees and charges), functions under this section may be discharged either by the Panel itself or by a committee of the Panel (but not otherwise).

(5) In relation to rules of any other description, the Panel must discharge its functions under this section by a committee of the Panel.

(6) Section 1 (meaning of "company") does not apply for the purposes of this section.

(7) In this section "takeover bid" includes a takeover bid within the meaning of the Takeovers Directive.

(8) In this Chapter "the Takeovers Directive" means Directive 2004/25/EC of the European Parliament and of the Council.

(9) A reference to rules in the following provisions of this Chapter is to rules under this section.

944. Further provisions about rules

(1) Rules may—

(a) make different provision for different purposes;

(b) make provision subject to exceptions or exemptions;

(c) contain incidental, supplemental, consequential or transitional provision;

(d) authorise the Panel to dispense with or modify the application of rules in particular cases and by reference to any circumstances.

Rules made by virtue of paragraph (d) must require the Panel to give reasons for acting as mentioned in that paragraph.

(2) Rules must be made by an instrument in writing.

(3) Immediately after an instrument containing rules is made, the text must be made available to the public, with or without payment, in whatever way the Panel thinks appropriate.

(4) A person is not to be taken to have contravened a rule if he shows that at the time of the alleged contravention the text of the rule had not been made available as required by subsection (3).

(5) The production of a printed copy of an instrument purporting to be made by the Panel on which is endorsed a certificate signed by an officer of the Panel authorised by it for that purpose and stating—

(a) that the instrument was made by the Panel,

(b) that the copy is a true copy of the instrument, and

(c) that on a specified date the text of the instrument was made available to the public as required by subsection (3),

is evidence (or in Scotland sufficient evidence) of the facts stated in the certificate.

(6) A certificate purporting to be signed as mentioned in subsection (5) is to be treated as having been properly signed unless the contrary is shown.

(7) A person who wishes in any legal proceedings to rely on an instrument by which rules are made may require the Panel to endorse a copy of the instrument with a certificate of the kind mentioned in subsection (5).

945. Rulings

(1) The Panel may give rulings on the interpretation, application or effect of rules.

(2) To the extent and in the circumstances specified in rules, and subject to any review or appeal, a ruling has binding effect.

946. Directions

Rules may contain provision conferring power on the Panel to give any direction that appears to the Panel to be necessary in order—

(1) to restrain a person from acting (or continuing to act) in breach of rules;

(2) to restrain a person from doing (or continuing to do) a particular thing, pending determination of whether that or any other conduct of his is or would be a breach of rules;

(3) otherwise to secure compliance with rules.

Information

947. Power to require documents and information

(1) The Panel may by notice in writing require a person—

(a) to produce any documents that are specified or described in the notice;

(b) to provide, in the form and manner specified in the notice, such information as may be specified or described in the notice.

(2) A requirement under subsection (1) must be complied with—

(a) at a place specified in the notice, and

(b) before the end of such reasonable period as may be so specified.

(3) This section applies only to documents and information reasonably required in connection with the exercise by the Panel of its functions.

(4) The Panel may require—

(a) any document produced to be authenticated, or

(b) any information provided (whether in a document or otherwise) to be verified,

in such manner as it may reasonably require.

(5) The Panel may authorise a person to exercise any of its powers under this section.

(6) A person exercising a power by virtue of subsection (5) must, if required to do so, produce evidence of his authority to exercise the power.

(7) The production of a document in pursuance of this section does not affect any lien that a person has on the document.

(8) The Panel may take copies of or extracts from a document produced in pursuance of this section.

(9) A reference in this section to the production of a document includes a reference to the production of—

(a) a hard copy of information recorded otherwise than in hard copy form, or

(b) information in a form from which a hard copy can be readily obtained.

(10) A person is not required by this section to disclose documents or information in respect of which a claim to legal professional privilege (in Scotland, to confidentiality of communications) could be maintained in legal proceedings.

948. Restrictions on disclosure

(1) This section applies to information (in whatever form)—

(a) relating to the private affairs of an individual, or

(b) relating to any particular business,

that is provided to the Panel in connection with the exercise of its functions.

(2) No such information may, during the lifetime of the individual or so long as the business continues to be carried on, be disclosed without the consent of that individual or (as the case may be) the person for the time being carrying on that business.

(3) Subsection (2) does not apply to any disclosure of information that—

(a) is made for the purpose of facilitating the carrying out by the Panel of any of its functions,

(b) is made to a person specified in Part 1 of Schedule 2,

(c) is of a description specified in Part 2 of that Schedule, or

(d) is made in accordance with Part 3 of that Schedule.

(4) The Secretary of State may amend Schedule 2 by order subject to negative resolution procedure.

(5) An order under subsection (4) must not—

(a) amend Part 1 of Schedule 2 by specifying a person unless the person exercises functions of a public nature (whether or not he exercises any other function);

(b) amend Part 2 of Schedule 2 by adding or modifying a description of disclosure unless the purpose for which the disclosure is permitted is likely to facilitate the exercise of a function of a public nature;

(c) amend Part 3 of Schedule 2 so as to have the effect of permitting disclosures to be made to a body other than one that exercises functions of a public nature in a country or territory outside the United Kingdom.

(6) Subsection (2) does not apply to—

(a) the disclosure by an authority within subsection (7) of information disclosed to it by the Panel in reliance on subsection (3);

(b) the disclosure of such information by anyone who has obtained it directly or indirectly from an authority within subsection (7).

(7) The authorities within this subsection are—

(a) the Financial Services Authority;

(b) an authority designated as a supervisory authority for the purposes of Article 4.1 of the Takeovers Directive;

(c) any other person or body that exercises functions of a public nature, under legislation in an EEA State other than the United Kingdom, that are similar to the Panel's functions or those of the Financial Services Authority.

(8) This section does not prohibit the disclosure of information if the information is or has been available to the public from any other source.

(9) Nothing in this section authorises the making of a disclosure in contravention of the Data Protection Act 1998 (c. 29).

949. **Offence of disclosure in contravention of section 948**

(1) A person who discloses information in contravention of section 948 is guilty of an offence, unless—

(a) he did not know, and had no reason to suspect, that the information had been provided as mentioned in section 948(1), or

(b) he took all reasonable steps and exercised all due diligence to avoid the commission of the offence.

(2) A person guilty of an offence under this section is liable—

(a) on conviction on indictment, to imprisonment for a term not exceeding two years or a fine (or both);

(b) on summary conviction—

(i) in England and Wales, to imprisonment for a term not exceeding twelve months or to a fine not exceeding the statutory maximum (or both);

(ii) in Scotland or Northern Ireland, to imprisonment for a term not exceeding six months, or to a fine not exceeding the statutory maximum (or both).

(3) Where a company or other body corporate commits an offence under this section, an offence is also committed by every officer of the company or other body corporate who is in default.

Co-operation

950. **Panel's duty of co-operation**

(1) The Panel must take such steps as it considers appropriate to co-operate with—

(a) the Financial Services Authority;

(b) an authority designated as a supervisory authority for the purposes of Article 4.1 of the Takeovers Directive;

(c) any other person or body that exercises functions of a public nature, under legislation in any country or territory outside the United Kingdom, that appear to the Panel to be similar to its own functions or those of the Financial Services Authority.

(2) Co-operation may include the sharing of information that the Panel is not prevented from disclosing.

Hearings and appeals

951. **Hearings and appeals**

(1) Rules must provide for a decision of the Panel to be subject to review by a committee of the Panel (the "Hearings Committee") at the instance of such persons affected by the decision as are specified in the rules.

(2) Rules may also confer other functions on the Hearings Committee.

(3) Rules must provide for there to be a right of appeal against a decision of the Hearings Committee to an independent tribunal (the "Takeover Appeal Board") in such circumstances and subject to such conditions as are specified in the rules.

(4) Rules may contain—

(a) provision as to matters of procedure in relation to proceedings before the Hearings Committee (including provision imposing time limits);

(b) provision about evidence in such proceedings;

(c) provision as to the powers of the Hearings Committee dealing with a matter referred to it;

(d) provision about enforcement of decisions of the Hearings Committee and the Takeover Appeal Board.

(5) Rules must contain provision—

(a) requiring the Panel, when acting in relation to any proceedings before the Hearings

Committee or the Takeover Appeal Board, to do so by an officer or member of staff of the Panel (or a person acting as such);

(b) preventing a person who is or has been a member of the committee mentioned in section 943(5) from being a member of the Hearings Committee or the Takeover Appeal Board;

(c) preventing a person who is a member of the committee mentioned in section 943(5), of the Hearings Committee or of the Takeover Appeal Board from acting as mentioned in paragraph (a).

Contravention of rules etc

952. Sanctions

(1) Rules may contain provision conferring power on the Panel to impose sanctions on a person who has—
  (a) acted in breach of rules, or
  (b) failed to comply with a direction given by virtue of section 946.

(2) Subsection (3) applies where rules made by virtue of subsection (1) confer power on the Panel to impose a sanction of a kind not provided for by the City Code on Takeovers and Mergers as it had effect immediately before the passing of this Act.

(3) The Panel must prepare a statement (a "policy statement") of its policy with respect to—
  (a) the imposition of the sanction in question, and
  (b) where the sanction is in the nature of a financial penalty, the amount of the penalty that may be imposed.
  An element of the policy must be that, in making a decision about any such matter, the Panel has regard to the factors mentioned in subsection (4).

(4) The factors are—
  (a) the seriousness of the breach or failure in question in relation to the nature of the rule or direction contravened;
  (b) the extent to which the breach or failure was deliberate or reckless;
  (c) whether the person on whom the sanction is to be imposed is an individual.

(5) The Panel may at any time revise a policy statement.

(6) The Panel must prepare a draft of any proposed policy statement (or revised policy statement) and consult such persons about the draft as the Panel considers appropriate.

(7) The Panel must publish, in whatever way it considers appropriate, any policy statement (or revised policy statement) that it prepares.

(8) In exercising, or deciding whether to exercise, its power to impose a sanction within subsection (2) in the case of any particular breach or failure, the Panel must have regard to any relevant policy statement published and in force at the time when the breach or failure occurred.

953. Failure to comply with rules about bid documentation

(1) This section applies where a takeover bid is made for a company that has securities carrying voting rights admitted to trading on a regulated market in the United Kingdom.

(2) Where an offer document published in respect of the bid does not comply with offer document rules, an offence is committed by—
  (a) the person making the bid, and
  (b) where the person making the bid is a body of persons, any director, officer or member of that body who caused the document to be published.

(3) A person commits an offence under subsection (2) only if—

    (a) he knew that the offer document did not comply, or was reckless as to whether it complied, and

    (b) he failed to take all reasonable steps to secure that it did comply.

(4) Where a response document published in respect of the bid does not comply with response document rules, an offence is committed by any director or other officer of the company referred to in subsection (1) who—

    (a) knew that the response document did not comply, or was reckless as to whether it complied, and

    (b) failed to take all reasonable steps to secure that it did comply.

(5) Where an offence is committed under subsection (2)(b) or (4) by a company or other body corporate ("the relevant body")—

    (a) subsection (2)(b) has effect as if the reference to a director, officer or member of the person making the bid included a reference to a director, officer or member of the relevant body;

    (b) subsection (4) has effect as if the reference to a director or other officer of the company referred to in subsection (1) included a reference to a director, officer or member of the relevant body.

(6) A person guilty of an offence under this section is liable—

    (a) on conviction on indictment, to a fine;

    (b) on summary conviction, to a fine not exceeding the statutory maximum.

(7) Nothing in this section affects any power of the Panel in relation to the enforcement of its rules.

(8) Section 1 (meaning of "company") does not apply for the purposes of this section.

(9) In this section—

    "designated" means designated in rules;

    "offer document" means a document required to be published by rules giving effect to Article 6.2 of the Takeovers Directive;

    "offer document rules" means rules designated as rules that give effect to Article 6.3 of that Directive;

    "response document" means a document required to be published by rules giving effect to Article 9.5 of that Directive;

    "response document rules" means rules designated as rules that give effect to the first sentence of Article 9.5 of that Directive;

    "securities" means shares or debentures;

    "takeover bid" has the same meaning as in that Directive;

    "voting rights" means rights to vote at general meetings of the company in question, including rights that arise only in certain circumstances.

954. Compensation

(1) Rules may confer power on the Panel to order a person to pay such compensation as it thinks just and reasonable if he is in breach of a rule the effect of which is to require the payment of money.

(2) Rules made by virtue of this section may include provision for the payment of interest (including compound interest).

955. Enforcement by the court

(1) If, on the application of the Panel, the court is satisfied—

    (a) that there is a reasonable likelihood that a person will contravene a rule-based requirement, or

    (b) that a person has contravened a rule-based requirement or a disclosure requirement,

the court may make any order it thinks fit to secure compliance with the requirement.

(2) In subsection (1) "the court" means the High Court or, in Scotland, the Court of Session.

(3) Except as provided by subsection (1), no person—

    (a) has a right to seek an injunction, or

(b) in Scotland, has title or interest to seek an interdict or an order for specific performance, to prevent a person from contravening (or continuing to contravene) a rule-based requirement or a disclosure requirement.

(4) In this section—

"contravene" includes fail to comply;

"disclosure requirement" means a requirement imposed under section 947;

"rule-based requirement" means a requirement imposed by or under rules.

956. No action for breach of statutory duty etc

(1) Contravention of a rule-based requirement or a disclosure requirement does not give rise to any right of action for breach of statutory duty.

(2) Contravention of a rule-based requirement does not make any transaction void or unenforceable or (subject to any provision made by rules) affect the validity of any other thing.

(3) In this section—

(a) "contravention" includes failure to comply;

(b) "disclosure requirement" and "rule-based requirement" have the same meaning as in section 955.

Funding

957. Fees and charges

(1) Rules may provide for fees or charges to be payable to the Panel for the purpose of meeting any part of its expenses.

(2) A reference in this section or section 958 to expenses of the Panel is to any expenses that have been or are to be incurred by the Panel in, or in connection with, the discharge of its functions, including in particular—

(a) payments in respect of the expenses of the Takeover Appeal Board;

(b) the cost of repaying the principal of, and of paying any interest on, any money borrowed by the Panel;

(c) the cost of maintaining adequate reserves.

958. Levy

(1) For the purpose of meeting any part of the expenses of the Panel, the Secretary of State may by regulations provide for a levy to be payable to the Panel—

(a) by specified persons or bodies, or persons or bodies of a specified description, or

(b) on transactions, of a specified description, in securities on specified markets.

In this subsection "specified" means specified in the regulations.

(2) The power to specify (or to specify descriptions of) persons or bodies must be exercised in such a way that the levy is payable only by persons or bodies that appear to the Secretary of State—

(a) to be capable of being directly affected by the exercise of any of the functions of the Panel, or

(b) otherwise to have a substantial interest in the exercise of any of those functions.

(3) Regulations under this section may in particular—

(a) specify the rate of the levy and the period in respect of which it is payable at that rate;

(b) make provision as to the times when, and the manner in which, payments are to be made in respect of the levy.

(4) In determining the rate of the levy payable in respect of a particular period, the Secretary of State—

(a) must take into account any other income received or expected by the Panel in respect of that period;

(b) may take into account estimated as well as actual expenses of the Panel in respect of that period.

(5) The Panel must—

(a) keep proper accounts in respect of any amounts of levy received by virtue of this section;

(b) prepare, in relation to each period in respect of which any such amounts are received, a statement of account relating to those amounts in such form and manner as is specified in the regulations.

Those accounts must be audited, and the statement certified, by persons appointed by the Secretary of State.

(6) Regulations under this section—

(a) are subject to affirmative resolution procedure if subsection (7) applies to them;

(b) otherwise, are subject to negative resolution procedure.

(7) This subsection applies to—

(a) the first regulations under this section;

(b) any other regulations under this section that would result in a change in the persons or bodies by whom, or the transactions on which, the levy is payable.

(8) If a draft of an instrument containing regulations under this section would, apart from this subsection, be treated for the purposes of the Standing Orders of either House of Parliament as a hybrid instrument, it is to proceed in that House as if it were not such an instrument.

959. Recovery of fees, charges or levy

An amount payable by any person or body by virtue of section 957 or 958 is a debt due from that person or body to the Panel, and is recoverable accordingly.

Miscellaneous and supplementary

960. Panel as party to proceedings

The Panel is capable (despite being an unincorporated body) of—

(a) bringing proceedings under this Chapter in its own name;

(b) bringing or defending any other proceedings in its own name.

961. Exemption from liability in damages

(1) Neither the Panel, nor any person within subsection (2), is to be liable in damages for anything done (or omitted to be done) in, or in connection with, the discharge or purported discharge of the Panel's functions.

(2) A person is within this subsection if—

(a) he is (or is acting as) a member, officer or member of staff of the Panel, or

(b) he is a person authorised under section 947(5).

(3) Subsection (1) does not apply—

(a) if the act or omission is shown to have been in bad faith, or

(b) so as to prevent an award of damages in respect of the act or omission on the ground that it was unlawful as a result of section 6(1) of the Human Rights Act 1998 (c. 42) (acts of public authorities incompatible with Convention rights).

962. Privilege against self-incrimination

(1) A statement made by a person in response to—

(a) a requirement under section 947(1), or

(b) an order made by the court under section 955 to secure compliance with such a requirement,

may not be used against him in criminal proceedings in which he is charged with an offence to which this subsection applies.

(2) Subsection (1) applies to any offence other than an offence under one of the following provisions (which concern false statements made otherwise than on oath)—

(a) section 5 of the Perjury Act 1911 (c. 6);

(b) section 44(2) of the Criminal Law (Consolidation) (Scotland) Act 1995 (c. 39);

(c) Article 10 of the Perjury (Northern Ireland) Order 1979 (S.I. 1979/1714 (N.I. 19)).

963. Annual reports

(1) After the end of each financial year the Panel must publish a report.

(2) The report must—

(a) set out how the Panel's functions were discharged in the year in question;

(b) include the Panel's accounts for that year;

(c) mention any matters the Panel considers to be of relevance to the discharge of its functions.

964. Amendments to Financial Services and Markets Act 2000

(1) The Financial Services and Markets Act 2000 (c. 8) is amended as follows.

(2) Section 143 (power to make rules endorsing the City Code on Takeovers and Mergers etc) is repealed.

(3) In section 144 (power to make price stabilising rules), for subsection (7) substitute—

"(7) "Consultation procedures" means procedures designed to provide an opportunity for persons likely to be affected by alterations to those provisions to make representations about proposed alterations to any of those provisions.".

(4) In section 349 (exceptions from restrictions on disclosure of confidential information), after subsection (3) insert—

"(3A) Section 348 does not apply to—

(a) the disclosure by a recipient to which subsection (3B) applies of confidential information disclosed to it by the Authority in reliance on subsection (1);

(b) the disclosure of such information by a person obtaining it directly or indirectly from a recipient to which subsection (3B) applies.

(3B) This subsection applies to—

(a) the Panel on Takeovers and Mergers;

(b) an authority designated as a supervisory authority for the purposes of Article 4.1 of the Takeovers Directive;

(c) any other person or body that exercises public functions, under legislation in an EEA State other than the United Kingdom, that are similar to the Authority's functions or those of the Panel on Takeovers and Mergers.".

(5) In section 354 (Financial Services Authority's duty to co-operate with others), after subsection (1) insert—

"(1A) The Authority must take such steps as it considers appropriate to co-operate with—

(a) the Panel on Takeovers and Mergers;

(b) an authority designated as a supervisory authority for the purposes of Article 4.1 of the Takeovers Directive;

(c) any other person or body that exercises functions of a public nature, under legislation in any country or territory outside the United Kingdom, that appear to the Authority to be similar to those of the Panel on Takeovers and Mergers.".

(6) In section 417(1) (definitions), insert at the appropriate place—

" "Takeovers Directive" means Directive 2004/25/EC of the European Parliament and of the Council;".

965. Power to extend to Isle of Man and Channel Islands

Her Majesty may by Order in Council direct that any of the provisions of this Chapter extend, with such modifications as may be specified in the Order, to the Isle of Man or any of the Channel Islands.

CHAPTER 2
IMPEDIMENTS TO TAKEOVERS

Opting in and opting out

966. Opting in and opting out

(1) A company may by special resolution (an "opting-in resolution") opt in for the purposes of this Chapter if the following three conditions are met in relation to the company.

(2) The first condition is that the company has voting shares admitted to trading on a regulated market.

(3) The second condition is that—

    (a) the company's articles of association—

        (i) do not contain any such restrictions as are mentioned in Article 11 of the Takeovers Directive, or

        (ii) if they do contain any such restrictions, provide for the restrictions not to apply at a time when, or in circumstances in which, they would be disapplied by that Article,

      and

    (b) those articles do not contain any other provision which would be incompatible with that Article.

(4) The third condition is that—

    (a) no shares conferring special rights in the company are held by—

        (i) a minister,

        (ii) a nominee of, or any other person acting on behalf of, a minister, or

        (iii) a company directly or indirectly controlled by a minister,

      and

    (b) no such rights are exercisable by or on behalf of a minister under any enactment.

(5) A company may revoke an opting-in resolution by a further special resolution (an "opting-out resolution").

(6) For the purposes of subsection (3), a reference in Article 11 of the Takeovers Directive to Article 7.1 or 9 of that Directive is to be read as referring to rules under section 943(1) giving effect to the relevant Article.

(7) In subsection (4) "minister" means—

    (a) the holder of an office in Her Majesty's Government in the United Kingdom;

    (b) the Scottish Ministers;

    (c) a Minister within the meaning given by section 7(3) of the Northern Ireland Act 1998 (c. 47);

and for the purposes of that subsection "minister" also includes the Treasury, the Board of Trade, the Defence Council and the National Assembly for Wales.

(8) The Secretary of State may by order subject to negative resolution procedure provide that subsection (4) applies in relation to a specified person or body that exercises functions of a public nature as it applies in relation to a minister.

"Specified" means specified in the order.

967. Further provision about opting-in and opting-out resolutions

(1) An opting-in resolution or an opting-out resolution must specify the date from which it is to have effect (the "effective date").

(2) The effective date of an opting-in resolution may not be earlier than the date on which the resolution is passed.

(3) The second and third conditions in section 966 must be met at the time when an opting-in resolution is passed, but the first one does not need to be met until the effective date.

(4) An opting-in resolution passed before the time when voting shares of the company are admitted to trading on a regulated market complies with the requirement in subsection (1) if, instead of specifying a particular date, it provides for the resolution to have effect from that time.

(5) An opting-in resolution passed before the commencement of this section complies with the requirement in subsection (1) if, instead of specifying a particular date, it provides for the resolution to have effect from that commencement.

(6) The effective date of an opting-out resolution may not be earlier than the first anniversary of the date on which a copy of the opting-in resolution was forwarded to the registrar.

(7) Where a company has passed an opting-in resolution, any alteration of its articles of association that would prevent the second condition in section 966 from being met is of no effect until the effective date of an opting-out resolution passed by the company.

Consequences of opting in

968. Effect on contractual restrictions

(1) The following provisions have effect where a takeover bid is made for an opted-in company.

(2) An agreement to which this section applies is invalid in so far as it places any restriction—

    (a) on the transfer to the offeror, or at his direction to another person, of shares in the company during the offer period;

    (b) on the transfer to any person of shares in the company at a time during the offer period when the offeror holds shares amounting to not less than 75% in value of all the voting shares in the company;

    (c) on rights to vote at a general meeting of the company that decides whether to take any action which might result in the frustration of the bid;

    (d) on rights to vote at a general meeting of the company that—

        (i) is the first such meeting to be held after the end of the offer period, and

        (ii) is held at a time when the offeror holds shares amounting to not less than 75% in value of all the voting shares in the company.

(3) This section applies to an agreement—

    (a) entered into between a person holding shares in the company and another such person on or after 21st April 2004, or

    (b) entered into at any time between such a person and the company,

and it applies to such an agreement even if the law applicable to the agreement (apart from this section) is not the law of a part of the United Kingdom.

(4) The reference in subsection (2)(c) to rights to vote at a general meeting of the company that decides whether to take any action which might result in the frustration of the bid includes a reference to rights to vote on a written resolution concerned with that question.

(5) For the purposes of subsection (2)(c), action which might result in the frustration of a bid is any action of that kind specified in rules under section 943(1) giving effect to Article 9 of the Takeovers Directive.

(6) If a person suffers loss as a result of any act or omission that would (but for this section) be a breach of an agreement to which this section applies, he is entitled to compensation, of such amount as the court considers just and equitable, from any person who would (but for this section) be liable to him for committing or inducing the breach.

(7) In subsection (6) "the court" means the High Court or, in Scotland, the Court of Session.

(8) A reference in this section to voting shares in the company does not include—

    (a) debentures, or

    (b) shares that, under the company's articles of association, do not normally carry rights to vote at its general meetings (for example, shares carrying rights to vote that, under those articles, arise only where specified pecuniary advantages are not provided).

969. Power of offeror to require general meeting to be called

(1) Where a takeover bid is made for an opted-in company, the offeror may by making a request

to the directors of the company require them to call a general meeting of the company if, at the date at which the request is made, he holds shares amounting to not less than 75% in value of all the voting shares in the company.

(2) The reference in subsection (1) to voting shares in the company does not include—

(a) debentures, or

(b) shares that, under the company's articles of association, do not normally carry rights to vote at its general meetings (for example, shares carrying rights to vote that, under those articles, arise only where specified pecuniary advantages are not provided).

(3) Sections 303 to 305 (members' power to require general meetings to be called) apply as they would do if subsection (1) above were substituted for subsections (1) to (3) of section 303, and with any other necessary modifications.

Supplementary

970. Communication of decisions

(1) A company that has passed an opting-in resolution or an opting-out resolution must notify—

(a) the Panel, and

(b) where the company—

(i) has voting shares admitted to trading on a regulated market in an EEA State other than the United Kingdom, or

(ii) has requested such admission,

the authority designated by that state as the supervisory authority for the purposes of Article 4.1 of the Takeovers Directive.

(2) Notification must be given within 15 days after the resolution is passed and, if any admission or request such as is mentioned in subsection (1)(b) occurs at a later time, within 15 days after that time.

(3) If a company fails to comply with this section, an offence is committed by—

(a) the company, and

(b) every officer of it who is in default.

(4) A person guilty of an offence under this section is liable on summary conviction to a fine not exceeding level 3 on the standard scale and, for continued contravention, a daily default fine not exceeding one-tenth of level 3 on the standard scale.

971. Interpretation of this Chapter

(1) In this Chapter—

"offeror" and "takeover bid" have the same meaning as in the Takeovers Directive;

"offer period", in relation to a takeover bid, means the time allowed for acceptance of the bid by—

(a) rules under section 943(1) giving effect to Article 7.1 of the Takeovers Directive, or

(b) where the rules giving effect to that Article which apply to the bid are those of an EEA State other than the United Kingdom, those rules;

"opted-in company" means a company in relation to which—

(a) an opting-in resolution has effect, and

(b) the conditions in section 966(2) and (4) continue to be met;

"opting-in resolution" has the meaning given by section 966(1);

"opting-out resolution" has the meaning given by section 966(5);

"the Takeovers Directive" means Directive 2004/25/EC of the European Parliament and of the Council;

"voting rights" means rights to vote at general meetings of the company in question, including rights that arise only in certain circumstances;

"voting shares" means shares carrying voting rights.

(2) For the purposes of this Chapter—

(a) securities of a company are treated as shares in the company if they are convertible into or entitle the holder to subscribe for such shares;

(b) debentures issued by a company are treated as shares in the company if they carry voting rights.

972. Transitory provision

(1) Where a takeover bid is made for an opted-in company, section 368 of the Companies Act 1985 (c. 6) (extraordinary general meeting on members' requisition) and section 378 of that Act (extraordinary and special resolutions) have effect as follows until their repeal by this Act.

(2) Section 368 has effect as if a members' requisition included a requisition of a person who—

(a) is the offeror in relation to the takeover bid, and

(b) holds at the date of the deposit of the requisition shares amounting to not less than 75% in value of all the voting shares in the company.

(3) In relation to a general meeting of the company that—

(a) is the first such meeting to be held after the end of the offer period, and

(b) is held at a time when the offeror holds shares amounting to not less than 75% in value of all the voting shares in the company,

section 378(2) (meaning of "special resolution") has effect as if "14 days' notice" were substituted for "21 days' notice".

(4) A reference in this section to voting shares in the company does not include—

(a) debentures, or

(b) shares that, under the company's articles of association, do not normally carry rights to vote at its general meetings (for example, shares carrying rights to vote that, under those articles, arise only where specified pecuniary advantages are not provided).

973. Power to extend to Isle of Man and Channel Islands

Her Majesty may by Order in Council direct that any of the provisions of this Chapter extend, with such modifications as may be specified in the Order, to the Isle of Man or any of the Channel Islands.

CHAPTER 3
"SQUEEZE-OUT" AND "SELL-OUT"

Takeover offers

974. Meaning of "takeover offer"

(1) For the purposes of this Chapter an offer to acquire shares in a company is a "takeover offer" if the following two conditions are satisfied in relation to the offer.

(2) The first condition is that it is an offer to acquire—

(a) all the shares in a company, or

(b) where there is more than one class of shares in a company, all the shares of one or more classes,

other than shares that at the date of the offer are already held by the offeror.

Section 975 contains provision supplementing this subsection.

(3) The second condition is that the terms of the offer are the same—

(a) in relation to all the shares to which the offer relates, or

(b) where the shares to which the offer relates include shares of different classes, in relation to all the shares of each class.

Section 976 contains provision treating this condition as satisfied in certain circumstances.

(4) In subsections (1) to (3) "shares" means shares, other than relevant treasury shares, that have been allotted on the date of the offer (but see subsection (5)).

(5) A takeover offer may include among the shares to which it relates—

(a) all or any shares that are allotted after the date of the offer but before a specified date;

(b) all or any relevant treasury shares that cease to be held as treasury shares before a specified date;

(c) all or any other relevant treasury shares.

(6) In this section—

"relevant treasury shares" means shares that—

(a) are held by the company as treasury shares on the date of the offer, or

(b) become shares held by the company as treasury shares after that date but before a specified date;

"specified date" means a date specified in or determined in accordance with the terms of the offer.

(7) Where the terms of an offer make provision for their revision and for acceptances on the previous terms to be treated as acceptances on the revised terms, then, if the terms of the offer are revised in accordance with that provision—

(a) the revision is not to be regarded for the purposes of this Chapter as the making of a fresh offer, and

(b) references in this Chapter to the date of the offer are accordingly to be read as references to the date of the original offer.

975. Shares already held by the offeror etc

(1) The reference in section 974(2) to shares already held by the offeror includes a reference to shares that he has contracted to acquire, whether unconditionally or subject to conditions being met.

This is subject to subsection (2).

(2) The reference in section 974(2) to shares already held by the offeror does not include a reference to shares that are the subject of a contract—

(a) intended to secure that the holder of the shares will accept the offer when it is made, and

(b) entered into—

(i) by deed and for no consideration,

(ii) for consideration of negligible value, or

(iii) for consideration consisting of a promise by the offeror to make the offer.

(3) In relation to Scotland, this section applies as if the words "by deed and" in subsection (2)(b)(i) were omitted.

(4) The condition in section 974(2) is treated as satisfied where—

(a) the offer does not extend to shares that associates of the offeror hold or have contracted to acquire (whether unconditionally or subject to conditions being met), and

(b) the condition would be satisfied if the offer did extend to those shares.

(For further provision about such shares, see section 977(2)).

976. Cases where offer treated as being on same terms

(1) The condition in section 974(3) (terms of offer to be the same for all shares or all shares of particular classes) is treated as satisfied where subsection (2) or (3) below applies.

(2) This subsection applies where—

(a) shares carry an entitlement to a particular dividend which other shares of the same class, by reason of being allotted later, do not carry,

(b) there is a difference in the value of consideration offered for the shares allotted earlier as against that offered for those allotted later,

(c) that difference merely reflects the difference in entitlement to the dividend, and

(d) the condition in section 974(3) would be satisfied but for that difference.

(3) This subsection applies where—

(a) the law of a country or territory outside the United Kingdom—

(i) precludes an offer of consideration in the form, or any of the forms, specified in the terms of the offer ("the specified form"), or

(ii) precludes it except after compliance by the offeror with conditions with which he is unable to comply or which he regards as unduly onerous,

(b) the persons to whom an offer of consideration in the specified form is precluded are able to receive consideration in another form that is of substantially equivalent value, and

(c) the condition in section 974(3) would be satisfied but for the fact that an offer of consideration in the specified form to those persons is precluded.

977. Shares to which an offer relates

(1) Where a takeover offer is made and, during the period beginning with the date of the offer and ending when the offer can no longer be accepted, the offeror—

(a) acquires or unconditionally contracts to acquire any of the shares to which the offer relates, but

(b) does not do so by virtue of acceptances of the offer,

those shares are treated for the purposes of this Chapter as excluded from those to which the offer relates.

(2) For the purposes of this Chapter shares that an associate of the offeror holds or has contracted to acquire, whether at the date of the offer or subsequently, are not treated as shares to which the offer relates, even if the offer extends to such shares.

In this subsection "contracted" means contracted unconditionally or subject to conditions being met.

(3) This section is subject to section 979(8) and (9).

978. Effect of impossibility etc of communicating or accepting offer

(1) Where there are holders of shares in a company to whom an offer to acquire shares in the company is not communicated, that does not prevent the offer from being a takeover offer for the purposes of this Chapter if—

(a) those shareholders have no registered address in the United Kingdom,

(b) the offer was not communicated to those shareholders in order not to contravene the law of a country or territory outside the United Kingdom, and

(c) either—

(i) the offer is published in the Gazette, or

(ii) the offer can be inspected, or a copy of it obtained, at a place in an EEA State or on a website, and a notice is published in the Gazette specifying the address of that place or website.

(2) Where an offer is made to acquire shares in a company and there are persons for whom, by reason of the law of a country or territory outside the United Kingdom, it is impossible to accept the offer, or more difficult to do so, that does not prevent the offer from being a takeover offer for the purposes of this Chapter.

(3) It is not to be inferred—

(a) that an offer which is not communicated to every holder of shares in the company cannot be a takeover offer for the purposes of this Chapter unless the requirements of paragraphs (a) to (c) of subsection (1) are met, or

(b) that an offer which is impossible, or more difficult, for certain persons to accept cannot be a takeover offer for those purposes unless the reason for the impossibility or difficulty is the one mentioned in subsection (2).

"Squeeze-out"

979. Right of offeror to buy out minority shareholder

(1) Subsection (2) applies in a case where a takeover offer does not relate to shares of different classes.

(2) If the offeror has, by virtue of acceptances of the offer, acquired or unconditionally contracted to acquire—

(a) not less than 90% in value of the shares to which the offer relates, and

(b) in a case where the shares to which the offer relates are voting shares, not less than 90% of the voting rights carried by those shares,

he may give notice to the holder of any shares to which the offer relates which the offeror has not acquired or unconditionally contracted to acquire that he desires to acquire those shares.

(3) Subsection (4) applies in a case where a takeover offer relates to shares of different classes.

(4) If the offeror has, by virtue of acceptances of the offer, acquired or unconditionally contracted to acquire—

(a) not less than 90% in value of the shares of any class to which the offer relates, and

(b) in a case where the shares of that class are voting shares, not less than 90% of the voting rights carried by those shares,

he may give notice to the holder of any shares of that class to which the offer relates which the offeror has not acquired or unconditionally contracted to acquire that he desires to acquire those shares.

(5) In the case of a takeover offer which includes among the shares to which it relates—

(a) shares that are allotted after the date of the offer, or

(b) relevant treasury shares (within the meaning of section 974) that cease to be held as treasury shares after the date of the offer,

the offeror's entitlement to give a notice under subsection (2) or (4) on any particular date shall be determined as if the shares to which the offer relates did not include any allotted, or ceasing to be held as treasury shares, on or after that date.

(6) Subsection (7) applies where—

(a) the requirements for the giving of a notice under subsection (2) or (4) are satisfied, and

(b) there are shares in the company which the offeror, or an associate of his, has contracted to acquire subject to conditions being met, and in relation to which the contract has not become unconditional.

(7) The offeror's entitlement to give a notice under subsection (2) or (4) shall be determined as if—

(a) the shares to which the offer relates included shares falling within paragraph (b) of subsection (6), and

(b) in relation to shares falling within that paragraph, the words "by virtue of acceptances of the offer" in subsection (2) or (4) were omitted.

(8) Where—

(a) a takeover offer is made,

(b) during the period beginning with the date of the offer and ending when the offer can no longer be accepted, the offeror—

(i) acquires or unconditionally contracts to acquire any of the shares to which the offer relates, but

(ii) does not do so by virtue of acceptances of the offer, and

(c) subsection (10) applies,

then for the purposes of this section those shares are not excluded by section 977(1) from those to which the offer relates, and the offeror is treated as having acquired or contracted to acquire them by virtue of acceptances of the offer.

(9) Where—

(a) a takeover offer is made,

(b) during the period beginning with the date of the offer and ending when the offer can no longer be accepted, an associate of the offeror acquires or unconditionally contracts to acquire any of the shares to which the offer relates, and

(c) subsection (10) applies,

then for the purposes of this section those shares are not excluded by section 977(2) from those to which the offer relates.

(10) This subsection applies if—

    (a) at the time the shares are acquired or contracted to be acquired as mentioned in subsection (8) or (9) (as the case may be), the value of the consideration for which they are acquired or contracted to be acquired ("the acquisition consideration") does not exceed the value of the consideration specified in the terms of the offer, or

    (b) those terms are subsequently revised so that when the revision is announced the value of the acquisition consideration, at the time mentioned in paragraph (a), no longer exceeds the value of the consideration specified in those terms.

980. Further provision about notices given under section 979

(1) A notice under section 979 must be given in the prescribed manner.

(2) No notice may be given under section 979(2) or (4) after the end of—

    (a) the period of three months beginning with the day after the last day on which the offer can be accepted, or

    (b) the period of six months beginning with the date of the offer, where that period ends earlier and the offer is one to which subsection (3) below applies.

(3) This subsection applies to an offer if the time allowed for acceptance of the offer is not governed by rules under section 943(1) that give effect to Article 7 of the Takeovers Directive. In this subsection "the Takeovers Directive" has the same meaning as in section 943.

(4) At the time when the offeror first gives a notice under section 979 in relation to an offer, he must send to the company—

    (a) a copy of the notice, and

    (b) a statutory declaration by him in the prescribed form, stating that the conditions for the giving of the notice are satisfied.

(5) Where the offeror is a company (whether or not a company within the meaning of this Act) the statutory declaration must be signed by a director.

(6) A person commits an offence if—

    (a) he fails to send a copy of a notice or a statutory declaration as required by subsection (4), or

    (b) he makes such a declaration for the purposes of that subsection knowing it to be false or without having reasonable grounds for believing it to be true.

(7) It is a defence for a person charged with an offence for failing to send a copy of a notice as required by subsection (4) to prove that he took reasonable steps for securing compliance with that subsection.

(8) A person guilty of an offence under this section is liable—

    (a) on conviction on indictment, to imprisonment for a term not exceeding two years or a fine (or both);

    (b) on summary conviction—

        (i) in England and Wales, to imprisonment for a term not exceeding twelve months or to a fine not exceeding the statutory maximum (or both) and, for continued contravention, a daily default fine not exceeding one-fiftieth of the statutory maximum;

        (ii) in Scotland or Northern Ireland, to imprisonment for a term not exceeding six months, or to a fine not exceeding the statutory maximum (or both) and, for continued contravention, a daily default fine not exceeding one-fiftieth of the statutory maximum.

981. Effect of notice under section 979

(1) Subject to section 986 (applications to the court), this section applies where the offeror gives a shareholder a notice under section 979.

(2) The offeror is entitled and bound to acquire the shares to which the notice relates on the terms of the offer.

(3) Where the terms of an offer are such as to give the shareholder a choice of consideration, the notice must give particulars of the choice and state—

(a) that the shareholder may, within six weeks from the date of the notice, indicate his choice by a written communication sent to the offeror at an address specified in the notice, and

(b) which consideration specified in the offer will apply if he does not indicate a choice.

The reference in subsection (2) to the terms of the offer is to be read accordingly.

(4) Subsection (3) applies whether or not any time-limit or other conditions applicable to the choice under the terms of the offer can still be complied with.

(5) If the consideration offered to or (as the case may be) chosen by the shareholder—

(a) is not cash and the offeror is no longer able to provide it, or

(b) was to have been provided by a third party who is no longer bound or able to provide it,

the consideration is to be taken to consist of an amount of cash, payable by the offeror, which at the date of the notice is equivalent to the consideration offered or (as the case may be) chosen.

(6) At the end of six weeks from the date of the notice the offeror must immediately—

(a) send a copy of the notice to the company, and

(b) pay or transfer to the company the consideration for the shares to which the notice relates.

Where the consideration consists of shares or securities to be allotted by the offeror, the reference in paragraph (b) to the transfer of the consideration is to be read as a reference to the allotment of the shares or securities to the company.

(7) If the shares to which the notice relates are registered, the copy of the notice sent to the company under subsection (6)(a) must be accompanied by an instrument of transfer executed on behalf of the holder of the shares by a person appointed by the offeror.

On receipt of that instrument the company must register the offeror as the holder of those shares.

(8) If the shares to which the notice relates are transferable by the delivery of warrants or other instruments, the copy of the notice sent to the company under subsection (6)(a) must be accompanied by a statement to that effect.

On receipt of that statement the company must issue the offeror with warrants or other instruments in respect of the shares, and those already in issue in respect of the shares become void.

(9) The company must hold any money or other consideration received by it under subsection (6)(b) on trust for the person who, before the offeror acquired them, was entitled to the shares in respect of which the money or other consideration was received.

Section 982 contains further provision about how the company should deal with such money or other consideration.

982. **Further provision about consideration held on trust under section 981(9)**

(1) This section applies where an offeror pays or transfers consideration to the company under section 981(6).

(2) The company must pay into a separate bank account that complies with subsection (3)—

(a) any money it receives under paragraph (b) of section 981(6), and

(b) any dividend or other sum accruing from any other consideration it receives under that paragraph.

(3) A bank account complies with this subsection if the balance on the account—

(a) bears interest at an appropriate rate, and

(b) can be withdrawn by such notice (if any) as is appropriate.

(4) If—

(a) the person entitled to the consideration held on trust by virtue of section 981(9) cannot be found, and

(b) subsection (5) applies,

the consideration (together with any interest, dividend or other benefit that has accrued from it) must be paid into court.

(5) This subsection applies where—

(a) reasonable enquiries have been made at reasonable intervals to find the person, and

(b) twelve years have elapsed since the consideration was received, or the company is wound up.

(6) In relation to a company registered in Scotland, subsections (7) and (8) apply instead of subsection (4).

(7) If the person entitled to the consideration held on trust by virtue of section 981(9) cannot be found and subsection (5) applies—

(a) the trust terminates,

(b) the company or (if the company is wound up) the liquidator must sell any consideration other than cash and any benefit other than cash that has accrued from the consideration, and

(c) a sum representing—

(i) the consideration so far as it is cash,

(ii) the proceeds of any sale under paragraph (b), and

(iii) any interest, dividend or other benefit that has accrued from the consideration,

must be deposited in the name of the Accountant of Court in a separate bank account complying with subsection (3) and the receipt for the deposit must be transmitted to the Accountant of Court.

(8) Section 58 of the Bankruptcy (Scotland) Act 1985 (c. 66) (so far as consistent with this Act) applies (with any necessary modifications) to sums deposited under subsection (7) as it applies to sums deposited under section 57(1)(a) of that Act.

(9) The expenses of any such enquiries as are mentioned in subsection (5) may be paid out of the money or other property held on trust for the person to whom the enquiry relates.

"Sell-out"

983. Right of minority shareholder to be bought out by offeror

(1) Subsections (2) and (3) apply in a case where a takeover offer relates to all the shares in a company.

For this purpose a takeover offer relates to all the shares in a company if it is an offer to acquire all the shares in the company within the meaning of section 974.

(2) The holder of any voting shares to which the offer relates who has not accepted the offer may require the offeror to acquire those shares if, at any time before the end of the period within which the offer can be accepted—

(a) the offeror has by virtue of acceptances of the offer acquired or unconditionally contracted to acquire some (but not all) of the shares to which the offer relates, and

(b) those shares, with or without any other shares in the company which he has acquired or contracted to acquire (whether unconditionally or subject to conditions being met)—

(i) amount to not less than 90% in value of all the voting shares in the company (or would do so but for section 990(1)), and

(ii) carry not less than 90% of the voting rights in the company (or would do so but for section 990(1)).

(3) The holder of any non-voting shares to which the offer relates who has not accepted the offer may require the offeror to acquire those shares if, at any time before the end of the period within which the offer can be accepted—

(a) the offeror has by virtue of acceptances of the offer acquired or unconditionally contracted to acquire some (but not all) of the shares to which the offer relates, and

(b) those shares, with or without any other shares in the company which he has acquired or contracted to acquire (whether unconditionally or subject to conditions being met), amount to not less than 90% in value of all the shares in the company (or would do so but for section 990(1)).

(4) If a takeover offer relates to shares of one or more classes and at any time before the end of the period within which the offer can be accepted—

    (a) the offeror has by virtue of acceptances of the offer acquired or unconditionally contracted to acquire some (but not all) of the shares of any class to which the offer relates, and

    (b) those shares, with or without any other shares of that class which he has acquired or contracted to acquire (whether unconditionally or subject to conditions being met)—

        (i) amount to not less than 90% in value of all the shares of that class, and

        (ii) in a case where the shares of that class are voting shares, carry not less than 90% of the voting rights carried by the shares of that class,

the holder of any shares of that class to which the offer relates who has not accepted the offer may require the offeror to acquire those shares.

(5) For the purposes of subsections (2) to (4), in calculating 90% of the value of any shares, shares held by the company as treasury shares are to be treated as having been acquired by the offeror.

(6) Subsection (7) applies where—

    (a) a shareholder exercises rights conferred on him by subsection (2), (3) or (4),

    (b) at the time when he does so, there are shares in the company which the offeror has contracted to acquire subject to conditions being met, and in relation to which the contract has not become unconditional, and

    (c) the requirement imposed by subsection (2)(b), (3)(b) or (4)(b) (as the case may be) would not be satisfied if those shares were not taken into account.

(7) The shareholder is treated for the purposes of section 985 as not having exercised his rights under this section unless the requirement imposed by paragraph (b) of subsection (2), (3) or (4) (as the case may be) would be satisfied if—

    (a) the reference in that paragraph to other shares in the company which the offeror has contracted to acquire unconditionally or subject to conditions being met were a reference to such shares which he has unconditionally contracted to acquire, and

    (b) the reference in that subsection to the period within which the offer can be accepted were a reference to the period referred to in section 984(2).

(8) A reference in subsection (2)(b), (3)(b), (4)(b), (6) or (7) to shares which the offeror has acquired or contracted to acquire includes a reference to shares which an associate of his has acquired or contracted to acquire.

984. Further provision about rights conferred by section 983

(1) Rights conferred on a shareholder by subsection (2), (3) or (4) of section 983 are exercisable by a written communication addressed to the offeror.

(2) Rights conferred on a shareholder by subsection (2), (3) or (4) of that section are not exercisable after the end of the period of three months from—

    (a) the end of the period within which the offer can be accepted, or

    (b) if later, the date of the notice that must be given under subsection (3) below.

(3) Within one month of the time specified in subsection (2), (3) or (4) (as the case may be) of that section, the offeror must give any shareholder who has not accepted the offer notice in the prescribed manner of—

    (a) the rights that are exercisable by the shareholder under that subsection, and

    (b) the period within which the rights are exercisable.

If the notice is given before the end of the period within which the offer can be accepted, it must state that the offer is still open for acceptance.

(4) Subsection (3) does not apply if the offeror has given the shareholder a notice in respect of the shares in question under section 979.

(5) An offeror who fails to comply with subsection (3) commits an offence.

If the offeror is a company, every officer of that company who is in default or to whose neglect the failure is attributable also commits an offence.

(6) If an offeror other than a company is charged with an offence for failing to comply with subsection (3), it is a defence for him to prove that he took all reasonable steps for securing compliance with that subsection.

(7) A person guilty of an offence under this section is liable—

    (a) on conviction on indictment, to a fine;

    (b) on summary conviction, to a fine not exceeding the statutory maximum and, for continued contravention, a daily default fine not exceeding one-fiftieth of the statutory maximum.

985. Effect of requirement under section 983

(1) Subject to section 986, this section applies where a shareholder exercises his rights under section 983 in respect of any shares held by him.

(2) The offeror is entitled and bound to acquire those shares on the terms of the offer or on such other terms as may be agreed.

(3) Where the terms of an offer are such as to give the shareholder a choice of consideration—

    (a) the shareholder may indicate his choice when requiring the offeror to acquire the shares, and

    (b) the notice given to the shareholder under section 984(3)—

        (i) must give particulars of the choice and of the rights conferred by this subsection, and

        (ii) may state which consideration specified in the offer will apply if he does not indicate a choice.

The reference in subsection (2) to the terms of the offer is to be read accordingly.

(4) Subsection (3) applies whether or not any time-limit or other conditions applicable to the choice under the terms of the offer can still be complied with.

(5) If the consideration offered to or (as the case may be) chosen by the shareholder—

    (a) is not cash and the offeror is no longer able to provide it, or

    (b) was to have been provided by a third party who is no longer bound or able to provide it,

the consideration is to be taken to consist of an amount of cash, payable by the offeror, which at the date when the shareholder requires the offeror to acquire the shares is equivalent to the consideration offered or (as the case may be) chosen.

Supplementary

986. Applications to the court

(1) Where a notice is given under section 979 to a shareholder the court may, on an application made by him, order—

    (a) that the offeror is not entitled and bound to acquire the shares to which the notice relates, or

    (b) that the terms on which the offeror is entitled and bound to acquire the shares shall be such as the court thinks fit.

(2) An application under subsection (1) must be made within six weeks from the date on which the notice referred to in that subsection was given.

If an application to the court under subsection (1) is pending at the end of that period, section 981(6) does not have effect until the application has been disposed of.

(3) Where a shareholder exercises his rights under section 983 in respect of any shares held by him, the court may, on an application made by him or the offeror, order that the terms on which the offeror is entitled and bound to acquire the shares shall be such as the court thinks fit.

(4) On an application under subsection (1) or (3)—

    (a) the court may not require consideration of a higher value than that specified in the terms of the offer ("the offer value") to be given for the shares to which the application relates unless the holder of the shares shows that the offer value would be unfair;

    (b) the court may not require consideration of a lower value than the offer value to be given for the shares.

(5) No order for costs or expenses may be made against a shareholder making an application under subsection (1) or (3) unless the court considers that—

    (a) the application was unnecessary, improper or vexatious,

    (b) there has been unreasonable delay in making the application, or

    (c) there has been unreasonable conduct on the shareholder's part in conducting the proceedings on the application.

(6) A shareholder who has made an application under subsection (1) or (3) must give notice of the application to the offeror.

(7) An offeror who is given notice of an application under subsection (1) or (3) must give a copy of the notice to—

    (a) any person (other than the applicant) to whom a notice has been given under section 979;

    (b) any person who has exercised his rights under section 983.

(8) An offeror who makes an application under subsection (3) must give notice of the application to—

    (a) any person to whom a notice has been given under section 979;

    (b) any person who has exercised his rights under section 983.

(9) Where a takeover offer has not been accepted to the extent necessary for entitling the offeror to give notices under subsection (2) or (4) of section 979 the court may, on an application made by him, make an order authorising him to give notices under that subsection if it is satisfied that—

    (a) the offeror has after reasonable enquiry been unable to trace one or more of the persons holding shares to which the offer relates,

    (b) the requirements of that subsection would have been met if the person, or all the persons, mentioned in paragraph (a) above had accepted the offer, and

    (c) the consideration offered is fair and reasonable.

This is subject to subsection (10).

(10) The court may not make an order under subsection (9) unless it considers that it is just and equitable to do so having regard, in particular, to the number of shareholders who have been traced but who have not accepted the offer.

987. Joint offers

(1) In the case of a takeover offer made by two or more persons jointly, this Chapter has effect as follows.

(2) The conditions for the exercise of the rights conferred by section 979 are satisfied—

    (a) in the case of acquisitions by virtue of acceptances of the offer, by the joint offerors acquiring or unconditionally contracting to acquire the necessary shares jointly;

    (b) in other cases, by the joint offerors acquiring or unconditionally contracting to acquire the necessary shares either jointly or separately.

(3) The conditions for the exercise of the rights conferred by section 983 are satisfied—

    (a) in the case of acquisitions by virtue of acceptances of the offer, by the joint offerors acquiring or unconditionally contracting to acquire the necessary shares jointly;

    (b) in other cases, by the joint offerors acquiring or contracting (whether unconditionally or subject to conditions being met) to acquire the necessary shares either jointly or separately.

(4) Subject to the following provisions, the rights and obligations of the offeror under sections 979 to 985 are respectively joint rights and joint and several obligations of the joint offerors.

(5) A provision of sections 979 to 986 that requires or authorises a notice or other document to be given or sent by or to the joint offerors is complied with if the notice or document is given or sent by or to any of them (but see subsection (6)).

(6) The statutory declaration required by section 980(4) must be made by all of the joint offerors and, where one or more of them is a company, signed by a director of that company.

(7) In sections 974 to 977, 979(9), 981(6), 983(8) and 988 references to the offeror are to be read as references to the joint offerors or any of them.

(8) In section 981(7) and (8) references to the offeror are to be read as references to the joint offerors or such of them as they may determine.

(9) In sections 981(5)(a) and 985(5)(a) references to the offeror being no longer able to provide the relevant consideration are to be read as references to none of the joint offerors being able to do so.

(10) In section 986 references to the offeror are to be read as references to the joint offerors, except that—

    (a) an application under subsection (3) or (9) may be made by any of them, and

    (b) the reference in subsection (9)(a) to the offeror having been unable to trace one or more of the persons holding shares is to be read as a reference to none of the offerors having been able to do so.

Interpretation

988. Associates

(1) In this Chapter "associate", in relation to an offeror, means—

    (a) a nominee of the offeror,

    (b) a holding company, subsidiary or fellow subsidiary of the offeror or a nominee of such a holding company, subsidiary or fellow subsidiary,

    (c) a body corporate in which the offeror is substantially interested,

    (d) a person who is, or is a nominee of, a party to a share acquisition agreement with the offeror, or

    (e) (where the offeror is an individual) his spouse or civil partner and any minor child or step-child of his.

(2) For the purposes of subsection (1)(b) a company is a fellow subsidiary of another body corporate if both are subsidiaries of the same body corporate but neither is a subsidiary of the other.

(3) For the purposes of subsection (1)(c) an offeror has a substantial interest in a body corporate if—

    (a) the body or its directors are accustomed to act in accordance with his directions or instructions, or

    (b) he is entitled to exercise or control the exercise of one-third or more of the voting power at general meetings of the body.

Subsections (2) and (3) of section 823 (which contain provision about when a person is treated as entitled to exercise or control the exercise of voting power) apply for the purposes of this subsection as they apply for the purposes of that section.

(4) For the purposes of subsection (1)(d) an agreement is a share acquisition agreement if—

    (a) it is an agreement for the acquisition of, or of an interest in, shares to which the offer relates,

    (b) it includes provisions imposing obligations or restrictions on any one or more of the parties to it with respect to their use, retention or disposal of such shares, or their interests in such shares, acquired in pursuance of the agreement (whether or not together with any other shares to which the offer relates or any other interests of theirs in such shares), and

    (c) it is not an excluded agreement (see subsection (5)).

(5) An agreement is an "excluded agreement"—

    (a) if it is not legally binding, unless it involves mutuality in the undertakings, expectations or understandings of the parties to it, or

    (b) if it is an agreement to underwrite or sub-underwrite an offer of shares in a company, provided the agreement is confined to that purpose and any matters incidental to it.

(6) The reference in subsection (4)(b) to the use of interests in shares is to the exercise of any rights or of any control or influence arising from those interests (including the right to enter

into an agreement for the exercise, or for control of the exercise, of any of those rights by another person).

(7) In this section—

    (a) "agreement" includes any agreement or arrangement;

    (b) references to provisions of an agreement include—

        (i) undertakings, expectations or understandings operative under an arrangement, and

        (ii) any provision whether express or implied and whether absolute or not.

989. Convertible securities

(1) For the purposes of this Chapter securities of a company are treated as shares in the company if they are convertible into or entitle the holder to subscribe for such shares.

References to the holder of shares or a shareholder are to be read accordingly.

(2) Subsection (1) is not to be read as requiring any securities to be treated—

    (a) as shares of the same class as those into which they are convertible or for which the holder is entitled to subscribe, or

    (b) as shares of the same class as other securities by reason only that the shares into which they are convertible or for which the holder is entitled to subscribe are of the same class.

990. Debentures carrying voting rights

(1) For the purposes of this Chapter debentures issued by a company to which subsection (2) applies are treated as shares in the company if they carry voting rights.

(2) This subsection applies to a company that has voting shares, or debentures carrying voting rights, which are admitted to trading on a regulated market.

(3) In this Chapter, in relation to debentures treated as shares by virtue of subsection (1)—

    (a) references to the holder of shares or a shareholder are to be read accordingly;

    (b) references to shares being allotted are to be read as references to debentures being issued.

991. Interpretation

(1) In this Chapter—

"the company" means the company whose shares are the subject of a takeover offer;

"date of the offer" means—

    (a) where the offer is published, the date of publication;

    (b) where the offer is not published, or where any notices of the offer are given before the date of publication, the date when notices of the offer (or the first such notices) are given;

    and references to the date of the offer are to be read in accordance with section 974(7) (revision of offer terms) where that applies;

"non-voting shares" means shares that are not voting shares;

"offeror" means (subject to section 987) the person making a takeover offer;

"voting rights" means rights to vote at general meetings of the company, including rights that arise only in certain circumstances;

"voting shares" means shares carrying voting rights.

(2) For the purposes of this Chapter a person contracts unconditionally to acquire shares if his entitlement under the contract to acquire them is not (or is no longer) subject to conditions or if all conditions to which it was subject have been met.

A reference to a contract becoming unconditional is to be read accordingly.

CHAPTER 4

AMENDMENTS TO PART 7 OF THE COMPANIES ACT 1985

992. Matters to be dealt with in directors' report

(1) Part 7 of the Companies Act 1985 (c. 6) (accounts and audit) is amended as follows.

(2) In Schedule 7 (matters to be dealt with in directors' report), after Part 6 insert—

"PART 7

DISCLOSURE REQUIRED BY CERTAIN PUBLICLY-TRADED COMPANIES

13 (1) This Part of this Schedule applies to the directors' report for a financial year if the company had securities carrying voting rights admitted to trading on a regulated market at the end of that year.

(2) The report shall contain detailed information, by reference to the end of that year, on the following matters—

(a) the structure of the company's capital, including in particular—

(i) the rights and obligations attaching to the shares or, as the case may be, to each class of shares in the company, and

(ii) where there are two or more such classes, the percentage of the total share capital represented by each class;

(b) any restrictions on the transfer of securities in the company, including in particular—

(i) limitations on the holding of securities, and

(ii) requirements to obtain the approval of the company, or of other holders of securities in the company, for a transfer of securities;

(c) in the case of each person with a significant direct or indirect holding of securities in the company, such details as are known to the company of—

(i) the identity of the person,

(ii) the size of the holding, and

(iii) the nature of the holding;

(d) in the case of each person who holds securities carrying special rights with regard to control of the company—

(i) the identity of the person, and

(ii) the nature of the rights;

(e) where—

(i) the company has an employees' share scheme, and

(ii) shares to which the scheme relates have rights with regard to control of the company that are not exercisable directly by the employees,

how those rights are exercisable;

(f) any restrictions on voting rights, including in particular—

(i) limitations on voting rights of holders of a given percentage or number of votes,

(ii) deadlines for exercising voting rights, and

(iii) arrangements by which, with the company's co-operation, financial rights carried by securities are held by a person other than the holder of the securities;

(g) any agreements between holders of securities that are known to the company and may result in restrictions on the transfer of securities or on voting rights;

(h) any rules that the company has about—

(i) appointment and replacement of directors, or

(ii) amendment of the company's articles of association;

      (i) the powers of the company's directors, including in particular any powers in relation to the issuing or buying back by the company of its shares;

      (j) any significant agreements to which the company is a party that take effect, alter or terminate upon a change of control of the company following a takeover bid, and the effects of any such agreements;

      (k) any agreements between the company and its directors or employees providing for compensation for loss of office or employment (whether through resignation, purported redundancy or otherwise) that occurs because of a takeover bid.

(3) For the purposes of sub-paragraph (2)(a) a company's capital includes any securities in the company that are not admitted to trading on a regulated market.

(4) For the purposes of sub-paragraph (2)(c) a person has an indirect holding of securities if—

      (a) they are held on his behalf, or

      (b) he is able to secure that rights carried by the securities are exercised in accordance with his wishes.

(5) Sub-paragraph (2)(j) does not apply to an agreement if—

      (a) disclosure of the agreement would be seriously prejudicial to the company, and

      (b) the company is not under any other obligation to disclose it.

(6) In this paragraph—

    "securities" means shares or debentures;

    "takeover bid" has the same meaning as in the Takeovers Directive;

    "the Takeovers Directive" means Directive 2004/25/EC of the European Parliament and of the Council;

    "voting rights" means rights to vote at general meetings of the company in question, including rights that arise only in certain circumstances.".

(3) In section 234ZZA (requirements of directors' reports), at the end of subsection (4) (contents of Schedule 7) insert—

"Part 7 specifies information to be disclosed by certain publicly-traded companies.".

(4) After that subsection insert—

"(5) A directors' report shall also contain any necessary explanatory material with regard to information that is required to be included in the report by Part 7 of Schedule 7.".

(5) In section 251 (summary financial statements), after subsection (2ZA) insert—

"(2ZB) A company that sends to an entitled person a summary financial statement instead of a copy of its directors' report shall—

      (a) include in the statement the explanatory material required to be included in the directors' report by section 234ZZA(5), or

      (b) send that material to the entitled person at the same time as it sends the statement.

For the purposes of paragraph (b), subsections (2A) to (2E) apply in relation to the material referred to in that paragraph as they apply in relation to a summary financial statement.".

(6) The amendments made by this section apply in relation to directors' reports for financial years beginning on or after 20th May 2006.

PART 29

FRAUDULENT TRADING

993. Offence of fraudulent trading

(1) If any business of a company is carried on with intent to defraud creditors of the company or creditors of any other person, or for any fraudulent purpose, every person who is knowingly a party to the carrying on of the business in that manner commits an offence.

(2) This applies whether or not the company has been, or is in the course of being, wound up.

(3) A person guilty of an offence under this section is liable—

    (a) on conviction on indictment, to imprisonment for a term not exceeding ten years or a fine (or both);

    (b) on summary conviction—

        (i) in England and Wales, to imprisonment for a term not exceeding twelve months or a fine not exceeding the statutory maximum (or both);

        (ii) in Scotland or Northern Ireland, to imprisonment for a term not exceeding six months or a fine not exceeding the statutory maximum (or both).

PART 30
PROTECTION OF MEMBERS AGAINST UNFAIR PREJUDICE

Main provisions

994. Petition by company member

(1) A member of a company may apply to the court by petition for an order under this Part on the ground—

    (a) that the company's affairs are being or have been conducted in a manner that is unfairly prejudicial to the interests of members generally or of some part of its members (including at least himself), or

    (b) that an actual or proposed act or omission of the company (including an act or omission on its behalf) is or would be so prejudicial.

(2) The provisions of this Part apply to a person who is not a member of a company but to whom shares in the company have been transferred or transmitted by operation of law as they apply to a member of a company.

(3) In this section, and so far as applicable for the purposes of this section in the other provisions of this Part, "company" means—

    (a) a company within the meaning of this Act, or

    (b) a company that is not such a company but is a statutory water company within the meaning of the Statutory Water Companies Act 1991 (c. 58).

995. Petition by Secretary of State

(1) This section applies to a company in respect of which—

    (a) the Secretary of State has received a report under section 437 of the Companies Act 1985 (c. 6) (inspector's report);

    (b) the Secretary of State has exercised his powers under section 447 or 448 of that Act (powers to require documents and information or to enter and search premises);

    (c) the Secretary of State or the Financial Services Authority has exercised his or its powers under Part 11 of the Financial Services and Markets Act 2000 (c. 8) (information gathering and investigations); or

    (d) the Secretary of State has received a report from an investigator appointed by him or the Financial Services Authority under that Part.

(2) If it appears to the Secretary of State that in the case of such a company—

    (a) the company's affairs are being or have been conducted in a manner that is unfairly prejudicial to the interests of members generally or of some part of its members, or

    (b) an actual or proposed act or omission of the company (including an act or omission on its behalf) is or would be so prejudicial,

he may apply to the court by petition for an order under this Part.

(3) The Secretary of State may do this in addition to, or instead of, presenting a petition for the winding up of the company.

(4) In this section, and so far as applicable for the purposes of this section in the other provisions of this Part, "company" means any body corporate that is liable to be wound up under the Insolvency Act 1986 (c. 45) or the Insolvency (Northern Ireland) Order 1989 (S.I. 1989/2405 (N.I. 19)).

996. Powers of the court under this Part

(1) If the court is satisfied that a petition under this Part is well founded, it may make such order as it thinks fit for giving relief in respect of the matters complained of.

(2) Without prejudice to the generality of subsection (1), the court's order may—

  (a) regulate the conduct of the company's affairs in the future;

  (b) require the company—

    (i) to refrain from doing or continuing an act complained of, or

    (ii) to do an act that the petitioner has complained it has omitted to do;

  (c) authorise civil proceedings to be brought in the name and on behalf of the company by such person or persons and on such terms as the court may direct;

  (d) require the company not to make any, or any specified, alterations in its articles without the leave of the court;

  (e) provide for the purchase of the shares of any members of the company by other members or by the company itself and, in the case of a purchase by the company itself, the reduction of the company's capital accordingly.

Supplementary provisions

997. Application of general rule-making powers

The power to make rules under section 411 of the Insolvency Act 1986 (c. 45) or Article 359 of the Insolvency (Northern Ireland) Order 1989 (S.I. 1989/2405 (N.I. 19)), so far as relating to a winding-up petition, applies for the purposes of a petition under this Part.

998. Copy of order affecting company's constitution to be delivered to registrar

(1) Where an order of the court under this Part—

  (a) alters the company's constitution, or

  (b) gives leave for the company to make any, or any specified, alterations to its constitution,

the company must deliver a copy of the order to the registrar.

(2) It must do so within 14 days from the making of the order or such longer period as the court may allow.

(3) If a company makes default in complying with this section, an offence is committed by—

  (a) the company, and

  (b) every officer of the company who is in default.

(4) A person guilty of an offence under this section is liable on summary conviction to a fine not exceeding level 3 on the standard scale and, for continued contravention, a daily default fine not exceeding one-tenth of level 3 on the standard scale.

999. Supplementary provisions where company's constitution altered

(1) This section applies where an order under this Part alters a company's constitution.

(2) If the order amends—

  (a) a company's articles, or

  (b) any resolution or agreement to which Chapter 3 of Part 3 applies (resolution or agreement affecting a company's constitution),

the copy of the order delivered to the registrar by the company under section 998 must be accompanied by a copy of the company's articles, or the resolution or agreement in question, as amended.

(3) Every copy of a company's articles issued by the company after the order is made must be accompanied by a copy of the order, unless the effect of the order has been incorporated into the articles by amendment.

(4) If a company makes default in complying with this section an offence is committed by—

    (a) the company, and

    (b) every officer of the company who is in default.

(5) A person guilty of an offence under this section is liable on summary conviction to a fine not exceeding level 3 on the standard scale.

PART 31
DISSOLUTION AND RESTORATION TO THE REGISTER

CHAPTER 1
STRIKING OFF

Registrar's power to strike off defunct company

1000. Power to strike off company not carrying on business or in operation

(1) If the registrar has reasonable cause to believe that a company is not carrying on business or in operation, the registrar may send to the company by post a letter inquiring whether the company is carrying on business or in operation.

(2) If the registrar does not within one month of sending the letter receive any answer to it, the registrar must within 14 days after the expiration of that month send to the company by post a registered letter referring to the first letter, and stating—

    (a) that no answer to it has been received, and

    (b) that if an answer is not received to the second letter within one month from its date, a notice will be published in the Gazette with a view to striking the company's name off the register.

(3) If the registrar—

    (a) receives an answer to the effect that the company is not carrying on business or in operation, or

    (b) does not within one month after sending the second letter receive any answer,

the registrar may publish in the Gazette, and send to the company by post, a notice that at the expiration of three months from the date of the notice the name of the company mentioned in it will, unless cause is shown to the contrary, be struck off the register and the company will be dissolved.

(4) At the expiration of the time mentioned in the notice the registrar may, unless cause to the contrary is previously shown by the company, strike its name off the register.

(5) The registrar must publish notice in the Gazette of the company's name having been struck off the register.

(6) On the publication of the notice in the Gazette the company is dissolved.

(7) However—

    (a) the liability (if any) of every director, managing officer and member of the company continues and may be enforced as if the company had not been dissolved, and

    (b) nothing in this section affects the power of the court to wind up a company the name of which has been struck off the register.

1001. Duty to act in case of company being wound up

(1) If, in a case where a company is being wound up—

    (a) the registrar has reasonable cause to believe—

        (i) that no liquidator is acting, or

        (ii) that the affairs of the company are fully wound up, and

    (b) the returns required to be made by the liquidator have not been made for a period of six consecutive months, the registrar must publish in the Gazette and send to the company or the liquidator (if any) a notice that at the expiration of three months from the date of the notice the name of the company mentioned in it will, unless cause is shown to the contrary, be struck off the register and the company will be dissolved.

(2) At the expiration of the time mentioned in the notice the registrar may, unless cause to the contrary is previously shown by the company, strike its name off the register.

(3) The registrar must publish notice in the Gazette of the company's name having been struck off the register.

(4) On the publication of the notice in the Gazette the company is dissolved.

(5) However—

(a) the liability (if any) of every director, managing officer and member of the company continues and may be enforced as if the company had not been dissolved, and

(b) nothing in this section affects the power of the court to wind up a company the name of which has been struck off the register.

1002. Supplementary provisions as to service of letter or notice

(1) A letter or notice to be sent under section 1000 or 1001 to a company may be addressed to the company at its registered office or, if no office has been registered, to the care of some officer of the company.

(2) If there is no officer of the company whose name and address are known to the registrar, the letter or notice may be sent to each of the persons who subscribed the memorandum (if their addresses are known to the registrar).

(3) A notice to be sent to a liquidator under section 1001 may be addressed to him at his last known place of business.

Voluntary striking off

1003. Striking off on application by company

(1) On application by a company, the registrar of companies may strike the company's name off the register.

(2) The application—

(a) must be made on the company's behalf by its directors or by a majority of them, and

(b) must contain the prescribed information.

(3) The registrar may not strike a company off under this section until after the expiration of three months from the publication by the registrar in the Gazette of a notice—

(a) stating that the registrar may exercise the power under this section in relation to the company, and

(b) inviting any person to show cause why that should not be done.

(4) The registrar must publish notice in the Gazette of the company's name having been struck off.

(5) On the publication of the notice in the Gazette the company is dissolved.

(6) However—

(a) the liability (if any) of every director, managing officer and member of the company continues and may be enforced as if the company had not been dissolved, and

(b) nothing in this section affects the power of the court to wind up a company the name of which has been struck off the register.

1004. Circumstances in which application not to be made: activities of company

(1) An application under section 1003 (application for voluntary striking off) on behalf of a company must not be made if, at any time in the previous three months, the company has—

(a) changed its name,

(b) traded or otherwise carried on business,

(c) made a disposal for value of property or rights that, immediately before ceasing to trade or otherwise carry on business, it held for the purpose of disposal for gain in the normal course of trading or otherwise carrying on business, or

(d) engaged in any other activity, except one which is—

    (i) necessary or expedient for the purpose of making an application under that section, or deciding whether to do so,

    (ii) necessary or expedient for the purpose of concluding the affairs of the company,

    (iii) necessary or expedient for the purpose of complying with any statutory requirement, or

    (iv) specified by the Secretary of State by order for the purposes of this sub-paragraph.

(2) For the purposes of this section, a company is not to be treated as trading or otherwise carrying on business by virtue only of the fact that it makes a payment in respect of a liability incurred in the course of trading or otherwise carrying on business.

(3) The Secretary of State may by order amend subsection (1) for the purpose of altering the period in relation to which the doing of the things mentioned in paragraphs (a) to (d) of that subsection is relevant.

(4) An order under this section is subject to negative resolution procedure.

(5) It is an offence for a person to make an application in contravention of this section.

(6) In proceedings for such an offence it is a defence for the accused to prove that he did not know, and could not reasonably have known, of the existence of the facts that led to the contravention.

(7) A person guilty of an offence under this section is liable—

    (a) on conviction on indictment, to a fine;

    (b) on summary conviction, to a fine not exceeding the statutory maximum.

1005. Circumstances in which application not to be made: other proceedings not concluded

(1) An application under section 1003 (application for voluntary striking off) on behalf of a company must not be made at a time when—

    (a) an application to the court under Part 26 has been made on behalf of the company for the sanctioning of a compromise or arrangement and the matter has not been finally concluded;

    (b) a voluntary arrangement in relation to the company has been proposed under Part 1 of the Insolvency Act 1986 (c. 45) or Part 2 of the Insolvency (Northern Ireland) Order 1989 (S.I. 1989/2405 (N.I. 19)) and the matter has not been finally concluded;

    (c) the company is in administration under Part 2 of that Act or Part 3 of that Order;

    (d) paragraph 44 of Schedule B1 to that Act or paragraph 45 of Schedule B1 to that Order applies (interim moratorium on proceedings where application to the court for an administration order has been made or notice of intention to appoint administrator has been filed);

    (e) the company is being wound up under Part 4 of that Act or Part 5 of that Order, whether voluntarily or by the court, or a petition under that Part for winding up of the company by the court has been presented and not finally dealt with or withdrawn;

    (f) there is a receiver or manager of the company's property;

    (g) the company's estate is being administered by a judicial factor.

(2) For the purposes of subsection (1)(a), the matter is finally concluded if—

    (a) the application has been withdrawn,

    (b) the application has been finally dealt with without a compromise or arrangement being sanctioned by the court, or

    (c) a compromise or arrangement has been sanctioned by the court and has, together with anything required to be done under any provision made in relation to the matter by order of the court, been fully carried out.

(3) For the purposes of subsection (1)(b), the matter is finally concluded if—

    (a) no meetings are to be summoned under section 3 of the Insolvency Act 1986 (c. 45) or Article 16 of the Insolvency (Northern Ireland) Order 1989,

    (b) meetings summoned under that section or Article fail to approve the arrangement with no, or the same, modifications,

    (c) an arrangement approved by meetings summoned under that section, or in consequence of a direction under section 6(4)(b) of that Act or Article 19(4)(b) of that Order, has been fully implemented, or

    (d) the court makes an order under section 6(5) of that Act or Article 19(5) of that Order revoking approval given at previous meetings and, if the court gives any directions under section 6(6) of that Act or Article 19(6) of that Order, the company has done whatever it is required to do under those directions.

(4) It is an offence for a person to make an application in contravention of this section.

(5) In proceedings for such an offence it is a defence for the accused to prove that he did not know, and could not reasonably have known, of the existence of the facts that led to the contravention.

(6) A person guilty of an offence under this section is liable—

    (a) on conviction on indictment, to a fine;

    (b) on summary conviction, to a fine not exceeding the statutory maximum.

1006. Copy of application to be given to members, employees, etc

(1) A person who makes an application under section 1003 (application for voluntary striking off) on behalf of a company must secure that, within seven days from the day on which the application is made, a copy of it is given to every person who at any time on that day is—

    (a) a member of the company,

    (b) an employee of the company,

    (c) a creditor of the company,

    (d) a director of the company,

    (e) a manager or trustee of any pension fund established for the benefit of employees of the company, or

    (f) a person of a description specified for the purposes of this paragraph by regulations made by the Secretary of State.

Regulations under paragraph (f) are subject to negative resolution procedure.

(2) Subsection (1) does not require a copy of the application to be given to a director who is a party to the application.

(3) The duty imposed by this section ceases to apply if the application is withdrawn before the end of the period for giving the copy application.

(4) A person who fails to perform the duty imposed on him by this section commits an offence. If he does so with the intention of concealing the making of the application from the person concerned, he commits an aggravated offence.

(5) In proceedings for an offence under this section it is a defence for the accused to prove that he took all reasonable steps to perform the duty.

(6) A person guilty of an offence under this section (other than an aggravated offence) is liable—

    (a) on conviction on indictment, to a fine;

    (b) on summary conviction, to a fine not exceeding the statutory maximum.

(7) A person guilty of an aggravated offence under this section is liable—

    (a) on conviction on indictment, to imprisonment for a term not exceeding seven years or a fine (or both);

    (b) on summary conviction—

        (i) in England and Wales, to imprisonment for a term not exceeding twelve months or to a fine not exceeding the statutory maximum (or both);

        (ii) in Scotland or Northern Ireland, to imprisonment for a term not exceeding six months, or to a fine not exceeding the statutory maximum (or both).

1007. Copy of application to be given to new members, employees, etc

    (1) This section applies in relation to any time after the day on which a company makes an application under section 1003 (application for voluntary striking off) and before the day on which the application is finally dealt with or withdrawn.

    (2) A person who is a director of the company at the end of a day on which a person (other than himself) becomes—

        (a) a member of the company,

        (b) an employee of the company,

        (c) a creditor of the company,

        (d) a director of the company,

        (e) a manager or trustee of any pension fund established for the benefit of employees of the company, or

        (f) a person of a description specified for the purposes of this paragraph by regulations made by the Secretary of State,

    must secure that a copy of the application is given to that person within seven days from that day.

    Regulations under paragraph (f) are subject to negative resolution procedure.

    (3) The duty imposed by this section ceases to apply if the application is finally dealt with or withdrawn before the end of the period for giving the copy application.

    (4) A person who fails to perform the duty imposed on him by this section commits an offence. If he does so with the intention of concealing the making of the application from the person concerned, he commits an aggravated offence.

    (5) In proceedings for an offence under this section it is a defence for the accused to prove—

        (a) that at the time of the failure he was not aware of the fact that the company had made an application under section 1003, or

        (b) that he took all reasonable steps to perform the duty.

    (6) A person guilty of an offence under this section (other than an aggravated offence) is liable—

        (a) on conviction on indictment, to a fine;

        (b) on summary conviction, to a fine not exceeding the statutory maximum.

    (7) A person guilty of an aggravated offence under this section is liable—

        (a) on conviction on indictment, to imprisonment for a term not exceeding seven years or a fine (or both);

        (b) on summary conviction—

            (i) in England and Wales, to imprisonment for a term not exceeding twelve months or to a fine not exceeding the statutory maximum (or both);

            (ii) in Scotland or Northern Ireland, to imprisonment for a term not exceeding six months, or to a fine not exceeding the statutory maximum (or both).

1008. Copy of application: provisions as to service of documents

    (1) The following provisions have effect for the purposes of—

    section 1006 (copy of application to be given to members, employees, etc), and

    section 1007 (copy of application to be given to new members, employees, etc).

    (2) A document is treated as given to a person if it is—

        (a) delivered to him, or

        (b) left at his proper address, or

        (c) sent by post to him at that address.

    (3) For the purposes of subsection (2) and section 7 of the Interpretation Act 1978 (c. 30) (service of documents by post) as it applies in relation to that subsection, the proper address of a person is—

        (a) in the case of a firm incorporated or formed in the United Kingdom, its registered or principal office;

(b) in the case of a firm incorporated or formed outside the United Kingdom—

   (i) if it has a place of business in the United Kingdom, its principal office in the United Kingdom, or

   (ii) if it does not have a place of business in the United Kingdom, its registered or principal office;

(c) in the case of an individual, his last known address.

(4) In the case of a creditor of the company a document is treated as given to him if it is left or sent by post to him—

(a) at the place of business of his with which the company has had dealings by virtue of which he is a creditor of the company, or

(b) if there is more than one such place of business, at each of them.

1009. Circumstances in which application to be withdrawn

(1) This section applies where, at any time on or after the day on which a company makes an application under section 1003 (application for voluntary striking off) and before the day on which the application is finally dealt with or withdrawn—

(a) the company—

   (i) changes its name,

   (ii) trades or otherwise carries on business,

   (iii) makes a disposal for value of any property or rights other than those which it was necessary or expedient for it to hold for the purpose of making, or proceeding with, an application under that section, or

   (iv) engages in any activity, except one to which subsection (4) applies;

(b) an application is made to the court under Part 26 on behalf of the company for the sanctioning of a compromise or arrangement;

(c) a voluntary arrangement in relation to the company is proposed under Part 1 of the Insolvency Act 1986 (c. 45) or Part 2 of the Insolvency (Northern Ireland) Order 1989 (S.I. 1989/2405 (N.I. 19));

(d) an application to the court for an administration order in respect of the company is made under paragraph 12 of Schedule B1 to that Act or paragraph 13 of Schedule B1 to that Order;

(e) an administrator is appointed in respect of the company under paragraph 14 or 22 of Schedule B1 to that Act or paragraph 15 or 23 of Schedule B1 to that Order, or a copy of notice of intention to appoint an administrator of the company under any of those provisions is filed with the court;

(f) there arise any of the circumstances in which, under section 84(1) of that Act or Article 70 of that Order, the company may be voluntarily wound up;

(g) a petition is presented for the winding up of the company by the court under Part 4 of that Act or Part 5 of that Order;

(h) a receiver or manager of the company's property is appointed; or

(i) a judicial factor is appointed to administer the company's estate.

(2) A person who, at the end of a day on which any of the events mentioned in subsection (1) occurs, is a director of the company must secure that the company's application is withdrawn forthwith.

(3) For the purposes of subsection (1)(a), a company is not treated as trading or otherwise carrying on business by virtue only of the fact that it makes a payment in respect of a liability incurred in the course of trading or otherwise carrying on business.

(4) The excepted activities referred to in subsection (1)(a)(iv) are—

(a) any activity necessary or expedient for the purposes of—

   (i) making, or proceeding with, an application under section 1003 (application for voluntary striking off),

  (ii) concluding affairs of the company that are outstanding because of what has been necessary or expedient for the purpose of making, or proceeding with, such an application, or

  (iii) complying with any statutory requirement;

 (b) any activity specified by the Secretary of State by order for the purposes of this subsection.

An order under paragraph (b) is subject to negative resolution procedure.

(5) A person who fails to perform the duty imposed on him by this section commits an offence.

(6) In proceedings for an offence under this section it is a defence for the accused to prove—

 (a) that at the time of the failure he was not aware of the fact that the company had made an application under section 1003, or

 (b) that he took all reasonable steps to perform the duty.

(7) A person guilty of an offence under this section is liable—

 (a) on conviction on indictment, to a fine;

 (b) on summary conviction, to a fine not exceeding the statutory maximum.

1010. Withdrawal of application

An application under section 1003 is withdrawn by notice to the registrar.

1011. Meaning of "creditor"

In this Chapter "creditor" includes a contingent or prospective creditor.

CHAPTER 2
PROPERTY OF DISSOLVED COMPANY

Property vesting as bona vacantia

1012. Property of dissolved company to be bona vacantia

(1) When a company is dissolved, all property and rights whatsoever vested in or held on trust for the company immediately before its dissolution (including leasehold property, but not including property held by the company on trust for another person) are deemed to be *bona vacantia* and—

 (a) accordingly belong to the Crown, or to the Duchy of Lancaster or to the Duke of Cornwall for the time being (as the case may be), and

 (b) vest and may be dealt with in the same manner as other *bona vacantia* accruing to the Crown, to the Duchy of Lancaster or to the Duke of Cornwall.

(2) Subsection (1) has effect subject to the possible restoration of the company to the register under Chapter 3 (see section 1034).

1013. Crown disclaimer of property vesting as bona vacantia

(1) Where property vests in the Crown under section 1012, the Crown's title to it under that section may be disclaimed by a notice signed by the Crown representative, that is to say the Treasury Solicitor, or, in relation to property in Scotland, the Queen's and Lord Treasurer's Remembrancer.

(2) The right to execute a notice of disclaimer under this section may be waived by or on behalf of the Crown either expressly or by taking possession.

(3) A notice of disclaimer must be executed within three years after—

 (a) the date on which the fact that the property may have vested in the Crown under section 1012 first comes to the notice of the Crown representative, or

 (b) if ownership of the property is not established at that date, the end of the period reasonably necessary for the Crown representative to establish the ownership of the property.

(4) If an application in writing is made to the Crown representative by a person interested in the property requiring him to decide whether he will or will not disclaim, any notice of disclaimer must be executed within twelve months after the making of the application or such further period as may be allowed by the court.

(5) A notice of disclaimer under this section is of no effect if it is shown to have been executed after the end of the period specified by subsection (3) or (4).

(6) A notice of disclaimer under this section must be delivered to the registrar and retained and registered by him.

(7) Copies of it must be published in the Gazette and sent to any persons who have given the Crown representative notice that they claim to be interested in the property.

(8) This section applies to property vested in the Duchy of Lancaster or the Duke of Cornwall under section 1012 as if for references to the Crown and the Crown representative there were respectively substituted references to the Duchy of Lancaster and to the Solicitor to that Duchy, or to the Duke of Cornwall and to the Solicitor to the Duchy of Cornwall, as the case may be.

1014. Effect of Crown disclaimer

(1) Where notice of disclaimer is executed under section 1013 as respects any property, that property is deemed not to have vested in the Crown under section 1012.

(2) The following sections contain provisions as to the effect of the Crown disclaimer—

sections 1015 to 1019 apply in relation to property in England and Wales or Northern Ireland;

sections 1020 to 1022 apply in relation to property in Scotland.

Effect of Crown disclaimer: England and Wales and Northern Ireland

1015. General effect of disclaimer

(1) The Crown's disclaimer operates so as to terminate, as from the date of the disclaimer, the rights, interests and liabilities of the company in or in respect of the property disclaimed.

(2) It does not, except so far as is necessary for the purpose of releasing the company from any liability, affect the rights or liabilities of any other person.

1016. Disclaimer of leaseholds

(1) The disclaimer of any property of a leasehold character does not take effect unless a copy of the disclaimer has been served (so far as the Crown representative is aware of their addresses) on every person claiming under the company as underlessee or mortgagee, and either—

(a) no application under section 1017 (power of court to make vesting order) is made with respect to that property before the end of the period of 14 days beginning with the day on which the last notice under this paragraph was served, or

(b) where such an application has been made, the court directs that the disclaimer shall take effect.

(2) Where the court gives a direction under subsection (1)(b) it may also, instead of or in addition to any order it makes under section 1017, make such order as it thinks fit with respect to fixtures, tenant's improvements and other matters arising out of the lease.

(3) In this section the "Crown representative" means—

(a) in relation to property vested in the Duchy of Lancaster, the Solicitor to that Duchy;

(b) in relation to property vested in the Duke of Cornwall, the Solicitor to the Duchy of Cornwall;

(c) in relation to property in Scotland, the Queen's and Lord Treasurer's Remembrancer;

(d) in relation to other property, the Treasury Solicitor.

1017. Power of court to make vesting order

(1) The court may on application by a person who—

(a) claims an interest in the disclaimed property, or

(b) is under a liability in respect of the disclaimed property that is not discharged by the disclaimer,

make an order under this section in respect of the property.

(2) An order under this section is an order for the vesting of the disclaimed property in, or its delivery to—

(a) a person entitled to it (or a trustee for such a person), or

(b) a person subject to such a liability as is mentioned in subsection (1)(b) (or a trustee for such a person).

(3) An order under subsection (2)(b) may only be made where it appears to the court that it would be just to do so for the purpose of compensating the person subject to the liability in respect of the disclaimer.

(4) An order under this section may be made on such terms as the court thinks fit.

(5) On a vesting order being made under this section, the property comprised in it vests in the person named in that behalf in the order without conveyance, assignment or transfer.

1018. Protection of persons holding under a lease

(1) The court must not make an order under section 1017 vesting property of a leasehold nature in a person claiming under the company as underlessee or mortgagee except on terms making that person—

(a) subject to the same liabilities and obligations as those to which the company was subject under the lease, or

(b) if the court thinks fit, subject to the same liabilities and obligations as if the lease had been assigned to him.

(2) Where the order relates to only part of the property comprised in the lease, subsection (1) applies as if the lease had comprised only the property comprised in the vesting order.

(3) A person claiming under the company as underlessee or mortgagee who declines to accept a vesting order on such terms is excluded from all interest in the property.

(4) If there is no person claiming under the company who is willing to accept an order on such terms, the court has power to vest the company's estate and interest in the property in any person who is liable (whether personally or in a representative character, and whether alone or jointly with the company) to perform the lessee's covenants in the lease.

(5) The court may vest that estate and interest in such a person freed and discharged from all estates, incumbrances and interests created by the company.

1019. Land subject to rentcharge

Where in consequence of the disclaimer land that is subject to a rentcharge vests in any person, neither he nor his successors in title are subject to any personal liability in respect of sums becoming due under the rentcharge, except sums becoming due after he, or some person claiming under or through him, has taken possession or control of the land or has entered into occupation of it.

Effect of Crown disclaimer: Scotland

1020. General effect of disclaimer

(1) The Crown's disclaimer operates to determine, as from the date of the disclaimer, the rights, interests and liabilities of the company, and the property of the company, in or in respect of the property disclaimed.

(2) It does not (except so far as is necessary for the purpose of releasing the company and its property from liability) affect the rights or liabilities of any other person.

1021. Power of court to make vesting order

(1) The court may—

(a) on application by a person who either claims an interest in disclaimed property or is under a liability not discharged by this Act in respect of disclaimed property, and

(b) on hearing such persons as it thinks fit,

make an order for the vesting of the property in or its delivery to any persons entitled to it, or to whom it may seem just that the property should be delivered by way of compensation for such liability, or a trustee for him.

(2) The order may be made on such terms as the court thinks fit.

(3) On a vesting order being made under this section, the property comprised in it vests accordingly in the person named in that behalf in the order, without conveyance or assignation for that purpose.

1022. Protection of persons holding under a lease

(1) Where the property disclaimed is held under a lease the court must not make a vesting order in favour of a person claiming under the company, whether—

(a) as sub-lessee, or

(b) as creditor in a duly registered or (as the case may be) recorded heritable security over a lease,

except on the following terms.

(2) The person must by the order be made subject—

(a) to the same liabilities and obligations as those to which the company was subject under the lease in respect of the property, or

(b) if the court thinks fit, only to the same liabilities and obligations as if the lease had been assigned to him.

In either event (if the case so requires) the liabilities and obligations must be as if the lease had comprised only the property comprised in the vesting order.

(3) A sub-lessee or creditor declining to accept a vesting order on such terms is excluded from all interest in and security over the property.

(4) If there is no person claiming under the company who is willing to accept an order on such terms, the court has power to vest the company's estate and interest in the property in any person liable (either personally or in a representative character, and either alone or jointly with the company) to perform the lessee's obligations under the lease.

(5) The court may vest that estate and interest in such a person freed and discharged from all interests, rights and obligations created by the company in the lease or in relation to the lease.

(6) For the purposes of this section a heritable security—

(a) is duly recorded if it is recorded in the Register of Sasines, and

(b) is duly registered if registered in accordance with the Land Registration (Scotland) Act 1979 (c. 33).

Supplementary provisions

1023. Liability for rentcharge on company's land after dissolution

(1) This section applies where on the dissolution of a company land in England and Wales or Northern Ireland that is subject to a rentcharge vests by operation of law in the Crown or any other person ("the proprietor").

(2) Neither the proprietor nor his successors in title are subject to any personal liability in respect of sums becoming due under the rentcharge, except sums becoming due after the proprietor, or some person claiming under or through him, has taken possession or control of the land or has entered into occupation of it.

(3) In this section "company" includes any body corporate.

CHAPTER 3
RESTORATION TO THE REGISTER

Administrative restoration to the register

1024. Application for administrative restoration to the register

(1) An application may be made to the registrar to restore to the register a company that has been struck off the register under section 1000 or 1001 (power of registrar to strike off defunct company).

(2) An application under this section may be made whether or not the company has in consequence been dissolved.

(3) An application under this section may only be made by a former director or former member of the company.

(4) An application under this section may not be made after the end of the period of six years from the date of the dissolution of the company.

For this purpose an application is made when it is received by the registrar.

1025. Requirements for administrative restoration

(1) On an application under section 1024 the registrar shall restore the company to the register if, and only if, the following conditions are met.

(2) The first condition is that the company was carrying on business or in operation at the time of its striking off.

(3) The second condition is that, if any property or right previously vested in or held on trust for the company has vested as *bona vacantia*, the Crown representative has signified to the registrar in writing consent to the company's restoration to the register.

(4) It is the applicant's responsibility to obtain that consent and to pay any costs (in Scotland, expenses) of the Crown representative—

(a) in dealing with the property during the period of dissolution, or

(b) in connection with the proceedings on the application,

that may be demanded as a condition of giving consent.

(5) The third condition is that the applicant has—

(a) delivered to the registrar such documents relating to the company as are necessary to bring up to date the records kept by the registrar, and

(b) paid any penalties under section 453 or corresponding earlier provisions (civil penalty for failure to deliver accounts) that were outstanding at the date of dissolution or striking off.

(6) In this section the "Crown representative" means—

(a) in relation to property vested in the Duchy of Lancaster, the Solicitor to that Duchy;

(b) in relation to property vested in the Duke of Cornwall, the Solicitor to the Duchy of Cornwall;

(c) in relation to property in Scotland, the Queen's and Lord Treasurer's Remembrancer;

(d) in relation to other property, the Treasury Solicitor.

1026. Application to be accompanied by statement of compliance

(1) An application under section 1024 (application for administrative restoration to the register) must be accompanied by a statement of compliance.

(2) The statement of compliance required is a statement—

(a) that the person making the application has standing to apply (see subsection (3) of that section), and

(b) that the requirements for administrative restoration (see section 1025) are met.

(3) The registrar may accept the statement of compliance as sufficient evidence of those matters.

1027. Registrar's decision on application for administrative restoration

(1) The registrar must give notice to the applicant of the decision on an application under section 1024 (application for administrative restoration to the register).

(2) If the decision is that the company should be restored to the register, the restoration takes effect as from the date that notice is sent.

(3) In the case of such a decision, the registrar must—

(a) enter on the register a note of the date as from which the company's restoration to the register takes effect, and

(b) cause notice of the restoration to be published in the Gazette.

(4) The notice under subsection (3)(b) must state—

(a) the name of the company or, if the company is restored to the register under a different name (see section 1033), that name and its former name,

(b) the company's registered number, and

(c) the date as from which the restoration of the company to the register takes effect.

1028. Effect of administrative restoration

(1) The general effect of administrative restoration to the register is that the company is deemed to have continued in existence as if it had not been dissolved or struck off the register.

(2) The company is not liable to a penalty under section 453 or any corresponding earlier provision (civil penalty for failure to deliver accounts) for a financial year in relation to which the period for filing accounts and reports ended—

(a) after the date of dissolution or striking off, and

(b) before the restoration of the company to the register.

(3) The court may give such directions and make such provision as seems just for placing the company and all other persons in the same position (as nearly as may be) as if the company had not been dissolved or struck off the register.

(4) An application to the court for such directions or provision may be made any time within three years after the date of restoration of the company to the register.

Restoration to the register by the court

1029. Application to court for restoration to the register

(1) An application may be made to the court to restore to the register a company—

(a) that has been dissolved under Chapter 9 of Part 4 of the Insolvency Act 1986 (c. 45) or Chapter 9 of Part 5 of the Insolvency (Northern Ireland) Order 1989 (S.I. 1989/2405 (N.I. 19)) (dissolution of company after winding up),

(b) that is deemed to have been dissolved under paragraph 84(6) of Schedule B1 to that Act or paragraph 85(6) of Schedule B1 to that Order (dissolution of company following administration), or

(c) that has been struck off the register—

(i) under section 1000 or 1001 (power of registrar to strike off defunct company), or

(ii) under section 1003 (voluntary striking off),

whether or not the company has in consequence been dissolved.

(2) An application under this section may be made by—

(a) the Secretary of State,

(b) any former director of the company,

(c) any person having an interest in land in which the company had a superior or derivative interest,

(d) any person having an interest in land or other property—

(i) that was subject to rights vested in the company, or

(ii) that was benefited by obligations owed by the company,

(e) any person who but for the company's dissolution would have been in a contractual relationship with it,

(f) any person with a potential legal claim against the company,

(g) any manager or trustee of a pension fund established for the benefit of employees of the company,

(h) any former member of the company (or the personal representatives of such a person),

(i) any person who was a creditor of the company at the time of its striking off or dissolution,

(j) any former liquidator of the company,

(k) where the company was struck off the register under section 1003 (voluntary striking off), any person of a description specified by regulations under section 1006(1)(f) or 1007(2)(f) (persons entitled to notice of application for voluntary striking off),

or by any other person appearing to the court to have an interest in the matter.

1030. When application to the court may be made

(1) An application to the court for restoration of a company to the register may be made at any time for the purpose of bringing proceedings against the company for damages for personal injury.

(2) No order shall be made on such an application if it appears to the court that the proceedings would fail by virtue of any enactment as to the time within which proceedings must be brought.

(3) In making that decision the court must have regard to its power under section 1032(3) (power to give consequential directions etc) to direct that the period between the dissolution (or striking off) of the company and the making of the order is not to count for the purposes of any such enactment.

(4) In any other case an application to the court for restoration of a company to the register may not be made after the end of the period of six years from the date of the dissolution of the company, subject as follows.

(5) In a case where—

(a) the company has been struck off the register under section 1000 or 1001 (power of registrar to strike off defunct company),

(b) an application to the registrar has been made under section 1024 (application for administrative restoration to the register) within the time allowed for making such an application, and

(c) the registrar has refused the application,

an application to the court under this section may be made within 28 days of notice of the registrar's decision being issued by the registrar, even if the period of six years mentioned in subsection (4) above has expired.

(6) For the purposes of this section—

(a) "personal injury" includes any disease and any impairment of a person's physical or mental condition; and

(b) references to damages for personal injury include—

(i) any sum claimed by virtue of section 1(2)(c) of the Law Reform (Miscellaneous Provisions) Act 1934 (c. 41) or section 14(2)(c) of the Law Reform (Miscellaneous Provisions) Act (Northern Ireland) 1937 (1937 c. 9 (N.I.)) (funeral expenses)), and

(ii) damages under the Fatal Accidents Act 1976 (c. 30), the Damages (Scotland) Act 1976 (c. 13) or the Fatal Accidents (Northern Ireland) Order 1977 (S.I. 1977/1251 (N.I. 18)).

1031. Decision on application for restoration by the court

(1) On an application under section 1029 the court may order the restoration of the company to the register—

(a) if the company was struck off the register under section 1000 or 1001 (power of registrar to strike off defunct companies) and the company was, at the time of the striking off, carrying on business or in operation;

(b) if the company was struck off the register under section 1003 (voluntary striking off) and any of the requirements of sections 1004 to 1009 was not complied with;

(c) if in any other case the court considers it just to do so.

(2) If the court orders restoration of the company to the register, the restoration takes effect on a copy of the court's order being delivered to the registrar.

(3) The registrar must cause to be published in the Gazette notice of the restoration of the company to the register.

(4) The notice must state—

(a) the name of the company or, if the company is restored to the register under a different name (see section 1033), that name and its former name,

(b) the company's registered number, and

(c) the date on which the restoration took effect.

1032. Effect of court order for restoration to the register

(1) The general effect of an order by the court for restoration to the register is that the company is deemed to have continued in existence as if it had not been dissolved or struck off the register.

(2) The company is not liable to a penalty under section 453 or any corresponding earlier provision (civil penalty for failure to deliver accounts) for a financial year in relation to which the period for filing accounts and reports ended—

(a) after the date of dissolution or striking off, and

(b) before the restoration of the company to the register.

(3) The court may give such directions and make such provision as seems just for placing the company and all other persons in the same position (as nearly as may be) as if the company had not been dissolved or struck off the register.

(4) The court may also give directions as to—

(a) the delivery to the registrar of such documents relating to the company as are necessary to bring up to date the records kept by the registrar,

(b) the payment of the costs (in Scotland, expenses) of the registrar in connection with the proceedings for the restoration of the company to the register,

(c) where any property or right previously vested in or held on trust for the company has vested as *bona vacantia*, the payment of the costs (in Scotland, expenses) of the Crown representative—

(i) in dealing with the property during the period of dissolution, or

(ii) in connection with the proceedings on the application.

(5) In this section the "Crown representative" means—

(a) in relation to property vested in the Duchy of Lancaster, the Solicitor to that Duchy;

(b) in relation to property vested in the Duke of Cornwall, the Solicitor to the Duchy of Cornwall;

(c) in relation to property in Scotland, the Queen's and Lord Treasurer's Remembrancer;

(d) in relation to other property, the Treasury Solicitor.

Supplementary provisions

1033. Company's name on restoration

(1) A company is restored to the register with the name it had before it was dissolved or struck off the register, subject to the following provisions.

(2) If at the date of restoration the company could not be registered under its former name without contravening section 66 (name not to be the same as another in the registrar's index of company names), it must be restored to the register—

(a) under another name specified—

(i) in the case of administrative restoration, in the application to the registrar, or

(ii) in the case of restoration under a court order, in the court's order, or

(b) as if its registered number was also its name.

References to a company's being registered in a name, and to registration in that context, shall be read as including the company's being restored to the register.

(3) If a company is restored to the register under a name specified in the application to the registrar, the provisions of—

section 80 (change of name: registration and issue of new certificate of incorporation), and

section 81 (change of name: effect),

apply as if the application to the registrar were notice of a change of name.

(4) If a company is restored to the register under a name specified in the court's order, the provisions of—

section 80 (change of name: registration and issue of new certificate of incorporation), and

section 81 (change of name: effect),

apply as if the copy of the court order delivered to the registrar were notice of a change a name.

(5) If the company is restored to the register as if its registered number was also its name—

    (a) the company must change its name within 14 days after the date of the restoration,

    (b) the change may be made by resolution of the directors (without prejudice to any other method of changing the company's name),

    (c) the company must give notice to the registrar of the change, and

    (d) sections 80 and 81 apply as regards the registration and effect of the change.

(6) If the company fails to comply with subsection (5)(a) or (c) an offence is committed by—

    (a) the company, and

    (b) every officer of the company who is in default.

(7) A person guilty of an offence under subsection (6) is liable on summary conviction to a fine not exceeding level 5 on the standard scale and, for continued contravention, a daily default fine not exceeding one-tenth of level 5 on the standard scale.

1034. Effect of restoration to the register where property has vested as bona vacantia

(1) The person in whom any property or right is vested by section 1012 (property of dissolved company to be *bona vacantia*) may dispose of, or of an interest in, that property or right despite the fact that the company may be restored to the register under this Chapter.

(2) If the company is restored to the register—

    (a) the restoration does not affect the disposition (but without prejudice to its effect in relation to any other property or right previously vested in or held on trust for the company), and

    (b) the Crown or, as the case may be, the Duke of Cornwall shall pay to the company an amount equal to—

        (i) the amount of any consideration received for the property or right or, as the case may be, the interest in it, or

        (ii) the value of any such consideration at the time of the disposition,

    or, if no consideration was received an amount equal to the value of the property, right or interest disposed of, as at the date of the disposition.

(3) There may be deducted from the amount payable under subsection (2)(b) the reasonable costs of the Crown representative in connection with the disposition (to the extent that they have not been paid as a condition of administrative restoration or pursuant to a court order for restoration).

(4) Where a liability accrues under subsection (2) in respect of any property or right which before the restoration of the company to the register had accrued as *bona vacantia* to the Duchy of Lancaster, the Attorney General of that Duchy shall represent Her Majesty in any proceedings arising in connection with that liability.

(5) Where a liability accrues under subsection (2) in respect of any property or right which before the restoration of the company to the register had accrued as *bona vacantia* to the Duchy of Cornwall, such persons as the Duke of Cornwall (or other possessor for the time being

of the Duchy) may appoint shall represent the Duke (or other possessor) in any proceedings arising out of that liability.

(6) In this section the "Crown representative" means—

    (a) in relation to property vested in the Duchy of Lancaster, the Solicitor to that Duchy;

    (b) in relation to property vested in the Duke of Cornwall, the Solicitor to the Duchy of Cornwall;

    (c) in relation to property in Scotland, the Queen's and Lord Treasurer's Remembrancer;

    (d) in relation to other property, the Treasury Solicitor.

PART 32
COMPANY INVESTIGATIONS: AMENDMENTS

1035. Powers of Secretary of State to give directions to inspectors

(1) In Part 14 of the Companies Act 1985 (c. 6) (investigation of companies and their affairs), after section 446 insert—

"Powers of Secretary of State to give directions to inspectors

446A General powers to give directions

(1) In exercising his functions an inspector shall comply with any direction given to him by the Secretary of State under this section.

(2) The Secretary of State may give an inspector appointed under section 431, 432(2) or 442(1) a direction—

    (a) as to the subject matter of his investigation (whether by reference to a specified area of a company's operation, a specified transaction, a period of time or otherwise), or

    (b) which requires the inspector to take or not to take a specified step in his investigation.

(3) The Secretary of State may give an inspector appointed under any provision of this Part a direction requiring him to secure that a specified report under section 437—

    (a) includes the inspector's views on a specified matter,

    (b) does not include any reference to a specified matter,

    (c) is made in a specified form or manner, or

    (d) is made by a specified date.

(4) A direction under this section—

    (a) may be given on an inspector's appointment,

    (b) may vary or revoke a direction previously given, and

    (c) may be given at the request of an inspector.

(5) In this section—

    (a) a reference to an inspector's investigation includes any investigation he undertakes, or could undertake, under section 433(1) (power to investigate affairs of holding company or subsidiary);

    (b) "specified" means specified in a direction under this section.

446B Direction to terminate investigation

(1) The Secretary of State may direct an inspector to take no further steps in his investigation.

(2) The Secretary of State may give a direction under this section to an inspector appointed under section 432(1) or 442(3) only on the grounds that it appears to him that—

    (a) matters have come to light in the course of the inspector's investigation which suggest that a criminal offence has been committed, and

    (b) those matters have been referred to the appropriate prosecuting authority.

(3) Where the Secretary of State gives a direction under this section, any direction already given to the inspector under section 437(1) to produce an interim report, and any

direction given to him under section 446A(3) in relation to such a report, shall cease to have effect.

(4) Where the Secretary of State gives a direction under this section, the inspector shall not make a final report to the Secretary of State unless—

    (a) the direction was made on the grounds mentioned in subsection (2) and the Secretary of State directs the inspector to make a final report to him, or

    (b) the inspector was appointed under section 432(1) (appointment in pursuance of order of the court).

(5) An inspector shall comply with any direction given to him under this section.

(6) In this section, a reference to an inspector's investigation includes any investigation he undertakes, or could undertake, under section 433(1) (power to investigate affairs of holding company or subsidiary).".

(2) In section 431 of that Act (inspectors' powers during investigation) in subsection (1) for "report on them in such manner as he may direct" substitute "report the result of their investigations to him".

(3) In section 432 of that Act (other company investigations) in subsection (1) for "report on them in such manner as he directs" substitute "report the result of their investigations to him".

(4) In section 437 of that Act (inspectors' reports)—

    (a) in subsection (1) omit the second sentence, and

    (b) subsections (1B) and (1C) shall cease to have effect.

(5) In section 442 of that Act (power to investigate company ownership), omit subsection (2).

1036. Resignation, removal and replacement of inspectors

After section 446B of the Companies Act 1985 (c. 6) (inserted by section 1035 above) insert—

"Resignation, removal and replacement of inspectors

446C Resignation and revocation of appointment

(1) An inspector may resign by notice in writing to the Secretary of State.

(2) The Secretary of State may revoke the appointment of an inspector by notice in writing to the inspector.

446D Appointment of replacement inspectors

(1) Where—

    (a) an inspector resigns,

    (b) an inspector's appointment is revoked, or

    (c) an inspector dies,

the Secretary of State may appoint one or more competent inspectors to continue the investigation.

(2) An appointment under subsection (1) shall be treated for the purposes of this Part (apart from this section) as an appointment under the provision of this Part under which the former inspector was appointed.

(3) The Secretary of State must exercise his power under subsection (1) so as to secure that at least one inspector continues the investigation.

(4) Subsection (3) does not apply if—

    (a) the Secretary of State could give any replacement inspector a direction under section 446B (termination of investigation), and

    (b) such a direction would (under subsection (4) of that section) result in a final report not being made.

(5) In this section, references to an investigation include any investigation the former inspector conducted under section 433(1) (power to investigate affairs of holding company or subsidiary).".

1037. **Power to obtain information from former inspectors etc**

    (1) After section 446D of the Companies Act 1985 (c. 6) (inserted by section 1036 above) insert—

"Power to obtain information from former inspectors etc

446E **Obtaining information from former inspectors etc**

    (1) This section applies to a person who was appointed as an inspector under this Part—

        (a) who has resigned, or

        (b) whose appointment has been revoked.

    (2) This section also applies to an inspector to whom the Secretary of State has given a direction under section 446B (termination of investigation).

    (3) The Secretary of State may direct a person to whom this section applies to produce documents obtained or generated by that person during the course of his investigation to—

        (a) the Secretary of State, or

        (b) an inspector appointed under this Part.

    (4) The power under subsection (3) to require production of a document includes power, in the case of a document not in hard copy form, to require the production of a copy of the document—

        (a) in hard copy form, or

        (b) in a form from which a hard copy can be readily obtained.

    (5) The Secretary of State may take copies of or extracts from a document produced in pursuance of this section.

    (6) The Secretary of State may direct a person to whom this section applies to inform him of any matters that came to that person's knowledge as a result of his investigation.

    (7) A person shall comply with any direction given to him under this section.

    (8) In this section—

        (a) references to the investigation of a former inspector or inspector include any investigation he conducted under section 433(1) (power to investigate affairs of holding company or subsidiary), and

        (b) "document" includes information recorded in any form.".

    (2) In section 451A of that Act (disclosure of information by Secretary of State or inspector), in subsection (1)(a) for "446" substitute "446E".

    (3) In section 452(1) of that Act (privileged information) for "446" substitute "446E".

1038. **Power to require production of documents**

    (1) In section 434 of the Companies Act 1985 (c. 6) (production of documents and evidence to inspectors), for subsection (6) substitute—

    "(6) In this section "document" includes information recorded in any form.

        (7) The power under this section to require production of a document includes power, in the case of a document not in hard copy form, to require the production of a copy of the document—

        (a) in hard copy form, or

        (b) in a form from which a hard copy can be readily obtained.

        (8) An inspector may take copies of or extracts from a document produced in pursuance of this section.".

    (2) In section 447 of the Companies Act 1985 (power of Secretary of State to require documents and information), for subsection (9) substitute—

    "(9) The power under this section to require production of a document includes power, in the case of a document not in hard copy form, to require the production of a copy of the document—

        (a) in hard copy form, or

        (b) in a form from which a hard copy can be readily obtained.".

1039. Disqualification orders: consequential amendments

In section 8(1A)(b)(i) of the Company Directors Disqualification Act 1986 (c. 46) (disqualification after investigation of company: meaning of "investigative material")—

(a) after "section" insert "437, 446E,", and

(b) after "448" insert ",451A".

PART 33

UK COMPANIES NOT FORMED UNDER COMPANIES LEGISLATION

CHAPTER 1

COMPANIES NOT FORMED UNDER COMPANIES LEGISLATION BUT
AUTHORISED TO REGISTER

1040. Companies authorised to register under this Act

(1) This section applies to—

    (a) any company that was in existence on 2nd November 1862 (including any company registered under the Joint Stock Companies Acts), and

    (b) any company formed after that date (whether before or after the commencement of this Act)—

        (i) in pursuance of an Act of Parliament other than this Act or any of the former Companies Acts,

        (ii) in pursuance of letters patent, or

        (iii) that is otherwise duly constituted according to law.

(2) Any such company may on making application register under this Act.

(3) Subject to the following provisions, it may register as an unlimited company, as a company limited by shares or as a company limited by guarantee.

(4) A company having the liability of its members limited by Act of Parliament or letters patent—

    (a) may not register under this section unless it is a joint stock company, and

    (b) may not register under this section as an unlimited company or a company limited by guarantee.

(5) A company that is not a joint stock company may not register under this section as a company limited by shares.

(6) The registration of a company under this section is not invalid by reason that it has taken place with a view to the company's being wound up.

1041. Definition of "joint stock company"

(1) For the purposes of section 1040 (companies authorised to register under this Act) "joint stock company" means a company—

    (a) having a permanent paid-up or nominal share capital of fixed amount divided into shares, also of fixed amount, or held and transferable as stock, or divided and held partly in one way and partly in the other, and

    (b) formed on the principle of having for its members the holders of those shares or that stock, and no other persons.

(2) Such a company when registered with limited liability under this Act is deemed a company limited by shares.

1042. Power to make provision by regulations

(1) The Secretary of State may make provision by regulations—

    (a) for and in connection with registration under section 1040 (companies authorised to register under this Act), and

    (b) as to the application to companies so registered of the provisions of the Companies Acts.

(2) Without prejudice to the generality of that power, regulations under this section may make provision corresponding to any provision formerly made by Chapter 2 of Part 22 of the Companies Act 1985 (c. 6).

(3) Regulations under this section are subject to negative resolution procedure.

CHAPTER 2
UNREGISTERED COMPANIES

1043. Unregistered companies

(1) This section applies to bodies corporate incorporated in and having a principal place of business in the United Kingdom, other than—

(a) bodies incorporated by, or registered under, a public general Act of Parliament;

(b) bodies not formed for the purpose of carrying on a business that has for its object the acquisition of gain by the body or its individual members;

(c) bodies for the time being exempted from this section by direction of the Secretary of State;

(d) open-ended investment companies.

(2) The Secretary of State may make provision by regulations applying specified provisions of the Companies Acts to all, or any specified description of, the bodies to which this section applies.

(3) The regulations may provide that the specified provisions of the Companies Acts apply subject to any specified limitations and to such adaptations and modifications (if any) as may be specified.

(4) This section does not—

(a) repeal or revoke in whole or in part any enactment, royal charter or other instrument constituting or regulating any body in relation to which provisions of the Companies Acts are applied by regulations under this section, or

(b) restrict the power of Her Majesty to grant a charter in lieu or supplementary to any such charter.

But in relation to any such body the operation of any such enactment, charter or instrument is suspended in so far as it is inconsistent with any of those provisions as they apply for the time being to that body.

(5) In this section "specified" means specified in the regulations.

(6) Regulations under this section are subject to negative resolution procedure.

PART 34
OVERSEAS COMPANIES

Introductory

1044. Overseas companies

In the Companies Acts an "overseas company" means a company incorporated outside the United Kingdom.

1045. Company contracts and execution of documents by companies

(1) The Secretary of State may make provision by regulations applying sections 43 to 52 (formalities of doing business and other matters) to overseas companies, subject to such exceptions, adaptations or modifications as may be specified in the regulations.

(2) Regulations under this section are subject to negative resolution procedure.

Registration of particulars

1046. Duty to register particulars

(1) The Secretary of State may make provision by regulations requiring an overseas company—

    (a) to deliver to the registrar for registration a return containing specified particulars, and

    (b) to deliver to the registrar with the return specified documents.

(2) The regulations—

    (a) must, in the case of a company other than a Gibraltar company, require the company to register particulars if the company opens a branch in the United Kingdom, and

    (b) may, in the case of a Gibraltar company, require the company to register particulars if the company opens a branch in the United Kingdom, and

    (c) may, in any case, require the registration of particulars in such other circumstances as may be specified.

(3) In subsection (2)—

"branch" means a branch within the meaning of the Eleventh Company Law Directive (89/666/EEC);

"Gibraltar company" means a company incorporated in Gibraltar.

(4) The regulations may provide that where a company has registered particulars under this section and any alteration is made—

    (a) in the specified particulars, or

    (b) in any document delivered with the return,

the company must deliver to the registrar for registration a return containing specified particulars of the alteration.

(5) The regulations may make provision—

    (a) requiring the return under this section to be delivered for registration to the registrar for a specified part of the United Kingdom, and

    (b) requiring it to be so delivered before the end of a specified period.

(6) The regulations may make different provision according to—

    (a) the place where the company is incorporated, and

    (b) the activities carried on (or proposed to be carried on) by it.

This is without prejudice to the general power to make different provision for different cases.

(7) In this section "specified" means specified in the regulations.

(8) Regulations under this section are subject to affirmative resolution procedure.

1047. Registered name of overseas company

(1) Regulations under section 1046 (duty to register particulars) must require an overseas company that is required to register particulars to register its name.

(2) This may be—

    (a) the company's corporate name (that is, its name under the law of the country or territory in which it is incorporated) or

    (b) an alternative name specified in accordance with section 1048.

(3) Subject only to subsection (5), an EEA company may always register its corporate name.

(4) In any other case, the following provisions of Part 5 (a company's name) apply in relation to the registration of the name of an overseas company—

    (a) section 53 (prohibited names);

    (b) sections 54 to 56 (sensitive words and expressions);

    (c) section 65 (inappropriate use of indications of company type or legal form);

    (d) sections 66 to 74 (similarity to other names);

    (e) section 75 (provision of misleading information etc);

    (f) section 76 (misleading indication of activities).

(5) The provisions of section 57 (permitted characters etc) apply in every case.

(6) Any reference in the provisions mentioned in subsection (4) or (5) to a change of name shall be read as a reference to registration of a different name under section 1048.

1048. Registration under alternative name

(1) An overseas company that is required to register particulars under section 1046 may at any time deliver to the registrar for registration a statement specifying a name, other than its corporate name, under which it proposes to carry on business in the United Kingdom.

(2) An overseas company that has registered an alternative name may at any time deliver to the registrar of companies for registration a statement specifying a different name under which it proposes to carry on business in the United Kingdom (which may be its corporate name or a further alternative) in substitution for the name previously registered.

(3) The alternative name for the time being registered under this section is treated for all purposes of the law applying in the United Kingdom as the company's corporate name.

(4) This does not—

(a) affect the references in this section or section 1047 to the company's corporate name,

(b) affect any rights or obligation of the company, or

(c) render defective any legal proceedings by or against the company.

(5) Any legal proceedings that might have been continued or commenced against the company by its corporate name, or any name previously registered under this section, may be continued or commenced against it by its name for the time being so registered.

Other requirements

1049. Accounts and reports: general

(1) The Secretary of State may make provision by regulations requiring an overseas company that is required to register particulars under section 1046—

(a) to prepare the like accounts and directors' report, and

(b) to cause to be prepared such an auditor's report,

as would be required if the company were formed and registered under this Act.

(2) The regulations may for this purpose apply, with or without modifications, all or any of the provisions of—

Part 15 (accounts and reports), and

Part 16 (audit).

(3) The Secretary of State may make provision by regulations requiring an overseas company to deliver to the registrar copies of—

(a) the accounts and reports prepared in accordance with the regulations, or

(b) the accounts and reports that it is required to prepare and have audited under the law of the country in which it is incorporated.

(4) Regulations under this section are subject to negative resolution procedure.

1050. Accounts and reports: credit or financial institutions

(1) This section applies to a credit or financial institution—

(a) that is incorporated or otherwise formed outside the United Kingdom and Gibraltar,

(b) whose head office is outside the United Kingdom and Gibraltar, and

(c) that has a branch in the United Kingdom.

(2) In subsection (1) "branch" means a place of business that forms a legally dependent part of the institution and conducts directly all or some of the operations inherent in its business.

(3) The Secretary of State may make provision by regulations requiring an institution to which this section applies—

(a) to prepare the like accounts and directors' report, and

(b) to cause to be prepared such an auditor's report,

as would be required if the institution were a company formed and registered under this Act.

(4) The regulations may for this purpose apply, with or without modifications, all or any of the provisions of—

Part 15 (accounts and reports), and

Part 16 (audit).

(5) The Secretary of State may make provision by regulations requiring an institution to which this section applies to deliver to the registrar copies of—

 (a) accounts and reports prepared in accordance with the regulations, or

 (b) accounts and reports that it is required to prepare and have audited under the law of the country in which the institution has its head office.

(6) Regulations under this section are subject to negative resolution procedure.

1051. Trading disclosures

(1) The Secretary of State may by regulations make provision requiring overseas companies carrying on business in the United Kingdom—

 (a) to display specified information in specified locations,

 (b) to state specified information in specified descriptions of document or communication, and

 (c) to provide specified information on request to those they deal with in the course of their business.

(2) The regulations—

 (a) shall in every case require a company that has registered particulars under section 1046 to disclose the name registered by it under section 1047, and

 (b) may make provision as to the manner in which any specified information is to be displayed, stated or provided.

(3) The regulations may make provision corresponding to that made by—

section 83 (civil consequences of failure to make required disclosure), and

section 84 (criminal consequences of failure to make required disclosure).

(4) In this section "specified" means specified in the regulations.

(5) Regulations under this section are subject to affirmative resolution procedure.

1052. Company charges

(1) The Secretary of State may by regulations make provision about the registration of specified charges over property in the United Kingdom of a registered overseas company.

(2) The power in subsection (1) includes power to make provision about—

 (a) a registered overseas company that—

   (i) has particulars registered in more than one part of the United Kingdom;

   (ii) has property in more than one part of the United Kingdom;

 (b) the circumstances in which property is to be regarded, for the purposes of the regulations, as being, or not being, in the United Kingdom or in a particular part of the United Kingdom;

 (c) the keeping by a registered overseas company of records and registers about specified charges and their inspection;

 (d) the consequences of a failure to register a charge in accordance with the regulations;

 (e) the circumstances in which a registered overseas company ceases to be subject to the regulations.

(3) The regulations may for this purpose apply, with or without modifications, any of the provisions of Part 25 (company charges).

(4) The regulations may modify any reference in an enactment to Part 25, or to a particular provision of that Part, so as to include a reference to the regulations or to a specified provision of the regulations.

(5) Regulations under this section are subject to negative resolution procedure.

(6) In this section—

"registered overseas company" means an overseas company that has registered particulars under section 1046(1), and

"specified" means specified in the regulations.

1053. Other returns etc

(1) This section applies to overseas companies that are required to register particulars under section 1046.

(2) The Secretary of State may make provision by regulations requiring the delivery to the registrar of returns—

    (a) by a company to which this section applies that—

        (i) is being wound up, or

        (ii) becomes or ceases to be subject to insolvency proceedings, or an arrangement or composition or any analogous proceedings;

    (b) by the liquidator of a company to which this section applies.

(3) The regulations may specify—

    (a) the circumstances in which a return is to be made,

    (b) the particulars to be given in it, and

    (c) the period within which it is to be made.

(4) The Secretary of State may make provision by regulations requiring notice to be given to the registrar of the appointment in relation to a company to which this section applies of a judicial factor (in Scotland).

(5) The regulations may include provision corresponding to any provision made by section 1154 of this Act (duty to notify registrar of certain appointments).

(6) Regulations under this section are subject to affirmative resolution procedure.

Supplementary

1054. Offences

(1) Regulations under this Part may specify the person or persons responsible for complying with any specified requirement of the regulations.

(2) Regulations under this Part may make provision for offences, including provision as to—

    (a) the person or persons liable in the case of any specified contravention of the regulations, and

    (b) circumstances that are, or are not, to be a defence on a charge of such an offence.

(3) The regulations must not provide—

    (a) for imprisonment, or

    (b) for the imposition on summary conviction of a fine exceeding level 5 on the standard scale and, for continued contravention, a daily default fine not exceeding one-tenth of level 5 on the standard scale.

(4) In this section "specified" means specified in the regulations.

1055. Disclosure of individual's residential address: protection from disclosure

Where regulations under section 1046 (overseas companies: duty to register particulars) require an overseas company to register particulars of an individual's usual residential address, they must contain provision corresponding to that made by Chapter 8 of Part 10 (directors' residential addresses: protection from disclosure).

1056. Requirement to identify persons authorised to accept service of documents

Regulations under section 1046 (overseas companies: duty to register particulars) must require an overseas company to register—

    (a) particulars identifying every person resident in the United Kingdom authorised to accept service of documents on behalf of the company, or

    (b) a statement that there is no such person.

1057. Registrar to whom returns, notices etc to be delivered

   (1) This section applies to an overseas company that is required to register or has registered particulars under section 1046 in more than one part of the United Kingdom.

   (2) The Secretary of State may provide by regulations that, in the case of such a company, anything authorised or required to be delivered to the registrar under this Part is to be delivered—

      (a) to the registrar for each part of the United Kingdom in which the company is required to register or has registered particulars, or

      (b) to the registrar for such part or parts of the United Kingdom as may be specified in or determined in accordance with the regulations.

   (3) Regulations under this section are subject to negative resolution procedure.

1058. Duty to give notice of ceasing to have registrable presence

   (1) The Secretary of State may make provision by regulations requiring an overseas company—

      (a) if it has registered particulars following the opening of a branch, in accordance with regulations under section 1046(2)(a) or (b), to give notice to the registrar if it closes that branch;

      (b) if it has registered particulars in other circumstances, in accordance with regulations under section 1046(2)(c), to give notice to the registrar if the circumstances that gave rise to the obligation to register particulars cease to obtain.

   (2) The regulations must provide for the notice to be given to the registrar for the part of the United Kingdom to which the original return of particulars was delivered.

   (3) The regulations may specify the period within which notice must be given.

   (4) Regulations under this section are subject to negative resolution procedure.

1059. Application of provisions in case of relocation of branch

   For the purposes of this Part—

      (a) the relocation of a branch from one part of the United Kingdom to another counts as the closing of one branch and the opening of another;

      (b) the relocation of a branch within the same part of the United Kingdom does not.

PART 35
THE REGISTRAR OF COMPANIES

The registrar

1060. The registrar

   (1) There shall continue to be—

      (a) a registrar of companies for England and Wales,

      (b) a registrar of companies for Scotland, and

      (c) a registrar of companies for Northern Ireland.

   (2) The registrars shall be appointed by the Secretary of State.

   (3) In the Companies Acts "the registrar of companies" and "the registrar" mean the registrar of companies for England and Wales, Scotland or Northern Ireland, as the case may require.

   (4) References in the Companies Acts to registration in a particular part of the United Kingdom are to registration by the registrar for that part of the United Kingdom.

1061. The registrar's functions

   (1) The registrar shall continue—

      (a) to perform the functions conferred on the registrar—

         (i) under the Companies Acts, and

         (ii) under the enactments listed in subsection (2), and

(b) to perform such functions on behalf of the Secretary of State, in relation to the registration of companies or other matters, as the Secretary of State may from time to time direct.

(2) The enactments are—

the Joint Stock Companies Acts;

the Newspaper Libel and Registration Act 1881 (c. 60);

the Limited Partnerships Act 1907 (c. 24);

section 53 of the Industrial and Provident Societies Act 1965 (c. 12) or, for Northern Ireland, section 62 of the Industrial and Provident Societies Act (Northern Ireland) 1969 (c. 24 (N.I.));

the Insolvency Act 1986 (c. 45) or, for Northern Ireland, the Insolvency (Northern Ireland) Order 1989 (S.I. 1989/2405 (N.I. 19));

section 12 of the Statutory Water Companies Act 1991 (c. 58);

sections 3, 4, 6, 63 and 64 of, and Schedule 1 to, the Housing Act 1996 (c. 52) or, for Northern Ireland, Articles 3 and 16 to 32 of the Housing (Northern Ireland) Order 1992 (S.I. 1992/1725 (N.I. 15));

sections 2, 4 and 26 of the Commonwealth Development Corporation Act 1999 (c. 20);

Part 6 and section 366 of the Financial Services and Markets Act 2000 (c. 8);

the Limited Liability Partnerships Act 2000 (c. 12);

section 14 of the Insolvency Act 2000 (c. 39) or, for Northern Ireland, Article 11 of the Insolvency (Northern Ireland) Order 2002 (S.I. 2002/3152 (N.I. 6));

section 121 of the Land Registration Act 2002 (c. 9);

section 1248 of this Act.

(3) References in this Act to the functions of the registrar are to functions within subsection (1)(a) or (b).

1062. The registrar's official seal

The registrar shall have an official seal for the authentication of documents in connection with the performance of the registrar's functions.

1063. Fees payable to registrar

(1) The Secretary of State may make provision by regulations requiring the payment to the registrar of fees in respect of—

(a) the performance of any of the registrar's functions, or

(b) the provision by the registrar of services or facilities for purposes incidental to, or otherwise connected with, the performance of any of the registrar's functions.

(2) The matters for which fees may be charged include—

(a) the performance of a duty imposed on the registrar or the Secretary of State,

(b) the receipt of documents delivered to the registrar, and

(c) the inspection, or provision of copies, of documents kept by the registrar.

(3) The regulations may—

(a) provide for the amount of the fees to be fixed by or determined under the regulations;

(b) provide for different fees to be payable in respect of the same matter in different circumstances;

(c) specify the person by whom any fee payable under the regulations is to be paid;

(d) specify when and how fees are to be paid.

(4) Regulations under this section are subject to negative resolution procedure.

(5) In respect of the performance of functions or the provision of services or facilities—

(a) for which fees are not provided for by regulations, or

(b) in circumstances other than those for which fees are provided for by regulations,

the registrar may determine from time to time what fees (if any) are chargeable.

(6) Fees received by the registrar are to be paid into the Consolidated Fund.

(7) The Limited Partnerships Act 1907 (c. 24) is amended as follows—
   (a) in section 16(1) (inspection of statements registered)—
      (i) omit the words ", and there shall be paid for such inspection such fees as may be appointed by the Board of Trade, not exceeding 5p for each inspection", and
      (ii) omit the words from "and there shall be paid for such certificate" to the end;
   (b) in section 17 (power to make rules)—
      (i) omit the words "(but as to fees with the concurrence of the Treasury)", and
      (ii) omit paragraph (a).

Certificates of incorporation

1064. Public notice of issue of certificate of incorporation

(1) The registrar must cause to be published—
   (a) in the Gazette, or
   (b) in accordance with section 1116 (alternative means of giving public notice),
   notice of the issue by the registrar of any certificate of incorporation of a company.
(2) The notice must state the name and registered number of the company and the date of issue of the certificate.
(3) This section applies to a certificate of incorporation issued under—
   (a) section 80 (change of name),
   (b) section 88 (Welsh companies), or
   (c) any provision of Part 7 (re-registration),
   as well as to the certificate issued on a company's formation.

1065. Right to certificate of incorporation

Any person may require the registrar to provide him with a copy of any certificate of incorporation of a company, signed by the registrar or authenticated by the registrar's seal.

Registered numbers

1066. Company's registered numbers

(1) The registrar shall allocate to every company a number, which shall be known as the company's registered number.
(2) Companies' registered numbers shall be in such form, consisting of one or more sequences of figures or letters, as the registrar may determine.
(3) The registrar may on adopting a new form of registered number make such changes of existing registered numbers as appear necessary.
(4) A change of a company's registered number has effect from the date on which the company is notified by the registrar of the change.
(5) For a period of three years beginning with that date any requirement to disclose the company's registered number imposed by regulations under section 82 or section 1051 (trading disclosures) is satisfied by the use of either the old number or the new.
(6) In this section "company" includes an overseas company whose particulars have been registered under section 1046, other than a company that appears to the registrar not to be required to register particulars under that section.

1067. Registered numbers of branches of overseas company

(1) The registrar shall allocate to every branch of an overseas company whose particulars are registered under section 1046 a number, which shall be known as the branch's registered number.
(2) Branches' registered numbers shall be in such form, consisting of one or more sequences of figures or letters, as the registrar may determine.

(3) The registrar may on adopting a new form of registered number make such changes of existing registered numbers as appear necessary.

(4) A change of a branch's registered number has effect from the date on which the company is notified by the registrar of the change.

(5) For a period of three years beginning with that date any requirement to disclose the branch's registered number imposed by regulations under section 1051 (trading disclosures) is satisfied by the use of either the old number or the new.

Delivery of documents to the registrar

1068. Registrar's requirements as to form, authentication and manner of delivery

(1) The registrar may impose requirements as to the form, authentication and manner of delivery of documents required or authorised to be delivered to the registrar under any enactment.

(2) As regards the form of the document, the registrar may—

(a) require the contents of the document to be in a standard form;

(b) impose requirements for the purpose of enabling the document to be scanned or copied.

(3) As regards authentication, the registrar may—

(a) require the document to be authenticated by a particular person or a person of a particular description;

(b) specify the means of authentication;

(c) require the document to contain or be accompanied by the name or registered number of the company to which it relates (or both).

(4) As regards the manner of delivery, the registrar may specify requirements as to—

(a) the physical form of the document (for example, hard copy or electronic form);

(b) the means to be used for delivering the document (for example, by post or electronic means);

(c) the address to which the document is to be sent;

(d) in the case of a document to be delivered by electronic means, the hardware and software to be used, and technical specifications (for example, matters relating to protocol, security, anti-virus protection or encryption).

(5) The registrar must secure that as from 1st January 2007 all documents subject to the Directive disclosure requirements (see section 1078) may be delivered to the registrar by electronic means.

(6) The power conferred by this section does not authorise the registrar to require documents to be delivered by electronic means (see section 1069).

(7) Requirements imposed under this section must not be inconsistent with requirements imposed by any enactment with respect to the form, authentication or manner of delivery of the document concerned.

1069. Power to require delivery by electronic means

(1) The Secretary of State may make regulations requiring documents that are authorised or required to be delivered to the registrar to be delivered by electronic means.

(2) Any such requirement to deliver documents by electronic means is effective only if registrar's rules have been published with respect to the detailed requirements for such delivery.

(3) Regulations under this section are subject to affirmative resolution procedure.

1070. Agreement for delivery by electronic means

(1) The registrar may agree with a company that documents relating to the company that are required or authorised to be delivered to the registrar—

(a) will be delivered by electronic means, except as provided for in the agreement, and

(b) will conform to such requirements as may be specified in the agreement or specified by the registrar in accordance with the agreement.

(2) An agreement under this section may relate to all or any description of documents to be delivered to the registrar.

(3) Documents in relation to which an agreement is in force under this section must be delivered in accordance with the agreement.

1071. Document not delivered until received

(1) A document is not delivered to the registrar until it is received by the registrar.

(2) Provision may be made by registrar's rules as to when a document is to be regarded as received.

Requirements for proper delivery

1072. Requirements for proper delivery

(1) A document delivered to the registrar is not properly delivered unless all the following requirements are met—

    (a) the requirements of the provision under which the document is to be delivered to the registrar as regards—

        (i) the contents of the document, and

        (ii) form, authentication and manner of delivery;

    (b) any applicable requirements under—

    section 1068 (registrar's requirements as to form, authentication and manner of delivery),

    section 1069 (power to require delivery by electronic means), or

    section 1070 (agreement for delivery by electronic means);

    (c) any requirements of this Part as to the language in which the document is drawn up and delivered or as to its being accompanied on delivery by a certified translation into English;

    (d) in so far as it consists of or includes names and addresses, any requirements of this Part as to permitted characters, letters or symbols or as to its being accompanied on delivery by a certificate as to the transliteration of any element;

    (e) any applicable requirements under section 1111 (registrar's requirements as to certification or verification);

    (f) any requirement of regulations under section 1082 (use of unique identifiers);

    (g) any requirements as regards payment of a fee in respect of its receipt by the registrar.

(2) A document that is not properly delivered is treated for the purposes of the provision requiring or authorising it to be delivered as not having been delivered, subject to the provisions of section 1073 (power to accept documents not meeting requirements for proper delivery).

1073. Power to accept documents not meeting requirements for proper delivery

(1) The registrar may accept (and register) a document that does not comply with the requirements for proper delivery.

(2) A document accepted by the registrar under this section is treated as received by the registrar for the purposes of section 1077 (public notice of receipt of certain documents).

(3) No objection may be taken to the legal consequences of a document's being accepted (or registered) by the registrar under this section on the ground that the requirements for proper delivery were not met.

(4) The acceptance of a document by the registrar under this section does not affect—

    (a) the continuing obligation to comply with the requirements for proper delivery, or

    (b) subject as follows, any liability for failure to comply with those requirements.

(5) For the purposes of—

    (a) section 453 (civil penalty for failure to file accounts and reports), and

    (b) any enactment imposing a daily default fine for failure to deliver the document,

the period after the document is accepted does not count as a period during which there is default in complying with the requirements for proper delivery.

(6) But if, subsequently—

    (a) the registrar issues a notice under section 1094(4) in respect of the document (notice of administrative removal from the register), and

    (b) the requirements for proper delivery are not complied with before the end of the period of 14 days after the issue of that notice,

any subsequent period of default does count for the purposes of those provisions.

1074. Documents containing unnecessary material

(1) This section applies where a document delivered to the registrar contains unnecessary material.

(2) "Unnecessary material" means material that—

    (a) is not necessary in order to comply with an obligation under any enactment, and

    (b) is not specifically authorised to be delivered to the registrar.

(3) For this purpose an obligation to deliver a document of a particular description, or conforming to certain requirements, is regarded as not extending to anything that is not needed for a document of that description or, as the case may be, conforming to those requirements.

(4) If the unnecessary material cannot readily be separated from the rest of the document, the document is treated as not meeting the requirements for proper delivery.

(5) If the unnecessary material can readily be separated from the rest of the document, the registrar may register the document either—

    (a) with the omission of the unnecessary material, or

    (b) as delivered.

1075. Informal correction of document

(1) A document delivered to the registrar may be corrected by the registrar if it appears to the registrar to be incomplete or internally inconsistent.

(2) This power is exercisable only—

    (a) on instructions, and

    (b) if the company has given (and has not withdrawn) its consent to instructions being given under this section.

(3) The following requirements must be met as regards the instructions—

    (a) the instructions must be given in response to an enquiry by the registrar;

    (b) the registrar must be satisfied that the person giving the instructions is authorised to do so—

        (i) by the person by whom the document was delivered, or

        (ii) by the company to which the document relates;

    (c) the instructions must meet any requirements of registrar's rules as to—

        (i) the form and manner in which they are given, and

        (ii) authentication.

(4) The company's consent to instructions being given under this section (and any withdrawal of such consent)—

    (a) may be in hard copy or electronic form, and

    (b) must be notified to the registrar.

(5) This section applies in relation to documents delivered under Part 25 (company charges) by a person other than the company as if the references to the company were to the company or the person by whom the document was delivered.

(6) A document that is corrected under this section is treated, for the purposes of any enactment relating to its delivery, as having been delivered when the correction is made.

(7) The power conferred by this section is not exercisable if the document has been registered under section 1073 (power to accept documents not meeting requirements for proper delivery).

1076. Replacement of document not meeting requirements for proper delivery

    (1) The registrar may accept a replacement for a document previously delivered that—

        (a) did not comply with the requirements for proper delivery, or

        (b) contained unnecessary material (within the meaning of section 1074).

    (2) A replacement document must not be accepted unless the registrar is satisfied that it is delivered by—

        (a) the person by whom the original document was delivered, or

        (b) the company to which the original document relates,

    and that it complies with the requirements for proper delivery.

    (3) The power of the registrar to impose requirements as to the form and manner of delivery includes power to impose requirements as to the identification of the original document and the delivery of the replacement in a form and manner enabling it to be associated with the original.

    (4) This section does not apply where the original document was delivered under Part 25 (company charges) (but see sections 873 and 888 (rectification of register of charges)).

Public notice of receipt of certain documents

1077. Public notice of receipt of certain documents

    (1) The registrar must cause to be published—

        (a) in the Gazette, or

        (b) in accordance with section 1116 (alternative means of giving public notice),

    notice of the receipt by the registrar of any document that, on receipt, is subject to the Directive disclosure requirements (see section 1078).

    (2) The notice must state the name and registered number of the company, the description of document and the date of receipt.

    (3) The registrar is not required to cause notice of the receipt of a document to be published before the date of incorporation of the company to which the document relates.

1078. Documents subject to Directive disclosure requirements

    (1) The documents subject to the "Directive disclosure requirements" are as follows.
The requirements referred to are those of Article 3 of the First Company Law Directive (68/151/EEC), as amended, extended and applied.

    (2) In the case of every company—

Constitutional documents

    1. The company's memorandum and articles.

    2. Any amendment of the company's articles (including every resolution or agreement required to be embodied in or annexed to copies of the company's articles issued by the company).

    3. After any amendment of the company's articles, the text of the articles as amended.

    4. Any notice of a change of the company's name.

Directors

    1. The statement of proposed officers required on formation of the company.

    2. Notification of any change among the company's directors.

    3. Notification of any change in the particulars of directors required to be delivered to the registrar.

Accounts, reports and returns

    1. All documents required to be delivered to the registrar under section 441 (annual accounts and reports).

    2. The company's annual return.

Registered office

Notification of any change of the company's registered office.

Winding up
1. Copy of any winding-up order in respect of the company.
2. Notice of the appointment of liquidators.
3. Order for the dissolution of a company on a winding up.
4. Return by a liquidator of the final meeting of a company on a winding up.

(3) In the case of a public company—

Share capital
1. Any statement of capital and initial shareholdings.
2. Any return of allotment and the statement of capital accompanying it.
3. Copy of any resolution under section 570 or 571 (disapplication of pre-emption rights).
4. Copy of any report under section 593 or 599 as to the value of a non-cash asset.
5. Statement of capital accompanying notice given under section 625 (notice by company of redenomination of shares).
6. Statement of capital accompanying notice given under section 627 (notice by company of reduction of capital in connection with redenomination of shares).
7. Notice delivered under section 636 (notice of new name of class of shares) or 637 (notice of variation of rights attached to shares).
8. Statement of capital accompanying order delivered under section 649 (order of court confirming reduction of capital).
9. Notification (under section 689) of the redemption of shares and the statement of capital accompanying it.
10. Statement of capital accompanying return delivered under section 708 (notice of cancellation of shares on purchase of own shares) or 730 (notice of cancellation of shares held as treasury shares).
11. Any statement of compliance delivered under section 762 (statement that company meets conditions for issue of trading certificate).

Mergers and divisions
1. Copy of any draft of the terms of a scheme required to be delivered to the registrar under section 906 or 921.
2. Copy of any order under section 899 or 900 in respect of a compromise or arrangement to which Part 27 (mergers and divisions of public companies) applies.

(4) Where a private company re-registers as a public company (see section 96)—

(a) the last statement of capital relating to the company received by the registrar under any provision of the Companies Acts becomes subject to the Directive disclosure requirements, and

(b) section 1077 (public notice of receipt of certain documents) applies as if the statement had been received by the registrar when the re-registration takes effect.

(5) In the case of an overseas company, such particulars, returns and other documents required to be delivered under Part 34 as may be specified by the Secretary of State by regulations.

(6) Regulations under subsection (5) are subject to negative resolution procedure.

1079. Effect of failure to give public notice

(1) A company is not entitled to rely against other persons on the happening of any event to which this section applies unless—

(a) the event has been officially notified at the material time, or

(b) the company shows that the person concerned knew of the event at the material time.

(2) The events to which this section applies are—

(a) an amendment of the company's articles,

(b) a change among the company's directors,

(c) (as regards service of any document on the company) a change of the company's registered office,

    (d) the making of a winding-up order in respect of the company, or

    (e) the appointment of a liquidator in a voluntary winding up of the company.

(3) If the material time falls—

    (a) on or before the 15th day after the date of official notification, or

    (b) where the 15th day was not a working day, on or before the next day that was,

the company is not entitled to rely on the happening of the event as against a person who shows that he was unavoidably prevented from knowing of the event at that time.

(4) "Official notification" means—

    (a) in relation to an amendment of the company's articles, notification in accordance with section 1077 (public notice of receipt by registrar of certain documents) of the amendment and the amended text of the articles;

    (b) in relation to anything else stated in a document subject to the Directive disclosure requirements, notification of that document in accordance with that section;

    (c) in relation to the appointment of a liquidator in a voluntary winding up, notification of that event in accordance with section 109 of the Insolvency Act 1986 (c. 45) or Article 95 of the Insolvency (Northern Ireland) Order 1989 (S.I.1989/2405 (N.I. 19)).

The register

1080. The register

(1) The registrar shall continue to keep records of—

    (a) the information contained in documents delivered to the registrar under any enactment,

    (b) certificates of incorporation issued by the registrar, and

    (c) certificates issued by the registrar under section 869(5) or 885(4) (certificates of registration of charge).

(2) The records relating to companies are referred to collectively in the Companies Acts as "the register".

(3) Information deriving from documents subject to the Directive disclosure requirements (see section 1078) that are delivered to the registrar on or after 1st January 2007 must be kept by the registrar in electronic form.

(4) Subject to that, information contained in documents delivered to the registrar may be recorded and kept in any form the registrar thinks fit, provided it is possible to inspect it and produce a copy of it.

This is sufficient compliance with any duty of the registrar to keep, file or register the document or to record the information contained in it.

(5) The records kept by the registrar must be such that information relating to a company is associated with that company, in such manner as the registrar may determine, so as to enable all the information relating to the company to be retrieved.

1081. Annotation of the register

(1) The registrar must place a note in the register recording—

    (a) the date on which a document is delivered to the registrar;

    (b) if a document is corrected under section 1075, the nature and date of the correction;

    (c) if a document is replaced (whether or not material derived from it is removed), the fact that it has been replaced and the date of delivery of the replacement;

    (d) if material is removed—

        (i) what was removed (giving a general description of its contents),

        (ii) under what power, and

        (iii) the date on which that was done.

(2) The Secretary of State may make provision by regulations—

    (a) authorising or requiring the registrar to annotate the register in such other circumstances as may be specified in the regulations, and

    (b) as to the contents of any such annotation.

(3) No annotation is required in the case of a document that by virtue of section 1072(2) (documents not meeting requirements for proper delivery) is treated as not having been delivered.

(4) A note may be removed if it no longer serves any useful purpose.

(5) Any duty or power of the registrar with respect to annotation of the register is subject to the court's power under section 1097 (powers of court on ordering removal of material from the register) to direct—

(a) that a note be removed from the register, or

(b) that no note shall be made of the removal of material that is the subject of the court's order.

(6) Notes placed in the register in accordance with subsection (1), or in pursuance of regulations under subsection (2), are part of the register for all purposes of the Companies Acts.

(7) Regulations under this section are subject to negative resolution procedure.

1082. Allocation of unique identifiers

(1) The Secretary of State may make provision for the use, in connection with the register, of reference numbers ("unique identifiers") to identify each person who—

(a) is a director of a company,

(b) is secretary (or a joint secretary) of a company, or

(c) in the case of an overseas company whose particulars are registered under section 1046, holds any such position as may be specified for the purposes of this section by regulations under that section.

(2) The regulations may—

(a) provide that a unique identifier may be in such form, consisting of one or more sequences of letters or numbers, as the registrar may from time to time determine;

(b) make provision for the allocation of unique identifiers by the registrar;

(c) require there to be included, in any specified description of documents delivered to the registrar, as well as a statement of the person's name—

(i) a statement of the person's unique identifier, or

(ii) a statement that the person has not been allocated a unique identifier;

(d) enable the registrar to take steps where a person appears to have more than one unique identifier to discontinue the use of all but one of them.

(3) The regulations may contain provision for the application of the scheme in relation to persons appointed, and documents registered, before the commencement of this Act.

(4) The regulations may make different provision for different descriptions of person and different descriptions of document.

(5) Regulations under this section are subject to affirmative resolution procedure.

1083. Preservation of original documents

(1) The originals of documents delivered to the registrar in hard copy form must be kept for three years after they are received by the registrar, after which they may be destroyed provided the information contained in them has been recorded in the register.

This is subject to section 1087(3) (extent of obligation to retain material not available for public inspection).

(2) The registrar is under no obligation to keep the originals of documents delivered in electronic form, provided the information contained in them has been recorded in the register.

(3) This section applies to documents held by the registrar when this section comes into force as well as to documents subsequently received.

1084. Records relating to companies that have been dissolved etc

(1) This section applies where—

(a) a company is dissolved,

(b) an overseas company ceases to have any connection with the United Kingdom by virtue of which it is required to register particulars under section 1046, or

(c) a credit or financial institution ceases to be within section 1050 (overseas institutions required to file accounts with the registrar).

(2) At any time after two years from the date on which it appears to the registrar that—

    (a) the company has been dissolved,

    (b) the overseas company has ceased to have any connection with the United Kingdom by virtue of which it is required to register particulars under section 1046, or

    (c) the credit or financial institution has ceased to be within section 1050 (overseas institutions required to file accounts with the registrar),

the registrar may direct that records relating to the company or institution may be removed to the Public Record Office or, as the case may be, the Public Record Office of Northern Ireland.

(3) Records in respect of which such a direction is given shall be disposed of under the enactments relating to that Office and the rules made under them.

(4) In subsection (1)(a) "company" includes a company provisionally or completely registered under the Joint Stock Companies Act 1844 (c. 110).

(5) This section does not extend to Scotland.

Inspection etc of the register

1085. Inspection of the register

(1) Any person may inspect the register.

(2) The right of inspection extends to the originals of documents delivered to the registrar in hard copy form if, and only if, the record kept by the registrar of the contents of the document is illegible or unavailable.

The period for which such originals are to be kept is limited by section 1083(1).

(3) This section has effect subject to section 1087 (material not available for public inspection).

1086. Right to copy of material on the register

(1) Any person may require a copy of any material on the register.

(2) The fee for any such copy of material derived from a document subject to the Directive disclosure requirements (see section 1078), whether in hard copy or electronic form, must not exceed the administrative cost of providing it.

(3) This section has effect subject to section 1087 (material not available for public inspection).

1087. Material not available for public inspection

(1) The following material must not be made available by the registrar for public inspection—

    (a) the contents of any document sent to the registrar containing views expressed pursuant to section 56 (comments on proposal by company to use certain words or expressions in company name);

    (b) protected information within section 242(1) (directors' residential addresses: restriction on disclosure by registrar) or any corresponding provision of regulations under section 1046 (overseas companies);

    (c) any application to the registrar under section 1024 (application for administrative restoration to the register) that has not yet been determined or was not successful;

    (d) any document received by the registrar in connection with the giving or withdrawal of consent under section 1075 (informal correction of documents);

    (e) any application or other document delivered to the registrar under section 1088 (application to make address unavailable for public inspection) and any address in respect of which such an application is successful;

    (f) any application or other document delivered to the registrar under section 1095 (application for rectification of register);

    (g) any court order under section 1096 (rectification of the register under court order) that the court has directed under section 1097 (powers of court on ordering removal of material from the register) is not to be made available for public inspection;

(h) the contents of—

    (i) any instrument creating or evidencing a charge and delivered to the registrar under section 860 (registration of company charges: England and Wales or Northern Ireland), or

    (ii) any certified copy of an instrument creating or evidencing a charge and delivered to the registrar under section 878 (registration of company charges: Scotland);

(i) any e-mail address, identification code or password deriving from a document delivered for the purpose of authorising or facilitating electronic filing procedures or providing information by telephone;

(j) the contents of any documents held by the registrar pending a decision of the Regulator of Community Interest Companies under section 36 or 38 of the Companies (Audit, Investigations and Community Enterprise) Act 2004 (c. 27) (decision on eligibility for registration as community interest company) and that the registrar is not later required to record;

(k) any other material excluded from public inspection by or under any other enactment.

(2) A restriction applying by reference to material deriving from a particular description of document does not affect the availability for public inspection of the same information contained in material derived from another description of document in relation to which no such restriction applies.

(3) Material to which this section applies need not be retained by the registrar for longer than appears to the registrar reasonably necessary for the purposes for which the material was delivered to the registrar.

1088. Application to registrar to make address unavailable for public inspection

(1) The Secretary of State may make provision by regulations requiring the registrar, on application, to make an address on the register unavailable for public inspection.

(2) The regulations may make provision as to—

    (a) who may make an application,

    (b) the grounds on which an application may be made,

    (c) the information to be included in and documents to accompany an application,

    (d) the notice to be given of an application and of its outcome, and

    (e) how an application is to be determined.

(3) Provision under subsection (2)(e) may in particular—

    (a) confer a discretion on the registrar;

    (b) provide for a question to be referred to a person other than the registrar for the purposes of determining the application.

(4) An application must specify the address to be removed from the register and indicate where on the register it is.

(5) The regulations may provide—

    (a) that an address is not to be made unavailable for public inspection under this section unless replaced by a service address, and

    (b) that in such a case the application must specify a service address.

(6) Regulations under this section are subject to affirmative resolution procedure.

1089. Form of application for inspection or copy

(1) The registrar may specify the form and manner in which application is to be made for—

    (a) inspection under section 1085, or

    (b) a copy under section 1086.

(2) As from 1st January 2007, applications in respect of documents subject to the Directive disclosure requirements may be submitted to the registrar in hard copy or electronic form, as the applicant chooses.

This does not affect the registrar's power under subsection (1) above to impose requirements in respect of other matters.

1090. Form and manner in which copies to be provided

    (1) The following provisions apply as regards the form and manner in which copies are to be provided under section 1086.

    (2) As from 1st January 2007, copies of documents subject to the Directive disclosure requirements must be provided in hard copy or electronic form, as the applicant chooses.

    This is subject to the following proviso.

    (3) The registrar is not obliged by subsection (2) to provide copies in electronic form of a document that was delivered to the registrar in hard copy form if—

        (a) the document was delivered to the registrar on or before 31st December 1996, or

        (b) the document was delivered to the registrar on or before 31st December 2006 and ten years or more elapsed between the date of delivery and the date of receipt of the first application for a copy on or after 1st January 2007.

    (4) Subject to the preceding provisions of this section, the registrar may determine the form and manner in which copies are to be provided.

1091. Certification of copies as accurate

    (1) Copies provided under section 1086 in hard copy form must be certified as true copies unless the applicant dispenses with such certification.

    (2) Copies so provided in electronic form must not be certified as true copies unless the applicant expressly requests such certification.

    (3) A copy provided under section 1086, certified by the registrar (whose official position it is unnecessary to prove) to be an accurate record of the contents of the original document, is in all legal proceedings admissible in evidence—

        (a) as of equal validity with the original document, and

        (b) as evidence (in Scotland, sufficient evidence) of any fact stated in the original document of which direct oral evidence would be admissible.

    (4) The Secretary of State may make provision by regulations as to the manner in which such a certificate is to be provided in a case where the copy is provided in electronic form.

    (5) Except in the case of documents that are subject to the Directive disclosure requirements (see section 1078), copies provided by the registrar may, instead of being certified in writing to be an accurate record, be sealed with the registrar's official seal.

1092. Issue of process for production of records kept by the registrar

    (1) No process for compelling the production of a record kept by the registrar shall issue from any court except with the permission of the court.

    (2) Any such process shall bear on it a statement that it is issued with the permission of the court.

Correction or removal of material on the register

1093. Registrar's notice to resolve inconsistency on the register

    (1) Where it appears to the registrar that the information contained in a document delivered to the registrar is inconsistent with other information on the register, the registrar may give notice to the company to which the document relates—

        (a) stating in what respects the information contained in it appears to be inconsistent with other information on the register, and

        (b) requiring the company to take steps to resolve the inconsistency.

    (2) The notice must—

        (a) state the date on which it is issued, and

        (b) require the delivery to the registrar, within 14 days after that date, of such replacement or additional documents as may be required to resolve the inconsistency.

    (3) If the necessary documents are not delivered within the period specified, an offence is committed by—

        (a) the company, and

        (b) every officer of the company who is in default.

(4) A person guilty of an offence under subsection (3) is liable on summary conviction to a fine not exceeding level 5 on the standard scale and, for continued contravention, a daily default fine not exceeding one-tenth of level 5 on the standard scale.

1094. Administrative removal of material from the register

(1) The registrar may remove from the register anything that there was power, but no duty, to include.

(2) This power is exercisable, in particular, so as to remove—

(a) unnecessary material within the meaning of section 1074, and

(b) material derived from a document that has been replaced under—

section 1076 (replacement of document not meeting requirements for proper delivery), or

section 1093 (notice to remedy inconsistency on the register).

(3) This section does not authorise the removal from the register of—

(a) anything whose registration has had legal consequences in relation to the company as regards—

(i) its formation,

(ii) a change of name,

(iii) its re-registration,

(iv) its becoming or ceasing to be a community interest company,

(v) a reduction of capital,

(vi) a change of registered office,

(vii) the registration of a charge, or

(viii) its dissolution;

(b) an address that is a person's registered address for the purposes of section 1140 (service of documents on directors, secretaries and others).

(4) On or before removing any material under this section (otherwise than at the request of the company) the registrar must give notice—

(a) to the person by whom the material was delivered (if the identity, and name and address of that person are known), or

(b) to the company to which the material relates (if notice cannot be given under paragraph (a) and the identity of that company is known).

(5) The notice must—

(a) state what material the registrar proposes to remove, or has removed, and on what grounds, and

(b) state the date on which it is issued.

1095. Rectification of register on application to registrar

(1) The Secretary of State may make provision by regulations requiring the registrar, on application, to remove from the register material of a description specified in the regulations that—

(a) derives from anything invalid or ineffective or that was done without the authority of the company, or

(b) is factually inaccurate, or is derived from something that is factually inaccurate or forged.

(2) The regulations may make provision as to—

(a) who may make an application,

(b) the information to be included in and documents to accompany an application,

(c) the notice to be given of an application and of its outcome,

(d) a period in which objections to an application may be made, and

(e) how an application is to be determined.

(3) An application must—

(a) specify what is to be removed from the register and indicate where on the register it is, and

    (b) be accompanied by a statement that the material specified in the application complies with this section and the regulations.

(4) If no objections are made to the application, the registrar may accept the statement as sufficient evidence that the material specified in the application should be removed from the register.

(5) Where anything is removed from the register under this section the registration of which had legal consequences as mentioned in section 1094(3), any person appearing to the court to have a sufficient interest may apply to the court for such consequential orders as appear just with respect to the legal effect (if any) to be accorded to the material by virtue of its having appeared on the register.

(6) Regulations under this section are subject to affirmative resolution procedure.

1096. Rectification of the register under court order

(1) The registrar shall remove from the register any material—

    (a) that derives from anything that the court has declared to be invalid or ineffective, or to have been done without the authority of the company, or

    (b) that a court declares to be factually inaccurate, or to be derived from something that is factually inaccurate, or forged,

and that the court directs should be removed from the register.

(2) The court order must specify what is to be removed from the register and indicate where on the register it is.

(3) The court must not make an order for the removal from the register of anything the registration of which had legal consequences as mentioned in section 1094(3) unless satisfied—

    (a) that the presence of the material on the register has caused, or may cause, damage to the company, and

    (b) that the company's interest in removing the material outweighs any interest of other persons in the material continuing to appear on the register.

(4) Where in such a case the court does make an order for removal, it may make such consequential orders as appear just with respect to the legal effect (if any) to be accorded to the material by virtue of its having appeared on the register.

(5) A copy of the court's order must be sent to the registrar for registration.

(6) This section does not apply where the court has other, specific, powers to deal with the matter, for example under—

    (a) the provisions of Part 15 relating to the revision of defective accounts and reports, or

    (b) section 873 or 888 (rectification of the register of charges).

1097. Powers of court on ordering removal of material from the register

(1) Where the court makes an order for the removal of anything from the register under section 1096 (rectification of the register), it may give directions under this section.

(2) It may direct that any note on the register that is related to the material that is the subject of the court's order shall be removed from the register.

(3) It may direct that its order shall not be available for public inspection as part of the register.

(4) It may direct—

    (a) that no note shall be made on the register as a result of its order, or

    (b) that any such note shall be restricted to such matters as may be specified by the court.

(5) The court shall not give any direction under this section unless it is satisfied—

    (a) that—

        (i) the presence on the register of the note or, as the case may be, of an unrestricted note, or

        (ii) the availability for public inspection of the court's order,

        may cause damage to the company, and

(b) that the company's interest in non-disclosure outweighs any interest of other persons in disclosure.

1098. Public notice of removal of certain material from the register

(1) The registrar must cause to be published—

(a) in the Gazette, or

(b) in accordance with section 1116 (alternative means of giving public notice),

notice of the removal from the register of any document subject to the Directive disclosure requirements (see section 1078) or of any material derived from such a document.

(2) The notice must state the name and registered number of the company, the description of document and the date of receipt.

The registrar's index of company names

1099. The registrar's index of company names

(1) The registrar of companies must keep an index of the names of the companies and other bodies to which this section applies.

This is "the registrar's index of company names".

(2) This section applies to—

(a) UK-registered companies;

(b) any body to which any provision of the Companies Acts applies by virtue of regulations under section 1043 (unregistered companies); and

(c) overseas companies that have registered particulars with the registrar under section 1046, other than companies that appear to the registrar not to be required to do so.

(3) This section also applies to—

(a) limited partnerships registered in the United Kingdom;

(b) limited liability partnerships incorporated in the United Kingdom;

(c) European Economic Interest Groupings registered in the United Kingdom;

(d) open-ended investment companies authorised in the United Kingdom;

(e) societies registered under the Industrial and Provident Societies Act 1965 (c. 12) or the Industrial and Provident Societies Act (Northern Ireland) 1969 (c. 24 (N.I.)).

(4) The Secretary of State may by order amend subsection (3)—

(a) by the addition of any description of body;

(b) by the deletion of any description of body.

(5) Any such order is subject to negative resolution procedure.

1100. Right to inspect index

Any person may inspect the registrar's index of company names.

1101. Power to amend enactments relating to bodies other than companies

(1) The Secretary of State may by regulations amend the enactments relating to any description of body for the time being within section 1099(3) (bodies other than companies whose names are to be entered in the registrar's index), so as to—

(a) require the registrar to be provided with information as to the names of bodies registered, incorporated, authorised or otherwise regulated under those enactments, and

(b) make provision in relation to such bodies corresponding to that made by—

section 66 (company name not to be the same as another in the index), and

sections 67 and 68 (power to direct change of company name in case of similarity to existing name).

(2) Regulations under this section are subject to affirmative resolution procedure.

1102. Application of language requirements

    (1) The provisions listed below apply to all documents required to be delivered to the registrar under any provision of—

        (a) the Companies Acts, or

        (b) the Insolvency Act 1986 (c. 45) or the Insolvency (Northern Ireland) Order 1989 (S.I. 1989/2405 (N.I. 19)).

    (2) The Secretary of State may make provision by regulations applying all or any of the listed provisions, with or without modifications, in relation to documents delivered to the registrar under any other enactment.

    (3) The provisions are—

        section 1103 (documents to be drawn up and delivered in English),

        section 1104 (documents relating to Welsh companies),

        section 1105 (documents that may be drawn up and delivered in other languages),

        section 1107 (certified translations).

    (4) Regulations under this section are subject to negative resolution procedure.

1103. Documents to be drawn up and delivered in English

    (1) The general rule is that all documents required to be delivered to the registrar must be drawn up and delivered in English.

    (2) This is subject to—

        section 1104 (documents relating to Welsh companies) and

        section 1105 (documents that may be drawn up and delivered in other languages).

1104. Documents relating to Welsh companies

    (1) Documents relating to a Welsh company may be drawn up and delivered to the registrar in Welsh.

    (2) On delivery to the registrar any such document must be accompanied by a certified translation into English, unless it is—

        (a) of a description excepted from that requirement by regulations made by the Secretary of State, or

        (b) in a form prescribed in Welsh (or partly in Welsh and partly in English) by virtue of section 26 of the Welsh Language Act 1993 (c. 38).

    (3) Where a document is properly delivered to the registrar in Welsh without a certified translation into English, the registrar must obtain such a translation if the document is to be available for public inspection.

    The translation is treated as if delivered to the registrar in accordance with the same provision as the original.

    (4) A Welsh company may deliver to the registrar a certified translation into Welsh of any document in English that relates to the company and is or has been delivered to the registrar.

    (5) Section 1105 (which requires certified translations into English of documents delivered to the registrar in another language) does not apply to a document relating to a Welsh company that is drawn up and delivered in Welsh.

1105. Documents that may be drawn up and delivered in other languages

    (1) Documents to which this section applies may be drawn up and delivered to the registrar in a language other than English, but when delivered to the registrar they must be accompanied by a certified translation into English.

    (2) This section applies to—

        (a) agreements required to be forwarded to the registrar under Chapter 3 of Part 3 (agreements affecting the company's constitution);

        (b) documents required to be delivered under section 400(2)(e) or section 401(2)(f) (company included in accounts of larger group: required to deliver copy of group accounts);

(c) instruments or copy instruments required to be delivered under Part 25 (company charges);

(d) documents of any other description specified in regulations made by the Secretary of State.

(3) Regulations under this section are subject to negative resolution procedure.

1106. Voluntary filing of translations

(1) A company may deliver to the registrar one or more certified translations of any document relating to the company that is or has been delivered to the registrar.

(2) The Secretary of State may by regulations specify—

(a) the languages, and

(b) the descriptions of document,

in relation to which this facility is available.

(3) The regulations must provide that it is available as from 1st January 2007—

(a) in relation to all the official languages of the European Union, and

(b) in relation to all documents subject to the Directive disclosure requirements (see section 1078).

(4) The power of the registrar to impose requirements as to the form and manner of delivery includes power to impose requirements as to the identification of the original document and the delivery of the translation in a form and manner enabling it to be associated with the original.

(5) Regulations under this section are subject to negative resolution procedure.

(6) This section does not apply where the original document was delivered to the registrar before this section came into force.

1107. Certified translations

(1) In this Part a "certified translation" means a translation certified to be a correct translation.

(2) In the case of any discrepancy between the original language version of a document and a certified translation—

(a) the company may not rely on the translation as against a third party, but

(b) a third party may rely on the translation unless the company shows that the third party had knowledge of the original.

(3) A "third party" means a person other than the company or the registrar.

Language requirements: transliteration

1108. Transliteration of names and addresses: permitted characters

(1) Names and addresses in a document delivered to the registrar must contain only letters, characters and symbols (including accents and other diacritical marks) that are permitted.

(2) The Secretary of State may make provision by regulations—

(a) as to the letters, characters and symbols (including accents and other diacritical marks) that are permitted, and

(b) permitting or requiring the delivery of documents in which names and addresses have not been transliterated into a permitted form.

(3) Regulations under this section are subject to negative resolution procedure.

1109. Transliteration of names and addresses: voluntary transliteration into Roman characters

(1) Where a name or address is or has been delivered to the registrar in a permitted form using other than Roman characters, the company may deliver to the registrar a transliteration into Roman characters.

(2) The power of the registrar to impose requirements as to the form and manner of delivery includes power to impose requirements as to the identification of the original document and the delivery of the transliteration in a form and manner enabling it to be associated with the original.

1110. Transliteration of names and addresses: certification

(1) The Secretary of State may make provision by regulations requiring the certification of transliterations and prescribing the form of certification.

(2) Different provision may be made for compulsory and voluntary transliterations.

(3) Regulations under this section are subject to negative resolution procedure.

Supplementary provisions

1111. Registrar's requirements as to certification or verification

(1) Where a document required or authorised to be delivered to the registrar under any enactment is required—

(a) to be certified as an accurate translation or transliteration, or

(b) to be certified as a correct copy or verified,

the registrar may impose requirements as to the person, or description of person, by whom the certificate or verification is to be given.

(2) The power conferred by section 1068 (registrar's requirements as to form, authentication and manner of delivery) is exercisable in relation to the certificate or verification as if it were a separate document.

(3) Requirements imposed under this section must not be inconsistent with requirements imposed by any enactment with respect to the certification or verification of the document concerned.

1112. General false statement offence

(1) It is an offence for a person knowingly or recklessly—

(a) to deliver or cause to be delivered to the registrar, for any purpose of the Companies Acts, a document, or

(b) to make to the registrar, for any such purpose, a statement,

that is misleading, false or deceptive in a material particular.

(2) A person guilty of an offence under this section is liable—

(a) on conviction on indictment, to imprisonment for a term not exceeding two years or a fine (or both);

(b) on summary conviction—

(i) in England and Wales, to imprisonment for a term not exceeding twelve months or to a fine not exceeding the statutory maximum (or both);

(ii) in Scotland or Northern Ireland, to imprisonment for a term not exceeding six months, or to a fine not exceeding the statutory maximum (or both).

1113. Enforcement of company's filing obligations

(1) This section applies where a company has made default in complying with any obligation under the Companies Acts—

(a) to deliver a document to the registrar, or

(b) to give notice to the registrar of any matter.

(2) The registrar, or any member or creditor of the company, may give notice to the company requiring it to comply with the obligation.

(3) If the company fails to make good the default within 14 days after service of the notice, the registrar, or any member or creditor of the company, may apply to the court for an order directing the company, and any specified officer of it, to make good the default within a specified time.

(4) The court's order may provide that all costs (in Scotland, expenses) of or incidental to the application are to be borne by the company or by any officers of it responsible for the default.

(5) This section does not affect the operation of any enactment making it an offence, or imposing a civil penalty, for the default.

1114. Application of provisions about documents and delivery

(1) In this Part—

    (a) "document" means information recorded in any form, and

    (b) references to delivering a document include forwarding, lodging, registering, sending, producing or submitting it or (in the case of a notice) giving it.

(2) Except as otherwise provided, this Part applies in relation to the supply to the registrar of information otherwise than in documentary form as it applies in relation to the delivery of a document.

1115. Supplementary provisions relating to electronic communications

(1) Registrar's rules may require a company to give any necessary consents to the use of electronic means for communications by the registrar to the company as a condition of making use of any facility to deliver material to the registrar by electronic means.

(2) A document that is required to be signed by the registrar or authenticated by the registrar's seal shall, if sent by electronic means, be authenticated in such manner as may be specified by registrar's rules.

1116. Alternative to publication in the Gazette

(1) Notices that would otherwise need to be published by the registrar in the Gazette may instead be published by such means as may from time to time be approved by the registrar in accordance with regulations made by the Secretary of State.

(2) The Secretary of State may make provision by regulations as to what alternative means may be approved.

(3) The regulations may, in particular—

    (a) require the use of electronic means;

    (b) require the same means to be used—

        (i) for all notices or for all notices of specified descriptions, and

        (ii) whether the company is registered in England and Wales, Scotland or Northern Ireland;

    (c) impose conditions as to the manner in which access to the notices is to be made available.

(4) Regulations under this section are subject to negative resolution procedure.

(5) Before starting to publish notices by means approved under this section the registrar must publish at least one notice to that effect in the Gazette.

(6) Nothing in this section prevents the registrar from giving public notice both in the Gazette and by means approved under this section.

In that case, the requirement of public notice is met when notice is first given by either means.

1117. Registrar's rules

(1) Where any provision of this Part enables the registrar to make provision, or impose requirements, as to any matter, the registrar may make such provision or impose such requirements by means of rules under this section.

This is without prejudice to the making of such provision or the imposing of such requirements by other means.

(2) Registrar's rules—

    (a) may make different provision for different cases, and

    (b) may allow the registrar to disapply or modify any of the rules.

(3) The registrar must—

    (a) publicise the rules in a manner appropriate to bring them to the notice of persons affected by them, and

    (b) make copies of the rules available to the public (in hard copy or electronic form).

1118. Payments into the Consolidated Fund

Nothing in the Companies Acts or any other enactment as to the payment of receipts into the Consolidated Fund shall be read as affecting the operation in relation to the registrar of section 3(1) of the Government Trading Funds Act 1973 (c. 63).

1119. Contracting out of registrar's functions

(1) Where by virtue of an order made under section 69 of the Deregulation and Contracting Out Act 1994 (c. 40) a person is authorised by the registrar to accept delivery of any class of documents that are under any enactment to be delivered to the registrar, the registrar may direct that documents of that class shall be delivered to a specified address of the authorised person.

Any such direction must be printed and made available to the public (with or without payment).

(2) A document of that class that is delivered to an address other than the specified address is treated as not having been delivered.

(3) Registrar's rules are not subordinate legislation for the purposes of section 71 of the Deregulation and Contracting Out Act 1994 (functions excluded from contracting out).

1120. Application of this Part to overseas companies

Unless the context otherwise requires, the provisions of this Part apply to an overseas company as they apply to a company as defined in section 1.

PART 36
OFFENCES UNDER THE COMPANIES ACTS

Liability of officer in default

1121. Liability of officer in default

(1) This section has effect for the purposes of any provision of the Companies Acts to the effect that, in the event of contravention of an enactment in relation to a company, an offence is committed by every officer of the company who is in default.

(2) For this purpose "officer" includes—

(a) any director, manager or secretary, and

(b) any person who is to be treated as an officer of the company for the purposes of the provision in question.

(3) An officer is "in default" for the purposes of the provision if he authorises or permits, participates in, or fails to take all reasonable steps to prevent, the contravention.

1122. Liability of company as officer in default

(1) Where a company is an officer of another company, it does not commit an offence as an officer in default unless one of its officers is in default.

(2) Where any such offence is committed by a company the officer in question also commits the offence and is liable to be proceeded against and punished accordingly.

(3) In this section "officer" and "in default" have the meanings given by section 1121.

1123. Application to bodies other than companies

(1) Section 1121 (liability of officers in default) applies to a body other than a company as it applies to a company.

(2) As it applies in relation to a body corporate other than a company—

(a) the reference to a director of the company shall be read as referring—

(i) where the body's affairs are managed by its members, to a member of the body,

(ii) in any other case, to any corresponding officer of the body, and

(b) the reference to a manager or secretary of the company shall be read as referring to any manager, secretary or similar officer of the body.

(3) As it applies in relation to a partnership—

(a) the reference to a director of the company shall be read as referring to a member of the partnership, and

(b) the reference to a manager or secretary of the company shall be read as referring to any manager, secretary or similar officer of the partnership.

(4) As it applies in relation to an unincorporated body other than a partnership—

    (a) the reference to a director of the company shall be read as referring—

        (i) where the body's affairs are managed by its members, to a member of the body,

        (ii) in any other case, to a member of the governing body, and

    (b) the reference to a manager or secretary of the company shall be read as referring to any manager, secretary or similar officer of the body.

Offences under the Companies Act 1985

1124. Amendments of the Companies Act 1985

Schedule 3 contains amendments of the Companies Act 1985 (c. 6) relating to offences.

General provisions

1125. Meaning of "daily default fine"

(1) This section defines what is meant in the Companies Acts where it is provided that a person guilty of an offence is liable on summary conviction to a fine not exceeding a specified amount "and, for continued contravention, a daily default fine" not exceeding a specified amount.

(2) This means that the person is liable on a second or subsequent summary conviction of the offence to a fine not exceeding the latter amount for each day on which the contravention is continued (instead of being liable to a fine not exceeding the former amount).

1126. Consents required for certain prosecutions

(1) This section applies to proceedings for an offence under any of the following provisions—

    section 458, 460 or 949 of this Act (offences of unauthorised disclosure of information);

    section 953 of this Act (failure to comply with rules about takeover bid documents);

    section 448, 449, 450, 451 or 453A of the Companies Act 1985 (c. 6) (offences in connection with company investigations);

    section 798 of this Act or section 455 of the Companies Act 1985 (offence of attempting to evade restrictions on shares).

(2) No such proceedings are to be brought in England and Wales except by or with the consent of—

    (a) in the case of an offence under—

        (i) section 458, 460 or 949 of this Act,

        (ii) section 953 of this Act, or

        (iii) section 448, 449, 450, 451 or 453A of the Companies Act 1985,

        the Secretary of State or the Director of Public Prosecutions;

    (b) in the case of an offence under section 798 of this Act or section 455 of the Companies Act 1985, the Secretary of State.

(3) No such proceedings are to be brought in Northern Ireland except by or with the consent of—

    (a) in the case of an offence under—

        (i) section 458, 460 or 949 of this Act,

        (ii) section 953 of this Act, or

        (iii) section 448, 449, 450, 451 or 453A of the Companies Act 1985,

        the Secretary of State or the Director of Public Prosecutions for Northern Ireland;

    (b) in the case of an offence under section 798 of this Act or section 455 of the Companies Act 1985, the Secretary of State.

1127. Summary proceedings: venue

(1) Summary proceedings for any offence under the Companies Acts may be taken—

    (a) against a body corporate, at any place at which the body has a place of business, and

    (b) against any other person, at any place at which he is for the time being.

(2) This is without prejudice to any jurisdiction exercisable apart from this section.

1128. Summary proceedings: time limit for proceedings

(1) An information relating to an offence under the Companies Acts that is triable by a magistrates' court in England and Wales may be so tried if it is laid—

    (a) at any time within three years after the commission of the offence, and

    (b) within twelve months after the date on which evidence sufficient in the opinion of the Director of Public Prosecutions or the Secretary of State (as the case may be) to justify the proceedings comes to his knowledge.

(2) Summary proceedings in Scotland for an offence under the Companies Acts—

    (a) must not be commenced after the expiration of three years from the commission of the offence;

    (b) subject to that, may be commenced at any time—

        (i) within twelve months after the date on which evidence sufficient in the Lord Advocate's opinion to justify the proceedings came to his knowledge, or

        (ii) where such evidence was reported to him by the Secretary of State, within twelve months after the date on which it came to the knowledge of the latter.

    Section 136 (3) of the Criminal Procedure (Scotland) Act 1995 (c. 46) (date when proceedings deemed to be commenced) applies for the purposes of this subsection as for the purposes of that section.

(3) A magistrates' court in Northern Ireland has jurisdiction to hear and determine a complaint charging the commission of a summary offence under the Companies Acts provided that the complaint is made—

    (a) within three years from the time when the offence was committed, and

    (b) within twelve months from the date on which evidence sufficient in the opinion of the Director of Public Prosecutions for Northern Ireland or the Secretary of State (as the case may be) to justify the proceedings comes to his knowledge.

(4) For the purposes of this section a certificate of the Director of Public Prosecutions, the Lord Advocate, the Director of Public Prosecutions for Northern Ireland or the Secretary of State (as the case may be) as to the date on which such evidence as is referred to above came to his notice is conclusive evidence.

1129. Legal professional privilege

In proceedings against a person for an offence under the Companies Acts, nothing in those Acts is to be taken to require any person to disclose any information that he is entitled to refuse to disclose on grounds of legal professional privilege (in Scotland, confidentiality of communications).

1130. Proceedings against unincorporated bodies

(1) Proceedings for an offence under the Companies Acts alleged to have been committed by an unincorporated body must be brought in the name of the body (and not in that of any of its members).

(2) For the purposes of such proceedings—

    (a) any rules of court relating to the service of documents have effect as if the body were a body corporate, and

    (b) the following provisions apply as they apply in relation to a body corporate—

        (i) in England and Wales, section 33 of the Criminal Justice Act 1925 (c. 86) and Schedule 3 to the Magistrates' Courts Act 1980 (c. 43),

        (ii) in Scotland, sections 70 and 143 of the Criminal Procedure (Scotland) Act 1995 (c. 46),

        (iii) in Northern Ireland, section 18 of the Criminal Justice Act (Northern Ireland) 1945 (c. 15 (N.I.)) and Article 166 of and Schedule 4 to the Magistrates' Courts (Northern Ireland) Order 1981 (S.I. 1981/1675 (N.I. 26)).

(3) A fine imposed on an unincorporated body on its conviction of an offence under the Companies Acts must be paid out of the funds of the body.

1131. Imprisonment on summary conviction in England and Wales: transitory provision

(1) This section applies to any provision of the Companies Acts that provides that a person guilty of an offence is liable on summary conviction in England and Wales to imprisonment for a term not exceeding twelve months.

(2) In relation to an offence committed before the commencement of section 154 (1) of the Criminal Justice Act 2003 (c. 44), for "twelve months" substitute "six months".

Production and inspection of documents

1132. Production and inspection of documents where offence suspected

(1) An application under this section may be made—

  (a) in England and Wales, to a judge of the High Court by the Director of Public Prosecutions, the Secretary of State or a chief officer of police;

  (b) in Scotland, to one of the Lords Commissioners of Justiciary by the Lord Advocate;

  (c) in Northern Ireland, to the High Court by the Director of Public Prosecutions for Northern Ireland, the Department of Enterprise, Trade and Investment or a chief superintendent of the Police Service of Northern Ireland.

(2) If on an application under this section there is shown to be reasonable cause to believe—

  (a) that any person has, while an officer of a company, committed an offence in connection with the management of the company's affairs, and

  (b) that evidence of the commission of the offence is to be found in any documents in the possession or control of the company,

an order under this section may be made.

(3) The order may—

  (a) authorise any person named in it to inspect the documents in question, or any of them, for the purpose of investigating and obtaining evidence of the offence, or

  (b) require the secretary of the company, or such other officer of it as may be named in the order, to produce the documents (or any of them) to a person named in the order at a place so named.

(4) This section applies also in relation to documents in the possession or control of a person carrying on the business of banking, so far as they relate to the company's affairs, as it applies to documents in the possession or control of the company, except that no such order as is referred to in subsection (3)(b) may be made by virtue of this subsection.

(5) The decision under this section of a judge of the High Court, any of the Lords Commissioners of Justiciary or the High Court is not appealable.

(6) In this section "document" includes information recorded in any form.

Supplementary

1133. Transitional provision

The provisions of this Part except section 1132 do not apply to offences committed before the commencement of the relevant provision.

PART 37
PART COMPANIES: SUPPLEMENTARY PROVISIONS

Company records

1134. Meaning of "company records"

In this Part "company records" means—

  (a) any register, index, accounting records, agreement, memorandum, minutes or other document required by the Companies Acts to be kept by a company, and

  (b) any register kept by a company of its debenture holders.

1135. Form of company records

    (1) Company records—

        (a) may be kept in hard copy or electronic form, and

        (b) may be arranged in such manner as the directors of the company think fit,

    provided the information in question is adequately recorded for future reference.

    (2) Where the records are kept in electronic form, they must be capable of being reproduced in hard copy form.

    (3) If a company fails to comply with this section, an offence is committed by every officer of the company who is in default.

    (4) A person guilty of an offence under this section is liable on summary conviction to a fine not exceeding level 3 on the standard scale and, for continued contravention, a daily default fine not exceeding one-tenth of level 3 on the standard scale.

    (5) Any provision of an instrument made by a company before 12th February 1979 that requires a register of holders of the company's debentures to be kept in hard copy form is to be read as requiring it to be kept in hard copy or electronic form.

1136. Regulations about where certain company records to be kept available for inspection

    (1) The Secretary of State may make provision by regulations specifying places other than a company's registered office at which company records required to be kept available for inspection under a relevant provision may be so kept in compliance with that provision.

    (2) The "relevant provisions" are—

    section 114 (register of members);

    section 162 (register of directors);

    section 228 (directors' service contracts);

    section 237 (directors' indemnities);

    section 275 (register of secretaries);

    section 358 (records of resolutions etc);

    section 702 (contracts relating to purchase of own shares);

    section 720 (documents relating to redemption or purchase of own shares out of capital by private company);

    section 743 (register of debenture holders);

    section 805 (report to members of outcome of investigation by public company into interests in its shares);

    section 809 (register of interests in shares disclosed to public company);

    section 877 (instruments creating charges and register of charges: England and Wales);

    section 892 (instruments creating charges and register of charges: Scotland).

    (3) The regulations may specify a place by reference to the company's principal place of business, the part of the United Kingdom in which the company is registered, the place at which the company keeps any other records available for inspection or in any other way.

    (4) The regulations may provide that a company does not comply with a relevant provision by keeping company records available for inspection at a place specified in the regulations unless conditions specified in the regulations are met.

    (5) The regulations—

        (a) need not specify a place in relation to each relevant provision;

        (b) may specify more than one place in relation to a relevant provision.

    (6) A requirement under a relevant provision to keep company records available for inspection is not complied with by keeping them available for inspection at a place specified in the regulations unless all the company's records subject to the requirement are kept there.

    (7) Regulations under this section are subject to negative resolution procedure.

1137. Regulations about inspection of records and provision of copies

(1) The Secretary of State may make provision by regulations as to the obligations of a company that is required by any provision of the Companies Acts—

    (a) to keep available for inspection any company records, or

    (b) to provide copies of any company records.

(2) A company that fails to comply with the regulations is treated as having refused inspection or, as the case may be, having failed to provide a copy.

(3) The regulations may—

    (a) make provision as to the time, duration and manner of inspection, including the circumstances in which and extent to which the copying of information is permitted in the course of inspection, and

    (b) define what may be required of the company as regards the nature, extent and manner of extracting or presenting any information for the purposes of inspection or the provision of copies.

(4) Where there is power to charge a fee, the regulations may make provision as to the amount of the fee and the basis of its calculation.

(5) Nothing in any provision of this Act or in the regulations shall be read as preventing a company—

    (a) from affording more extensive facilities than are required by the regulations, or

    (b) where a fee may be charged, from charging a lesser fee than that prescribed or none at all.

(6) Regulations under this section are subject to negative resolution procedure.

1138. Duty to take precautions against falsification

(1) Where company records are kept otherwise than in bound books, adequate precautions must be taken—

    (a) to guard against falsification, and

    (b) to facilitate the discovery of falsification.

(2) If a company fails to comply with this section, an offence is committed by every officer of the company who is in default.

(3) A person guilty of an offence under this section is liable on summary conviction to a fine not exceeding level 3 on the standard scale and, for continued contravention, a daily default fine not exceeding one-tenth of level 3 on the standard scale.

(4) This section does not apply to the documents required to be kept under—

    (a) section 228 (copy of director's service contract or memorandum of its terms); or

    (b) section 237 (qualifying indemnity provision).

Service addresses

1139. Service of documents on company

(1) A document may be served on a company registered under this Act by leaving it at, or sending it by post to, the company's registered office.

(2) A document may be served on an overseas company whose particulars are registered under section 1046—

    (a) by leaving it at, or sending it by post to, the registered address of any person resident in the United Kingdom who is authorised to accept service of documents on the company's behalf, or

    (b) if there is no such person, or if any such person refuses service or service cannot for any other reason be effected, by leaving it at or sending by post to any place of business of the company in the United Kingdom.

(3) For the purposes of this section a person's "registered address" means any address for the time being shown as a current address in relation to that person in the part of the register available for public inspection.

(4) Where a company registered in Scotland or Northern Ireland carries on business in England and Wales, the process of any court in England and Wales may be served on the company by leaving it at, or sending it by post to, the company's principal place of business in England and Wales, addressed to the manager or other head officer in England and Wales of the company. Where process is served on a company under this subsection, the person issuing out the process must send a copy of it by post to the company's registered office.

(5) Further provision as to service and other matters is made in the company communications provisions (see section 1143).

1140. Service of documents on directors, secretaries and others

(1) A document may be served on a person to whom this section applies by leaving it at, or sending it by post to, the person's registered address.

(2) This section applies to—

    (a) a director or secretary of a company;

    (b) in the case of an overseas company whose particulars are registered under section 1046, a person holding any such position as may be specified for the purposes of this section by regulations under that section;

    (c) a person appointed in relation to a company as—

        (i) a judicial factor (in Scotland),

        (ii) a receiver and manager appointed under section 18 of the Charities Act 1993 (c. 10), or

        (iii) a manager appointed under section 47 of the Companies (Audit, Investigations and Community Enterprise) Act 2004 (c. 27).

(3) This section applies whatever the purpose of the document in question.

It is not restricted to service for purposes arising out of or in connection with the appointment or position mentioned in subsection (2) or in connection with the company concerned.

(4) For the purposes of this section a person's "registered address" means any address for the time being shown as a current address in relation to that person in the part of the register available for public inspection.

(5) If notice of a change of that address is given to the registrar, a person may validly serve a document at the address previously registered until the end of the period of 14 days beginning with the date on which notice of the change is registered.

(6) Service may not be effected by virtue of this section at an address—

    (a) if notice has been registered of the termination of the appointment in relation to which the address was registered and the address is not a registered address of the person concerned in relation to any other appointment;

    (b) in the case of a person holding any such position as is mentioned in subsection (2)(b), if the overseas company has ceased to have any connection with the United Kingdom by virtue of which it is required to register particulars under section 1046.

(7) Further provision as to service and other matters is made in the company communications provisions (see section 1143).

(8) Nothing in this section shall be read as affecting any enactment or rule of law under which permission is required for service out of the jurisdiction.

1141. Service addresses

(1) In the Companies Acts a "service address", in relation to a person, means an address at which documents may be effectively served on that person.

(2) The Secretary of State may by regulations specify conditions with which a service address must comply.

(3) Regulations under this section are subject to negative resolution procedure.

1142. Requirement to give service address

Any obligation under the Companies Acts to give a person's address is, unless otherwise expressly provided, to give a service address for that person.

Sending or supplying documents or information

1143. The company communications provisions

(1) The provisions of sections 1144 to 1148 and Schedules 4 and 5 ("the company communications provisions") have effect for the purposes of any provision of the Companies Acts that authorises or requires documents or information to be sent or supplied by or to a company.

(2) The company communications provisions have effect subject to any requirements imposed, or contrary provision made, by or under any enactment.

(3) In particular, in their application in relation to documents or information to be sent or supplied to the registrar, they have effect subject to the provisions of Part 35.

(4) For the purposes of subsection (2), provision is not to be regarded as contrary to the company communications provisions by reason only of the fact that it expressly authorises a document or information to be sent or supplied in hard copy form, in electronic form or by means of a website.

1144. Sending or supplying documents or information

(1) Documents or information to be sent or supplied to a company must be sent or supplied in accordance with the provisions of Schedule 4.

(2) Documents or information to be sent or supplied by a company must be sent or supplied in accordance with the provisions of Schedule 5.

(3) The provisions referred to in subsection (2) apply (and those referred to in subsection (1) do not apply) in relation to documents or information that are to be sent or supplied by one company to another.

1145. Right to hard copy version

(1) Where a member of a company or a holder of a company's debentures has received a document or information from the company otherwise than in hard copy form, he is entitled to require the company to send him a version of the document or information in hard copy form.

(2) The company must send the document or information in hard copy form within 21 days of receipt of the request from the member or debenture holder.

(3) The company may not make a charge for providing the document or information in that form.

(4) If a company fails to comply with this section, an offence is committed by the company and every officer of it who is in default.

(5) A person guilty of an offence under this section is liable on summary conviction to a fine not exceeding level 3 on the standard scale and, for continued contravention, a daily default fine not exceeding one-tenth of level 3 on the standard scale.

1146. Requirement of authentication

(1) This section applies in relation to the authentication of a document or information sent or supplied by a person to a company.

(2) A document or information sent or supplied in hard copy form is sufficiently authenticated if it is signed by the person sending or supplying it.

(3) A document or information sent or supplied in electronic form is sufficiently authenticated—

(a) if the identity of the sender is confirmed in a manner specified by the company, or

(b) where no such manner has been specified by the company, if the communication contains or is accompanied by a statement of the identity of the sender and the company has no reason to doubt the truth of that statement.

(4) Where a document or information is sent or supplied by one person on behalf of another, nothing in this section affects any provision of the company's articles under which the company may require reasonable evidence of the authority of the former to act on behalf of the latter.

1147. Deemed delivery of documents and information

(1) This section applies in relation to documents and information sent or supplied by a company.

(2) Where—

(a) the document or information is sent by post (whether in hard copy or electronic form) to an address in the United Kingdom, and

(b) the company is able to show that it was properly addressed, prepaid and posted,

it is deemed to have been received by the intended recipient 48 hours after it was posted.

(3) Where—

(a) the document or information is sent or supplied by electronic means, and

(b) the company is able to show that it was properly addressed,

it is deemed to have been received by the intended recipient 48 hours after it was sent.

(4) Where the document or information is sent or supplied by means of a website, it is deemed to have been received by the intended recipient—

(a) when the material was first made available on the website, or

(b) if later, when the recipient received (or is deemed to have received) notice of the fact that the material was available on the website.

(5) In calculating a period of hours for the purposes of this section, no account shall be taken of any part of a day that is not a working day.

(6) This section has effect subject to—

(a) in its application to documents or information sent or supplied by a company to its members, any contrary provision of the company's articles;

(b) in its application to documents or information sent or supplied by a company to its debentures holders, any contrary provision in the instrument constituting the debentures;

(c) in its application to documents or information sent or supplied by a company to a person otherwise than in his capacity as a member or debenture holder, any contrary provision in an agreement between the company and that person.

1148. Interpretation of company communications provisions

(1) In the company communications provisions—

"address" includes a number or address used for the purposes of sending or receiving documents or information by electronic means;

"company" includes any body corporate;

"document" includes summons, notice, order or other legal process and registers.

(2) References in the company communications provisions to provisions of the Companies Acts authorising or requiring a document or information to be sent or supplied include all such provisions, whatever expression is used, and references to documents or information being sent or supplied shall be construed accordingly.

(3) References in the company communications provisions to documents or information being sent or supplied by or to a company include references to documents or information being sent or supplied by or to the directors of a company acting on behalf of the company.

Requirements as to independent valuation

1149. Application of valuation requirements

The provisions of sections 1150 to 1153 apply to the valuation and report required by—

section 93 (re-registration as public company: recent allotment of shares for non-cash consideration);

section 593 (allotment of shares of public company in consideration of non-cash asset);

section 599 (transfer of non-cash asset to public company).

1150. Valuation by qualified independent person

(1) The valuation and report must be made by a person ("the valuer") who—

(a) is eligible for appointment as a statutory auditor (see section 1212), and

(b) meets the independence requirement in section 1151.

(2) However, where it appears to the valuer to be reasonable for the valuation of the consideration, or part of it, to be made by (or for him to accept a valuation made by) another person who—

    (a) appears to him to have the requisite knowledge and experience to value the consideration or that part of it, and

    (b) is not an officer or employee of—

        (i) the company, or

        (ii) any other body corporate that is that company's subsidiary or holding company or a subsidiary of that company's holding company,

or a partner of or employed by any such officer or employee,

he may arrange for or accept such a valuation, together with a report which will enable him to make his own report under this section.

(3) The references in subsection (2)(b) to an officer or employee do not include an auditor.

(4) Where the consideration or part of it is valued by a person other than the valuer himself, the latter's report must state that fact and shall also—

    (a) state the former's name and what knowledge and experience he has to carry out the valuation, and

    (b) describe so much of the consideration as was valued by the other person, and the method used to value it, and specify the date of that valuation.

1151. The independence requirement

(1) A person meets the independence requirement for the purposes of section 1150 only if—

    (a) he is not—

        (i) an officer or employee of the company, or

        (ii) a partner or employee of such a person, or a partnership of which such a person is a partner;

    (b) he is not—

        (i) an officer or employee of an associated undertaking of the company, or

        (ii) a partner or employee of such a person, or a partnership of which such a person is a partner; and

    (c) there does not exist between—

        (i) the person or an associate of his, and

        (ii) the company or an associated undertaking of the company,

a connection of any such description as may be specified by regulations made by the Secretary of State.

(2) An auditor of the company is not regarded as an officer or employee of the company for this purpose.

(3) In this section—

    "associated undertaking" means—

        (i) a parent undertaking or subsidiary undertaking of the company, or

        (ii) a subsidiary undertaking of a parent undertaking of the company; and

    "associate" has the meaning given by section 1152.

(4) Regulations under this section are subject to negative resolution procedure.

1152. Meaning of "associate"

(1) This section defines "associate" for the purposes of section 1151 (valuation: independence requirement).

(2) In relation to an individual, "associate" means—

    (a) that individual's spouse or civil partner or minor child or step-child,

    (b) any body corporate of which that individual is a director, and

    (c) any employee or partner of that individual.

(3) In relation to a body corporate, "associate" means—

    (a) any body corporate of which that body is a director,

    (b) any body corporate in the same group as that body, and

    (c) any employee or partner of that body or of any body corporate in the same group.

(4) In relation to a partnership that is a legal person under the law by which it is governed, "associate" means—

    (a) any body corporate of which that partnership is a director,

    (b) any employee of or partner in that partnership, and

    (c) any person who is an associate of a partner in that partnership.

(5) In relation to a partnership that is not a legal person under the law by which it is governed, "associate" means any person who is an associate of any of the partners.

(6) In this section, in relation to a limited liability partnership, for "director" read "member".

1153. Valuer entitled to full disclosure

(1) A person carrying out a valuation or making a report with respect to any consideration proposed to be accepted or given by a company, is entitled to require from the officers of the company such information and explanation as he thinks necessary to enable him to—

    (a) carry out the valuation or make the report, and

    (b) provide any note required by section 596 (3) or 600(3) (note required where valuation carried out by another person).

(2) A person who knowingly or recklessly makes a statement to which this subsection applies that is misleading, false or deceptive in a material particular commits an offence.

(3) Subsection (2) applies to a statement—

    (a) made (whether orally or in writing) to a person carrying out a valuation or making a report, and

    (b) conveying or purporting to convey any information or explanation which that person requires, or is entitled to require, under subsection (1).

(4) A person guilty of an offence under subsection (2) is liable—

    (a) on conviction on indictment, to imprisonment for a term not exceeding two years or a fine (or both);

    (b) on summary conviction—

        (i) in England and Wales, to imprisonment for a term not exceeding twelve months or to a fine not exceeding the statutory maximum (or both);

        (ii) in Scotland or Northern Ireland, to imprisonment for a term not exceeding six months, or to a fine not exceeding the statutory maximum (or both).

Notice of appointment of certain officers

1154. Duty to notify registrar of certain appointments etc

(1) Notice must be given to the registrar of the appointment in relation to a company of—

    (a) a judicial factor (in Scotland),

    (b) a receiver and manager appointed under section 18 of the Charities Act 1993 (c. 10), or

    (c) a manager appointed under section 47 of the Companies (Audit, Investigations and Community Enterprise) Act 2004 (c. 27).

(2) The notice must be given—

    (a) in the case of appointment of a judicial factor, by the judicial factor;

    (b) in the case of appointment of a receiver and manager under section 18 of the Charities Act 1993 (c. 10), by the Charity Commission;

    (c) in the case of appointment of a manager under section 47 of the Companies (Audit, Investigations and Community Enterprise) Act 2004, by the Regulator of Community Interest Companies.

(3) The notice must specify an address at which service of documents (including legal process) may be effected on the person appointed.

Notice of a change in the address for service may be given to the registrar by the person appointed.

(4) Where notice has been given under this section of the appointment of a person, notice must also be given to the registrar of the termination of the appointment.

This notice must be given by the person specified in subsection (2).

1155. Offence of failure to give notice

(1) If a judicial factor fails to give notice of his appointment in accordance with section 1154 within the period of 14 days after the appointment he commits an offence.

(2) A person guilty of an offence under this section is liable on summary conviction to a fine not exceeding level 5 on the standard scale and, for continued contravention, a daily default fine not exceeding one-tenth of level 5 on the standard scale.

Courts and legal proceedings

1156. Meaning of "the court"

(1) Except as otherwise provided, in the Companies Acts "the court" means—

(a) in England and Wales, the High Court or (subject to subsection (3)) a county court;

(b) in Scotland, the Court of Session or the sheriff court;

(c) in Northern Ireland, the High Court.

(2) The provisions of the Companies Acts conferring jurisdiction on "the court" as defined above have effect subject to any enactment or rule of law relating to the allocation of jurisdiction or distribution of business between courts in any part of the United Kingdom.

(3) The Lord Chancellor may, with the concurrence of the Lord Chief Justice, by order—

(a) exclude a county court from having jurisdiction under the Companies Acts, and

(b) for the purposes of that jurisdiction attach that court's district, or any part of it, to another county court.

(4) The Lord Chief Justice may nominate a judicial office holder (as defined in section 109 (4) of the Constitutional Reform Act 2005 (c. 4)) to exercise his functions under subsection (3).

1157. Power of court to grant relief in certain cases

(1) If in proceedings for negligence, default, breach of duty or breach of trust against—

(a) an officer of a company, or

(b) a person employed by a company as auditor (whether he is or is not an officer of the company),

it appears to the court hearing the case that the officer or person is or may be liable but that he acted honestly and reasonably, and that having regard to all the circumstances of the case (including those connected with his appointment) he ought fairly to be excused, the court may relieve him, either wholly or in part, from his liability on such terms as it thinks fit.

(2) If any such officer or person has reason to apprehend that a claim will or might be made against him in respect of negligence, default, breach of duty or breach of trust—

(a) he may apply to the court for relief, and

(b) the court has the same power to relieve him as it would have had if it had been a court before which proceedings against him for negligence, default, breach of duty or breach of trust had been brought.

(3) Where a case to which subsection (1) applies is being tried by a judge with a jury, the judge, after hearing the evidence, may, if he is satisfied that the defendant (in Scotland, the defender) ought in pursuance of that subsection to be relieved either in whole or in part from the liability sought to be enforced against him, withdraw the case from the jury and forthwith direct judgment to be entered for the defendant (in Scotland, grant decree of absolvitor) on such terms as to costs (in Scotland, expenses) or otherwise as the judge may think proper.

PART 38
COMPANIES: INTERPRETATION

Meaning of "UK-registered company"

1158. Meaning of "UK-registered company"
In the Companies Acts "UK-registered company" means a company registered under this Act. The expression does not include an overseas company that has registered particulars under section 1046.

Meaning of "subsidiary" and related expressions

1159. Meaning of "subsidiary" etc
(1) A company is a "subsidiary" of another company, its "holding company", if that other company—
    (a) holds a majority of the voting rights in it, or
    (b) is a member of it and has the right to appoint or remove a majority of its board of directors, or
    (c) is a member of it and controls alone, pursuant to an agreement with other members, a majority of the voting rights in it,
    or if it is a subsidiary of a company that is itself a subsidiary of that other company.
(2) A company is a "wholly-owned subsidiary" of another company if it has no members except that other and that other's wholly-owned subsidiaries or persons acting on behalf of that other or its wholly-owned subsidiaries.
(3) Schedule 6 contains provisions explaining expressions used in this section and otherwise supplementing this section.
(4) In this section and that Schedule "company" includes any body corporate.

1160. Meaning of "subsidiary" etc: power to amend
(1) The Secretary of State may by regulations amend the provisions of section 1159 (meaning of "subsidiary" etc) and Schedule 6 (meaning of "subsidiary" etc: supplementary provisions) so as to alter the meaning of the expressions "subsidiary", "holding company" or "wholly-owned subsidiary".
(2) Regulations under this section are subject to negative resolution procedure.
(3) Any amendment made by regulations under this section does not apply for the purposes of enactments outside the Companies Acts unless the regulations so provide.
(4) So much of section 23 (3) of the Interpretation Act 1978 (c. 30) as applies section 17 (2) (a) of that Act (effect of repeal and re-enactment) to deeds, instruments and documents other than enactments does not apply in relation to any repeal and re-enactment effected by regulations under this section.

Meaning of "undertaking" and related expressions

1161. Meaning of "undertaking" and related expressions
(1) In the Companies Acts "undertaking" means—
    (a) a body corporate or partnership, or
    (b) an unincorporated association carrying on a trade or business, with or without a view to profit.
(2) In the Companies Acts references to shares—
    (a) in relation to an undertaking with capital but no share capital, are to rights to share in the capital of the undertaking; and

    (b) in relation to an undertaking without capital, are to interests—

        (i)   conferring any right to share in the profits or liability to contribute to the losses of the undertaking, or

        (ii) giving rise to an obligation to contribute to the debts or expenses of the undertaking in the event of a winding up.

(3) Other expressions appropriate to companies shall be construed, in relation to an undertaking which is not a company, as references to the corresponding persons, officers, documents or organs, as the case may be, appropriate to undertakings of that description.

This is subject to provision in any specific context providing for the translation of such expressions.

(4) References in the Companies Acts to "fellow subsidiary undertakings" are to undertakings which are subsidiary undertakings of the same parent undertaking but are not parent undertakings or subsidiary undertakings of each other.

(5) In the Companies Acts "group undertaking", in relation to an undertaking, means an undertaking which is—

    (a) a parent undertaking or subsidiary undertaking of that undertaking, or

    (b) a subsidiary undertaking of any parent undertaking of that undertaking.

1162. Parent and subsidiary undertakings

(1) This section (together with Schedule 7) defines "parent undertaking" and "subsidiary undertaking" for the purposes of the Companies Acts.

(2) An undertaking is a parent undertaking in relation to another undertaking, a subsidiary undertaking, if—

    (a) it holds a majority of the voting rights in the undertaking, or

    (b) it is a member of the undertaking and has the right to appoint or remove a majority of its board of directors, or

    (c) it has the right to exercise a dominant influence over the undertaking—

        (i)   by virtue of provisions contained in the undertaking's articles, or

        (ii) by virtue of a control contract, or

    (d) it is a member of the undertaking and controls alone, pursuant to an agreement with other shareholders or members, a majority of the voting rights in the undertaking.

(3) For the purposes of subsection (2) an undertaking shall be treated as a member of another undertaking—

    (a) if any of its subsidiary undertakings is a member of that undertaking, or

    (b) if any shares in that other undertaking are held by a person acting on behalf of the undertaking or any of its subsidiary undertakings.

(4) An undertaking is also a parent undertaking in relation to another undertaking, a subsidiary undertaking, if—

    (a) it has the power to exercise, or actually exercises, dominant influence or control over it, or

    (b) it and the subsidiary undertaking are managed on a unified basis.

(5) A parent undertaking shall be treated as the parent undertaking of undertakings in relation to which any of its subsidiary undertakings are, or are to be treated as, parent undertakings; and references to its subsidiary undertakings shall be construed accordingly.

(6) Schedule 7 contains provisions explaining expressions used in this section and otherwise supplementing this section.

(7) In this section and that Schedule references to shares, in relation to an undertaking, are to allotted shares.

Other definitions

1163. "Non-cash asset"

    (1) In the Companies Acts "non-cash asset" means any property or interest in property, other than cash.

    For this purpose "cash" includes foreign currency.

    (2) A reference to the transfer or acquisition of a non-cash asset includes—

        (a) the creation or extinction of an estate or interest in, or a right over, any property, and

        (b) the discharge of a liability of any person, other than a liability for a liquidated sum.

1164. Meaning of "banking company" and "banking group"

    (1) This section defines "banking company" and "banking group" for the purposes of the Companies Acts.

    (2) "Banking company" means a person who has permission under Part 4 of the Financial Services and Markets Act 2000 (c. 8) to accept deposits, other than—

        (a) a person who is not a company, and

        (b) a person who has such permission only for the purpose of carrying on another regulated activity in accordance with permission under that Part.

    (3) The definition in subsection (2) must be read with section 22 of that Act, any relevant order under that section and Schedule 2 to that Act.

    (4) References to a banking group are to a group where the parent company is a banking company or where—

        (a) the parent company's principal subsidiary undertakings are wholly or mainly credit institutions, and

        (b) the parent company does not itself carry on any material business apart from the acquisition, management and disposal of interests in subsidiary undertakings.

    "Group" here means a parent undertaking and its subsidiary undertakings.

    (5) For the purposes of subsection (4)—

        (a) a parent company's principal subsidiary undertakings are the subsidiary undertakings of the company whose results or financial position would principally affect the figures shown in the group accounts, and

        (b) the management of interests in subsidiary undertakings includes the provision of services to such undertakings.

1165. Meaning of "insurance company" and related expressions

    (1) This section defines "insurance company", "authorised insurance company", "insurance group" and "insurance market activity" for the purposes of the Companies Acts.

    (2) An "authorised insurance company" means a person (whether incorporated or not) who has permission under Part 4 of the Financial Services and Markets Act 2000 (c. 8) to effect or carry out contracts of insurance.

    (3) An "insurance company" means—

        (a) an authorised insurance company, or

        (b) any other person (whether incorporated or not) who—

            (i) carries on insurance market activity, or

            (ii) may effect or carry out contracts of insurance under which the benefits provided by that person are exclusively or primarily benefits in kind in the event of accident to or breakdown of a vehicle.

    (4) Neither expression includes a friendly society within the meaning of the Friendly Societies Act 1992 (c. 40).

    (5) References to an insurance group are to a group where the parent company is an insurance company or where—

        (a) the parent company's principal subsidiary undertakings are wholly or mainly insurance companies, and

(b) the parent company does not itself carry on any material business apart from the acquisition, management and disposal of interests in subsidiary undertakings.

"Group" here means a parent undertaking and its subsidiary undertakings.

(6) For the purposes of subsection (5)—

(a) a parent company's principal subsidiary undertakings are the subsidiary undertakings of the company whose results or financial position would principally affect the figures shown in the group accounts, and

(b) the management of interests in subsidiary undertakings includes the provision of services to such undertakings.

(7) "Insurance market activity" has the meaning given in section 316 (3) of the Financial Services and Markets Act 2000.

(8) References in this section to contracts of insurance and to the effecting or carrying out of such contracts must be read with section 22 of that Act, any relevant order under that section and Schedule 2 to that Act.

1166. "Employees' share scheme"

For the purposes of the Companies Acts an employees' share scheme is a scheme for encouraging or facilitating the holding of shares in or debentures of a company by or for the benefit of—

(a) the bona fide employees or former employees of—

(i) the company,

(ii) any subsidiary of the company, or

(iii) the company's holding company or any subsidiary of the company's holding company, or

(b) the spouses, civil partners, surviving spouses, surviving civil partners, or minor children or step-children of such employees or former employees.

1167. Meaning of "prescribed"

In the Companies Acts "prescribed" means prescribed (by order or by regulations) by the Secretary of State.

1168. Hard copy and electronic form and related expressions

(1) The following provisions apply for the purposes of the Companies Acts.

(2) A document or information is sent or supplied in hard copy form if it is sent or supplied in a paper copy or similar form capable of being read.

References to hard copy have a corresponding meaning.

(3) A document or information is sent or supplied in electronic form if it is sent or supplied—

(a) by electronic means (for example, by e-mail or fax), or

(b) by any other means while in an electronic form (for example, sending a disk by post).

References to electronic copy have a corresponding meaning.

(4) A document or information is sent or supplied by electronic means if it is—

(a) sent initially and received at its destination by means of electronic equipment for the processing (which expression includes digital compression) or storage of data, and

(b) entirely transmitted, conveyed and received by wire, by radio, by optical means or by other electromagnetic means.

References to electronic means have a corresponding meaning.

(5) A document or information authorised or required to be sent or supplied in electronic form must be sent or supplied in a form, and by a means, that the sender or supplier reasonably considers will enable the recipient—

(a) to read it, and

(b) to retain a copy of it.

(6) For the purposes of this section, a document or information can be read only if—

(a) it can be read with the naked eye, or

(b) to the extent that it consists of images (for example photographs, pictures, maps, plans or drawings), it can be seen with the naked eye.

(7) The provisions of this section apply whether the provision of the Companies Acts in question uses the words "sent" or "supplied" or uses other words (such as "deliver", "provide", "produce" or, in the case of a notice, "give") to refer to the sending or supplying of a document or information.

1169. Dormant companies

(1) For the purposes of the Companies Acts a company is "dormant" during any period in which it has no significant accounting transaction.

(2) A "significant accounting transaction" means a transaction that is required by section 386 to be entered in the company's accounting records.

(3) In determining whether or when a company is dormant, there shall be disregarded—

    (a) any transaction arising from the taking of shares in the company by a subscriber to the memorandum as a result of an undertaking of his in connection with the formation of the company;

    (b) any transaction consisting of the payment of—

        (i) a fee to the registrar on a change of the company's name,

        (ii) a fee to the registrar on the re-registration of the company,

        (iii) a penalty under section 453 (penalty for failure to file accounts), or

        (iv) a fee to the registrar for the registration of an annual return.

(4) Any reference in the Companies Acts to a body corporate other than a company being dormant has a corresponding meaning.

1170. Meaning of "EEA State" and related expressions

In the Companies Acts—

"EEA State" means a state which is a Contracting Party to the Agreement on the European Economic Area signed at Oporto on 2nd May 1992 (as it has effect from time to time);

"EEA company" and "EEA undertaking" mean a company or undertaking governed by the law of an EEA State.

1171. The former Companies Acts

In the Companies Acts—

"the former Companies Acts" means—

    (a) the Joint Stock Companies Acts, the Companies Act 1862 (c. 89), the Companies (Consolidation) Act 1908 (c. 69), the Companies Act 1929 (c. 23), the Companies Act (Northern Ireland) 1932 (c. 7 (N.I.)), the Companies Acts 1948 to 1983, the Companies Act (Northern Ireland) 1960 (c. 22 (N.I.)), the Companies (Northern Ireland) Order 1986 (S.I. 1986/1032 (N.I. 6)) and the Companies Consolidation (Consequential Provisions) (Northern Ireland) Order 1986 (S.I. 1986/1035 (N.I. 9)), and

    (b) the provisions of the Companies Act 1985 (c. 6) and the Companies Consolidation (Consequential Provisions) Act 1985 (c. 9) that are no longer in force;

"the Joint Stock Companies Acts" means the Joint Stock Companies Act 1856 (c. 47), the Joint Stock Companies Acts 1856, 1857 (20 & 21 Vict. c. 14), the Joint Stock Banking Companies Act 1857 (c. 49), and the Act to enable Joint Stock Banking Companies to be formed on the principle of limited liability (1858 c. 91), but does not include the Joint Stock Companies Act 1844 (c. 110).

General

1172. References to requirements of this Act

References in the company law provisions of this Act to the requirements of this Act include the requirements of regulations and orders made under it.

1173. Minor definitions: general

(1) In the Companies Acts—

"body corporate" and "corporation" include a body incorporated outside the United Kingdom, but do not include—

(a) corporation sole, or

(b) partnership that, whether or not a legal person, is not regarded as a body corporate under the law by which it is governed;

"credit institution" means a credit institution as defined in Article 4.1(a) of Directive 2006/48/EC of the European Parliament and of the Council relating to the taking up and pursuit of the business of credit institutions;

"financial institution" means a financial institution within the meaning of Article 1.1 of the Council Directive on the obligations of branches established in a Member State of credit and financial institutions having their head offices outside that Member State regarding the publication of annual accounting documents (the Bank Branches Directive, 89/117/EEC);

"firm" means any entity, whether or not a legal person, that is not an individual and includes a body corporate, a corporation sole and a partnership or other unincorporated association;

"the Gazette" means—

(a) as respects companies registered in England and Wales, the London Gazette,

(b) as respects companies registered in Scotland, the Edinburgh Gazette, and

(c) as respects companies registered in Northern Ireland, the Belfast Gazette;

"hire-purchase agreement" has the same meaning as in the Consumer Credit Act 1974 (c. 39);

"officer", in relation to a body corporate, includes a director, manager or secretary;

"parent company" means a company that is a parent undertaking (see section 1162 and Schedule 7);

"regulated activity" has the meaning given in section 22 of the Financial Services and Markets Act 2000 (c. 8);

"regulated market" has the same meaning as in Directive 2004/39/EC of the European Parliament and of the Council on markets in financial instruments (see Article 4.1(14));

"working day", in relation to a company, means a day that is not a Saturday or Sunday, Christmas Day, Good Friday or any day that is a bank holiday under the Banking and Financial Dealings Act 1971 (c. 80) in the part of the United Kingdom where the company is registered.

(2) In relation to an EEA State that has not implemented Directive 2004/39/EC of the European Parliament and of the Council on markets in financial instruments, the following definition of "regulated market" has effect in place of that in subsection (1)—

"regulated market" has the same meaning as it has in Council Directive 93/22/EEC on investment services in the securities field.

1174. Index of defined expressions

Schedule 8 contains an index of provisions defining or otherwise explaining expressions used in the Companies Acts.

PART 39
COMPANIES: MINOR AMENDMENTS

1175. Removal of special provisions about accounts and audit of charitable companies

(1) Part 7 of the Companies Act 1985 (c. 6) and Part 8 of the Companies (Northern Ireland) Order 1986 (accounts and audit) are amended in accordance with Schedule 9 to this Act so as to remove the special provisions about companies that are charities.

(2) In that Schedule—

Part 1 contains repeals and consequential amendments of provisions of the Companies Act 1985;

Part 2 contains repeals and consequential amendments of provisions of the Companies (Northern Ireland) Order 1986.

1176. Power of Secretary of State to bring civil proceedings on company's behalf

(1) Section 438 of the Companies Act 1985 (power of Secretary of State to bring civil proceedings on company's behalf) shall cease to have effect.

(2) In section 439 of that Act (expenses of investigating company's affairs)—

(a) in subsection (2) omit ", or is ordered to pay the whole or any part of the costs of proceedings brought under section 438,";

(b) omit subsections (3) and (7) (which relate to section 438);

(c) in subsection (8)—

(i) for "subsections (2) and (3)" substitute "subsection (2)", and

(ii) omit "; and any such liability imposed by subsection (2) is (subject as mentioned above) a liability also to indemnify all persons against liability under subsection (3)".

(3) In section 453 (1A) of that Act (investigation of overseas companies: provisions not applicable), omit paragraph (b) (which relates to section 438).

(4) Nothing in this section affects proceedings brought under section 438 before the commencement of this section.

1177. Repeal of certain provisions about company directors

The following provisions of Part 10 of the Companies Act 1985 shall cease to have effect—

section 311 (prohibition on tax-free payments to directors);

sections 323 and 327 (prohibition on directors dealing in share options);

sections 324 to 326 and 328 to 329, and Parts 2 to 4 of Schedule 13 (register of directors' interests);

sections 343 and 344 (special procedure for disclosure by banks).

1178. Repeal of requirement that certain companies publish periodical statement

The following provisions shall cease to have effect—

section 720 of the Companies Act 1985 (c. 6) (certain companies to publish periodical statement), and

Schedule 23 to that Act (form of statement under section 720).

1179. Repeal of requirement that Secretary of State prepare annual report

Section 729 of the Companies Act 1985 (annual report to Parliament by Secretary of State on matters within the Companies Acts) shall cease to have effect.

1180. Repeal of certain provisions about company charges

Part 4 of the Companies Act 1989 (c. 40) (registration of company charges), which has not been brought into force, is repealed.

1181. Access to constitutional documents of RTE and RTM companies

(1) The Secretary of State may by order—

(a) amend Chapter 1 of Part 1 of the Leasehold Reform, Housing and Urban Development Act 1993 (c. 28) for the purpose of facilitating access to the provisions of the articles or any other constitutional document of RTE companies;

(b) amend Chapter 1 of Part 2 of the Commonhold and Leasehold Reform Act 2002 (c. 15) (leasehold reform) for the purpose of facilitating access to the provisions of the articles or any other constitutional document of RTM companies.

(2) References in subsection (1) to provisions of a company's articles or any other constitutional document include any provisions included in those documents by virtue of any enactment.

(3) An order under this section is subject to negative resolution procedure.

(4) In this section—

"RTE companies" has the same meaning as in Chapter 1 of Part 1 of the Leasehold Reform, Housing and Urban Development Act 1993;

"RTM companies" has the same meaning as in Chapter 1 of Part 2 of the Commonhold and Leasehold Reform Act 2002.

PART 40
COMPANY DIRECTORS: FOREIGN DISQUALIFICATION ETC

Introductory

1182. Persons subject to foreign restrictions

(1) This section defines what is meant by references in this Part to a person being subject to foreign restrictions.

(2) A person is subject to foreign restrictions if under the law of a country or territory outside the United Kingdom—

(a) he is, by reason of misconduct or unfitness, disqualified to any extent from acting in connection with the affairs of a company,

(b) he is, by reason of misconduct or unfitness, required—

(i) to obtain permission from a court or other authority, or

(ii) to meet any other condition,

before acting in connection with the affairs of a company, or

(c) he has, by reason of misconduct or unfitness, given undertakings to a court or other authority of a country or territory outside the United Kingdom—

(i) not to act in connection with the affairs of a company, or

(ii) restricting the extent to which, or the way in which, he may do so.

(3) The references in subsection (2) to acting in connection with the affairs of a company are to doing any of the following—

(a) being a director of a company,

(b) acting as receiver of a company's property, or

(c) being concerned or taking part in the promotion, formation or management of a company.

(4) In this section—

(a) "company" means a company incorporated or formed under the law of the country or territory in question, and

(b) in relation to such a company—

"director" means the holder of an office corresponding to that of director of a UK company; and

"receiver" includes any corresponding officer under the law of that country or territory.

1183. Meaning of "the court" and "UK company"

In this Part—

"the court" means—

(a) in England and Wales, the High Court or a county court;

(b) in Scotland, the Court of Session or the sheriff court;

(c) in Northern Ireland, the High Court;

"UK company" means a company registered under this Act.

Power to disqualify

1184. Disqualification of persons subject to foreign restrictions

(1) The Secretary of State may make provision by regulations disqualifying a person subject to foreign restrictions from—

(a) being a director of a UK company,

(b) acting as receiver of a UK company's property, or

    (c) in any way, whether directly or indirectly, being concerned or taking part in the promotion, formation or management of a UK company.

(2) The regulations may provide that a person subject to foreign restrictions—

    (a) is disqualified automatically by virtue of the regulations, or

    (b) may be disqualified by order of the court on the application of the Secretary of State.

(3) The regulations may provide that the Secretary of State may accept an undertaking (a "disqualification undertaking") from a person subject to foreign restrictions that he will not do anything which would be in breach of a disqualification under subsection (1).

(4) In this Part—

    (a) a "person disqualified under this Part" is a person—

        (i) disqualified as mentioned in subsection (2)(a) or (b), or

        (ii) who has given and is subject to a disqualification undertaking;

    (b) references to a breach of a disqualification include a breach of a disqualification undertaking.

(5) The regulations may provide for applications to the court by persons disqualified under this Part for permission to act in a way which would otherwise be in breach of the disqualification.

(6) The regulations must provide that a person ceases to be disqualified under this Part on his ceasing to be subject to foreign restrictions.

(7) Regulations under this section are subject to affirmative resolution procedure.

1185. Disqualification regulations: supplementary

(1) Regulations under section 1184 may make different provision for different cases and may in particular distinguish between cases by reference to—

    (a) the conduct on the basis of which the person became subject to foreign restrictions;

    (b) the nature of the foreign restrictions;

    (c) the country or territory under whose law the foreign restrictions were imposed.

(2) Regulations under section 1184 (2) (b) or (5) (provision for applications to the court)—

    (a) must specify the grounds on which an application may be made;

    (b) may specify factors to which the court shall have regard in determining an application.

(3) The regulations may, in particular, require the court to have regard to the following factors—

    (a) whether the conduct on the basis of which the person became subject to foreign restrictions would, if done in relation to a UK company, have led a court to make a disqualification order on an application under the Company Directors Disqualification Act 1986 (c. 46) or the Company Directors Disqualification (Northern Ireland) Order 2002 (S.I. 2002/3150 (N.I. 4));

    (b) in a case in which the conduct on the basis of which the person became subject to foreign restrictions would not be unlawful if done in relation to a UK company, the fact that the person acted unlawfully under foreign law;

    (c) whether the person's activities in relation to UK companies began after he became subject to foreign restrictions;

    (d) whether the person's activities (or proposed activities) in relation to UK companies are undertaken (or are proposed to be undertaken) outside the United Kingdom.

(4) Regulations under section 1184 (3) (provision as to undertakings given to the Secretary of State) may include provision allowing the Secretary of State, in determining whether to accept an undertaking, to take into account matters other than criminal convictions notwithstanding that the person may be criminally liable in respect of those matters.

(5) Regulations under section 1184 (5) (provision for application to court for permission to act) may include provision—

    (a) entitling the Secretary of State to be represented at the hearing of the application, and

    (b) as to the giving of evidence or the calling of witnesses by the Secretary of State at the hearing of the application.

1186. Offence of breach of disqualification

    (1) Regulations under section 1184 may provide that a person disqualified under this Part who acts in breach of the disqualification commits an offence.

    (2) The regulations may provide that a person guilty of such an offence is liable—

        (a) on conviction on indictment, to imprisonment for a term not exceeding two years or a fine (or both);

        (b) on summary conviction—

            (i) in England and Wales, to imprisonment for a term not exceeding twelve months or to a fine not exceeding the statutory maximum (or both);

            (ii) in Scotland or Northern Ireland, to imprisonment for a term not exceeding six months, or to a fine not exceeding the statutory maximum (or both).

    (3) In relation to an offence committed before the commencement of section 154 (1) of the Criminal Justice Act 2003 (c. 44), for "twelve months" in subsection (2)(b)(i) substitute "six months".

Power to make persons liable for company's debts

1187. Personal liability for debts of company

    (1) The Secretary of State may provide by regulations that a person who, at a time when he is subject to foreign restrictions—

        (a) is a director of a UK company, or

        (b) is involved in the management of a UK company,

is personally responsible for all debts and other liabilities of the company incurred during that time.

    (2) A person who is personally responsible by virtue of this section for debts and other liabilities of a company is jointly and severally liable in respect of those debts and liabilities with—

        (a) the company, and

        (b) any other person who (whether by virtue of this section or otherwise) is so liable.

    (3) For the purposes of this section a person is involved in the management of a company if he is concerned, whether directly or indirectly, or takes part, in the management of the company.

    (4) The regulations may make different provision for different cases and may in particular distinguish between cases by reference to—

        (a) the conduct on the basis of which the person became subject to foreign restrictions;

        (b) the nature of the foreign restrictions;

        (c) the country or territory under whose law the foreign restrictions were imposed.

    (5) Regulations under this section are subject to affirmative resolution procedure.

Power to require statements to be sent to the registrar of companies

1188. Statements from persons subject to foreign restrictions

    (1) The Secretary of State may make provision by regulations requiring a person who—

        (a) is subject to foreign restrictions, and

        (b) is not disqualified under this Part,

to send a statement to the registrar if he does anything that, if done by a person disqualified under this Part, would be in breach of the disqualification.

    (2) The statement must include such information as may be specified in the regulations relating to—

        (a) the person's activities in relation to UK companies, and

        (b) the foreign restrictions to which the person is subject.

    (3) The statement must be sent to the registrar within such period as may be specified in the regulations.

(4) The regulations may make different provision for different cases and may in particular distinguish between cases by reference to—

(a) the conduct on the basis of which the person became subject to foreign restrictions;

(b) the nature of the foreign restrictions;

(c) the country or territory under whose law the foreign restrictions were imposed.

(5) Regulations under this section are subject to affirmative resolution procedure.

1189. Statements from persons disqualified

(1) The Secretary of State may make provision by regulations requiring a statement or notice sent to the registrar of companies under any of the provisions listed below that relates (wholly or partly) to a person who—

(a) is a person disqualified under this Part, or

(b) is subject to a disqualification order or disqualification undertaking under the Company Directors Disqualification Act 1986 (c. 46) or the Company Directors Disqualification (Northern Ireland) Order 2002 (S.I. 2002/3150 (N.I. 4)),

to be accompanied by an additional statement.

(2) The provisions referred to above are—

(a) section 12 (statement of a company's proposed officers),

(b) section 167 (2) (notice of person having become director), and

(c) section 276 (notice of a person having become secretary or one of joint secretaries).

(3) The additional statement is a statement that the person has obtained permission from a court, on an application under section 1184 (5) or (as the case may be) for the purposes of section 1 (1) (a) of the Company Directors Disqualification Act 1986 (c. 46) or Article 3(1) of the Company Directors Disqualification (Northern Ireland) Order 2002 (S.I. 2002/3150 (N.I. 4)), to act in the capacity in question.

(4) Regulations under this section are subject to affirmative resolution procedure.

1190. Statements: whether to be made public

(1) Regulations under section 1188 or 1189 (statements required to be sent to registrar) may provide that a statement sent to the registrar of companies under the regulations is to be treated as a record relating to a company for the purposes of section 1080 (the companies register).

(2) The regulations may make provision as to the circumstances in which such a statement is to be, or may be—

(a) withheld from public inspection, or

(b) removed from the register.

(3) The regulations may, in particular, provide that a statement is not to be withheld from public inspection or removed from the register unless the person to whom it relates provides such information, and satisfies such other conditions, as may be specified.

(4) The regulations may provide that section 1081 (note of removal of material from the register) does not apply, or applies with such modifications as may be specified, in the case of material removed from the register under the regulations.

(5) In this section "specified" means specified in the regulations.

1191. Offences

(1) Regulations under section 1188 or 1189 may provide that it is an offence for a person—

(a) to fail to comply with a requirement under the regulations to send a statement to the registrar;

(b) knowingly or recklessly to send a statement under the regulations to the registrar that is misleading, false or deceptive in a material particular.

(2) The regulations may provide that a person guilty of such an offence is liable—

(a) on conviction on indictment, to imprisonment for a term not exceeding two years or a fine (or both);

   (b) on summary conviction—

    (i) in England and Wales, to imprisonment for a term not exceeding twelve months or to a fine not exceeding the statutory maximum (or both);

    (ii) in Scotland or Northern Ireland, to imprisonment for a term not exceeding six months, or to a fine not exceeding the statutory maximum (or both).

  (3) In relation to an offence committed before the commencement of section 154 (1) of the Criminal Justice Act 2003 (c. 44), for "twelve months" in subsection (2)(b)(i) substitute "six months".

PART 41
BUSINESS NAMES

CHAPTER 1 RESTRICTED OR PROHIBITED NAMES

Introductory

1192. Application of this Chapter

  (1) This Chapter applies to any person carrying on business in the United Kingdom.

  (2) The provisions of this Chapter do not prevent—

   (a) an individual carrying on business under a name consisting of his surname without any addition other than a permitted addition, or

   (b) individuals carrying on business in partnership under a name consisting of the surnames of all the partners without any addition other than a permitted addition.

  (3) The following are the permitted additions—

   (a) in the case of an individual, his forename or initial;

   (b) in the case of a partnership—

    (i) the forenames of individual partners or the initials of those forenames, or

    (ii) where two or more individual partners have the same surname, the addition of "s" at the end of that surname;

   (c) in either case, an addition merely indicating that the business is carried on in succession to a former owner of the business.

Sensitive words or expressions

1193. Name suggesting connection with government or public authority

  (1) A person must not, without the approval of the Secretary of State, carry on business in the United Kingdom under a name that would be likely to give the impression that the business is connected with—

   (a) Her Majesty's Government, any part of the Scottish administration or Her Majesty's Government in Northern Ireland,

   (b) any local authority, or

   (c) any public authority specified for the purposes of this section by regulations made by the Secretary of State.

  (2) For the purposes of this section—

   "local authority" means—

   (a) a local authority within the meaning of the Local Government Act 1972 (c. 70), the Common Council of the City of London or the Council of the Isles of Scilly,

   (b) a council constituted under section 2 of the Local Government etc. (Scotland) Act 1994 (c. 39), or

   (c) a district council in Northern Ireland;

   "public authority" includes any person or body having functions of a public nature.

(3) Regulations under this section are subject to affirmative resolution procedure.

(4) A person who contravenes this section commits an offence.

(5) Where an offence under this section is committed by a body corporate, an offence is also committed by every officer of the body who is in default.

(6) A person guilty of an offence under this section is liable on summary conviction to a fine not exceeding level 3 on the standard scale and, for continued contravention, a daily default fine not exceeding one-tenth of level 3 on the standard scale.

1194. Other sensitive words or expressions

(1) A person must not, without the approval of the Secretary of State, carry on business in the United Kingdom under a name that includes a word or expression for the time being specified in regulations made by the Secretary of State under this section.

(2) Regulations under this section are subject to approval after being made.

(3) A person who contravenes this section commits an offence.

(4) Where an offence under this section is committed by a body corporate, an offence is also committed by every officer of the body who is in default.

(5) A person guilty of an offence under this section is liable on summary conviction to a fine not exceeding level 3 on the standard scale and, for continued contravention, a daily default fine not exceeding one-tenth of level 3 on the standard scale.

1195. Requirement to seek comments of government department or other relevant body

(1) The Secretary of State may by regulations under—

(a) section 1193 (name suggesting connection with government or public authority), or

(b) section 1194 (other sensitive words or expressions),

require that, in connection with an application for the approval of the Secretary of State under that section, the applicant must seek the view of a specified Government department or other body.

(2) Where such a requirement applies, the applicant must request the specified department or other body (in writing) to indicate whether (and if so why) it has any objections to the proposed name.

(3) He must submit to the Secretary of State a statement that such a request has been made and a copy of any response received from the specified body.

(4) If these requirements are not complied with, the Secretary of State may refuse to consider the application for approval.

(5) In this section "specified" means specified in the regulations.

1196. Withdrawal of Secretary of State's approval

(1) This section applies to approval given for the purposes of—

section 1193 (name suggesting connection with government or public authority), or

section 1194 (other sensitive words or expressions).

(2) If it appears to the Secretary of State that there are overriding considerations of public policy that require such approval to be withdrawn, the approval may be withdrawn by notice in writing given to the person concerned.

(3) The notice must state the date as from which approval is withdrawn.

Misleading names

1197. Name containing inappropriate indication of company type or legal form

(1) The Secretary of State may make provision by regulations prohibiting a person from carrying on business in the United Kingdom under a name consisting of or containing specified words, expressions or other indications—

(a) that are associated with a particular type of company or form of organisation, or

(b) that are similar to words, expressions or other indications associated with a particular type of company or form of organisation.

(2) The regulations may prohibit the use of words, expressions or other indications—

    (a) in a specified part, or otherwise than in a specified part, of a name;

    (b) in conjunction with, or otherwise than in conjunction with, such other words, expressions or indications as may be specified.

(3) In this section "specified" means specified in the regulations.

(4) Regulations under this section are subject to negative resolution procedure.

(5) A person who uses a name in contravention of regulations under this section commits an offence.

(6) Where an offence under this section is committed by a body corporate, an offence is also committed by every officer of the body who is in default.

(7) A person guilty of an offence under this section is liable on summary conviction to a fine not exceeding level 3 on the standard scale and, for continued contravention, a daily default fine not exceeding one-tenth of level 3 on the standard scale.

1198. Name giving misleading indication of activities

(1) A person must not carry on business in the United Kingdom under a name that gives so misleading an indication of the nature of the activities of the business as to be likely to cause harm to the public.

(2) A person who uses a name in contravention of this section commits an offence.

(3) Where an offence under this section is committed by a body corporate, an offence is also committed by every officer of the body who is in default.

(4) A person guilty of an offence under this section is liable on summary conviction to a fine not exceeding level 3 on the standard scale and, for continued contravention, a daily default fine not exceeding one-tenth of level 3 on the standard scale.

Supplementary

1199. Savings for existing lawful business names

(1) This section has effect in relation to—

sections 1192 to 1196 (sensitive words or expressions), and

section 1197 (inappropriate indication of company type or legal form).

(2) Those sections do not apply to the carrying on of a business by a person who—

    (a) carried on the business immediately before the date on which this Chapter came into force, and

    (b) continues to carry it on under the name that immediately before that date was its lawful business name.

(3) Where—

    (a) a business is transferred to a person on or after the date on which this Chapter came into force, and

    (b) that person carries on the business under the name that was its lawful business name immediately before the transfer,

those sections do not apply in relation to the carrying on of the business under that name during the period of twelve months beginning with the date of the transfer.

(4) In this section "lawful business name", in relation to a business, means a name under which the business was carried on without contravening—

    (a) section 2 (1) of the Business Names Act 1985 (c. 7) or Article 4(1) of the Business Names (Northern Ireland) Order 1986 (S.I. 1986/1033 N.I. 7)), or

    (b) after this Chapter has come into force, the provisions of this Chapter.

CHAPTER 2
DISCLOSURE REQUIRED IN CASE OF INDIVIDUAL OR PARTNERSHIP

Introductory

1200. Application of this Chapter

(1) This Chapter applies to an individual or partnership carrying on business in the United Kingdom under a business name.

References in this Chapter to "a person to whom this Chapter applies" are to such an individual or partnership.

(2) For the purposes of this Chapter a "business name" means a name other than—

    (a) in the case of an individual, his surname without any addition other than a permitted addition;

    (b) in the case of a partnership—

        (i) the surnames of all partners who are individuals, and

        (ii) the corporate names of all partners who are bodies corporate,

    without any addition other than a permitted addition.

(3) The following are the permitted additions—

    (a) in the case of an individual, his forename or initial;

    (b) in the case of a partnership—

        (i) the forenames of individual partners or the initials of those forenames, or

        (ii) where two or more individual partners have the same surname, the addition of "s" at the end of that surname;

    (c) in either case, an addition merely indicating that the business is carried on in succession to a former owner of the business.

1201. Information required to be disclosed

The "information required by this Chapter" is—

(a) in the case of an individual, his name;

(b) in the case of a partnership, the name of each member of the partnership;

and in relation to each person so named, an address in the United Kingdom at which service of any document relating in any way to the business will be effective.

Disclosure requirements

1202. Disclosure required: business documents etc

(1) A person to whom this Chapter applies must state the information required by this Chapter, in legible characters, on all—

    (a) business letters,

    (b) written orders for goods or services to be supplied to the business,

    (c) invoices and receipts issued in the course of the business, and

    (d) written demands for payment of debts arising in the course of the business.

This subsection has effect subject to section 1203 (exemption for large partnerships if certain conditions met).

(2) A person to whom this Chapter applies must secure that the information required by this Chapter is immediately given, by written notice, to any person with whom anything is done or discussed in the course of the business and who asks for that information.

(3) The Secretary of State may by regulations require that such notices be given in a specified form.

(4) Regulations under this section are subject to negative resolution procedure.

1203. Exemption for large partnerships if certain conditions met

(1) Section 1202 (1) (disclosure required in business documents) does not apply in relation to a document issued by a partnership of more than 20 persons if the following conditions are met.

(2) The conditions are that—

(a) the partnership maintains at its principal place of business a list of the names of all the partners,

(b) no partner's name appears in the document, except in the text or as a signatory, and

(c) the document states in legible characters the address of the partnership's principal place of business and that the list of the partners' names is open to inspection there.

(3) Where a partnership maintains a list of the partners' names for the purposes of this section, any person may inspect the list during office hours.

(4) Where an inspection required by a person in accordance with this section is refused, an offence is committed by any member of the partnership concerned who without reasonable excuse refused the inspection or permitted it to be refused.

(5) A person guilty of an offence under subsection (4) is liable on summary conviction to a fine not exceeding level 3 on the standard scale and, for continued contravention, a daily default fine not exceeding one-tenth of level 3 on the standard scale.

1204. Disclosure required: business premises

(1) A person to whom this Chapter applies must, in any premises—

(a) where the business is carried on, and

(b) to which customers of the business or suppliers of goods or services to the business have access,

display in a prominent position, so that it may easily be read by such customers or suppliers, a notice containing the information required by this Chapter.

(2) The Secretary of State may by regulations require that such notices be displayed in a specified form.

(3) Regulations under this section are subject to negative resolution procedure.

Consequences of failure to make required disclosure

1205. Criminal consequences of failure to make required disclosure

(1) A person who without reasonable excuse fails to comply with the requirements of—

section 1202 (disclosure required: business documents etc), or

section 1204 (disclosure required: business premises),

commits an offence.

(2) Where an offence under this section is committed by a body corporate, an offence is also committed by every officer of the body who is in default.

(3) A person guilty of an offence under this section is liable on summary conviction to a fine not exceeding level 3 on the standard scale and, for continued contravention, a daily default fine not exceeding one-tenth of level 3 on the standard scale.

(4) References in this section to the requirements of section 1202 or 1204 include the requirements of regulations under that section.

1206. Civil consequences of failure to make required disclosure

(1) This section applies to any legal proceedings brought by a person to whom this Chapter applies to enforce a right arising out of a contract made in the course of a business in respect of which he was, at the time the contract was made, in breach of section 1202 (1) or (2) (disclosure in business documents etc) or section 1204 (1) (disclosure at business premises).

(2) The proceedings shall be dismissed if the defendant (in Scotland, the defender) to the proceedings shows—

(a) that he has a claim against the claimant (pursuer) arising out of the contract that he has been unable to pursue by reason of the latter's breach of the requirements of this Chapter, or

    (b) that he has suffered some financial loss in connection with the contract by reason of the claimant's (pursuer's) breach of those requirements,

unless the court before which the proceedings are brought is satisfied that it is just and equitable to permit the proceedings to continue.

(3) References in this section to the requirements of this Chapter include the requirements of regulations under this Chapter.

(4) This section does not affect the right of any person to enforce such rights as he may have against another person in any proceedings brought by that person.

CHAPTER 3
SUPPLEMENTARY

1207. Application of general provisions about offences

The provisions of sections 1121 to 1123 (liability of officer in default) and 1125 to 1131 (general provisions about offences) apply in relation to offences under this Part as in relation to offences under the Companies Acts.

1208. Interpretation

In this Part—

"business" includes a profession;

"initial" includes any recognised abbreviation of a name;

"partnership" means—

(a) a partnership within the Partnership Act 1890 (c. 39), or

(b) a limited partnership registered under the Limited Partnerships Act 1907 (c. 24),

or a firm or entity of a similar character formed under the law of a country or territory outside the United Kingdom;

"surname", in relation to a peer or person usually known by a British title different from his surname, means the title by which he is known.

PART 42
STATUTORY AUDITORS

CHAPTER 1
INTRODUCTORY

1209. Main purposes of Part

The main purposes of this Part are—

(a) to secure that only persons who are properly supervised and appropriately qualified are appointed as statutory auditors, and

(b) to secure that audits by persons so appointed are carried out properly, with integrity and with a proper degree of independence.

1210. Meaning of "statutory auditor" etc

(1) In this Part "statutory auditor" means—

(a) a person appointed as auditor under Part 16 of this Act,

(b) a person appointed as auditor under section 77 of or Schedule 11 to the Building Societies Act 1986 (c. 53),

(c) a person appointed as auditor of an insurer that is a friendly society under section 72 of or Schedule 14 to the Friendly Societies Act 1992 (c. 40),

(d) a person appointed as auditor of an insurer that is an industrial and provident society under section 4 of the Friendly and Industrial and Provident Societies Act 1968 (c. 55) or under section 38 of the Industrial and Provident Societies Act (Northern Ireland) 1969 (c. 24 (N.I.)),

    (e) a person appointed as auditor for the purposes of regulation 3 of the Insurance Accounts Directive (Lloyd's Syndicate and Aggregate Accounts) Regulations 2004 (S.I. 2004/3219) or appointed to report on the "aggregate accounts" within the meaning of those Regulations,

    (f) a person appointed as auditor of an insurer for the purposes of regulation 3 of the Insurance Accounts Directive (Miscellaneous Insurance Undertakings) Regulations 1993 (S.I. 1993/3245),

    (g) a person appointed as auditor of a bank for the purposes of regulation 4 of the Bank Accounts Directive (Miscellaneous Banks) Regulations 1991 (S.I. 1991/2704), and

    (h) a person appointed as auditor of a prescribed person under a prescribed enactment authorising or requiring the appointment;

and the expressions "statutory audit" and "statutory audit work" are to be construed accordingly.

(2) In this Part "audited person" means the person in respect of whom a statutory audit is conducted.

(3) In subsection (1)—

"bank" means a person who—

    (a) is a credit institution within the meaning given by Article 4.1(a) of Directive 2006/48/EC of the European Parliament and of the Council relating to the taking up and pursuit of the business of credit institutions, and

    (b) is a company or a firm as defined in Article 48 of the Treaty establishing the European Community;

"friendly society" means a friendly society within the meaning of the Friendly Societies Act 1992 (c. 40);

"industrial and provident society" means—

    (a) a society registered under the Industrial and Provident Societies Act 1965 (c. 12) or a society deemed by virtue of section 4 of that Act to be so registered, or

    (b) a society registered under the Industrial and Provident Societies Act (Northern Ireland) 1969 or a society deemed by virtue of section 4 of that Act to be so registered;

"insurer" means a person who is an insurance undertaking within the meaning given by Article 2.1 of Council Directive 1991/674/EEC on the annual accounts and consolidated accounts of insurance undertakings;

"prescribed" means prescribed, or of a description prescribed, by order made by the Secretary of State for the purposes of subsection (1)(h).

(4) An order under this section is subject to negative resolution procedure.

1211. Eligibility for appointment as a statutory auditor: overview

A person is eligible for appointment as a statutory auditor only if the person is so eligible—

(a) by virtue of Chapter 2 (individuals and firms), or

(b) by virtue of Chapter 3 (Comptroller and Auditor General, etc).

CHAPTER 2
INDIVIDUALS AND FIRMS

Eligibility for appointment

1212. Individuals and firms: eligibility for appointment as a statutory auditor

(1) An individual or firm is eligible for appointment as a statutory auditor if the individual or firm—

    (a) is a member of a recognised supervisory body, and

    (b) is eligible for appointment under the rules of that body.

(2) In the cases to which section 1222 applies (individuals retaining only 1967 Act authorisation) a person's eligibility for appointment as a statutory auditor is restricted as mentioned in that section.

1213. Effect of ineligibility

(1) No person may act as statutory auditor of an audited person if he is ineligible for appointment as a statutory auditor.

(2) If at any time during his term of office a statutory auditor becomes ineligible for appointment as a statutory auditor, he must immediately—
  (a) resign his office (with immediate effect), and
  (b) give notice in writing to the audited person that he has resigned by reason of his becoming ineligible for appointment.

(3) A person is guilty of an offence if—
  (a) he acts as a statutory auditor in contravention of subsection (1), or
  (b) he fails to give the notice mentioned in paragraph (b) of subsection (2) in accordance with that subsection.

(4) A person guilty of an offence under subsection (3) is liable—
  (a) on conviction on indictment, to a fine;
  (b) on summary conviction, to a fine not exceeding the statutory maximum.

(5) A person is guilty of an offence if—
  (a) he has been convicted of an offence under subsection (3)(a) or this subsection, and
  (b) he continues to act as a statutory auditor in contravention of subsection (1) after the conviction.

(6) A person is guilty of an offence if—
  (a) he has been convicted of an offence under subsection (3)(b) or this subsection, and
  (b) he continues, after the conviction, to fail to give the notice mentioned in subsection (2)(b).

(7) A person guilty of an offence under subsection (5) or (6) is liable—
  (a) on conviction on indictment, to a fine;
  (b) on summary conviction, to a fine not exceeding one-tenth of the statutory maximum for each day on which the act or the failure continues.

(8) In proceedings against a person for an offence under this section it is a defence for him to show that he did not know and had no reason to believe that he was, or had become, ineligible for appointment as a statutory auditor.

Independence requirement

1214. Independence requirement

(1) A person may not act as statutory auditor of an audited person if one or more of subsections (2), (3) and (4) apply to him.

(2) This subsection applies if the person is—
  (a) an officer or employee of the audited person, or
  (b) a partner or employee of such a person, or a partnership of which such a person is a partner.

(3) This subsection applies if the person is—
  (a) an officer or employee of an associated undertaking of the audited person, or
  (b) a partner or employee of such a person, or a partnership of which such a person is a partner.

(4) This subsection applies if there exists, between—
  (a) the person or an associate of his, and
  (b) the audited person or an associated undertaking of the audited person,

a connection of any such description as may be specified by regulations made by the Secretary of State.

(5) An auditor of an audited person is not to be regarded as an officer or employee of the person for the purposes of subsections (2) and (3).

(6) In this section "associated undertaking", in relation to an audited person, means—

    (a) a parent undertaking or subsidiary undertaking of the audited person, or

    (b) a subsidiary undertaking of a parent undertaking of the audited person.

(7) Regulations under subsection (4) are subject to negative resolution procedure.

1215. Effect of lack of independence

(1) If at any time during his term of office a statutory auditor becomes prohibited from acting by section 1214(1), he must immediately—

    (a) resign his office (with immediate effect), and

    (b) give notice in writing to the audited person that he has resigned by reason of his lack of independence.

(2) A person is guilty of an offence if—

    (a) he acts as a statutory auditor in contravention of section 1214(1), or

    (b) he fails to give the notice mentioned in paragraph (b) of subsection (1) in accordance with that subsection.

(3) A person guilty of an offence under subsection (2) is liable—

    (a) on conviction on indictment, to a fine;

    (b) on summary conviction, to a fine not exceeding the statutory maximum.

(4) A person is guilty of an offence if—

    (a) he has been convicted of an offence under subsection (2)(a) or this subsection, and

    (b) he continues to act as a statutory auditor in contravention of section 1214(1) after the conviction.

(5) A person is guilty of an offence if—

    (a) he has been convicted of an offence under subsection (2)(b) or this subsection, and

    (b) after the conviction, he continues to fail to give the notice mentioned in subsection (1)(b).

(6) A person guilty of an offence under subsection (4) or (5) is liable—

    (a) on conviction on indictment, to a fine;

    (b) on summary conviction, to a fine not exceeding one-tenth of the statutory maximum for each day on which the act or the failure continues.

(7) In proceedings against a person for an offence under this section it is a defence for him to show that he did not know and had no reason to believe that he was, or had become, prohibited from acting as statutory auditor of the audited person by section 1214(1).

Effect of appointment of a partnership

1216. Effect of appointment of a partnership

(1) This section applies where a partnership constituted under the law of—

    (a) England and Wales,

    (b) Northern Ireland, or

    (c) any other country or territory in which a partnership is not a legal person,

is by virtue of this Chapter appointed as statutory auditor of an audited person.

(2) Unless a contrary intention appears, the appointment is an appointment of the partnership as such and not of the partners.

(3) Where the partnership ceases, the appointment is to be treated as extending to—

    (a) any appropriate partnership which succeeds to the practice of that partnership, or

    (b) any other appropriate person who succeeds to that practice having previously carried it on in partnership.

(4) For the purposes of subsection (3)—

    (a) a partnership is to be regarded as succeeding to the practice of another partnership only if the members of the successor partnership are substantially the same as those of the former partnership, and

    (b) a partnership or other person is to be regarded as succeeding to the practice of a partnership only if it or he succeeds to the whole or substantially the whole of the business of the former partnership.

(5) Where the partnership ceases and the appointment is not treated under subsection (3) as extending to any partnership or other person, the appointment may with the consent of the audited person be treated as extending to an appropriate partnership, or other appropriate person, who succeeds to—

    (a) the business of the former partnership, or

    (b) such part of it as is agreed by the audited person is to be treated as comprising the appointment.

(6) For the purposes of this section, a partnership or other person is "appropriate" if it or he—

    (a) is eligible for appointment as a statutory auditor by virtue of this Chapter, and

    (b) is not prohibited by section 1214(1) from acting as statutory auditor of the audited person.

Supervisory bodies

1217. Supervisory bodies

(1) In this Part a "supervisory body" means a body established in the United Kingdom (whether a body corporate or an unincorporated association) which maintains and enforces rules as to—

    (a) the eligibility of persons for appointment as a statutory auditor, and

    (b) the conduct of statutory audit work,

which are binding on persons seeking appointment or acting as a statutory auditor either because they are members of that body or because they are otherwise subject to its control.

(2) In this Part references to the members of a supervisory body are to the persons who, whether or not members of the body, are subject to its rules in seeking appointment or acting as a statutory auditor.

(3) In this Part references to the rules of a supervisory body are to the rules (whether or not laid down by the body itself) which the body has power to enforce and which are relevant for the purposes of this Part.

This includes rules relating to the admission or expulsion of members of the body, so far as relevant for the purposes of this Part.

(4) Schedule 10 has effect with respect to the recognition of supervisory bodies for the purposes of this Part.

1218. Exemption from liability for damages

(1) No person within subsection (2) is to be liable in damages for anything done or omitted in the discharge or purported discharge of functions to which this subsection applies.

(2) The persons within this subsection are—

    (a) any recognised supervisory body,

    (b) any officer or employee of a recognised supervisory body, and

    (c) any member of the governing body of a recognised supervisory body.

(3) Subsection (1) applies to the functions of a recognised supervisory body so far as relating to, or to matters arising out of, any of the following—

    (a) rules, practices, powers and arrangements of the body to which the requirements of Part 2 of Schedule 10 apply;

    (b) the obligations with which paragraph 20 of that Schedule requires the body to comply;

    (c) any guidance issued by the body;

    (d) the obligations imposed on the body by or by virtue of this Part.

(4) The reference in subsection (3)(c) to guidance issued by a recognised supervisory body is a reference to any guidance or recommendation which is—

(a) issued or made by it to all or any class of its members or persons seeking to become members, and

(b) relevant for the purposes of this Part,

including any guidance or recommendation relating to the admission or expulsion of members of the body, so far as relevant for the purposes of this Part.

(5) Subsection (1) does not apply—

(a) if the act or omission is shown to have been in bad faith, or

(b) so as to prevent an award of damages in respect of the act or omission on the ground that it was unlawful as a result of section 6(1) of the Human Rights Act 1998 (c. 42) (acts of public authorities incompatible with Convention rights).

Professional qualifications

1219. Appropriate qualifications

(1) A person holds an appropriate qualification for the purposes of this Chapter if and only if—

(a) he holds a recognised professional qualification obtained in the United Kingdom,

(b) immediately before the commencement of this Chapter, he—

(i) held an appropriate qualification for the purposes of Part 2 of the Companies Act 1989 (c. 40) (eligibility for appointment as company auditor) by virtue of section 31(1)(a) or (c) of that Act, or

(ii) was treated as holding an appropriate qualification for those purposes by virtue of section 31(2), (3) or (4) of that Act,

(c) immediately before the commencement of this Chapter, he—

(i) held an appropriate qualification for the purposes of Part III of the Companies (Northern Ireland) Order 1990 (S.I. 1990/593 (N.I. 5)) by virtue of Article 34(1)(a) or (c) of that Order, or

(ii) was treated as holding an appropriate qualification for those purposes by virtue of Article 34(2), (3) or (4) of that Order,

(d) he is within subsection (2),

(e) he has been authorised to practise the profession of statutory auditor pursuant to the European Communities (Recognition of Professional Qualifications) (First General System) Regulations 2005 (S.I. 2005/18) and has fulfilled any requirements imposed pursuant to regulation 6 of those Regulations, or

(f) subject to any direction under section 1221(5), he is regarded for the purposes of this Chapter as holding an approved overseas qualification.

(2) A person is within this subsection if—

(a) before 1st January 1990, he began a course of study or practical training leading to a professional qualification in accountancy offered by a body established in the United Kingdom,

(b) he obtained that qualification on or after 1st January 1990 and before 1st January 1996, and

(c) the Secretary of State approves his qualification as an appropriate qualification for the purposes of this Chapter.

(3) The Secretary of State may approve a qualification under subsection (2)(c) only if he is satisfied that, at the time the qualification was awarded, the body concerned had adequate arrangements to ensure that the qualification was awarded only to persons educated and trained to a standard equivalent to that required, at that time, in the case of a recognised professional qualification under Part 2 of the Companies Act 1989 (c. 40) (eligibility for appointment as company auditor).

1220. Qualifying bodies and recognised professional qualifications

(1) In this Part a "qualifying body" means a body established in the United Kingdom (whether a body corporate or an unincorporated association) which offers a professional qualification in accountancy.

(2) In this Part references to the rules of a qualifying body are to the rules (whether or not laid down by the body itself) which the body has power to enforce and which are relevant for the purposes of this Part.

This includes, so far as so relevant, rules relating to—

(a) admission to or expulsion from a course of study leading to a qualification,

(b) the award or deprivation of a qualification, or

(c) the approval of a person for the purposes of giving practical training or the withdrawal of such approval.

(3) Schedule 11 has effect with respect to the recognition for the purposes of this Part of a professional qualification offered by a qualifying body.

1221. Approval of overseas qualifications

(1) The Secretary of State may declare that the following are to be regarded for the purposes of this Chapter as holding an approved overseas qualification—

(a) persons who are qualified to audit accounts under the law of a specified foreign country, or

(b) persons who hold a specified professional qualification in accountancy obtained in a specified foreign country.

(2) A declaration under subsection (1)(b) may be expressed to be subject to the satisfaction of any specified requirement or requirements.

(3) The Secretary of State may make a declaration under subsection (1) only if he is satisfied that—

(a) in the case of a declaration under subsection (1)(a), the fact that the persons in question are qualified to audit accounts under the law of the specified foreign country, or

(b) in the case of a declaration under subsection (1)(b), the specified professional qualification taken with any requirement or requirements to be specified under subsection (2),

affords an assurance of professional competence equivalent to that afforded by a recognised professional qualification.

(4) The Secretary of State may make a declaration under subsection (1) only if he is satisfied that the treatment that the persons who are the subject of the declaration will receive as a result of it is comparable to the treatment which is, or is likely to be, afforded in the specified foreign country or a part of it to—

(a) in the case of a declaration under subsection (1)(a), some or all persons who are eligible to be appointed as a statutory auditor, and

(b) in the case of a declaration under subsection (1)(b), some or all persons who hold a corresponding recognised professional qualification.

(5) The Secretary of State may direct that persons holding an approved overseas qualification are not to be treated as holding an appropriate qualification for the purposes of this Chapter unless they hold such additional educational qualifications as the Secretary of State may specify for the purpose of ensuring that such persons have an adequate knowledge of the law and practice in the United Kingdom relevant to the audit of accounts.

(6) The Secretary of State may give different directions in relation to different approved overseas qualifications.

(7) The Secretary of State may, if he thinks fit, having regard to the considerations mentioned in subsections (3) and (4), withdraw a declaration under subsection (1) in relation to—

(a) persons becoming qualified to audit accounts under the law of the specified foreign country after such date as he may specify, or

    (b) persons obtaining the specified professional qualification after such date as he may specify.

(8) The Secretary of State may, if he thinks fit, having regard to the considerations mentioned in subsections (3) and (4), vary or revoke a requirement specified under subsection (2) from such date as he may specify.

(9) In this section "foreign country", in relation to any time, means a country or territory that, at that time, is not a "relevant State" within the meaning of the European Communities (Recognition of Professional Qualifications) (First General System) Regulations 2005 (S.I. 2005/18) or part of such a State.

1222. Eligibility of individuals retaining only 1967 Act authorisation

(1) A person whose only appropriate qualification is based on his retention of an authorisation originally granted by the Board of Trade or the Secretary of State under section 13(1) of the Companies Act 1967 (c. 81) is eligible only for appointment as auditor of an unquoted company.

(2) A company is "unquoted" if, at the time of the person's appointment, neither the company, nor any parent undertaking of which it is a subsidiary undertaking, is a quoted company within the meaning of section 385(2).

(3) References to a person eligible for appointment as a statutory auditor by virtue of this Part in enactments relating to eligibility for appointment as auditor of a person other than a company do not include a person to whom this section applies.

Information

1223. Matters to be notified to the Secretary of State

(1) The Secretary of State may require a recognised supervisory body or a recognised qualifying body—
    (a) to notify him immediately of the occurrence of such events as he may specify in writing and to give him such information in respect of those events as is so specified;
    (b) to give him, at such times or in respect of such periods as he may specify in writing, such information as is so specified.

(2) The notices and information required to be given must be such as the Secretary of State may reasonably require for the exercise of his functions under this Part.

(3) The Secretary of State may require information given under this section to be given in a specified form or verified in a specified manner.

(4) Any notice or information required to be given under this section must be given in writing unless the Secretary of State specifies or approves some other manner.

1224. The Secretary of State's power to call for information

(1) The Secretary of State may by notice in writing require a person within subsection (2) to give him such information as he may reasonably require for the exercise of his functions under this Part.

(2) The persons within this subsection are—
    (a) any recognised supervisory body,
    (b) any recognised qualifying body, and
    (c) any person eligible for appointment as a statutory auditor by virtue of this Chapter.

(3) The Secretary of State may require that any information which he requires under this section is to be given within such reasonable time and verified in such manner as he may specify.

Enforcement

1225. Compliance orders

(1) If at any time it appears to the Secretary of State—

    (a) in the case of a recognised supervisory body, that any requirement of Schedule 10 is not satisfied,

    (b) in the case of a recognised professional qualification, that any requirement of Schedule 11 is not satisfied, or

    (c) that a recognised supervisory body or a recognised qualifying body has failed to comply with an obligation to which it is subject under or by virtue of this Part,

he may, instead of revoking the relevant recognition order, make an application to the court under this section.

(2) If on an application under this section the court decides that the requirement in question is not satisfied or, as the case may be, that the body has failed to comply with the obligation in question, it may order the body to take such steps as the court directs for securing that the requirement is satisfied or that the obligation is complied with.

(3) In this section "the court" means the High Court or, in Scotland, the Court of Session.

CHAPTER 3

AUDITORS GENERAL

Eligibility for appointment

1226. Auditors General: eligibility for appointment as a statutory auditor

(1) In this Part "Auditor General" means—

    (a) the Comptroller and Auditor General,

    (b) the Auditor General for Scotland,

    (c) the Auditor General for Wales, or

    (d) the Comptroller and Auditor General for Northern Ireland.

(2) An Auditor General is eligible for appointment as a statutory auditor.

(3) Subsection (2) is subject to any suspension notice having effect under section 1234 (notices suspending eligibility for appointment as a statutory auditor).

Conduct of audits

1227. Individuals responsible for audit work on behalf of Auditors General

An Auditor General must secure that each individual responsible for statutory audit work on behalf of that Auditor General is eligible for appointment as a statutory auditor by virtue of Chapter 2.

The Independent Supervisor

1228. Appointment of the Independent Supervisor

(1) The Secretary of State must appoint a body ("the Independent Supervisor") to discharge the function mentioned in section 1229(1) ("the supervision function").

(2) An appointment under this section must be made by order.

(3) The order has the effect of making the body appointed under subsection (1) designated under section 5 of the Freedom of Information Act 2000 (c. 36) (further powers to designate public authorities).

(4) A body may be appointed under this section only if it is a body corporate or an unincorporated association which appears to the Secretary of State—

    (a) to be willing and able to discharge the supervision function, and

  (b) to have arrangements in place relating to the discharge of that function which are such as to be likely to ensure that the conditions in subsection (5) are met.

 (5) The conditions are—

  (a) that the supervision function will be exercised effectively, and

  (b) where the order is to contain any requirements or other provisions specified under subsection (6), that that function will be exercised in accordance with any such requirements or provisions.

 (6) An order under this section may contain such requirements or other provisions relating to the exercise of the supervision function by the Independent Supervisor as appear to the Secretary of State to be appropriate.

 (7) An order under this section is subject to negative resolution procedure.

Supervision of Auditors General

1229. Supervision of Auditors General by the Independent Supervisor

 (1) The Independent Supervisor must supervise the performance by each Auditor General of his functions as a statutory auditor.

 (2) The Independent Supervisor must discharge that duty by—

  (a) entering into supervision arrangements with one or more bodies, and

  (b) overseeing the effective operation of any supervision arrangements entered into by it.

 (3) For this purpose "supervision arrangements" are arrangements entered into by the Independent Supervisor with a body, for the purposes of this section, in accordance with which the body does one or more of the following—

  (a) determines standards relating to professional integrity and independence which must be applied by an Auditor General in statutory audit work;

  (b) determines technical standards which must be applied by an Auditor General in statutory audit work and the manner in which those standards are to be applied in practice;

  (c) monitors the performance of statutory audits carried out by an Auditor General;

  (d) investigates any matter arising from the performance by an Auditor General of a statutory audit;

  (e) holds disciplinary hearings in respect of an Auditor General which appear to be desirable following the conclusion of such investigations;

  (f) decides whether (and, if so, what) disciplinary action should be taken against an Auditor General to whom such a hearing related.

 (4) The Independent Supervisor may enter into supervision arrangements with a body despite any relationship that may exist between the Independent Supervisor and that body.

 (5) The Independent Supervisor must notify each Auditor General in writing of any supervision arrangements that it enters into under this section.

 (6) Supervision arrangements within subsection (3)(f) may, in particular, provide for the payment by an Auditor General of a fine to any person.

 (7) Any fine received by the Independent Supervisor under supervision arrangements is to be paid into the Consolidated Fund.

1230. Duties of Auditors General in relation to supervision arrangements

 (1) Each Auditor General must—

  (a) comply with any standards of the kind mentioned in subsection (3)(a) or (b) of section 1229 determined under the supervision arrangements,

  (b) take such steps as may be reasonably required of that Auditor General to enable his performance of statutory audits to be monitored by means of inspections carried out under the supervision arrangements, and

  (c) comply with any decision of the kind mentioned in subsection (3)(f) of that section made under the supervision arrangements.

(2) Each Auditor General must pay to the body or bodies with which the Independent Supervisor enters into the supervision arrangements such proportion of the costs incurred by the body or bodies for the purposes of the arrangements as the Independent Supervisor may notify to him in writing.

(3) Expenditure under subsection (2) is—

    (a) in the case of expenditure of the Comptroller and Auditor General, to be regarded as expenditure of the National Audit Office for the purposes of section 4(1) of the National Audit Act 1983 (c. 44);

    (b) in the case of expenditure of the Comptroller and Auditor General for Northern Ireland, to be regarded as expenditure of the Northern Ireland Audit Office for the purposes of Article 6(1) of the Audit (Northern Ireland) Order 1987 (S.I. 1987/460 (N.I. 5)).

(4) In this section "the supervision arrangements" means the arrangements entered into under section 1229.

Reporting requirement

1231. Reports by the Independent Supervisor

(1) The Independent Supervisor must, at least once in each calendar year, prepare a report on the discharge of its functions.

(2) The Independent Supervisor must give a copy of each report prepared under subsection (1) to—

    (a) the Secretary of State;

    (b) the First Minister in Scotland;

    (c) the First Minister and the deputy First Minister in Northern Ireland;

    (d) the Assembly First Secretary in Wales.

(3) The Secretary of State must lay before each House of Parliament a copy of each report received by him under subsection (2)(a).

(4) In relation to a calendar year during which an appointment of a body as the Independent Supervisor is made or revoked by an order under section 1228, this section applies with such modifications as may be specified in the order.

Information

1232. Matters to be notified to the Independent Supervisor

(1) The Independent Supervisor may require an Auditor General—

    (a) to notify the Independent Supervisor immediately of the occurrence of such events as it may specify in writing and to give it such information in respect of those events as is so specified;

    (b) to give the Independent Supervisor, at such times or in respect of such periods as it may specify in writing, such information as is so specified.

(2) The notices and information required to be given must be such as the Independent Supervisor may reasonably require for the exercise of the functions conferred on it by or by virtue of this Part.

(3) The Independent Supervisor may require information given under this section to be given in a specified form or verified in a specified manner.

(4) Any notice or information required to be given under this section must be given in writing unless the Independent Supervisor specifies or approves some other manner.

1233. The Independent Supervisor's power to call for information

(1) The Independent Supervisor may by notice in writing require an Auditor General to give it such information as it may reasonably require for the exercise of the functions conferred on it by or by virtue of this Part.

(2) The Independent Supervisor may require that any information which it requires under this section is to be given within such reasonable time and verified in such manner as it may specify.

Enforcement

1234. Suspension notices

(1) The Independent Supervisor may issue—

    (a) a notice (a "suspension notice") suspending an Auditor General's eligibility for appointment as a statutory auditor in relation to all persons, or any specified person or persons, indefinitely or until a date specified in the notice;

    (b) a notice amending or revoking a suspension notice previously issued to an Auditor General.

(2) In determining whether it is appropriate to issue a notice under subsection (1), the Independent Supervisor must have regard to—

    (a) the Auditor General's performance of the obligations imposed on him by or by virtue of this Part, and

    (b) the Auditor General's performance of his functions as a statutory auditor.

(3) A notice under subsection (1) must—

    (a) be in writing, and

    (b) state the date on which it takes effect (which must be after the period of three months beginning with the date on which it is issued).

(4) Before issuing a notice under subsection (1), the Independent Supervisor must—

    (a) give written notice of its intention to do so to the Auditor General, and

    (b) publish the notice mentioned in paragraph (a) in such manner as it thinks appropriate for bringing it to the attention of any other persons who are likely to be affected.

(5) A notice under subsection (4) must—

    (a) state the reasons for which the Independent Supervisor proposes to act, and

    (b) give particulars of the rights conferred by subsection (6).

(6) A person within subsection (7) may, within the period of three months beginning with the date of service or publication of the notice under subsection (4) or such longer period as the Independent Supervisor may allow, make written representations to the Independent Supervisor and, if desired, oral representations to a person appointed for that purpose by the Independent Supervisor.

(7) The persons within this subsection are—

    (a) the Auditor General, and

    (b) any other person who appears to the Independent Supervisor to be affected.

(8) The Independent Supervisor must have regard to any representations made in accordance with subsection (6) in determining—

    (a) whether to issue a notice under subsection (1), and

    (b) the terms of any such notice.

(9) If in any case the Independent Supervisor considers it appropriate to do so in the public interest it may issue a notice under subsection (1), without regard to the restriction in subsection (3)(b), even if—

    (a) no notice has been given or published under subsection (4), or

    (b) the period of time for making representations in pursuance of such a notice has not expired.

(10) On issuing a notice under subsection (1), the Independent Supervisor must—

    (a) give a copy of the notice to the Auditor General, and

    (b) publish the notice in such manner as it thinks appropriate for bringing it to the attention of persons likely to be affected.

(11) In this section "specified" means specified in, or of a description specified in, the suspension notice in question.

1235. Effect of suspension notices

(1) An Auditor General must not act as a statutory auditor at any time when a suspension notice issued to him in respect of the audited person has effect.

(2) If at any time during an Auditor General's term of office as a statutory auditor a suspension notice issued to him in respect of the audited person takes effect, he must immediately—

(a) resign his office (with immediate effect), and

(b) give notice in writing to the audited person that he has resigned by reason of his becoming ineligible for appointment.

(3) A suspension notice does not make an Auditor General ineligible for appointment as a statutory auditor for the purposes of section 1213 (effect of ineligibility: criminal offences).

1236. Compliance orders

(1) If at any time it appears to the Independent Supervisor that an Auditor General has failed to comply with an obligation imposed on him by or by virtue of this Part, the Independent Supervisor may make an application to the court under this section.

(2) If on an application under this section the court decides that the Auditor General has failed to comply with the obligation in question, it may order the Auditor General to take such steps as the court directs for securing that the obligation is complied with.

(3) In this section "the court" means the High Court or, in Scotland, the Court of Session.

Proceedings

1237. Proceedings involving the Independent Supervisor

(1) If the Independent Supervisor is an unincorporated association, any relevant proceedings may be brought by or against it in the name of any body corporate whose constitution provides for the establishment of the body.

(2) For this purpose "relevant proceedings" means proceedings brought in or in connection with the exercise of any function by the body as the Independent Supervisor.

(3) Where an appointment under section 1228 is revoked, the revoking order may make such provision as the Secretary of State thinks fit with respect to pending proceedings.

Grants

1238. Grants to the Independent Supervisor

In section 16 of the Companies (Audit, Investigations and Community Enterprise) Act 2004 (c. 27) (grants to bodies concerned with accounting standards etc), after subsection (2)(k) insert—

"(ka) exercising functions of the Independent Supervisor appointed under Chapter 3 of Part 42 of the Companies Act 2006;".

CHAPTER 4
THE REGISTER OF AUDITORS ETC

1239. The register of auditors

(1) The Secretary of State must make regulations requiring the keeping of a register of—

(a) the persons eligible for appointment as a statutory auditor, and

(b) third country auditors (see Chapter 5) who apply to be registered in the specified manner and in relation to whom specified requirements are met.

(2) The regulations must require each person's entry in the register to contain—

(a) his name and address,

(b) in the case of an individual eligible for appointment as a statutory auditor, the specified information relating to any firm on whose behalf he is responsible for statutory audit work,

(c) in the case of a firm eligible for appointment as a statutory auditor, the specified information relating to the individuals responsible for statutory audit work on its behalf,

(d) in the case of an individual or firm eligible for appointment as a statutory auditor by virtue of Chapter 2 the name of the relevant supervisory body, and

(e) in the case of a firm eligible for appointment as a statutory auditor by virtue of Chapter 2 or a third country auditor, the information mentioned in subsection (3),

and may require each person's entry to contain other specified information.

(3) The information referred to in subsection (2)(e) is—

(a) in relation to a body corporate, except where paragraph (b) applies, the name and address of each person who is a director of the body or holds any shares in it;

(b) in relation to a limited liability partnership, the name and address of each member of the partnership;

(c) in relation to a corporation sole, the name and address of the individual for the time being holding the office by the name of which he is the corporation sole;

(d) in relation to a partnership, the name and address of each partner.

(4) The regulations may provide that different parts of the register are to be kept by different persons.

(5) The regulations may impose such obligations as the Secretary of State thinks fit on—

(a) recognised supervisory bodies,

(b) any body designated by order under section 1252 (delegation of Secretary of State's functions),

(c) persons eligible for appointment as a statutory auditor,

(d) third country auditors,

(e) any person with whom arrangements are made by one or more recognised supervisory bodies, or by any body designated by order under section 1252, with respect to the keeping of the register, or

(f) the Independent Supervisor appointed under section 1228.

(6) The regulations may include—

(a) provision requiring that specified entries in the register be open to inspection at times and places specified or determined in accordance with the regulations;

(b) provision enabling a person to require a certified copy of specified entries in the register;

(c) provision authorising the charging of fees for inspection, or the provision of copies, of such reasonable amount as may be specified or determined in accordance with the regulations.

(7) The Secretary of State may direct in writing that the requirements imposed by the regulations in accordance with subsections (2)(e) and (3), or such of those requirements as are specified in the direction, are not to apply, in whole or in part, in relation to a particular registered third country auditor or class of registered third country auditors.

(8) The obligations imposed by regulations under this section on such persons as are mentioned in subsection (5)(b) or (e) are enforceable on the application of the Secretary of State by injunction or, in Scotland, by an order under section 45 of the Court of Session Act 1988 (c. 36).

(9) In this section "specified" means specified by regulations under this section.

(10) Regulations under this section are subject to negative resolution procedure.

1240. Information to be made available to public

(1) The Secretary of State may make regulations requiring a person eligible for appointment as a statutory auditor, or a member of a specified class of such persons, to keep and make available to the public specified information, including information regarding—

    (a) the person's ownership and governance,

    (b) the person's internal controls with respect to the quality and independence of its audit work,

    (c) the person's turnover, and

    (d) the audited persons of whom the person has acted as statutory auditor.

(2) Regulations under this section may—

    (a) impose such obligations as the Secretary of State thinks fit on persons eligible for appointment as a statutory auditor;

    (b) require the information to be made available to the public in a specified manner.

(3) In this section "specified" means specified by regulations under this section.

(4) Regulations under this section are subject to negative resolution procedure.

CHAPTER 5
REGISTERED THIRD COUNTRY AUDITORS

Introductory

1241. Meaning of "third country auditor", "registered third country auditor" etc

(1) In this Part—

    "third country auditor" means the auditor of the accounts of a traded non-Community company, and the expressions "third country audit" and "third country audit work" are to be construed accordingly;

    "registered third country auditor" means a third country auditor who is entered in the register kept in accordance with regulations under section 1239(1).

(2) In subsection (1) "traded non-Community company" means a body corporate—

    (a) which is incorporated or formed under the law of a country or territory which is not a member State or part of a member State,

    (b) whose transferable securities are admitted to trading on a regulated market situated or operating in the United Kingdom, and

    (c) which has not been excluded, or is not of a description of bodies corporate which has been excluded, from this definition by an order made by the Secretary of State.

(3) For this purpose—

    "regulated market" has the meaning given by Article 4.1(14) of Directive 2004/39/EC of the European Parliament and of the Council on markets in financial instruments;

    "transferable securities" has the meaning given by Article 4.1(18) of that Directive.

(4) An order under this section is subject to negative resolution procedure.

Duties

1242. Duties of registered third country auditors

(1) A registered third country auditor must participate in—

    (a) arrangements within paragraph 1 of Schedule 12 (arrangements for independent monitoring of audits of traded non-Community companies), and

    (b) arrangements within paragraph 2 of that Schedule (arrangements for independent investigation for disciplinary purposes of public interest cases).

(2) A registered third country auditor must—

    (a) take such steps as may be reasonably required of it to enable its performance of third country audits to be monitored by means of inspections carried out under the arrangements mentioned in subsection (1)(a), and

    (b) comply with any decision as to disciplinary action to be taken against it made under the arrangements mentioned in subsection (1)(b).

(3) Schedule 12 makes further provision with respect to the arrangements in which registered third country auditors are required to participate.

(4) The Secretary of State may direct in writing that subsections (1) to (3) are not to apply, in whole or in part, in relation to a particular registered third country auditor or class of registered third country auditors.

Information

1243. Matters to be notified to the Secretary of State

(1) The Secretary of State may require a registered third country auditor—

    (a) to notify him immediately of the occurrence of such events as he may specify in writing and to give him such information in respect of those events as is so specified;

    (b) to give him, at such times or in respect of such periods as he may specify in writing, such information as is so specified.

(2) The notices and information required to be given must be such as the Secretary of State may reasonably require for the exercise of his functions under this Part.

(3) The Secretary of State may require information given under this section to be given in a specified form or verified in a specified manner.

(4) Any notice or information required to be given under this section must be given in writing unless the Secretary of State specifies or approves some other manner.

1244. The Secretary of State's power to call for information

(1) The Secretary of State may by notice in writing require a registered third country auditor to give him such information as he may reasonably require for the exercise of his functions under this Part.

(2) The Secretary of State may require that any information which he requires under this section is to be given within such reasonable time and verified in such manner as he may specify.

Enforcement

1245. Compliance orders

(1) If at any time it appears to the Secretary of State that a registered third country auditor has failed to comply with an obligation imposed on him by or by virtue of this Part, the Secretary of State may make an application to the court under this section.

(2) If on an application under this section the court decides that the auditor has failed to comply with the obligation in question, it may order the auditor to take such steps as the court directs for securing that the obligation is complied with.

(3) In this section "the court" means the High Court or, in Scotland, the Court of Session.

1246. Removal of third country auditors from the register of auditors

(1) The Secretary of State may, by regulations, confer on the person keeping the register in accordance with regulations under section 1239(1) power to remove a third country auditor from the register.

(2) Regulations under this section must require the person keeping the register, in determining whether to remove a third country auditor from the register, to have regard to the auditor's compliance with obligations imposed on him by or by virtue of this Part.

(3) Where provision is made under section 1239(4) (different parts of the register to be kept by different persons), references in this section to the person keeping the register are to the person keeping that part of the register which relates to third country auditors.

(4) Regulations under this section are subject to negative resolution procedure.

1247. Grants to bodies concerned with arrangements under Schedule 12

In section 16 of the Companies (Audit, Investigations and Community Enterprise) Act 2004 (c. 27) (grants to bodies concerned with accounting standards etc), after subsection (2)(ka) (inserted by section 1238) insert—

"(kb) establishing, maintaining or carrying out arrangements within paragraph 1 or 2 of Schedule 12 to the Companies Act 2006;".

CHAPTER 6
SUPPLEMENTARY AND GENERAL

Power to require second company audit

1248. Secretary of State's power to require second audit of a company

(1) This section applies where a person appointed as statutory auditor of a company was not an appropriate person for any part of the period during which the audit was conducted.

(2) The Secretary of State may direct the company concerned to retain an appropriate person—
   (a) to conduct a second audit of the relevant accounts, or
   (b) to review the first audit and to report (giving his reasons) whether a second audit is needed.

(3) For the purposes of subsections (1) and (2) a person is "appropriate" if he—
   (a) is eligible for appointment as a statutory auditor or, if the person is an Auditor General, for appointment as statutory auditor of the company, and
   (b) is not prohibited by section 1214(1) (independence requirement) from acting as statutory auditor of the company.

(4) The Secretary of State must send a copy of a direction under subsection (2) to the registrar of companies.

(5) The company is guilty of an offence if—
   (a) it fails to comply with a direction under subsection (2) within the period of 21 days beginning with the date on which it is given, or
   (b) it has been convicted of a previous offence under this subsection and the failure to comply with the direction which led to the conviction continues after the conviction.

(6) The company must—
   (a) send a copy of a report under subsection (2)(b) to the registrar of companies, and
   (b) if the report states that a second audit is needed, take such steps as are necessary for the carrying out of that audit.

(7) The company is guilty of an offence if—
   (a) it fails to send a copy of a report under subsection (2)(b) to the registrar within the period of 21 days beginning with the date on which it receives it,
   (b) in a case within subsection (6)(b), it fails to take the steps mentioned immediately it receives the report, or
   (c) it has been convicted of a previous offence under this subsection and the failure to send a copy of the report, or take the steps, which led to the conviction continues after the conviction.

(8) A company guilty of an offence under this section is liable on summary conviction—
   (a) in a case within subsection (5)(a) or (7)(a) or (b), to a fine not exceeding level 5 on the standard scale, and

     (b) in a case within subsection (5)(b) or (7)(c), to a fine not exceeding one-tenth of level 5 on the standard scale for each day on which the failure continues.

    (9) In this section "registrar of companies" has the meaning given by section 1060.

1249. Supplementary provision about second audits

    (1) If a person accepts an appointment, or continues to act, as statutory auditor of a company at a time when he knows he is not an appropriate person, the company may recover from him any costs incurred by it in complying with the requirements of section 1248.

    For this purpose "appropriate" is to be construed in accordance with subsection (3) of that section.

    (2) Where a second audit is carried out under section 1248, any statutory or other provision applying in relation to the first audit applies also, in so far as practicable, in relation to the second audit.

    (3) A direction under section 1248(2) is, on the application of the Secretary of State, enforceable by injunction or, in Scotland, by an order under section 45 of the Court of Session Act 1988 (c. 36).

False and misleading statements

1250. Misleading, false and deceptive statements

    (1) A person is guilty of an offence if—

      (a) for the purposes of or in connection with any application under this Part, or

      (b) in purported compliance with any requirement imposed on him by or by virtue of this Part,

    he knowingly or recklessly furnishes information which is misleading, false or deceptive in a material particular.

    (2) It is an offence for a person whose name does not appear on the register of auditors kept under regulations under section 1239 in an entry made under subsection (1)(a) of that section to describe himself as a registered auditor or so to hold himself out as to indicate, or be reasonably understood to indicate, that he is a registered auditor.

    (3) It is an offence for a person whose name does not appear on the register of auditors kept under regulations under that section in an entry made under subsection (1)(b) of that section to describe himself as a registered third country auditor or so to hold himself out as to indicate, or be reasonably understood to indicate, that he is a registered third country auditor.

    (4) It is an offence for a body which is not a recognised supervisory body or a recognised qualifying body to describe itself as so recognised or so to describe itself or hold itself out as to indicate, or be reasonably understood to indicate, that it is so recognised.

    (5) A person guilty of an offence under subsection (1) is liable—

      (a) on conviction on indictment, to imprisonment for a term not exceeding two years or to a fine (or both);

      (b) on summary conviction—

        (i) in England and Wales, to imprisonment for a term not exceeding twelve months or to a fine not exceeding the statutory maximum (or both),

        (ii) in Scotland or Northern Ireland, to imprisonment for a term not exceeding six months or to a fine not exceeding the statutory maximum (or both).

    In relation to an offence committed before the commencement of section 154(1) of the Criminal Justice Act 2003 (c. 44), for "twelve months" in paragraph (b)(i) substitute "six months".

    (6) Subject to subsection (7), a person guilty of an offence under subsection (2), (3) or (4) is liable on summary conviction—

      (a) in England and Wales, to imprisonment for a term not exceeding 51 weeks or to a fine not exceeding level 5 on the standard scale (or both),

(b) in Scotland or Northern Ireland, to imprisonment for a term not exceeding six months or to a fine not exceeding level 5 on the standard scale (or both).

In relation to an offence committed before the commencement of section 281(5) of the Criminal Justice Act 2003, for "51 weeks" in paragraph (a) substitute "six months".

(7) Where a contravention of subsection (2), (3) or (4) involves a public display of the offending description, the maximum fine that may be imposed is an amount equal to level 5 on the standard scale multiplied by the number of days for which the display has continued.

(8) It is a defence for a person charged with an offence under subsection (2), (3) or (4) to show that he took all reasonable precautions and exercised all due diligence to avoid the commission of the offence.

Fees

1251. Fees

(1) An applicant for a recognition order under this Part must pay such fee in respect of his application as the Secretary of State may by regulations prescribe; and no application is to be regarded as duly made unless this subsection is complied with.

(2) The Secretary of State may by regulations prescribe periodical fees to be paid by—

(a) every recognised supervisory body,

(b) every recognised qualifying body,

(c) every Auditor General, and

(d) every registered third country auditor.

(3) Fees received by the Secretary of State by virtue of this Part are to be paid into the Consolidated Fund.

(4) Regulations under this section are subject to negative resolution procedure.

Delegation of Secretary of State's functions

1252. Delegation of the Secretary of State's functions

(1) The Secretary of State may make an order under this section (a "delegation order") for the purpose of enabling functions of the Secretary of State under this Part to be exercised by a body designated by the order.

(2) The body designated by a delegation order may be either—

(a) a body corporate which is established by the order, or

(b) subject to section 1253, a body (whether a body corporate or an unincorporated association) which is already in existence ("an existing body").

(3) A delegation order has the effect of making the body designated by the order designated under section 5 of the Freedom of Information Act 2000 (c. 36) (further powers to designate public authorities).

(4) A delegation order has the effect of transferring to the body designated by it all functions of the Secretary of State under this Part—

(a) subject to such exceptions and reservations as may be specified in the order, and

(b) except—

(i) his functions in relation to the body itself, and

(ii) his functions under section 1228 (appointment of Independent Supervisor).

(5) A delegation order may confer on the body designated by it such other functions supplementary or incidental to those transferred as appear to the Secretary of State to be appropriate.

(6) Any transfer of functions under the following provisions must be subject to the reservation that the functions remain exercisable concurrently by the Secretary of State—

     (a) section 1224 (power to call for information from recognised bodies etc);

     (b) section 1244 (power to call for information from registered third country auditors);

     (c) section 1254 (directions to comply with international obligations).

(7) Any transfer of—

     (a) the function of refusing to make a declaration under section 1221(1) (approval of overseas qualifications) on the grounds referred to in section 1221(4) (lack of comparable treatment), or

     (b) the function of withdrawing such a declaration under section 1221(7) on those grounds,

must be subject to the reservation that the function is exercisable only with the consent of the Secretary of State.

(8) A delegation order may be amended or, if it appears to the Secretary of State that it is no longer in the public interest that the order should remain in force, revoked by a further order under this section.

(9) Where functions are transferred or resumed, the Secretary of State may by order confer or, as the case may be, take away such other functions supplementary or incidental to those transferred or resumed as appear to him to be appropriate.

(10) Where a delegation order is made, Schedule 13 has effect with respect to—

     (a) the status of the body designated by the order in exercising functions of the Secretary of State under this Part,

     (b) the constitution and proceedings of the body where it is established by the order,

     (c) the exercise by the body of certain functions transferred to it, and

     (d) other supplementary matters.

(11) An order under this section which has the effect of transferring or resuming any functions is subject to affirmative resolution procedure.

(12) Any other order under this section is subject to negative resolution procedure.

1253. Delegation of functions to an existing body

(1) The Secretary of State's power to make a delegation order under section 1252 which designates an existing body is exercisable in accordance with this section.

(2) The Secretary of State may make such a delegation order if it appears to him that—

     (a) the body is able and willing to exercise the functions that would be transferred by the order, and

     (b) the body has arrangements in place relating to the exercise of those functions which are such as to be likely to ensure that the conditions in subsection (3) are met.

(3) The conditions are—

     (a) that the functions in question will be exercised effectively, and

     (b) where the delegation order is to contain any requirements or other provisions specified under subsection (4), that those functions will be exercised in accordance with any such requirements or provisions.

(4) The delegation order may contain such requirements or other provision relating to the exercise of the functions by the designated body as appear to the Secretary of State to be appropriate.

(5) An existing body—

     (a) may be designated by a delegation order under section 1252, and

     (b) may accordingly exercise functions of the Secretary of State in pursuance of the order, despite any involvement of the body in the exercise of any functions under arrangements within paragraph 21, 22, 23(1) or 24(1) of Schedule 10 or paragraph 1 or 2 of Schedule 12.

International obligations

1254. Directions to comply with international obligations

(1) If it appears to the Secretary of State—

    (a) that any action proposed to be taken by a recognised supervisory body or a recognised qualifying body, or a body designated by order under section 1252, would be incompatible with Community obligations or any other international obligations of the United Kingdom, or

    (b) that any action which that body has power to take is required for the purpose of implementing any such obligations,

he may direct the body not to take or, as the case may be, to take the action in question.

(2) A direction may include such supplementary or incidental requirements as the Secretary of State thinks necessary or expedient.

(3) A direction under this section given to a body designated by order under section 1252 is enforceable on the application of the Secretary of State by injunction or, in Scotland, by an order under section 45 of the Court of Session Act 1988 (c. 36).

General provision relating to offences

1255. Offences by bodies corporate, partnerships and unincorporated associations

(1) Where an offence under this Part committed by a body corporate is proved to have been committed with the consent or connivance of, or to be attributable to any neglect on the part of, an officer of the body, or a person purporting to act in any such capacity, he as well as the body corporate is guilty of the offence and liable to be proceeded against and punished accordingly.

(2) Where an offence under this Part committed by a partnership is proved to have been committed with the consent or connivance of, or to be attributable to any neglect on the part of, a partner, he as well as the partnership is guilty of the offence and liable to be proceeded against and punished accordingly.

(3) Where an offence under this Part committed by an unincorporated association (other than a partnership) is proved to have been committed with the consent or connivance of, or to be attributable to any neglect on the part of, any officer of the association or any member of its governing body, he as well as the association is guilty of the offence and liable to be proceeded against and punished accordingly.

1256. Time limits for prosecution of offences

(1) An information relating to an offence under this Part which is triable by a magistrates' court in England and Wales may be so tried if it is laid at any time within the period of twelve months beginning with the date on which evidence sufficient in the opinion of the Director of Public Prosecutions or the Secretary of State to justify the proceedings comes to his knowledge.

(2) Proceedings in Scotland for an offence under this Part may be commenced at any time within the period of twelve months beginning with the date on which evidence sufficient in the Lord Advocate's opinion to justify proceedings came to his knowledge or, where such evidence was reported to him by the Secretary of State, within the period of twelve months beginning with the date on which it came to the knowledge of the Secretary of State.

(3) For the purposes of subsection (2) proceedings are to be deemed to be commenced on the date on which a warrant to apprehend or cite the accused is granted, if the warrant is executed without undue delay.

(4) A complaint charging an offence under this Part which is triable by a magistrates' court in Northern Ireland may be so tried if it is made at any time within the period of twelve months beginning with the date on which evidence sufficient in the opinion of the Director of

Public Prosecutions for Northern Ireland or the Secretary of State to justify the proceedings comes to his knowledge.

(5) This section does not authorise—

(a) in the case of proceedings in England and Wales, the trial of an information laid,

(b) in the case of proceedings in Scotland, the commencement of proceedings, or

(c) in the case of proceedings in Northern Ireland, the trial of a complaint made,

more than three years after the commission of the offence.

(6) For the purposes of this section a certificate of the Director of Public Prosecutions, the Lord Advocate, the Director of Public Prosecutions for Northern Ireland or the Secretary of State as to the date on which such evidence as is referred to above came to his knowledge is conclusive evidence.

(7) Nothing in this section affects proceedings within the time limits prescribed by section 127(1) of the Magistrates' Courts Act 1980 (c. 43), section 331 of the Criminal Procedure (Scotland) Act 1975 or Article 19 of the Magistrates' Courts (Northern Ireland) Order 1981 (S.I. 1981/1675 (N.I. 26)) (the usual time limits for criminal proceedings).

1257. Jurisdiction and procedure in respect of offences

(1) Summary proceedings for an offence under this Part may, without prejudice to any jurisdiction exercisable apart from this section, be taken—

(a) against a body corporate or unincorporated association at any place at which it has a place of business, and

(b) against an individual at any place where he is for the time being.

(2) Proceedings for an offence alleged to have been committed under this Part by an unincorporated association must be brought in the name of the association (and not in that of any of its members), and for the purposes of any such proceedings any rules of court relating to the service of documents apply as in relation to a body corporate.

(3) Section 33 of the Criminal Justice Act 1925 (c. 86) and Schedule 3 to the Magistrates' Courts Act 1980 (c. 43) (procedure on charge of offence against a corporation) apply in a case in which an unincorporated association is charged in England and Wales with an offence under this Part as they apply in the case of a corporation.

(4) Section 18 of the Criminal Justice Act (Northern Ireland) 1945 (c. 15 (N.I.)) and Article 166 and Schedule 4 to the Magistrates' Courts (Northern Ireland) Order 1981 (S.I. 1981/1675 (N.I. 26)) (procedure on charge of offence against a corporation) apply in a case in which an unincorporated association is charged in Northern Ireland with an offence under this Part as they apply in the case of a corporation.

(5) In relation to proceedings on indictment in Scotland for an offence alleged to have been committed under this Part by an unincorporated association, section 70 of the Criminal Procedure (Scotland) Act 1995 (proceedings on indictment against bodies corporate) applies as if the association were a body corporate.

(6) A fine imposed on an unincorporated association on its conviction of such an offence must be paid out of the funds of the association.

Notices etc

1258. Service of notices

(1) This section has effect in relation to any notice, direction or other document required or authorised by or by virtue of this Part to be given to or served on any person other than the Secretary of State.

(2) Any such document may be given to or served on the person in question—

(a) by delivering it to him,

(b) by leaving it at his proper address, or

(c) by sending it by post to him at that address.

(3) Any such document may—

    (a) in the case of a body corporate, be given to or served on an officer of that body;

    (b) in the case of a partnership, be given to or served on any partner;

    (c) in the case of an unincorporated association other than a partnership, be given to or served on any member of the governing body of that association.

(4) For the purposes of this section and section 7 of the Interpretation Act 1978 (c. 30) (service of documents by post) in its application to this section, the proper address of any person is his last known address (whether of his residence or of a place where he carries on business or is employed) and also—

    (a) in the case of a person who is eligible under the rules of a recognised supervisory body for appointment as a statutory auditor and who does not have a place of business in the United Kingdom, the address of that body;

    (b) in the case of a body corporate or an officer of that body, the address of the registered or principal office of that body in the United Kingdom;

    (c) in the case of an unincorporated association other than a partnership or a member of its governing body, its principal office in the United Kingdom.

1259. Documents in electronic form

(1) This section applies where—

    (a) section 1258 authorises the giving or sending of a notice, direction or other document by its delivery to a particular person ("the recipient"), and

    (b) the notice, direction or other document is transmitted to the recipient—

        (i) by means of an electronic communications network, or

        (ii) by other means but in a form that requires the use of apparatus by the recipient to render it intelligible.

(2) The transmission has effect for the purposes of this Part as a delivery of the notice, direction or other document to the recipient, but only if the recipient has indicated to the person making the transmission his willingness to receive the notice, direction or other document in the form and manner used.

(3) An indication to a person for the purposes of subsection (2)—

    (a) must be given to the person in such manner as he may require,

    (b) may be a general indication or an indication that is limited to notices, directions or other documents of a particular description,

    (c) must state the address to be used,

    (d) must be accompanied by such other information as the person requires for the making of the transmission, and

    (e) may be modified or withdrawn at any time by a notice given to the person in such manner as he may require.

(4) In this section "electronic communications network" has the same meaning as in the Communications Act 2003 (c. 21).

Interpretation

1260. Meaning of "associate"

(1) In this Part "associate", in relation to a person, is to be construed as follows.

(2) In relation to an individual, "associate" means—

    (a) that individual's spouse, civil partner or minor child or step-child,

    (b) any body corporate of which that individual is a director, and

    (c) any employee or partner of that individual.

(3) In relation to a body corporate, "associate" means—

    (a) any body corporate of which that body is a director,

    (b) any body corporate in the same group as that body, and

    (c) any employee or partner of that body or of any body corporate in the same group.

(4) In relation to a partnership constituted under the law of Scotland, or any other country or territory in which a partnership is a legal person, "associate" means—

(a) any body corporate of which that partnership is a director,

(b) any employee of or partner in that partnership, and

(c) any person who is an associate of a partner in that partnership.

(5) In relation to a partnership constituted under the law of England and Wales or Northern Ireland, or the law of any other country or territory in which a partnership is not a legal person, "associate" means any person who is an associate of any of the partners.

(6) In subsections (2)(b), (3)(a) and (4)(a), in the case of a body corporate which is a limited liability partnership, "director" is to be read as "member".

1261. Minor definitions

(1) In this Part, unless a contrary intention appears—

"address" means—

(a) in relation to an individual, his usual residential or business address;

(b) in relation to a firm, its registered or principal office in the United Kingdom;

"company" means any company or other body the accounts of which must be audited in accordance with Part 16;

"director", in relation to a body corporate, includes any person occupying in relation to it the position of a director (by whatever name called) and any person in accordance with whose directions or instructions (not being advice given in a professional capacity) the directors of the body are accustomed to act;

"firm" means any entity, whether or not a legal person, which is not an individual and includes a body corporate, a corporation sole and a partnership or other unincorporated association;

"group", in relation to a body corporate, means the body corporate, any other body corporate which is its holding company or subsidiary and any other body corporate which is a subsidiary of that holding company;

"holding company" and "subsidiary" are to be read in accordance with section 1159 and Schedule 6;

"officer", in relation to a body corporate, includes a director, a manager, a secretary or, where the affairs of the body are managed by its members, a member;

"parent undertaking" and "subsidiary undertaking" are to be read in accordance with section 1162 and Schedule 7.

(2) For the purposes of this Part a body is to be regarded as "established in the United Kingdom" if and only if—

(a) it is incorporated or formed under the law of the United Kingdom or a part of the United Kingdom, or

(b) its central management and control are exercised in the United Kingdom;

and any reference to a qualification "obtained in the United Kingdom" is to a qualification obtained from such a body.

(3) The Secretary of State may by regulations make such modifications of this Part as appear to him to be necessary or appropriate for the purposes of its application in relation to any firm, or description of firm, which is not a body corporate or a partnership.

(4) Regulations under subsection (3) are subject to negative resolution procedure.

1262. Index of defined expressions

The following Table shows provisions defining or otherwise explaining expressions used in this Part (other than provisions defining or explaining an expression used only in the same section)—

Expression	Provision
address	section 1261(1)
appropriate qualification	section 1219
associate	section 1260
audited person	section 1210(2)
Auditor General	section 1226(1)
company	section 1261(1)
delegation order	section 1252(1)
director (of a body corporate)	section 1261(1)
enactment	section 1293
established in the United Kingdom	section 1261(2)
firm	section 1261(1)
group (in relation to a body corporate)	section 1261(1)
holding company	section 1261(1)
main purposes of this Part	section 1209
member (of a supervisory body)	section 1217(2)
obtained in the United Kingdom	section 1261(2)
officer	section 1261(1)
parent undertaking	section 1261(1)
qualifying body	section 1220(1)
recognised, in relation to a professional qualification	section 1220(3) and Schedule 11
recognised, in relation to a qualifying body	paragraph 1(2) of Schedule 11
recognised, in relation to a supervisory body	section 1217(4) and Schedule 10
registered third country auditor	section 1241(1)
rules of a qualifying body	section 1220(2)
rules of a supervisory body	section 1217(3)
statutory auditor, statutory audit and statutory audit work	section 1210(1)
subsidiary	section 1261(1)
supervisory body	section 1217(1)
subsidiary undertaking	section 1261(1)
third country auditor, third country audit and third country audit work	section 1241(1)

Miscellaneous and general

1263. Power to make provision in consequence of changes affecting accountancy bodies

    (1) The Secretary of State may by regulations make such amendments of enactments as appear to him to be necessary or expedient in consequence of any change of name, merger or transfer of engagements affecting—

        (a) a recognised supervisory body or recognised qualifying body, or

        (b) a body of accountants referred to in, or approved, authorised or otherwise recognised for the purposes of, any other enactment.

    (2) Regulations under this section are subject to negative resolution procedure.

1264. Consequential amendments

    Schedule 14 contains consequential amendments relating to this Part.

PART 43
TRANSPARENCY OBLIGATIONS AND RELATED MATTERS

Introductory

1265. The transparency obligations directive

In Part 6 of the Financial Services and Markets Act 2000 (c. 8) (which makes provision about official listing, prospectus requirements for transferable securities, etc), in section 103(1) (interpretation), at the appropriate place insert—

" "the transparency obligations directive" means Directive 2004/109/EC of the European Parliament and of the Council relating to the harmonisation of transparency requirements in relation to information about issuers whose securities are admitted to trading on a regulated market;".

Transparency obligations

1266. Transparency rules

(1) After section 89 of the Financial Services and Markets Act 2000 insert—

"Transparency obligations

89A Transparency rules

(1) The competent authority may make rules for the purposes of the transparency obligations directive.

(2) The rules may include provision for dealing with any matters arising out of or related to any provision of the transparency obligations directive.

(3) The competent authority may also make rules—

(a) for the purpose of ensuring that voteholder information in respect of voting shares traded on a UK market other than a regulated market is made public or notified to the competent authority;

(b) providing for persons who hold comparable instruments (see section 89F(1)(c)) in respect of voting shares to be treated, in the circumstances specified in the rules, as holding some or all of the voting rights in respect of those shares.

(4) Rules under this section may, in particular, make provision—

(a) specifying how the proportion of—

(i) the total voting rights in respect of shares in an issuer, or

(ii) the total voting rights in respect of a particular class of shares in an issuer,

held by a person is to be determined;

(b) specifying the circumstances in which, for the purposes of any determination of the voting rights held by a person ("P") in respect of voting shares in an issuer, any voting rights held, or treated by virtue of subsection (3)(b) as held, by another person in respect of voting shares in the issuer are to be regarded as held by P;

(c) specifying the nature of the information which must be included in any notification;

(d) about the form of any notification;

(e) requiring any notification to be given within a specified period;

(f) specifying the manner in which any information is to be made public and the period within which it must be made public;

(g) specifying circumstances in which any of the requirements imposed by rules under this section does not apply.

(5) Rules under this section are referred to in this Part as "transparency rules".

(6) Nothing in sections 89B to 89G affects the generality of the power to make rules under this section.

89B Provision of voteholder information

(1) Transparency rules may make provision for voteholder information in respect of voting shares to be notified, in circumstances specified in the rules—

    (a) to the issuer, or

    (b) to the public,

    or to both.

(2) Transparency rules may make provision for voteholder information notified to the issuer to be notified at the same time to the competent authority.

(3) In this Part "voteholder information" in respect of voting shares means information relating to the proportion of voting rights held by a person in respect of the shares.

(4) Transparency rules may require notification of voteholder information relating to a person—

    (a) initially, not later than such date as may be specified in the rules for the purposes of the first indent of Article 30.2 of the transparency obligations directive, and

    (b) subsequently, in accordance with the following provisions.

(5) Transparency rules under subsection (4)(b) may require notification of voteholder information relating to a person only where there is a notifiable change in the proportion of—

    (a) the total voting rights in respect of shares in the issuer, or

    (b) the total voting rights in respect of a particular class of share in the issuer,

    held by the person.

(6) For this purpose there is a "notifiable change" in the proportion of voting rights held by a person when the proportion changes—

    (a) from being a proportion less than a designated proportion to a proportion equal to or greater than that designated proportion,

    (b) from being a proportion equal to a designated proportion to a proportion greater or less than that designated proportion, or

    (c) from being a proportion greater than a designated proportion to a proportion equal to or less than that designated proportion.

(7) In subsection (6) "designated" means designated by the rules.

89C Provision of information by issuers of transferable securities

(1) Transparency rules may make provision requiring the issuer of transferable securities, in circumstances specified in the rules—

    (a) to make public information to which this section applies, or

    (b) to notify to the competent authority information to which this section applies,

    or to do both.

(2) In the case of every issuer, this section applies to—

    (a) information required by Article 4 of the transparency obligations directive;

    (b) information relating to the rights attached to the transferable securities, including information about the terms and conditions of those securities which could indirectly affect those rights; and

    (c) information about new loan issues and about any guarantee or security in connection with any such issue.

(3) In the case of an issuer of debt securities, this section also applies to information required by Article 5 of the transparency obligations directive.

(4) In the case of an issuer of shares, this section also applies to—

    (a) information required by Article 5 of the transparency obligations directive;

    (b) information required by Article 6 of that directive;

    (c) voteholder information—

        (i) notified to the issuer, or

        (ii) relating to the proportion of voting rights held by the issuer in respect of shares in the issuer;

    (d) information relating to the issuer's capital; and

    (e) information relating to the total number of voting rights in respect of shares or shares of a particular class.

89D Notification of voting rights held by issuer

(1) Transparency rules may require notification of voteholder information relating to the proportion of voting rights held by an issuer in respect of voting shares in the issuer—

    (a) initially, not later than such date as may be specified in the rules for the purposes of the second indent of Article 30.2 of the transparency obligations directive, and

    (b) subsequently, in accordance with the following provisions.

(2) Transparency rules under subsection (1)(b) may require notification of voteholder information relating to the proportion of voting rights held by an issuer in respect of voting shares in the issuer only where there is a notifiable change in the proportion of—

    (a) the total voting rights in respect of shares in the issuer, or

    (b) the total voting rights in respect of a particular class of share in the issuer,

held by the issuer.

(3) For this purpose there is a "notifiable change" in the proportion of voting rights held by a person when the proportion changes—

    (a) from being a proportion less than a designated proportion to a proportion equal to or greater than that designated proportion,

    (b) from being a proportion equal to a designated proportion to a proportion greater or less than that designated proportion, or

    (c) from being a proportion greater than a designated proportion to a proportion equal to or less than that designated proportion.

(4) In subsection (3) "designated" means designated by the rules.

89E Notification of proposed amendment of issuer's constitution

Transparency rules may make provision requiring an issuer of transferable securities that are admitted to trading on a regulated market to notify a proposed amendment to its constitution—

    (a) to the competent authority, and

    (b) to the market on which the issuer's securities are admitted,

at times and in circumstances specified in the rules.

89F Transparency rules: interpretation etc

(1) For the purposes of sections 89A to 89G—

    (a) the voting rights in respect of any voting shares are the voting rights attached to those shares,

    (b) a person is to be regarded as holding the voting rights in respect of the shares—

        (i) if, by virtue of those shares, he is a shareholder within the meaning of Article 21(e) of the transparency obligations directive;

(ii) if, and to the extent that, he is entitled to acquire, dispose of or exercise those voting rights in one or more of the cases mentioned in Article 10(a) to (h) of the transparency obligations directive;

(iii) if he holds, directly or indirectly, a financial instrument which results in an entitlement to acquire the shares and is an Article 13 instrument, and

(c) a person holds a "comparable instrument" in respect of voting shares if he holds, directly or indirectly, a financial instrument in relation to the shares which has similar economic effects to an Article 13 instrument (whether or not the financial instrument results in an entitlement to acquire the shares).

(2) Transparency rules under section 89A(3)(b) may make different provision for different descriptions of comparable instrument.

(3) For the purposes of sections 89A to 89G two or more persons may, at the same time, each be regarded as holding the same voting rights.

(4) In those sections—

"Article 13 instrument" means a financial instrument of a type determined by the European Commission under Article 13.2 of the transparency obligations directive;

"UK market" means a market that is situated or operating in the United Kingdom;

"voting shares" means shares of an issuer to which voting rights are attached.

89G Transparency rules: other supplementary provisions

(1) Transparency rules may impose the same obligations on a person who has applied for the admission of transferable securities to trading on a regulated market without the issuer's consent as they impose on an issuer of transferable securities.

(2) Transparency rules that require a person to make information public may include provision authorising the competent authority to make the information public in the event that the person fails to do so.

(3) The competent authority may make public any information notified to the authority in accordance with transparency rules.

(4) Transparency rules may make provision by reference to any provision of any rules made by the Panel on Takeovers and Mergers under Part 28 of the Companies Act 2006.

(5) Sections 89A to 89F and this section are without prejudice to any other power conferred by this Part to make Part 6 rules.".

(2) The effectiveness for the purposes of section 155 of the Financial Services and Markets Act 2000 (c. 8) (consultation on proposed rules) of things done by the Financial Services Authority before this section comes into force with a view to making transparency rules (as defined in the provisions to be inserted in that Act by subsection (1) above) is not affected by the fact that those provisions were not then in force.

1267. Competent authority's power to call for information

In Part 6 of the Financial Services and Markets Act 2000 after the sections inserted by section 1266 above insert—

"Power of competent authority to call for information

89H Competent authority's power to call for information

(1) The competent authority may by notice in writing given to a person to whom this section applies require him—

(a) to provide specified information or information of a specified description, or

(b) to produce specified documents or documents of a specified description.

(2) This section applies to—

(a) an issuer in respect of whom transparency rules have effect;

(b) a voteholder;

(c) an auditor of—

(i) an issuer to whom this section applies, or

(ii) a voteholder;

(d) a person who controls a voteholder;

(e) a person controlled by a voteholder;

(f) a director or other similar officer of an issuer to whom this section applies;

(g) a director or other similar officer of a voteholder or, where the affairs of a voteholder are managed by its members, a member of the voteholder.

(3) This section applies only to information and documents reasonably required in connection with the exercise by the competent authority of functions conferred on it by or under sections 89A to 89G (transparency rules).

(4) Information or documents required under this section must be provided or produced—

(a) before the end of such reasonable period as may be specified, and

(b) at such place as may be specified.

(5) If a person claims a lien on a document, its production under this section does not affect the lien.

89I **Requirements in connection with call for information**

(1) The competent authority may require any information provided under section 89H to be provided in such form as it may reasonably require.

(2) The competent authority may require—

(a) any information provided, whether in a document or otherwise, to be verified in such manner as it may reasonably require;

(b) any document produced to be authenticated in such manner as it may reasonably require.

(3) If a document is produced in response to a requirement imposed under section 89H, the competent authority may—

(a) take copies of or extracts from the document; or

(b) require the person producing the document, or any relevant person, to provide an explanation of the document.

(4) In subsection (3)(b) "relevant person", in relation to a person who is required to produce a document, means a person who—

(a) has been or is a director or controller of that person;

(b) has been or is an auditor of that person;

(c) has been or is an actuary, accountant or lawyer appointed or instructed by that person; or

(d) has been or is an employee of that person.

(5) If a person who is required under section 89H to produce a document fails to do so, the competent authority may require him to state, to the best of his knowledge and belief, where the document is.

89J **Power to call for information: supplementary provisions**

(1) The competent authority may require an issuer to make public any information provided to the authority under section 89H.

(2) If the issuer fails to comply with a requirement under subsection (1), the competent authority may, after seeking representations from the issuer, make the information public.

(3) In sections 89H and 89I (power of competent authority to call for information)—

"control" and "controlled" have the meaning given by subsection (4) below;

"specified" means specified in the notice;

"voteholder" means a person who—

    (a) holds voting rights in respect of any voting shares for the purposes of sections 89A to 89G (transparency rules), or

    (b) is treated as holding such rights by virtue of rules under section 89A(3)(b).

(4) For the purposes of those sections a person ("A") controls another person ("B") if—

    (a) A holds a majority of the voting rights in B,

    (b) A is a member of B and has the right to appoint or remove a majority of the members of the board of directors (or, if there is no such board, the equivalent management body) of B,

    (c) A is a member of B and controls alone, pursuant to an agreement with other shareholders or members, a majority of the voting rights in B, or

    (d) A has the right to exercise, or actually exercises, dominant influence or control over B.

(5) For the purposes of subsection (4)(b)—

    (a) any rights of a person controlled by A, and

    (b) any rights of a person acting on behalf of A or a person controlled by A,

    are treated as held by A.".

1268. Powers exercisable in case of infringement of transparency obligation

In Part 6 of the Financial Services and Markets Act 2000 (c. 8), after the sections inserted by section 1267 above insert—

"Powers exercisable in case of infringement of transparency obligation

89K Public censure of issuer

(1) If the competent authority finds that an issuer of securities admitted to trading on a regulated market is failing or has failed to comply with an applicable transparency obligation, it may publish a statement to that effect.

(2) If the competent authority proposes to publish a statement, it must give the issuer a warning notice setting out the terms of the proposed statement.

(3) If, after considering any representations made in response to the warning notice, the competent authority decides to make the proposed statement, it must give the issuer a decision notice setting out the terms of the statement.

(4) A notice under this section must inform the issuer of his right to refer the matter to the Tribunal (see section 89N) and give an indication of the procedure on such a reference.

(5) In this section "transparency obligation" means an obligation under—

    (a) a provision of transparency rules, or

    (b) any other provision made in accordance with the transparency obligations directive.

(6) In relation to an issuer whose home State is a member State other than the United Kingdom, any reference to an applicable transparency obligation must be read subject to section 100A(2).

89L Power to suspend or prohibit trading of securities

(1) This section applies to securities admitted to trading on a regulated market.

(2) If the competent authority has reasonable grounds for suspecting that an applicable transparency obligation has been infringed by an issuer, it may—

    (a) suspend trading in the securities for a period not exceeding 10 days,

    (b) prohibit trading in the securities, or

    (c) make a request to the operator of the market on which the issuer's securities are traded—

        (i) to suspend trading in the securities for a period not exceeding 10 days, or

        (ii) to prohibit trading in the securities.

(3) If the competent authority has reasonable grounds for suspecting that a provision required by the transparency obligations directive has been infringed by a voteholder of an issuer, it may—

    (a) prohibit trading in the securities, or

    (b) make a request to the operator of the market on which the issuer's securities are traded to prohibit trading in the securities.

  (4) If the competent authority finds that an applicable transparency obligation has been infringed, it may require the market operator to prohibit trading in the securities.

  (5) In this section "transparency obligation" means an obligation under—

    (a) a provision contained in transparency rules, or

    (b) any other provision made in accordance with the transparency obligations directive.

  (6) In relation to an issuer whose home State is a member State other than the United Kingdom, any reference to an applicable transparency obligation must be read subject to section 100A(2).

89M Procedure under section 89L

  (1) A requirement under section 89L takes effect—

    (a) immediately, if the notice under subsection (2) states that that is the case;

    (b) in any other case, on such date as may be specified in the notice.

  (2) If the competent authority—

    (a) proposes to exercise the powers in section 89L in relation to a person, or

    (b) exercises any of those powers in relation to a person with immediate effect,

  it must give that person written notice.

  (3) The notice must—

    (a) give details of the competent authority's action or proposed action;

    (b) state the competent authority's reasons for taking the action in question and choosing the date on which it took effect or takes effect;

    (c) inform the recipient that he may make representations to the competent authority within such period as may be specified by the notice (whether or not he had referred the matter to the Tribunal);

    (d) inform him of the date on which the action took effect or takes effect;

    (e) inform him of his right to refer the matter to the Tribunal (see section 89N) and give an indication of the procedure on such a reference.

  (4) The competent authority may extend the period within which representations may be made to it.

  (5) If, having considered any representations made to it, the competent authority decides to maintain, vary or revoke its earlier decision, it must give written notice to that effect to the person mentioned in subsection (2).

89N Right to refer matters to the Tribunal

A person—

    (a) to whom a decision notice is given under section 89K (public censure), or

    (b) to whom a notice is given under section 89M (procedure in connection with suspension or prohibition of trading),

may refer the matter to the Tribunal.".

Other matters

1269. Corporate governance rules

In Part 6 of the Financial Services and Markets Act 2000 (c. 8), after the sections inserted by section 1268 above insert—

"Corporate governance

89O Corporate governance rules

  (1) The competent authority may make rules ("corporate governance rules")—

    (a) for the purpose of implementing, enabling the implementation of or dealing with matters arising out of or related to, any Community obligation relating to the corporate governance of issuers who have requested or approved admission of their securities to trading on a regulated market;

(b) about corporate governance in relation to such issuers for the purpose of implementing, or dealing with matters arising out of or related to, any Community obligation.

(2) "Corporate governance", in relation to an issuer, includes—

(a) the nature, constitution or functions of the organs of the issuer;

(b) the manner in which organs of the issuer conduct themselves;

(c) the requirements imposed on organs of the issuer;

(d) the relationship between the different organs of the issuer;

(e) the relationship between the organs of the issuer and the members of the issuer or holders of the issuer's securities.

(3) The burdens and restrictions imposed by rules under this section on foreign-traded issuers must not be greater than the burdens and restrictions imposed on UK-traded issuers by—

(a) rules under this section, and

(b) listing rules.

(4) For this purpose—

"foreign-traded issuer" means an issuer who has requested or approved admission of the issuer's securities to trading on a regulated market situated or operating outside the United Kingdom;

"UK-traded issuer" means an issuer who has requested or approved admission of the issuer's securities to trading on a regulated market situated or operating in the United Kingdom.

(5) This section is without prejudice to any other power conferred by this Part to make Part 6 rules.".

1270. Liability for false or misleading statements in certain publications

In Part 6 of the Financial Services and Markets Act 2000 (c. 8), after section 90 insert—

"90A Compensation for statements in certain publications

(1) The publications to which this section applies are—

(a) any reports and statements published in response to a requirement imposed by a provision implementing Article 4, 5 or 6 of the transparency obligations directive, and

(b) any preliminary statement made in advance of a report or statement to be published in response to a requirement imposed by a provision implementing Article 4 of that directive, to the extent that it contains information that it is intended—

(i) will appear in the report or statement, and

(ii) will be presented in the report or statement in substantially the same form as that in which it is presented in the preliminary statement.

(2) The securities to which this section applies are—

(a) securities that are traded on a regulated market situated or operating in the United Kingdom, and

(b) securities that—

(i) are traded on a regulated market situated or operating outside the United Kingdom, and

(ii) are issued by an issuer for which the United Kingdom is the home Member State within the meaning of Article 2.1(i) of the transparency obligations directive.

(3) The issuer of securities to which this section applies is liable to pay compensation to a person who has—

    (a) acquired such securities issued by it, and

    (b) suffered loss in respect of them as a result of—

        (i) any untrue or misleading statement in a publication to which this section applies, or

        (ii) the omission from any such publication of any matter required to be included in it.

(4) The issuer is so liable only if a person discharging managerial responsibilities within the issuer in relation to the publication—

    (a) knew the statement to be untrue or misleading or was reckless as to whether it was untrue or misleading, or

    (b) knew the omission to be dishonest concealment of a material fact.

(5) A loss is not regarded as suffered as a result of the statement or omission in the publication unless the person suffering it acquired the relevant securities—

    (a) in reliance on the information in the publication, and

    (b) at a time when, and in circumstances in which, it was reasonable for him to rely on that information.

(6) Except as mentioned in subsection (8)—

    (a) the issuer is not subject to any other liability than that provided for by this section in respect of loss suffered as a result of reliance by any person on—

        (i) an untrue or misleading statement in a publication to which this section applies, or

        (ii) the omission from any such publication of any matter required to be included in it, and

    (b) a person other than the issuer is not subject to any liability, other than to the issuer, in respect of any such loss.

(7) Any reference in subsection (6) to a person being subject to a liability includes a reference to another person being entitled as against him to be granted any civil remedy or to rescind or repudiate an agreement.

(8) This section does not affect—

    (a) the powers conferred by section 382 and 384 (powers of the court to make a restitution order and of the Authority to require restitution);

    (b) liability for a civil penalty;

    (c) liability for a criminal offence.

(9) For the purposes of this section—

    (a) the following are persons "discharging managerial responsibilities" in relation to a publication—

        (i) any director of the issuer (or person occupying the position of director, by whatever name called),

        (ii) in the case of an issuer whose affairs are managed by its members, any member of the issuer,

        (iii) in the case of an issuer that has no persons within subparagraph (i) or (ii), any senior executive of the issuer having responsibilities in relation to the publication;

    (b) references to the acquisition by a person of securities include his contracting to acquire them or any interest in them.

90B Power to make further provision about liability for published information

(1) The Treasury may by regulations make provision about the liability of issuers of securities traded on a regulated market, and other persons, in respect of information published to holders of securities, to the market or to the public generally.

(2) Regulations under this section may amend any primary or subordinate legislation, including any provision of, or made under, this Act.".

1271. Exercise of powers where UK is host member State

In Part 6 of the Financial Services and Markets Act 2000 (c. 8), after section 100 insert—

"**100AExercise of powers where UK is host member state**

(1) This section applies to the exercise by the competent authority of any power under this Part exercisable in case of infringement of—

(a) a provision of prospectus rules or any other provision made in accordance with the prospectus directive, or

(b) a provision of transparency rules or any other provision made in accordance with the transparency obligations directive,

in relation to an issuer whose home State is a member State other than the United Kingdom.

(2) The competent authority may act in such a case only in respect of the infringement of a provision required by the relevant directive.

Any reference to an applicable provision or applicable transparency obligation shall be read accordingly.

(3) If the authority finds that there has been such an infringement, it must give a notice to that effect to the competent authority of the person's home State requesting it—

(a) to take all appropriate measures for the purpose of ensuring that the person remedies the situation that has given rise to the notice, and

(b) to inform the authority of the measures it proposes to take or has taken or the reasons for not taking such measures.

(4) The authority may not act further unless satisfied—

(a) that the competent authority of the person's home State has failed or refused to take measures for the purpose mentioned in subsection (3)(a), or

(b) that the measures taken by that authority have proved inadequate for that purpose.

This does not affect exercise of the powers under section 87K(2), 87L(2) or (3) or 89L(2) or (3) (powers to protect market).

(5) If the authority is so satisfied, it must, after informing the competent authority of the person's home State, take all appropriate measures to protect investors.

(6) In such a case the authority must inform the Commission of the measures at the earliest opportunity.".

1272. Transparency obligations and related matters: minor and consequential amendments

(1) Schedule 15 to this Act makes minor and consequential amendments in connection with the provision made by this Part.

(2) In that Schedule-

Part 1 contains amendments of the Financial Services and Markets Act 2000 (c. 8);

Part 2 contains amendments of the Companies (Audit, Investigations and Community Enterprise) Act 2004 (c. 27).

1273. Corporate governance regulations

(1) The Secretary of State may make regulations—

(a) for the purpose of implementing, enabling the implementation of or dealing with matters arising out of or related to, any Community obligation relating to the corporate governance of issuers who have requested or approved admission of their securities to trading on a regulated market;

(b) about corporate governance in relation to such issuers for the purpose of implementing, or dealing with matters arising out of or related to, any Community obligation.

(2) "Corporate governance", in relation to an issuer, includes—

(a) the nature, constitution or functions of the organs of the issuer;

(b) the manner in which organs of the issuer conduct themselves;

(c) the requirements imposed on organs of the issuer;

(d) the relationship between different organs of the issuer;

(e) the relationship between the organs of the issuer and the members of the issuer or holders of the issuer's securities.

(3) The regulations may—

(a) make provision by reference to any specified code on corporate governance that may be issued from time to time by a specified body;

(b) create new criminal offences (subject to subsection (4));

(c) make provision excluding liability in damages in respect of things done or omitted for the purposes of, or in connection with, the carrying on, or purported carrying on, of any specified activities.

"Specified" here means specified in the regulations.

(4) The regulations may not create a criminal offence punishable by a greater penalty than—

(a) on indictment, a fine;

(b) on summary conviction, a fine not exceeding the statutory maximum or (if calculated on a daily basis) £100 a day.

(5) Regulations under this section are subject to negative resolution procedure.

(6) In this section "issuer", "securities" and "regulated market" have the same meaning as in Part 6 of the Financial Services and Markets Act 2000 (c. 8).

PART 44

MISCELLANEOUS PROVISIONS

Regulation of actuaries etc

1274. Grants to bodies concerned with actuarial standards etc

(1) Section 16 of the Companies (Audit, Investigations and Community Enterprise) Act 2004 (c. 27) (grants to bodies concerned with accounting standards etc) is amended as follows.

(2) In subsection (2) (matters carried on by bodies eligible for grants) for paragraph (l) substitute—

"(l) issuing standards to be applied in actuarial work;

(m) issuing standards in respect of matters to be contained in reports or other communications required to be produced or made by actuaries or in accordance with standards within paragraph (l);

(n) investigating departures from standards within paragraph (l) or (m);

(o) taking steps to secure compliance with standards within paragraph (l) or (m);

(p) carrying out investigations into public interest cases arising in connection with the performance of actuarial functions by members of professional actuarial bodies;

(q) holding disciplinary hearings relating to members of professional actuarial bodies following the conclusion of investigations within paragraph (p);

(r) deciding whether (and, if so, what) disciplinary action should be taken against members of professional actuarial bodies to whom hearings within paragraph (q) related;

(s) supervising the exercise by professional actuarial bodies of regulatory functions in relation to their members;

(t) overseeing or directing any of the matters mentioned above.".

(3) In subsection (5) (definitions) at the appropriate places insert—

""professional actuarial body" means—

(a) the Institute of Actuaries, or

(b) the Faculty of Actuaries in Scotland,

and the "members" of a professional actuarial body include persons who, although not members of the body, are subject to its rules in performing actuarial functions;"

""regulatory functions", in relation to professional actuarial bodies, means any of the following—

(a) investigatory or disciplinary functions exercised by such bodies in relation to the performance by their members of actuarial functions,

(b) the setting by such bodies of standards in relation to the performance by their members of actuarial functions, and

(c) the determining by such bodies of requirements in relation to the education and training of their members;".

1275. Levy to pay expenses of bodies concerned with actuarial standards etc

(1) Section 17 of the Companies (Audit, Investigations and Community Enterprise) Act 2004 (c. 27) (levy to pay expenses of bodies concerned with accounting standards etc) is amended in accordance with subsections (2) to (5).

(2) In subsection (3)(a) after "to which" insert ", or persons within subsection (3A) to whom,".

(3) After subsection (3) insert—

"(3A) The following persons are within this subsection—

(a) the administrators of a public service pension scheme (within the meaning of section 1 of the Pension Schemes Act 1993);

(b) the trustees or managers of an occupational or personal pension scheme (within the meaning of that section).".

(4) After subsection (4)(b) insert—

"(c) make different provision for different cases.".

(5) After subsection (12) insert—

"(13) If a draft of any regulations to which subsection (10) applies would, apart from this subsection, be treated for the purposes of the standing orders of either House of Parliament as a hybrid instrument, it is to proceed in that House as if it were not such an instrument.".

(6) The above amendments have effect in relation to any exercise of the power to make regulations under section 17 of the Companies (Audit, Investigations and Community Enterprise) Act 2004 after this section comes into force, regardless of when the expenses to be met by the levy in respect of which the regulations are made were incurred.

(7) In Schedule 3 to the Pensions Act 2004 (c. 35) (disclosure of information held by the Pensions Regulator), in the entry relating to the Secretary of State, in the second column, for "or" at the end of paragraph (g) substitute—

"(ga) Section 17 of the Companies (Audit, Investigations and Community Enterprise) Act 2004 (levy to pay expenses of bodies concerned with accounting standards, actuarial standards etc), or".

1276. Application of provisions to Scotland and Northern Ireland

(1) Section 16 of the Companies (Audit, Investigations and Community Enterprise) Act 2004 (grants to bodies concerned with accounting standards etc) is amended as follows.

(2) For subsection (6) (application of section to Scotland) substitute—

"(6) In their application to Scotland, subsection (2)(a) to (t) are to be read as referring only to matters provision relating to which would be outside the legislative competence of the Scottish Parliament.".

(3) In subsection (2) in paragraph (c), after "1985 (c. 6)" insert "or the 1986 Order".

(4) In subsection (5)—

(a) in the definition of "company" after "1985 (c. 6)" insert "or the 1986 Order",

(b) in the definition of "subsidiary" after "1985" insert "or Article 4 of the 1986 Order", and

(c) after that definition insert—
> ""the 1986 Order" means the Companies (Northern Ireland) Order 1986 (S.I. 1986/1032 (N.I. 6)).".

(5) In section 66 of that Act (extent), in subsection (2) (provisions extending to Northern Ireland, as well as England and Wales and Scotland) for "17" substitute "16 to 18".

Information as to exercise of voting rights by institutional investors

1277. Power to require information about exercise of voting rights

(1) The Treasury or the Secretary of State may make provision by regulations requiring institutions to which this section applies to provide information about the exercise of voting rights attached to shares to which this section applies.

(2) This power is exercisable in accordance with—
> section 1278 (institutions to which information provisions apply),
> section 1279 (shares to which information provisions apply), and
> section 1280 (obligations with respect to provision of information).

(3) In this section and the sections mentioned above—
> (a) references to a person acting on behalf of an institution include—
>> (i) any person to whom authority has been delegated by the institution to take decisions as to any matter relevant to the subject matter of the regulations, and
>> (ii) such other persons as may be specified; and
> (b) "specified" means specified in the regulations.

(4) The obligation imposed by regulations under this section is enforceable by civil proceedings brought by—
> (a) any person to whom the information should have been provided, or
> (b) a specified regulatory authority.

(5) Regulations under this section may make different provision for different descriptions of institution, different descriptions of shares and for other different circumstances.

(6) Regulations under this section are subject to affirmative resolution procedure.

1278. Institutions to which information provisions apply

(1) The institutions to which section 1277 applies are—
> (a) unit trust schemes within the meaning of the Financial Services and Markets Act 2000 (c. 8) in respect of which an order is in force under section 243 of that Act;
> (b) open-ended investment companies incorporated by virtue of regulations under section 262 of that Act;
> (c) companies approved for the purposes of section 842 of the Income and Corporation Taxes Act 1988 (c. 1) (investment trusts);
> (d) pension schemes as defined in section 1(5) of the Pension Schemes Act 1993 (c. 48) or the Pension Schemes (Northern Ireland) Act 1993 (c. 49);
> (e) undertakings authorised under the Financial Services and Markets Act 2000 to carry on long-term insurance business (that is, the activity of effecting or carrying out contracts of long-term insurance within the meaning of the Financial Services and Markets (Regulated Activities) Order 2001 (S.I. 2001/544);
> (f) collective investment schemes that are recognised by virtue of section 270 of that Act (schemes authorised in designated countries or territories).

(2) Regulations under that section may—
> (a) provide that the section applies to other descriptions of institution;
> (b) provide that the section does not apply to a specified description of institution.

(3) The regulations must specify by whom, in the case of any description of institution, the duty imposed by the regulations is to be fulfilled.

1279. Shares to which information provisions apply

   (1) The shares to which section 1277 applies are shares—

      (a) of a description traded on a specified market, and

      (b) in which the institution has, or is taken to have, an interest.

      Regulations under that section may provide that the section does not apply to shares of a specified description.

   (2) For this purpose an institution has an interest in shares if the shares, or a depositary certificate in respect of them, are held by it, or on its behalf.

      A "depositary certificate" means an instrument conferring rights (other than options)—

      (a) in respect of shares held by another person, and

      (b) the transfer of which may be effected without the consent of that person.

   (3) Where an institution has an interest—

      (a) in a specified description of collective investment scheme (within the meaning of the Financial Services and Markets Act 2000 (c. 8)), or

      (b) in any other specified description of scheme or collective investment vehicle,

      it is taken to have an interest in any shares in which that scheme or vehicle has or is taken to have an interest.

   (4) For this purpose a scheme or vehicle is taken to have an interest in shares if it would be regarded as having such an interest in accordance with subsection (2) if it was an institution to which section 1277 applied.

1280. Obligations with respect to provision of information

   (1) Regulations under section 1277 may require the provision of specified information about—

      (a) the exercise or non-exercise of voting rights by the institution or any person acting on its behalf,

      (b) any instructions given by the institution or any person acting on its behalf as to the exercise or non-exercise of voting rights, and

      (c) any delegation by the institution or any person acting on its behalf of any functions in relation to the exercise or non-exercise of voting rights or the giving of such instructions.

   (2) The regulations may require information to be provided in respect of specified occasions or specified periods.

   (3) Where instructions are given to act on the recommendations or advice of another person, the regulations may require the provision of information about what recommendations or advice were given.

   (4) The regulations may require information to be provided—

      (a) in such manner as may be specified, and

      (b) to such persons as may be specified, or to the public, or both.

   (5) The regulations may provide—

      (a) that an institution may discharge its obligations under the regulations by referring to information disclosed by a person acting on its behalf, and

      (b) that in such a case it is sufficient, where that other person acts on behalf of more than one institution, that the reference is to information given in aggregated form, that is—

         (i) relating to the exercise or non-exercise by that person of voting rights on behalf of more than one institution, or

         (ii) relating to the instructions given by that person in respect of the exercise or non-exercise of voting rights on behalf of more than one institution, or

         (iii) relating to the delegation by that person of functions in relation to the exercise or non-exercise of voting rights, or the giving of instructions in respect of the exercise or non-exercise of voting rights, on behalf of more than one institution.

   (6) References in this section to instructions are to instructions of any description, whether general or specific, whether binding or not and whether or not acted upon.

Disclosure of information under the Enterprise Act 2002

1281. Disclosure of information under the Enterprise Act 2002

In Part 9 of the Enterprise Act 2002 (c. 40) (information), after section 241 insert—

"241A Civil proceedings

(1) A public authority which holds prescribed information to which section 237 applies may disclose that information to any person—

(a) for the purposes of, or in connection with, prescribed civil proceedings (including prospective proceedings) in the United Kingdom or elsewhere, or

(b) for the purposes of obtaining legal advice in relation to such proceedings, or

(c) otherwise for the purposes of establishing, enforcing or defending legal rights that are or may be the subject of such proceedings.

(2) Subsection (1) does not apply to—

(a) information which comes to a public authority in connection with an investigation under Part 4, 5 or 6 of the 1973 Act or under section 11 of the Competition Act 1980;

(b) competition information within the meaning of section 351 of the Financial Services and Markets Act 2000;

(c) information which comes to a public authority in connection with an investigation under Part 3 or 4 or section 174 of this Act;

(d) information which comes to a public authority in connection with an investigation under the Competition Act 1998 (c. 41).

(3) In subsection (1) "prescribed" means prescribed by order of the Secretary of State.

(4) An order under this section—

(a) may prescribe information, or civil proceedings, for the purposes of this section by reference to such factors as appear to the Secretary of State to be appropriate;

(b) may prescribe for the purposes of this section all information, or civil proceedings, or all information or civil proceedings not falling within one or more specified exceptions;

(c) must be made by statutory instrument subject to annulment in pursuance of a resolution of either House of Parliament.

(5) Information disclosed under this section must not be used by the person to whom it is disclosed for any purpose other than those specified in subsection (1).".

Expenses of winding up

1282. Payment of expenses of winding up

(1) In Chapter 8 of Part 4 of the Insolvency Act 1986 (c. 45) (winding up of companies: provisions of general application), before section 176A (under the heading "*Property subject to floating charge*") insert—

"176ZA   Payment of expenses of winding up (England and Wales)

(1) The expenses of winding up in England and Wales, so far as the assets of the company available for payment of general creditors are insufficient to meet them, have priority over any claims to property comprised in or subject to any floating charge created by the company and shall be paid out of any such property accordingly.

(2) In subsection (1)—

(a) the reference to assets of the company available for payment of general creditors does not include any amount made available under section 176A(2)(a);

(b) the reference to claims to property comprised in or subject to a floating charge is to the claims of—

(i) the holders of debentures secured by, or holders of, the floating charge, and

(ii) any preferential creditors entitled to be paid out of that property in priority to them.

(3) Provision may be made by rules restricting the application of subsection (1), in such circumstances as may be prescribed, to expenses authorised or approved—

    (a) by the holders of debentures secured by, or holders of, the floating charge and by any preferential creditors entitled to be paid in priority to them, or

    (b) by the court.

(4) References in this section to the expenses of the winding up are to all expenses properly incurred in the winding up, including the remuneration of the liquidator.".

(2) In Chapter 8 of Part 5 of the Insolvency (Northern Ireland) Order 1989 (S.I. 1989/2405 (N.I. 19)) (winding up of companies: provisions of general application), before Article 150A (under the heading "*Property subject to floating charge*") insert—

"150ZA   Payment of expenses of winding up

(1) The expenses of winding up, so far as the assets of the company available for payment of general creditors are insufficient to meet them, have priority over any claims to property comprised in or subject to any floating charge created by the company and shall be paid out of any such property accordingly.

(2) In paragraph (1)—

    (a) the reference to assets of the company available for payment of general creditors does not include any amount made available under Article 150A(2)(a);

    (b) the reference to claims to property comprised in or subject to a floating charge is to the claims of—

        (i) the holders of debentures secured by, or holders of, the floating charge, and

        (ii) any preferential creditors entitled to be paid out of that property in priority to them.

(3) Provision may be made by rules restricting the application of paragraph (1), in such circumstances as may be prescribed, to expenses authorised or approved—

    (a) by the holders of debentures secured by, or holders of, the floating charge and by any preferential creditors entitled to be paid in priority to them, or

    (b) by the Court.

(4) References in this Article to the expenses of the winding up are to all expenses properly incurred in the winding up, including the remuneration of the liquidator.".

Commonhold associations

1283. Amendment of memorandum or articles of commonhold association

In paragraph 3(1) of Schedule 3 to the Commonhold and Leasehold Reform Act 2002 (c. 15) (alteration of memorandum or articles by commonhold association to be of no effect until altered version registered with Land Registry) for "An alteration of the memorandum or articles of association" substitute "Where a commonhold association alters its memorandum or articles at a time when the land specified in its memorandum is commonhold land, the alteration".

PART 45
NORTHERN IRELAND

1284. Extension of Companies Acts to Northern Ireland

(1) The Companies Acts as defined by this Act (see section 2) extend to Northern Ireland.

(2) The Companies (Northern Ireland) Order 1986 (S.I. 1986/1032 (N.I. 6)), the Companies Consolidation (Consequential Provisions) (Northern Ireland) Order 1986 (S.I. 1986/1035 (N.I. 9)) and Part 3 of the Companies (Audit, Investigations and Community Enterprise) Order 2005 (S.I. 2005/1967 (N.I. 17)) shall cease to have effect accordingly.

1285. Extension of GB enactments relating to SEs

(1) The enactments in force in Great Britain relating to SEs extend to Northern Ireland.

(2) The following enactments shall cease to have effect accordingly—

(a) the European Public Limited-Liability Company Regulations (Northern Ireland) 2004 (SR 2004/417), and

(b) the European Public Limited-Liability Company (Fees) Regulations (Northern Ireland) 2004 (SR 2004/418).

(3) In this section "SE" means a European Public Limited-Liability Company (or Societas Europaea) within the meaning of Council Regulation 2157/2001/EC of 8 October 2001 on the Statute for a European Company.

1286. Extension of GB enactments relating to certain other forms of business organisation

(1) The enactments in force in Great Britain relating to—

(a) limited liability partnerships,

(b) limited partnerships,

(c) open-ended investment companies, and

(d) European Economic Interest Groupings,

extend to Northern Ireland.

(2) The following enactments shall cease to have effect accordingly—

(a) the Limited Liability Partnerships Act (Northern Ireland) 2002 (c. 12 (N. I.));

(b) the Limited Partnerships Act 1907 (c. 24) as it formerly had effect in Northern Ireland;

(c) the Open-Ended Investment Companies Act (Northern Ireland) 2002 (c. 13 (N.I.));

(d) the European Economic Interest Groupings Regulations (Northern Ireland) 1989 (SR 1989/216).

1287. Extension of enactments relating to business names

(1) The provisions of Part 41 of this Act (business names) extend to Northern Ireland.

(2) The Business Names (Northern Ireland) Order 1986 (S.I. 1986/1033 (N.I. 7)) shall cease to have effect accordingly.

PART 46
GENERAL SUPPLEMENTARY PROVISIONS

Regulations and orders

1288. Regulations and orders: statutory instrument

Except as otherwise provided, regulations and orders under this Act shall be made by statutory instrument.

1289. Regulations and orders: negative resolution procedure

Where regulations or orders under this Act are subject to "negative resolution procedure" the statutory instrument containing the regulations or order shall be subject to annulment in pursuance of a resolution of either House of Parliament.

1290. Regulations and orders: affirmative resolution procedure

Where regulations or orders under this Act are subject to "affirmative resolution procedure" the regulations or order must not be made unless a draft of the statutory instrument containing them has been laid before Parliament and approved by a resolution of each House of Parliament.

1291. Regulations and orders: approval after being made

(1) Regulations or orders under this Act that are subject to "approval after being made"—

(a) must be laid before Parliament after being made, and

(b) cease to have effect at the end of 28 days beginning with the day on which they were made unless during that period they are approved by resolution of each House.

(2) In reckoning the period of 28 days no account shall be taken of any time during which Parliament is dissolved or prorogued or during which both Houses are adjourned for more than four days.

(3) The regulations or order ceasing to have effect does not affect—

    (a) anything previously done under them or it, or

    (b) the making of new regulations or a new order.

1292. Regulations and orders: supplementary

(1) Regulations or orders under this Act may—

    (a) make different provision for different cases or circumstances,

    (b) include supplementary, incidental and consequential provision, and

    (c) make transitional provision and savings.

(2) Any provision that may be made by regulations under this Act may be made by order; and any provision that may be made by order under this Act may be made by regulations.

(3) Any provision that may be made by regulations or order under this Act for which no Parliamentary procedure is prescribed may be made by regulations or order subject to negative or affirmative resolution procedure.

(4) Any provision that may be made by regulations or order under this Act subject to negative resolution procedure may be made by regulations or order subject to affirmative resolution procedure.

Meaning of "enactment"

1293. Meaning of "enactment"

In this Act, unless the context otherwise requires, "enactment" includes—

    (a) an enactment contained in subordinate legislation within the meaning of the Interpretation Act 1978 (c. 30),

    (b) an enactment contained in, or in an instrument made under, an Act of the Scottish Parliament, and

    (c) an enactment contained in, or in an instrument made under, Northern Ireland legislation within the meaning of the Interpretation Act 1978.

Consequential and transitional provisions

1294. Power to make consequential amendments etc

(1) The Secretary of State or the Treasury may by order make such provision amending, repealing or revoking any enactment to which this section applies as they consider necessary or expedient in consequence of any provision made by or under this Act.

(2) This section applies to—

    (a) any enactment passed or made before the passing of this Act,

    (b) any enactment contained in this Act or in subordinate legislation made under it, and

    (c) any enactment passed or made before the end of the session after that in which this Act is passed.

(3) Without prejudice to the generality of the power conferred by subsection (1), orders under this section may—

    (a) make provision extending to other forms of organisation any provision made by or under this Act in relation to companies, or

    (b) make provision corresponding to that made by or under this Act in relation to companies, in either case with such adaptations or other modifications as appear to the Secretary of State or the Treasury to be necessary or expedient.

(4) The references in subsection (3) to provision made by this Act include provision conferring power to make provision by regulations, orders or other subordinate legislation.

(5) Amendments and repeals made under this section are additional, and without prejudice, to those made by or under any other provision of this Act.

(6) Orders under this section are subject to affirmative resolution procedure.

1295. Repeals

The enactments specified in Schedule 16, which include enactments that are no longer of practical utility, are repealed to the extent specified.

1296. Power to make transitional provision and savings

(1) The Secretary of State or the Treasury may by order make such transitional provision and savings as they consider necessary or expedient in connection with the commencement of any provision made by or under this Act.

(2) An order may, in particular, make such adaptations of provisions brought into force as appear to be necessary or expedient in consequence of other provisions of this Act not yet having come into force.

(3) Transitional provision and savings made under this section are additional, and without prejudice, to those made by or under any other provision of this Act.

(4) Orders under this section are subject to negative resolution procedure.

1297. Continuity of the law

(1) This section applies where any provision of this Act re-enacts (with or without modification) an enactment repealed by this Act.

(2) The repeal and re-enactment does not affect the continuity of the law.

(3) Anything done (including subordinate legislation made), or having effect as if done, under or for the purposes of the repealed provision that could have been done under or for the purposes of the corresponding provision of this Act, if in force or effective immediately before the commencement of that corresponding provision, has effect thereafter as if done under or for the purposes of that corresponding provision.

(4) Any reference (express or implied) in this Act or any other enactment, instrument or document to a provision of this Act shall be construed (so far as the context permits) as including, as respects times, circumstances or purposes in relation to which the corresponding repealed provision had effect, a reference to that corresponding provision.

(5) Any reference (express or implied) in any enactment, instrument or document to a repealed provision shall be construed (so far as the context permits), as respects times, circumstances and purposes in relation to which the corresponding provision of this Act has effect, as being or (according to the context) including a reference to the corresponding provision of this Act.

(6) This section has effect subject to any specific transitional provision or saving contained in this Act.

(7) References in this section to this Act include subordinate legislation made under this Act.

(8) In this section "subordinate legislation" has the same meaning as in the Interpretation Act 1978 (c. 30).

PART 47
FINAL PROVISIONS

1298. Short title

The short title of this Act is the Companies Act 2006.

1299. Extent

Except as otherwise provided (or the context otherwise requires), the provisions of this Act extend to the whole of the United Kingdom.

1300. Commencement

    (1) The following provisions come into force on the day this Act is passed—

        (a) Part 43 (transparency obligations and related matters), except the amendment in paragraph 11(2) of Schedule 15 of the definition of "regulated market" in Part 6 of the Financial Services and Markets Act 2000 (c. 8),

        (b) in Part 44 (miscellaneous provisions)—

            section 1274 (grants to bodies concerned with actuarial standards etc), and

            section 1276 (application of provisions to Scotland and Northern Ireland),

        (c) Part 46 (general supplementary provisions), except section 1295 and Schedule 16 (repeals), and

        (d) this Part.

    (2) The other provisions of this Act come into force on such day as may be appointed by order of the Secretary of State or the Treasury.

SCHEDULES

SCHEDULE 1 Sections 254 and 255

CONNECTED PERSONS: REFERENCES TO AN INTEREST IN SHARES OR DEBENTURES

Introduction

1. (1) The provisions of this Schedule have effect for the interpretation of references in sections 254 and 255 (directors connected with or controlling a body corporate) to an interest in shares or debentures.

    (2) The provisions are expressed in relation to shares but apply to debentures as they apply to shares.

General provisions

2. (1) A reference to an interest in shares includes any interest of any kind whatsoever in shares.

    (2) Any restraints or restrictions to which the exercise of any right attached to the interest is or may be subject shall be disregarded.

    (3) It is immaterial that the shares in which a person has an interest are not identifiable.

    (4) Persons having a joint interest in shares are deemed each of them to have that interest.

Rights to acquire shares

3. (1) A person is taken to have an interest in shares if he enters into a contract to acquire them.

    (2) A person is taken to have an interest in shares if—
       (a) he has a right to call for delivery of the shares to himself or to his order, or
       (b) he has a right to acquire an interest in shares or is under an obligation to take an interest in shares,
       whether the right or obligation is conditional or absolute.

    (3) Rights or obligations to subscribe for shares are not to be taken for the purposes of sub-paragraph (2) to be rights to acquire or obligations to take an interest in shares.

    (4) A person ceases to have an interest in shares by virtue of this paragraph—
       (a) on the shares being delivered to another person at his order—
          (i) in fulfilment of a contract for their acquisition by him, or
          (ii) in satisfaction of a right of his to call for their delivery;
       (b) on a failure to deliver the shares in accordance with the terms of such a contract or on which such a right falls to be satisfied;
       (c) on the lapse of his right to call for the delivery of shares.

Right to exercise or control exercise of rights

4. (1) A person is taken to have an interest in shares if, not being the registered holder, he is entitled—
       (a) to exercise any right conferred by the holding of the shares, or
       (b) to control the exercise of any such right.

    (2) For this purpose a person is taken to be entitled to exercise or control the exercise of a right conferred by the holding of shares if he—
       (a) has a right (whether subject to conditions or not) the exercise of which would make him so entitled, or
       (b) is under an obligation (whether or not so subject) the fulfilment of which would make him so entitled.

    (3) A person is not by virtue of this paragraph taken to be interested in shares by reason only that—

(a) he has been appointed a proxy to exercise any of the rights attached to the shares, or

(b) he has been appointed by a body corporate to act as its representative at any meeting of a company or of any class of its members.

Bodies corporate

5. (1) A person is taken to be interested in shares if a body corporate is interested in them and—

   (a) the body corporate or its directors are accustomed to act in accordance with his directions or instructions, or

   (b) he is entitled to exercise or control the exercise of more than one-half of the voting power at general meetings of the body corporate.

   (2) For the purposes of sub-paragraph (1)(b) where—

   (a) a person is entitled to exercise or control the exercise of more than one-half of the voting power at general meetings of a body corporate, and

   (b) that body corporate is entitled to exercise or control the exercise of any of the voting power at general meetings of another body corporate,

   the voting power mentioned in paragraph (b) above is taken to be exercisable by that person.

Trusts

6. (1) Where an interest in shares is comprised in property held on trust, every beneficiary of the trust is taken to have an interest in shares, subject as follows.

   (2) So long as a person is entitled to receive, during the lifetime of himself or another, income from trust property comprising shares, an interest in the shares in reversion or remainder or (as regards Scotland) in fee shall be disregarded.

   (3) A person is treated as not interested in shares if and so long as he holds them—

   (a) under the law in force in any part of the United Kingdom, as a bare trustee or as a custodian trustee, or

   (b) under the law in force in Scotland, as a simple trustee.

   (4) There shall be disregarded any interest of a person subsisting by virtue of—

   (a) an authorised unit trust scheme (within the meaning of section 237 of the Financial Services and Markets Act 2000 (c. 8));

   (b) a scheme made under section 22 or 22A of the Charities Act 1960 (c. 58), section 25 of the Charities Act (Northern Ireland) 1964 (c. 33 (N.I.)) or section 24 or 25 of the Charities Act 1993 (c. 10), section 11 of the Trustee Investments Act 1961 (c. 62) or section 42 of the Administration of Justice Act 1982 (c. 53); or

   (c) the scheme set out in the Schedule to the Church Funds Investment Measure 1958 (1958 No. 1).

   (5) There shall be disregarded any interest—

   (a) of the Church of Scotland General Trustees or of the Church of Scotland Trust in shares held by them;

   (b) of any other person in shares held by those Trustees or that Trust otherwise than as simple trustees.

   "The Church of Scotland General Trustees" are the body incorporated by the order confirmed by the Church of Scotland (General Trustees) Order Confirmation Act 1921 (1921 c. xxv), and "the Church of Scotland Trust" is the body incorporated by the order confirmed by the Church of Scotland Trust Order Confirmation Act 1932 (1932 c. xxi).

SCHEDULE 2   Section 948

SPECIFIED PERSONS, DESCRIPTIONS OF DISCLOSURES ETC FOR THE
PURPOSES OF SECTION 948

PART 1
SPECIFIED PERSONS

1.   The Secretary of State.
2.   The Department of Enterprise, Trade and Investment for Northern Ireland.
3.   The Treasury.
4.   The Bank of England.
5.   The Financial Services Authority.
6.   The Commissioners for Her Majesty's Revenue and Customs.
7.   The Lord Advocate.
8.   The Director of Public Prosecutions.
9.   The Director of Public Prosecutions for Northern Ireland.
10. A constable.
11. A procurator fiscal.
12. The Scottish Ministers.

PART 2
SPECIFIED DESCRIPTIONS OF DISCLOSURES

13. A disclosure for the purpose of enabling or assisting a person authorised under section 457 of this
     Act (persons authorised to apply to court) to exercise his functions.
     Until the coming into force of section 457, the reference to that section is to be read as a reference
     to section 245C of the Companies Act 1985 (c. 6).
14. A disclosure for the purpose of enabling or assisting an inspector appointed under Part 14 of the
     Companies Act 1985 (investigation of companies and their affairs, etc) to exercise his functions.
15. A disclosure for the purpose of enabling or assisting a person authorised under section 447 of the
     Companies Act 1985 (power to require production of documents) or section 84 of the Companies
     Act 1989 (c. 40) (exercise of powers by officer etc) to exercise his functions.
16. A disclosure for the purpose of enabling or assisting a person appointed under section 167 of the
     Financial Services and Markets Act 2000 (c. 8) (general investigations) to conduct an investigation
     to exercise his functions.
17. A disclosure for the purpose of enabling or assisting a person appointed under section 168 of
     the Financial Services and Markets Act 2000 (investigations in particular cases) to conduct an
     investigation to exercise his functions.
18. A disclosure for the purpose of enabling or assisting a person appointed under section 169(1)(b)
     of the Financial Services and Markets Act 2000 (investigation in support of overseas regulator) to
     conduct an investigation to exercise his functions.
19. A disclosure for the purpose of enabling or assisting the body corporate responsible for adminis-
     tering the scheme referred to in section 225 of the Financial Services and Markets Act 2000 (the
     ombudsman scheme) to exercise its functions.
20. A disclosure for the purpose of enabling or assisting a person appointed under paragraph 4 (the
     panel of ombudsmen) or 5 (the Chief Ombudsman) of Schedule 17 to the Financial Services and
     Markets Act 2000 to exercise his functions.

21. A disclosure for the purpose of enabling or assisting a person appointed under regulations made under section 262(1) and (2)(k) of the Financial Services and Markets Act 2000 (investigations into open-ended investment companies) to conduct an investigation to exercise his functions.

22. A disclosure for the purpose of enabling or assisting a person appointed under section 284 of the Financial Services and Markets Act 2000 (investigations into affairs of certain collective investment schemes) to conduct an investigation to exercise his functions.

23. A disclosure for the purpose of enabling or assisting the investigator appointed under paragraph 7 of Schedule 1 to the Financial Services and Markets Act 2000 (arrangements for investigation of complaints) to exercise his functions.

24. A disclosure for the purpose of enabling or assisting a person appointed by the Treasury to hold an inquiry into matters relating to financial services (including an inquiry under section 15 of the Financial Services and Markets Act 2000 (c. 8)) to exercise his functions.

25. A disclosure for the purpose of enabling or assisting the Secretary of State or the Treasury to exercise any of their functions under any of the following—
    (a) the Companies Acts;
    (b) Part 5 of the Criminal Justice Act 1993 (c. 36) (insider dealing);
    (c) the Insolvency Act 1986 (c. 45);
    (d) the Company Directors Disqualification Act 1986 (c. 46);
    (e) Part 42 of this Act (statutory auditors);
    (f) Part 3 (investigations and powers to obtain information) or 7 (financial markets and insolvency) of the Companies Act 1989 (c. 40);
    (g) the Financial Services and Markets Act 2000.
    Until the coming into force of Part 42 of this Act, the reference to it in paragraph (e) is to be read as a reference to Part 2 of the Companies Act 1989.

26. A disclosure for the purpose of enabling or assisting the Scottish Ministers to exercise their functions under the enactments relating to insolvency.

27. A disclosure for the purpose of enabling or assisting the Department of Enterprise, Trade and Investment for Northern Ireland to exercise any powers conferred on it by the enactments relating to companies or insolvency.

28. A disclosure for the purpose of enabling or assisting a person appointed or authorised by the Department of Enterprise, Trade and Investment for Northern Ireland under the enactments relating to companies or insolvency to exercise his functions.

29. A disclosure for the purpose of enabling or assisting the Pensions Regulator to exercise the functions conferred on it by or by virtue of any of the following—
    (a) the Pension Schemes Act 1993 (c. 48);
    (b) the Pensions Act 1995 (c. 26);
    (c) the Welfare Reform and Pensions Act 1999 (c. 30);
    (d) the Pensions Act 2004 (c. 35);
    (e) any enactment in force in Northern Ireland corresponding to any of those enactments.

30. A disclosure for the purpose of enabling or assisting the Board of the Pension Protection Fund to exercise the functions conferred on it by or by virtue of Part 2 of the Pensions Act 2004 or any enactment in force in Northern Ireland corresponding to that Part.

31. A disclosure for the purpose of enabling or assisting—
    (a) the Bank of England,
    (b) the European Central Bank, or
    (c) the central bank of any country or territory outside the United Kingdom,
    to exercise its functions.

32. A disclosure for the purpose of enabling or assisting the Commissioners for Her Majesty's Revenue and Customs to exercise their functions.

33. A disclosure for the purpose of enabling or assisting organs of the Society of Lloyd's (being organs constituted by or under the Lloyd's Act 1982 (c. xiv)) to exercise their functions under or by virtue of the Lloyd's Acts 1871 to 1982.

34. A disclosure for the purpose of enabling or assisting the Office of Fair Trading to exercise its functions under any of the following—
    (a) the Fair Trading Act 1973 (c. 41);
    (b) the Consumer Credit Act 1974 (c. 39);
    (c) the Estate Agents Act 1979 (c. 38);
    (d) the Competition Act 1980 (c. 21);
    (e) the Competition Act 1998 (c. 41);
    (f) the Financial Services and Markets Act 2000 (c. 8);
    (g) the Enterprise Act 2002 (c. 40);
    (h) the Control of Misleading Advertisements Regulations 1988 (S.I. 1988/915);
    (i) the Unfair Terms in Consumer Contracts Regulations 1999 (S.I. 1999/2083).

35. A disclosure for the purpose of enabling or assisting the Competition Commission to exercise its functions under any of the following—
    (a) the Fair Trading Act 1973;
    (b) the Competition Act 1980;
    (c) the Competition Act 1998;
    (d) the Enterprise Act 2002.

36. A disclosure with a view to the institution of, or otherwise for the purposes of, proceedings before the Competition Appeal Tribunal.

37. A disclosure for the purpose of enabling or assisting an enforcer under Part 8 of the Enterprise Act 2002 (enforcement of consumer legislation) to exercise its functions under that Part.

38. A disclosure for the purpose of enabling or assisting the Charity Commission to exercise its functions.

39. A disclosure for the purpose of enabling or assisting the Attorney General to exercise his functions in connection with charities.

40. A disclosure for the purpose of enabling or assisting the National Lottery Commission to exercise its functions under sections 5 to 10 (licensing) and 15 (power of Secretary of State to require information) of the National Lottery etc. Act 1993 (c. 39).

41. A disclosure by the National Lottery Commission to the National Audit Office for the purpose of enabling or assisting the Comptroller and Auditor General to carry out an examination under Part 2 of the National Audit Act 1983 (c. 44) into the economy, effectiveness and efficiency with which the National Lottery Commission has used its resources in discharging its functions under sections 5 to 10 of the National Lottery etc. Act 1993.

42. A disclosure for the purpose of enabling or assisting a qualifying body under the Unfair Terms in Consumer Contracts Regulations 1999 (S.I. 1999/2083) to exercise its functions under those Regulations.

43. A disclosure for the purpose of enabling or assisting an enforcement authority under the Consumer Protection (Distance Selling) Regulations 2000 (S.I. 2000/2334) to exercise its functions under those Regulations.

44. A disclosure for the purpose of enabling or assisting an enforcement authority under the Financial Services (Distance Marketing) Regulations 2004 (S.I. 2004/2095) to exercise its functions under those Regulations.

45. A disclosure for the purpose of enabling or assisting a local weights and measures authority in England and Wales to exercise its functions under section 230(2) of the Enterprise Act 2002 (c. 40) (notice of intention to prosecute, etc).

46. A disclosure for the purpose of enabling or assisting the Financial Services Authority to exercise its functions under any of the following—
    (a) the legislation relating to friendly societies or to industrial and provident societies;

(b) the Building Societies Act 1986 (c. 53);

(c) Part 7 of the Companies Act 1989 (c. 40) (financial markets and insolvency);

(d) the Financial Services and Markets Act 2000 (c. 8).

47. A disclosure for the purpose of enabling or assisting the competent authority for the purposes of Part 6 of the Financial Services and Markets Act 2000 (official listing) to exercise its functions under that Part.

48. A disclosure for the purpose of enabling or assisting a body corporate established in accordance with section 212(1) of the Financial Services and Markets Act 2000 (compensation scheme manager) to exercise its functions.

49. A disclosure for the purpose of enabling or assisting a recognised investment exchange or a recognised clearing house to exercise its functions as such.

"Recognised investment exchange" and "recognised clearing house" have the same meaning as in section 285 of the Financial Services and Markets Act 2000.

50. A disclosure for the purpose of enabling or assisting a person approved under the Uncertificated Securities Regulations 2001 (S.I. 2001/3755) as an operator of a relevant system (within the meaning of those regulations) to exercise his functions.

51. A disclosure for the purpose of enabling or assisting a body designated under section 326(1) of the Financial Services and Markets Act 2000 (designated professional bodies) to exercise its functions in its capacity as a body designated under that section.

52. A disclosure with a view to the institution of, or otherwise for the purposes of, civil proceedings arising under or by virtue of the Financial Services and Markets Act 2000.

53. A disclosure for the purpose of enabling or assisting a body designated by order under section 1252 of this Act (delegation of functions of Secretary of State) to exercise its functions under Part 42 of this Act (statutory auditors).

Until the coming into force of that Part, the references to section 1252 and Part 42 are to be read as references to section 46 of the Companies Act 1989 (c. 40) and Part 2 of that Act respectively.

54. A disclosure for the purpose of enabling or assisting a recognised supervisory or qualifying body, within the meaning of Part 42 of this Act, to exercise its functions as such.

Until the coming into force of that Part, the reference to it is to be read as a reference to Part 2 of the Companies Act 1989.

55. A disclosure for the purpose of enabling or assisting an official receiver (including the Accountant in Bankruptcy in Scotland and the Official Assignee in Northern Ireland) to exercise his functions under the enactments relating to insolvency.

56. A disclosure for the purpose of enabling or assisting the Insolvency Practitioners Tribunal to exercise its functions under the Insolvency Act 1986 (c. 45).

57. A disclosure for the purpose of enabling or assisting a body that is for the time being a recognised professional body for the purposes of section 391 of the Insolvency Act 1986 (recognised professional bodies) to exercise its functions as such.

58. A disclosure for the purpose of enabling or assisting an overseas regulatory authority to exercise its regulatory functions.

"Overseas regulatory authority" and "regulatory functions" have the same meaning as in section 82 of the Companies Act 1989.

59. A disclosure for the purpose of enabling or assisting the Regulator of Community Interest Companies to exercise functions under the Companies (Audit, Investigations and Community Enterprise) Act 2004 (c. 27).

60. A disclosure with a view to the institution of, or otherwise for the purposes of, criminal proceedings.

61. A disclosure for the purpose of enabling or assisting a person authorised by the Secretary of State under Part 2, 3 or 4 of the Proceeds of Crime Act 2002 (c. 29) to exercise his functions.

62. A disclosure with a view to the institution of, or otherwise for the purposes of, proceedings on an application under section 6, 7 or 8 of the Company Directors Disqualification Act 1986 (c. 46) (disqualification for unfitness).

63. A disclosure with a view to the institution of, or otherwise for the purposes of, proceedings before the Financial Services and Markets Tribunal.

64. A disclosure for the purposes of proceedings before the Financial Services Tribunal by virtue of the Financial Services and Markets Act 2000 (Transitional Provisions) (Partly Completed Procedures) Order 2001 (S.I. 2001/3592).

65. A disclosure for the purposes of proceedings before the Pensions Regulator Tribunal.

66. A disclosure for the purpose of enabling or assisting a body appointed under section 14 of the Companies (Audit, Investigations and Community Enterprise) Act 2004 (supervision of periodic accounts and reports of issuers of listed securities) to exercise functions mentioned in subsection (2) of that section.

67. A disclosure with a view to the institution of, or otherwise for the purposes of, disciplinary proceedings relating to the performance by a solicitor, barrister, advocate, foreign lawyer, auditor, accountant, valuer or actuary of his professional duties.
  "Foreign lawyer" has the meaning given by section 89(9) of the Courts and Legal Services Act 1990 (c. 41).

68. A disclosure with a view to the institution of, or otherwise for the purposes of, disciplinary proceedings relating to the performance by a public servant of his duties.
  "Public servant" means an officer or employee of the Crown or of any public or other authority for the time being designated for the purposes of this paragraph by the Secretary of State by order subject to negative resolution procedure.

69. A disclosure for the purpose of the provision of a summary or collection of information framed in such a way as not to enable the identity of any person to whom the information relates to be ascertained.

70. A disclosure in pursuance of any Community obligation.

PART 3
OVERSEAS REGULATORY BODIES

71. A disclosure is made in accordance with this Part of this Schedule if—
  (a) it is made to a person or body within paragraph 72, and
  (b) it is made for the purpose of enabling or assisting that person or body to exercise the functions mentioned in that paragraph.

72. The persons or bodies that are within this paragraph are those exercising functions of a public nature, under legislation in any country or territory outside the United Kingdom, that appear to the Panel to be similar to its own functions or those of the Financial Services Authority.

73. In determining whether to disclose information to a person or body in accordance with this Part of this Schedule, the Panel must have regard to the following considerations—
  (a) whether the use that the person or body is likely to make of the information is sufficiently important to justify making the disclosure;
  (b) whether the person or body has adequate arrangements to prevent the information from being used or further disclosed otherwise than for the purposes of carrying out the functions mentioned in paragraph 72 or any other purposes substantially similar to those for which information disclosed to the Panel could be used or further disclosed.

AMENDMENTS OF REMAINING PROVISIONS OF THE COMPANIES ACT 1985 RELATING TO OFFENCES

Failure to give information about interests in shares etc

1. (1) In subsection (3) of section 444 of the Companies Act 1985 (c. 6) (failure to give information requested by Secretary of State relating to interests in shares etc) for "is liable to imprisonment or a fine, or both" substitute "commits an offence".

   (2) At the end of that section add—

   "(4) A person guilty of an offence under this section is liable—

   (a) on conviction on indictment, to imprisonment for a term not exceeding two years or a fine (or both);

   (b) on summary conviction—

   (i) in England and Wales, to imprisonment for a term not exceeding twelve months or to a fine not exceeding the statutory maximum (or both) and, for continued contravention, a daily default fine not exceeding one-fiftieth of the statutory maximum;

   (ii) in Scotland or Northern Ireland, to imprisonment for a term not exceeding six months, or to a fine not exceeding the statutory maximum (or both) and, for continued contravention, a daily default fine not exceeding one-fiftieth of the statutory maximum.".

Obstruction of rights conferred by a warrant or failure to comply with requirement under section 448

2. (1) In section 448(7) of the Companies Act 1985 (obstruction of rights conferred by or by virtue of warrant for entry and search of premises) omit the words "and liable to a fine." to the end.

   (2) After that provision insert—

   "(7A) A person guilty of an offence under this section is liable—

   (a) on conviction on indictment, to a fine;

   (b) on summary conviction, to a fine not exceeding the statutory maximum.".

Wrongful disclosure of information to which section 449 applies

3. (1) Section 449 of the Companies Act 1985 (wrongful disclosure of information obtained in course of company investigation) is amended as follows.

   (2) For subsection (6)(a) and (b) substitute "is guilty of an offence."

   (3) After subsection (6) insert—

   "(6A) A person guilty of an offence under this section is liable—

   (a) on conviction on indictment, to imprisonment for a term not exceeding two years or a fine (or both);

   (b) on summary conviction—

   (i) in England and Wales, to imprisonment for a term not exceeding twelve months or to a fine not exceeding the statutory maximum (or both);

   (ii) in Scotland or Northern Ireland, to imprisonment for a term not exceeding six months, or to a fine not exceeding the statutory maximum (or both).".

   (4) Omit subsection (7).

Destruction, mutilation etc of company documents

4. (1) For subsection (3) of section 450 of the Companies Act 1985 (offence of destroying, etc company documents) substitute—

   "(3) A person guilty of an offence under this section is liable—

   (a) on conviction on indictment, to imprisonment for a term not exceeding seven years or a fine (or both);

(b) on summary conviction—

    (i) in England and Wales, to imprisonment for a term not exceeding twelve months or to a fine not exceeding the statutory maximum (or both);

    (ii) in Scotland or Northern Ireland, to imprisonment for a term not exceeding six months, or to a fine not exceeding the statutory maximum (or both).".

(2) Omit subsection (4) of that section.

Provision of false information in purported compliance with section 447

5. (1) For subsection (2) of section 451 of the Companies Act 1985 (c. 6) (provision of false information in response to requirement under section 447) substitute—

"(2) A person guilty of an offence under this section is liable—

    (a) on conviction on indictment, to imprisonment for a term not exceeding two years or a fine (or both);

    (b) on summary conviction—

        (i) in England and Wales, to imprisonment for a term not exceeding twelve months or to a fine not exceeding the statutory maximum (or both);

        (ii) in Scotland or Northern Ireland, to imprisonment for a term not exceeding six months, or to a fine not exceeding the statutory maximum (or both).".

(2) Omit subsection (3) of that section.

Obstruction of inspector, etc exercising power to enter and remain on premises

6. (1) Section 453A of the Companies Act 1985 (obstruction of inspector etc exercising power to enter and remain on premises) is amended as follows.

(2) For subsection (5)(a) and (b) substitute "is guilty of an offence."

(3) After subsection (5) insert—

"(5A) A person guilty of an offence under this section is liable—

    (a) on conviction on indictment, to a fine;

    (b) on summary conviction, to a fine not exceeding the statutory maximum.".

(4) Omit subsection (6).

Attempted evasion of restrictions under Part 15

7. (1) In subsection (1) of section 455 of the Companies Act 1985 (attempted evasion of restrictions under Part 15) for "is liable to a fine if he" substitute "commits an offence if he".

(2) In subsection (2) of that section for the words "the company" to the end substitute "an offence is committed by—

(a) the company, and

(b) every officer of the company who is in default."

(3) After that subsection insert—

"(2A) A person guilty of an offence under this section is liable—

    (a) on conviction on indictment, to a fine;

    (b) on summary conviction, to a fine not exceeding the statutory maximum.".

SCHEDULE 4 Section 1144(1)

DOCUMENTS AND INFORMATION SENT OR SUPPLIED TO A COMPANY

PART 1
INTRODUCTION

Application of Schedule

1. (1) This Schedule applies to documents or information sent or supplied to a company.
    (2) It does not apply to documents or information sent or supplied by another company (see section 1144(3) and Schedule 5).

PART 2
COMMUNICATIONS IN HARD COPY FORM

Introduction

2. A document or information is validly sent or supplied to a company if it is sent or supplied in hard copy form in accordance with this Part of this Schedule.

Method of communication in hard copy form

3. (1) A document or information in hard copy form may be sent or supplied by hand or by post to an address (in accordance with paragraph 4).
    (2) For the purposes of this Schedule, a person sends a document or information by post if he posts a prepaid envelope containing the document or information.

Address for communications in hard copy form

4. A document or information in hard copy form may be sent or supplied—
    (a) to an address specified by the company for the purpose;
    (b) to the company's registered office;
    (c) to an address to which any provision of the Companies Acts authorises the document or information to be sent or supplied.

PART 3
COMMUNICATIONS IN ELECTRONIC FORM

Introduction

5. A document or information is validly sent or supplied to a company if it is sent or supplied in electronic form in accordance with this Part of this Schedule.

Conditions for use of communications in electronic form

6. A document or information may only be sent or supplied to a company in electronic form if—
    (a) the company has agreed (generally or specifically) that the document or information may be sent or supplied in that form (and has not revoked that agreement), or
    (b) the company is deemed to have so agreed by a provision in the Companies Acts.

Address for communications in electronic form

7. (1) Where the document or information is sent or supplied by electronic means, it may only be sent or supplied to an address—
    (a) specified for the purpose by the company (generally or specifically), or
    (b) deemed by a provision in the Companies Acts to have been so specified.

693

(2) Where the document or information is sent or supplied in electronic form by hand or by post, it must be sent or supplied to an address to which it could be validly sent if it were in hard copy form.

PART 4
OTHER AGREED FORMS OF COMMUNICATION

8. A document or information that is sent or supplied to a company otherwise than in hard copy form or electronic form is validly sent or supplied if it is sent or supplied in a form or manner that has been agreed by the company.

SCHEDULE 5   Section 1144(2)

COMMUNICATIONS BY A COMPANY

PART 1
INTRODUCTION

Application of this Schedule

1. This Schedule applies to documents or information sent or supplied by a company.

PART 2
COMMUNICATIONS IN HARD COPY FORM

Introduction

2. A document or information is validly sent or supplied by a company if it is sent or supplied in hard copy form in accordance with this Part of this Schedule.

Method of communication in hard copy form

3. (1) A document or information in hard copy form must be—
    (a) handed to the intended recipient, or
    (b) sent or supplied by hand or by post to an address (in accordance with paragraph 4).

    (2) For the purposes of this Schedule, a person sends a document or information by post if he posts a prepaid envelope containing the document or information.

Address for communications in hard copy form

4. (1) A document or information in hard copy form may be sent or supplied by the company—
    (a) to an address specified for the purpose by the intended recipient;
    (b) to a company at its registered office;
    (c) to a person in his capacity as a member of the company at his address as shown in the company's register of members;
    (d) to a person in his capacity as a director of the company at his address as shown in the company's register of directors;
    (e) to an address to which any provision of the Companies Acts authorises the document or information to be sent or supplied.

    (2) Where the company is unable to obtain an address falling within subparagraph (1), the document or information may be sent or supplied to the intended recipient's last address known to the company.

PART 3
COMMUNICATIONS IN ELECTRONIC FORM

Introduction

5. A document or information is validly sent or supplied by a company if it is sent in electronic form in accordance with this Part of this Schedule.

Agreement to communications in electronic form

6. A document or information may only be sent or supplied by a company in electronic form—

(a) to a person who has agreed (generally or specifically) that the document or information may be sent or supplied in that form (and has not revoked that agreement), or

(b) to a company that is deemed to have so agreed by a provision in the Companies Acts.

Address for communications in electronic form

7. (1) Where the document or information is sent or supplied by electronic means, it may only be sent or supplied to an address—

(a) specified for the purpose by the intended recipient (generally or specifically), or

(b) where the intended recipient is a company, deemed by a provision of the Companies Acts to have been so specified.

(2) Where the document or information is sent or supplied in electronic form by hand or by post, it must be—

(a) handed to the intended recipient, or

(b) sent or supplied to an address to which it could be validly sent if it were in hard copy form.

PART 4
COMMUNICATIONS BY MEANS OF A WEBSITE

Use of website

8. A document or information is validly sent or supplied by a company if it is made available on a website in accordance with this Part of this Schedule.

Agreement to use of website

9. A document or information may only be sent or supplied by the company to a person by being made available on a website if the person—

(a) has agreed (generally or specifically) that the document or information may be sent or supplied to him in that manner, or

(b) is taken to have so agreed under—

(i) paragraph 10 (members of the company etc), or

(ii) paragraph 11 (debenture holders),

and has not revoked that agreement.

Deemed agreement of members of company etc to use of website

10. (1) This paragraph applies to a document or information to be sent or supplied to a person—

(a) as a member of the company, or

(b) as a person nominated by a member in accordance with the company's articles to enjoy or exercise all or any specified rights of the member in relation to the company, or

(c) as a person nominated by a member under section 146 to enjoy information rights.

(2) To the extent that—

(a) the members of the company have resolved that the company may send or supply documents or information to members by making them available on a website, or

(b) the company's articles contain provision to that effect, a person in relation to whom the following conditions are met is taken to have agreed that the company may send or supply documents or information to him in that manner.

(3) The conditions are that—

    (a) the person has been asked individually by the company to agree that the company may send or supply documents or information generally, or the documents or information in question, to him by means of a website, and

    (b) the company has not received a response within the period of 28 days beginning with the date on which the company's request was sent.

(4) A person is not taken to have so agreed if the company's request—

    (a) did not state clearly what the effect of a failure to respond would be, or

    (b) was sent less than twelve months after a previous request made to him for the purposes of this paragraph in respect of the same or a similar class of documents or information.

(5) Chapter 3 of Part 3 (resolutions affecting a company's constitution) applies to a resolution under this paragraph.

Deemed agreement of debenture holders to use of website

11. (1) This paragraph applies to a document or information to be sent or supplied to a person as holder of a company's debentures.

(2) To the extent that—

    (a) the relevant debenture holders have duly resolved that the company may send or supply documents or information to them by making them available on a website, or

    (b) the instrument creating the debenture in question contains provision to that effect,

a debenture holder in relation to whom the following conditions are met is taken to have agreed that the company may send or supply documents or information to him in that manner.

(3) The conditions are that—

    (a) the debenture holder has been asked individually by the company to agree that the company may send or supply documents or information generally, or the documents or information in question, to him by means of a website, and

    (b) the company has not received a response within the period of 28 days beginning with the date on which the company's request was sent.

(4) A person is not taken to have so agreed if the company's request—

    (a) did not state clearly what the effect of a failure to respond would be, or

    (b) was sent less than twelve months after a previous request made to him for the purposes of this paragraph in respect of the same or a similar class of documents or information.

(5) For the purposes of this paragraph—

    (a) the relevant debenture holders are the holders of debentures of the company ranking *pari passu* for all purposes with the intended recipient, and

    (b) a resolution of the relevant debenture holders is duly passed if they agree in accordance with the provisions of the instruments creating the debentures.

Availability of document or information

12. (1) A document or information authorised or required to be sent or supplied by means of a website must be made available in a form, and by a means, that the company reasonably considers will enable the recipient—

    (a) to read it, and

    (b) to retain a copy of it.

(2) For this purpose a document or information can be read only if—

    (a) it can be read with the naked eye, or

    (b) to the extent that it consists of images (for example photographs, pictures, maps, plans or drawings), it can be seen with the naked eye.

Notification of availability

13. (1) The company must notify the intended recipient of—
    (a) the presence of the document or information on the website,
    (b) the address of the website,
    (c) the place on the website where it may be accessed, and
    (d) how to access the document or information.

    (2) The document or information is taken to be sent—
    (a) on the date on which the notification required by this paragraph is sent, or
    (b) if later, the date on which the document or information first appears on the website after that notification is sent.

Period of availability on website

14. (1) The company must make the document or information available on the website throughout—
    (a) the period specified by any applicable provision of the Companies Acts, or
    (b) if no such period is specified, the period of 28 days beginning with the date on which the notification required under paragraph 13 is sent to the person in question.

    (2) For the purposes of this paragraph, a failure to make a document or information available on a website throughout the period mentioned in subparagraph (1) shall be disregarded if—
    (a) it is made available on the website for part of that period, and
    (b) the failure to make it available throughout that period is wholly attributable to circumstances that it would not be reasonable to have expected the company to prevent or avoid.

PART 5
OTHER AGREED FORMS OF COMMUNICATION

15. A document or information that is sent or supplied otherwise than in hard copy or electronic form or by means of a website is validly sent or supplied if it is sent or supplied in a form or manner that has been agreed by the intended recipient.

PART 6
SUPPLEMENTARY PROVISIONS

Joint holders of shares or debentures

16. (1) This paragraph applies in relation to documents or information to be sent or supplied to joint holders of shares or debentures of a company.

    (2) Anything to be agreed or specified by the holder must be agreed or specified by all the joint holders.

    (3) Anything authorised or required to be sent or supplied to the holder may be sent or supplied either—
    (a) to each of the joint holders, or
    (b) to the holder whose name appears first in the register of members or the relevant register of debenture holders.

    (4) This paragraph has effect subject to anything in the company's articles.

Death or bankruptcy of holder of shares

17. (1) This paragraph has effect in the case of the death or bankruptcy of a holder of a company's shares.

    (2) Documents or information required or authorised to be sent or supplied to the member may be sent or supplied to the persons claiming to be entitled to the shares in consequence of the death or bankruptcy—

    (a) by name, or

    (b) by the title of representatives of the deceased, or trustee of the bankrupt, or by any like description,

at the address in the United Kingdom supplied for the purpose by those so claiming.

(3) Until such an address has been so supplied, a document or information may be sent or supplied in any manner in which it might have been sent or supplied if the death or bankruptcy had not occurred.

(4) This paragraph has effect subject to anything in the company's articles.

(5) References in this paragraph to the bankruptcy of a person include—

    (a) the sequestration of the estate of a person;

    (b) a person's estate being the subject of a protected trust deed (within the meaning of the Bankruptcy (Scotland) Act 1985 (c. 66)).

In such a case the reference in sub-paragraph (2)(b) to the trustee of the bankrupt is to be read as the permanent or interim trustee (within the meaning of that Act) on the sequestrated estate or, as the case may be, the trustee under the protected deed.

SCHEDULE 6   Section 1159

MEANING OF "SUBSIDIARY" ETC: SUPPLEMENTARY PROVISIONS

Introduction

1. The provisions of this Part of this Schedule explain expressions used in section 1159 (meaning of "subsidiary" etc) and otherwise supplement that section.

Voting rights in a company

2 In section 1159 (1) (a) and (c) the references to the voting rights in a company are to the rights conferred on shareholders in respect of their shares or, in the case of a company not having a share capital, on members, to vote at general meetings of the company on all, or substantially all, matters.

Right to appoint or remove a majority of the directors

3 (1) In section 1159 (1) (b) the reference to the right to appoint or remove a majority of the board of directors is to the right to appoint or remove directors holding a majority of the voting rights at meetings of the board on all, or substantially all, matters.

(2) A company shall be treated as having the right to appoint to a directorship if—

    (a) a person's appointment to it follows necessarily from his appointment as director of the company, or

    (b) the directorship is held by the company itself.

(3) A right to appoint or remove which is exercisable only with the consent or concurrence of another person shall be left out of account unless no other person has a right to appoint or, as the case may be, remove in relation to that directorship.

Rights exercisable only in certain circumstances or temporarily incapable of exercise

4 (1) Rights which are exercisable only in certain circumstances shall be taken into account only—

    (a) when the circumstances have arisen, and for so long as they continue to obtain, or

    (b) when the circumstances are within the control of the person having the rights.

(2) Rights which are normally exercisable but are temporarily incapable of exercise shall continue to be taken into account.

Rights held by one person on behalf of another

5 Rights held by a person in a fiduciary capacity shall be treated as not held by him.

6 (1) Rights held by a person as nominee for another shall be treated as held by the other.

  (2) Rights shall be regarded as held as nominee for another if they are exercisable only on his instructions or with his consent or concurrence.

Rights attached to shares held by way of security

7 Rights attached to shares held by way of security shall be treated as held by the person providing the security—

  (a) where apart from the right to exercise them for the purpose of preserving the value of the security, or of realising it, the rights are exercisable only in accordance with his instructions, and

  (b) where the shares are held in connection with the granting of loans as part of normal business activities and apart from the right to exercise them for the purpose of preserving the value of the security, or of realising it, the rights are exercisable only in his interests.

Rights attributed to holding company

8 (1) Rights shall be treated as held by a holding company if they are held by any of its subsidiary companies.

  (2) Nothing in paragraph 6 or 7 shall be construed as requiring rights held by a holding company to be treated as held by any of its subsidiaries.

  (3) For the purposes of paragraph 7 rights shall be treated as being exercisable in accordance with the instructions or in the interests of a company if they are exercisable in accordance with the instructions of or, as the case may be, in the interests of—

 (a) any subsidiary or holding company of that company, or

 (b) any subsidiary of a holding company of that company.

Disregard of certain rights

9 The voting rights in a company shall be reduced by any rights held by the company itself.

  Supplementary

10 References in any provision of paragraphs 5 to 9 to rights held by a person include rights falling to be treated as held by him by virtue of any other provision of those paragraphs but not rights which by virtue of any such provision are to be treated as not held by him.

SCHEDULE 7

Section 1162

PARENT AND SUBSIDIARY UNDERTAKINGS: SUPPLEMENTARY PROVISIONS

Introduction

1. The provisions of this Schedule explain expressions used in section 1162 (parent and subsidiary undertakings) and otherwise supplement that section.

Voting rights in an undertaking

2. (1) In section 1162(2)(a) and (d) the references to the voting rights in an undertaking are to the rights conferred on shareholders in respect of their shares or, in the case of an undertaking not having a share capital, on members, to vote at general meetings of the undertaking on all, or substantially all, matters.

  (2) In relation to an undertaking which does not have general meetings at which matters are decided by the exercise of voting rights the references to holding a majority of the voting rights in the undertaking shall be construed as references to having the right under the constitution

of the undertaking to direct the overall policy of the undertaking or to alter the terms of its constitution.

Right to appoint or remove a majority of the directors

3. (1) In section 1162(2)(b) the reference to the right to appoint or remove a majority of the board of directors is to the right to appoint or remove directors holding a majority of the voting rights at meetings of the board on all, or substantially all, matters.

   (2) An undertaking shall be treated as having the right to appoint to a directorship if—

      (a) a person's appointment to it follows necessarily from his appointment as director of the undertaking, or

      (b) the directorship is held by the undertaking itself.

   (3) A right to appoint or remove which is exercisable only with the consent or concurrence of another person shall be left out of account unless no other person has a right to appoint or, as the case may be, remove in relation to that directorship.

Right to exercise dominant influence

4. (1) For the purposes of section 1162(2)(c) an undertaking shall not be regarded as having the right to exercise a dominant influence over another undertaking unless it has a right to give directions with respect to the operating and financial policies of that other undertaking which its directors are obliged to comply with whether or not they are for the benefit of that other undertaking.

   (2) A "control contract" means a contract in writing conferring such a right which—

      (a) is of a kind authorised by the articles of the undertaking in relation to which the right is exercisable, and

      (b) is permitted by the law under which that undertaking is established.

   (3) This paragraph shall not be read as affecting the construction of section 1162(4)(a).

Rights exercisable only in certain circumstances or temporarily incapable of exercise

5. (1) Rights which are exercisable only in certain circumstances shall be taken into account only—

      (a) when the circumstances have arisen, and for so long as they continue to obtain, or

      (b) when the circumstances are within the control of the person having the rights.

   (2) Rights which are normally exercisable but are temporarily incapable of exercise shall continue to be taken into account.

Rights held by one person on behalf of another

6. Rights held by a person in a fiduciary capacity shall be treated as not held by him.

7. (1) Rights held by a person as nominee for another shall be treated as held by the other.

   (2) Rights shall be regarded as held as nominee for another if they are exercisable only on his instructions or with his consent or concurrence.

Rights attached to shares held by way of security

8. Rights attached to shares held by way of security shall be treated as held by the person providing the security—

      (a) where apart from the right to exercise them for the purpose of preserving the value of the security, or of realising it, the rights are exercisable only in accordance with his instructions, and

      (b) where the shares are held in connection with the granting of loans as part of normal business activities and apart from the right to exercise them for the purpose of preserving the value of the security, or of realising it, the rights are exercisable only in his interests.

Rights attributed to parent undertaking

9. (1) Rights shall be treated as held by a parent undertaking if they are held by any of its subsidiary undertakings.

   (2) Nothing in paragraph 7 or 8 shall be construed as requiring rights held by a parent undertaking to be treated as held by any of its subsidiary undertakings.

(3) For the purposes of paragraph 8 rights shall be treated as being exercisable in accordance with the instructions or in the interests of an undertaking if they are exercisable in accordance with the instructions of or, as the case may be, in the interests of any group undertaking.

Disregard of certain rights

10. The voting rights in an undertaking shall be reduced by any rights held by the undertaking itself.

Supplementary

11. References in any provision of paragraphs 6 to 10 to rights held by a person include rights falling to be treated as held by him by virtue of any other provision of those paragraphs but not rights which by virtue of any such provision are to be treated as not held by him.

SCHEDULE 8   Section 1174

INDEX OF DEFINED EXPRESSIONS

abbreviated accounts (in Part 15)	sections 444(4) and 445(3)
accounting reference date and accounting reference period	section 391
accounting standards (in Part 15)	section 464
accounts meeting	section 437(3)
acquisition, in relation to a non-cash asset	section 1163(2)
address	
—generally in the Companies Acts	section 1142
—in the company communications provisions	section 1148(1)
affirmative resolution procedure, in relation to regulations and orders	section 1290
allotment (time of)	section 558
allotment of equity securities (in Chapter 3) of Part 17)	section 560(2)
allotted share capital and allotted shares	section 546(1)(b) and (2)
annual accounts (in Part 15)	section 471
annual accounts and reports (in Part 15)	section 471
annual general meeting	section 336
annual return	section 854
appropriate audit authority (in sections 522, 523 and 524)	section 525(1)
appropriate rate of interest	
—in Chapter 5 of Part 17	section 592
—in Chapter 6 of Part 17	section 609
approval after being made, in relation to regulations and orders	section 1291
arrangement	
—in Chapter 7 of Part 17	section 616(1)
—in Part 26	section 895(2)
articles	section 18
associate (in Chapter 3 of Part 28)	section 988
associated bodies corporate and associated company (in Part 10)	section 256
authenticated, in relation to a document or information sent or supplied to a company	section 1146
authorised group, of members of a company (in Part 14)	section 370(3)
authorised insurance company	section 1165(2)

authorised minimum (in relation to share capital of public company)	section 763
available profits (in Chapter 5 of Part 18)	sections 711 and 712
banking company and banking group	section 1164
body corporate	section 1173(1)
called-up share capital	section 547
capital redemption reserve	section 733
capitalisation in relation to a company's profits (in Part 23)	section 853(3)
cash (in relation to paying up or allotting shares)	section 583
cause of action, in relation to derivative proceedings (in Chapter 2 of Part 11)	section 265(7)
certified translation (in Part 35)	section 1107
charge (in Chapter 1 of Part 25)	section 861(5)
circulation date, in relation to a written resolution (in Part 13)	section 290
class of shares	section 629
the Companies Acts	section 2
Companies Act accounts	sections 395(1)(a) and 403(2)(a)
Companies Act group accounts	section 403(2)(a)
Companies Act individual accounts	section 395(1)(a)
companies involved in the division (in Part 27)	section 919(2)
company	
—generally in the Companies Acts	section 1
—in Chapter 7 of Part 17	section 616(1)
—in Chapter 1 of Part 25	section 861(5)
—in Chapter 2 of Part 25	section 879(6)
—in Part 26	section 895(2)
—in Chapter 3 of Part 28	section 991(1)
—in the company communications provisions	section 1148(1)
the company communications provisions	section 1143
the company law provisions of this Act	section 2(2)
company records (in Part 37)	section 1134
connected with, in relation to a director (in Part 10)	sections 252 to 254
constitution, of a company	
—generally in the Companies Acts	section 17
—in Part 10	section 257
controlling, of a body corporate by a director (in Part 10)	section 255
corporation	section 1173(1)
the court	section 1156
credit institution	section 1173(1)
credit transaction (in Chapter 4 of Part 10)	section 202
creditor (in Chapter 1 of Part 31)	section 1011
daily default fine	section 1125
date of the offer (in Chapter 3 of Part 28)	section 991(1)
debenture	section 738
derivative claim (in Chapter 1 of Part 11)	section 260
derivative proceedings (in Chapter 2 of Part 11)	section 265
Directive disclosure requirements	section 1078
director	
—generally in the Companies Acts	section 250
—in Chapter 8 of Part 10	section 240(3)
—in Chapter 1 of Part 11	section 260(5)
—in Chapter 2 of Part 11	section 265(7)
—in Part 14	section 379(1)
directors' remuneration report	section 420
directors' report	section 415
distributable profits	

—in Part 15	section 474(1)
—in Part 16	section 539
issued share capital and issued shares	section 546(1)(a) and (2)
the issuing company (in Chapter 7 of Part 17)	section 610(6)
the Joint Stock Companies Acts	section 1171
liabilities (in Part 27)	section 941
liability, references to incurring, reducing or discharging (in Chapter 2 of Part 18)	section 683(2)
limited by guarantee	section 3(3)
limited by shares	section 3(2)
limited company	section 3
the main register (of members) (in Chapter 3 of Part 8)	section 131(1)
major audit (in sections 522 and 525)	section 525(2)
market purchase, by a company of its own shares (in Chapter 4 of Part 18)	section 693(4)
member, of a company	
—generally in the Companies Acts	section 112
—in Chapter 1 of Part 11	section 260(5)
—in Chapter 2 of Part 11	section 265(7)
memorandum of association	section 8
merger (in Part 27)	section 904
merging companies (in Part 27)	section 904(2)
merger by absorption (in Part 27)	section 904(1)(a)
merger by formation of a new company (in Part 27)	section 904(1)(b)
negative resolution procedure, in relation to regulations and orders	section 1289
net assets (in Part 7)	section 92
new company (in Part 27)	section 902(2)
non-cash asset	section 1163
non-voting shares (in Chapter 3 of Part 28)	section 991(1)
number, in relation to shares	section 540(4)(b)
off-market purchase, by a company of its own shares (in Chapter 4 of Part 18)	section 693(2)
offer period (in Chapter 2 of Part 28)	section 971(1)
offer to the public (in Chapter 1 of Part 20)	section 756
offeror	
—in Chapter 2 of Part 28	section 971(1)
—in Chapter 3 of Part 28	section 991(1)
officer, in relation to a body corporate	section 1173(1)
officer in default	section 1121
official seal, of registrar	section 1062
opted-in company (in Chapter 2 of Part 28)	section 971(1)
opting-in resolution (in Chapter 2 of Part 28)	section 966(1)
opting-out resolution (in Chapter 2 of Part 28)	section 966(5)
ordinary resolution	section 282
ordinary shares (in Chapter 3 of Part 17)	section 560(1)
organisation (in Part 14)	section 379(1)
other relevant transactions or arrangements (in Chapter 4 of Part 10)	section 210
overseas company	section 1044
overseas branch register	section 129(1)
paid up	section 583
the Panel (in Part 28)	section 942
parent company	section 1173(1)
parent undertaking	section 1162 (and see Schedule 7)
payment for loss of office (in Chapter 4 of Part 10)	section 215
pension scheme (in Chapter 1 of Part 18)	section 675
period for appointing auditors, in relation to a private company	section 485(2)

website, communication by a company by means of	Part 4 of Schedule 5
Welsh company	section 88
wholly-owned subsidiary	section 1159(2) (and see section 1160 and Schedule 6)
working day, in relation to a company	section 1173(1)
written resolution	section 288

SCHEDULE 9   Section 1175

REMOVAL OF SPECIAL PROVISIONS ABOUT ACCOUNTS AND AUDIT OF CHARITABLE COMPANIES

PART 1
THE COMPANIES ACT 1985 (C. 6)

1. In section 240 (requirements in connection with publication of accounts)—
   (a) in subsection (1) omit from "or, as the case may be," to "section 249A(2)";
   (b) in subsection (3)(c) omit from "and, if no such report" to "any financial year";
   (c) after subsection (3)(c) insert ", and";
   (d) omit subsection (3)(e) and the ", and" preceding it;
   (e) in the closing words of subsection (3) omit from "or any report" to "section 249A(2)".
2. In section 245 (voluntary revision of annual accounts or directors' report), in subsection (4)(b) omit "or reporting accountant".
3. In section 249A (exemptions from audit)—
   (a) omit subsections (2), (3A) and (4);
   (b) in subsection (6) for "figures for turnover or gross income" substitute "figure for turnover";
   (c) in subsection (6A) omit "or (2)";
   (d) in subsection (7) omit the definition of "gross income" and the ", and" preceding it.
4. In section 249B (cases where exemptions not available)—
   (a) in the opening words of subsection (1) omit "or (2)";
   (b) in subsection (1C)(b) omit from "where the company referred to" to "is not a charity";
   (c) in subsection (3) omit "or (2)";
   (d) in subsection (4), in the opening words and in paragraph (a), omit "or (2)".
5. Omit section 249C (report required for purposes of section 249A(2)).
6. Omit section 249D (the reporting accountant).
7. In section 249E (effect of exemptions) omit subsection (2).
8. In section 262A (index of defined expressions) omit the entry for "reporting accountant".

PART 2
THE COMPANIES (NORTHERN IRELAND) ORDER 1986 (S.I. 1986/1032 (N.I. 6)

9. In Article 248 (requirements in connection with publication of accounts)—
   (a) in paragraph (1) omit from "or, as the case may be," to "Article 257A(2)";
   (b) in paragraph (3)(c) omit from "and, if no such report" to "any such financial year";
   (c) after paragraph (3)(c) insert ", and";
   (d) omit paragraph (3)(e) and the word ", and" preceding it;
   (e) in the closing words of paragraph (3) omit from "or any report" to "Article 257A(2)".
10. In Article 253 (voluntary revision of annual accounts or directors' report), in paragraph (4)(b) omit "or reporting accountant".

11. In Article 257A (exemptions from audit)—
    (a) omit paragraphs (2), (3A) and (4);
    (b) in paragraph (6) for "figures for turnover or gross income" substitute "figure for turnover";
    (c) in paragraph (6A) omit "or (2)";
    (d) in paragraph (7) omit the definition of "gross income" and the ", and" preceding it.

12. In Article 257B (cases where exemptions not available)—
    (a) in the opening words of paragraph (1) omit "or (2)";
    (b) in paragraph (1C)(b) omit from "where the company referred to" to "is not a charity";
    (c) in paragraph (3) omit "or (2)";
    (d) in paragraph (4), in the opening words and in sub-paragraph (a), omit "or (2)".

13. Omit Article 257C (report required for purposes of Article 257A(2)).

14. Omit Article 257D (the reporting accountant).

15. In Article 257E (effect of exemptions) omit paragraph (2).

16. In Article 270A (index of defined expressions) omit the entry for "reporting accountant".

SCHEDULE 10   Section 1217

RECOGNISED SUPERVISORY BODIES

PART 1
GRANT AND REVOCATION OF RECOGNITION OF A SUPERVISORY BODY

Application for recognition of supervisory body

1. (1) A supervisory body may apply to the Secretary of State for an order declaring it to be a recognised supervisory body for the purposes of this Part of this Act ("a recognition order").

    (2) Any such application must be—
        (a) made in such manner as the Secretary of State may direct, and
        (b) accompanied by such information as the Secretary of State may reasonably require for the purpose of determining the application.

    (3) At any time after receiving an application and before determining it the Secretary of State may require the applicant to furnish additional information.

    (4) The directions and requirements given or imposed under sub-paragraphs (2) and (3) may differ as between different applications.

    (5) The Secretary of State may require any information to be furnished under this paragraph to be in such form or verified in such manner as he may specify.

    (6) Every application must be accompanied by—
        (a) a copy of the applicant's rules, and
        (b) a copy of any guidance issued by the applicant in writing.

    (7) The reference in sub-paragraph (6)(b) to guidance issued by the applicant is a reference to any guidance or recommendation—
        (a) issued or made by it to all or any class of its members or persons seeking to become members,
        (b) relevant for the purposes of this Part, and
        (c) intended to have continuing effect,
    including any guidance or recommendation relating to the admission or expulsion of members of the body, so far as relevant for the purposes of this Part.

Grant and refusal of recognition

2. (1) The Secretary of State may, on an application duly made in accordance with paragraph 1 and after being furnished with all such information as he may require under that paragraph, make or refuse to make a recognition order in respect of the applicant.

(2) The Secretary of State may make a recognition order only if it appears to him, from the information furnished by the body and having regard to any other information in his possession, that the requirements of Part 2 of this Schedule are satisfied in the case of that body.

(3) The Secretary of State may refuse to make a recognition order in respect of a body if he considers that its recognition is unnecessary having regard to the existence of one or more other bodies which—

(a) maintain and enforce rules as to the appointment and conduct of statutory auditors, and

(b) have been or are likely to be recognised.

(4) Where the Secretary of State refuses an application for a recognition order he must give the applicant a written notice to that effect—

(a) specifying which requirements, in the opinion of the Secretary of State, are not satisfied, or

(b) stating that the application is refused on the ground mentioned in sub-paragraph (3).

(5) A recognition order must state the date on which it takes effect.

Revocation of recognition

3. (1) A recognition order may be revoked by a further order made by the Secretary of State if at any time it appears to him—

(a) that any requirement of Part 2 of this Schedule is not satisfied in the case of the body to which the recognition order relates ("the recognised body"),

(b) that the body has failed to comply with any obligation imposed on it by or by virtue of this Part of this Act, or

(c) that the continued recognition of the body is undesirable having regard to the existence of one or more other bodies which have been or are to be recognised.

(2) An order revoking a recognition order must state the date on which it takes effect, which must be after the period of three months beginning with the date on which the revocation order is made.

(3) Before revoking a recognition order the Secretary of State must—

(a) give written notice of his intention to do so to the recognised body,

(b) take such steps as he considers reasonably practicable for bringing the notice to the attention of the members of the body, and

(c) publish the notice in such manner as he thinks appropriate for bringing it to the attention of any other persons who are in his opinion likely to be affected.

(4) A notice under sub-paragraph (3) must—

(a) state the reasons for which the Secretary of State proposes to act, and

(b) give particulars of the rights conferred by sub-paragraph (5).

(5) A person within sub-paragraph (6) may, within the period of three months beginning with the date of service or publication of the notice under sub-paragraph (3) or such longer period as the Secretary of State may allow, make written representations to the Secretary of State and, if desired, oral representations to a person appointed for that purpose by the Secretary of State.

(6) The persons within this sub-paragraph are—

(a) the recognised body on which a notice is served under sub-paragraph (3),

(b) any member of the body, and

(c) any other person who appears to the Secretary of State to be affected.

(7) The Secretary of State must have regard to any representations made in accordance with sub-paragraph (5) in determining whether to revoke the recognition order.

(8) If in any case the Secretary of State considers it essential to do so in the public interest he may revoke a recognition order without regard to the restriction imposed by sub-paragraph (2), even if—

(a) no notice has been given or published under sub-paragraph (3), or

(b) the period of time for making representations in pursuance of such a notice has not expired.

(9) An order revoking a recognition order may contain such transitional provision as the Secretary of State thinks necessary or expedient.

(10) A recognition order may be revoked at the request or with the consent of the recognised body and any such revocation is not subject to—

  (a) the restrictions imposed by sub-paragraphs (1) and (2), or

  (b) the requirements of sub-paragraphs (3) to (5) and (7).

(11) On making an order revoking a recognition order in respect of a body the Secretary of State must—

  (a) give written notice of the making of the order to the body,

  (b) take such steps as he considers reasonably practicable for bringing the making of the order to the attention of the members of the body, and

  (c) publish a notice of the making of the order in such manner as he thinks appropriate for bringing it to the attention of any other persons who are in his opinion likely to be affected.

Transitional provision

4. A recognition order made and not revoked under—

  (a) paragraph 2(1) of Schedule 11 to the Companies Act 1989 (c. 40), or

  (b) paragraph 2(1) of Schedule 11 to the Companies (Northern Ireland) Order 1990 (S.I. 1990/593 (N.I. 5)),

before the commencement of this Chapter of this Part of this Act is to have effect after the commencement of this Chapter as a recognition order made under paragraph 2(1) of this Schedule.

Orders not statutory instruments

5. Orders under this Part of this Schedule shall not be made by statutory instrument.

PART 2

REQUIREMENTS FOR RECOGNITION OF A SUPERVISORY BODY

Holding of appropriate qualification

6. (1) The body must have rules to the effect that a person is not eligible for appointment as a statutory auditor unless—

  (a) in the case of an individual, he holds an appropriate qualification,

  (b) in the case of a firm—

    (i) each individual responsible for statutory audit work on behalf of the firm is eligible for appointment as a statutory auditor, and

    (ii) the firm is controlled by qualified persons (see paragraph 7 below).

(2) Sub-paragraph (1) does not prevent the body from imposing more stringent requirements.

(3) A firm which has ceased to comply with the conditions mentioned in sub-paragraph (1)(b) may be permitted to remain eligible for appointment as a statutory auditor for a period of not more than three months.

7. (1) This paragraph explains what is meant in paragraph 6(1)(b) by a firm being "controlled by qualified persons".

(2) In this paragraph references to a person being qualified are—

  (a) in relation to an individual, to his holding—

    (i) an appropriate qualification, or

    (ii) a corresponding qualification to audit accounts under the law of a member State, or part of a member State, other than the United Kingdom;

  (b) in relation to a firm, to its—

    (i) being eligible for appointment as a statutory auditor, or

    (ii) being eligible for a corresponding appointment as an auditor under the law of a member State, or part of a member State, other than the United Kingdom.

(3) A firm is to be treated as controlled by qualified persons if, and only if—
    (a) a majority of the members of the firm are qualified persons, and
    (b) where the firm's affairs are managed by a board of directors, committee or other management body, a majority of that body are qualified persons or, if the body consists of two persons only, at least one of them is a qualified person.

(4) A majority of the members of a firm means—
    (a) where under the firm's constitution matters are decided upon by the exercise of voting rights, members holding a majority of the rights to vote on all, or substantially all, matters;
    (b) in any other case, members having such rights under the constitution of the firm as enable them to direct its overall policy or alter its constitution.

(5) A majority of the members of the management body of a firm means—
    (a) where matters are decided at meetings of the management body by the exercise of voting rights, members holding a majority of the rights to vote on all, or substantially all, matters at such meetings;
    (b) in any other case, members having such rights under the constitution of the firm as enable them to direct its overall policy or alter its constitution.

(6) Paragraphs 5 to 11 of Schedule 7 to this Act (rights to be taken into account and attribution of rights) apply for the purposes of this paragraph.

Auditors to be fit and proper persons

8. (1) The body must have adequate rules and practices designed to ensure that the persons eligible under its rules for appointment as a statutory auditor are fit and proper persons to be so appointed.

(2) The matters which the body may take into account for this purpose in relation to a person must include—
    (a) any matter relating to any person who is or will be employed by or associated with him for the purposes of or in connection with statutory audit work;
    (b) in the case of a body corporate, any matter relating to—
        (i) any director or controller of the body,
        (ii) any other body corporate in the same group, or
        (iii) any director or controller of any such other body; and
    (c) in the case of a partnership, any matter relating to—
        (i) any of the partners,
        (ii) any director or controller of any of the partners,
        (iii) any body corporate in the same group as any of the partners, or
        (iv) any director or controller of any such other body.

(3) Where the person is a limited liability partnership, in sub-paragraph (2)(b) "director" is to be read as "member".

(4) In sub-paragraph (2)(b) and (c) "controller", in relation to a body corporate, means a person who either alone or with an associate or associates is entitled to exercise or control the exercise of 15% or more of the rights to vote on all, or substantially all, matters at general meetings of the body or another body corporate of which it is a subsidiary.

Professional integrity and independence

9. (1) The body must have adequate rules and practices designed to ensure that—
    (a) statutory audit work is conducted properly and with integrity, and
    (b) persons are not appointed as statutory auditors in circumstances in which they have an interest likely to conflict with the proper conduct of the audit.

(2) The body must participate in arrangements within paragraph 21, and the rules and practices mentioned in sub-paragraph (1) must include provision requiring compliance with any standards for the time being determined under such arrangements.

(3) The body must also have adequate rules and practices designed to ensure that no firm is eligible under its rules for appointment as a statutory auditor unless the firm has arrangements to prevent a person to whom sub-paragraph (4) applies from being able to exert any influence over the way in which a statutory audit is conducted in circumstances in which that influence would be likely to affect the independence or integrity of the audit.

(4) This sub-paragraph applies to—

    (a) any individual who is not a qualified person within the meaning of paragraph 7, and

    (b) any person who is not a member of the firm.

Technical standards

10. (1) The body must have rules and practices as to—

    (a) the technical standards to be applied in statutory audit work, and

    (b) the manner in which those standards are to be applied in practice.

(2) The body must participate in arrangements within paragraph 22, and the rules and practices mentioned in sub-paragraph (1) must include provision requiring compliance with any standards for the time being determined under such arrangements.

Procedures for maintaining competence

11. The body must have rules and practices designed to ensure that persons eligible under its rules for appointment as a statutory auditor continue to maintain an appropriate level of competence in the conduct of statutory audits.

Monitoring and enforcement

12. (1) The body must have adequate arrangements and resources for the effective monitoring and enforcement of compliance with its rules.

(2) The arrangements for monitoring may make provision for that function to be performed on behalf of the body (and without affecting its responsibility) by any other body or person who is able and willing to perform it.

Independent monitoring of audits of listed companies and other major bodies

13. (1) The body must—

    (a) participate in arrangements within paragraph 23(1), and

    (b) have rules designed to ensure that members of the body who perform any statutory audit functions in respect of major audits take such steps as may be reasonably required of them to enable their performance of any such functions to be monitored by means of inspections carried out under the arrangements.

(2) Any monitoring of such persons under the arrangements is to be regarded (so far as their performance of statutory audit functions in respect of major audits is concerned) as monitoring of compliance with the body's rules for the purposes of paragraph 12(1).

(3) In this paragraph—

    "major audit" means a statutory audit conducted in respect of—

        (a) a company any of whose securities have been admitted to the official list (within the meaning of Part 6 of the Financial Services and Markets Act 2000 (c. 8)), or

        (b) any other person in whose financial condition there is a major public interest;

    "statutory audit function" means any function performed as a statutory auditor.

Membership, eligibility and discipline

14. The rules and practices of the body relating to—

    (a) the admission and expulsion of members,

    (b) the grant and withdrawal of eligibility for appointment as a statutory auditor, and

    (c) the discipline it exercises over its members,

must be fair and reasonable and include adequate provision for appeals.

Investigation of complaints

15. (1) The body must have effective arrangements for the investigation of complaints against—

    (a) persons who are eligible under its rules for appointment as a statutory auditor, and

    (b) the body in respect of matters arising out of its functions as a supervisory body.

  (2) The arrangements mentioned in sub-paragraph (1) may make provision for the whole or part of that function to be performed by and to be the responsibility of a body or person independent of the body itself.

Independent investigation for disciplinary purposes of public interest cases

16. (1) The body must—

    (a) participate in arrangements within paragraph 24(1), and

    (b) have rules and practices designed to ensure that, where the designated persons have decided that any particular disciplinary action should be taken against a member of the body following the conclusion of an investigation under such arrangements, that decision is to be treated as if it were a decision made by the body in disciplinary proceedings against the member.

  (2) In sub-paragraph (1) "the designated persons" means the persons who, under the arrangements, have the function of deciding whether (and if so, what) disciplinary action should be taken against a member of the body in the light of an investigation carried out under the arrangements.

Meeting of claims arising out of audit work

17. (1) The body must have adequate rules or arrangements designed to ensure that persons eligible under its rules for appointment as a statutory auditor take such steps as may reasonably be expected of them to secure that they are able to meet claims against them arising out of statutory audit work.

  (2) This may be achieved by professional indemnity insurance or other appropriate arrangements.

Register of auditors and other information to be made available

18. The body must have rules requiring persons eligible under its rules for appointment as a statutory auditor to comply with any obligations imposed on them by—

    (a) requirements under section 1224 (Secretary of State's power to call for information);

    (b) regulations under section 1239 (the register of auditors);

    (c) regulations under section 1240 (information to be made available to the public).

Taking account of costs of compliance

19. The body must have satisfactory arrangements for taking account, in framing its rules, of the cost to those to whom the rules would apply of complying with those rules and any other controls to which they are subject.

Promotion and maintenance of standards

20. The body must be able and willing—

    (a) to promote and maintain high standards of integrity in the conduct of statutory audit work, and

    (b) to co-operate, by the sharing of information and otherwise, with the Secretary of State and any other authority, body or person having responsibility in the United Kingdom for the qualification, supervision or regulation of auditors.

PART 3

ARRANGEMENTS IN WHICH RECOGNISED SUPERVISORY BODIES ARE
REQUIRED TO PARTICIPATE

Arrangements for setting standards relating to professional integrity and independence

21. The arrangements referred to in paragraph 9(2) are appropriate arrangements—
    (a) for the determining of standards for the purposes of the rules and practices mentioned in paragraph 9(1), and
    (b) for ensuring that the determination of those standards is done independently of the body.

Arrangements for setting technical standards

22. The arrangements referred to in paragraph 10(2) are appropriate arrangements—
    (a) for the determining of standards for the purposes of the rules and practices mentioned in paragraph 10(1), and
    (b) for ensuring that the determination of those standards is done independently of the body.

Arrangements for independent monitoring of audits of listed companies and other major bodies

23. (1) The arrangements referred to in paragraph 13(1) are appropriate arrangements—
    (a) for enabling the performance by members of the body of statutory audit functions in respect of major audits to be monitored by means of inspections carried out under the arrangements, and
    (b) for ensuring that the carrying out of such monitoring and inspections is done independently of the body.
    (2) In this paragraph "major audit" and "statutory audit function" have the same meaning as in paragraph 13.

Arrangements for independent investigation for disciplinary purposes of public interest cases

24. (1) The arrangements referred to in paragraph 16(1) are appropriate arrangements—
    (a) for the carrying out of investigations into public interest cases arising in connection with the performance of statutory audit functions by members of the body,
    (b) for the holding of disciplinary hearings relating to members of the body which appear to be desirable following the conclusion of such investigations,
    (c) for requiring such hearings to be held in public except where the interests of justice otherwise require,
    (d) for the persons before whom such hearings have taken place to decide whether (and, if so, what) disciplinary action should be taken against the members to whom the hearings related, and
    (e) for ensuring that the carrying out of those investigations, the holding of those hearings and the taking of those decisions are done independently of the body.
    (2) In this paragraph—
    "public interest cases" means matters which raise or appear to raise important issues affecting the public interest;
    "statutory audit function" means any function performed as a statutory auditor.

Supplementary: arrangements to operate independently of body

25. (1) This paragraph applies for the purposes of—
    (a) paragraph 21(b),
    (b) paragraph 22(b),
    (c) paragraph 23(1)(b), or
    (d) paragraph 24(1)(e).

(2) Arrangements are not to be regarded as appropriate for the purpose of ensuring that a thing is done independently of the body unless they are designed to ensure that the body—

(a) will have no involvement in the appointment or selection of any of the persons who are to be responsible for doing that thing, and

(b) will not otherwise be involved in the doing of that thing.

(3) Sub-paragraph (2) imposes a minimum requirement and does not preclude the possibility that additional criteria may need to be satisfied in order for the arrangements to be regarded as appropriate for the purpose in question.

Supplementary: funding of arrangements

26. The body must pay any of the costs of maintaining any arrangements within paragraph 21, 22, 23 or 24 which the arrangements provide are to be paid by it.

Supplementary: scope of arrangement

27. Arrangements may qualify as arrangements within any of paragraphs 21, 22, 23 and 24 even though the matters for which they provide are more extensive in any respect than those mentioned in the applicable paragraph.

SCHEDULE 11   Section 1220

RECOGNISED PROFESSIONAL QUALIFICATIONS

PART 1
GRANT AND REVOCATION OF RECOGNITION OF A PROFESSIONAL
QUALIFICATION

Application for recognition of professional qualification

1 (1) A qualifying body may apply to the Secretary of State for an order declaring a qualification offered by it to be a recognised professional qualification for the purposes of this Part of this Act ("a recognition order").

(2) In this Part of this Act "a recognised qualifying body" means a qualifying body offering a recognised professional qualification.

(3) Any application must be—

(a) made in such manner as the Secretary of State may direct, and

(b) accompanied by such information as the Secretary of State may rasonably require for the purpose of determining the application.

(4) At any time after receiving an application and before determining it the Secretary of State may require the applicant to furnish additional information.

(5) The directions and requirements given or imposed under sub-paragraphs (3) and (4) may differ as between different applications.

(6) The Secretary of State may require any information to be furnished under this paragraph to be in such form or verified in such manner as he may specify.

(7) In the case of examination standards, the verification required may include independent moderation of the examinations over such a period as the Secretary of State considers necessary.

(8) Every application must be accompanied by—

(a) a copy of the applicant's rules, and

(b) a copy of any guidance issued by the applicant in writing.

(9) The reference in sub-paragraph (8)(b) to guidance issued by the applicant is a reference to any guidance or recommendation—

    (a) issued or made by it to all or any class of persons holding or seeking to hold a qualification, or approved or seeking to be approved by the body for the purposes of giving practical training,

    (b) relevant for the purposes of this Part of this Act, and

    (c) intended to have continuing effect,

including any guidance or recommendation relating to a matter within sub-paragraph (10).

(10) The matters within this sub-paragraph are—

    (a) admission to or expulsion from a course of study leading to a qualification,

    (b) the award or deprivation of a qualification, and

    (c) the approval of a person for the purposes of giving practical training or the withdrawal of such an approval,

so far as relevant for the purposes of this Part of this Act.

Grant and refusal of recognition

2 (1) The Secretary of State may, on an application duly made in accordance with paragraph 1 and after being furnished with all such information as he may require under that paragraph, make or refuse to make a recognition order in respect of the qualification in relation to which the application was made.

(2) The Secretary of State may make a recognition order only if it appears to him, from the information furnished by the applicant and having regard to any other information in his possession, that the requirements of Part 2 of this Schedule are satisfied in relation to the qualification.

(3) Where the Secretary of State refuses an application for a recognition order he must give the applicant a written notice to that effect specifying which requirements, in his opinion, are not satisfied.

(4) A recognition order must state the date on which it takes effect.

Revocation of recognition

3 (1) A recognition order may be revoked by a further order made by the Secretary of State if at any time it appears to him—

    (a) that any requirement of Part 2 of this Schedule is not satisfied in relation to the qualification to which the recognition order relates, or

    (b) that the qualifying body has failed to comply with any obligation imposed on it by or by virtue of this Part of this Act.

(2) An order revoking a recognition order must state the date on which it takes effect, which must be after the period of three months beginning with the date on which the revocation order is made.

(3) Before revoking a recognition order the Secretary of State must—

    (a) give written notice of his intention to do so to the qualifying body,

    (b) take such steps as he considers reasonably practicable for bringing the notice to the attention of persons holding the qualification or in the course of studying for it, and

    (c) publish the notice in such manner as he thinks appropriate for bringing it to the attention of any other persons who are in his opinion likely to be affected.

(4) A notice under sub-paragraph (3) must—

    (a) state the reasons for which the Secretary of State proposes to act, and

    (b) give particulars of the rights conferred by sub-paragraph (5).

(5) A person within sub-paragraph (6) may, within the period of three months beginning with the date of service or publication or such longer period as the Secretary of State may allow, make written representations to the Secretary of State and, if desired, oral representations to a person appointed for that purpose by the Secretary of State.

(6) The persons within this sub-paragraph are—
    (a) the qualifying body on which a notice is served under sub-paragraph (3),
    (b) any person holding the qualification or in the course of studying for it, and
    (c) any other person who appears to the Secretary of State to be affected.

(7) The Secretary of State must have regard to any representations made in accordance with sub-paragraph (5) in determining whether to revoke the recognition order.

(8) If in any case the Secretary of State considers it essential to do so in the public interest he may revoke a recognition order without regard to the restriction imposed by sub-paragraph (2), even if—
    (a) no notice has been given or published under sub-paragraph (3), or
    (b) the period of time for making representations in pursuance of such a notice has not expired.

(9) An order revoking a recognition order may contain such transitional provision as the Secretary of State thinks necessary or expedient.

(10) A recognition order may be revoked at the request or with the consent of the qualifying body and any such revocation is not subject to—
    (a) the restrictions imposed by sub-paragraphs (1) and (2), or
    (b) the requirements of sub-paragraphs (3) to (5) and (7).

(11) On making an order revoking a recognition order the Secretary of State must—
    (a) give written notice of the making of the order to the qualifying body,
    (b) take such steps as he considers reasonably practicable for bringing the making of the order to the attention of persons holding the qualification or in the course of studying for it, and
    (c) publish a notice of the making of the order in such manner as he thinks appropriate for bringing it to the attention of any other persons who are in his opinion likely to be affected.

Transitional provision

4   A recognition order made and not revoked under—
    (a) paragraph 2(1) of Schedule 12 to the Companies Act 1989 (c. 40), or
    (b) paragraph 2(1) of Schedule 12 to the Companies (Northern Ireland) Order 1990 (S.I. 1990/593 (N.I. 5)),
before the commencement of this Chapter of this Part of this Act is to have effect after the commencement of this Chapter as a recognition order made under paragraph 2(1) of this Schedule.

Orders not statutory instruments

5   Orders under this Part of this Schedule shall not be made by statutory instrument.

PART 2
REQUIREMENTS FOR RECOGNITION OF A PROFESSIONAL QUALIFICATION

Entry requirements

6 (1) The qualification must only be open to persons who—
    (a) have attained university entrance level, or
    (b) have a sufficient period of professional experience.

(2) In relation to a person who has not been admitted to a university or other similar establishment in the United Kingdom, "attaining university entrance level" means—
    (a) being educated to such a standard as would entitle him to be considered for such admission on the basis of—
        (i) academic or professional qualifications obtained in the United Kingdom and recognised by the Secretary of State to be of an appropriate standard, or
        (ii) academic or professional qualifications obtained outside the United Kingdom which the Secretary of State considers to be of an equivalent standard, or

(b) being assessed, on the basis of written tests of a kind appearing to the Secretary of State to be adequate for the purpose (with or without oral examination), as of such a standard of ability as would entitle him to be considered for such admission.

(3) The assessment, tests and oral examination referred to in sub-paragraph (2)(b) may be conducted by—

(a) the qualifying body, or

(b) some other body approved by the Secretary of State.

(4) The reference in sub-paragraph (1)(b) to "a sufficient period of professional experience" is to not less than seven years' experience in a professional capacity in the fields of finance, law and accountancy.

Requirement for theoretical instruction or professional experience

7 (1) The qualification must be restricted to persons who—

(a) have completed a course of theoretical instruction in the subjects prescribed for the purposes of paragraph 8, or

(b) have a sufficient period of professional experience.

(2) The reference in sub-paragraph (1)(b) to "a sufficient period of professional experience" is to not less than seven years' experience in a professional capacity in the fields of finance, law and accountancy.

Examination

8. (1) The qualification must be restricted to persons who have passed an examination (at least part of which is in writing) testing—

(a) theoretical knowledge of the subjects prescribed for the purposes of this paragraph by regulations made by the Secretary of State, and

(b) ability to apply that knowledge in practice,

and requiring a standard of attainment at least equivalent to that required to obtain a degree from a university or similar establishment in the United Kingdom.

(2) The qualification may be awarded to a person without his theoretical knowledge of a subject being tested by examination if he has passed a university or other examination of equivalent standard in that subject or holds a university degree or equivalent qualification in it.

(3) The qualification may be awarded to a person without his ability to apply his theoretical knowledge of a subject in practice being tested by examination if he has received practical training in that subject which is attested by an examination or diploma recognised by the Secretary of State for the purposes of this paragraph.

(4) Regulations under this paragraph are subject to negative resolution procedure.

Practical training

9 (1) The qualification must be restricted to persons who have completed at least three years' practical training of which—

(a) part was spent being trained in statutory audit work, and

(b) a substantial part was spent being trained in statutory audit work or other audit work of a description approved by the Secretary of State as being similar to statutory audit work.

(2) For the purpose of sub-paragraph (1) "statutory audit work" includes the work of a person appointed as the auditor of a person under the law of a country or territory outside the United Kingdom where it appears to the Secretary of State that the law and practice with respect to the audit of accounts is similar to that in the United Kingdom.

(3) The training must be given by persons approved by the body offering the qualification as persons whom the body is satisfied, in the light of undertakings given by them and the supervision to which they are subject (whether by the body itself or some other body or organisation), will provide adequate training.

(4) At least two-thirds of the training must be given by a person—

(a) eligible for appointment as a statutory auditor, or

(b) eligible for a corresponding appointment as an auditor under the law of a member State, or part of a member State, other than the United Kingdom.

Supplementary provision with respect to a sufficient period of professional experience

10 (1) Periods of theoretical instruction in the fields of finance, law and accountancy may be deducted from the required period of professional experience, provided the instruction—

(a) lasted at least one year, and

(b) is attested by an examination recognised by the Secretary of State for the purposes of this paragraph;

but the period of professional experience may not be so reduced by more than four years.

(2) The period of professional experience together with the practical training required in the case of persons satisfying the requirement in paragraph 7 by virtue of having a sufficient period of professional experience must not be shorter than the course of theoretical instruction referred to in that paragraph and the practical training required in the case of persons satisfying the requirement of that paragraph by virtue of having completed such a course.

The body offering the qualification

11 (1) The body offering the qualification must have—

(a) rules and arrangements adequate to ensure compliance with the requirements of paragraphs 6 to 10, and

(b) adequate arrangements for the effective monitoring of its continued compliance with those requirements.

(2) The arrangements must include arrangements for monitoring—

(a) the standard of the body's examinations, and

(b) the adequacy of the practical training given by the persons approved by it for that purpose.

SCHEDULE 12 Section 1242

ARRANGEMENTS IN WHICH REGISTERED THIRD COUNTRY AUDITORS ARE REQUIRED TO PARTICIPATE

Arrangements for independent monitoring of audits of traded non-Community companies

1 (1) The arrangements referred to in section 1242 (1) (a) are appropriate arrangements—

(a) for enabling the performance by the registered third country auditor of third country audit functions to be monitored by means of inspections carried out under the arrangements, and

(b) for ensuring that the carrying out of such monitoring and inspections is done independently of the registered third country auditor.

(2) In this paragraph "third country audit function" means any function performed as a third country auditor.

Arrangements for independent investigations for disciplinary purposes

2 (1) The arrangements referred to in section 1242 (1)(b) are appropriate arrangements—

(a) for the carrying out of investigations into matters arising in connection with the performance of third country audit functions by the registered third country auditor,

(b) for the holding of disciplinary hearings relating to the registered third country auditor which appear to be desirable following the conclusion of such investigations,

(c) for requiring such hearings to be held in public except where the interests of justice otherwise require,

(d) for the persons before whom such hearings have taken place to decide whether (and, if so, what) disciplinary action should be taken against the registered third country auditor, and

(e) for ensuring that the carrying out of those investigations, the holding of those hearings and the taking of those decisions are done independently of the registered third country auditor.

(2) In this paragraph—

"disciplinary action" includes the imposition of a fine; and

"third country audit function" means any function performed as a third country auditor.

Supplementary: arrangements to operate independently of third country auditor

3 (1) This paragraph applies for the purposes of—

(a) paragraph 1(1)(b), or

(b) paragraph 2(1)(e).

(2) Arrangements are not to be regarded as appropriate for the purpose of ensuring that a thing is done independently of the registered third country auditor unless they are designed to ensure that the registered third country auditor—

(a) will have no involvement in the appointment or selection of any of the persons who are to be responsible for doing that thing, and

(b) will not otherwise be involved in the doing of that thing.

(3) Sub-paragraph (2) imposes a minimum requirement and does not preclude the possibility that additional criteria may need to be satisfied in order for the arrangements to be regarded as appropriate for the purpose in question.

Supplementary: funding of arrangements

4 (1) The registered third country auditor must pay any of the costs of maintaining any relevant arrangements which the arrangements provide are to be paid by it.

(2) For this purpose "relevant arrangements" are arrangements within paragraph 1 or 2 in which the registered third country auditor is obliged to participate.

Supplementary: scope of arrangements

5 Arrangements may qualify as arrangements within either of paragraphs 1 and 2 even though the matters for which they provide are more extensive in any respect than those mentioned in the applicable paragraph.

Specification of particular arrangements by the Secretary of State

6 (1) If there exist two or more sets of arrangements within paragraph 1 or within paragraph 2, the obligation of a registered third country auditor under section 1242 (1) (a) or (b), as the case may be, is to participate in such set of arrangements as the Secretary of State may by order specify.

(2) An order under sub-paragraph (1) is subject to negative resolution procedure.

SCHEDULE 13   Section 1252

SUPPLEMENTARY PROVISIONS WITH RESPECT TO DELEGATION ORDER

Operation of this Schedule

1. (1) This Schedule has effect in relation to a body designated by a delegation order under section 1252 as follows—

(a) paragraphs 2 to 12 have effect in relation to the body where it is established by the order;

(b) paragraphs 2 and 6 to 11 have effect in relation to the body where it is an existing body;

(c) paragraph 13 has effect in relation to the body where it is an existing body that is an unincorporated association.

(2) In their operation in accordance with sub-paragraph (1)(b), paragraphs 2 and 6 apply only in relation to—

(a) things done by or in relation to the body in or in connection with the exercise of functions transferred to it by the delegation order, and

(b) functions of the body which are functions so transferred.

(3) Any power conferred by this Schedule to make provision by order is a power to make provision by an order under section 1252.

Status

2. The body is not to be regarded as acting on behalf of the Crown and its members, officers and employees are not to be regarded as Crown servants.

Name, members and chairman

3. (1) The body is to be known by such name as may be specified in the delegation order.

(2) The body is to consist of such persons (not being less than eight) as the Secretary of State may appoint after such consultation as he thinks appropriate.

(3) The chairman of the body is to be such person as the Secretary of State may appoint from among its members.

(4) The Secretary of State may make provision by order as to—

(a) the terms on which the members of the body are to hold and vacate office;

(b) the terms on which a person appointed as chairman is to hold and vacate the office of chairman.

Financial provisions

4. (1) The body must pay to its chairman and members such remuneration, and such allowances in respect of expenses properly incurred by them in the performance of their duties, as the Secretary of State may determine.

(2) As regards any chairman or member in whose case the Secretary of State so determines, the body must pay or make provision for the payment of—

(a) such pension, allowance or gratuity to or in respect of that person on his retirement or death, or

(b) such contributions or other payment towards the provision of such a pension, allowance or gratuity,

as the Secretary of State may determine.

(3) Where—

(a) a person ceases to be a member of the body otherwise than on the expiry of his term of office, and

(b) it appears to the Secretary of State that there are special circumstances which make it right for that person to receive compensation,

the body must make a payment to him by way of compensation of such amount as the Secretary of State may determine.

Proceedings

5. (1) The delegation order may contain such provision as the Secretary of State considers appropriate with respect to the proceedings of the body.

(2) The delegation order may, in particular—

(a) authorise the body to discharge any functions by means of committees consisting wholly or partly of members of the body;

(b) provide that the validity of proceedings of the body, or of any such committee, is not affected by any vacancy among the members or any defect in the appointment of any member.

Fees

6. (1) The body may retain fees payable to it.

    (2) The fees must be applied for—

        (a) meeting the expenses of the body in discharging its functions, and

        (b) any purposes incidental to those functions.

    (3) Those expenses include any expenses incurred by the body on such staff, accommodation, services and other facilities as appear to it to be necessary or expedient for the proper performance of its functions.

    (4) In prescribing the amount of fees in the exercise of the functions transferred to it the body must prescribe such fees as appear to it sufficient to defray those expenses, taking one year with another.

    (5) Any exercise by the body of the power to prescribe fees requires the approval of the Secretary of State.

    (6) The Secretary of State may, after consultation with the body, by order vary or revoke any regulations prescribing fees made by the body.

Legislative functions

7. (1) Regulations or an order made by the body in the exercise of the functions transferred to it must be made by instrument in writing, but not by statutory instrument.

    (2) The instrument must specify the provision of this Part of this Act under which it is made.

    (3) The Secretary of State may by order impose such requirements as he thinks necessary or expedient as to the circumstances and manner in which the body must consult on any regulations or order it proposes to make.

    (4) Nothing in this Part applies to make regulations or an order made by the body subject to negative resolution procedure or affirmative resolution procedure.

8. (1) Immediately after an instrument is made it must be printed and made available to the public with or without payment.

    (2) A person is not to be taken to have contravened any regulation or order if he shows that at the time of the alleged contravention the instrument containing the regulation or order had not been made available as required by this paragraph.

9. (1) The production of a printed copy of an instrument purporting to be made by the body on which is endorsed a certificate signed by an officer of the body authorised by it for the purpose and stating—

        (a) that the instrument was made by the body,

        (b) that the copy is a true copy of the instrument, and

        (c) that on a specified date the instrument was made available to the public as required by paragraph 8,

    is evidence (or, in Scotland, sufficient evidence) of the facts stated in the certificate.

    (2) A certificate purporting to be signed as mentioned in sub-paragraph (1) is to be deemed to have been duly signed unless the contrary is shown.

    (3) Any person wishing in any legal proceedings to cite an instrument made by the body may require the body to cause a copy of it to be endorsed with such a certificate as is mentioned in this paragraph.

Report and accounts

10. (1) The body must, at least once in each calendar year for which the delegation order is in force, make a report to the Secretary of State on—

        (a) the discharge of the functions transferred to it, and

        (b) such other matters as the Secretary of State may by order require.

(2) The delegation order may modify sub-paragraph (1) as it has effect in relation to the calendar year in which the order comes into force or is revoked.

(3) The Secretary of State must lay before Parliament copies of each report received by him under this paragraph.

(4) The following provisions of this paragraph apply as follows—

(a) sub-paragraphs (5) and (6) apply only where the body is established by the order, and

(b) sub-paragraphs (7) and (8) apply only where the body is an existing body.

(5) The Secretary of State may, with the consent of the Treasury, give directions to the body with respect to its accounts and the audit of its accounts.

(6) A person may only be appointed as auditor of the body if he is eligible for appointment as a statutory auditor.

(7) Unless the body is a company to which section 394 (duty to prepare individual company accounts) applies, the Secretary of State may, with the consent of the Treasury, give directions to the body with respect to its accounts and the audit of its accounts.

(8) Whether or not the body is a company to which section 394 applies, the Secretary of State may direct that any provisions of this Act specified in the directions are to apply to the body, with or without any modifications so specified.

Other supplementary provisions

11. (1) The transfer of a function to a body designated by a delegation order does not affect anything previously done in the exercise of the function transferred; and the resumption of a function so transferred does not affect anything previously done in exercise of the function resumed.

(2) The Secretary of State may by order make such transitional and other supplementary provision as he thinks necessary or expedient in relation to the transfer or resumption of a function.

(3) The provision that may be made in connection with the transfer of a function includes, in particular, provision—

(a) for modifying or excluding any provision of this Part of this Act in its application to the function transferred;

(b) for applying to the body designated by the delegation order, in connection with the function transferred, any provision applying to the Secretary of State which is contained in or made under any other enactment;

(c) for the transfer of any property, rights or liabilities from the Secretary of State to that body;

(d) for the carrying on and completion by that body of anything in the process of being done by the Secretary of State when the order takes effect;

(e) for the substitution of that body for the Secretary of State in any instrument, contract or legal proceedings.

(4) The provision that may be made in connection with the resumption of a function includes, in particular, provision—

(a) for the transfer of any property, rights or liabilities from that body to the Secretary of State;

(b) for the carrying on and completion by the Secretary of State of anything in the process of being done by that body when the order takes effect;

(c) for the substitution of the Secretary of State for that body in any instrument, contract or legal proceedings.

12. Where a delegation order is revoked, the Secretary of State may by order make provision—

(a) for the payment of compensation to persons ceasing to be employed by the body established by the delegation order;

(b) as to the winding up and dissolution of the body.

13. (1) This paragraph applies where the body is an unincorporated association.

(2) Any relevant proceedings may be brought by or against the body in the name of any body corporate whose constitution provides for the establishment of the body.

(3) In sub-paragraph (2) "relevant proceedings" means proceedings brought in or in connection with the exercise of any transferred function.

(4) In relation to proceedings brought as mentioned in sub-paragraph (2), any reference in paragraph 11(3)(e) or (4)(c) to the body replacing or being replaced by the Secretary of State in any legal proceedings is to be read with the appropriate modifications.

SCHEDULE 14   Section 1264

STATUTORY AUDITORS: CONSEQUENTIAL AMENDMENTS

Companies (Audit, Investigations and Community Enterprise) Act 2004 (c. 27)

1 (1) Section 16 of the Companies (Audit, Investigations and Community Enterprise) Act 2004 (c. 27) (grants to bodies concerned with accounting standards etc) is amended as follows.

(2) In subsection (2)—

    (a) in paragraph (f) for "paragraph 17" to the end substitute "paragraph 21, 22, 23(1) or 24(1) of Schedule 10 to the Companies Act 2006;",

    (b) in paragraph (g) for "Part 2 of that Act" substitute "Part 42 of that Act".

(3) In subsection (5), in the definition of "professional accountancy body"—

    (a) in paragraph (a) for "Part 2 of the Companies Act 1989 (c. 40)" substitute "Part 42 of the Companies Act 2006", and

    (b) in paragraph (b) for "section 32" substitute "section 1220".

SCHEDULE 15   Section 1272

TRANSPARENCY OBLIGATIONS AND RELATED MATTERS: MINOR AND CONSEQUENTIAL AMENDMENTS

PART 1
AMENDMENTS OF THE FINANCIAL SERVICES AND MARKETS ACT 2000

1. Part 6 of the Financial Services and Markets Act 2000 (listing and other matters) is amended as follows.

2. In section 73 (general duty of competent authority), after subsection (1) insert—

    "(1A) To the extent that those general functions are functions under or relating to transparency rules, subsection (1)(c) and (f) have effect as if the references to a regulated market were references to a market."

3. In section 73A (Part 6 Rules), after subsection (5) insert—

    "(6) Transparency rules and corporate governance rules are not listing rules, disclosure rules or prospectus rules, but are Part 6 rules."

4. For the cross-heading before section 90 substitute "*Compensation for false or misleading statements etc*".

5. For the heading to section 90 substitute "**Compensation for statements in listing particulars or prospectus**".

6. (1) Section 91 (penalties for breach of Part 6 rules) is amended as follows.

    (2) For subsection (1) substitute—

        "(1) If the competent authority considers that—

            (a) an issuer of listed securities, or

            (b) an applicant for listing,

has contravened any provision of listing rules, it may impose on him a penalty of such amount as it considers appropriate.

(1ZA) If the competent authority considers that—

(a) an issuer who has requested or approved the admission of a financial instrument to trading on a regulated market,

(b) a person discharging managerial responsibilities within such an issuer, or

(c) a person connected with such a person discharging managerial responsibilities,

has contravened any provision of disclosure rules, it may impose on him a penalty of such amount as it considers appropriate.".

(3) After subsection (1A) insert—

"(1B) If the competent authority considers—

(a) that a person has contravened—

(i) a provision of transparency rules or a provision otherwise made in accordance with the transparency obligations directive, or

(ii) a provision of corporate governance rules, or

(b) that a person on whom a requirement has been imposed under section 89L (power to suspend or prohibit trading of securities in case of infringement of applicable transparency obligation), has contravened that requirement,

it may impose on the person a penalty of such amount as it considers appropriate.".

(4) In subsection (2) for "(1)(a), (1)(b)(i) or (1A)" substitute "(1), (1ZA)(a), (1A) or (1B)".

7. In section 96B (persons discharging managerial responsibilities and connected persons)—

(a) for the heading substitute "**Disclosure rules: persons responsible for compliance**";

(b) in subsection (1) for "For the purposes of this Part" substitute "for the purposes of the provisions of this Part relating to disclosure rules".

8. In section 97 (1) (appointment by the competent authority of persons to carry out investigations), for paragraphs (a) and (b) substitute—

"(a) there may have been a contravention of—

(i) a provision of this Part or of Part 6 rules, or

(ii) a provision otherwise made in accordance with the prospectus directive or the transparency obligations directive;

(b) a person who was at the material time a director of a person mentioned in section 91 (1), (1ZA)(a), (1A) or (1B) has been knowingly concerned in a contravention by that person of—

(i) a provision of this Part or of Part 6 rules, or

(ii) a provision otherwise made in accordance with the prospectus directive or the transparency obligations directive;".

9. In section 99 (fees) after subsection (1B) insert—

"(1C) Transparency rules may require the payment of fees to the competent authority in respect of the continued admission of financial instruments to trading on a regulated market.".

10. (1) Section 102A (meaning of "securities" etc) is amended as follows.

(2) After subsection (3) insert—

"(3A) "Debt securities" has the meaning given in Article 2.1(b) of the transparency obligations directive.".

(3) In subsection (3) (meaning of "transferable securities") for "the investment services directive" substitute "Directive 2004/39/EC of the European Parliament and of the Council on markets in financial instruments".

(4) In subsection (6) (meaning of "issuer"), after paragraph (a) insert—

"(aa) in relation to transparency rules, means a legal person whose securities are admitted to trading on a regulated market or whose voting shares are admitted to trading on a UK market other than a regulated market, and in the case of depository receipts representing securities, the issuer is the issuer of the securities represented;".

11. (1) Section 103 (1) (interpretation of Part 6) is amended as follows.

(2) In the definition of "regulated market" for "Article 1.13 of the investment services directive" substitute "Article 4.1(14) of Directive 2004/39/EC of the European Parliament and of the Council on markets in financial instruments".

(3) At the appropriate place insert—

" "transparency rules" has the meaning given by section 89A (5);

"voteholder information" has the meaning given by section 89B (3);".

12. In section 429 (2) (Parliamentary control of statutory instruments: affirmative procedure) of the Financial Services and Markets Act 2000 (c. 8) after "section" insert "90B or".

PART 2

AMENDMENTS OF THE COMPANIES (AUDIT, INVESTIGATIONS AND COMMUNITY ENTERPRISE) ACT 2004

13. Chapter 2 of Part 1 of the Companies (Audit, Investigations and Community Enterprise) Act 2004 (accounts and reports) is amended as follows.

14. (1) Section 14 (supervision of periodic accounts and reports of issuers of listed securities) is amended as follows.

(2) In subsection (2)(a)—

(a) for "listed" substitute "transferable";

(b) for "listing" substitute "Part 6".

(3) In subsection (3)(a)—

(a) for "listed" substitute "transferable";

(b) for "listing" substitute "Part 6".

(4) In subsection (7)(b) for "listed" substitute "transferable".

(5) In subsection (12)—

(a) for " "listed securities" and "listing rules" have" substitute ""Part 6 rules" has";

(b) for the definition of "issuer" substitute—

" "issuer" has the meaning given by section 102A (6) of that Act;";

(c) in the definition of "periodic" for "listing" substitute "Part 6";

(d) at the end add—

" "transferable securities" has the meaning given by section 102A (3) of that Act.".

15. (1) Section 15 (application of certain company law provisions to bodies appointed under section 14) is amended as follows.

(2) In subsection (5)(a)—

(a) for "listed" substitute "transferable";

(b) for "listing" substitute "Part 6".

(3) In subsection (5B)(a)—

(a) for "listed" substitute "transferable";

(b) for "listing" substitute "Part 6".

(4) In subsection (6)(b) for ""listing rules" and "security"" substitute ""Part 6 rules" and "transferable securities"".

REPEALS

Company law repeals (Great Britain)

Short title and chapter	Extent of repeal
Companies Act 1985 (c. 6)	Sections 1 to 430F.
	In section 437—
	(a) in subsection (1), the second sentence, and
	(b) subsections (1B) and (1C).
	Section 438.
	In section 439—
	(a) in subsection (2), ",or is ordered to pay the whole or any part of the costs of proceedings brought under section 438",
	(b) subsections (3) and (7), and
	(c) in subsection (8), ";and any such liability imposed by subsection (2) is (subject as mentioned above) a liability also to indemnify all persons against liability under subsection (3)".
	Section 442(2).
	Section 446.
	In section 448(7), the words "and liable to a fine." to the end.
	Section 449(7).
	Section 450(4).
	Section 451(3).
	In section 453(1A)—
	(a) paragraph (b), and
	(b) paragraph (d) and the word "and" preceding it.
	Section 453A(6).
	Sections 458 to 461.
	Sections 651 to 746.
	Schedules 1 to 15B.
	Schedules 20 to 25.

Short title and chapter	Extent of repeal
Insolvency Act 1985 (c. 65)	Schedule 6.
Insolvency Act 1986 (c. 45)	In Schedule 13, in Part 1, the entries relating to the following provisions of the Companies Act 1985—
	(a) section 13(4),
	(b) section 44(7),
	(c) section 103(7),
	(d) section 131(7),
	(e) section 140(2),
	(f) section 156(3),
	(g) section 173(4),
	(h) section 196,
	(i) section 380(4),
	(j) section 461(6),
	(k) section 462(5),
	(l) section 463(2),
	(m) section 463(3),
	(n) section 464(6),
	(o) section 657(2),
	(p) section 658(1), and
	(q) section 711(2).
Building Societies Act 1986 (c. 53)	Section 102C(5).
Finance Act 1988 (c. 39)	In section 117(3), from the beginning to "that section";".
	In section 117(4), the words "and (3)".
Water Act 1989 (c. 15)	In Schedule 25, paragraph 71(3).
Companies Act 1989 (c. 40)	Sections 1 to 22.
	Section 56(5).
	Sections 57 and 58.
	Section 64(2).
	Section 66(3).
	Section 71.
	Sections 92 to 110.
	Sections 113 to 138.
	Section 139(1) to (3).
	Sections 141 to 143.
	Section 144(1) to (3) and (6).
	Section 207.
	Schedules 1 to 9.
	In Schedule 10, paragraphs 1 to 24.
	Schedules 15 to 17.
	In Schedule 18, paragraphs 32 to 38.

Short title and chapter	Extent of repeal
	In Schedule 19, paragraphs 1 to 9 and 11 to 21.
Age of Legal Capacity (Scotland) Act 1991 (c. 50)	In Schedule 1, paragraph 39.
Water Consolidation (Consequential Provisions) Act 1991 (c. 60)	In Schedule 1, paragraph 40(2).
Charities Act 1992 (c. 41)	In Schedule 6, paragraph 11.
Charities Act 1993 (c. 10)	In Schedule 6, paragraph 20.
Criminal Justice Act 1993 (c. 36)	In Schedule 5, paragraph 4.
Welsh Language Act 1993 (c. 38)	Section 30.
Pension Schemes Act 1993 (c. 48)	In Schedule 8, paragraph 16.
Trade Marks Act 1994 (c. 26)	In Schedule 4, in paragraph 1(2), the reference to the Companies Act 1985.
Deregulation and Contracting Out Act 1994 (c. 40)	Section 13(1).
	Schedule 5.
	In Schedule 16, paragraphs 8 to 10.
Requirements of Writing (Scotland) Act 1995 (c. 7)	In Schedule 4, paragraphs 51 to 56.
Criminal Procedure (Consequential Provisions) (Scotland) Act 1995 (c. 40)	In Schedule 4, paragraph 56(3) and (4).
Disability Discrimination Act 1995 (c. 50)	In Schedule 6, paragraph 4.
Financial Services and Markets Act 2000 (c. 8)	Section 143.
	Section 263.
Limited Liability Partnerships Act 2000 (c. 12)	In the Schedule, paragraph 1.
Political Parties, Elections and Referendums Act 2000 (c. 41)	Sections 139 and 140.
	Schedule 19.
	In Schedule 23, paragraphs 12 and 13.
Criminal Justice and Police Act 2001 (c. 16)	Section 45.
	In Schedule 2, paragraph 17.
Enterprise Act 2002 (c. 40)	In Schedule 17, paragraphs 3 to 8.
Companies (Audit, Investigations and Community Enterprise) Act 2004 (c. 27)	Sections 7 to 10.
	Section 11(1).
	Sections 12 and 13.
	Sections 19 and 20.
	Schedule 1.
	In Schedule 2, paragraphs 5 to 10, 22 to 24 and 26.

Short title and chapter	Extent of repeal
	In Schedule 6, paragraphs 1 to 9.
Civil Partnership Act 2004 (c. 33)	In Schedule 27, paragraphs 99 to 105.
Constitutional Reform Act 2005 (c. 4)	In Schedule 11, in paragraph 4(3), the reference to the Companies Act 1985.

Repeals and revocations relating to Northern Ireland

Short title and chapter	Extent of repeal or revocation
Companies (Northern Ireland) Order 1986 (S.I. 1986/1032 (N.I. 6))	The whole Order.
Companies Consolidation (Consequential Provisions) (Northern Ireland) Order 1986 (S.I. 1986/1035 (N.I. 9))	The whole Order.
Business Names (Northern Ireland) Order 1986 (S.I. 1986/1033 (N.I. 7))	The whole Order.
Industrial Relations (Northern Ireland) Order 1987 (S.I. 1987/936 N.I. 9))	Article 3.
Finance Act 1988 (c. 39)	In section 117(3), the words from "and for" to the end.
Companies (Northern Ireland) Order 1989 (S.I. 1989/2404 (N.I. 18))	The whole Order.
Insolvency (Northern Ireland) Order 1989 (S.I. 1989/2405 (N.I. 19))	In Schedule 7, in the entry relating to Article 166(4), the word "office". In Schedule 9, Part I.
European Economic Interest Groupings Regulations (Northern Ireland) 1989 (S.R. 1989/216)	The whole Regulations.
Companies (Northern Ireland) Order 1990 (S.I. 1990/593 (N.I. 5))	The whole Order.
Companies (No. 2) (Northern Ireland) Order 1990 (S.I. 1990/1504 (N.I. 10))	Parts II to IV. Part VI. Schedules 1 to 6.
Criminal Justice Act 1993 (c. 36)	In Schedule 5, Part 2. Schedule 6.
Financial Provisions (Northern Ireland) Order 1993 (S.I. 1993/1252 (N.I. 5))	Article 15.
Deregulation and Contracting Out Act 1994 (c. 40)	Section 13(2). Schedule 6.

Short title and chapter	Extent of repeal
Pensions (Northern Ireland) Order 1995 (S.I. 1995/3213 (N.I. 22))	In Schedule 3, paragraph 7.
Deregulation and Contracting Out (Northern Ireland) Order 1996 (S.I. 1996/1632 (N.I. 11))	Article 11. Schedule 2. In Schedule 5, paragraph 4.
Youth Justice and Criminal Evidence Act 1999 (c. 23)	In Schedule 4, paragraph 18.
Limited Liability Partnerships Act (Northern Ireland) 2002 (c. 12 (N.I.))	The whole Act.
Open-Ended Investment Companies Act (Northern Ireland) 2002 (c. 13)	The whole Act.
Company Directors Disqualification (Northern Ireland) Order 2002 (S.I. 2002/3150 (N.I. 4))	In Schedule 3, paragraphs 3 to 5.
Companies (Audit, Investigations and Community Enterprise) Act 2004 (c. 27)	Section 11(2). In Schedule 2, paragraphs 11 to 15.
Law Reform (Miscellaneous Provisions) (Northern Ireland) Order 2005 (S.I. 2005/1452 (N.I. 7))	Article 4(2).
Companies (Audit, Investigations and Community Enterprise) (Northern Ireland) Order 2005 (S.I. 2005/1967 (N.I. 17))	The whole Order.

Other repeals

Short title and chapter	Extent of repeal or revocation
Limited Partnerships Act 1907 (c. 24)	In section 16(1)— (a) the words ", and there shall be paid for such inspection such fees as may be appointed by the Board of Trade, not exceeding 5p for each inspection", and

Short title and chapter	Extent of repeal
	(b) the words from "and there shall be paid for such certificate" to the end.
	In section 17—
	(a) the words "(but as to fees with the concurrence of the Treasury)", and
	(b) paragraph (a).
Business Names Act 1985 (c. 7)	The whole Act.
Companies Act 1989 (c. 40)	Sections 24 to 54.
	Schedules 11 to 13.
Criminal Procedure (Consequential Provisions) (Scotland) Act 1995 (c. 40)	In Schedule 4, paragraph 74(2).
Companies (Audit, Investigations and Community Enterprise) Act 2004 (c. 27)	Sections 1 to 6.
	In Schedule 2, Part 1.
Civil Partnership Act 2004 (c. 33)	In Schedule 27, paragraph 128.

APPENDIX 2

Table of Destinations

Notes

1. The table identifies the provisions of the Companies Act 1985 (c. 6) that are repealed and re-enacted (with or without changes) by the Companies Act 2006 and identifies the corresponding provisions in that Act.
2. The table is based on the table of origins. So it only shows a provision of the Companies Act 2006 as a destination of a provision of the Companies Act 1985 if the latter is cited in that table as an origin for the new provision.
3. A repealed provision of the Companies Act 1985 may not be listed in this table because the provision is spent or it is otherwise unnecessary to re-enact it, because the new provision is fundamentally different from the existing provision or because as a matter of policy it has been decided to repeal the existing provision without replacing it.
4. There is no entry for Schedule 24 to the Companies Act 1985 (punishment of offences) in the table. This is cited in the table of origins as the origin for a large number of provisions in the Companies Act 2006.
5. A section at the end of the table identifies the substantive provisions of the Companies Act 1989 (c. 40) that are repealed and re-enacted by the Companies Act 2006.

COMPANIES ACT 1985

Provision of Companies Act 1985	Destination in Companies Act 2006
s.1 Mode of forming incorporated company	
(1)	s.7(1) and (2) (changed)
(2)	s.3(1) to (4)
(3)	s.4(1) to (3)
(4)	s.5(1) and (2)
s.2 Requirements with respect to memorandum	
(1)	s.9(2)
(2)	ss.9(2), 88(2)
(3)	s.9(2) (changed)
(4)	s.11(3) (changed)
s.3 Forms of memorandum	
(1)	s.8(2)
s.7 Articles prescribing regulations for companies	
(1)	s.18(2) (changed)
(3)	s.18(3) (changed)
s.8 Tables A, C, D and E	
(1)	s.19(1) to (3) (changed)
(2)	s.20(1) and (2) (changed)
(3)	s.19(4)
(4)	s.19(1) to (3) (changed)

733

Provision of Companies Act 1985	Destination in Companies Act 2006
(5)	s.19(5)
s.9 Alteration of articles by special resolution	
(1) and (2)	s.21(1)
s.10 Documents to be sent to registrar	
(1)	s.9(1), (5) and (6) (changed)
(2)	s.12(1) (changed)
(3)	s.12(3)
(4)	s.9(3)
(6)	s.9(5)
s.12 Duty of registrar	
(1) and (2)	s.14
(3) and (3A)	s.13(1) and (2) (changed)
s.13 Effect of registration	
(1)	s.15(1)
(2)	s.15(3)
(3)	s.16(2) (changed)
(4)	s.16(3)
(5)	s.16(6)
(7)	s.15(4)
s.14 Effect of memorandum and articles	
(1)	s.33(1) (changed)
(2)	s.33(2) (changed)
s.15 Memorandum and articles of company limited by guarantee	
(1)	s.37
(2)	s.5(3)
s.16 Effect of alteration on company's members	
(1)	s.25(1)
(2)	s.25(2)
s.18 Amendments of memorandum or articles to be registered	
(1)	s.34(2) (changed)
(2)	ss.26(1), 34(3) (changed)
(3)	ss.26(3) and (4), 34(5) and (6)
s.19 Copies of memorandum and articles to be given to members	
(1)	s.32(1) (changed)
(2)	s.32(3) and (4) (changed)
s.22 Definition of "member"	
(1)	s.112(1) (changed)
(2)	s.112(2)
s.23 Membership of holding company	
(1)	s.136(1)
(2)	s.138(1) and (2)
(3)	s.141(1) and (2)
(3A)	s.141(3)
(3B)	s.141(4)
(3BA)	s.141(5)
(3C)	s.142(1) and (2)
(4) and (5)	s.137(1) and (2)
(6)	s.137(3) and (4)
(7)	s.144
(8)	s.143

Provision of Companies Act 1985	Destination in Companies Act 2006
s.25 Name as stated in memorandum	
(1)	s.58(1) and (2)
(2)	s.59(1), (2) and (3)
s.26 Prohibition on registration of certain names	
(1)	ss.53, 65(1) to (5), 66(1)(changed)
(2)	ss.54(1) to (3) and 55(1) (changed)
(3)	s.66(2) and (3) (changed)
s.27 Alternatives of statutory designations	
(4)	ss.58(1) and (2), 59(1) and (2)
s.28 Change of name	
(1)	s.77(1)
(2)	ss.67(1), 68(2) and (3)
(3)	s.75(1), (2) and (4)
(4)	ss.68(3), 75(3)
(5)	ss.68(5) and (6), 75(5) and (6)
(6)	ss.80(1) to (3), 81(1)
(7)	s.81(2) and (3)
s.29 Regulations about names	
(1)	ss.55(1), 56(1)
(2)	s.56(2)
(3)	s.56(3) and (4) (changed)
(6)	s.55(2)
s.30 Exemption from requirement of "limited" as part of the name	
(2) and (3)	ss.61(1) to (4), 62(1) to (3) (changed)
(4)	s.60(3)
(5B)	s.60(2)
s.31 Provisions applying to company exempt under s.30	
(1)	s.63(1)
(2)	s.64(1) to (4) (changed)
(3)	s.64(7)
(5)	s.63(2) and (3)
(6)	s.64(5) and (6)
s.32 Power to require company to abandon misleading name	
(1)	s.76(1)
(2)	s.76(3)
(3)	s.76(4) and (5)
(4)	s.76(6) and (7) (changed)
(5)	ss.80(1) to (3), 81(1)
(6)	s.81(2) and (3)
s.35 A company's capacity not limited by its memorandum	
(1)	s.39(1) (changed)
(4)	s.39(2)
s.35A Power of directors to bind the company	
(1)	s.40(1)
(2)	s.40(2)
(3)	s.40(3)
(4)	s.40(4)
(5)	s.40(5)
(6)	s.40(6)

Provision of Companies Act 1985	Destination in Companies Act 2006
s.35B No duty to enquire as to capacity of company or authority of directors	
	s.40(2)
s.36 Company contracts: England and Wales	
(1) and (2)	s.43(1) and (2)
s.36A Execution of documents: England and Wales	
(2)	ss.44(1)
(3)	s.45(1)
(4)	s.44(2), (3) and (4)
(4A)	s.44(6)
(6)	s.44(5)
(7)	s.44(8)
(8)	s.44(7)
s.36AA Execution of deeds: England and Wales	
(1)	s.46(1)
(2)	s.46(2)
s.36B Execution of documents by companies	
(1)	s.48(2)
(2)	s.48(3)
s.36C Pre-incorporation contracts, deeds and obligations	
(1)	s.51(1)
(2)	s.51(2)
s.37 Bills of exchange and promissory notes	
	s.52
s.38 Execution of deeds abroad	
(1)	s.47(1) (changed)
(2)	s.47(2)
(3)	s.47(1)
s.39 Power of company to have official seal for use abroad	
(1)	s.49(1) and (2) (changed)
(2) and (2A)	s.49(3)
(3)	s.49(4)
(4)	s.49(5)
(5)	s.49(6)
s.40 Official seal for share certificates, etc	
(1)	s.50(1) and (2)
s.42 Events affecting a company's status	
(1)	s.1079(1) to (3)
s.43 Re-registration of private company as public	
(1)	s.90(1) and (2) (changed)
(2)	s.90(3)
(3)	ss.92(1) and (2), 94(2) and (3)
(4)	s.92(1)
s.44 Consideration for shares recently allotted to be valued	
(1)	s.93(1)
(2)	s.93(2) and (7)
(4) and (5)	s.93(3) to (5)
(6)	s.93(6)
(7)	s.93(6) and (7)

Provision of Companies Act 1985	Destination in Companies Act 2006
s.45 Additional requirements relating to share capital	
(1) to (4)	s.91(1)
s.46 Meaning of "unqualified report" in s 43(3)	
(2)	s.92(3)
(3)	s.92(4)
(4)	s.92(5) and (6)
s.47 Certificate of re-registration under s 43	
(1)	s.96(1) and (2)
(2)	s.94(4)
(3)	s.91(5) (changed)
(4)	s.96(4)
(5)	s.96(5)
s.48 Modification for unlimited company re-registering	
(1) and (2)	s.90(4)
(5)	s.91(2)
(6)	s.91(3)
(7)	s.91(4)
s.49 Re-registration of limited company as unlimited	
(1)	s.102(1)
(2)	s.102(2)
(4)	s.102(1)
(5) to (7)	s.102(3)
(8)	ss.102(1), 103(2) to (4) (changed)
(8A)	s.103(3) and (4) (changed)
(9)	s.102(4)
s.50 Certificate of re-registration under s 49	
(1)	s.104(1) and (2)
(2)	s.104(4)
(3)	s.104(5)
s.51 Re-registration of unlimited company as limited	
(1)	s.105(1) (changed)
(2)	s.105(2)
(3)	s.105(3) and (4)
(5)	s.106(2)
s.52 Certificate of re-registration under s 51	
(1)	s.107(1) and (2)
(2)	s.107(4)
(3)	s.107(5)
s.53 Re-registration of public company as private	
(1)	ss.97(1), 100(2) (changed)
(2)	s.97(3)
s.54 Litigated objection to resolution under s 53	
(1)	s.98(1)
(2)	ss.98(1), 370(3) (changed)
(3)	s.98(2)
(4)	s.99(1) and (2) (changed)
(5)	s.98(3) and (4)
(6)	s.98(5) and (6)
(7)	s.99(3)
(8)	s.98(6)
(10)	s.99(4) and (5)

Provision of Companies Act 1985	Destination in Companies Act 2006
s.55 Certificate of re-registration under s 53	
(1)	s.101(1) and (2)
(2)	s.101(4)
(3)	s.101(5)
s.58 Document offering shares etc for sale deemed a prospectus	
(3)	s.755(2)
s.80 Authority of company required for certain allotments	
(1)	s.549(1), s.551(1) (changed)
(2)	ss.549(1) to (3), 551(1), 559
(3)	s.551(2)
(4)	s.551(3) and (4)
(5)	s.551(5)
(6)	s.551(6)
(7)	s.551(7)
(8)	s.551(8)
(9)	s.549(4) and (5)
(10)	s.549(6) (changed)
s.81 Restriction on public offers by private company	
(1)	s.755(1)
(3)	s.760
s.84 Allotment where issue not fully subscribed	
(1)	s.578(1)
(2)	s.578(2)
(3)	s.578(3) (changed)
(4)	s.578(4) and (5)
(5)	s.578(5)
(6)	s.578(6)
s.85 Effect of irregular allotment	
(1)	s.579(1) and (2)
(2)	s.579(3)
(3)	s.579(4)
s.88 Return as to allotments, etc	
(1)	s.555(1)
(2)	s.555(2) (changed)
(5)	s.557(1) and (2)
(6)	ss.557(3), 597(5) and (6)
s.89 Offers to shareholders to be on pre-emptive basis	
(1)	s.561(1)
(2)	s.568(1)
(3)	s.568(1) and (2)
(4)	ss.561(2), 565
(5)	s.566
(6)	s.561(4)
s.90 Communication of pre-emption offers to shareholders	
(1)	s.562(1)
(2)	s.568(3)
(5)	s.562(3) (changed)
(6)	s.562(4) and (5) (changed)

Provision of Companies Act 1985	Destination in Companies Act 2006
s.91 Exclusion of ss 89, 90 by private company	
(1)	s.567(1) and (2)
(2)	s.567(3) and (4)
s.92 Consequences of contravening ss 89, 90	
(1)	ss.563(1) and (2), 568(4)
(2)	ss.563(3), 568(5)
s.93 Saving for other restrictions as to offers	
(1)	s.575(1)
(2)	s.575(2)
s.94 Definitions for ss 89–96	
(2)	ss.560(1), 564, 577
(3)	ss.560(2), 561(3)
(3A)	s.560(2)
(5)	s.560(1)
(7)	s.574(1) and (2)
s.95 Disapplication of pre-emption rights	
(1)	ss.570(1) and (2), 573(2), (3) and (5)
(2)	ss.571(1) and (2), 573(4)
(2A)	s.573(1) to (5|)
(3)	ss.570(3), 571(3)
(4)	ss.570(4), 571(4), 573(3) and (5)
(5)	ss.571(5) to (7), 573(5) (changed)
(6)	572(1) to (3)
s.96 Saving for company's pre-emption procedure operative before 1982	
(1) and (2)	s.576(1)
(3)	s.576(2)
(4)	s.576(3)
s.97 Power of company to pay commissions	
(1)	s.553(1)
(2)	s.553(2)
s.98 Apart from s 97, commissions and discounts barred	
(1)	s.552(1)
(2)	s.552(2)
(3)	s.552(3)
(4)	s.553(3)
s.99 General rules as to payment for shares on allotment	
(1)	s.582(1) and (3)
(2)	s.585(1)
(3)	s.585(2)
(4)	s.582(2)
(5)	s.585(3)
s.100 Prohibition on allotment of shares at a discount	
(1)	s.580(1)
(2)	s.580(2)
s.101 Shares to be allotted as at least one-quarter paid-up	
(1)	s.586(1)
(2)	s.586(2)

Provision of Companies Act 1985	Destination in Companies Act 2006
(3) and (4)	s.586(3)
(5)	s.586(4)
s.102 Restriction on payment by long-term undertaking	
(1)	s.587(1)
(2)	s.587(2)
(3) and (4)	s.587(3)
(5) and (6)	s.587(4)
(7)	s.587(5)
s.103 Non-cash consideration to be valued before allotment	
(1)	s.593(1)
(2)	s.593(2)
(3)	s.594(1) to (3)
(4)	s.594(4) and (5)
(5)	s.595(1) and (2)
(6)	s.593(3)
(7)	ss.594(6), 595(3)
s. 104 Transfer to public company of non-cash asset in initial period	
(1)	s.598(1)
(2)	s.598(2)
(3)	s.603
(4)	ss.599(1) and (3), 601(1) to (3) (changed)
(5)	s.599(2) and (4)
(6)	s.598(4) and (5)
s.105 Agreements contravening s 104	
(1)	s.604(1)
(2)	s.604(2)
(3)	s.604(3)
s.106 Shares issued to subscribers of memorandum	
	s.584
s.107 Meaning of "the appropriate rate"	
	ss.592(1) and (2), 609(1) and (2)
s.108 Valuation and report (s 103)	
(1)	s.1150(1) (changed)
(2)	s.1150(2)
(3)	s.1150(3)
(4)	s.596(2)
(5)	s.1150(4)
(6)	ss.596(3), 600(3)
(7)	s.596(4) and (5)
s.109 Valuation and report (s 104)	
(2)	s.600(2) and (3)
(3)	s.600(4) and (5)
s.110 Entitlement of valuer to full disclosure	
(1)	s.1153(1)
(2)	s.1153(2) and (4)
(3)	s.1153(3)
s.111 Matters to be communicated to registrar	
(1)	s.597(1) and (2)
(2)	s.602(1)

Provision of Companies Act 1985	Destination in Companies Act 2006
(3)	s.597(3) to (6)
(4)	s.602(2) and (3)
s.111A Right to damages, &c not affected	
	s.655
s.112 Liability of subsequent holders of shares allotted	
(1)	ss.588(1), 605(1)
(2)	s.605(2)
(3)	ss.588(2), 605(3)
(4)	ss.588(3), 605(4)
(5)	s.588(1) and (4)
s.113 Relief in respect of certain liabilities under ss 99 ff	
(1)	ss.589(1) and (2), 606(1)
(2)	ss.589(3), 606(2) (changed)
(3)	ss.589(3), 606(2)
(4)	ss.589(4), 606(3)
(5)	ss.589(5), 606(4)
(6) and (7)	ss.589(6), 606(5)
(8)	s.606(6)
s.114 Penalty for contravention	
	ss.590(1) and (2), 607(2) and (3)
s.115 Undertakings to do work, etc	
(1)	ss.591(1) and (2), 608(1) and (2)
s.117 Public company share capital requirements	
(1)	s.761(1)
(2)	s.761(2) (changed)
(3)	s.762(1) (changed)
(4)	s.761(3)
(5)	s.762(3)
(6)	s.761(4) (changed)
(7)	s.767(1) and (2)
(8)	s.767(3)
s.118 The authorised minimum	
(1)	ss.763(1), 764(1) (changed)
(2)	s.764(3)
(3)	s.764(4)
s.119 Provision for different amounts to be paid on shares	
	s.581
s.121 Alteration of share capital (limited companies)	
(1)	s.617(1) (changed)
(2)	ss.617(2) and (3), 618(1), 620(1) (changed)
(3)	s.618(2)
(4)	ss.618(3), 620(2) (changed)
s.122 Notice to registrar of alteration	
(1)	ss.619(1) to (3), 621(1), 663(1), 689(1) (changed)
(2)	ss.619(4) and (5), 621(4) and (5), 663(4) and (5), 689(4) and (5)
s.125 Variation of class rights	
(1)	s.630(1)
(2)	s.630(2) to (4) (changed)

Provision of Companies Act 1985	Destination in Companies Act 2006
(6)	s.334(1) to (4) and (6) (changed)
(7)	ss.334(7), 630(5)
(8)	s.630(6)
s.126 Saving for court's powers under other provisions	
	s.632
s.127 Shareholders' right to object to variation	
(1)	s.633(1)
(2)	s.633(2) and (3)
(2A)	s.633(2)
(3)	s.633(4)
(4)	s.633(5)
(5)	s.635(1) to (3)
(6)	s.633(6)
s.128 Registration of particulars of special rights	
(1)	s.556(1) to (3) (changed)
(2)	ss.556(1) and (4), 629(2)
(3)	s.637(1) (changed)
(4)	s.636(1) (changed)
(5)	ss.557(1) and (2), 636(2) and (3), 637(2) and (3) (changed)
s.129 Registration of newly created class rights	
(1)	s.638(1) (changed)
(2)	s.640(1) (changed)
(3)	s.639(1) (changed)
(4)	ss.638(2) and (3), 639(2) and (3), 640(2) and (3)
s.130 Application of share premiums	
(1)	s.610(1)
(2)	s.610(2) and (2) (changed)
(3)	s.610(4)
(4)	s.610(5) and (6)
s.131 Merger relief	
(1)	s.612(1) and (4)
(2)	s.612(2)
(3)	s.612(3)
(4)	s.613(2) and (3)
(5)	s.613(4)
(6)	s.613(5)
(7)	s.616(1)
s.132 Relief in respect of group reconstructions	
(1)	s.611(1)
(2)	s.611(2)
(3)	s.611(3)
(4)	s.611(4)
(5)	s.611(5)
(8)	s.612(4)
s.133 Provisions supplementing ss 131, 132	
(1)	s.615
(2)	s.616(2)
(3)	s.616(3)
(4)	s.616(1)

Provision of Companies Act 1985	Destination in Companies Act 2006
s.134 Provision for extending or restricting relief from s 130	
(1)	s.614(1)
(3)	s.614(2)
s.135 Special resolution for reduction of share capital	
(1)	s.641(1) to (3) (changed)
(2)	s.641(4)
s.136 Application to court for order of confirmation	
(1)	s.645(1)
(2)	ss.645(2) and (4), 646(4)
(3)	s.646(1)
(4)	s.646(2) and (3)
(5)	s.646(4) and (5)
(6)	s.645(2) and (3)
s.137 Court order confirming reduction	
(1)	s.648(1) and (2)
(2)	s.648(3) and (4)
(3)	s.648(4)
s.138 Registration of order and minute of reduction	
(1)	s.649(1) (changed)
(2)	s.649(3) (changed)
(3)	s.649(4) (changed)
(4)	s.649(5) and (6) (changed)
s.139 Public company reducing capital below authorised minimum	
(1)	s.650(1)
(2)	s.650(2)
(3)	s.651(1) and (2)
(4)	s.651(3) (changed)
(5)	s.651(4), (6) and (7)
s.140 Liability of members on reduced shares	
(1)	s.652(1) (changed)
(2)	s.653(1)
(3)	s.653(2)
(4)	s.653(3)
(5)	s.653(3)
s.141 Penalty for concealing name of creditor, etc	
	s.647(1), (2) (changed)
s.142 Duty of directors on serious loss of capital	
(1)	s.656(1) to (3)
(2)	s.656(4) and (5) (changed)
(3)	s.656(6)
s.143 General rule against company acquiring own shares	
(1)	s.658(1)
(2)	s.658(2) and (3)
(2A)	s.725(4)
(3)	s.659(1) and (2)
s.144 Acquisition of shares by company's nominee	
(1)	s.660(1) and (2) (changed)
(2)	s.661(1) and (2) (changed)

Provision of Companies Act 1985	*Destination in Companies Act 2006*
(3)	s.661(3)
(4)	s.661(4)
s.145 Exceptions from s 144	
(1)	s.660(3)
(2)	ss.660(3), 661(5)
(3)	s.671
s.146 Treatment of shares held by or for public company	
(1)	ss.662(1), 671
(2)	s.662(2) and (3)
(3)	s.662(3)
(4)	s.662(5) and (6)
s.147 Matters arising out of compliance with s 146(2)	
(2)	s.664(1) and (2)
(3)	s.664(4) (changed)
(4)	s.665(1), (2), (4) and (5) (changed)
s.148 Further provisions supplementing ss 146, 147	
(1)	s.668(1) and (2)
(2)	s.668(3)
(3)	s.671
(4)	s.669(1) and (2)
s.149 Sanctions for non-compliance	
(1)	s.666(1) and (2)
(2)	s.667(1) to (3)
s.150 Charges of public companies on own shares	
(1)	s.670(1)
(2)	s.670(2)
(3)	s.670(3)
(4)	s.670(4)
s.151 Financial assistance generally prohibited	
(1)	ss.678(1), 679(1) (changed)
(2)	ss.678(3), 679(3) (changed)
(3)	s.680(1) and (2)
s.152 Definitions for this Chapter	
(1)	ss.677(1), 683(1)
(2)	s.677(2) and (3)
(3)	s.683(2)
s.153 Transactions not prohibited by s 151	
(1)	ss.678(2), 679(2) (changed)
(2)	ss.678(4), 679(4)
(3)	s.681(1) and (2)
(4)	s.682(1) and (2)
(5)	s.682(5)
s.154 Special restriction for public companies	
(1)	s.682(1)
(2)	ss.682(3) and (4), 840(4) and (5)
s.159 Power to issue redeemable shares	
(1)	s.684(1) and (3) (changed)
(2)	s.684(4)
(3)	ss.686(1) to (3) (changed), 691(1) and (2)

Provision of Companies Act 1985	Destination in Companies Act 2006
s.160 Financing etc of redemption	
(1)	ss.687(1) to (3) and (6), 692(1), (2) and (5)
(2)	ss.687(4) and (5), 692(3) and (4)
(4)	ss.688, 706 (changed)
s.162 Power of company to purchase own shares	
(1)	s.690(1) (changed)
(2)	ss.691(1) and (2), 692(1) to (5)
(2A)	s.706
(2B)	ss.706, 724(1)
(3)	s.690(2)
(4)	s.724(2)
s.162A Treasury shares	
(1)	s.724(3)
(2)	s.724(4)
(3)	s.724(5)
s.162B Treasury shares: maximum holdings	
(1)	s.725(1)
(2)	s.725(2)
(3)	s.725(4)
s.162C Treasury shares: voting and other rights	
(1)	s.726(1)
(2) and (3)	s.726(2)
(4)	s.726(3)
(5)	s.726(4)
(6)	s.726(5)
s.162D Treasury shares: disposal and cancellation	
(1)	ss.727(1), 729(1)
(2)	s.727(2) (changed)
(3)	s.727(3)
(4)	s.729(4)
(5)	s.729(5)
s.162E Treasury shares: mandatory cancellation	
(1)	s.729(2)
(2)	s.729(3)
s.162F Treasury shares: proceeds of sale	
(1)	s.731(1)
(2)	s.731(2)
(3)	s.731(3)
(4) and (5)	s.731(4)
s.162G Treasury shares: penalty for contravention	
	s.732(1) and (2) (changed)
s.163 Definitions of "off-market" and "market" purchase	
(1)	s.693(2)
(2)	s.693(3)
(3)	s.693(4)
(4) and (5)	s.693(5)
s.164 Authority for off-market purchase	
(1)	ss.693(1), 694(1)
(2)	s.694(2) (changed)
(3)	ss.694(4), 697(3), 700(3)
(4)	ss.694(5), 697(4), 700(4)

Provision of Companies Act 1985	Destination in Companies Act 2006
(5)	ss.694(1), (3) and (4), 698(1), (3) and (4), 700(5)
(6)	ss.696(1) to (5), 699(1) to (6), 700(5) (changed)
(7)	ss.697(1) to (4), 698(1), (3) and (4), 699(1) to (6), 700(3) to (5)
s.165 Authority for contingent purchase contract	
(1)	s.694(3)
(2)	ss.694(2), (4) and (5), 695(1), (3) and (5), 696(1) to (5)
s.166 Authority for market purchase	
(1)	ss.693(1), 701(1)
(2)	s.701(2)
(3)	s.701(3) and (5)
(4)	s.701(4) and (5)
(5)	s.701(6)
(6)	s.701(7)
(7)	s.701(8)
s.167 Assignment or release of company's right to purchase own shares	
(1)	s.704
(2)	s.700(1) to (5)
s.168 Payments apart from purchase price to be made out of distributable profits	
(1)	s.705(1)
(2)	s.705(2)
s.169 Disclosure by company of purchase of own shares	
(1)	ss.707(1) to (3), 708(1) (changed)
(1A)	ss.707(1) to (3), 708(1) (changed)
(1B)	ss.707(1) to (3), 708(1) (changed)
(2)	s.707(4)
(3)	s.707(5)
(4)	s.702(1) to (4) (changed)
(5)	s.702(6)
(6)	ss.707(6) and (7), 708(4) and (5)
(7)	s.703(1) and (2) (changed)
(8)	s.703(3)
(9)	s.702(7)
s.169A Disclosure by company of cancellation or disposal of treasury shares	
(1)	ss.728(1), 730(1)
(2)	ss.728(2), 730(2)
(3)	ss.728(3), 730(3)
(4)	ss.728(4) and (5), 730(6) and (7)
s.170 The capital redemption reserve	
(1)	s.733(1), (2) and (4)
(2) and (3)	s.733(3)
(4)	s.733(5) and (6)
s.171 Power of private companies to redeem or purchase own shares out of capital	
(1)	s.709(1) (changed)
(2)	s.709(2)
(3)	s.710(1) and (2)

Provision of Companies Act 1985	Destination in Companies Act 2006
(4)	s.734(2)
(5)	s.734(3)
(6)	s.734(4)
s.172 Availability of profits for purposes of s 171	
(1)	s.711(1) and (2)
(2)	s.712(2)
(3)	s.712(6)
(4)	s.712(3)
(5)	s.712(4)
(6)	s.712(7)
s.173 Conditions for payment out of capital	
(1)	s.713(1) and (2)
(2)	s.716(1)
(3)	s.714(1) to (3)
(4)	s.714(4) (changed)
(5)	s.714(5) and (6) (changed)
(6)	s.715(1) and (2)
s.174 Procedure for special resolution under s 173	
(1)	ss.716(2), 723(1)
(2)	s.717(3)
(3)	s.717(4)
(4)	s.718(2) and (3) (changed)
(5)	s.717(5)
s.175 Publicity for proposed payment out of capital	
(1)	s.719(1)
(2)	s.719(2)
(3)	s.719(3)
(4)	ss.719(4), 720(1)
(5)	s.719(4)
(6)	s.720(1), (2) and (4) (changed)
(7)	s.720(5) and (6)
(8)	s.720(7)
s.176 Objections by company's members or creditors	
(1)	s.721(1) and (2)
(2)	s.721(2)
(3)	s.722(2) and (3)
(4)	s.722(4) and (5)
s.177 Powers of court on application under s 176	
(1)	s.721(3)
(2)	s.721(4) and (5)
(3)	s.721(6)
(4)	s.721(7)
s.178 Effect of company's failure to redeem or purchase	
(1)	s.735(1)
(2)	s.735(2)
(3)	s.735(2) and (3)
(4)	s.735(4)
(5)	s.735(5)
(6)	s.735(6)
s.181 Definitions for Chapter VII	
	s.736

Provision of Companies Act 1985	Destination in Companies Act 2006
s.182 Nature, transfer and numbering of shares	
(1)	ss.541, 544(1) and (2)
(2)	s.543(1) and (2)
s.183 Transfer and registration	
(1)	s.770(1)
(2)	s.770(2)
(3)	s.773
(4)	s.772
s.184 Certification of transfers	
(1)	s.775(1) and (2)
(2)	s.775(3)
(3)	s.775(4)
s.185 Duty of company as to issue of certificates	
(1)	ss.769(1) and (2), 776(1) and (3)
(2)	s.776(2)
(3)	s.777(1) and (2)
(4)	ss.769(2), 776(3), 778(1)
(4A)	s.778(1)
(4B) and (4C)	s.778(2)
(4D)	s.778(3)
(5)	ss.769(3) and (4), 776(5) and (6)
(6)	s.782(1)
(7)	s.782(2) and (3)
s.186 Certificate to be evidence of title	
(1)	s.768(1) and (2)
(2)	s.768(2)
s.187 Evidence of grant of probate or confirmation as executor	
	s.774
s.188 Issue and effect of share warrant to bearer	
(1)	s.779(1)
(2)	s.779(2)
(3)	s.779(3)
s.189 Offences in connections with share warrants (Scotland)	
(1)	s.781(1) and (3)
(2)	s.781(2) and (4)
s.190 Register of debenture holders	
(1)	s.743(6)
(5)	s.743(2) and (6) (changed)
(6)	s.743(3)
s.191 Right to inspect register	
(1)	s.744(1)
(2)	s.744(2)
(3)	s.749(1)
(4)	ss.746(1) and (2), 749(2) and (3)
(5)	ss.746(3), 749(4)
(6)	s.744(5)
(7)	s.748(1) and (2) (changed)
s.192 Liability of trustees of debentures	
(1)	s.750(1) and (3)
(2)	s.750(2)

Provision of Companies Act 1985	Destination in Companies Act 2006
(3)	s.751(1) and (2)
(4)	s.751(3) and (4)
s.193 Perpetual debentures	
	s.739(1) and (2)
s.194 Power to re-issue redeemed debentures	
(1)	s.752(1)
(2)	s.752(2)
(3)	s.753
(4)	s.752(3)
(5)	s.752(4)
s.195 Contract to subscribe for debentures	
	s.740
s.196 Payment of debts out of assets subject to floating charge (England and Wales)	
(1)	s.754(1)
(2)	s.754(2)
(3)	s.754(3)
(4)	s.754(4)
s.197 Debentures to bearer (Scotland)	
	s.742
s.198 Obligation of disclosure: the cases in which it may arise and "the relevant time"	
(2)	s.792(1) and (2) (changed)
s.203 Notification of family and corporate interests	
(1)	s.822(1) and (2)
(2)	s.823(1)
(3)	s.832(2)
(4)	s.823(3)
s.204 Agreement to acquire interests in a particular company	
(1)	s.824(1)
(2)	ss.824(1) and (2), 988(4)
(3)	ss.824(3), 988(6)
(4)	s.824(4)
(5)	ss.824(5), 988(7)
(6)	ss.824(6), 988(5)
s.205 Obligation of disclosure arising under s 204	
(1)	s.825(1)
(2)	s.825(2)
(3)	s.825(3)
(4)	s.825(4)
s.207 Interests in shares by attribution	
(1)	ss.783, 785(1)
(2)	s.785(2)
(3)	s.785(3)
(4)	s.785(4)
(5)	s.785(5)
(6)	s.785(6)
(7)	s.788
(9)	s.784(3)
(10)	s.783

Provision of Companies Act 1985	Destination in Companies Act 2006
s.208 Interests in shares which are to be notified	
(1)	s.820(1)
(2)	s.820(2)
(3)	s.820(3)
(4)	s.820(4)
(5)	s.820(6)
(6)	s.820(5)
(7)	s.820(7)
(8)	s.820(8)
s.210A Power to make further provision by regulations	
(1)	s.828(1) and (2)
(5)	s.828(3)
s.211 Register of interests in shares	
(3)	s.808(2)
(4)	s.808(7)
(5)	s.808(4)
(6)	s.810(1) to (3)
(7)	s.819(1)
(8)	ss.809(1), 810(4), 811(1) and (2), 813(1) to (3) (changed)
(9)	s.826(1)
(10)	ss.808(5) and (6), 819(2) and (3)
s.212 Company investigations	
(1)	s.793(1) and (2) (changed)
(2)	s.793(3), (4) and (6)
(3)	s.793(5)
(4)	s.793(7)
(5)	ss.820(1) to (8), 822(1) and (2), 823(1) to (3), 824(1) to (6), 825(1) to (4)
(6)	s.821(1) and (2)
s.213 Registration of interests disclosed under s 212	
(1)	s.808(1) to (3) (changed)
(3)	ss.808(2) and (4) to (7), 809(1), 810(1) to (4), 811(1) and (2), 813(1) to (3), 819(1) to (3), 826(1)
s.214 Company investigation on requisition by members	
(1)	s.803(1) and (2) (changed)
(2)	s.803(3) (changed)
(4)	s.804(1)
(5)	s.804(2) and (3) (changed)
s.215 Company report to members	
(1)	s.805(1)
(2)	s.805(2) and (3)
(3)	s.805(1) and (3)
(4)	s.826(1) and (2)
(5)	s.805(6)
(6)	s.805(7)
(7)	ss.805(4), 807(1) to (5)
(8)	s.806(3) and (4)
s.216 Penalty for failure to provide information	
(1)	s.794(1)
(1A)	s.794(3)
(1B)	s.794(2)

Provision of Companies Act 1985	Destination in Companies Act 2006
(3)	s.795(1) and (3)
(4)	s.795(2)
(5)	s.796(1) and (2)
s.217 Removal of entries from register	
(1)	s.816 (changed)
(2)	s.817(1) (changed)
(3)	s.817(2) and (3)
(4)	s.818(1) and (2)
(5)	ss.817(4), 818(3)
s.218 Otherwise, entries not to be removed	
(1)	s.815(1)
(2)	s.815(2)
(3)	s.815(3) and (4)
s.219 Inspection of register and reports	
(1)	s.807(1), 811(1)
(2)	s.807(2), 811(2)
(3)	ss.807(3) and (4), 813(1) and (2) (changed)
(4)	ss.807(5), 813(3)
s.220 Definitions for Part VI	
(2)	s.827
s.221 Duty to keep accounting records	
(1)	s.386(1) and (2)
(2) to (4)	s.386(3) to (5)
(5)	s.387(1) and (2)
(6)	s.387(3)
s.222 Where and for how long records to be kept	
(1) to (3)	s.388(1) to (3)
(4)	s.389(1), (2) and (4)
(5)	s.388(4) and (5)
(6)	s.389(3) and (4)
s.223 A company's financial year	
(1) to (5)	s.390(1) to (5)
s.224 Accounting reference periods and accounting reference date	
(1)	s.391(1)
(2) and (3)	s.391(2)
(3A)	s.391(4)
(4) to (6)	s.391(5) to (7)
s.225 Alteration of accounting reference date	
(1)	s.392(1)
(3) to (7)	s.392(2) to (6)
s.226 Duty to prepare individual accounts	
(1)	s.394
(2) to (6)	s.395(1) to (5)
s.226A Companies Act individual accounts	
(1) and (2)	s.396(1) and (2)
(3)	s.396(3) (changed)
(4)	s.396(4)
(5) and (6)	s.396(5)
s.226B IAS individual accounts	
	s.397

Provision of Companies Act 1985	Destination in Companies Act 2006
s.227 Duty to prepare group accounts	
(1)	s.399(2)
(2) to (7)	s.403(1) to (6)
(8)	s.399(2) and (3)
s.227A Companies Act group accounts	
(1) and (2)	s.404(1) and (2)
(3)	s.404(3) (changed)
(4)	s.404(4)
(5) and (6)	s.404(5)
s.227B IAS group accounts	
	s.406
s.227C Consistency of accounts	
(1) to (5)	s.407(1) to (5)
s.228 Exemption for parent companies included in accounts of larger group	
(1) and (2)	s.400(1) and (2)
(3)	s.400(4)
(4)	s.400(5)
(5)	s.400(3)
(6)	s.400(6)
s.228A Exemption for parent companies included in non-EEA group accounts	
(1) and (2)	s.401(1) and (2)
(3)	s.401(4)
(4)	s.401(5)
(5)	s.401(3)
(6)	s.401(6)
s.229 Subsidiary undertakings included in the consolidation	
(1) and (2)	s.405(1) and (2)
(3)	s.405(3) and (4)
(5)	s.402
s.230 Treatment of individual profit and loss account where group accounts prepared	
(1)	s.408(1) (changed)
(2)	s.408(2) (changed)
(3) and (4)	s.408(3) and (4)
s.231 Disclosure required in notes to accounts: related undertakings	
(1) and (2)	s.409(1) and (2) (changed)
(3)	s.409(3) and (4) (changed)
(4)	s.409(5)
(5)	s.410(1) and (2)
(6)	s.410(3)
(7)	s.410(4) and (5)
s.231A Disclosure required in notes to annual accounts: particulars of staff	
(1)	s.411(1)
(2) to (4)	s.411(3) to (5)
(5)	s.411(2)
(6)	s.411(7)
(7)	s.411(6)

Provision of Companies Act 1985	Destination in Companies Act 2006
s.232 Disclosure required in notes to accounts: emoluments and other benefits of directors and others	
(3)	s.412(5)
(4)	s.412(6)
s.233 Approval and signing of accounts	
(1) and (2)	ss.414(1) and (2), 450(1) and (2)
(3)	ss.433(1) to (3), 436(1) and (2)
(4)	ss.444(6), 445(5), 446(3), 447(3) (changed)
(5)	ss.414(4) and (5) (changed)
(6)(a)	s.433(4) and (5)
s.234 Duty to prepare directors' report	
(1)	ss.415(1), 417(1), 418(2)
(2) and (3)	s.415(2) and (3)
(5)	ss.415(4) and (5), 419(3) and (4)
s.234ZZA Directors' report: general requirements	
(1)	s.416(1) and (3)
(2)	s.416(2)
(3) and (4)	s.416(4) (changed)
s.234ZZB Directors' report: business review	
(1) and (2)	s.417(3) and (4)
(3)	s.417(6)
(4)	s.417(8)
(5)	s.417(6)
(6)	s.417(9)
s.234ZA Statement as to disclosure of information to auditors	
(1) to (4)	s.418(1) to (4)
(6)	s.418(5) and (6)
s.234A Approval and signing of directors' report	
(1)	s.419(1)
(2)	ss.433(1) to (3), 436(1) and (2)
(3)	ss.444(6), 445(5), 446(3), 447(3)
(4)	ss.419(3) and (4), 433(4) and (5)
s.234B Duty to prepare directors' remuneration report	
(1)	ss.420(1), 421(1) and (2)
(2)	s.421(1) and (2)
(3) and (4)	s.420(2) and (3)
(5) and (6)	s.421(3) and (4)
s.234C Approval and signing of directors' remuneration report	
(1)	s.422(1)
(2)	ss.433(1) to (3), 436(1) and (2)
(3)	s.447(3)
(4)	s.422(2) and (3)
s.235 Auditors' report	
(1)	ss.475(1), 495(1)
(1A)	s.495(2)
(1B) and (2)	s.495(3)
(2A)	s.495(4)
(3)	s.496
(4) and (5)	s.497(1) and (2)

Provision of Companies Act 1985	Destination in Companies Act 2006
s.236 Signature of auditors' report	
(1)	s.503(1) and (2)
(2)	s.505(1) and (2) (changed)
(3)	s.444(7) (changed)
(4)	s.505(3) and (4)
s.237 Duties of auditors	
(1) to (4)	s.498(1) to (4)
(4A)	s.498(5)
s.238 Persons entitled to receive copies of accounts and reports	
(1) and (1A)	ss.423(1), 424(1) to (3) (changed)
(3)	s.423(4)
(4)	s.424(4) (changed)
(5)	s.425(1) and (2)
(6)	s.423(5)
s.239 Right to demand copies of accounts and reports	
(1) and (2)	ss.431(1) and (2), 432(1) and (2)
(3)	ss.431(3) and (4), 432(3) and (4)
s.240 Requirements in connection with publication of accounts	
(1)	s.434(1) (changed)
(2)	s.434(2) (changed)
(3)	s.435(1) and (2) (changed)
(4)	s.436(1) and (2) (changed)
(5)	ss.434(3), 435(3) (changed)
(6)	s.435(5) and (6)
s.241 Accounts and reports to be laid before company in general meeting	
(1)	s.437(1) (changed)
(2)	ss.437(2), 438(1) and (4)
(3) and (4)	s.438(2) and (3)
s.241A Members' approval of directors' remuneration report	
(1) and (3)	s.439(1)
(4)	s.439(2)
(5)	s.439(3)
(6)	s.439(4)
(7)	s.439(3)
(8)	s.439(5)
(9)	s.440(1) and (4)
(10)	s.440(2) to (4)
(11)	s.440(2) and (3)
(12)	s.439(6)
s.242 Accounts and reports to be delivered to the registrar	
(1)	s.441(1), 444(1) and (2), 445(1) and (2), 446(1) and (2), 447(1) and (2) (changed)
(2)	s.451(1)
(3)	s.452(1) and (2)
(4) and (5)	s.451(2) and (3)

Provision of Companies Act 1985	Destination in Companies Act 2006
s.242A Civil penalty for failure to deliver accounts	
(1)	s.453(1)
(2)	s.453(2) (changed)
(3) and (4)	s.453(3) and (4)
s.242B Delivery and publication of accounts in ECUs	
(1) to (4)	s.469(1) to (4)
s.244 Period allowed for laying and delivering accounts and reports	
(1) and (2)	s.442(2) and (3) (changed)
(4) and (5)	s.442(4) and (5)
(6)	s.442(7)
s.245 Voluntary revision of annual accounts or directors' report	
(1) to (3)	s.454(1) to (3)
(4)	s.454(4) (changed)
(5)	s.454(5)
s.245A Secretary of State's notice in respect of annual accounts	
(1)	s.455(1) and (2)
(2) to (4)	s.455(3) to (5)
s.245B Application to court in respect of defective accounts	
(1) to (3)	s.456(1) to (3)
(3A)	s.456(4)
(4) to (7)	s.456(5) to (8)
s.245C Other persons authorised to apply to court	
(1)	s.457(1)
(1A)	s.457(5)
(2) and (3)	s.457(2) and (3)
(4)	s.457(7)
(4A)	s.457(5)
(4B)	s.457(4)
(5)	s.457(6)
s.245D Disclosure of information held by Inland Revenue to persons authorised to apply to court	
(1)	s.458(1)
(2)	s.458(2)
(3)	s.458(1)
s.245E Restrictions on use and further disclosure of information disclosed under section 245D	
(1) and (2)	s.458(3)
(3)	s.458(4) and (5)
(4)	s.458(4) (changed)
(5)	ss.1126, 1130
s.245F Power of authorised persons to require documents, information and explanations	
(1) to (8)	s.459(1) to (8)
s.245G Restrictions on further disclosure of information obtained under section 245F	
(1) and (2)	s.460(1) and (2)
(3)	ss.460(3), 461(1) to (6)

Provision of Companies Act 1985	Destination in Companies Act 2006
(4) to (6)	s.462(1) to (3)
(7)	s.460(4) and (5)
(8)	s.460(4)
(9)	ss.1126, 1130
(10)	s.460(3)
(11)	s.461(7)
s.246 Special provisions for small companies	
(3)	s.411(1)
(4)	ss.416(3), 417(1)
(5)	s.444(1) and (3) (changed)
(6)	s.444(3) (changed)
(7)	ss.444(6), 450(1) and (2)
(8)	ss.414(3), 419(2), 444(5), 450(3)
s.246A Special provisions for medium-sized companies	
(1)	s.445(1)
(2)	s.445(3) (changed)
(2A)	s.417(7)
(3)	s.445(3) (changed)
(4)	s.450(3)
s.247 Qualification of company as small or medium-sized	
(1)(a)	ss.382(1), 465(1)
(1)(b) and (2)	ss.382(2), 465(2)
(3) and (4)	ss.382(3) and (4), 465(3) and (4)
(5)	ss.382(5), 465(5) (changed)
(6)	ss.382(6), 465(6)
s.247A Cases in which special provisions do not apply	
(1) to (1B)	ss.384(1), 467(1)
(2)	ss.384(2), 467(2) (changed)
(2A)	ss.384(3), 467(3)
(3)	ss.383(1), 466(1)
s.247B Special auditors' report	
(1)	s.449(1)
(2)	ss.444(4), 445(4), 449(2)
(3) to (5)	s.449(3) to (5)
s.248 Exemption for small and medium-sized groups	
(1) and (2)	ss.398, 399(1) and (2) (changed)
s.249 Qualification of group as small or medium-sized	
(1)(a)	s.466(2)
(1)(b) and (2)	s.466(3)
(3)	s.466(4)
(4)	s.466(5) and (6)
(5) and (6)	s.466(7)
s.249A Exemptions from audit	
(1)	s.477(1)
(3)	s.477(2) and (4)
(6)	s.477(3)
(7)	s.477(4)
s.249AA Dormant companies	
(1) and (2)	s.480(1) and (2)
(3)	s.481

Provision of Companies Act 1985	Destination in Companies Act 2006
(4)	s.1169(1)
(5) to (7)	s.1169(2) and (3)
s.249B Cases where exemptions not available	
(1)	ss.478, 479(1) to (3)
(1A)	s.479(3)
(1B)	s.479(1) to (3)
(1C)	s.479(2), (5) and (6)
(2) and (3)	s.476(1) to (3)
(4)	s.475(2) and (3)
(5)	s.475(4)
s.249E Effect of exemptions	
(1)(b)	ss.444(2), 445(2), 446(2) (changed)
s.251 Provision of summary financial statement to shareholders	
(1)	ss.426(1), 427(1)
(2)	s.426(2) and (3)
(3)	ss.427(2), 428(2)
(3A)	ss.427(3), 428(3)
(4)	ss.427(4), 428(4)
(5)	ss.427(6), 428(6)
(6)	s.429(1) and (2)
(7)	ss.434(6), 435(7)
s.254 Exemption from requirement to deliver accounts and reports	
(1) to (3)	s.448(1) to (3)
(4)	s.448(4)
s.255A Special provisions for banking and insurance groups	
(4)	s.1164(5)
(5)	s.1165(5)
(5A)	ss.1164(5), 1165(6)
s.255D Power to apply provisions to banking partnerships	
(1)	s.470(1)
(2) and (2A)	s.470(2)
(4)	s.470(4)
(5)	s.470(3)
s.256 Accounting standards	
(1) and (2)	s.464(1) and (2)
(4)	s.464(3)
s.257 Power of Secretary of State to alter accounting requirements	
(1)	s.484(1)
(2)	ss.473(1) to (4) (changed), 484(3)
(3)	s.484(4)
(4)(c)	s.484(2)
s.258 Parent and subsidiary undertakings	
(1) to (6)	s.1162(1) to (6)
s.259 Meaning of "undertaking" and related expressions	
(1)	ss.1161(1), 1173 "parent company"
(2) to (5)	s.1161(2) to (5)

Provision of Companies Act 1985	Destination in Companies Act 2006
s.261 Notes to the accounts	
(1) and (2)	s.472(1) and (2)
s.262 Minor definitions	
(1)	ss.474(1), 539, 835(6), 1173 "credit institution" (changed)
(2)	s.474(2)
(3)	s.853(4) and (5)
s.263 Certain distributions prohibited	
(1)	s.830(1)
(2)	s.829(1) and (2)
(3)	s.830(2) and (3)
(4)	s.849
(5)	s.850(1) to (3)
s.264 Restriction on distribution of assets	
(1)	s.831(1) and (6)
(2)	s.831(2) and (3)
(3)	s.831(4)
(4)	s.831(5)
s.265 Other distributions by investment companies	
(1)	s.832(1) to (3)
(2)	s.832(4)
(3)	s.832(7)
(4)	s.832(5)
(4A)	s.832(6)
(5)	s.832(6)
(6)	s.832(5)
s.266 Meaning of "investment company"	
(1)	s.833(1)
(2)	ss.833(2), 834(1)
(2A)	s.833(3)
(3)	s.833(4) and (5)
(4)	s.834(2) to (5)
s.267 Extension of ss 265, 266 to other companies	
(1)	s.835(1)
(2)	s.835(2)
s.268 Realised profits of insurance company with long term business	
(1)	s.843(1), (2), (4) and (5)
(2)	s.843(3) and (4)
(3)	s.843(6) and (7)
(4)	s.843(7)
s.269 Treatment of development costs	
(1)	s.844(1)
(2)	s.844(2) and (3)
s.270 Distribution to be justified by reference to company's accounts	
(1) and (2)	s.836(1)
(3)	ss.836(2), 837(1)
(4)	ss.836(2), 838(1), 839(1)
(5)	s.836(3) and (4)
s.271 Requirements for last annual accounts	
(2)	s.837(2)
(3)	s.837(3) and (4)

Provision of Companies Act 1985	Destination in Companies Act 2006
(4)	s.837(4)
(5)	s.837(5)
s.272 Requirements for interim accounts	
(1)	s.838(2)
(2)	s.838(3)
(3)	ss.838(4) and (5), 839(4)
(4) and (5)	s.838(6)
s.273 Requirements for initial accounts	
(1)	s.839(2)
(2)	s.839(3)
(3)	s.839(4)
(4)	s.839(5) and (6)
(5)	s.839(6)
(6) and (7)	s.839(7)
s.274 Method of applying s 270 to successive distributions	
(1)	s.840(1)
(2)	s.840(1) and (2)
(3)	s.840(3) to (5)
s.275 Treatment of assets in the relevant accounts	
(1)	s.841(1) and (2)
(1A)	s.841(3)
(2)	s.841(5)
(3)	s.842
(4) to (6)	s.841(4)
s.276 Distributions in kind	
	s.846(1) and (2) (changed)
s.277 Consequences of unlawful distribution	
(1)	s.847(1) and (2)
(2)	s.847(3) and (4)
s.278 Saving for provision in articles operative before Act of 1980	
	s.848(1) and (2)
s.280 Definitions for Part VIII	
(1)	s.853(1)
(2)	s.853(2)
(3)	s.853(3)
s.281 Saving for other restraints on distribution	
	ss.851, 852 (changed)
s.282 Directors	
(1)	s.154(2) (changed)
(3)	s.154(1)
s.283 Secretary	
(1)	s.271 (changed)
(3)	ss.270(3), 274 (changed)
s.284 Acts done by person in dual capacity	
	s.280
s.285 Validity of acts of directors	
	s.161(1) and (2) (changed)
s.286 Qualifications of company secretaries	
(1)	s.273(1) and (2) (changed)
(2)	s.273(3)

Provision of Companies Act 1985	Destination in Companies Act 2006
s.287 Registered office	
(1)	s.86
(3)	s.87(1)
(4)	s.87(2)
(5)	s.87(3)
(6)	s.87(4)
s.288 Register of directors and secretaries	
(1)	ss.162(1) to (3), 275(1) to (3) (changed)
(2)	ss.167(1) and (2), 276(1) and (2)
(3)	ss.162(5), 275(5)
(4)	ss.162(6) and (7), 167(4) and (5), 275(6) and (7), 276(3) and (4)
(5)	ss.162(8), 275(8)
(6)	s.162(6), 167(4), 275(6), 276(3)
s.289 Particulars of directors to be registered under s 288	
(1)	ss.163(1), 164 (changed)
(2)	ss.163(2) and (4), 277(2) and (4) (changed)
s.290 Particulars of secretaries to be registered under s 288	
(1)	ss.277(1), 278(1) (changed)
(2)	s.278(2)
(3)	s.277(2) and (4)
s.292 Appointment of directors to be voted on individually	
(1)	s.160(1)
(2)	s.160(2)
(3)	s.160(3)
(4)	s.160(4)
s.303 Resolution to remove director	
(1)	s.168(1) (changed)
(2)	s.168(2)
(3)	s.168(3)
(4)	s.168(4)
(5)	s.168(5)
s.304 Director's right to protest removal	
(1)	s.169(1) and (2)
(2)	s.169(3)
(3)	s.169(4)
(4)	s.169(5)
(5)	s.169(6)
s.309 Directors to have regard to interests of employees	
(1)	s.172(1)
s.309A Provisions protecting directors from liability	
(1)	s.232(1) and (2)
(2)	s.232(1)
(3)	s.232(2)
(4)	s.234(1)
(5)	s.233
(6)	s.232(3)
s.309B Qualifying third party indemnity provisions	
(1) and (2)	s.234(2)
(3)	s.234(3)

Provision of Companies Act 1985	Destination in Companies Act 2006
(4)	s.234(3) and (6)
(5)	s.234(4)
(6) and (7)	s.234(5)
s.309C Disclosure of qualifying third party indemnity provisions	
(1)	s.236(1) (changed)
(2)	s.236(2) and (3)
(3)	s.236(4) and (5) (changed)
(4)	s.237(1)
(5)	ss.237(1) to (3) and (5) to (8), 238(1) and (3) to (5)
s.310 Provisions protecting auditors from liability	
(1)	s.532(1) and (3) (changed)
(2)	s.532(2)
(3)	s.533
s.312 Payment to director for loss of office, etc	
	ss215(1), 217(1) and (3) (changed)
s.313 Company approval for property transfer	
(1)	ss.215(1), 218(1) and (3) (changed)
(2)	s.222(2)
s.314 Director's duty of disclosure on takeover, etc	
(1)	ss.215(1), 219(1) (changed)
s.315 Consequences of non-compliance with s 314	
(1)	ss.219(1) and (2), 222(3) (changed)
(3)	s.219(5)
s.316 Provisions supplementing ss 312 to 315	
(1)	ss.218(5), 219(7)
(2)	s.216(1) and (2) (changed)
(3)	s.220(1)
s.317 Directors to disclose interest in contracts	
(1)	s.182(1) (changed)
(2)	s.182(2) (changed)
(3)	s.185(1) and (2) (changed)
(4)	s.185(4)
(5)	s.185(1) (changed)
(7)	s.183(1) and (2)
(8)	s.187(1) to (4)
s.318 Director's service contracts to be open to inspection	
(1)	ss.228(1), 237(2)
(2) and (3)	ss.228(2), 237(3) (changed)
(4)	ss.228(4), 237(5)
(6)	s.230
(7)	ss.229(1), 238(1)
(8)	ss.228(5) and (6), 229(3) and (4), 237(6) and (7), 238(3) and (4) (changed)
(9)	ss.229(5), 238(5) (changed)
(10)	ss.228(7), 237(8)
s.319 Director's contract of employment for more than 5 years	
(1)	s.188(1) and (3) (changed)
(2)	s.188(4) (changed)
(3)	s.188(2) (changed)
(4)	s.188(6)

Provision of Companies Act 1985	Destination in Companies Act 2006
(5)	s.188(5)
(6)	s.189
(7)	ss.188(7), 223(1)
s.320 Substantial property transactions involving directors, etc	
(1)	s.190(1) and (2) (changed)
(2)	s.191(1) to (5) (changed)
(3)	s.223(1)
s.321 Exceptions from s 320	
(1)	s.190(4)
(2)	ss.192, 193(1) and (2) (changed)
(3)	s.192
(4)	s.194(1) and (2)
s.322 Liabilities arising from contravention of s 320	
(1)	s.195(1) and (2)
(2)	ss.195(2) and 196
(3)	s.195(1), (3) and (4)
(4)	s.195(3), (5) and (8)
(5)	s.195(6)
(6)	s.195(7)
s.322A Invalidity of certain transactions involving directors, etc	
(1)	s.41(1) and (2)
(2)	s.41(2)
(3)	s.41(3)
(4)	s.41(1)
(5)	s.41(4)
(6)	s.41(5)
(7)	s.41(6)
(8)	s.41(7)
s.322B Contracts with sole members who are directors	
(1)	s.231(1) and (2) (changed)
(2)	s.231(1)
(3)	s.231(5)
(4)	s.231(3) and (4) (changed)
(5)	s.231(7)
(6)	s.231(6)
s.325 Register of directors' interests notified under s 324	
(5)	s.809(2) and (3)
s.330 General restriction on loans etc to directors and persons connected with them	
(2)	s.197(1) (changed)
(3)	ss.198(1) and (2) (changed), 200(1) and (2)
(4)	s.201(1) and (2) (changed)
(5)	s.223(1)
(6)	s.203(1) and (6) (changed)
(7)	s.203(1) (changed)
s.331 Definitions for ss 330 ff	
(3)	s.199(1)
(4)	s.199(2) and (3)
(6)	ss.198(1), 200(1), 201(1)
(7)	s.202(1)

Provision of Companies Act 1985	Destination in Companies Act 2006
(8)	s.202(3)
(9)	ss.202(2), 212
(10)	s.202(3)
s.333 Inter-company loans in same group	
	s.208(1) (changed)
s.334 Loans of small amounts	
	s.207(1) (changed)
s.335 Minor and business transactions	
(1)	s.207(2) (changed)
(2)	s.207(3)
s.336 Transactions at behest of holding company	
	208(1) and (2) (changed)
s.337 Funding of director's expenditure on duty to company	
(1) and (2)	s.204(1) (changed)
(3)	s.204(2) (changed)
s.337A Funding of director's expenditure on defending proceedings	
(1)	s.205(1) (changed)
(2)	s.205(5)
(3)	s.205(1) (changed)
(4)	s.205(2)
(5)	s.205(3)
(6)	s.205(4)
s.338 Loan or quasi-loan by money-lending company	
(1)	s.209(1)
(2)	s.209(2)
(3)	s.209(1)
(6)	s.209(3) and (4)
s.339 "Relevant amounts" for purposes of ss 334 ff	
(1)	ss.204(2), 207(1) and (2), 210(1)
(2)	ss.204(2), 207(1) and (2), 210(2) to (4)
(3)	s.210(3) and (4)
(5)	s.210(5)
(6)	s.211(1)
s.340 "Value" of transactions and arrangements	
(2)	s.211(2)
(3)	s.211(3)
(4)	s.211(5)
(5)	s.211(6)
(6)	s.211(4)
(7)	s.211(7) (changed)
s.341 Civil remedies for breach of s 330	
(1)	s.213(1) and (2)
(2)	s.213(3) and (4)
(3)	s.213(5) and (8)
(4)	s.213(6)
(5)	s.213(7)
s.345 Power to increase financial limits	
(1)	s.258(1)
(2)	s.258(2)
(3)	s.258(3)

Provision of Companies Act 1985	Destination in Companies Act 2006
s.346 "Connected persons", etc	
(1)	ss.252(1), 254(1), 255(1)
(2) and (3)	ss.252(2) and (3), 253(2) (changed)
(4)	s.254(2) and (5)
(5)	s.255(2) and (5)
(6)	ss.254(6), 255(6)
(7)	ss.254(3), 255(3)
(8)	ss.254(4), 255(4)
s.347 Transactions under foreign law	
	s.259
s.347 A Introductory provisions	
(1)	s.362 (changed)
(3)	s.379(1)
(4)	s.364(2)
(5)	s.365(1) (changed)
(6)	s.363(1) and (2)
(7)	s.363(1) and (2) (changed)
(8)	s.379(1)
(9)	s.363(1)
(10)	ss.366(5), 379(2)
s.347B Exemptions	
(1)	s.375(1)
(2)	s.375(2) (changed)
(3)	s.376(1) and (2)
(4)	s.378(1) (changed)
(5)	s.378(3)
(6) and (7)	s.378(1) (changed)
(8)	s.377(1)
(9)	s.377(3)
(10)	s.377(2)
(11)	s.377(4)
s.347C Prohibition on donations and political expenditure by companies	
(1)	s.366(1), (2) and (5) (changed)
(2)	s.367(3) and (6) (changed)
(3)	s.368(1) and (2)
(4)	s.367(5)
(6)	s.366(6)
s.347D Special rules for subsidiaries	
(1)	s.366(2)
(2)	s.366(2) and (5) (changed)
(3)	s.366(2), (3) and (5) (changed)
(4)	s.367(3) and (6) (changed)
(5)	s.368(1) and (2)
(6)	s.367(5)
(9)	s.366(6)
s.347F Remedies for breach of prohibitions on company donations etc	
(1)	s.369(1)
(2)	s.369(2) and (3) (changed)
(3)	s.369(2) and (5)
(4)	s.369(2)
(5)	s.369(6)
(6)	s.369(3) (changed)

Provision of Companies Act 1985	Destination in Companies Act 2006
s.347I Enforcement of directors' liabilities by shareholder action	
(1)	s.370(1) and (2) (changed)
(2)	s.370(3)
(3)	ss.370(4), 371(1)
(4) and (5)	s.371(2)
(6)	s.371(3)
(7)	s.371(4)
(8)	s.371(5)
s.347J Costs of shareholder action	
(1)	s.372(1)
(2)	s.372(2)
(3)	s.372(3)
(4) and (5)	s.372(4)
(6)	s.372(5)
s.347K Information for purposes of shareholder action	
(1)	s.373(1)
(2)	s.373(2)
s.348 Company name to appear outside place of business	
(1)	s.82(1) and (2)
(2)	s.84(1) and (2)
s.349 Company's name to appear in its correspondence, etc	
(1)	s.82(1) and (2)
(2) and (3)	s.84(1) and (2)
s.350 Company seal	
(1)	s.45(2) and (3) (changed)
(2)	s.45(4) and (5)
s.351 Particulars in correspondence etc	
(1) and (2)	s.82(1) and (2)
(5)	s.84(1) and (2)
s.352 Obligation to keep and enter up register	
(1)	s.113(1)
(2)	s.113(2)
(3)	s.113(3) and (4)
(4)	s.113(6)
(5)	s.113(7) and (8)
(6)	s.121 (changed)
(7)	s.128(1) and (2)
s.352A Statement that company has only one member	
(1)	s.123(2) (changed)
(2)	s.123(3) (changed)
(3)	s.123(4) and (5)
(3A)	s.124(1) and (2)
s.353 Location of register	
(1)	s.114(1) (changed)
(2)	s.114(2)
(3)	s.114(3) and (4)
(4)	s.114(5) and (6)

Table of Destinations

Provision of Companies Act 1985	Destination in Companies Act 2006
s.354 Index of members	
(1)	s.115(1) and (2)
(2)	s.115(3)
(3)	s.115(4) (changed)
(4)	s.115(5) and (6)
s.355 Entries in register in relation to share warrants	
(1)	s.122(1) (changed)
(2)	s.122(4)
(3)	s.122(5)
(4)	s.122(2) and (6)
(5)	s.122(3)
s.356 Inspection of register and index	
(1)	s.116(1) (changed)
(3)	s.116(2)
(5)	s.118(1) and (2) (changed)
(6)	s.118(3)
s.359 Power of court to rectify register	
(1)	s.125(1)
(2)	s.125(2)
(3)	s.125(3)
(4)	s.125(4)
s.360 Trusts not to be entered on register in England and Wales	
	s.126
s.361 Register to be evidence	
	s.127
s.362 Overseas branch registers	
(1)	s.129(1)
(2)	s.129(1) and (5)
(3)	ss.130(1) to (3), 131(1) and (4), 132(1) to (4), 133(1) to (3), 134(1) to (3), 135(1) to (5)
s.363 Duty to deliver annual returns	
(1)	s.854(1) and (2)
(2)	s.854(3) (changed)
(3)	s.858(1) to (3)
(4)	s.858(1), (2) and (4) (changed)
s.364 Contents of annual return: general	
(1)	s.855(1) (changed)
(2)	s.855(2)
(3)	s.855(3)
s.364A Contents of annual return: particulars of share capital and shareholders	
(1)	s.856(1)
(2)	s.856(2)
(3)	s.856(2) (changed)
(4)	s.856(3)
(5)	s.856(4)
(6)	s.856(5)
(8)	s.856(6)

Provision of Companies Act 1985	Destination in Companies Act 2006
s.365 Supplementary provisions: regulations and interpretation	
(1)	s.857(1) and (2)
(2)	s.857(3)
(3)	s.859
s.366 Annual general meeting	
(1)	ss.336(1), 337(1)
(4)	s.336(3) and (4)
s.368 Extraordinary general meeting on members' requisition	
(1)	s.303(1) and (2)
(2)	s.303(2) and (3) (changed)
(2A)	s.303(2)
(3)	s.303(4) and (6) (changed)
(4)	ss.304(1), 305(1) and (3)
(5)	s.305(4)
(6)	s.305(6) and (7)
(7)	s.304(4)
(8)	s.304(1)
s.369 Length of notice for calling meetings	
(1) and (2)	s.307(2) and (3) (changed)
(3)	ss.307(4), 337(2) (changed)
(4)	s.307(5) and (6) (changed)
(4A)	s.308 (changed)
(4B)	ss.308, 309(1) and (3) (changed)
(4C)	s.309(2)
s.370 General provisions as to meetings and votes	
(1)	ss.284(4), 310(4), 318(2), 319(2)
(2)	s.310(1)
(4)	s.318(2) (changed)
(5)	s.319(1)
(6)	s.284(1) and (3)
s.370A Quorum at meetings of the sole member	
	s.318(1) and (3) (changed)
s.371 Power of court to order meeting	
(1)	s.306(1) and (2)
(2)	s.306(3) and (4)
(3)	s.306(5)
s.372 Proxies	
(1)	s.324(1)
(2)	s.324(2) (changed)
(3)	s.325(1) (changed)
(4)	s.325(3) and (4)
(5)	s.327(1) and (2) (changed)
(6)	s.326(1) to (4) (changed)
s.373 Right to demand a poll	
(1)	s.321(1) and (2) (changed)
(2)	s.329(1) and (2) (changed)
s.374 Voting on a poll	
	s.322

Provision of Companies Act 1985	Destination in Companies Act 2006
s.375 Representation of corporations at meetings	
(1)	s.323(1)
(2)	s.323(2) and (3) (changed)
s.376 Circulation of members' resolutions	
(1)	ss.314(1) and (4), 315(2), 316(2), 338(1) and (4), 339(2), 340(2)
(2)	ss.314(2) and (3), 338(3)
(3)	ss.315(1), 339(1)
(5)	ss.315(1), 339(1)
(6)	s.339(3)
(7)	ss.315(3) and (4), 339(4) and (5)
s.377 In certain cases, compliance with s 376 not required	
(1)	ss.314(4), 316(2), 338(4), 340(2) (changed)
(3)	s.317(1) and (2) (changed)
s.378 Extraordinary and special resolutions	
(1)	s.283(1), (4) and (5) (changed)
(2)	s.283(1) and (4) to (6) (changed)
(4)	s.320(1) and (3)
(5)	s.283(5) (changed)
(6)	s.301 (changed)
s.379 Resolution requiring special notice	
(1)	s.312(1)
(2)	s.312(2) and (3) (changed)
(3)	s.312(4)
s.380 Registration, etc of resolutions and agreements	
(1)	s.30(1)
(2)	s.36(1) and (2) (changed)
(4)	s.29(1) (changed)
(4A)	s.29(2)
(5)	s.30(2) and (3)
(6)	s.36(3) and (4) (changed)
(7)	ss.30(4), 36(5)
s.381 Resolution passed at adjourned meeting	
	s.332
s.381A Written resolutions of private companies	
(1)	ss.288(1), 289(1) (changed)
(2)	s.296(1) (changed)
(4)	s.288(5)
(7)	s.288(2)
s.381C Written resolutions: supplementary provisions	
(1)	s.300
s.382 Minutes of meetings	
(1)	ss.248(1), 355(1)
(2)	ss.249(1), 356(4)
(4)	ss.249(2), 356(5)
(5)	ss.248(3) and (4), 355(3) and (4) (changed)
s.382A Recording of written resolutions	
(1)	s.355(1) (changed)
(2)	s.356(2) and (3)

Provision of Companies Act 1985	Destination in Companies Act 2006
s.382B Recording of decisions by the sole member	
(1)	s.357(1) and (2)
(2)	s.357(3) and (4)
(3)	s.357(5)
s.383 Inspection of minute books	
(1)	s.358(1) and (3) (changed)
(3)	s.358(4) (changed)
(4)	s.358(5) and (6) (changed)
(5)	s.358(7)
s.384 Duty to appoint auditors	
(1)	ss.485(1), 489(1) (changed)
(2)	s.489(2)
s.385 Appointment at general meeting at which accounts laid	
(2)	ss.489(2) and (4), 491(1) (changed)
(3)	s.489(3) (changed)
(4)	s.489(4) (changed)
s.387 Appointment by Secretary of State in default of appointment by company	
(1)	ss.486(1), 490(1)
(2)	ss.486(2) to (4), 490(2) to (4)
s.388 Filling of casual vacancies	
(1)	ss.489(3), 526
s.389A Rights to information	
(1)	s.499(1)
(2)	s.499(2)
(3)	s.500(1)
(4)	s.500(2)
(5)	s.500(3)
(6)	ss.499(3), 500(4)
(7)	ss.499(4) 500(5)
s.389B Offences relating to the provision of information to auditors	
(1)	s501(1) and (2)
(2)	s.501(3)
(3)	s.501(3) (changed)
(4)	s.501(4) and (5)
(5)	s.501(6)
s.390 Right to attend company meetings, &c	
(1)	s.502(2)
(2)	s.502(1)
(3)	s.502(2)
s.390A Remuneration of auditors	
(1)	s.492(1)
(2)	s.492(2) and (3)
(4)	s.492(4)
(5)	s.492(5)
s.390B Disclosure of services provided by auditors or associates and related remuneration	
(1)	ss.494(1), 501(1) and (2)
(2)	s.494(2)

Provision of Companies Act 1985	Destination in Companies Act 2006
(3)	s.494(3)
(4)	s.494(4)
(5)	s.494(5)
(8)	s.494(1)
(9)	s.494(6)
s.391 Removal of auditors	
(1)	s.510(1) and (2)
(2)	s.512(1) to (3)
(3)	s.510(3)
(4)	s.513(1) and (2)
s.391A Rights of auditors who are removed or not re-appointed	
(1)	ss.511(1), 515(1) and (2) (changed)
(2)	ss.511(2), 515(3)
(3)	ss.511(3), 515(4)
(4)	ss.511(4), 515(5)
(5)	ss.511(5), 515(6)
(6)	ss.511(6), 515(7)
s.392 Resignation of auditors	
(1)	s.516(1) and (2)
(2)	s.516(3)
(3)	s.517(1) to (3)
s.392A Rights of resigning auditors	
(1)	s.518(1)
(2)	s.518(2)
(3)	s.518(3)
(4)	s.518(4)
(5)	s.518(5) to (7)
(6)	s.518(8)
(7)	s.518(9)
(8)	s.518(10)
s.394 Statement by person ceasing to hold office as auditor	
(1)	s.519(1) to (3) and (7) (changed)
(2)	s.519(4) (changed)
(3)	s.520(2)
(4)	s.520(3)
(5)	s.521(1)
(6)	s.520(4)
(7)	ss.520(5), 521(2) (changed)
s.394A Offences of failing to comply with s 394	
(1)	ss.519(5), 521(3) to (5)
(2)	ss.519(6), 521(4)
(4)	s.520(6) and (8) (changed)
s.395 Certain charges void if not registered	
(1)	ss.860(1), 861(5), 870(1), 874(1) and (2)
(2)	s.874(3)
s.396 Charges which have to be registered	
(1)	ss.860(7), 861(2)
(2)	s.861(3)
(3)	s.861(1)
(3A)	s.861(4)
(4)	s.861(5)

Provision of Companies Act 1985	*Destination in Companies Act 2006*
s.397 Formalities of registration (debentures)	
(1)	ss.863(1) to (4), 870(3)
(2)	s.864(1) and (3)
(3)	s.864(2)
s.398 Verification of charge on property outside United Kingdom	
(1)	s.866(1)
(2)	s.870(1)
(3)	s.866(2)
(4)	s.867(1) and (2)
s.399 Company's duty to register charges it creates	
(1)	ss.860(1) and (2), 863(5)
(2)	ss.860(3), 863(5)
(3)	ss.860(4) to (6), s.863(5)
s.400 Charges existing on property acquired	
(1)	ss.861(5), 862(1)
(2)	ss.862(2) and (3), 870(2)
(3)	s.870(2)
(4)	s.862(4) and (5) (changed)
s.401 Register of charges to be kept by registrar of companies	
(1)	s.869(1), (2) and (4)
(2)	s.869(5) and (6)
(3)	s.869(7)
s.402 Endorsement of certificate on debentures	
(1)	s.865(1)
(2)	s.865(2)
(3)	s.865(3) and (4)
s.403 Entries of satisfaction and release	
(1)	s.872(1) and (2) (changed)
(2)	s.872(3)
s.404 Rectification of register of charges	
(1)	s.873(1)
(2)	s.873(2)
s.405 Registration of enforcement of security	
(1)	s.871(1) and (3)
(2)	s.871(2) and (3)
(4)	s.871(4) and (5)
s.406 Companies to keep copies of instrument creating charges	
(1)	ss.875(1), 877(2) (changed)
(2)	s.875(2)
s.407 Company's register of charges	
(1)	ss.876(1), 877(2) (changed)
(2)	s.876(2)
(3)	s.876(3) and (4)
s.408 Right to inspect instruments which create charges, etc	
(1)	s.877(1), (2) and (4) (changed)
(2)	s.877(2) (changed)
(3)	s.877(5) and (6)
(4)	s.877(7)

Provision of Companies Act 1985	Destination in Companies Act 2006
s.410 Charges void unless registered	
(1)	s.878(1)
(2)	ss.886(1), 889(1)
(3)	s.889(2)
(4)	ss.878(7), 879(1) and (3)
(5)	s.879(5) and (6)
s.411 Charges on property outside United Kingdom	
(1)	s.886(1)
(2)	s.884
s.412 Negotiable instrument to secure book debts	
	s.879(4)
s.413 Charges associated with debentures	
(1)	s.879(2)
(2)	ss.882(1) to (4), 886(3)
(3)	s.883(1) to (3)
s.414 Charge by way of ex facie absolute disposition, etc	
(1)	s.881(1)
(2)	s.881(2) and (3)
s.415 Company's duty to register charges created by it	
(1)	ss.878(1) and (2), 882(5)
(2)	s.878(3), 882(5)
(3)	s.878(4) to (6), 882(5)
s.416 Duty to register charges existing on property acquired	
(1)	ss.880(1) and (2), 886(2)
(2)	s.886(2)
(3)	s.880(3) and (4) (changed)
s.417 Register of charges to be kept by registrar of companies	
(1)	s.885(1)
(2)	s.885(2)
(3)	s.885(3)
(4)	s.886(6)
s.418 Certificate of registration to be issued	
(1)	s.885(4)
(2)	s.885(4) and (5)
s.419 Entries of satisfaction and release	
(1)	s.887(1) and (3) (changed)
(1B)	s.887(2)
(2)	s.887(4)
(3)	s.887(2) (changed)
(4)	s.887(5)
s.420 Rectification of register	
	s.888(1) and (2)
s.421 Copies of instruments creating charges to be kept by company	
(1)	ss.890(1), 892(2) (changed)
(2)	s.890(2)

Provision of Companies Act 1985	Destination in Companies Act 2006
s.422 Company's register of charges	
(1)	ss.891(1), 892(2) (changed)
(2)	s.891(2)
(3)	s.891(3) and (4)
s.423 Right to inspect copies of instruments, and company's register	
(1)	s.892(1), (2) and (4) (changed)
(2)	s.892(4) (changed)
(3)	s.892(5) and (6)
(4)	s.892(7)
s.425 Power of company to compromise with creditors and members	
(1)	ss.895(1), 896(1) and (2)
(2)	ss.899(1) and (3), 907(1), 922(1)
(3)	s.899(4), 901(3) and (4) (changed)
(4)	s.901(5) and (6)
(6)	s.895(2)
s.426 Information as to compromise to be circulated	
(1)	s.897(1)
(2)	s.897(1) and (2)
(3)	s.897(1)
(4)	s.897(3)
(5)	s.897(4)
(6)	ss.895(1), 897(5) to (8)
(7)	s.898(1) to (3)
s.427 Provisions for facilitating company reconstruction or amalgamation	
(1)	s.900(1)
(2)	s.900(1) and (2)
(3)	s.900(2)
(4)	s.900(3) and (4)
(5)	s.900(6) to (8)
(6)	ss.900(5), 941
s.427 A Application of ss 425-427 to mergers and divisions of public companies	
(1)	ss.902(1), 903(1), 907(2), 922(2)
(2)	ss.904(1), 919(1)
(3)	s.938(1) and (2)
(4)	s.902(3)
(8)	s.941
s.428 Takeover offers	
(1)	s.974(1) to (3)
(2)	s.974(4) and (5)
(2A)	s.974(6)
(3)	s.976(1)
(4)	s.976(3)
(5)	s.975(1) and (2) (changed)
(6)	s.975(3) (changed)
(7)	s.974(7)
(8)	s.991(1)
s.429 Right of offeror to buy out minority shareholders	
(1)	s.979(1) and (2) (changed)
(2)	s.979(3) and (4) (changed)

Provision of Companies Act 1985	Destination in Companies Act 2006
(3)	s.980(2) (changed)
(4)	s.980(1) and (4)
(5)	s.980(5)
(6)	s.980(6) and (8)
(7)	s.980(7)
(8)	ss.977(1), 979(8) to (10) (changed)
s.430 Effect of notice under s 429	
(1)	s.981(1)
(2)	s.981(2)
(3)	s.981(3)
(4)	s.981(4) and (5) (changed)
(5)	s.981(6)
(6)	s.981(7)
(7)	s.981(8)
(8)	s.981(6)
(9)	s.981(9)
(10)	s.982(2) and (3)
(11)	s.982(4) and (5)
(12)	s.982(6)
(13)	s.982(7)
(14)	s.982(8)
(15)	s.982(9)
s.430A Right of minority shareholder to be bought out by offeror	
(1)	ss.983(1) to (3), 984(1)
(1A)	s.983(1)
(2)	s.983(4)
(2A)	s.983(5)
(3)	s.984(3)
(4)	s.984(2)
(5)	s.984(4)
(6)	s.984(5) and (7)
(7)	s.984(6)
s.430B Effect of requirement under s 430A	
(1)	s.985(1)
(2)	s.985(2)
(3)	s.985(3)
(4)	s.985(4) and (5) (changed)
s.430C Applications to the court	
(1)	s.986(1) and (2)
(2)	s.986(2)
(3)	s.986(3)
(4)	s.986(5)
(5)	s.986(9) and (10)
s.430D Joint offers	
(1)	s.987(1)
(2)	s.987(2) and (3) (changed)
(3)	s.987(5) and (6)
(4)	s.987(4) and (7)
(5)	s.987(8)
(6)	s.987(9)
(7)	s.987(10)
s.430E Associates	
(1)	ss.975(4), 977(2) (changed)
(2)	s.979(9)

Provision of Companies Act 1985	Destination in Companies Act 2006
(3)	s.983(8)
(4)	s.988(1) and (4)
(5)	s.988(2)
(6)	s.988(3)
(7)	s.988(3), (5) and (7)
(8)	s.988(1)
s.430F Convertible securities	
(1)	s.989(1)
(2)	s.989(2)
s.458 Punishment for fraudulent trading	
	s.993(1) to (3)
s.459 Order on application of company member	
(1)	s.994(1)
(2)	s.994(2)
(3)	s.994(3)
s.460 Order on application of Secretary of State	
(1)	s.995(2) and (3)
(1A)	s.995(1)
(2)	s.995(4)
s.461 Provisions as to petitions and orders under this Part	
(1)	s.996(1)
(2)	s.996(2)
(3)	s.996(2)
(5)	s.998(1) to (4)
(6)	s.997
s.652 Registrar may strike defunct company off register	
(1)	s.1000(1)
(2)	s.1000(2)
(3)	s.1000(3)
(4)	s.1001(1)
(5)	ss.1000(4) to (6), 1001(2) to (4)
(6)	ss.1000(7), 1001(5)
(7)	s.1002(1) to (3)
s.652A Registrar may strike private company off register on application	
(1)	s.1003(1) (changed)
(2)	s.1003(2) (changed)
(3)	s.1003(3)
(4)	s.1003(4)
(5)	s.1003(5)
(6)	s.1003(6)
(7)	s.1003(6)
s.652B Duties in connection with making application under section 652A	
(1)	s.1004(1)
(2)	s.1004(2)
(3)	s.1005(1)
(4)	s.1005(2)
(5)	s.1005(3)
(6)	s.1006(1)
(7)	s.1006(2)

Provision of Companies Act 1985	Destination in Companies Act 2006
(8)	s.1006(3)
(9)	s.1004(3)
s.652C Directors' duties following application under section 652A	
(1)	s.1007(1)
(2)	s.1007(2)
(3)	s.1007(3)
(4)	s.1009(1)
(5)	s.1009(2)
(6)	s.1009(4)
(7)	s.1009(3)
s.652D Sections 652B and 652C: supplementary provisions	
(1)	s.1008(1) and (2)
(2)	s.1008(3)
(3)	s.1008(3)
(4)	s.1008(4)
(5)(c)	ss.1004(4), 1006(1), 1007(2), 1009(4)
(6)	s.1010
(8)	s.1011
s.652E Section 652B and 652C: enforcement	
(1)	ss.1004(5) and (7), 1005(4) and (6), 1006(4) and (6), 1007(4) and (6), 1009(5) and (7)
(2)	ss.1006(4) and (7), 1007(4) and (7)
(3)	ss.1004(6), 1005(5)
(4)	s1006(5)
(5)	ss 1007(5), 1009(6)
s654 Property of dissolved company to be bona vacantia	
(1)	s.1012(1)
(2)	s.1012(2)
s.655 Effect on s.654 of company's revival after dissolution	
(1)	s.1034(1)
(2)	s.1034(2)
(3)	s.1034(4)
(4)	s.1034(5)
s.656 Crown disclaimer of property vesting as bona vacantia	
(1)	s.1013(1)
(2)	s.1013(2) (changed)
(3)	s.1013(3) to (5) (changed)
(5)	s.1013(6) and (7)
(6)	s.1013(8)
s.657 Effect of Crown disclaimer under s 656	
(1)	s.1014(1)
(2)	ss.1015(1) and (2), 1016(1) and (2), 1017(1) to (5), 1018(1) to (5), 1019
(4)	s.1020(1) and (2)
(5)	s.1021(1) and (2)
(6)	s.1021(3)

Provision of Companies Act 1985	Destination in Companies Act 2006
s.658 Liability for rentcharge on company's land after dissolution	
(1)	s.1023(1) and (2)
(2)	s.1023(3)
s.680 Companies capable of being registered under this Chapter	
(1)(a) and (b)	s.1040(1)
(1) (closing words)	s.1040(2), (3) and (6)
(1A)	s.1040(1)
(2)	s.1040(1)
(3)	s.1040(4)
(4)	s.1040(4)
(5)	s.1040(5)
s.683 Definition of "joint stock company"	
(1)	s.1041(1)
(2)	s.1041(2)
s.694 Regulation of oversea companies in respect of their names	
(4)	s.1048(1) and (2) (changed)
(5)	s.1048(3) to (5)
s.695 Service of documents on oversea company	
(1) and (2)	s.1139(2) (changed)
s.695A Registrar to whom documents to be delivered: companies to which section 690A applies	
(4)	s.1059
s.699A Credit and financial institutions to which the Bank Branches Directive (89/117/EEC) applies	
(3) ("financial institution")	s.1173(1)
s.704 Registration offices	
(2)	s.1060(1) and (2)
(4)	s.1062 (changed)
(7) and (8)	s.1119(1) and (2)
s.705 Companies' registered numbers	
(1) to (3)	s.1066(1) to (3)
(4)	s.1066(4) and (5)
(5)(za)	s.1066(6)
s.705A Registration of branches of oversea companies	
(1)	s.1067(1) (changed)
(2)	s.1067(1)
(3)	s.1067(2)
(4)	s.1067(3)
(5)	s.1067(4) and (5)
s.707A The keeping of company records by the registrar	
(1)	s.1080(4)
(2)	s.1083(1) (changed)
(3)	s.1084(1) to (3) (changed) and (5)
(4)	s.1084(4)

Provision of Companies Act 1985	Destination in Companies Act 2006
s.708 Fees payable to registrar	
(1)	s.1063(1) to (3) (changed)
(2) and (3)	s.1063(4) (changed)
(4)	s.1063(6)
(5)	s.1063(5) (changed)
s.709 Inspection, &c. of records kept by the registrar	
(1) opening words	s.1085(1) and s.1100
(1)(a) and (b)	s.1086(1)
(2)	s.1085(2) (changed)
(3)	s.1091(3)
(4)	s.1091(5)
(5)	s.1092(1) and (2)
s.710 Certificate of incorporation	
	s.1065
s.710A Provision and authentication by registrar of documents in non-legible form	
(2)	s.1115(2)
s.710B Documents relating to Welsh companies	
(1) to (3)	s.1104(1) and (2)
(4)	s.1104(3)
(5)	s.1104(4)
s.711 Public notice by registrar of receipt and issue of certain documents	
(1)	ss.1064(1) to (3), 1077(1) to (3), 1078(2) and (3) (changed)
(2)	s.1079(4) (changed)
s.713 Enforcement of company's duty to make returns	
(1)	s.1113(1) to (3)
(2) and (3)	s.1113(4) and (5)
s.714 Registrar's index of company and corporate names	
(1)	s.1099(1) to (3) (changed)
(2)	s.1099(4) and (5)
s.715A Interpretation	
(1) ("document") and (2)	s.1114(1)
s.718 Unregistered companies	
(1)	s.1043(1), (3) and (5) (changed)
(2)	s.1043(1)
(3)	s.1043(2) and (5) (changed)
(5)	s.1043(4)
(6)	s.1043(6)
s.719 Power of company to provide for employees on cessation or transfer of business	
(1)	s.247(1)
(2)	s.247(2) (changed)
(3)	s.247(4) to (6) (changed)
(4)	s.247(7) (changed)
s.721 Production and inspection of books where offence suspected	
(1)	s.1132(1) and (2)
(2) to (4)	s.1132(3) to (5)

Provision of Companies Act 1985	Destination in Companies Act 2006
s.722 Form of company registers, etc	
(1)	ss.1134 and 1135(1) (changed)
(2)	s.1138(1)
(3)	s.1138(2) and (3)
s.723 Use of computers for company records	
(1)	s.1135(1) (changed)
(2)	s.1135(5)
s.723A Obligations of company as to inspections of registers, &c.	
(1)	s.1137(1) and (2)
(2)	s.1137(3)
(3)	s.1137(3)
(4)	s.1137(4)
(6) and (7)	s.1137(5) and (6)
s.725 Service of documents	
(1)	s.1139(1)
(2)	s.1139(4)
(3)	s.1139(4)
s.727 Power of court to grant relief in certain cases	
(1) to (3)	s.1157(1) to (3)
s.730 Punishment of offences	
(4)	s.1125(2)
(5)	ss.1121(1) and (3) (changed)
s.731 Summary proceedings	
(1)	s.1127(1) and (2)
(2)	s.1128(1)
(3)	s.1128(2)
(4)	s.1128(4)
s.732 Prosecution by public authorities	
(1)	s.1126(1)
(2)	s.1126(2) (changed)
(3)	s.1129 (changed)
s.734 Criminal proceedings against unincorporated bodies	
(1)	s.1130(1) and (2) (changed)
(2)	s.1130(3)
(3)	s.1130(2)
(4)	s.1130(2)
s.735 "Company", etc	
(1)(a) and (b)	s.1(1)
(1)(c)	s.1171 (changed)
(3)	s.1171
s.736 "Subsidiary"; "holding company" and "wholly-owned subsidiary"	
(1) and (2)	s.1159(1) and (2)
(3)	s.1159(4)
s.736A Provisions supplementing s 736	
(1) to (11)	s.1159(3), Sch.6
s.736B Power to amend ss 736 and 736A	
(1)	s.1160(1)
(3) to (5)	s.1160(2) to (4)

Provision of Companies Act 1985	Destination in Companies Act 2006
s.737 "Called-up share capital"	
(1) and (2)	s.547
s.738 "Allotment" and "paid up"	
(1)	s.558
(2)	s.583(2) to (3)(d)
(3)	s.583(5)
(4)	s.583(6)
s.739 "Non-cash asset"	
(1) and (2)	s.1163(1) and (2)
s.741 "Director" and "shadow director"	
(1)	s.250
(2)	s.251(1) and (2)
(3)	s.251(3)
s.742 Expressions used in connection with accounts	
(1) ("fixed assets")	s.853(6)
(1) ("parent company")	s.1173(1)
(2)	s.853(4) and (5)
s.742A Meaning of "offer to the public"	
(1)	s.756(1) and (2)
(2)	s.756(3)
(3)	s.756(4) and (5)(a) to (d) (changed)
(4)	s.756(4)
(5)	s.756(4)
(6)	s.756(5)(e) and (6)
s.742B Meaning of "banking company"	
(1) to (3)	s.1164(1) to (3)
s. 742C Meaning of "insurance company" and "authorised insurance company"	
(1) to (4)	s.1165(2) to (4)
(5)	s.1165(8)
s.743 "Employees' share scheme"	
	s.1166
s.744 Expressions used generally in this Act	
"articles"	s.18(4)
"the Companies Acts"	s.2(1) and (2) (changed)
"the court"	s.1156(1) to (3) (changed)
"debenture"	s.738
"EEA State"	s.1170
"equity share capital"	s.548
"the Gazette"	s.1173(1)
"hire-purchase agreement"	s.1173(1)
"insurance market activity"	s.1165(7)
"officer"	ss.1121(2), 1173(1)
"oversea company"	s.1044 (changed)
"prescribed"	s.1167
"the registrar of companies" and "the registrar"	s.1060(3)
"regulated activity"	s.1173(1)
"share"	s.540(1) and (4)
s.744A Index of defined expressions	
	Sch.8

Provision of Companies Act 1985	Destination in Companies Act 2006
Sch.2 Interpretation of references to "beneficial interest"	
Part 1 References in sections 23, 145, 146 and 148	
para.1(1)	ss.139(1), 672(1)
para.1(2)	ss.139(2), 672(2)
para.1(3)	ss.139(3), 672(3)
para.1(4)	ss.139(4), 672(4)
para.2(3)	s.672(5)
para.2(4)	s.672(6)
para.3(1) and (2)	ss.140(1) and (2), 673(1) and (2)
para.4(1)	ss.138(1) and (2), 674
para.4(2)	s.138(1)
para.4(3)	s.674
para.5(1)	ss.675(1) and (2), 676
para.5(2)	ss.139(5) and (6), 140(3), 675(1) and (2)
para.5(3)	ss.139(6), 140(4), 676
Sch.4 Form and content of company accounts	
Part 3 Notes to the accounts	
para.56(2) and (3)	ss.382(6), 465(6)
Part 7 Interpretation of Schedule	
para.94(1) and (2)	s.411(6)
Sch.7B Specified persons, descriptions of disclosures etc for the purposes of section 245G	
Part 1 Specified persons	
	s.461(1)
Part 2 Specified descriptions of disclosures	
	s.461(4)
Part 3 Overseas regulatory bodies	
	s.461(5) and (6)
Sch.10A Parent and subsidiary undertakings: supplementary provisions	
para.1	Sch.7 para.1
para.2(1)	Sch.7 para.2(1)
para.2(2)	Sch.7 para.2(2)
para.3(1)	Sch.7 para.3(1)
para.3(2)	Sch.7 para.3(2)
para.3(2)	Sch.7 para.3(3)
para.4(1)	Sch.7 para.4(1)
para.4(2)	Sch.7 para.4(2)
para.4(3)	Sch.7 para.4(3)
para.5(1)	Sch.7 para.5(1)
para.5(2)	Sch.7 para.5(2)
para.6	Sch.7 para.6
para.7(1)	Sch.7 para.7(1)
para7(2)	Sch.7 para.7(2)
para.8	Sch.7 para.8
para.9(1)	Sch.7 para.9(1)
para.9(2)	Sch.7 para.9(2)
para.9(3)	Sch.7 para.9(3)
para.10	Sch.7 para.10
para.11	Sch.7 para.11

Provision of Companies Act 1985	Destination in Companies Act 2006
Sch.13 Provisions supplementing and interpreting sections 324 to 328	
Part 4 Provisions with respect to register of directors' interests to be kept under section 325	
para.27	s.809(2) and (3)
Sch.14 Overseas branch registers	
Part 1 Countries and territories in which overseas branch register may be kept	
	s.129(2)
Part 2 General provisions with respect to overseas branch registers	
para.1(1) and (2)	ss.130(1), 135(3)
para.1(3)	ss.130(2) and (3), 135(4) and (5)
para.2(1)	s.131(1)
para.3(1)	s.134(1) and (2) (changed)
para.3(2)	s.134(3)
para.4(1)	s.132(1) and (2) (changed)
para.4(2)	s.132(3) and (4)
para.5	s.133(1) and (2)
para.6	s.135(1) and (2)
para.7	s.131(4)
Sch.15A Written resolutions of private companies	
Part 1 Exceptions	
para.1	s.288(2)
Part 2 Adaptation of procedural requirements	
para.3(1) and (2)	ss.571(7), 573(5)
para.5(1) and (2)	ss.695(2), 698(2)
para.5(3) and (4)	ss.696(2), 699(2)
para.6(1)	ss.717(2), 718(2)
para.6(2)	s.717(2)
para.6(3)	s.718(2)
para.7	s.188(5)
Sch.15B Provisions subject to which ss 425-427 have effect in their application to mergers and divisions of public companies	
para.1	ss.907(1) and (2), 922(1) and (2)
para.2(1)	ss.905(1), 906(1) to (3), 920(1), 921(1) to (4)
para.2(2)	ss.905(2) and (3), 920(2)
para.2(3)	s.920(3)
para.3	ss.908(1) and (3), 909(1) and (7), 911(1), (2) and (4), 912, 923(1) and (4), 924(1) and (7), 925(5), 926(1), (2) and (4), 927(1) to (3), 928
para.4(1)	ss.908(2), 923(2)
para.4(2)	s.923(3)
para.5(1)	ss.909(2) and (3), 924(2) and (3)
para.5(2)	ss.909(3), 924(3)
para.5(3)	ss.909(4), 924(4)
para.5(4)	s.935(1) (changed)
para.5(6)	s.935(2)
para.5(7)	ss.909(5), 924(5)
para.5(8)	ss.909(6), 924(6)
para.6(1)	ss.910(1), 911(3), 925(1), 926(3)
para.6(2)	ss.910(2), 925(2)
para.6(3)	ss.910(3), 925(3) (changed)

Provision of Companies Act 1985	Destination in Companies Act 2006
para.6(4)	ss.910(4), 925(4)
para.7	ss.914, 930
para.8(1)	ss.913(1), 929(1)
para.8(2)	ss.913(2), 929(2)
para.9(1)	s.939(1)
para.9(2)	s.939(1) and (2)
para.9(3)	s.939(3) and (4)
para.9(4)	s.939(5)
para.10(1)	ss.918(1), 932(1)
para.10(2)	ss.916(3) to (5), 918(2) to (4), 932(2) to (5)
para.11(1)	s.933(1) to (3), 934(1)
para.11(2)	s.933(1) to (3)
para.11(3)	s.934(1)
para.11(4)	s.934(2) to (4)
para.12(1)	ss.915(1) and (6), 917(1) and (6)
para.12(2)	s.915(2)
para.12(3)	s.915(3) to (5)
para.12(4)	s.917(2)
para.12(5)	ss.917(3) to (5), 931(3) and (5)
para.13(1)	s.931(1)
para.13(2)	s.931(2)
para.13(3)	s.931(3), (4) and (6)
para.14(1)	s.916(1)
para.14(2)	s.916(2)
para.14(3)	s.916(3) to (5)
para.15(1)	s.940(1)
para.15(2)	s.940(2)
para.15(3)	s.940(3)
Sch.20 Vesting of disclaimed property; protection of third parties	
Part 2 Crown disclaimer under section 656 (Scotland only)	
para.5	s.1022(1)
para.6	s.1022(2)
para.7	s.1022(3)
para.8	s.1022(4) and (5)
para.9	s.1022(6)

COMPANIES ACT 1989

1. Section 130(6) of the Companies Act 1989 (power by regulations to apply provisions relating to company contracts and execution of documents by companies to overseas companies) is re-enacted in section 1045 of the Companies Act 2006.
2. Section 207 of the Companies Act 1989 (transfer of securities) is re-enacted in sections 783, 784(3), 785 and 788 of the Companies Act 2006.

Index

References are to Paragraph Numbers